THE HANDBOOK
OF SCHOOL VIOLENCE
AND SCHOOL SAFETY

THE HANDBOOK
OF SCHOOL VIOLENCE
AND SCHOOL SAFETY

From Research to Practice

Edited by

Shane R. Jimerson
and
Michael J. Furlong
University of California
Santa Barbara

LEA
LAWRENCE ERLBAUM ASSOCIATES, PUBLISHERS
2006 Mahwah, New Jersey London

Director, Editorial:	Lane Akers
Editorial Assistant:	Rebecca Larsen
Cover Design:	Tomai Maridou
Full-Service Compositor:	TechBooks
Text and Cover Printer:	Hamilton Printing Company

This book was typeset in 10/12 pt. Times Roman, Italic, Bold, and Bold Italic.
The heads were typeset in Helvetica, Helvetica Italic, Helvetica Bold, Helvetica Bold Italic.

Lawrence Erlbaum Associates, Inc., Publishers
10 Industrial Avenue
Mahwah, New Jersey 07430
www.erlbaum.com

Library of Congress Cataloging-in-Publication Data

The handbook of school violence and school safety : from research to practice / edited by
    Shane R. Jimerson and Michael J. Furlong.
        p.   cm.
    Includes bibliographical references and index.
    ISBN 0-8058-5223-9 (clothbound : alk. paper)—ISBN 0-8058-5224-7 (pbk. : alk. paper)
    1. School violence—Prevention—Handbooks, manuals, etc.   2. School improvement
programs—Handbooks, manuals, etc.   I. Jimerson, Shane R.   II. Furlong, Michael J., 1951–
LB3013.3.H346   2006
    371.7′82—dc22   2006000394

Books published by Lawrence Erlbaum Associates are printed on
acid-free paper, and their bindings are chosen for strength and durability.

Printed in the United States of America
10 9 8 7 6 5 4 3 2 1

Dedicated to

Gavin O'Brien Jimerson   Devin and Leiana Furlong
Kathryn O'Brien   Flora Furlong

and to all those who are victims of violence at school, the dedicated professionals who promote school safety through efforts to prevent acts of violence and provide support for victims of violence, and the scholars who inform our understanding of important facets of school violence and school safety. Through bringing the best of science to professional practice, it is hoped that the information presented in this handbook serves as an impetus to prevent school violence and promote safe and effective schools.

Contents

Preface

Schools are typically safe places, but the reality of school violence cannot be ignored. Research reveals that students regularly report witnessing and experiencing violence in and around their schools, which ranges from harassment and bullying to serious physical assaults. Thus, *The Handbook of School Violence and School Safety* provides the conceptual, empirical, and practical foundation for implementing effective prevention and intervention programs to reduce school violence and promote safe and effective schools. This handbook provides both scholars and practitioners with essential knowledge about both school violence and school safety that draws on the best thinking of school violence researchers. This volume emphasizes the evidence-based research that informs professional practice and offers fundamental and comprehensive information. Clearly, when it comes to school violence prevention and intervention "one size does not fit all" and schools need to be able to consider an array of appropriate strategies. Being able to provide effective prevention and intervention requires knowledge of the factors associated with school violence and school safety. Providing such knowledge is the primary goal of *The Handbook of School Violence and School Safety*.

The timing for the development of *The Handbook of School Violence and School Safety* is ideal. The early era of school violence and safety research and practice was dominated by understandably reflexive responses to school violence crises and public demands for actions. For this reason, education policy and education practice raced ahead of empirical research, until recently. Consequently, it is now possible to identify high-quality school violence research and to organize the researchers who have carried it out to bring core school violence and safety knowledge to a single volume. *The Handbook of School Violence and School Safety* brings science to practice in a format that is designed so that it will be highly valued by educators and researchers.

The 41 chapters in The *Handbook of School Violence and School Safety* are organized into four sections: I: Foundations of School Violence and Safety, II: Assessment and Measurement, III: Research-Based Prevention and Intervention, and IV: Implementing Comprehensive Safe School Plans. This collection of chapters provides information and insights from scholars and practitioners around the world. In developing the contents of *The Handbook of School Violence and School Safety* it was essential to emphasize an appropriate balance of both breadth and depth, thus, providing information on numerous facets of school violence and school safety, while also emphasizing particular facets as appropriate (e.g., bullying). A particularly important component included in each chapter is a summary table delineating *implications for practice*.

About the Contributors

Chapter 1

Shane R. Jimerson, PhD, is an associate professor in the Counseling, Clinical, and School Psychology Program and an associate professor of child and adolescent development at the University of California, Santa Barbara. <jimerson@education.ucsb.edu>

Gale M. Morrison, PhD, is a professor in the Counseling, Clinical, and School Psychology Program at the University of California, Santa Barbara. <gale@education.ucsb.edu>

Sarah W. Pletcher, MEd, is a doctoral student in the Counseling, Clinical, and School Psychology Program at the University of California, Santa Barbara. <swoehr@education.ucsb.edu>

Michael J. Furlong, PhD, is a professor in the Counseling, Clinical, and School Psychology Program at the University of California, Santa Barbara. <mfurlong@education.ucsb.edu>

Chapter 2

Michelle Kilpatrick Demaray, PhD, is an associate professor in the Department of Psychology at Northern Illinois University. <mkdemaray@niu.edu>

Christine Kerres Malecki, PhD, is an associate professor in the Department of Psychology at Northern Illinois University. <cmalecki@niu.edu>

Lauren K. DeLong is a doctoral student in the Department of Psychology at Northern Illinois University. <ldelong@niu.edu>

Chapter 3

Kirk A. Bailey, JD, is counsel at Smith, Dawson & Andrews, a public affairs firm in Washington, DC. <kirk@sda-inc.com>

Chapter 4

David Osher, PhD, is Managing Research Scientist at the American Institutes For Research, Washington, DC. <dosher@air.org>

Kevin P. Dwyer, MA, is a school psychologist and education and mental health consultant affiliated with the American Institutes for Research, Washington, DC. <ekdwyer@aol.com>

Shane R. Jimerson, PhD, is an associate professor in the Counseling, Clinical, and School Psychology Program and an associate professor of child and adolescent development at the University of California, Santa Barbara. <jimerson@education.ucsb.edu>

Chapter 5

Jim Larson, PhD, is professor of psychology in the School Psychology Program at the University of Wisconsin-Whitewater. <larsonj@uww.edu>

R. T. Busse, PhD, is an associate professor in the Counseling and School Psychology Program at Chapman University. <rtsian@juno.com>

Chapter 6

Amanda B. Nickerson, PhD, is an assistant professor of school psychology at the University at Albany, State University of New York. <anickerson@uamail.albany.edu>

Kristina M. Osborne, MS, is a doctoral student in school psychology at the University at Albany, State University of New York. <surrealist326@yahoo.com>

Chapter 7

Ron Avi Astor, PhD, is a professor in the Schools of Social Work and Education at the University of Southern California. <rastor@usc.edu>

Rami Benbenishty, PhD, is a professor in the School of Social Work and Social Welfare at the Hebrew University of Jerusalem. <msrami@mscc.huji.ac.il>

Roxana Marachi, PhD, is an assistant professor in the Department of Child & Adolescent Development at California State University, Northridge. <marachi@csun.edu>

Chapter 8

Jill D. Sharkey, PhD, is an assistant researcher at the Center for School-Based Youth Development, University of California, Santa Barbara. <jsharkey@education.ucsb.edu>

Michael J. Furlong, PhD, is a professor in the Counseling, Clinical, and School Psychology Program at the University of California, Santa Barbara. <mfurlong@education.ucsb.edu>

Georgette Yetter, PhD, is an assistant professor of school psychology at Oklahoma State University, Stillwater, OK. <gyetter@okstate.edu>

Chapter 9

Douglas Smith, PhD, is an associate professor and coordinator of the school counseling specialization in the Department of Counselor Education at the University of Hawaii, Manoa. <smithdou@hawaii.edu>

Michael J. Furlong, PhD, is a professor in the Counseling, Clinical, and School Psychology Program at the University of California, Santa Barbara. <mfurlong@education.ucsb.edu>

Peter Boman, PhD, is a coordinator in educational psychology and school counseling at the James Cook University, Cairns, Australia. <Peter.Boman@jcu.edu.au>

Chapter 10

Marisa Reddy Randazzo, PhD, is a senior expert, behavioral intelligence and risk management, with BIA Security Services and former chief research psychologist with the U.S. Secret Service. <marisa_randazzo@yahoo.com>

Randy Borum, PsyD, is associate professor, Department of Mental Health Law and Policy at the University of South Florida. <borum@fmhi.usf.edu>

Bryan Vossekuil, BA, is a director with the National Violence Prevention and Study Center. <bvossekuil@nvpsc.org>

Robert Fein, PhD, is a forensic psychologist with the National Violence Prevention and Study Center. <rfein@nvpsc.org>

William Modzeleski, MA, is associate assistant deputy secretary of the Office of Safe and Drug Free Schools, with the U.S. Department of Education. <bill.modzeleski@ed.gov>

William S. Pollack, PhD, is assistant clinical professor, Department of Psychiatry, Harvard Medical School and director, The Centers for Men and Young Men, McLean Hospital, Belmont, MA. <wpollack@mclean.harvard.edu>

Chapter 11

Russell J. Skiba, PhD, is a professor in the Department of Counseling and Educational Psychology at Indiana University, Bloomington. <skiba@indiana.edu>

Ada B. Simmons, EdD, is executive associate director of the Center for Evaluation and Education Policy at Indiana University, Bloomington. <adsimmon@indiana.edu>

Reece L. Peterson, PhD, is a professor in the Department of Special Education and Communication Disorders at the University of Nebraska, Lincoln. <rpeterson1@unl.edu>

Susan Forde, MEd, is a doctoral student at the University of South Florida. <sforde@alumni.indiana.edu>

Chapter 12

Matthew J. Mayer, PhD, is an assistant professor of special education at Michigan State University. <mayerma@msu.edu>

Chapter 13

Dewey G. Cornell, PhD, is professor of education in the Curry Programs in Clinical and School Psychology at the University of Virginia. <dcornell@virginia.edu>

Peter L. Sheras, PhD, is professor of Education in the Curry Programs in Clinical and School Psychology at the University of Virginia. <pls@virginia.edu>

Joanna C. M. Cole, MEd, is a graduate student in the Curry Programs in Clinical and School Psychology at the University of Virginia. <jcc8f@virginia.edu>

Chapter 14

Gale M. Morrison, PhD, is a professor in the Counseling, Clinical, and School Psychology Program at the University of California, Santa Barbara. <gale@education.ucsb.edu>

Megan Redding, MEd, is a doctoral student in the Counseling, Clinical, and School Psychology Program at the University of California, Santa Barbara. <mredding@education.ucsb.edu>

Emily Fisher, PhD, is an assistant professor of school psychology at Loyola Marymount University, Los Angeles. <emilysfisher@yahoo.com>

Reece L. Peterson, PhD, is a professor in the Department of Special Education and Communication Disorders at the University of Nebraska, Lincoln. <rpeterson1@unl.edu>

Chapter 15

Ron Avi Astor, PhD, is a professor in the Schools of Social Work and Education at the University of Southern California. <rastor@usc.edu>

Rami Benbenishty, PhD, is a professor in the School of Social Work and Social Welfare at the Hebrew University of Jerusalem. <msrami@mscc.huji.ac.il>

Roxana Marachi, PhD, is an assistant professor in the Department of Child and Adolescent Development at California State University, Northridge. <marachi@csun.edu>

Heather A. Meyer, PhD, is a lecturer at Skidmore College, New York.

Chapter 16

Michael J. Furlong, PhD, is a professor in the Counseling, Clinical, and School Psychology Program at the University of California, Santa Barbara. <mfurlong@education.ucsb.edu>

Jill D. Sharkey, PhD, is an assistant researcher at the Center for School-Based Youth Development, University of California, Santa Barbara. <jsharkey@education.ucsb.edu>

Chapter 17

Susan M. Swearer, PhD, is an associate professor of school psychology at the University of Nebraska, Lincoln. <sswearer@unlserve.unl.edu>

James Peugh, MA, is a graduate student in the Department of Educational Psychology University of Nebraska, Lincoln. <oaktreetx@yahoo.com>

Dorothy L. Espelage, PhD, is an associate professor of counseling psychology at the University of Illinois, Urbana-Champaign. <espelage@uiuc.edu>

Amanda B. Siebecker, MA, is a graduate student in the Department of Educational Psychology at the University of Nebraska, Lincoln. <mandasiebecker@yahoo.com>

Whitney Kingsbury, MS, is a graduate student in the Department of Educational Psychology at the University of Illinois, Urbana-Champaign. <kingsbur@uiuc.edu>

Katherine S. Bevins, BA, is a graduate student in the Department of Educational Psychology at the University of Nebraska, Lincoln. <kbevins2@bigred.unl.edu>

Chapter 18

Richard J. Hazler, PhD, is a professor of counselor education at Penn State University. <hazler@psu.edu>

JoLynn V. Carney, PhD, is an associate professor of counselor education at Penn State University. <jcarney@psu.edu>

Chapter 19

Susan P. Limber, PhD, is associate director of the Institute on Family and Neighborhood Life and professor of psychology at Clemson University. <slimber@clemson.edu>

Chapter 20

Miriam K. Hirschstein, PhD, is a research scientist at the Committee for Children, Seattle, WA. <mhirschstein@cfchildren.org>

Karin S. Frey, PhD, was a research scientist at the Committee for Children and is an associate research professor in educational psychology at the University of Washington, Seattle, WA. <karinf@u.washington.edu>

Chapter 21

Ken Rigby, PhD, is adjunct professor (Research) in the School of Education at the University of South Australia, Adelaide, Australia. <ken.rigby@unisa.edu.au>

Chapter 22

Richard J. DioGuardi, PhD, is an assistant professor in the Department of Psychology at Iona College. <rdioguardi@iona.edu>

Lea A. Theodore, PhD, is an assistant professor at the City University of New York, Queens College. <Lea_Theodore@qc.edu>

Chapter 23

Eva L. Feindler, PhD, is a professor of psychology and director of the Psychological Services Center at the University of Long Island, C. W. Post Campus, New York. <elfphd@aol.com>

Scott A. Weisner, PsyD, JD, recently received his doctorate from the Long Island University, C.W. Post Clinical Psychology Program, New York. <weisesq@aol.com>

Chapter 24

Douglas Smith, PhD, is an associate professor and coordinator of the school counseling specialization in the Department of Counselor Education at the University of Hawaii, Manoa. <smithdou@hawaii.edu>

Jim Larson, PhD, is professor of psychology in the School Psychology Program at the University of Wisconsin, Whitewater. <larsonj@uww.edu>

DeAnne R. Nuckles, MSE, is a graduate student in the School Psychology Program at the University of Wisconsin, Whitewater. <deanne_nuckles@yahoo.com>

Susan P. Giancola, PhD, is president of Giancola Research Associates, Inc. and an adjunct professor of education at the University of Delaware, Newark. <Giancola@comcast.net>

Lindsay S. Goetz, MA, is a school psychologist in the Colonial School District, New Castle DE. <goetz@colonial.k12.de.us>

Jennifer Parisella Veach, MA, is a school psychologist in the Appoquinimink School District, Newark, DE. <veachj@christina.k12.de.us>

Chapter 36

Leslie Z. Paige, EdS, NCSP, is the grants facilitator for the Graduate School and the Docking Institute of Public Affairs at Fort Hays State University, Hays, KS. <lpaige@fhsu.edu>

Stephen N. Kitzis, PhD, is an associate professor of psychology and policy fellow of the Docking Institute of Public Affairs at Fort Hays State University, Hays, KS. <skitzis@fhsu.edu>

Joyce Wolfe, MS, is a research scientist at the Docking Institute of Public Affairs at Fort Hays State University, Hays, KS. <jwolfe@fhsu.edu>

Jennifer Kitson, EdS, is a senior research/development associate for the Education Development Center, Inc., Newton, MA. <jkitson@edc.org>

Chapter 37

Sharon L. Telleen, PhD, is a research associate professor, Department of Sociology and Institute for Research on Race and Public Policy, University of Illinois at Chicago. <telleen@uic.edu>

Helen Stewart-Nava, MSW is a lead case manager, Community Care Options, Berwyn, IL. <HStewart-Nava@CCOptions.org>

Young Ok Rhee Kim, PhD, RN, is a research specialist, College of Nursing University of Illinois at Chicago. <ykim2@uic.edu>

Rosario C. Pesce, PhD, is a school psychologist and student assistance coordinator, Morton High School District 201, Cicero, IL. <VPpsych@aol.com>

Susan Maher, PhD, is coordinator of School Health Programs, Massachusetts Department of Education, Malden. <susanmaher98@yahoo.com>

Chapter 38

Dewey G. Cornell, PhD, is professor of education in the Curry Programs in Clinical and School Psychology at the University of Virginia. <dcornell@virginia.edu>

Farah E. Williams, MEd, is a graduate student in the Curry Programs in Clinical and School Psychology at the University of Virginia. <farah@virginia.edu>

Chapter 39

Russell B. Van Dyke, PhD, is a school psychologist at Panama-Buena Vista Union School District in Bakersfield, CA. <rvandyke@pbvusd.net>

Jennifer L. Schroeder, PhD, is an assistant professor of psychology and special education at Texas A & M University, Commerce. <Jennifer_Schroeder@tamucommerce.edu>

Chapter 40

Laura Delizonna, PhD, is on the clinical faculty at Stanford University Medical School in addition to being an instructor at Stanford University. She has a private practice conducting evidence-based psychotherapy and consulting in San Francisco, CA. <delizonna@stanford.edu>

Ivan Alan, MA, is a doctoral candidate at Pacific Graduate School of Psychology, Palo Alto, CA. <ialan@pgsp.edu>

Hans Steiner, MD, is a professor of psychiatry and behavioral sciences, Child Psychiatry and Child Development, Stanford University School of Medicine, Stanford, CA. <steiner@stanford.edu>

Chapter 41

Russell J. Skiba, PhD, is a professor in the Department of Counseling and Educational Psychology at Indiana University, Bloomington. <skiba@indiana.edu>

Shana Ritter, BA, is coordinator of the Initiative on Equity and Opportunity at the Indiana University Center for Evaluation and Education Policy, Bloomington, IN. <rritter@indiana.edu>

Ada B. Simmons, EdD, is executive associate director of the Center for Evaluation and Education Policy at Indiana University, Bloomington, IN. <adsimmon@indiana.edu>

Reece L. Peterson, PhD, is a professor in the Department of Special Education and Communication Disorders at the University of Nebraska, Lincoln. <rpeterson1@unl.edu>

Courtney K. Miller, EdS, is a doctoral student in the School Psychology Program at the University of Nebraska, Lincoln. <ckm@unlserve.unl.edu>

About the Editors

Shane R. Jimerson, PhD, is an associate professor of counseling, clinical, and school psychology and an associate professor of child and adolescent development at the University of California, Santa Barbara (UCSB), in the Gevirtz Graduate School of Education. Among more than 100 professional publications, he is a co-author of a five-book grief support group curriculum series, *The Mourning Child Grief Support Group Curriculum* (Taylor and Francis) and a co-editor of *Best Practices in School Crisis Prevention and Intervention* (National Association of School Psychologists). He is a board certified expert in traumatic stress, (BCETS) and diplomat of The American Academy of Experts in Traumatic Stress. He serves as the editor of *The California School Psychologist* journal, associate editor of the *School Psychology Review* journal, and is on the editorial boards of the *Journal of School Psychology* and *School Psychology Quarterly*. Dr. Jimerson has chaired and served on numerous boards and advisory committees at the state, national, and international levels, including co-chair of the international school violence and crisis response network and the research committee of the International School Psychology Association. His scholarly publications and presentations have provided further insights regarding developmental pathways, the efficacy of early prevention and intervention programs, and school crisis prevention and intervention. During the past decade, Dr. Jimerson has led a series of studies examining delinquency among adolescents, including a longitudinal study of a family-focused, neighborhood-based supervision, intervention for youths in the juvenile justice system. Each of these studies has included a particular emphasis on understanding similarities and differences in the experiences and appropriate support services for females and males. The quality and contributions of his scholarship are reflected in the numerous awards and recognition that he has received. Dr. Jimerson received the Best Research Article of the Year Award from the Society for the Study of School Psychology in 1998 and then again in 2000. He also received the 2001 Outstanding Article of the Year Award from the National Association of School Psychologists', *School Psychology Review*. Dr. Jimerson's scholarly efforts were also recognized by the American Educational Research Association with the 2002 Early Career Award in Human Development. He and his UCSB research team received the 2003 Outstanding Research Award from the California Association of School Psychologists. Also during 2003, Dr. Jimerson received the Lightner Witmer Early Career Contributions Award from Division 16 (School Psychology) of the American Psychological Association. His scholarship continues to highlight the importance of early experiences on subsequent development and emphasize the importance of research informing professional practice to promote the social and cognitive competence of children.

Michael J. Furlong, PhD, is a professor at the University of California, Santa Barbara in the Gevirtz Graduate School of Education. He is the program leader for the Counseling/Clinical/School Psychology Program and director of the Center for School-Based Youth Development. Among more than 200 professional publications, Dr. Furlong is the lead editor of *Appraisal and Prediction of School Violence: Issues, Methods and Contexts.* He is also the editor of several special issues of *Psychology in the Schools* issues addressing the implementation of school violence prevention and intervention programs including Addressing Aggression and Anger in School Settings, Appraisal and Prediction of School Violence, and Lessons Learned from Implementing the Safe Schools/Healthy Students Projects. Dr. Furlong's research examines factors associated with the occurrence of violence on school campuses, patterns and influences of substance use by youths; implementation of interagency coordinated, family-focused programs to help children with emotional and behavioral disorders; delinquency prevention; truancy prevention; and developmental and health impacts of chronic hostility in youth. Dr. Furlong has served as the president of the California Association of School Psychologists and is currently an advisory panel member for the California Healthy KIDS Survey program. In recognition of his distinguished leadership and contributions to the field of school psychology, he received the 2001 Goff Award from the California Association of School Psychologists. He serves as an associate editor of *Psychology in the Schools* and the *California School Psychologist* and is on the editorial boards of the *Journal of Emotional and Behavioral Disorders* and the *Journal of School Violence.*

I

Foundations of School Violence and Safety

Violence and aggressive behaviors have challenged humans even before the advent of mandatory public education. As such, at the foundation of preventing school violence and promoting school safety is knowledge and awareness of the numerous and multifaceted influences associated with acts of violence in general and, in particular, those that occur at school. The chapters in this first section provide valuable information regarding the foundations of school violence and safety.

Chapter 1 provides a brief synthesis of information describing the diverse group of youth who engage in antisocial and aggressive behaviors. Chapter 2 offers valuable insights regarding the social support among aggressive youth, their victims, and their peers. Chapter 3, presents a thorough review of legal facets related to school violence and school safety. Recognizing that schools are generally safe places, Chapter 4 advocates that the best means of violence prevention is to promote school success and provides a comprehensive review of research informing the development of safe, supportive, and effective schools. Considering the importance of a pragmatic strategy to prevent school violence, Chapter 5 offers a problem-solving approach. Chapter 6 discusses the results of surveys of school professionals, examining their preparation for responding to school violence. The final chapter in this section, Chapter 7, provides an international perspective on school violence.

1

Youth Engaged in Antisocial and Aggressive Behaviors: Who Are They?

Shane R. Jimerson
Gale M. Morrison
Sarah W. Pletcher
Michael J. Furlong
University of California, Santa Barbara

In contrast to the extensive media coverage devoted to isolated events of violence on school campuses, careful consideration of the facts reveals that schools are among the safest places for youth. The annual *Indicators of School Crime and Safety* provides a yearly snapshot of specific crime and safety indicators in the United States, including victimization, fights, bullying, classroom disorder, teacher injury, weapons, and student perceptions of school safety (DeVoe et al., 2004). These indicators demonstrate that during the years 1992–2002, improvements occurred in the safety of students. For instance, the violent crime victimization rate at school declined from 48 violent victimizations per 1,000 students in 1992 to 24 such victimizations in 2002, a 50% reduction. Despite these encouraging trends, violence, bullying, and firearms are still prevalent at school. Findings from the report on school crime and safety specify that students ages 12 to 18 were victims of about 1.8 million nonfatal crimes of violence or theft at school in 2002 (DeVoe et al., 2004). Moreover, a larger number of serious violent victimizations among youths (e.g., rape, sexual assault, robbery, and aggravated assault) take place away from school than at school.

The 2003 administration of the Youth Risk Behavior Surveillance Survey (YRBS; Grunbaum et al., 2002) in the United States (DeVoe et al., 2004) found that 27% of males and 7% of females (in Grades 9–12) in the United States reported they had carried a gun during the previous 30 days (at school 9% and 3%, respectively). In addition, 41% of males and 25% of females indicated they had been in a physical fight in the previous year (at school 17% and 8%, respectively). The rates of antisocial behavior reported in the 2003 YRBS were lower than in previous years, nonetheless, they continue to show the high incidence of antisocial and aggression-related behaviors among American adolescents. Additionally, although less than 1% of all homicides among school-aged children (5 to 19 years old) occur in or around school

Portions of this chapter were adapted, with permission from Guilford Press, from: Furlong, M., Morrison, G., & Jimerson, S. (2004). Externalizing behaviors of aggression and violence and the school context. In R. B. Rutherford, M. M. Quinn, & S. R. Mathur (Eds.), *Handbook of Research in Emotional and Behavioral Disorders*. (pp. 243–261). New York: Guilford Press.

grounds or on the way to and from school, in raw numbers this included more than 234 deaths between July 1, 1992 and June 30, 2002, which compares to more than 24,000 homicides away from school. Although these events are not the most pressing youth violence problem, they have resulted in increased attention by educators to the origins and occurrence of antisocial behavior disorders among students. This, of course, is related to the very high standards held for schools with respect to the incidence of violence. Schools, like family homes, are places that should provide nurturance and care and any form of violence on a school campus is anathema with this overwhelming, positive student development objective.

As a first step in understanding and addressing violence that occurs at school, it is important to consider the factors associated with the characteristics and contexts of youth who engage in antisocial and aggressive behaviors, which have heterogeneous origins. Careful consideration of the factors associated with antisocial behaviors reveals that there is no single profile of factors associated with aggressive behavior. Thus, the following sections discuss these important considerations, with an emphasis on developmental, contextual, and mental health factors. The first section provides an overview of aggressive diagnostic patterns as delineated in the *Diagnosis and Statistical Manual of Mental Disorders* (4th ed; text revision [*DSM–IV–TR*]; American Psychiatric Association, 2000). Subsequent sections explore research-derived models of how antisocial and aggressive behaviors emerge from the developmental process. A central tenet drawn from this review of relevant literature is that youth engaged in antisocial and behaviors have many needs that community and school-based professionals may address.

DIAGNOSTIC AND DEVELOPMENTAL PATTERNS OF ANTISOCIAL AND AGGRESSIVE BEHAVIORS

Antisocial and aggressive behaviors associated with conduct disorder constitute the most frequent bases for referral of children and adolescents for psychological, criminal behaviors, and social maladjustment (Doll, 1996; Kazdin, 1995, 1997). Conduct disorder encompasses a breadth of chronic antisocial behaviors that typically begins in early childhood and extends into adulthood (Moffitt, Caspi, Rutter, & Silva, 2001; Robins & Ratcliff, 1979). Youth who exhibit such problematic behaviors usually present challenges in the traditional classroom environment, often being associated with poor academic performance. Youth manifesting behavioral problems may also have learning disabilities and sometimes are previously diagnosed with attention deficit hyperactivity disorder (ADHD). Research also indicates that antisocial behavior is related to increased rates of truancy and dropping out (Rumberger, 1987). During adolescence, concurrent exacerbating experiences include the use of alcohol and substance abuse. Knowledge and research pertaining to this childhood disorder can serve as a useful tool to clinicians, professionals, teachers, and the community.

DSM–IV–TR Criteria of Conduct Disorder

Behaviors among youth diagnosed with conduct disorder may vary. The following provides the list of criteria relevant to this particular disorder according to the *DSM–V–TR* (American Psychiatric Association, 2000).

1. A repetitive and persistent pattern in which the rights or societal norms or rules are violated as manifested by the presence of at least three of the following criteria in the past 12 months (with at least one criterion present in the past 6 months).

2. *Aggression to people and animals*, for example, bullying, threatening, or intimidating others, initiating physical fights, using a weapon that can cause serious physical harm to others

(e.g., a bat, brick, broken bottle, knife, gun), being physically cruel to people or animals, or has stolen while confronting a victim (e.g., mugging, purse snatching, extortion, armed robbery), or has forced someone into sexual activity.

3. *Destruction of property*, such as having deliberately engaged in fire setting with the intention of causing serious damage, or has deliberately destroyed others' property (other than by fire setting).

4. *Deceitfulness or theft*, for instance, has broken into someone else's house, building or car, having often lied to obtain goods or favors or to avoid obligations (i.e., "cons" others) or has stolen items of nontrivial value without confronting a victim (e.g., shoplifting, but without breaking and entering; forgery).

5. *Serious violation of rules such as,* staying out at night despite parental prohibitions (beginning before age 13 years), running away from home overnight (at least twice while living in parental or parental surrogate home or once without returning for a lengthy period), or is often truant from school (beginning before age 13 years).

DSM–IV–TR specifies that there is a "Childhood-Onset Type" wherein onset of at least one criterion characteristic of conduct disorder occurs prior to age 10 years, and also an "Adolescent-Onset Type," which occurs when there is an absence of any criteria characteristic of conduct disorder prior to age 10 years. The prevalence of conduct disorder is estimated at about 2% for girls with an onset typically between 14 and 16 years old and 9% in boys with onset generally before age 10 years (Russo & Beidel, 1994). Conduct disorders differ from other childhood challenges due to the antisocial behavior, the chronic nature of such behavior, as well as the impairment of functioning of those exhibiting such behaviors. Although it is possible for a youth to be given a diagnosis of conduct disorder without a record of overt physical aggression, the symptoms commonly include these behaviors.

Co-Morbidity Among Youth Diagnosed With Conduct Disorders

Youth meeting the criteria for conduct disorder classification often present symptoms of ADHD, Oppositional Defiant Disorder (ODD), and anxiety disorders. As highlighted in a review of epidemiological studies by Russo and Beidel (1994), there is significant co-morbidity between anxiety disorders, externalizing disorders, and depression. Co-morbidity of ADHD with conduct disorder (50%), ODD, anxiety disorders, speech and language disorders (78%), and learning disabilities (LD; 40%–70%) is extremely high (Mayes, Calhoun, & Crowell, 2000). In fact, the *DSM–IV–TR* includes aggression as one criteria for the diagnosis of depression during childhood. It is notable that ADHD is the most commonly diagnosed behavioral disorder during childhood (Tannock & Schachar, 1996). The symptoms of this disorder are closely tied to behavioral difficulties. ADHD includes a heterogeneous array of symptoms, which overlap markedly with ODD, conduct disorder, affective disorders such as depression, anxiety, LDs, and communication disorders. As characteristics of conduct disorder, emotional disturbance, and ADHD are often interrelated, the distinctions become blurred and these definitions continue to evolve (Forness & Kavale, 2000). As Achenbach (1998) emphasized previously, often it is more important to understand the individual's developmental history and constellation of behaviors, as there is a great degree of overlap among youth who are identified as having conduct disorder and other classifications.

Early-Onset Versus Adolescent-Onset of Antisocial Behaviors

There has been considerable scholarship examining the diverse developmental pathways associated with antisocial behaviors. For instance, Moffitt and Caspi (2001) provided a thorough review of childhood predictors that differentiate life-course-persistent and adolescence-limited antisocial pathways. Their scholarship provides a comparison between childhood risk factors of males and females exhibiting childhood-onset and adolescent-onset antisocial behavior, utilizing data from the Dunedin, New Zealand longitudinal study. The results reveal that outcomes associated with early-onset are much more deleterious relative to those youth who initiate behavior problems during adolescence. It has been suggested that this may not be the case among females (Frick, 1998); however, there have been few systematic comparisons of developmental trajectories by gender (Kratzer & Hodgins, 1999; Mazerolle, Brame, Paternoster, Piquero, & Dean, 2000). Results of the Moffitt and Caspi (2001) study indicate that both males and females with childhood-onset delinquency had childhoods of inadequate parenting, neurocognitive problems, and behavior problems, whereas adolescent-onset delinquents did not have these pathological backgrounds (Burke, Lahey, Loeber, & Rathouz, 2002). Considering the developmental trajectories of children displaying behavior problems, which indicate that early aggressive behaviors are characteristic of chronic life-course persisters (Burke et al., 2002; Stanger, Achenbach, & Verhulst, 1997), early antisocial and aggressive behaviors warrant serious attention in order to provide appropriate early interventions that address both behavioral and underlying emotional problems.

PATHWAYS TO ANTISOCIAL AND AGGRESSIVE BEHAVIORS

A review of the relevant literature and theories indicates that there is not one single developmental trajectory that leads to long-term antisocial and aggressive behavior, but that it evolves through periods of quiescence and more dynamic increases (Patterson & Yoerger, 2002). Moreover, aggressive behavior pattern subtypes have been proffered (e.g., instrumental–hostile, predatory–affective, and offensive–defensive). The distinctions between *overt* (observable behaviors such as fighting) versus *covert* (more hidden behaviors such as vandalism), and the *reactive* (angry, defensive responses) versus *proactive* (purposeful goal-directed acts) subtypes have the strongest internal and external validation (Connor, 2002). Developmental and ecological models of how antisocial and aggressive behavior patterns emerge (whether in overt behavior, covert behavior, or both) among youth have focused on the family, the peer group, and the school as the primary settings in which aggression is modeled and learned. The next section provides a brief overview of the predominant research-based perspectives about the emergence of aggressive behavior in youth with externalizing disorders.

Multiple Factors and the Convergence of Theoretical Perspectives

Social Learning Model

The social learning model emphasizes the importance of multiple proximal factors related to aggression, particularly antecedents and consequences of behaviors occurring in daily social exchanges between children and their siblings and parents within dysfunctional families (Patterson, Capaldi, & Bank, 1991; Patterson & Yoerger, 2002). The foundation of the social learning model is that youth begin to learn aggressive behaviors through these everyday social exchanges between family members, as well as through exposure to parenting styles that include inconsistent discipline, with both negative and positive reinforcement of antisocial behaviors and cognitions. The family environment and interactions of aggressive youth are characterized by coercion, typified by a family member using physical or verbal aggression to stop another family member from aggravating him or her or from interfering with his or her goals. These coercive behaviors become cyclical and reinforced such that children do not comply with their parents' requests, parents then create harsher demands, children's noncompliance becomes more escalated, and parents eventually submit to their child's noncompliance.

Thus, parents of aggressive children do not model prosocial and appropriate problem-solving behaviors but instead, inadvertently teach aggressive behaviors.

Social Information-Processing Model

The social information-processing model focuses on the cognitive role in social adjustment (Crick & Dodge, 1994) in that social cognitive skills, deficits, and biases are learned through the same social learning processes as noncompliance and coercive behavior. This theory differs from the social learning model in that the social information-processing model emphasizes the role of the youth's own social cognitions that account for various antisocial behaviors rather than placing primary influence on external modeling and reinforcement of behaviors (Dodge, Price, Bachorowski, & Newman, 1990).

Dodge's developmental model of social information-processing (Crick & Dodge, 1994) offers a foundation for understanding behaviors. Six cognitive processing steps elucidate the types of information a youth retrieves from memory and how the information is interpreted. It is hypothesized that flaws in this information-processing procedure lead to antisocial behavior, including aggression. The first two steps are encoding and interpreting social cues, in which the youth reads specific cues in the situation. Here, the youth may compare the immediate situation cues to those already stored in memory, analyze the potential problem and why the problem exists, infer what others might be thinking or intending to do, compare the present social exchange with the previous one, and consider the importance of the exchange to the self and the peer. Habitually aggressive children tend to concentrate more on hostile or aversive social cues, have memory difficulties that interfere with their ability to process social information, and interpret cues from their existing aggressive schema (Dodge & Tomlin, 1987; Slaby & Guerra, 1988).

The third step is determining goals in a given situation. Children determine their personal goals or desired outcomes for a given situation, based on their previous experiences and pre-existing cognitive scripts (habitual ways of interpreting social encounters; Crick & Dodge, 1994). Aggressive children, although desiring to be socially accepted, often seek goals such as getting what they want and retaliating against those who present obstacles to those goals (Erdley & Asher, 1998; Slaby & Guerra, 1988).

The next step in the model is constructing a response. Alternative behavioral or emotional responses are drawn from memory and past experiences, but when confronted with novel situations, form new alternative responses. Aggressive children tend to generate fewer prosocial alternative solutions compared to socially adjusted children (Slaby & Guerra, 1988). Specifically, these responses tend to be more atypical, maladaptive, and aggressive (Rubin, Bream, & Rose-Krasnor, 1991), with the latter viewed as socially acceptable and not immoral (Boldizar, Perry, & Perry, 1989; Crick & Ladd, 1990).

The fifth step of the social information-processing model is response decision. This refers to the process by which the individual evaluates the alternative responses. Aggressive children tend to consider immediate egotistical gains when using moral reasoning rather than considering others' needs or long-term consequences. Research indicates that aggressive children believe their aggressive behaviors will indeed "work" and that their choices will lead to more favorable outcomes than prosocial alternatives (Quiggle, Garber, Panak, & Dodge, 1992).

The final step of the model is enacting or committing an aggressive act. Deficits at this step are apparent when a student is aware of the prosocial act yet is unable to perform this act.

"Life-Course-Persistent" and "Adolescent-Limited" Models of Aggression

Aggressors who continue their aggressive behaviors from childhood throughout are considered "life-course persistent." A large proportion of aggressors commit their one and only crime between the ages of 14 and 17, and are considered "adolescent-limited" aggressors. Moffitt (1993a) suggests that social learning, social information-processing, and emotion-based theories do not explain or differentiate those who are life-course-persistent or adolescent-limited aggressors and, instead, proposes two new theories that account for such differences in etiology, developmental course, prognosis, and pathology or normality.

Life-course-persistent aggression is based on research from neuropsychology, temperament, and ADHD. Moffitt and colleagues (Caspi & Moffitt, 1995; Moffitt, 1993a, 1993b) suggested that chronic aggression begins with neurological impairment. Sources of neurological impairment such as genetics, maternal drug abuse, exposure to toxic agents, brain injury, poor nutrition, lack of stimulation or affection, and child abuse have been associated with children's antisocial behavior. However, neurological effects are not viewed as deterministic. Instead, research has demonstrated the malleability in neuropsychological functioning and how neurological and environmental factors interact in determining aggression. The primary role of neuropsychological impairment in influencing the development of aggression is its effects on language-based verbal skills and executive functions of the brain (Moffitt, 1990). A deficiency in these areas can lead to poor academics, poor social information processing, impulsive behavior, a restricted behavioral repertoire, social rejection, and poor self-concept; thus, furthering the continuity in aggressive behaviors. These deficits can also place the child at risk for more negative outcomes such as substance abuse, dropping out of school, and gang membership. Together, it is suggested these factors contribute to the development and maintenance of life-course-persistent aggression.

Adolescent-limited aggression involves those youth who engage in antisocial behaviors between early adolescence and young adulthood, who tend to commit less violent crimes than those of the life-course-persistent aggressors. Such crimes include fighting, theft, vandalism, and drug use. Although Moffitt (1993a) suggested that neither social learning nor social information-processing models explain the sudden onset and discontinuity of aggressive behaviors in adolescence, her model agrees that reinforcement and punishment contingencies contribute to adolescent-limited aggression. Adolescents' desires to gain adult status lead them to seek less constructive or social ways by committing aggressive acts. Thus, it is the adolescent's quest for maturity and autonomy that is viewed as a primary factor of aggression (Moffitt, 1993a).

Social Development Model

Integrating social learning theory, control theory, and differential association theory, Catalino and Hawkins' (1996) social development model focuses on explaining and predicting the onset of delinquency (both violent and nonviolent behaviors) and illegal drug use. Catalino and Hawkins assert that two general developmental pathways exist, with shared underlying processes—prosocial and antisocial. Additionally, acknowledging the influential factors that take hold at different stages of development, submodels are postulated for four transitional periods in social development: preschool, elementary school, middle school, and high school. Outcomes from each period of development, or submodel, are considered to influence subsequent developmental periods (Catalino & Hawkins, 1996; Laundra, Kiger, & Bahr, 2002). These submodels outline the importance of interactions that occur over time (i.e., transactions) among individuals and various contextual factors—family, peers, school, and the greater community. Each submodel places greater emphasis on certain contextual factors that are posited to influence prosocial or antisocial development, depending on the developmental period (e.g., the role of the family is stressed during the preschool period; Catalino & Hawkins, 1996).

Risk and protective factors are further proposed to be involved in either the prevention or development of delinquent behaviors and as such, are key components within this model (Catalino

& Hawkins, 1996). Three related concepts that are thought to influence prosocial/antisocial development, but were not accounted for in the theories from which this model was derived, are also included—social structure position (i.e., one's position in his or her social context), biological factors, and external feedback to one's behavior (Catalino & Hawkins, 1996; Laundra et al., 2002).

Transactional–Ecological Developmental Model

Sameroff (1995, 2000) proposed a transactional-ecological developmental model that incorporates key components of both general systems theory and Bronfenbrenner's ecological model of development, as well as the fields of biology and sociology. This model asserts that individuals cannot be accurately studied outside of the contexts in which they develop and that development is a complex and dynamic process (Sameroff, 2000). The transactional-ecological developmental model views individuals within a contextual framework, which translates to studying human development on multiple levels. These levels are labeled the *genotype*, the *phenotype*, and the *environtype* (Sameroff, 1995). The genotype is the microlevel, focusing on the individual's biology and unique characteristics that factor into development (i.e., genetic makeup; Sameroff, 1995). The phenotype may be construed as the channel, or mid-level, through which the genotype and environtype are expressed at any given time. This is not to assert that the phenotype is a passive element, but rather it is the active representation of the self at any point in time based on transactions that have taken place at the environtype and genotype levels (Sameroff, 1995). The environtype would be considered the macrolevel, influencing the phenotype through various external factors such as family dynamics, peer relationships, and school environment (Sameroff, 1995).

What tie these three levels together are the transactions that take place among them. For example, a child's biological background may predispose him or her to poor decision-making skills (genotype). The family environment may be one characterized by chaotic, volatile interactions (environtype). The child may then behave in a certain manner that further elicits negative responses, based on the contextual factors in place (phenotype). Over time, the dynamic interplay among these various influences could lead the child down a pathway to develop conduct disorder or other antisocial behaviors. Although this may be an oversimplified example of the complex developmental process that is emphasized in this model, it provides a snapshot of the way this process evolves over time. Individuals are to be viewed across time periods rather than at any one point in time in order to best understand their adaptive patterns, based on the transactions (i.e., interactions that occur over time) that influence the subsequent developmental trajectory (Sameroff, 2000). Additionally, these contextual factors (e.g., biological characteristics, family, school, and societal norms) are viewed in terms of their potential negative (i.e., risk) or positive (i.e., promotive) effect on a child (Pianta, 2001; Sameroff, 1995). The accumulation of and interplay among, as opposed to merely the presence of, risk and promotive factors are purported to influence the developmental trajectory, with more of one or the other altering a child's outcome in either a negative or positive direction. In essence, these various contextual factors serve as regulatory mechanisms that create a relatively stable course of development (Pianta, 2001). In the field of developmental psychopathology this has been referred to as a *homeorhetic tendency*, such that the confluence of factors influencing development is often relatively consistent, for better or worse.

Sameroff (1995) outlined three key types of regulatory mechanisms that influence child development: macroregulations (environmental changes that occur during key developmental periods), miniregulations (actions taken by caregiver/family that impact child behavior on a daily basis and vice versa), and microregulations (brief exchanges between child and caregiver during which their responses are in sync). Finally, a strong emphasis is placed on the reciprocity of relationships among individuals with respect to its impact on development. Children are not viewed as sponges, merely soaking up information, but rather as individuals who give and receive information that subsequently influences future developmental opportunities.

In addition to the relationship between harsh discipline and children's aggression, qualities of parent–child relationships such as lack of warmth with a primary caregiver (Doll & Lyon, 1998) can also contribute to children's aggression. Another possible factor leading to poor parenting and parent–child relationships includes family life stressors related to socioeconomic disadvantage. Parents of children with conduct problems reported a greater degree of stress than parents of typically developing children (Webster-Stratton, 1990). The stressors, in turn, further impact their parenting styles.

In short, the transactional–ecological developmental model aims to promote the understanding of developmental outcomes through exploration of developmental trajectories. These developmental trajectories are composed of multiple transactions, occurring over time, between the individual and various contextual factors, which consist of both risk and promotive factors that serve to structure or regulate behavior, and influence subsequent behaviors and relationships. Various studies have examined the phenomenon of antisocial and violent behaviors from a transactional-ecological developmental perspective (Kashani, Jones, Bumby, & Thomas, 1999; Sameroff, 1995; Tolan, 2001). Taking into account the many levels of contextual factors, from biological makeup to societal norms, the transactional-ecological developmental model offers a compelling framework through which to study school violence, in particular, as it articulates the complex pathway that leads to such. An important strength of this model is that individuals are not solely, or inherently, responsible for their developmental outcome. Instead, it is the confluence, or additive effects, of risk and promotive factors (i.e., the child's transactions with various contextual factors) that dictate adaptation to one's environment (Sameroff, 1995). This model views the youth's behavior as being adaptive to his or her environment. As such, the behaviors of youth should be examined within all of his or her contexts, including the environmental systems in which the child operates in order to inform effective interventions.

Research examining the emergence of externalizing behavior disorders involving aggressive behavior has suggested that there are multiple pathways and that the meaning and stability of aggression is different depending on the age at which the behavior fist emerges (Connor, 2002). Of great concern to educators is the need to better understand how to recognize and respond to those youth who show early signs of externalizing behavior symptoms as well as how to respond effectively with prevention efforts to deflect these youth from what can be a long-term pattern of aggression (Patterson & Yoerger, 2002).

ANTISOCIAL AND AGGRESSIVE BEHAVIORS AND THE SCHOOL CONTEXT

The boundaries for antisocial and aggressive behavior are often first met within classroom, peer, or schoolwide contexts where the behavior goes beyond a norm for acceptable behavior. Schools are also the most likely origin for intervention for antisocial and aggressive behaviors. As such, in order to better understand the development of antisocial and aggressive behaviors among youth, it is important to consider how these behaviors interact within school systems. This section focuses on how schools react to antisocial and aggressive behaviors and how these reactions help to reduce or exacerbate the behavior.

School disciplinary systems and the systems for identification and education for students with disabilities impact how schools address the needs of youth manifesting antisocial and aggressive behaviors. Antisocial and aggressive behaviors are most often seen within the special education category of emotional disturbance (ED). However, many states use the narrow definition of ED (as opposed to emotionally and behaviorally disturbed [EBD]) and exclude students who may be exhibiting aggressive or antisocial behavior, and therefore are considered to be socially maladjusted (Forness & Kavale, 2000), although it is important to point out that there is no official definition of "social maladjustment" in the *DSM–IV–TR* nor in educational law. Students who are considered by schools to be socially maladjusted are more likely to be seen on the lists for school exclusion (i.e., suspension and expulsion). Students who have LDs and who also exhibit antisocial or aggressive behavior are likely to be served under the LD category unless the behavior becomes a primary focus for school intervention, in which case they are at risk for being determined "ineligible" under Individuals with Disabilities Education Act (IDEA) categories (Morrison & D'Incau, 2000). Because of the conflicting attitudes about serving students who might be considered socially maladjusted under special education, it is important to focus on the disciplinary system as one of the primary school responses to aggressive and violent behavior.

The school disciplinary system usually consists of office referrals, suspensions, and expulsions as outcomes or consequences for behavior that breaks school rules. The behaviors punished by these mechanisms get progressively worse (i.e., an office referral may result from pushing or shoving behavior, while suspension and expulsion are used for state-defined rule breaking behaviors). For example, aggressive and violent behavior such as weapon use or possession, fighting, vandalism, sexual harassment, and stealing are typically included in state education codes as suspendable offenses (Civil Rights Project, 2000). Zero-tolerance policies have led to variations in how strictly and comprehensively these codes are applied, sometimes leading to a rigidity of implementation that ignores extenuating circumstances related to the offense.

Physical fights and aggression are the most common reasons for student suspension (Costenbader & Markson, 1994; Skiba, Peterson, & Williams, 1997). Youths who engage in harassment, bullying, or other aggressive behavior are at greater risk for being caught in a disciplinary action (Tobin, Sugai, & Colvin, 1996). Leonne, Mayer, Malmgren, and Meisel (2000) reviewed data from a number of state and national databases and found that students with disability represent about 20% of all students suspended, although their representation in the overall population is around 11%.

Once a youth engages in antisocial behaviors, the reactions of school officials, teachers, parents, and others may or may not facilitate positive outcomes (Caspi, Elder, & Bem, 1988). Developmental psychopathology provides a model for exploring the complex, multifaceted issues that impact students as they move through their school years. Sroufe and Rutter (1984) defined *developmental psychopathology* as the "study of the origins and course of individual patterns of behavioral maladaptation" (p. 18). This conceptualization has relevance to the discussion of school discipline in that the developmental perspective views the onset, course, and outcome of problematic behaviors across the developmental span from a broad perspective and examines the context in which these behaviors occur.

Recognizing that behavior interacts with critical contexts across time, it is important to examine the likely impacts of these contexts on students who struggle with behavioral issues of aggression and antisocial behavior. These contexts provide opportunities to improve behavior or lead to continued misbehavior; thus, the following highlights protective and risk factors associated within each context (Masten, Best, & Garmezy, 1990).

Individual Characteristics Associated With Antisocial and Aggressive Behaviors

Students who act out at school often show early signs of aggression and difficult temperament (Loeber, 1990; Moffitt, 1993a; Tubman & Windle, 1995). These youth may show deficits in social skills such as awkward initiations of social interactions, poor perspective taking, and deficits in conflict resolution (Coie, Dodge, & Kupersmidt, 1990; Walker, Ramsey, & Gresham, 2004). Behavioral impulsivity is also a strong predictor of antisocial behavior in the preadolescent years (White, Moffitt, Earls, Robins, & Silva, 1990). McFadden, Marsh, Price, and Hwang (1992) noted that students with disabilities differed from their typically developing classmates, with a higher incidence of office referrals for "bothering others" and "unacceptable physical contact." School failure is a strong correlate of later psychological disturbance and delinquency (Cernkovich & Giordano, 1992; Gold & Osgood, 1992; Hawkins & Lishner, 1987; Roff, Sells, & Golden, 1972; Walker et al., 2004). In general, antisocial or aggressive behaviors may result from a combination of traumatic experiences, a history of poor behavior control, and heightened negative emotions (Shields, Cicchetti, & Ryan, 1994). The latter characteristics point to the importance of considering the contexts within school that are likely to trigger aggressive actions.

In contrast, resilience factors that may counterbalance some of the deficits just cited include constitutional dispositions (i.e., sociability, problem-solving ability, planning ability, and internal locus of control) that help the child establish relationships with parents, teachers, and other critical adults as well as make positive life-course decisions (Clarke & Clarke, 1994). Within the individual and behavioral domains, critical variables include students' perceptions of their self-control, cooperation, self-efficacy, cognitive abilities, and social problem solving. Personal control and cooperation were significant protective factors in the Jessor study (Jessor et al., 1995), whereas self-efficacy was suggested by the foundational research of Garmezy, Rutter, and Werner (Garmezy, Masten, & Tellegen, 1984; Rutter, 1979; Werner & Smith, 1982). Elias and Branden (1988) identified problem-solving skills as important in maintaining positive coping in the face of stressful situations.

One of the reasons that students with the characteristics just described find themselves involved in the disciplinary system is that they experience difficulty in negotiating the demands, rules, and norms of the school context with regard to being a student. They may use disrespectful language with the teacher or may lack the verbal skills to explain their way out of an offense committed on campus. As such, it is necessary to examine the peer influences that may positively or negatively impact antisocial, aggressive student behavior in the school setting.

Peer Influences Associated With Antisocial and Aggressive Behaviors

The influence of social or peer affiliations in the trajectory toward delinquent behavior is important (Cairnes & Cairnes, 1994). Peer social clusters are highly influential and supporting of behaviors considered "normative" for the group. The personal impact of these peer associations is carried forward, even after their group affiliation changes. Research has found that peer social networks can influence negative behaviors such aggression, bullying, and ostracism (Rodkin, Farmer, Pearl, & Van Acker, 2000). However, they can also influence positive behaviors in the academic and social realms. Specifically, a prosocial peer group that provides social support can have a stress-buffering function (Clarke & Clarke, 1994; Dubow & Tisak, 1989).

The Classroom Context for Antisocial and Aggressive Behaviors

The classroom is a primary context where a youth's behavior may come into conflict with the rules and norms of the school. The skills of the teacher to handle misbehavior and encourage positive behavior are critical setting characteristics for student behavior (Osher et al., 2004; Scott, Nelson, & Liaupsin, 2001; Stage, 1997). Some of the risk factors for students who struggle with behavior issues in the classroom include a teacher who has few strategies for addressing developmental lags (La Paro, Pianta, & Cox, 2000), and an increase of negative attention that works against the establishment of a positive relationship (Blankemeyer, Flannery, & Vazsonyi, 2002; Reinke & Herman, 2002). Teachers vary in their ability to handle student misbehavior in their classroom. In one investigation at the middle school level, two thirds of all disciplinary referrals came from 25% of the school's teachers (Skiba et al., 1997). Classrooms that are characterized by low rates of academic engagement, praise, and reinforcement and high rates of reprimand are associated with high rates of misbehavior, setting up a cycle of negative student–teacher interactions (Farmer, Farmer, & Gut, 1999; Reinke & Herman, 2002). Osher and colleagues (2004) referred to these characteristics as "warning signs" for unsafe classrooms.

In contrast, teacher management strategies, effective instructional techniques (e.g., class-wide peer tutoring), early intervention for students with learning problems and teacher–student relationships are critical components for keeping students in the classroom or avoiding the necessity of excluding them for disciplinary reasons (Reinke & Herman, 2002; Scott et al., 2001). Effective instruction and positive student–teacher relationships should be accompanied by opportunities for students to be involved in activities that promote the development of desired social and emotional skills.

Schoolwide Context for Antisocial and Aggressive Behaviors

Considerable literature has been published on school effectiveness and school reform (Levine & Lezotte, 1990; Reynolds, Teddlie, Creemers, Scheerens, & Townsend, 2000). Information from this research provides valuable information regarding the way schoolwide practices can help or harm students who are at risk for behavior problems. One indicator of an ineffective school is a disorderly school environment with vague rules and expectations; this situation is likely to place students at risk who are especially in need of clear expectations and structure (Gottfredson, 1989). A disorderly school environment is associated with high suspension and expulsion rates (Civil Rights Project, 2000). McEvoy and Welker (2000) noted that schools that have low academic achievement and high antisocial behavior often rely on suspension and expulsion as a preferred method of maintaining control. "Get tough" school expulsion policies place a student who is struggling with behavior and compliance issues at risk for school exclusion (Morrison et al., 2001); school exclusion being a policy that virtually lacks evidence about its effectiveness (Skiba & Peterson, 2000). Mayer and Leonne (1999) found that ambiguous sanctions, punitive teacher attitudes, poor high school teacher–administrator cooperation, and use of physical restrictions (metal detectors, high fencing, etc.) can increase rates of problem behavior as well as alienate students.

Suspension rates are influenced by a variety of school factors. Schools with higher rates of suspension often have higher student–teacher ratios, negative teacher attitudes and low expectations of students, and a lower level of academic quality (Ostroff, 1992; Wu, Pink, Crain, & Moles, 1982). Also, in such schools, school personnel spend more time on discipline-related matters and pay significantly less attention to issues of school climate (Bickel & Qualls, 1980). As a result of such interactions, adult and student relationships are often further fractured in the process of these disciplinary actions, leading to a negative cycle.

In contrast, a protective school environment for these students would be one where there are effective schoolwide discipline practices that include a clear statement of rules and expectations, consistently communicated and applied consequences for rule-breaking behavior, concrete efforts to teach students appropriate behavior, and positive consequences available for positive behavior (Sugai & Horner, 1999). Characteristics of programs that contribute to the development and enhancement of positive behavior include the use of multiple strategies to reduce negative behavior and support positive behavior, early intervention, targeting students with specific needs, building a positive school climate, and the involvement of families, students, and community (Flay, Allred, & Ordway, 2001; Skiba & Peterson, 2000).

Support from the leadership of the school is critical in creating and maintaining the school-level characteristics in support of positive behavior (Safran & Oswald, 2003). Teachers need the support of school administrators through consistent disciplinary practice and technical assistance provided for classroom management in order to keep problematic students in their classrooms (Chaney, Osher, & Caesar, 2002). Administrators can also provide leadership through use of data analysis to examine disciplinary office referrals (number, type of offense, who refers, and who offends) that may then provide insight into patterns of problem behavior and situations that result in disciplinary referrals (Sugai, Sprague, Horner, & Walker, 2000).

An important component of a protective school environment is the constructive involvement of parents in the education of their children and in the determination of the overall school mission and function (Henderson & Berla, 1996). Communication and cooperation between families and schools is particularly difficult when there are barriers of race, ethnicity, language, and social class (Osher, 2000) and when families and schools do not perceive each other as having the same goals for their individual students (Bryk & Schneider, 2002). When behavior is an issue, it is particularly important to have open and positive communication between parents and school officials. This is particularly difficult because by definition, behavior problems at school require that information about the negative behavior of the child be communicated. When a youth's behavior is dangerous, parents, school officials, and community agencies need to work together to support the child and family in receiving appropriate assessment and targeted intervention.

The amendments to IDEA indicate that the individualized education plan (IEP) team is to focus on addressing behavioral problems of children with disabilities in order to enhance their success in the classroom. In particular, it has been dictated that (a) the IEP team should explore the need for strategies and support systems to address any behavior that may impede the learning of the child with the disability or the learning of his or her peers; and (b) states shall address the needs of in-service and preservice personnel (including professionals and paraprofessionals who provide special education, general education, related services, or early intervention services) as they relate to developing and implementing positive intervention strategies. Intervention plans emphasizing skills students need in order to behave in a more appropriate manner, or plans providing motivation to conform to required standards, are generally more effective than plans that simply serve to control behavior (Hinshaw, 1996, 2000). Such plans often include positive strategies, program or curricular modifications, and supplementary support to address problem behaviors. The implications of prior scholarship for practice are listed in Table 1.1.

CONCLUDING COMMENTS REGARDING YOUTH WITH ANTISOCIAL AND AGGRESSIVE BEHAVIORS

Youths engaged in antisocial and aggressive behaviors represent a heterogeneous group of individuals. Moreover, there are numerous factors that have been associated with developmental pathways toward manifesting antisocial and aggressive behaviors. The simple response to the question, "Who are they?" is that these are youth with considerable needs. The specific constellation of needs varies considerably; however, there are numerous factors that warrant careful consideration, including (a) individual factors such as problem solving, language, processing, self-regulation skills, and mental health; (b) family factors such as interaction, discipline, and communication patterns; (c) school factors such as support and discipline programs; (d) the interplay among the multiple contexts; and (e) the age of onset and history of

TABLE 1.1

Implications for Practice: Toward an Understanding of Youth Engaging in Antisocial
and Aggressive Behaviors

1. Youth engaged in antisocial and aggressive behaviors represent a diverse group, there is no single profile.
2. Many youth engaged in antisocial and aggressive behaviors face numerous challenges, for instance, at home, with peers, at school, and have many needs to be addressed.
3. Early antisocial and aggressive behaviors warrant serious attention to provide appropriate early interventions to address both behavioral and underlying emotional problems.
4. There is no single theory to explain the patterns of antisocial and aggressive behaviors among youth.
5. The transactional–ecological developmental perspective incorporates numerous considerations to enhance understanding of the complex interplay among factors influencing antisocial and aggressive trajectories.
6. Each of the theories recognizes the importance of early identification and intervention to address the needs of youth engaged in antisocial and aggressive behaviors.
7. Research focusing on the interface of antisocial developmental patterns and the schooling process has the potential support screening, prevention, and intervention efforts.
8. School policies, practices, and relationships have important influences on the well-being of youth engaged in antisocial and aggressive behaviors.
9. Intervention plans emphasizing skills students need in order to behave in a more appropriate manner, or plans providing motivation to conform to required standards, are generally most effective.
10. The school is a social setting in which to systematically screen for youth with such behavioral patterns.
11. Schools are generally among the safest places for youth and provide an important context to address their needs (e.g., academic, cognitive, social, emotional, and mental health).

behaviors of the youth. The primary objective of early identification of youth with antisocial and aggressive behaviors should be to explore and address their specific needs. Early prevention and intervention programs aimed at enhancing the social and cognitive competence of youths are necessary to promote the well-being and academic success of students. Such efforts will result in healthier communities, families, children, and schools. Schools are generally among the safest places for youth and provide an important context for support and services to address their needs.

REFERENCES

Achenbach, T. (1998). Diagnosis, assessment, taxonomy, and case formulations. In T. Ollendick & M. Hersen (Eds.), *Handbook of child psychopathology* (3rd ed., pp. 63–87). New York: Plenum Press.

American Psychiatric Association. (2000). *Diagnostic and statistical manual of mental disorders* (4th ed., text rev.). Washington, DC: Author.

Bickel, F., & Qualls, R. (1980). The impact of school climate on suspension rates in the Jefferson County Public Schools. *The Urban Review, 12*, 79–86.

Blankemeyer, M., Flannery, D. J., & Vazsonyi, A. T. (2002). The role of aggression and social competence in children's perceptions of the child-teacher relationship. *Psychology in the Schools, 39*, 293–304.

Boldizar, J. P., Perry, D. G., & Perry, L. C. (1989). Outcome values and aggression. *Child Development, 60*, 571–579.

Bryk, A. S., & Schneider, B. (2002). *Trust in schools: A core resource for improvement*. New York: Russell Sage Foundation.

Burke, J., Lahey, B. B., Loeber, R., & Rathouz, P. J. (2002). Adolescent outcomes of childhood conduct disorder among clinic-referred boys: Predictors of improvement. *Journal of Abnormal Child Psychology, 30*, 333–348.

Cairns, R. B., & Cairns, B. D. (1994). *Lifelines and risks: Pathways of youth of our time*. New York: Cambridge University Press.

Caspi, A., Elder, G. H., & Bem, D. (1988). Moving against the world: Life course patterns of explosive children. *Developmental Psychopathology, 24*, 824–831.

Caspi, A., & Moffitt, T. E. (1995). The continuity of maladaptive behavior: From description to explanation in the study of antisocial behavior. In D. Cicchetti & D. Cohen (Eds.), *Developmental psychopathology* (Vol. 2, pp. 472–511). New York: Wiley.

Catalino, R. F., & Hawkins, J. D. (1996). The social development model: A theory of antisocial behavior. In J. D. Hawkins (Ed.), *Delinquency and crime: Current theories* (pp. 149–197). New York: Cambridge University Press.

Chaney, D., Osher, T. W., & Caesar, M. (2002). Providing ongoing skill development and support for educators and parents of students with emotional and behavioral disabilities. *Journal of Child and Family Studies, 11*, 79–90.

Civil Rights Project. (2000). *Opportunities suspended: The devastating consequences of zero tolerance and school discipline policies.* Cambridge, MA: Harvard University Press.

Cernkovich, S. A., & Giordano, P. G. (1992). School bonding, race, and delinquency. *Criminology, 30*, 261–290.

Clarke, A. M., & Clarke, A. D. B. (1994). Individual differences as risk factors: Development, birth weight, and chronic illness. In W. B. Carey & S. C. McDevitt (Eds.), *Prevention and early intervention: Individual differences as risk factors for the mental health of children* (pp. 83–91). New York: Brunner/Mazel.

Coie, J. D., Dodge, K. A., & Kupersmidt, J. B. (Eds.). (1990). *Peer group behavior and social status.* New York: Cambridge University Press.

Conner, D. F. (2002). *Aggression & antisocial behavior in children and adolescents: Research and treatment.* New York: Guilford.

Costenbader, V. K., & Markson, S. (1994). School suspension: A survey of current policies and practices. *NASSP Bulletin, 78*, 103–107.

Crick, N. R., & Dodge, K. A. (1994). A review and reformulation of social information-processing mechanisms in children's social adjustment. *Psychological Bulletin, 115*, 74–101.

Crick, N. R., & Ladd, G. W. (1990). Children's perceptions of the outcomes of social strategies: Do the ends justify being mean? *Developmental Psychology, 26*(4), 612–620.

DeVoe, J. F., Peter, K., Kaufman, P., Miller, A., Noonan, M., Snyder, T. D., & Baum, K. (2004). *Indicators of school crime and safety: 2004* (NCES 2005–002/NCJ 205290). U.S. Departments of Education and Justice. Washington, DC: U.S. Government Printing Office. Available: http://nces.ed.gov or http://www.ojp.usdoj.gov/bjs.

Dodge, K. A., Price, J. M., Bachorowski, J., & Newman, J. P. (1990). Hostile attributional biases in severely aggressive adolescents. *Journal of Abnormal Psychology, 99*, 385–392.

Dodge, K. A., & Tomlin, A. M. (1987). Utilization of self-schemas as a mechanism of interpretational bias in aggressive children. *Social Cognition, 5*(3), 280–300.

Doll, B. (1996). Prevalence of psychiatric disorders in children and youth: An agenda for advocacy by school psychology. *School Psychology Quarterly, 11*, 20–47.

Doll, B., & Lyon, M. A. (1998). Risk and resilience: Implications for the delivery of educational and mental health services in schools. *School Psychology Review, 27*, 348–363.

Dubow, E. F., & Tisak, J. (1989). The relation between stressful life events and adjustment in elementary school children: The role of social support and social problem-solving skills. *Child Development, 60*, 1412–1423.

Elias, M. J., & Branden, L. R. (1988). Primary prevention of behavioral and emotional problems in school-aged populations. *School Psychology Review, 17*, 581–592.

Erdley, C. A., & Asher, S. R. (1998). Linkages between children's beliefs about the legitimacy of aggression and their behavior. *Social Development, 7*, 321–339.

Farmer, T. W., Farmer, E. M. Z., & Gut, D. M. (1999). Implications for social development research for school-based interventions for aggressive youth with EBD. *Journal of Emotional and Behavioral Disorders, 7*, 130–136.

Flay, B. R., Allred, C. G., & Ordway, N. (2001). Effects of the positive action program on achievement and discipline: Two matched-control comparisons. *Prevention Science, 2*(2), 71–89.

Forness, S. R., & Kavale, K. A. (2000). Emotional or behavioral disorders: Background and current status of the E/BD terminology and definition. *Behavior Disorders, 25*, 264–269.

Frick, P. J. (1998). *Conduct disorders and severe antisocial behavior.* New York: Plenum Press.

Garmezy, N., Masten, A. S., & Tellegen, A. (1984). The study of stress and competence in children: A building block for developmental psychopathology. *Child Development, 55*, 97–111.

Gold, M., & Osgood, D. (1992). *Personality and peer influence in juvenile corrections.* Westport, CT: Greenwood Press.

Gottfredson, G. D. (1989). *Reducing disorderly behavior in middle schools.* Baltimore, MD: Center for Research on Elementary and Middle Schools.

Grunbaum, J., Kann, L., Kinchen, S. A., Williams, B., Ross, J. G., Lowry, R., & Kolbe, L. (2002). Youth Risk Behavior Surveillance—United States, 2001: Surveillance summaries. *Morbidity and Mortality Weekly Report, 51*(SS04), 1–64.

Hawkins, J. D., & Lishner, D. (1987). Etiology and prevention of antisocial behavior in children and adolescents. In D. H. Crowell, I. M. E. Clifford, & R. O. Donnell (Eds.), *Childhood aggression and violence: Sources of influence, prevention, and control. Applied clinical psychology* (pp. 263–282). New York: Plenum Press.

Henderson, A. T., & Berla, N. (1996). *A new generation of evidence: The family is critical to student achievement.* Washington, DC: Center for Law and Education.

Hinshaw, S. P. (1996). Enhancing social competence: Integrating self-management strategies with behavioral procedures for children with ADHD. In E. D. Hibbs & P. S. Jensen (Eds.), *Child and adolescent disorders: Empirically based strategies for clinical practice* (pp. 285–310). Washington, DC: American Psychological Association.

Hinshaw, S. P. (2000). Attention-deficit/hyperactivity disorder: The search for viable treatments. In P. C. Kendall (Ed.), *Child and adolescent therapy: Cognitive-behavioral procedures* (2nd ed., pp. 88–128). New York: Guilford.

Jessor, R., Van Den Bos, J., Vanderryn, J., Costa, F. M., & Turbin, M. S. (1995). Protective factors in adolescent problem behavior: Moderator effects and developmental change. *Developmental Psychology, 31*, 923–933.

Kashani, J. H., Jones, M. R., Bumby, K. M., & Thomas, L. A. (1999). Youth violence: Psychosocial risk factors, treatment, prevention, and recommendations. *Journal of Emotional & Behavioral Disorders, 7*(4), 200–210.

Kazdin, A. E. (1995). Risk factors, onset, and course of dysfunction. In A. Kazdin (Ed.), *Conduct Disorders in childhood and adolescence* (2nd ed., pp. 50–74). Thousand Oaks, CA: Sage.

Kazdin, A. E. (1997). Practitioner review: Psychosocial treatments for conduct disorder in children. *Journal of Child Psychology and Psychiatry, 38*, 161–178.

Kratzer, L., & Hodgins, S. (1999). A typology of offenders: A test of Moffitt's theory among males and females from childhood to age 30. *Developmental Psychology, 29*, 19–30.

La Paro, K. M., Pianta, R. C., & Cox, M. (2000). Teachers' reported transition practices for children transitioning into kindergarten and first grade. *Exceptional Children, 67*, 7–20.

Laundra, K. H., Kiger, G., & Bahr, S. J. (2002). A social development model of serious delinquency: Examining gender differences. *The Journal of Primary Prevention, 22*, 389–407.

Leone, P. E., Mayer, M., Malmgren, K., & Meisel, S. M. (2000). School violence and disruption: Rhetoric, reality, and reasonable balance. *Focus on Exceptional Children, 33*(1), 1–20.

Levine, D. U., & Lezotte, L. W. (1990). *Unusually effective schools: A review and analysis of unusually effective schools.* Madison, WI: National Center for Effective Schools Research and Development.

Loeber, R. (1990). Developmental and risk factors of juvenile antisocial behavior and delinquency. *Clinical Psychology Review, 10*, 1–41.

Masten, A. S., Best, K. M., & Garmezy, N. (1990). Resilience and development: Contributions from the study of children who overcome adversity. *Development & Psychopathology, 2*, 425–444.

Mayer, M. J., & Leone, P. E. (1999). A structural analysis of school violence and disruption: Implications for creating safer schools. *Education & Treatment of Children, 22*, 333–356.

Mayes, S. D., Calhoun, S. L., & Crowell, E. W. (2000). Learning disabilities and ADHD: Overlapping spectrum disorders. *Journal of Learning Disabilities, 33*, 417–424.

Mazerolle, P., Brame, R., Paternoster, R., Piquero, A., & Dean, C. (2000). Onset age, persistence, and offending versatility: Comparisons across gender. *Criminology, 38*, 1143–1172.

McEvoy, A., & Welker, R. (2000). Antisocial behavior, academic failure, and school climate: A critical review. *Journal of Emotional & Behavioral Disorders, 8*, 130–140.

McFadden, A. C., Marsh, G. E., Price, B. J., & Hwang, Y. (1992). A study of race and gender bias in the punishment of handicapped school children. *Urban Review, 24*, 239–251.

Moffitt, T. E. (1990). The neuropsychology of juvenile delinquency: A critical review. In M. Tonry & N. Morris (Eds.), *Crime and justice: A review of research* (Vol. 12, pp. 99–169). Chicago: University of Chicago Press.

Moffitt, T. E. (1993a). Adolescence-limited and life-course persistent antisocial behavior: A developmental taxonomy. *Psychological Review, 100*, 674–701.

Moffitt, T. E. (1993b). The neuropsychology of conduct disorder. *Development & Psychopathology, 5,* 135–151.

Moffitt, T. E., & Caspi, A. (2001). Childhood predictors differentiate life-course persistent and adolescence-limited antisocial pathways among males and females. *Development and Psychopathology, 13*, 355–375.

Moffitt, T. E., Caspi, A., Rutter, M., & Silva, P. A. (2001). *Sex difference in antisocial behaviour: Conduct disorder, delinquency, and violence in the Dunedin Longitudinal Study.* New York: Cambridge University Press.

Morrison, G. M., Anthony, S., Storino, M., Cheng, J., Furlong, M. J., & Morrison, R. L. (2001). School expulsion as a process and an event: Before and after effects on children at-risk for school discipline. *New Directions for Youth Development: Theory, Practice, Research, 92*, 45–72.

Morrison, G. M., & D'Incau, B. (2000). Developmental and service trajectories of students with disabilities recommended for expulsion from school. *Exceptional Children, 66*, 257–272.

Osher, D. (Ed.). (2000). *Breaking the cultural disconnect: Working with families to improve outcomes for students placed at risk of school failure.* Miami: Florida International University.

Osher, D., Van Acker, R., Morrison, G., Gable, R., Dwyer, K., & Quinn, M. M. (2004). Warning signs of problems in schools: Ecological perspectives and effective practices for combating school aggression and violence. *Journal of School Violence, 3,* 13–37.

Ostroff, C. (1992). The relationship between satisfaction, attitudes and performance: An organizational level analysis. *Journal of Applied Psychology, 77*, 963–974.

Patterson, G. R., Capaldi, D., & Bank, L. (1991). An early starter model for predicting delinquency. In D. J. Pepler & K. H. Rubin (Eds.), *The development and treatment of childhood aggression* (pp. 139–168). Hillsdale, NJ: Lawrence Erlbaum Associates.

Patterson, G. R., & Yoerger, K. (2002). A developmental model for early- and late-onset delinquency. In J. B. Reid, G. R. Patterson, & J. Snyder (Eds.), *Antisocial behavior in children and adolescents: A development analysis and model for intervention* (pp. 147–172). Washington, DC: American Psychological Association.

Pianta, R. C. (2001). Implications of a developmental systems model for preventing and treating behavioral disturbances in children and adolescents. In J. N. Hughes, A. M. La Greca, & J. C. Conoley (Eds.), *Handbook of psychological services for children and adolescents* (pp. 23–41). New York: Oxford University Press.

Quiggle, N. L., Garber, J., Panak, W. F., & Dodge, K. A. (1992). Social information processing in aggressive and depressed children. *Child Development, 63,* 1305–1320.

Reinke, W. M., & Herman, K. C. (2002). Creating school environments that deter antisocial behaviors in youth. *Psychology in the Schools, 39,* 549–560.

Reynolds, D., Teddlie, C., Creemers, B., Scheerens, J., & Townsend, T. (2000). An introduction to school effectiveness research. In C. Teddlie & D. Reynolds (Eds.), *The international handbook of school effectiveness research* (pp. 3-25). London: Falmer Press.

Robins, L., & Ratcliff, K. (1979). Risk factors in the continuation of childhood antisocial behavior into adulthood. *International Journal of Mental Health, 7,* 96–116.

Rodkin, P., Farmer, T. W., Pearl, R., & Van Acker, R. (2000). Heterogeneity of popular boys: Antisocial and prosocial configurations. *Developmental Psychology, 36,* 14–24.

Roff, M., Sells, S. B., & Golden, M. M. (1972). *Social adjustment and personality development in children*: Minneapolis: University of Minnesota Press.

Rubin, K. H., Bream, L. A., & Rose-Krasnor, L. (1991). Social problem solving and aggression in childhood. In D. J. Pepler & K. H. Rubin (Eds.), *The development and treatment of childhood aggression* (pp. 219–248). Hillsdale, NJ: Lawrence Erlbaum Associates.

Rumberger, R. W. (1987). High school dropouts: A review of issues and evidence. *Review of Educational Research, 57,* 101–121.

Russo, M. F., & Beidel, D. C. (1994). Comorbidity of childhood anxiety and externalizing disorders: Prevalence, associated characteristics, and validation issues. *Clinical Psychology Review, 14,* 199–221.

Rutter, M. (Ed.). (1979). *Protective factors in children's responses to stress and disadvantage*. Hanover, NH: University Press of New England.

Safran, S., & Oswald, K. (2003). Positive behavior supports: Can schools reshape disciplinary practices? *Exceptional Children, 69,* 361–373.

Sameroff, A. J. (1995). General systems theories and developmental psychopathology. In D. Cicchetti & D. Cohen (Eds.), *Developmental psychopathology* (pp. 659–689). New York: Wiley.

Sameroff, A. J. (2000). Dialectical processes in developmental psychopathology. In A. J. Sameroff, M. Lewis, & S. M. Miller (Eds.), *Handbook of developmental psychopathology* (2nd ed., pp. 23–40). New York: Kluwer Academic/Plenum.

Scott, T., Nelson, C. M., & Liaupsin, C. J. (2001). Effective instruction: The forgotten component in preventing school violence. *Education and Treatment of Children, 24,* 309–322.

Shields, A. M., Cicchetti, D., & Ryan, R. M. (1994). The development of emotional and behavioral self-regulation and social competence among maltreated school-age children. *Development & Psychopathology, 6,* 57–75.

Skiba, R. J., & Peterson, R. (2000). School discipline at a crossroads: From zero tolerance to early response. *Exceptional Children, 66,* 335–346.

Skiba, R. J., Peterson, R. L., & Williams, T. (1997). Office referrals and suspension: Disciplinary intervention in middle schools. *Education and Treatment of Children, 20,* 295–315.

Slaby, R. G., & Guerra, N. G. (1988). Cognitive mediators of aggression in adolescent offenders: I. Assessment. *Developmental Psychology, 24,* 580–588.

Sroufe, L. A., & Rutter, M. (1984). The domain of developmental psychopathology. *Child Development, 55,* 17–29.

Stage, S. A. (1997). A preliminary investigation of the relationship between in-school suspension and the disruptive classroom behavior of student with behavior disorders. *Behavioral Disorders, 23,* 57–76.

Stanger, C., Achenbach, T., & Verhulst, F. C. (1997). Accelerated longitudinal comparisons of aggressive versus delinquent syndromes. *Development and Psychopathology, 9,* 43–58.

Sugai, G., & Horner, R. (1999). Discipline and behavioral support: Practices, pitfalls, and promises. *Effective School Practices, 17*(4), 10–22.

Sugai, G., Sprague, J. R., Horner, R. H., & Walker, H. M. (2000). Preventing school violence: The use of office discipline referrals to assess and monitor school-wide discipline interventions. *Journal of Emotional and Behavioral Disorders, 8,* 94–101.

Tannock, R., & Schachar R. (1996). Executive dysfunction as an underlying mechanism of behavior and language problems in attention deficit hyperactivity disorder. In J. H. Beitchman, N. Cohen, M. M. Konstantareas, & R. Tannock (Eds.), *Language, learning, and behavior disorders: Developmental, biological, and clinical perspectives* (pp. 128–155). New York: Cambridge University Press.

Tobin, T., Sugai, G., & Colvin, G. (1996). Patterns in middle school discipline records. *Journal of Emotional and Behavioral Disorders, 4*, 82–94.

Tolan, P. (2001). Youth violence and its prevention in the United States: An overview of current knowledge. *Injury Control and Safety Promotion, 8*(1), 1–12.

Tubman, J. G., & Windle, M. (1995). Continuity of difficult temperament in adolescence: Relations with depression, life events, family support, and substance use across a one-year period. *Journal of Youth and Adolescence, 24*, 133–153.

Walker, H. M., Ramsey, E., & Gresham, F. (2004). *Antisocial behavior in school: Evidence-based practices* (2nd ed.). Pacific Grove, CA: Brooks/Cole.

Webster-Stratton, C. (1990). Long-term follow-up of families with young conduct problem children: From preschool to grade school. *Journal of Clinical Child Psychology, 19*, 144–149.

Werner, E., & Smith, R. S. (1982). *Vulnerable but invincible: A longitudinal study of resilient children and youth*. New York: McGraw-Hill.

White, J. L., Moffitt, T. E., Earls, F., Robins, L., & Silva, P. A. (1990). How early can we tell? Predictors of childhood conduct disorder and adolescent delinquency. *Criminology, 28*, 507–533.

Wu, S. C., Pink, W. T., Crain, R. L., & Moles, O. (1982). Student suspension: A critical reappraisal. *The Urban Review, 14*, 245–303.

2

Support in the Lives of Aggressive Students, Their Victims, and Their Peers

Michelle Kilpatrick Demaray
Christine Kerres Malecki
Lauren K. DeLong
Northern Illinois University

Violence in American schools has been identified as a concern to educators across the country. For example, one large-scale study in the United States has identified that at least 30% of students in Grades 6–10 are involved in bullying either as a bully, a victim, or both (Nansel et al., 2001) in their school. Bullying behavior is a risk factor for even more serious school violence (Hazler & Carney, 2000; Nansel, Overpeck, Haynie, Ruan, & Scheidt, 2003). Because of these problems, it has been suggested that "schools simply cannot wait for violence to occur ... [they] must be prepared to respond appropriately when it does occur and take efforts to prevent it whenever possible" (Furlong, Kingery, & Bates, 2001, p. 91). Thus, researchers have been moving forward to study this phenomenon and identify the contextual factors surrounding bullying and school violence (Espelage & Swearer, 2004). One such contextual factor is social support. For example, do students who perpetrate aggression or violence on others have adequate support in their lives? Do victims receive support from adults or from peers before or after a bullying or school violence incident? What kind of support do bystanders provide or not provide? Are teachers and staff provided adequate support in the schools with which to deal with school violence? Answering these questions may help us further understand a salient factor surrounding school violence.

SOCIAL SUPPORT

When asked to define social support, most people typically think of the type of support they receive from friends and family that involves caring. They may say it is "when someone cares about you or when someone is there for you when you need to talk." However, the definition of social support is much broader than that. In fact, Tardy (1985) defined a broad conceptual model that includes five aspects of social support. First, *direction* describes whether the support is being given or received. Second, *disposition* describes whether the supportive behaviors are just available or if they are actually being enacted or used. *Description/evaluation* refers to whether a person describes the support they receive or evaluates that support. Fourth,

Tardy describes one's *network* or the source(s) of an individual's support network (parents, teachers, friends, etc.). Finally, Tardy describes the *content* or type of support, which includes emotional, instrumental, informational, and/or appraisal support. As mentioned previously, most people think only of the emotional support they receive that refers to caring support. However, the other types of support are also important. Instrumental support refers to spending time with someone or providing necessary resources. For example, a parent spending time with a child to work on math homework or to practice soccer is instrumental support. Providing the necessary resources, such as a calculator for a math class or a soccer ball to practice soccer, is also instrumental support. Informational support involves providing someone with valuable information or advice. Finally, people we care about provide appraisal support when they give feedback or evaluation that is beneficial. For perpetrators and/or their victims, various types of social support from different sources may play a role in the aggressive dynamic or in the aftermath of violent school behavior.

Social support may play a role in school violence in several ways. Two theoretical models generally describe how social support may function. First, the main effect model (Cohen, Gottlieb, & Underwood, 2000) suggests that positive social support is beneficial for all people. This theory posits that if individuals have adequate levels of social support, they will function more effectively and be healthier in general. The stress-buffering theory (Cohen et al., 2000) suggests that when individuals are under stress, social support plays a protective role resulting in more positive outcomes than if they did not have adequate social support. For victims of school violence, the stress-buffering model of support seems most salient. Students who are victims of violence or bullying may be under more stress and social support may buffer them from more negative outcomes. For perpetrators or potential perpetrators, the main effect model may make more sense. That is, if students do not have adequate social support in their lives, and thus do not enjoy the positive benefits, one negative outcome may be that they lash out at others.

THE IMPORTANCE OF RESEARCH ON SOCIAL SUPPORT IN RELATION TO SCHOOL VIOLENCE

Many researchers believe that social support may be a salient factor in preventing school violence. For instance, one focus of the National School Safety Center (NSSC) in recent years has been to expand the role of student support services in schools (Stephens, 2002). Creating supportive student environments includes establishing a sense of student ownership and pride in the school and offering services for troubled youth. The NSSC strategies for increasing school safety not only include providing social support for students, but also for teachers, parents, and community members (Stephens, 2002). The creation and implementation of these programs rely on an understanding of various social support systems (i.e., family, peer group, and school) that may affect students' behavior (Espelage & Swearer, 2003). For example, Furlong, Pavelski, and Saxton (2002) suggested that the examination of supportive connections of students to their school is a useful way to identify the level of violence-prevention programs needed. Therefore, an understanding of the relation between social support and school violence is one that must be understood if efforts to decrease violence are to be successful.

Despite the fact that policies meant to address violent behavior in schools often focus on creating meaningful relationships between students and supportive peers and adults (Austin, 2003), the research on social support and violent or aggressive behaviors remains somewhat scarce. Although some previous investigations have included students' significant others as a factor in the lives of victims (Furlong, Chung, Bates, & Morrison, 1995; Morrison, Furlong, & Smith, 1994), only a handful have investigated social support as a primary construct related to aggressive and violent behaviors in schools (Cowie & Olafsson, 2000; Demaray & Malecki, 2003; Malecki & Demaray, 2003; Naylor & Cowie, 1999; Rigby, 2000). The use of socially supportive behaviors is often suggested as a method to decrease and prevent violence (Reinke & Herman, 2002; Scott, Nelson, & Liaupsin, 2001; Stephens, 1994), yet these suggestions are based on assumptions rather than scientific data. Thus, numerous questions remain to be answered.

BULLYING AND SCHOOL VIOLENCE

Although the term *school violence* may bring to mind extreme behaviors, such as school shootings, violence in schools encompasses a much wider range of behaviors including bullying, teasing, harassment, and assault (Furlong et al., 2002). These low-level forms of violence have been largely overlooked in previous decades of research, despite their potential to greatly influence the school environment (Dupper & Meyer-Adams, 2002). This oversight is troubling given that seemingly benign behaviors, like teasing or bullying, can lead to more serious, violent behaviors (Spivak & Prothrow-Stith, 2001). In order to effectively intervene and prevent violence, all behaviors must be viewed on a continuum, with actions like bullying and teasing at the lower end and behaviors such as murder and suicide at the upper end (Hazler & Carney, 2000). Given the pervasive and highly underrated problem of bullying in the United States (Stephens, 2002), a review of the literature on social support and school violence without research on bullying would be incomplete.

BENEFITS OF SOCIAL SUPPORT

Previous research has established that the presence of social support in one's life is related to emotional and physical health benefits (DuBois, Bull, Sherman, & Roberts, 1998; Meehan, Durlak, & Bryant, 1993; Shumaker & Brownell, 1984; Vandervoort, 1999). Conversely, the lack of support is associated with negative outcomes including stress (Camp, Holman, & Ridgway, 1993; Dumont, & Provost, 1999; Israel, Farquhar, Schulz, James, & Parker, 2002), depression (Hoard & Anderson, 2004; Reddy, Rhodes, & Mulhall, 2003; Windle, 1992), and substance use (Frauenglass, Routh, Pantin, & Mason, 1997; Windle & Davies, 1999). Furthermore, low support has been related significantly to various violent and delinquent behaviors in youth (DuBois, Felner, Meares, & Krier, 1994; Windle, 1992).

Given the abundance of evidence indicating the positive outcomes associated with social support, it is reasonable to expect that these benefits would extend to victims and perpetrators of violent and aggressive behaviors in the schools. Crime patterns in the United States appear to support this assumption. Statistics indicate that juvenile crime and delinquent behavior are related to a lack of adult presence in the lives of children and adolescents (Stephens, 2002), suggesting that increasing adult support could decrease such behaviors. Furthermore, students report that their feelings of safety are related to the number of adult confidants they have in their lives (Morrison et al., 1994). Thus, the existing research on social support can provide valuable guidance in how we respond and prevent violence and aggressive behaviors in schools.

Victims' Levels of Support

When attempting to understand why certain students are victimized, it is helpful to identify risk factors that may make them vulnerable to attack. One risk factor appears to be the lack of support, as previous research indicates that victims typically have poor support from adults and peers in their lives (Duncan, 2004; Hanish, Kochenderfer-Ladd, Fabes, Martin, Denning, 2004; Hazler & Carney, 2000). Furlong et al. (1995) compared students in Grades 5–12 who were victims of multiple incidents of school violence with those who were not victimized. Victims sought teacher and peer support significantly less than nonvictimized students. Additionally, victims reported feeling less connected to their schools than nonvictims. Similarly, using a sample of more than 18,000 parents and students, Schreck, Miller, and Gibson (2003) found that students who felt alienated from school were more likely to be victims of violent and nonviolent crimes. Victims of school bullying exhibit similar patterns of low support as victims of violence. For instance, in a sample of 12- to 16-year-old students, status as a victim of peer bullying was related to low levels of support from best friends and classmates. For females, victimization was also related to low teacher support (Rigby, 2000). In their investigation of bullying and social support in sixth- through eighth-grade students, Demaray and Malecki (2003) found that students classified as victims had low support from their classmates, whereas students who exhibited characteristics of both bullies and victims (i.e., bully/victims) also had low support from the people in their lives. Bully/victims reported low support from their parents, classmates, and people in their schools, suggesting that students who are both the perpetrators and victims of such behaviors are at the greatest risk for negative outcomes (Demaray & Malecki, 2003). The overlap of the bully and victim categories and the great risk for students who are both bullies and victims presents concerns that some victims may become violent in an attempt to protect themselves. Kingery, Pruitt, and Heuberger (1996) reported that adolescents who brought guns to school were much more likely than non gun-carriers to have been the victim of violent behavior in the previous year. These bully/victims appear to be especially vulnerable to negative outcomes, as they report lower levels of support than nonaggressive victims (Brockenbrough, Cornell, & Loper, 2002).

Perpetrators' Levels of Support

It is not only students who are at the receiving end of violent and bully behaviors who present a concern for schools; perpetrators of these behaviors have similarly low levels of support (Boulton & Smith, 1994; Duncan, 2004; Hanish et al., 2004). This could indicate that violent and aggressive students may be disengaged from the very individuals who can help decrease their problem behaviors. In an investigation of the determinants of violent behavior in inner-city youth, Powell (1997) found that support from adults outside the family was able to protect against student involvement in violent behavior. Behaviors that could potentially lead to violent incidents, such as weapon carrying, also appear to be related to low support. Malecki and Demaray (2003) investigated the social support of early adolescents who self-reported bringing a weapon to school and found that low support from parents, teachers, and peers was predictive of weapon carrying. Similarly, McNabb, Farley, Powell, Rolka, and Horan (1996) reported that adolescent gun carrying was correlated with the lack of an employed male role model in the home. Other low-level forms of aggressive behavior, such as bullying, have been linked to low support. Demaray and Malecki (2003) found that students who were classified as bullies had low amounts of support from parents, classmates, and people in their schools.

The Protective Effects of Social Support After Victimization

The stress-buffering model of social support, which states that social support has a beneficial effect on well-being for individuals under stress (Cohen & Wills, 1985), suggests that the provision of support may be a valuable tool in helping students cope with and recover from incidents of school violence and bullying. Accordingly, previous research indicates that social support resources have been successful in protecting individuals against the harmful consequences of traumatic experiences (McNally, Bryant, & Ehlers, 2003; Regehr, Hill, & Glancy, 2000). Rigby (2000) found that students who were frequent victims of school bullying and had low social support had the greatest risk of poor mental health, suggesting that an increase in social support would protect victims' future well-being. Peer support programs for victimized students based on this assumption have not yet been proven responsible for decreasing overall levels of school bullying (Cowie & Olafsson, 2000; Naylor & Cowie, 1999). However, preliminary results suggest that these programs prompt more victims to seek help and victims feel a greater strength to overcome their victimization than before participation in the program (Naylor & Cowie, 1999).

Social Support Benefits Everyone in the School System

Peer support systems for students are not the only type of school-based intervention to include a social support component. A myriad of school prevention and intervention programs are based on the idea that support for all members of the school community improves student outcomes. Osher, Sandler, and Nelson (2002) suggested schools that are most effective at preventing behavior problems and violence are those that provide innovative social support for teachers, students, and staff. School climates that reflect a sense of community and encourage tight relationships among students and teachers are safer and more welcoming (Dupper & Meyer-Adams, 2002; Reinke & Herman, 2002). Academic support also appears to be important for keeping students from falling into cycles that end in delinquent and violent behavior (Scott et al., 2001). Consequently, safe schools not only provide social support for the emotional needs of students, but for their academic needs as well.

Social Support From Negative Sources and Peer Groups

One factor that sometimes is overlooked when examining the relationship between social support and violent or aggressive behaviors is the impact of the specific source of social support being received. Just as social support from positive sources such as teachers, parents, and school staff, can keep students from becoming involved in violent behaviors (McNabb et al., 1996; Schreck et al., 2003) and protect against the negative impact of victimization (Rigby, 2000), support from negative sources can have a harmful impact on students' lives. The influence of delinquent peers, siblings, or family members has been related to a variety of aggressive and violent behaviors. In fact, it appears that although peers reject some aggressive children, others are popular and may gain support for engaging in aggressive acts from classmates (Estell, Cairns, Farmer, & Cairns, 2002). Powell (1997) reported that peer social support and family member involvement in gangs were risk factors for inner-city students' involvement in violent behavior. Similarly, social support may have the undesired effect of perpetuating low-level aggressive behavior. Recently, Sutton and Smith (1999) identified a role in the bullying process called *participant*. Participants in the bullying process are those students who provide social support for the bullies and may perpetuate such behavior. Therefore, it is important to be aware of the positive and potentially negative impact of various types of social support on school violence and aggressive behavior.

IMPLICATIONS OF SOCIAL SUPPORT RESEARCH FOR SCHOOL VIOLENCE VICTIMIZATION

Based on the current research, many potential implications for practice can be inferred. First, the research indicates that social support from many sources in a student's life may influence or be related to the occurrence of violence in schools. Parents, teachers, peers, and students' school environments all seem to play a role in the complex set of factors that surround school violence. For example, teachers could be trained to create and maintain socially supportive classrooms and classmates could be trained how to intervene in a socially supportive manner if they witness violence or bullying. Additionally, although the research is not as specific when discussing how varying types of support may be related to school violence in students' lives, this is another area where potential interventions may be inferred. For example, parents could be provided with *informational* support to help them learn how to recognize signs that their children may be experiencing violence or may be perpetrating violence at school. Peer support groups could provide *emotional* support for victimized students. More potential implications for the inclusion of social support in schools to reduce school violence are listed in Table 2.1. These ideas are starting points to think about applying the knowledge that has been learned about social support for victims and perpetrators of violence in the schools. It is important to note that these ideas are hypothesized based on current research findings, however, further research is needed.

TABLE 2.1
Implications for Practice: Social Support and School Violence

Source of Support	Implications for Practice
Parents	Provide parents with informational support about recognizing signs that their children are either perpetrators or victims of violence in the schools.
	Provide parents with supportive contacts if they suspect their child is either a perpetrator or victim of school violence. These contacts should be people in the school whom they can contact for emotional and informational support.
	Have trained staff at the school conduct support groups for parents whose children have been involved in school violence to obtain emotional support from other parents.
	Encourage parents to take an active, supportive role in the lives of their children.
Teachers	Provide teachers with informational support about recognizing signs that students are either perpetrators or victims of violence in the schools.
	Train teachers how to provide support to students who are bullies or victims of bullying.
	Train teachers to respond in supportive ways to an observance of school violence or bullying.
	Train teachers how to, in general, encourage and create socially supportive classrooms.
Schools	Assess the perceptions of students with regard to level of social support in schools or school climate.
	Train entire school staff in ways to be socially supportive to students, especially victims of bullying or school violence.
	Create a sense of connectedness within the school.
	Have a system in place so that victims of violence get services from supportive staff in the school to increase the connectedness victims of violence feel to the school.
Classmates/friends	Train students how to intervene in a socially supportive manner when they witness violence or bullying acts.
	Train students to communicate their *lack* of support for violent or aggressive behavior in the school.
	Have trained staff at the school conduct support groups with students who have been victims of violence to gain emotional support from other students.

Although researchers are beginning to understand perceptions of social support among victims and perpetrators of school violence, the next step is to investigate the role social support may play in intervening or preventing school violence. The research clearly documenting the effectiveness of social support as an intervention and prevention tool is lacking. The focus of future research in this area needs to be on investigating specific types of social support from various sources as an intervention or prevention method for reducing school violence or aiding victims of school violence.

CONCLUSIONS

Several questions were posed early in this chapter. Although we do not have definitive answers to these questions, the research provides initial understanding of some of these factors.

1. *Do students who perpetrate aggression or violence on others have adequate support in their lives?* Researchers have begun to recognize that not only victims, but also perpetrators of violent and aggressive behaviors in the schools, have lower levels of support (Boulton & Smith, 1994; Demaray & Malecki, 2003; Duncan, 2004; Hanish et al., 2004; Malecki & Demaray, 2003; McNabb et al., 1996) and should not be forgotten when discussing a needed increase in social support.
2. *Do victims receive support from adults or from peers before or after a bullying or school violence incident?* Researchers are beginning to understand that one risk factor for victims of violence appears to be the lack of support from people in one's life including parents, teachers, peers, and the school (Demaray & Malecki, 2003; Duncan, 2004; Furlong et al., 1995; Hanish et al., 2004; Hazler & Carney, 2000; Schreck et al., 2003). Little is known about socially supportive responses to victims.
3. *What kind of support do bystanders provide or not provide?* The research is not clear in this area, but does suggest that bystanders often do not provide support or may even provide unintended negative support (Sutton & Smith, 1999).
4. *Are teachers and staff provided adequate support in the schools with which to deal with school violence?* Overall, social support appears to have a beneficial effect on all individuals in the school community, not just students (Dupper & Meyer-Adams, 2002; Osher et al., 2002), thus a broad approach to social support interventions in the schools would be beneficial.

Given current research, it seems logical to recommend implementing social support resources as a potential intervention for victims of school violence and for the prevention of violent behaviors in the schools (Reinke & Herman, 2002; Scott et al., 2001; Stephens, 1994). Further research will help to guide this work more directly and can help lead educators to specific interventions.

REFERENCES

Austin, V. L. (2003). Fear and loathing in the classroom: A candid look at school violence and the policies and practices that address it. *Journal of Disability Policy Studies, 14,* 17–22.

Boulton, M. J., & Smith, P. K. (1994). Bully/victim problems in middle-school children: Stability, self-perceived competence, peer perceptions and peer acceptance. *British Journal of Developmental Psychology, 12,* 315–329.

Brockenbrough, K. K., Cornell, D. G., & Loper, A. B. (2002). Aggressive attitudes among victims of violence at school. *Education and Treatment of Children, 25,* 273–287.

Camp, B. W., Holman, S., & Ridgway, E. (1993). The relationship between social support and stress in adolescent mothers. *Journal of Developmental and Behavioral Pediatrics, 14,* 369–374.

Cohen, S., Gottlieb, B. H., & Underwood, L. G. (2000). Social relationships and health. In S. Cohen, L. G. Underwood, & B. H. Gottlieb (Eds.), *Social support measurement and intervention: A guide for health and social scientists* (pp. 3–25). New York: Oxford University Press.

Cohen, S., & Wills, T. A. (1985). Stress, social support, and the buffering hypothesis. *Psychological Bulletin, 98,* 310–357.

Cowie, H., & Olafsson, R. (2000). The role of peer support in helping the victims of bullying in a school with high levels of aggression. *School Psychology International, 21,* 79–95.

Demaray, M. K., & Malecki, C. K. (2003). Perceptions of the frequency and importance of social support by students classified as victims, bullies, and bully/victims in an urban middle school. *School Psychology Review, 32,* 471–489.

DuBois, D. L., Bull, C. A., Sherman, M. D., & Roberts, M. (1998). Self-esteem and adjustment in early adolescence: A social-contextual perspective. *Journal of Youth and Adolescence, 27,* 557–583.

DuBois, D. L., Felner, R. D., Meares, H., & Krier, M. (1994). Prospective investigation of the effects of socioeconomic disadvantage, life stress, and social support on early adolescent adjustment. *Journal of Abnormal Psychology, 103,* 511–522.

Dumont, M., & Provost, M. A. (1999). Resilience in adolescents: Protective role of social support, coping strategies, self-esteem, and social activities on experience of stress and depression. *Journal of Youth and Adolescence, 28,* 343–363.

Duncan, R. D. (2004). The impact of family relationships on school bullies and victims. In D. L. Espelage & S. M. Swearer (Eds.), *Bullying in American schools: A social-ecological perspective on prevention and intervention* (pp. 227–244). Mahwah, NJ: Lawrence Erlbaum Associates.

Dupper, D. R., & Meyer-Adams, N. (2002). Low-level violence: A neglected aspect of school culture. *Urban Education, 37,* 350–364.

Espelage, D. L., & Swearer, S. M. (2003). Research on school bullying and victimization: What have we learned and where do we go from here? *School Psychology Review, 32,* 365–383.

Espelage, D. L., & Swearer, S. M. (Eds.). (2004). *Bullying in American schools: A social-ecological perspective on prevention and intervention.* Mahwah, NJ: Lawrence Erlbaum Associates.

Estell, D. B., Cairns, R. B., Farmer, T. W., & Cairns, B. D. (2002). Aggression and inner-city early elementary classrooms: Individual and peer-group configurations. *Merrill-Palmer Quarterly, 48,* 52–76.

Frauenglass, S., Routh, D. K., Pantin, H. M., & Mason, C. A. (1997). Family support decreases influence of deviant peers on Hispanic adolescents' substance use. *Journal of Clinical Child Psychology, 26,* 15–23.

Furlong, M. J., Chung, A., Bates, M., & Morrison, R. L. (1995). Who are the victims of school violence? A comparison of student non-victims and multi-victims. *Education and Treatment of Children, 18,* 282–298.

Furlong, M. J., Kingery, P. M., & Bates, M. P. (2001). Introduction to the special issue on the appraisal and prediction of school violence. *Psychology in the Schools, 38,* 89–91.

Furlong, M. J., Pavelski, R., & Saxton, J. (2002). The prevention of school violence. In S. E. Brock, P. J. Lazarus, & S. R. Jimerson (Eds.), *Best practices in school crisis prevention and intervention* (pp. 131–149). Bethesda, MD: National Association of School Psychologists.

Hanish, L. D., Kochenderfer-Ladd, B., Fabes, R. A., Martin, C. L., & Denning, D. (2004). Bullying among young children: The influence of peers and teachers. In D. L. Espelage & S. M. Swearer (Eds.), *Bullying in American schools: A social-ecological perspective on prevention and intervention* (pp. 141–159). Mahwah, NJ: Lawrence Erlbaum Associates.

Hazler, R. J., & Carney, J. V. (2000). When victims turn aggressors: Factors in the development of deadly school violence. *Professional School Counseling, 4,* 105–112.

Hoard, L. R., & Anderson, E. A. (2004). Factors related to depression in rural and urban noncustodial, low-income fathers. *Journal of Community Psychology, 32,* 103–119.

Israel, B., Farquhar, S. A., Schulz, A. J., James, S. A., & Parker, E. A. (2002). The relationship between social support, stress, and health among women on Detroit's east side. *Health Education and Behavior, 29,* 342–360.

Kingery, P. M., Pruitt, B. E., & Heuberger, G. (1996). A profile of rural Texas adolescents who carry handguns. *Journal of School Health, 66,* 18–22.

Malecki, C. K., & Demaray, M. K. (2003). Carrying a weapon to school and perceptions of social support in an urban middle school. *Journal of Emotional and Behavioral Disorders, 11,* 169–178.

McNabb, S. J. N., Farley, T. A., Powell, K. E., Rolka, H. R., & Horan, J. M. (1996). Correlates of gun-carrying among adolescents in south Louisiana. *American Journal of Preventive Medicine, 12,* 96–102.

McNally, R. J., Bryant, R. A., & Ehlers, A. (2003). Does early psychological intervention promote recovery from posttraumatic stress? *Psychological Science in the Public Interest, 4,* 45–79.

Meehan, M. P., Durlak, J. A., & Bryant, F. B. (1993). The relationship of social support to perceived control and subjective mental health in adolescents. *Journal of Community Psychology, 21,* 49–55.

Morrison, G. M., Furlong, M. J., & Smith, G. (1994). Factors associated with the experience of school violence among general education, leadership class, opportunity class, and special day class pupils. *Education and Treatment of Children, 17,* 356–369.

Nansel, T. R., Overpeck, M. D., Haynie, D. L., Ruan, J., & Scheidt, P. C. (2003). Relationships between bullying and violence among US youth. *Archives of Pediatrics and Adolescent Medicine, 157,* 348–353.

Nansel, T. R., Overpeck, M. P., Ramani, S., Ruan, W. J., Simons-Morton, B. & Scheidt, P. (2001). Bullying behaviors among US youth: Prevalence and association with psychosocial adjustment. *Journal of the American Medical Association, 285,* 2094–2100.

Naylor, P., & Cowie, H. (1999). The effectiveness of peer support systems in challenging school bullying: The perspectives and experiences of teachers and pupils. *Journal of Adolescence, 22,* 467–479.

Osher, D. M., Sandler, S., & Nelson, C. L. (2002). The best approach to school safety is to fix schools and support children and staff. In R. J. Skiba & G. G. Noam (Eds.), *New directions for youth development, special issue on zero tolerance: Can suspension and expulsion keep school safe?* (pp. 127–153). San Francisco, CA: Jossey-Bass.

Powell, K. B. (1997). Correlates of violent and nonviolent behavior among vulnerable inner-city youths. *Family and Community Health, 20,* 38–47.

Reddy, R., Rhodes, J. E., & Mulhall, P. (2003). The influence of teacher support on student adjustment in the middle school years: A latent growth curve study. *Development and Psychopathology, 15,* 119–138.

Regehr, C., Hill, J., & Glancy, G. D. (2000). Individual predictors of traumatic reactions in firefighters. *Journal of Nervous and Mental Disease, 188,* 333–339.

Reinke, W. M., & Herman, K. C. (2002). Creating school environments that deter antisocial behaviors in youth. *Psychology in the Schools, 39,* 549–559.

Rigby, K. (2000). Effects of peer victimization in schools and perceived social support on adolescent well-being. *Journal of Adolescence, 23,* 57–68.

Schreck, C. J., Miller, J. M., & Gibson, C. L. (2003). Trouble in the school yard: A study of the risk factors of victimization at school. *Crime and Delinquency, 49,* 460–484.

Scott, T. M., Nelson, C. M., & Liaupsin, C. J. (2001). Effective instruction: The forgotten component in preventing school violence. *Education and Treatment of Children, 24,* 309–322.

Shumaker, S. A., & Brownell, A. (1984). Toward a theory of social support: Closing conceptual gaps. *Journal of Social Issues, 40,* 11–36.

Spivak, H., & Prothrow-Stith, D. (2001). The need to address bullying: An important component of violence prevention. *Journal of the American Medical Association*, 285, 2131–2132.

Stephens, R. D. (1994). Planning for safer and better schools: School violence prevention and intervention strategies. *School Psychology Review, 23,* 204–216.

Stephens, R. D. (2002). Promoting school safety. In S. E. Brock, P. J. Lazarus, & S. R. Jimerson (Eds.), *Best practices in school crisis prevention and intervention* (pp. 47–65). Bethesda, MD: National Association of School Psychologists.

Sutton, J., & Smith, P. K. (1999). Bullying as a group process: An adaptation of the participant role approach. *Aggressive Behavior, 25,* 97–111.

Tardy, C. H. (1985). Social support measurement. *American Journal of Community Psychology, 13,* 187–202.

Vandervoort, D. (1999). Quality of social support in mental and physical health. *Current Psychology, 18,* 205–222.

Windle, M. (1992). Temperament and social support in adolescence: Interrelations with depressive symptoms and delinquent behaviors. *Journal of Youth and Adolescence, 21,* 1–21.

Windle, M., & Davies, P. T. (1999). Depression and heavy alcohol use among adolescents: Concurrent and prospective relations. *Development and Psychopathology, 11,* 823–844.

3

Legal Knowledge Related to School Violence and School Safety

Kirk A. Bailey
Smith, Dawson & Andrews

As they have been throughout history, schools are the crucible of society where the causes, effects, and experiments of human interaction first manifest. Whether the first Socratic classroom or the horror of Columbine High School, schools see the cutting edge of each new societal trend, whether for good or ill. No wonder then that the violence that so seems to pervade modern American society would express itself vividly in America's educational institutions. Schools must address this violence and associated school safety concerns in the context of the larger legal institutions, procedures, and knowledge that underpin American society. In the course of these activities, teachers, school leaders, and counselors will face important legal questions that impact many lives. These questions center on issues involving privacy and school records, discipline and due process (including zero-tolerance polices), search and seizure, dress codes, security measures and school resource officers, and general liability. When appropriate measures are taken in all these areas, the risk of violence at school or the effects of its aftermath will be minimized. The law is a powerful tool for school officials, allowing them to proactively develop clear and consistent polices that help teachers and parents manage student expectations and promote a stable school setting, leading to a safe educational environment.

At the same time, the philosophical perspective of any youth violence prevention effort is important to the results that are anticipated. In other words, even while promoting school safety and meeting legal requirements, schools, parents, teachers, and communities will reap what they sow. The important foundational principle to bear in mind is that policies set the tone of school administration and shape the culture of each classroom, school, and school district. Accordingly, although it is important to focus on the legal implications and issues of school safety efforts, it must be balanced by a strong sense of fairness and concern for the dignity and integrity of every member of the school community. Youth experiences with law enforcement and the justice system subtly influence their perceptions of the relationships between individuals and society and likely affect their compliance with the law, and the progress of their learning.[1] Allowing youth to learn that true justice is less about the effort to exact punishment and retribution but about working to repair a safe and secure vision for their school in order to create healing, restoration, and peace; will build their sense of values, personal integrity, and accountability to the larger community.

GENERAL PRINCIPLES OF SCHOOL SAFETY EFFORTS

There are numerous important points to consider when addressing the legal issues related to school safety and youth violence. School officials need to consider the process for developing such school safety policies, implement and maintain that process, ensure consistency with state law and local regulations, incorporate best practices whenever possible, and ensure the reasonableness and practicality of the policies. It has been a long-standing belief that the government has a compelling interest in ensuring a strong system of education; necessarily implying it is free of violence. In *Brown v. Board of Education* (1954)[2], the Supreme Court observed:

> Education is perhaps the most important function of state and local governments. . . . It is a principal instrument in awakening the child to cultural values, in preparing him for later professional training, and in helping him to adjust normally to his environment. . . . It is doubtful that any child may reasonably be expected to succeed in life if he is denied the opportunity of an education.

For this reason, school officials have a strong obligation, both moral and legal, to take action in dealing with undisciplined youths, who may potentially threaten the welfare and safety of the other children in attendance.

Reasonableness

Generally, school districts will be required to adopt policies that are reasonably designed to address whatever problem they face. A school's actions will be valid provided they rest on some rational basis, meaning that it is reasonably related to achieving a legitimate state purpose.[3] It is not necessary for the state to utilize the best possible methods to achieve its goals; rather all that is required is that the methods actually used be reasonable.[4] The reasonableness standard requires that school officials balance the need to make the school environment safe and maintain order and control, with student's interest in privacy, access to education, and autonomy. Schools should then design policies that match the problem in scope. In other words, a school safety policy must bear some rational relationship to the problem it attempts to solve.

A key example is the use of metal detectors, which are clearly a rational and reasonable method of locating weapons in a school. However, cameras placed in boys and girls locker rooms to monitor potential drug sales may not be reasonable when students' rightly expect some degree of privacy and the problem might be addressed just as easily by the presence of coaches, monitors, or other school officials. In addition, it is reasonable for a school to share disciplinary records with local police, but it is probably not reasonable to share a student's school records showing poor attendance, unsatisfactory academic performance, and low-income levels as part of a profile of potentially antisocial students. Moreover, although it is reasonable to expel a student for bringing a handgun to school, it is not reasonable to expel that same student for writing a story about bringing a handgun to school for a classroom creative writing project. Fortunately, the reasonableness standard offers a great deal of latitude for school policymakers. Most conceivable school safety efforts will be rationally related to preventing violence, intercepting weapons, responding to antisocial behavior, and prohibiting drug use or theft. School safety and violence prevention policies and plans will be upheld by the legal system in most cases, provided they meet this standard.

Publication of School Safety Efforts

Of course, school safety efforts are only effective if students, teachers, and parents are aware of standards and requirements. Schools are advised to make every effort to ensure that students and parents are aware of the existence of a school safety plan and are familiar with the provisions of the school conduct code. School leaders need to be careful to design their publications and outreach to account for the different developmental stages of their students so that information is accessible and understandable to elementary-, middle school-, or high school-age youth. To this end, schools might ask both students and parents to sign forms stating they have read the school conduct code as a part of school procedures related to student enrollment, participation in extracurricular activities, or notification of grades. In addition, teachers may find appropriate opportunities to reference the school conduct code or safety plan as a part of parent–teacher conferences. Moreover, schools would benefit from frequent references and overviews of the school safety plan in board meetings, school newsletters, or other outreach efforts to parents, students, and the community. Although no specific measures are required of schools in this regard, any effort to certify that students and parents are aware of the school's safety plans will heighten awareness and enhance the security of the school.

SPECIFIC SCHOOL SAFETY ISSUES

The following sections provide some additional discussion of key policy areas and legal issues.[5] Currently, no specific measures are required of schools to enhance safety on school grounds. Courts are reluctant to impose such requirements and consequently have not required schools to provide security officers, conduct routine searches, or adopt supervisory programs.[6] Constant supervision is also not required.[7] At their discretion, schools often employ a standard set of security measures, including metal detectors, cameras, student searches, and in one, even lie detector tests.

Threats of Violence

Disciplinary actions may be taken simply for the threat of harm to another person. Students sometimes will threaten to hurt fellow students out of frustration, fear, or a genuine intent to harm. Threats may take several forms including direct threats ("I'm going to kill you"); indirect threats ("If I wanted to, I could blow the school up"); veiled threats ("If you want to settle this, let's go outside."); or conditional threats ("If I don't get out of detention, I'm going to cut you.").[8] Schools may discipline a student for a threat if it can reasonably be inferred that the threat is a serious expression of intent to harm or assault another person.[9] A student may be punished where he or she has "directly and unambiguously threatened physical harm" to a fellow student or teacher.[10] In addition, any threat that rises to the level of a crime in the jurisdiction will provide a basis for disciplining a student. It is imperative, however, that schools distinguish between school discipline and custodial arrest by law enforcement for speech that may be interpreted as a threat of violence. Courts have overturned disciplinary sanctions (arrest and felony convictions) on students for expressing violent themes such as bringing guns to school or wishing harm on fellow students and teachers in poetry and other creative writing efforts.[11] Although it may be appropriate for schools to investigate, provide psychological evaluations and treatment, and impose lesser school punishments for such speech, arrest and detention by law enforcement is probably unreasonable in light of recent court decisions.

Accordingly, students' speech rights may be limited where they infringe on the rights of others to be secure and left alone, such as disrupting class work, causing substantial disorder, or invading the personal rights of others.[12] Students have been appropriately disciplined for voicing threats of violence in a variety of circumstances, including the following:

1. Threatening to shoot a high school guidance counselor if a class schedule was not changed.[13]
2. Threatening to rape a teacher and the teacher's daughter and bragging to other students about the threats.[14]
3. Verbally assaulting school officials and using "veiled threats" after an erroneous identification of a gun in a student's car.[15]

School conduct codes should clearly identify the behavior related to threats that could result in discipline. This will provide teachers, students, and parents with an enforceable understanding of the appropriate conduct in school. In fact, many states have adopted detailed disciplinary codes that apply to school districts statewide, so all members of the school community are encouraged to become familiar with the requirements in their state.

Risk Factors: "Profiles"

In some circumstances, a list of risk factors for youth violence or a profile of a potentially dangerous student may be used as grounds to stop a student for questioning or to search his or her possessions or person. The U.S. Supreme Court has expressly approved the use of "probabilistic" profiles in other settings (namely airports) to identify potential drug couriers or terrorists.[16] In these circumstances, the fact that lists of factors giving rise to reasonable suspicion are also part of a profile "does not somehow detract from their evidentiary significance.[17] Generally, individuals may be searched based on their identification through the use of a profile because the profile provides the officers with reasonable suspicion to stop a suspect.[18] Profiles are treated as an objective and useful tool and are valid as long as they leave no room for subjective interpretation by security authorities and are not applied in a discriminatory fashion.[19] The usefulness of profiles is limited, however, by fundamental concerns about their tendency to be over-inclusive of innocent individuals, and their general validity as scientific tools, including their objectivity, accuracy, sensitivity, and general acceptance in the scientific community.[20]

In contrast, a joint effort of the U.S. Secret Service and U.S. Department of Education produced a threat assessment guide entitled, *Threat Assessment in Schools: A Guide to Managing Threatening Situations and to Creating Safe School Climates*, which provides a more effective method of assessing potential violence in a school setting. The key findings of this report clearly state, "[t]here is no accurate or useful "profile" of students who engage in targeted school violence."[21] A profile, therefore, should not stand alone as the only factor justifying a search. School officials might use a profile to stop students to inquire about their activities, but probably need other suspicious behavior or other corroborating information in order to conduct a full search of the student's person or property. Characteristics, such as those in a risk-factor list, which appear benign as an initial matter but when utilized in school policies have the effect of selecting individuals who are disproportionately members of a protected class (such as race, gender, age, religion), complicate matters considerably. Among the characteristics that might work as proxies in this way are poverty, poor school achievement or skills, weapons possession, and/or history of suspension. A school official needs reasonable grounds for suspecting a search will reveal contraband or evidence that a student is violating school rules under the circumstances. A profile match on a student tells a school official nothing regarding the presence of contraband or whether a student is violating school rules in a specific instance, so it should not be the only basis for the search or detention of a student.

School Search and Seizure

Generally, school officials may search a student "if the search is justified at its inception and is conducted in a manner reasonably related in scope to the circumstances.[22] The reasonableness standard, as set forth by the U.S. Supreme Court in *New Jersey v. T.L.O.*, is intended "to ensure student's rights [will] be invaded no more than necessary to maintain order in schools," not to authorize all searches conceivable to school officials.[23] Any school official may make this determination depending on the circumstances, but will usually be made by an assistant principal or another school official with responsibility for school conduct matters. A search will be justified where there are reasonable grounds for suspecting a search will reveal contraband or evidence that a student is violating school rules.[24] The permissible scope of a search depends on whether the measures used are reasonably related to the objective of the search and not excessively intrusive given the age and sex of the student and nature of the infraction.[25] General exploratory or sweep searches are usually impermissible.[26]

School officials may inspect a student's bag (purse, backpack, or duffel) and clothing for hidden weapons, cigarettes, and drugs when they have reason to do so (e.g., a tip that appears to be reliable, observation of materials associated with drug use, or bulges in clothing characteristic of weapons). In addition, school officials may search a student for weapons when they notice a bulge in a student's clothing characteristic of knives *and* the officials received an anonymous tip that a student had a weapon. School officials may frisk a student and proceed on reasonable suspicion resulting from the stop. It is also worth noting that in a situation where a student is on court-ordered probation, school officials may request the student's parole officer conduct a search because, in most cases, consent to a search is a condition of the probation. Moreover, searches may be conducted when a student does not possess the proper school pass and acts excited, aggressive, or exhibits other signs of potential drug use when confronted by school officials.[27] Teachers and school officials should be careful to document their preliminary observations, sources of information, tips, investigative steps, or other evidence that leads to reasonable grounds for a search.

Student Tips

In the case of student tips about illegal behavior, school officials must take steps to verify the reliability of the information.[28] They need to subject the student informant to extensive questioning regarding the student's motives and perception or source of knowledge. In addition, they should conduct their own investigation of the accused student's activities through direct observations, questioning classmates, or using other methods, in an effort to corroborate the tip. Either approach ensures school officials have reasonable grounds to believe a search will produce contraband or evidence of illegal behavior.

Locker Searches

Generally, locker searches are permissible as a function of the orderly administration of a school. Schools should adopt and carry out a policy informing students that the school owns the locker and may search it from time to time.[29] In such cases, courts have found that schools do not need the same reasonable suspicion in order to justify a search. In contrast, a locker search should not extend to a student's private articles, such as jackets, purses, and backpacks, within the locker. The student rightly considers these items private and has a greater expectation of privacy involving those items, so a school official must possess individualized reasonable suspicion to search them.[30] School officials may ask the student for permission to search the items found in the locker, but school officials need to be careful that consent is not obtained through coercion or undue influence. Without a student's consent, a search of a student's personal effects found in a locker must be "justified at its inception and conducted in a manner reasonably related in scope to the circumstances."[31]

Strip Searches

A strip search should be used rarely and as a last resort in light of the serious invasion of privacy it represents. Such a search is permissible if it is "justified at its inception and reasonably related in scope to the circumstances which justified the search in the first place."[32] Generally, a reasonable search under the circumstances requires that school officials have reasonable suspicion that the student in question possessed drugs or other contraband.[33] A strip search may be reasonable when (a) the item cannot be found in other locations, (b) there is reason to believe the student possessed the item, and (c) a policy outlining the strip-search procedure exists, and is followed.

Allegations of previous illegal activity (as old as 6 months) may contribute to the reasonable suspicion, particularly when new incidents of suspected illegal behavior are present.[34] Strip searches in cases of imminent physical harm to students or school personnel are probably justified, especially when weapons are involved. Imminent circumstances would mean that a student presents an immediate and impending threat to him or herself or others, such as when a student threatens to use a weapon that he or she appears to possess (e.g., as indicated by a characteristic bulge in clothing), but is detained before carrying out the threat.

As the intrusiveness of the search increases, so does the concern regarding whether the search is reasonable. School officials must consider the age and sex of the student involved. Accordingly, if school officials plan to make a student disrobe to locate contraband items, they are encouraged to pursue an exhaustive search of possible alternative locations for the contraband item (weapon/drugs), establish with reasonable certainty that the student possessed the item (e.g., through a reliable witness, or the elimination of all other possibilities), and thoroughly explain the search to the student in accordance with a pre-existing policy. Despite these general guidelines, strip searches should be very rare and pursued only under the most extreme circumstances.

Metal Detectors

Metal detector searches are clearly permissible security measures. Although individualized suspicion is normally required for a search, general searches are permissible when the search is minimally intrusive and the individual has a low reasonable expectation of privacy, such as at the entrance to a school. Metal detector searches are valid when notice (e.g., a posted sign) has been given stating that such searches will be conducted at that school, and when a school policy governing such searches is in place. It is not required that the actual date of the metal detector search be provided.[35]

The use of other metal-detecting methods may be somewhat more problematic, such as the random "wanding" of students using a hand-held magnometer to inspect students for metallic objects, in particular, guns or weapons. Random searches may be permissible provided arbitrary discretion is not employed. Consequently, pre-established procedures should be implemented, such as searching every third student for example, in order to avoid arbitrary discretion and the misuse of hand-held metal detection devices.[36] In any case, the *T.L.O.* reasonableness standard will still apply, so a search must be "justified at its inception and conducted in a manner reasonably related in scope to the circumstances."[37] If wand searches are conducted at the entrance of school or at the entry to a school event (e.g., a dance or sporting event), as a matter of ordinary administration, then they will be permitted because they are minimally intrusive and students have a low expectation of privacy. If the "wanding" applies only to an individual student, the school probably needs reasonable suspicion that the search will reveal a weapon. The use of a metal detector wand itself is a reasonable method under the circumstances, provided the school meets the first requirement that there be reasonable suspicion.

Cameras

Technology increases the ability of school officials to monitor the activity of the student population through advanced camera and recording systems. The key question is whether a student has an expectation of privacy in the area being filmed. Accordingly, photographing public areas such as buses, hallways, classrooms, and cafeterias is permissible, whereas the use of a camera in a locker room or bathroom is normally unacceptable.[38]

Lie Detectors/Polygraph Tests

In one instance, an Illinois school used lie detector (polygraph) tests to determine if students were complying with school drug and alcohol use policies.[39] Guidance is difficult to provide in this area because there are very few examples of polygraph tests given to students, children, or youth, except in juvenile sexual abuse cases or where a juvenile might be on probation. In the unlikely case that a polygraph test might be useful, schools need to inform all students that lie detector tests may be given for violations of specific school policies. In addition, when a polygraph test is to be administered in a particular case, school officials need to fully inform the student and his or her parents of the nature of the test, the charges or rule violations justifying the test, and the student's right not to take the test; and obtain consent to proceed with test from parents, and the student. Finally, school officials need to guarantee and maintain the results of the test in accordance with the requirements for school records under the Family Educational and Privacy Rights Act (FERPA); see discussion later in this chapter.

In addition, polygraph tests and post-polygraph interviews may constitute custodial detention, and therefore, create a possible right to counsel under the Sixth Amendment, or implicate the application of Miranda rights under the Fourth Amendment. Furthermore, schools must know that even if obtained validly, the results of the polygraph test may not be admissible in disciplinary hearings.[40] Particularly where criminal activity is involved, the results of polygraph tests are usually inadmissible if its value as evidence is "substantially outweighed by the danger of unfair prejudice, confusion of the issues, or misleading a jury."[41] Consequently, even if a polygraph test is given under these circumstances, it may not be admissible in certain disciplinary actions against a student.

Dress Codes and School Uniforms

In the exercise of its general authority to enact and endorse school regulations, a school may adopt rules regarding personal appearance, dress codes, and school uniforms.[42] These rules must bear some reasonable relationship to the educational mission of the school and its interest in promoting a safe and secure learning environment, and not simply represent a mere matter of preference or taste.[43] Generally, these rules reflect community values and serve to create a positive educational environment. They will be upheld as long as they are consistently applied to achieve the schools' inherent educational mission, such as improving school attendance, dropout rates, academic performance, or school safety.[44] Dress codes may include provisions related to specific types of clothing, gender-appropriate clothing, correctly sized clothing, clothing that contains obscene, profane, lewd, or vulgar statements, cosmetics, jewelry, clothing that promotes drugs or contains logos, clothing that is discourteous of school officials or authority, and clothing that is disrespectful of religion.[45]

Dress and appearance, however, may function as purely expressive speech related to political, religious, or social purposes. Some statements and words printed on clothing are protected by the First Amendment as pure speech. Consequently, students may wear clothing with messages related to political candidates, social causes, symbols of ethnic heritage, religious symbols, and words to express ideas or opinions.[46] For example, schools have been prevented from implementing hair regulations prohibiting Native American students from wearing their hair long as a symbol of moral and spiritual strength.[47]

Content-laden clothing of this type may be prohibited only to prevent a substantial and material interference with schoolwork or discipline, and must be neutral regarding the views expressed.[48] When the content does not create disruption or disorder, however, it may not be prohibited.[49] The protection of free speech, however, is not a blanket opportunity for students to say whatever they wish. Schools may restrict lewd, indecent, or offensive speech, and conduct that runs counter to essential lessons of civil, mature conduct. They are not required to allow speech that undermines the school's basic educational mission. Consequently, they may prohibit clothing containing information that promotes the use of illegal substances or criminal activity.[50] At a minimum, schools should support dress codes with a determination that the policy furthers the school's educational mission. In addition, schools should adopt findings, as necessary, that indicate school dress codes help reduce gang activity or other antisocial/violent behavior, ease tensions between students, aid schools in identifying campus visitors/intruders, and promote school safety in general.[51] Moreover, schools should adopt opt-out policies in uniform requirements, to allow parents to preserve their right to direct the upbringing of their children, particularly where traditional ethnic or religious dress is an important part of family life.[52]

School Resource/School Safety Officers

School resource officers (SROs) serve an important purpose in maintaining a safe and secure environment for students, teachers, and school officials. However, their quasi-law enforcement role complicates some security questions, such as searching students or seizing weapons or other contraband. Understanding the best approach for SROs requires a clear picture of their role in the school: namely do they serve a law enforcement purpose, or do they serve to maintain a safe and proper educational environment? In addition, it is helpful to clarify whether they are acting at their own discretion or at the request of school officials.[53]

Law Enforcement Purposes

Where the law enforcement features of an SRO are emphasized, regardless of their status as a police officer, sheriff, or other law enforcement personnel, their investigatory or search activities must meet probable cause requirements.[54] Of course, this is especially true if the SRO is actually a police officer assigned to a school. Consequently, the reasonableness of a search conducted at a school by a police officer or at their request will be governed by the probable cause standard. Probable cause requires that a security officer must consider whether "a reasonably prudent police officer, considering the total circumstances confronting him/her based on experience, would be warranted in the belief that an offense has been or is being committed."[55] Stated another way, probable cause requires that a search or arrest be objectively reasonable under the totality of the circumstances, and that the policy officer actually had probable cause to believe a crime had been committed. This is a fluid concept based on an independent assessment of the facts in each situation. Probable cause does not mean the security officer is correct or even more likely true than false, but it does mean more than a hunch, feeling, or vague suspicion. There must be specific, identifiable facts that can be stated to support the officer's conclusion. For these reasons, the reasonableness balancing factors applying to school officials do not apply to police operating in a school environment.[56] The lower standard is usually reserved for professional school staff, but not security officers who perform no educational function.

Educational or Violence Prevention Purposes

In many schools, SROs are hired to serve an educational and preventive function within the school, and to develop a more cooperative and trusting relationship among students, school officials, and law enforcement. These officers may or may not be police or law enforcement personnel.

Accordingly, where a security officer conducts a search at the request of school officials in conjunction with these purposes, generally probable cause and a warrant are not required. The security officer needs only a reasonable suspicion in this case. This is true in the clear majority of cases, reflecting the usual situation where an SRO will be acting at the request or behest of school officials.[57] This lesser standard is applied based on the assumption that the officer has only limited involvement and discretion in the decision to search a student.[58] In essence, the security officer is acting as an agent of the school, and only exercises the authority delegated from school officials.[59] This standard applies even where the security officer is a police officer, whether on or off duty.[60]

Discipline and Due Process

Discipline may take many forms, from a simple rebuke to expulsion from school. Generally, schools have great flexibility to determine and establish disciplinary methods, provided they are consistent with local community values and are not shocking to constitutional standards such as due process, equal protection, free speech, freedom from discrimination based on race, religion, gender, disability, or national origin. Schools may implement almost any reasonable method of discipline provided it is directed at controlling, training, or educating students. Schools should endeavor to ensure their methods are not capricious, oppressive, arbitrary, or contrary to law. The essential relationship to remember is that the amount of process that is due is proportional to the severity of the penalty. Overall, most disciplinary methods employed by schools are considered valid and draw little attention from courts, including detention, time-out or isolation, alternative education programs, denial of participation in school activities, and verbal reprimand or chastisement.

Moreover, a student generally may be disciplined for off-campus conduct if school authorities can show that the student's actions have a direct and immediate effect on either school discipline or the safety and welfare of students and staff.[61] Usually, if the off-campus activity involves two or more students from the same school, then a sufficient connection will be established to warrant school discipline. However, this type of direct connection is not required.

Suspension and Expulsion: Zero-Tolerance Policies

Perhaps the most significant discipline issues currently faced by schools are suspension and expulsion penalties under zero-tolerance policies. In light of the state's clear responsibility to ensure the safety of teachers and students, school officials may expect zero-tolerance sanctions to survive legal challenges so long as the school guarantees the student the necessary due process protections.[62] Such policies are not a violation of state compulsory education laws.[63] Schools may ban weapons and impose suspension or expulsion for possessing a weapon, but should exercise discretion in other circumstances.

Federal zero-tolerance policies generally require mandatory suspension or expulsion for students caught possessing a weapon. Increasingly, students have been suspended or expelled for incidents not involving firearms or weapons, such as engaging in violent behavior or using/possessing drugs, allegedly threatening violence,[64] writing about or describing violent acts, and even bringing a nail clipper to school.[65] The expansion of zero tolerance to such cases has carried the policy into uncertain, potentially unreasonable, legal territory.

Zero-tolerance policies in the states draw their inspiration from the federal Gun Free Schools Act (GFSA) of 1994. In essence, the GFSA requires each state receiving federal funds under the Elementary and Secondary Education Act to expel, for a period of not less than 1 year, any student found with a weapon on school grounds.[66] Weapons may include firearms designed to propel a projectile by an explosive reaction, including starter guns, the components of any such device, silencers or other destructive devices such as bombs, poison gas, grenades, rockets, missiles, or mines.[67]

Under the GFSA, federal funds may be denied to states that fail to adopt a zero-tolerance policy for firearms. The GFSA allows local school officials to modify firearm-related expulsion requirements on a case-by-case basis, but does not define modification or outline the circumstances under which such modifications would be appropriate.[68] The federal mandate applies only to firearms, meaning that federal law for other weapons, substance abuse, or other infractions does not require a zero-tolerance policy. A number of states, however, have broadened the definition of "weapons" well beyond firearms to include knives, razors, slingshots, brass knuckles, and any other inherently dangerous object.[69] In addition, some schools view threats of violence from students, including assaults not involving the use of a weapon, as a reason for expulsion.[70] The GFSA also allows schools to arrange alternative educational opportunities for expelled students at their discretion.

DUE PROCESS: SUSPENSION AND EXPULSION

Certain procedural requirements must be followed if a student is to be suspended for a substantial period of time or expelled from a school. The U.S. Supreme Court noted in a famous line from the case of *Tinker v. Des Moines School District* that students do not "shed their constitutional rights . . . at the school house gate."[71]

Suspensions

In cases involving suspensions of 10 days or less, a student must be provided with the following due process:

1. Oral or written notice of the charges against him or her.
2. An explanation of the reasons for the charges, (i.e., the evidence).
3. An opportunity to present his or her side of the story.[72]

The requirement of a hearing does not mean it must be as formal as a trial; an informal review of the evidence will be sufficient. In addition, no delay between notice to the student and the hearing is necessary, because a school official "may informally discuss the alleged misconduct with the student minutes after it has occurred."[73]

Expulsions

Suspensions for a substantial period of time (more than 10 days) or expulsions typically involve a greater level of procedural protection,[74] which may include the following:

1. Notice to the student and parents.
2. A fair hearing and right to appeal.
3. An impartial hearing board.
4. Right to be represented by counsel.
5. Reasonable time to prepare for the hearing.
6. An opportunity to review evidence against the student.
7. An opportunity to examine witnesses against the student.
8. Opportunity to present evidence and witnesses on the student's behalf.
9. Recorded proceedings.
10. Requirement that board's decision be based on substantial evidence.

A school board should make an independent assessment of the facts and circumstances of the case in light of any adopted zero-tolerance policy and not simply endorse the decision of a school official or the effect of the policy.[75] Of course, an expulsion policy should be developed in compliance with the GFSA, but schools must be careful in implementing zero-tolerance policies, as expulsion may be an excessive consequence in circumstances when weapons are brought to school unknowingly and without a threat of harm to others.[76] Generally, expulsion is warranted only in cases of repeated or extreme misconduct, such as attacking a fellow student or teacher, repeatedly pulling fire alarms without cause, drug use, and weapons possession or use.[77]

Emergency Situations

Generally, notice and a hearing must precede a student's removal from school, except when the student presents an imminent threat to him or herself or the safety of others. Emergency situations justifying the immediate suspension or expulsion of a student may include conduct that seriously disrupts the academic atmosphere of the school; endangers other students, teachers, or school officials; or damages property.[78]

In emergency situations, a two-step approach may be employed: first, immediately impose a temporary suspension or expulsion; and second, enforce a permanent expulsion after the proper notice and hearing. In these scenarios, notice and a hearing must be provided as soon as practicable. Notice should be sent to the student's parents within 24 hours of a decision to conduct disciplinary proceedings, and a hearing should be held within 72 hours (3 days) of the student's removal.

Individuals With Disabilities Education Act Considerations[79]

A critical area of school discipline policy includes the appropriate treatment and procedures related to misconduct by children with disabilities. The Individuals with Disabilities Education Act (IDEA) provides the primary source of guidance for educational agencies in this area.

The threshold question is whether the youth actually engaged in misconduct. Alleged misconduct by students with disabilities should be investigated in the same manner as alleged misconduct by students without disabilities. Substantive and procedural requirements for investigations will be the same as those generally applicable to all students, as described in this chapter.

The next critical question involves whether the IDEA applies to the circumstances of any particular student. Obviously, it will apply to students who have been assessed with a disability eligible for special education services and placed on an individualized education program (IEP). In addition, an educational agency will be deemed to have knowledge that a child is one with a disability if, before the behavior that precipitated the disciplinary action occurred, a parent expressed concern in writing to an administrator or a teacher; a parent of the child requested an evaluation of the child pursuant to IDEA; or a teacher or other school personnel expressed specific concerns about a pattern of behavior demonstrated to an administrator.[80]

Generally, IDEA allows that where "the behavior of the child with a disability was not a manifestation of the child's disability, the relevant disciplinary procedures applicable to children without disabilities may be applied to the child in the same manner in which they would be applied to children without disabilities."[81] Under such circumstances, schools must provide adequate alternative educational services in order to assure the progress of learning.

Schools also may discipline students with disabilities in circumstances where a conduct violation was a manifestation of the student's disability provided certain procedural safeguards are followed. Courts have uniformly held that disciplinary removal of a student with disabilities from a placement may be a change of placement under the IDEA. Removal of a student for 10 or fewer days is not a change of placement. New IDEA provisions state that within 10 school days of any decision to change the placement of a child with a disability because of a violation of a code of student conduct, the local educational agency, parent and relevant members of the IEP team must review all relevant information in the student's file, including the child's IEP, any teacher observations, and any relevant information provided by the parents to determine if conduct was caused by, or in direct and substantial relationship to, the child's disability; or a direct result of the school's failure to implement the IEP.[82]

School personnel may consider any unique circumstances on a case-by-case basis when deciding to order a change in placement for a child with a disability who violates a student conduct code.[83]

Procedurally, where disciplinary removal constitutes a change of placement and exceeds 10 days, a student must be provided written notice of the decision and procedural rights. These rights include the right to appeal a decision to a hearings officer, and thereafter to a court, if necessary. In addition, after the 10 days, a school must provide an alternative educational setting.[84]

Recent IDEA revisions establish a new standard for special circumstances justifying immediate removal for behavior while at school, on school premises, or at a school function under the jurisdiction of a state or local education agency. A school is permitted to remove a child with a disability to an alternative educational setting for not more than 45 school days without regard to whether the behavior is determined to be a manifestation of the child's disability, in cases where a child (a) carries or possesses a weapon; (b) knowingly possesses or uses illegal drugs, or sells or solicits the sale of a controlled substance; or (c) has inflicted serious bodily injury on another person.[85]

Overall, schools have great flexibility to appropriately discipline students with disabilities for misconduct, provided they recognize that the provisions of IDEA were enacted to address the disturbing trend of excluding disabled students from proper public education services. The goals of school safety and guaranteeing the rights of students with disabilities are not mutually exclusive. Schools will find these goals compatible so long as they adhere to the protections established by IDEA and supporting case law.

GENERAL LIABILITY ISSUES

Generally, schools cannot guarantee safety for all students or teachers while at school. Yet, schools do have a duty to provide reasonable supervision of students and maintain the safety of the school grounds, especially because students are required to be at school under compulsory attendance rules. Acts of violence involving schools may make school officials, teachers, or the school board liable for civil damages for those harmed. This liability may arise from a variety of circumstances and may depend on actions taken (or not taken) by the school itself.

Civil Liability

School districts face potential liability for the violent acts of students or non-students when they fail to do the following:

1. Supervise a specific area at school where prior instances of violence occurred.
2. Warn faculty, potential targets, or school personnel about a pre-existing danger, including the violent propensities of a student.
3. Establish/adhere to a school safety plan.[86]

Generally, schools are required to show the same degree of care and supervision that a reasonably prudent parent would employ under the circumstances.[87] The absence of supervision must have caused the violence or crime for the school to be liable.[88] School boards may be liable for failure to establish adequate supervisory procedures, even if their employees are not liable.[89] This general duty of care and supervision extends to preventing a foreseeable suicide. School officials with knowledge or notice of suicidal intent on the part of the student must exercise care to prevent the student from carrying out his or her intent.[90] Recall, however, no specific security measures are required of schools to enhance safety on school grounds. Schools are urged to do so, but so long as the school's efforts display the same care as a reasonably prudent parent, they will not be penalized for not adopting specific measures.

In addition, even when a school may have a duty to supervise, the school will not be liable for sudden, spontaneous violence. Courts generally agree that "spontaneous or planned acts of violence by students on school grounds do not create liability on behalf of the school board if the school ground is otherwise well supervised."[91]

Time and Location of Incident

Liability may depend on the time and location of the incident. For example, a school may be liable for violence suffered by students while in the school parking lot, or while on their way to and from the school grounds. Normally, however, a school will not be liable when an incident occurs off campus, during non-school hours, and is not related to school-sponsored activities.[92] For example, a school incurred no liability for the assault of a young female student after an evening of drinking at a local bar and the activity had no relation to school-sponsored events, or where an elementary school student wandered from school grounds and was subsequently kidnapped and murdered.[93]

A school may have a duty to supervise a particular area of school grounds depending on whether similar acts have occurred in that area previously. The recency, frequency, location, and nature of the prior crimes will be factors in determining whether the crimes establish a duty to supervise.[94] Common sense dictates that a school will be liable if a person is injured in an area where attacks of the same type occur often. Schools should develop monitoring plans for these "hot spots" and are especially urged to adopt a school safety plan where there is a generally high level of violence at a school or the school is in a high crime area. The most effective school safety plans will include an assessment of the time and location of incidents and increase monitoring and resources during that time.

Attacker's Dangerous Propensities

A school will be liable when it fails to safeguard other students or teachers from someone with a known propensity to violence. This includes those students engaging in bullying behaviors as well as other person crimes, in particular, sexual offenders. School officials must warn intended and identifiable victims where serious danger from a known suspect exists, and the warning must be specific (time, place, identity of suspect, and motivation) and complete (all these factors, if known).[95]

PRIVACY ISSUES AND FAMILY EDUCATIONAL AND PRIVACY RIGHTS ACT

Creating a safe school environment requires extensive communications among schools, law enforcement, and social service agencies. Such cooperation involves significant record-keeping about disciplinary and counseling matters between schools, law enforcement agencies, counseling and health organizations, research groups, and parents. The appropriate use of these records is essential for schools and the educational process. The confidentiality of student records (educational, medical, and disciplinary) has long been regarded as a compelling state interest, requiring courts, state agencies, and school districts to take reasonable steps to ensure that confidentiality is maintained. The leading framework on the appropriate use of student records is the Family Educational and Privacy Rights Act (FERPA), passed by Congress in 1999.[96]

Generally, FERPA allows schools to collect information concerning disciplinary action taken against a student for conduct that "poses a significant risk to the safety or well-being of that student, other students or other members of the school community."[97] In addition, schools may disclose that information to teachers or school officials who have a "legitimate interest in the behavior of the student."[98]

Accordingly, a school may track the type and severity of violent incidents through regular reports included in a student's school records. These records would be considered disciplinary records because they involve reports of actual incidents of behavior requiring disciplinary action. Moreover, to the extent these records are maintained by a law enforcement office within the school, they will be considered law enforcement records, similar to crime reports that include investigation reports and incident data. Neither law enforcement records nor crime reports are educational records under the statute.[99] In contrast, education records may include psychological evaluations and the results of psychological tests used for diagnostic purposes.[100]

Sharing Disciplinary Records[101]

Juvenile education records are generally regarded as confidential, even after being provided to other agencies in accordance with law, and may be sealed in court proceedings despite a presumption that such proceedings are open to the public and media.[102] The delicate matter of reporting student information to an outside agency or another school or institution is addressed directly by FERPA. It is important to remember that a school is not required to disclose information related to wrongdoing by a student, but schools have the discretion to do so.[103] FERPA governs both the request for information received by a school and the school's voluntary interest in providing information to an outside agency, such as law enforcement, social service agencies, or mental health counseling services.[104] Consequently, the following guidelines apply where a school receives a request for student information or where the school may wish to volunteer student information.

Schools or Educational Institutions

Generally, a school that discloses an education record must make a reasonable attempt to notify the parent or the student, provide a copy of the record that it proposes to release, and provide a hearing if requested.[105] A school may disclose education or disciplinary records to another school or institution that the student is attending if the student is enrolled or receives services from the other institution, and the preceding conditions are met. Student disciplinary records may be shared between schools attended by the student in question, with the appropriate notice to parents.

Non-School Agencies or Organizations: Law Enforcement and Social Service Agencies

FERPA generally restricts access to student records by non-school individuals or organizations. Generally, funds will be denied to any school that allows disclosure of student records without written consent from the parents, with a few exceptions. The statute's exceptions allow disclosure of even personally identifiable information from student records without the consent of the student or parents to state or local juvenile justice officials, to organizations conducting educational studies, in health and safety emergencies, or if they are disciplinary records.[106]

Information on Specific Acts in Student Records

FERPA allows the reporting of violent acts such as homicide, rape, assault, or the imminent threat of such acts.[107] Information regarding such actions by students may be reported voluntarily by the school or on request by an outside agency.[108] FERPA allows the reporting of information related to the possession of drugs or weapons by students on school grounds, voluntarily or at the request of outside agencies.[109] To the extent disruptive or antisocial behavior includes the destruction of property or vandalism, it may be reported to law enforcement, voluntarily or on request.[110] Other forms of antisocial or disruptive behavior that do not fall into any of the previously mentioned categories will require notification to and consent of the student's parents before the information can be released to a third party. This type of behavior might include yelling in class, name-calling, disrespect for teachers or other school officials, bullying, intimidation, or similar behavior that does not reach the level of destruction of property or assault of fellow students or school personnel.

Risk-Factor/Behavioral/Threat Assessments

FERPA does not address this area directly and does not provide an exception for this type of information in a student's record. Therefore, the general provisions of FERPA govern the release of information on student achievement, behavioral or academic history, personal interests, extracurricular activity, or similar background information on a student. This means that the release must be accompanied by notification and consent of the student's parents or guardians.

CONCLUSION

In summary, school safety is a critical endeavor for any school community. Generally, school districts are empowered to pursue this mission with great latitude provided they adopt policies that are reasonably designed to address whatever problem they face. It is not necessary for the state to utilize the best possible methods to achieve its goals; rather all that is required is that the methods actually used be reasonable. Most conceivable school safety efforts will be rationally related to preventing violence, intercepting weapons, responding to antisocial behavior, and prohibiting drug use or theft. For this reason, schools may employ metal detectors and cameras, school uniform policies, school resource officers, and they may search students provided they have reasonable grounds to do so. They may proceed based on student tips and respond with discipline to threats of violence made by students. They may suspend or expel students for infractions of school rules, especially for possession of weapons or drugs, or violent behavior— provided they meet the due process rights of students to notice and an opportunity to address the charges against them. School officials will keep records of these matters and may share these records with other schools, law enforcement, or health agencies in order to improve school safety efforts.

Implementation of these efforts, however, needs to be balanced by a school's central and primary mission of education. Thus, school officials must bear in mind that policies set the tone of school administration and shape the culture of each classroom, school and school district. School leaders would be wise to practice the greatest care possible and employ the best practices available to ensure the safety of a school environment. In addition, cultivating a strong sense of justice as the repair of a safe and secure school environment and concern for the dignity of every member of the school community will build students' sense of values, personal integrity, and accountability to the larger community. Ultimately, policies and the law are only guideposts for human activity and cannot substitute for its basic humanity. This humanity requires each of us to engage our common sense, common compassion, and common creativity to build a more secure environment for learning.

ACKNOWLEDGMENTS

I thank Robert Schwartz, executive director, Juvenile Law Center; and Kamala Shugar, assistant district attorney, Lane County, Oregon for their contributions and suggestions for this chapter. The strength of the work is a result of their clarifying arguments, editorial acumen, and expansive legal knowledge, while any deficiencies remain those of the author.

NOTES

[1] This developmental mechanism, known as *legal socialization*, is the "process through which individuals acquire attitudes and beliefs about the law and the justice system." MacArthur Foundation Research Network on Adolescent Development and Juvenile Justice (http://www.mac-adoldev-juvjustice.org/page33.html). The MacArthur Foundation is conducting extensive pilot research on this area, with results expected in 2005.

[2] Brown v. Board of Education, 347 U.S. 483 (1954).

[3] Reynolds v. Sims, 377 U.S. 533 (1964), and Cleburne v. Cleburne Living Center, 473 U.S. 432 (1985).

While the reasonableness standard is the norm, it is important to note that U.S. Supreme Court decisions have established other, sometimes more stringent, standards in certain areas, namely student speech, general school discipline, suspension and expulsion (discussed further in this chapter), search and seizure (discussed further in this chapter), and arrest. School officials are urged to consult with their school or district legal representation, and state educational agency for a full review of the applicable standards and procedures.

[4] Tyler v. Vickery, 517 F.2d 1089 (5th Cir. 1975), *cert. denied*, 426 U.S. 940 (1976). Note: from a policy perspective, however, schools are urged to implement the best practices available in order to ensure the safety of the school community, even if they are only required to implement policies and procedures reasonably related to school safety.

[5] Additional materials on many of these topics may be found at 6 Rapp Chapter F5—Student Control & Discipline, Chapter F7—Education Records (2004); 7 Rapp Table T1: Statutes Regulating Methods of Investigating Student Conduct, Table T2: Statutes Regulating Student Disciplinary Standards, Procedures & Related Practices, and Table T3: Statutes Regulating Methods of Student Discipline other than Suspension and Expulsion (1995).

[6]Legal Guidelines for Curbing School Violence, March 1995, National School Boards Association Council of School Attorneys, p. 13. (Hereinafter Legal Guidelines)

[7]*See,* 5 Rapp at 12.12 (2004).

[8]See Department of Justice, Federal Bureau of Investigations, "The School Shooter: A Threat Assessment Perspective" 5 (2000).

[9]Swem, Lisa, L., *Preventing Threats of Violence in Schools from Turning into a Tragedy,* School Law in Review 1999, National School Boards Association (1999); *citing* U.S. v. Orozco-Santillan, 903 F.2d 1262, 1265 (9th Cir. 1990)

[10]3 James A. Rapp §9.04[4][c][iv][B] (2004) (hereafter 3 Rapp), *citing* Lovell v. Poway Unified Sch. Dist., 90 F.3d 367, 374 (9th Cir. 1996)

[11]*See,* In re GEORGE T., People v. George T., California Supreme Court Op. S111780, Ct.App. 6 H023080, Santa Clara County Super. Ct. No. J122537 (July 22, 2004); In the Interest of Douglas D., State v. Douglas D., No. 99-1767-FT (Wis. Sup. Ct., May 16, 2001), *motion for reconsideration denied,* June 28, 2001.

[12]3 Rapp at 9.04[4][a](2004), *citing* Tinker v. Des Moines Indep. Comm. Sch. Dist., 393 U.S. 503 (1969); See also, Hazelwood Sch. Dist v. Kuhlmeier 484 U.S. 260 (1988).

[13]3 Rapp at 9.04 [4][c][iv][B] (2004), *citing* Lovell v. Poway Unified Sch. Dist., 90 F.3d 367 (9th Cir. 1996), rev'g 847 F. Supp. 780 (S.D. Cal. 1994).

[14]Achman v. Chicago Lakes Indep. Sch. Dist. No. 2144, 45 F. Supp. 2d 664 (D.C. Minn. March 31, 1999).

[15]Turner v. South-Western City School District, 82 F. Supp. 2d 757; 1999 U.S. Dist. LEXIS 20680 (S.D. Ohio, December 22, 1999).

[16]U.S. v. Sokolow, 490 U.S. 1 (1989).

[17]U.S. v. Sokolow, 490 U.S. 1, at 19.

[18]United States v. Riggs, 347 F. Supp. 1098, (E.D.N.Y. 1972), United States v. Lopez, 328 F. Supp. 1077 (E.D.N.Y. 1971), U.S. v. Moreno, 475 F.2d 44 (5th Cir. 1973), U.S. v. Bell, 464 F.2d 667 (2nd Cir. N.Y. 1972).

[19]*See,* U.S. v. Bell, 464 F.2d 667.

[20]*Software Can't Make School Safe,* Laurence Steinberg, New York Times, April 22, 2000; *Legal Implications of Profiling Students for Violence,* Kirk A. Bailey, Psychology in the Schools, Vol. 38(2), 2001, John Wiley & Sons, Inc.

[21]*Threat Assessment in Schools: A Guide to Managing Threatening Situations and to Creating Safe School Climates,* U.S. Secret Service & U.S. Department of Education, May 2002, p. 17.

[22]New Jersey v. T.L.O., 469 U.S. 325 (1985).

[23]New Jersey v. T.L.O., 469 U.S. 325 (1985).

[24]3 Rapp 9.08[1][c] (2004); Please note, excellent guidelines, forms and model conduct codes may be found at 6 James A. Rapp, Education Law Chapter F5: Student Control and Discipline.

[25]T.L.O., at 342. *See* 3 Rapp at 9.08[1][c] (2004).

[26]3 Rapp at 9.08[6][c][i] (2004), *citing* Burnham v. West, 681 F. Supp. 1160 (E.D. Va. 1988).

[27]3 Rapp at 9.08[6][c][ii] (2004), citations omitted.

[28]Legal Guidelines, p. 2, *citing* Williams v. Ellington, 936 F2d 881 (6th Cir. 1991).

[29]Legal Guidelines, n. 2 at p. 4, *citing* Zamora v. Pomeroy, 639 F.2d 662 (10th Cir. 1981).

[30]People v. Scott, 34 N.Y. 2d 483, 315 N.E. 2d 466 (1974, *cited in* 3 Rapp §9.08[10][g][ii] (2004). *See also,* New Jersey v. T.L.O., 469 U.S. 325 (1985), 3 Rapp §9.08[10][f][iii] (2004).

[31]New Jersey v. T.L.O., 469 U.S. 325 (1985)

[32]Sostarecz by & through Sostarecz v. Misko, 1999 U.S. Dist. Lexis 4065 (E.D. Pa. March 26, 1999), *citing* New Jersey v. T.L.O., 469 U.S. 325 (1985).

[33]Sostarecz, *citing* Cornfield v. School District No. 230, 991 F.2d 1316 (7th Cir. 1993), Widener v. Frye, 809 F. Supp. 35 (S.D. Ohio 1992), *aff'd* 12 F.3d 215 (6th Cir. 1993), Williams v. Ellington, 936 F.2d 881 (6th Cir. 1991).

[34]Legal Guidelines, p. 2, *citing* Cornfield v. School District No. 230, 991 F.2d 1316 (7th Cir. 1993).

[35]Legal Guidelines, n. 2 at p. 3, *citing* People v. Dukes, 151 Misc.2d 295, 580 N.Y.S.2d 850 (Crim.Ct. 1992)

[36]See 92 Cal. Att'y Gen. Op. 201 (October 6, 1992), *cited in* 3 Rapp §9.08[10][h][iii] (2004).

[37]New Jersey v. T.L.O., 469 U.S. 325 (1985).

[38]Preventing Threats of Violence, supra n. 6 at p. 7.

[39]See Jay Hughes, *Illinois School Uses Lie Detectors,* Associated Press, November 6, 2001.

[40]See O'Hartigan v. State Dep't of Personnel, 118 Wasgh.2d 111, 821 P.2d 44 (1991). *See also,* 2 Rapp §6.09[5][d] and 3 Rapp §9.08[10][d][iv] (2004).

[41]U.S. v. Cordoba, 194 F.3d 1053 (9th Cir. 1999); 1999 U.S. App. LEXIS 29687., *See* Fed. R. Evid. 403

[42]Hicks v. Halifax County Bd. of Educ., 93 F.Supp.2d 649, 143 Educ. L.R. 861 (E.D.N.C. 1999).

[43]*See* Rapp 9.04[8][b] (2002), *citing* L. Bartlett, *Hair and Dress Codes Revisited,* 33 Educ. L.R. 7 (1986); Annot., 58 A.L.R.5th 1.

[44]Hines v. Caston Sch. Corp., 651 N.E.2d 330, 101 Educ. L.R. 392 (Ind. Ct. App. 1995), *cited in* Rapp 9.04[8][b] (2002).

48   BAILEY

⁴⁵*See,* Rapp §9.04[8][c][iii] (2004), citations omitted.

⁴⁶Canady v. Bossier Parish Sch. Bd., 240 F.3d 437, 151 Educ. L.R. 110 (5th Cir. 2001); *See also,* Alabama & Coushatta Tribes of Tex. v. Big Sandy Sch. Dist., 817 F.Supp. 1319, 82 Educ. L.R. 442 (E.D. Tex. 1993), cited in Rapp 9.04[8][b][ii] (2002).

⁴⁷Alabama & Coushatta Tribes of Tex. v. Big Sandy Sch. dist., 817 F. Supp. 1319 (E.D. Tex. 1993).

⁴⁸Tinker v. Des Moines Indep. Cmty. Sch. Dist. 393 U.S. 503 (1969), *See also,* Castorina v. Madison County Sch. Bd., 246 F.3d 536, 152 Educ. L.R. 524 (6th Cir. 2001) (issues over regulation of display of Confederate flag and clothing related to Malcolm X and/or Black Muslims).

⁴⁹*See* Pyle v. South Hadley School Committee, 423 Mass. 283, 667 NE2d 869 (1996).

⁵⁰*See,* Bethel Sch. Dist. No. 403 v. Fraser, 478 U.S. 675, 32 Educ. L.R. 1243 (1986), cited in 3 Rapp 9.08[8][c][iii] (2002), additional citations omitted.

⁵¹Long v. Board of Educ., 121 F. Supp.2d 621, 149 Educ. L.R. 157 (W.D. Ky. 2000), *see also,* Bethel School Dist. No. 403 v. Fraser, 478b U.S. 675 (1986).

⁵²*See* Hicks v. Halifax County Bd. of Educ. 93 F.Supp.2d 649, 143 Educ. L. R. 861 (E.D.N.C. 1999).

⁵³*See,* 3 Rapp §9.08[9] (2004), *citing* T.L.O, 469 U.S. 325 at 341, n.7.

⁵⁴*See* Picha v. Wielgos, 410 F. Supp. 1214 (N.D. Ill. 1976), *cited in* 3 Rapp §9.08 [9] (2004) and T.L.O, 469 U.S. 325 at 341, n.7.

⁵⁵Davis v. U.S., 781 A.2d 729 (D.C. App. 2001), *citing* Peterkin v. United States, 281 A.2d 567, 568 (D.C. 1971); *see also* Hill v. United States, 627 A.2d 975, 979 (D.C. 1993).

⁵⁶Waters v. United States, 311 A.2d 835 (D.C. 1973), cited in 3 Rapp §9.08[9][c][i] (2004).

⁵⁷*See* Rapp 9.08[9][c][ii] (2004), *citing In re* Angelia D.B., 564 N.W.2d 682, 118 Educ. L.R. 1191 (Wis. 1997).

⁵⁸*See* Tarter v. Raybuck, 742 F.2d 977, 19 Educ. L.R. 952 (6th Cir. 1984), *cert. denied,* 470 U.S. 1051 (1985) (school officials were not acting on direction of police); Martens v. District No. 220, 620 F. Supp. 298, 28 Educ. L. R. 471 (N.D. Ill. 1985) (applying reasonable suspicion where an officer's role in the search of a student was limited); Coronado v. State, 835 S.W.2d 636, 77 Educ. L.R. 582 (Tex. Crim. App. 1992) (applying reasonable suspicion where a school official, along with a sheriff's officer assigned to the school, conducted various searches of a student); *cited* in 3 Rapp §9.08[9][c][i] (2004).

⁵⁹*See* State v. Serna, 860 P.2d 1320, 86 Educ. L.R. 480 (Ariz. Ct. App. 1993), *cited in* Rapp 9.08[9][d] (2004).

⁶⁰*See* Salazar v. Luty, 761 F. Supp. 45, 67 Educ. L.R. 158 (S.D. Tex. 1991), *cited in* 3 Rapp 9.08[9][d] (2004).

⁶¹Legal Guidelines, p. 10.

⁶²*See,* 3 Rapp §9.10[2][b][i] (2004).

⁶³3 Rapp, 9.10[6][c][ii] (2004).

⁶⁴The Columbine Effect, John Cloud, Time Magazine, DECEMBER 6, 1999, VOL. 154 NO. 23.

⁶⁵*Id.*

⁶⁶Gun Free Schools Act of 1994, 20 USCA Section 8921 (1994).

⁶⁷18 USCS §§921 (3), (4) (1999), stating as follows: The term "firearm" means (A) any weapon (including a starter gun) which will or is designed to or may readily be converted to expel a projectile by the action of an explosive; (B) the frame or receiver of any such weapon; (C) any firearm muffler or firearm silencer; or (D) any destructive device. Such term does not include an antique firearm.

(4) The term "destructive device" means—
A) any explosive, incendiary, or poison gas—
(i) bomb,
(ii) grenade,
(iii) rocket having a propellant charge of more than four ounces,
(iv) missile having an explosive or incendiary charge of more than one-quarter ounce,
(v) mine, or
(vi) device similar to any of the devices described in the preceding clauses

⁶⁸20 USCS Section 8921 (b)(1) (1999).

⁶⁹In California, for example, knives have a specific legal definition (length and locking) related to expulsion decisions. [California Education Code, 48915 (g)]. Expulsion is not mandated—a recommendation to the school board for expulsion by the site principal is the mandated procedure. *See* California Education Code 48900–48927.

⁷⁰Please refer to discussion regarding *Threats of Violence.*

⁷¹Tinker v. Des Moines School Dist., 393 U.S. 503, 506 (1969). The Supreme Court held in a later case, Goss v. Lopez, that a "student's legitimate entitlement to a public education [is] a property interest which is protected by the Due Process Clause and may not be taken away for misconduct without adherence to the minimum procedure required by that clause." Goss v. Lopez, 419 U.S. 565 (1975).

⁷²3 Rapp 9.00[5][b] (2004).

⁷³Goss v. Lopez, at 582.

[74]Givens v. Poe, 346 F. Supp. 202, 209 (1972); Legal Guidelines, p. 9; *See also*, 3 Rapp 9.09[6][b] (2002), *citing* Dixon v. Alabama State Board of Education, 294 F.2d 150 (5th Cir.), *cert. denied*, 368 U.S. 930 (1961).

[75]Colvin by and Through Colvin v. Lowndes County, 2000 U.S. Dist. LEXIS 2403 (N.D. Miss. Feb. 24, 2000), *See also*, 3 Rapp §9.10[2][b][ii] (2004).

[76]Seal v. Morgan, 229 F. 3d 567 (6th Cir. 2000), *See also* 3 Rapp 9.10[2][b][ii] (2004).

[77]3 Rapp 9.10[6][c][i] (2004), citations omitted.

[78]Goss v. Lopez, 419 U.S. 565, at 572.

[79]Although this brief overview provides the basic outline of disciplinary procedures covered by IDEA, school officials are urged to consult with their school or district legal representation, state educational agency and the U.S. Department of Education for a full review of the applicable IDEA standards and procedures. The Office of Special Education and Rehabilitative Services (OSERS) in the U.S. Department of Education has published an excellent set of materials that may be found on their website at www.ed.gov/about/offices/list/osers/index.html.

[80]IDEA [615(k)(5)(B)]

[81]20 U.S.C. §1415(k)(5)(A).

[82]IDEA [615(k)(1)(E)(i)]

[83]IDEA [615(k)(1)(A)]

[84]20 U.S.C. §1415(k)(4)(A)(i), 34 CFR §300.520(a)(1)(ii).

[85]IDEA [615(k)(1)(G)]

[86]Legal Guidelines, p.11.

[87]5 James A. Rapp, Education Law 12.12[2][a] (2004), citations omitted.

[88]*Id.*

[89]5 Rapp at 12.12[2][b] (2004).

[90]5 Rapp at 12.12[6] (2002).

[91]5 Rapp at 12.12[2][b] (2004), *citing* Nicolosi v. Livingston Parish School Bd. 441 So.2d 1261, 1265 (La. Ct. App. 1983).

[92]Legal Guidelines at p. 12.

[93]Legal Guidelines at p. 12, *citing* Hartman v. Bethany College, 778 F. Supp. 286 (N.D. W.Va. 1991) and Chavez v. Tolleson Elementary School District, 595 P.2d 1017 (1979).

[94]Legal Guidelines, p.12.

[95]5 Rapp at 12.12[3] (2004).

[96]Family Education and Privacy Act, 20 USCS §1232g. (1999).

[97]20 USCS §1232g (h).

[98]20 USCS §1232g (h).

[99]20 USCS §1232g (a)(4)(B)(ii); *See also,* John Theumann, Annotation: *Validity, Construction and Application of the Family Educational and Privacy Rights Act of 1974,* 112 A.L.R. Fed. 1, 23 (1993) (hereinafter, Theumann).

[100]Theumann, *supra* n. 80, at 22.

[101]An excellent guide to student record sharing and forms may be found at 6 James A. Rapp Education Law, Section F7.04: Student Record Sharing (2004). This section outlines a reciprocal reporting system for schools and law enforcement.

[102]*See* FERPA, 20 USCS §1232g (b)(4); See also, State ex rel. Garden State Newspapers, Inc. v. Hoke, 205 W. Va. 611, 520 S.E. 2d 186 1999.

[103]*See* 209 U.S.C. §1232g (b)(1), *See also* 34 C.F.R. §99.31, and 6 Rapp 13.04[8][b][i] (2003).

[104]It is worth noting that many states now have laws in place requiring courts to notify schools of juvenile adjudications for serious offenses. Generally, notification is limited to the school principal and the information can only be shared on a need-to-know basis. School officials should consult with their school or district legal representation, state educational agency, or state court administrator for a full review of the applicable laws and procedures in this area.

[105]34 CFR 99.30 - .34

[106]6 James A. Rapp, Education Law, Sec. 13.04[8][b][i] (2003); *See also*, Rapp, Stephens, and Clantz, *The Need to Know, Juvenile Record Sharing* (National School Safety Center 1989); FERPA, 20 USCS §1232g (b)(4); State *ex rel.* Garden State Newspapers, Inc. v. Hoke, 205 W. Va. 611, 520 S.E. 2d 186 1999.

[107]20 USC §1232g (a)(4)(B)(ii), (b)(6)(A), (b)(1)(E), (h).

[108]20 USC §1232g (b)(1)(E), (h).

[109]20 USC §1232g (b)(1)(E)

[110]20 USC §1232g (b)(1)(E), (h); *See also* 6 Rapp 13.04 [8][b][xii][A] (2001).

4

Safe, Supportive, and Effective Schools: Promoting School Success to Reduce School Violence

David Osher
Kevin Dwyer
American Institutes for Research

Shane R. Jimerson
University of California, Santa Barbara

Too often, school safety, school violence, student support, and academic achievement are treated as separate domains. A safe and effective school framework aligns school safety, student support, and academic achievement at an individual, classroom, school, and ideally, community level. The risk and protective factors for academic, social, and behavioral problems are often intertwined; thus, interventions that target one domain frequently impact on the other domains (Skinner & Smith, 1992; Slavin & Fashola, 1998). This chapter describes a comprehensive three-level approach to align student support, school safety, and academic achievement. The first section provides an overview of the connections between and among student support, school safety, and academic achievement. The second section provides the conceptual underpinnings for implementing a comprehensive approach. The final section provides a brief description of how to apply this model to students and schools that have different needs and strengths. Creating safe, supportive, and effective schools will result in reduced school violence.

ALIGNING SAFETY, SUPPORT, AND ACHIEVEMENT

Although student support, school safety, and academic achievement are often discussed independently, they are interactive and often interdependent. For example, a review by the Educational Testing Service emphasized that school safety was one of the correlates of academic achievement (Barton, 2003), and the work of Kellam and his colleagues suggests that improvements in academic performance can reduce depressive symptoms (Kellam, Rebok, Mayer, Ialongo, & Kalodner, 1994). Bandura (1991) and Harter (1990) illustrated how academic success can enhance student self-concept, and analyses of data from the National Longitudinal Study of Adolescent Health (AddHealth) suggest that youth who have problems with school, who are doing poorly in school, who are failing school, and who are skipping school are at much higher risk of early health-risk behavior (Blum, 2001). Similarly, an analysis of the National Assessment of Educational Progress (NAEP) 2000 school questionnaire on school climate (student behavior; parent involvement; and schoolwide morale, attitudes, and expectations) found that at three grade levels (4, 8, and 12), students in schools reporting an above average climate on any one of the three measures had higher mean NAEP mathematics scale scores than students in schools reporting average or below average school climate on the same measure (Greenberg, Skidmore, & Rhodes, 2004). Furthermore, analyses of the AddHealth data found that at schools where students get along with each other, pay attention, and hand in assignments on time, teenagers report substantially stronger feelings of connectedness (Blum, 2001). The efforts of Wang, Haertel, and Walberg (1997) to identify influences on learning suggest the impact of major features of what can be conceptualized as student support. Their analysis examined the content of 179 handbook chapters and reviews and 91 research syntheses and surveyed 61 educational researchers. Eight of the top 11 (out of 28) influences were classroom management, parental support, student–teacher social interactions, sociobehavioral attributes, motivational–affective attributes, the peer group, school culture, and classroom climate factors. A strong positive relationship appears to exist among and between school climate, student support factors, and academic achievement.

Although some school safety approaches focus on threat assessment or physical safety, a comprehensive approach emphasizes and addresses the social and emotional as well as the physical aspects of safety. For example, although students may miss school because of fears for their physical safety, they may also do so out of fear of emotional ridicule or threat (Garbarino & deLara, 2002), including being bullied or harassed by students and staff for their gender, appearance, disability, sexual orientation, race, language, behavior, clothes, or other matters. Social and emotional threats are far more common than physical attacks (Bear, Webster-Stratton, Furlong, & Rhee, 2000). Feeling emotionally safe is critical to learning, and although learning depends on an orderly environment, it also involves asking for help and acknowledging mistakes, which often depend on whether students feel emotionally safe (Lee, Smith, Perry, & Smylie, 1999). This climate of safety can contribute to students seeking help for themselves and others and, in doing so, reducing the risk of violence (Osher & Dwyer, 2005).

Effective schools foster and support high academic and behavioral standards, making achievement within these schools both a collective and an individual phenomenon. Collective components of achievement involve the characteristics of the school community, including its culture, structure, human resources, and student members. These factors vary considerably across schools. Individual components include the characteristics of both the adults and the students. Adult characteristics include the knowledge, skills, beliefs, attitudes, and behaviors of administrators, teachers, student services personnel, and other staff. Student characteristics include the cognitive and behavioral strengths and needs of students. These include student academic and socioemotional skills as well as their behavioral and psychological characteristics, including their attitudes and motivation. Collective and individual characteristics of both adults and students may be analytically distinguishable, but they interact in a dynamic and reciprocal manner. For example, a teacher's health, the physical arrangement of the classroom, curricular demands placed on the student, and peer influences can affect student–teacher transactions (Sutherland & Wehby, 2001), and these transactions are nested in, as well as affect, the broader school context (Sameroff, 2000).

Adults have characteristics that include their beliefs and attitudes regarding themselves, other adults, and students. This also includes their capacity, knowledge, and ability to act in a way that promotes a high-performing school community, as well as high achievement and appropriate behavior among all students. Beliefs and attitudes include adults' sense of their role; for example, does a teacher view student support, or even support of other teachers, as part of his or her role? It also includes the beliefs and attitudes that teachers hold toward students and one another (Bryk & Schneider, 2002). For example, do teachers, administrators, and families trust one another, believe that every child can achieve to high standards, and believe that they have the individual and collective capacity to do the individual and organizational things necessary to help students realize these standards? These beliefs and the behaviors that are related to them are also transactional, resulting in an ongoing dynamic influence across time. For example, capacity is the ability to act and involves an ongoing interaction between the individual and the school. Although caring teachers are very important, the challenge is whether or not teachers have and sustain the capacity to care (Quinn, Osher, Hoffman, & Hanley, 1998). Their professional demeanor and positive interactions with parents influence student success and enhance parent involvement. However, parent involvement may be diminished by inappropriate communications. For instance, Harry, Allen, and McLaughlin (1995) found that school personnel decreased African-American parental involvement by using technical jargon, ignoring parents' questions and concerns, and scheduling conferences without parental input.

The capacity of adults also includes their experiences, knowledge, skills, and ability to integrate these and draw on them in a productive manner. Capacity to meet the many challenges that adults face requires ongoing training and support of skills and practices. Training should be focused, support necessary attitudinal change, and be delivered in a manner that develops or enhances the capacity of administrators, teachers, other staff, and families to collaborate and employ effective strategies and approaches. Adults should be prepared to be both interpersonally and culturally competent. Administrative support is vital, including the moral, logistical, and technical support needed to implement these approaches effectively (e.g., principal leadership, scheduling planning and meeting times, instructional support, monitoring, and coaching). Capacity is moderated (and in some cases mediated) by peer support groups, problem-solving teams, and peer pressure to act appropriately (or inappropriately). Although capacity is often thought of in technical terms, it also has an emotional component; it includes the ability of adults to regulate their behavior, which appears to be mediated by their emotional capital, which, in turn, is influenced by all things that occur at the school and in their life.

Student behavioral characteristics include their preparedness, attendance, attentiveness, and behavioral engagement while in school, including time on task (Connell, Spencer, & Aber, 1994). Psychological characteristics include motivation, psychological engagement, and perseverance, the absence of which has been related to dropping out (Fredricks, Blumenfeld, Friedel, & Paris, in press). Cairns and Cairns' (1994) longitudinal analyses demonstrated the connection between behavioral and emotional disengagement and discipline problems. Bryk and Thum's (1989) analysis of the effects of high school organization on dropping out found that absenteeism was higher in schools with more discipline problems and where principals reported teacher problems. This study also noted that the drop-out rate is lower when students feel safe and academic emphasis is greater, faculty are interested in and engaged with students, students feel that discipline policies are fair, and there is less internal differentiation among students. Strong academic emphasis without social support and connectedness may put students who are already at risk at even greater levels of risk of failure, frustration, and even school removal for academic noncompliance (McDill, Natriello, & Pallas, 1986; Morrison, 2002). Alternatively, the combination of student support and academic press is promising (Ancess, 2003). Analyses of Chicago school data indicated that regardless of their backgrounds, students learn more when they experience both high levels of student support and academic press, and schools that have high levels of student support and academic press make larger gains in math and reading scores than do those that do not combine student support and academic press (Lee et al., 1999).

Because students need appropriate support to facilitate learning and address the barriers to learning, academically effective schools often have high levels of academic emphasis in combination with student support (Adelman & Taylor, 2000). This may particularly be the case in schools that serve students who are challenged by multiple risk factors (Ancess,

2003; Pianta & Walsh, 1996; Shouse, 1996). Academic emphasis includes (a) instructional leadership, (b) effective pedagogy, (c) well-trained teachers, and (d) an explicit focus on teaching and learning. Student support includes (a) positive connections to adults, (b) explicit support of prosocial student interactions in an inclusive school community, (c) teaching of and support for social and emotional learning (SEL) skills, (d) use of positive behavioral supports, and (e) appropriate and engaging opportunities to learn. Effective schools provide students and staff with the support necessary to promote high achievement, and the intensity of support is varied to address student and school needs. Connecting resources maximizes the chances for success by aligning school—and community—student support resources.

Conceptual Basis for a Three-Level Approach to Align Safety, Support, and Achievement

The conceptual roots of a comprehensive approach are grounded in a variety of disciplines, frameworks, and fields related to children's learning and behavior.

- *Public health* focuses on population-based (as opposed to individual) approaches to problems, which include a focus on variation of effect and impact. A public health approach aligns promotion and prevention and includes universal, early (selective and indicated), and intensive interventions (Davis, 2002; Mrazek & Haggerty, 1994; World Health Organization, 2002).
- *Prevention and developmental science* (including developmental psychopathology) identify risk and protective factors and factors that mediate and moderate outcomes (e.g., Hawkins et al., 1998; Jessor, 1998; Kendziora & Osher, 2004).
- *Positive youth development* (including research on social competence) points to the importance of promoting resilience, social emotional learning (SEL), and developmental assets (Catalano et al., 2004; Cicchetti, Rappaport, Sandler, & Weissberg, 2000).
- *Behavioral research in special education and psychology* has led to the development of positive behavioral supports, classroom management techniques, and functional behavior analysis (Walker, Colvin, & Ramsey, 1995).
- *Mental health services and treatment research* identify effective approaches and therapeutic interventions for mental health disorders (Burns & Hoagwood, 2002).
- *Life course/social field theory* points to the key role of social fields and natural raters and how the fields and raters change through people's life course (Kellam & Rebok, 1992).
- *Ecological theory* (Bronfenbrenner, 1977) points to the importance of focusing on multiperson systems of interaction: an immediate setting (e.g., a school); interrelations among major settings (e.g., home–school); other social structures that influence what goes on in the major settings (e.g., the presence of a system of care); and overarching institutional patterns (community resources and how they are allocated).
- *Transactional analyses* emphasize that developmental outcomes are the result of an ongoing dynamic interplay among child behavior, adult responses, and environmental variables that may influence both the child and youth and those who interact with him or her (Sameroff, 2000; Sutherland, 2000; Sutherland, Wehby, & Yoder, 2002).

Although the models that come out of each of these knowledge areas are distinct, the models and the empirical data that ground them can be aligned (e.g., Dryfoos, 1990). For example, school-related transactions take place in nested environments (e.g., home, community, school, and classroom) and change over the life span as the importance of social fields change, and developmental epidemiological approaches can study the impact of interventions among populations over time (Kellam, 1994). Similarly, a public health model can integrate both promotion of positive youth development and prevention of problems (Davis, 2002).

Research suggests that risk and protective factors underlying problem behavior predict positive youth development, suggesting that an approach that reduces risk and enhances protection is likely to enhance youth wellness while reducing future problem behaviors (Catalano et al., 2004; Catalano, Hawkins, Berglund, Pollard, & Arthur, 2002). Further, although the intellectual foundations of work in positive youth development is not necessarily based in behavioral theory, the behavioral principles of reinforcement and social learning can be aligned with youth development approaches (Bandura, 1995). This does not mean that a hodgepodge approach should be taken; the nuances and specifics of each framework must be addressed. For example, a focus on risk factors alone does not produce high-quality outcomes (Pittman, 1991), but research on risk and protection suggests that an exclusive focus on developmental assets will not eliminate the impact of risk factors (Pollard, Hawkins, & Arthur, 1999). Further syntheses of research from different paradigms will help coordinate problem solving and help schools better predict and prevent individual and system failures.

In addition to these considerations, a number of relevant fields of inquiry exist. They include research on the following:

- *School effectiveness* includes research regarding school effects, improvement, reform, and size, which describe what is necessary to transform and enhance schools (Teddlie & Reynolds, 2000).
- *School safety, discipline, and violence prevention* provide data on effective approaches and identify the problems associated with punitive approaches and the potential benefits of a three-level approach to prevention and intervention (Gottfredson et al., 2000; U.S. Public Health Service, 2000).
- *Research on instruction, curriculum, and assessment* identifies effective and less effective approaches to working with different groups of students (Marzano, 2003).
- *Research on safe, supportive, and successful schools* identifies the characteristics of such schools (Ancess, 2003; Murphy, Beck, Crawford, Hodges, & McGaughy, 2002; Osher, Sandler, & Nelson, 2001).
- *Research on consultation and team problem-solving theory* assists in the application of these foundations to systems and their application to learning. Interventions are supported through training, modeling, and ongoing coaching. Effects on systems and individuals are monitored and solutions measured through formative and standardized assessments (Kratochwill & Bergan, 1990).
- *Research on cultural competence, culturally responsive teaching, and multicultural education* examines the nature of disparities among youth of diverse cultural backgrounds and identifies what works and what does not work in the education of children of color (Cross, Bazron, Isaacs, & Dennis, 1989; Gay, 2000; Osher, Cartledge, et al., 2004; U.S. Public Health Service, 2001).

There is a good deal of convergence across these areas on five matters:

1. There are school effects (Osher, Woodruff, & Sims, 2002; Rutter, Maughan, Mortimore, Outson, & Smith, 1979; Teddlie & Reynolds, 2000). Research indicates there are numerous important school factors that matter, including (a) teacher beliefs and expectations that relationships with students matter; (b) leadership; (c) collaboration and coordination; (d) academic press; and (e) a commitment to doing what is necessary to help students succeed (Ancess, 2003; Evans, 2001; Lee et al., 1999).

2. Students benefit from and need high-quality teaching and effective social support that engages them in the learning process. Effective instruction includes the ability to connect with students, help them regulate their behavior, manage the classroom, and engage students at the zone of proximal development (Ancess, 2003; Marzano, 2003; Murphy et al., 2002; Osher et al., 2001).

3. Rigid and unflexible approaches to discipline do not work and disproportionately harm students of color and students with disabilities, and positive and relational approaches to discipline do the opposite (Osher et al., 2001; Skiba, Michael, Nardo, & Peterson, 2000; Sugai et al., 2000; U.S. Public Health Service, 2000).

4. Culture matters and must and can be addressed (Allen & Boykin, 1992; Cross et al., 1989; Gay, 2000; U.S. Public Health Service, 2001).

5. Change is hard, takes time, and requires facilitation, trust, and support (Bryk & Schneider, 2002; Evans, 2001).

The convergence of literature as described earlier supports the comprehensive framework, which is presented in the next section.

Student support is key to a comprehensive approach to student safety and achievement. This support can be understood from both a risk and an asset-based perspective. From a risk-based perspective, student support addresses barriers to learning as well as factors that set the stage for or reinforce behavioral problems (e.g., alienating environments, bullying, punitive discipline, and inappropriate pedagogy). From an asset-based perspective, student support provides youth with the personal resources and social capital needed to help them succeed in school, handle problematic situations, meet the schools' behavioral expectations, and learn. Some interventions focus on risk and protection and aim at decreasing problem behaviors, and others focus on the development of assets that provide building blocks for healthy development; however, they can be aligned. Prevention efforts that target risks are most successful when they are coordinated with explicit attempts to enhance children's competence, connection to others, and ability to contribute to their community (Eccles & Appleton-Gootman, 2002; Greenberg et al., 2003; Pittman, Irby, Tolman, Yohalem, & Ferber, 2001). For example, Durlak and Wells' (1997) meta-analysis of 177 primary prevention programs, which were designed to prevent behavioral and social problems among youth under age 18, showed improved assertiveness, communication skills, self-confidence, and academic performance as well as reduced internalizing and externalizing problems.

A COMPREHENSIVE FRAMEWORK FOR STUDENT SUPPORT, SAFETY, AND ACHIEVEMENT

Supportive schools as conceptualized in this chapter provide students with social support (supportive relationship with individuals; Lee et al., 1999) and other forms of support (e.g., behavioral and mental health support) that facilitate achievement and address barriers to learning (Osher, Dwyer, & Jackson, 2004). Student support can be conceptualized as having four dimensions, each of which involves a cluster of attributes:

1. Connection within caring schools
2. Self-regulation and teaching SEL skills
3. Positive behavioral supports
4. Engaging and appropriate learning opportunities (Osher, Dwyer, & Jackson, 2004)

These four dimensions are interactive and interdependent.

There is some overlap between and among dimensions, both in terms of what each dimension includes and the impact of some interventions across multiple dimensions. For example, there is a connection between helping students regulate their behavior (Dimension 2) and teaching them the skills necessary to meet the schools' behavioral demands (Dimension 3); however, there are differences. Dimension 2 explicitly targets SEL and focuses on internalization, application, and generalization of SEL skills. Skill instruction under the positive behavioral supports dimension, on the other hand, focuses on meeting the schools' behavioral demands. SEL, when taught and reinforced in natural settings in school and home, is far more likely to be generalized and internalized than behavior modifications requiring token reinforcements (Greenberg et al., 2003; McConnell, Missall, Silberglitt, & McEvoy, 2002; Nelson & Rutherford, 1988). Effective interventions may also cross multiple dimensions or combine interventions that cross multiple dimensions. For example, the Child Development Project involves Dimensions 1, 2, and 4 (Solomon, Battistich, Watson, Schaps, & Lewis, 2000) and BEST combines Second Step (Dimension 2) with Effective Behavioral Support (Dimension 3) (Sprague et al., 2001).

This section explores the four dimensions (and related clusters) and then illustrates how they can be addressed for all students, for some students who are at a greater level of risk, and for a smaller number of students who are at an even greater level of need.

The Four Dimensions

Belonging, Connection, and Care

Dimension 1 involves feelings of belonging at schools, connection to students and adults in both the classroom and school, and caring school environments. Resnick and his colleagues (1997) called this phenomenon *connectedness* and included within it an adolescent's perception of safety, belonging, respect, and feeling cared for at school. Other researchers have pointed to the importance of bonding to the school (Hawkins & Weis, 1985), sense of community (Battistich & Horn, 1997), and school membership (Wehlage, Rutter, Smith, Lesko, & Fernandez, 1989) and linked them to both positive and negative academic and behavioral outcomes (McNeely & Falci, 2004; McNeely, Nonnemaker, & Blum, 2002; Metz, 2003; Valenzuela, 1999). School engagement and related constructs and measures have recently been reviewed by Jimerson, Campos, and Greif (2003).

Schools, particularly large ones, can be alienating places, which students, particularly those who are socially disadvantaged or are not doing well, experience as uncaring (e.g., Page, 1991). Successful schools are often places of connection and engagement for all students (e.g., Bensman, 2000; Maeroff, 1999; National Research Council, 2004). Osterman's (2000) review of research on student belongingness found that it influences achievement through its effects on engagement. Other research suggests that students' sense of belonging is related to their course grades and academic self-efficacy (Roeser, Midgley, & Urdan, 1996). Resnick, Harris, and Blum's (1993) multivariate analyses of data on 36,000 students in Grades 7–12 found that school connectedness was the most salient protective factor for both boys and girls against acting-out behaviors and was second in importance after family connectedness for internalizing behaviors (e.g., withdrawal, despondence, and panic, which are frequently associated with depression and anxiety disorders). Further analyses of the AddHealth data (Blum, 2001) suggest that adolescents who feel connected to adults at school are less likely to use alcohol or substances, experience less emotional distress, attempt suicide less, and engage in less deviant and violent behaviors. School connectedness was the only school-related variable that was protective for every single outcome measured (Resnick et al., 1993).

Research suggests that students who believe that they are cared for and matter put more effort into their schooling, which, in turn, positively affects their learning (Smerdon, 1999). For example, examinations of National Longitudinal Study of 1988 (NELS:88) data established that students are more likely to perform well on tests when they believe that their teachers care about them (Muller, 2001; Ryan & Patrick, 2001). Similarly, Croninger and Lee (2001) examined NELS:88 data regarding students' beliefs about how much their Grade-10 teachers support their efforts to succeed in school and teachers' reports about whether individual Grade-10 students receive guidance from them about school or personal matters. They found that teachers served as an important source of social capital for students, which reduced the probability of a student's dropping out by nearly half. Students from socially disadvantaged backgrounds as well as those who had academic difficulties in the past benefited most, a finding that others have also made (e.g., Ancess, 2003). In a meta-analysis of more than 100 studies, Waters, Marzano, and McNulty (2003) found that the quality of teacher–student relationships drove other aspects of classroom management. Teachers who had high-quality relationships with their students had 31% fewer discipline problems, rule violations, and related problems over a year's time than did teachers who lacked high-quality relationships with their students. This finding is supported by a set of studies that range from preschool through high school. They suggest that supportive relationships between teachers and students promote student engagement, positive attitudes, a sense of belonging toward school, motivation, and academic achievement (Birch & Ladd, 1997; Connell, Halpern-Felsher, Clifford, Crichlow, & Usinger, 1995; Haamre & Pianta, 2001; NRC, 2004; Sinclair, Christenson, Lehr, & Anderson, 2003; Wentzel, 1997, 1998; Wentzel & Wigfield, 1998).

Social Emotional Learning

Dimension 2 involves support for students' ability to regulate their emotions as well as their social and academic behavior through developing their social and emotional skills. Effective SEL programming helps students develop skills that enable them to recognize and manage their emotions, understand and appreciate others' perspectives, establish positive goals, make responsible decisions, and handle interpersonal situations effectively (CASEL, 2003; Lemerise & Arsenio, 2000). Wilson, Gottfredson, and Najaka's (2001) meta-analysis of 165 studies of school-based prevention found that self-control or social competency programming that employed cognitive–behavioral and behavioral instructional methods consistently was effective in reducing dropout, nonattendance, conduct problems, and substance use.

Analyses by Zins, Weissberg, Wang, and Walberg (2004) suggest that SEL contributes to school-related attitudes, behavior, and performance.

- Attitudes include (a) stronger sense of community (bonding), (b) more academic motivation and higher aspirations, and (c) positive attitudes toward school.
- Behavior includes (a) understanding the consequences of behavior, (b) coping effectively with middle school stressors, (c) more prosocial behavior, (d) fewer or reduced absences, (e) more classroom participation, (f) greater effort to achieve, (g) reductions in aggression and disruptions, (h) lower rate of conduct problems, (i) fewer hostile negotiations at school, (j) fewer suspensions, (k) better transition to middle school, and (l) increased engagement.
- Performance includes (a) increased grades and achievement, (b) on track to graduate, and (c) fewer dropouts.

Positive Behavioral Approaches

Dimension 3 involves reducing inappropriate use of punitive responses and the use of positive behavioral supports. Schools sometimes emphasize punitive measures to manage student behavior, and teachers often use disapproval more frequently than approval as a consequence for student behavior (Mayer & Sulzer-Azaroff, 1991). Educators may respond to student behavioral problems in a reactive, negative, and harsh manner, which includes hostile adult responses, disciplinary referrals, punishment, segregation, and removal from the school environments (Mayer, 2001; Noguera, 2003; Page, 1991). Punitive responses can include paddling, other forms corporal punishment, and even denial of bathroom privileges (Hyman & Snook, 1999). These responses are often disproportionately applied to students of color and students with emotional and behavioral disabilities (Skiba et al., 2000). Mayer and his colleagues have demonstrated that a heavy reliance on punishment as a management tool can promote vandalism and disruption (Mayer, 2002). These negative responses can also affect the learning process; students with behavioral problems and disorders are provided with lower levels of instruction, praised less, called on less frequently than other students, and provided with less wait time (Gunter & Denny, 1998; Sutherland & Wehby, 2001; Sutherland et al., 2002; Van Acker, Grant, & Henry, 1996; Wehby, Symons, & Shores, 1995).

In fact, what Gunter and his colleagues have conceptualized as a negative-reinforcement cycle (Gunter, Denny, Jack, Shores, & Nelson, 1993) reduces a student's opportunity to learn (Gunter & Coutinho, 1997; Osher, Morrison, & Bailey, 2003), which is dependent on instructional time (Greenwood, Carta, & Maheady, 1991). These ongoing transactions contribute to a self-sustaining cycle of classroom disruption and negative consequences (Dumas, Prinz, Smith, & Laughlin, 1999; Farmer, Quinn, Hussey, & Holohan, 2001; Osher et al., 2002) that includes academic failure, as teachers ignore, remove, or in other ways fail to address the academic needs of students with behavioral problems, and forced segregation with antisocial peers, which may reinforce problem behavior (Dishion, McCord, & Poulin, 1999; Maag, 2001; Murphy et al., 2002; Powell, Farrar, & Cohen, 1985). These responses also contribute to student disaffection and disengagement (Noguera, 2003) and may increase the frequency and intensity of problematic behavior (Dishion, et al., 1999; Mayer, Butterworth, Nafpaktitis, & Sulzer-Azaroff, 1983).

Positive behavioral supports (PBS) can be employed at a schoolwide level. For example, PBS as a universal intervention may include a limited number of schoolwide behavioral rules that can be clearly identified, stating them positively, displaying them visibly, and structuring the school environment so that students can meet behavioral expectations. PBS as an early intervention may be in the form of functional behavioral assessment. PBS can also be incorporated within an intensive intervention, such as school-based wrap-around services. Positive supports also include the physical structure of the school (e.g., its size, layout, and lighting), as well as administrative practices.

This dimension is based on research grounded in applied behavioral analysis and environmental design that demonstrates the following: (a) how teachers and schools can proactively reduce the incidence of problem behavior and respond in a proactive manner, (b) the ineffectiveness of punishment as an intervention, and (c) how schools can successfully use alternatives to punishment. For example, Mayer and his colleagues reduced vandalism and vandalism-related costs in some Los Angeles County elementary and junior high schools by matching academic materials to student skill levels, increasing positive reinforcement for appropriate classroom behavior and academic progress, and educating school counselors and psychologists about behavioral consultation methods (Mayer et al., 1983). Similarly, results of a study by Sutherland, Alder, and Gunter (2003), which examined the impact of an intervention aimed at increasing the opportunity to respond (OTR) for fourth graders who have emotional or behavioral disorders, suggest that increased rates of OTR contributed to increased rates of student correct responses, increased task engagement, and decreased disruptive behavior. This research has demonstrated inefficiencies of inconsistent and punitive school and classroom management systems including (a) punitive and inconsistent school and classroom behavior management practices and unclear, invisible, or unachievable rules and expectations regarding appropriate behavior; (b) lack of adequate supervision and monitoring of student behavior; (c) the failure to effectively correct rule violations and reward adherence to them; and (d) the failure to individualize consequences (Colvin, Kameenui, & Sugai, 1993; Hawkins, Catalano, Kosterman, Abbott, & Hill, 1999; Mayer & Sulzer-Azaroff, 1991; Walker et al., 1996).

Academic Engagement and Support

Dimension 4 includes all the things schools do to ensure that every child succeeds academically. This dimension can be conceptualized as having technical, cultural-structural, and student-specific dimensions. These dimensions interact with one another as well as with the other three dimensions. For example, in schools that lack community and PBS, it is more likely that the enacted curriculum will be a curriculum of control (Knitzer, Steinberg, & Fleisch, 1990) or teaching for order (what some call *defensive teaching*) where teachers lower the academic press and accept disengagement as long as it is not disruptive (Murphy et al., 2002).

Technical Factors.   Some students may learn regardless of the quality of the academic opportunities, but others require effective instruction, and still others require additional academic supports. Technical issues include the quality of organization, sequencing, presentation, and pacing of the curriculum as well as the manner in which learning is regularly assessed and feedback is provided. This includes the management of instructional time (Greenwood et al., 1991) and the extent to which students are actively involved in learning (Murphy et al., 2002). Technical issues also include the efficient and appropriate use of effective instructional strategies such as advance organizers, mastery learning approaches, homework and practice, direct instruction, peer tutoring, curriculum-based assessment, and cooperative learning. They also involve the availability of additional supports (e.g., tutoring) for students who need those supports. Finally, they include the use of research-based educational strategies and the decision not to employ strategies that do not work for many students.

School Cultural and Structural Factors.   Successful schools are ones in which (a) there is a teacher community that focuses on learning, (b) individual teachers have high expectations for all students and believe that all students can learn and that they as teachers can teach them, and (c) teachers as a group believe that they are collectively accountable for student success (Lee, Smith, & Croninger, 1995; Murphy et al., 2002; Wehlage et al., 1989). Teachers in these schools do not blame students, their families, or their social failure for student failure. For this to happen, there needs to be a culture of problem solving rather than a culture of blame or avoidance and principal leadership that supports that culture (Murphy et al., 2002; Quinn et al., 1998). For example, it is harder for teachers to maintain high standards for every student, have community among themselves, and feel collective responsibility for learning in large schools and in schools that track students (Ancess, 2003; Metz, 1997). Structural factors also include efficient school and community systems that connect students and families to prevention and treatment resources (Blechman, Fishman, Fishman, & Lewis, 2004; Osher, 2002; Rappaport et al., 2002).

Student-Specific Factors.   For learning to take place, teachers must engage and connect with the students (NRC, 2004). Students learn best when learning is active, aligns with their experiences and goals, and builds on their strengths as well as builds strengths. Hence, individualization (personalization) is important. This includes using multiple modalities for learning and scaffolding the learning process so that there is an appropriate balance between challenge and support (Moll & Greenberg, 1990). Effective instruction and assessment require cultural competency, both in content and delivery, to successfully address student epistemology, student-language proficiency, cultural worldviews, cultural communication and socialization styles, and student life context and values (Solano-Flores & Nelson-Barber, 2001).

ADDRESSING DIFFERENT LEVELS OF NEED

Effective intervention should address the nature and intensity of student needs, and a three-level public health approach provides a way for organizing supportive resources. Because student needs are related to environmental factors that place them at risk, as well as the presence of protective factors and assets in the community, the percentage of students in a school who require early or intensive interventions will vary (Scales & Leffert, 1999). Hence, although it may be useful to parse out interventions by percentages of students for triaging purposes, the percentages of students who actually require early and intensive interventions will vary based on the configuration of risk and protective factors in and among the members of the school community.

The three levels of intervention are interactive. Universal approaches and interventions create a schoolwide foundation. When a strong foundation is in place, it is easier to identify students who require early interventions and also makes it more likely that early interventions, which often are done in groups or are not provided at a high dosage level, will work. Similarly, universal interventions reduce the incidence of problem behavior in the school population. This, in turn means, that fewer (and hopefully no) students will be available to tease or harass other students or to induce other students to participate in problematic activities or to reinforce students when they do act in an antisocial manner (Espelage & Swearer, 2004; Patterson, Reid, & Dishion, 1992). Furthermore, a reduction in problematic behaviors at a universal level will free adults to teach and connect with students, while reducing the likelihood that they will respond to students in a counteraggressive manner, which would reinforce inappropriate behaviors.

The more risk factors a child has, the more likely it is that he or she will experience poor outcomes (Kendziora & Osher, 2004). Schools can function as additional risk factors. School attributes that appear to be risk factors include alienation, academic frustration, chaotic transitions, negative relationships with adults and peers, teasing, bullying, gangs, segregation with antisocial peers, school-driven mobility, harsh discipline, suspension, and expulsion. A healthy, solid schoolwide foundation and effective early interventions reduce the alienation and chaos level of bullying that can be particularly harmful to students who are at a high level of need. Empirical data suggest the power of universal interventions on students who are at greater level of risk. For example, disaggregated data from the Good Behavior Game suggest that the students who benefit most are boys with the highest level of behavioral problems (Kellam et al., 1994). Similarly, disaggregated data from the Child Development Project and the Tennessee statewide Class Size Reduction Experiment suggest that students of color as well as students from economically disadvantaged families benefited the most from these interventions (Pate-Bain, Fulton, & Boyd-Zaharias, 1999; Solomon et al., 2000).

All children require connection, need self-regulation, and benefit from effective, engaging instruction and PBS. However, what is done to support individual students—both the intensity and type of intervention—differs as a function of student strengths, assets, and needs. The following sections illustrate how these supports can be implemented.

There are some common characteristics of interventions at each level. Universal interventions include both promotion efforts that build assets and protective factors (e.g., connection to adults in the school) and risk-targeted interventions that address risk factors (e.g., behavioral problems in the classroom). As in the case of adding fluoride to water to prevent tooth decay, universal interventions (they are sometimes referred to as primary prevention) are provided to everyone in a population whether it is a grade or the school—even though every one may not require them. This is important because no matter how effective screening for risk factors is, there will always be false-negatives (Derzon, 2001), and the purpose of primary prevention is to reduce the incidence of a problem (e.g., tooth decay) in a population. However, universal interventions will not be sufficient to protect all children, hence the need for early and intensive intervention.

Early interventions include both selective and indicated interventions. Selective interventions are for individuals who, although they are not displaying early warning signs, are members of a population that research suggests are at a higher level of risk for a particular problem such as an emotional disorder (e.g., a child who has be exposed to violence). Indicated interventions address the needs of students whose behavior indicates that they are at a higher level of risk than other children (e.g., a child who exhibits early warning signs). Early interventions are often provided in group contexts, often focused on one ecological domain (e.g., the school) or even one dimension (e.g., reading). Compared with intensive interventions, early interventions are less demanding in the amount of time involved. Because early interventions should take place before an intensive problem manifests itself, it important to intervene in a nonstigmatizing manner, to build on strengths, and to avoid self-fulfilling prophecies, where teachers, staff, students, or parents confound information about a risk of a bad outcome happening (or a label) with a belief in its inevitability, and act on that belief (Weinstein, 2002). This is particularly the case for selective interventions, where, although group patterns warrant an intervention, there are no or insufficient data to definitively support the conclusion that a youth may develop a serious problem.

Intensive interventions should be individualized and focus on multiple ecological domains (e.g., family and school) as well as dimensions (e.g., academics, self-regulation, and behavior). To be effective, they must be strength-based, capacity-building, able to address multiple risk factors, linguistically and culturally competent, child-and family-driven, monitored in an ongoing manner, and intensive and sustained.

Caring and Connection

Although social connection is a universal need, some students may find it harder to connect to others because of temperament, learning or behavioral disabilities that affect their thought processes, cultural differences, and prior attachment issues. Some students are also more vulnerable to teasing or harassment, again due to temperament, disability, their personal characteristics, or lack of social skills. Small classes where teachers have more opportunity to connect with individual students, and small schools (or academies) where every adult is expected to connect with and follow some of the students, provide a platform to support social connections. Programs like the Child Development Program, which intentionally builds a school community, extend this connection at a classroom level, but some students may still require more intensive efforts at connection, for example, to help their transition into high school or to prevent them from dropping out of school (Felner, Ginter, & Primavera, 1982; Osher et al., 2003). The more students experience risks in their lives, the more it is important to engage families in a family-driven and respectful manner and in a culturally competent manner (Osher, 2000; Osher et al., 2004; Osher & Osher, 2002). Families and Schools Together (FAST) exemplifies such an approach for families (McDonald & Sayger, 1998).

Self-Regulation and SEL Skills

All students require self-regulation and SEL skills, but some students require additional support in developing these skills. Just as most students need to learn how to read in school, they must also learn how to interact appropriately with peers and adults and how to address academic challenges (e.g., frustration) and interpersonal conflicts (e.g., teasing). Effective SEL programs are developmentally appropriate and cover all age ranges. They aim at developing five core competencies: self-awareness, interpersonal and social awareness, self-regulation and management, relationship skills, and responsible decision making. Many good programs address universal needs in a developmentally appropriate way, and they can be found in *Safe and Sound: An Education Leader's Guide to Social and Emotional Learning Programs* (CASEL, 2003). However, some students require more intensive interventions, for example, those who have experienced trauma or struggle with depression or attention deficit hyperactivity disorder. In other instances, some students have an inability to control anger when provoked, cannot express their feelings, or have a particularly hard time handling failure or group pressure. Aggression replacement therapy, which is provided in a group and includes skill-streaming, anger-control training, and moral-reasoning training is a good example of an early intervention (Goldstein & Glick, 1987). Some students, such as those with anxiety disorder and depression, may need more support than group counseling can provide. Some may benefit from cognitive–behavioral treatments where they learn to deal with fears by modifying the way they think and behave; others may require medication, and still others may require both (Substance Abuse and Mental Health Services Administration, 2005). Schools are rarely involved with medication management; hence, cross-agency collaboration and coordination are very important.

Positive Behavioral Supports

All students can benefit from schoolwide systems and school–community members that support a positive and proactive approach to discipline. This strategy is likely to include articulating positive behavioral expectations, teaching students desired behaviors, and providing procedures to encourage appropriate behavior and discourage inappropriate behaviors. Positive Behavioral Interventions and Supports (PBIS), Effective Behavioral Support (EBS), and Achieve are models that provide schoolwide systems (Knoff & Batsche, 1995; Lewis & Sugai, 1999; Quinn et al., 1998; Sugai et al., 2000). However, some students (sometimes estimated at less than 15% to 20%; Sugai et al., 2000) require more intensive support, which is provided in small groups (e.g., a planning center) or individually (e.g., functional assessment; Quinn et al., 1998; Scott & Eber, 2003). Like universal approaches, these approaches are useful because adults use data to identify and respond to what they may be doing to create or reinforce any student behavior problems, as well as what supports can be put in place to address the problems (Gable, Quinn, Rutherford, & Howell, 1998; Osher, Van Aker, et al., 2004). An even smaller number of students require more intensive support, such as school-based wrap-around, which might even include an aide in the classroom (Scott & Eber, 2003). Wrap-around and other effective intensive behavioral interventions must be youth- and family-driven, must be implemented in a culturally competent manner, and, when school-based, must address the concerns and training needs of school staff (Poduska, Kendziora, & Osher, 2004; Woodruff et al., 1999).

Providing Effective Academic Support

All students require opportunities to learn. They learn best when schools provide them with effective, well-designed learning tasks that are presented in a meaningful manner and actively engage them. Effective teachers set and communicate explicit learning goals; connect learning to student experiences; present new content multiple times and through a variety of modalities; provide opportunities for practice and additional challenges after students master content; employ a quick pace; monitor student progress; provide students with ongoing feedback; and recognize efforts and celebrate progress. Effective interventions that facilitate this process include Class-wide Peer Tutoring (Greenwood, Terry, Utley, Montagna, & Walker, 1993) and Success For All (Slavin & Madden, 2001), which enable children to experience a high rate of success on meaningful academic tasks and to practice new skills. Although all students can benefit from effective instruction, some students will require group support that targets their

TABLE 4.1

Implications for Practice: Comprehensive Plans to Promote Student Safety, Support, and Achievement

1. Understand that student safety and student support are essential features in facilitating student achievement.
2. Implement strategies and programs that promote student support.
3. Use efficient, appropriate, and effective instructional strategies such as advance organizers, mastery learning approaches, homework and practice, direct instruction, peer tutoring, and cooperative learning.
4. Carefully consider the quality of organization, sequencing, presentation, and pacing of the curriculum as well as the manner in which learning is regularly assessed and feedback is provided.
5. Promote a school community that has high expectations for all students and is collectively accountable for student success.
6. Develop a school context where learning is active, aligns with student experiences and goals, and builds on students' strengths.
7. Incorporate effective instruction and assessment that require cultural competency, both in content and in delivery.
8. Implement effective intervention to address the nature and intensity of student needs.
9. Establish a school culture that reflects caring and connectedness to promote school engagement and active participation among students.
10. Provide programs that help students learn how to interact appropriately with peers and adults and how to solve academic problems and interpersonal conflicts, including self-awareness, interpersonal and social awareness, self-regulation and management, relationship skills, and responsible decision making.
11. Organize schoolwide systems and school–community members who support a positive and proactive approach to discipline.
12. Apply effective, well-designed learning tasks that are presented in a meaningful manner and actively engage students.
13. Recognize that some students will require group support that targets their linguistic background, and others may require individualized supports that address their specific learning disabilities.

linguistic background, and others may require individualized supports that address their specific learning disabilities or problems. Interventions will be most effective when they leverage student strengths and assets (e.g., interests and parental support) and when they align with the student's experiences and goals. Traditional approaches to addressing the needs of students (and teachers) involve tracking, pull-out, and separate classes. Research (Oakes & Lipton, 1994; Page, 1991) suggests that such approaches are counterproductive, and techniques have been developed to bring needed support into the classroom, such as teaming special and regular educators, employing assistive technology, and leveraging service learning to scaffold learning and engage students (Muscott, 2000; Quinn et al., 1998).

Given the numerous demands on educators, it is important to recognize that challenges are likely in aligning safety, support, and achievement. Among the most salient is the disproportionate emphasis of student evaluation on test scores. Within the current context of high-stakes testing, too often resources are invested only in those programs that purport to directly impact student achievement. Thus, many factors related to school safety and student support are ignored. Limited resources must be invested wisely. As discussed earlier, safety and student support are essential features in facilitating student achievement. Table 4.1 briefly delineates important implications for implementing comprehensive plans to promote student safety, support, and achievement.

Each school and community has unique values, needs, and strengths, which will affect how schools move forward. For some schools, the starting point may be universal youth development, for others, comprehensive behavioral approaches, and still for others, intensive mental health support. Thus, there is no single strategy or program that can be systematically implemented in all schools. This presents challenges for administrators and school personnel in determining appropriate strategies and making sure that they align. Selection criteria can be found in Osher, Dwyer, and Jackson (2004). This chapter provides a conceptual foundation for educators to build on in promoting safety, support, and achievement at school.

REFERENCES

Adelman, H. S., & Taylor, L. (2000). Moving prevention from the fringes into the fabric of school improvement. *Journal of Educational and Psychological Consultation, 11*, 7–36.

Allen, B. A., & Boykin, A. W. (1992). African American children and the educational process: Alleviating cultural discontinuity through prescriptive pedagogy. *School Psychology Review, 21*(4), 586–596.

Ancess, J. (2003). *Beating the odds: High schools as communities of commitment.* New York: Teachers College Press.

Bandura, A. (1991). Social cognitive theory of self-regulation. *Organizational Behavior and Human Decision Processes, 50*(2), 248–287.

Bandura, A. (1995). *Self-efficacy in changing societies.* Melbourne: Cambridge University Press.

Barton, P. (2003). *Parsing the achievement gap: Baselines for tracking progress.* Princeton, NJ: Educational Testing Service.

Battistich, V., & Horn, A. (1997). The relationship between students' sense of their school as a community and their involvement in problem behaviors. *American Journal of Public Health, 87*(12), 1997–2001.

Bear, G., Webster-Stratton, C., Furlong, M., & Rhee, S. (2000). Preventing aggression and violence. In G. Bear & K. Minke (Eds.), *Preventing school problems—Strategies and programs that work* (pp. 1–70). Bethesda, MD: National Association of School Psychologists.

Bensman, D. (2000). *Central Park East and its graduates: Learning by heart.* New York: Teachers College Press.

Birch, S. H., & Ladd, G. W. (1997). The teacher–child relationship and children's early school adjustment. *Journal of School Psychology, 35*(1), 61–79.

Blechman, E. A., Fishman, D. B., Fishman, C. A., & Lewis, J. E. (2004). *Caregiver alliances for at-risk and dangerous youth: Establishing school and agency coordination and accountability.* Champaign, IL: Research Press.

Blum, R. (2001). Early transitions: Risk and protective factors. *The Center,* 38–41.

Bronfenbrenner, U. (1977). Toward an experimental ecology of human development. *American Psychologist, 32,* 513–531.

Bryk, A. S., & Schneider, B. (2002). *Trust in schools: A core resource for improvement.* New York: Russell Sage Foundation.

Bryk, A. S., & Thum, Y. M. (1989). The effects of high school organization on dropping out: An exploratory investigation. *American Educational Research Journal, 26,* 353–384.

Burns, B., & Hoagwood, K. (Eds.). (2002). *Community treatment for youth: Evidence-based interventions for severe emotional and behavioral disorders.* New York: Oxford University Press.

Cairns, R., & Cairns, B. (1994). *Lifelines and risks: Pathways in our lifetime.* Cambridge University Press.

Catalano, R. F., Berglund, M. L., Ryan, J. A. M., Lonczak, H. S., & Hawkins, J. D. (2004). Positive youth development in the United States: Research findings on evaluations of positive youth development programs. *Annals of the American Academy of Political and Social Science, 591,* 98–124.

Catalano, R. F., Hawkins, J. D., Berglund, L., Pollard, J., & Arthur, M. (2002). Prevention science and positive youth development: Competitive or cooperative frameworks? *Journal of Adolescent Health, 31,* 230–239.

Cicchetti, D., Rappaport, I., Sandler, I. N., & Weissberg, R. P. (Eds.). (2000). *The promotion of wellness in children and adolescents.* Washington, DC: Child Welfare League of America Press.

Collaborative for Academic, Social, and Emotional Learning (CASEL). (2003). *Safe and sound: An education leader's guide to evidence-based social and emotional learning (SEL) programs.* Chicago, IL: Author.

Colvin, G., Kameenui, E. J., & Sugai, G. (1993). Reconceptualizing behavior management and schoolwide discipline in general education. *Education and Treatment of Children, 16,* 361–381.

Connell, J. P., Halpern-Felsher, B. L., Clifford, E., Crichlow, W., & Usinger, P. (1995). Hanging in there: Behavioral, psychological, and contextual factors affecting whether African American adolescents stay in high school. *Journal of Adolescent Research, 10*(1), 41–63.

Connell, J. P., Spencer, M. B., & Aber, J. L. (1994). Educational risk and resilience in African American youth: Context, self, actions, and outcomes in school. *Child Development, 65,* 493–506.

Croninger, R. G., & Lee, V. E. (2001). Social capital and dropping out of high school: Benefits to at-risk students of teachers' support and guidance. *Teachers College Record, 1034,* 548–581.

Cross, T. L., Bazron, B. J., Isaacs, M. R., & Dennis, K. W. (1989). *Towards a culturally competent system of care: A monograph on effective services for minority children who are severely emotionally disturbed.* Washington DC: Georgetown University Center for Child Health and Mental Health Policy, CASSP Technical Assistance Center.

Davis, N. J. (2002). The promotion of mental health and the prevention of mental and behavioral disorders: Surely the time is right. *International Journal of Mental Health, 4*(1), 3–29.

Derzon, J. H. (2001). Antisocial behavior and the prediction of violence: A meta-analysis. *Psychology in the Schools, 38*(2), 93–106.

Dishion, T. J., McCord, J., & Poulin, F. (1999). When interventions harm: Peer groups and problem behavior. *American Psychologist, 54*, 755–764.

Dryfoos, J. G. (1990). *Adolescents at risk: Prevalence and prevention.* New York: Oxford University Press.

Dumas, J. E., Prinz, R. J., Smith, E. P., & Laughlin, J. (1999). The EARLY ALLIANCE prevention trial: An integrated set of interventions to promote competence and reduce risk for conduct disorder, substance abuse, and school failure. *Clinical Child and Family Psychology Review, 2*(2), 37–53.

Durlak, J. A., & Wells, A. M. (1997). Primary prevention programs for children and adolescents: A meta-analytic review. *American Journal of Community Psychology, 25*, 115–152.

Eccles, J., & Appleton-Gootman, J. (Eds.). (2002). *Community programs to promote youth development.* Washington, DC: National Academy Press.

Espelage, D. L., & Swearer, S. M. (Eds.). (2004). *Bullying in American schools: A social-ecological perspective on prevention and intervention.* Mahwah, NJ: Lawrence Erlbaum Associates.

Evans, R. (2001). *The human side of school change: Reform, resistance, and the real-life problems of innovation.* San Francisco, CA: Jossey-Bass.

Farmer, T. W., Quinn, M. M., Hussey, W., & Holohan, T. (2001). The development of disruptive behavior disorders and correlated constraints: Implications for intervention. *Behavioral Disorders, 26*, 117–130.

Felner, R. D., Ginter, M., & Primavera, J. (1982). Primary prevention during school transition: Social support and environmental structure. *American Journal of Community Psychology, 10*, 277–290.

Fredricks, J., Blumenfeld, P., Friedel, J., & Paris, A. (in press). School engagement. In K. A. Moore & L. Lippman (Eds.), *Conceptualizing and measuring indicators of positive development: What do children need to flourish?* New York: Kluwer Academic Press.

Gable, R. A., Quinn, M. M., Rutherford, R. B., & Howell, K. (1998). Addressing problem behaviors in schools: Use of functional assessments and behavior intervention plans. *Preventing School Failure, 42*(3), 106–119.

Garbarino, J., & deLara, E. (2002). *And words can hurt forever: How to protect adolescents from bullying, harassment, and emotional violence.* New York: The Free Press.

Gay, G. (2000). *Culturally responsive teaching: Theory, research & practice.* New York: Teachers College Press.

Goldstein, A. P., & Glick, B. (1987). *Aggression replacement training: A comprehensive intervention for aggressive youth.* Champaign, IL: Research Press.

Gottfredson, G. D., Gottfredson, D. C., Czeh, E. R., Cantor, D., Crosse, S. B., & Hantman, I. (2000). *National study of delinquency prevention in schools.* Ellicott City, MD: Gottfredson Associates, Inc. Available: http://www.gottfredson.com/national.htm.

Greenberg, E., Skidmore, D., & Rhodes, D. (2004, April). *Climates for learning: mathematics achievement and its relationship to schoolwide student behavior, schoolwide parental involvement, and school morale.* Presented at the Annual Meeting of the American Educational Researchers Association, San Diego, CA.

Greenberg, M. T., Weissberg, R. P., O'Brien, M. U., Zins, J. E., Fredericks, L., Resnik, H., & Elias, M. J. (2003). Enhancing school-based prevention and youth development through coordinated social, emotional, and academic learning. *American Psychologist, 58*, 466–474.

Greenwood, C. R., Carta, J. J., & Maheady, L. (1991). Peer tutoring programs in the regular education classroom. In G. Stoner, M. R. Shinn, & H. M. Walker (Eds.), *Interventions for achievement and behavior problems* (pp. 179–200). Silver Spring, MD: National Association of School Psychologists.

Greenwood, C. R., Terry, B., Utley, C. A., Montagna, D., & Walker, D. (1993). Achievement, placement, and services: Middle school benefits of classwide peer tutoring used at the elementary school. *School Psychology Review, 22*, 497–516.

Gunter, P. L., & Coutinho, M. J. (1997). Negative reinforcement in classrooms: What we're beginning to learn. *Teacher Education and Special Education, 20*(3), 249–264.

Gunter, P. L., & Denny, R. K. (1998). Trends and issues in research regarding academic instruction of students with emotional and behavioral disorders. *Behavioral Disorders, 24*, 44–50.

Gunter, P. L., Denny, K., Jack, S. L., Shores, R. E., & Nelson, C. M. (1993). Aversive stimuli in academic interactions between students with serious emotional disturbance and their teachers. *Behavioral Disorders, 18*(4), 265–274.

Haamre, B. K., & Pianta, R. C. (2001). Early teacher–child relationships and the trajectory of children's school outcomes through eighth grade. *Child Development, 72*, 625–638.

Harry, B., Allen, N., & McLaughlin, M. (1995). Communication vs. compliance: African American parents' involvement in special education. *Exceptional Children, 61*, 364–377.

Harter, S. (1990). Processes underlying adolescent self-concept formation. In R. Montemayor, G. R. Adams, & T. P. Gulotta (Eds.), *From childhood to adolescence: A transition period?* (pp. 205–239). Newbury Park, CA: Sage.

Hawkins, J. D., Catalano, R. F., Kosterman, R., Abbott, R., & Hill, K. G. (1999). Preventing adolescent health-risk behaviors by strengthening protection during childhood. *Archives of Pediatrics and Adolescent Medicine, 153,* 226–234.

Hawkins, J. D., Herrenkohl, T., Farrington, D. P., Brewer, D., Catalano, R. F., & Harachi, T. W. (1998). A review of predictors of youth violence. In R. Loeber & D. P. Farrington (Eds.), *Serious and violent juvenile offenders: Risk factors and successful interventions* (pp. 106–146).Thousand Oaks, CA: Sage.

Hawkins, J. D., & Weis, J. G. (1985). The social development model: An integrated approach to delinquency prevention. *Journal of Primary Prevention, 6,* 73–97.

Hyman, I., & Snook, P. (1999) *Dangerous schools: What we can do about the physical and emotional abuse of our children.* San Francisco, CA: Jossey-Bass.

Jessor, R. (Ed.). (1998). *New perspectives on adolescent risk behavior.* New York: Cambridge University Press.

Jimerson, S. R., Campos, E., & Greif, J. (2003). Toward an understanding of definitions and measures of school engagement and related terms. *The California School Psychologist, 8,* 7–27.

Kellam, S., Rebok, G., Mayer, L., Ialongo, N., & Kalodner, C. (1994). Depressive symptoms over first grade and their response to a developmental epidemiologically based preventive trial aimed at improving achievement. *Development and Psychopathology, 6,* 463–481.

Kellam, S. G. (1994). The social adaptation of children in classrooms: A measure of family childrearing effectiveness. In R. D. Parke & S. G. Kellam (Eds.), *Exploring family relationships with other social contexts* (pp. 147–168). Hillsdale, NJ: Lawrence Erlbaum Associates.

Kellam, S. G., & Rebok, G. W. (1992). Building developmental and etiological theory through epidemiologically based preventive intervention trials. In J. McCord & R. E. Tremblay (Eds.), *Preventing antisocial behavior: Interventions from birth through adolescence* (pp. 162–195). New York: Guilford.

Kellam, S. G., Rebok, G. W., Wilson, R., & Mayer, L. S. (1994). The social field of the classroom: Context for the developmental epidemiological study of aggressive behavior. In R. K. Silbereisen & E. Todt (Eds.), *Adolescence in context: The interplay of family, school, peers and work in adjustment* (pp. 390–408). New York: Springer-Verlag.

Kendziora, K., & Osher, D. (2004). Fostering resilience among youth in the juvenile justice system. In C. C. Clauss-Ehlers & M. Weist (Eds.), *Community planning to foster resiliency in children* (pp. 177–196). New York: Kluwer.

Knitzer, J., Steinberg, Z., & Fleisch, B. (1990). *At the schoolhouse door: An examination of programs and policies for children with behavioral and emotional problems.* New York: Bank Street College of Education.

Knoff, H. M., & Batsche, G. M. (1995). Project ACHIEVE: Analyzing a school reform process for at-risk and underachieving students. *School Psychology Review, 24,* 579–608.

Kratochwill T. R., & Bergan, J. R. (1990). *Behavioral consultation in applied settings: An individual guide.* New York: Plenum.

Lee, V. E., Smith, J. B., & Croninger, R. G. (1995). Another look at high school restructuring: More evidence that it improves student achievement, and more insight into why. *Issues in restructuring schools* (vol. 9). Madison: WI: Center on Organization and Restructuring of School, University of Wisconsin-Madison.

Lee, V. E., Smith, J., Perry, T., & Smylie, M. A. (1999, October). *Social support, academic press, and student achievement: A view from the middle grades in Chicago.* Chicago: Consortium on Chicago School Research, Chicago Annenberg Research Project. Available: http://www.consortium-chicago.org/publications/p0e01.html

Lemerise, E., & Arsenio, W. (2000). An integrated model of emotion processes and cognition in social information processing. *Child Development, 71,* 107–118.

Lewis, T. J., & Sugai, G. (1999). Effective behavior support: A systems approach to proactive school-wide management. *Focus on Exceptional Children, 31*(6), 1–24.

Maag, J. W. (2001). Rewarded by punishment: Reflections on the disuse of positive reinforcement in schools. *Exceptional Children, 67*(2), 173–186.

Maeroff, G. I. (1999). *Altered destinies: Making life better for schoolchildren in need.* New York: St. Martin's Griffin.

Marzano, R. (2003). *What works in schools: Translating research into action.* Alexandria, VA: Association for Supervision and Curriculum Development.

Mayer, G. R. (2001). Antisocial behavior: Its causes and prevention within our schools. *Education and Treatment of Children, 24,* 414–429.

Mayer, G. R. (2002). Behavioral strategies to reduce violence. *Child and Family Behavior Therapy, 24,* 83–100.

Mayer, G. R., Butterworth, T., Nafpaktitis, & Sulzer-Azaroff, B. (1983). Preventing school vandalism and increasing discipline: A three year study. *Journal of Applied Behavior Analysis, 16,* 355–369.

Mayer, G. R., & Sulzer-Azaroff, B. (1991). Interventions for vandalism. In G. Stoner, M. R. Shinn, & H. M. Walker (Eds.), *Interventions for achievement and behavior problems* (pp. 559–580). Bethesda, MD: National Association of School Psychologists.

McConnell, S. R., Missall, K. N., Silberglitt, B., & McEvoy, M. A. (2002). Promoting social development in preschool classrooms. In M. Shinn, G. Stoner, & H. M. Walker (Eds.), *Interventions for academic and behavior problems II: Preventive and remedial approaches* (pp. 501–536). Bethesda, MD: National Association of School Psychologists.

McDill, E. L., Natriello, G., & Pallas, A. (1986). A population at risk: Potential consequences of tougher school standards for student dropouts. *American Journal of Education, 94,* 135–181.

McDonald, L., & Sayger, T. (1998). Impact of a family and school based prevention program on protective factors for high risk youth. *Drugs and Society, 12,* 61–86.

McNeely, C. A., & Falci, C. (2004). School connectedness and the transition into and out of health risk behavior among adolescents: A comparison of social belonging and teacher support. *Journal of School Health, 74*(7), 284–292.

McNeely, C.A., Nonnemaker, J. M., & Blum, R. W. (2002). Promoting student connectedness to school: Evidence from the National Longitudinal Study of Adolescent Health. *Journal of School Health, 72*(4), 138–146.

Metz, M. H. (1997). *Keeping students in, gangs out, scores up, alienation down, and the copy machine in working order: Pressures that make urban schools in poverty different.* Paper presented at the annual meeting of the American Educational Research Association, Chicago. IL.

Metz, M. H. (2003). *Different by design: The context and character of three magnet schools.* New York: Teachers College Press.

Moll, L. C., & Greenberg, J. B. (1990). Creating zones of possibilities: Creating social contexts for instruction. In L. C. Moll (Ed.), *Vygotsky and education: Instruction implications and applications of sociohistorical psychology* (pp. 319–348). New York: Cambridge University Press.

Morrison, G. (2002). *Characteristcs of students who are suspended from school.* Paper presented at the annual meeting of the American Educational Research Association, New Orleans, LA.

Mrazek, P. J., & Haggerty, R. J. (Eds.). (1994). *Reducing risks for mental disorders: Frontiers for prevention intervention research.* Washington, DC: National Academy Press.

Muller, C. (2001). The role of caring in the teacher–student relationship for at-risk students. *Sociological Inquiry, 71*(2), 241–255.

Murphy, J., Beck, L., Crawford, M., Hodges, A., & McGaughy, C. (2002). *The productive high school: Creating personalized academic communities.* Thousand Oaks, CA: Corwin Press.

Muscott, H. (2000). A review and analysis of service-learning programs involving students with emotional/behavioral disorders. *Education and Treatment of Children, 23,* 346–368.

National Research Council (NRC). (2004). *Engaging schools: Fostering high school students' motivation to learn.* Washington, DC: National Academy Press.

Nelson, C. M., & Rutherford, R. B., Jr. (1988). Behavioral interventions with behaviorally disordered students. In M. C. Wang, M. C. Reynolds, & H. J. Walberg (Eds.), *Handbook of special education: Research and practice: Vol. 2. Mildly handicapped conditions* (pp. 125–153). New York: Pergamon.

Noguera, P. (2003). *City schools and the American dream: Reclaiming the promise of public education.* New York: Teachers College Press.

Oakes, J., & Lipton, M. (1994). Tracking and ability grouping. In G. Keating (Ed.), *Access to knowledge* (pp. 43–58). New York: College Board.

Osher, D. (2000). Breaking the cultural disconnect: Working with families to improve outcomes for students placed at risk of school failure. In I. Goldenberg (Ed.), *Urban education: Possibilities and challenges confronting colleges of education* (pp. 4–11). Miami: Florida International University.

Osher, D. (2002). Creating comprehensive and collaborative systems. *Journal of Child and Family Studies, 11*(1), 91–101.

Osher, D., Cartledge, G., Oswald, D., Sutherland, K., Artiles, A. J., & Coutinho, M. (2004). Issues of cultural and linguistic competency and disproportionate representation. In R. Rutherford, M. Quinn, & S. Mather (Eds.), *Handbook of research in behavioral disorders* (pp. 54–77). New York: Guilford.

Osher, D., & Dwyer, K. (2005). *Safeguarding our children: An action guide revised and expanded.* Longmont, CO: Sopris West.

Osher, D., Dwyer, K., & Jackson, S. (2004). *Safe, supportive, and successful schools step by step.* Longmont, CO: Sopris West.

Osher, D., Morrison, G., & Bailey, W. (2003). Exploring the relationship between students: Mobility and dropout among students with emotional and behavioral disorders. *Journal of Negro Education, 72*(1), 79–96.

Osher, D., Sandler, S., & Nelson, C. (2001). The best approach to safety is to fix schools and support children and staff. *New Directions in Youth Development, 92,* 127–154.

Osher, D., Woodruff, D., & Sims, A. (2002). Schools make a difference: The relationship between education services for African American children and youth and their overrepresentation in the juvenile justice system. In D. Losen (Ed.), *Minority issues in special education* (pp. 93–116). Cambridge, MA: Harvard University, The Civil Rights Project.

Osher, D., Van Aker, R., Morrison, G., Gable, R., Dwyer, K., & Quinn, M. (2004). Warning signs of problems in schools: Ecological perspectives and effective practices for combating school aggression and violence. In M. J. Furlong, G. M. Morrison., D. Cornell, & R. Skiba, R. (Eds.), *Issues in school violence research* (pp. 13–37). Binghamton, NY: Haworth Press.

Osher, T. W., & Osher, D. (2002). The paradigm shift to true collaboration with families. *Journal of Child and Family Studies, 11*(1), 47–60.

Osterman, K. F. (2000). Students' need for belonging in the school community. *Review of Educational Research, 70*(3), 323–367.

Page, R. N. (1991). *Lower track classrooms: A curricular and cultural perspective.* New York: Teachers College Press.

Pate-Bain, H., Fulton, B. D., & Boyd-Zaharias, J. (1999). *Effects of class-size reduction in the early grades (k-3) on high school performance. Preliminary results (1999) from Project STAR, Tennessee's longitudinal class-size study.* Lebanon, PA: HEROS, Inc.

Patterson, G. R., Reid, J. B., & Dishion, T. J. (1992). *Antisocial boys: A social interactional approach.* Eugene, OR: Castalia.

Pianta, R. C., & Walsh, D. J. (1996). *High-risk children in the schools: Constructing sustaining relationships.* New York: Routledge.

Pittman, K. (1991). *Promoting youth development: Strengthening the role of youth-serving and community organizations.* Washington DC: Academy for Educational Development.

Pittman, K., Irby, M., Tolman, J., Yohalem, N., & Ferber, T. (2001). *Preventing problems, promoting development, encouraging engagement: Competing priorities or inseparable goals?* Washington, DC: The Forum for Youth Investment.

Poduska, J., Kendziora, K., & Osher, D. (2004). *Coordinated and individualized services within systems of care.* Washington, DC: Center for Effective Collaboration and Practice, American Institutes for Research.

Pollard, J. A., Hawkins, J. D., & Arthur, M. W. (1999). Risk and protection: Are both necessary to understand diverse behavioral outcomes in adolescence? *Social Work Research, 23,* 145–158.

Powell, A. G., Farrar, E., & Cohen, D. K. (1985). *The shopping mall high school:* Boston: Houghton Mifflin.

Quinn, M. M., Osher, D., Hoffman, C. C., & Hanley, T. V. (1998). *Safe, drug-free, and effective schools for all students: What works!* Washington, DC: American Institutes for Research.

Rappaport, N., Osher, D., Dwyer, K., Garrison, E., Hare, I., Ladd, J., & Anderson-Ketchmark, C. (2002). Enhancing collaborations within and across disciplines to advance mental health programs in schools. In M. D. Weist, S. Evans, & N. Tashman (Eds.), *School mental health handbook* (pp. 107–118). New York: Kluwer Academic.

Resnick, M. D., Harris, L. J., & Blum, R. W. (1993). The impact of caring and connectedness on adolescent health and well-being. *Journal of Child and Pediatric Health, 29,* 3–9.

Resnick, M. D., Bearman, P. S., Blum, R. W., Bauman, K. E., Harris, K. M., Jones, J., et al. (1997). Protecting adolescents from harm: Findings from the National Longitudinal Study of Adolescent Health. *The Journal of the American Medical Association, 278*(10), 795–878.

Roeser, R., Midgley, C., & Urdan, T. C. (1996). Perception of the school psychological environment and early adolescents' psychological and behavioural functioning in school: The mediating role of goals and belonging. *Journal of Educational Psychology, 88,* 408–422.

Rutter, M., Maughan, B., Mortimore, P., Outson, J., & Smith, A. (1979). *Fifteen thousand hours: Secondary schools and their effects on children.* Cambridge, MA: Harvard University Press.

Ryan, A., & Patrick, H. (2001). The classroom social environment and changes in adolescents' motivation and engagement during middle school. *American Educational Research Journal, 38*(2), 437–460.

Sameroff, A. J. (2000). Developmental systems and psychopathology. *Development and Psychopathology, 12,* 297–312.

Scales, P. C., & Leffert, N. (1999). *Developmental assets: A synthesis of the scientific research on adolescent development.* Minneapolis, MN: Search Institute.

Scott, T. M., & Eber, L. (2003). Functional assessment and wraparound as systemic school processes: Primary, secondary, and tertiary systems examples. *Journal of Positive Behavior Interventions, 5,* 131–143.

Shouse, R. (1996). Academic press and sense of community: Conflict and congruence in American high schools. *Research in Sociology of Education and Socialization, 11,* 173–202.

Sinclair, M. F., Christenson, S. L., Lehr, C. A., & Anderson, A. R. (2003). Facilitating student engagement: Lessons learned from Check & Connect longitudinal studies. *The California School Psychologist, 8*(1), 29–42.

Skiba, R. J., Michael R., Nardo, A., & Peterson, R. (2000). *The color of discipline: Gender and racial disparities in school punishment.* Bloomington: Indiana Education Policy Center.

Skinner, C. H., & Smith, E. S. (1992). Issues surrounding the use of self-management interventions for increasing academic performance. *School Psychology Review, 21,* 202–210.

Slavin, R. E., & Fashola, O. S. (1998). *Show me the evidence: Proven & promising programs for America's schools.* Thousand Oaks, CA: Sage.

Slavin, R. E., & Madden, N. A. (2001). *One million children: Success for all.* Newbury Park, CA: Corwin.

Smerdon, B. A. (1999). *How perceptions of school membership influence high school students' academic development: Implications for adolescents at risk of educational failure.* Unpublished dectoral dissertation, University of Michigan, Ann Arbor.

Solano-Flores, G., & Nelson-Barber, S. (2001). On the cultural validity of science assessments. *Journal of Research in Science Teaching, 38,* 553–573.

Solomon, D., Battistich, V., Watson, M., Schaps, E., & Lewis, C. (2000). A six-district study of educational change: Direct and mediated effects of the Child Development Project. *Social Psychology of Education, 4,* 3–51.

Sprague, J., Walker, H., Golly, A., White, K., Myers, D. R., & Shannon, T. (2001). Translating research into effective practice: The effects of a universal staff and student intervention on indicators of discipline and school safety. *Education and Treatment of Children, 24*(4), 495–511.

Substance Abuse and Mental Health Services Administration. (2005). *Children and adolescents with anxiety disorders.* Available: http://www.mentalhealth.samhsa.gov/publications/allpubs/CA-0007/default.asp

Sugai, G., Horner, R. H., Dunlap, G., Hieneman, M., Lewis, T. J., Nelson, C. M., Scott, T., Liaupsin, C., Sailor, W., Turnbull, A. P., Turnbull, H. R., III, Wickham, D., Reuf, M., & Wilcox, B. (2000). Applying positive behavioral support and functional behavioral assessment in schools. *Journal of Positive Behavioral Interventions, 2,* 131–143.

Sutherland, K. S. (2000). Promoting positive interactions between teachers and students with emotional and behavioral disorders. *Preventing School Failure, 44,* 110–115.

Sutherland, K. S., Alder, N., & Gunter, P. L. (2003). The effect of varying rates of OTR on the classroom behavior of students with EBD. *Journal of Emotional and Behavioral Disorders, 11,* 239–248.

Sutherland, K. S., & Wehby, J. H. (2001). Exploring the relation between increased opportunities to respond to academic requests and the academic and behavioral outcomes of students with emotional and behavioral disorders: A review. *Remedial and Special Education, 22,* 113–121.

Sutherland, K. S., Wehby, J. H., & Yoder, P. J. (2002). Examination of the relationship between teacher praise and opportunities for students with EBD to respond to academic requests. *Journal of Emotional and Behavioral Disorders, 10,* 5–13.

Teddlie, C., & Reynolds, D. (2000). School effectiveness research and the social and behavioral sciences. In C. Teddlie & D. Reynolds (Eds.), *The international handbook of school effectiveness research* (pp. 301–321). London: Falmer Press.

U.S. Public Health Service. (2000). *Youth violence: A report of the surgeon general.* Washington, DC: Author.

U.S. Public Health Service. (2001). *Mental health: Culture, race, ethnicity: A supplement to the Surgeon General's Report on Mental Health.* Washington, DC: Author.

Valenzuela, A. (1999). *Subtractive schooling: U.S.—Mexican youth and the politics of caring.* Albany: State University of New York Press.

Van Acker, R., Grant, S., & Henry, D. (1996). Teacher and student behavior as a function of risk for aggression. *Education and Treatment of Children, 19*(3), 316–334.

Walker, H. M., Colvin, G., & Ramsey, E. (1995). *Antisocial behavior in school: Strategies and best practices.* Pacific Grove, CA: Brooks/Cole.

Walker, H. M., Horner, R. H., Sugai, G., Bullis, M., Sprague, J. R., Bricker, D., & Kaufman, M. J. (1996). Integrated approaches to preventing antisocial behavior patterns among school-age children and youth. *Journal of Emotional & Behavioral Disorders, 4*(4), 194–209.

Wang, M. C., Haertel, G. D., & Walberg, H. J. (1997). *What do we know? Widely implemented school improvement programs.* Philadelphia, PA: Temple University Center for Research in Human Development and Education.

Waters, T., Marzano, B., & McNulty, B. (2003). Balanced leadership: What 30 years of research tells us about the effect of leadership on student achievement. Aurora, CO: Mid-continent Research for Education and Learning. Available: http://www.mcrel.org/

Wehby, J. H., Symons, F. J., & Shores, R. E. (1995). A descriptive analysis of aggressive behavior in classrooms for children with emotional and behavioral disorders. *Behavioral Disorders, 20*(2), 87–105.

Wehlage, G. G., Rutter, R. A., Smith, G. A., Lesko, N., & Fernandez, R. R. (1989). *Reducing the risk: Schools as communities of support.* London: The Falmer Press.

Weinstein, R. S. (2002). Overcoming inequality in schooling: A call to action for community psychology. *American Journal of Community Psychology, 30,* 21–42.

Wentzel, K. R. (1997). Student motivation in middle school: The role of perceived pedagogical caring. *Journal of Educational Psychology, 89,* 411–419.

Wentzel, K. R. (1998). Social relationships and motivation in middle school: The role of parents, teachers and peers. *Journal of Educational Psychology, 90,* 202–209.

Wentzel, K. R., & Wigfield, A. (1998). Academic and social motivational influences on students' academic performance, *Educational Psychology Review, 10*(2), 155–175.

Wilson, D. B., Gottfredson, D. C., & Najaka, S. S. (2001). School-based prevention of problem behaviors: A meta-analysis. *Journal of Quantitative Criminology, 17,* 247–272.

Woodruff, D. W., Osher, D., Hoffman, C. C., Gruner, A., King, M., Snow, S., & McIntire, J. C. (1999). *The role of education in a system of care: Effectively serving children with emotional or behavioral disorders.* Washington, DC: Center for Effective Collaboration and Practice, American Institutes for Research.

World Health Organization. (2002). *The world health report 2002—Reducing risks, promoting healthy life.* Geneva: Author.

Zins, J. E., Weissberg, R. P., Wang, M. C., & Walberg, H. J. (2004). *Building academic success on social and emotional learning: What does the research say?* New York: Teachers College Press.

5

A Problem-Solving Approach to School Violence Prevention

Jim Larson
University of Wisconsin-Whitewater

R. T. Busse
Chapman University

Virtually all plans to prevent the expression of aggressive or violent behavior in and around any school building arise out of some form of problem-solving process. Because violence is anathema to the educational process, the actuality or even the potential for it creates a problem in the school setting.

> A problem is a situation, which is experienced by an agent as different from the situation which the agent ideally would like to be in. A problem is solved by a sequence of actions that reduce the difference between the initial situation and the goal. (Heylighen, 1998)

Simply stated, and using Heylighen's definition, while in the course of normal activities educators will become aware of situations in the school that are different from the way they desire them to be. Within the problems of school violence, this may be new awareness of escalating incidences of bullying, finding a gun in a locker, or as was the case following the Columbine High School shootings in 1999 and other high-profile school shootings, frantic parental and media calls to hyper-protect children in school. Action will then be taken to reach a goal that reduces the difference between the way things are (e.g., too much bullying and too much parental concern) and the way educators want them to be. At least, one hopes so.

The elegance of the problem-solving process lies in its heuristic simplicity; the complexity lies in its execution. This chapter examines how educators concerned with violence prevention can proceed most effectively from the first recognition of a need to act to the final goal attainment using a structured problem-solving methodology.

CONCEPTUAL BASIS

The conceptual origins of problem solving as a process for service delivery in a system such as a school can be traced within modern psychology to theory and research in cognitive psychology, and more specifically, information processing psychology. In their seminal work, *Human*

Problem Solving, Newell and Simon (1972) postulated that human beings are information-processing organisms who, when presented with a stimulus, engage in a sequence of sensory reception, data transformation, memory integration, and behavioral output. When applied specifically to the process of cognitive problem solving, Newell and Simon theorized that the information must be further organized into a sequence of four tasks:

1. Identification of the problem space, which is the boundary between what is known and what the eventual goal is to be.
2. Identification of the intermediate states or subgoals that must be attained to reach the final goal state.
3. Identification of the moves or action that must be enacted by the problem solver to move from one goal state to the next.
4. Identification of the resources necessary (e.g., time, knowledge, skills, and people) to move from one goal state to the next.

These theoretical constructs have served as the foundation for applied work in clinical social problem solving, including therapy with adults (e.g., D'Zurrilla & Nezu, 1999), understanding aggressive children (e.g., Crick & Dodge, 1994; Dodge, 1986), and social skills training with children (e.g., Spivak, Platt, & Shure, 1976). Simon (1976) advanced the information-processing model to administrative decision making in the workplace, and set the stage for the application of problem solving to larger systems.

Brody (1982) described a problem-solving methodology applied to the needs of community-based organizations that address problems such as crime, poverty, and other social ills. A problem at this level was defined as "a deviation between what should be and what actually is" (p. 34). Brody stressed the need to clarify and systematically analyze the problem by (a) defining any vague or abstract terms, (b) avoiding premature focus on a solution, (c) considering multiple perspectives of all stakeholders, (d) narrowing the problem focus to specific factors, and (e) articulating impact of the problem to aid in program evaluation.

In the last decade, problem solving as a model for service delivery in general and special education has expanded (Allen & Graden, 2002; Deno, 2002). In the mid-1990s, the Heartland Area Education Agency in Iowa spearheaded a statewide reformation of special education service delivery that systematized a problem-solving model to address learning and behavioral needs of students (Ikeda et al., 2003; Ikeda, Tilly, Stumme, Volmer, & Allison, 1996). This model subsequently was adopted by other school districts around the country, including the Milwaukee public schools (Haubner, Staum, & Potter, 2002) and the Minneapolis public schools (Marston, Cantor, Lau, & Muyskens, 2002). Cuban (2001) expanded the education problem-solving model to building- and school system-level decision making and defined the process as a series of stages involving problem solving, decision making, and changing:

> To solve problems, an individual or group must stake some initiative—even risk—by first identifying the problem, framing it, generating solutions, deciding on a solution, and taking action that alters what routinely occurs in order to solve the problem. Moving through these various steps involves solutions becoming planned changes that have to be implemented. (p. 5)

In the remainder of this chapter we discuss how a problem-solving process can be effectively employed in the context of team decision making to design, implement, and evaluate a comprehensive school violence prevention program.

PROBLEM SOLVING AND SCHOOL VIOLENCE PREVENTION

In the period after the tragic school shootings between 1997 and 2000, and in the aftermath of the September 11, 2001 attacks on the World Trade Center and the Pentagon, the professional literature offered numerous organizational structures for educators to use as they approach the issue of school violence prevention (e.g., Dwyer & Jimerson, 2002; Dwyer, & Osher, 2000; Dwyer, Osher, & Warger, 1998; Larson, Smith, & Furlong, 2002). Central to each of these structures is the employment of a broadly representative, school-based team to initiate and oversee the effort. When forming a school safety team, building representation should be secured from among diverse segments of the faculty as well as administration, pupil services, and unclassified staff. At the middle and high school levels, student representatives should be included. This core team should subsequently identify which community and parent candidates will have the interest, expertise, and time to be a part of the team. A diverse team structure such as this can facilitate (a) topic-focused, data-based decision making; (b) enhanced buy-in and shared responsibility among stakeholders; (c) perspective sharing among stakeholders; and (d) centralized coordination of multiple services and programs. By its nature, problem solving thrives in a framework wherein ideas are freely exchanged and fully analyzed from multiple perspectives, and a team format offers such a context. Dwyer and Jimerson (2002) put forward a comprehensive and practical guide to the design and organization of teams for school safety decision making. We recommend readers consult their work.

The application of a problem-solving process to school violence prevention initially was proposed by Larson et al. (2003). These authors identified a five-step process: (a) Problem identification, (b) problem analysis, (c) problem response proposals, (d) response implementation, and (e) evaluation of prevention strategies. In the remainder of this chapter, we further articulate and expand this format with a special emphasis on procedures to acquire and analyze local school-based data to assist in decision making at each step. As a vehicle to enhance understanding at a practical level, we frame this discussion in part along the efforts of a hypothetical school safety team working at a school we will call Kennedy Elementary. Kennedy is a K–5 school of 600 students located in an ethnically diverse, major metropolitan area. Forty percent of its students qualify for the free or reduced-fee lunch program. Under the provisions of the federal No Child Left Behind legislation, states are required to enact policies that define the criteria for designating a school as "persistently dangerous." When a school is found to meet those criteria, students who attend that school must be allowed to transfer to another school within the district. Kennedy Elementary has been informed by its state Department of Education that it is at risk to be designated a persistently dangerous school.

Step 1: Problem Identification

A high-profile event such as the discovery of a firearm in the school building can trigger school board and media pressure for school personnel to "do something," sometimes regardless of any linkage to the actual problem. In this case, a knee-jerk focus on the weapon security problem may completely ignore what may be the real issue of widespread bully victimization. Conversely, taking the time to systematically identify the problem in a manner conducive to effective action can allow for a markedly improved chance at resolution.

Effective problem identification involves two essential processes: (a) understanding through assessment and (b) reframing for action. The school safety team must first gather enough reliable information to be able to frame the problems that the school is experiencing in language that lends itself to action plans. To accomplish this goal, the team needs to know the extent and nature of the gap that exists between the current reality and the desired reality. The current reality can be defined as an interaction between the nature and extent of existing violence-related behaviors in the school and the effectiveness of existing programs and procedures to prevent them. The essential questions are as follow:

1. What are the personal experiences of school violence from the perspective of students, staff, and parents? What are the nature, frequency, and other pertinent characteristics of interpersonal aggression in the school?
2. What is the context of school violence (e.g., in the classroom, noninstructional areas, exterior grounds)? In what way does the context increase or decrease the likelihood of aggressive behavior?
3. What has been the impact of current prevention measures? Are there efficacy data on current approaches?

Archival Data

To begin this process, the school safety team needs to seek out and analyze relevant information regarding the problem. An appropriate starting place is with data already in archival form within school records. Disciplinary office referrals can be a useful index of day-to-day student behaviors that contribute to an unsafe learning environment (Morrison, Peterson, O'Farrell, & Redding, 2004). The team should examine the records for information regarding incident frequency within a defined time period, at a minimum within the most recently completed school year and continuing up to the present date. The team should graph the frequency of behavior problems such as fist fights, bully perpetration (including relational aggression), gang-related behaviors, "hate crime" behaviors that target specific groups, weapon possession, vandalism, inappropriate sexual conduct, and drug possession. Precision and reliability of discipline records can be enhanced by following the proposals described in the *Recommendations of the Crime, Violence, and Discipline Reporting Task Force* (National Center for Educational Statistic, 1996). These recommendations offer a structure for incident reporting and propose useful definitions of persons, incidents, and consequences associated with school discipline. For example, definitions are provided for "fighting" as well as for "battery" so that incidences of either can be distinguished from one another and recorded appropriately.

Morrison et al. (2004) recommended that a disciplinary reporting system contain the following information: (a) demographic data on the referred student, such as academic status, special education status, ethnicity, and gender; (b) a full description of the nature of the problem behavior; (c) the location of the problem behavior; (d) the identity of the referring person; (e) date and time of the incident; and (f) the effectiveness of the consequences. Software is commercially available to assist schools in collecting, maintaining, and analyzing discipline data. *School Safety Software: SSP* (GBA Systems; http://www.schoolsafetysoftware.com/default.htm) is a sophisticated data collection and analysis program for schools that "meets or exceeds most of the recommendations by the National Forum on Educational Statistics with its ability to collect, report, and analyze incidents of crime and violence at school" (Minogue, Kingery, & Murphy, 1999, p. 11). Additionally, the School Wide Information System (SWIS; http://www.swis.org/index.php) is a Web-based office referral organization and monitoring system designed to help school personnel use office referral data in the development of student interventions.

Additionally, the team should gather available data on existing programs and procedures of a preventative nature that function both in the school and in the community. This examination must differentiate those resources that are genuine and active from those that may be only "paper programs"; that is, those programs that are carried on the books but seldom accessed (Dwyer & Jimerson, 2002). This assessment may ask the following questions:

1. Who are the targets of this program?
2. How are those individuals identified?
3. What is the scientific support for this program?
4. How many individuals have accessed this program in the most recent school year?
5. What are the real costs of this program (e.g., staffing, supplies, and facilities)?
6. Is there a well-designed, ongoing program evaluation?
7. What do the outcome data indicate with regard to program efficacy?

A comprehensive examination of existing prevention programs can help direct needed resources toward demonstrably effective efforts as well as identify needed improvements for promising programs. Additionally, a wide-ranging examination of all of the prevention programs in the schools can provide the necessary documentation to eliminate those programs that fail to demonstrate a positive effect and may be usurping valuable resources that could be reallocated elsewhere.

Needs Assessment Surveys

Personal experience and context data can be most efficiently obtained through carefully considered needs assessment surveys and self-reports. Peterson and Skiba (n.d.- a, n.d.- b) designed a set of assessment tools for use within a school safety team that allow members to self-assess their own understanding of current prevention procedures in the school, and to organize their thoughts about what their colleagues outside of the committee believe about the problems. These tools are a useful starting point as the team prepares to assemble a wider needs assessment survey and are available for download at http://www.unl.edu/srs/index.html.

Once the school safety team has discussed its own thinking about the directions for change, the opinions of others in the school must be solicited and analyzed. Fig. 5.1 contains the School Violence Needs Assessment Survey, a form developed by the first author that allows staff members the opportunity to express their opinions on the current status of a variety of school violence-related elements and to put each one into priority for action. This survey form should be adapted to meet the specific needs of individual schools by adding or removing prevention elements as needed. Two additional useful assessment tools for staff members are worth noting. The California School Climate and Safety Survey—Staff Form (Furlong, Morrison, & Boles, 1991), is a 62-item survey that examines school staff members' opinions and experiences with safety-related issues. The measure is comprised of three major sections: perceptions of school climate, perceptions of school danger, and reports of victimization. This instrument is available for download at http://www.education.ucsb.edu/school-pscyhology/. The California Healthy Kids Survey (http://www.wested.org/pub/docs/chks_home.html) has a Staff School Climate Survey that examines a broad range of potential staff concerns, including those related to school violence and student discipline issues.

Students also are an essential source of information and their input into the problem definition undertaking can provide the school safety team with substantial clarification and direction. The California School Climate and Safety Survey—Short Form (Furlong et al., 2005) is a 52-item revision of an original 102-item form (see Furlong et al., 1991). The scale yields self-report information from students in three principal areas: school danger, school climate, and school victimization. This measure is available for download at http://www.education.ucsb.edu/school-psychology.

Our hypothetical school safety team at Kennedy Elementary School used these assessment methods to gather survey data from all staff members and all students in the fourth and fifth

Current Status			Prevention Level - Primary	Priority for Improvement		
In Place	Partially in Place	Not in Place		High	Med	Low
			School code of conduct has been examined for currency, is educational more than punitive, and defines desirable as well as undesirable behavior for all stakeholders			
			Building and grounds have security measures adequate to prevent and respond to reasonably anticipated problems			
			All areas of the building and grounds are supervised and there are no obvious "dead zones" where problems can occur			
			Interior of building is well-lit, clean, and shows pride in school identity and accomplishments of its student body			
			Parents are welcomed into the building and provided opportunities and information in order to be full partners in their child's education			
			All teachers have received training in classroom behavior management and office referrals are minimized			
			Academic standards are high and pride in achievement is emphasized and publicly expressed through multiple outlets			
			All students receive evidence-based classroom instruction in anger management, social problem solving, and/or conflict resolution across multiple grade levels			
			Cultural, ethnic, and other minority groups are valued, and there are evident procedures and action provided to address their particular needs and concerns			
			All building staff members are valued as part of the school community and prevention efforts			

FIG. 5.1.   School Violence Needs Assessment Survey.

grades. They also examined office disciplinary forms that helped them identify "hot spots" in the school for problem behavior, periods in the week and school year that occasioned the most aggressive behavior, and the referral rates of individual teachers. The team now needs to convert the accumulated data into practical information that can be useful for prevention planning.

Step 2: Problem Analysis and Hypothesis Development

This phase of the problem-solving process necessitates that the school safety team organize the data in a manner such that converging trends become evident. The main foci of the

Current Status			Prevention Level – Secondary	Priority for Improvement		
In Place	Partially in Place	Not in Place		High	Med	Low
			Effective procedures are in place for early and valid identification of students at risk for behavioral and academic difficulties			
			Teachers and supportive services staff have training in evidence-based interventions for academic and behavioral problems			
			Teachers and supportive services staff are provided adequate time and support to implement interventions for identified students at risk			
			There is an effective schoolwide program in place to prevent and respond to bullying and harassment that includes a classroom instruction component			
			Existing interventions for at-risk students have undergone recent program evaluations to demonstrate effectiveness			
			Students are suspended out of school only as a last resort and only for reasons of their safety or that of others			
			In-school suspension is used sparingly, only for the most serious offenses, and contains an academic support component			
			Administrators treat office referrals as teaching opportunities to augment appropriate disciplinary procedures			

FIG. 5.1. Continued.

problem-analysis phase are validation of the problem definition(s) and subsequent generation of hypotheses for responding to the problem. Care must be taken to avoid over- or under-interpretation, which can be accomplished by using a systematic process of data analysis. We suggest that the school safety team adopt a gating procedure to validate the problems identified through the first gate (i.e., the initial data collection). In the second gate, the problem is validated within a test–retest method. The retest can be accomplished by a second administration of the assessment methods to the initial sample, or by randomly selecting a subset of respondents for follow-up validation surveys or interviews. Although a second assessment is time-consuming, the gating method allows for more systematic identification of those areas in need of intervention by compensating for temporal or transient variables, and validating perceptions of problems as identified in the initial assessment data. The use of a gating procedure also provides for more focused problem response proposals, thereby offsetting potential wasted time and resources. Once the data are gathered, a simple component or item analysis can be conducted to identify and prioritize problem areas.

With analyzed data in front of them, the team next must convert the data to behaviorally worded action hypotheses. Hypothesis development involves translating what the data indicate into workable propositions about environmental or individual variables that mediate the

Current Status			Prevention Level – Tertiary	Priority for Improvement		
In Place	Partially in Place	Not in Place		High	Med	Low
			There are effective policies and procedures for keeping weapons out of the school			
			There are effective policies and procedures for keeping gang-related behaviors out of the school			
			There are effective policies and procedures to prevent vandalism and crimes against both the person and property of all individuals			
			There is a broadly representative crisis management team that has been trained in crisis response and management			
			All building staff members have been trained relative to their roles and obligations in a variety of potential crisis situations			
			There are staff members professionally trained in student restraint and safe transport and their identities are known by everyone			
			There are staff members professionally trained in emergency first aid and cardio-pulmonary resuscitation and their identities are known by everyone			
			Students with acute and chronic anger management and aggression problems are provided with evidence-based skills training by supportive services staff			
			Students with acute and chronic anger management and aggression problems are provided with assessment-driven positive behavioral supports around the school			
			Effective partnerships or wraparound arrangements with families, community mental health, law enforcement, and social service agencies are maintained to support highest risk students			

FIG. 5.1. Continued.

problem. For example, data that showed high frequencies of lunchroom fights may be hypothesized to be a function of overcrowding, inadequate supervision, poor environmental design of the facility, student anger management deficits, lousy food, or some combination of any or all of these variables. Each action hypothesis should contain implications for intervention that are practical and testable.

A useful method for creating testable action hypotheses is goal attainment scaling (GAS; Kirusek, Smith, & Cardillo, 1994). GAS is a criterion-referenced approach to operationalizing problem definitions that also can be used to document intervention effectiveness. The basic methodology, can be used at either an individual or group level and involves operationally defining successive levels of program progress on a 5 or 6-point scale (i.e., -2 to $+2$, wherein -2 indicates that a problem is much worse and $+2$ indicates a program

TABLE 5.1

Example of Action Hypothesis

Problem Analysis	Action Hypothesis
The data indicate that slightly more than 18% of our third- to fifth-grade students reported having "stayed home to avoid being bullied" at least once in the past year and the absentee rate for that group was up 7% for the same period	*The students' repertoire of effective responses to bully behavior and the staff's efforts to create an environment that is not conducive to bully behavior are in need of knowledge and skill building. Training in these areas will result in a reduction of bullying-related absences.*
The number of student fights on the property has increased 40% over the past year, with 85% occurring among fourth- and fifth-grade boys at recess or before school. The number of physical fights between girls only has increased 120% in 2 years.	*The current external setting events in the school in combination with the conflict response skills of some students increase the probability that too many students will choose physical aggression to resolve interpersonal conflicts. General conflict- resolution education for all student and skills training for some students, paired with increased supervision of common areas will reduce incidences of fighting behavior.*
In response to the item, "All building staff members have been trained relative to their roles and obligations in a variety of potential crisis situations," 82% of staff responded "not in place" and 63% rated it "high priority" for improvement (validated in randomized staff interviews).	*The current knowledge and skills of staff members to respond to a crisis situation is inadequate and staff development training is indicated. Subsequent assessment on this item should show at least 80% of staff members reporting "in place."*
In response to the item "School code of conduct has been examined for currency, is educational more than punitive, and defines desirable as well as undesirable behavior for all stakeholders," 97% of the staff responded "not in place" and 93% rated it "high priority" for improvement (validated in randomized staff interviews).	*Staff members want a more visible and functional code of conduct, and an administration request for volunteers to draft a revision will identify a satisfactory work team for the project.*

goal is attained). For example, consider the survey item "I have stayed at home to avoid being bullied." Baseline data indicate that 18% of third- to fifth-grade students responded to the item (GAS rating 0). The student safety team agreed that a decrease to a rate of 10% would indicate progress toward the program goal (GAS = 1), and a decrease to less than 1% would indicate the program goal was attained (GAS = 2). An increase to 25% indicates a moderately worse problem (GAS = −1), and an increase to above 30% indicates the problem has significantly worsened. As shown in this example, the GAS method is simple to use, provides a format for writing testable hypotheses, is readily understandable, and can be used to gather outcome data on a number of different action hypotheses. Finally, the GAS method reflects the criterion-based nature of data that can be most useful in individual school settings.

The school safety team at Kennedy Elementary found multiple sources of assessment data that converged on three major areas of concern: (a) bullying in the third through fifth grades, (b) fighting across all grade levels, (c) staff dissatisfaction with professional development opportunities in numerous areas associated with violence prevention, and (d) staff desire to re-invigorate the building code of conduct. Table 5.1 provides examples of their data analysis statements and corresponding action hypotheses.

Step 3: Problem Response Proposals

With the data now organized into focused student, staff, and environmental needs, school safety team members must consider options regarding how the building should address the identified needs. In recent years, a three-tiered public health schema for classifying prevention outcomes has been applied to the schools (Walker, Ramsey, & Gresham, 2004; see also Furlong, Morrison, Austin, Huh-Kim, & Skager, 2001; Larson et al., 2003). Using this model, prevention planners apply a primary, secondary, and tertiary needs hierarchy to the school population. At the primary level, universal interventions are designed and implemented to prevent the development and occurrences of antisocial, aggressive behavior. Universal interventions are considered necessary for all children in the school population, regardless of individual risk status. Universal procedures may take the form of schoolwide initiatives, such as a building code of conduct or a peer-mediation program, or they may include classroom-level instruction in anger management or conflict resolution.

Secondary prevention employs selected measures to target a smaller group of students who, because of individual exposure to risk factors, already are exhibiting behaviors considered precursor or marker behaviors for more serious problems in the school. The goal of these interventions is to prevent these less serious problems from evolving into more serious aggressive or violent behaviors in later grades. These students typically are identified through the use of formal or informal screening procedures (see Walker et al., 2004, for a discussion). Selected intervention procedures often take the form of individual or group behavioral skills training, parent management training, or assessment-driven academic and behavioral supports.

Prevention Realm → Action Elements ↓	Primary Prevention	Secondary Prevention	Tertiary Prevention
Which Students?			
What Needs?			
Data Source			
Desired Goals			
Intervention			
Timeline			
Budget Factors			
Responsibilities			
Evaluation			

FIG. 5.2.   Framework for Problem Response Proposals.

At the tertiary level of the prevention hierarchy, indicated programs target the smallest group of students whose high level of risk involvement are manifested in severe emotional-behavioral disabilities, mental illness, or other forms of dangerous or aggressive behavior. Students receiving indicated-level prevention often require the support of every resource that the school, family, and community can bring together, and the major focus is on the provision of support to retard the worsening of the problem and to move the student forward in a positive direction (Larson et al., 2003). Indicated prevention measures are best conceptualized as a structure of interacting supports under the direction of a collaborative team that figuratively "wrap" services around the student and often the family (see Eber, Sugai, Smith, & Scott, 2002, for a review and useful discussion).

At this juncture in the problem-solving process, the school safety team must align appropriate universal, selected, and indicated prevention measures with the action hypotheses developed from the assessment data. The focus of the programs and procedures that will comprise a comprehensive schoolwide violence prevention program will be guided by the assessment data from Steps 1 and 2 in the problem-solving process. Effective decisions about which particular program or procedure will be used to successfully address the action hypothesis demand that school safety team members become informed consumers of the research. It is common for schools to implement well-intentioned programs that have no evidentiary support in professional journals because of the following:

1. *Sunk costs and budget restraints.* The school may have previously purchased a program or have a currently funded program in place. In an era of ever-tightening school budgets, educators often select or are forced to make do.
2. *Effective product marketing.* Educators often are persuaded by well-designed, aggressive marketing procedures and published testimonials from fellow educators.
3. *Success at another school.* News reports of one school's experience can have undue influence on some decision makers despite evident differences between the two environments.
4. *Lack of a tradition in research-based decision making.* It is often the case that there is no one in an influential position on staff who will routinely ask the question, "What does the research say?" Consequently, budget, marketing, and hearsay rule the day.

Whereas many public school professionals are cognizant of the array of high-quality, research-supported programs and procedures to address violence in the school, this is not always the case. The team should not hesitate to further its expertise by consulting with experts at a local university, the state department of education, or by accessing reputable Websites such as the What Works Clearinghouse (http://www.w-w-c.org/), the Hamilton Fish Institute (http://www.hamfish.org/), and the Center for the Prevention and Study of Violence (http://www.colorado.edu/cspv/index.html). Additional discussion on the topic of evidenced-based interventions in schools can be found in Kratochwill (2002) and Kratochwill and Shernoff (2004).

The use of a guiding framework such as displayed in Fig. 5.1 can bring needed organization and structure to this process:

1. *Which students?* The team needs to consider the entire prevention hierarchy. What do all the students need? What do some specific students need? Team members should systematically address each level, starting with primary prevention.
2. *What needs?* The action hypotheses will provide the proposed areas for intervention.
3. *Data source.* Proposed interventions should be driven by well-analyzed data that emerged from the Step 1 and Step 2 assessments. As a consequence, data-based

accountability for intervention decisions is maintained, and the team has potentially useful baseline data for use in program evaluations.

4. *Desired goals.* In this frame, the team defines the outcomes that when met, will eliminate the gap between the current situation and the desired situation. Use of the GAS procedure (described earlier) will assist in monitoring progress toward the goals.

5. *Interventions.* In addition to the need for a strong evidence base, proposed interventions should connect rationally and supportively to one another. How are prevention activities at the secondary and tertiary levels logically connected to those at the primary level? For example, in what ways will a pull-out anger management group interface with and connect to a revised discipline policy? Employing the capacity that the school environment has for connectivity, communication, and mutual support enhances the potential power of school-based interventions and prevents the growth of a confusing archipelago of free-floating intervention efforts.

6. *Time line.* The team should render the intervention plan to a feasible time line for implementation, review, and evaluation. The team should distinguish between larger initiatives that need to be phased-in over a period of years (e.g., a schoolwide anger management curriculum or bully prevention program) and more immediate intervention opportunities (e.g., increased supervision of common areas).

7. *Budget factors.* The true initial and continuing costs need to be considered, including those associated with reallocation of staff time, equipment purchases, and required training. For school board-funded initiatives, Knoff (2003) offered a practical discussion on strategy. For available grant opportunities, teams should consult the listing of local private granting agencies, the state department of education, or consider a partnership with a local university on a multiyear federal grant (e.g., Safe and Drug-Free Schools, Substance Abuse and Mental Health Services Administration, or the Office of Juvenile Justice and Delinquency Prevention).

8. *Responsibilities.* For this frame, the team must allocate leadership for the necessary tasks to move the plan along. Necessary duties include (a) intervention program research and design, (b) funding, (c) information sharing and team-building with other stakeholders, and (d) evaluation design.

9. *Evaluation.* Each initiative should have an evaluation design built in at the onset. The evaluation should be linked to the assessment methods used in the problem identification and problem analysis phases. Furthermore, the evaluation should contain a method for assessing *intervention integrity* (i.e., ensuring that the intervention[s] is implemented as intended).

Our hypothetical school safety team at Kennedy Elementary School consulted with experts from a local university, visited a neighboring school district to observe a number of intervention programs in action, conducted an Internet search for exemplar codes of conduct, and examined the literature for bullying prevention programs and anger management interventions. Using the *Framework for Problem Response Proposals*, team members aligned the primary, secondary, and tertiary needs of all their students in the areas identified in their action hypotheses. This process allowed the team to establish reasonable time lines so that it could meet budgetary and staff development imperatives.

Step 4: Response Implementation

This phase of the problem-solving process is a critical step because the success or failure of the best-planned violence prevention program rests squarely on the quality of its implementation. Fundamental to successful implementation are issues of *social acceptability* and *intervention integrity*. Social acceptability refers to "judgments by laypersons, clients, and others of whether treatment procedures are appropriate, fair, and reasonable" (Kazdin, 2001, p. 401). The school safety team needs to consider the impact that the proposed intervention will have on the students, the staff directly involved in the implementation, and the larger body of additional stakeholders in and out of the building.

Intervention programs that students find embarrassing, demeaning, or excessively harsh may be met with resistance. For example, a middle school may find that although the hallway behavior of the sixth-grade students was positively influenced by the staff distribution of "Positive Behavior Lottery" tickets during passing time, the eighth-grade students found the intervention childish and tore up the tickets. The management of aggressive behavior in the school setting can entail the use of out of the ordinary or controversial procedures such as exclusionary time-out, pull-out anger management skills training, or even physical restraint. Consequently, schools may find that the use of a district-level oversight body to review proposed interventions for possible legal, ethical, or student and staff acceptability concerns will help avoid potential problems.

When a teacher or pupil services professional puts into practice an evidence-supported intervention, there is a presumption that the procedures will be implemented in the same manner as was done in the supporting research. When this happens, the intervention is said to have high treatment integrity (Gresham, 1989). Integrity problems may arise if teachers or other personnel are asked to engage in intervention practices that they perceive as ineffective, overly complex, or poorly related to their own understanding of the problem. It is not enough for the school safety team alone to understand and be convinced of the merits of a school violence prevention plan; effective implementation demands that the personnel charged with carrying out that plan also share that understanding and conviction. The integrity of a prevention plan can be enhanced with thorough staff development training, assessment of training competencies, ongoing support and follow-through, and ongoing evaluation of adherence to the intervention program.

Schools also need to be cognizant of the impact that any new program will have on parents and on the greater community outside of the school. For instance, do all parents understand why instruction time is being taken away from traditional subjects in order to implement a new anger management curriculum? Is the prevention program targeting a specific group of students such that it could be perceived from the outside as racist, sexist, or otherwise discriminatory, despite benign, data-supported intentions? Are there significant budget issues to which taxpayers may object? Additionally, the age-old question "How will this play in the press?" is one worth asking. For example, a well-designed intervention that allows high-risk youth to earn fast food coupons for identified positive behaviors may turn up in the newspaper as "Desperate School Now Paying Delinquents to Behave."

These issues underscore the importance of effective communication, training, and team-building throughout the problem-solving process. The broadly representative school safety team structure stressed earlier gives voice to the various constituencies affected by the plan and helps ensure that potential problems are proactively addressed.

The school safety team at Kennedy Elementary presented its comprehensive school violence prevention plan to the school board, providing opportunities to begin the budget request process and to receive citizen input. The team sent a press release to the local media outlets that described the rationale for its plan and the anticipated benefits for the school community. An informational parent meeting was held at the school, and additional flyers were sent home with all the children. In consultation with the faculty and pupil services staff, the team constructed a phased implementation plan over a 2-year span that allowed for (a) the most critical needs to be addressed first, (b) adequate funding from grants and the regular budget to be accumulated, and (c) sufficient opportunities for staff development.

Step 5: Evaluation of Prevention Strategies

The final phase of the problem-solving model involves both formative and summative evaluations of the response programs. A formative evaluation component is important for monitoring ongoing progress toward program goals and allows for changes to be made in the response implementation as dictated by the outcome assessment methods. For example, it may be that intervention integrity data indicate that the response protocol is too difficult to consistently implement. One then must analyze the reasons for this difficulty (e.g., insufficient training or insufficient program support) and perhaps recycle to an earlier problem-solving phase. Ongoing assessment also will help with decisions about program goal attainment and subsequent implementation to address the next problem as prioritized by the team. We suggest that a sub-sample of staff and students complete ongoing, formative assessments at least once per month to evaluate progress toward the outcome goals. The GAS method can be readily applied to both formative and summative evaluations in a time-efficient manner by assessing only those variables that have been identified as problems.

A summative evaluation can be achieved by evaluating the level of convergence of the outcome goals. A simple method is to average the GAS ratings for each problem variable to provide an overall convergent evidence rating. Traditional statistical methods also may be used to evaluate change; however, we believe that a criterion-referenced approach is most useful in applied school settings. A statistically significant change from pre- to postintervention may not reflect the desired magnitude of change and, as such, may not demonstrate social or educational significance. Regardless of the evaluation method, several aspects of the prevention program will be continuously implemented; therefore, the assessment will be an ongoing enterprise to ensure that the program goals have been maintained.

After 4 months of the phased implementation, the school safety team at Kennedy School collected evaluation data using average GAS ratings and authentic disciplinary data. They found that bullying continued at near baseline rates, but was beginning to demonstrate a positive trend. Fighting was less of a problem, but still below program goals. Following a staff development in-service conducted by a team from the local university, staff satisfaction with crisis response obligations showed significant improvement. The work team for the revised code of conduct had been productive, and the initial draft was distributed to the faculty.

TABLE 5.2
Implications for Practice: Using a Problem-Solving Approach to Prevent School Violence

---

Develop a school safety team to enhance buy-in and shared responsibilities among stakeholders Use the five-step problem-solving approach:
1. Problem identification
   - Collect systematic data using archival data, surveys, and interviews to enhance specificity
2. Problem analysis and hypothesis development
   - Use a gating assessment procedure to validate the problem(s)
   - Generate testable hypotheses
3. Problem response protocols
   - Employ data-based response protocols for primary, secondary, and tertiary prevention
4. Response implementation
   - Collect systematic data with the measures used in problem identification
   - Ensure intervention integrity
5. Evaluation of prevention strategies
   - Engage in frequent formative evaluations
   - Use a criterion-based approach to evaluation

ADVANTAGES AND DISADVANTAGES
OF THE PROBLEM-SOLVING MODEL

The major advantage of applying the problem-solving model to school safety concerns is the team-based approach toward systematic assessment and intervention (Table 5.2 delineates implications for practice). The problem-solving model provides focus that can maximize resources and enhance intervention outcomes. That focus, however, has initial cost due to the significant amount of time, effort, and resources required to engage in a complete problem-solving process. Among these costs are the potential difficulties with buy-in from the staff and community when solutions are not immediately evident. Educators, however, must systematically approach school safety and violence prevention. School professionals often set up themselves and their constituents for failure in problem solving when specificity is lacking. If the data are too general, the intervention vague, and follow-through lacking, the likelihood is high that the prevention efforts will be ineffective.

REFERENCES

Allen, S., & Graden, J. (2002). Best practices in collaborative problem solving for intervention design. In A. Thomas & J. Grimes (Eds.), *Best practices in school psychology* (Vol. 4, pp. 565–582). Bethesda, MD: National Association of School Psychologists.

Brody, R. (1982). *Problem solving: Concepts and methods for community organizations.* New York: Human Science Press.

Crick, N. R., & Dodge, K. A. (1994). A review and reformulation of social information-processing mechanisms in children's social adjustment. *Psychological Bulletin, 115,* 74–101

Cuban, L. (2001). *How can I fix it? Finding solutions and managing dilemmas.* New York: Teachers College Press.

Deno, S. L. (2002). Problem solving as "best practice." In A. Thomas & J. Grimes (Eds.), *Best practices in school psychology* (Vol. 4, pp. 37–56). Bethesda, MD: National Association of School Psychologists.

Dodge, K. A. (1986). A social information processing model of social competence in children. In M. Perlmutter (Ed.), *Cognitive perspectives on children's social and behavioral development: The Minnesota symposium on child psychology* (Vol. 18, pp. 77–125). Hillsdale, NJ: Lawrence Erlbaum Associates.

Dwyer, K. P., & Jimerson, S. R. (2002). Enabling prevention through planning. In S. E. Brock, P. J. Lazerus, & S. R. Jimerson (Eds.), *Best practices in school crisis prevention and intervention* (pp. 23–46). Bethesda, MD: National Association of School Psychologists.

Dwyer, K., & Osher, D. (2000). *Safeguarding our children: An action guide.* Washington, DC: U.S. Departments of Education and Justice, American Institutes for Research.

Dwyer, K., Osher, D., & Warger, C. (1998). *Early warning, timely response: A guide to safe schools.* Washington, DC: U.S. Department of Education.

D'Zurilla, T. J., & Nezu, A. M. (1999). *Problem-solving therapy: A social competence approach to clinical intervention* (2nd ed.). New York: Springer.

Eber, L., Sugai, G., Smith, C., & Scott, T. M. (2002). Wraparound and positive behavioral interventions and supports in the schools. *Journal of Emotional and Behavioral Disorders, 10,* 136–173.

Furlong, M. J., Greif, J. L., Bates, M. P., Whipple, A. D., Jimenez, T. C., & Morrison, R. (2005). Development of the California School Climate and Safety Survey–Short Form. *Psychology in the Schools, 42,* 137–149.

Furlong, M., Morrison, G. M., Austin, G., Huh-Kim, J., & Skager, R. (2001). Using student risk factors in school violence surveillance reports: Illustrative examples for enhanced policy formation, implementation, and evaluation. *Law & Policy, 23,* 271–296.

Furlong, M. J., Morrison, R., & Boles, S. (1991). *California School Climate and Safety Survey.* Paper presented at the annual meetings of the California Association of School Psychologists. Los Angeles, April.

Gresham, F. M. (1989). Assessment of treatment integrity in school consultation and prereferral intervention. *School Psychology Review, 18,* 37–50.

Haubner, C., Staum, M., & Potter, A. (2002, June). Optimizing success through problem solving: School reform in Milwaukee Public Schools. *Communiqué, 30*(8), pp. 31–33.

Heylighen, F. (1998). *Problem solving.* Availlable: http://pespmc1.vub.ac.be/PROBSOLV.html

Ikeda, M., Grimes, J., Tilly, W. D., III, Allison, R., Kurns, S., & Stumme, J. (2003). Implementing an intervention-based approach to service delivery: A case example. In M. Shinn, H. M. Walker, & G. Stoner (Eds.), *Interventions for academic and behavior problems II: Preventive and remedial approaches* (pp. 53–70). Bethesda, MD: National Association of School Psychologists.

Ikeda, M., Tilly, W. D., III, Stumme, J., Volmer, L., & Allison, R. (1996). Agency-wide implementation of problem-solving consultation. *School Psychology Quarterly, 11*, 228–243.

Kazdin, A. E. (2001). *Behavior modification in applied settings* (6th ed.). Belmont, CA: Wadsworth/Thomson Learning.

Kirusek, T. J., Smith, A., & Cardillo, J. E. (Eds.). (1994). *Goal attainment scaling: Application, theory, and measurement.* Hillsdale, NJ: Lawrence Erlbaum Associates.

Knoff, H. (2003). Best practices in facilitating school reform, organizational change, and strategic planning. In A. Thomas & J. Grimes (Eds.), *Best practices in school psychology* (Vol. 4, pp. 235–245). Bethesda, MD: National Association of School Psychologists.

Kratochwill, T. R. (2002). Evidence-based interventions in school psychology: Thoughts on thoughtful commentary. *School Psychology Quarterly, 17*, 518–532.

Kratochwill, T. R., & Shernoff, E. S. (2004). Evidence-based practice: Promoting evidence-based interventions in school psychology. *School Psychology Quarterly, 18*, 1–21.

Larson, J., Smith, D. C., & Furlong, M. J. (2003). Best practices in school violence prevention. In A. Thomas & J. Grimes (Eds.), *Best practices in school psychology* (Vol. 4, pp. 1081–1098). Bethesda, MD: National Association of School Psychologists.

Marston, D., Cantor, A., Lau, M., & Muyskens, P. (2002). Problem-solving: Implementation and Evaluation in Minneapolis Schools. *Communiqué, (30)*8, pp. 15–17.

Minogue, N., Kingery, P., & Murphy, L. (1999). *Approaches to assessing violence among youth.* Rosslyn, VA: Hamilton Fish Institute on School and Community Violence.

Morrison, G. M., Peterson, R., O'Farrell, S., & Redding, M. (2004). Using office referrals records in school violence research: Possibilities and limitations. *Journal of School Violence, 3*, 39–61.

National Center for Educational Statistics. (1996). *Recommendation of the crime, violence, and discipline reporting task force* (NCES Publication no. 97–581). Washington, DC: Author.

Newell, A., & Simon, H. A. (1972). *Human problem solving.* Englewood Cliffs, NJ: Prentice-Hall.

Peterson, R. L., & Skiba, R. J. (n.d.-a). *Needs assessment questionnaire.* Available: http://www.unl.edu/srs/index.html

Peterson, R. L., & Skiba, R. J. (n.d.-b). *Practices and program inventory.* Available: http://www.unl.edu/srs/index.html

Simon, H. A. (1976). *Administrative behavior: A study of decision-making processes in administrative behavior.* New York: The Free Press.

Spivack, G., Platt, J. J., & Shure, M. B. (1976). *The problem-solving approach to adjustment.* San Francisco, CA: Jossey-Bass.

Walker, H. M., Ramsey, E., & Gresham, F. M. (2004). *Antisocial behavior in school: Evidence-based practices* (2nd ed.). Belmont, CA: Wadsworth/Thomson Learning.

6

Crisis Preparedness, Response, and Management: Surveys of School Professionals

Amanda B. Nickerson
Kristina M. Osborne
University at Albany, State University of New York

Preparing for and responding to crises has become one of the most pressing issues facing our nation's schools. The attention given to this topic is reflected in the number of publications that have emerged in the last decade (e.g., Brock, Lazarus, & Jimerson, 2002; Brock, Sandoval, & Lewis, 2001; Dwyer, Osher, & Warger, 1998; Klingman, 1996). Additionally, recent legislation has required school districts to take preventative and remedial measures to address school crises, with 33 states requiring schools to develop crisis plans (Allen, 2003). Despite this increased professional, political, and public interest in crisis prevention and intervention, research in this area is limited (Brock & Jimerson, 2004; Pagliocca & Nickerson, 2001; Pagliocca, Nickerson, & Williams, 2002; Vernberg, 2002).

There are several reasons for the lack of crisis prevention and intervention research, largely due to the nature of crises as sudden, uncontrollable events that have the potential to impact an entire school community (Brock, 2002). This raises methodological challenges, such as feasibility problems in conducting controlled studies and the high degree of variability in behavioral and emotional responses to, and recovery from, traumatic experience (Pagliocca et al., 2002). From a practical perspective, researchers have noted the difficulty in gaining approval from school administration when attempting to evaluate the effectiveness of interventions following disasters (Blom, 1986; Vernberg, 1994), perhaps due to concern over possible effects on students and the need to attend to the immediacy of the crisis situation.

Given the importance of school crisis prevention and intervention and the need for research in this area, it is important to identify methodologies that provide accurate information with minimal disruption to crisis response when studying these situations. Survey methodology is proposed as a promising means for beginning to systematically research school professionals' crisis prevention, response, and management practices. This chapter provides an overview of the importance of preparedness, response, and management of school crises. A framework of comprehensive school crisis planning and response is presented, including the following phases: (a) predisaster, (b) impact, (c) short-term adaptation, and (d) long-term adaptation. Survey methodology is reviewed as a promising approach for studying school crisis preparedness, response, and management. A recent national survey is presented as an example of survey methodology in this area, followed by a review of relevant research from surveys of a wide range of school professionals. Advantages and disadvantages of surveys are reviewed, and implications for conducting surveys and for preventing and intervening with crises are summarized.

CONCEPTUAL BASIS OF SCHOOL CRISIS PREPAREDNESS AND RESPONSE

Many frameworks have been proposed to guide the conceptualization of school crisis preparedness and response, including Caplan's (1964) three-part model of preventive mental health: primary, secondary, and tertiary prevention. In Israel, Avigdor Klingman (1978) developed perhaps the best multifaceted conceptual model of school crisis preparedness and response. This model, which has evolved since the late 1970s (Klingman, 1978, 1985, 1987, 1988, 1996; Klingman & Ben Eli, 1981) was designated as an exemplary service-delivery program by the American Psychological Association (Roberts, 1996). The model describes a four-phase preventive intervention for disasters, including school violence. The four phases are (a) predisaster, (b) impact, (c) short-term adaptation, and (d) long-term adaptation.

The predisaster phase involves anticipation of the event, including activities such as developing intervention plans, identifying and training responders, and rehearsing response procedures. The impact phase, which occurs in the early stages of a crisis, focuses on organization and intervention, such as coordination of services, mental health consultation to school leaders and service providers, initial classroom intervention, and the provision of crisis intervention to those assessed to be at risk for further psychological harm. In the short-term adaptation phase, the focus shifts to assisting individuals, groups, and families adapt to its impact. Finally, in the long-term adaptation phase, strategies such as relapse prevention and reintegration of students into the school community are used, with the expectation that children will resume their roles as students (Klingman, 1996). Additionally, individual, group, and family treatment may be provided. This comprehensive model may be useful for guiding research and the development of surveys.

Use of Survey Methodology

Surveys can be used for purposes of description, explanation, and exploration. This methodology is being increasingly used to study sensitive topics such as violence, abuse, and crises. If used properly, surveys are guided by a rigorous data-collection procedure that applies common questions and answer choices and is systematically conducted on a sample rigorously drawn from a known population (Jackson & Antonucci, 1994). It is critical to develop a high-quality survey questionnaire, which can be guided by the recommendations of Dillman (2000) and Mangione (1995), such as developing unambiguous questions, writing specific instructions, and pretesting.

Traditionally, the three major approaches to survey data collection have been personal interviews, mail questionnaires, and telephone interviews. Reflecting societal change and advances in technology, survey methods increasingly include e-mail, Web, and interactive voice response surveys, where a computer plays recorded questions over the phone (Tourangeau, 2004). Each of these approaches to survey data collection has its advantages and disadvantages, discussion of which is beyond the scope of this chapter. For in-depth coverage of these topics, the reader is encouraged to consult Dillman (2000), Mangione (1995), and Tourangeau (2004).

School Survey on Crime and Safety

One of the most recent, comprehensive, and well-designed surveys addressing crisis prepared-ness and management is the National Center for Educational Statistics (NCES) School Survey on Crime and Safety (SSOCS). In the 1970s, the U.S. Department of Education funded the Safe Schools Study, the first large-scale study, with the purpose of assessing the quality of safety in our nation's school systems (NCES, 2001). This survey was administered to principals, teachers, and students. For the past several decades, the federal government has periodically continued to collect crime and violence data from school principals. The SSOCS, the most recent expansion of the original Safe Schools Study, was conducted during the 1999–2000 school year. It was designed to gather current information on crime, violence, and disorder in America's public schools. A nationally representative sample of 2,270 public elementary, middle, and secondary school principals completed a series of questions in regard to school policies, school violence prevention programs and practices, frequency of crime and violence in their schools, disciplinary problems and actions, and school characteristics associated with school crime and violence.

The NCES summarized selected findings of the SSOCS study in its *Crime and Safety in America's Public Schools* (NCES, 2004) report. Respondents indicated that the most fre-quently incorporated components of violence prevention programs for their students included counseling, social work, psychological, or therapeutic activities (66%); behavior modification interventions (66%); prevention curriculum, instruction, or training (65%); and individual at-tention, mentoring, tutoring, or coaching by students or adults (63%). The most infrequent component used as part of violence prevention programs was a hotline or a tip-line for students to report problems, used by only 22% of responding school principals.

The SSOCS included questions about supportive violence prevention training programs offered to teachers, staff, and parents. Sixty-six percent of principals reported that training, supervision, or technical assistance in classroom management programs were provided for teachers. Of the respondents, 35% indicated training teachers and staff to identify early warning signs in potentially violent students, whereas 31% of the schools reported training faculty in crime prevention. Many schools encouraged parental involvement in crime reduction efforts. For example, 54% of the principals reported obtaining input from parents about school crime and discipline policies and 45% of the schools provided parental training or assistance in coping with their child's behavioral problems. Only 21% of the schools reported involving parents in maintaining discipline within the school setting.

School principals also were asked about the specific procedures or practices employed during the 1999–2000 school year to ensure the safety of their school communities. The most common practice intended to limit access to the school campus was the requirement of a visitor sign-in when entering the school building, which was used by 97% of respondents. Few schools required students (1%) and visitors (1%) to regularly pass through metal detectors when entering the school buildings. Furthermore, schools used a variety of specific security measures to prevent or reduce potential violent or crisis-related behaviors. The most commonly used practice reported was not providing students with school lockers (54%); the most infrequent practices used when monitoring the school campus were drug testing for any student (4%) and requiring students to wear picture identification (4%).

The vast majority (96%) of schools indicated having a crisis management plan for at least one of the following crises: shooting, riots or large-scale fights, schoolwide threats such as bomb or anthrax scares, natural disasters, or hostages. Principals also reported common barriers reducing their efforts to ensure safe schools. Inadequate alternative programs for disruptive students (67%), funds (62%), and federal policies on disciplining disabled students (60%) were the most frequently reported factors limiting schools' preventive efforts and attempts to reduce crime. Furthermore, half of the respondents indicated that lack of teacher training in classroom management was an impediment. Lack of teacher support for school policies (19%) and fear of district or state reprisal (19%) were the least frequently reported barriers to safe schools.

Survey Research on Crisis Preparedness, Response, and Management

In addition to the SSOCS, findings from surveys of a variety of school professionals provide useful sources of information when examining school crisis preparedness and management approaches and needs. Selected common themes from these surveys, organized by Klingman's conceptual model of predisaster, impact, short-term adaptation, and long-term adaptation, are summarized here, with more specific details about each study provided in Table 6.1. It should be noted that this conceptual model is provided to organize survey information, however, it is unlikely that the actual research and schools' implementation of these strategies proceed with such purpose and coordination.

Predisaster Phase

The majority of existing surveys of school professionals with regard to crisis preparedness, response, and management address content related to the predisaster phase of crisis response. A major topic of surveys has been the preparation of school professionals for crisis prevention and intervention. Consistent results have been found in terms of university training, with fewer than 10% of survey respondents across disciplines such as teaching (Nims & Wilson, 1998), social work (Astor, Behre, Wallace, & Fravil, 1998), and school psychology (Allen et al., 2002; Wise, Smead, & Huebner, 1987) indicating that they had taken a course specific to crisis prevention and intervention. It should be noted, however, that some states have passed recent legislation requiring preservice training for all school personnel. For example, New York's Project Safe Schools Against Violence in Education Act (SAVE, 2000) requires 2 hours of violence prevention training for teachers and other school personnel seeking certification and the California Student Safety and Violence Prevention Act of 2000 requires preservice training in discrimination and harassment based on sexual orientation and gender identity.

In-service training results have been more variable across disciplines and content areas. For instance, 47% of school resource officers reported not receiving terrorism-specific training and more than 71% of these respondents indicated that other school personnel had not received this training (Trump, 2003). This latter finding is consistent with results from the SSOCS, where 35% of principals indicated that their schools provide staff training to identify early warning signs in potentially violent students and 31% train faculty in crime prevention (NCES, 2004). More school social workers (62%) have reported receiving in-service training in school violence education (Astor et al., 1998). Training of school psychologists has been variable; 85% of school psychologists surveyed by Furlong, Babinski, Poland, Munoz, and Boles (1996) indicated that they received no specialized training in school violence, whereas Larson and Busse's (1998) survey found that 67% of specialist-level school psychology programs indicated that they covered violence prevention and safe schools in coursework. It is possible that practicing school psychologists define specialized training as more in-depth than coverage across coursework. Studies of school counselors' in-service training on suicide prevention and intervention have suggested that about half receive this training (Malley & Kush, 1994), whereas slightly less than half indicated their school has not offered in-service programs on suicide prevention to staff in the previous 5 years (King, Price, Telljohann, & Wahl, 1999).

When asked about perceived level of preparation for crisis situations, 76% of school resource officers indicated their schools were not well prepared to respond to a terrorist attack (Trump, 2003) and between 45% (Furlong et al., 1996) to 58% (Allen et al., 2002) of school psychologists reported feeling minimally prepared to respond to crisis situations, such as violence.

TABLE 6.1
Summary of Surveys of School Professionals in Crisis Prevention and Intervention

Study	Respondent	Findings
		Predisaster Phase
Nickerson and Zhe (2004)	School psychologists ($N = 197$)	• 81% had police/resource officer • 72% used crisis drills • 33% had suicide prevention • 9% used metal detectors
Nims and Wilson (1998)	College deans and department heads of teacher education programs ($N = 350$)	• 44% reported that violence prevention content is a part of other teacher curriculum • 4%–7% of institutions offer specific violence prevention courses • 5%–6% indicated that this type of course should be implemented
Trump (2003)	School-based police officers ($N = 728$)	• More than 55% reported that their school crisis plans are not adequate • More than 62% indicated that their school crisis plans have not been adequately practiced
Allen et al. (2002)	School psychologists ($N = 276$)	• 2% considered themselves "well prepared" to deal with crisis situations • 30% had experience in crisis intervention during practicum or internship (68% of this training was by on-site practitioner) • 81% of the respondents received local training after graduation (64% gained information from books and journal articles, 27% attended relevant presentations at NASP conventions) • 53% reported having practice drills within the last year
King, Price, Telljohann, and Wahl (1999)	High school counselors ($N = 243$)	• 34% of the high schools provided teaching about suicide prevention (1–15 hours annually) • 44% of high schools had not offered in-service on suicide prevention in past 5 years • 38% believed they could recognize a student at risk of committing suicide (79% could offer effective support to a suicidal student; 74% could offer support to an at-risk student) • 85% were confident in referring a suicidal student to a mental health professional
National Center for Education Statistics (2004)	School principals ($N = 2,270$)	• 57% of respondents reported that their school included programs to promote a sense of community/social integration among students (22% indicated the inclusion of a hotline) • 35% indicated their schools provided staff training to identify early warning signs in potentially violent students (31% reported training faculty in crime prevention) • 75% reported controlled access to the school building (65% closed the campus during lunch, 34% controlled access to school grounds) • Security measures included no school lockers (54%), random dog sniffs (21%), security cameras (19%), drug testing for students (4%), student picture identification (4%)
Astor, Behre, Wallace, and Fravil (1998)	School social workers ($N = 576$)	• 71% of inner-city social workers, 36% urban, 37% suburban, and 31% rural social workers reported a fear for their personal safety (35% were physically assaulted or threatened) • Common precautions to protect themselves included: 33% left money at home, 24% avoided the school after dark, and 11% avoided wearing certain types or colors of clothing

(Continued)

TABLE 6.1
(Continued)

		• 68% of the respondents felt adequately prepared to respond effectively to school violence (19% reported being highly prepared)
		• Prevention and intervention training sources included: 70% conferences, 56% self-education, 27% continuing education, 17% other sources, and 5% university training
		• 89% preferred more violence education in graduate school (59% preferred in-services)
Furlong, Babinski, Poland, Munoz, and Boles (1996)	School psychologists ($N = 123$)	• 78% worried about their personal safety at school less than once a year
		• 85.4% reported that they had received no specialized school violence training
		• 26.8% indicated feeling prepared to address this issue (27.7% gave a neutral response, 45.5% felt some level of being unprepared)
Malley and Kush (1994)	School counselors ($N = 325$)	• 51% of schools had formal suicide policy statement (52% had procedure for at-risk students)
		• 51% indicated that schools provided suicide prevention/intervention training for counselors (42% reported their schools provided in-service training for staff)
		• 56% of school counselors provided with suicide reference materials
		• 50% reported their schools distribute prevention materials to students (28% distributed materials to parents)
		• 42% of schools hold prevention discussions in the classroom.
Wise, Smead, and Huebner (1987)	School psychologists ($N = 193$)	• 8% had taken a course devoted to the topic
		• 42% indicated that the area of child abuse training was inadequate
Ballard (1998)	Rural school superintendents ($N = 81$)	• 74% reported school violence was a priority
		• 96% said school safety was growing concern
		• 46% reported school violence policy would be implemented in new school year
		• 75% authorized searches to prevent drugs/violence (77% locker searches, 73% use of dogs)
		• All superintendents reported the use of video cameras on school buses (39% live cameras)
		• 80% had not installed metal detectors (64% used hand-held metal detectors, not regularly)
		• 75% of the school systems used security alarm system (mostly administrative buildings, followed by high schools, and then middle schools)
		• 85% used alternative school programs to maintain discipline and promote safety
Mansfield and Farris (1992)	Elementary and secondary school principals ($N = 830$)	• 33% considered general discipline programs/policies to be highly effective in reducing disruptive behavior (45% considered these moderately effective, 4% considered them not very effective, 17% did not consider disruptive behavior a problem in their schools)
		• Half reported that social service agencies and parent groups provided same level of support

(Continued)

TABLE 6.1

(Continued)

Impact Phase

Nickerson and Zhe (2004)	School psychologists ($N = 197$)	• Interventions used with teachers included providing information about referring students (93%), providing general information about crises (90%), debriefing (73%) • Interventions with students after a crisis included psychological first aid (87%), group to process event (80%), debriefing (73%), triage (72%) • Parent interventions included providing information about crises (74%), debriefing (32%)
Bolnik and Brock (2004)	School psychologists ($N = 200$)	• 86% had been involved in a school crisis intervention • 90% reported having experienced at least one physical, emotional, behavioral, cognitive, or work performance reaction to their school intervention work • 94% said self-care strategies were important/very important during crisis intervention work

Short-Term Adaptation Phase

Nickerson and Zhe (2004)	School psychologists ($N = 197$)	• After a crisis, 95% of schools referred students for mental health and 88% referred families for mental health services (60% helped families secure resources)

Long-term Adaptation Phase

Astor, Behre, Wallace, and Fravil (1998)	School social workers ($N = 576$)	• Most effective violence services reported: social skills training (37%), conflict management (37%), child abuse education (31%), after-school sports/clubs (30%), classroom management (30%), individual/family counseling (30%), crisis intervention (28%) • 91% reported home visits to be most effective intervention for children with aggression issues (although 74% viewed the home visits to be potentially dangerous)
Mansfield and Farris (1992)	Elementary and secondary school principals ($N = 830$)	• Types of services provided to disruptive students: referrals to social service agencies outside school (91%), individual/group counseling (82%), parent participation in decisions (82%), procedure to identify at-risk students (81%), in-school suspension (75%), health services (73%), academic assistance programs. (71%), referal to alternative program (67%), conflict management instruction (54%)
NCES (2004)	School principals ($N = 2,270$)	• 66% used counseling, social work, psychological, or therapeutic activities (behavior modification interventions [66%]; prevention curriculum, instruction, or training [65%]; and individual attention, mentoring, tutoring, or coaching by students or adults [63%]1)
Nickerson and Zhe (2004)	School psychologists ($N = 197$)	• 89% used anger management/social skills • 89% used individual counseling • 72% used peer mediation or conflict resolution • 53% of schools held memorials • 16% had parent support groups

Focus groups with school personnel in California revealed that educators reported feeling ill-prepared to address school violence, leading to the implementation of preservice and in-service training for educators (Attorney General and State Superintendent of Public Instruction Safe Schools Task Force, 2000). In contrast to the lack of preparation reported by many school professionals, only 10% of school social workers in one study indicated being minimally prepared to respond effectively to school violence (Astor et al., 1998). With regard to crisis intervention for suicidal students, 38% of high school counselors indicated they could recognize a student at risk of committing suicide, 74%–79% believed they could offer effective support to an at-risk or suicidal student, and 85% were confident in referring a suicidal student to another mental health professional (King et al., 1999). Results of these surveys suggest that professionals may feel more at ease with suicide than they do with other types of violent aggression.

In addition to surveying school professionals about their preparation and training for crisis prevention and intervention, information has been gathered about the predisaster procedures in place, such as crisis plans and teams, as well as the use of policing and therapeutic or educational measures to prevent violence and other crises. Nearly all (96%) of school principals reported that their schools had a crisis management plan for at least one crisis (NCES, 2004). Recent surveys of school psychologists have indicated that 91% of schools had crisis plans (Allen et al., 2002) and 78% reported that the schools used the plans (Nickerson & Zhe, 2004). When asked specifically about formal written plans or policies for suicidal and at-risk students, only 51%–52% of school counselors indicated that their schools had these (Malley & Kush, 1994). With regard to crisis response teams, 93% of school psychologists in the Nickerson and Zhe study indicated that their schools used these, whereas 76% of school psychologists in Allen et al.'s study indicated that their districts had these teams. Only 66% of high school counselors indicated that their school had a crisis team to handle suicide attempts (King et al., 1999).

Surveys have also assessed schools' safety practices. Ninety-seven percent of school principals reported using visitor sign-ins, 25% required faculty and staff to wear identification badges, and 7% used metal detectors (NCES, 2004). It should be noted that the use of metal detectors was consistent with Nickerson and Zhe's (2004) finding that 9% of school psychologists reported their use in the schools, but differed substantially from Ballard's (1998) finding that 64% of superintendents reported the use of metal detectors in their schools. This discrepant finding may be because superintendents are responsible for a large number of schools, whereas principals and school psychologists likely reported only on the one or two schools in which they have worked. Alternatively, district administrators may perceive violence in schools to be more under control than it actually is. Surveys indicate that students more frequently report violent behavior in schools, such as weapon carrying, than do school administrators, suggesting differing perceptions about school violence (Coggeshall & Kingery, 2001). The use of police or resource officers on campus was widespread, with 81% of school psychologists (Nickerson & Zhe, 2004) and 85% of superintendents reporting the presence of officers on their school campuses (Ballard, 1998). When surveyed about the perceived helpfulness of the police in promoting safe schools, 69% of principals indicated that they provided moderate to great support (Mansfield & Farris, 1992).

Impact Phase

In contrast to the research on the predisaster phase, there is a paucity of survey research examining school professionals' response in the early stages of a crisis. Nickerson and Zhe (2004) surveyed school psychologists and found that at least 90% of respondents provided teachers with general information about crises and procedures for referring students in the early response phase, whereas 75% used debriefing with teachers. Common interventions with students in the early phase included psychological first aid (87%), running groups to process the event (80%), debriefing (73%), and triage (72%). There was less involvement with parents, with 75% of respondents indicating that they provided general information to parents and only 32% debriefing parents. In their survey of school psychologists, Bolnik and Brock (2004) found that 86% had been involved in a school crisis intervention, with 90% having experienced at least one physical, emotional, behavioral, cognitive, or work performance reaction to the work. Additionally, nearly all respondents indicated that self-care strategies were "important" or "very important" during crisis intervention work.

Short-Term Adaptation Phase

Assisting individuals, groups, and families in adapting to the impact of the crisis, and referring students and families for mental health services have been found to be common practices (Mansfield & Farris, 1992; Nickerson & Zhe, 2004). Additionally, Nickerson and Zhe (2004) found that 60% of school psychologists surveyed reported that their schools helped parents secure resources in the aftermath of a crisis. Malley and Kush (1994) found that nearly 50% of school counselors surveyed indicated that their schools had a postvention component when a suicide occurred.

Long-Term Adaptation Phase

This phase focuses on preventing relapse and may include individual, group, and family counseling. For the purposes of this chapter, this section includes survey results across a wide variety of strategies, such as counseling, conflict management, and support groups. It should be noted that many of these strategies could also be included in the predisaster phase of crisis intervention, as they can be used as preventive efforts. Mental health counseling was a commonly used long-term intervention in schools, used by more than 80% of schools, as reported by school counselors (Malley & Kush, 1994), principals (Mansfield & Farris, 1992), and school psychologists (Nickerson & Zhe, 2004). Other strategies included conflict-management instruction (Mansfield & Farris, 1992; Nickerson & Zhe, 2004), social skills training (Astor et al., 1998; Nickerson & Zhe, 2004), and academic assistance programs (Mansfield & Farris, 1992; NCES, 2001). Far fewer school professionals indicated using outreach and support groups for parents (Mansfield & Farris, 1992; Nickerson & Zhe, 2004). Findings from two surveys (Mansfield & Farris, 1992; NCES, 2001) indicated that school principals perceive a lack of alternative programs for disruptive students to be a barrier to maintaining a safe school environment. Despite widespread use of crisis prevention and intervention strategies, surveys have revealed that evaluation of these strategies rarely occurs (Malley & Kush, 1994; Nickerson & Zhe, 2004).

Relative Advantages/Disadvantages of Survey Methods to Study School Crisis Preparation and Response

There are several advantages of using surveys as a research methodology. First, surveys allow researchers to describe a wide range of phenomena based on the self-reported opinions, attitudes, or behaviors of a group of people (Stangor, 2004). Surveys are capable of generating large amounts of data (Jackson & Antonucci, 1994), allowing the scope of inquiry to be broadened from a patient base to a population base, which is important for epidemiological research (Willis & Gonzalez, 1998). Additionally, the large sample size is beneficial for statistical power. Surveys have the capacity for secondary and historical data analyses, and can be used as measured variables in to test research hypotheses in correlational or experimental designs (Stangor, 2004). Well-designed surveys with standardized questions minimize subjectivity and allow for comparisons across groups of people. Finally, from a practical perspective, surveys are a relatively portable and cost-effective methodology (Jackson & Antonucci, 1994; Mangione, 1995).

Traditionally, disadvantages of survey methodology have focused on sampling error, including coverage, nonresponse and sampling errors (Groves, 1987). All of these errors concern discrepancies between results of the survey sample and results from the full population under study, although reasons for the discrepancies differ. Coverage error concerns the fact that some members of the population are not covered under the list from which the samples were drawn, nonresponse errors can occur when a significant number of people in the sample do not respond to the survey, and sampling errors may arise if some members of the population are deliberately excluded from the survey through a selection of a subset (Dillman, 2000; Groves, 1987). These errors are especially problematic if the people who are not sampled or who do not respond have different characteristics from the people who do respond.

The field of survey methodology has undergone a paradigm shift in the past two decades. The new paradigm, sometimes referred to as the Cognitive Aspects of Survey Measurement (CASM) movement, focuses on measurement error (Tourangeau, 2004). Measurement error occurs when a respondent's answers are inaccurate or imprecise (Dillman, 2000). According to the CASM model, response errors in surveys arise from underlying cognitive processes. In CASM research, an effort is made to ensure that respondents interpret the meaning of survey questions in the same way, thereby enhancing reliability and validity (Wright & Loftus, 1998). Much of the work on respondent error focuses on influences such as social desirability, motivation, and cognitive demands (Krosnick, 1999). Measurement errors arising from the questionnaire include question order, structure, wording, and whether multiple questions measure the same concept.

With respect to existing surveys of school professionals regarding crisis prevention and intervention, an advantage is that there are many descriptive surveys that provide consistent information about strategies used to prevent a wide variety of crises. Additionally, these descriptive surveys have identified needs in this area, such as the need for more university and in-service preparation in crisis prevention and intervention. Survey findings also indicated the need for implementing ways to support school professionals currently working in this field. A disadvantage of existing surveys is the lack of information on what happens in the impact and short-term adaptation phases in actual crises, which would be particularly useful for school practitioners. Aditionally, there is less information on perceived effectiveness of the various strategies and survey respondents have indicated that evaluation of crisis prevention and intervention efforts rarely occurs.

IMPLICATIONS FOR SCHOOL CRISIS PREPAREDNESS AND PRACTICE

Because this chapter has focused on the two primary areas of surveys and crisis prevention and intervention, implications for practice are summarized for both of these areas. Although comprehensive books have been written to guide researchers in designing surveys to reduce common survey errors (see Dillman, 2000; Mangione, 1995), we have summarized some key variables to guide practitioners and researchers in conducting effective surveys, with consideration of both general survey issues and also those pertaining to crises (see Table 6.2). Perhaps most importantly, surveys of school professionals have yielded a wealth of information about common practices and areas of need in preparedness, response, and management that can be used to guide practitioners' work, which are summarized in Table 6.3. It should be noted that these implications for practice are limited to those revealed through survey research. For crisis prevention and intervention implications based on other research methodologies, the

TABLE 6.2

Implications for Conducting Crisis Prevention and Intervention Surveys

---

Preventing Coverage Error
- Evaluate lists from which sample will be drawn to ensure that everyone in the survey population is on the list and that others not in the population are excluded; find out how list is maintained and updated (Dillman, 2000; Mangione, 1995)

Preventing Nonresponse Error
- Establish trust with potential respondents (e.g., have legitimate authority sponsor the survey; Dillman, 2000)
- Motivate respondents/increase expectations for rewards (e.g., "thank you" or give reward; Dillman, 2000; Mangione, 1995)
- If interviews about sensitive topics are used, make a special effort to develop trust and safety (Brush, 1990)
- Incorporate data collection into more general assistance in adapting after a crisis (Willis & Gonzalez, 1998)
- Reduce respondents' expectations for social costs: make survey easy to complete (Dillman, 2000; Mangione, 1995) and explain why collecting sensitive information is important (Mangione, 1995; Willis & Gonzalez, 1998)

Preventing Sampling Error
- Use formulas for selecting sample size (see Dillman, 2000; Mangione, 1995); use random samples (see Mangione, 1995 for discussion)

Preventing Measurement Error
- Write good questions with few words, equal numbers of positive and negative response options, and specified time periods (Dillman, 2000; Mangione, 1995); ask questions beyond posttraumatic stress symptoms (Willis & Gonzalez, 1998)
- Place instructions exactly where needed, creating visual navigation guides, and pretesting (Dillman, 2000)
- Make sensitive questions less threatening by placing them in contexts with other questions (Dillman, 2000; Mangione, 1995), asking several questions to allow for desensitization (Brush, 1990), and considering self-administered rather than interview-administered questionnaire (Willis & Gonzalez, 1998)

TABLE 6.3

Implications for Practice From Surveys to Guide Practitioners' Work in Crisis Prevention
and Intervention

- Increase exposure to topics of crisis prevention and intervention at the graduate level of training by dedicating an entire course to this area and/or practicum and internship experiences providing practice of appropriate prevention and intervention skills.
- Encourage the school community to provide a mandatory in-service training in emergency preparedness for all school professionals.
- Take opportunities to read literature and attend workshops on crisis prevention and intervention; share this information with colleagues in other disciplines (e.g., social workers, counselors, teachers, administrators) and encourage them to do the same.
- Work as part of an interdisciplinary team to establish, exercise, and evaluate crisis management plans within the school community.
- Work with students in class and/or develop parent workshops to share knowledge of crisis prevention and intervention skills in order to raise awareness, prevent crisis situations from occurring, and provide useful coping skills in dealing with a crisis situation if one should occur.
- Assist administrators in creating, implementing, and evaluating programs to reduce violence for students with disruptive behavior.
- Encourage the use of safety precautions and measures, combined with educational and therapeutic interventions to prevent crises.
- Recognize the critical nature of naturally occurring social support systems (e.g., parents) and ensure that they are an integral part of the school's crisis prevention and intervention efforts.
- Assist in developing and implementing strategies to provide support for the emotional, behavioral, and cognitive reactions experienced by professionals involved in crisis intervention.
- Engage in self-care strategies after intense crisis intervention work.

reader should see Brock and Jimerson (2004). As illustrated in these tables, survey research has provided us with some useful information to guide future research and practitioners' work, although there is much work to be done to gain a comprehensive understanding of what occurs and how best to intervene in the predisaster, impact, short and long-term adaptation phases of a school crisis.

REFERENCES

Allen, M. (2003). [State mandated crisis plans]. Unpublished raw data.

Allen, M., Jerome, A., White, A., Marston, S., Lamb, S., Pope, D., & Rawlins, C. (2002). The preparation of school psychologists for crisis intervention. *Psychology in the Schools, 39*, 427–439.

Astor, R. A., Behre, W. J., Wallace, J. M., & Fravil, K. A. (1998). School social workers and school violence: Personal safety, training, and violence programs. *Social Work, 43*, 223–232.

Attorney General and State Superintendent of Public Instruction Safe Schools Task Force. (2000, June). *Final report.* Available: http://caag.state.ca.us/publications/safeschool.pdf

Ballard, C. (1998). Violence prevention in Georgia's rural public school systems: Perceptions of school superintendents. *Southern Rural Sociology, 14*, 91–109.

Blom, G. E. (1986). A school disaster—Intervention and research aspects. *Journal of the American Academy of Child Psychiatry, 25*, 336–345.

Bolnik, L., & Brock, S. E. (2004). *The effects of crisis intervention work on school psychologists.* Unpublished manuscript, California State University, Sacramento.

Brock, S. E. (2002). Crisis theory: A foundation for the comprehensive crisis prevention and intervention team. In S. E. Brock, P. J. Lazarus, & S. R. Jimerson (Eds.), *Best practices in school crisis prevention and intervention* (pp. 5–17). Washington, DC: National Association of School Psychologists.

Brock, S. E., & Jimerson, S. R. (2004). School crisis interventions: Strategies for addressing the consequences of crisis events. In E. R. Gerler (Ed.), *Handbook of school violence.(pp. 285–332).* Binghamton, NY: Haworth Press.

Brock, S. E., Lazarus, P. J., & Jimerson, S. R. (Eds.). (2002). *Best practices in school crisis prevention and intervention.* Bethesda, MD: National Association of School Psychologists.

Brock, S. E., Sandoval, J., & Lewis, S. (2001). *Preparing for crises in the schools: A manual for building school crisis response teams* (2nd ed.). New York: Wiley.

Brush, L. D. (1990). Violent acts and injurious outcomes in married couples: Methodological issues in the National Survey of Families and Households. *Gender and Society, 4*, 56–67.

California Student Safety and Violence Prevention Act of 2000, A.B. 537. 587 Cal. Stat. §§ 422.6 et seq. (Kuehl 1999).

Caplan, G. (1964). *Principles of preventive psychiatry.* New York: Basic Books.

Coggeshall, M. B., & Kingery, P. M. (2001). Cross-survey analysis of school violence and disorder. *Psychology in the Schools, 38*, 107–116.

Comprehensive School Safety Plans, S.B. 187, 736 Cal. Stat., §§ 35294.2 (Hughes 1997).

Dillman, D. A. (2000). *Mail and internet surveys* (2nd ed.). New York: Wiley.

Dwyer, K., Osher, D., & Warger, C. (1998). *Early warning, timely response: A guide to safe schools.* Washington, DC: U. S. Department of Education. Available http://www.ed.gov/offices/OSERS/OSEP/Products/earlywrn.html

Furlong, M., Babinski, L., Poland, S., Munoz, J., & Boles, S. (1996). Factors associated with school psychologists' perceptions of campus violence. *Psychology in the Schools, 33*, 28–37.

Groves, R. M. (1987). Research on survey data quality. *The Public Opinion Quarterly, 51*, S156–S172.

Jackson, J. S., & Antonucci, T. C. (1994). Survey methodology in life-span human development research. In S. H. Cohen & H. W. Reese (Eds.), *Life-span developmental psychology: Methodological contributions* (pp. 65–94). Hillsdale, NJ: Lawrence Erlbaum Associates.

King, K. A., Price, J. H., Telljohann, S. K., & Wahl, J. (1999). How confident do high school counselors feel in recognizing students at risk for suicide? *American Journal of Health Behavior, 23*, 457–467.

Klingman, A. (1978). Children in stress: Anticipatory guidance in the framework of the educational system. *Personnel and Guidance Journal, 57*, 22–26.

Klingman, A. (1985). Free writing: Evaluation of a preventive program with elementary school children. *Journal of School Psychology, 23*, 167–175.

Klingman, A. (1987). A school-based emergency crisis intervention in a mass school disaster. *Professional Psychology: Research and Practice, 18*, 604–612.

Klingman, A. (1988). School community in disaster: Planning for intervention. *Journal of Community Psychology, 16*, 205–215.

Klingman, A. (1996). School-based intervention in disaster and trauma. In M. C. Roberts (Ed.), *Model programs in child and family mental health* (pp. 149–171). Mahwah, NJ: Lawrence Erlbaum Associates.

Klingman, A., & Ben Eli, Z. (1981). A school community in disaster: Primary and secondary prevention in situational crisis. *Professional Psychology: Research and Practice, 12*, 523–533.

Krosnick, J. A. (1999). Survey research. *Annual Review of Psychology, 50*, 537–567.

Larson, J., & Busse, R. T. (1998). Specialist-level preparation in school violence and youth gang intervention. *Psychology in the Schools, 35*, 373–379.

Malley, P., & Kush, F. (1994). School-based adolescent suicide prevention and intervention programs: A survey. *School Counselor, 42*, 130–138.

Mangione, T. W. (1995). *Mail surveys: Improving the quality*. Thousand Oaks, CA: Sage.

Mansfield, W., & Farris, E. (1992). *Public school survey on safe, disciplined, and drug-free schools* (NCES Publication no. 92–007). Washington, DC: U.S. Department of Education, National Center for Education Statistics.

National Center for Education Statistics (NCES). (2001). *Indicators of School Crime and Safety, 2001*. Available; http://nces.ed.gov/pubs2002/crime2001/11.asp

National Center for Education Statistics (NCES). (2004). *Crime and safety in America's public schools: Selected findings from the school survey on crime and safety*. Available; http://nces.ed.gov/pubs2004/2004370.pdf

Nickerson, A. B., & Zhe, E. J. (2004). Crisis prevention and intervention: A survey of school psychologists. *Psychology in the Schools, 41*, 777–788.

Nims, D., & Wilson, R. W. (1998, February). *Violence prevention preparation: A survey of colleges of education and departments of teacher education*. Paper presented at the annual meeting of the American Association of Colleges for Teacher Education, New Orleans, LA.

Pagliocca, P. M., & Nickerson, A. B. (2001). Legislating school crisis response: Good policy or just good politics? *Law and Policy, 23*, 373–407.

Pagliocca, P. M., Nickerson, A. B., & Williams, S. (2002). Research and evaluation directions in crisis intervention. In S. E. Brock, P. J. Lazarus, & S. R. Jimerson (Eds.), *Best practices in school crisis prevention and intervention* (pp. 771–790). Washington, DC: National Association of School Psychologists.

Roberts, M. C. (Ed.). (1996). *Model programs in child and family mental health*. Mahwah, NJ: Lawrence Erlbaum Associates.

Safe Schools Against Violence in Education Act (Project SAVE), New York. §§ 55-2801–2814 (2000).

Stangor, C. (2004). *Research methods for the behavioral sciences* (2nd ed.). Boston: Houghton Mifflin.

Tourangeau, R. (2004). Survey research and societal change. *Annual Review of Psychology, 55*, 775–801.

Trump, K. (2003). *School safety threats persist, funding decreasing: NASRO 2003 national school-based law enforcement survey*. Available http://www.nasro.org/2003NASROsurvey.pdf

Vernberg, E. M. (1994). Evaluating the effectiveness of school-based interventions after large-scale disasters: An achievable goal? *Child, Youth, and Family Services Quarterly, 17*, 11–13.

Vernberg, E. M. (2002). Intervention approaches following disasters. In A. M. La Greca, W. K. Silverman, E. M. Vernberg, & M. C. Roberts (Eds.), *Helping children cope with disasters and terrorism* (pp. 55–72). Washington, DC: American Psychological Association.

Willis, G. B., & Gonzalez, A. (1998). Methodological issues in the use of survey questionnaires to assess the health effects of torture. *The Journal of Nervous and Mental Disease, 186*, 283–289.

Wise, P. S., Smead, V. S., & Huebner, E. S. (1987). Crisis intervention: Involvement and training needs of school psychology personnel. *Journal of School Psychology, 25*, 185–187.

Wright, D. B., & Loftus, E. F. (1998). How memory research can benefit from CASM. *Memory, 6*, 467–474.

7

Making the Case for an International Perspective on School Violence: Implications for Theory, Research, Policy, and Assessment

Ron Avi Astor
University of Southern California

Rami Benbenishty
Hebrew University

Roxana Marachi
California State University Northridge

SCHOOL VIOLENCE AS A GLOBAL PHENOMENON

Concerns about school violence are shared around the world. Although lethal shootings in the United States have attracted most of the international media coverage (Herda-Rapp, 2003), reports from other parts of the world reveal that school violence is a serious global problem. Time and again the public in countries with cultures as diverse as Japan, Jordan, Brazil, Norway, Israel, Malaysia, the United States, and Ethiopia are alarmed by atrocious acts of senseless violence in their own country's schools. Since Columbine, the U.S. media has attempted to frame this dilemma as an American problem affecting mainly middle-and upper middle-class White students. Nevertheless, the data suggest that an array of heinous acts of violence occur across all segments of U.S. society and in many countries across the globe (i.e., decapitations in Japan, hangings in Norway, group stabbings in Israel, etc.; Kachur et al., 1996; Smith, 2003; Smith & Morita et al., 1999; see also Astor et al., 2004 on the role of the media in defining what is considered school violence and where the problem exists.) According to Ohsako (1997), "violence is occurring at a high rate in developing countries and its impact on schooling, learning and living is certainly serious, which refutes the commonly-held view that violence is primarily an issue of industrialized countries" (p. 7).

TABLE 7.1
Countries Included in Review of School Violence

Australia	Hong Kong	Nicaragua
Austria	Hungary	Norway
Belgium (French/Flemish)	Ireland	Peru
Canada	Iceland	Philippines
Colombia	Iran	Poland
Croatia	Ireland	Portugal
Cyprus	Israel	Romania
Czech Republic	Italy	Russian Federation
Denmark	Japan	Scotland
El Salvador	Jordan	Singapore
England	Korea	Slovakia
Estonia	Kuwait	Slovenia
Ethiopia	Latvia	South Africa
Finland	Lithuania	Spain
France	Macedonia	Sweden
Germany	Malaysia	Switzerland
Greece	Malta	Thailand
Greenland	Netherlands	United States
Guatemala	New Zealand	Wales

Akiba and associates also put forth a global perspective stating that "school violence is a global phenomenon that affects one of the core institutions of modern society to some degree in virtually all nation-states" (Akiba, LeTendre, Baker, & Goesling, 2002, p. 830).

School violence has been a global phenomena for decades prior to being "discovered" by the media in the post-Columbine era. Given the current review of empirical data in many countries, we strongly support a global perspective on the phenomena of school violence. Currently, many societies are developing an awareness of the uniqueness of school violence as an independent form of context-oriented violence.

This chapter is based on analyses of numerous empirical studies and publications that examine school violence in a wide range of countries (e.g., Akiba et al., 2002; Currie et al., 2004; Eslea et al., 2003; Ohsako, 1997; Smith, 2003; Smith, Cowie, Olafsson, & Liefooghe, 2002; Smith et al., 1999). All the conclusions are based on research reports related to more than 60 countries. Table 7.1 lists the names of the countries that had reports or reviews that formed the basis for this chapter.

Although comprehensive, this review is far from exhaustive—many programs and interventions are published and discussed in languages other than English. This review is limited to English-language publications. In addition to reviews of studies indexed in major scientific indexes (such as Web of Science and PsychInfo), this review also incorporated the Internet. This added quite significantly to the review because many reports on countries that were never published in English-language academic journals were available on the Internet. In some instances, automatic translation facilities available on the Internet were utilized.

This review is also limited by the extent of information provided by reports from various countries. One of the most challenging aspects of cross-national comparisons is the fact that reports often do not provide detailed information about the methods and instruments used to obtain the figures being reported. Except for reports in academic journals and of bodies such as the World Health Organization, the details about surveys are quite sporadic and it is quite difficult to gauge important study characteristics such as methodological rigor, how representative are the samples, and what types of instruments were used.

This chapter discusses the potential contributions of international and cross-cultural perspectives. It lists a range of questions and issues that should be addressed by international studies. A proposal for an international collaborative study of school violence that could address these issues is also provided. Finally, this chapter includes recommendations for a conceptual and methodological framework to design an international monitoring system for school violence.

WHY AN INTERNATIONAL
AND CROSS-CULTURAL PERSPECTIVES?

Raising Awareness and Establishing Priorities

One of the important functions of examining school violence in different countries is to develop cross-country comparisons. Such comparative data could be used to gain a perspective on how extreme the school safety situation is in a given country, and in which countries the situation is less severe than others. This greatly facilitates policy creation surrounding school violence in specific counties. For instance, in Israel, the findings of comparative international studies have been used to dramatize the situation. Thus, in the wake of a series of reports on youth violence, the front page of the largest daily newspaper presented a chart derived from an Trends in International Mathematics and Science Study (TIMMS) depicting the Israeli students as victims of high levels of bullying compared with the rest of the world. This greater awareness helped mobilize the government, teacher organizations, and select governing committees to create policy, training, and interventions designed to reduce Israel's prevalence rates. Using the same TIMMS data, on the other side of the ocean, Akiba and associates (2002) made the argument to the U.S. educational research audience and the American public that many other countries are experiencing either similar or higher levels of school violence than the United States. This kind of global contextualization helps countries situate their standings independent of media stories associated with school violence.

Such comparisons may also have a strong impact on the public within countries. For instance, Menesini and Modiano (2003) reported that comparative research showed that school violence in Italy was reported at a higher level than in other European and Western countries (being about as twice as high as in England and almost three times higher than in Norway). The authors claimed that the major response of newspapers and television programs to these data brought about awareness in Italian schools. School heads and staff began to be interested in Italian-based interventions and to study school safety issues in depth. This type of narrative has been repeated in many countries across the globe when the media has reported high rates of school violence compared with other countries.

Creating a Global Inventory of Interventions and Policy

A cross-cultural perspective of school violence provides a rich source of insights about policies and interventions. Understanding why certain cultures endorse or reject specific interventions would be very helpful for understanding the cultural dynamics surrounding school violence. For example, mediation programs are mentioned in almost every national school safety report we reviewed (see Table 7.1 for a list of countries). By contrast, Olweus and Smith's anti-bullying programs are more common in Europe, the United States, and Australia, whereas programs of restorative justice are more common in Australia and New Zealand. Zero-tolerance policies and the use of electronic security (i.e., video cameras, sensors, metal detectors, and professional guards) are more common in the United States. Even so, in this global era of communications, numerous international conferences, and the reliance on empirical evaluations, almost all the school safety interventions listed here are present in multiple countries. Still, an inventory of interventions used in each country and information on their success would be helpful in understanding the spread and adoption of certain interventions across the globe and in identifying which interventions may be more effective in some countries and not in others.

Increasing Contributions to Theory

An international perspective can contribute significantly to theories of school violence. On the most basic level, theories advanced to explain school violence in one culture can inform and stimulate comparative research in other countries. For instance, Yoneyama and Naito (2003) advanced the theory on factors contributing to bullying by examining the Japanese literature on school factors that contribute to *ijime* (bullying in Japanese). Their analysis connects between aspects of the role and structure of the Japanese educational system and characteristics of bullying behavior. They see a relationship between the class as a social group and the fact that most bullying behavior is carried out by a group of classmates against individual students. Also, they analyze the role expectations of Japanese teachers and show how teacher–student practices contribute to both teacher and student bullying behaviors. Such hypotheses and theoretical propositions advanced in the Japanese context should inform and enrich theory development in other countries that differ in specific characteristics of the educational system. For instance, one would expect to find different patterns of bullying (i.e., more individuals bullying other individuals) in educational systems that emphasize more individualistic ethos rather than the collectivistic ethos of the Japanese system.

Akiba and colleagues (2002) utilized TIMMS data on student victimization in 37 countries to test theoretical assumptions about the nature of school violence in different countries. They tested two sets of nation-level variables: (a) known predictors of crime (both general and juvenile) and (b) factors related to the educational system itself. Their work shows that factors inherent in the educational system (e.g., academic achievement, school climate, and teacher–child relationships) are better predictors of school violence than predictors of general crime, basic national economic conditions, and demographic characteristics. However, they note that certain kinds of school victimization (e.g., sexual assaults) are related to community crime levels more than other kinds. This pattern was also found in a study in Israel (Khoury-Kassabri, Benbenishty, Astor, & Zeira, 2004) in which severe types of school victimization were related to poor neighborhoods much more than mild/moderate types of victimization. Such findings and more extensive testing in other countries may help refine a theory on the "spill over" of political and community violence into schools (Benbenishty & Astor, 2005). These kinds of cross-cultural empirical findings advance existing theories on the relationships between victimization and structural factors associated with the school and its environment.

THEORETICAL ISSUES THAT COULD BE ADDRESSED BY A GLOBAL PERSPECTIVE

The Relative Influences of School, Family, Neighborhood, and Cultural Context in School Violence

In recent years, there have been many calls urging scholars to move from a focus on individual characteristics of victims and bullies to an understanding of how contexts, both within and outside school impact school violence (e.g., Akiba et al., 2002; Benbenishty & Astor, 2005; Furlong & Morrison, 2000; Yoneyama & Naito, 2003). These approaches examine how external contexts in which a school is embedded interact with internal school and student characteristics to influence levels of victimization in schools. These layered and nested contexts include the *school* (e.g., structural characteristics, social climate, and policies against violence), the *neighborhood* (e.g., poverty, social organization, and crime), the students' *families* (e.g., education and family structure), *cultural* aspects of student and teacher population (e.g., religion and ethnic affiliation) and the *economic*, social, and political makeup of the country as a whole. An international system will help clarify both theoretically and practically the role of these nested contexts.

The issue of social and physical context is relevant to international perspectives for several important reasons. First, it is essential to view results of comparisons among cultures with an understanding of the circumstances that lead to differences, so that popularly intuitive and often misleading interpretations can be avoided. Within the popular media, there is frequently a tendency to attribute findings related to violence in certain countries and cultures to (a) a "national character," (b) a "cultural acceptance of violence," or (c) to other unidimensional causal explanations (i.e., religious affiliations, racial compositions, or educational attainment). Attention to the role of multiple contexts is not only better scientific practice, but is also more ethical because explanations that focus on one salient characteristic may be stereotypic and demeaning.

To illustrate, in the National Study of School Violence in Israel, rates of school violence were compared between religious and nonreligious Jewish students, Arab, and Bedouin students. This was socially, politically, and ethically very dangerous. On the other hand, without accurate data, the scope of the problem and interventions would have been based on stereotypes and news media reports, which tended to be extremely sensational and had no representational validity. Still, it is unclear if the Israeli public was ready to objectively interpret any statistics regarding group differences. There was concern that segments of the Israel public would interpret results as supporting their preconceived ideas and stereotypes concerning which cultures are more violent. It was anticipated that more politically conservative and religious populations would focus on the role of religious education in instilling discipline and "moral" values in students. Therefore, in analyses and interpretation, it was very important to examine group differences together with the socioeconomic contexts in which these groups are being educated.

With these ethical considerations in mind, in a study of staff victimization of students, the roles of ethnic/cultural affiliation and socioeconomic status (SES) of the students' families were examined (Benbenishty, Astor, Zeira, & Khoury-Kassabri, 2002). According to the analyses, SES is far more important than cultural practices. The results indicated that lower levels of school violence among religious Jewish junior high schools were not associated with the "religious education of students" but with the fact that Jewish religious schools are separated by gender. Thus, whereas all-girl religious junior high schools were low in school violence, the all-boy religious schools were considerably more violent than the secular mixed-gender Jewish schools. These findings have profound implications for school violence theories. They also help in better understanding how social hierarchy, patriarchy, and more traditional religious societies interact with school, community, and family variables.

A Deeper Theoretical Understanding of History, Oppression, Social Hierarchy, and Prejudice in Relation to School Violence

Quite often, factors such as minority status, ethnic, and cultural affiliation are strongly correlated within a given society with other important factors, especially poverty, education, deprivation, and oppression. These high correlations limit the ability to isolate and assess the independent role that each of these conceptually different factors play. However, the same ethnic or cultural group that is associated with poverty and crime in one country may have a different status in another location (e.g., Jewish youth when compared in the United States vs. Israel or other countries, or among "Asian" and "Hispanic" youths from various countries or regions). Careful comparison of such groups embedded in different social contexts may help sort out and isolate the relative cultural role of different aspects of group membership in contributing to school violence. For instance, immigrant and minority groups that are associated with economic and social marginality in one educational system may be the majority population in their native country. Comparing levels and characteristics of school violence within cultural groups that have different socio-political circumstances may contribute to a better understanding of the relative role of each context factor. One way to do this is to conduct more studies involving within-group comparisons. For example, if samples are stratified by economic levels, educational levels, and perhaps religion, theories and interventions could have more information on differences within cultures based on these characteristics.

There is evidence that there may be huge structural and organizational differences between schools in different countries (see Currie et al., 2004). As an example, Smith's (2003) compendium of school violence in 24 European countries revealed major differences in the age levels students begin schooling and the actual structure of the education system by student age and by school types (i.e., elementary, middle school, and high school). Whereas in Italy there are three age sectors (6–11, 11–14, and 15–19), in Ireland there are only two (4–11 and 12–18). In some countries, students begin schooling at a very young age, whereas in other countries they enter the formal educational setting significantly later (Benbenishty & Astor, 2003). Similarly, it is noted that in some European countries the percentage of *repeaters* (term used in Europe for children held back a grade) differs widely. The informative UNESCO publications (e.g., UNESCO, 2004) provide educational statistics for countries around the world. These statistics reveal even greater unexplored variations among educational systems of many countries in the world.

Structural differences across countries are likely to have far-reaching consequences on the levels and characteristics of school violence. One would expect that having children that range widely in age in the same building (such as a K–8 school) might influence age-related patterns of bullying and victimization. As another example, the presence of many repeaters in a class due to academic failure may have a crucial impact on how safe other students feel because these older students may bully the younger students. A cross-national perspective brings attention to such contextual factors that are mostly hidden from awareness when studies are done within a single national education system.

Clarifying the Contributions of Age, Gender, Context, and Culture

Smith, Madsen, and Moody (1999) reviewed the literature on bullying and showed that there is a clear decline in victimization as students grow older. These findings were replicated in many studies carried out in Western countries (Craig & Harel, 2004). Still, the question remains whether this pattern is true in other parts of the world. The volume edited by Ohsako (1997) provides some indications that in countries such as Ethiopia and Malaysia, this age pattern replicated in many European and Anglo countries may not hold in other cultures. Perhaps in countries where the culture emphasizes the importance of seniority and age, older students are more involved in bullying their younger peers. According to the accounts of Terefe and Mengistu (1997), school authorities view this form of bullying as normative and accept this kind of behavior. However, readers are cautioned not to make national or cultural interpretations without a convergence of data that is both representative and qualitative. Hypotheses about different national norms in non-European and Anglo/English-speaking cultures should be tested in future international research.

International studies may also shed new light on the relationships between gender and school violence. Currently, there is wide consensus that more males are both perpetrators and victims of physical violence in school than females. Findings from several European countries regarding gender differences related to relational and indirect violence seem to be less consistent (see recent reviews and studies by Currie et al., 2004; Salmivalli & Kaukiainen, 2004; Tapper & Boulton, 2004). For instance, Craig and Harel (2004) noted that although males tend to bully others more than females in most countries surveyed in the Health Behavior in School-Age Children (HBSC) study (Currie et al., 2004), patterns of gender differences in bully victimization are far less consistent. The picture is even more complicated with regard to the interaction between age and gender. Benbenishty and Astor (2005) reported that the gap between victimization rates of males and females grows with age such that older students tend to experience less victimization. In contrast, Craig and Harel (2004) concluded that in most of the 24 countries surveyed in the HBSC study, the trend was in the opposite direction and gender gaps were smaller among older students.

The literature on violence from other parts of the world raises many questions. Is this gender pattern a global phenomenon or does it reflect societal norms that vary across the world? For instance, Terefe and Mengistu (1997) reported that in some schools in Addis Ababa, Ethiopia, female students were victims of extensive violence in school. They found that 72% of their respondents agreed that girls were the main victims at these schools. Victimization of female students ranged from snatching of minor property to attempted rape and intimidation. It is possible that international patterns of gender violence may be more a function of education, modernity, and economics than cultural variables alone. This means that there may be more gender similarities across similarly developed countries.

Exploring the Relationships Between Different Forms of Violence: Rankings and Linearity

We previously proposed this theoretical proposition (Benbenishty & Astor, 2005): the base rates of school violence victimization differ across groups (genders, cultures, and nations), but the rank order of the frequency of these behaviors is stable across groups. Comparisons among groups in Israel and in the United States found support for this proposition. We suggested that dissimilarities in rank order to frequency of victimization may provide important clues as to how cultural and gender factors operate differently in various contexts. Furthermore, international comparisons may help assess to what extent this proposition could be confirmed and generalized.

Comparisons across the globe have also been used to test the underlying assumption that the relationship between context characteristics and school violence is linear. For instance, it is often assumed that the more crime ridden, poor, and disorganized communities will have higher levels of violence in the neighborhood schools. Akiba et al. (2002) examined the *linear* correlations between national gross domestic product per capita, national rates of assault on women, and national levels of victimization and found that national patterns of school violence are not strongly related to general patterns of violence and social integration in society.

As an alternative, we propose that these relationships may not be linear. Many reports (mainly from developing countries) describe extreme situations that are not familiar to most of us. For instance, reports from Ethiopia describe stabbings and intentional killing of helpless students (Terefe & Mangistu, 1997). A child in South America said: "Because I failed to pass the course, they hanged me by the throat and lit fire under my feet, in order to burn them" (Salas, 1997, p. 115). A Human Rights Watch (2001) report on sexual violence against girls in South Africa cites alarming statistics on the proportion of schoolgirls raped, most often by young male schoolchildren and their teachers. Girls who encountered sexual violence at school were raped in school washrooms, in empty classrooms and hallways, and in hostels and dormitories. Girls were also fondled, subjected to aggressive sexual advances, and verbally degraded at school. Teachers have raped, sexually assaulted, and otherwise sexually abused girls, sometimes reinforcing sexual demands with threats of physical violence or corporal punishment.

These reports describe situations that can be considered qualitatively different than the ones usually studied in Europe, the United States, and Australia. It is possible that within a certain range of variation, there is no relationship between certain context characteristics and school violence. However, when the circumstances are extreme and cross a certain threshold, they may have a stronger impact on school violence. For instance, a certain range of deprivation, inequality, and marginality of the school community may not have a strong influence on certain types of school violence, but when there is a complete breakdown of the community and students' families, the school may be devastated by these outside circumstances and violence may be rampant.

Examination of the Role of Religion and Religiosity

A review of the international literature reveals that there are very few references to the role of religion and religiosity in school violence. It is possible that value systems and ideology related to religion and to education in parochial schools may have strong influences on violence-related issues. For instance, in Israel, students in religious Jewish primary schools reported more staff physical maltreatment than children in Jewish non-religious schools (Benbenishty & Astor, 2005). It was also found that ultra-orthodox religious schools tended to address the issue of school violence very differently than other schools. For instance, principals in these schools refused to even discuss school violence issues with their students, believing that these discussions would have negative effects by "bringing bad ideas to students' heads." It would be interesting to see whether prevalence of school violence and the school responses toward these phenomena are influenced by how the school ideology and practices are influenced by religion and religiosity.

Careful Explorations of Within Country Variability Between Different Groups

The few international studies that compare levels of school violence in different countries, such as the HBSC (Currie et al., 2004), focused on whole-country patterns. This approach, however, overlooks important variability within the participating countries. There is much to be learned about the factors associated with variance among schools within the same country that is lost when data are aggregated across a whole country. One of the interesting questions that should be addressed is how different countries are in their variability in levels of school violence. Why are certain countries more homogenous in levels of school violence, whereas others are much more heterogeneous? Is this phenomenon related to measures of inequality in these countries? Furthermore, it is possible that certain groups of schools in different countries have much more in common than they have with other schools in their own country. For instance, private or parochial schools in different countries may be more similar to each other than they are to public schools in their own country.

Such cross-cultural empirical findings would advance existing theories on the relationships between victimization and structural factors associated with the school and its environment.

OUR PROPOSAL: A WORLD WIDE STUDY OF SCHOOL VIOLENCE

Based on a review of reports on school violence from across the world and the analysis presented here, we recommend a proactive research agenda for an international perspective on school violence—a worldwide study to monitor school violence. Such a study would follow examples of international studies on academic achievements (e.g., TIMMS) and health behaviors (HBSC) and would utilize standardized measures and methods to serve as a platform for global learning and monitoring of school violence over time. It is also proposed that this study address the multiple perspectives of students, teachers, principals, and whenever possible, parents. Each of these constituents should be asked questions about aspects of school victimization and climate that are relevant to its specific position in the school community in addition to a set of questions that will be identical to all participating schools. This combination would help understand each separate perspective, as well as the degree of congruence among these perspectives.

To better test hypotheses on the role of contexts in school violence, it is suggested that sampling and analysis occur at both student- and school-level perspectives (see chap. 15, this volume). This design will enable the measurement of school- and neighborhood-level variables and test hypotheses on the role of contexts in explaining levels of school violence. This approach also creates the foundation for examining how different countries vary in their level of homogeneity in terms of levels of violence in their schools. Furthermore, such a design allows the examination of what is similar and different in schools that are either very high or very low on school violence across the world.

Finally, such an international endeavor cannot rely solely on quantitative source of information. As Devine and Lawson (2003) suggested, research in this area should go beyond exact measurement of reports of individual students and search for larger social factors. In order to better understand these aspects of social and cultural contexts, it is important to expand the range of methodologies used. In addition to quantitative studies that provide vital and representative statistical information on many aspects of the phenomenon, sociological and ethnographic qualitative methods are needed to understand the ways in which the social fabric and culture of society shape school violence. For instance, Yoneyama and Naito's (2003) sociological analysis of the Japanese schools is a prime example of how the analysis of the role of education and schools in society can help us understand and interpret quantitative data.

In-depth and detailed qualitative study can help identify differences and similarities among schools and cultures. For 2 years, Mateo-Gelabert (2000) studied the bi-directional conflict flow between the school and the neighborhood focusing on one middle school in New York City. Some of the narratives regarding the issue of violence erupting over issues of territory are quite similar to stories from Malaysia (Ahmed & Salleh, 1997). Similarly, Devine and Lawson (2003) cited that some of Debarbieux's qualitative observations in France (Debarbieux, Blaya, & Vidal, 2003) are in the same direction as their findings in the United States.

The National Study of School Violence in Israel employed a mixed-method design. The initial findings seem to strongly support the advantages of a mixed-method study for cross-cultural comparisons. Different patterns of interpersonal, peer, and staff violence were found in Jewish, Bedouin, and Arab schools. For instance, "violence games" that were not part of interpersonal conflict were much more frequent in Jewish schools than in other ethnic groups. In Bedouin schools, there was a unique pattern in which students tried to avoid escalation of interpersonal conflicts in schools, so that the situation would not deteriorate into violent clashes among tribal clans. Although quantitative methods are more often used, qualitative aspects of the school contexts are also critical in *explaining* differences between cultures and should also be included in international studies of school violence.

Practical and Conceptual Considerations in an International Study on School Violence

Definitions, Connotations, Interpretations, and Meanings

When cross-cultural comparisons are made, very often, different forms of violence are inappropriately compared. The two most used terms in the English literature are *bullying* and *school violence*. In many publications, they are often used interchangeably, even though they are not conceptually or theoretically the same. There is a pressing need to either distinguish between what is school violence and bullying, or better explain the relationship between the two terms. As Devine and Lawson (2003) noted, bullying is more often used in European countries, whereas school violence is a term used more often in the United States. School violence is a general term that may include many different aspects of victimization. It is practically impossible to compare reports that use school violence as a generic term without providing the kinds of specific behaviors that are included under this term. Bullying, on the other hand, has had a quite precise theoretical definition (e.g., Olweus, 1991), to the point that it could allow direct international comparisons. Hence, the World Health Organization (WHO) conducts a cross-national study of HBSC that uses and defines the term *bully* (Currie et al., 2004). Nevertheless, most current, large-scale international research does not strictly use the formal theoretical definitions of bullying (e.g., that the bully have asymmetrical power over the victim, that the bullying event be part of a large repeating pattern of events, etc). Instead, bullying studies often list similar behaviors that are commonly used in school violence studies. Yet, inferences are made about bullying. Our view is that bullying is a specific subset of school violence that could overlap with a wide array of school violence behaviors (e.g., sexual harassment, weapon use, and school fights). However, those behaviors may not be considered bullying if they do not conform to the definition of bullying (power differential, repeated intentional targeting of victim, etc). Furlong and colleagues also made this similar and important point (Furlong, Morrison, & Greif, 2003; Greif, Furlong, & Morrison, 2003).

Even with a more precise research definition of *bullying,* the review of the literature suggests that most international bullying researchers employ diverse meanings, measures, and the understandings of which behaviors should be included in the term bully (Benbenishty & Astor, 2003). This could have a dramatic impact on the interpretation of cross-national comparisons. For example, Harel, Kenny, and Rahav (1997) asked Israeli students whether they were bullied. The questions (in Hebrew) stated that they were being asked about *hatrada* (harassment), *hatzaka* (teasing), and *biryonoot* (mainly physical bullying). Each of these words in Hebrew has quite a specific meaning. The direct word for bullying in Hebrew strongly implies physical force exerted by a strong, well-built student (an antisocial "thug"). By contrast, in reports from Japan, bullying is often equated with the Japanese term *ijime* (e.g., Yoneyama & Naito, 2003). The overall term *bullying* in Japan has a strong connotation of social isolation, impurity, and shame. In some ways, the set of behaviors, connotations, and cultural interpretations associated with *ijime* seems distant from the term *biryonot* for the Israeli bully. How might students in different cultures with different connotations for the word bullying synthesize and integrate these different terms in order to respond to questions about bullying?

Indeed, Smith et al. (2002) studied school children (ages 8–14) from 14 countries and found significant differences in the ways the term *bullying* was understood in the different countries. Similarly, a study among parents of schoolaged children in five countries (Italy, Spain, Portugal, England, and Japan) found clear differences in the ways the term bullying was understood by the parents. Cultures also varied on the extent to which the term *bullying* was used in everyday language (Smorti, Menesini, & Smith, 2003).

One potential solution is to use the same scientific definition, and agreed upon instruments, across many countries. Indeed, the WHO uses the HBSC instruments that provide the definition of bullying. This effort could be coupled with smaller qualitative studies that aim toward understanding the social and cultural meanings of bullying in each country. It should be noted, however, that policymakers and the public in different countries are likely to have diverse understandings and interpretations of the same concept, regardless of formal scientific definitions. Hence, Israeli policymakers interpreting high levels of bullying will have a very different image of the problem than South African, Brazilian, Canadian, or Japanese policymakers. Nevertheless, the more clear researchers are in definitions and instruments, the more cultural variations of interpretation and nuance can be explored. Understanding similarities and differences in cultural nuances can also help target specific cultural norms within each country.

Reduce Over-Reliance on Police, School, or Discipline Board Reports: Move Toward Representative Surveys

Government educational statistics based on organizational reporting are usually problematic. Most countries keep records of reports on students' violent behaviors. However, countries vary greatly in what incidents are reported and to what extent these reports are representative of the actual prevalence of these violent acts. Thus, for instance, Obeidat (1997) reported on violence in Jordanian schools and analyzed the documents and minutes of "school discipline boards." This analysis includes behaviors such as "circulating obscene photos" and "rioting," in addition to other behaviors more common in other countries, such as assaulting teachers and bullying colleagues. According to this analysis, rioting and screaming accounted for 33.7% of the reported cases, destroying property 22.8%, bullying others 15.6%, and swearing and threatening 7.3%. Such a distribution raises the question of whether the figures reflect school violence in Jordan or the role of school discipline boards in this country's educational system. Similarly, in Malaysia, schools are required to complete a student school discipline report. These reports reflect different cultural assumptions and emphases than the reports in Jordan, including aspects of "personal neatness," and "dishonesty," along with categories such as "criminality" and "destructive behavior" (Ahmad & Salleh, 1997). One can assume that official records across the world reflect the cultural context and are therefore difficult to compare directly.

Furthermore, there are many indications that the validity of these reports may vary across countries and times. For instance, in Malaysia, students tend to report to the authorities severe victimization perpetrated by older students less frequently because they do not expect any action taken and see these behaviors as part of the culture of respect to their elders (Ahmad & Salleh, 1997). In Malaysia, and probably in many countries across the globe, according to these authors, such official reports are manipulated to preserve the reputation of the school and prevent any further outside inquiries that may tarnish the school's name and point a blaming finger at the school management. In contrast, in countries in which awareness has increased and there are less punitive outcomes for reporters, one would expect more extensive reporting. Hence, comparing between "official" figures obtained from such diverse educational systems may be quite misleading. This leads us to believe that direct surveying of students using a random sample of schools or students is the best method to have accurate incidence levels across countries or regions (see a discussion of the merits of self-report on school victimization in the report from the Surgeon General, Department of Health and Human Services, 2001).

An Operational Solution: Using Self-Reports
of a Wide Range of Specific School Violence Behaviors

A parallel approach that could reduce variability in cultural definitions and interpretations is to create instruments that highlight very specific behaviors and refrain as much as possible from using abstract labels (such as bully) that may have different meanings and connotations in different countries. Hence, asking students whether larger or stronger students pushed them is probably understood more similarly across cultures than the question of whether or not they were bullied. The work by Furlong and associates (e.g., Furlong, Chung, Bates, & Morrison, 1995; Furlong et al., 2004) provides a good example of the suggested approach. The California School Climate and Safety Survey contains questions about victimization to an extensive list of concrete and specific victimization types. In the design process of the first National Study of School Violence in Israel, we chose to use this instrument because we thought that cross-national comparisons of specific behaviors would be much more meaningful than comparisons of the general term *bullying*. Indeed, translating the specific and concrete behaviors in the instrument and the comparisons with available U.S. data were quite straightforward (Benbenishty & Astor, 2005). The findings of the study showed the advantages of using this wide range of victimization types. The findings portrayed a complex and rich picture and highlighted the multifaceted nature of school victimization. It enabled analysis and description of which forms of victimization are more frequent in Israeli schools and which behaviors are quite rare. The findings in Israel were then comparable with data in Furlong and colleagues' studies in Southern California.

Furthermore, the findings that included a wide range of behaviors showed that various aspects of victimization have different patterns of association with student characteristics, such as gender and age, and with school context variables, such as poverty in the school neighborhood. These patterns have important implications for developing theories of school violence (see Benbenishty & Astor, 2005). Without the large number of behaviors examined, we would not be able to ascertain how forms of school violence were related to each other in Israeli culture. These patterns may or may not be similar in other cultures. It is suggested, therefore, that school violence studies examine the prevalence of a wide range of concrete and specific victimization types.

Correct Interpretation/Analyses of Subjective Judgments of Context
Versus Objective Measures of Victimization

Quite often, international studies do not distinguish between self-reports on specific victimization behaviors in school and students' assessments and feelings about their school as a whole. They also do not carefully distinguish between time lines for victimization reports. For example, in the Harel et al. (1997) study, Israeli students were asked: "During this school year has any student hit you, slapped you, or pushed you hard?" In contrast, Akiba and associates utilized as a measure of school violence the question: "How often did you think another student might hurt you last month in school?" The authors assumed that such assessment is a proxy for reporting of self-victimization. A comparison between studies using these different measures would be impossible. In other studies, students were asked global questions surrounding the existence of school violence in their school (e.g., Obeidat, 1977), or the size of the violence problem (Astor, Behre, Fravil, & Wallace, 1997). These incompatible approaches may yield different results and interpretation of differences across countries and may therefore be misleading both in how questions are asked and in the methods used to collect them.

A series of studies by Astor and associates (Astor, Benbenishty, Vinokur, & Zeira, in press; Astor, Benbenishty, Zeira, & Vinokur, 2002; Benbenishty, Astor, Zeira, & Vinokur, 2002) strongly suggest that there are significant and important differences between behavioral reports of peer victimization and (a) subjective assessments of fear in school and (b) assessments of the severity of the violence problem in school. In three very large-scale studies including elementary, middle, and high school students, fear was associated more with severe personal victimization by peers, whereas observing risky peer behaviors (e.g., school fights, drug use on campus, or seeing peers with weapons on school grounds) is associated with assessing the school as having a problem. Clearly, caution should be exercised when inferences are made from subjective and schoolwide global types of questions (e.g., on fear or view of their school) to specific behavioral events that personally happened to the student (e.g., victimization). Therefore, we suggest that international studies include subjective feelings (e.g., fear) and assessments (e.g., seriousness of the problem) in addition to self-reports on victimization, and ensure that each of these dimensions is considered separately.

Including a Focus on Staff-Initiated Victimization

Studies of school violence across the world differ regarding whether they include staff victimization of students. Studies on prevalence of school violence in the United States rarely address victimization by staff. Although there have been state and federal mandates to survey school staff, few if any have asked about staff maltreatment of students. The extensive work by Hyman and associates (e.g., Hyman, 1990; Hyman & Perone, 1998) on the role of staff in inducing trauma among students is the exception rather than the norm. Similarly, a review of reports from 24 European countries reveals minimal reference to staff victimizing students (Smith, 2003). In contrast, reports from other parts of the world address the role of staff in understanding school violence. Staff may play direct and indirect roles in victimizing students. The international literature reveals how teacher behaviors may actually promote bullying of certain students by their peers (Yoneyama & Naito, 2003). Other studies, mainly from developing countries, present teachers as one of the main sources of victimization of students. Hence, in places like Malaysia, Ethiopia, Brazil, and other countries in Latin America (e.g., Salas, 1997), teachers may use physical and verbal means to hurt students as a common means of discipline. Given that staff may play such an important role in victimizing students, it seems imperative that reference to staff-initiated violence be included in international comparisons of school violence.

Summary of Need for International Studies

A reader of reports on school violence from across the globe is struck by contradictions. On one hand, there is a degree of similarity surrounding stories told about school safety in diverse places in the world. At the same time, it is surprising how different, varied, and unique school violence narrative can be within each of these nations and cultures. A cross-national examination can contribute to an understanding of which school violence variables are unique to each culture and which variables are shared by many cultures. Explicating similarities and differences between and within countries would greatly inform theory, public policy, and interventions. Empirical work conducted across different countries can serve as the foundation for major international collaborative efforts to promote worldwide safety in schools.

CONCLUDING COMMENTS

School violence is a global phenomenon. A review of the literature from across the world shows both the similarities across diverse cultures and the many different patterns that reflect the unique characteristics of each cultural and national context. This richness provides unique opportunities for comparisons and mutual learning that can expand the repertoire of interventions and help examine and develop theories of school violence. Although reviews of existing studies from across the world can be quite fruitful, there is a clear need to initiate an ongoing worldwide study of school violence. We propose a collaborative study that will bring together researchers and policymakers from across the world and employ methods and instruments that will help further theory and global efforts to reduce school violence.

REFERENCES

Ahmad, R. H., & Salleh, N. M. (1997). Bullying and violence in the Malaysian school. In T. Ohsako (Ed.), *Violence at school: Global issues and interventions* (pp. 57–71). Paris: UNESCO.

Akiba, M., Letendre, G. K., Baker, D. P., & Goesling, B. (2002). Student victimization: National and school systems effects on school violence in 37 nations. *American Educational Research Journal, 39*, 829–853.

Astor, R. A., Benbenishty, R., Vinokur, A., & Zeira, A. (in press). Arab and Jewish elementary school students' perceptions of fear and school violence: Understanding the influence of school context. *British Journal of Educational Psychology.*

Astor, R. A., Benbenishty, R., Zeira, A., & Vinokur, A. (2002). School climate, observed risk behaviors, and victimization as predictors of high school students' fear and judgments of school violence as a problem. *Health Education and Behavior, 29*, 716–736.

Astor, R. A., Benbenishty, R., & Marachi, R. (2004). Violence in schools. In P. A. Meares (Ed.). *Social Work Services in Schools, Fourth Editions* (pp. 149–182). Boston, MA: Allyn & Bacon.

Astor, R. A., Behre, W. J., Fravil, K. A., & Wallance, J. M. (1997). Perceptions of school violence as a problem and reports of violent events: A national survey of school social workers. *Social Work, 42*, 55–68.

Astor, R. A., Benbenishty, R., Pitner, R. O., & Meyer, H. A. (2004). Bullying and peer victimization in schools. In P. A. & Meares, M. W., Fraser (Eds.). *Intervention with Children & Adolescents: An Interdisciplinary Perspective* (pp. 471–448). Boston: MA: Allyn & Bacon.

Benbenishty, R., & Astor, R. A. (2003). Cultural specific and cross-cultural bully/ victim patterns: The response from Israel. In P. K. Smith, (Ed.), *Violence in schools: The response in Europe* (pp. 317–331). New York: RoutledgeFalmer.

Benbenishty, R., & Astor R. A. (2005). *School violence in context: Culture, neighborhood, family, school, and gender.* New York: Oxford University Press.

Benbenishty, R., Astor, R. A., Zeira, A., & Vinokur, A. (2002). Perceptions of violence and fear of school attendance among junior high school students' in Israel. *Social Work Research, 26*, 71–87.

Benbenishty, R., Astor, R. A., Zeira, A., & Khoury-Kassabri, M. (2002). Maltreatment of primary school students by educational staff in Israel. *Child Abuse and Neglect, 26*, 1291–1309.

Craig, W. M., & Harel, Y. (2004). Bullying, physical fighting and victimization. In C. Currie, C. Roberts, A. Morgan, R. Smith, W. Settertobulte, O. Samdal, & V. B. Rasmussen (Eds.), *Young people's health in context: Health behavior in school-aged children (HBSC) study: International report from the 2001/2002 survey* (pp. 133–144). Copenhagen, Sweden: World Health Organization.

Currie, C., Roberts, C., Morgan, A., Smith, R., Settertobulte, W., Samdal, O., & Rasmussen, V. B. (Eds.). (2004). *Young people's health in context: Health behavior in school-aged children (HBSC) study: International report from the 2001/2002 survey.* Copenhagen, Sweden: World Health Organization.

Debarbieux, E., Blaya, C., & Vidal, D. (2003). Tackling violence in schools: A report from France. In P. K. Smith (Ed.), *Violence in schools: The response in Europe* (pp. 17–32). London: RoutledgeFalmer.

Department of Health and Human Services (DHHS). (2001). *Youth violence: A report from the Surgeon General.* Available: http://www.surgeongeneral.gov/library/youthviolence/report.html#foreward

Devine, J., & Lawson, H. A. (2003). The complexity of school violence: Commentary from the US. In P. K. Smith (Ed.), *Violence in schools: The response in Europe* (pp. 332–350). London: RoutledgeFalmer.

Eslea, M., Menesini, E., Morita, Y., O'Moore, M., Mora-Merchan, J. A., Pereira, B., & Smith, P. K. (2003). Friendship and loneliness among bullies and victims: Data from seven countries. *Aggressive Behavior, 30*, 71–83.

Furlong, M. J., Chung, A., Bates, M., & Morrison, R. L. (1995). Profiles of non-victims and multiple-victims of school violence. *Education and Treatment of Children, 18*, 282–298.

Furlong, M. J., Greif, J. L., Bates, M. P., Whipple, A. D., Jimenez, T. C., & Morrison, R. (2004). *Development of the California School Climate and Safety Survey–Short Form. Psychology in the Schools, 43, 137–150.*

Furlong, M. J., & Morrison, G. (2000). The *school* in school violence: Definitions and facts. *Journal of Emotional and Behavioral Disorders, 8*, 71–82.

Furlong, M. J., Morrison, G. M., & Greif, J. (2003). Reaching an American coherence on bullying prevention: Reactions to the *School Psychology Review* special issue on school bullying. *School Psychology Review, 32*, 456–470.

Greif, J. L., Furlong, M. J., & Morrison, G. (2003, November). Operationally defining "bullying" [Letter to the editor]. *Archives of Pediatrics and Adolescent Medicine, 157*, 1134–1135.

Harel, Y., Kenny, D., & Rahav, G. (1997). *Youth in Israel: Social welfare, health and risk behaviors from international perspectives.* Jerusalem: Joint Distribution Committee.

Herda-Rapp, H. (2003). The social construction of local school violence threats by the news media and professional organizations. *Sociological Enquiry, 73*, 545–574.

Human Rights Watch. (2001). *Scared at school: Sexual violence against girls in South African schools.* New York: Author.

Hyman, I. A. (1990). *Reading, writing, and the hickory stick.* Lexington, MA: Lexington Books.

Hyman I., A., & Perone, D. C. (1998). The other side of school violence: Educator policies and practices that may contribute to student misbehavior. *Journal of School Psychology*, 36, 7–27.

Kachur, P., Stennies, G., Powell, K., Modzeleski, W., Stephens, R., Murphy, R., Kresnow, M., Sleet, D., & Lowry, R. (1996). School-associated violent deaths in the United States, 1992 to 1994. *Journal of the American Medical Association, 275*, 1729–1733.

Khoury-Kassabri, M. (2002). *The relationship between school ecology and students victimization.* Unpublished doctoral dissertation, The Hebrew University, Jerusalem.

Khoury-Kassabri, M., Benbenishty, R., Astor, R. A., & Zeira, A. (2004). The contribution of community, family and school variables on student victimization. *American Journal of Community Psychology, 34*, 187–204.

Mateo-Gelabert, P. (2000). *School violence: The bi-directional conflict flow between neighborhood and school.* New York: Vera Institute of Justice.

Menesini, E., & Modiano, R. (2003). A multifaceted reality: A report from Italy. In P. K. Smith (Ed.), *Violence in schools: The response in Europe* (pp. 153–168). London: RoutledgeFalmer.

Obeidat, Z. (1997). Bullying and violence in the Jordanian school. In T. Ohsako (Ed.), *Violence at school: Global issues and interventions* (pp. 20–33). Paris: UNESCO.

Ohsako, T. (Ed.). (1997). *Violence at school: Global issues and interventions.* Paris: UNESCO.

Olweus, D. (1991). Bully/victim problems among school children: Some basic facts and effects of a school-based intervention program. In D. Pepler & K. Rubin (Eds.), *The development and treatment of childhood aggression* (pp. 411–448). Hillsdale, NJ: Lawrence Erlbaum Associates.

Salas, L. M. (1997). Violence and aggression in the schools of Columbia, El Salvador, Guatemala, Nicaragua and Peru. In T. Ohsako (Ed.), *Violence at school: Global issues and interventions* (pp.110–127). Paris: UNESCO.

Salmivalli, C., & Kaukiainen, A. (2004). "Female aggression" revisited: Variable and person-centered approaches to studying gender differences in different types of aggression. *Aggressive Behavior, 30*, 158–163.

Smith, P. K. (2003). *Violence in schools: The response in Europe.* London: RoutledgeFalmer.

Smith, P. K., Cowie, H., Olafsson, R. F., & Liefooghe, A. P. (2002). Definitions of bullying: A comparison of terms used, and age and gender differences, in a fourteen-country international comparison, *Child Development, 73*, 1119–1133.

Smith, P. K., Madsen K. C., & Moody J. C. (1999). What causes the age decline in reports of being bullied at school? Towards a developmental analysis of risks of being bullied. *Educational Research, 41*, 267–285.

Smith, P. K., Morita, Y., Junger-Tas, J., Olweus, D., Catalano, R., & Slee, P. (1999). *The nature of school bullying: A cross-national perspective.* New York: Routledge.

Smorti, A., Menesini, E., & Smith, P. K. (2003). Parents' definitions of children's bullying in a five-country comparison. *Journal of Cross-Cultural Psychology, 34*, 417–432.

Tapper, K., & Boulton, M. (2004). Sex differences in levels of physical, verbal and indirect aggression amongst primary school children and their associations with beliefs about aggression. *Aggressive Behavior, 30*, 123–145.

Terefe, D., & Mengistu, D. (1997). Violence in Ethiopian schools: A study of some school in Addis-Ababa. In T. Ohsako (Ed.), *Violence at school: Global issues and interventions* (pp. 34–56). Paris: UNESCO.

UNESCO (United Nations). (2004). *Global education digest 2004.* Montreal: UNESCO Institute for Statistics.

Yoneyama, S., & Naito, A. (2003). Problems with the paradigm: The school as a factor in understanding bullying (with special reference to Japan). *British Journal of Sociology of Education, 24*, 315–330.

II

Assessment and Measurement

Assesssment and measurement are two very important topics related to both scholarship and practice aimed at understanding school violence and school safety. The chapters in this section address an array of important topics including anger, threat assessment, safe school surveys, bullying, discipline, victimization, and weapons. Accuracy and precision in the development and use of school violence and safety-related surveys and questionnaires have not kept pace with the need for high-quality needs assessment and research tools. This section provides acccess to critical reviews of school violence and safety measures with the objective of advancing research and practice.

Chapter 8 provides an overview of measurement issues related to school violence and safety research. Chapter 9 highlights important considerations in assessing anger and hostility in school settings. The assessment of violent threat potential at school is a topic that has received considerable attention, and chapter 10 clarifies the concept of threat assessment and presents a review of empirical support for threat assessment. In advancing a broader perspective on school violence prevention, chapter 11 provides a review of the Safe and Responsive Schools safe school survey. Given the emphasis on evidence-based practices, chapter 13 provides an important synthesis of applications to school violence prevention research. A very popular topic, the assessment of bullying warrants further scrutiny, and chapter 14 highlights important considerations about the accuracy of current bully assessment practices. School discipline records represent a potential valuable source of information to inform both prevention and evaluation of effort, however, caution is suggested to avoid the shortcomings of discipline data that are typically available. With an emphasis on the social context at school, chapter 15 offers insights regarding the monitoring and mapping of student victimization at school. The final chapter in this section, chapter 16, provides a thoughtful analysis of methods to assess self-report methods to examine weapons on school campuses, often the source of the public's greatest concerns about school safety.

8

An Overview of Measurement Issues in School Violence and School Safety Research

Jill D. Sharkey
Michael J. Furlong
University of California, Santa Barbara

Georgette Yetter
Oklahoma State University

For too long, topics of school violence and safety have been primarily investigated from a social problem perspective and not as a coherent topic of high-quality scientific research. Recently, however, significant gains have been made in understanding measurement issues associated with examining school violence and school safety. These efforts have grown out of significant national efforts to implement school violence prevention programs such as the Safe School/Healthy Students (SS/HS) initiative (Furlong, Paige, & Osher, 2003; Safe Schools Healthy Students, 2004) as well as emerging efforts to more critically examine the methodological procedures implemented by researchers (e.g., Cross & Newman-Gonchar, 2004; Furlong, Sharkey, Bates, & Smith, 2004; Mayer, 2004). Because the measurement procedures used by researchers are a core aspect of high-quality research, the findings of any study can be no more reliable and valid than the instruments used to measure key variables. This is a core issue for school violence research because this field cannot progress rapidly without increasing the precision with which key dependent variables are measured. Hence, the purpose of this chapter is to provide an overview of the status of school violence and safety measurement issues.

After introducing the history of measurement of school violence and safety concerns, this chapter provides a review of various procedures commonly used to measure school safety- and violence-related variables. It describes prominent threats to the validity of these procedures and suggests mechanisms whereby future self-report school safety and violence measures can be improved. Several threats to the valid interpretation and use of survey data are discussed and recommendations are provided for using survey results to inform school- and district-level intervention decision-making efforts.

HISTORICAL CONTEXT OF EXAMINING SCHOOL VIOLENCE
AND SAFETY MEASUREMENT PRACTICES

Current school violence and safety instruments are predominately based on a public health model that develops items to establish population trends (e.g., Youth Risk Behavior Surveillance [YRBS] survey; Centers for Disease Control and Prevention [CDC], 2004a). Although items have undergone careful content scrutiny by researchers, they are not typically subjected to rigorous psychometric analyses. This is due, in part, to their original intended purpose, which was to obtain population estimates of behaviors. Despite the fact that the YRBS was developed as a population-based surveillance instrument, researchers often use it to examine individual differences in youth behavior and the association between risk and health behaviors. Because items were not developed for this purpose, their sensitivity and validity for such measurement purposes have not been established. Nonetheless, these instruments provide the best information available about school violence and safety and there is overwhelming momentum to continue their use, raising them to the status of a "gold standard." Although the collection of population-based surveillance information is necessary and valuable, there is a need to also examine and enhance current measurement practices as research about school safety and violence causes, correlates, and outcomes proceeds.

Appropriate consideration of the measurement practices commonly applied to school safety and violence research is a vital and necessary aspect of moving this field of inquiry forward. In doing so, it should be acknowledged that pioneers of school safety research have already provided the impetus to many others in invaluable ways. However, no single national survey has been originally and specifically designed to assess school safety and violence conditions. Nevertheless, although efforts to refine school safety and violence research practices move forward, the essential past and ongoing contributions of previous efforts to science and public interest should be appreciated and recognized. In fact, the CDC is continuing its efforts to provide high-quality data as evidenced by a vigorous methodology research effort (e.g., Brener, Billy, & Grady, 2003; Brener, Grunbaum, Kann, McManus, & Ross, 2004; Brener, Kann, et al., 2004).

The Departments of Education, Health and Human Services and Justice created the SS/HS initiative, the most extensive effort yet to address school safety and violence prevention/ intervention (Furlong et al., 2003). SS/HS was launched in April 1999 to support primary prevention of school violence through the implementation of evidence-based practices to enhance child development. Each of the more than 150 community-based programs funded to date are required to evaluate activities, both at the local and national levels. A core principle guiding these programs is that they "implement science-based programs with demonstrated outcomes" (Safe Schools Healthy Students, 2004, p. 5). Such large-scale school–community programs face many challenges, including those related to demonstrating changes in large-scale school–community conditions. SS/HS evaluation strategies are dependent on local research questions and focused on treatment integrity, systematic attitudes and knowledge, and academic, social, and behavioral change (Welsh, Domitrovich, Bierman, & Lang, 2003). In this context of increased outcome scrutiny, selecting instruments/procedures to measure outcomes is a critical endeavor.

Given the expectation that programs implement "science-based" prevention/intervention strategies, evaluations would presumably include the use of high-quality, psychometrically sound outcome assessment. Although the national evaluation is using an impressive array of instruments designed to assess program process implementation, coalition building, school policy development, changes in school climate, changes in school safety-related behaviors, and student social-emotional status (Research Triangle Institute, 2004), most of the items used in these surveys were developed specifically for the SS/HS national evaluation or were taken from other national surveys (e.g., the YRBS; Furlong, Sharkey, et al., 2004), that have not had extensive psychometric scrutiny. Considering the scarcity of school safety and school violence measurement tools, many sites used surveys developed by their local evaluation teams. For example, the Riverside, California SS/HS site implemented schoolwide data collection using a "Student Wellness Questionnaire" created by local evaluators to assess positive identity, personal agency, self-regulation, social relationship skills, prosocial system of belief, victim-ization, aggression, and drug and alcohol use (Guerra & Williams, 2003). A rural Kansas county compiled school and community climate surveys by combining questions not found together in existing measures of school climate (Paige, Kitzis, & Wolfe, 2003). Although tailor-made assessments are of great interest to local programs, rarely are adequate psychometric prop-erties reported to allow definitive conclusions to be drawn, and when psychometric analyses are provided they are not conducted prior to their use. There is a need for expanded efforts to validate measures of school violence and school safety before they are widely disseminated or used in research and evaluation studies.

GENERAL SCHOOL VIOLENCE AND SAFETY MEASUREMENT ISSUES

Various methods have been used to assess school violence and safety concerns. This section provides an overview of frequently used procedures. The most common way of measuring safety and violence-related concerns has been through self-report surveys. These include large-scale surveillance surveys, such as the YRBS (CDC; 2004a, 2004b) and the California Healthy Kids Survey (CHKS; WestEd, 2004). Other methods include mandated districtwide reporting and examining school discipline referrals.

Large-Scale Surveillance Surveys

National surveys of students' self-reported behaviors and experiences are the most typical form of school violence data collection. National surveillance approaches provide information about the widespread prevalence of a problem. However, because this information is not applicable to individual school sites and is aggregated over broad contexts, its applicability to local conditions is limited. National (and state) surveillance data provide limited information about important cultural differences between schools and communities (Benbenishty, Astor, & Zeira, 2003). Benbenishty and colleagues argued that school- and district-level assessment of school violence indicators is crucial for indicating specific local needs, as well as for providing a baseline against which treatment efficacy can later be evaluated. Measures appropriate for understanding the constellation of factors affecting aggressive and violent behavior should assess influences at a variety of ecological levels, including community, school, and family, that are believed to make up the developmental pathways to violence.

Identifying the environmental predictors of aggressive and violent behavior for individuals is a difficult task. First, findings regarding which factors are most salient in their association with school violence vary according to survey and geographic location. For instance, Sullivan (2002) noted that studies vary in the degree to which individual and contextual variables predict school violence, and that some of these differences are attributable to differences in the amount of variance inherent in the individual-versus school-level constructs that were measured using participant samples from geographically disparate locations. Second, individual development occurs within the context of school and community influences, and large-scale survey reports rarely take contextual variables (other than geographic region and city size) into account. Therefore, a person's characteristics inherently reflect many environmental influences over a protracted time period, so that attempts to partition out the effects of environment from individual-level variables are unlikely to yield large effects. Often, the sophistication of the analytic methods used to examine predictors of aggression and violence (such as hierarchical linear modeling) supercedes the psychometric sophistication of the measures that are used to gather the data (Sullivan, 2002).

Mandated Districtwide Reporting

The federal Gun-Free Schools Act of 1994 (GFSA, 1994) imposed specific reporting require-ments for each state regarding the number of students who engage in a variety of violent behaviors. Unfortunately, data submitted by districts were not comparable (Kingery & Cogge-shall, 2001) because (a) some states reported more detailed information than others, (b) dis-tricts differed in how they categorized violent behavior, (c) inconsistencies in time periods assessed interfered with comparing data from different locations, and (d) federally mandated definitions of the classifications of weapons and violent behavior were often not specified in student surveys (for instance, the GFSA definitions included bombs and gas as firearms). Kingery and Coggeshall also cited other problems that interfered with a clear understand-ing of these data. They noted that (a) students may hide serious incidents from staff, (b) school personnel may fail to detect many violence incidents or to only document observed infractions, (c) staff are not often trained in a standardized fashion, and (d) school personnel may feel pressured to underreport violence so as not to reflect negatively on their school or district.

Using Discipline Referrals to Measure Outcomes

Insofar as past behavior is the most useful predictor of future behavior, school discipline data, such as office referrals, suspensions, and expulsions, have the potential to provide valuable information about student risk for future infractions. Sugai, Sprague, Horner, and Walker (2000) observed that all schools collect discipline data to some extent, so that discipline data may be the most effective way for school systems to understand the relationships and behavioral contexts that disrupt schools. Discipline data can inform multiple dimensions of inquiry, including (a) which student behaviors are of greatest concern; (b) whether or not there are disproportionate referrals by gender, ethnicity, or special education status; and (c) whether or not there are disproportionate referrals made by certain teachers or during certain periods of instruction (e.g., recess, gym class, reading, and math). This information may be used to identify targets for intervention at schoolwide, staff, individual staff, student group, or individual student levels. However, methods for collecting discipline data need to be carefully considered and procedures need to be standardized across classroom, playground, and other school settings. Morrison, Peterson, O'Farrell, and Redding (2004) noted that although these data are easily obtained, little is known about the reliability or validity for predicting future aggressive acts with either school- or individual-level data.

Studies have demonstrated that patterns of school discipline predict future engagement in delinquent activities (Morrison & Skiba, 2001). However, Morrison and Skiba cautioned that school discipline data are not as straightforward a measure as they might appear. Behavior referrals, suspensions, and other disciplinary actions reflect not only student behavior, but also teacher tolerance for disruptive behavior, teacher skills in classroom management, adminis-trative discipline policies, and other classroom, school, and community factors, although they often fail to document the contribution of these environmental influences. Thus, predicting disruptive and violent behavior from school discipline data is problematic because it must account for these multiple levels of influence.

SCHOOL VIOLENCE AND SAFETY INSTRUMENT
MEASUREMENT ISSUES

In a relevant review of methodological research related to youth self-reports of risk behaviors, including violence items, Brener et al. (2003) examined studies pertaining to the influences of cognitive (e.g., item comprehension and memory retrieval) and situational (e.g., privacy and social desirability) factors on youth self-reports. They found that although there were numerous studies examining factors affecting the measurement accuracy of other health-risk behaviors, such as substance use and dietary behavior, studies examining behaviors related to violence were scarce. Nonetheless, a number of threats to the validity of school violence survey data have been identified. Researchers have recommended a variety of design practices for enhancing survey accuracy. These strategies include maintaining confidentiality or anonymity of responses, verifying the survey's reading level, checking for the honesty of answers, including sufficient numbers of items to measure a given construct, and taking steps to ask questions about past experiences in ways that are most likely to elicit accurate recall. Nonetheless, information about the reliability and validity of methods used to collect self-report surveys is limited.

Implausible Responding Patterns

Investigators need to address the possibility that students may not respond honestly. Data screening methods should detect response inconsistencies or implausibly extreme patterns of responding. Although data screening should be an essential element of all large-scale student surveys, unfortunately, few school violence surveys have included such safeguards (Cornell & Loper, 1998; Kingery & Coggeshall, 2001), and many others do not report whether, or how they evaluated the quality of student responses (Furlong, Sharkey, et al., 2004). To investigate this issue, researchers from the University Oregon examined dubious and inconsistent responders to a state survey and found that 1.88% of the cases were eliminated (Oregon Healthy Teens 2001: Methodology, 2004). This finding supports the general utility of using students self-reports, however, it suggests that surveys that do not apply such standards may produce results that overestimate very low-incident, at-risk behaviors because inconsistent responders have been found to report higher rates of risk behaviors (Cornell & Loper, 1998; Rosenblatt & Furlong, 1997).

Another survey that uses high-quality data screening is the CHKS (WestEd, 2004), mandated for use throughout California. The CHKS is one of the most carefully developed surveillance instruments, having undergone more than 6 years of rigorous development and review by a standing panel of independent experts. Analysis of CHKS data includes a data-cleansing procedure that screens records from the data set that meet a combination of criteria, including inconsistent patterns of responding, implausible reports of drug use, the endorsement of using a fictitious drug, or failure to assent to having answered survey questions honestly.

Although surveyors are often concerned with participants responding in a socially desirable manner, few researchers have taken into consideration the possibility that alternative response sets may apply with school violence surveys. In this research, the concern is that youths involved with antisocial and aggressive peers will exaggerate their involvement in delinquent activities as an alternative form of social desirability. For instance, Cornell and Loper (1998) administered the Safe School Survey to students in Grades 7, 9, and 11. They found that approximately 9% of the participants reported implausibly extreme amounts of aggression (i.e., they engaged in all six target behaviors, including carrying various weapons, fighting, and using drugs and alcohol). Students who failed either of two validity checks ("I am reading this survey carefully" and "I am telling the truth on this survey") were two to three times more likely to claim that they carried a weapon, fought, and used substances at school. Eliminating the extreme responders and students who failed the validity check significantly decreased incidence rates for these behaviors.

In an investigation using data from the public access YRBS data files, Furlong, Sharkey, and colleagues (2004) reported that about 3% of the participants indicated that they had brought a weapon to school six or more times in the previous 30 days. This group of frequent weapon carriers was also significantly more likely to endorse the most extreme response options on all of the school-related items, even positive health behaviors. This finding is particularly noteworthy because most published studies using the YRBS neither report evaluating data for the quality of responses nor screening for implausible response patterns.

In a related study, Cross and Newman-Gonchar (2004) examined responses on three surveys: the Colorado Youth Survey, the SS/HS survey, and a perception survey. When examining the pattern of extreme and inconsistent responses, Cross and Newman-Gonchar found that not only did rates vary substantially by survey and by school, but extreme and inconsistent responses inflated rates of violent behavior much more at one school than at the other school. Even small percentages of questionable responses had the ability to inflate estimates of risk behavior substantially, so that by excluding the fewer than 3% of responses to the Colorado Youth Survey that were suspect, Cross and Newman-Gonchar eliminated 70% of reported incidents of gun carrying. It is important to note than such small differences in rates are important for low incidence behaviors (such as school gun possession) because even high-quality, large-scale surveys such as the YRBS are designed to have a 5% confidence interval (Brener, Kann et al., 2004).

In their examination of responses to the California School Climate and Safety Survey (CSCSS), Rosenblatt and Furlong (1997) compared a group of students who failed reliability and validity checks to a matched control group. They found systematic bias in the way failed students responded to the survey, including higher ratings of school violence victimization, campus danger, poor grades, and few good friends. By contrast, comparison students were more likely to be caught by the social desirability item. Results did not differ by gender, dislike of school, or number of close relationships with teachers.

Importantly, although youth who respond in what seem to be implausibly extreme ways endorse unlikely seeming behavior patterns (e.g., daily marijuana and alcohol use, while still attending school on the day of the survey), it is possible that there is, in fact, a true correlation between these response patterns and a tendency to engage in aggressive behavior. Should this be the case, these extreme responses truly reflect extreme levels of key behaviors experienced by this small subset of youths, and removing these individuals from the data pool could bias results (Cross & Newman-Gonchar, 2004; Skiba et al., 2004). More research is needed to better understand extreme responders.

Survey Administration Procedures

Cross and Newman-Gonchar (2004) examined the impact of survey administrator training on student response patterns. District prevention specialists coached a group of teachers about the importance of collecting quality data, and they were taught to explain the uses and importance of the data to their students and to ask them to respond honestly. Cross and Newman-Gonchar compared rates of invalid responses to surveys administered by trained versus untrained teachers. Results indicated that the trained administrators obtained far lower rates of highly suspect responses (3%) than the untrained administrators (28%).

In addition to administration procedures, evidence indicates responses are influenced by the survey format. Turner et al. (1998) provided one of few investigations regarding how traditional paper-and-pencil formats and computer-assisted presentation influence response rates.

Based on similar studies about youth substance use, computer presentations were expected to produce higher self-report rates. Turner and colleagues found that the computer format produced substantially higher prevalence rates than did the paper-and-pencil format for weapon carrying, acts of violence, and threatened violence. The authors explained that the computer format, with the benefit of audio presentation and computerization was likely to promote more accurate responding for sensitive questions. This explanation is supported by evidence of similarly high rates from studies that rely on retrospective accounts by adults regarding sensitive adolescent behaviors.

In one important study by Hilton, Harris, and Rice (2003), the authors examined the consistency of youth self-reports of violence victimization and perpetration (not school violence) and compared prevalence rates derived from traditional paper-and-pencil reports with those provoked by the same experience modeled in an audio vignette. They found that the same youths reported two to three times more violence perpetration and victimization using the self-report format. This finding, considered in relation to other studies (e.g., Hilton, Harris, & Rice, 1998), led these researchers to conclude that, "although we would not suggest that standard paper-and-pencil surveys yield completely inaccurate data, the accumulated evidence, including these results, calls on researchers in the field of interpersonal violence to redouble efforts to demonstrate and improve the factual accuracy of their primary dependent measures" (p. 235). In the context of assessing school bullying, Cornell and Brockenbrough (2004) also suggested that self-reports may be less meaningful than peer or teacher ratings.

Despite findings that presentation and response conditions may influence youth self-reports of school violence, limited research attention has been given to how school violence and safety surveys are presented to students. More research is needed on the effects of administrator training on student motivation and responses (Cross & Newman-Gonchar, 2004).

Item Wording

It is also important to evaluate whether or not all respondents understand school violence survey questions in the same way. Of concern, Brener, Grunbaum, et al. (2004) found that differences in item wording across three national surveys resulted in significantly different rates of behavior. One challenge with surveys of school violence and safety is that questions are worded so broadly as to leave a great deal of interpretation to individual responders (Cornell & Loper, 1998). A survey question that asks students if they carry a weapon without defining the word "weapon" has the potential to result in students inappropriately reporting their hunting rifles or pocketknives as weapons. For example, the CHKS item, "During the past 12 months, how often have you been picked on or bullied by a student on school property?" is ambiguous for several reasons. First, it is unclear whether being picked on and being bullied are to be interpreted as separate experiences, or if they are implied to be equivalent. Beyond this, the item does not define "bullying" in a way that is consistent with best research practices. It could be argued that this item does not measure "bullying" victimization per se, but rather each student's understanding of this word, which may or may not fit with research definitions. To promote consistent and accurate responses, items should be unambiguous and easy to read, and all terms should be clearly defined (Fowler, 1993).

Item Response Time Frames

Many commonly used school violence and safety instruments, such as the YRBS and the CHKS, include items that refer to past behavior using a variety of time frames (e.g., 30 days, 6 months, 1 year). It would seem quite logical to presume that survey responses in any given month provide a cross-section (in time) of student behaviors and experiences and that the reported incidence of these behaviors would be higher over the longer periods of time. For example, if 10% of students report carrying a weapon to school in the previous 30 days, one might expect this percentage to be higher if the same group of students was asked to report about past-year weapon possession. However, no published research has confirmed that this is the case.

Another issue is that respondents can interpret response time frames as providing subtle cues about the types of events the researchers are asking about. The YRBS, for example, includes the following items: "During the past 30 days, on how many days did you carry a gun on school property?" and "During the past 12 months, how many times were you in a physical fight on school property?" According to Schwartz (1999), asking about past-month incidents is likely to convey to respondents that researchers want to know about less serious but common events. In contrast, students might interpret asking about fights in the past year as seeking information about less frequent but more serious fights.

To explore this issue, Furlong, Felix, and Sharkey (2005) administered the research version of the California School Climate and Safety Survey (CSCSS-R; Furlong, Chung, Bates, & Morrison, 1995) to 475 students at a comprehensive high school (Grades 9–12). The CSCSS-R includes 102 items that ask students to report on school safety-related experiences. Two versions of the survey were randomly administered to the students. Approximately half of the students received a survey that asked them to indicate the occurrence of these experiences "during the past year (12 months)" and the remaining students were asked about their experiences "during the month (30 days)." Given that these students attended the same school and were randomly assigned surveys, it was hypothesized that the incidence of these experiences would be higher for the students reporting on past-year events.

The results, however, were unexpected. The 30-day and 12-month groups did not differ on their general perceptions of the campus (e.g., danger, safety, and climate—indicating that they perceived their campus in similar ways), but surprisingly, they also did not differ in their reported rates of school violence victimization and related experiences. That is, they reported experiencing similar numbers of violence victimization instances in 30 days as in the 12-month period. These results point to the need for school violence researchers to develop a better understanding of the factors that influence student recollections of school safety-related experiences and their interpretation of what types of information researchers are requesting.

Although not specifically focusing on reported school violence, Hilton and colleagues (1998) also examined differences in self-reports across 1-month, 6-month, and 1-year time periods. They reported "that standard self-reports of interpersonal violence were insensitive to the specified time frame; for example, participants reported almost the same number of violent acts in the past month as in the past year, something that could not be factually true" (p. 234). Similarly, based on their review of what is known about influences of response-time referents, Brener et al. (2003) concluded that multiple factors affect student recollection of school violence experiences.

Survey designers should be mindful that respondents can find it difficult to accurately remember past events (Cornell & Loper, 1998; Fowler, 1993). For this reason, survey questions that ask about past behavior or experiences can incorporate any of a variety of techniques for enhancing recall. Converse and Presser (1986) recommend (a) using simple language, (b) asking about experiences within a narrow reference period (within no more than a 6-month period), (c) using memory landmarks (e.g., asking about behavior "since the beginning of the school year" or "since New Year's"), and (d) stimulating recall by describing concrete events ("Instead of asking respondents if they have experienced 'assaults,' for instance, . . . ask if anyone . . . used force by grabbing, punching, choking, scratching, or biting," p. 22). Unfortunately, school violence and safety research has not yet thoroughly attended to these measurement concerns.

Item-Response Options

Not only do surveys differ in the response time frame, but they also vary in the number and type of response options they offer. Often, items that appear on one survey are included on other questionnaires with a different number of response options, without stating a rationale for the change in response options. For example, the YRBS asks, "During the past 30 days, on how many days did you carry a weapon such as a gun, knife, or club on school property?" The following five response options are offered; *0 days, 1 day, 2 or 3 days, 4 or 5 days,* and *6 or more days.* When applied by Farrell and Meyer (1997) to evaluate the effectiveness of a violence prevention program, however, the item included six response options: *never, 1–2 times, 3–5 times, 6–9 times, 10–19 times,* and *20 times or more.* Although it might appear that similar items with different numbers of response options yield equivalent results, in fact, this is not the case (Schwartz, 1999). Additionally, Schwartz noted that survey respondents also are most likely to choose response options near the middle of Likert-type scales.

Taken together, these findings suggest that although comparing data obtained using different instruments may appear straightforward it is, in fact, complicated. Responses to items having different numbers of response options or response options that span different time periods may not be comparable.

SCHOOL VIOLENCE AND SAFETY INSTRUMENT PSYCHOMETRIC PROPERTIES

The survey method typically used to assess school safety and school violence seeks to identify indicators that increase the likelihood of negative outcomes. This practice differs substantially from that most often used in educational research, which establishes in advance the psychometric properties of a scale for identification or diagnosis purposes (Cornell & Loper, 1998). Unfortunately, some reports have used survey instruments for identification purposes without adequately examining the psychometric properties of the scales. There has been very limited research examining the reliability and validity of school violence and safety instruments.

Reliability

As with any self-report measure, measures of violence and safety should have rigorous psychometric testing to establish reliability and validity (Rosenblatt & Furlong, 1997). Unfortunately, such testing has not been widespread. Brener et al. (2002) completed the only study to date that has examined the reliability of the YRBS items that inquired about school-associated behaviors. They examined the responses of 4,619 of 6,802 eligible students, derived from a convenience sample, who completed the YRBS twice over a 2-week time period. They subsequently converted the responses to all items into binary format to compute a kappa statistic, a measure of response consistency that is corrected for chance agreement. The kappa statistic ranges in value from 0 to 1 with qualitative labels of "fair" (.2 to .4), "moderate" (.4–.6), "substantial" (.6–.8), and "almost perfect" (.8–1.0) (Landis & Koch, 1977). Kappa coefficients ranged from .41 to .68 for the four YRBS items that directly assess school violence content. The incidence of one behavior ("Injured in a physical fight one time in the past 12 months") was significantly higher at Time 2 compared with Time 1. Although Brener et al. concluded that in general the YRBS is a reliable instrument and this study is cited often to justify the use of the YRBS, there are several methodological questions with this study, particularly when school violence items are examined. These issues pertain to the appropriateness of excluding inconsistent responses prior to analysis; converting responses to binary format and using the kappa statistic;

using a 14-day (average) retest period for items with 30-day or 12-month reference time frames; and interpreting *kappa* coefficients for items with different reference time frames (e.g., past 30 days and past 12 months). As a result, this analysis likely generated the most favorable possible test–retest reliability. Even so, the reliability coefficients for the school items were only in the moderate range.

Validity of Measures

Skiba and colleagues (2004) noted that instruments can contribute significantly to the field of school violence and safety only when they include a more complex and representative set of factors involved. They recommended using empirical methods such as factor analysis to justify inclusion of items in surveys, rather than relying only on professional judgment, as has been done in the past. Regarding the content of school safety and school violence measures, Skiba and colleagues pointed out that many surveys focus on significant acts of violence, such as weapon carrying. However, although extreme violence is the end result within a context of unsafe school climate, it may not provide enough variance to yield meaningful comparisons, particularly for typical schools. For this reason, Skiba and colleagues stated that researchers need to focus less on serious violent acts, especially as smaller discipline problems are more frequent and are part of a common trajectory toward future antisocial behavior. However, there has been no research to ascertain which are the most important indicators of school climate in this regard, and whether or not indicators such as bringing a weapon to school are indeed the most important ones to measure.

To test the validity of one particular school safety measure, the Safe and Responsive Schools Safe Schools Survey, Skiba and colleagues (2004) examined the relative importance of several subscales of school safety. They conducted a factor analysis of items and identified four scales, which they called Connection/Climate, Incivility and Disruption, Personal Safety, and Delinquency/Major Safety. Using hierarchical linear regression, Skiba et al. looked for variables that predicted student perceptions of school safety. Perhaps surprisingly, the single most significant predictor of school safety was not among the items related to violent and criminal behavior, but rather, consisted of the single item, "I feel welcome when I am at school." These findings suggest that examining victimization and violence issues alone is insufficient; rather, to understand school safety it is essential to include measures of school climate and connectedness.

The work of Skiba and colleagues (2004) and Furlong et al. (California School Climate and Safety Survey; 2005) presents school violence and safety instruments that are being developed using psychometric approaches to scale development. Although these instruments are not appropriate for large-scale national surveys, they have potential to provide options when used as outcome measures in local evaluations and studies using controlled experimental designs. Recently, Greif and Furlong (2004a, 2004b) extended the psychometric approach by using item-response analysis to create a unidimensional school violence victim scale. Such a scale could be used to measure true change in victimization experiences across time.

IMPLICATIONS FOR RESEARCH AND PRACTICE

Given the lack of information about factors influencing student reports of violence, confidence in the quality of these data can be improved in several ways. One way to enhance the accuracy of this information is to solicit responses from multiple informants. Hence, as is now required in federal No Child Left Behind procedures, it is particularly helpful to gain the perspectives of both students and staff, although even less is known about the psychometric properties of staff safety and violence surveys than about student self-report measures.

Another step that can be taken to improve the quality of school violence survey data is to ensure anonymity, particularly when surveys are conducted at the school or classroom level. This can be accomplished by using multiple-choice rather than handwritten response formats to avoid detection of handwriting, by excluding demographic questions that would make it easier to identify members of minority groups, and by distributing surveys an adequate distance from peers and administrators (Coggeshall & Kingery, 2001). Anonymous self-report data have been reported to indicate higher rates of weapon possession than either discipline data or teacher reports (Furlong & Morrison, 2000). It is unclear, however, whether or not this was because these self-report data were more accurate than the other methods (Furlong, Sharkey, et al., 2004).

It is essential that school personnel be cautious when drawing inferences at the local level based on their students' responses to national surveillance surveys. To illustrate, although the YRBS results are broadly representative of the U.S. secondary school population, having been collected from sites across the country, they do not represent all 50 states. That is, some states did not participate in the survey (e.g., California, Pennsylvania, and Washington), and other states' samples could not be used for weighting adjustments (e.g., Colorado, Oregon, and South Carolina; CDC, 2004b). Although the information such surveys gather is useful for estimating national trends, they have relatively little sensitivity and relevance for addressing local school district conditions and needs. (It should be noted that CDC researchers do not suggest that the YRBS be used for this purpose.) To make valid inferences regarding local conditions, schools and districts should interpret their students' responses to these surveys by comparison with regional, state, and local data. Additionally, schools should supplement these survey data by debriefing with students to better understand how the students interpreted the survey items and specifically which school conditions and experiences they considered when responding.

A second caution to school staff pertaining to the use of items from national surveillance surveys is that these large-scale instruments query a wide range of experiences and conditions. Because their focus is broad, these measures include only a limited number of items pertaining specifically to school violence and safety matters (e.g., school fights and weapon carrying), so they cannot provide a comprehensive, in-depth measure of specific safety-related conditions or needs for any particular school. Thus, there is a need to refine validated instruments that assess safety-related variables. Practitioners need to be especially mindful that data used to measure school- and district-level safety and violence issues for decision-making purposes should be gathered using instruments that are known to be valid for measuring the specific variables of interest for their particular population of students.

After results have been tallied, they should be presented separately to the students, their parents, and the school staff. A collaborative team atmosphere can be maintained by soliciting interpretations of the findings and ideas for taking action from all three groups (students, parents, and school staff). After an intervention is implemented, the students should be periodically re-assessed to evaluate its effectiveness. Table 8.1 presents a summary of recommendations for the use of school safety self-report procedures.

The study of school violence needs to move beyond measuring the prevalence of the problem using large-scale surveys toward applying more advanced standards for multidisciplinary examination. Newly developed surveys should attend to both theoretical and psychometric principles before being used to evaluate programs or guide policy. Existing measures need to be more rigorously evaluated to demonstrate their psychometric properties and to better understand the effects of measurement issues specific to the nature of the field of school safety and violence, such as implausible responding patterns, the effects of survey administration procedures, item wording, item-response procedures, item-response time frames, and item-response

TABLE 8.1

Implications for Practice: Recommendations for the Use of School Violence
Self-Report Procedures

Constructing surveys
    Clearly define key terms
    Keep questions concrete
    Use memory aids or referent points when asking about past events
    Include multiple questions to measure each main construct
    Check survey's reading level for the target population
    Include items that screen for honesty and accuracy
Selecting existing surveys
    Check reliability and validity for the population to be tested
Administering surveys
    Ensure confidentiality/anonymity
    Train staff to adhere to a standard protocol
    Explain purpose of survey to students and how results will be used
    If needed, read questions aloud to students and to clarify content
    Debrief students afterward: What were they thinking?
Reporting survey results
    Present information in a format appropriate for students, staff, and parents
    Solicit perceptions of survey data
    Brainstorm alternative courses of action
    Maintain a collaborative, team-oriented stance
Next steps
    Link assessment to planning and intervention
    Choose activities and programs with empirical support
    Re-assess students periodically to measure program effectiveness

options. Finally, results of surveys should be only applied within their scope; for example, national surveillance surveys may inform national trends, whereas individually administered surveys may inform individual-level decisions. By attending to basic principles of sound measurement, assessments will have the potential to advance knowledge and understanding of school safety and school violence.

REFERENCES

Benbenishty, R., Astor, R. A., & Zeira, A. (2003). Monitoring school violence: Linking national-, district-, and school-level data over time. *Journal of School Violence, 2*, 29–50.

Brener, N. D., Billy, J. O. G., & Grady, W. R. (2003). Assessment of factors affecting the validity of self-reported health-risk behavior among adolescents: evidence from the scientific literature. *Journal of Adolescent Health, 33*, 436–457.

Brener, N. D., Grunbaum, J. A., Kann, L., McManus, T., & Ross, J. (2004). Assessing health risk behaviors among adolescents: The effect of question wording and appeals for honesty. *Journal of Adolescent Health, 35*, 91–100.

Brener, N. D., Kann, L., Kinchen, S. A., Grunbaum, J., Whalen, L., Eaton, D., Hawkins, J., & Ross, J. G. (2004, September 24). Methodology of the Youth Risk Behavior Surveillance System. *Morbidity and Mortality Weekly Reports (Recommendations and Reports), 53*(RR12), 1–13.

Brener, N. D., Kann, L., McManus, T., Kinchen, S. A., Sundberg, E. C., & Ross, J. G. (2002). Reliability of the 1999 Youth Risk Behavior Survey Questionnaire. *Journal of Adolescent Health, 31*, 336–342.

Centers for Disease Control and Prevention. (2004a). Data & statistics: Youth Risk Behavior Surveillance System. Available: http://www.cdc.gov/HealthyYouth/yrbs/index.htm

Centers for Disease Control and Prevention. (2004b). Data & statistics: YRBS Survey participation map, 2003. Available: http://www.cdc.gov/HealthyYouth/yrbs/map.htm

Coggeshall, M. B., & Kingery, P. M. (2001). Cross-survey analysis of school violence and disorder. *Psychology in the Schools, 38*, 107–116.

Converse, J. M., & Presser, S. (1986). *Survey questions: Handcrafting the standardized questionnaire.* Newbury Park, CA: Sage.

Cornell, D. G., & Brockenbrough, K. (2004). Identification of bullies and victims: A comparison of methods. *Journal of School Violence, 3*, 63–88.

Cornell, D. G., & Loper, A. B. (1998). Assessment of violence and other high-risk behaviors with a school survey. *School Psychology Review, 27*, 317–330.

Cross, J. E., & Newman-Gonchar, R. (2004). Data quality in student risk behavior surveys and administrator training. *Journal of School Violence, 3*, 89–108.

Farrell, A. D., & Meyer, A. L. (1997). The effectiveness of a school-based curriculum for reducing violence among urban sixth-grade students. *American Journal of Public Health, 87*, 979–984.

Fowler, F. J., Jr. (1993). *Survey research methods* (2nd ed.). Newbury Park, CA: Sage.

Furlong, M. J., Bates, M. P., Sharkey, J. D., & Smith, D. C. (2004). The accuracy of school and non-school risk behaviors as predictors of school weapons possession. In M. J. Furlong, M. Bates, D. C. Smith, & P. Kingery (Eds.), *Appraisal and prediction of school violence: Issues, methods and contexts* (pp. 193–214). Hauppauge, NY: Nova Science.

Furlong, M. J., Chung, A., Bates, M., & Morrison, R. L. (1995). Who are the victims of school violence? *Education and Treatment Children, 18*, 1–17.

Furlong, M. J., Felix, E., & Sharkey, J. (2005). *The effects of 30-day and 1-year time intervals on students' reported school violence victimization.* Manuscript submitted for publication, University of California, Santa Barbara.

Furlong, M. J., Greif, J. L., Bates, M. P., Whipple, A. D., Jimenez, T. C., & Morrison, R. (2005). Development of California School Climate and Safety Survey—Short Form. *Psychology in the Schools, 42*, 1–13.

Furlong, M. J., & Morrison, G. M. (2000). The school in school violence. *Journal of Emotional and Behavioral Disorders, 8*, 71–82.

Furlong, M. J., Morrison, G. M., Cornell, D., & Skiba, R. (2004). Methodological and measurement issues in school violence research: Moving beyond the social problem era. *Journal of School Violence, 3*(2/3), 5–12.

Furlong, M. J., Paige, L. Z., & Osher, D. (2003). The safe schools/healthy students (SS/HS) initiative: Lessons learned from implementing comprehensive youth development programs. *Psychology in the Schools, 40*, 447–456.

Furlong, M. J., Sharkey, J. D., Bates, M. P., & Smith, D. C. (2004). An examination of the reliability, data screening procedures, and extreme response patterns for the Youth Risk Behavior Surveillance Survey. *Journal of School Violence, 3*(2/3), 109–130.

Greif, J. L., & Furlong, M. J. (2004a). *Towards precision in measuring school violence victimization using IRT.* Paper presented at the 20th annual meeting of the International Society for Traumatic Stress Studies, New Orleans, LA.

Greif, J. L., & Furlong, M. J. (2004b). Using item response analysis to develop a unidimensional school violence victimization scale. In *Persistently safe schools: The National Conference of the Hamilton Fish Institute on School and Community Violence* (pp. 123–136). Washington, DC: Hamilton Fish Institute, George Washington University.

Guerra, N. G., & Williams, K. R. (2003). Implementation of school-based wellness centers. *Psychology in the Schools, 40*, 473–487.

Gun-Free Schools Act (GFSA). 20 USC §8921. (1994).

Hilton, N. Z., Harris, G. T., & Rice, M. E. (1998). On the validity of self-reported rates of interpersonal violence. *Journal of Interpersonal Violence, 13*, 58–72.

Hilton, N. Z., Harris, G. T., & Rice, M. E. (2003). Correspondence between self-reports of interpersonal violence. *Journal of Interpersonal Violence, 18*, 223–239.

Kingery, P. M., & Coggeshall, M. B. (2001). Surveillance of school violence, injury, and disciplinary actions. *Psychology in the Schools, 38*, 117–126.

Landis, J. R., Koch, G. G. (1977). The measurement of observer agreement for categorical data. *Biometrics, 33*, 159–74.

Mayer, M. J. (2004). Structural equation modeling of school violence data: Methodological considerations. *Journal of School Violence, 3*(2/3), 131–148.

Morrison, G. M., Peterson, R., O'Farrell, S., & Redding, M. (2004). Using office referral records in school violence research: Possibilities and limitations. *Journal of School Violence, 3*(2/3), 139–149.

Morrison, G. M., & Skiba, R. (2001). Predicting violence from school misbehavior: Promises and perils. *Psychology in the Schools, 38*, 173–184.

Oregon Healthy Teens 2001: Methodology. (2004). Available: www.dhs.state.or.us/publichealth/chs/ohteens/2001/methods2001.pdf

Paige, L. Z., Kitzis, S. N., & Wolfe, J. (2003). Rural underpinnings for resiliency and linkages (RURAL): A Safe Schools/Healthy Students project. *Psychology in the Schools, 40*, 531–547.

Research Triangle Institute. (2004). National evaluation surveys. Available: http://www.sshsevaluation.org/resources/

Rosenblatt, J. A., & Furlong, M. J. (1997). Assessing the reliability and validity of student self-reports of campus violence. *Journal of Youth and Adolescence, 26*, 187–202.

Safe Schools Healthy Students. (2004). *The faces of the Safe Schools/Healthy Students.* Available: http://www.sshs.samhsa.gov/initiative/faces.aspx

Schwartz, N. (1999). Self reports: How the questions shape the answers. *American Psychologist, 54*, 93–105.

Skiba, R., Simmons, A. B., Peterson, R., McKelvey, J., Ford, S., & Gallini, S. (2004). Beyond guns, drugs, and gangs: The structure of student perceptions of school safety. *The Journal of School Violence, 3*(2/3), 149–171.

Sugai, G., Sprague, J. R., Horner, R. H., & Walker, H. M. (2000). Preventing school violence: The use of office discipline referrals to assess and monitor school-wide discipline interventions. *Journal of Emotional and Behavioral Disorders, 8*, 94–101.

Sullivan, M. L. (2002). Exploring layers: Extended case method as a tool for multilevel analysis of school violence. *Sociological Methods & Research, 31*, 255–285.

Turner, C. F., Ku, L., Rogers, S. M., Lindberg, L. D., Pleck, J. H., & Sonenstein, F. L. (1998). Adolescent sexual behavior, drug use, and violence: Increased reporting with computer survey technology. *Science, 280*, 867–873.

Welsh, J., Domitrovich, C. E., Bierman, K., & Lang, J. (2003). Promoting safe schools and healthy students in rural Pennsylvania. *Psychology in the Schools, 40*, 457–472.

WestEd. (2004). *California Healthy Kids Survey.* Available: www.wested.org/hks

9

Assessing Anger and Hostility in School Settings

Douglas C. Smith
University of Hawaii

Michael J. Furlong
University of California, Santa Barbara

Peter Boman
James Cook University

Chronically high levels of anger and hostility have been identified as important contributors to violence potential at school (Dwyer, Osher, & Warger, 1998; McGee & DeBernardo, 1999; Reddy et al., 2001; Verlinden, Hersen, & Thomas, 2000). In published lists of warning signs posted by the American Psychological Association (APA, 1999) and the U.S. Departments of Justice and Education (Dwyer et al., 1998), for example, aspects of uncontrolled anger and hostility are among the key indices of violence potential. Additionally, profiles of perpetrators of serious acts of violence at school, such as those developed by the FBI (O'Toole, 2000), frequently cite intense anger and resentment toward others as common characteristics of violence-prone youth.

Given the potential impact of anger and hostility on aggressive and violent behavior, it is imperative that educators, psychologists, and other mental health personnel have reliable and valid methods for assessing anger in school settings. The purpose of this chapter is to provide an overview of selected instruments designed to measure levels of anger and hostility in school-age populations. This review begins with a brief discussion of some of the fundamental concerns associated with measuring anger and hostility and then provides a description and critique of selected instruments of interest to school personnel. The chapter concludes with a summary of best practices in anger assessment as well as some of the limitations and other obstacles associated with measuring students' anger in school environments.

ASSESSMENT OF ANGER AND HOSTILITY AT SCHOOL

Theoretical and Definitional Issues

Systematic appraisal of anger and hostility is a fairly recent phenomenon. Because each construct represents a highly personalized experience, most assessment efforts rely almost exclusively on self-report procedures. Some instruments utilize behavior ratings by teachers, parents, and others, but these run the risk of confusing internal feelings and attitudes with external behaviors, most notably aggression.

Considerable conceptual ambiguity surrounds the use of the terms anger and hostility in the literature. At its most basic level, anger refers to an emotional reaction to a perceived internal or external provocation (Miller, Smith, Turner, Guijarro, & Hallett, 1996; Novaco, 1994, 2003) and it varies in intensity from mild irritation to extreme rage. Anger can be viewed as a transitory state or a stable and general disposition to experience this emotion more frequently and intensely (Spielberger, 1999; Spielberger, Reheiser, & Sydeman, 1995). Research has distinguished between state anger, or the degree of angry affect experienced at a particular moment in response to a particular situation, and trait anger, or one's disposition to experience angry affect across a range of situations.

Research has also distinguished between *anger-in, anger-out,* and *anger control* (Spielberger et al., 1995; Thomas & Williams, 1991). Each of these terms refers to a characteristic mode of anger expression. Anger-in refers to the tendency of some individuals to restrain or stifle the expression of angry feelings. Anger-out refers to the tendency to express anger overtly, usually through verbal or physical aggression. Anger control refers to the ability of some individuals to express anger in a controlled fashion, usually in what many would consider a socially appropriate manner, such as discussing their feelings with another. Whether it is best to withhold expression of angry feelings or to express these emotions outwardly is a matter of some controversy. Some studies (e.g., Julkunen, Salonen, Kaplan, Chesney, & Salonen, 1994) suggest that frequent anger-out is a risk factor for a number of serious medical conditions including coronary heart disease (CHD), whereas others (e.g., Mills, Schneider, & Dimsdale, 1989) propose that outward expressions of anger may serve a protective function by reducing tension and pent-up frustration.

The term *hostility* (*cynicism* is a term also used in the literature) refers to a cognitive process whereby other people are perceived in essentially negativistic terms (Miller et al., 1996; T. Smith, 1994). As such, hostility constitutes an attitude or worldview in which the actions of others are often perceived as intentionally harmful or intrusive, there is an expectation that negative outcomes are highly probable, and there is a desire to inflict harm on others or to see others harmed. Given the pervasive nature of these beliefs, hostility is thought to constitute a stable disposition or personality attribute. In this sense, it is similar to what was referred to earlier as "trait anger" (Martin, Watson, & Wan, 2000).

Both anger and hostility have been linked to aggressive behavior and this presents another point of contention for those concerned with the measurement of these constructs. It is difficult to identify the existence and intensity of angry feelings and hostile beliefs without considering how such feelings and beliefs are expressed behaviorally. In fact, there is substantial support for the notion that high levels of anger, hostile beliefs, and proneness to aggression co-exist in many individuals (Bushman, Cooper, & Lemke, 1991; Musante, MacDougall, Dembroski, & Costa, 1989). The degree to which these constitute separate and distinct constructs is unclear at this point. A number of researchers over the past decade have proposed multidimensional inventories designed to measure affective, cognitive, and behavioral dimensions of anger and hostility (e.g., Martin et al., 2000; Siegel, 1986; D. Smith, Furlong, Bates, & Laughlin, 1998; Thomas, 1993). In general, these measures demonstrate moderate correlations among subscales, suggesting that anger, hostility, and aggression constitute separate but related factors. Martin et al. in a cross-instrument factor analysis of scales involving a sample of college students, found strong evidence supporting a multidimensional model of anger than includes affective, cognitive, and behavioral elements.

Anger and Hostility as Predictors of School Violence

As a fundamental human emotion, anger clearly plays a vital role in the overall adaptive process. Chronic high levels of anger and hostility are associated with a wide range of negative developmental outcomes including physical and mental illness, academic and occupational distress, poor peer relationships, and aggressive and violent behavior both in and out of school. Thus, there is certainly ample reason for schools to not only be concerned about the challenges that aggressive students present, but to recognize that these students' behavior indicates their risk status for various negative developmental outcomes.

In recent years, there have been several attempts to identify behaviors associated with school violence that might help inform educators of the risks posed by specific students within specific contexts (e.g., DeBecker, 1999; McCann, 2002; Mohandie, 2002). Among the best known of these are the warning signs proposed by the Departments of Justice and Education (Dwyer et al., 1998; distributed to every school in the United States) and the APA (1999). Each of these documents contains an array of personal, social, school, and family factors thought to increase the odds that a youth might engage in acts of violence at school. These documents do not claim to be "checklists" that can be used to assess the level of risk of future school violence. Rather, they were developed with the intention that they be used to broadly assess the contexts in a youth's life that might push them toward or away from committing an extreme act of violence (for an extended review see Furlong, Bates, Smith, & Kingery, 2004).

INSTRUMENTS DESIGNED TO ASSESS YOUTH ANGER AND HOSTILITY

Although there is an increasing array of instruments purporting to measure angry emotions and hostile attitudes in child and adolescent populations, a number of these focus almost exclusively on expression of anger; that is, aggression. This review focuses exclusively on those instruments that adhere to a multidimensional model of anger, which includes affective, cognitive, and behavioral components of anger and hostility.

Adolescent Anger Rating Scale

The Adolescent Anger Rating Scale (AARS; Burney & Kromrey, 2001) is designed to assist clinicians and researchers in identifying specific subtypes of anger problems in adolescents. It is a brief self-report scale assessing the intensity and frequency of angry reactions in youth aged 11–19.

The AARS measures two distinct types of anger: instrumental and reactive, as well as students' ability to control their anger. Instrumental anger is defined as negative affect oriented toward achieving a specific goal or purpose. It often results in retaliatory behavior that is planned, malicious, and goal-directed. Reactive anger, on the other hand, is defined as an immediate emotional response to an anger-provoking event that is perceived as threatening, hurtful, or intentional. It is characterized by its immediacy, lack of foresight, and apparent insensitivity to cognitive considerations facilitating self-control. Anger control is defined as one's ability to engage in proactive behaviors in the face of anger provocations. In addition to subscale scores for Instrumental Anger, Reactive Anger, and Anger Control, the AARS yields a Total Anger score, which is the sum of Instrumental and Reactive anger scores.

The AARS includes 41 items utilizing a 4-point, Likert-type response scale on which respondents indicate the frequency with which they engage in behaviors representative of instrumental anger, reactive anger, and anger control. Items within each subscale are totaled to yield representative subscale scores.

Normative data are provided based on the responses of 4,187 males and females in middle and high schools. Five ethnic groups were represented in the normative sample. Additional information is provided on grade-point average, suspensions in the past year, number of friends, friends' behavior, and primary caretaker for students within the normative sample.

Burney and Kromrey (2001) report AARS reliability data based on the initial development of the scale. Utilizing an earlier 16-item version of the scale, coefficient alphas were .83, .70, and .80 for Instrumental, Reactive, and Anger Control subscales, respectively. Test–retest reliabilities over a 2-week interval, based on the responses of 155 participants, were .58, .69, and .65 for the same three subscales.

Validity data reported by Burney and Kromrey (2001) during initial development of the AARS was based on the responses of 792 students in Grades 7–12. Exploratory factor analysis utilizing a 20-item revised version of the scale resulted in three factors corresponding to the hypothesized underlying structure of the scale: Reactive Anger, Instrumental Anger, and Anger Control. Construct validity for the AARS was further established by comparing mean subscale scores for groups expected to differ in terms of the constructs measured by this scale. As expected, male students, members of ethnic minority groups, older students, and those receiving special education services scored significantly higher on both Reactive and Instrumental Anger and significantly lower on Anger Control. Additionally, discriminant validity for the AARS was established by comparing subscale scores with another anger scale, the Multidimensional Anger Inventory (Siegel, 1986), which, according to the author, measures different aspects of anger. Subscale correlations between these two measures ranged from minus −.11 to .46 for the three AARS subscales.

AARS Summary

Given its fourth-grade reading level, the AARS would usually be easily understandable by the majority of students ages 11–19. The manual provides information on conversion of obtained raw scores to percentiles and T-scores according to students' gender and age group.

The AARS is a time-efficient, cost-effective measure for assessing modes of anger expression in adolescents. It offers the practitioner a concise and practical method of determining a youth's characteristic response to anger-provoking situations and also offers information on the likelihood of an individual's ability to control negative expressions of anger. Outstanding questions relate to its overall reliability and its ability to discriminate between various types of anger disorders in adolescent populations. At this time, there are no studies linking the AARS with future aggression potential among adolescents.

Anger Response Inventory, Child and Adolescent Versions

The Anger Response Inventories, Child and Adolescent Versions (ARI-C; Tangney, Wagner, Hansbarger, & Gramzow, 1991 and ARI-A; Tangney, Wagner, Gavias, & Gramzow, 1991a) are self-report instruments that present children with a range of potentially frustrating situations and ask how angry they would feel, what they would want to do, what they actually would do, and how their actions might affect themselves and others. Results from the ARI-C and ARI-A indicate children's levels of anger, their intentions, their likely cognitive and behavioral responses in similar frustrating situations, and the long-term consequences that they perceive as a result of their chosen responses.

The ARI-C and ARI-A consist of several scales divided into four main components: Anger Arousal, Intentions, Behavioral and Cognitive Responses to Anger, and Long-Term

Consequences. The Anger Arousal scale measures the level of anger children experience in a given situation. The Intentions component assesses what children initially may think about doing in response to a frustrating or problematic situation. The Intentions component includes the following scales: Constructive Intentions (intent to remedy the problem situation), Malevolent Intentions (intent to seek revenge; a potentially important element within the threat assessment context), and Fractious Intentions (intent to express or diffuse one's anger). The Fractious Intentions scale is included in the ARI-A only.

The Behavioral and Cognitive Reponses to Anger component assesses what children actually will choose to do in response to a frustrating or problematic situation. The chosen responses often are directed at the "target," or the person whom the child believes played a central role in the problem situation. The Behavioral and Cognitive Responses to Anger component includes the following scales: Direct Physical Aggression (attempts to physically hurt or harm the target), Direct Verbal Aggression (attempts to verbally hurt or harm the target), Direct Symbolic Aggression (attempts to express anger toward the target in a symbolic way; for example, by slamming a door in the target's face), Malediction (talking negatively about the target to a third party), Indirect Harm (damaging something important to the target or withholding something the target finds enjoyable), Displaced Physical Aggression (physical aggression directed at a person other than the target), Displaced Verbal Aggression (verbal aggression directed at a person other than the target), Displaced Aggression To Object (aggression directed at a non-human object not connected to the target), Self-Aggression (aggression directed toward the self), Anger Held In (withholding one's anger), Discussion With Target (engaging in a rational and neutral discussion with the target), Corrective Action (attempts to remedy the situation), Diffusion (attempts to lessen one's anger), Minimization (minimizing the importance of the incident), Removal (leaving the situation), Doing Nothing, Cognitive Reappraisals of Target's Role (reevaluating the motives or actions of the target), and Cognitive Reappraisals of Self's Role (reevaluating one's own role in the situation). These scales provide a very detailed picture of the multiple ways in which youths may express their anger either adaptively or aggressively.

Finally, the Long-Term Consequences component assesses the consequences that children perceive may occur as a result of their chosen behavioral or cognitive responses. This component includes the following scales: Long-Term Consequences for Self, Long-Term Consequences for Target, and Long-Term Consequences for Relationship. The Long-Term Consequences for Relationship scale is included in the ARI-A only.

Both the ARI-C and ARI-A are self-report measures consisting of 20 common and developmentally appropriate scenarios that, in everyday life, could trigger frustration or anger in children. Children imagine themselves in each situation and rate on a 5-point Likert scale (a) their level of anger (anger arousal), (b) what they would feel like doing (their intentions), (c) what they would likely do (their behavioral and cognitive responses), and (d) their perception of the long-term consequences that would result from their behavioral or cognitive responses.

Standardization of the ARI-C and ARI-A was based on normative samples of 302 children and 427 adolescents. The children and adolescents attended primarily public schools in suburban areas on the east coast of the United States. They were from African-American and white backgrounds and their socioeconomic status (SES) levels were diverse.

Internal consistencies of the ARI-C and ARI-A were assessed using samples of 307 children (Grades 4–6) and 434 adolescents (Grades 7–11; Tangney, Hill-Barlow, et al., 1996). The internal consistencies of the ARI-C and ARI-A total scores were high (0.91 and 0.94, respectively). The internal consistencies for the ARI-C scales ranged from 0.35 to 0.93 (average 0.72). The Anger Arousal, Intentions, and Long-Term Consequences scales demonstrated the highest internal consistencies, ranging from 0.90 to 0.93. The internal consistencies for the ARI-A scales ranged from 0.47 to 0.94 (average 0.77). The Anger Arousal, Intentions, and Long-Term Consequences scales demonstrated the highest internal consistencies, ranging from 0.85 to 0.94. Test–retest reliabilities and interrater reliabilities for the ARI-C and ARI-A were not assessed.

The authors of the ARI-C and ARI-A developed the tests by collaborating with other professionals to generate pools of items from which they selected the most appropriate and representative scenarios and item responses. These scenarios and item responses were revised and refined as necessary and were included in preliminary versions of the instruments. These pilot versions were then presented via individual interviews to 29 children in Grades 4–6 and 29 adolescents in Grades 7–12. Based on the information gathered from these interviews, the ARI-C and ARI-A were again revised. The newly revised instruments were then administered to 163 public school children in Grades 4–6 and 223 public school adolescents in Grades 7–12. Based on the results of these administrations, the ARI-C and ARI-A were each reduced to 20 scenarios. These revisions are reflected in the current versions of the instruments.

Tangney, Hill-Barlow, et al. (1996) investigated the convergent validity of the ARI-C and ARI-A. The study involved 309 children (ages 8–14) and 373 adolescents (ages 12–20). These two groups were comprised mostly of white and African-American students of low to moderate SES. The students completed the ARI-C or ARI-A, and their teachers completed the Child Behavior Checklist—Teacher Report Form (CBCL-TRF; Achenbach & Edelbrock, 1986). Results indicated that the CBCL-TRF Aggression and Delinquency scales were significantly and positively correlated with most of the ARI-C and ARI-A Aggression scales. The largest correlations were found between the Aggression and Delinquency scales of the CBCL-TRF and the Direct Physical Aggression, Direct Symbolic Aggression, Displaced Physical Aggression, and Displaced Aggression to Object scales of the ARI-C and ARI-A. In addition, the researchers found significant inverse relationships between the CBCL-TRF Aggression and Delinquency scales and the ARI-C and ARI-A adaptive response scale, Discuss With Target, and the Long-Term Consequences for Self scale. The inverse relationship obtained with the latter scale indicates that as TRF Aggression and Delinquency decrease, the perception of positive long-term consequences for oneself increases.

Tangney, Wagner, Hill-Barlow, Marschall, and Gramzow (1996) also investigated the concurrent validity of the ARI-C and ARI-A. The study involved 307 children and 434 adolescents. They completed either the ARI-C or ARI-A and either the Test of Self-Conscious Affect for Children (TOSCA-C; Tangney, Wagner, Burggraf, Gramzow, & Fletcher, 1990) or the Test of Self-Conscious Affect for Adolescents (TOSCA-A; Tangney, Wagner, Gavlas, & Gramzow, 1991b). Results indicated that the tendency to feel shame, as reported on the TOSCA-C or TOSCA-A, was significantly related to maladaptive and destructive anger responses on the ARI-C and ARI-A. The study also found that the tendency to feel guilt about one's inappropriate behavior generally was related to adaptive and constructive responses on the ARI-C and ARI-A.

Summary of Anger Response Inventory

The ARI-C and ARI-A are self-report instruments that assess how children and adolescents feel and respond in a variety of potentially frustrating or anger-provoking situations. The scenarios presented in the instruments cover a variety of settings and situations with which children can relate, and the instruments are relatively quick and easy to administer. The instruments provide a comprehensive assessment of various factors related to anger, although working with the relatively large number of scales may seem confusing and complicated to some. The ARI-C and ARI-A have strong internal consistency and have demonstrated evidence of content validity and convergent validity. As such, they provide useful information when working with a specific child in a school-based anger management intervention. Nonetheless, additional data are needed on other types of reliability and validity, including test–retest reliability, concurrent validity, and discriminant validity.

Qualified school personnel and professionals may use the ARI-C and ARI-A as a screening tool to identify children or adolescents who have problems with anger or aggression. The large number of scales utilized in the instruments can provide a lot of information on how a particular child feels, thinks, and behaves in various anger-provoking situations, which is of obvious interest in threat assessment situations. High scores on the Anger Arousal, Malevolent Intentions, and Aggression scales may indicate the presence of emotional or behavioral concerns that warrant further evaluation. The attention given by the ARI-C and ARI-A to multiple aspects of the anger experience provides information that can assist in assessment, intervention planning, and evaluation.

Multidimensional School Anger Inventory

The Multidimensional School Anger Inventory (MSAI; D. Smith et al., 1998) is designed to assess the affective, cognitive, and behavioral dimensions of anger pertinent to the school setting and context. As a multidimensional scale, it attempts to measure the intensity of angry feelings in response to hypothetical school situations, levels of hostility with regard to school, and both positive and negative expressions of angry feelings.

Purpose and Nature of the MSAI

Construct(s) Measured. Development of the MSAI was based on a three-component model of the global anger process that involves an emotional-affective component, a cognitive hostility-cynicism component, and a behavioral-expressive component. The model is consistent with conceptual definitions of anger proposed by Spielberger et al. (1995). The behavioral-expressive component of the scale is further subdivided into positive and negative expressions of anger.

Subtests and Scores Obtained. The MSAI includes four subscales that the authors designate as Anger Experience, Hostile/Cynical Attitudes, Destructive Expression, and Positive Coping. Principal components factor analysis supported each of the four subscales as relatively independent measures of the general construct of anger in adolescent populations. This instrument has been used with children and adolescents ages 10–18 (fourth-grade reading level). It can be administered in 15–20 minutes either individually or in groups.

Items, Scaling Method, Sources of Information. The revised version of the MSAI (Furlong, Smith, & Bates, 2002) consists of 36 items utilizing a Likert-type response options (the current research version includes 54 items, see www.education.ucsb.edu/school-psychology for more information). The first 13 items comprise the Anger Experience subscale and respondents are asked to indicate the intensity of angry feelings they would experience as a result of a variety of frustrating school-related experiences. The 13 items include both peer- and teacher-initiated conflicts and are scored on a 4 point scale ranging from 1 (I *wouldn't be mad at all*) to 4 (I *would be furious*). Scores on these 13 items are totaled to yield an Anger Experience scale score that ranges from 13 to 42.

Items 14–19 are included as part of the Hostility subscale. On this subscale, respondents are asked to indicate their level of disagreement/agreement with a series of statements pertaining to the value of school, grades, rules, and attitudes of adults such as teachers. These items are also scored on a Likert-type scale from 1 (*strongly agree*) to 4 (*strongly disagree*). Individual subscale items are again totaled to yield a Hostility Index score ranging from 6 to 24.

Finally, Items 20 to 36 pertain to customary modes of expressing angry affect. About half of these items (9 out of 17) refer to Destructive Modes of Expression such as physical and verbal aggression, property destruction, and planned acts of retribution. The remaining eight items refer to Positive Modes of Coping such as talking it out, physical activity, use of humor, or cognitive reframing. Each item is scored according to a Likert-type scale from 1 (*never*) to 4 (*always*). Scores on both the Destructive Expression and Positive Coping subscales are summed to yield subscale total scores that range from 9 to 36 and 8 to 32, respectively.

MSAI Technical Evaluation

Norms.   The revised version of the MSAI (Furlong et al., 2002) was normed on a sample of 1,166 adolescents in Grades 9–12. Mean subscale scores for Anger Experience, Hostility, Destructive Expression, and Positive Coping were 30.8, 12.4, 14.5, and 17.3, respectively. Corresponding standard deviations were 6.8, 3.3, 4.8, and 4.1, respectively. Mean scores for male students were significantly higher than for females on Anger Experience, Hostility, and Destructive Expression. Females, on the other hand, scored significantly higher than males on the Positive Coping subscale. Subscale mean scores and standard deviations are also provided by grade level and by ethnicity for students in the normative sample.

Reliability Data.   Alpha coefficients for the four MSAI subscales based on the sample of 1,166 adolescents in Grades 9–12 were .86 for Anger Experience, .80 for Hostility, .82 for Destructive Expression, and .68 for Positive Coping. In addition, test–retest reliabilities over a 6-month period based on a subsample of 508 students ranged from .56 to .62 for the four subscales.

Validity Data.   A principal components factor analysis based on the responses of 1,166 adolescents in Grades 9–12 yielded a four-factor structure that supported the theoretical model on which the scale was based. Intrascale loadings ranged between .44 and .69 with no item having a between-subscale loading greater than .40. Thus, the factor analysis suggests four relatively independent subscales assessing affective, cognitive, and behavioral components of anger.

Recent studies support the construct and predictive validity of the MSAI. D. Smith et al. (1998) found moderately positive correlations between the MSAI and other measures of oppositional behavior at school including the Connors' Teacher Rating Scale (CTRS; Connors, 1990) and the Aggression Questionnaire (AQ; Buss & Warren, 2000). Additionally, these authors reported that students referred for special education services, due to emotional and behavioral difficulties, reported significantly higher levels of angry affect and cynical attitudes on the MSAI than did comparable students in regular education. Boman, Smith, and Curtis (2003) found that Australian secondary students who manifested helpless atttributional styles and a general sense of pessimism were more likely on the MSAI to experience higher levels of anger, express greater hostility toward school, and to more readily engage in acts of destructive expression. Boman and Yates (2001) found that students who entered high school with expectations for negative outcomes also demonstrated high levels of hostility as measured by the MSAI. Finally, Furlong and Smith (1998) used the MSAI to develop an empirically derived typology of anger responses in an effort to identify subgroups of students with specific intervention needs with regard to anger management and control.

In a more recent cross-national investigation, Furlong et al. (2004), compared the responses of students from the United States, Guatemala, Peru, and Australia. They found that the responses of students were more similar than dissimilar but that (a) males, regardless of nationality, tended to score higher; (b) the Australian students tended to have higher scores on the Anger Expression and Destructive Expression subscales; (c) the Peruvian students had the lowest scores on the Hostility subscale and the highest on Positive Coping scores; and (d) the U.S. males were highest on scores overall on the Hostility subscale and had the lowest scores on the Positive Coping subscale. While acknowledging the on-going need to consider nuances related to the translation of the MSAI items (into Spanish used in two cultures and even to better match Australian English), a Rasch analysis provided good support for the integrity of the items across cultural groups.

Summary of the MSAI

The MSAI offers researchers and practitioners an efficient and psychometrically sound instrument for identifying students with anger-related problems in school settings. One of the strengths of the scale, with regard to assessing a youth's emotional status, is its specific application to the school context. Another is its multidimensional framework, which allows researchers and practitioners to attend to affective, cognitive, and behavioral components of anger among school-age youth. Such a distinction may have significant implications for anger management strategies and interventions. Additional research is needed to evaluate the utility of the MSAI for this and other purposes within school settings. The authors recommend that the MSAI is best used as part of a comprehensive assessment battery, which evaluates not only angry feelings, attitudes, and behaviors but the context and setting in which these occur.

SUMMARY AND RECOMMENDATIONS FOR PRACTITIONERS

This chapter reviewed several instruments designed to measure aspects of anger and hostility in school-age youth. Each of these constructs has been demonstrated by prior research to be related to a variety of negative physical, interpersonal, academic, and behavioral outcomes. More importantly, chronic anger and hostility have been related to aggressive behavior, both within and outside school settings. As such, individual levels of anger and hostility should be considered in any school-based threat assessment. A number of professional organizations have, in fact, published lists of risk factors or warning signs that include chronic anger and hostility among other key factors.

Despite these encouraging findings, it is cautioned that assessment of anger and hostility, particularly in the school context, is still in its early stages and the vast majority of contemporary instruments rely almost exclusively upon self-report. Additionally, both anger and hostility are highly personalized experiences, often beyond the purview of informed adults such as parents or teachers. Angry feelings and hostile attitudes are often confused with aggressive behavior, which is much more observable. Students who may be developing chronic, cynical attitudes about school, family, and community may not aggressively act out these developing beliefs, but they are nonetheless often in need of counseling and other support services.

Assessment of anger and hostility is important if educators are to understand what motivates student behavior at school from everyday conflicts/hassles to more serious acts of violence. A summary of Anger Assessment implications for practitioners is included in Table 9.1. Such

TABLE 9.1
Anger Assessment: Implications for Practitioners

1. Chronically high levels of anger and hostility may frequently underlie acts of violence and aggression at school
2. Assessment of anger should be considered as part of a comprehensive evaluation of both externalizing and internalizing disorders in children
3. Anger is a multidimensional construct with affective, cognitive, and behavioral dimensions
4. Anger, hostility, and aggression constitute separate but related factors
5. Multidimensional assessment of anger can provide specific directions for intervention efforts
6. Comprehensive assessment of anger and related constructs should include not only within child characteristics and behaviors but aspects of the environment as well

assessments are potentially of vital importance in determining the level of threat for violence exhibited by particular students. These instruments are best used as part of a more comprehensive battery designed to assess not only individual and personal factors but situational and contextual variables as well.

REFERENCES

Achenbach, T. M., & Edelbrock, C. (1986). *Manual for the teacher's report form and teacher version of the Child Behavior Profile*. Burlington, VT: T. M. Achenbach.

Achenbach, T. M., & Edelbrock, C. S. (1988). *Manual for the Child Behavior Checklist and Revised Child Behavior Profile*. Burlington, VT: T. M. Achenbach.

American Psychological Association. (1999). *Warning signs: A violence prevention guide for youth*. Available: http://helping.apa.org/warningsigns/index.html

Boman, P., Smith, D. C., & Curtis, D. (2003). Effects of pessimism and explanatory style on development of anger in children. *School Psychology International, 24*, 80–94.

Boman, P., & Yates, G. (2001). Optimism, hostility, and adjustment in the first year of high school. *British Journal of Educational Psychology, 71*, 401–412.

Burney, D. A., & Kromrey, J. (2001). Initial development and score validation of the adolescent anger rating scale. *Educational and Psychological Measurement, 61*, 446–460.

Bushman, B. J., Cooper, H. M., & Lemke, K. M. (1991). Meta-analysis of factor analyses: An illustration using the Buss-Durkee Hostility Inventory. *Personality and Social Psychology Bulletin, 17*, 344–349.

Buss, A. H., & Warren, W. L. (2000). *Aggression Questionnaire: Manual*. Los Angeles: Western Psychological Services.

Connors, C. K. (1990). *Manual for the Connors' Teacher Rating Scales*. North Tonowanda, NY: Multi-Health Systems.

DeBecker, G. (1999). *MOSAIC for the Assessment of Student Threats (MAST)*. Available: http://www.mosaicsystem.com/

Dwyer, K., Osher, D., & Warger, C. (1998). *Early warning, timely response: A guide to safe schools*. Washington, DC: U.S. Department of Education.

Furlong, M. J., Bates, M. P., Smith, D. C., & Kingery, P. (Eds.). (2004). *Appraisal and Prediction of school violence: Issues, methods and contexts*. Hauppauge, NY: Nova Science Publishers.

Furlong, M. J., & Smith, D. C. (1994). Assessment of youth's anger, hostility, and aggression using self-report and rating scales. In M. J. Furlong & D. C. Smith (Eds.), *Anger, hostility, and aggression: Assessment, prevention and intervention strategies for youth* (pp. 167–244). New York: Wiley.

Furlong, M. J., & Smith, D. C. (1998). Raging Rick to tranquil Tom: An empirically based multidimensional anger typology for adolescent males. *Psychology in the Schools, 35*, 229–245.

Furlong, M. J., Smith, D. C., & Bates, M. P. (2002). Further development of the Multidimensional School Anger Inventory: Construct validation, extension to female adolescents, and preliminary norms. *Journal of Psychoeducational Assessment, 20*, 46-65.

Furlong, M. J., Smith, D. C., Boman, P., Gonzalez, M., Grazioso, M. P., & Merino Soto, C. (2004, July). *Multidimensional School Anger Inventory: A cross-national comparison*. Poster presented at the, American Psychological Association, Honolulu, HI.

Julkunen, J., Salonen, R., Kaplan, G. A., Chesney, M. A., & Salonen, J. T. (1994). Hostility and the progression of carotid Artherosclerosis. *Psychosomatic Medicine, 56*, 519–525.

Martin, R., Watson, D., & Wan, C. K. (2000). A three-factor model of trait anger: Dimensions of affect, behavior, and cognition. *Journal of Personality, 68*, 869–897.

McCann, J. T. (2002). *Threats in schools: A practical guide for managing violence*. Binghamton, NY: Haworth Press.

McGee, J., & DeBernardo, C. R. (1999, May/June). The classroom avenger: A behavioral profile of school based shootings. *The Forensic Examiner*, 16–18.

Miller, T. Q., Smith, T. W., Turner, C. W., Guijarro, M. L., & Hallett, A. J. (1996). A meta-analytic review of research on hostility and physical health. *Psychological Bulletin, 19*, 322–348.

Mills, P. J., Schneider, R. H., & Dimsdale, J. E. (1989). Anger assessment and reactivity to stress. *Journal of Psychosomatic Research, 33*, 379–382.

Mohandie, K. (2002). *School violence threat management*. San Diego, CA: Specialized Training Services.

Musante, L., MacDougall, J. M., Dembroski, T. M., & Costa, P. T. (1989). Potential for hostility and dimenstions of anger. *Health psychology, 8*, 343–354.

Novaco, R. (1994). *Novaco Anger Scale*. Los Angeles: Western Psychological Services.

Novaco, R. (2003). *Novaco Anger Scale and Provocation Inventory: manual*. Los Angeles: Western Psychological Services.

O'Toole, M. E. (2000). *The school shooter: A threat assessment perspective.* Quantico, VA: Federal Bureau of Investigation, Critical Response Group, National Center for the Analysis of Violent Crime.

Reddy, M., Borum, R., Berglund, J., Vossekuil, B., Fein, R., & Modzeleski, W. (2001). Evaluating risk for targeted violence in schools: Comparing risk assessment, threat assessment, and other approaches. *Psychology in the Schools, 38,* 157–172.

Siegel, J. M. (1986). The Multidimensional Anger Inventory. *Journal of Personality and Social Psychology, 51,* 191–200.

Smith, D. C., Furlong, M. J., Bates, M., & Laughlin, J. (1998). Development of the Multidimensional School Anger Inventory for males. *Psychology in the Schools, 35,* 1–15.

Smith, T. W. (1994). Concepts and methods in the study of anger, hostility and health. In A. W. Siegman & T. W. Smith (Eds.), *Anger, hostility and the heart* (pp. 23–42). Hillsdale, NJ: Lawrence Erlbaum Associates.

Spielberger, C. D. (1999). *State-Trait Anger Expression Inventory-2 (STAXI-2).* Lutz, FL: Psychological Assessment Resources.

Spielberger, C. D., Reheiser, E. C., & Sydeman, S. J. (1995). Measuring the experience, expression, and control of anger. In H. Kassinove (Ed.), *Anger disorders: Definition, diagnosis, and treatment* (pp. 49–67). Washington, DC: Taylor & Francis.

Tangney, J. P., Hill-Barlow, D., Wagner, P. E., Marschall, D. E., Borenstein, J. K., Sanftner, J., Mohr, T., & Gramzow, R. (1996). Assessing individual differences in constructive versus destructive responses to anger across the lifespan. *Journal of Personality and Social Psychology, 70,* 780–796.

Tangney, J. P., Wagner, P. E., Burggraf, S. A., Gramzow, R., & Fletcher, C. (1990). *The Test of Self-Conscious Affect for Children (TOSCA-C).* Fairfax, VA: George Mason University.

Tangney, J. P., Wagner, P. E., Galvas, J., & Gramzow, R. (1991a). *The Anger Response Inventory for Adolescents (ARI-A).* Fairfax, VA: George Mason University.

Tangney, J. P., Wagner, P. E., Gavlas, J., & Gramzow, R. (1991b). *The Test of Self-Conscious Affect for Adolescents (TOSCA-A).* Fairfax, VA: George Mason University.

Tangney, J. P., Wagner, P. E., Hansbarger, A., & Gramzow, R. (1991). *The Anger Response Inventory for Children (ARI-C).* Fairfax, VA: George Mason University.

Tangney, J. P., Wagner, P. E., Hill-Barlow, D., Marschall, D. E., & Gramzow, R. (1996). Relation of shame and guilt to constructive versus destructive responses to anger across the lifespan. *Journal of Personality and Social Psychology, 70,* 797–809.

Thomas, S. P. (Ed.). (1993). *Women and anger.* New York: Springer.

Thomas, S. P., & Williams, R. (1991). Perceived stress, trait anger, modes of anger expression and health status of college men and women. *Nursing Research, 40,* 303–307.

Verlinden, S., Hersen, M., & Thomas, J. (2000). Risk factors in school shootings. *Clinical Psychology Review, 20,* 3–56.

10

Threat Assessment in Schools: Empirical Support and Comparison With Other Approaches

Marisa Reddy Randazzo
*Business Intelligence
Advisors, Inc.*

Randy Borum
University of South Florida

Bryan Vossekuil
Robert Fein
*National Violence Prevention
and Study Center*

William Modzeleski
U.S. Department of Education

William Pollack
Harvard Medical School

The vast majority of the nation's students will complete their schooling without ever being touched by school shootings. Nevertheless, some high-profile school attacks carried out by students have shaken the image of schools as reliably safe and secure environments (Fein et al., 2002). A recent study released by the Centers for Disease Control and Prevention (2004) notes that between 1991 and 2003 there was a significant increase in the number of students who reported not going to school because they felt too unsafe to attend. Although the U.S. Department of Education (2000) reports that approximately 53 million children attend the nation's 119,000 schools, available statistics indicate that few of these students will fall prey to serious violence in school settings. With respect to school shootings in particular, recent research by the U.S. Secret Service and U.S. Department of Education found that incidents of such school-based attacks, which we refer to as *targeted violence* in school, occurred in only 37 schools across the United States between December 1974 and May 2000 (Vossekuil, Fein, Reddy, Borum, & Modzeleski, 2002). We have conceptualized targeted violence as violent incidents where both the perpetrator and target(s) are identified or identifiable prior to the incident (Borum, Fein, Vossekuil, & Berglund, 1999; Fein & Vossekuil, 1998; Fein, Vossekuil, & Holden, 1995). The defining element of targeted violence is that the perpetrator selects a target prior to engaging in the violent incident. In this chapter, we focus specifically on approaches for preventing targeted violence in school—school shootings and other school-based attacks—rather than on other more common and recurring forms of school violence.

Compared with the other types of violence and crime that children face both in and outside of school, school-based attacks are extremely rare (Fein et al., 2002; Vossekuil et al., 2002). Nevertheless, to incorporate the necessary lessons from past attacks and ensure a safe environment, it is useful to reflect on two central questions: "Could we have known that these attacks were being planned?" and, if so, "What could we have done to prevent these attacks from occurring?" (Brooks, Schiraldi, & Ziedenberg, 2000; Fein et al., 2002; Lawrence, 2000; Sugai, Sprague, Horner, & Walker, 2000). This chapter addresses these questions by reviewing available options for evaluating risk of targeted violence in schools. The following sections examine the three assessment approaches currently advocated and used in some jurisdictions for evaluating risk of targeted violence in schools. These are profiling; mental health assessments; and automated decision making, which includes the use of actuarial formulas and expert systems (see Reddy et al., 2001, for a detailed description of each approach). It is not currently known how many schools use which type of assessment and no data yet exist that describe the prevalence of any of these three approaches (or others) schools may currently use, nor of their effectiveness—perceived or actual. An alternative fact-based threat assessment approach, for identifying, evaluating, and managing threats and other inappropriate behaviors is also described (Borum et al., 1999; Fein & Vossekuil, 1998; Fein et al., 1995). After describing the principles of threat assessment, empirical support is presented for its utility among school administrators, law enforcement professionals, mental health professionals, and others to determine the risk of targeted school violence posed by a student who has engaged in threatening or otherwise concerning behavior.

CURRENT APPROACHES TO TARGETED VIOLENCE ASSESSMENT

Profiling

The term *profiling* carries a number of different meanings, and has been used to characterize a range of identification techniques or assessment strategies used in both law enforcement and non-law enforcement settings (Homant & Kennedy, 1998; Turvey, 1999a). For purposes of this discussion, it is useful to distinguish profiling from criminal investigative analysis (CIA), an investigative technique developed by the FBI's Behavioral Science Unit. CIA uses information gathered from a crime scene to generate a set of hypotheses about the characteristics—physical, demographic, personality, and others—of the person most likely to have committed the crime (Douglas, Ressler, Burgess, & Hartman, 1986; Holmes & Holmes, 1996; Homant & Kennedy, 1998). CIA works retrospectively from a behavior (i.e., the crime and crime scene evidence) backward to infer the type of person who committed the crime.

In the context of school-based threat assessments, the strategy of profiling is prospective. A profile or description of the typical "school shooter" is compiled from characteristics shared by known previous perpetrators (Homant & Kennedy, 1998; McGee & DeBernardo, 1999; Pinizzotto, 1984). This prospective profile is then sometimes used both to identify types of individuals likely to become perpetrators (even absent a behavior or communication that brings someone to official attention) and to assess the degree of risk posed by a given individual who has come to someone's attention for some troubling communication or behavior. The threat is assessed by determining the degree of "fit" or similarity between the characteristics of prior perpetrators and those of the person under consideration. No data exist demonstrating the validity or effectiveness of prospective profiling to identify potential perpetrators for any type of crime (Reddy et al., 2001).

Numerous concerns have arisen over the use of use of demographic or behavioral profiles to identify types of students likely to become school shooters (Cooper, 2000; Morse, 2000; Reddy et al., 2001). First, the use of static profiles for threat assessment will cause errors of overidentifying students who will not engage in targeted violence and underidentifying students who may pose a serious risk. Because targeted violence in school is such a rare event, most youth who "fit" a profile or share some set of common characteristics (e.g., wearing dark clothing or listening to certain kinds of music) will not engage in acts of targeted school violence (Reddy et al., 2001; Sewell & Mendelsohn, 2000). Conversely, the profile may inappropriately exclude students who do not have the designated characteristics, but who may, in fact, pose a risk of targeted violence. For example the profile of a male attending public school would have failed to identify Elizabeth Bush prior to her school shooting at a parochial school in Williamsport, Pennsylvania in 2001. Richard W. Riley, while serving as the U.S. secretary of education, publicly opposed the use of profiling in schools to identify potentially violent students, saying that we "simply cannot put student behaviors into a formula to come up with the appropriate response" (Cooper, 2000, p. A11).

Mental Health Assessment

The second approach used in schools to evaluate the risk of violence posed by a student is to refer them to mental health professionals. Although most mental health professionals are competent and compassionate, many have no formal training in violence risk assessment (Borum, 1996). Even those that do often fail to understand the distinction between assessing risk for general violence and assessing risk for targeted violence, and the implications for threat assessment.

A conscientious mental health practitioner, faced with such a referral from the school, might seek to examine the research literature for information on known risk factors for violence among young people. After determining the base rate for the type of violence in question, among individuals with similar demographic or clinical characteristics, the evaluator would assess whether and which risk factors apply to the instant case and potentially adjust the probability estimate (base rate) accordingly. Although this approach may be reasonable for assessing risk of general aggression, in school as well as in other settings, it has limited value for determining the risk that a student poses for targeted violence in school (Borum, 2000; Borum et al., 1999; Reddy et al., 2001).

It is unclear whether or how aggregate data from research studies on other types of youth-perpetrated violence will generalize to specific targeted violence fact patterns (Borum, 2000). Most of the research on risk factors for youth violence has examined only general violence recidivism as a criterion. Moreover, most of this research has been conducted on criminal offenders and psychiatric patients, populations to which the perpetrators of targeted school violence may not belong (Vossekuil et al., 2002). Moreover, because the incidence of targeted school violence is so small, an evaluation of its risk or probability cannot be driven primarily by the base rate (Sewell & Mendelsohn, 2000; Reddy et al., 2001; Vossekuil et al., 2002). The baseline probability would be so low that it would be nearly impossible—even adding relevant risk factors—ever to approach a threshold of statistical likelihood.

Similarly, standard psychological tests and other instruments traditionally used in guided professional judgments are of questionable utility to school-based targeted violence risk assessments. Many clinical psychological tests are designed primarily to assess mental disorders; yet, initial evidence on the prevalence of mental disorders among perpetrators of targeted violence suggests that few school attackers had any history of mental disorders prior to their attack (Vossekuil et al., 2002). Nor has research demonstrated any useful relationship between the results of standard psychological tests and instruments and the risk of targeted violence in schools (Borum, 2000).

Automated Decision Making

The two final approaches to assessing risk of targeted violence in schools fall under the heading of what we term *automated decision making*. They are actuarial formulas and expert systems and other artificial intelligence/artificial intuition approaches. These are reviewed together because both procedures produce a decision (although one that can be framed in more or less definitive terms), rather than leaving the decision to the person conducting the assessment (Reddy et al., 2001).

Actuarial tools are equations or formulae consisting of risk and/or protective factors that are statistically or mechanically combined (and may or may not be weighted) to yield a decision about the likelihood of a condition or outcome (see, e.g., Dawes, Faust, & Meehl, 1989). Where such actuarial equations can be standardized and validated, they have been shown generally to perform as well or better than human judgments in a range of decision tasks (Borum, 2000; Borum, Otto, & Golding, 1993; Dawes et al., 1989; Grove & Meehl, 1996; Grove, Zald, Lebow, Snitz, & Nelson, 2000). Expert systems and artificial intelligence/intuition are defined here as computer-based or automated applications of expert knowledge on a particular issue to solve a problem or render a decision in an instant case. Through various methods and structures, expertise that has been compiled on a particular topic or issue is represented in a computer program through the use of algorithms or other computer-based rules (see Beaumont, 1991; Fox, 1996). The computer then applies the input of information about the instant case to its programmed rules and arrives at a decision or predicted outcome.

At present, the application of actuarial formulae to questions of school violence is essentially hypothetical. Actuarial equations purported to determine risk of targeted violence, particularly school-based targeted violence, have not been developed. Additionally, the base rate of targeted school violence is likely too low for any statistically derived equation ever to attain any reasonable degree of discriminative accuracy (Sewell & Mendelsohn, 2000). Expert systems and artificial intuition programs that claim to compare the case in question with thousands of known cases (e.g., Morse, 2000; Steinberg, 2000) are not making comparisons only against other cases of targeted school violence, because the incidence of such cases is far lower (see Henry, 2000; Reddy et al., 2001; Vossekuil et al., 2002).

Regarding expert systems, it is unclear that expert consensus on evaluating risk of targeted violence generally, and targeted school violence in particular, has yet been reached, particularly at a level of specificity that would allow the creation of decision rules. This area of research is clearly in its infancy, with the first known empirical study of targeted violence in schools published in 2002 (Vossekuil et al., 2002). Research on the use of expert systems in other contexts has raised concerns regarding the creation of expectations that exceed what expert systems can reasonably accomplish (Winegrad & Flores, 1987). To the extent that existing actuarial formulas and expert systems are not yet informed by empirical research on targeted violence in schools, they may fail to gather information on the student or situation that may be most relevant to appraising risk and thus produce a flawed assessment. Still other research has documented that users of expert systems may rely inappropriately on the decisions produced by a computer (Will, 1991). In one study, users of an expert system (both experts and novices for the task in question) reported considerable satisfaction with what were, in fact, flawed decisions the system produced (only one participant figured out the decision was fundamentally flawed; Will, 1991). By extension, when an expert systems approach is used to determine risk of targeted school violence, there is a risk the user may discount their own knowledge of the situation and student in question and rely primarily, if not solely, on the computer-generated decision instead (Reddy et al., 2001).

THREAT ASSESSMENT APPROACH

The common conceptual element in each of these approaches is that they focus exclusively or nearly exclusively on information about the student, with the assumption that certain traits or characteristics will indicate which students or "type" of students are most likely to engage in targeted violence at the school. In our view, what is needed instead to evaluate the risk of school-based targeted violence is an approach that focuses primarily on the facts of the particular case and on the student's behavior (rather than shared traits) to guide inferences and conclusions; that examines closely the progression of ideas and planning behaviors over time; and that corroborates key information gathered in the case from multiple sources (see Fein et al., 2002).

Based on their empirical research on assassinations and attacks of public officials and public figures, Fein and Vossekuil (1998, 1999) and Fein et al. (1995) developed the threat assessment approach, a framework for identifying, assessing, and managing persons who pose a risk for targeted violence. This fact-based threat assessment approach is guided by certain operational principles and relies on key questions that this research suggests are important to ask when evaluating the risk of targeted violence (Borum et al., 1999; Fein & Vossekuil, 1998, 1999; Fein et al., 1995).

Guiding Principles of the Threat Assessment Approach

Certain guiding principles derived from the research on public official violence underlie the threat assessment approach. First among these is that there is no profile or single "type" of perpetrator of targeted violence. Rather, violence is seen as the product of an interaction among the perpetrator, situation, target, and the setting. Vossekuil, Fein, and their colleagues (Fein et al., 1995; Fein & Vossekuil, 1998, 1999; Vossekuil et al., 2002) found the attackers were quite diverse. This is similar to what has been sought—and found—with juvenile delinquents more generally. As Herbert Quay (1987) noted more than a decade ago:

> The assumption that all delinquents exhibit some common set of psychological characteristics has been the basis for most of the early research into the psychological characteristics of delinquents ... and unfortunately, remains so.... If, in fact, delinquent youth are behaviorally and psychologically heterogeneous, the search for single psychological variables that can reliably separate delinquents from non-delinquents is not an effective research strategy. (p. 118)

We extend this comment by suggesting that it is also not a useful clinical assumption or an effective assessment strategy.

The second key guiding principle underlying the threat assessment approach is that there is a distinction between making a threat (expressing, to the target or others, an intent to harm the target) and posing a threat (engaging in behaviors that further a plan to harm the target). Many people who make threats do not pose a serious risk of harm to a target. Conversely, many who pose a serious risk of harm will not issue direct threats prior to an attack. The first empirical analysis of school-based attacks, the Safe School Initiative, found very few school attackers ever directed threats to their targets in advance of the incident (Vossekuil et al., 2002). The implication derived from these findings is that although all threats (direct, indirect, conditional, or otherwise) should be taken seriously, they are not the most reliable indicator of risk and therefore should not be a necessary condition to initiate an inquiry or preliminary evaluation. Indeed, a youth who is committed to mounting an attack may be less inclined to threaten a potential target directly, particularly if he or she does not want to be stopped. The youth may, however, discuss ideas of harm among friends and peers, as most school shooters did prior to their attacks (Vossekuil et al., 2002).

The third principle underlying the approach is that targeted violence is neither random nor spontaneous; it does not occur because someone "just snapped." Targeted violence, rather, is seen as the result of an understandable, and an often discernible, pattern of thinking and behavior (Borum et al., 1999; Fein & Vossekuil, 1998; Fein et al., 1995; Vossekuil et al., 2002). What this finding suggests is that incidents of targeted violence may be preventable. Conceptually, this principle is very important because assessing risk for events that are considered to be random would seem to be a contradiction. If, however, they are viewed as the result of a behavioral process, then a fact-based assessment makes sense.

Utility of Threat Assessment to Evaluate Risk of Targeted School Violence

The threat assessment approach appears to hold promise for assessing risk of targeted violence in school. Data from the first empirical study of school-based attacks further support it utility (Fein et al., 2002; Vossekuil et al., 2002). In an analysis of 37 incidents of targeted school violence that occurred between December 1974 and May 2000, researchers from the U.S. Secret Service and U.S. Department of Education, collaborating on the Safe School Initiative, found that school-based attacks are rarely impulsive but instead are typically thought out and planned in advance. The researchers further found that prior to most school attacks, other children knew the attack was going to occur. In most cases, these pre-attack planning and communications were observed by others or were potentially detectable. Few attackers, however, ever directed any threats to their targets (Vossekuil et al., 2002).

Empirically validating the concerns about profiling (Fein et al., 2002; Reddy et al., 2001; Vossekuil et al., 2002), the researchers also determined that there was no accurate or useful profile of a school shooter and that one cannot tell simply by looking at a student whether he or she may pose a risk of targeted violence in school (Vossekuil et al., 2002). What the researchers found to be more informative were the behaviors the attackers engaged in prior to their school attack. For example, the researchers found that nearly all of the attackers had engaged in some behavior prior to their attacks that seriously concerned at least one adult in their life—and most attackers engaged in various behaviors that concerned three or more different adults in their life. The attackers were already on someone's "radar screen" prior to their incidents (Vossekuil et al., 2002).

Many attackers felt bullied or persecuted by others prior to the attack and, in a number of cases, had experienced bullying that had gone on for long periods of time and carried out by many fellow students. Strikingly, not only did other students often know of the planned attack, in more than half of the attacks other children encouraged, dared, or assisted the attacker in some manner (e.g., by adding to a target list or showing the attacker how to load a weapon).

What Constitutes Threat Assessment in School?

In general, the threat assessment approach comprises a set of operational activities that combine the use of an investigative process and information-gathering strategies to inform a set of relevant questions, which are used to determine whether the student/situation poses a serious risk of targeted violence (see Borum et al., 1999, for a detailed description of the general threat assessment approach; see also IACP, 1999, p. 67; see Fein et al., 2002, for a detailed description of threat assessment in schools; see Jimerson and Brock, 2004, for a discussion of the importance of threat assessment in preparing for and preventing a school crisis). In essence, these activities are designed to identify, assess, and manage students who pose a risk of violence to an identified, or identifiable, target.

A threat assessment may be initiated by any communication or behavior of concern. Threats are not a necessary threshold for concern; in fact, the threat assessment approach strongly encourages not waiting for a threat before initiating an inquiry when a student has already raised some concern through other behaviors. This does not mean that threats should ever be ignored. If there is a threat, it is important to respond to the threat and launch an inquiry, because some students who threaten may take a lack of response to their threat as tacit permission to proceed with a violent plan.

The process of gathering information about the student includes an investigative emphasis on corroboration of facts to establish their veracity (in contrast with the typical clinical reliance on self-report and subjective perceptions). The focus of the inquiry is on the student's behavior in the instant case, and what the progression of their behaviors may suggest (i.e., movement from development of an idea to implementation of a plan and efforts to acquire a weapon to carry out the attack). The threshold for concern is evidence suggesting that the student may be on a pathway toward violent action. The threshold is deliberately set low enough to facilitate early intervention, as the emphasis of this approach is on prevention and the development of effective case management strategies.

Although much discussion in the violence risk assessment literature has focused on the accuracy of predictions (Borum, 1996; Monahan, 1981; Mossman, 1994; Otto, 1992), we see an important distinction between *predicting* violence and *preventing* it. The central difference lies in the outcome implied by each term. With the frame of "violence prediction" or even "violence risk assessment," the implicit outcome is maximizing the accuracy of the assessor's predictions—to be able to gauge accurately who is more likely to be violent, and the circumstances under which the probability is greatest (Sewell & Mendelsohn, 2000). With a frame of "violence prevention," however, the outcome emphasis shifts from optimizing predictive accuracy to effecting appropriate interventions. By emphasizing prevention as the outcome, the need to provide necessary services takes precedence over the need to be "right" about whether a given child will in fact become violent. More importantly, we would argue that the need to intervene permits school officials and others to consider options that are less punitive (e.g., counseling, establishing a friendship with the child, and finding a mentor) than those available when the emphasis is placed on the child's danger to others.

The threat assessment approach requires the person or team conducting the inquiry to gather information, answer key questions about the instant case, and evaluate the evidence suggesting movement toward violent action. These questions focus on the following:

1. Motivation for the behavior that brought the student being evaluated to official attention.
2. Communication about ideas and intentions.
3. Unusual interest in targeted violence.
4. Evidence of attack-related behaviors and planning.
5. A capacity to carry out an act of targeted violence.
6. Feelings of hopelessness or despair (including suicidal ideation or attempts) or recent losses, real or perceived (including losses of status).
7. A trusting relationship with a responsible adult (a protective factor).
8. A belief that violence is a solution to his or her problems.
9. Consistency between communications and behaviors.
10. Concern by others about the student's potential for harm.
11. Factors in the student's life and/or environment or situation that might increase or decrease the likelihood of attack.

Fein et al. (2002) present a full discussion of key questions for a school threat assessment.

Taken together, the information learned from these questions—as gathered from the student and from corroborating sources (e.g., family members, friends, teachers, classmates, and school and mental health records)—should provide evidence to answer the more global concern of whether the student is moving on a path toward violent action. In addition, the answer to Item 11 can inform the development of a risk management plan by highlighting conditions in the student's life that could be monitored for changes, enhanced to provide the student support, and/or reduced to help the student solve a problem. For example, school officials could decide to take active steps to minimize factors that are considered to put the student at greater risk to make an attack, such as through referral to appropriate services. Alternatively, they could opt instead to monitor the student (perhaps with assistance from family and others close to the student) for changes in conditions that could increase the student's targeted violence risk.

CONCLUSION

When considering how best to prevent (rather than optimally predict) targeted violence in circumstances where a student has come to the attention of the school because of threatening or concerning behavior, traditional trait-based approaches are unlikely to be helpful. The use of profiles is ineffective and inefficient, carries with it a considerable risk of false-positives (most youth who "fit" the profile are not a targeted violence risk), has a potential for bias (by encouraging a search for confirming evidence that the student fits the profile rather than disconfirming evidence that the student does not), and has been sharply criticized for its potential to stigmatize students and deprive them of civil liberties. The use of clinical risk assessments may be inappropriate for assessing risk of targeted violence in school, as many mental health professionals do not have requisite training in risk assessment or understand critical distinctions between assessing risk of general aggression and targeted violence. Finally, because targeted school violence is such an infrequent event, it is not amenable

TABLE 10.1

Implications for Practice: Developing a School Threat Assessment Plan

---

1. Identify one person to conduct threat assessments for the school or, preferably, assemble a multidisciplinary team to do the same. The team should involve representatives from various systems that have contact with the students—including at a minimum members from the school and local law enforcement agency. Others systems can include the mental health community, after-school (and weekend) programs and teams, juvenile justice system, social services, and so on.
2. Establish the *authority* and *capacity* to conduct threat assessments in school. If the team only has members from the school and local law enforcement, it should develop and maintain relationships with other key systems in the community (see Item 1).
3. Establish mechanisms to *identify*, *assess*, and *manage* students who may pose a threat to the school or someone at school. Having relationships with other systems—or having them represented on the team—helps all three threat assessment components. Having relationships can (a) facilitate earlier identification (e.g., when a student is arrested over the weekend, the school may not learn about it); (b) enable more efficient information gathering (e.g., those who coach the student on a weekend sports team may be aware of a tough family situation the student is facing); and (c) assist in finding ways to manage or reduce the risk a student may pose by intervening or monitoring a student. With multiple systems already involved in the assessment process, chances are higher that the team can find an adult whom the student already trusts to initiate efforts to move the student away from thoughts or plans of violence.

Source: Fein et al. (2002).

to statistical prediction by actuarial tools. Nor is it amenable to evaluation by expert systems or artificial intuition programs because expert consensus on this topic has not yet been reached and the validity (i.e., accuracy) of the programs or their decision rules is not yet established.

Based on the limitations of these competing approaches, we suggest that a fact-based approach is needed to investigate and assess the risk for targeted violence in schools. The fact-based threat assessment approach (Borum et al., 1999; Fein & Vossekuil, 1998; Fein et al., 1995, 2002) represents a good first step toward identifying and assessing risk posed by students for targeted violence in schools. Implementing threat assessment procedures in school can address both the actual risk of targeted school violence and fear of such attacks as well. Table 10.1 sets out steps professionals can take to implement a threat assessment plan in school. We suggest further that a threat assessment approach can be most effective when placed in the context of larger efforts to create safe school climates and to reduce bullying within schools (see, e.g., Fein et al., 2002; Pollack, 1998; Pollack & Shuster, 2000). We recommend that schools adopt policies, practices, and procedures that promote a school culture and climate that increase students' connectedness to adults and where differences are respected (Fein et al., 2002). Particularly when used in conjunction with broader efforts to assess a school's climate, address problem areas, reduce bullying, and establish relationships with every student in the school, a threat assessment approach can provide a solid answer to the question of what can be done to prevent school-based attacks from occurring.

REFERENCES

Beaumont, J. G. (1991). Expert systems and the clinical psychologist. In A. Ager (Ed.), *Microcomputers and clinical psychology: Issues, applications and future developments* (pp. 175–193). Chichester, UK: Wiley.

Borum, R. (1996). Improving the clinical practice of violence risk assessment: Technology, guidelines and training. *American Psychologist, 51*, 945–956.

Borum, R. (2000). Assessing violence risk among youth. *Journal of Clinical Psychology, 56*, 1263–1288.

Borum, R., Fein, R., Vossekuil, B., & Berglund, J. (1999). Threat assessment: Defining an approach for evaluating risk of targeted violence. *Behavioral Sciences & the Law, 17*, 323–337.

Borum, R., Otto, R., & Golding, S. (1993). Improving clinical judgement and decision making in forensic evaluation. *Journal of Psychiatry and Law, 21*, 35–76.

Brooks, K., Schiraldi, V., & Ziedenberg, J. (2000). *School house hype: Two years later.* Washington, DC: Justice Policy Institute/Children's Law Center. Available: http://www.cjcj.org/schoolhousehype/shh2.html.

Centers for Disease Control and Prevention. (2004). Violence-related behaviors among high school students—United States, 1991–2003. *Morbidity and Mortality Weekly Report (MMWR), 53*, 651–655.

Cooper, K. J. (2000, April 19). Riley rejects schools' profiling of potentially violent students. *The Washington Post*, p. A11.

Dawes, R., Faust, D., & Meehl, P. (1989). Clinical versus actuarial judgement. *Science, 243*, 1668–1674.

Douglas, J. E., Ressler, R. K., Burgess, A. W., & Hartman, C. R. (1986). Criminal profiling from crime scene analysis. *Behavioral Sciences & the Law, 4*, 401–421.

Fein, R. A., & Vossekuil, B. (1998). *Protective intelligence & threat assessment investigations: A guide for state and local law enforcement officials* (NIJ/OJP/DOJ Publication No. 170612). Washington, DC: U.S. Department of Justice.

Fein, R. A., & Vossekuil, B. V. (1999). Assassination in the United States: An operational study of recent assassins, attackers, and near-lethal approachers. *Journal of Forensic Sciences, 44*, 321–333.

Fein, R. A., Vossekuil, B., & Holden, G. A. (1995, September). Threat assessment: An approach to prevent targeted violence. *National Institute of Justice: Research in Action*, 1–7.

Fein, R. A., Vossekuil, B., Pollack, W. S., Borum, R., Modzeleski, W., & Reddy, M. (2002). *Threat assessment in schools: A guide to managing threatening situations and creating safe school climates.* Washington, DC: U.S. Department of Education, Office of Elementary and Secondary Education, Safe and Drug-Free Schools Program and U.S. Secret Service, National Threat Assessment Center.

Fox, J. (1996). Expert systems and theories of knowledge. In M. A. Boden (Ed.), *Artificial intelligence* (pp. 157–181). San Diego, CA: Academic Press.

Grove, W., & Meehl, P. (1996). Comparative efficiency of informal (subjective, impressionistic) and formal (mechanical, algorithmic) prediction procedures: The clinical-statistical controversy. *Psychology, Public Policy and Law, 2*, 293–323.

Grove, W., Zald, D., Lebow, B., Snitz, B., & Nelson, C. (2000). Clinical versus mechanical prediction: A meta-analysis. *Psychological Assessment, 12*, 19–30.

Henry, T. (2000, April 11). Scared at school: Fear encourages an anti-violence fervor that may be short on facts. *USA Today.*

Holmes, R. M., & Holmes, S. T. (1996). *Profiling violent crimes: An investigative tool* (2nd ed.). Thousand Oaks, CA: Sage.

Homant, R., & Kennedy, D. (1998). Psychological aspects of crime scene profiling: Validity research. *Criminal Justice & Behavior, 25*, 319–343.

International Association of Chiefs of Police. (1999). *Guidelines for preventing and responding to school violence.* Alexandria, VA: Author.

Jimerson, S. & Brock, S. (2004). Threat assessment, school crisis preparation, and crisis response. In M. J. Furlong, M. P. Bates. D. C. Smith, & P. M. Kingery (Eds), *Appraisal and prediction of school violence: Methods, issues, and contexts* (pp. 63–82). Hauppauge, NY: Nova Science.

Lawrence, R. (2000, May/June). School violence, the media, and the ACJS. *ACJS Today, 20*, 1, 4–6. Alexandria, VA: Academy of Criminal Justice Sciences.

McGee, J., & DeBernardo, C. R. (1999, May/June). The classroom avenger: A behavioral profile of school based shootings. *The Forensic Examiner*, 16–18.

Monahan, J. (1981). *The clinical prediction of violent behavior.* Rockville, MD: National Institute of Mental Health.

Morse, J. (2000, April 24). Looking for trouble: More and more schools are trying to spot the potential killers in their midst. But what about the innocents? Time, p. 50.

Mossman, D. (1994). Assessing predictions of violence: Being accurate about accuracy. *Journal of Consulting and Clinical Psychology, 62*, 783–792.

Otto, R. (1992). The prediction of dangerous behavior: A review and analysis of "second generation" research. *Forensic Reports, 5*, 103–133.

Pinizzotto, A. J. (1984). Forensic psychology: Criminal personality profiling. *Journal of Police Science & Administration, 12*, 32–40.

Pollack, W. (1998*). Real boys: Rescuing our sons from the myths of boyhood.* New York: Random House.

Pollack, W., & Shuster, T. (2000). *Real boys' voices.* New York: Random House.

Quay, H. C. (1987). Patterns of delinquent behavior. In H. C. Quay (Ed.), *Handbook of juvenile delinquency* (pp. 118–138). New York: Wiley.

Reddy, M., Borum, R., Vossekuil, B., Fein, R., Berglund, J., & Modzeleski, W. (2001). Evaluating risk for targeted violence in schools: Comparing risk assessment, threat assessment, and other approaches. *Psychology in the Schools, 38*, 157–172.

Sewell, K. W., & Mendelsohn, M. (2000). Profiling potentially violent youth: Statistical and conceptual problems. *Children's Services: Social Policy, Research, and Practice, 3*, 147–169.

Steinberg, L. (2000, April 22). Software can't make school safe. *The New York Times*, p. A13.

Sugai, G., Sprague, J. R., Horner, R., & Walker, H. M. (2000). Preventing school violence: The use of office discipline referrals to assess and monitor school-wide discipline interventions. *Journal of Emotional and Behavioral Disorders, 8*, 94–101.

Turvey, B. E. (1999a). An overview of criminal profiling. In B. Turvey (Ed.), *Criminal profiling* (pp. 1–11). San Diego, CA: Academic Press.

U.S. Department of Education, National Center for Education Statistics. (2000). *Digest of Education Statistics 2000.* Washington, DC: Authors.

Vossekuil, B., Fein, R., Reddy, M., Borum, R., & Modzeleski, W. (2002). *The final report and findings of the Safe School Initiative: Implications for the prevention of school attacks in the United States.* Washington, DC: U.S. Department of Education, Office of Elementary and Secondary Education, Safe and Drug-Free Schools Program and U.S. Secret Service, National Threat Assessment Center.

Will, R. (1991). True and false dependence on technology: Evaluation with an expert system. *Computers in Human Behavior, 7*, 171–183.

Winegrad, T., & Flores, F. (1987). *Understanding computers and cognition.* New York: Addison-Wesley.

11

The SRS Safe Schools Survey:
A Broader Perspective
on School Violence Prevention

Russell Skiba
Ada B. Simmons
Indiana University

Reece Peterson
Susan Forde
University of Nebraska-Lincoln

Self-report school safety surveys, in which students rate their perceptions of violence and their personal sense of safety at school, are among the most important tools in school violence assessment (Furlong & Morrison, 1994, 2000). The direct approach represented by student surveys offers a more practical measure that also affords a measure of anonymity to students (Fitzgerald & Mulford, 1986; Kingery, Coggeshall, & Alford, 1998); yet the use of self-report as a measure of school violence is not without criticism. In addition to general concerns about the accuracy of self-report (Bruce & Desmond, 1997), particular concerns have also been raised about high rates of incomplete or unreliable responding (Cornell & Loper, 1998; Rosenblatt & Furlong, 1997).

An important yet relatively unexplored issue for school safety survey may be *construct validity*; that is, the extent to which the measure fully and accurately captures the domain of school safety and school violence. National surveys of school violence (Chandler, Chapman, Rand, & Taylor, 1998; Kann et al., 2000) tend to focus primarily on more dramatic violence (e.g., fights with weapons, drug usage). Yet, national reports and consensually validated models of school violence prevention suggest that lower intensity, higher frequency events such as minor disruption, bullying, or incivility may be more important in predicting overall school safety (Heaviside, Rowand, Williams, & Farris, 1998; Vossekuil, Fein, Reddy, Borum, & Modzeleski, 2002). Additionally, although it is typically assumed that certain events or behaviors, such as weapons possession, are highly influential in determining whether a school is perceived to be safe, little is actually known about which factors contribute the most to students' perceptions of safety or violence.

Description of current levels of functioning is but one use to which any measurement data can be put. Locally gathered assessment data can also provide information enabling schools to examine their practices reflectively and can act as a baseline for evaluating reform. To date, however, there has been little examination of the extent to which locally gathered school safety data can be useful in motivating or tracking school reform efforts. The Safe and Responsive Schools (SRS) model (Skiba et al., chap. 40, this volume) posits that by assessing both major disruption and minor misbehavior, school teams can develop more comprehensive approaches to school safety and school discipline that better address local needs.

The following describes the development, characteristics, and use of the *SRS Safe Schools Survey,* designed to provide a comprehensive assessment of variables related to school safety and violence prevention. In order to assess the overlap between the measurement of school safety and school climate, we begin by reviewing some existing school safety and school climate surveys.

HISTORICAL USE OF SCHOOL SAFETY AND SCHOOL CLIMATE SURVEYS

School Safety Surveys

Definitions of school violence have broadened considerably in the last decade beyond juvenile justice violation or physical assault (Flannery, 1997; Furlong & Morrison, 2000). Yet, the majority of available school safety surveys (see Table 11.1) maintain a narrow focus on actual or potential criminal violations and occurrences of physical harm. With some exceptions (Cornell & Loper, 1998; Furlong et al., 2005), the most common items and factors across these scales address the frequency and/or severity of school-related serious violence or criminal

TABLE 11.1
Inclusion of Climate Variables on School Safety Surveys

Survey	Factors	Climate Addressed
Youth Risk Behavior Inventory [a] (Kann et al., 2000)	Serious violent incidents, drugs/alcohol/tobacco, weapons, avoidance	No
School Crime Supplement [a] (Chandler et al., 1998)	School characteristics, Serious violent incidents, drugs/alcohol/tobacco, weapons, avoidance, prevention programs/ practices, policies	No
California School Climate and Safety Survey [b] (Furlong et al., 2005)	Climate, school violence, victimization, hostility, social support	Yes
School Safety Survey [a] (Cornell & Loper, 1998)	Aggressive behaviors, high-risk behaviors, weapon carrying, fighting, substance abuse	No
Inviting School Safety Survey [a] (Shoffner & Vacc, 1999)	Valuing influence of teacher and staff feelings of fear and lack of safety, stressors and daily discomforts, positive attitude toward school environment and school community	Yes

[a] Subscales reported are not based on factor analysis.
[b] Subscales reported are based on factor analysis.

TABLE 11.2

Inclusion of Major Safety Issues on School Climate Surveys

Survey	Factors	Items on Major Acts of Violence?
Charles F. Kettering Climate Profile[a] (Fox et al., 1973)	Teachers in the school, school renewal cohesiveness, school involvement–growth, school input, student perceptions	No
Comprehensive Assessment of School Environment [b] (NASSP, 1986)	Teacher–student relationships, security and maintenance, administration, student academic orientation, student behavioral values, guidance, student–peer relationships, parent and community–school relationships, instructional management, student activities	No
School Climate Survey[b] (Haynes Emmons, Ben-Avie, & Comer, 1996)	Fairness, order and discipline, parent involvement, sharing of resources, student interpersonal relations, student–teacher relations, achievement motivation, school building, and general school climate	No
Quality of School Life Survey[b] (Karatzias, Power, & Swanson, 2001)	Curriculum, attainment, teaching methods, teaching style, learning, personal needs, assessment, ethos/school factors, ethos/individual factors, support, career, relationships, environmental/objective and subjective factors	No
Effective School Battery[a] (Gottfredson, 1991)	Safety, respect for students, planning and action, fairness of rules, clarity of rules, and student influence	Yes

[a] Subscales reported are not based on factor analysis.
[b] Subscales reported are based on factor analysis.

violation, including possession and use of weapons, physical assault, substance abuse, rape, and murder; school safety scales typically do not include items assessing the contribution of school climate to student perceptions of school safety. Additionally, few of the school violence surveys currently reported in the literature report using factor analysis or other multivariate procedures to derive subscales.

School Climate Scales

Just as commonly available school safety surveys do not address the construct of school climate, school climate scales do not typically address school violence issues. Table 11.2 presents an analysis of the most commonly used scales in the literature used to assess the construct of school climate (Lehr & Christenson, 2002). Typical factors in these school climate surveys include teacher–student relationships, student–peer relationships, order and discipline, environmental and school building characteristics, parent involvement, support, fairness of rules, and overall student perceptions; with the exception of Gottfredeson (1991), the scales do not include items or dimensions designed specifically to address the presence or absence of violence as part of a school's climate. The use of empirically derived subscales is more common among measures of school climate than among measures of school safety. Of the five commonly used scales in Table 11.2, three reported the results of a factor analysis for identifying the structure of the subscales.

IMPORTANCE OF THE ISSUE

Most current theoretical models of the prediction and prevention of youth violence inherently recognize the importance of day-to-day interactions and school climate in shaping both the perception and reality of school violence or school safety. In the field of school violence prevention, a comprehensive three-tiered prevention model (primary, secondary, and tertiary) is emerging as the most widely accepted framework for understanding school violence and organizing violence prevention efforts (Dwyer, Osher, & Warger, 1998; Furlong & Morrison, 2000; Larson, 1994; Leone, Mayer, Malmgren, & Meisel, 2000; Walker et al., 1996). Emphasizing prevention and early intervention, that model highlights the relationship of school climate and school violence, and the role of day-to-day disruption and feelings of school connection in predicting or preventing disruption and violence.

As knowledge of the predictors of school violence has grown, so too has an understanding of the relationship between day-to-day disruption and serious violence. National reports have found a strong positive relationship between the presence of discipline problems and the presence of crime (Heaviside et al., 1998). The most extensive available analysis of school shooting incidents, completed by the U.S. Secret Service (Vossekuil et al., 2002) found that, in more than two thirds of all school shootings, the perpetrator viewed his act as retribution for bullying and harassment; the report concluded that the shootings may have been the final outcome of a chain of events set in motion by excessive student harassment and incivility.

Given the emerging emphasis in the field of school violence prevention on a comprehensive model, the lack of focus on day-to-day disciplinary disruption or school climate in school safety surveys appears to pose a serious threat to the validity of those measures. Additionally, although school safety surveys have been used to describe current levels of violence and disruption at schools, there has been less attention paid to the possible contribution of such surveys to the reform of current disciplinary or school safety practices.

This chapter reports on the development, technical characteristics, and use of a comprehensive measure of school safety, the SRS Safe Schools Survey, constructed specifically to assess both serious violence and daily disruption/school climate. Description of multivariate analyses conducted using the scale illustrates the importance of an expanded focus in the measurement and school violence and school safety. In addition, we describe the use of the scale by schools as an aid in restructuring school discipline and school safety practices.

DESCRIPTION OF THE SURVEY

Development and Structure of the Survey

The SRS Safe Schools Survey is a self-report scale designed to assess perceptions concerning school safety and school climate. Intended to be representative of a comprehensive model of school safety, the survey drew on previous national surveys of school violence that emphasize serious violence or criminal acts (e.g., Chandler et al., 1998), as well as existing school climate surveys (e.g., Kelly et al., 1986; Swearer & Paulk, 1998). More specific descriptions of the development, administration procedures, and technical adequacy of the measure may be found in Skiba et al. (2004).

Separate versions of the survey were developed for use with parents, school staff, and students (elementary and secondary versions). The secondary student version had 45 items, the teacher/administrator version 65 items, and the parent and elementary student version each had 25 items. Responses were recorded using a Likert-type scale ranging from 1 (*strongly disagree*) to 5 (*strongly Agree*).

A principal components factor analysis of the secondary student version of the *SRS Safe Schools Survey* (Skiba et al., 2004) revealed four underlying factors to the scale (specific items comprising each factor may be found in Table 11.3):

- *Connection/Climate*: This factor contains 19 items describing the degree of connection students feel with the school and their perception of the responsiveness of the school environment.
- *Incivility and Disruption*: This factor consists of seven variables focused on the civility of interpersonal relationships among students as expressed by the frequency of name calling, arguments, and conflicts.
- *Personal Safety*: The third factor consisted of eight items pertaining to feelings of personal safety in a variety of settings. The contribution of seeing a gun at school to this factor suggests that that particular experience impacts feelings of personal safety.
- *Delinquency/Major Safety*: This factor contained six variables reflecting students' awareness of the presence of drugs, alcohol, knives, and smoking on school property.

Together, the four-factor solution accounted for 51.67% of the variance in the variables. Reliability of the scales was high, ranging from .83 (Incivility and Disruption) to .94 (Connection/Climate).

Administration of the Survey

Surveys were administered during the spring semester of three successive school years, (1999, 2000, and 2001) to schools in two midwestern states as part of a comprehensive planning process for school restructuring in those schools (see chap. 40, this volume, for description of the SRS project and participating schools). Students completed either a paper-and-pencil version of the survey, or an online version of the survey in the school computer lab. Staff surveys were distributed through school mailboxes and then mailed directly to the project. Parent surveys were mailed directly to the students' home, and return envelopes were mailed directly to the project.

FINDINGS OF THE SCHOOL SAFETY SURVEY

Descriptive Data

Table 11.3 presents the means for each question on the survey organized by factor. For purposes of consistency of interpretation, items with a negative weighting (e.g., "name calling, insults, or teasing happen regularly at school") have been rescaled in a positive directions. Thus, for all items, lower scores represent a negative perception and positive scores indicate a positive perception. In general, the secondary students responding to the survey felt their schools were safe, with a mean of 3.55 and 58% of students agreeing or strongly agreeing with the statement "Overall, I feel that this school is a safe school." Across the four factors, students tended to rate items connected with their feelings of personal safety most highly. They felt safest coming and going from school (3.88), in the lunchroom (3.87), in their classrooms (3.78), and on school grounds (3.76). In contrast, students were far less satisfied with their schools on items contained in the Incivility and Disruption scale. Items included in this factor—name calling, insults, and teasing (1.74) and frequent arguments among students (1.92)—were among the most negatively rated on the scale.

TABLE 11.3

Mean Ratings on Items on SRS Safe Schools Survey by Factor

Factor and Variable	Mean	SD	N
Connection/Climate *(Cronbach's α = .94)*			
I feel that teachers care about my learning	3.48	1.07	2,446
School rules are clearly defined and explained so that I can understand them	3.44	1.16	2,446
Teachers and staff accept me for who I am	3.43	1.15	2,457
I am getting a good education at this school	3.36	1.06	2,459
I am generally treated fairly at this school	3.35	1.14	2,449
I feel that I belong at this school	3.30	1.18	2,448
Teachers praise students when they have done well	3.28	1.00	2,458
I feel welcome when I am at school	3.27	1.12	2,459
I am learning a lot at this school	3.26	1.11	2,456
I feel that I can talk to a teacher or an administrator if I have a problem	3.25	1.19	2,462
I feel that the teachers care about me as a person	3.15	1.12	2,457
I am proud of this school	3.15	1.19	2,451
Teachers enjoy teaching here	3.13	1.05	2,455
Teachers listen carefully to what I have to say	3.04	1.05	2,455
I feel comfortable telling a teacher or an administrator about potential violence	2.95	1.19	2,458
School rules seem reasonable	2.94	1.21	2,454
Teachers work hard to make every student successful	2.93	1.14	2,454
Students enjoy learning here	2.70	1.09	2,460
Most students are proud of this school	2.60	1.08	2,454
Incivility and Disruption *(Cronbach's α = .83)*			
Physical fighting or conflicts happen regularly at school	2.84[a]	1.08	2,453
Threats by one student against another are common at school	2.47[a]	1.08	2,461
Groups of students cause problems or conflicts at school	2.46[a]	1.11	2,458
Students regularly cheat on tests or assignments	2.38[a]	1.13	2,452
Some students are regularly hassled by other students	2.12[a]	1.01	2,452
Arguments among students are common at school	1.92[a]	0.97	2,444
Name calling, insults, or teasing happen regularly at school	1.74[a]	0.91	2,455
Personal Safety *(α = .89)*			
I feel safe going to and coming from school	3.88	1.02	2,444
I feel safe in the lunchroom	3.87	1.03	2,454
I feel safe in my classrooms	3.78	1.00	2,454
I feel safe before and after school while on school grounds	3.76	1.03	2,457
I feel safe in the school hallways	3.65	1.05	2,454
I feel safe in the bathrooms at school	3.58	1.13	2,459
Overall, I feel that this school is a safe school	3.55	1.07	2,449
I have seen a gun at school this year	4.50[a]	0.94	2,454
Delinquency/Major Safety *(Cronbach's α = .85)*			
I have seen a knife at school (not including a cafeteria knife)	3.18[a]	1.43	2,448
Students use alcohol or drugs at school	3.01[a]	1.28	2,451
Sale of drugs occurs on school grounds	2.95[a]	1.35	2,453
I have seen students with drugs or alcohol at school	2.90[a]	1.45	2,454
Robbery or theft of school property over $10 in value is common	2.79[a]	1.18	2,459
I have seen students smoking at school or on school grounds	2.47[a]	1.49	2,454
Students cut classes or are absent regularly	2.38[a]	1.14	2,451
Students use drugs or alcohol outside of school	1.80[a]	1.10	2,458

[a]Item has been rescaled in the opposite direction by subtracting scores from 5, in order to make all items more comparable. Thus, items with a rating closer to 5 are viewed more positively, whereas items closer to 1 are viewed more negatively. Notice that when these items are rescaled, they no longer assess relative frequency. Thus, the low rescaled rating on "Students use drugs or alcohol outside of school" should be interpreted as student assent that drugs or alcohol *are* widely used outside of school, a negative perception. The high rating for "I have seen a gun at school," scaled in a positive direction, should be interpreted to mean that few students have seen guns at school.

TABLE 11.4
Discrepancies Between Secondary Staff and Student Responses on 2001 School Safety Survey

Item[a]	Teachers	Students	Discrepancy[c]
	Strongly Agree/Agree Responses[b]		
Teachers enjoy teaching here.	72.2%	36.6%	35.6%
Teachers praise students when they have done well.	90.2%	42.9%	47.3%
I am proud of this school.	85.8%	40.2%	45.6%
Teachers work hard to make every student successful.	74.3%	32.8%	41.5%
I feel that I belong at this school.	87.7%	46.6%	41.1%
I am getting a good education at this school. *(Staff: Most students are...)[d]*	87.0%	48.3%	38.7%
I feel teachers care about my learning. *(Staff: Teachers care...)*	91.1%	53.9%	37.2%
Most students are proud of this school.	55.2%	18.5%	36.7%
Students enjoy learning here.	57.6%	21.7%	35.9%
Overall, I feel that this school is a safe school.	91.1%	56.3%	34.8%
I feel safe in the school hallways.	95.6%	61.4%	34.2%
I have seen students with drugs or alcohol at school.	12.3%	42.9%	−30.6%
I am generally treated fairly at this school. *(Staff: Students are...)*	82.3%	52.1%	30.2%
Teachers listen carefully to what I have to say. *(Staff: ...to what students...)*	64.4%	35.0%	29.4%
I feel safe in my classrooms.	92.5%	66.1%	26.4%
Threats by one student against another are common at school.	24.0%	50.3%	−26.3%
I feel safe before and after school while on school grounds.	91.8%	66.2%	25.6%
Arguments among students are common at school.	49.8%	74.7%	−24.9%
Physical fighting or conflicts happen regularly at school.	16.8%	36.6%	−19.8%
I have seen a knife at school (not including a cafeteria knife).	19.1%	38.0%	−18.9%
I have seen students smoking at school or on school grounds.	42.7%	55.6%	−12.9%
Robbery or theft of school property over $10 in value is common.	25.9%	37.6%	−11.7%
Students regularly cheat on tests or assignments.	40.9%	52.7%	−11.8%
Groups of students cause problems or conflicts at school.	62.6%	51.8%	10.8%

[a] Items presented are those on which there was greater than 10% difference between staff and student respondents.
[b] Percentages represent those respondents who indicated "Strongly Agree" or "Agree" on their surveys in response to the item.
[c] Positive values represent higher (more positive) teacher ratings. Negative values represent higher student ratings.
[d] In cases where wording differed on student and teacher versions of the survey, changed staff wording is presented in parentheses following the wording on the student version.

Discrepancies Between Student and Staff Ratings

One of the unexpected findings from the survey was a high degree of discrepancy between student and teacher ratings on the scale. Table 11.4 presents the items on which there was the greatest discrepancy between student and teacher ratings. These fell into two categories. First, students provided substantially lower ratings than teachers on many of the items from the Connection/Climate scale; ratings on a number of items on this scale showed a discrepancy greater than 40%. On none of these items did students rate climate or connectedness higher than teachers. Second, students perceived higher rates of dangerous or disruptive behavior than teachers in such areas as threats, fighting, possession of guns or knives, robbery or theft, and cheating.

What Determines Students' Perceptions of School Safety?

What are the strongest predictors students' perceptions of school safety? The results of two multivariate procedures were analyzed in order to address that question.

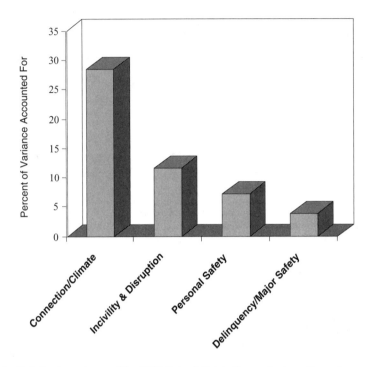

FIG. 11.1.   Relative importance of the SRS School Safety Survey factors. Percentages represent the varience contributed (pesent of varience explained) by each factor to the overall variance of the survey

As noted, a principal component factor analysis identified four factors on the secondary school version of the SRS Safe Schools Survey. The relative contribution of the four factors to the total variance of the survey is represented in Fig. 11.1. The Connection/Climate factor made the strongest contribution to the overall scale, accounting for 28.6% of the variance. Delinquency/Major Safety was the last factor to be extracted and accounted for only 4.1% of the total variance.

The inclusion of multiple dimensions of school violence prevention on the SRS School Safety Survey also allowed us to examine which dimensions or variables are most predictive of students' perceptions of school safety or school violence (Skiba et al., 2004). Thus, items from the Connection, Major Safety, and Incivility scales were entered into a regression equation predicting students' rating of the item "Overall I feel this school is a safe school." All variables in the Personal Safety scale were excluded from this analysis because of their obvious overlap with perceptions of general safety, with the exception of "I have seen a gun at school this year," due to its theoretical importance in perceptions of school safety. Results showed that together and individually, these variables make a strong contribution to student perceptions of school safety. All three of the factors were significant at all steps of the model, and together they accounted for 46.4% of the variance in predicting student overall feelings of safety.

The results also provided additional support for the importance of connectedness as a key factor in school safety planning. Of the three factors, the largest contribution to predicting overall feelings of school safety among the secondary students was Connection/Climate, accounting for 26.6% of the variance in the model. Of the seven strongest predictors, four were from the Connection/Climate scale: *"I am getting a good education at this school," "I am proud of this school," "I am generally treated fairly at this school,"* and *"I feel welcome when I am at school."* Two items came from the Incivility and Disruption scale: "Physical fighting or conflicts happen regularly at school," and "Threats by one student against another are common at school." Although *"I have seen a gun at school"* was among the strongest predictors of overall feelings of school safety, no items from the Delinquency/Major Safety scale were among the strongest predictors. It is important to note that the strongest single predictor of student overall feelings of safety was the item "I feel welcome when I am at school."

APPLICATIONS OF THE SRS SAFE SCHOOLS SURVEY

Results across various analyses supported the primary assumption of the Safe Schools Survey that inclusion of both high-intensity serious disruption and lower level minor disruption and climate issues is necessary in order to accurately assess school safety. This shift in perspective also had implications for the use of the scale among a group of schools participating in an effort to restructure their school discipline and violence prevention efforts. This section describes the use of the SRS Safe Schools Survey as a tool in a process of school reform and restructuring.

Once the surveys were completed, results for each school for all groups (elementary students, secondary students, staff, and parents) were analyzed by means of a spreadsheet program. These results were returned to the schoolwide planning team charged with needs assessment and development of a safe schools plan. Teams were guided to interpret the results through four questions:

1. What are important themes that emerged across the surveys?
2. What discrepancies emerged among the responses of students, staff, and parents?
3. What were the most highly rated items and areas indicating current strengths in our school safety planning?
4. What were the lowest rated areas that may indicate areas to target in school safety planning?

The teams then used this information, plus needs assessment data from other sources, to develop a comprehensive school safety plan to address local concerns. The only stipulation of the plan was that it include one component each of a primary prevention model: Creating a Positive Climate, Early Idenification and Assessment, and Effective Responses.

Case Study: River Valley Middle School

In the following sections, the experience of one middle school (named River Valley Middle School for purposes of this chapter) in using the results of the Safe Schools Survey for planning and reform efforts is described.

School Description

River Valley is a middle school in rural Indiana. In the second year of participation in the project, the elementary/middle school configuration in the district changed. Thus, in the first year of the project, the school served 727 students in Grades 6–8, whereas in Year 2, it served 487 students in Grades 7–8. The school is almost entirely White (99.6%) and 13.9% of families in the district live below the poverty line.

Safe Schools Survey Results

Results at River Valley Middle School were in some ways representative of the survey results at the majority of participating schools. The most highly rated items for both students and staff were in the area of Personal Safety, whereas the most negative perceptions were in the area of Incivility and Disruption. More than 75% of students and more than 80% of teachers agreed or strongly agreed that name calling, insults, or teasing happen regularly at school; there was a similar high rate of agreement that some students are regularly hassled by other students. Team members felt the survey results indicated an unacceptably high level of drug use at the school. Unlike some other schools, there was a high rate of disagreement between students and faculty regarding Personal Safety: whereas 92.5% of staff agreed or strongly that the school was safe overall, only 37.8% of students agreed or strongly agreed. This discrepancy may have been due in part to high rates of discrepancy between staff and students on items in the Connection/Climate scale. Although 70.7% of staff agreed that students enjoyed learning at the school, only 20.5% of students agreed or strongly agreed. Similar disagreements were in evidence for a number of other items from this scale, including "I feel that I belong at this school" (staff: 92.7% agreement; students: 38.6% agreement), and "Teachers praise students when they have done well" (staff: 90% agreement; students: 42.6% agreement).

Using the Survey Information for School Safety Planning

Based on these results and other needs assessment planning, the SRS team at River Valley Middle School concluded that the rate of verbal abuse and incivility at the school was unacceptable, and that the school did not have a good system of taking care of such incidents.

The plan as developed by the team included three components. To address issues of school climate, the team decided to focus on issues of parent involvement. The first step to be taken in that regard was the development of a detailed monthly newsletter to parents. For issues of early identification and intervention, the team decided to implement the Second Step Violence Prevention Curriculum (Grossman et al., 1997) to address issues of verbal harassment, incivility and drug awareness. Finally, to address concerns about safety at the school, the school planned to re-institute and reform an in-school suspension program that had lapsed.

Staff Reactions to the Survey

Surveys and focus group data were collected at participating schools to determine the treatment acceptability of the SRS Safe Schools Survey. As part of a broader survey of the treatment acceptability of the SRS process, team members were asked to rate the usefulness of the survey for their planning efforts; the mean rating across participating schools was 4.2 on a 5-point scale. Focus group interviews also showed a good level of satisfaction with the survey. The most common responses among teachers after the first year of the project was that the survey was "helpful," "informative," and provided "concrete information." As one teacher said, "The survey was very scientific. I liked looking at the school through staff, parent, and student eyes."

Other teachers and administrators noted that the survey was "a real eye-opener" about areas that the school staff had not previously considered:

> I think the surveys have helped us a lot. They've opened up discussion on some concerns in our school. It made some people realize that there are some things going on. I think some of those issues have been addressed and I think we have a good plan going into first-day [of the school year] activities to try to make the kids feel better about the school and have a more positive environment.

Finally, a number of team members noted that the discrepancies between student and staff ratings of school safety and school climate proved valuable in developing their school safety plan:

> The survey was very informative. We were kind of surprised by some of the results we got, especially with regards to belongingness and a caring environment. We had the idea that we are providing that, but we found the kids saying that we're not.

LIMITATIONS OF THE STUDY

The most important limitation of this study is the limited demographics of the original sample. Although the sample was representative of the school context in which the study was situated, it was not racially diverse, and represented only suburban and rural, not urban, locales. Thus, the descriptive results for students and staff form the survey cannot be assumed to generalize to urban settings. Whether the relationships described in the multivariate analyses hold in more diverse urban school settings remains to be tested. Further analyses of the SRS Safe Schools Survey in urban schools with moderate to high minority representation will test the generalizability of the reported factor structure and prediction coefficients.

CONCLUSIONS

The field of school violence prevention has been characterized by a progressive broadening of focus, from models based in criminal justice that place a primary emphasis on criminal violation and physical assault, to more comprehensive school-based models (Furlong & Morrison, 1994; Leone et al., 2000; Peterson, Larson, & Skiba, 2002). However, the majority of published surveys of school violence, in particular the most widely reported of those surveys—the School Crime Supplement (Chandler et al., 1998) and the Youth Risk Behavior Surveillance (Kann et al., 2000) have tended to maintain a narrow focus on juvenile delinquency and physical acts of violence. The SRS Safe Schools Survey was designed as an alternative, including a broader range of variables representing more current models of school safety and school violence prevention. Multivariate analyses of the survey results provided a test of the construct validity of the measure, while implementation of the measure as part of a school restructuring process provided an examination of the extent to which the scale could provide useable and practical information for practitioners.

Quantitative analyses provided strong and consistent evidence that students' perceptions of school violence and school safety are determined by a broader range of factors than have been traditionally assessed. Factor analysis of the items yielded four strong factors—Connection/Climate, Incivility and Disruption, Personal Safety, and Delinquency/Major Safety. All four factors contributed significantly to the overall factor analysis, suggesting that student perceptions of school safety are multiply determined by a variety of variables ranging from incivility and name calling to climate issues to weapons infractions.

In fact, these data suggest that day-to-day disruption and issues of climate and connection make a stronger contribution to overall feelings of safety than criminal violations or serious physical violence. The Connection/Climate scale provided the most important information both in the overall structure of perceptions of school violence, and in predicting overall feelings of safety. The Delinquency/Major Safety scale proved least predictive in both sets of analyses. Indeed, the item making the single most important contribution to the prediction of overall feelings of safety was "I feel welcome at this school." In the field of criminology, school connection or alienation has emerged as among the most important variables in predicting juvenile delinquency (Hawkins, Farrington, & Catalano, 1998). These results suggest that connectedness is also among the most important predictors of school safety.

The expanded focus provided by the survey also provided increased information to school teams seeking to reform practices in the areas of school discipline and school violence prevention. School teams charged with developing school safety plans found that the survey enabled them to address a broad range of issues that could threaten the safety of their schools. National studies of deadly school violence have led to an emerging understanding of the way in which school climate issues such as bullying can serve as a predictor or precursor to more serious violence (Vossekuil et al., 2002). For schools using the SRS Safe Schools Survey, substantial

TABLE 11.5

Implications for Practice: What Educational Professionals Should Do to Adequately Assess
School Safety

---

1. Be aware of a broad range of professional opinion supporting comprehensive primary prevention models as a guide to school discipline and violence prevention efforts.
2. Be aware of and evaluate the technical adequacy of all measures used to assess school safety at the local level.
3. Examine the technical characteristics of the measurement of school safety presented in national reports on school violence and school violence prevention to assure that the data support the conclusions of the report, and that those conclusions are generalizable to the local level.
4. Examine the scale being used to measure school safety or school violence to determine whether it includes items relating to serious disruption/criminal violation, as well as to issues of day-to-day disruption or belongingness that may make a *greater* contribution to overall perceptions of school safety.
5. Insist that all efforts to address school discipline and school violence concerns, whether zero tolerance, bullying prevention, or positive behavior supports, are evaluated by sound data that can enable school personnel to judge whether those interventions are working.

---

discrepancies between student and staff ratings in the areas of climate and connection motivated the teams to address climate and connection issues. This broadened perspective would of course not have been possible without an assessment tool that provided information about both serious and day-to-day disruption.

Implications for Practitioners

Table 11.5 presents implications for practice and suggests a number of questions practitioners can ask in choosing a scale to measure school safety. Does the scale contain a broad enough range of items in order to adequately represent current best thinking on school violence stressing a comprehensive three-tiered model of prevention? Does the survey control for potential errors or purposeful inaccuracy on the part of some students (Cornell & Loper, 1998)? What is the reliability and validity of the scale, and if there are separate scale scores, were these empirically derived from factor analysis? Are the characteristics of the sample on which the scale was developed similar enough to our local situation to be generalizable to our school or our district? Finally, is the survey sufficiently broad, including attention to all relevant dimensions of school safety, to be able to accurately capture the full complexity of student perceptions of school safety and school violence?

The emergence of the field of school violence from fields (e.g., criminal justice) outside of education may have weighted the study of school violence toward an emphasis on criminal violation and physical assault (Furlong & Morrison, 1994). As the field has grown, however, more sophisticated data and more comprehensive models have converged on a broader perspective and an increased awareness of the centrality of school climate and day-to-day disruption. The current results suggest that serious violent incidents may be, in fact, less important contributors to perceptions of school safety than perceptions of student connectedness and climate in some school environments. If school practitioners are to have information necessary to respond to current thinking in school violence that stresses a broader perspective, school violence assessment must move beyond a focus on "guns, gangs, and drugs" to include all variables that may pose a potential threat to school safety.

ACKNOWLEDGMENTS

This chapter and the products it describes were developed with support from grant H325N990009 from the Office of Special Education Programs, U.S. Department of Education.

We wish to acknowledge the assistance of Janet McKelvey, Sarah Gallini, Kimberly Boone, Angela Fontanini, and Becky Perez, graduate research assistants at the Indiana University Center for Evaluation and Education Policy, and Courtney Miller at the University of Nebraska for their assistance in data collection and analysis. We are most grateful to Cyndi Skoog, Forest Hills Special Education Cooperative, for her assistance in school district coordination.

REFERENCES

Bruce, A. S., & Desmond, S. A. (1997). Limitations of self-report delinquency surveys: A "hands-on" approach. *Teaching Sociology, 25*, 315–321.

Chandler, K. A., Chapman, C. D., Rand, M. R., & Taylor, B. M. (1998). *Students' reports of school crime: 1989 and 1995* (NCJRS Document Reproduction Service No. 169607). Washington, DC: Bureau of Justice Statistics, U.S. Department of Justice and National Center for Education Statistics, U.S. Department of Education.

Cornell, D. G., & Loper, A. B. (1998). Assessment of violence and other high-risk behaviors with a school survey. *School Psychology Review, 27*, 317–330.

Dwyer, K., Osher, D., & Warger, C. (1998). *Early warning, Timely response: A guide to safe schools.* Washington, DC: U.S. Department of Education.

Fitzgerald, J. L., & Mulford, H. A. (1986). Self-report validity issues. *Journal of Studies on Alcohol, 48*, 207–211.

Flannery, D. J. (1997). *School violence: Risk preventive intervention and policy* (Urban Diversity Series, No. 109). New York: ERIC Clearinghouse on Urban Education. (ERIC Document Reproduction Service No. ED 416 272)

Fox, R. S., Boies, H. E., Brainard, E., Feltcher, E., Huge, J. S., Martin, C. L., Maynard, W., Monasmith, J., Olivero, J., Schmuck, R., Shaheen, T. A., & Stegeman, W. H. (1973). *School climate improvement: A challenge to the school administrator.* Bloomington, IN: Phi Delta Kappa Educational Foundation.

Furlong, M. J., Greif, J. L., Bates, M. P., Whipple, A. D., Jimenez, T. C., & Morrison, R. (2005). Development of the California School Climate and Safety Survey—Short Form. *Psychology in the Schools, 42*, 137–149.

Furlong, M. J., Chung, A., Bates, M., & Morrison, R. L. (1995). Who are the victims of school violence? *Education and Treatment Children, 18*, 1–17.

Furlong, M., & Morrison, G. (1994). Introduction to the miniseries: School violence and safety in perspective. *School Psychology Review, 23*, 139–150.

Furlong, M., & Morrison, G. (2000). The school in school violence: Definitions and facts. *Journal of Emotional & Behavioral Disorders, 8*(2), 71–87.

Gottfredson, G. D. (1991). *The Effective School Battery.* Odessa, FL: Psychological Assessment Resources.

Grossman, D. C., Neckerman, H. J., Koepsell, T. D., Liu, P-Y., Asher, K. N., Beland, K., Frey, K., & Rivera, F. P. (1997). Effectiveness of a violence prevention curriculum among children in elementary school. *Journal of the American Medical Association, 277*, 1605–1611.

Hawkins, J. D., Farrington, D. P., & Catalano, R. F. (1998). Reducing violence through the schools. In D. S. Elliott, B. A. Hamburg, & K. R. Williams (Eds.), *Violence in American schools* (pp. 188–216). New York: Cambridge University Press.

Haynes, N. M., Emmons, C. L., Ben-Avie, M., & Comer, J. P. (1996). *The school development program: Student, staff and parent school climate surveys.* New Haven, CT: Yale Child Study Center.

Heaviside, S., Rowand, C., Williams, C., & Farris, E. (1998). *Violence and discipline problems in U.S. Public Schools: 1996–97,* (NCES 98-030). Washington, DC: U.S. Department of Education, National Center for Education Statistics.

Kann, L., Kinchen, S. A., Williams, B. I., Ross, J. G., Lowry, R., Hill, C. V., Grunbaum, J. A., & Kolge, L. J. (2000). Youth risk behavior surveillance—United States, 1999. *Morbidity and Mortality Weekly Report, 49*(SS-5), 1–94.

Karatzias, A., Power, K. G., & Swanson, V. (2001). Quality of school life: Development and preliminary standardization of an instrument based on performance indicators in Scottish secondary schools. *School Effectiveness and School Improvement, 12*(3), 265–284.

Kelly, E. A., Glover, J. A., Keefe, J. W., Halderson, C., Sorenson, C., & Speth, C. (1986). *School Climate Survey (Form A).* Reston, VA: National Association of Secondary School Principals.

Kingery, P. M., Coggeshall, M. B., & Alford, A. A. (1998). Violence at school: Recent evidence from four national surveys. *Psychology in the Schools, 35*, 247–258.

Larson, J. D. (1994). Violence prevention in the schools: A review of selected programs and procedures. *School Psychology Review, 23*, 151–164.

Lehr, C., & Christenson, S. (2002). Best practices in promoting a positive school climate. In A. Thomas & J. Grimes (Eds.), *Best practices in school psychology* (Vol. 4, pp. 929–947). Bethesda, MD: The National Association of School Psychologists.

Leone, P. E., Mayer, M. J., Malmgren, K., & Meisel, S. M. (2000). School violence and disruption: Rhetoric, reality, and reasonable balance. *Focus on Exceptional Children, 33*(1), 1–20.

National Association of Secondary School Principals (NASSP). (1986). *School Climate Survey.* Reston, VA: Author.

Peterson, R. L., Larson, J., & Skiba, R. (2002) School violence prevention. Current status and policy recommendations. *Law and Policy, 23*, 345–371.

Rosenblatt, J. A., & Furlong, M. J. (1997). Assessing the reliability and validity of student self-reports of campus violence. *Journal of Youth and Adolescence, 26*, 187–202.

Shoffner, M. F., & Vacc, N. A. (1999). Psychometric analysis of the Inviting School Safety Survey. *Measurement and Evaluation in Counseling and Development, 32*, 66–74.

Skiba, R., & Peterson, R. (2003). Teaching the social curriculum: School discipline as instruction. *Preventing School Failure, 47*(2), 66–73.

Skiba, R., Simmons, A. B., Peterson, R., McKelvey, J., Forde, S., & Gallini, S. (2004). Beyond guns, drugs and gangs: The structure of student perceptions of school safety. *Journal of School Violence, 3*, 149–171.

Swearer, S. M., & Paulk, D. L. (1998). *The Bully Survey.* Lincoln, NE: Author.

U.S. Department of Education. (1998). *Principal/disciplinarian survey on school violence, Fast Response Survey System.* Washington, DC: Author.

U.S. Department of Justice, Bureau of Justice Statistics. (1995). *National Crime Victimization Survey: 1995 school crime supplement.* Ann Arbor, MI: Interuniversity Consortium for Political and Social Research (ICPSR).

Vossekuil, B., Fein, R., Reddy, M., Borum, R., & Modzeleski, W. (2002). *The final report and findings of the Safe School Initiative: Implications for the prevention of school attacks in the United States.* Washington, DC: U.S. Department of Education and U.S. Secret Service, National Threat Assessment Center.

Walker, H. M., Horner, R. H., Sugai, G., Bullis, M., Sprague, J. R., Bricker, D., & Kaufman, M. J. (1996). Integrated approaches to preventing antisocial behavior patterns among school-age children and youth. *Journal of Emotional and Behavioral Disorders, 4*, 194–209.

12

The Current State of Methodological Knowledge and Emerging Practice in Evidence-Based Evaluation: Applications to School Violence Prevention Research

Matthew J. Mayer
Michigan State University

Researchers and practitioners in fields such as school psychology, special education, social work, and juvenile justice are continually working on issues of service provision to youth clients who are or will be involved in school violence prevention and intervention programs from one or more of these allied disciplines. Many of these professionals incorporate each other's disciplines to some degree, and tools that they use for evidence-based evaluation of prevention and intervention programs vary. In turn, studies of the effectiveness of school violence prevention and safe schools programming may be subject to somewhat differing standards for evidence-based research, depending on the orientation of the investigators.

In concert with the mandates of the Government Performance and Results Act of 1993 (GRPA) and the No Child Left Behind Act (2001), standards for evaluating effective prevention and intervention have received much attention across multiple disciplines in recent years (Centers for Disease Control, 1999; Kratochwill & Stoiber, 2002; Schinke, Brounstein, & Gardner, 2002; Valentine & Cooper, 2004). This is evidenced by the recently increased level of discussion of evidence-based interventions in professional journals and texts (Chambless & Hollon, 1998; Chorpita, 2003; Clingempeel & Henggeler, 2002; Weisz & Hawley, 1998).

This chapter focuses on developments during the last 10 years across these disciplines with respect to evidence-based interventions and professional practice. This chapter aims to (a) provide an overview of recent developments (theoretical and applied) in evidence-based intervention evaluation and practice across the disciplines of education, mental health, juvenile justice, and social work; (b) highlight key issue areas among current approaches across these disciplines; (c) connect the discussion of these developments on prevention and intervention programming for school violence and school safety issues, discussing implications for that research and resultant real-world practices; and (d) highlight critical issues requiring further study and attention with regard to evidence-based research on school violence prevention.

171

The first section provides a synopsis of recent evidence-based developments in education, special education, school and clinical psychology, public health, social work, and juvenile justice, from a discipline-specific point of view, as well as an overview of two key evidence-based organizations—the Cochrane and Campbell Collaborations. Although some of the developments discussed are unique to the respective disciplines, it is important to note the crossover involvement and cross-influences for many of these fields. For example, public health research on violence prevention has often involved researchers and practitioners in allied professions such as psychology, juvenile justice, education, and social work. The second section of the chapter discusses several critical issue areas for evidence-based research that cut across these disciplines, including efficacy/effectiveness research (including transportability and dissemination issues); use of meta-analysis, developmental levels of child and adolescent clients, manualized treatments; and, relating to dissemination of research results subject to these evolving review standards, editors' space constraints for research manuscripts. Implications for research in school violence prevention are discussed for each of these issues. The final section discusses overall implications for current and future research and practice.

RECENT EVIDENCE-BASED DEVELOPMENTS
IN MULTIPLE DISCIPLINES

Education

The No Child Left Behind Act (2001), using the terminology, *scientifically based research*, signaled a significant shift in educational intervention research, placing an increased emphasis on more rigorous methodology. This emphasis has been recently reinforced with requirements for evidence of intervention effectiveness among most federally funded K–12 intervention research programs. Several important developments since 1999 have fed into this stream of change. In 1999, the National Research Council (NRC) formed the Center for Education, with the purpose of improving their education research efforts. The NRC concurrently launched the Strategic Education Research Partnership, whose focus was infrastructure and capacity development to better bridge educational research and practice (NRC, 2002). An outgrowth of these changes was the NRC book, *Scientific Research in Education* (2002), an important influence in current education research thinking. At about the same time, the 1998 Congressional Comprehensive School Reform appropriation of $150 million included a requirement to use "proven, comprehensive reform models." This is credited by Slavin (2002) as the first federal education research effort explicitly requiring effectiveness research as part of funding.

During the same period, following enactment of the No Child Left Behind Law, the Department of Education reorganized its research branch, creating the Institute for Educational Sciences (IES), influenced in part by prior work by the American Institutes for Research, and the work and report by the Coalition for Evidence-Based Policy. Presentations by IES Director Grover Whitehurst began to emphasize a new approach to educational research, with a strong commitment to randomized controlled trials. The IES created the What Works ClearingHouse (WWC), a joint federally funded venture, contracted to American Institutes for Research and the Campbell Collaboration. The purpose of the WWC is to develop and implement standards for evaluating educational research and disseminate evidence on educational interventions. The WWC will produce three types of reports: (a) study reports that address individual intervention research projects; (b) intervention reports that evaluate bodies of evidence on particular interventions; and (c) topic reports that provide a summary of knowledge on interventions aligned with a particular topical area. As part of its initial efforts, the WWC launched a task force to develop instrumentation to aid in the assessment of published research, resulting in the Study Design and Implementation Assessment Device (Study DIAD). The Study DIAD work formed the foundation for the WWC Study Review Standards.

These standards articulate a three-stage process of (a) screening studies for relevance and eligibility for review; (b) determining that the reviewed study (i) "meets evidence standards," (ii) "meets evidence standards with reservations," or (iii) "does not meet evidence standards"; and (c) further review as outlined below. The review process is based on providing strong evidence of causal validity. The causal validity standards (WWC Study Review Standards, 2003) state the following:

> Studies that "Meet Evidence Standards" are randomized trials that did not have problems with randomization, attrition, or disruption, and regression discontinuity designs without attrition or disruption problems. Studies that "Meet Evidence Standards with Reservations" are quasi-experiments with equivalent groups and no attrition or disruption problems, as well as randomized trials with randomization, attrition, or disruption problems and regression discontinuity designs with attrition or disruption problems. (p. 5)

For studies meeting the criteria for demonstrating causal evidence, the standards, third stage, further addresses: (a) intervention fidelity; (b) outcome measures; (c) the extent to which relevant people, settings, and timings are included in the study; (d) the extent to which the study allowed testing of the intervention's effect within subgroups; (e) statistical analysis; and (f) statistical reporting. As of mid-2005, the WWC moved to include single subject research designs in its list of methodologies that can meet evidence standards. The WWC is developing the Cumulative Research Assessment Device (CREAD), a tool to assess larger bodies of research that accrue over time, and is also crafting a set of standards for reviewing test instruments.

There are emerging indications that future federal funding of educational research will require significant adherence to more rigorous standards. For example, on January 25, 2005, the Department of Education posted a formal notice in the Federal Register (Scientifically based evaluation methods; Notice, 2005), announcing that effective February 24, 2005, research funding proposals that meet department standards for scientifically based evaluation methods will receive preferential priority in funding awards. This notice was a refinement of a prior proposed notice from 2003. The notice included the statement: "proposed evaluation strategies that use neither experimental designs with random assignment nor quasiexperimental designs using a matched comparison group nor regression discontinuity designs will not be considered responsive to the priority when sufficient numbers of participants are available to support these designs" (p. 3586).

Special Education

A significant proportion of students requiring academic, social, emotional, and behavioral interventions—including violence prevention efforts—are served by special education. The Council for Exceptional Children Division of Research (CEC-DR) created a task force in early 2003 to (a) identify and establish quality indicators for specific research methodologies appropriate for rigorous scientific investigation in special education and (b) determine how research results from each methodology could inform effective practice. Toward that end, the task force identified four types of research for which quality indicators would be developed: experimental group, correlational, single subject, and qualitative (Odom et al., 2005). Odom and colleagues noted some challenges facing researchers in special education: (a) heterogeneity of special education students can make equivalent group designs problematic; (b) some disabilities are very low incidence, making subject availability for large group designs impossible; (c) federal disability law may preclude the use of no-treatment groups that might deny legally mandated entitlements to students; and (d) the widely used grouping practices within special education may prevent investigators from using individuals as the unit of analysis.

Due to space limitations, this discussion is limited to CEC-DR task force work on quality indicators for experimental and quasi-experimental design (Gersten et al., 2005). The task force crafted two sets of quality indicators: "essential quality indicators" and "desirable quality indicators." These two sets of indicators are proposed for selecting "high-" and "acceptable-" quality research publications. High-quality research must meet all but one of the 10 essential indicators and at least 4 of the 8 desirable indicators. Acceptable research must meet all but one of the essential indicators and at least one of the desirable indicators. The essential quality indicators require detailed information on participant description, comparable group design, intervention implementers, intervention details, fidelity of implementation, comparison condition services, multiple appropriate measures, timing of outcome measurement, appropriate data-analysis techniques, and effect size calculations. The desirable quality indicators addressed attrition data, reliability and validity measures, follow-up measurements, qualitative aspects of fidelity of implementation, documentation on comparison conditions, audio/video documentation of intervention, and appropriate and clear presentation of results. The work of the CEC-DR task force will continue as these standards are further defined.

Clinical and School Psychology

The psychology community, particularly researchers in school and child clinical psychology, has been at the forefront of developments in the evidence-based intervention movement. The American Psychological Association (APA) Division 12 (clinical) Taskforce on Promotion and Dissemination of Psychological Procedures articulated standards for "well-established," "probably efficacious," and "experimental" treatments (Hoagwood & Johnson, 2002; Lonigan, Elbert, & Johnson, 1998; Ollendick & King, 2004; see Table 12.1).

TABLE 12.1
Criteria for Empirically Validated Treatments

I. Well-established treatments
  A. At least two good between-group design experiments demonstrating efficacy in one or more of the following ways:
    1. Superior to pill or psychological placebo or to another treatment
    2. Equivalent to an already established treatment in experiments with adequate statistical power (about 30 per group)
or
  B. A large series of single case design experiments ($n > 9$) demonstrating efficacy. These experiments must have:
    1. Used good experimental designs, and
    2. Compared the intervention to another treatment as in A.1.

Further criteria for both A and B:
  C. Experiments must be conducted with treatment manuals.
  D. Characteristics of the client samples must be clearly specified.
  E. Effects must have been demonstrated by at least two different investigators or investigatory teams.

II. Probably efficacious treatments
  A. Two experiments showing the treatment is more effective than a waiting-list control group
or
  B. One or more experiments meeting the well-established treatment criteria A, C, D, but not E
or
  C. A small series of single case design experiments ($n > 3$) otherwise meeting well-established treatment criteria B, C, and D.

Note: From Barrett and Ollendick (2004). Copyright © 2004 by John Wiley & Sons. Reprinted with permission.

The APA Taskforce had previously introduced the term, *empirically validated*, which was contentious, especially because it could imply that the question of effectiveness was finalized (Chorpita, 2003; Ollendick & King, 2004). Both the well-established and probably efficacious criteria required at least two experimental demonstrations of effect, but the well-established criterion required superior effect compared to a placebo or alternate treatment, where the probably efficacious criterion required the effect to be superior to a wait-list control group. The well-established criterion also had stricter requirements for a well-designed study. Both standards required an intervention treatment manual and sample characteristic information. Additional criteria were identified for single-case designs, with stricter standards for the well-established criterion. So-called experimental treatments were those not meeting the probably efficacious standard.

The Division 12 Taskforce report was oriented mainly to questions of "efficacy" as opposed to "effectiveness" (Chambless & Hollon, 1998). Efficacy addresses whether the experimental treatment works, usually tested under well-controlled laboratory-like conditions. Effectiveness studies test whether and how well treatments work under more real-world conditions where the treatments are typically provided (Lonigan et al., 1998). Efficacy studies are indicative of internal validity, as evidenced in randomized clinical trials. Several researchers have spoken to the substantive differences between research-based, and real-world clinical experiments and implications for developing a knowledge base on effective interventions, demonstrating external validity (Chorpita, 2003; Ollendick & King, 2004; Schoenwald & Hoagwood, 2001; Weisz & Hawley, 1998).

Building on work by the Division 12 Taskforce in the early- to mid-1990s, as well as input from APA Division 17 (Counseling Psychology), the APA Division 16 (School Psychology) Taskforce developed the *Procedural and Coding Manual for Review of Evidence-Based Interventions*. There were concerns regarding the Division 12 criteria that led to an independent criteria development effort by Division 16 (Kratochwill & Stoiber, 2002). These concerns included overreliance on randomized clinical trials, *Diagnostic and Statistical Manual* (DSM) diagnostic categories, and manualized treatments, as well as insufficient attention to comorbidity issues.

The Division 16 approach addressed four types of research: group designs, single-subject, qualitative, and program evaluation. Three thematic areas of coding are used for all types of research design: (a) empirical/theoretical basis, design, and statistical characteristics; (b) evidence components; and (c) additional explanatory details (Kratochwill & Stoiber, 2002). The first area ascertains the linkage to established theory and prior research, along with well-conceived research methodology, and appropriate outcome measures and related statistical procedures. The second area, key evidence components or key features, addresses the following:

(a) outcome measurement procedures that are valid, reliable, multimethod, and multisource; (b) a comparison group demonstrating the same target problem to test outcome differences when a group design is used (i.e., group equivalence established); (c) key outcomes that are statistically significant; (d) equivalent mortality for participants; (e) evidence of durability of effects, (f) identifiable components indicating what aspects of the intervention produced which outcomes; (g) evidence of intervention fidelity/integrity; and (h) information regarding replication. (p. 346)

The third area addresses the quality of match to the research setting and circumstances, including information on participants, contextual factors surrounding the intervention, how the intervention was applied, and so forth.

The larger clinical child, developmental, counseling, and school psychology community has been very actively engaged since the late 1990s, contributing to an enlarged literature on evidenced-based interventions (Chambless & Ollendick, 2001; Kazdin & Weisz, 2003; Kratochwill & Shernoff, 2004; Kratochwill & Stoiber, 2000; Lonigan et al., 1998; Ollendick

& King, 2004; Schoenwald & Hoagwood, 2001; Stoiber & Kratochwill, 2000; Wampold, Lichtenberg, & Waehler, 2002; Weisz & Hawley, 1998).

Social Work

Although the field of social work often interfaces with that of education and school psychology, recent evidence-based research developments in social work have been markedly different from the former fields of study. Many in the theorist, researcher, and practitioner trainer community in the field of social work have embraced a perspective of evidence-based practice (EBP), an outgrowth of the evidence-based medicine movement, typically associated with the work of David Sackett and the Evidence-Based Medicine Working Group at Canada's McMaster University (Sackett, Rosenberg, Gray, Haynes, & Richardson, 1996). As opposed to the more discrete and targeted efforts (discussed previously) in education and school psychology to create and use tools to measure the value of specific intervention research studies, EBP is a systemic approach (see Fig. 12.1) that integrates clinical expertise, best scientific evidence, and client needs and preferences, to support more well-attuned and effective service delivery (Shonsky & Gibbs, 2004). The EBP model incorporates a multistep procedure of (a) asking an answerable question regarding the need, (b) locating the best evidence, (c) ascertaining the validity and utility of the evidence, (d) deciding if the presenting problem can be addressed, (e) advising and conferring with stakeholders, (f) developing an integrated action plan, and (g) implementing the plan with ongoing process and outcome monitoring and evaluation.

As part of the EBP process, Gibbs (2004) outlined the Client-Oriented Practical Evidence Search (COPES) model, which assists practitioners in posing and then answering critical questions that will guide their intervention efforts. The COPES model parallels the EBP model in being client-oriented, having practical relevance in the context of daily practice, and supporting efficient searches for evidence-based methods. The model supports five types of questions: effectiveness, prevention, assessment, risk/prognosis, and description. Effectiveness questions address actual outcomes for clients based on particular interventions. Prevention questions focus on how well interventions prevent the onset of a problem. Assessment questions consider standardized measurement of client conditions, intervention procedures, and outcomes. Risk/prognosis questions concern the likelihood and nature of client outcomes over time. Description questions, which are sometimes qualitative in nature, seek to explain client experiences and perceptions, often considering client needs and levels of satisfaction.

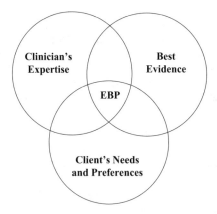

FIG. 12.1.   Evidence-based practice (EBP) model.

Proponents of the EBP model note that a sizable segment of the social work practitioner community "rely primarily on the advice of their colleagues and supervisors, personal experiences, relevant theory, and authoritative texts for practice" (Howard, McMillen, & Pollio, 2003, p. 235) and don't necessarily follow "practice-related research findings" (Gibbs & Gambrill, 2002, p. 452). Rosen (2003) discussed challenges to the field in adopting the EBP model, citing three fundamental barriers to implementation of EBP in social work: (a) personal attitudes, beliefs, and experiential knowledge among social workers that may conflict with evidence-based practice; (b) differing orientations to knowledge, related in part to a resistance to a logical positivist paradigm, along with an orientation to relative constructs of social justice and reform; and (c) ideographic and intuitive applications of empirically generalized knowledge, where practitioners deal with uncertainties arising from inferential research by avoiding or supplanting implementation of empirically based interventions.

Although the EBP model has been a defining feature in social work, other significant develops have occurred since 1990. In 1991, the Task Force on Social Work Research (created in 1988 by the director of the National Institutes of Mental Health [NIMH]) presented a report—*Building Social Work Knowledge for Effective Services and Policies: A Plan for Research Development*—to a committee of the NIMH (Austin, 1998; Zlotnik, Biegel, & Solt, 2002). As a result of that work, several social work research centers were created as well as the Institute for the Advancement of Social Work Research (IASWR), originally, a collaboration among five social work professional bodies. All of these efforts have led to further best practices research, coordination of large-scale intervention studies, training, and related dissemination activities in the field of social work (IASWR, 2003).

Juvenile Justice

The field of juvenile justice has benefited from multiple distributed efforts to support evidence-based practice, but on a whole, there has been a less well-focused effort within the field in this regard. Juvenile justice as a field has not pursued the development of instruments to evaluate specific research publications as have the fields of education and school psychology. There have been multiple efforts along these lines in the past decade, such as the Maryland Scale of Scientific Methods (no longer in use), and the Standardized Program Evaluation Protocol (discussed later). Also, the field in large part, has not subscribed to a widely accepted theoretical framework such as EBP, as has been the case in social work. At the same time, there have been multiple developments in the research literature and the establishment of and use of evaluation research centers to guide evidence-based best practices.

The Justice Statistics and Research Association, a project funded by the Office of Juvenile Justice and Delinquency Prevention (OJJDP) in the U.S. Department of Justice, created the Juvenile Justice Evaluation Center (JJEC). The JJEC provides technical assistance to the states, online publications on evaluation issues, referral to other evaluation resources, summary information on evaluations of interventions that are organized topically, funding seed projects, and related activities. Likewise, the Bureau of Justice Assistance manages the Center for Program Evaluation, a similar organizational resource.

The JJEC has developed a briefing series of nontechnical publications to assist administrators and practitioners in addressing evaluation issues. For example, JJEC's seventh briefing publication, *Approaches to Assessing Juvenile Justice Program Performance* (JJEC, 2004), discussed types of performance assessment, factors guiding selection of an assessment methodology, and appropriate use of measures to meet OJJDP assessment requirements. This and other documents in the briefing series have offered little or no guidance to researchers and do not provide end-users with technical methods to assess the value of specific research on interventions. The juvenile justice research and practitioner community has also relied on a combination of resources for guidance, including the Society for Prevention Research, the Cochrane and Campbell Collaborations, the Center for Evaluation Research and Methodology at Vanderbilt University, and similar evaluation research efforts at other universities. The Campbell Crime and Justice Coordinating Group, a component of the Campbell Collaboration, is an international effort among scholars from more than 10 nations to provide rigorous systematic reviews and evaluations of research in criminology and justice-related areas.

Howell and Lipsey (2004) discussed efforts to use research on evidence-based programs for juvenile delinquency. They identified three basic approaches: (a) replication of model programs, such as the "Blueprints" program at the Center for the Study and Prevention of Violence at University of Colorado; (b) conducting evaluations of many individual programs; and (c) defining characteristics of successful program principles and practices from research and applying them. In addition to discussing the benefits of meta-analysis, Howell and Lipsey described the Standardized Program Evaluation Protocol (SPEP), an instrument that applies principles gathered from characteristics of effective intervention programs and scores individual programs, relative to the instrument's domains. These domains include supplementary services, duration of service, face-to-face contact days, risk level for juvenile clients, and age of juveniles.

As has been the case in allied fields (Shavelson & Towne, 2002), evaluations of intervention programs funded by the National Institute of Justice (NIJ) have come under scrutiny and criticism. For example, a Government Accountability Office (GAO) study (GAO, 2003), *Justice Outcome Evaluations: Design and Implementation of Studies Require More NIJ Attention*, raised serious criticism of evaluations of a sample of 15 (out of 96) NIJ-funded evaluation studies. The methodological review of the NIJ studies found that sufficiently sound information about program outcomes was not available for 10 of the 15 program evaluations reviewed. Of the 15 studies, 11 were launched with sound evaluation designs. Of these 11 studies, 5 were also well implemented, including use of random assignment, use of adequate control groups, baseline data, and follow-up measures. Of these 11 studies, 6 suffered implementation problems, such as incomplete or different implementation, and inability to obtain reliable outcome data, sometimes related to participating agency cooperation. These issues are not unique to the field of juvenile justice and are indicative of some of the challenges facing allied disciplines in ensuring quality evaluation studies.

Public Health

The field of public health maintains a long tradition of ongoing monitoring and analysis of public health events along with a commitment to developing and refining research standards.

With regard to youth violence prevention research, the Centers for Disease Control and Prevention (CDC) launched a series of 15 CDC-funded evaluation projects in the early 1990s (Powell et al., 1996), with a strong emphasis on rigorous science, including use of randomization and control groups. Descriptions and baseline data for these projects were presented in a 1996 special issue of the *American Journal of Preventive Medicine*.

Using the term *program* to represent any public health action, from a highly focused direct intervention with individual clients to more broad-based community-level mobilization, the CDC Evaluation Working Group developed the Framework for Program Evaluation in Public Health (Centers for Disease Control, 1999). The framework identifies the following steps in evaluation practice: engage stakeholders, describe the program, focus the evaluation design, gather credible evidence, justify conclusions, and ensure use and sharing of lessons learned (see Fig. 12.2). This framework applies the Joint Committee on Evaluation Standards' four core concepts: utility, feasibility, propriety, and accuracy (Joint Committee on Standards for Educational Evaluation, 1994).

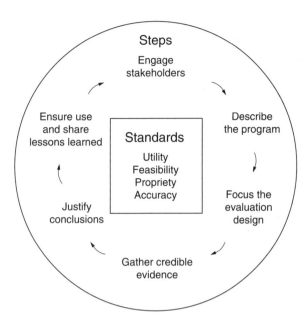

FIG. 12.2.   CDC framework for program evaluation.

The framework includes specific standards for research methods, including experimental, quasi-experimental, and observational designs, with an acknowledgment of the relative strengths and weaknesses of all methods and a suggestion that mixed-method approaches can offer advantages to the researcher. Unlike some recent developments in fields such as education and school psychology, where specific instrumentation has been developed to rate the strength of evidence of published research, this framework does not provide a scoring rubric as such; rather, it is a more general structure to drive the process of quality evaluation. Although there have been many developments in crafting standards for scientifically based research in the broader field of public health (a discussion of which is beyond the scope of this chapter), a few additional recent developments are noteworthy.

The CDC Epidemiology Program Office (EPO) directs multiple activities that support best practices in evidence-based research. The EPO maintains a Prevention Effectiveness Branch and a Statistics and Epidemiology Branch, which address evidence-based research methods, including standards development, training, and partnerships in related projects such as the Cochrane Collaboration (discussed later). Along with other related publications, the CDC has supported high-quality research in violence prevention through publications of supporting materials such as the National Center for Injury Prevention and Control's *Measuring Violence-Related Attitudes, Beliefs, and Behaviors Among Youths: A Compendium of Assessment Tools.*

The Substance Abuse and Mental Health Services Administration (SAMHSA) has been very active in developing protocols for reviewing effective science-based prevention programs (Schinke, et al., 2002). SAMHSA's Center for Substance Abuse Prevention (CSAP) created the National Registry of Effective Programs (NREP), which reviews and identifies efficacious and effective programs, based on experimental, quasi-experimental, time-series, and ethnographic research. The interventions are reviewed, drawing on (a) current scientific literature, (b) other governmental and private review organizations with rigorous review standards comparable to those of the NREP (discussed later), (c) CSAP grantee reports, and (d) documentation of program effectiveness submitted directly to NREP.

SAMHSA reviewed programs are classified into promising programs, effective programs, and model programs. The NREP uses a scoring rubric to assess program merit that includes the following:

1. Theoretical/conceptual framework.
2. Intervention fidelity.
3. Process evaluation.
4. Design.
5. Method of assignment.
6. Sample size.
7. Attrition.
8. Analysis of attrition effects.
9. Methods to correct biases.
10. Outcome measures and their psychometric properties.
11. Missing data.
12. Treatment of missing data.
13. Outcome data collection.
14. Analysis techniques.
15. Outcome effects.
16. Other plausible threats to validity.

Following the multi-item scoring, programs are subsequently scored on (a) integrity, (b) utility, (c) dissemination capability, (d) cultural appropriateness, (e) replications, (f) consumer involvement, and (g) summative appropriateness criteria. Studies are also reviewed and evaluated (but not scored numerically) on research design, use of comparison/control groups, and sample size.

Another important development in public health supporting evidence-based research is the Evidence-Based Practice for Public Health Project, administered through the University of Massachusetts Medical School. This project is developing an evidence-based resource Website for public health research as well as related electronic publications and training programs. Their electronic publication, *Models of Information Summary, Synthesis, and Dissemination: Sources and Organization of Evidence-Based Knowledge*, provides a collection of broad and deep linkages into evidence-based public health research evaluation resources.

Cochrane and Campbell Collaborations/CONSORT Protocol

The Cochrane Collaboration takes its name from Archibald Cochrane, who, in the 1970s, pointed to a disconnect between research and effective medical practice, citing a lack of consistent application of scientific principles (Smith, 1996). The Cochrane Collaboration is an international effort among researchers to provide structured reviews of interventions in the medicine and healthcare related fields. A Cochrane systematic review of a collection of studies provides concise and accessible information in the following format: (a) background, (b) study objectives, (c) search strategy, (d) selection criteria, (e) data collection and analysis, (f) main results, and (g) reviewers' conclusions. The Cochrane reviews provide details on interventions from reviewed studies, along with conclusions regarding methodological quality and implications for research and practice, and potential conflicts of interest. The Cochrane reviews tend to be focused on randomized clinical trials (Schuerman et al., 2002).

The Campbell Collaboration, or "C2," named after American researcher, Donald Campbell, was launched in 2000 and has emulated the work of the Cochrane Collaborative. C2 seeks to be all-inclusive in its reviews of research, avoiding sources of study selection bias, including lack of international focus, and publication bias regarding nonsignificant results. Extra measures that include hand searches and communication with experts in a field of study are used to support this mission. C2 will offer a registry of evaluations of social interventions, called "C2-SPECTR" (Social, Psychological, Educational, and Criminological Trials Register; Schuerman et al., 2002). As is the case with the Cochrane Collaboration, C2 uses a systematic protocol in its reviews.

The Consolidated Standards of Reporting Trials (CONSORT), a protocol for reporting the results of randomized controlled trials (Moher, Schulz, & Altman, 2001), relates in part to the structured reviews provided through the Cochrane and Campbell Collaborations. Developed in the mid-1990s by an international task force of experts in clinical research, statistics, and epidemiology, the CONSORT provides a flow chart and 22-item checklist to guide presentation of research using randomized controlled trials. CONSORT addresses a wide range of study issues, including, but not limited to sample design, allocation of participants to interventions, intervention details, specific hypotheses, details of outcome measures, randomization procedures, baseline and follow-up data procedures, and so forth. The CONSORT standard has been adopted by an increasing number of journals in the health care and allied fields.

There are other organizations in the United States and internationally that have made major contributions to evidence-based research. Space limitations do not permit discussion of many of these organizations, but noteworthy among them are the ESRC UK Centre for Evidence Based Policy and Practice, and the Centre for Evidence-Based Social Services, also located in the United Kingdom. Although the former is more broad-based in its efforts and the latter has more of a local researcher–practitioner partnership focus, both are exemplary of the recent emergence of evidence-based support organizations internationally.

CROSS-CUTTING ISSUES IN EVIDENCE-BASED RESEARCH

Although developments in evidence-based intervention research review and practice have varied across disciplines, as illustrated earlier, a number of broader cross-cutting issues emerge that have a bearing on school violence prevention and school safety programming. This section examines efficacy/effectiveness research (including transportability and dissemination issues), use of meta-analysis, developmental levels of child and adolescent clients, manualized treatments, and editors' space constraints for research manuscripts. Although beyond the scope of this chapter, it is also important to acknowledge a number of critical issues that are foundational to a discussion of evidence-based research: (a) defining treatment; (b) sample design; (c) training interventionists; (d) allocation of treatment to participants; (e) fidelity of implementation; (f) baseline, outcome, and follow-up measures; (g) comparison group issues; (h) statistical analysis techniques; (i) moderating and mediating variables; (j) statistical reporting; and (k) client acceptance and compliance.

Efficacy/Effectiveness Research

There are substantial differences in experimental results from efficacy and effectiveness research, with research-based therapy (efficacy research) usually faring better than real-world clinical therapy (effectiveness research) (Hoagwood & Johnson, 2003; Lonigan et al., 1998; Weisz, Donenberg, Han, & Weiss, 1995; Weisz & Hawley, 1998). Ollendick and King (2004) and others have noted fairly consistent differences in characteristics of study samples, interventionists, settings, and research conditions (see Table 12.2). At the same time, Ollendick and King, using a brief discussion of three studies, explicated how the lines between efficacy and effectiveness research can become blurred. There are many implications to consider

TABLE 12.2
Characteristics of Research and Clinic Therapy

Research Therapy	Recruited cases (less severe, study volunteers)
	Homogeneous groups
	Narrow or single-problem focus
	Treatment in lab, school settings
	Researcher as therapist
	Very small caseloads
	Heavy pre-therapy preparation
	Pre-planned, highly structured treatment (manualized)
	Monitoring of therapist behaviour
	Behavioural methods
Clinic Therapy	Clinic-referred cases (more severe, some coerced into treatment)
	Heterogeneous groups
	Broad, multiproblem focus
	Treatment in clinic, hospital settings
	Professional career therapists
	Very large caseloads
	Little/light pre-therapy preparation
	Flexible, adjustable treatment (no treatment manual)
	Little monitoring of therapist behaviour
	Nonbehavioural methods

Note: From Barrett and Ollendick (2004). Copyright 2004 by John Wiley & Sons. Reprinted with permission.

for intervention research generally as well as school safety research with regard to efficacy–effectiveness issues. Three of these issues are highlighted here.

First, study subjects often differ, with efficacy research participants often demonstrating milder presenting problems and limited comorbid conditions, as compared with most subjects receiving interventions in real-world settings (Chambless & Hollon, 1998; Lonigan et al., 1998). School violence prevention efforts at the indicated level (Institute of Medicine, 1994) target youngsters with the highest degree of need. For children and adolescents with entrenched patterns of antisocial behavior, co-morbid conditions (e.g., conduct disorder, oppositional defiant disorder, attention deficit hyperactivity disorder), and a combination of harsh family and school-failure experiences, there are many variables in play that may not even be approximated in much of the efficacy research on school violence prevention measures. As a result, the generalizability of such efficacy research to these high-needs students remains questionable.

Second, the intervention training and caseloads of the interventionists can differ considerably between efficacy and effectiveness studies (Chorpita, 2003; Ollendick & King, 2004). Chorpita suggested that most organizations that deliver interventions lack the resources to train staff in intervention delivery in as thorough a manner as staff working for an efficacy research study. The implications of this difference for school safety interventions relates directly to fidelity of implementation. With less training and less time to devote (as a result of relatively heavy caseloads), interventionist staff in schools and clinics are prone to offer less thorough service delivery, resulting in diminished outcome effects. This theme is paralleled in some of the meta-analytic findings suggesting that fidelity of implementation was a critical issue for effective programs (Gottfredson & Gottfredson, 2002; Wilson, Lipsey, & Derzon, 2003).

Third, intervention settings can differ greatly, resulting in varied research outcomes (Chambless & Hollon, 1998; Hoagwood, Burns, Kiser, Ringeisen, & Schoenwald, 2001; Ollendick & King, 2004; Shoenwald & Hoagwood, 2001). Chambless and Hollon noted that, "All things being equal, those studies that most faithfully reproduce the conditions found in actual clinical practice are most likely to produce findings that generalize to those settings" (p. 15). Greenberg (2004) noted the importance of focusing on the "quality and nature of adaptations," rather than engaging in the "polarizing debate regarding fidelity versus adaptation." (p. 9) The lack of "fit" between efficacy studies and real-world settings is reflected in the mismatch between (a) the strictly defined intervention and related research requirements and (b) the philosophy, policies, procedures, and staff scheduling and service delivery requirements found in real-world settings (Hoagwood et al., 2001; Shoenwald & Hoagwood, 2001). One example of this can be found in the GAO study on NIJ evaluations previously discussed that pointed to researchers' problems obtaining outcome data as a result of difficulties working with local service delivery agencies. Similar setting-related problems can easily compromise school violence intervention research. For example, given the pressures of demonstrating adequate yearly progress under the mandates of the No Child Left Behind Act, schools would be hard pressed for purposes of testing a school violence intervention, despite the obvious advantages of reducing school violence and disruption, to take time and resources away from focused academic programs aimed at raising schoolwide scores.

Chorpita (2003) suggested reframing the efficacy–effectiveness issue along a continuum of evidentiary research: (a) Type I—efficacy research, demonstrating internal validity under strict experimental conditions; (b) Type II—transportability, where the research is conducted with a more representative group of clients, allowing some degree of generalizability; (c) Type III—dissemination, in which the intervention is implemented within the natural context and framework of a system (e.g., school) by the actual service providers in that system; and (d) Type IV—system evaluation, in which the research is conducted in a system, independent of the investigatory team. Chorpita noted that Types II, III, and IV research are relatively rare, contributing to the evidence–practice gap.

Meta-Analysis

Meta-analysis has been widely used to assess the efficacy of interventions in education, psychology, and allied fields (Lipsey & Wilson, 1993). Examining the results of more than 300 meta-analytic studies, Lipsey and Wilson demonstrated how broad patterns in intervention research could inform the research and practitioner community and how meta-analysis has repeatedly produced clear evidence regarding treatment efficacy. Lipsey and Wilson (2001) articulated four specific strengths of meta-analysis: (a) meta-analysis uses a well-structured approach to synthesizing research, with documented criteria and procedural steps that can be fully audited and evaluated; (b) meta-analysis uses sophisticated techniques for integrating effect size and significance statistics that help differentiate contributions among included studies, more so than conventional reviews of research; (c) meta-analysis provides the tools to detect effects and relationships that may be hidden or difficult to determine using other research review approaches; and (d) meta-analysis offers a systematic and well-defined approach and set of data-management tools to process large volumes of information from studies under review.

Along a similar vein, Hunter and Schmidt (1990) discussed contributions of meta-analysis to the advancement of scientific knowledge: (a) meta-analysis in the social and behavioral sciences has demonstrated that prior research findings have not been as ambiguous or conflicting as previously thought and that valuable conclusions could be drawn from these bodies of research, (b) the "cumulativeness of research findings in the behavioral sciences is probably as great as in the physical sciences" (p. 37), and (c) findings from meta-analysis provide critically important direction for future theory development and research efforts.

While appealing in its ability to provide syntheses of prior research, cautions and concerns have been raised with regard to this technique. Lipsey and Wilson (1993) offered cautionary discussion of the following: (a) assessing methodological quality of included studies,

(b) availability bias, (c) small sample bias, and (d) generalized placebo effect. The authors also commented that pre- and posttest designs typically overestimate effects compared to random samples, and publication bias regarding excluded studies with negative results can inflate effect size results. Later research by Wilson and Lipsey (2001) found that among 319 meta-analyses, study methods explained almost as much variability in meta-analysis results as did the analyzed data on the respective interventions.

Other researchers have also raised concerns about use of meta-analyses in effectiveness research (Kazdin & Weisz, 1998; Kratochwill, 2002; Weisz et al., 1995; Weisz & Hawley, 1998). These concerns included the following: (a) screening criteria for including studies; (b) imbalanced coverage of specific techniques (e.g., behavioral/cognitive–behavioral more so than psychodynamic); (c) varying approaches to effect size calculation; (d) representativeness of subjects, interventionists, and treatment conditions to real-world practice; (e) common omission of single-subject research; (f) confounding of treatment–outcome interactions; and (g) outcome reporting sources relative to knowledge of subject treatment status.

Meta-analysis, by its very nature, often sifts through large volumes of data. As a result, differences across study characteristics can constrain the fineness of common detail found, resulting in more broad-based findings. For school safety and related research, there can be a trade-off between (a) a more inclusive approach to meta-analysis that taps into a large body of relevant research, often yielding only general findings; and (b) preserving the ability to uncover the effectiveness of more specific intervention components, based on an analysis of a more focused subset of the research literature. Also obscuring the view provided by meta-analytic techniques into specific intervention mechanisms that can effectively reduce school violence and disruption problems are confounds among variables that influence outcomes (Kazdin & Weisz, 1998; Weisz & Hawley, 1998). For example, where a meta-analysis may determine that a stand-alone anger management curriculum may have resulted in reduced incidents of violence in school, an interaction effect involving increased teacher attention (outside of the intervention) to, and in support of participating students, may also have significantly contributed to the outcomes.

Developmental Levels

Many psychotherapeutic interventions for children and adolescents have not been developmentally targeted, taking into account specific age-related tasks and milestones that account for developmental differences (Holmbeck, Greenley, & Franks, 2003; Weisz & Hawley, 2002). Holmbeck and colleagues suggested that effect sizes for child and adolescent interventions that have been in the moderate range would be even larger if these interventions were developmentally oriented. Interestingly, many interventions for adolescents have been adapted upward from those originally designed for children, and downward from those originally designed for adults (Weisz & Hawley, 2002).

Several meta-analyses of cognitive–behavioral interventions have demonstrated significantly larger (about double) effect sizes for interventions targeted at adolescents, compared to younger children. These results may reflect differences in cognitive abilities, or possibly other related developmental attributes. Holmbeck et al. (2003) explicated models in which developmental attributes may serve as either moderating or mediating variables, affecting outcomes. For example, according to Piagetian theory, a student's cognitive-developmental level would be linked to his or her ability to engage in perspective-taking and develop empathy for others, core skill components common to several empirically supported school violence reduction programs. As such, a student's developmental level could act as a moderating variable. A mediating variable is tied to some type of mechanism that leads from a causal variable to an outcome. As discussed by Holmbeck and colleagues, Treadwell and Kendall (1996) demonstrated that improvements in self-statements acted as a mediator between intervention and the outcome measure—level of anxiety.

The implications for school violence prevention, particularly with interventions that involve cognitive–behavioral techniques, are clear. Specific techniques that are well-aligned with the child's development are more likely to succeed. Well-validated interventions such as Second Step and Olweus' Bully Prevention Program have developed multiple sets of intervention procedures with supporting materials targeted at different developmental levels.

Manualized Treatments

Documentation of treatment protocols in manual form (a) provides a clear definition of the treatment, (b) standardizes procedures, (c) facilitates assessment of implementation fidelity, (d) provides researchers and practitioners with a clear understanding of what was done, and (e) allows others to engage in replication research (Kratochwill & Stoiber, 2000; Ollendick & King, 2004). As discussed previously, treatment manuals were required by the APA Division 12 Taskforce draft document for an intervention to be classified as either "probably efficacious" or "well-established." The Division 16 protocols require use of a manual along with other conditions in order to earn the higher component scores of "2" or "3" for implementation fidelity.

Practitioners have expressed concerns that mandatory manualization of treatment, prescribing a "lockstep" process, is impractical and will harm clients. Real-life clinical practice also involves working with clients and families who may not fully invest in treatment, requiring modification of procedures (Kratochwill & Stoiber, 2000; Weisz & Hawley, 1998). Kendall and colleagues (1998) argued that treatment manuals can be effectively used in a flexible manner.

Strict manualization of interventions in school violence prevention programs could compromise effectiveness in cases where the local context and changing conditions demand some flexibility. As discussed by Kratochwill and Stoiber (2002) and Ollendick and King (2004), applied intervention settings typically have barriers to treatment that must be accommodated as well as idiosyncratic attributes of local populations. For example, consider a situation where an after-school social skills training program is implemented, and a group of students must leave the sessions early due to parents pulling them out for participation in a local sports team or other activity. The treatment manual may be designed around working with groups of students for a given minimum time and with a given number of students making up the group, for purposes of group activities that comprise part of the training. Without the ability to modify the program to accommodate the changing circumstances, the outcomes may be severely compromised.

Editors' Space Constraints for Research Manuscripts

The What Works ClearingHouse *Study Review Standards*, APA's Division 16 *Procedural and Coding Manual*, as well as SAMHSA's NREP protocols and requirements of the Cochrane and Campbell collaborations, all articulate varying, yet significant levels of documentation of high-quality research and strict adherence to scientific standards. Authors of prospective manuscripts seeking publication of intervention research results must develop rather extensive and lengthy written explanations to satisfy these reviewing organizations. Although a laudable goal and supportive of establishing quality reviews of evidence-based intervention research, these requirements may clash with journal editors' typically strict limitations on manuscript length. Many journals advise prospective authors to limit submitted manuscripts to about 25 to 30 pages, double-spaced. It seems questionable whether the research review protocols can be satisfied, given such constraints. Research journal editors and affiliated professional groups may need to revisit these guidelines in view of this issue.

IMPLICATIONS FOR CURRENT AND FUTURE
RESEARCH AND PRACTICE

There are several important implications for research and practice to be drawn from this review (see Table 12.3). Considering the many protocols in development and in use that can guide the review and evaluation of intervention research, the reader may feel as though he or she is walking through a carnival house of mirrors, seeing varied reflections of a core concept—scientifically based evidence of effective intervention. Using a different metaphor, one can

TABLE 12.3
Implications for Research and Practice Based on Developments in Evidence-Based Evaluation

	Positive	*Possibly Problematic*
Research	Increasing attention to and dissemination of articles, other media, and funding organization procedures regarding rigorous evaluation may help educate more researchers, gradually changing the overall research landscape.	Studies of interventions for students with high intensity needs may preclude randomized controlled trials in favor of alternate methods such as single subject design due to limited sample sizes.
	The quality of intervention evaluation efforts may gradually improve.	Limited heterogeneity of special populations may constrain research designs with regard to assignment to groups and related randomization efforts.
	Use of emerging standards for more rigorous evaluation research may drive more efficient use of research funds.	Increasingly scarce school-based resources to support staff release time for training and reluctance to modify academic programming due to academic accountability mandates may interfere with effectiveness research designs.
	A greater proportion of published intervention evaluation research may be of higher quality.	
	Greater attention to relatively neglected areas, such as effectiveness research, and related issues of transportability and dissemination may be better addressed.	The relative paucity of effectiveness research, as compared to efficacy research, suggests the need for a greatly increased investment in the former.
Practice	Due to resources such as the What Works Clearinghouse and National Registry of Effective Prevention Programs, practitioners may focus more on the need to verify that proposed interventions are evidence-based, resulting in less implementation of ineffective interventions.	A plethora of Web-based clearinghouses and information centers on evidence-based program evaluation may overwhelm end-users, leaving them confused or discouraged, limiting how they access and later adopt evidence-based practices.
	Because of a more widespread evidence-based perspective, the field of nonevidence-based interventions should thin somewhat, leaving practitioners a more manageable set of choices to consider.	Limitations on evidence-based research designs may result in fewer effective options being made available to practitioners for meeting needs of high-risk youth.
	With an increased focus on manualization and explicit documentation of intervention procedures, training practitioners to implement intervention practices appropriately may be more efficient.	Continuing challenges with transportability and dissemination of interventions limits the practical utility for school personnel to employ many interventions.
	Scarce school and community funding to provide interventions for high-risk youth may be spent more efficiently.	Continuing budgetary constraints in schools and pressures for demonstrating adequate yearly progress under the No Child Left Behind Act may limit the widespread use of evidence-based interventions for violence prevention in favor of academically oriented programming.

consider the historical fragmentation across the human service disciplines, each embracing different theoretical frameworks, organizational philosophies, targeting different goals, utilizing different service delivery models, employing varying measurement and accountability tools, and using similar sounding, yet distinct technical terminology.

This issue of differing orientations and practices is not new to the school violence research community. Definitional and measurement issues have led to varying reports of school violence data (Furlong & Morrison, 1994, 2000; Leone, Mayer, Malmgren, & Meisel, 2000; Reiss & Roth, 1993; U.S. Library of Congress, 1994). These definitional and measurement challenges remain as does the need to reconcile the admissibility of varying research designs in evidence-based practice. For example, single-subject research has contributed key understandings of effective behavioral interventions with low incidence and other groups in special education environments that have major implications for school safety research and practice (Horner et al., 2005). Yet, in the current zeitgeist of scientifically based research, single-subject research is generally not acknowledged as contributing strong evidentiary support for interventions.

The implications for researchers in school violence also relate to studying interventions with those students who are most often involved in school violence. Students who are at highest risk, receiving indicated interventions (Institute of Medicine, 1994), may comprise about 1%–7% of a school's population (Sugai et al., 1999). Discussing adolescent violence, Dodge and Pettit (2003) noted, "over 50% of violent behaviors are perpetrated by only 6% of the population" (p. 350). This points to a need to examine highly focused interventions for a relatively small and unique group within the school. Owing to a lack of heterogeneity and limited availability for group assignments, evaluation for group differences using randomized clinical trials that depend on group assignment would not be practical for these high-risk students in many educational settings. This presents serious challenges for effectiveness research in real-world settings.

Given the relatively bleak state of K–12 funding nationally, combined with mandates to produce improved test scores for adequate yearly progress pursuant to the requirements of the No Child Left Behind Act, schools are struggling to use their personnel in the most efficient ways possible. This leaves little room for releasing and paying for staff training in new intervention programs designed to reduce school violence. More likely, schools will provide marginally adequate support for such staff training. This will severely compromise effectiveness research in school violence prevention, as problems may occur with fidelity of implementation, outcome measurements, and related concerns tied to appropriate staff training.

Practitioners face challenges on several levels with regard to violence prevention programming and service delivery. First, although there are a growing number of information clearinghouses (e.g., What Works ClearingHouse, National Registry of Effective Programs, Cochrane and Campbell Collaborations) available to the practitioner community, the standards of research evaluation underpinning these endorsed programs vary. The end user is forced to "fly on faith," assuming that despite differing approaches, the approved programs are worth implementing. Second, research design constraints will limit the availability of evidence for interventions addressing special education populations, and especially, the 6% or so of chronic, high-risk adolescents. However, chronic, high-risk students are precisely the group for whom we need to develop more effective school violence prevention programs. Third, continuing disconnects between efficacy and effectiveness research, the difficulty of conducting effectiveness research in settings where high-risk students typically exist, and the tendency favoring efficacy research, all totaled, will likely limit the availability of proven intervention approaches that are rigorously tested in real world environments. As previously noted by Chorpita (2003), research in transportability, generalizability, and system effectiveness is rare. In summary, the consuming public will probably have limited choices of thoroughly researched interventions. These points are not made to suggest a purely negative scenario. Rather, they draw attention to continuing challenges the research and practice community face in more strategically responding to competing requirements and constraints in evidence-based research.

Developments since the mid-1990s in building improved intervention research evaluation protocols and models have yielded several viable approaches that continue to evolve. Although still problematic, and far from perfect, they signal an important shift in our collective thinking. Given our limited resources and significant social problems, especially in reducing school violence and promoting school safety practices, we can no longer afford to implement interventions without a solid foundation of research-based evidence. The research and practitioner community needs to continue to invest in the concept of evidence-based practice and to support continued development efforts so that future research will benefit the clients that need these interventions.

REFERENCES

Austin, D. (1998). *A Report on Progress. Institute for the Advancement of Social Work Research.* Austin: University of Texas at Austin, School of Social Work.

Barrett, P. M., & Ollendick, T. H. (2004), Handbook of interventions that work with children and adolescents: Prevention and treatment. West Sussex, England: Wiley.

Centers for Disease Control and Prevention. (1999). Framework for program evaluation in public health. *Morbidity and Mortality Weekly Report, 48* (No. RR-11): [i-41]

Chambless, D. L., & Hollon, S. D. (1998). Defining empirically supported therapies. *Journal of Consulting and Clinical Psychology, 66*, 7–18.

Chambless, D. L., & Ollendick, T. H. (2001). Empirically supported psychological interventions: Controversies and evidence. *Annual Review of Psychology, 52*, 685–716.

Chorpita, B. F. (2003). The frontier of evidence-based practice. In A. E. Kazdin & J. R. Weisz (Eds.), *Evidence-based psychotherapies for children and adolescents* (pp. 42–59). New York: Guilford.

Clingempeel, W. G., & Henggeler, S. W. (2002). Randomized clinical trials, developmental theory, and antisocial youth: Guidelines for research. *Development and Psychopathology, 14*, 695–711.

Dodge, K. A., & Pettit, G. S. (2003). A biopsychosocial model of the development of chronic conduct problems in adolescence. *Developmental Psychology, 39*, 349–371.

Furlong, M. J., & Morrison, G. M. (1994). Introduction to Miniseries: School violence and safety in perspective. *School Psychology Review, 23*, 139–150.

Furlong, M. J., & Morrison, G. M. (2000). The school in school violence: Definitions and facts. *Journal of Emotional and Behavioral Disorders, 8*, 71–82.

General Accounting Office (CAO). (2003). *Justice outcome evaluations: Design and implementation of studies require more NIJ attention* (GAO-03-1091) Washington, DC: Author.

Gersten, R., Fuchs, L., Compton, D., Coyne, M., Greenwood, C., & Innocenti, M.S. (2005). Quality indicators for group experimental and quasi-experimental research in special education. *Exceptional Children, 71*(2), 149–164.

Gibbs, L. (2004). *Evidence-based practice for the helping professions.* Available: www.evidence.brookscole.com/moredetails.html

Gibbs, L., & Gambrill, E. (2002). Evidence-based practice: Counterarguments to objections. *Research on Social Work Practice, 12*, 452–476.

Gottfredson, D. C., & Gottfredson, G. D. (2002). Quality of school-based prevention programs: Results from a national survey. *Journal of Research on Crime and Delinquency, 39*, 3–35.

Greenberg, M. T. (2004). Current and future challenges in school-based prevention: The researcher perspective. *Prevention Science, 5*, 5–13.

Hoagwood, K., Burns, B. J., Kiser, L., Ringeisen, H., & Schoenwald, S. K. (2001). Evidence-based practice in child and adolescent mental health services. *Psychiatric Services, 52*, 1179–1189.

Hoagwood, K., & Johnson, J. (2003). School psychology: A public health framework I. From evidence-based practices to evidence-based policies. *Journal of School Psychology, 41*, 3–21.

Holmbeck, G. N., Greenley, R. N., & Franks, E. (2003). Developmental issues and considerations in child and adolescents therapy: Research and practice. In A. E. Kazdin & J. R. Weisz (Eds.), *Evidence-based psychotherapies for children and adolescents* (pp. 21–41). New York: Guilford.

Horner, R. H., Carr, E. G., Halle, J., McGee, G., Odom, S., & Wolery, M. (2005). The use of single-subject research to identify evidence-based practice in special education. *Exceptional Children, 71*(2), 165–179.

Howard, M. O., McMillen, C. J., & Pollio, D. E. (2003). Teaching evidence-based practice: Toward a new paradigm for social work education. *Research on Social Work Practice, 13*, 234–259.

Howell, J. C., & Lipsey, M. W. (2004). A practical approach to evaluating and improving juvenile justice programs. *Juvenile and Family Court Journal, 55*, 35–48.

Hunter, J. E., & Schmidt, F. L. (1990). *Methods of meta-analysis: Correcting error and bias in research findings.* Thousand Oaks, CA: Sage.

Institute for the Advancement of Social Work Research (IASWR). (2003). *1993–2003: A decade of linking policy, practice, and education through the advancement of research.* Washington, DC: Author.

Institute of Medicine. (1994). *Reducing risks for mental disorders: Frontiers for preventive intervention research.* Washington, DC: National Academy Press.

Joint Committee on Standards for Educational Evaluation. (1994). *The program evaluation standards.* Thousand Oaks, CA: Sage.

Juvenile Justice Evaluation Center (JJEC). (2004). *Approaches to assessing juvenile justice program performance.* Washington, DC: Author.

Kazdin, A. E., & Weisz, J. R. (1998). Identifying and developing empirically supported child and adolescent treatments. *Journal of Consulting and Clinical Psychology, 66*, 19–36.

Kazdin, A. E., & Weisz, J. R. (2003). Context and background of evidence-based psychotherapies for children and adolescents. In A. E. Kazdin & J. R. Weisz (Eds.), *Evidence-based psychotherapies for children and adolescents* (pp. 3–20). New York: Guilford.

Kendall, P. C., Chu, B. C., Gifford, A., Hayes, C., & Nauta, M. (1998). Breathing life into a manual: Flexibility and creativity with manual-based treatments. *Cognitive and Behavioral Practice, 5*, 177–198.

Kratochwill, T. R. (2002). Evidence-based interventions in school psychology: Thoughts on thoughtful commentary. *School Psychology Quarterly, 17*, 518–532.

Kratochwill, T. R., & Shernoff, E. S. (2004). Evidence-based practice: Promoting evidence-based interventions in school psychology. *School Psychology Quarterly, 18*(4), 1–21.

Kratochwill, T. R., & Stoiber, K. C. (2000). Empirically supported interventions and school psychology: Conceptual and practice issues—Part II. *School Psychology Quarterly, 15*, 233–253.

Kratochwill, T. R., & Stoiber, K. C. (2002). Evidence-based interventions in school psychology: Conceptual foundations of the *Procedural and Coding Manual* of Division 16 and the Society for the Study of School Psychology Task Force. *School Psychology Quarterly, 17*, 341–389.

Leone, P. E., Mayer, M. J., Malmgren, K., & Meisel, S. M. (2000). School violence and disruption: Rhetoric, reality, and reasonable balance. *Focus on Exceptional Children, 33*, 1–20.

Lipsey, M. W., & Wilson, D. B. (1993). The efficacy of psychological, education, and behavioral treatment: Confirmation from meta-analysis. *American Psychologist, 48*, 1181–1209.

Lipsey, M. W., & Wilson, D. B. (2001). *Practical meta-analysis.* Thousand Oaks, CA: Sage.

Lonigan, C. J., Elbert, J. C., & Johnson, S. B. (1998). Empirically supported psychosocial interventions for children: An overview. *Journal of Clinical Child Psychology, 27*, 138–145.

Moher D., Schulz, K. F., & Altman, D., for the CONSORT Group. (2001). The CONSORT statement: Revised recommendations for improving the quality of reports of parallel-group randomized trials. *Journal of the American Medical Association, 285*(15), 1987–1991.

No Child Left Behind Act of 2001, P.L. 107–110, 115 Stat. 1425 (2002).

Odom, S. L., Brantlinger, E., Gersten, R., Horner, R. H., Thompson, B., & Harris, K. R. (2005). Research in special education: Scientific methods and evidenced-based practices. *Exceptional Children, 71*(2), 137–148.

Ollendick, T. H., & King, N. J. (2004). Empirically supported treatments for children: Advances toward evidence-based practice. In P. M. Barrett & T. H. Ollendick (Eds.), *Handbook of interventions that work with children and adolescents: From prevention to treatme*nt (pp. 3–26). London: Wiley.

Powell, K. E., Dahlberg, L. L., Friday, J., Mercy, J. A., Thornton, T., & Crawford. S. (1996). Prevention of youth violence: Rationale and characteristics of 15 evaluation projects. *American Journal of Preventive Medicine*, Supplement to *12*(5), 3–12

Reiss, A. J., & Roth, J. A. (Eds.). (1993). *Understanding and preventing violence.* Washington, DC: National Academy Press.

Rosen, A. (2003). Evidence-based social work practice: Challenges and promise. *Social Work Research, 27*, 197–208.

Sackett, D. L., Rosenberg, W. M. C., Gray, J. A. M., Haynes, R. B., & Richardson, W. S. (1996). Evidence based medicine: What it is and what it isn't. *British Medical Journal, 312*, 71–72.

Schinke, S., Brounstein, P., & Gardner, S. (2002). *Science-based prevention programs and principles, 2002.* DHHS Pub. No. (SMA) 03-3764. Rockville, MD: Center for Substance Abuse Prevention, Substance Abuse and Mental Health Services Administration.

Schoenwald, S. K., & Hoagwood, K., (2001). Effectiveness, transportability, and dissemination of interventions: What matters when? *Journal of Psychiatric Services, 52*, 1190–1197.

Schuerman, J., Soydan, H., Macdonald, G., Forslund, M., de Moya, D., & Boruch, R. (2002). The Campbell collaboration. *Research on Social Work Practice, 12*, 309–317.

Scientifically based evaluation methods; Notice, 70 Fed. Reg. 3,586 (January 25, 2005).

Shavelson, R. J., Towne, L., & the Committee on Scientific Principles for Education Research. (Eds.). (2002). *Scientific research in education*. Washington, DC: National Academy Press.

Shonsky, A., & Gibbs, L. (2004). Will the real evidence-based practice please stand up? Teaching the process of evidence-based practice to the helping professions. *Brief Treatment and Crisis Intervention, 4*, 137–153.

Slavin, R. E. (2002). Evidence-based education policies: Transforming educational practice and research. *Educational Researcher, 31*(7), 15–21.

Smith, A. (1996). Mad cows and ecstasy. *Journal of the Royal Statistical Society, 159*, 367–383.

Stoiber, K. C., & Kratochwill, T. R. (2000). Empirically supported interventions and school psychology: Rationale and methodological issues—Part I. *School Psychology Quarterly, 15*,75–105.

Sugai, G., Horner, R. H., Dunlap, G., Hieneman, M., Lewis, T. J., Nelson, C. M., Scott, T., Liaupsin, C. J., Sailor, W., Turnbull, A. P., Turnbull, H. R. III, Wickham, D., Ruef, M., & Wilcox, B. (1999). *Applying positive behavioral support and functional assessment in schools. Technical assistance guide #1 (TAG 1)*. Washington, DC: OSEP Center on Positive Behavioral Interventions and Support.

Treadwell, K. R., & Kendall, P. C. (1996). Self-talk in youth with anxiety disorders: States of mind, content specificity, and treatment outcome. *Journal of Consulting and Clinical Psychology, 64*, 941–950.

U.S. Library of Congress, Congressional Research Service. (1994). *Violence in schools: An overview* (CRS Report for Congress No. 94–141 EPW). Washington, DC: Author.

Valentine, J. C., & Cooper, H. (2004). *What Works Clearinghouse Study Design and Implementation Assessment Device* (Version 1.1). Washington, DC: U.S. Department of Education.

Wampold, B. E., Lichtenberg, J. W., & Waehler, C. A. (2002). Principles of empirically supported interventions in counseling psychology. *The Counseling Psychologist, 30*, 197–217.

Weisz, J., Donenberg, G., Han, S., & Weiss, B. (1995). Bridging the gap between lab and clinic in child and adolescent psychotherapy. *Journal of Consulting and Clinical Psychology, 63*, 688–701.

Weisz, J. R., & Hawley, K. M. (1998). Finding, evaluating, refining, and applying empirically supported treatments for children and adolescents. *Journal of Clinical Child Psychology, 27*, 206–216.

Weisz, J. R., & Hawley, K. M. (2002). Developmental factors in the treatment of adolescents. *Journal of Consulting and Clinical Psychology, 70*, 21–43.

Wilson, D. B., & Lipsey, M. W. (2001). The role of method in treatment effectiveness research: Evidence from meta-analysis. *Psychological Methods, 6*, 413–429.

Wilson, S. J., Lipsey, M. W., & Derzon, J. H. (2003). The effects of school-based intervention programs on aggressive behavior: A Meta-Analysis. *Journal of Consulting and Clinical Psychology, 71*, 136–149.

WWC Study Review Standards. (2004). What Works Clearinghouse, U.S. Department of Education. Available: www.w-w-c.org/reports/studystandardsfinal.pdf

Zlotnik, J., Biegel, D. E., & Solt, B. (2002). The Institute for the Advancement of Social Work Research: Strengthening social work research in practice and policy. *Research on Social Work Practice, 12*, 318–337.

13

Assessment of Bullying

Dewey G. Cornell
Peter L. Sheras
Joanna C. M. Cole
University of Virginia

After decades of neglect, bullying has become widely recognized as an important and pervasive problem in American schools (Espelage & Swearer, 2004). A national study revealed that 30% of students (Grades 6–10) reported moderate or frequent involvement in bullying as a bully or victim (Nansel et al., 2001). Studies of school shootings found that most of the perpetrators experienced chronic teasing and harassment by their classmates and perceived themselves as victims (O'Toole, 2000; Vossekuil, Fein, Reddy, Borum, & Modzeleski, 2002). Organizations such as the National Crime Prevention Council (2003), the National Youth Violence Prevention Resource Center (2003), and the U.S. Department of Education (2002) have published reports urging more attention to bully prevention. At least 15 states have passed laws to address bullying (Limber & Small, 2003).

In response to this newly acknowledged problem, many programs have been developed to prevent or reduce bullying (e.g., Garrity, Jens, Porter, Sager, & Short-Camilli, 1994; Horne, Bartolomucci, Newman-Carlson, 2003; Olweus, Limber, & Mihalic, 1999; Whitaker, Rosen-bluth, Valle, & Sanchez, 2004). Not surprisingly, research on bullying has grown dramatically; a PsycINFO search using keywords *bully* or *bullying* located 300 published articles in the past 30 years (1975–2004), however, 90% (271) of these studies were published in the past 10 years and more than three-fourths (229) were published in the past 5 years.

Despite the overdue attention being paid to the problem of bullying, there are already indications that the movement to reduce bullying is not making good progress. The U.S. Surgeon General's report on youth violence (U.S. Department of Health and Human Services, 2001) identified 29 best practices in youth violence prevention; the only bullying program to make the list was the Olweus Bullying Prevention Program (Olweus et al., 1999), and it was ranked as a "promising" rather than a "model" program. A more recent listing of 32 "effective programs" produced the same result; only the Olweus program made the list (Osher, Dwyer, & Jackson, 2004).

A team of Canadian and English researchers (Smith, Schneider, Smith, & Ananiadou, 2004) reviewed 14 studies that either used the Olweus Bullying Prevention Program or shared its core features. Eight studies used control groups, including four studies that randomly assigned either classes or schools to intervention and control conditions. All but one study relied on student self-reports of bullying and victimization as their outcome measures, What did the researchers find? Overall, bullying prevention programs had little or no effect on bullying. The largest effect observed was a single condition in one study that produced a medium effect size. For self-reported bullying, all of the studies produced effects that were negligible or negative (meaning that bullying increased).

There are so few rigorous, controlled studies of bullying programs that bullying prevention was not recognized in recent scientific reviews of violence prevention. Mytton, DiGuiseppi, Gough, Taylor, and Logan (2002) conducted a systematic review of 44 randomized trials of school-based violence prevention programs; none of them involved programs focused on bullying or were identified as bullying prevention efforts. Wilson, Lipsey, and Derzon (2003) reported a meta-analysis of 221 studies of school-based violence prevention programs; there were categories of interventions involving social competence training, classroom management, peer mediation, and other types of interventions, but no category for bullying prevention.

Undoubtedly, many of the school violence prevention programs identified in official lists of effective programs have an impact on bullying, and many of the intervention studies focused on the reduction of peer aggression are treating youths who engage in bullying; nevertheless, bullying is not recognized as a critical construct in these efforts. Why is there so little published research on the effectiveness of bullying prevention programs and why is bullying so conspicuously absent from studies concerned with peer aggression? One critical problem is that bullying is difficult to conceptualize and measure (Griffin & Gross, 2004). The assessment of bullying has not been adequately studied, and as a result there is a lack of reliable and valid measures of many aspects of bullying and related constructs.

Why is bullying so difficult to assess? First, bullying is a broad category that encompasses physical, verbal, and social behaviors. Physical bullying seems most easy to identify because it involves discrete acts of violence and can be readily observed. However, physical bullying often involves the threat of violence, and threats can be conveyed in words or even implied with a gesture or a glance. Verbal bullying refers to statements that tease or insult the victim, but do not threaten physical injury. Social or relational bullying is the subtlest form of bullying and involves the manipulation of friendship patterns and social interactions to demean or exclude the victim from peers (Bjorkqvist, Lagerspetz, & Kaukinian, 1992; Crick & Grotpeter, 1995; Olweus, 1991).

A natural question is whether all these forms of bullying are psychologically equivalent. Does physical bullying occur in the same circumstances and have the same impact as verbal or social bullying? Do all forms of bullying respond to the same interventions? Instruments that measure bullying with a definition that encompasses all forms of bullying run the risk of collecting heterogeneous data that obscure trends and correlations. It may be necessary to develop separate measures of each type of bullying so that these questions can be investigated.

A second problem in the assessment of bullying is that it must be judged in its social context, and as a result, is often difficult to distinguish from playful behavior. Common horseplay and teasing among friends can seem like bullying to an observer. Even the participants may have differing perceptions of their behavior; teasing remarks can be misunderstood or taken more seriously than they were intended, and sometimes playful wrestling can escalate into physical bullying. Accused bullies may rely on the defense that they were "just playing around" or "didn't mean" what they said. Problem behaviors such as drug use, gang membership, and weapon possession are sufficiently discrete that they can be readily identified as present or absent, but bullying requires an assessment of the social circumstances, meaning, and intent of the behavior.

One way to deal with the ambiguity of bullying is to place less emphasis on individual incidents and focus on patterns of behavior over time. In this respect, it is helpful that the Olweus definition requires that bullying must take place frequently (Solberg & Olweus, 2003). Nevertheless, standards for the frequency of bullying are not well established, and conceivably, a severe incident such as a brutal beating should be considered bullying even it occurs only once. And it is not clear whether the threshold frequencies for physical, verbal, and social bullying should be the same.

Finally, it is difficult to distinguish bullying from other forms of peer conflict. All forms of fighting, teasing, and social conflict are not bullying. Bullying requires a power imbalance between aggressor and victim, and specifically excludes a conflict or fight between students of equal strength (Solberg & Olweus, 2003). The difference in power may be a function of physical size, as in the stereotype of the "big bully" who physically dominates a smaller victim, but more subtle forms of social bullying may result when the aggressor has an advantage in social status or popularity. The power imbalance between bully and victim could result simply from a disparity in self-confidence or verbal skills. These observations suggest that an adequate measure of bullying must encompass several different forms of bullying as well as the ability to distinguish bullying from ordinary peer conflict between students of relatively equal status. Many studies use self-report measures of hitting, teasing, or relational conflict that are presumed to indicate bullying, but that may be reports of peer aggression between students of comparable status.

Despite these formidable problems, accurate assessment of bullying is essential to the success of bullying prevention efforts. Assessment is the Achilles heel of bullying prevention efforts, and overlooking this weakness can result in the failure of bullying prevention efforts. Researchers understand the need to have reliable and valid instruments in order to obtain meaningful data and generate positive findings; a weak or unreliable instrument will always generate poor quality data that result in an underestimate of the effectiveness of a program, and may even lead to the false conclusion that a program is not effective. School practitioners implementing prevention programs for nonresearch purposes may not appreciate that this concern applies to their efforts as well. School practitioners may devise their own surveys, or indiscriminately choose a conveniently available survey, without consideration of the instrument's validity.

Accurate assessment of bullying is essential from the outset and throughout the course of a school-based prevention effort. An initial assessment of the nature and scope of bullying in a school is valuable in galvanizing staff support for a bullying prevention initiative. Without a credible instrument providing trustworthy data, some staff members (as well as students and parents) will doubt the significance of the problem or the need for action. And without a baseline assessment, it is not possible to demonstrate the program's effect. Post-intervention assessment is essential in order to document the program's effectiveness, which is a requirement of schools making use of funding from the U.S. Office of Safe and Drug-Free Schools (2001).

Programs may take time to have an impact, and a timely reassessment of bullying can be helpful in identifying areas for improvement. For example, a mid-year assessment of bullying in one middle school found that the program was successful in reducing bullying among sixth- and eighth-grade students, but that seventh-grade girls were experiencing a spike in social and verbal bullying (Posey & Cornell, 2003). The middle school staff responded by focusing more attention on the rivalries and conflicts among a core group of seventh-grade girls. Assessment should become a routine component of bullying prevention programs.

This chapter reviews current methods for the assessment of bullying. Particular attention is given to the issue of self-report versus peer report in estimating the prevalence of bullying and bully victimization. Additionally, this chapter includes measures of bully victimization, characteristics of bullies, and aspects of school climate that influence bullying (Table 13.1).

TABLE 13.1
Selected Measures for the Assessment of Bullying

Measures and Citations	Constructs Measured	Number of Items	Ages
General measures of bullying and school climate			
Peer Relations Questionnaire (Rigby & Slee, 1993)	Tendency to bully, tendency to be victimized, and prosocial tendency	12	12–18
Bully-Victimization Scale (Reynolds, 2003)	Scales to measure frequency of engaging in bullying behaviors and being the victim of bullying	46	8–18
California School Climate and School Safety Scales-Short Form (Furlong et al., 2005)	School climate, personal safety	54	10–18
Peer Nomination Inventory (Eron, Walder, & Lefkowitz, 1971)	Aggression, hyperactivity, victimization, prosocial behaviors, and rejection	26	5–18
Revised Olweus Bully/Victim Questionnaire (Olweus, 1996)	Frequency of being bullied and bullying others, covering different kinds of bullying and duration of bullying	40	8–18
Self-reported Bullying, Fighting, and Victimization (Espelage & Holt, 2001)	Bullying behaviors, fighting, and victim experiences	18	11–13
SRS Safe Schools Survey (Skiba et al., 2004)	Feelings of connection to school, perceptions of incivility and delinquent behavior at school, concerns about personal safety at school	45	10–18
Assessment of Victims			
Bully-Victimization Distress Scale (Reynolds, 2003)	Measures externalizing and internalizing symptoms in response to being bullied	35	8–18
Juvenile Victimization Questionnaire (Finkelhor, Hamby, Ormrod, & Turner, 2004)	Crime, maltreatment, and other victimization experiences during childhood	34	10–17
Multidimensional Peer-Victimization Scale (Mynard & Joseph, 2000)	Physical and verbal victimization, social manipulation, and attacks on property	24	11–16
School Violence Anxiety Scale (Reynolds, 2003)	Symptoms of anxiety in response to fears of school violence and bullying	29	10–18
Social Experience Questionnaire (Crick & Grotpeter, 1996)	Overt and relational victimization, and receipt of prosocial behavior	15	8–11
Assessment of bullying and aggression			
Adolescent Violence Survey (Kingery, 1998)	Common, inventive, and impulsive violence, passive aggression, and menacing behavior	41	12–18
Aggressive Behavior Teacher Checklist (Dodge & Coie, 1987)	Reactive and proactive aggression	6	6–12
Attitudes Toward Peer Aggression Scale (McConville & Cornell, 2003)	Beliefs supportive of peer aggression and bullying	11	10–14

TABLE 13.1
(Continued)

Measures and Citations	Constructs Measured	Number of Items	Ages
Beliefs Questionnaire (Slaby & Guerra, 1988)	Beliefs that fighting is appropriate and that victims deserve what happens to them	8	6–8
Beliefs Supportive of Violence (Bosworth Espelage, & Simon, 1999)	Attitudes toward fighting and aggression	6	11–14
Bullying Behaviour Scale (Austin & Joseph, 1996)	Physical and verbal bullying	6	8–11
Direct and Indirect Aggression Scales (Bjorkqvist, Lagerspetz, & Osterman, 1992)	Physical, verbal, and indirect aggression	24	8–15
Modified Aggression Scale (Bosworth, Espelage, & Simon, 1999)	Fighting, bullying, anger, and cooperative/caring behavior	15	11–14
Normative Beliefs about Aggression Scale (Huesmann, Guerra, Miller, & Zelli, 1989)	Beliefs that aggression is appropriate	20	6–30
Peer Rating of Aggression (Walder, Abelson, Eron, Banta, & Laulicht, 1961)	Physical, verbal, indirect, acquisitive, and unclassified aggression; popularity and aggression anxiety	14	8–10
Peer Nomination Instrument (Crick & Grotpeter, 1995)	Overt and relational aggression, prosocial behavior and isolation	19	8–12
Self-Reported Bullying, Fighting, and Victimization (Espelage & Holt, 2001)	Bullying, fighting, and victimization	18	10–14

SELF-REPORT ASSESSMENT

Research on bullying intervention and prevention owes much to the groundbreaking work of Norwegian researcher Daniel Olweus who, in 1983, implemented a nationwide program to reduce bullying in Norway. His program has served as the model for bully prevention efforts throughout the world, including the United States (Olweus et al., 1999). The Olweus program received international recognition because it produced reductions in bullying of 50% or more. Critical to this recognition is that Olweus had an assessment instrument that could document the success of his program. Without a reliable measure of bullying, Olweus would not have received due credit for the success of his program. Because bullying is so often undetected by adults, the success of any bullying reduction effort is always in question without a good assessment instrument to measure its prevalence before and after program implementation.

Olweus assessed the prevalence of bullying and bully victimization in schools with an anonymous self-report questionnaire that has become the most widely used instrument in bullying research. The Olweus Bully/Victim Questionnaire (Olweus, 1996; Solberg & Olweus, 2003) has undergone several changes over the years; the current version has 36 main questions that encompass bullying and aggressive behavior, involvement in antisocial activities, victim experiences, feelings of acceptance by classmates, negative self-evaluations, and depressive tendencies. A critical feature of this questionnaire is that students are presented with a standard definition of bullying and then asked two key questions: "How often have you been bullied

TABLE 13.2

Implications for Practice: Recommendations for the Assessment of Bullying

---

1. The use of instruments that have uncertain reliability and validity will undermine the integrity of bully prevention programs. Without good assessment data, no program can demonstrate its effectiveness.
2. Teachers should be well prepared for survey administration and motivated to engage the students in taking the survey seriously.
3. Student surveys should be screened for careless, exaggerated, or flagrantly dishonest responding.
4. Peer nominations can be a useful and compelling source of information in identifying bullies and victims.
5. Assessment measures should clearly distinguish bullying from other forms of peer aggression.
6. Assessment of bullying should move beyond questions of prevalence to identify characteristics of bullies and victim.
7. Assessment of school climate may yield valuable information about the context and conditions that promote or prevent bullying.

---

at school in the past couple of months?" and "How often have you taken part in bullying another student(s) at school in the past couple of months?" Students can choose among five possible responses: "I haven't been bullied/bullied other students at school in the past couple of months," "only once or twice," " two or three times a month," "about once a week," and "several times a week."

Subsequent bullying researchers frequently relied on variations of the Olweus instrument, or their own, similar self-report questionnaires to measure bullying (Nansel et al., 2001; Rigby & Slee, 1993; Smith, Madsen, & Moody, 1999). Unfortunately, instruments vary in how they define *bullying*, the wording of questions asking about bullying, and the time periods and frequencies of bullying that students are asked to recall. Even when studies use the Olweus questionnaire, it must be translated into the student's language, and there may be meaningful differences in wording as well as cultural differences in the conceptualization of bullying. Not surprisingly, studies have produced wide differences in the prevalence of bullying across samples, even in studies using modifications of the Olweus questionnaire. Smith et al. (1999) reviewed data from studies in Norway, Sweden, England, Australia, and Ireland, and found considerable variation in the percent of children who reported being bullied both within and across countries. For example, the percent of 11-year-old children who reported being bullied ranged from 3.1% in one Irish sample to 22% in one of the English samples. At age 13, the percentages ranged from 3.3% in a Norwegian sample to 21.3% in an Australian sample. It is not possible to determine whether these differences reflect true national differences or represent artifacts of measurement.

Eslea et al. (2003) compared rates of bullying and victimization in seven countries, all using some form of the Olweus questionnaire. The percent of students classified as bullies ranged from 2% in China to 16.9% in Spain. The percent of students classified as victims ranged from 5.2% in Ireland to 25.6% in Italy. Similarly, the percent of students who claimed no involvement in bullying ranged from 91% in Ireland to just 50.8% in Spain. The researchers pointed out that these differences are so large that it is unlikely they indicate true national differences in behavior.

In an effort to bring more consistency to the assessment of bullying, Solberg and Olweus (2003) defined cutoff points for estimating the prevalence of bullying using the Olweus Bully/Victim Questionnaire. They analyzed response patterns in 5,171 students in Grades 5 through 9 enrolled in 37 schools in Bergen, Norway, and found that 68.2% of students had not been bullied in the past couple of months, and that nearly 22% had been bullied only once or twice. The remaining 10% of students were regarded as victims of bullying because they reported frequencies of "two or three times a month" (4.3%), "about once a week"

(3%), or "several times a week" (2.8%). Solberg and Olweus (2003) concluded that a frequency of "two or three times a month" should be the lower bound for identifying a student as a victim of bullying or as someone who bullies others. It remains for future research to determine whether these cutoffs are equally valid in other countries and different ethnic backgrounds. Another question is whether there should be different cutoffs for different forms of bullying.

Assessment of Program Effectiveness

Student self-report is often used to measure the effectiveness of bullying prevention programs. These studies typically survey students at the outset of the program to determine the prevalence of bullying—usually defined as the percent of students who report bullying others and the percent who report being victims of bullying—and then assess the change in prevalence at some later time, usually after one or more years. Unfortunately, many of these studies have yielded weak or inconsistent results. Roland and Munthe (1997) reported survey results from 37 schools in southwest Norway that were part of the same nationwide campaign studied by Olweus. In contrast to Olweus, they found an increase in bullying among boys and no change among girls. Olweus (1999) hypothesized that the discrepancy between his positive results and those reported by Roland and Munthe were due in part to differences in data quality and times of measurement.

D. Smith and Ananiadou (2003) reviewed bullying prevention programs in England, Canada, Germany, Belgium, and the United States. Each program made use of a modified Olweus questionnaire to assess program effects. The results of each study were largely disappointing; researchers generally found small or statistically nonsignificant reductions in student reports of being bullied or bullying others. In some cases, bullying appeared to increase. One of the more successful programs, the Sheffield project in England, did find a 7% reduction in students who reported bullying others and a 17% increase in the number of pupils who reported not being bullied, but in secondary schools there were reductions of only 37–5% (P. Smith, 1997). Another English program produced reductions of just 1%–4% in five secondary schools (Arora, 1994). Similarly modest results were found in bully prevention programs implemented in Toronto (Pepler, Craig, Ziegler, & Charach, 1994), Germany (Hanewinkel & Eichler, 1999, cited in D. Smith & Ananiadou, 2003), and South Carolina (Melton et al., 1998). Most notably, the Belgian study (Stevens, De Bourdeaudhuij, & Van Oost, 2000) used an experimental design with random assignment of schools to intervention and control conditions, and took special effort to train school personnel and help them implement the program properly. The study found a slight difference between treatment and control schools in self-reported bullying and no differences in self-reports of being bullied. The effects were limited to primary rather than secondary schools.

D. Smith and Ananiadou (2003) pointed out that the use of student self-report to evaluate program effects could be problematic because the intervention tends to sensitize students to recognize and report bullying. The initial baseline assessment might underestimate bullying because students are not fully aware of the different forms of bullying or tend to deny bullying, whereas after participating in the prevention program, students might be more aware of bullying and more willing to report it. In this regard, it is noteworthy that the Sheffield project found a 32% increase in student willingness to report being bullied to teachers (P. Smith, 1997). Ironically, the more effective the program, the more pronounced the sensitization—resulting in the paradoxical conclusion that bullying had increased rather than decreased. Clearly, program evaluations should consider additional ways to assess the impact of their interventions, perhaps by monitoring office referrals for bullying or some other indicator that is less likely to be confounded with the intervention.

Weaknesses in Student Self-Report

Despite the widespread reliance on student self-report to measure bullying, there has been relatively little attention to psychometric issues (Griffin & Gross, 2004; Leff, Power, & Goldstein, 2004). Several researchers have questioned the lack of information on the reliability and validity of self-report instruments used to measure bullying and other high-risk behavior at school (Cornell & Loper, 1998; Cross & Newman-Gonchar, 2004; Rosenblatt & Furlong, 1997). For example, several bully prevention programs provide survey instruments, but report little information on their reliability and validity (Beane, 1999; Garrity et al., 1994; Horne et al., 2003).

Even evidence in support of the Olweus instruments has been slow to emerge. The package of materials accompanying the Olweus Bully/Victim Questionnaire states, "We have made lots of analyses on the internal consistency (reliability), the test–retest reliability and the validity of the Olweus Bully/Victim Questionnaire on large representative samples (more than 5,000 students). The results are generally quite good.... Unfortunately, most of this psychometric information has not yet been published, due to lack of time" (Olweus, 2002; p. 1).

As many researchers have pointed out (Cross & Newman-Gonchar, 2004; Furlong, Sharkey, Bates, & Smith, 2004; Griffin & Gross, 2004; Leff, et al., 2004), self-report measures depend on the student's understanding of the survey questions and his or her memory for events that may be unpleasant to recall. Some students may be tempted to give inflated accounts of their experiences, whereas others may want to minimize or deny their involvement in bullying, whether as perpetrator or victim.

Both careless and dishonest responding could inflate estimates of bullying and bully victimization. Because bullying and victimization generally occur in a small percentage of students, careless or inattentive marking by students will increase their frequency (e.g., random responses to a yes–no question will generate a 50% prevalence rate). Provocative adolescents will produce even higher rates if they intentionally choose the most extreme or unexpected response. Furlong et al. (2004) identified a group of respondents on the Youth Risk Behavior Surveillance survey (YRBS) who claimed to have carried a weapon to school six or more times in the previous month (the most extreme response). Although this might be a credible response in some cases, as a group these students tended to give extreme responses indiscriminately on both healthy and high-risk items. A disproportionate number of the weapon-carrying students claimed to exercise every day, eat plenty of carrots, and drink lots of milk, but also to make frequent suicide attempts, use heroin, sniff glue, and take steroids. The researchers concluded that a group of students gave extreme responses to survey questions regardless of item content.

The time frame for recalling events may influence student responses in unexpected ways. For example, Morrison and Furlong (2002) compared two versions of the California School Climate and Safety Survey (CSCSS), one version inquiring about victim experiences in the past 30 days and the other asking about the same experiences in the past year. Surprisingly, for many items students reported *more* victim experiences in the past 30 days than in the past year. Perhaps the time frame of the question affects the standards that students use to judge whether an event qualifies for reporting, and a shorter time frame prompts students to consider less serious, more frequent events.

Validity screening procedures can substantially reduce estimates of the prevalence of student involvement in high-risk behavior such as fights, drug use, and gangs. In a survey of 10,909 middle and high school students, Cornell and Loper (1998) found that approximately one-fourth of the surveys failed to meet validity screening criteria that included detection of students who omitted demographic information, marked a series of items all in the same way, and gave inappropriate answers to validity questions (e.g., answering "No" to "I am telling the truth on this survey"). The deletion of invalid self-report surveys reduced the estimated 30-day prevalence of fighting at school from 28.7% to 19.2%. Similarly, the estimated prevalence of self-reported drug use at school dropped from 25.1% to 14.8%, gang membership dropped from 8.4% to 5.2%, and carrying a knife at school dropped from 18.4% to 7.7%. Similar research is needed with bullying surveys.

Cross and Newman-Gonchar (2004) screened three different school surveys for the presence of inconsistent responses to items with the same content (e.g., answering "never" when asked what age they belonged to a gang and "yes" to the question, "Have you ever belonged to a gang?") and extreme responses (e.g., claiming to have used LSD 20 or more times in the past 30 days). Surveys with three or more inconsistent and/or extreme responses were identified as "suspect." Although only a small percentage of surveys were identified as suspect—2.7% in one sample and 4.4% in another sample using a different survey—the presence of these suspect surveys inflated estimates of victimization and high-risk behaviors. For example, estimates of the percent of students carrying a handgun at school in the past 30 days jumped by a magnitude of 30—from 0.1% to 3.2%—in one survey; in another survey, reports of physically attacking or harming someone went from 9.9% to 15.8%. Even reports of being physically attacked at school rose from 24.5% to 37.8%.

In one high school, the proportion of students who reported having been bullied was 45.7%, but after suspect surveys were removed from the sample, the proportion dropped to 25%, which is a reduction of more than 45% (Cross & Newman-Gonchar, 2004). In other words, the error in survey results that could be attributable to inconsistent and extreme responding—not considering other forms of error such as limitations in memory or concentration—is larger than the typical reductions reported by many bully prevention programs (D. Smith & Ananiadou, 2003). As a comparison, imagine a medical treatment study in which the instrument used to determine a successful outcome was prone to measurement errors that were larger than the expected treatment effect.

Finally, Cross and Newman-Gonchar (2004) raised an important concern about the effects of administration procedures on student compliance with survey instructions and motivation to give valid answers. They pointed out the lack of standards for classroom administration of surveys. Teachers must be well prepared and motivated to administer the survey, they must have clear instructions and adequate time, and they must be willing and able to engage the students so that they take the survey seriously and put forth a reasonable effort to complete it accurately. The survey should not be so laborious that students lose interest, fail to concentrate, or begin marking answers at random.

Cross and Newman-Gonchar (2004) observed that there were striking differences in survey results between schools that used trained versus untrained survey administrators. In some cases, the teachers were not given adequate instructions or advance notice that they would be administering a lengthy survey in their classroom. Although this was not a controlled study, their post hoc observations were provocative; 28% of surveys obtained by untrained administrators failed to meet validity standards, whereas only 3% of those obtained by trained administrators were considered invalid. The findings by Cross and Newman-Gonchar (2004) do not demonstrate that all self-report surveys are prone to such errors, but they raise concern that teachers should be appropriately prepared to administer any classroom survey and that survey results should be carefully scrutinized for invalid responses.

PEER NOMINATION

Peer reports of bullying are a viable alternative to student self-report. Although Solberg and Olweus (2003) raised objections to the use of peer nominations in the assessment of bullying— because of the arbitrariness in deciding on the number of nominations needed to identify a student as a bully or victim of bullying, and the potential influences of class size and administration procedures—these legitimate concerns could be overcome with systematic measurement research. Moreover, these issues have been addressed in the related field of peer aggression research, where peer nomination is a highly regarded, standard method of identifying aggressive students and their victims (Hawker & Boulton, 2000; Ladd & Kochenderfer-Ladd, 2002; Leff, Kupersmidt, Patterson, & Power, 1999; Pellegrini, Bartini, & Brooks, 1999; Perry, Kusel, & Perry, 1988).

The peer nomination method typically involves surveying a classroom of students and asking each of them independently to identify classmates who match a descriptive statement, such as "someone who gets hit, pushed, or kicked by other kids" (Ladd & Kochenderfer-Ladd, 2002, p. 95). The number of times a student is nominated by peers is used as an index of the student's victim status, and a cutoff may be used to classify a student as a victim or nonvictim. In variations of this method, students are asked to assess their classmates on a series of descriptive statements, to nominate a fixed number of classmates, or to assign frequency ratings (e.g., *never, sometimes*, or *often*) to each of their classmates.

The simple advantage of peer report over self-report is that scores are based on data aggregated from multiple sources, which tends to decrease measurement error and produce a more reliable result. Although some children may make an erroneous judgment about a classmate's involvement in bullying, the combined judgment of the class should be more accurate. The most common reservation about peer nomination is that teachers are reluctant to ask students to make judgments about one another, fearing that the exercise will stimulate teasing or cause anxiety. With appropriate classroom supervision, a peer nomination survey can be administered without such problems.

Several studies have supported the reliability and validity of peer-report measures of child victimization in middle and high school-age children (Achenbach, McConaughy, & Howell, 1987; Ladd & Kochenderfer-Ladd, 2002; Nabuzoka, 2003; Perry, et al. 1988). Peer nomination inventories have been developed to identify both externalizing and internalizing conditions, including aggression, delinquency, and hyperactivity, as well as anxiety and depression (Eron, Walder, & Lefkowitz, 1971; Weiss, Harris, & Catron, 2004).

Researchers have found only moderate correspondence between self and peer reports, generally in the range of .14 to .42 (Achenbach et al., 1987; Juvonen, Nishina, & Graham, 2001; Ladd & Kochenderfer-Ladd, 2002; Perry et al., 1988). Ladd and Kochenderfer-Ladd compared self- and peer reports of peer victimization among primary (Grades K–4) children. They examined student self-reports of being the victim of peer aggression, including physical, verbal, and social forms of aggression that correspond with the types of peer aggression included in most definitions of bullying. They found that concordance between self and peer reports was virtually zero at the kindergarten level, but increased with age and reached .50 among fourth-grade students. In a follow-up study with children in Grades 2–4, Ladd and Kochenderfer-Ladd (2002) examined the concordance among self-, peer, and teacher report measures of child victimization. Once again they observed increasing levels of concordance in higher grades. For fourth-grade students, self-reports correlated .47 with peer reports and .30 with teacher reports, whereas peer and teacher reports correlated .47.

In perhaps the most ambitious comparison of methods, Pellegrini (2001) assessed 367 sixth graders with peer nominations and self-report rating scales (but not self-identification as a victim) from one of the earlier Olweus questionnaires. Trained observers conducted regular observations throughout an entire school year, and once a month for the whole school year students wrote in a diary recounting any victim experiences in the past 24 hours. The range of correlations among the four measures was .07 to .34. Peer nominations correlated significantly with all three of the other measures (.21 to .32, all $p < .05$) and the Olweus self-report scales correlated .34 with diary entries. Direct observation did not correlate significantly with self-report or the diary measure.

Juvonen et al. (2001) argued that self-report and peer nomination methods are complementary and assess different constructs. They asserted that self-reports capture the student's self-perception, and this may not correspond with his or her social reputation, which is measured by peer perceptions. From this perspective, researchers should use both methods. Indeed, some studies have used both methods and identified students who perceive themselves to be (a) victims who are not perceived as victims by peers, (b) students who do not report themselves to be victims but are perceived as victims by peers, and (c) students who are identified as victims by both self-report and peer-report methods (Crick & Bigbee, 1998; Graham, Bellmore, & Juvonen, 2003; Pellegrini et al., 1999). There is validational evidence to support both methods in these studies.

There are many examples of successful use of peer nomination inventories for research purposes. Eron et al. (1971) developed a 26-item peer nomination inventory to assess aggression, hyperactivity, and victimization in school-age children. This well-established inventory has been used repeatedly in longitudinal studies of childhood aggression, including predictions of aggressive and criminal behavior for periods up to 22 years (Huesmann, Eron, Guerra, & Crawshaw, 1994).

Crick and Grotpeter (1995) developed a 19-item peer nomination instrument to assess overt (physical aggression and threatening behavior) and relational (social exclusion) aggression in 9- to 12-year-old children. Students are given a class roster and asked to select up to three classmates who fit descriptions such as "children who say mean things to other kids." Crick and Bigbee (1998) found that girls experienced more relational victimization, whereas boys experienced more overt victimization. Both peer and self-reported victims scored as more maladjusted than nonvictims in self-reported measures of social-psychological adjustment; students identified as victims by both methods were least well adjusted.

Fox and Boulton (2003) demonstrated how a peer nomination inventory could be used to evaluate the effectiveness of a social skills training program for victims of bullying. The peer nomination inventory assessed social skills problems, peer victimization, friendship, and peer acceptance. A small group of children were identified as victims of bullying if they received more than 33% of classroom nominations for being a victim of verbal, physical, or social bullying. Evaluation data for a small group ($N = 15$) were collected from classmates at the conclusion of treatment and again at a follow-up several months later, but yielded little evidence of treatment effects. What is needed is a large-scale peer nomination study with adequate statistical power to identify the effects of bullying interventions. In collecting peer nomination data for evaluation purposes, it may be especially important to direct students to attend to a recent time period, so that they are not overly influenced by longstanding reputations or victimization experiences that preceded the intervention.

The choice of instrument to assess bullying can have a powerful effect on the nature and course of the intervention. If school authorities or researchers choose to measure the baseline prevalence of bullying with an anonymous self-report measure, they may learn how much bullying is occurring, but they will not know who is being bullied and by whom. With this limited knowledge, interventions naturally focus on schoolwide rules and curriculum units on bullying. Meanwhile, counselors must wait for bullying to be reported before they can intervene with specific students. Unfortunately, many students do not seek help for bullying and teachers often do not detect it (Unnever & Cornell, 2003, 2004).

The peer nomination method may be especially valuable for school counselors attempting to reduce bullying because it can focus and expedite their intervention efforts by identifying specific students who are perceived to be victims and perpetrators of bullying. Assisted by this information, counselors can observe or interview these students to confirm their involvement. Peer nomination data in which one or more students are identified as a victim by a large number of classmates can be useful in convincing teachers that bullying is a problem in their classroom and motivating them to take action.

OBSERVATIONAL AND INTERVIEW METHODS

Direct behavioral observations of children and adolescents at school have yielded valuable insights into the circumstances and frequency of bullying, and provided information about the role of bystanders as well as direct participants in bullying incidents (Craig & Pepler, 1997; Salmivalli, Lagerspetz, Bjorkqvist, Osterman, & Kaukianien, 1996). Unfortunately, observational methods are laborious and costly to undertake because they must be conducted across a long period of time and in a variety of settings (e.g., playground, cafeteria, and classroom) to yield reliable scores (Pellegrini, 2001). As noted previously, even with systematic surveillance by a team of observers over an entire school year, observational ratings correlated .22 with peer nominations and failed to correlate significantly with student self-report or diary entries (Pellegrini, 2001).

Another potential problem is that because bullying often occurs when adults are not present, students who know they are being observed will be less likely to engage in it. More subtle forms of social bullying may not be apparent to observers. Pellegrini (2001) reported that students do habituate to observers and behave more naturally, at least in their use of language and play behavior, but it seems unlikely that serious bullying would occur in plain view.

Can teachers identify bullying? Teachers are reliable sources of ratings for many standard measures of child behavior and adjustment (e.g., Achenbach, 1991; Reynolds & Kamphaus, 2004) and for specialized scales to measure aggressive behavior (e.g., Dodge & Coie, 1987; Shapiro, 2000). Several studies have used teacher reports to identify bullies and victims (Hazler, Miller, Carney, & Greek, 2001; Leff et al., 1999; Nabuzoka, 2003). Nevertheless, there is some question about the reliance on teachers to identify bullying. An observational study by Craig, Pepler, and Atlas (2000) found that teachers often overlook or ignore bullying. In some cases, the teacher may be simply unaware of the bullying; for example, Cornell and Brockenbrough (2004) found that many middle school students identified as victims of bullying by their peers were not recognized as victims by teachers. In one middle school, 12 students were identified as victims of bullying by 10 or more classmates, yet only 4 of these students were identified by their teachers. Leff et al. (1999) found that elementary and middle school teachers identified just 44% of peer-reported bullies and 41% of peer-reported victims.

Another approach is to interview students directly about their involvement in bullying. Although schools more often rely on questionnaires for practical reasons, we know of one elementary school where the principal decided to interview each student in the younger grades by calling them aside one at a time during their physical education class. Each interview lasted just a few minutes while the principal or an assistant principal presented a brief definition of bullying and asked the child if he or she was being treated that way by anyone. The principal was able to interview more than 100 students in a few class periods and identified several previously unknown cases of chronic bullying.

Although research on bullying relies primarily on school-based questionnaires, research on juvenile victimization makes extensive use of direct interviewing, often via home visits or telephone calls. Interviews permit the researcher to interact with the youth, clarify questions, and generally pursue more complete and accurate information. On the other hand, some youth may be uncomfortable discussing sensitive topics in an interview. By comparing interview and questionnaire data, juvenile victimization researchers have generally concluded that adequate information can be obtained with both face-to-face and telephone interviews (Hamby & Finkelhor, 2000). For particularly sensitive subjects (e.g., sexual abuse), researchers have experimented with audio-enhanced, computer-assisted self-interviewing (audio-CASI), which permits interviewees to listen on headphones and type their answers on a laptop computer (Hamby & Finkelhor, 2000).

ASSESSMENT OF VICTIM CHARACTERISTICS

Bullying represents one of many forms of child victimization, a field that has received considerable attention from researchers in multiple disciplines (Hamby & Finkelhor, 2000). Childhood victimization is linked to subsequent emotional disorder, social maladjustment, academic difficulties, and other adverse outcomes (Hawker & Boulton, 2000; Ladd & Ladd, 2001; Rigby, 2001). Rigby demonstrated that both self-reported and peer-reported victimization was associated with suicidal ideation in Australian adolescents.

In recent years, a large number of scales have been designed to go beyond identification of victims to assess their experiences and reactions in more detail. Although these scales may be supported by factor analyses and demonstrate adequate internal consistency, more evidence is needed for their validity. Frequently, self-report victim scales are correlated with other self-report measures, but the modest correlations obtained in such studies could be attributable to shared method variance or mere consistency in student self-report.

Mynard and Joseph (2000) developed the Multidimensional Peer-Victimization scale to distinguish direct from indirect bullying. The scale contains 45 items asking how often a student has experienced various forms of bullying (*not at all, once*, or *more than once*) during the school year. A factor analysis based on a sample of 812 English secondary students (ages 11 to 16) resulted in four factors: physical victimization, verbal victimization, social manipulation, and attacks on property, all with internal consistency (α) of at least .73. Convergent validity for the scale was limited to comparisons between students who responded "yes" or "no" to the question, "Have you ever been bullied?"

Reynolds (2003) recently introduced three brief self-report scales designed to measure bullying and anxiety over school violence in Grade 3–12 students. The Bully-Victimization scale contains items to measure bullying behaviors and victim experiences, the Bully-Victimization Distress scale measures externalizing and internalizing symptoms related to bullying, and the School Violence Anxiety scale measures anxiety associated with perceiving the school to be unsafe. The scales were standardized on a national sample of more than 2,400 students in Grades 3–12 (1,850 students in grades 5–12 for School Violence Anxiety). Reynolds converted raw scores into T-scores and judged that students scoring over T-58—approximately 14% of the standardization sample—"demonstrated a meaningful level of bullying behavior," but he cautioned that the scores are "not indications of who has or has not bullied or been bullied" (p. 58). This caution is well justified, because scores on the Bully-Victimization scale could be inflated by reports of aggression and conflict between peers of equal status, which would not meet the definition of bullying. Reynolds (2003) reported good test–retest reliability for scores on all three scales and found that scores correlated moderately with teacher ratings (e.g., the Bullying scale correlated .46 with teacher ratings of bullying and .47 with past school disciplinary violations).

Hamby and Finkelhor (2000) articulated specific standards and recommendations for the assessment of child victimization, which although largely concerned with the broad range of criminal offenses against children, have useful applications to bullying. They recommended collecting data that permits victimization experiences to be mapped onto standard crime categories, which would enhance links to research using national databases and national surveys such as the National Crime Victimization Survey. They also recommended assessment of specific behaviors over more ambiguous global categories such as "assault." They pointed out that adult victims are sometimes reluctant to label their experiences with emotionally laden terms such as *rape* and *abuse*; perhaps a similar reluctance affects victims of *bullying*. Finally, they offered valuable practical advice on the use of clear, simple language and time concepts in assessing younger children.

Finkelhor, Hamby, Ormrod, and Turner (2004) recently developed the Juvenile Victimization Questionnaire (JVQ) to cover 34 offenses against youth. The JVQ is administered to children or, in the case of children under age 10, their parents. They identify one question in the Peer and Sibling Victimization section as an indication of bullying ("In the last year, did any kids, even a brother or sister, pick on you by chasing you or grabbing your hair or clothes or by making you do something you didn't want to do?") and another as "emotional bullying" ("In the last year, did you get scared or feel really bad because kids were calling you names, saying mean things to you, or saying they didn't want you around?"). Two items are likely not adequate to measure bullying accurately, but in the context of a broader survey of victim experiences, they help demonstrate the importance of bullying in comparison to other forms of victimization. In their standardization study of 1,000 children (ages 10–17) and parent/caregivers of an additional 1,030 children ages 2–9, Finkelhor et al. (2004) found that the two bullying items identified 21.7% of children as victims of physical bullying and 24.9% as victims of emotional bullying in the past year. A test–retest reliability study on 100 youth over a 3- to 4-week period indicated adequate reliability for both physical bullying (81% agreement, $\kappa = .33$) and emotional bullying (85% agreement and $\kappa = .51$). Interestingly, the researchers correlated the incidence of 34 types of victimization with self-report measures of anxiety, depression, and anger (for 992 youth ages 10–17). Among these 34 victim experiences, physical bullying and emotional bullying produced the highest correlations with anxiety and depression (range .18 to .33).

ASSESSMENT OF AGGRESSIVE AND BULLYING BEHAVIOR

It is important to distinguish bullying from broader forms of peer aggression. Bullying must be a repeated activity and does not include conflicts between peers of comparable strength or power (Olweus, 1996). In some studies, items that measure hitting, teasing, or relational conflict are treated as indices of bullying, although student responses could refer to conflict between peers of comparable strength or status. Assessment of aggression is discussed in other chapters in this book.

In an influential study, Dodge and Coie (1987) found that boys identified by teachers as engaging primarily in proactive aggression enjoyed a favorable and more dominant peer status in comparison with boys who engaged in reactive aggression. When asked to make judgments about provocative peer interactions presented in videotaped skits, reactively aggressive boys displayed a tendency to misjudge the interaction and to attribute hostile motives or intentions to others, which was termed *hostile attributional bias*. Subsequent studies have confirmed the link between hostile attributional bias and reactive aggression in juvenile offenders (Dodge, Price, Bachorowski, & Newman, 1990). Pellegrini, et al. (1999) found that bullies scored higher in both reactive and proactive aggression, but that only proactive aggression was associated with higher peer status. The strategy of presenting students with videotaped scenarios is an intriguing assessment method that might be used in investigations of bullies and bully victims.

Examination of aggressive attitudes has identified a subgroup of victims who are themselves highly aggressive and are sometimes referred to as *bully-victims* or *aggressive victims* (Schwartz, Proctor, & Chien, 2001). These victims rate highly on measures of reactive aggression, they are unpopular with their peers and feel unsupported by adults at school, and they report more high-risk behavior such as weapon carrying and substance use than other students (Brockenbrough, Cornell, & Loper, 2002; Pellegrini et al. 1999). Such findings underscore the need to move beyond global identification of bullies and victims to assess psychological characteristics and needs that should be considered in intervention planning.

ASSESSMENT OF SCHOOL CLIMATE

Espelage and Swearer (2004) have championed a social ecological approach to bullying that emphasizes the role of contextual factors that influence bullying. From this perspective, it is important to assess prevailing attitudes and values in a school that can affect bully prevention efforts. Unnever and Cornell (2003) referred to a "culture of bullying" in middle schools where bullying behavior and unwarranted acts of aggression are regarded as normal events and there is a prevailing belief that teachers will not intervene. Using a scale derived from the Olweus Bully/Victim Questionnaire, Unnever and Cornell found that attitudes supporting a culture of bullying were prevalent throughout the student bodies of six middle schools. Students with aggressive attitudes and high levels of anger were most likely to hold this perception of the school climate. A subsequent study found that students who perceive their school as accepting of bullying are less likely than other students to seek help when they are bullied (Unnever & Cornell, 2004). Such findings can be used to identify areas for school improvement that could bolster bullying prevention efforts.

Holt and Keyes (2004) developed a 50-item survey of teacher attitudes toward bullying that measured constructs such as teacher support for equity and diversity and assessing teacher perceptions of how much hostility is expressed through jokes and disrespectful behavior toward others. The next step with these kinds of measures is to show how teacher attitudes affect the prevalence of bullying and what kinds of interventions can alter teacher attitudes.

The CSCSS (Furlong et al., 1991) has been used in a series of studies to measure perceptions of school climate, danger at school, and victim experiences. The CSCSS is reviewed in more detail elsewhere in this book. A noteworthy feature of the CSCSS is that it included two validity items (e.g., "In the past month you took 10 field trips") to identify students who were not responding appropriately to the survey and three items to measure the tendency of students to present themselves in an unrealistically favorable light (e.g., "I like everyone I meet").

The original 102-item survey has been reduced to a 54-item short form (CSCSS–SF) to facilitate routine use by schools (Furlong, Greif, Bates, Whipple, Jimenez, & Morrison, 2005). The new short form has a School Danger section based on seven items to measure how often students fight, steal, bully, destroy things, use drugs, drink alcohol, and carry weapons at school. The School Climate section has two subscales, one to assess whether students view teachers as supportive and rules as fair, and another that asks about the presence of gang members, crime, and school and community violence. The School Victimization section has subscales to measure physical–verbal harassment, weapons and physical attacks, and sexual harassment. Another measure of school climate is the newly developed Safe and Responsive Safe Schools Survey (Skiba et al., 2004).

FUTURE DIRECTIONS IN BULLYING ASSESSMENT

Although assessment is the Achilles heel of bullying prevention, improved measurement of the nature and extent of bullying could be a powerful source of support for implementing and sustaining a school intervention program. Self-report undoubtedly will continue to be the most popular means of measuring the prevalence of school bullying, so it is critically important that researchers tackle the measurement issues that cloud the results obtained with current self-report instruments. Self-report instruments are vulnerable to intentional biases and unintentional errors in student reporting. Students may not carefully distinguish bullying from other forms peer aggression.

To overcome the potential shortcomings of student self-report, there should be wider use of peer nomination measures—in concert with self-report—to gain a more complete and compelling picture of the prevalence of bullying in schools. If the prevalence of bullying is assessed only by anonymous self-report, school authorities will not know which students are involved in bullying. Supplemental use of a peer nomination measure will give counselors immediate direction in identifying the participants in bullying as part of an overall effort to provide support for bully victims as well as to intervene constructively with bully perpetrators.

To address questions that go beyond prevalence, there are a wide variety of instruments to measure psychological characteristics of bullying and victims of bullying. The field of bullying prevention would benefit from greater integration with the extensive research literatures on childhood aggression and victimization, although it is important to maintain the distinction between bullying and other forms of peer aggression. Finally, the assessment of school climate may be especially helpful in identifying the conditions that permit bullying to flourish, and the sorts of interventions that will reduce it.

REFERENCES

Achenbach, T. M. (1991). *Integrative guide for the 1991 CBCL/4-18, YSR, and TRF profiles.* Burlington, VT: Department of Psychiatry, University of Vermont.

Achenbach, T. M., McConaughy, S. H., & Howell, C. T. (1987). Child/adolescent behavioral and emotional problems: Implications of cross-informant correlations for situational specificity. *Psychological Bulletin, 101*, 213–232.

Arora, C. M. J. (1994). *Measuring bullying with the "Life in School Checklist."* Sheffield, UK: Education Division, Sheffield University.

Austin, S., & Joseph, S. (1996). Assessment of bully/victim problems in 8 to 11-year-olds. *British Journal of Educational Psychology, 66*, 447–456.

Beane, A. (1999). *The bully-free classroom.* Minneapolis, MN: Free Spirit.

Bjorkqvist, K., Lagerspetz, K., & Kaukinian, A. (1992). Do girls manipulate and boys fight?: Developmental trends in regard to direct and indirect aggression. *Aggressive Behavior, 18*, 117–127.

Bjorkqvist, K., Lagerspetz, K. M. J., & Osterman, K. (1992). *The direct and indirect aggression Scales.* Vasa, Finlad: Department of Social Sciences, Abo Akademi University.

Bosworth, K., Espelage, D. L., & Simon, T. R. (1999). Factors associated with bullying behavior in middle school students. *Journal of Early Adolescence, 19*, 341–362.

Brockenbrough, K., Cornell, D., & Loper, A. (2002). Aggressive victims of violence at school. *Education and Treatment of Children, 25*, 273–287.

Cornell, D. G., & Brockenbrough, K. (2004). Identification of bullies and victims: A comparison of methods. *Journal of School Violence, 3*, 63–87.

Cornell, D. G., & Loper, A. B. (1998). Assessment of violence and other high-risk behaviors with a school survey. *School Psychology Review, 27*, 317–330.

Craig, W., & Pepler, D. (1997). Observations of bullying and victimization in the schoolyard. *Canadian Journal of School Psychology, 13*, 41–59.

Craig, W. M., Pepler, D., & Atlas, R. (2000). Observations of bullying in the playground and in the classroom. *School Psychology International, 21*, 22–36.

Crick, N., & Bigbee, M. (1998). Relational and overt forms of peer victimization: A multi-informant approach. *Journal of Consulting and Clinical Psychology, 66*, 337–347.

Crick, N., & Grotpeter, J. (1995). Relational aggression, gender, and social-psychological adjustment. *Child Development, 66*, 710–722.

Crick, N., & Grotpeter, J. (1996). Children's treatment by peers: Victims of relational and overt aggression. *Development and psychopathology, 8*, 367–380.

Cross, J., & Newman-Gonchar, R. (2004). Data quality in student risk behavior surveys and administrator training. *Journal of School Violence, 3*, 89–108.

Dodge, K. A., & Coie, J. D. (1987). Social-information-processing factors in reactive and proactive aggression in children's peer groups. *Journal of Personality and Social Psychology, 53*, 1146–1158.

Dodge, K. A., Price, J., Bachorowski, J., & Newman, J. (1990). Hostile attributional biases in severely aggressive adolescents. *Journal of Abnormal Psychology, 99*, 385–392.

Eron, L. D., Walder, L. O., & Lefkowitz, M. M. (1971). *Learning of aggression in children.* Boston, MA: Little, Brown.

Eslea, M., Menesini, E., Morita, Y., O'Moore, M., Mora-Merchan, J., Pereira, B., & Smith, P. (2003). Friendship and loneliness among bullies and victims: Data from seven countries. *Aggressive Behavior, 30*, 71–83.

Espelage, D. L., & Holt, M. K. (2001). Bullying and victimization during early adolescence: Peer influences and psychosocial correlates. *Journal of Emotional Abuse, 2*, 123–142.

Espelage, D., & Swearer, S. (Eds.). (2004). *Bullying in American schools: A social-ecological perspective on prevention and intervention.* Mahwah, NJ: Lawrence Erlbaum Associated.

Finkelhor, D., Hamby, S., Ormrod, R., & Turner, H. (2004). *The Juvenile Victimization Questionnaire: Reliability, validity, and national norms.* Unpublished report. Crimes against Children Research Center, University of New Hampshire, Durham, NH.

Fox, C., & Boulton, M. (2003). Evaluating the effectiveness of a social skills training (SST) programme for victims of bullying. *Educational Research, 45*, 231–247.

Furlong. M., Greif, J., Bates, M., Whipple, A., Jimenez, T., & Morrison, R. (2005). *California School Climate & Safety Survey-Short Form. Psychology in the Schools, 43*, 137–150.

Furlong, M., & Morrison, R., & Boles, S. (1991). *California School Climate and Safety Survey.* Santa Barbara: University of California, Santa Barbara, UCSB School Climate & Safety Partnership.

Furlong, M., Sharkey, J., Bates, M. P., & Smith, D. (2004). An examination of reliability, data screening procedures, and extreme response patterns for the Youth Risk Behavior Surveillance Survey. *Journal of School Violence, 3*, 109–130.

Garrity, C., Jens, K., Porter, W., Sager, N., & Short-Camilli, C. (1994). *Bully-proofing your school.* Longmont, CO: Sopris West.

Graham, S., Bellmore, A., & Juvonen, J. (2003). Peer victimization in middle school: When self and peer views diverge. *Journal of Applied Psychology, 19,* 117–137.

Griffin, R. S., & Gross, A. M. (2004). Childhood bullying: Current empirical findings and future directions for research. *Aggression and Violent Behavior, 9*, 379–400.

Hamby, S., & Finkelhor, D. (2000). The victimization of children: Recommendations for assessment and instrument development. *Journal of the American Academy of Child & Adolescent Psychiatry, 39*, 829–840.

Hanewinkel, R., & Eichler, D. (1999). Ergebnisse enier Interventionsstudie zur Prävention schulischer Gewalt [Study of an intervention on presenting violence in schools]. In M. Schäfer & D. Frey (Eds.), *Aggression und gewlat unter kindern und jugendlichen* (pp. 245–264). Göttingern: Hogrefe-Verlag.

Hawker, D., & Boulton, M. (2000). Twenty years' research on peer victimization and psychosocial maladjustment: A meta-analytic review of cross-sectional studies. *Journal of Child Psychology & Psychiatry & Allied Disciplines, 41*, 441–455.

Hazler, R., Miller, D., Carney, J., & Green, S. (2001). Adult recognition of school bullying situations. *Educational Research, 43,* 133–146.

Holt, M., & Keyes, M. (2004). Teachers' attitudes toward bullying. In D. Espelage & S. Swearer (Eds.), *Bullying in American schools: A social-ecological perspective on prevention and intervention* (pp. 121–140). Mahwah, NJ: Lawrence Erlbaum Assocites.

Horne, A. M., Bartolomucci, C. L., & Newman-Carlson, D. (2003). *Bully Busters: A teacher's manual for helping bullies, victims, and bystanders (Grades K-5).* Champaign, IL: Research Press.

Huesmann, L., Eron, L., Guerra, N., & Crawshaw, B. (1994). Measuring children's aggression with teachers' predictions of peer nominations. *Psychological Assessment, 6*, 329–336.

Huesmann, L., Guerra, N., Miller, L., & Zelli, A. (1989). The role of social norms in the development of aggression. In H. Zumkley & A. Fraczek (Eds.), *Socialization and aggression* (pp. 139–151). New York: Springer.

Juvonen, J., Nishina, A., & Graham, S. (2001). Self-views versus peer perceptions of victim status among early adolescents. In J. Juvonen & S. Graham (Eds.), *Peer harassment in school: A plight of the vulnerable and victimized* (pp. 105–124). New York: Guilford.

Kingery, P. M. (1998). The adolescent violence survey. *School Psychology International, 19,* 43–59.

Ladd, B., & Ladd, G. (2001). Variations in peer victimization: Relations to children's maladjustment. In J. Juvonen & S. Graham (Eds.). *Peer harassment in school: The plight of the vulnerable and victimized* (pp. 25-48). New York: Guilford.

Ladd, G. W., & Kochenderfer-Ladd, B. (2002). Identifying victims of peer aggression from early to middle childhood: Analysis of cross-informant data from concordance, estimation of relational adjustment, prevalence of victimization, and characteristics of identified victims. *Psychological Assessment, 14*, 74–96.

Leff, S., Kupersmidt, J., Patterson, C., & Power, T. (1999). Factors influencing teacher identification of peer bullies and victims. *School Psychology Review, 28*, 505–517.

Leff, S., Power, T., & Goldstein, A. (2004). Outcome measures to assess the effectiveness of bullying prevention programs in the schools. In D. Espelage & S. Swearer (Eds.), *Bullying in American schools: A social-ecological perspective on prevention and intervention* (pp. 269-293). Mahwah, NJ: Lawrence Erlbaum Associates.

Limber, S., & Small, M. (2003). State laws and policies to address bullying in schools. *School Psychology Review, 32,* 445–455.

McConville, D., & Cornell, D. (2003). Attitudes toward aggression and aggressive behavior among middle school students. *Journal of Emotional and Behavioral Disorders, 11,* 179–187.

Melton, G. B., Limber, S. P., Cunningham, P., Osgood, D. W., Chambers, J., Flerx, V., Henggeler, S., & Nation, M. (1998). *Violence among rural youth.* Final report to the Office of Juvenile Justice and Delinquency Prevention Washington, DC.

Morrison, G., & Furlong, M. J. (2002, June). *Understanding the turning points in students' school discipline histories.* Paper presented at Safe Schools for the 21st Century, National Conference of the Hamilton Fish Institute, Monterey, CA.

Mynard, H., & Joseph, S. (2000). Development of the Multidimensional Peer-Victimization Scale. *Aggressive Behavior, 26,* 169–178.

Mytton, J. A., DiGuiseppi, C., Gough, D. A., Taylor, R. S., & Logan, S. (2002). School-based violence prevention programs: Systematic review of secondary prevention trials. *Archives of Pediatrics & Adolescent Medicine, 156,* 752–762.

Nabuzoka, D. (2003). Teacher ratings and peer nominations of bullying and other behaviour of children with and without learning difficulties. *Educational Psychology, 23,* 307–321.

Nansel, T., Overpeck, M., Pilla, R., Ruan, W., Simons-Morton, B., & Scheidt, P. (2001). Bullying behaviors among US youth: Prevalence and association with psychosocial adjustment. *American Medical Association, 285,* 2094–2100.

National Crime Prevention Council. (2003). *Fight crime: Invest in kids.* Available: http://www.fightcrime.org

National Youth Violence Prevention Resource Center. (2003). *Take action against bullying.* Available: http://media.shs.net/ken/pdf/svp-0056/svp-0056.pdf

Olweus, D. (1991). Bully/victim problems among schoolchildren: Basic facts and effects of a school based intervention program. In D. Pepler & K. Rubin (Eds.), *The development and treatment of childhood aggression* (pp. 411–448). Hillsdale, NJ: Lawrence Erlbaum Associates.

Olweus, D. (1996). The Revised Olweus Bully/Victim Questionnaire. Bergen, Norway: Mimeo, Research Center for Health Promotion (HEMIL), University of Bergen.

Olweus, D. (1999). Norway. In P. K. Smith, Y. Morita, J. Junger-Tas, D. Olweus, R. Catalano, & P. Slee (Eds.), *The nature of school bullying: A cross-national perspective* (pp. 28–48). New York: Routledge.

Olweus, D. (2002). *General information about the Revised Olweus Bully/Victim Questionnaire, PC program and teacher handbook* (pp. 1–12). Bergen, Norway: Mimeo, Research Center for Health Promotion (HEMIL), University of Bergen.

Olweus, D., Limber, S., & Mihalic, S. F. (1999). *Blueprints for violence prevention, book nine: Bullying Prevention Program.* Boulder, CO: Center for the Study and Prevention of Violence.

Osher, D., Dwyer, K., & Jackson, S. (2004). *Safe, supportive and successful schools: Step by step.* Longmont, CO: Sopris West.

O'Toole, M. E. (2000). *The school shooter: A threat assessment perspective.* Quantico, VA: National Center for the Analysis of Violent Crime, Federal Bureau of Investigation.

Pellegrini, A. D. (2001). Sampling instances of victimization in middle school: A methodological comparison. In J. Juvonen & S. Graham (Eds.), *Peer harassment in school: The plight of the vulnerable and victimized* (pp. 125–146). New York: Guilford.

Pellegrini, A. D., Bartini, M., & Brooks, F. (1999). School bullies, victims, and aggressive victims: Factors relating to group affiliation and victimization in early adolescence. *Journal of Educational Psychology, 91,* 216–224.

Pepler, D. J., Craig, W. M., Ziegler, S., & Charach, A. (1994). An evaluation of an anti-bullying intervention in Toronto schools. *Canadian Journal of Community Mental Health, 13,* 95–110.

Perry, D., Kusel, S., & Perry, L. (1988). Victims of peer aggression. *Developmental Psychology, 24,* 807–814.

Posey, J., & Cornell, D. (2003). *Lessons learned from research on a middle school bullying prevention program.* Unpublished manuscript, Curry School of Education, University of Virginia.

Reynolds, W. (2003). *Reynolds Bully Victimization Scales for Schools.* San Antonio, TX: Psychological Corp.

Reynolds, C. R., & Kamphaus, R. W. (2004). *Behavioral Assessment System for Children, Second Edition.* Circle Pines, MN: American Guidance Services.

Rigby, K. (2001). Health consequences of bullying and its prevention in schools. In J. Juvonen & S. Graham (Eds.), *Peer harassment in school* (pp. 310–331). New York: Guilford.

Rigby, K., & Slee, P. (1993). Dimensions of interpersonal relating among Australian schoolchildren and their implications for psychological well-being. *Journal of Social Psychology, 133,* 33–42.

Roland, E., & Munthe, E. (1997). The 1996 Norwegian program for preventing and managing bullying in schools. *Irish Journal of Psychology, 18,* 233–247.

Rosenblatt, J. A., & Furlong, M. J. (1997). Assessing the reliability and validity of student self-reports of campus violence. *Journal of Youth and Adolescence, 26,* 187–202.

Salmivalli, C., Lagerspetz, K., Bjorkqvist, K., Osterman, K., & Kaukianien, A. (1996). Bullying as a group process: Participant roles and their relations to social status within the group. *Aggressive Behavior, 22,* 1–15.

Schwartz, D., Proctor, L. J., & Chien, D. H. (2001). The aggressive victim of bullying: Emotional and behavioral dysregulation as a pathway to victimization by peers. In J. Juvonen & S. Graham (Eds.), *Peer harassment in school: The plight of the vulnerable and victimized* (pp. 147–174). New York: Guilford.

Shapiro, J. P. (2000). *Attitudes toward guns and violence questionnaire: Manual.* Los Angeles, CA: Western Psychological Services.

Skiba, R., Simmons, A. B., Peterson, R., McKelvey, J., Ford, S., & Gallini, S. (2004). Beyond guns, drugs, and gangs: The structure of student perceptions of school safety. *Journal of School Violence, 3,* 149–171.

Slaby, R., & Guerra, N. (1988). Cognitive mediators of aggression in adolescent offenders: 1. Assessment. *Developmental Psychology, 24,* 580–588.

Smith, J. D., Schneider, B. H., Smith, P. K., & Ananiadou, K. (2004). The effectiveness of whole-school antibullying programs: A synthesis of evaluation research. *School Psychology Review, 33,* 547–560.

Smith, D., & Ananiadou, K. (2003). The nature of school bullying and the effectiveness of school-based interventions. *Journal of Applied Psychoanalytic Studies, 5,* 189–209.

Smith, D., Madsen, K., & Moody, J. (1999). What causes the age decline in reports of being bullied at school? Towards a developmental analysis of risks of being bullied. *Educational research, 41,* 267–285.

Smith, P. (1997). Bullying in schools: The UK experience and the Sheffield Anti-Bullying project. *The Irish Journal of Psychology, 18,* 191–201.

Solberg, M., & Olweus, D. (2003). Prevalence estimation of school bullying with the Olweus Bully/Victim Questionnaire. *Aggressive Behavior, 29,* 239–268.

Stevens, V., De Bourdeaudhuij, I., & Van Oost, P. (2000). *Pesten op school: Een actieprogrammema* [An intervention against bully/victim problems at school]. Kessel-Lo, Belguim: Garant Uitgevers.

Tremblay, R. E., Loeber, R., Gagnon, C., Charlebois, P., Larivee, S., & LeBlanc, M. (1991). Disruptive boys with stable and unstable high fighting behavior patterns during junior elementary school. *Journal of Abnormal Child Psychology, 19,* 285–300.

U.S. Department of Education. (2002). *Preventing bullying.* Available: www.ericfacility.net/databases/ERICDigests/ed463563.html

U.S. Department of Health and Human Services. (2001). *Youth violence: A report of the Surgeon General.* Rockville, MD: Author.

U.S. Office of Safe and Drug-Free Schools. (2001). *Principles of effectiveness.* Available: www.ed.gov/index.jhtml

Unnever J., & Cornell, D. (2003). The culture of bullying in middle school. *Journal of School Violence, 2,* 5–27.

Unnever, J., & Cornell, D. (2004). Middle school victims of bullying: Who reports being bullied? *Aggressive Behavior, 30,* 373–388.

Vossekuil, B., Fein, R. A., Reddy, M., Borum, R., & Modzeleski, W. (2002). *The final report and findings of the Safe School Initiative: Implications for the prevention of school attacks in the United States.* Washington, DC: U.S. Secret Service and U.S. Department of Education.

Walder, L. O., Abelson, R. P., Eron, L. D., Banta, T. J., & Laulicht, J. H. (1961). Development of a peer-rating measure of aggression. *Psychological Reports, 9,* 497–556.

Weiss, B., Harris, V., & Catron, T. (2004). Development and initial validation of the peer-report measure of internalizing and externalizing behavior. *Journal of Abnormal Child Psychology, 30,* 285–294.

Whitaker, D., Rosenbluth, B., Valle, L., & Sanchez, E. (2004). Expect Respect: A school-based intervention to promote awareness and effective responses to bullying and sex harassment. In D. Espelage & S. Swearer (Eds.), *Bullying in American schools: A social-ecological perspective on prevention and intervention* (pp. 327–350). Mahwah, NJ: Lawrence Erlbaum Associates.

Wilson, S. J., Lipsey, M. W., & Derzon, J. H. (2003). The effects of school-based intervention programs on aggressive behavior: A meta-analysis. *Journal of Consulting and Clinical Psychology, 71,* 136–149.

14

Assessing School Discipline

Gale M. Morrison
Megan Redding
University of California, Santa Barbara

Emily Fisher
Loyola Marymount University

Reece Peterson
University of Nebraska

In the search for predictors of school violence, attention has often rested on school discipline, both as an indicator of safe and orderly school campuses and as individual student predisposition to committing acts of violence. The indexes that have garnered attention are counts of office referrals, suspensions, and expulsions. In the 1999 National Center for Education Statistics report, a high association was found between principal perceptions of discipline problems and school crime statistics (U.S. Department of Education, 1999). More recently, attention has been drawn to "low-level" violence or incidents of behavior such as bullying, peer sexual harassment, and victimization. These behaviors occur with greater frequency and potentially have long-lasting negative impact on students (Dupper & Meyer-Adams, 2002). As a result of heightened awareness of the negative impact of incidents of low-level violence, such behaviors have been added to lists of suspendable offenses, along with more physical forms of threat and aggression. These changes in school discipline policy indicate an enhanced concern about behaviors that threaten psychological and developmental safety as well as physical safety (Morrison, Furlong, & Morrison, 1994). Zero-tolerance policies have taken some of these policies to an extreme, broadening the scope of exclusion to behavior that, although related, may not be associated with greater likelihood of violence and disorder (e.g., plastic knifes, Midol tablets—interpreted as a "substance" being abused). Although such zero-tolerance applications loosen the association between disciplinary counts and associated school disorder or violence, there are other sources of error involved with these metrics that are highlighted here.

USES OF DISCIPLINE STATISTICS

School districts track suspensions and expulsions for state-level reports. For example, in California, schools are required to report suspensions and expulsions as part of a School Accountability Report Card, with the intention to communicate to parents and the public about various indices of school performance and conditions. At the federal level, Title IX of the No Child Left Behind Act of 2001 requires that each state establish a method for identifying schools that are "persistently dangerous." The California State Board of Education defined a "persistently dangerous school" as one in which more than 1% of the student body is expelled for any of nine serious offenses, each year for 3 consecutive years.

Within and between districts, the assumption often is that higher numbers of disciplinary incidents are associated with higher rates of misbehavior. Numbers of suspensions have been associated with negative academic indicators such as grade retention, school dropout, alienation from school, juvenile delinquency, and drug use (Brooks, Schiraldi, & Ziedenberg, 1999; Costenbader & Markson, 1998; Skiba & Peterson, 2000). Positive behavior support programs use office referrals as indicators of the impact of systematic use of schoolwide discipline practices (Sugai, Sprague, Horner, & Walker, 2000). Similarly, Putnam, Luiselli, Handler, and Jefferson (2003) and Sugai et al. (2000) argued for the use of office referrals as an outcome index to measure effectiveness of programs targeting problem behavior, as these data are naturally occurring data sources commonly collected by school personnel.

At the individual level, researchers and practitioners have used these indices to determine the prevalence and chronicity of problem behavior to predict later problem behavior. School discipline metrics have also been used as correlates of problem behavior (Walker, Zeller, Close, Webber, & Gresham, 1999). Researchers suggest a strong association between early discipline problems and later adjustment problems, inside and outside of school (Sprague, Walker, Stieber, Simonsen, & Nishioka, 2001; Tobin & Sugai, 1999). Sprague et al., however, found that the actual count of discipline referrals in schools had a low association with offenses within the community, although a higher correlation was found for the severity of the community offense.

Despite attempts to associate group- and individual-level statistics with negative, risky outcomes, these indices are not necessarily intended to serve as reliable and valid measures of misbehavior. Rather, they have been have developed as legal and record-keeping measures. Office referrals help communicate between teacher and principal about student misbehavior. Suspension and expulsion data result from legal due process procedures for excluding students from school. Because these indices were not necessarily intended to be used for group and individual summary and prediction, these systems are fraught with error in design and implementation (Morrison & Skiba, 2003). This chapter describes potential variations in practices and corresponding sources of error in school discipline indexes, specifically office referrals and suspensions. This analysis leads to recommendations about how to improve these important sources of information as reliable and valid measures of school discipline.

OFFICE REFERRALS

Recently, a body of research has begun to focus on the strengths and weaknesses of using office referral data for analyzing school safety, for predicting later problem behavior, and as a way of documenting improvements in schoolwide discipline practices (Morrison, Peterson, O'Farrell, & Redding, 2004; Putnam et al., 2003; Sprague et al., 2001; Tobin & Sugai, 1999). Although data on suspensions and expulsions can give information on the most severe behaviors that occurs on school campuses, office referral data can provide information about the day-to-day behavior on school campuses. These data, when carefully analyzed, also give information on the discipline policies and philosophies of schools (e.g., which behaviors are considered as serious offenses and what consequences are used). An example of office referrals "as practice" is the situation where teachers and students consider office referrals a "consequence" for misbehavior, not just a data mechanism. In other words, an office referral implies that the student will be called to the administrator's office for a discussion of the cause for the referral. Teachers may view this as an adequate consequence for the misdeed, particularly if it is minor. Moreover, teachers may use the threat of an office referral as a lever to change student behavior.

Similarly, administrators may exchange the opportunity remove the office referral from the student's record for improved behavior. Both of these circumstances use the referral itself as a disciplinary consequence.

Sugai et al. (2000) defined an office discipline referral as "an event in which (a) a student engaged in a behavior that violated a rule or social norm in the school, (b) the problem behavior was observed or identified by a member of the school staff, and (c) the event resulted in a consequence delivered by administrative staff who produced a permanent (written) product defining the whole event" (p. 96). Office referral data varies across schools and within schools as a function of the school, teacher, or policy, as opposed to actual student misbehavior (Morrison et al., 2004).

One way of using office referral data is to look at the type of behavior that is described as a behavior or rule offense. Looking at this metric *within schools* (even with the same discipline policy), variability in teacher office referral rates may be less a measure of student misbehavior across classrooms and more an indicator of which teachers are struggling with their teaching and classroom management skills. Between teachers there are variations in instructional effectiveness, (Scott, Nelson, & Liaupsin, 2001), classroom management abilities (Blankemeyer, Flannery, & Vazsonyi, 2002; Reinke & Herman, 2002), and tolerance levels for student activity and learning levels (Gerber, 1988; Wright & Dusek, 1998), all of which may be related to problem behaviors. These factors are linked to variation in a teacher's likelihood of sending students to the office for behavioral offenses. The types of behavior that would cause a student to be referred to the office in one classroom may be treated differently in another classroom. In addition, the schoolwide discipline policy may be ambiguous, so teachers may not be informed as to what behaviors should result in office referrals. Consequently, some teachers may overrefer, whereas others may not-refer often enough. There is variability in office referral rates *within schools* as a function of teachers' ability to manage the class, effectively engage students in academic lessons, interpret the school discipline system, and tolerate misbehavior.

Information about numbers of office referrals can also be a target of analysis. Morrison et al. (2004) looked at office discipline practices across elementary schools and found extreme variability in the number of office referrals at each school. For example, at one school, the ratio of office referrals to school population was 1.07, whereas in a comparison school with similar student demographics, the ratio was 0.14. Given different rates of misbehavior indicated through office referrals, did students misbehave at higher rates in the first school? Possibly; however, the likely answer is that formal discipline policies, as well as informal practices, differed significantly between these schools. In the second school, misbehavior may have been dealt with at a classroom level rather than at the schoolwide level. Classroom teachers may have used practices such as timeouts, missed recess, or community service to deal with misbehavior, as opposed to sending these students to the office. At the first school, however, teachers may have referred students to the office for any type of misbehavior, thus leaving discipline up to the school, rather than dealing with it at a classroom level. Much of how a school deals with discipline depends on the principal's approach to discipline; that is, whether it is punitive and controlling, or preventative (Mukuria, 2002; Reimers, Wacker, & Koeppl, 1987). As well, these practices depend on the administrators' willingness to deal with school discipline problems. Teachers do not refer to the office if they feel that "nothing will happen" or if they feel that a referral will reflect poorly on their teaching or behavioral management skills. Administrators also have different tolerances for misbehavior and may encourage referral for certain behaviors, and discourage referral for other behaviors. Thus, interpretation of office referral counts must be made in light of knowledge about the context and discipline practices at the school.

Another potential threat to the validity and reliability of office referrals as an index involves the extent to which all possible offenses are recorded. Considering there are numerous unsupervised areas on school campuses such as hallways, cafeterias, or bathrooms; behaviors that occur in these areas that warrant an office referral, may not be recorded because of the absence of an adult observing the behavior. Research suggests that during transition times or unstructured times, misbehavior is more likely to occur (Colvin, Sugai, Good, & Lee, 1997). Some schools organize staff to supervise during these times; however, other schools still leave these areas unsupervised. Therefore, using office referral data as an index of school safety may not adequately capture the real safety at a school because behaviors that occur in unsupervised areas are not recorded.

Variation in recording procedures is a potential source or error. Morrison et al. (2004) also looked at the "written document" that may or may not accompany a referral to the office. There is no standardized instrument that constitutes an office referral, and many elementary schools either do not use a formal office referral form or use such a form only for the most severe behaviors. Additionally, even in schools that do use these forms, variation occurs in what is recorded on the form as well as in the actual format of the office referral form. For example, Morrison et al. (2004) found that in a sample of eight schools, two elementary schools used multiple forms to record office referrals. One of the schools had seven possible forms in use over a 2-year period of time. Given the use of multiple forms, confusion among staff about the overall discipline system seems unavoidable. In looking at the written document, the purpose of the office referral system can be interpreted. For example, this document may serve the purpose of information for the administrator, as data to keep track of particular student's misbehavior, or as a system within which to record consequences.

Clearly, there is much variability in office referral practices within schools and across schools. Therefore, it is imperative for researchers to closely examine the disciplinary practices at schools before making interpretations of office referral data. School-to-school and within-school comparisons (across time) are unwise unless standard information about the types of information collected and the fidelity of that collection are ensured. However, office referral data have much to offer researchers and school administrators. First, these data can be used to assess who is being referred to the office, as well as which teachers are doing the referring. It can be useful to understand patterns in office referrals as a function of gender, ethnicity, special education status, or academic status. As well, these data may provide evidence on who is referring in order to assess whether staff should be trained on which offenses warrant the referral to the office. Data may also provide evidence for which behaviors teachers are referring students to the office. This again could provide evidence for the necessity of staff training, as well as provide evidence for behavioral training that may be effective or necessary for students. These data also provide evidence for where these problems occur, thus informing the school where supervision is necessary. Accurate recording of office referral data across time can provide information on the effectiveness of interventions designed to reduce office referrals.

SUSPENSIONS

Suspension from school is a widely used disciplinary action; it involves legal actions taken by school officials to exclude students from school on a temporary basis for breaking the rules of the school. Offenses are generally defined by state education codes. Common to most states are the following offenses: possession of a firearm or deadly weapon, possession or selling of illegal drugs, physical harm to others, willful disobedience, destruction of property, disruption of school activities and threat of harm (Kingery & Coggeshall, 2001). The most common reasons for suspension do not tend to be violent and destructive offenses such as weapon possession and drug selling or possession, rather offenses such as defiance of authority and

TABLE 14.1

Suspension Indices Across 2 Years

Index	Year 1	Year 2
Enrollment-Population	646	562
Incidents	176	234
Students	109	129
Repeaters	20.5%	22.6%
Ratio of suspended students to population	0.17	0.23

class disruption (Heaviside, Rowand, Williams, & Farris, 1998; Skiba, Peterson, & Williams, 1997).

Implementation of zero-tolerance policies in our nations schools in the past 15 years has resulted in high rates of suspension and expulsions. Brooks et al. (1999) note that 6.84% of students nationwide were suspended in 1997. Skiba et al. (1997) reported that 41% of students in middle schools in 19 midwestern schools were involved in disciplinary actions (office referrals or suspension). When examining state or national statistics, it is important to note some of the possible variations in reporting traditions. For example, it is critical to know whether the rate reported is the number of incidents or the number of students. Incidents involve redundancies in students; students will often be "repeat offenders." Costenbader and Markson (1994) reported that 42% of suspended students in their survey of 10 states were repeat offenders. Leone et al. (2000) cautioned about interpreting suspension statistics unless "incident" versus "person" counts is specified. Raffaele-Mendez, Knoff, and Ferron (2002) referred to these as duplicated (number of suspensions) and unduplicated counts (number of students who experienced suspension at least once during the school year). These authors recommended the use of unduplicated counts for analysis of school practices because this index indicates number of times suspension being used.

Table 14.1 displays data from a junior high school (Weissglass & Morrison, 2004) and shows the number of disciplinary offenses and the number of students involved in these offenses. Repeat offenders are indicated to the extent that there are fewer students than incidents. Overall, there was a significant increase from one year to the next in terms of the number of offenses, the percentage of students involved in offenses and the number of repeat offenders. These trends existed despite declining enrollment. Between Years 1 and 2 of the study, this school underwent key administrative changes (change in principal and assistant principal[s]). These changes were accompanied by discipline policy changes, which led to an increase in referrals and application of consequences. Reports about the current year indicate that referrals have gone down as a result of students understanding the new rules and consequences. Thus, although it is tempting to attribute changes to student behavior, policy and administrative actions need to be factored into the explanation as well.

In the case of repeat offenders, these data may inform school officials about the behavioral trajectories of students in their schools as they interact with school policies. For repeat offenders, it is evident that suspension is not serving as an effective intervention (Skiba & Knesting, 2001). These students warrant further attention to academic, social, and familial factors that are impacting their behavior.

As another example of reporting variations that threaten the reliability and validity of suspension summaries, Raffaele-Mendez et al. (2002) noted high variability in the number of days of exclusion from schools associated with suspensions used by administrators. It is typical to see exclusions vary from 1 to 5 days. Standards for deciding on number of days are not always explicit. Another variation that may occur is when multiple students are involved in one incident; for example, several students may be involved and therefore suspended if they are involved in a fight. Does this get counted as one incident or multiple incidents?

Variations also occur in how many offenses are reported for any one incident. On the district reporting forms that display the state education code list of suspendable offenses, school administrators may check off more than one offense. For example, on suspension forms used in California school districts, if a student is involved in a fight, the administrator may choose to check both "disrupting school activities" and "attempting physical injury" (fighting), which are both listed in California's as suspendable offenses. So, although one school administrator may not duplicate his or her reporting across categories, another may. The disruption category of the latter school would look exceptionally high, not because there was more disruption, but because the administrator would duplicate the offense reporting (fighting and disrupting). In the Weissglass and Morrison (2004) study, the duplicative use of disruption with another offense category accounted for the following increases within the disruption category for 4 consecutive years: 13.6%, 2.2%, 7.3%, 10.3%. These variations were likely due to changes in administrative staff. When reporting data to an external agency, this possible complication in "counts" should be taken into consideration. As with incidents versus students, this is a potential source of error in reporting and therefore interpreting data.

The importance of having confidence in suspension counts is highlighted in the use of group level suspension statistics to describe disproportionality issues in the exclusion of students from different racial-ethnic minority groups and students with disabilities (Civil Rights Project, 2000). The importance of this issue is highlighted the suspension risk indices for different ethnic/racial groups calculated from U.S. Department of Education Office of Civil Rights (OCR) Elementary and Secondary School Survey (2000) data. A risk index is calculated by dividing the number of students in a racial group suspended by the total number of student in that racial group. Minnesota and South Carolina had the highest risk indices for suspension of African-American students (34% and 22%, respectively). Hispanic students were most at risk in Connecticut (14%) and Pennsylvania (11%). Despite interesting variations between states, conclusions based on these comparisons are suspect unless there is a high degree of confidence that data were gathered and reported in a standard fashion. Ensuring that busy school-level personnel are reporting suspension numbers that are standard in terms of how "repeat offenses," number of days suspended, and multiple categories of offenses are treated is a challenge at best. Some of the variations in data and reporting are described in the document *Collection and Using Crime, Violence, and Discipline Incident Data to Make a Difference in Schools* (http://ncews.ed.gov/pubs2002/safety/chapter4_2.asp#piece) published by the National Center for Education Statistics. The National Center for Education Statistics surveyed respondents about the ease of reporting on school discipline information for the U.S. Department of Education OCR 2000 Elementary and Secondary School (2000). A large percentage (range of approximately 66% to 75%) of schools reported that it would be easy or very easy to report frequencies and unduplicated counts of students disciplined. The level of difficulty was higher for larger districts. Although this percentage is relatively high, the fact that between 25% and 34% of the districts would experience challenges in accurate reporting gives reduces the confidence for interpretation of the resulting data.

Another source of variation occurs when local schools decide to add a category above and beyond the state suggested categories of suspendable offenses. In Morrison (2004), one of the junior high schools in the sample had a suspension category for "obligations." Students were suspended for failing to bring their books (multiple times) and other academically related issues. In the third year, despite a growing student population (Year 1 = 1,116; Year 2 = 1,234; Year 3 = 1,327), the suspensions declined (Year 1 = 495; Year 2 = 433; Year 3 = 374).

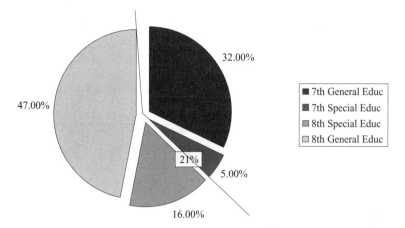

FIG. 14.1.   Suspension data disaggregated by special education status and gender.

In Years 1 and 2 of the study, the "obligations" suspension category account for 18% and 22% of the total suspensions, respectively. This decline paralleled a change in the use of "obligations" as a suspension category (the school had a change in principal that paralleled the discontinuation of this practice). In another district, during the same time period, two high schools were suspending students for tardies and truancies under the category of "disruption of school activities." The tardy and truancy offenses accounted for 27% and 59% of all suspensions at these two high schools. The point to be emphasized here is that school policy changes may impact reported suspension rates, making conclusions about student behavior difficult to make with confidence.

In some schools, suspensions are recorded for issues that have no connection of our usual understanding of discipline or behavior. Notably, some schools suspend students when parents have not provided proof of immunization or when students have head lice. Although some schools may keep records of these types of suspensions distinct from behavior-related suspensions, other schools may not; thus, these types of suspensions may confound the compiled data. Where this situation occurs, it may also bias the racial or socioeconomic disaggregation of data reported to the state since these types of suspensions may be related to poverty and access to health care

Potential Uses of Suspension Data

Disaggregating the "types" of individual demographic information recorded with suspension may be helpful for schoolwide information. For example, suspension databases often include information about ethnicity, gender, grade, and disability status. These patterns help with an understanding of where potential targets for further intervention might be. For example, Raffaelle-Mendez and Knoff (2003) noted that the greatest rates of out-of-school suspensions tend to be at the middle and high school levels, peaking at the ninth grade. Figure 14.1 displays suspension data disaggregated by grade and special education status (Weissglass & Morrison, 2004). Eighth graders account for the largest proportion of suspensions during one year, with the relative representation of special education students being larger at the eighth-grade level as well. Clearly, special education students and older students are in need of more effective behavioral interventions at this school.

Relating suspension statistics to office referral statistics offers some potentially interesting information. For example, Morrison et al. (2004) found that schools that had high office referrals did not necessarily have high suspension rates and visa versa. A high office referral rate and low

TABLE 14.2

Implications for Practice: Recommendations for Using Disciplinary Referrals
to Assess School Safety

Office Referrals
1. Involve staff in the development of discipline policies and procedures (rules and referral standards).
2. Provide a standard form for recording office referrals.
3. Record actions taken as a result of the referral.
4. Analyze office referral data on a yearly basis and provide feedback to teachers. (levels of analysis may include by child, by grade, by special population, by teacher, by type and location of offense)
5. When reporting discipline data across years or schools, provide information about existing or changing policies or key implementers (school administrators, and teachers).

Suspensions
1. Decide on a standard procedure to marking offense categories (to avoid duplicate or inflated categories).
2. Decide on guidelines for number of days suspended.
3. Note when additional "local" offense categories for offenses are added to state-mandated or suggested categories.
4. Disaggregate incidents and students in the suspension counts.
5. Note when there have been changes in personnel and policy with regard to school discipline.
6. Disaggregate data by grade, ethnic group, special population, and behavioral offense category.
7. Compare suspension rates to office referral and expulsion rates.

---

suspension rate as opposed to a high suspension and low office referral rate indicate differences in school discipline practices. The former could reflect low teacher tolerance for minor offenses and a tendency to use other alternatives for offenses that could lead to suspension. The latter pattern may indicate that teachers handle minor offenses in the classroom and when the student commits a suspendable offense other alternative are not used.

Although these patterns contribute to school-level considerations, office referral/ suspension relationships can be explored at the individual level as well. Morrison, Anthony, Storino, and Dillon (2001) found differences in student characteristics between students who were suspended and had previous office referrals and those who had no previous discipline history, with previous office referral history being associated with poorer personal social status. Also, this study found that office referrals that followed suspensions tended to be more associated with attitudinal rather than aggressive offenses, indicating that school officials may be responding differently to students after they have committed suspendable offenses.

RECOMMENDATIONS

The information presented here highlights sources of error that may be found in the collection of school discipline data, specifically office referrals and suspensions. Despite these limitations, these data remain potentially important indicators of student behavior and implementation of school discipline policies. Because these data are reflections of behavior and policy implementation, extreme caution should be used in interpreting and comparing schoolwide totals on office referral and suspensions. Given this caution, the Table 14.2 lists recommendations are suggested to increase the reliability and validity of these data.

School safety and order is key to a successful school and are foundational to providing a productive learning environment for students. An effective schoolwide discipline system will contribute to safety and order. Collecting and analyzing data (office referrals and suspensions) is an important part of monitoring and adjusting a schoolwide discipline system. This chapter has provided a discussion about sources of error that may limit the ability to draw conclusions from these data. By identifying and controlling these sources of error, these data become more useful. However, at all times these data will reflect both the behaviors of students and the systems that support or modify these behaviors. Thus, school discipline data should always be interpreted in light of the important contexts that have been highlighted in this chapter.

REFERENCES

Blankemeyer, M., Flannery, D. J., & Vazsonyi, A. T. (2002). The role of aggression and social competence in children's perceptions of the child-teacher relationship. *Psychology in the Schools, 39*, 293–304.

Brooks, K., Schiraldi, V., & Ziedenberg, J. (1999). *School house hype: Two years later*. San Francisco, CA: Justice Policy Institute/Children's Law Center.

Civil Rights Project. (2000). *Opportunities suspended: The devastating consequences of zero tolerance and school discipline policies*. Cambridge, MA: Harvard University.

Colvin, G., Sugai, G., Good, R. H., & Lee, Y. (1997). Using active supervision and precorrection to improve transition behavior in an elementary school. *School Psychology Quarterly, 12*, 344–363.

Costenbader, V., & Markson, S. (1998). School suspension: A study with secondary school students. *Journal of School Psychology, 36*, 59–82.

Dupper, D. R., & Meyer-Adams, N. (2002). Low-level violence: A neglected aspect of school culture. *Urban Education, 37*, 350–364.

Gerber, M. M. (1988). Tolerance and technology of instruction: Implications for special education reform. *Exceptional Children, 54*, 309–314.

Heaviside, S., Rowand, C., Williams, C., & Farris, E. (1998). *Violence and discipline problems in U.S. Public Schools: 1996-97* (No. NCES 98-030). Washington, DC: U.S. Department of Education, National Center for Education Statistics.

Kingery, P. M., & Coggeshall, M. B. (2001). Surveillance of school violence, injury, and disciplinary actions. *Psychology in the Schools, 38*, 117–112.

Leone, P. E., Mayer, M., Malmgren, K. R., & Meisel, S. M. (2000). School violence and disruption: Rhetoric, reality, and reasonable balance. *Focus on Exceptional Children, 33*, 1–20.

Morrison, G., Peterson, R., O'Farrell, S., & Redding, M. (2004). Using office referral records in school violence research: Possibilities and limitations. In M. J. Furlong, G. Morrison, R. J. Skiba, & D. Cornell (Eds.), *Issues in school violence research* (pp. 39–61). Binghamton, NY: Haworth Press.

Morrison, G. M. (2004). *Turning Point Effects for Students With and Without Disabilities Who are Involved in School Disciplinary Actions*. Washington, DC: U.S. Department of Education, Office of Special Education Programs (Award # H324C000072).

Morrison, G. M., Anthony, S., Storino, M., & Dillon, C. (2001). An examination of the disciplinary histories and the individual and educational characteristics of students who participate in an in-school suspension program. *Education & Treatment of Children, 24*, 276–293.

Morrison, G. M., Furlong, M. J., & Morrison, R. L. (1994). School violence to school safety: Reframing the issue for school psychologists. *School Psychology Review, 23*, 236–256.

Morrison, G. M., & Skiba, R. J. (2003). School discipline indices and school violence: An imperfect correspondence. In M. J. Furlong, M. Bates, D. Smith, & P. Kingery (Eds.), *Appraisal and prediction of school violence* (pp. 111–133). Hauppauge, NY: Nova Science.

Mukuria, G. (2002). Disciplinary challenges: How do principals address this dilemma? *Urban Education, 37*, 432–452.

Putnam, R. F., Luiselli, J. K., Handler, M. W., & Jefferson, G. (2003). Evaluating student discipline practices in a public school through behavioral assessment of office referrals. *Behavior Modification, 27*, 505–523.

Leone, P. E, Mayer, M. Malmgren, KH. r. & Meisel, S. M. (2000). School violence and disruption: Rhetoric, reality, and reasonable balance, *Focus on Exceptional Children, 33*, 1–20.

Raffaele-Mendez, L. M., Knoff, H. M., & Ferron, J. M. (2002). School demographic variables and out-of-school suspension rates: A quantitative and qualitative analysis of a large, ethnically diverse school district. *Psychology in the Schools, 39*, 259–277.

Raffaele-Mendez, L. M., *Knoff, H. M.*, (2003). Who gets suspended from school and why: A demographic analysis of schools and disciplinary infractions in a large school district. *Education and Treatment of Children, 26*, 30–51.

Reimers, T. M., Wacker, D. P., & Koeppl, G. (1987). Acceptability of behavioral interventions: A review of the literature. *School Psychology Review, 16*, 212–227.

Reinke, W. M., & Herman, K. C. (2002). Creating school environments that deter antisocial behaviors in youth. *Psychology in the Schools, 39*, 549–560.

Scott, T., Nelson, C. M., & Liaupsin, C. J. (2001). Effective instruction: The forgotten component in preventing school violence. *Education and Treatment of Children, 24,* 309–322.

Skiba, R. J., & Knesting, K. (2001). Zero tolerance, zero evidence: An analysis of school disciplinary practice. *New Directions for Youth Development: Theory, Practice, Research, 92,* 17–44.

Skiba, R. J., & Peterson, R. (2000). School discipline at a crossroads: From zero tolerance to early response. *Exceptional Children, 66,* 335–346.

Skiba, R. J., Peterson, R. L., & Williams, T. (1997). Office referrals and suspension: Disciplinary intervention in middle schools. *Education and Treatment of Children, 20,* 295–315.

Sprague, J., Walker, H. M., Stieber, S., Simonsen, B., & Nishioka, V. (2001). Exploring the relationship between school discipline referrals and delinquency. *Psychology in the Schools, 38,* 197–206.

Sugai, G., Sprague, J. R., Horner, R. H., & Walker, H. M. (2000). Preventing school violence: The use of office discipline referrals to assess and monitor school-wide discipline interventions. *Journal of Emotional and Behavioral Disorders, 8,* 94–101.

Tobin, T., & Sugai, G. (1999). Using sixth-grade school records to predict school violence, chronic discipline problems, and high school outcomes. *Journal of Emotional and Behavioral Disorders, 7,* 40–53.

U.S. Department of Education, National Center for Education Statistics and the U.S. Department of Justice, Bureau of Justice Statistics. (1999). *Indicators of school crime and safety, 1999.* Washington, DC: U.S. Department of Education.

Walker, H. M., Zeller, R. W., Close, D. W., Webber, J., & Gresham, F. (1999). The present unwrapped: Change and challenge in the field of behavioral disorders. *Behavior Disorders, 24,* 293–304.

Weissglass, T. & Morrison, G. M. (2004). *Evaluation of the La Cumbre Middle School Healthy Start Program* (ID#42-10-265). Sacramento: California Department of Education.

Wright, J. A., & Dusek, J. B. (1998). Compiling school base rates for disruptive behaviors from student disciplinary referral data. *School Psychology Review, 27,* 138–147.

15

The Social Context of Schools: Monitoring and Mapping Student Victimization in Schools

Ron Avi Astor
University of Southern California

Rami Benbenishty
Hebrew University of Jerusalem

Roxana Marachi
California State University, Northridge

Heather Ann Meyer
Skidmore College

There is mounting evidence that interventions focusing on school social contexts can be powerful mediators of school victimization (Benbenishty & Astor, 2005). Educators can play a critical role in shaping and implementing policy, interventions, and procedures that make U.S. schools safer. This chapter provides a discussion of two processes—monitoring and mapping—in order to help school professionals create grassroots programs, empower students and teachers, and use school site data to adapt programs, evaluate interventions, and debate school safety issues.

District-level monitoring is the first method that is described. This process produced strong reductions in school violence for the schools in a school district in Israel. The Israeli Government Accounting Office (GAO) recently recommended this district-level monitoring as a model program for all Israeli schools. More specifically, the monitoring process encouraged each school in the district to conduct a thorough assessment of school violence and their school climate. All schools in the district used the same instruments and methods so that all of the information could be aggregated on the district level. This process was repeated over time, on a regular basis. The information was analyzed, and detailed feedback was provided to all participants within each school (parents, students, teachers, administrators, community organizations, police, etc.). This information derived from the monitoring then went through a democratic process that was designed to empower the school leadership, teachers, parents, and students, to plan interventions for the school on the basis of valid and reliable data. On the district level, a comprehensive and detailed picture of the region emerged. It described both the district as a whole and the relative situation of each school site within the district. Hence, the district leadership and other school constituents could make both policy decisions and choices regarding which programs to adopt for the district as a whole and for particular schools based on this comprehensive and comparable data. This methodology and conceptualization also provided an empirical basis for the evaluation of interventions.

The second method described in this chapter involves mapping violence-prone areas. This process can lead to grassroots problem solving in schools. Studies from criminology,

architecture, environmental psychology, and urban planning have documented that certain public locations tend to be more prone to violence than others (Day, 1994; Fisher & Nasar, 1992;
Greenberg, Rohe, & Williams, 1982; Newman, 1973; Perkins, Meeks, & Taylor, 1992; Stokols,
1995). Because most schools tend to share a similar physical layout (e.g., a gym, hallways, a
cafeteria, and classrooms), the mapping method has been adapted to identify problem areas in
elementary, middle, or high school, and create solutions to reclaim them. However, both the
monitoring and mapping methods share a common set of assumptions and processes that distinguish them from many other school safety "programs." These assumptions are described here.

UTILIZING MONITORING AND MAPPING TO DEVELOP
AND IMPLEMENT SCHOOL SAFETY PROGRAMS

Given the vast array of behaviors considered to be school "violence," how do school officials
know what kind of violence problem they might have? When does a specific school cross
the threshold from having an average level of school violence to having a "high" level of
violence? Conversely, how do we know when a school should be considered a "model" safe
school? What kind of violence prevention program should a school select? If a violence
prevention program is implemented, how do we know if it was effective? These are not abstract,
moral, or academic issues alone. The U.S. No Child Left Behind legislation requires states to
report school safety data and to provide mechanisms for students to leave "unsafe schools."
Despite these developments, no one yet has put forth a uniform set of empirically based criteria
on what would constitute an "unsafe" school district or school. Educators' participation in
these philosophical discussions could add to the national dialogue because as a society, as
practitioners, and as researchers, it is essential to have agreed on ways to understand what is
a safe or unsafe school. Without this shared understanding, it will be difficult to assess the
success or failure of prevention and intervention programs.

A review of the school safety literature strongly suggests that programs should be developed
and implemented in a process that would ensure their relevance and applicability to each specific
site. It appears that one reason for the promising results of anti-bullying programs in Europe and
Australia has to do with the implementation process and underlying philosophical approaches
of the programs (e.g., Sharp & Smith, 1994; Smith et al., 1999). Important assumptions of
the bullying programs center on the following: (a) the belief that the efforts to "fit" a program
to a school involves grassroots participation, (b) a belief that students and teachers in the
school need to be empowered to deal with the problem, (c) a belief that democracy is the
core of a good school safety programs, and (d) a belief that schools should demonstrate
a proactive vision surrounding the violence problem in their school. The implementation
of interventions or components of the program are slightly different for each school site.
These beliefs enable each school to adapt the program or general principles to their unique
demographic, philosophical, and organizational needs. This is a very different process than
many "skills-oriented" curricular approaches used in the United States (Alexander & Curtis,
1995; Astor, Benbenishty, & Marachi, 2004; Guerra & Tolan, 1994; Larson, 1998).

One other major difference exists between the international school safety programs and
programs in the United States. Many international prevention efforts begin with an overriding
belief that school social context data are necessary for the successful adaptation of the program
to each school, whereas U.S. programs are more focused on curricular interventions without
data as their foundation (Astor, Pitner, Benbenishty, & Meyer, 2002; Benbenishty, Astor, &
Zeira, 2003; Olweus, Limber, & Mihalic, 1999; Rigby, 1996; Smith et al., 1999). Hence,
an important element of successful school safety programs is the use of data in an ongoing
and interactive manner. Figure 15.1 represents our interpretation of the cycle of monitoring

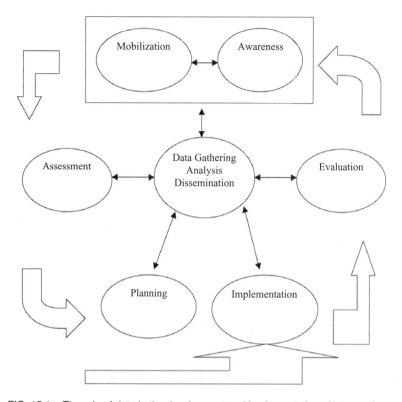

FIG. 15.1.   The role of data in the development and implementation of interventions.

and how data should be used to maintain successful school safety programs. This perspective proposes that the continuous and ongoing analysis and interpretation of data is an essential part of the intervention process. Data are used to create awareness, mobilize different school constituents, assess the extent of the problem, plan and implement interventions, and conduct evaluations. Information is provided on a continuous basis to different groups in each step of the intervention process. By contrast, many U.S. schools tend to purchase evidence-based programs, but rarely actually collect data about their own district or school. Schools in the United States rarely use data to inform the process described in Fig. 15.1.

For example, the process of introducing data allows each school to identify its specific needs, limitations, strengths, and resources so that choices can be made regarding which specific interventions and components to implement. Moreover, the process of building and implementing school safety programs is continuous and cyclical, always changing to respond to new circumstances and emerging needs. Hence, the evaluation of the program progress after implementation becomes a reassessment of the situation, leading to a new cycle of awareness building, planning, the modification of programs, and evaluation of their success. Not having site-specific and comparative data at the individual school site level could be a significant obstacle in (a) assessing whether or not that specific school has a school violence problem, (b) adapting a school safety program to a specific school, and (c) evaluating the implementation process and outcomes of the program over time. Given how important site-specific and comparative data are for the success of creating safe schools, we believe this warrants further elaboration. Also, with a few exceptions, it is rare to find research or theory published about the creation of a school district-level policy based on district data on victimization.

Most of the intervention literature remains primarily at the individual or school site level. Most often, it is the school district that has the expendable resources to implement districtwide interventions. The next portion of this chapter presents two schoolwide data-based approaches to bullying prevention programs that depart from a focus on changing the individual student. The following sections on monitoring and school mapping are presented as quantitative and qualitative processes that help create a "whole-school response" and help the school identify, create, and/or adapt programs to the site.

Concepts Surrounding Monitoring

Description and Comparison

The value of the monitoring approach for schools comes from the two levels of information processing involved: description and comparison. The *description* of the frequency of certain behaviors may be quite instructive. Consider, for instance, the students' perceptions of their teachers' responses when a student complains about bullying. The description of these responses may reveal that 25% of the students describe the response as "ignoring the complaint," another 33% portrays the response as "blaming the victim," and the rest describe a variety of caring and effective responses. This distribution is informative and has direct implications for training of school staff.

In general, comparisons enhance the value of information by putting it in context. In order to design an intervention plan and prioritize resource allocation, it is imperative to ascertain which violent acts are more prevalent than others, which grade levels are victimized more, how violence levels in a specific school compare with other schools in the district, and how a particular district compares with the state/nation in terms of the severity of its school violence. Furthermore, after resources are allocated, it is important to examine how current levels of violence compare with those reported a year ago. In our model, comparisons are made across several dimensions.

Within-School Comparisons. Two types of comparisons are made within each school. They are as follow:

1. *Across areas.* Compare across areas of interest within the same school. For instance, examine how dangerous various places and times in school are perceived to be, and identify the school contexts that are perceived as most dangerous and require immediate attention (Astor, Meyer, & Pitner, 1999). Also, compare various types of victimization to ascertain whether, for instance, verbal threats are more prevalent than actual physical victimization.

2. *Across groups.* Within the school, also compare among groups of students. For instance, when examining the issue of relational aggression in school, ask whether there are gender differences in victimization, which grade levels are most susceptible to this type of victimization, and whether it is more frequent among particular ethnic groups.

Between-School Comparisons. At least two levels of comparisons are valuable.

1. *Within a district.* Compare the schools within the district to identify schools that show significantly high and low levels of victimization in order to prioritize the allocation of programs addressing this issue.

2. *With national-level data.* Whenever national data are available, link and compare them with the district- and school-level data. Each school and the district as a whole are seen within the context of the larger national picture.

Temporal Comparisons.   The monitoring model is based on measuring school violence information over time, using similar instruments and methods. The comparisons across points in time help detect changes and identify trends.

1. *Identifying changes.* Comparisons help identify whether changes occur over time. For instance, compare levels of relational aggression collected in the past 2 years with current data.
2. *Comparing degrees of change across areas.* Ask whether there are differences in the magnitude of change across different forms of school violence. For instance, examine how the drop in relational aggression compares with changes in serious victimization.
3. *Comparing degrees of change across schools.* Compare levels of change over time among the schools in the district. Identify schools that show significantly high or low levels of change in violence so that we can focus our ongoing efforts on schools that have difficulty making significant progress.

MONITORING AT THE SCHOOL DISTRICT LEVEL: PRACTICAL EXAMPLES FROM THE HERTZELIA SCHOOL DISTRICT, ISRAEL

The two lead authors of this chapter conducted a multiyear project examining the uses of data (as shown in Fig. 15.1) for an entire school district in Israel. The district annually surveyed all of their students. Therefore, each school had comparative data for specific types of perpetration and victimization involved with bullying. The school violence and bullying data were then provided to each of 29 schools in the district to inform assessment, planning, and evaluation of grassroots projects developed by the teachers and students in each school. Schools in this

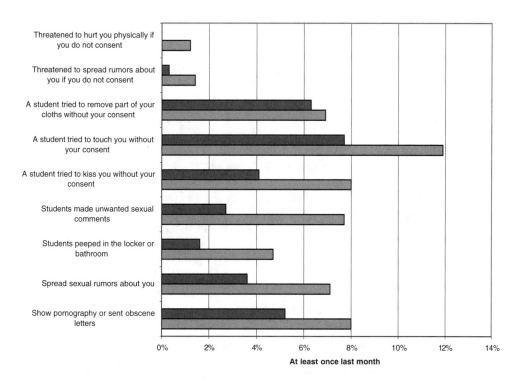

FIG. 15.2.   Sexual harassment: A comparison between the school and district.

project were able to compare themselves by grade, gender groups, and between other schools in their district. The following section highlights the advantages of such an approach for school safety interventions.

Comparing a School Site to District Student Victimization Norms

One school wanted to know how it compared with other schools in its district on specific kinds of bullying/victim behaviors. The local media was suggesting that this specific school had problems with sexual harassment. Prior to monitoring, the school staff was not sure if its school had similar or higher rates than the school district norms. Consequently, the information from Fig. 15.2 was helpful because it showed that the school was lower than the district average on every sexual harassment item. This information helped teachers, parents, and the media situate the extent of the school problem within their district and counter harmful media stereotypes about this school with regards to sexual harassment. The data also raised awareness in the school as to which types of behaviors were most prevalent in their school (e.g., unwanted sexual touching and unwanted removal of parts of clothing). The issues presented in the data were brought to the teachers, students, and principal in forums where they could discuss what could/should be done to address the issue. The school then focused on developing interventions around these data. After several months of interventions, these behaviors were measured again to examine whether the new policies and grassroots interventions reduced the prevalence of sexual harassment behaviors in their school.

Assessment: Identifying Target Groups

Identifying specific target groups for interventions is another way data can/should be used. District administrators were particularly interested in knowing if students in their district who were victimized were also perpetrators. Students who were both bullies and victims could require different types of interventions. Some of this concern came from the numerous U.S. school shootings that received media attention in the late 1990s (Bragg, 1997; Gegax, Adler, & Petersen, 1998; Sack, 1999; Verhovek, 1999).

Figure 15.3 shows the percent of students in this district that reported being both *victims and perpetrators* of violence by grade and gender. It demonstrates two distinct patterns for boys and girls who fit the criteria of "high" victimization and perpetration in their district. It suggests that far more boys than girls fit the dual criteria. Girls who were both victims and perpetrators had relatively stable rates over time. Boys who fit the criteria had greater variability from a high of 30% in Grade 7 to a low of 15% in Grade 12. This suggests that there may be a need to have gender-specific strategies when targeting students who were both victims and perpetrators. It also suggests that prevention programs should begin at least by Grade 4. This information was extremely helpful for the district in addressing its particular concerns surrounding students who were both bullies and victims. As a result, teachers and parents decided to develop policies and procedures focused on the process of provocation and retribution. They also had forums in which teachers and students could address ways to help students who were both bullies and victims. Students revealed that bully/victims were an easy target because they already had a reputation as a bully and teachers would not believe them when there was an altercation. This information made teachers more responsive to situations where children (who were bullies) suggested that other students were also bullying them.

Evaluation: Assessing Change Following Interventions

School administrations could use such a monitoring system to identify particular problem areas in their school. They could then track progress in reducing bullying in this location over time. For example, one junior high school wanted to know where violence occurred most frequently.

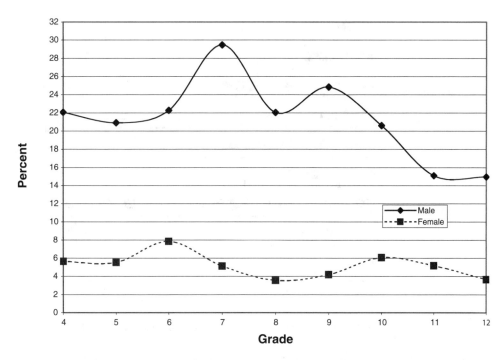

FIG. 15.3.   Percent of students in district who report high victimization and perpetration by grade and gender.

Using the process outlined in Fig. 15.1, this school used the data to develop specific interventions generated by teachers and students around certain locations (e.g., increased monitoring, school beautification projects, and alterations to the schedule so there were less students in the hallways at the same time). Then the progress in terms of reducing violence in specific areas in their school over time was monitored. Figure 15.4 represents a comparison between the 1999–2000 and 2000–2001 academic years in a school that implemented intervention programs during 2000–2001. Figure 15.4 suggests that the students' perceptions of danger decreased in all the targeted areas when compared to the prior year, before the intervention was initiated. This was not readily evident by data collected from focus groups. Figure 15.4 represented the views of the entire student body.

Each of the 29 school sites in the district used this flexible monitoring system in different ways depending on the specific kinds of bully/victim problems. The programs adopted by schools were quite diverse but included (a) school beautification projects (murals, planting grass/plants, targeting violence-prone locations); (b) increasing staff–student ratios at key times and in vulnerable locations; (c) efforts to improve staff and school morale, traditional bully/victim programs; (d) the creation of policies and procedure surrounding bullying; and (e) community interventions that targeted locations where students felt unsafe walking to and from schools due to bullies.

Concepts Surrounding Mapping Violence-Prone Locations

Undefined Public Spaces

There are many spaces in schools such as auditoriums, playgrounds, and lunchrooms where both staff and students congregate. However, because of the social hierarchy, mission, and professional roles/structure of schools, these spaces may not foster informal interactions among students or between students and staff. Furthermore, professionals in schools may not believe

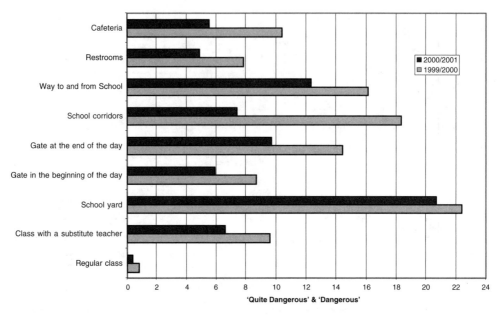

FIG. 15.4.   Specific places perceived by students to be dangerous in a school by school year.

it is their role to interact with students in these spaces unless administrators have assigned them to monitor those times/spaces.

Consequently, an important concept in understanding school violence is undefined public space (Newman, 1973, 1995; Newman & Franck, 1982). This concept asserts that within any community there are physical areas that may not be seen as anyone's responsibility to monitor or maintain (see Cisnernos, 1995). In his early studies of housing projects, Newman (1973, 1995) found that most criminal activity occurred in semipublic, "undefined" areas of buildings (e.g., lobbies, stairwells, halls, and elevators). Since the 1980s, numerous studies have documented undefined community locations that are seen as dangerous or violence-prone (e.g., Day, 1994; Fisher & Nasar, 1992; Goldstein, 1994; Greenberg et al., 1982; Newman & Franck, 1982; Perkins et al., 1992).

The concepts of *territoriality* and *undefined space* could have theoretical and practical implications for school-related spaces such as hallways, cafeterias, playgrounds, or routes to and from school. One obvious and important strategy implied by this approach is to identify these locations and work with members of the community to "reclaim" them. Are certain school spaces violence-prone because of a lack of perceived student or adult responsibility for keeping these areas safe? If so, can these spaces be reclaimed by students or teachers simply by identifying them and developing strategies around the behaviors that occur in those spaces?

Evidence for Undefined and Dangerous Areas in Schools

Previous studies on school violence have suggested that violent events occur repeatedly in specific places in and around school buildings (American Association of University Women, 2001; Arnette & Walsleben, 1998; Astor & Meyer, 1999; Astor, Meyer, & Behre, 1999; Carnegie Council on Adolescent Development, 1993; Chandler, Chapman, Rand, & Taylor, 1998; Goldstein, 1994; Lockwood, 1997; National Institute of Education & U.S. Department of Health, Education, & Welfare, 1978). Some studies in the United States and abroad have suggested that students who attend urban schools report the highest rates of avoiding particular areas in and around their school due to fear (e.g., Astor, Benbenishty, Zeira, & Vinokur, 2002;

Benbenishty & Astor, 2005; Benbenishty, Astor, Zeira, & Vinokur, 2002; Chandler et al., 1998). Astor, Meyer, and Behre (1999) found that violence-prone areas in high schools were also "undefined" and "unowned" by members of the school community (i.e., students, teachers, staff, and parents). Students and teachers voiced concerns about personal/professional responsibility and safety in specific violence-prone locations, such as hallways, bathrooms, and playgrounds. Even though most individuals in the school community were aware of these locations, neither the students nor the teachers thought that monitoring those areas was their personal or professional role/responsibility (Astor, Meyer, & Behre, 1999; Behre, Astor, & Meyer, 2001; Meyer, Astor, & Behre, 2002).

Applications of Mapping

This procedure is designed to involve school constituents in revealing how bully/victim issues and other forms of violence within a school building interact with locations, patterns of the school day, and social organizational variables (e.g., teacher and student relationships, teachers' professional roles, and the school's organizational response to violence; for more detail see Astor & Meyer, 1999; Astor, Meyer, & Behre, 1999; Astor, Meyer, & Pitner, 2001). An important goal of this procedure is to allow students and teachers to convey their personal theories about why specific locations and times in their schools are more dangerous. This approach assumes that students, teachers, school staff, and administrators have important information that should be the foundation for setting-specific interventions. Usually, interventions emerge from the information presented by the students, teachers, staff, and administrators in each school. Most successful bullying prevention programs involve a spatial and temporal analysis because many of the interventions are centered on specific bullying/victim prone locations.

Mapping, Interviews, and Interventions

The first step in this assessment procedure is obtaining a map of the school. Ideally, the map should contain all internal school territory, including the areas surrounding the school and playground facilities. In some communities where the routes to and from school are dangerous, a simple map of the surrounding neighborhood may be added to the assessment process (see Astor et al., 2004, for a description of this process). The school maps are an essential part of the interviewing process in order to anchor discussions to places and times in ways that interviews about "issues" alone cannot. The focus groups should begin with the facilitator distributing two sets of identical school maps to each individual.

Two photocopied maps of the school are needed for each student and teacher (map A and B). A first map should be used to determine what students and teachers believe to be the location of the most events involving bullying in or around the school building. Participants should be asked to identify the locations (on the maps) of up to three of the most violent events that have occurred within the past academic year. Next to each marked event on the map, participants should be asked to write the following information: (a) the general time frame of the event (e.g., before school, after school, morning period, afternoon period, evening sports event, between classes, etc.); (b) the grade and gender of those involved in the violence; and (c) their knowledge of any organizational response to the event (e.g., sent to principal's office, suspended, sent to peer counselor, nothing, etc.). On the second map, members should be asked to circle areas or territories that they perceive to be unsafe or potentially dangerous. This second map provides information about areas within the school that participants avoid or fear even though they may not possess knowledge of a particular event.

Discussion of Violent Events and Areas

The first part of the group discussion should center on the specific bullying events and the areas marked as unsafe or dangerous on their personal maps. We have asked questions such as the following:

- Are there times when those places you've marked on the maps are less safe?
- Is there a particular group of students that is more likely to get hurt there?
- Why do you think that area has so many incidents involving bullies and victims?

The overall purpose of the group interviews is to explore why bullying or victimization occurs at those specific times and in those specific spaces. Consequently, the interviews should also focus on gathering information regarding the following:

1. The organizational response to the event (e.g., "What happened to the two students after the event?" or "Did the hall monitors intervene when they saw what happened?").
2. Procedures (e.g., "What happens when the students are sent to the office after a fight?" or "Did anyone call the parents of the bully or victim?").
3. Follow-up (e.g., "Do the teachers, hall monitors, and/or administrators follow-up on any consequences given to the students?" or "Did anyone check on the welfare of the victim?").
4. Clarity of procedures (e.g., "Does it matter who stops the bullying?" e.g., a volunteer, security guard, teacher, or principal).

Interviewers should also explore participants' ideas for solutions to the specific bully problems (e.g., "Can you think of ways to avoid bullying or victimization in that place?" or "If you were the principal what would you do to make that place safer?"). Additionally, the interviewer should explore any obstacles participants foresee with implementation (e.g., "Do you think that type of plan is realistic?", "Has that been tried before? What happened?", or "Do you think that plan would work?"). Such obstacles could range from issues related to roles (e.g., "It's not my job to monitor students during lunch"), to discipline policy, and to issues of personal safety (e.g., "I don't want to intervene because I may get hurt").

In schools that already have programs designed to address school violence, specific questions should be asked about the effectiveness of those interventions, why they work or do not work, and what could be done to make the current measures more effective. We recommend that the interviewer ask both subjective questions (e.g., "Do you think the anti-bullying program is working?" or "Why do you think it works or why does it not work?") as well as specific questions related to the reduction of bullying/victimization (e.g., "Do you believe the anti-bully program has reduced the number of bullying events on the playground? Why or why not?").

Transferring all of the reported events onto one large map of the school enables students and staff to locate specific "hot spots" for violence and dangerous time periods within each individual school. The combined data are presented to all school constituents and they are asked to once again discuss and interpret the maps. Teachers and students use the maps and interviews to suggest ways to improve the settings. For example, in one school, events were clustered by time, age, gender, and location. In the case of older students (Grades 11 and 12), events were clustered in the parking lot outside of the auxiliary gym immediately after school, whereas for younger students (Grades 9 and 10), events were reported in the lunchroom and hallways during transition periods. For this school, the map suggested that interventions be geared specifically toward older students, directly after school, by the main entrance, and in the school parking lot. Students and teachers agreed that increasing the visible presence of school staff in and around the parking lot for the 20 minutes after school had great potential for reducing many violent events. Younger students were experiencing violence mainly before, during, and after lunch, near the cafeteria. Many students expressed feelings of being unsafe between classes in the hallways.

Compiling all the interview suggestions into themes is an important second step in creating context relevant interventions. Students, teachers, and administrators may have differing viewpoints regarding the organizational response of the school when victimization happened. Relaying the diversity of responses to students, teachers, and administrators can provide an opportunity for reflection and may generate ways to remedy the bully/victim problem in certain situations. When the data are presented to students, teachers, and administrators, they can center their discussions on why those areas are dangerous and what kinds of interventions could make the location safer. The data are collected and used in different stages of the process outlined in Fig. 15.1. Both the monitoring and mapping methods provide data-based approaches to gathering information about bullying/victimization in schools. Moreover, they provide site-specific information, which makes it easier for schools to address these problems.

CONCLUSION

Although some violence prevention programs are focused on altering the whole school climate, policy, and procedures, more work is needed on these contextually based approaches. One major commonality between effective programs is that they are based on school site data. Therefore, with effective programs, all interventions are created and adapted to fit the school site and involve the entire school setting. This requires a high degree of commitment and awareness of school staff to change the organizational response of the school to bullying. Although many of the currently popular anti-school violence programs are curricular-based and geared at improving students' social skills, it is important to highlight recent efforts at incorporating contextual perspectives into violence prevention as well. Moreover, successful programs appear to involve the principal and the entire teaching staff during the adaptation and implementation phase (for an example of a risk behavior program that includes some components of school-level system changes see Hawkins, Catalano, Kosterman, Abbott, & Hill, 1999). Programs that focus on the entire school social context have a greater likelihood of being sustained over time and showing significant reductions in victimization.

REFERENCES

Alexander, R., & Curtis, C. M. (1995). A critical review of strategies to reduce school violence. *Social Work in Education, 17*, 73–82.

American Association of University Women. (2001). *Hostile hallways: Bullying, teasing, and sexual harassment.* Washington, DC: Author.

Arnette, J., & Walsleben, M. (1998). *Combating fear and restoring safety in schools.* (NCJ-167888). Washington, DC: Office of Juvenile Justice and Delinquency Prevention.

Astor, R. A., Benbenishty, R., & Marachi, R. (2004). Violence in schools. In P. A. Meares (Ed.), *Social work services in schools, fourth edition* (pp. 149–182). Boston, MA: Allyn & Bacon.

Astor, R. A., Benbenishty, R., Zeira, A., & Vinokur, A. (2002). School climate, observed risky behaviors, and victimization as predictors of high school students' fear and judgments of school violence as a problem. *Health Education and Behavior, 29*, 716–736.

Astor, R., & Meyer, H. (1999). Where girls and women won't go: Female students', teachers', and school social workers' views of school safety. *Social Work in Education, 21*, 201–219.

Astor, R. A., & Meyer, H. (2001). The conceptualization of violence prone school sub contexts: Is the sum of the parts greater than the whole? *Urban Education, 36*, 374–399.

Astor, R. A., Meyer, H. A., & Behre, W. J. (1999). Unowned places and times: Maps and interviews about violence in high schools. *American Educational Research Journal, 36*, 3–42.

Astor, R. A., Meyer, H. A., & Pitner, R. (1999). Mapping school violence with students, teachers, and administrators. In L. Davis (Ed.), *Working with African American males: A guide to practice* (pp. 129–144). Thousand Oaks, CA: Sage.

Astor, R. A., Meyer, H., & Pitner, R. (2001). Elementary and middle school students' perceptions of violence-prone school sub-contexts. *The Elementary School Journal, 101*, 511–528.

Astor, R. A., Pitner, R. O., Benbenishty, R., & Meyer, H. A. (2002). Public concern and focus on school violence. In L. A. Rapp-Paglicci, A. R. Roberts, & J. S. Wodarski (Eds.) *Handbook of violence* (pp. 262–302) New York: Wiley.

Behre, W. J., Astor, R. A., & Meyer, H. A. (2001). Elementary and middle school teachers' reasoning about intervening in school violence: An examination of violence-prone school subcontexts. *The Journal of Moral Education, 2*, 131–153.

Benbenishty, R., & Astor R. A. (2005). *School violence in context: Culture, neighborhood, family, school, and gender.* New York: Oxford University Press.

Benbenishty, R., & Astor, R. A. (2003). Cultural specific and cross-cultural bully/victim patterns: The response from Israel. In P. K. Smith (Ed), *Violence in schools: The response in Europe* (pp. 317–331). London: RoutledgeFalmer.

Benbenishty, R., Astor, R. A., & Zeira, A. (2003). Monitoring school violence at the site level: Linking national, district and school-level data. *Journal of School Violence, 2*, 29–50.

Benbenishty, R., Astor, R. A., Zeira, A., & Vinokur, A. (2002). Perceptions of violence and fear of school attendance among junior high school students' in Israel. *Social Work Research, 26*, 71–88

Benbenishty, R., Zeira, A., & Astor, R.A. (2002). Children reports of emotional, physical and sexual maltreatment by educational staff in Israel. *Child Abuse and Neglect, 26*, 763–782.

Bragg, R. (1997, December 3). Forgiveness, after 3 die in Kentucky shooting; M. Carneal opens fire on fellow students at Heath High School in West Paducah. *The New York Times*, p. A16.

Cairns, R. B., & Cairns, B. D. (1991). Social cognition and social networks: A developmental perspective. In D. J. Pepler & K. H. Rubin (Eds.), *The development and treatment of childhood aggression* (pp. 249–278). Hillsdale, NJ: Lawrence Erlbaum Associates.

Carnegie Council on Adolescent Development. (1993). *A matter of time: Risk and opportunity in nonschool hours.* New York: Author.

Chandler, K., Chapman, C., Rand, M., & Taylor, B. (1998). *Students' reports of school crime: 1989 and 1995* (National Center for Education Statistics 98–241). Washington DC: U.S. Departments of Education and Justice.

Cisnernos, H. G. (1995). *Defensible space: Deterring crime and building community* (HUD-1512-PDR). Washington, DC: U.S. Department of Housing and Urban Development.

Day, K. (1994). Conceptualizing women's fear of sexual assault on campus: A review of causes and recommendations for change. *Environment and Behavior, 26*, 742–765.

Fisher, B., & Nasar, J. (1992). Fear of crime in relation to three exterior site features: Prospect, refuge, and escape. *Environment and Behavior, 24*, 35–65.

Gegax, T., Adler, J., & Pedersen, D. (1998, April 6). The boys behind the ambush. *Newsweek, 131*, 21–24.

Goldstein, A. (1994). *The ecology of aggression.* New York: Plenum.

Greenberg, A., Rohe, W. M., & Williams, K. R. (1982). Safety in urban neighborhoods: A comparison of physical characteristics and informal territorial control in high and low crime neighborhoods. *Population and Environment, 5*, 141–165.

Guerra, N., & Tolan, P. (1994). *What works in reducing adolescent violence: An empirical review of the field* (Report No. F-888). Boulder: University of Colorado, Center for the Study and Prevention of Violence.

Hawkins, J. D., Catalano, R. F., Kosterman, R., Abbott, R., & Hill, K. G. (1999). Preventing adolescent health-risk behaviors by strengthening protection during childhood. *Archives of Pediatric and Adolescent Medicine, 153*, 226–234.

Larson, J. (1998). Managing student aggression in high schools: Implications for practice. *Psychology in the Schools, 35*, 283–295.

Lockwood, D. (1997). *Violence among middle school and high school students: An analysis of implications for prevention.* Washington DC: U.S. Department of Justice, Office of Justice Programs, National Institute for Justice.

Meyer, H. A., Astor, R. A., & Behre, W. J. (2002). Teachers' reasoning about school violence: The role of gender and location. *Contemporary Educational Psychology, 27*, 499–528.

Nansel, T., Overpeck, M., Pilla, R., Ruan, W., Simons-Morton, B., & Scheidt, P. (2001). Bullying behaviors among U.S. youth: Prevalence and association with psychosocial adjustment. *Journal of the American Medical Association, 285*, 2094–2100.

National Institute of Education & U.S. Department of Health, Education, and Welfare. (1978). *Violent schools-safe schools: The safe school study report to Congress* (No. 1). Washington, DC: U.S. Government Printing Office.

Newman, O. (1973). *Architectural design for crime prevention.* Washington, DC: U.S. Department of Justice.

Newman, O. (1995). Defensible space: A new physical planning tool for urban revitalization. *Journal of the American Planning Association, 61*, 149–155.

Newman, O., & Franck, K. A. (1982). The effect of building size on personal crime and fear of crime. *Population and Environment, 5*, 203–220.

Olweus, D. (1993). *Bullying at school*. Cambridge, MA: Blackwell Publishers.

Olweus, D., Limber, S., & Mihalic, S. F. (1999). *Blueprints for violence prevention, book nine: Bullying prevention program*. Boulder, CO: Center for the Study and Prevention of Violence.

Perkins, D. D., Meeks, J. W., & Taylor, R. B. (1992). The physical environment of street block and resident perceptions of crime and disorder: Implications for theory and measurement. *Journal of Environmental Psychology, 12*, 21–34.

Rigby, K. (1996). *Bullying in schools: And what to do about it*. Melbourne, Victoria: Australian Council for Educational Research.

Sack, K. (1999, May 21). Youth with 2 guns shoots 6 at Georgia school. *The New York Times*, p. 1.

Sharp, S., & Smith, P. (1994). *Tackling bullying in your school: A practical handbook for teachers*. London: Routledge.

Smith, P., Morita, Y., Junger-Tas, J., Olweus, D., Catalano, R., & Slee, P. (1999). *The nature of school bullying: A cross-national perspective*. New York: Routledge.

Stokols, D. (1995). The paradox of environmental psychology. *American Psychologist, 50*, 821–837.

Verhovek, S. (1999, April 23). Terror in Littleton: The Overview. *The New York Times*, p. A1.

16

A Review of Methods to Assess Student Self-Report of Weapons on School Campuses

Michael Furlong
Jill Sharkey
University of California, Santa Barbara

The occurrence of multivictim shootings in recent years increased attention and concern about the prevalence of weapons on school campus. These events punctuate the importance of having complete and accurate information about the prevalence and correlates of weapon possession at schools. Fortunately, since peaking in the early-mid 1990s, youth violence in general, and school violence in particular, has declined (Furlong, Nyborg, & Sharkey, 2005). Previous reviews have examined the topic of school weapon possession (e.g., May, 2004), summarizing what is known of its incidence and factors associated with students bringing weapons to school. However, what is known about student weapon possession is limited by current methods of evaluation. To address a fundamental yet neglected aspect of youth violence research, this chapter focuses on how researchers have approached the task of measuring school weapon-related behaviors and experiences and implications regarding the validity of these data. In summary, this chapter provides (a) a review the importance of assessing school weapons possession, (b) a summary of the history of such assessment, (c) a description of specific approaches used, (c) a review and critique of methodology, and (d) a summary of implications for future practice.

Importantly, this review focuses on student reports of school-based weapon possession. Therefore, it does not include studies focused more broadly on youth weapon possession in other community contexts (e.g., Behrman, 2002; Ding, Nelsen, & Lassonde, 2002; Martin et al., 2001; Sheley & Wright, 1998). Moreover, this chapter examines student self-report methods and not other available strategies such as surveys of school personnel (e.g., National School Principal Survey; National Center for Education Statistics [NCES], 2004b) or official state-mandated school crime reports that include counts of weapon-related discipline (e.g., California Department of Education, 2000). Student self-reports are by far the most common measurement method for this topic, and it has even been argued that self-report methods provide more accurate information about the presence of weapons on school campuses than other methods (see Coggeshall, Kingery, & Berg, 2004).

IMPORTANCE OF ASSESSING WEAPONS
ON SCHOOL CAMPUSES

A weapon is used to inflict injury or death, and thus, when brought to school poses obvious danger to members of a school campus. Weapons on campus threaten a school's climate and may contribute to feelings of danger and concern among students and staff. Thus, information about the presence of weapons is an important focus of school safety evaluation. In order to appropriately address this safety concern, it is important to understand the presence of weapons from an ecological viewpoint, acknowledging family, school, and community factors that influence weapon-carrying behavior. All schools need to evaluate the presence of weapons because large-scale surveys indicate that weapon carrying by students in urban, suburban, and rural schools is common regardless of student socioeconomic status (May, 2004).

Concern about school site weapon possession has motivated the federal government to promote zero-tolerance policies regarding the possession of firearms at school. The federal Gun-Free Schools Act of 1994 (20 U.S.C. Chapter 70, Section 8921) and subsequent updates require that local education agencies expel students for at least 1 year who have brought a firearm to school. Each state was obligated to integrate this law into practice in order to continue to receive related federal funding. California, for instance, implemented this law by requiring mandatory suspension and recommendation for expulsion whenever a student commits any of the following behaviors: (a) possesses, sells, or otherwise furnishes a firearm; (b) brandishes a knife at another person; (c) sells a controlled substance; (d) commits or attempts to commit a sexual assault or sexual battery; and (e) possesses an explosive (California Department of Education, 2004b). If a student is caught with a weapon at school, staff must invest a tremendous amount of resources to investigate the purported crime, negative public attention is focused on the school, and the student often enters the juvenile justice system. Compounding the consequences of possessing a weapon is the possibility that it can be used to do harm, hence it is important to thoroughly understand this behavior. Despite concern over the limitations of zero-tolerance policies, the assessment of weapon carrying on school campus is crucial to understand the prevalence of the problem and the various multilevel factors related to the behavior.

HISTORICAL INTEREST ABOUT SCHOOL WEAPON POSSESSION

Although public awareness of violence at school followed from a series of multiple homicides in the mid-to-late 1990s, it is less well recalled that original interest in school violence came in the mid-1970s leading to the Violent School Safe School National Study (see Furlong & Morrison, 2000). This large-scale, national study was initiated because of concern by the U.S. Congress that schools were inundated by crime. It was expected that the study would expose the breadth and depth of this problem. Although some problems in schools were found, close inspection indicated that the incidence of school crime was not as pronounced as the public feared. Thus, interest in the topic diminished and was hardly addressed by researchers for almost a decade (Furlong & Morrison, 2000). By the late 1980s, however, there was substantial increase in the incidence of adolescent homicide, culminating in the Columbine High School tragedy of 1999 and continuing with the Red Lake, Minnesota crisis in 2005. These events were followed by increased attention to the problem of school violence, in general, and to school-based weapon possession in particular.

Amidst what is perceived to be a social crisis (Behrman, 2002), there have been efforts to assess the prevalence of weapon possession at school. Initial efforts to understand weapon-carrying behaviors were not focused primarily on school weapon possession, rather school weapon possession items were added to existing instruments that were designed to asses broader aspects of youth health and risk behaviors. These efforts have been primarily defined within a public health model, and the Centers for Disease Control and Prevention (CDC) were originally charged with the task of gathering this information. Since these initial efforts, others have used a similar strategy of adding school weapon possession and exposure items to surveys originally focused on alternative risk behaviors, such as substance abuse.

The first and what has become the predominant source of information about of the presence of weapons on school campuses was the CDC's Youth Risk Behavior Surveillance Survey (YRBS), systematically implemented in 1991. Although the first version of the YRBS did not include any items that specifically asked about weapon possession at school, the biennial administration of the YRBS since 1993 has included two items regarding school weapon experiences. One item questions the frequency of weapon possession (gun, knife, or club) on school property in the past 30 days and a second item inquires about the frequency of being threatened with a weapon by someone on school property in the past 12 months. These two items have formed the foundation of information about weapons on school campuses and have subsequently been included in U.S. safe school reports (e.g., NCES, 2004a, 2004b). By the early 2000s, the YRBS had become the most widely used source of information about weapons on school campuses, primarily because it provided a series of databases from which to estimate trends related to school weapon possession and exposure.

DESCRIPTION OF THE SPECIFIC
APPROACH/SCALES/MEASURES

With respect to school weapon possession, there is, at this time, no instrument comprehensive enough to assess all school weapon-related behaviors and experiences. Rather, studies have used single items or a series of a few items embedded within more general surveys. There is limited consensus regarding how questions about school weapon behaviors and experiences should be framed. In fact, there has been only one attempt to examine the psychometric properties of the most widely used YRBS school weapon items (see Furlong, Sharkey, Bates, & Smith, 2004, for a discussion). Thus, for researchers and school-based mental health service providers to evaluate research and to assess individual student experiences related to school weapon possession, it is necessary to draw on information across existing assessment instruments.

Items Used in National Surveys

Individual items, derived from national surveillance studies, state and regional surveillance studies, as part of general school safety surveys, and within empirical research studies, are summarized in Table 16.1. The instruments are presented in the order of the prominence of their use in assessing school weapon possession across the United States.

Youth Risk Behavior Surveillance Survey

The YRBS was developed as a youth health-risk surveillance system (e.g., see Kann et al., 1996, 2000). The YRBS instrument is an anonymous self-report for adolescents administered to students within their classroom. It was initially administered to a national sample in 1990, and was later revised and re-administered in 1991. Since then, the YRBS has been administered biennially across the nation with students in Grades 9–12. The YRBS focuses on health-risk behaviors in youth that may result in later disability, mortality, morbidity, and/or significant social problems. Such behaviors include alcohol and drug use, unintended pregnancies, dietary

TABLE 16.1
Items Used to Assess School Weapon-Related Experiences

Survey	Weapons	Responses
	National Surveillance Surveys	
Youth Risk Behavior Surveillance Survey (YRBS) (Centers for Disease Control and Prevention) (http://www.cdc.gov/Healthy Youth/yrbs/index.htm)	During the past 30 days, on how many days did you carry a weapon such as a gun, knife, or club on school property?	0 days 1 day 2 or 3 days 4 or 5 days 6 or more days
	During the past 12 months, how many times has someone threatened or injured you with a weapon such as a gun, knife, or club on school property?	0 times 1 time 2 or 3 times 4 or 5 times 6 or 7 times 8 or 9 times 10 or 11 times 12 or more times
Parents Resource Institute for Drug Education (PRIDE) Survey GRADES 4–6 (http://www. pridesurveys.com/)	While at school, have you (in the past year) . . . carried a real gun? . . . carried a knife? . . . carried other weapons for protection?	No One time Two or more
Parents Resource Institute for Drug Education (PRIDE) Survey GRADES 6–12 (http://www. pridesurveys.com/)	While at school have you. . . (time not specified, from list) . . . carried a gun? . . . carried a knife, club, or other weapon? . . . threatened a student with a gun, knife, or club? . . . hurt a student by using a gun, knife, or club? . . . been threatened with a gun, knife, or club by a student? . . . been hurt by a student using a gun, knife, or club?	Never One time 2–5 times 6 or more times
Monitoring the Future (MTF) (http://monitoringthefuture.org/)	During the last 4 weeks, on how many days (if any) were you carrying a weapon such as a gun, knife, or club to school?	None One day Two days 3–5 days 6–9 days 10 or more days
	During the last four weeks, on how many days (if any) did you carry a gun to school? (Note. This question was asked in a different questionnaire than question 4 above)	None One day Two days 3–5 days 6–9 days 10 or more days
The National School Crime and Safety Survey (http://www. hamfish.org/resources/record/21/)	Have you brought any of the following weapons to school in the past 30 days? a. knife b. handgun c. other	Yes No
	If yes, the last time I brought a weapon to school, it was: a. to hurt someone before or after school b. to defend myself c. to be prepared for anything that might happen	Important Somewhat Important Not important
	In the past 30 days, how many times (if at all) has anyone done any of the following to you on purpose at school	Never 1–2 times

TABLE 16.1

Continued

Survey	Weapons	Responses
	National Surveillance Surveys	
	or on school grounds? (from list)	3–5 times
	... hit you with an object	6–9 times
		10 or more times
	In the past 30 days, how many times have you done any	Never
	of the following to someone else on purpose at school or	1–2 times
	on school grounds? (from list)	3–5 times
	... hit someone with an object	6–9 times
	... shot at someone	10 or more times
National Crime Victimization Survey (NCVS)—School Crime Supplement (2001) (http://nces.ed.gov/pubsearch/ pubsinfo.asp?pubid=2001017)	During the last 6 months, that is since————1st, did you ever bring a gun to school or onto school grounds? During the last 6 months, did you ever bring a knife to school or onto school grounds? Include only knives brought as weapons.	Yes No Yes No
	During the last 6 months, did you ever bring some other weapon to school or on to school grounds?	Yes No
	Do you know any (other) students who have brought a gun to your school in the last 6 months?	Yes No
	Have you actually seen another student with a gun at school in the last 6 months?	Yes No
	During the last 6 months could you have gotten a loaded gun without adult supervision, either at school or away from school?	
National Crime Victimization Survey (NCVS)—School Crime Supplement (1995) (http://www.ojp.usdoj.gov/ bjs/abstract/srsc.htm)	During this school year, did you ever bring something to school to protect yourself from being attacked or harmed? (If yes to previous question) Did you bring ... ... a gun ... a knife ... brass knuckles ... razor blade ... spiked jewelry ... mace ... nunchucks	Yes No Yes No
	Examples of State Surveillance Surveys	
California Student Survey Grade 7 and Grades 9, 11 versions (http://safestate.org/ index-print.cfm?navid=254)	During the past 12 months, how many times on school property have you been threatened or injured with a weapon, such as a gun, knife, or club?	0 times 1 time 2–3 times 4 or more times
	During the past 12 months, how many times on school property have you seen someone carrying a gun, knife, or club?	0 times 1 times 2–3 times 4 or more times
	During the past 12 months, how many times on school property have you used any a weapon to threaten or bully someone?	0 times 1 time 2–3 times 4 or more times

Continued

TABLE 16.1
Continued

Survey	Weapons	Responses
	National Surveillance Surveys	
	During the past 12 months, how many times on school property have you carried a gun?	0 times 1 times 2–3 times 4 or more times
	During the past 12 months, how many times on school property have you carried any weapon, such as a knife or club?	0 times 1 time 2–3 times 4 or more times
	How much would your friends disapprove of you for carrying a weapon to school?	A lot Some Not much Not at all
	Examples of Empirical Research Items	
Bailey et al. (1997) (see References)	How often in the past month did you bring something to school to protect yourself from being attacked or harmed?	Never Rarely Sometimes Most of the time
	Do you think that other students brought guns to school today?	Yes No
National Longitudinal Study of Adolescent Health (http://www.cpc.unc.edu/addhealth/)	During the past 12 months, how often did each of the following things happen? (from list) ... carried a weapon to school	No Yes Refused Don't know
	During the past 30 days, on how many days did you carry a weapon—such as a gun, knife, or club—to school?	None 1 day 2 or 3 days 4 or 5 days 6 or more days
	During the past 30 days, what one kind of weapon did you carry most often to school?	A handgun Other kind of gun A club, stick, bat, or pipe A knife or razor Some other kind of weapon
Wilcox and Clayton (2001) (see References)	Have you ever (from a list of experiences) ... taken a weapon to school?	Never Ever in lifetime In the past 12 months In the past 30 days
California School Climate and Safety Survey-Short Form (Furlong, Greif, et al., 2005) (www.education.ucsb.edu/csbyd)	How often do these things happen at your school? (from list) ... students carrying weapons	Not at all A little Some Quite a bit Very often

TABLE 16.1
Continued

Survey	Weapons	Responses
	National Surveillance Surveys	
	Have any of these things happened to you at school during the past month? (from list) ... you personally saw another student with a gun on campus ... you personally saw another student with a knife or razor on campus ... you were threatened by a student with a gun and you saw the gun ... you were threatened by a student with a knife and you saw the knife	No Yes
	Examples of Comprehensive Safe School Survey Items	
Safe and Responsive Schools Safe School Survey (Skiba et al., 2004) (see References)	I have seen a gun at school this year. (Personal Safety Factor) I have seen a knife at school this year. (Delinquency/Major Safety Factor)	5-point Likert 1 = *strongly disagree* 5 = *strongly agree*
Cornell and Loper, (1998) (see References)	Did any of these things happen to you at school in the past month (30 days)? At school means anywhere in school buildings, on school property, on a school bus, or at a school bus stop. (from list) ... someone threatened you with a weapon at school ... you carried a knife from protection at school ... you carried a gun from protection at school ... you carried another weapon (not a gun or knife) for protection at school ... you personally saw someone (not police) with a gun at school ... you personally saw someone (not police) with a knife at school	No Once More than once
Demaray and Malecki, 2002 (see References)	How many times in the last year have you (from list) ... carried a knife to school ... carried a gun to school ... carried another weapon to school	Never 1 or 2 times 3–5 times 6–9 times 10+ times
	How many times in the last 30 days have you (from list) ... carried a knife to school ... carried a gun to school ... carried another weapon to school	Never 1 or 2 times 3–5 times 6–9 times 10+ times

behaviors, physical activity, and sexual activity. The CDC uses results from the YRBS to monitor health-risk behaviors among high school students, evaluate the impact of various efforts to decrease the prevalence of health-risk behaviors, and to monitor the progress of national health objectives.

The YRBS includes two items that inquire about weapon experiences on school campuses; these items ask about the frequency of weapon possession at school in the previous 30 days using the following frequency response options: 0, 1, 2–3, 4–5, and 6+. The term *weapon* is not defined except by using the examples of "gun, knife, and club." This weapon item is used to assess national trends in school weapon possession and has been used to estimate the number of weapons brought to school in a given month (e.g., Kingery, Coggeshall, & Alford, 1998). This single item has also been used as a variable in published studies (e.g., Simon, Crosby, & Dahlberg, 1999) to evaluate school weapon-carrying behavior. Despite this status, there is only one published study that has examined the reliability of this item (Brener et al., 2002). Results of this investigation indicated inadequate reliability and validity data to support the use of the YRBS (beyond its epidemiological purpose) to describe characteristics of youths who engage in high-risk behaviors. For instance, the stability of weapon-carrying items, as measured through test–retest reliability, was low. Additionally, reliability analyses did not address the different time frames of items (30-day vs. lifetime). Finally, the validity of the responses of youth who selected the most extreme response options was not supported (see Furlong, Sharkey, et al., 2004).

Monitoring the Future

Monitoring the Future (MTF; Bachman, Johnston, & O'Malley, 2001) is a national study of secondary and college students regarding their behaviors, attitudes, and values and is funded by the National Institute on Drug Abuse. The Institute for Social Research at the University of Michigan conducts the annual administration of the surveys with students directly in the schools. The project began in 1975 with the purpose of examining changes in young people's beliefs, attitudes, and behaviors in the United States over time, while also monitoring trends in youth substance use and abuse. Multiple forms are used at each grade level with fewer forms in the lower grades—this strategy is used in order to monitor more variables than can be addressed within a single questionnaire during one class period (Bachman, Johnston, & O'Malley, 2001).

Nationwide, approximately 50,000 students in Grades 8, 10, and 12 are surveyed annually in approximately 420 secondary schools (both public and private). The focus of the survey is on substance use; however, a number of items regarding participation in violence, such as physical fighting at school or at work, intentional infliction of injury with a weapon and without a weapon, and threats made against others are also included (Kingery et al., 1998). Monitored behaviors related to issues of school violence and safety include delinquent and other deviant behaviors (carrying a weapon to school) and victimization (theft, vandalism, and interpersonal aggression). School experiences that relate to school violence and safety issues include feeling safe at school, reporting problems at school, and victimization in school (Bachman et al., 2001). Surveys have been completed both anonymously and confidentially during different years of administration and at different grade levels.

A recent report on the MTF survey provides results on the reliability, and stability of the measure on items pertaining to drug use (Johnston, O'Malley, & Bachman, 2001) but not specifically on those items related to delinquency and victimization in school. Bachman and colleagues (2001) reported that although their study fails to provide any direct, objective validation of the measure of drug use, much inferential evidence exits to support its validity including items pertaining to delinquency and their relationship with drug use. However, this evidence does not specifically provide an analysis of the validity of the items (e.g., factor analysis or discriminate analysis) but attempts to explain the degree of truthfulness in youths' responses to items. Kingery and Coggeshall (2001) have noted problems with the wording of a specific item asking students about carrying a gun "to school." This item wording confounds those students who carry a gun to school but not onto the school campus with those who do carry the firearm onto school property. Thus, it is unknown how well these items, including those related to violence and safety, actually measure what they are intended to measure.

National Crime Victimization Survey (School Crime Supplement)

Since 1972, the National Crime Victimization Survey (NCVS) has been collected through ongoing surveys of household members (12 years and older) for the purpose of collecting information on criminal victimization (Chandler, Chapman, Rand, & Taylor, 1998). The NCVS is sponsored by the U.S. Department of Justice and conducted by the Bureau of the Census (Coggeshall & Kingery, 2001). The main function of the survey is to obtain information about the victims and consequences of crime, estimate the number and types of unreported crimes to police, provide uniform measures for specific crimes, and provide comparisons of this information over time. The NCVS has a national U.S. sample of approximately 58,000 households.

The School Crime Supplement (SCS) of the NCVS (Bastian & Taylor, 1991) is an additional questionnaire that obtains information directly from students regarding their experiences of victimization. The 1989 SCS, for example, contained 35 items, of which 18 specifically pertain to school violence and safety. The 1995 SCS contained 33 items, of which 16 pertain to school violence and safety. The development of the supplement was a joint effort between the Department of Education's NCES and the Department of Justice's Bureau of Justice Statistics. A national sample of approximately 10,000 students between the ages of 12 and 19 first completed the supplement between January and June 1989 and then again in 1995 and 1999 (Chandler et al., 1998). These students were attending either a primary or secondary school program for at least 6 months prior to the interview. Students were either interviewed personally in their home or by telephone and only after completing their initial NCVS interview (Kaufman et al., 2001). Interviews with proxy respondents were permitted only when the child was unable to complete the interview or if the parents refused to allow an interview with the child. Students were only asked to report about crimes that had occurred inside a school, on school grounds, or on a school bus within the last 6 months (Chandler et al., 1998). Information obtained in the supplement includes the availability of drugs at school, prevalence of gang fights, existence of street gangs, presence of guns at school, victimization, and fear of being attacked or harmed (Chandler et al., 1998). In 1989, 10,449 interviews were completed in 1989; 9,728 were completed during the 1995 supplement, and 8,398 in 1999. The completion rate for 1989 was 86%, and 78% in 1995 and 1999 (Kaufman et al., 2001). Comparisons made between the 1989, 1995, and 1999 data should be made with caution due to design changes that were made in the measure in 1992 (Kaufman et al., 2001). Various studies have been published using the NCVS SCS data, however, no literature could be obtained regarding the measure's psychometric properties. Given the context of a government representative interviewing students about school crime perpetration and victimization, it is not surprising that this survey produces the lowest reported rates of school violence (Kingery, Berg, & Coggeshall, 2004).

Parents Resource Institute for Drug Education Survey

The Parents Resource Institute For Drug Education (PRIDE) surveys have been used since 1982 by more than 8,000 school systems (PRIDE, 2004). The questionnaire identifies level of student drug use, violence, and other behaviors and it takes 25–30 minutes to administer. It can assess changes in student behavior allowing for the measurement of goals and objectives related to school-based prevention programs. Survey collection is anonymous and voluntary. The PRIDE survey was field-tested and then implemented in 1982. It has been modified regularly to respond to the changing interests of parents, schools, and communities. Procedures and means for reporting results have also been updated and refined. Survey procedures standardize data collection including directions for pre-survey preparation, how to administer the survey, and how to collect and return the questionnaires to PRIDE for data processing. PRIDE provides consumers with a comprehensive summary of the results via a 70-page report including tables, charts, and statistics. Survey results are based on opportunity samples and not scientifically derived stratified random samples.

Metze (2001) examined the 1-week test–retest reliability of the PRIDE survey with a group of fourth through sixth graders. Using an earlier version of the survey, he found the reliability for aggression items was much lower than for drug use items. The aggression items have stability correlations below .70. However, given the low incidence on these items (skewed response distributions), 82% of students provided the same response on both occasions. There are no known psychometric studies of the weapon-related items included in the elementary version of the PRIDE survey.

Metze (2000) also provided reliability information for a sample of 631 students in Grades 6–12 using the secondary version of the PRIDE survey. One-week stability coefficients (in parentheses) for the following school weapon related items were found: "Carried a gun" (.472); "Carried a knife, club, or other weapon" (.695); "Threatened a student with a gun, knife or club" (.465); " Hurt a student by using a gun, knife, or club" (.520); "Been threatened with a gun, knife, or club by a student" (.458); and "Been hurt by a student using a gun, knife, or club" (.775). The time frame used in the secondary version items is not specified, so presumably it reflects lifetime experiences, which should not change markedly over a 1-week period. It is noteworthy that the one weapon-carrying item had a very low stability coefficient.

National School Crime and Safety Survey

The National School Crime and Safety Survey (NSCSS; Kingery, Minogue, Murphy, & Coggeshall, 1998) includes both a staff and student form. The student form contains 15 items. The Motivation for Fighting scale is composed of five items on which students indicate, using a 1–5 scale, if they agree or disagree with a list of given statements (e.g., "I would probably get into a fight if someone: shoved me, tried to start a fight with me, bullied me, spread rumors about me or disrespected or insulted me"). The Perceived Ability to Fight scale consists of three items on which the student indicates if a statement is either true or false ("If I fight, I am likely to win," "I am a better fighter than most students are in my school," and "I'm a good fist-fighter"). The Victimization by Common Aggression scale contains six items on which the student chooses the frequency of times anyone else had purposely done any one of a list of actions at school or on school grounds in the past 30 days. The list includes being (a) "hit, punched, or slapped"; (b) "kicked or tripped"; (c) "pushed or shoved"; (d) "hit with an object"; (e) "sat on or pinned down"; and (f) "pulled, twisted, squeezed, or pinched." The Common Perpetration scale has five items on which the student chooses the frequency of times that he or she has purposely done any one of a list of actions to someone else at school or on school grounds in the past 30 days. This list includes the same behaviors included in the Victimization subscale. The internal consistency coefficients for each of the subscales fell between .53 and .86, with test-retest reliability coefficients falling between .42 and .69. (see http://hamfish.org/pub/nscss/relval.html). No recent studies using the NSCSS are available.

Items Used in State Surveys

A number of states conduct systematic school safety and violence surveys that include items that inquire about school weapon possession (e.g., Texas, North Carolina, Oregon, and Washington). Since 1997, California has devoted significant resources to develop and refine a comprehensive safe and drug-free school assessment system that includes school weapon items.

California Healthy Kids Survey

The California Healthy Kids Survey (CHKS) is series of assessment modules developed by WestEd's Human Development Program in collaboration with Duerr Evaluation Resources for the California Department of Education (California Department of Education, 2004a). The CHKS provides schools with a method of collecting ongoing youth health and risk behavior data. Items for the measures were taken from the YRBS and the California Student Substance Use Survey, also developed by WestEd. Since 1998, it has been successfully administered in California, Oregon, Arkansas, New Hampshire, Maryland, Kansas, and Virginia. Groups in Australia and South Africa have also administered the survey. In California, the CHKS is mandated statewide. By Spring 2003, the survey had been administered in 820 school districts in more than 5,500 schools to more than 1.3 million students, representing 94% of the state's enrollment.

Three separate versions of the CHKS are available for use at the elementary, middle school, and high school levels (California Department of Education, 2004a). The middle and high school versions contain modules that can be added to the core survey covering supplemental topics. The surveys contain items concerning youth nutrition and physical activity, sexual behavior, exposure to prevention and intervention activities, risk and protective factors, alcohol, tobacco and other drug use as well as items specific to violence, school safety, gang involvement, and delinquency (California Department of Education, 2004a). Items measuring school violence and safety on both the middle school and high school measures are identical.

The core module takes approximately one class period to administer by school staff and completed by students. Student participation is voluntary and responses are anonymous. The surveys include items to assess how truthful each respondent has been. The results can be compared to results from the YRBS, and various health-risk surveys. A few of the benefits of using the CHKS include meeting categorical program requirements (such as Title IV), identifying risk and protective factors (through its Resiliency and Youth Development Module), and identifying program goals and high-risk groups (California Department of Education, 2004a). As a recently developed survey system, the CHKS and its various modules are currently undergoing various psychometric analyses. The school weapon items included in the CHKS are shown in the Table 16.1.

Comprehensive Safe School Instruments

Safe and Responsive Schools Safe Schools Survey

The Safe and Responsive (SRS) Safe Schools Survey (Skiba et al., 2004) has developed a school-based survey that can be used to assess aspects of school climate and students' safety-related experiences. As reported by the authors, it represents a comprehensive model of school safety, providing data concerning perceptions of both serious/violent offenses as well as more routine interactions among individuals in the school community. The survey drew on previous national surveys of school violence that emphasize serious violence or criminal acts and from other school climate surveys. A set of 120 items was reduced to 65 items after accounting for redundancy and tested in five schools that were part of a federal school safety-planning project. Basic psychometric item analysis techniques reduced the scale to 45 items. The final secondary student version included 43 items related to school climate and safety with two additional items included as a check on the veracity and seriousness of responding. Questions were framed as a point Likert-type scale ranging from 1 (*strongly disagree*) to 5 (*strongly agree*). Seven additional demographic items included school name, student's race, age, grade level, length of time at the school, and mode of transportation to school. Among these 45 items, the SRS Safe Schools Survey includes just two items that ask about students' perceptions of the frequency with which weapons are visible on their school campus: "I have seen a gun at school this year" (an item in the Personal Safety Factor) and "I have seen a knife at school this year" (an item in the Delinquency/Major Safety Factor). There are no items that specifically target weapon-carrying behavior, but two items ask about students' exposure to weapons on campus (see Table 16.1).

California School Climate and Safety Survey–Short Form

The California School Climate and Safety Survey–Short Form (CSCSS-SF) was derived from an earlier research version (Furlong, Morrison, & Boles, 1991) used in various studies (e.g., Bates, Chung, & Chase, 1997; Furlong, Morrison, Chung, & Bates, 1998, Furlong, Sharma, & Rhee, 2000), The original 102 items were reduced through a series of independent exploratory factor analyses and further validated with a confirmatory factor analysis with the school climate items centered on validating the four factors derived from the previous exploratory factor analyses. The final version included a School Danger subscale (general perceptions of dangerous campus conditions); a School Climate subscale (level of positive support); a School Safety subscale (level of safety at school); and School Victimization subscales (personal experiences related to physical–verbal harassment, sexual harassment, and weapons and physical attacks). In addition, two critical items ask students whether they observed other students with a knife or gun on campus, as well as whether they were involved in ethnic or racial conflicts with other students. Although they are not computed as part of a subscale, these two critical items are important for schools that are assessing the safety of their students. In summary, the CSCSS-SF includes items that measure students' perceptions of weapons on their school campus and their personal exposure and victimization by weapons (see Furlong, Greif, et al., 2005, and Table 16.1).

APPLICATION: WHERE AND HOW TO USE SCHOOL
WEAPON ASSESSMENTS

Within this chapter's broader discussion of school safety and violence-related assessment issues, it is proposed that a lack of consensus among researchers about how to measure school weapon possession and its related experiences (possession, exposure, and victimization) makes it difficult to compare incidence rates across studies and has led to inconsistent research findings regarding the correlates of weapon carrying at school. This section provides a review of how assessments of weapon carrying have been applied in the literature.

One of the primary purposes of surveys questioning school-based weapon carrying is to determine the prevalence of the problem. Given the prominent status of the YRBS, the following summary provides information reflecting the response trends to its school weapon items from 1993 to 2003, as an estimate of the prevalence of this behavior. As shown in Table 16.2, nationally representative samples of students have reported that they possessed weapons at school (exemplified as gun, knife, or club) less often in 2003 than in 1993. Although weapon possession decreased, students were actually slightly more likely to report that they had been threatened with a weapon at school, as shown in Table 16.3.

In addition to forming a baseline for school weapon prevalence, other studies have used school weapon items to explore correlates of students bringing guns to school. This early wave of opportunistic research used large existing databases to look for associations between school weapon possession and other risk behaviors. Wilcox and Clayton (2001) and May (2004) summarized this research as focusing on individual student characteristics (e.g., gender, race, socioeconomic status, age, family influences, peer influences, and previous victimization) to

TABLE 16.2
Responses to the Youth Risk Behavior Surveillance (YRBS) Survey Items: During the Past 30
Days, on How Many Days Did You Carry a Weapon Such as a Gun, Knife, or Club? (Anywhere)
and During the Past 30 Days, on How Many Days Did You Carry a Weapon Such as a Gun,
Knife, or Club on School Property? (School) Percentage of Valid Responses
by Response Option and 1993–2003 Trend

Response No.	YRBS Survey Year							Comment
Days/Location	1993	1995	1997	1999	2001	2003	Trend	
0 times								
Anywhere	76.1	78.7	80.7	82.7	82.6	82.9	+8.5%	Traditionally YRBS weapon
School	87.9	90.3	91.9	93.1	93.6	93.9	+6.8%	responses have been
1 time								dichotomized to show those
Anywhere	4.4	4.4	4.1	3.5	3.2	3.7	−15.9%	youths who reported zero or
School	2.6	2.4	2.2	1.7	1.5	1.7	−34.6%	any weapon carrying in the
2–3 times								previous month. As shown,
Anywhere	5.6	5.4	4.6	3.9	3.8	4.0	−28.6%	since 1993, fewer students
School	2.6	2.2	1.7	1.2	1.2	1.2	−53.8%	report any previous month
4–5 times								school weapon possession
Anywhere	2.1	1.9	1.9	1.1	1.6	1.5	−28.6%	
School	1.0	0.8	0.6	0.5	0.6	0.4	−60.0%	
6+ times								
Anywhere	11.9	9.6	8.8	8.8	8.7	8.0	−32.8%	
School	5.9	4.4	3.7	3.6	3.2	2.8	−52.5%	

Note: Derived from YRBS code books for each survey year, downloaded from www.cdc.gov.us.

TABLE 16.3
Responses to the Youth Risk Behavior Surveillance Survey Items: During the Past 12 Months.
How Many Times Has Someone Threatened or Injured You With a Weapon Such as a Gun,
Knife, or Club on School Property? Percentage of Valid Responses
by Response Option and 1993–2003 Trend

Response	YRBS Survey Year							Comment
No. Times	1993	1995	1997	1999	2001	2003	Trend	
0	91.7	91.0	92.2	92.3	91.1	90.8	−1.0%	This YRBS item does not ask
1	3.9	4.1	3.2	3.7	4.1	4.1	+5.1%	if the victim actually saw the
2–3	2.4	2.4	2.2	1.9	2.2	2.0	−16.7%	weapon, as is done in some
4–5	0.8	0.7	0.6	0.7	0.8	0.9	+12.5%	other studies. Although weapon
6–7	0.3	0.4	0.3	0.4	0.4	0.5	+40.0%	carrying has decreased, there
8–9	0.2	0.3	0.2	0.1	0.1	0.3	+50.0%	has been an increase in the
10–11	0.1	0.1	0.1	0.1	0.1	0.1	0.0%	proportion of students reporting
12+	0.6	1.0	0.7	0.8	1.1	1.4	+133.3%	very frequent threats

Note: Derived from YRBS code books for each survey year, downloaded from www.cdc.gov.us.

explain why some students bring weapons to schools and others do not. Much of this research is based on a conceptual model that links individual student risks with increased probability of bring weapons to school campuses. Data regarding prevalence rates and correlates of school weapon possession have been disseminated to school districts, media, and national policymakers as describing students' experiences with weapons on campus without a thorough examination of what has been measured.

More recently, researchers have conducted studies that attempt to expand on this research by co-administering school safety surveys with measures of other relevant constructs such as trusting school relationships (Bates et al., 1997), school social support (Demaray & Malecki, 2003), and attachment to school and family (e.g., DuRant, Kahn, Beckford, & Woods, 1997). Some researchers have also been able to examine school weapon possession across time using longitudinal methods (e.g., Litardo, 2001) and to compare the relative influences of school structure, individual student characteristics, and school climate on weapon possession using multilevel constructions and analysis (Wilcox & Clayton, 2001). These studies are useful in that they have extended the range of variables included in cross-sectional designs using national databases and they have begun to provide valuable information regarding the stability of school weapon possession, highlighting that some youth are episodic carriers and that persistent carriers show the most extreme patterns of risk behavior (Estell, Farmer, Cairns, & Clemmer, 2003; Litardo, 2002; Steinman & Zimmerman, 2003).

Although several studies have examined the influences of various individual and contextual factors on weapon-carrying behavior, Wilcox and Clayton (2001) were the first to propose a multilevel conceptual model to address the hierarchical effects of individual and school factors. Highlighting the lack of investigation into the link between school bonding, school safety, and in-school weapon possession, these sociologists examined the relationships between (a) individual characteristics (e.g., problem behavior, gun ownership, family dysfunction, and school attachment); (b) school structural characteristics (e.g., proportion free lunch and proportion male); (c) school deficits (e.g., proportion students afraid at school and mean problem behavior); (d) school capital (e.g., mean school attachment and mean church attendance); and (e) a dichotomous indicator of weapon-carrying (i.e., taken a weapon to school in the last 30 days). Using the Kentucky Youth Survey, Wilcox and Clayton examined data from 6,000 students Grades 6 through 12 in 21 middle and high schools. With a 4% rate of weapon carrying, they found significant interindividual and intercontextual variation in weapon carrying. Individual problem behavior had a significant positive relationship with school-based weapon carrying and explained most of the variance in weapon-carrying behavior. Nonetheless, school factors, particularly school-level socioeconomic status, had a significant effect, although it was mediated by school deficit and school capital constructs. Importantly, this study acknowledges the complex relationships between individual and ecological factors in understanding weapon-carrying behaviors. Further research should expand and refine this approach to consider a wide variety of individual, family, peer, school, and community variables in a comprehensive model of weapon-carrying behavior.

CRITIQUE, LIMITATIONS, AND ADVANTAGES OF CURRENT SCHOOL WEAPON ASSESSMENT PRACTICES

In order to better understand the factors associated with carrying weapons in school, researchers need to more thoroughly examine the context, environment, and foundation of the problem. To date, researchers have not demonstrated that items they use have enough reliability to unambiguously understand why students bring weapons to school. Most assessments have focused on epidemiological approaches to answer how prevalent weapons possession is, and thus, do not have adequate psychometric properties to draw conclusions about individual level experiences. Consequently, there is great need to better understand why students carry weapons to school. School weapon researchers should develop a consensus on how to comprehensively measure school weapon-related behaviors, attitudes, and experiences. Fundamental issues still need to be addressed, including the following: (a) verifying the psychometric properties of measures used, (b) defining the behaviors under investigation, (c) understanding the causes and correlates of weapon carrying through longitudinal examination, and (d) moving beyond the assumption that weapon carrying is exclusively part of a constellation of high-risk behaviors. These efforts would help researchers and practitioners to more accurately understand why students, both those who engage in delinquent and antisocial behaviors, and others, who have no obvious risk factors, bring weapons to school.

There is a clear need for a comprehensive school weapon instrument that assesses the following: (a) what objects students bring to school that pose a danger regardless of their intended use (e.g., guns and large knives); (b) any other objects that student bring that they consider to be a "weapon" as defined by the researcher; (c) the reasons students give for bringing these objects to school; (d) students' beliefs and attitudes related to weapons on their school campus (e.g., Shapiro, Dorman, Burkey, Welker, & Clough, 1997) ; (e) their perceptions of the impacts these objects have on their campus; and (f) weapons-related exposure/victimization they may have personally had on their campus. Such an instrument would allow for a more thorough investigation of the reasons why students carry weapons to school, and allow for more psychometrically sound investigations that do not rely on single-item responses.

A consistent definition of *weapon* needs to be developed and included in the assessment of weapon carrying. The YRBS item uses examples of objects to convey a meaning of weapon. This approach suggests that the trait of being a weapon lies within the object itself. In contrast, *weapon* is defined in the *Indicators of School Crime and Safety: 2003* as, "Any instrument or object used with the intent to threaten, injure, or kill, includes look-alikes if they are used to threaten others" (U.S. Departments of Education and Justice, 2004, p. 160). This definition implies that the quality of an object being a weapon lies within its intended use and includes many potential objects that are not typically mentioned in school weapons research (e.g., cigarette lighters, rocks, pencils, and geometry compasses). It is likely that both perspectives are of interest in certain contexts and for differing purposes. Clarity, in terms of understanding what has been or may be used as weapons, is needed to move school weapon research and related prevention efforts forward. Although some studies have included examples or some clarification in asking about weapons possession, this practice is not standard and no consistent definition has been offered by researchers.

In addition to examining the correlates to school weapon possession and exposure, researchers have found evidence for a link between various high-risk behaviors and school weapon possession (e.g., Kulig, Valentine, Griffith, & Ruthazer, 1998). Some have sought explanations in existing theories such as Differential Association Theory (Wilcox & Clayton, 2001) and Social Disorganization Theory (May, 2004). However, the preponderance of research has used cross-sectional designs to assess correlates of weapon possession by examining the association between school weapon possession and various school and community risk behaviors (such as being in fight and using illegal substances) (Furlong, Bates, & Smith, 2001; Furlong, Sharkey, et al., 2004). To investigate this relationship using combined YRBS samples, one study developed an index of school and community-related risk behaviors to assess their relationship with school weapon possession (Furlong et al., 2001). As reported in numerous other studies using YRBS data, there were strong associations between the number of risk behaviors and the frequency of weapon possession. It was also found that community risk factors did not enhance prediction of school weapon possession above school risk behaviors. Although the association between school risk behaviors and weapon possession was confirmed in that 84% of those with seven or more risk factors also reported carrying a weapon (gun, knife, or club) to school one or more times in the previous month, it was also found that 3% of students with no risk factors reported carrying a weapon to school. What has not been commonly recognized in research, importantly, is that in terms of raw numbers there were actually more students with zero risk behaviors who carried weapons to school ($n = 565$) than students with six or more risk factors ($n = 206$). Moreover, in another study regarding the validity of extreme responses to the gun carrying item, it was found that those who most often carried a weapon to school were not only the most likely to engage in a variety of risky behaviors (e.g., smoked marijuana 40 or more times at school in the past 30 days), they were also more likely to engage in a variety of healthy behaviors (e.g., eats carrots four or more times a day; Furlong, Sharkey, et al., 2004). This result suggests that extreme responses may not be accurate, and that without psychometric evidence of validity, results should be interpreted with caution. In summary, although research has searched for explanations in deviant behavior patterns and contexts to understand school weapon possession, it has relied on surveys that are not valid for this purpose. Additionally, research has largely ignored the numerically larger group of students who carry weapons to school and have no known pattern of other high-risk behaviors.

The combination of using single items on national surveillance systems with zero-tolerance reactions to the act of weapon possession on school campuses has attenuated views of this risk behavior. In order to fully understand the various motives and consequences of weapon carrying, it is important to create measurement tools that adequately address questions posed about this behavior. Limited research has examined those influences that act as protective buffers against weapon possession. There has also been little done in the school environment to understand the social context in which the possession occurs. Further investigation should focus on understanding the consequences of zero-tolerance policies and what interventions are most appropriate for creating a safe school climate to both prevent and intervene with

TABLE 16.4

Implications for Practice: How to Assess Weapon Possession at School

---

Create a school-based safety planning team to discuss the issue of weapon carrying at school consisting of key stakeholders such as administrators, teachers, students, parents, and community members

Determine which questions are of primary interest and carefully define them

Consider the following that may be of concern:
  (a) Objects students bring to school that pose a danger regardless of their use (e.g., guns)
  (b) Any other objects that student bring that they consider to be a "weapon" as defined by the safety planning team (e.g., mace)
  (c) Reasons students give for bringing these objects to school
  (d) Student beliefs and attitudes related to weapons on their school campus
  (e) Perceptions of the impacts these objects have on their campus
  (f) Weapons-related exposure/victimization they may have personally had on their campus

Create a local survey and administer this to students

Planning team should examine the results and discuss the meaning and implications of what is found among themselves and with students, staff, parents, and community members

Research clearly shows that youth who have multiple risk factors in their lives (e.g., substance use, delinquency, poor academic performance, and weak positive social bonds) are much more likely than other students to carry weapons—this issue should be openly discussed with such students

In raw numbers, other students without known risks may carry more weapons to school—this possibility should be considered by the school planning team

Interventions should build on enhancing a safe school climate with the goal to re-engage rather than disengage at-risk students

Recognize that although many high-risk students report carrying and/or being exposed to weapons at school, most school weapon behaviors involve students with no known risk factors weapons on campus, not just on the outcome of surveillance surveys based on individual items of unverified reliability and validity. National policies that require a severe and unwavering punishment for a student behavior assume a single motivation for school weapon possession. Research is needed to elucidate the reasons why students carry weapons on campus to help educators intervene most effectively. For example, expelling an academically engaged student for accidentally carrying a knife to school in the trunk of his or her car most likely does harm to that student and the school climate overall.

SUMMARY OF IMPLICATIONS FOR RESEARCH AND PRACTICE

Given the status of school weapon-related assessment practices, it is clear that existing research provides only a preliminary understanding of this behavior. Although the YRBS is being used to provide a national barometer for weapon-carrying trends, we urge individual schools and districts that might use YRBS weapon items to avoid comparing local rates to national rates because these items were not developed or validated for such a purpose. Practitioners should not assume that these surveys provide definitive information about the danger that weapons pose to their campus. To rely on current assessment information does not produce a thorough picture of the problem. For example, most surveys define weapons as a gun, knife, or club. To date, there is no research to inform us about how students actually interpret such language about "weapons." Practitioners should not automatically presume that all students who have a knife at school, for example, brought it with the conscious intention of using it as a weapon. An 11th-grade boy who brought a knife to school to slice an apple may not report that he brought a weapon to school, although he could have used it for that purpose given the right circumstances. Moreover, to assume that the weapons students bring to school are mostly guns or knives and to implement a metal wand program to detect them would obviously be inappropriate if students were bringing other types of weapons to school. Current best practice would be to develop a site-based team of stakeholders to investigate the issue locally and to respond to local interests and needs. Table 16.4 provides a summary of implications for practice to guide schools toward a better understanding the nature of weapon possession on their campuses. Such a site-based approach is recommended given the lack of psychometrically sound assessment tools.

REFERENCES

Bachman, J. G., Johnston, L. D., & O'Malley, P. M. (2001). *The Monitoring the Future Project after twenty-seven years: Design and procedures.* (Monitoring the Future Occasional Paper No. 54). Ann Arbor, MI: Institute for Social Research.

Bastian, L., & Taylor, B. (1991). *School crime: A National Crime Victimization Survey Report.* Washington, DC: Bureau of Justice Statistics.

Bailey, S. L., Flewelling, R. L., & Rosenbaum, D. P. (1997). Characteristics of students who bring weapons to school. *Journal of Adolescent Health, 20,* 261–270.

Bates, M. P., Chung, A., & Chase, M. (1997). Where has the trust gone? The protective role of interpersonal trust and connections with adults in the school. *California School Psychologist, 2,* 39–52.

Behrman, R. E. (Ed.). (2002). Special Issue: Children, youth, and gun violence. *The Future of Children, 12*(2), 1–176.

Brener, N. D., Kann, L., McManus, T., Kinchen, S. A., Sundberg, E. C., & Ross, J. G. (2002). Reliability of the 1999 Youth Risk Behavior Survey Questionnaire. *Journal of Adolescent Health, 31,* 336–342.

California Department of Education. (2000). *California Safe School Assessment Report, 1998–99 report.* Sacramento, CA: Author. Available: http://www.cde.ca.gov/re/pn/fd/cssa9899-pdf.asp

California Department of Education. (2004a). *California Healthy Kids Survey web site.* Available: http://www.wested.org/hks

California Department of Education. (2004b, May 7). *Zero tolerance.* Available: http://www.cde.ca.gov/ls/ss/se/zerotolerance.asp

Chandler, K. A., Chapman, C. D., Rand, M. R., & Taylor, B. M. (1998). *Students' reports of school crime: 1989 and 1995*. Washington, DC: Bureau of Justice Statistics, U.S. Department of Justice and National Center for Education Statistics, U.S. Department of Education (NCJRS Document Reproduction Service No. 169607).

Coggeshall, M. B., & Kingery, P. M. (2001). Cross–survey analysis of school violence and disorder. *Psychology in the Schools, 38*, 107–116.

Coggeshall, M. B., Kingery, P. M., & Berg, K. F. (2004). Improving the accuracy of school violence surveys. In M. J. Furlong, M. P. Bates, D. C. Smith, & P. M. Kingery (Eds.). *Appraisal and prediction of school violence: Issues, methods and contexts* (pp. 253–266). Hauppauge, NY: Nova Science.

Cornell, D. G., & Loper, A. B. (1998). Assessment of violence and other high-risk behaviors with a school survey. *School Psychology Review, 27*, 317–330.

Demaray, M. K., & Malecki, C. K. (2003). Perceptions of the frequency and importance of social support by students classified as victims, bullies, and bully/victims in an urban middle school. *School Psychology Review, 32*, 471–489.

Dennis, D., Massie, J. E., Wycoff-Horn, M., Mouzon, L., Pleban, F. T., & Monge, E., & Sarvela, P. D. (2002). Weapon carrying among rural southern Illinois elementary school children. *Journal of Health Care for the Poor & Underserved, 13*, 413–424.

Ding, C. S., Nelsen, E. A., & Lassonde, C. T. (2002). Correlates of gun involvement and aggressiveness among adolescents. *Youth & Society, 34*, 195–213.

DuRant, R. H., Kahn, J., Beckford, P. H., & Woods, E. R. (1997). The association of weapon carrying and fighting on school property and other health risk and problem behaviors among high school students. *Archives Pediatric Adolescent Medicine, 151*, 360–366.

Estell, D. B., Farmer, T. W., Cairns, B. D., & Clemmer, J. T. (2003). Self-reported weapon possession in school and patterns of early adolescent adjustment in rural African American youth. *Journal of Clinical Child & Adolescent Psychology, 32*, 442–452.

Furlong, M. J., Bates, M. P., Sharkey, J. D., & Smith, D. C. (2004). The accuracy of school and non-school risk behaviors as predictors of school weapons possession. In M. J. Furlong, M. Bates, D. C. Smith, & P. Kingery (Eds.), *Appraisal and prediction of school violence: Issues, methods and contexts* (pp. 193–214). Hauppauge, NY: Nova Science.

Furlong, M. J., Bates, M. P., & Smith, D. C. (2001). Predicting school weapon possession: A secondary analysis of the Youth Risk Behavior Surveillance Survey. *Psychology in the Schools, 38*, 127–140.

Furlong, M. J., Greif, J. L., Bates, M. P., Whipple, A. D., Jimenez, T. C., & Morrison, R. (2005). Development of the California School Climate and Safety Survey—Short Form. *Psychology in the Schools, 42*, 137–150.

Furlong, M. J., & Morrison, G. M. (2000). The SCHOOL in school violence: Definitions and facts. *Journal of Emotional & Behavioral Disorders, 8*, 71–82.

Furlong, M., J., Morrison, R., Chung, A., & Bates, M. (1998). School violence victimization among secondary students in California: Grade, gender, and racial-ethnic group incidence patterns. *California School Psychologist, 3*, 71–87.

Furlong, M. J., Nyborg, V. M., & Sharkey, J. D. (2005). Homicide and the adolescent: Prevention approaches. In T. P. Gullotta & G. Adams (Eds.), Handbook of adolescent behavioral problems: Evidence-based approaches to prevention and treatment (in press). New York: Springer.

Furlong, M. J., Sharkey, J. D., Bates, M. P., & Smith, D. C. (2004). An examination of the reliability, data screening procedures, and extreme response patterns for the Youth Risk Behavior Surveillance Survey. In M. J. Furlong, G. M. Morrison, R. Skiba, & D. Cornell (Eds.), *Issues in school violence research* (pp. 109–130). New York: Haworth Press.

Furlong, M. J., Morrison, R., & Boles, S. (1991). *California School Climate and Safety Survey*. Paper presented at the annual meeting of the California Association of School Psychologists. Los Angeles, April.

Furlong, M. J., Sharma, B., & Rhee, S. S. (2000). Defining school violence victim subtypes: A step toward adapting prevention and intervention programs to match student needs. In D. S. Sandhu & C. B. Aspy (Eds.). *Violence in American schools: A practical guide for counselors* (pp. 67–87). Alexandria, VA: American Counseling Association.

Johnston, L. D., O'Malley, P. M., & Bachman, J. G. (2001). *Monitoring the Future national survey results on drug use, 1975–2000. Vol. 1. secondary school students*. Publication No. 99-4660. Bethesda, MD: National Institute of Drug Abuse.

Kann, L., Warren, C. W., Harris, W. A., Collins, J. L., Williams, B. I., Ross, J. G., & Kolbe, L. J. (1996). Youth Risk Behavior Surveillance-United States, 1995. *Morbidity and Mortality Weekly Report, 45*(SS-4), 1–84.

Kann, L., Kinchen, S, A., Williams, B. I., Ross, J. G., Lowry, R., Hill, C. V., Grunbaum, J. A., & Kolbe, L. J. (2000). Youth Risk Behavior Surveillance-United States, 1999. *Morbidity and Mortality Weekly Report, 49*(SS-5), 1–94.

Kaufman, P., Chen, X., Choy, S. P., Peter, K., Ruddy, S. A., Miller, A. K., Fleury, J. K., Chandler, K. A., Planty, M. G., & Rand, M. R. (2001). *Indicators of school crime and safety: 2001*. Washington, DC: U.S. Departments of Education and Justice. NCES 2002-113/NCJ-190075.

Kingery; P. M., Minogue, N., Murphy, L., & Coggeshall, M. (1998). *The National School Crime and Safety Survey: Student Form.* Washington, DC: Hamilton Fish National Institute on School and Community Violence. Available: http://.hamfish.org/

Kingery, P. M., Berg, K. F., & Coggeshall, M. B. (2004). Examining the incidence of weapon carrying in America's schools. In M. J. Furlong, M. P. Bates, D. C. Smith, & P. M. Kingery (Eds.), *Appraisal and prediction of school violence: Issues, methods and contexts* (pp. 267–284). Hauppauge, NY: Nova Science.

Kingery, P. M., & Coggeshall, M. B. (2001). Surveillance of school violence, injury, and disciplinary actions. *Psychology in the Schools, 38*, 117–126.

Kingery, P. M., Coggeshall, M. B., & Alford, A. A. (1998). Violence at school: Recent evidence from four national surveys. *Psychology in the Schools, 35*, 247–258.

Kulig, J., Valentine, J., Griffith, J., & Ruthazer, R. (1998). Predictive model of weapon carrying among urban high school students: Results and validation. *Journal of Adolescent Health, 22*, 312–319.

Litardo, H. A. (2002). *Adolescent predictors of weapon carrying behavior in schools: A longitudinal perspective.* (Doctoral dissertation). Dissertation Abstracts International: Section B: The Sciences & Engineering, *62*(7-B), 3411.

Litardo, H. A. (2001). *Adolescent predictors of weapon-carrying behaviors in schools: A longitudinal perspective.* Unpublished doctoral dissertation, University of Albany, State University of New York. (Digital Dissertations, No. AAT 3019537).

Martin, C. A., Mainous, A. G., III, Ford, H. H., Mainous, R., Slade, S., Martin, D., & Omar, H. (2001). Attitudes towards guns: Associations with alcohol use and impulsive behavior. *International Journal of Adolescent Medicine & Health, 13*, 205–210.

May, D. C. (2004). Weapons in schools. In E. R. Gerler (Ed.), *Handbook of school violence* (pp. 227–268). New York: Haworth Press.

Metze, L. (2000, October). *PRIDE technical report: The PRIDE questionnaire for grades 6–12 validity and reliability study.* Western Kentucky University, Bowling Green, KY: Author.

Metze, L. (2001). *PRIDE technical report: The PRIDE questionnaire for grades 4–6 reliability study.* Western Kentucky University, Bowling Green, KY: Author.

National Center for Education Statistics (NCES). (2004a). *Crime and safety in America's public schools: Selected findings from the School Survey on Crime and Safety.* Washington, DC: U.S. Department of Education, Institute of Education Sciences (NCES 2004–370).

National Center for Education Statistics (NCES). (2004). *Indicators of school crime and safety: 2003.* Washington, DC: Author and Bureau of Justice Statistics and the U.S. Departments of Education and Justice (NCES 2004–004).

PRIDE. (2004). *PRIDE surveys.* Website retrieved August 16, 2004, from http://www.pridesurveys.com/

Shapiro, J. P., Dorman, R. L., Burkey, W. M., Welker, C. J., & Clough, J. B. (1997). Development and factor analysis of a measure of youth attitudes toward guns and violence. *Journal of Clinical Child Psychology, 26*, 311–320.

Sheley, J. F., & Wright, J. D. (1998, October). High school youth, weapons, and violence: A national survey. *National Institute of Justice Research in Brief.* Washington, DC: National Institute of Justice.

Simon, T. R., Crosby, A. E., & Dahlberg, L. L. (1999). Students who carry weapons to high school: Comparison with other weapon-carriers. *Journal of Adolescent Health, 24*, 340–348.

Skiba, R., Simmons, A. B., Peterson, R., McKelvey, J., Ford, S., & Gallini, S. (2004). Beyond guns, drugs and gangs: The structure of student perceptions of school safety. In M. J. Furlong, M. P. Bates, D. C. Smith, & P. Kingery (Eds.), *Appraisal and prediction of school violence: Issues, methods and contexts* (pp. 149–171). Hauppauge, NY: Nova Science.

Steinman, K. J., & Zimmerman, M. A. (2003). Episodic and persistent gun carrying among urban African American adolescents. *Journal of Adolescent Health, 32*, 356–364.

U.S. Department of Education, National Center for Education Statistics. (2004). *Crime and safety in America's public schools: Selected findings from the School Survey on Crime and Safety* (NCES 2004–370). Washington, DC: Author.

Wilcox, P., & Clayton, R. R. (2001). A multilevel analysis of school-based weapon possession. *Justice Quarterly, 18*, 501–533.

III

Research-Based Prevention and Intervention Programs

The implementation of evidence-based prevention and intervention strategies are essential to reduce acts of violence that impact schools, and promote safe, supportive, and effective schools. Chapters in this section highlight a variety of valuable strategies, including anger management, bullying prevention, addressing peer victimization, positive behavioral supports, and comprehensive multifaceted programs to promote the well-being of students.

The first five chapters address the topic of bullying, including a socioecological model for bullying prevention and intervention (chap. 17), critical characteristics of effective bullying programs (chap. 18), an overview of the internationally implemented Olweus Bullying Prevention Program (chap. 19), a synthesis of the Steps to Respect program to promote behaviors and beliefs that reduce bullying (chap. 20), and a critical review of studies examining school-based programs to reduce bullying (chap. 21). Chapter 22 offers information regarding peer victimization among students. Chapters 23 and 24 address anger management programs, including a focus on youth anger management treatments as a means to prevent school violence and a critical analysis of school-based anger management programs. Chapters 25 through 28 address important facets of school-wide prevention programs, including a review of a Second Step violence prevention program, an overview of the PATHS curriculum for building social and emotional competence, a synthesis of schoolwide positive behavioral supports, and a meta-analysis examining the effectiveness of school-based violence prevention programs in preventing and reducing violence. Chapter 29 incorporates the Standardized Emergency Management System in preventing, preparing, for, and responding to school violence.

17

A Socioecological Model for Bullying Prevention and Intervention in Early Adolescence: An Exploratory Examination

Susan M. Swearer
James Peugh
University of Nebraska—Lincoln

Dorothy L. Espelage
*University of Illinois,
Urbana-Champaign*

Amanda B. Siebecker
University of Nebraska—Lincoln

Whitney L. Kingsbury
*University of Illinois,
Urbana-Champaign*

Katherine S. Bevins
University of Nebraska—Lincoln

Involvement in bullying and victimization is the result of the complex interplay between individuals and their broader social environment. In this chapter, Bronfenbrenner's (1979) classic ecological theory is used as a base to illustrate the interrelated nature between the individual, multiple environments, and engagement in bullying and victimization behaviors. First, the bullying literature across the social ecology is reviewed, a socioecological model of bullying is proposed and evaluated, and implications for effective bullying intervention are discussed.

Socioecological theory has been previously applied to the conceptualization of bullying and victimization (Garbarino & deLara, 2002; Newman, Horne, & Bartolomucci, 2000; Olweus, 1993; Swearer & Doll, 2001; Swearer & Espelage, 2004). It is clear from both theory and research that bullying and victimization are phenomena that are reciprocally influenced by the individual, family, school, peer group, community, and society. One major task facing bullying researchers is how to empirically examine these reciprocal influences. Although it is beyond the scope of this chapter to examine each area in depth, a brief overview of selected socioecological variables associated with bullying and victimization is provided and followed by an empirical examination of these multiple and reciprocal influences.

INDIVIDUAL VARIABLES ASSOCIATED WITH BULLYING
AND VICTIMIZATION

Much of the extant literature on bullying and victimization has focused on the individuals involved in bullying and victimization. Researchers and educators are understandably interested in the reasons why an individual either engages in bullying others and/or might be bullied by others. Previous research has found that individuals involved in bullying (e.g., a victim, bully, or bully-victim), are more likely to experience significant depressive symptomatology (Austin & Joseph, 1996; Craig, 1998; Kaltiala-Heino, Rimpela, Marttunen, Rimpela, & Rantanen, 1999; Swearer, Song, Cary, Eagle, & Mickelson, 2001). Individuals who are victimized (e.g., a victim or a bully-victim) report significant anxious symptomatology (Craig, 1998; Hodges & Perry, 1996; Swearer et al., 2001). Although it is evident that individuals involved in bullying and victimization may experience greater levels of depression and anxiety than individuals not involved in bullying, the temporal relation between involvement and bullying and internalizing problems is less clear. Do the bullying behaviors precede depression/anxiety or does the depression/anxiety precede the bullying? Despite this unanswered temporal relationship, internalizing factors appear to influence an individual's experience with bullying and/or victimization.

The relationship between caregivers and children functions as a model for the child's interactions with others. A child with an insecure attachment learns to expect inconsistent and insensitive interactions with others, whereas a child with a secure attachment style comes to expect consistent and sensitive interactions (Bowlby, 1969). Troy and Sroufe (1987) found that children who had insecure, anxious-avoidant, or anxious-resistant attachments at the age of 18 months were more likely than children with secure attachments to become a victim of bullying by age 5. Perry, Hodges, and Egan (2001) found that anxious-resistant children tended to cry easily, were manifestly anxious, and were hesitant to explore—all causal characteristics for victimization. Furthermore, Perry et al. (2001) found that the self-concepts of children with resistant attachments often included feelings of low self-worth, helplessness, and incompetence, which are attributes targeted by bullies. Each individual brings his or her own characteristics to the bullying interaction. Temperamental, personality, and psychological variables are individual traits that interact with other contexts in the social-ecology of bullying.

PEER VARIABLES ASSOCIATED WITH BULLYING
AND VICTIMIZATION

Although individual variables play a prominent role in bullying and victimization, it is the peer group that becomes a major socialization force during early adolescence. Researchers have consistently documented that the transition from elementary school to middle school is a potential stressor associated with negative emotional and psychological outcomes for some students. In the limited available research on the trend of bullying during this transition it appears that there is a temporary increase in bullying during early adolescence (NCES, 1995; Pellegrini, 2002; Pellegrini & Bartini, 2001; Pellegrini & Long, 2002). Indeed, Akso (2002) found that fifth graders identified bullying as one of their primary concerns about starting sixth grade.

The peer context is a powerful and salient force in contributing to bullying and victimization and several theories permeate the literature, including dominance theory (Pellegrini, 2002), attraction theory (Bukowski, Sippola, & Newcomb, 2000) and the homophily hypothesis (Cairns & Cairns, 1994; Espelage, Holt, & Henkel, 2003). Research has also focused on the various participant roles that peer group members adopt and how the instrumentality of these participant roles contributes to the bully/victim phenomena (Craig & Pepler, 1995; Salmivalli, 2001).

Dominance Theory

Pellegrini (2002) argued that the transition to middle school requires students to renegotiate their dominance relationships, and bullying is thought to be a deliberate strategy used to attain dominance in newly formed peer groups. From a social dominance perspective, individuals are ordered along a vertical hierarchy where each position represents varying access to resources (e.g., friendship and status). In a longitudinal study of 87 boys, Pellegrini and Bartini (2001) found strong correlations between aggression and dominance at the beginning of the first year of middle school. These authors conjectured that aggression is used to establish dominance within a peer group and then initial aggression diminishes because the peer group understands who occupies higher status. Bullying behaviors ebb and flow depending on the need to assert and maintain dominance within the peer group. Thus, the inclusion or exclusion of peers provides fertile ground for bullying behaviors.

Attraction Theory

The instrumentality of aggression during early adolescence has been well documented (Bukowski et al., 2000). Attraction theory argues that adolescents attempt to establish independence from parents by affiliating or wanting to affiliate with peers who possess characteristics that reflect greater independence (e.g., aggression) and less compliant behaviors (e.g., prosocial behavior; Bukowski et al., 2000; Moffitt, 1993). For example, through nominations for play characters, Bukowski and colleagues found that girls' and boys' attraction to aggressive peers (i.e., mean, cruel, or picks on smaller kids) increased on the entry to middle school, whereas attraction to students who had high classroom competence (i.e., smart and helps everyone) decreased.

Homophily Hypothesis

Peer groups during early adolescence typically consist of members who share common attributes (e.g., "homophily," Berndt, 1982; Kandel, 1978), including sex, race, and behavioral characteristics (e.g., academic focus or delinquency). Studies examining peer networks and aggression have found support for the homophily hypothesis (Cairns & Cairns, 1994). Peers not only affiliate with students with similar levels of aggression, but they also influence each other over time. In particular, in a short-term investigation of verbal aggression among middle school students, the amount of peer group aggression was predictive of individual youths' verbal aggression over a school year, even after controlling for baseline levels, a finding that held true for both males and females (Espelage et al., 2003). Aggression is relatively stable over time, but an increase among some students during early adolescence can be explained in part by their peer group membership.

   These developmental theories provide an understanding of how bullying might be promoted within or by peer groups, but says little about the exact roles that students take in bullying encounters. Observational studies conducted by Canadian researchers provided rich empirical data of how students participated or did not participate in bullying episodes on the playground (Craig & Pepler, 1995, 1997; O'Connell, Pepler, & Craig, 1999). Although the participants in these studies included elementary school children, it would be remiss to not include a discussion of this seminal work because it contributed to a shift away from the individual child to the larger social context. For example, it was evident that bullying was a group phenomena because peers were present 85% of the time (Craig & Pepler, 1997), peers reinforced bullies' behaviors 81% of the time (Craig & Pepler, 1995), and intervened to help the victim only 11% of the time (Craig & Pepler, 1997). Salmivalli (2001) developed descriptors for the various roles that students take during bullying episodes, including reinforcers, assisters, and passive bystanders.

SCHOOL VARIABLES ASSOCIATED WITH BULLYING AND VICTIMIZATION

Although much of the research on bullying has focused on individuals and peers, the broader issue of school climate has largely been ignored. Individuals interact within peer groups for the majority of each day in the school setting. The school setting affects the academic, social, and emotional functioning of all students and is integrally connected to the overall climate of the school. School climate has long been recognized as an important factor in student outcomes, resulting in the identification of a number of factors that affect and are affected by school climate. Anderson's (1982) comprehensive review of the literature identified several important factors influencing school climate. These factors were categorized into three groups: milieu (i.e., characteristics of the individuals and groups in the school); social system (i.e., the variables which address the relationships within the school); and culture (i.e., variables which include group beliefs and values).

School personnel play a key role in creating a positive or negative school climate. Recent research suggests that teachers may actually tolerate bullying, resulting in increases in bullying behaviors (Yoneyama & Naito, 2003). Teachers have also been found to be inaccurate in estimating the amount of bullying that occurs in their schools (Holt & Keyes, 2004). Additionally, teachers may lack knowledge about how to effectively respond when they observe bullying (Espelage & Swearer, 2003). Teachers' ability to respond to bullying has implications for student perceptions of intervention. Adair, Dixon, Moore, and Sutherland (2000) found that almost half of the students surveyed believed that bullying could not be stopped. When students observe a lack of awareness and responsiveness on the part of teachers, they may feel hopeless and believe that effective solutions are impossible (Dupper & Meyer-Adams, 2002; Houndoumadi & Pateraki, 2001). Unnever and Cornell (2003) also found that the majority of students felt that their peers and their teachers would not stop bullying.

FAMILY VARIABLES ASSOCIATED WITH BULLYING AND VICTIMIZATION

Although much of the bullying and victimization reported by adolescents occurs in the schools, researchers have recently begun to examine the early developmental processes such as family socialization that may contribute to bullying and victimization. The role of parenting style and sibling relationships contributes to our understanding of the family connection to bullying. According to Lickel, Schmader, and Hamilton's (2003) investigation of the Columbine shootings in Littleton, Colorado, parents were considered to have the most responsibility for the tragedy. The authors contend that parents are often held responsible by the public because they are expected to be close to and have authority over their children. Although some research has investigated the impact of the family on bullies and victims there is less research investigating the parent responsiveness to bullying. However, numerous news reports detail parents' attempts to talk with school personnel about bullying incidents. When schools respond ineffectively, parents take matters into their own hands by either transferring their child to another school or pursuing legal action. Research suggests that students tend to report bullying to their parents instead of teachers, suggesting that students believe their parents will be more effective than their teachers in addressing the bullying (Houndoumadi & Pateraki, 2001).

Parents serve as important models upon which children base their expectations of future interactions with others. In examining the family connection to bullying, more is known about families of bullies versus families of victims (Finnegan, Hodges, & Perry, 1998; Rodkin & Hodges, 2003). Olweus (1993) found that caregivers of boys who bully tend to lack involvement and warmth, use "power-assertive" practices such as physical punishment and violent emotional outbursts, and demonstrate a permissive attitude with regard to their child's aggressive behaviors. Bowers, Smith, and Binney (1994) confirmed this finding, emphasizing the high need for power demonstrated by bully's families. High marital conflict between parents has also been found to influence the child's instrumentality of aggressive behavior (Olweus, 1993).

Generally speaking, for bullies, victims, or bully-victims, these children have been found to have relatively authoritarian parents (Baldry & Farrington, 1998). In a study conducted by Bowers and colleagues (1994), differences in parenting style were further examined, with parents of bully-victims demonstrating characteristics demonstrative of the indifferent-uninvolved style. Specifically, bully-victims reported troubled relationships with their parents characterized by low warmth, abusive and inconsistent discipline, neglect, and low in support. In light of findings that bullying tends to occur when parents are absent or unaware of their child's actions, Olweus (1993) highlighted the importance of parental monitoring of children's activities both inside and outside of school.

In contrast to the lack of warmth and involvement often demonstrated in families of bullies, victims' families have been characterized by overinvolved and overprotective mothers (Bowers et al., 1994; Olweus, 1993). Olweus theorized that victimized boys reported more positive relationships with their mothers than nonvictimized boys, but the controlling nature of these mothers could inhibit their child's development of self-confidence, independence, and the ability to be assertive. In a review of the literature on fathers of victims, Duncan (2004) concluded that fathers of victims were often critical and distant.

Maltreatment by parents, including physical, sexual, emotional abuse, and neglect (Shields & Cicchetti, 2001) has also been linked to both bullying and victimization in children. These authors proposed that maltreatment fosters emotional dysregulation, which is then transferred to interactions with the peer group. Relatedly, Schwartz, Dodge, Pettit, and Bates (1997) found that aggressive victims were often frequently exposed to violence in the home by being physically abused and, although nonvictimized aggressive boys did not share the same experience of physical abuse, they had higher ratings of exposure to aggressive role models.

Few studies have examined the role of sibling relationships and involvement in bullying. Wolke and Samara (2004) found a significant connection between being bullied by siblings and being bullied at school. Duncan (1999) surveyed 375 middle school students and of the 336 children with siblings, 42% reported that they often bullied their siblings, 24% reported they often push or hit their brothers and sisters, and 11% stated that they often beat up their siblings. A smaller group (30%) reported siblings frequently victimized them, with 22% stating they were often hit or pushed around, and 8% reporting a sibling often beat them up. As for concordance rates between bullying siblings and bullying peers at school, 57% of those who bullied their peers and 77% of bully-victims reported also bullying their siblings. A previous study by Bowers and colleagues (1994) detected a similar pattern of relationships, finding that bullies reported negative and ambivalent relationships with siblings and viewed their siblings as more powerful then themselves. The opposite was found for victims, who reported enmeshed and positive relationships with their siblings (Bowers et al., 1994).

COMMUNITY VARIABLES ASSOCIATED WITH BULLYING
AND VICTIMIZATION

Just as individual, peer, and family characteristics clearly impact bullying and victimization, the characteristics of the community in which children live and go to school also have direct and indirect influences on these behaviors. Rates of child maltreatment, delinquency, violence, aggression, and general externalizing behavior in youth have all been linked to community-level variables (Coulton, Korbin, Su, & Chow, 1995; Kupersmidt, Griesler, DeRosier, Patterson, & Davis, 1995; Jonson-Reid, 1998; Plybon & Kliewer, 2001; Stern & Smith, 1995). However, few studies directly connect community structure to the phenomenon of bullying. Bullying differs from other aggressive behaviors in that it is chronic, involves a power differential, and is often covert (Olweus, 1993). Many bullying prevention programs incorporate components addressing community factors (Cox, 1997); however, an analysis of community variables and bullying is sparse.

Aggregate community demographics using census and police data are often used in the study of the relation between community and developmental outcomes for children and adolescents (Brooks-Gunn, Duncan, Klebanov, & Sealand, 1993). Debate has ensued about how communities and neighborhoods are defined and measured. Although alternative methods have been proposed (Coulton, Korbin, & Su, 1996), census and police data continue to be widely used. Measures of poverty, mobility, crime, single-parent families, and racial diversity have all been examined and linked to youth outcomes. Overwhelmingly, indicators of high levels of poverty within a community are most strongly and directly linked to undesirable youth outcomes including aggression and delinquency (Brooks-Gunn et al., 1993; Kupersmidt et al., 1995; Plybon & Kliewer, 2001; Stern & Smith, 1995).

Aggregate measures of community structure have also been shown to have an indirect influence on outcomes through mediating and moderating factors. Such factors include family cohesion, parenting behavior, social support, and stress. Plybon and Kliewer (2001) demonstrated that family cohesion might serve as a protective factor for children. Youth living in neighborhoods characterized by high levels of poverty and moderate levels of crime tend to develop fewer externalizing behaviors when families are highly cohesive. These authors have also shown that family stress may mediate the effect between neighborhood risk and externalizing behavior (Plybon & Kliewer, 2001). Stern and Smith (1995) showed that neighborhood disadvantage affects rates of delinquency indirectly through social isolation and parental involvement. These studies indicate that a lack of community resources may isolate families from support and financial opportunities.

There exists a solid body of literature indicating that children who are exposed to high levels of community violence tend to become violent themselves, however, little is known about this connection with bullying. In one study of Swedish middle school students, Andershed, Kerr, and Stattin (2001) found that students involved in school bullying were likely to be the same students perpetrating violence in the community. Students involved in bullying at school were also more likely to be the victims of community violence. Bullies were more likely to carry weapons in the community and loiter on the streets. The direction of these relations was not clarified by the study but it did link bullying in school to the broader expression of violence in the community.

Based on the brief review of individual, peer, family, school, and community variables that impact involvement in bullying and victimization, it is easy to see that the interaction between these multiple systems is critical to understanding the socioecological framework of bullying and victimization in early adolescence. During the transition from elementary school to middle school, students enter a new environment where the nature of peer groups are changing, teachers are less connected to students, academic work becomes more rigorous, and biological changes occur within the individual. Additionally, the family becomes a less salient force in the life of middle school students. The community that surrounds the home and the school becomes more important as students may walk to and from school and become more involved in community activities. Some students may use aggressive behaviors, in the form of bullying, to establish a higher position on the hierarchy of social dominance within their peer group. Attraction theory suggests that these students will be seen as attractive by their peers and potentially could have a socializing effect on other students, as bullying may be viewed as "cool" (Rodkin, 2004). Attachment theory suggests that young adolescents who are insecurely attached may have problematic relationships with their peers and/or teachers. These changes across multiple contexts present fertile ground for bullying during this developmental period.

In the remainder of this chapter, a socioecological model of bullying and victimization in early adolescence is proposed and parts of this model are empirically examined. In this model, influences of individual negative *affect* (i.e., depression, anxiety, and aggression), *peer factors* (i.e., being bullied by peers and status attached to bullying), *family factors* (i.e., being bullied at home, socioeconomic status, and living arrangement), *school factors* (i.e., perceived school climate and school responsiveness), and *community factors* (i.e., crime statistics, family mobility, and being bullied to and from school) are proposed. Given the fact that data from only three communities were collected, community factors were not analyzed in the full model.

METHOD

Participants

Data were collected from students in Grades 6–9 as part of a larger longitudinal study on bullying and victimization (i.e., Target Bullying). Data were collected ($N = 469$) across three middle schools ($n = 121$, 194, and 154, respectively) in a mid-sized midwestern town. Data from these three middle schools were used in this study because these schools represent different communities within an urban town. Thus, the diversity of the schools included in this study aids in the generalization of the model. Participant demographics can be found in Table 17.1.

Procedure and Measures

Due to space limitations, a detailed explanation of procedures and measures are not provided. The reader is encouraged to see Swearer and Cary (2003) and Swearer et al. (2001) for more detail regarding procedures and measures used in the Target Bullying project. All students with parental consent (28% participation at School A; 29% participation at School B; and 22% participation at School C) and youth assent were administered a series of counterbalanced instruments assessing bullying and psychosocial functioning.

The following measures were used in these analyses: (a) *The Bully Survey* (Swearer, 2001)[1] is a three-part, 31-question survey that queries students regarding their experiences with bullying, perceptions of bullying, and attitudes toward bullying. There are two questions about being bullied at home and the final section contains a scale that measures peer attitudes toward bullying (PEER). Higher total scores on the PEER scale indicate greater acceptance of bullying ($r = .76$); (b) *Thoughts about School* (TAS; Song & Swearer, 1999) is a 32-item scale that is based on a previous school climate measure (Kasen, Johnson, & Cohen, 1990; $r = .80$);

---

[1]The Bully Survey (Swearer, 2001) can be obtained from the first author.

TABLE 17.1
Participant Descriptive Statistics

	School A (n = 121)	School B (n = 194)	School C (n = 154)
Gender			
Male	57 (47%)	83 (43%)	64 (42%)
Female	64 (53%)	109 (56%)	90 (58%)
Ethnicity			
Caucasian	75 (62%)	177 (91%)	140 (91%)
African American	16 (13.2%)	5 (2.6%)	1 (.6%)
Hispanic/Latino	7 (5.8%)	2 (1%)	
Asian American	8 (6.6%)	3 (1.5%)	7 (4.5%)
Native American	3 (2.5%)	2 (1%)	
Middle Eastern	3 (2.5%)		
Eastern European		1 (.5%)	1 (.6%)
Mixed Ethnicity	9 (7.4%)	4 (2.4%)	5 (3.3%)
Grade			
Sixth Grade	35 (29%)		
Seventh Grade	51 (42%)	74 (38%)	64 (42%)
Eighth Grade	35 (29%)	73 (38%)	43 (28%)
Ninth Grade	47 (24%)	47 (30%)	
Age			
Mean	12.67	13.32	13.05
Standard deviation	0.87	0.93	0.69

(c) *The Children's Depression Inventory* (CDI; Kovacs, 1992; $r = .87$); (d) *The Multidimensional Anxiety Scale for Children* (MASC; March, 1997; $r = .92$); (e) *The Aggression Questionnaire* (AQ; Buss & Warren, 2000; $r = .92$); and (f) *Family Demographics*. School records were examined and data on free/reduced fee lunch, paying for lunch, and living arrangement at home were obtained. Information on being bullied at home was analyzed from the *Bully Survey*.

Descriptive Community and Crime Data

Community-level data were collected from the U.S. Bureau of the Census (2000) for each of the three schools. These data were collected for the zip code in which each school was located in order to approximate school attendance area. The local school district provided the student mobility index for each school. Crime statistics were also collected for each school attendance area through the local police department. Although many studies use census tracts to approximate neighborhood boundaries (Brooks-Gunn et al., 1993), in this analysis student residence zip codes were the best measure of overall community conditions.

RESULTS

Descriptive statistics for participants are shown in Table 17.1 and summary statistics for variables included in the analyses are presented in Table 17.2. Because data were collected at only three schools, statistical analyses could not be performed for community or crime variables, however, observed trends are described. Table 17.3 displays community level variables for

TABLE 17.2
Variable Descriptive Statistics

	School A (n = 121)	School B (n = 194)	School C (n = 154)
AQ			
Mean	81.86	78.36	77.39
(standard deviation)	(24.53)	(22.05)	(19.34)
CDI			
Mean	8.64	8.97	8.31
(standard deviation)	(7.65)	(6.89)	(7.10)
MASC			
Mean	43.17	41.54	41.44
(standard deviation)	(19.43)	(16.06)	(18.22)
Peer attitudes Toward bullying			
Mean	26.64	26.06	25.34
(standard deviation)	(7.55)	(7.53)	(7.17)
TAS			
Mean	60.27	56.71	57.14
(standard deviation)	(7.56)	(7.60)	(7.78)
SES			
Free/reduced lunch	60 (50%)	26 (16%)	11 (7%)
Pays for Lunch	58 (48%)	163 (84%)	143 (93%)
Living arrangement			
Lives with mother and father	70 (58%)	76 (39.2%)	117 (76%)
Other	48 (39.5%)	44 (22.6%)	36 (23.3%)
Home bullying different from school?			
Yes	19 (16%)	41 (21%)	34 (22%)
No	12 (10%)	9 (4.6%)	9 (6%)
Bully-victim status			
Bully	10 (8.2%)	12 (6.2%)	6 (3.9%)
Victim	40 (33.1%)	76 (39.2%)	52 (33.8%)
Bully-victim	24 (19.8%)	43 (22.2%)	44 (28.6%)
Bystander	36 (29.8%)	53 (27.3%)	36 (23.4%)
No status	11 (9.1%)	10 (5.2%)	15 (9.7%)
Involvement in bullying			
Involved	74 (61.2%)	131 (67.5%)	102 (66.2%)
Not Involved	47 (38.8%)	63 (32.5%)	52 (33.8%)

each of the three schools included in this analysis. These variables were chosen based on community factors shown in previous research and theory to affect outcomes for children and adolescents (e.g., poverty, family structure, and mobility; Coulton et al., 1995; Wandersman & Nation, 1998). Schools A and B are similar in community characteristics. The greatest discrepancy appears to be between Schools A and C. School C has low student mobility and a median household income almost twice that in the community surrounding School A. For School C, poverty rates, the proportion of single-parent families, and unemployment are low, whereas the number of adults with at least a high school education is high. Thus, it could be hypothesized that stress might be lower and social support higher for the families of students attending School C. The proportion of single-parent families, people living in poverty, and student mobility in the community surrounding School A is noticeably larger than for the community surrounding School C. This may indicate greater levels of stress and lower levels of social support for families living in the community surrounding School A.

TABLE 17.3
U.S. Census Data (2000) for Each School Zip Code

	Single-[a] Parent Families	Adults with [b] at Least a High School Education	Unemployment [b] Household	Median [c] Income	Below [d] Poverty	Student [e] Mobility Index
School A	20.4	86.3	5.0	$30,481	14.1	27.0
School B	15.8	89.1	3.1	$35,627	12.7	11.8
School C	5.9	97.2	1.5	$64,415	3.2	8.6

[a] Percent of total families.
[b] Percent of total adults.
[c] Absolute value in dollars.
[d] Percent of total population.
[e] Percent of total students.

TABLE 17.4
Total Number of Crimes Committed in Each School Attendance Area by Crime Type

	Assaults	Auto Theft	Burglary	Larceny	Rapes and Attempted Rapes	Attempted Suicide	Robbery	Murder
School A	608	103	286	1,852	12	3	20	0
School B	444	54	246	1,224	3	4	17	2
School C	133	16	78	538	2	0	2	1

Table 17.4 displays the total number of property and violent crimes committed in each school attendance area. These data do not yield crime rates (i.e., crimes committed per unit population), but the data provide an illustration of the total amount of crime occurring in the surrounding community. Estimates of the total population for each attendance area using census data show that School C has the largest estimated population followed by Schools A and B. Notice that overall, crime rates are lowest for the School C attendance area and highest for the School A attendance area. Like the community data discussed previously, these crime data suggest greater life stress for students attending School A than School C.

Psychometric Analyses of Study Instruments

Preliminary analyses were conducted to establish the measurement scale properties of the TAS and PEER items. After deleting 12 TAS items (2, 4, 6, 11, 12, 18, 22, 23, 24, 28, 29, and 30) and 2 PEER items ("Bullies are popular" and "I can understand why someone would bully other kids") to eliminate redundancy and maintain parsimony, the remaining TAS and the PEER items showed acceptable levels of internal consistency (TAS $r = .80$; PEER $r = .76$). Combination exploratory/confirmatory factor analyses (e.g., see Muthen & Muthen, 1998–2004) were performed with the 20 TAS and 12 PEER items, respectively. Based on fit indices, parsimony, and factor interpretability, one-factor solutions best explained both sets of items (TAS: $r^2[152, 171] = 380.62$, root mean square error of approximation [RMSEA] = .06, Standardized root mean squared residual [SRMR] = .05, comparative fit index [CFI] = .82, factor determinacy $= .91$; PEER: $r^2[55, 66] = 307.43$, RMSEA $= .09$, SRMR $= .18$, CFI $= .76$, factor determinacy$= .93$). Although CFI values of 0.96 or greater are considered indicative of model fit, two points are noteworthy. First, the RMSEA and factor determinacy values for both scales are acceptable (Hu & Bentler, 1999; Muthen & Muthen, 1998–2004). Second, this study represents a first attempt to empirically establish the construct validity of a school climate measure and a "peer attitudes toward bullying" scale. As such, these fit indices can be considered adequate for exploratory research purposes.

A multigroup measurement invariance analysis was conducted to determine if school climate and peer attitude latent factors and the individual negative affect latent factor (measured by AQ, CDI, MASC total scores), were measured identically across the three middle schools. Results indicated variance/covariance matrices were invariant, but three factor loadings based on the Total score for the Aggression Questionnaire (AQSUM, TAS 21, and a peer attitude item, "I feel sorry for kids who are bullied") were noninvariant. Assuming equal scores for these items for students from each school, School C students would show slightly lower peer attitude and individual negative affect latent variable scores, whereas School B students would show slightly higher school climate factor scores. The 20 TAS and 12 peer attitude items were combined and analyzed as summative scale scores assuming the measurement invariance analysis results would not impact latent variable model results significantly. School climate and peer attitudes toward bullying latent factors were specified for analysis using single-indicator techniques that allow for the specification of measurement error, resulting in latent factors for school climate and peer attitudes toward bullying that are comprised of true score variance only (e.g., see Bollen, 1989; Kline, 1998).

Latent Variable Models

Figure 17.1 illustrates the multinomial logistic regression analysis performed with the "no status" bully/victim classification (i.e., not involved in bullying) used as the reference group for

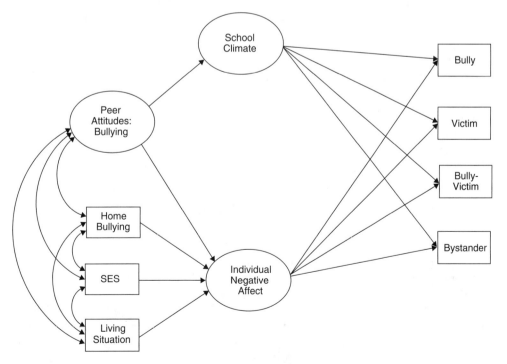

FIG. 17.1. Proposed Social-Ecological Model of Bullying.

TABLE 17.5
Multinomial Logistic Regression Results

	Estimate	Standardized	S.E.	Wald	Odds Ratio
Regressions					
Peer attitudes_School climate	−0.26	−0.24	0.07	**−3.80**	NA
Peer attitudes_Individual affect	−0.01	−0.22	0.04	−0.32	NA
Living arrangement_Individual affect	−0.06	−0.07	0.19	−0.31	NA
SES_Individual affect	0.10	0.11	0.33	0.32	NA
Home bullying_Individual affect	0.13	0.14	0.40	0.32	NA
Individual affect_Bully	0.69	0.97	2.32	0.30	1.99
Individual affect_Victim	0.54	0.93	1.78	0.30	1.72
Individual affect_Bully/victim	0.65	0.93	2.13	0.31	1.92
Individual affect_Bystander	0.57	0.71	1.84	0.31	1.77
School climate_Bully	0.01	0.18	0.05	0.16	1.01
School climate_Victim	−0.01	−0.43	0.03	−0.41	0.99
School climate_Bully/victim	−0.02	−0.42	0.04	−0.48	0.98
School climate_Bystander	−0.03	−0.74	0.03	−0.98	0.97

Note: **Bold** = $p < .05$.

TABLE 17.6
Binary Logistic Regression Results

	Estimate	Standardized	S.E.	Wald	Odds Ratio
Model 2					
Peer attitudes_School climate	−0.26	−0.24	0.07	**−3.83**	NA
Peer attitudes_Individual affect	−0.01	−0.22	0.04	−0.32	NA
Living arrangement_Individual affect	−0.06	−0.07	0.19	−0.31	NA
SES_Individual affect	0.10	0.11	0.31	0.33	NA
Home bullying_Individual affect	0.11	0.12	0.35	0.32	NA
School climate_Involvement in bullying	0.01	0.79	0.02	0.80	1.01
Individual affect_Involvement in bullying	0.17	0.58	0.61	0.28	1.19

Note: **Bold** = $p < .05$.

comparison. Results are presented in Table 17.5 and indicate a significant inverse relationship ($p < .001$) between peer attitudes toward bullying and school climate scores; school climate scores will decrease .25 points for every 1-point increase in peer attitude towards bullying scores, on average. For all subsequent analyses, the bully-victim categories were collapsed into a binary "involvement in bullying" dependent variable. Specifically, bullies, bully-victims, and victims were classified as 1 (*involved*) in bullying and bystanders and no status categories were classified as 0 (*not involved*) in bullying. The *not involved* group served as the baseline for comparison. Results of the binary logistic regression analyses presented in Table 17.6 also

TABLE 17.7
Binary Logistic Regression Results by School—School A

	Estimate	Standardized	S.E.	Wald	Odds Ratio
School A					
Peer attitudes_School climate	−0.43	−0.42	0.15	**−2.82**	NA
Peer attitudes_Individual affect	−0.01	−0.13	0.07	−0.10	NA
Living arrangement_Individual affect	−0.20	−0.27	1.94	−0.10	NA
SES_Individual affect	0.11	0.16	1.09	0.10	NA
Home Bullying_Individual affect	0.37	0.50	3.71	0.10	NA
School climate_Involvement in bullying	−0.01	−0.12	0.04	−0.35	0.99
Individual affect_Involvement in bullying	2.17	1.00	21.9	0.10	8.76

Note: **Bold** = $p < .05$.

TABLE 17.8
Binary Logistic Regression Results by School—School C

	Estimate	Standardized	S.E.	Wald	Odds Ratio
School C					
Peer attitudes_School climate	−0.36	−0.32	0.12	**−3.14**	NA
Peer attitudes_Individual affect	−0.01	−0.24	0.01	−1.72	NA
Living arrangement_Individual affect	−0.05	−0.09	0.05	−1.05	NA
Home Bullying_Individual affect	−0.02	−0.03	0.07	0.27	NA
School climate_Involvement in bullying	0.06	0.73	0.03	1.90	1.06
Individual affect_Involvement in bullying	−1.79	−0.74	1.14	−1.57	.17
					(5.88)

Note: **Bold** = $p < .05$.

showed a significant inverse relationship between peer attitudes toward bullying and school climate scores similar to results shown in Table 17.5.

Further binary logistic regression analyses were performed within each of the three middle schools. Results for School A are presented in Table 17.7 and indicate the significant inverse relationship between peer attitudes toward bullying and school climate scores was slightly more pronounced ($p < .01$). School climate scores decreased .43 points on average for every 1-point increase in peer attitudes toward bullying scores. Finally, Table 17.8 indicates the relationship between peer attitudes toward bullying and bullying involvement was statistically significant ($p < .01$) for School C students; school climate scores decreased .36 points for every one unit increase in peer attitudes toward bullying scores. One nonsignificant finding was noteworthy. The relationship between school climate scores and bullying involvement (.06; $p = .06$, odds ratio = 1.06) suggests the odds are 1.06 times higher for students at School C to become involved in bullying on average for every one unit increase in school climate scores.

Therefore, students in School C who have positive perceptions of school climate are more likely to bully others. No significant path coefficients were observed for School B. Follow-up analyses examining the direct effect of peer attitude scores on bullying for all multinomial and binomial logistic models showed no significant path coefficients.

Currently, traditional indices of model fit are not available for dependent variables measured on a categorical scale (i.e., bully-victim status). As such, the adequacy of the proposed socioecological model of bullying prevention can only be evaluated by the extent to which the estimated model parameters conform to current theories of school bullying and victimization. Aside from a significant relationship between peer attitudes towards bullying and school climate scores, none of the remaining parameter estimates confirmed our hypothesized socioecological model of bullying.

DISCUSSION AND LIMITATIONS

Results from this study support previous research that has found students who are involved in bullying and victimization hold more supportive attitudes toward bullying and perceive the school climate to be more negative (Pellegrini, Bartini, & Brooks, 1999; Swearer & Cary, 2003). The relationship between pro-bullying attitudes and negative school climate supports the notion that high levels of bullying are associated with negative school climate. Although the proposed socioecological model of bullying did not hold up in the analyses, some interesting methodological issues were raised from the attempt.

One major limitation in this attempt is due to the categorical nature of the bully-victim status dependent variable. Specifically, many structural equation modeling analysis features, such as multiple group comparisons, significance tests of indirect effects, model fit indices, and model modification indices are not available for categorical dependent variables (e.g., see Muthen & Muthen, 1998–2004). Thus, continuous measures of bully-victim status should be considered for future model testing. However, accurate measurement of bullying, which is a reciprocal relationship problem, is a difficult task via self-report items (Furlong, Morrison, & Greif, 2003).

None of the direct effects of the binary covariates (living arrangement, socioeconomic status, bullying occurring in the home) on bully/victim status or bullying involvement could be tested. Latent variable statistical software packages (e.g., Mplus) require near-complete data for categorical models in general and specifically for testing the direct effects of covariates on categorical dependent variables because listwise deletion is the default setting for the needed parameter estimation algorithm (see Muthen & Muthen, 1998–2004). However, although these covariates were not testable in the proposed model, the relationships between these variables remain an area of empirical interest and should be tested in future research.

The implications of a socioecological model for bullying prevention and intervention programming are delineated in Table 17.9. One interesting outcome from the attempt to test a socioecological model of bullying is an increased understanding of how to examine the community context surrounding schools. A reasonable hypothesis might be made that higher rates of poverty, violent crime, and mobility might be related to higher rates of bullying in any given school. Census and crime data can be collected in an attempt to study these influences. Previous research suggests that the characteristics of neighborhoods directly adjacent to a school are more closely related to school climate than the neighborhoods in which students live (Welsh, Stokes, & Greene, 2000). Thus, smaller units of community analysis may yield useful findings in relation to bullying. While in many respects, our analysis of a socioecological model raised more questions than it answered, there is much to be learned about the relationship

TABLE 17.9
Implications for Practice: What Educational Professionals Should Do to Effectively Intervene
in Bullying and Victimization.

Use the "CIRCLE" metaphor to illustrate the socioecology of bullying and victimization:
Community—Involve community leaders, police officers, and clergy in the effort to reduce
  bullying and victimization.
Individual—Utilize individual counseling interventions to address internalizing and
  externalizing problems when working with students involved in bullying and
  victimization.
PaRent—Get involved with families and include parents in intervention efforts.
SChool—Conduct school-wide assessments and staff meetings to analyze the scope of the
  bullying problem. Address staff issues with bullying. If there is a bullying culture at the
  adult level, chances are there will be bullying at the student level.
SibLing—School personnel have a unique generational perspective on many families. Work
  with siblings to help foster healthy sibling relationships.
PEer—Observe and get involved in the peer groups. Determine if the peer group is supportive
  of bullying and work with peer groups to dispel the notion that bullying is "cool."

between multiple contexts and influences on bullying and victimization. Understanding these
reciprocal relationships is an important step in preventing bullying in our schools, homes, and
communities.

REFERENCES

Adair, V. A., Dixon, R. S., Moore, D. W., & Sutherland, C. M. (2000). Ask your mother not to make yummy sandwiches: Bullying in New Zealand secondary schools. *New Zealand Journal of Educational Studies, 35*, 207–221.

Akos, P. (2002). Student Perceptions of the transition to middle school. *Professional School Counseling, 5*(5), 339–345.

Andershed, H., Kerr, M., & Stattin, H. (2001). Bullying in school and violence on the streets: Are the same people involved? *Journal of Scandinavian Studies in Criminology and Crime Prevention, 2*, 31–49.

Anderson, C. S. (1982). The search for school climate: A review of the research. *Review of Educational Research, 52*, 368–420.

Austin, S., & Joseph, S. (1996). Assessment of bully/victim problems in 8- to 11-year-olds. *British Journal of Educational Psychology, 66*, 447–456.

Baldry, A. C., & Farrington, D. P. (1998). Parenting influences on bullying and victimization. *Criminal and Legal Psychology, 3*, 237–254.

Berndt, T. J. (1982). The features and effects of friendship in early adolescence. *Child Development, 53*, 1447–1460.

Bollen, K. A. (1989). *Structural equations with latent variables.* New York: Wiley.

Bowers, L., Smith, P. K., & Binney, V. (1994). Perceived family relationship of bullies, victims and bully/victims in middle childhood. *Journal of Social and Personal Relationships, 11*, 215–232.

Bowlby, J. (1969). *Attachment and loss* (Vol. 1). New York: Basic Books.

Bronfenbrenner, U. (1979). *The ecology of human development: Experiments by nature and design.* Cambridge, MA: Harvard University Press.

Brooks–Gunn, J., Duncan, G. J., Klebanov, P. K., & Sealand, N. (1993). Do neighborhoods influence child and adolescent development? *American Journal of Sociology, 99*, 353–395.

Bukowski, W. M., Sippola, L. K., & Newcomb, A. F. (2000). Variations in patterns of attraction to same- and other-sex peers during early adolescence. *Developmental Psychology, 36*, 147–154.

Buss, A. H., & Warren, W. L. (2000). *Aggression Questionnaire manual.* Los Angeles, CA: Wosten Psychological Services.

Cairns, R. B., & Cairns, B. D. (1994). *Lifelines and risks: Pathways of youth in our time.* Cambridge, England: Cambridge University.

Coulton, C., Korbin, J., & Su, M. (1996). Measuring neighborhood context for young children in an urban area. *American Journal of Community Psychology, 24*, 5–32.

Coulton, C. J., Korbin, J. E., Su, M., & Chow, J. (1995). Community level factors and child maltreatment rates. *Child Development, 66*, 1262–1276.

Cox, A. D. (1997). Preventing child abuse; a review of community-based projects 1: Intervening on processes and outcomes of reviews. *Child Abuse Review, 6*, 243–256.

Craig, W. M. (1998). The relationship among bullying, victimization, depression, anxiety, and aggression in elementary school children. *Personality and Individual Differences, 24*, 123–130.

Craig, W. M., & Pepler, D. J. (1995). Peer process in bullying and victimization: An observational study. *Exceptionality Education Canada, 5*, 81–95.

Craig, W. M., & Pepler, D. J. (1997). Observations of bullying and victimization in the schoolyard. *Canadian Journal of School Psychology, 13*, 41–59.

Duncan, R. D. (1999). Peer and sibling aggression: An investigation of intra- and extra-familial bullying. *Journal of Interpersonal Violence, 14*, 871–886.

Duncan, R. D. (2004). The impact of family relationships on school bullies and their victims. In D. L. Espelage & S. M. Swearer (Eds.), *Bullying in American schools: A socialecological perspective on prevention and intervention* (pp. 227–244). Mahwah, NJ: Lawrence Erlbaum Associates.

Dupper, D. R., & Meyer-Adams, N. (2002). Low-level violence: A neglected aspect of school culture. *Urban Education, 37*, 350–364.

Espelage, D. L., Holt, M. K., & Henkel, R. R. (2003). Examination of peer-group contextual effects on aggression during early adolescence. *Child Development, 74*, 205–220.

Espelage, D. L., & Swearer, S. M. (2003). Research on school bullying and victimization: What have we learned and where to we go from here? *School Psychology Review, 32*, 365–383.

Finnegan, R. A., Hodges, E. V. E., & Perry, D. G. (1998). Victimization by peers: Associations with children's reports of mother-child interaction. *Journal of Personality and Social Psychology, 75*, 1076–1086.

Furlong, M. J., Morrison, G. M., & Greif, J. L. (2003). Reaching an American consensus: Reactions to the special issue on school bullying. *School Psychology Review, 3*, 456–470.

Garbarino, J., & deLara, E. (2002). *And words can hurt forever: How to protect adolescents from bullying, harassment, and emotional violence.* New York: The Free Press.

Hodges, E., & Perry, D. (1996). Victims of peer abuse: An overview. *Journal of Emotional and Behavioral Disorders, 5*, 23–28.

Holt, M. K., & Keyes, M. A. (2004). Teachers' attitudes toward bullying. In D. L. Espelage & S. M. Swearer (Eds.), *Bullying in American schools: A socialecological perspective on prevention and intervention* (pp. 121–139). Mahwah, NJ: Lawrence Erlbaum Associates.

Houndoumadi, A., & Pateraki, L. (2001). Bullying and bullies in Greek elementary schools: Pupils' attitudes and teachers'/parents' awareness. *Educational Review, 53*, 19–26.

Hu, L., & Bentler, P.M. (1999). Cutoff criteria for fit indexes in covariance structure analysis: Conventional criteria versus new alternatives. *Structural Equation Modeling, 6*, 1–55.

Jonson-Reid, M. (1998). Youth violence and exposure to violence in childhood: An ecological review. *Aggression and Violent Behavior, 3*, 159–179.

Kaltiala-Heino, R., Rimpela, M., Marttunen, M., Rimpela, A., & Rantanen, P. (1999). Bullying, depression, and suicidal ideation in Finnish adolescents: School survey. *British Medical Journal, 319*, 348–351.

Kandel, D. B. (1978). Homophily, selection, and socialization in adolescent friendships. *American Journal of Sociology, 84*, 427–436.

Kasen, S., Johnson, J., & Cohen, P. (1990). The impact of school emotional climate on student psychopathology. *Journal of Abnormal Child Psychology, 18*, 165–177.

Kline, R. B. (1998). *Principles and practice of structural equation modeling.* New York: Guilford.

Kovacs, M. (1992). *Children's Depression Inventory.* North Tonawanda, NY: Multi-Health Systems.

Kupersmidt, J. B., Griesler, P. C., DeRosier, M. E., Patterso, C. J., & Davis, P. W. (1995). Childhood aggression and peer relations in the context of family and neighborhood factors. *Child Development, 66*, 360–375.

Lickel, B., Schmader, T., & Hamilton, D. L. (2003). A case of collective responsibility: Who else was to blame for the Columbine High School shootings? *Personality and Social Psychology Bulletin, 29*, 194–204.

March, J. S. (1997). *Multidimensional Anxiety Scale for Children.* North Tonawanda, NY: Multi-Health Systems.

Moffitt, T. E. (1993). Adolescence-limited and life-course-persistent antisocial behavior: A developmental taxonomy. *Psychological Review, 100*, 674-701.

Muthen, B. O., & Muthen, L. K. (1998–2004). *Mplus user's guide: Third edition.* Los Angeles: Muthen & Muthen.

National Center for Educational Statistics (NCES). (1995, October). *Strategies to avoid harm at school.* Washington, DC: U.S. Department of Education, Office of Educational Research and Improvement.

Newman, D. A., Horne, A. M., & Bartolomucci, C. L. (2000). *Bully busters: A teacher's manual for helping bullies, victims, and bystanders.* Champaign, IL: Research Press.

O'Connell, P., Pepler, D., & Craig, W. (1999). Peer involvement in bullying: Insights and challenges for intervention. *Adolescence, 22*, 437–452.

Olweus, D. (1993). *Bullying at school.* Oxford, UK: Blackwell.

Pellegrini, A. D. (2002). Bullying, victimization, and sexual harassment during the transition to middle school. *Educational Psychologist, 37,* 151–163.

Pellegrini, A. D., & Bartini, M. (2001). Dominance in early adolescent boys: Affiliative and aggressive dimensions and possible functions. *Merrill-Palmer Quarterly, 47,* 142–163.

Pellegrini, A. D., Bartini, M., & Brooks, F. (1999). School bullies, victims, and aggressive victims: Factors relating to group affiliation and victimization in early adolescence. *Journal of Educational Psychology, 91,* 216–224.

Pellegrini, A. D., & Long, J. (2002). A longitudinal study of bullying, dominance, and victimization during the transition from primary to secondary school. *British Journal of Developmental Psychology, 20,* 259–280.

Perry, D. G., Hodges, E. V. E., & Egan, S. K. (2001). Determinants of chronic victimization by peers. In J. Juvonen & S. Graham (Eds.), *Peer harassment in schools: The plight of the vulnerable and victimized* (pp. 73–104). New York: Guilford.

Plybon, L. E., & Kliewer, W. (2001). Neighborhood types and externalizing behavior in urban school-age children: Tests of direct, mediated and moderated effects. *Journal of Child and Family Studies, 10,* 419–437.

Rodkin, P. C. (2004). Peer ecologies of aggression and bullying. D. L. Espelage & S. M. Swearer (Eds.), *Bullying in American schools: A socialecological perspective on prevention and intervention* (pp. 87–106). Mahwah, NJ: Lawrence Erlbaum Associates.

Rodkin, P. C., & Hodges, E. V. E. (2003). Bullies and victims in the peer ecology: Four questions for psychologists and school professionals. *School Psychology Review, 32,* 384–400.

Salmivalli, C. (2001). Group view on victimization: Empirical findings and their implications. In J. Juvonen & S. Graham (Eds.), *Peer harassment in school: The plight of the vulnerable and victimized* (pp. 398–419). New York: Guilford.

Schwartz, D. Dodge, K. A., Pettit, G. S., & Bates, J. E. (1997). The early socialization of aggressive victims of bullying. *Child Development, 68,* 665–675.

Shields, A., & Cicchetti, D. (2001). Parental maltreatment and emotion dysregulation as risk factors for bullying and victimization in middle childhood. *Journal of Clinical Child Psychology, 30,* 349–363.

Song, S. Y., & Swearer, S. M. (1999). *Thoughts about school.* Unpublished manuscript, The University of Nebraska, Lincoln.

Stern, S. B., & Smith, C. A. (1995). Family processes and delinquency in an ecological context. *Social Service Review, 69,* 703–731.

Swearer, S. M. (2001). *The Bully Survey.* Unpublished manuscript, The University of Nebraska, Lincoln.

Swearer, S. M., & Cary, P. T. (2003). Attitudes toward bullying in middle school youth: A developmental examination across the bully/victim continuum. *Journal of Applied School Psychology, 19,* 63–79.

Swearer, S. M., & Doll, B. (2001). Bullying in schools: An ecological framework. *Journal of Emotional Abuse, 2,* 7–23.

Swearer, S. M., & Espelage, D. L. (2004). Introduction: A socialecological framework of bullying among youth. In D. L. Espelage & S. M. Swearer (Eds.), *Bullying in American schools: A socialecological perspective on prevention and intervention* (pp. 1–12). Mahwah, NJ: Lawrence Erlbaum Associates.

Swearer, S. M., Song, S. Y., Cary, P. T., Eagle, J. W., & Mickelson, W. T. (2001). Psychosocial correlates in bullying and victimization: The relationship between depression, anxiety, and bully/victim status. *Journal of Emotional Abuse, 2,* 95–121.

Troy, M., & Sroufe, L. A. (1987). Victimization among preschoolers: Role of attachment relationship history. *Journal of the American Academy of Child and Adolescent Psychiatry, 26,* 166–172.

Unnever, J. D., & Cornell, D. G. (2003). The culture of bullying in middle school. *Journal of School Violence, 2,* 5–28.

U.S. Bureau of the Census. (2000). *Summary file 3.* Washington DC: Author.

Wandersman, A., & Nation, M. (1998). Urban neighborhoods and mental health: Psychological contributions to understanding toxicity, resilience, and interventions. *American Psychologist, 53,* 647–656.

Welsh, W., Stokes, R., & Greene, J. R. (2000). A macro–level model of school disorder. *Journal of Research in Crime and Delinquency, 37,* 243–283.

Wolke, D., & Samara, M. M. (2004). Bullied by siblings: Association with peer victimisation and behaviour problems in Israeli lower secondary school children. *Journal of Child Psychology and Psychiatry, 45,* 1015–1029.

Yoneyama, S., & Naito, A. (2003). Problems with the paradigm: The school as a factor in understanding bullying (with special reference to Japan). *British Journal of Sociology of Education, 24,* 316–330.

18

Critical Characteristics of Effective Bullying Prevention Programs

Richard J. Hazler
JoLynn V. Carney
Pennsylvania State University

Activities such as bullying and harassment, once referred to primarily as child's play, are now recognized as important elements in problems of youth violence, (Hazler & Carney, 2000). This connection to youth violence, as well as social (Ross, 2002), emotional (Orpinas, Horne, & Staniszewski, 2003), and health related problems (Rigby, 1999), has prompted funding for research and program development. Published research on amounts, types, causes, and impact of bullying from numerous countries demonstrate the international concern for the problem (Carney, Hazler, & Higgins, 2002; Smith et al., 1999).

Prevention programs and published materials designed to reduce the increasing concern over problems of bullying and school violence have become numerous, whereas they were virtually nonexistent in the United States prior to 1990 (Hoover & Hazler, 1990). The programs designed in the 1990s began focusing on strategies like teaching interpersonal skills and involving students in prevention efforts. These new models augmented or replaced the more traditional emphases on simplistic discipline enforcement and full school assemblies that had been the primary tactics in the past (Scheckner & Rollin, 2003; Tolan & Guerra, 1994).

Schools continue to be among the safest places for children to be, but that does not reflect the anxiety and tension experienced by students because of bullying and school climates that tolerate these abuses. Whether it is a bully, victim, or bystander, everyone is affected by situations that have them focus attention on self-protection rather than the knowledge and skills schools are designed to provide. Students cannot focus on learning mathematics when they are anxiously thinking about being bullied (victims), how to avoid it (victims and bystanders), or how to maintain their domination of someone (bullies). Schools and funding agencies have gotten the message and now provide substantial funding to develop programs for interventions with individual student problems and prevention models that involve the entire school population. The question for school personnel is no longer whether programs are available, but instead, what differentiates the best program(s) for a given school or school district from ones that will be less effective or less likely to be appropriately implemented?

Just as students lose academic concentration when their anxieties and thoughts are focused on bullying, school personnel also lose time and energy that could be put toward student academic development when implementing intervention/prevention efforts to deal with a culture of peer abuse. When faculty must intervene in individual bullying situations, valuable time and energy are taken away from the immediate process of academic learning, while the emotional toll from the intervention can hinder educational interactions long after the event itself is concluded. Schoolwide prevention efforts also require students and staff to reduce academic study time in order to learn about these socioemotional issues and how to deal with them. Time, energy, and motivation are precious in today's closely evaluated schools, so it is important that schools not only be effective in their intervention/prevention efforts, but they must also be efficient in their delivery of services.

Efficiency of effort is a major concern for today's schools, which are much more pressed for time and money than at any time in the past. Many schools may not be able to afford prevention programming because resources that have been commonly available from local, state, and federal resources are not available in current tight budget climates (Limber & Small, 2003). Further exacerbating the problem are new pressures on teachers, administrators, and parents to continually increase academic accomplishments as evaluated by standardized tests. Taken together, these pressures have demanded increased time for concentrated academic instruction, practice, and testing on academic issues that have resulted in much less time for developing social abilities, character building, and physical dimensions of students. Balancing these pressures requires schools to make sound choices in terms of time required and available, costs, commitment of school personnel, and program quality. This chapter provides those selecting and implementing bullying prevention programs with the critical characteristics that drive effectiveness and efficiency.

CONCEPTUAL BASIS

Local, state, and national communities have developed programs designed to reverse the trend of increasing youth violence like bullying (Furlong, Morrison, & Greif, 2003). Government-sponsored materials at times offer some detail about funded projects that have found some level of success, although these generally lack attention to the needs of a specific school community. New privately produced materials appear almost daily in the forms of videotapes such as *but Names Will Never Hurt Me* (Brown, 1997), *Scars* (Brown, 2004), and books (Geffner, Loring, & Young, 2001; Hazler, 1996; Miller, Martin, & Schamess 2003; Rigby, 2002). There are also packaged programs such as Don't Laugh at Me (Operation Respect, 2000), Steps to Respect: A Bullying Prevention Program (Committee for Children, 2002), and Bully/Victim Program, Olweus (1993). These packaged programs can include consultations and speakers, but also require a significantly greater financial investment than government or journal materials.

The vast majority of programs and materials available have had little if any quality research done on them to determine there value (U.S. Department of Health and Human Services, 2001) and even the underlying design of many programs are not empirically based. Instead, they often rely on what appear to be good ideas and logical suggestions that come from the integration of personal experiences and recent literature. A much smaller number of programs have actually documented forms of success through published research: (a) Second Step: A Violence Prevention Curriculum (Committee for Children, 1993; Grossman, Neckerman, Koepsell, & Liu, 1997; Samples & Aber, 1998); (b) Peace Builders (Dusenbury, Falco, Lake, Brannigan, & Bosworth, 1997; Heartsprings, Inc., 1992; Sample & Aber, 1998); (c) Promoting Alternative THinking Skills Curriculum (PATHS; Greenberg, 1993; Greenberg, Kusche, Cook, & Quamma, 1995; Kam, Greenberg, & Kusche, 2004; Kam, Greenberg, & Walls, 2003); and (d) Bully/Victim Program (Kallestad & Olweus, 2003; Melton et al., 1998; Olweus, 1993;

Olweus, Limber, & Mihalic, 1999; Samples & Aber, 1998). Thoughtful studies with quality research designs have provided credibility to such programs' claims of initial outcome and sustained effectiveness in reducing bullying.

There are two different conceptual approaches to prevention programming—targeted and universal. Targeted programs focus on select groups of students who have demonstrated a high risk of perpetuating inappropriately aggressive behaviors and/or those who have a high probability of becoming victims of such aggressive behaviors. Although many of these students are involved in bullying, few of the targeted programs are directly focused on bullying. Such programs are generally limited to select staff and often parents who plan and implement organized behavior change and social skill development for specific students without widespread involvement of others in the school system. Targeted programs can be very useful for individual students, but they are not intended to impact the overall prevention of bullying in a school or community.

Universal bullying programs are the most common variety that has been developed over the past decade. Virtually all youth will be exposed to peer abuse either as bullies, victims, bystanders, or combinations of the three such as the so-called bully-victim. This widespread exposure to bullying promotes a less-than-safe climate that impacts everyone in the school community, reduces the ability of the system to effectively carry out its educational function, and therefore calls for a comprehensive approach to promote systemic change. Universal anti-bullying programs are given primary attention in this chapter because they are the ones designed to produce the greatest amount of overall change for the most students, they are the vast majority of ones in use today, and they take the most financial and human resources to effectively implement. It is therefore vitally important that those educators making decisions about program selection, development, and implementation be knowledgeable of the principle program characteristics that will influence what they will need to do and the potential success they can experience.

There are many differences in quality programs including age groups, placing more emphasis on student, teacher, staff, or parent involvement, and requirements of more or less commitment from a school or district. The differences do not change the fact that each program applies a consistent set of themes and stages that produce the potential for success. One key local decision that impacts successful implementation in a classroom, school, or school system is to identify the programs that have the necessary components and present them in ways that those involved can buy into and apply consistently over time.

SUCCESSFUL BULLYING PROGRAM CHARACTERISTICS

Program descriptions tend to focus on the specific techniques used to help change cognitions, behaviors, and overall school climate. Schools and individuals who attempt to utilize these techniques can find them to be effective only in certain circumstances, for limited periods of time, or not effective at all. This ineffectiveness of overall and long-term program implementation is often caused by implementation of the techniques that do not attend to the full compliment of quality bullying program characteristics applied in an appropriate local context. These key characteristics include the program themes of a socioecological perspective model, empathic involvement, and reducing isolation of people and ideas. They also include sequential program stages of awareness building, policy development, skill development, continuing involvement, assessment, adjustment, and recycling (see Fig. 18.1).

Individually, these characteristics will have more appeal to some people than to others. Administrators, for example, tend to be attracted to policy development, counselors and teachers to skill development, boards of education to assessment of outcomes, and students will want quick

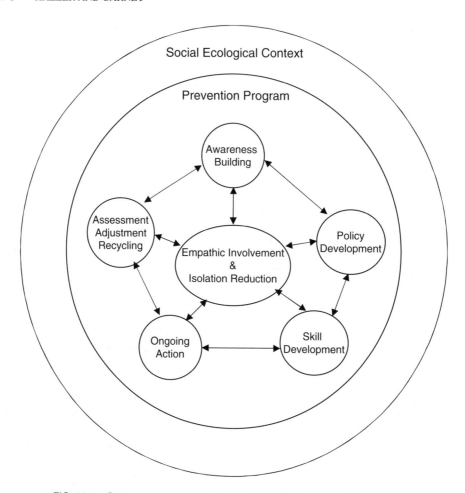

FIG. 18.1.   Socioecological perspective model of bullying prevention programs.

action where their feelings and situations are fully taken into account. These understandable preferences point to the need for involvement of representatives of all parties in selection and implementation of programs. The characteristics become effective only when they are all considered collectively and where specific aspects are presented in a progression that builds one step upon the other.

PROGRAM THEMES

Socioecological Perspective

Quality programs have evolved to recognize the critical nature of interactions between individual characteristics and ecological contexts (Orpinas, et al., 2003). Peers, schools, families, and communities all interact with individual student characteristics to create the variety of individual behavioral, emotional, and cognitive reactions as well as the dynamics between individuals. This socioecological perspective emphasizes that no one individual or pair of individuals alone creates a bullying situation. Instead, it is the combination of individuals plus the ecological situation that will foster or discourage bullying over time (Swearer & Doll, 2001).

Recognition that prevention programs need to take a socioecological perspective has emphasized the appropriateness of designing and implementing universal programs that impact
entire systems rather than ones targeted at select groups. In order to help individuals, it has
become clear that prevention efforts must develop an understanding of and focus actions on
the complexities of the ecological system. The larger the group that can be successfully integrated into prevention efforts the better. Communities and school systems that can organize
and coordinate prevention efforts provide the most valued models.

The difficulties of bringing large groups together in effective collaboration often results in
smaller and more manageable working groups taking initial steps to set the process in motion.
Peer groups, classrooms, select grade levels, or individual schools have advantages in finding
the commonalities of problems and day-to-day interactions that promote the kind motivation
and purpose needed to sustain such an effort over time.

This socioecological perspective and universal approach can be found in prevention programs that have the most support from researchers (Espelage & Swearer, 2003). They seek to
involve as many individuals and groups in the largest possible viable communities to develop
and implement the program. Those involved in developing prevention efforts need to recognize
that even the best programs will not offer a quick or easy fix that can be implemented by one or
two motivated professionals. One or two committed individuals can and normally do initiate
efforts, but degree of success over time will be related to how many individuals and groups
become invested as active participants in a coordinated program.

Reducing Isolation of People and Ideas

A common theme that runs throughout successful prevention programs is the overall emphasis
on reducing the social and conceptual isolation of people. Bullying occurs most often during
unstructured times (Craig, Pepler, & Atlas, 2000) because social support is a key factor in
determining the frequency and severity of bullying (Demaray & Malecki, 2003; Rigby, 2000).
Bullies are not seeking a fair fight, but instead an interaction in which they know they will
dominate an individual or group. When victims increase their numbers or gain new constructive
ideas regarding possible actions, the bully's potential to dominate is diminished and the likelihood of bullying decreases. Prevention programs give on-going emphasis to increasing social
connections between people and to helping victims, bystanders, and bullies conceptualize their
situations in new, more productive ways.

The Columbine, Colorado shootings demonstrate one well-known extreme example of how
isolation caused in part by being bullied, is related to a lack of interactions with others. Over
time, the shooters were ostracized from more and more peer groups and had dropped out
of extra-curricular activities. The circle of people with whom they communicated became
increasingly smaller. They had even become too different for continuing interaction with the
small group known as the trench coat mafia, so that the only ideas that might come from
peers were their own. The result was physical, social, and conceptual isolation from peers, an
increasing sense that they were alone in their struggles, and no new ideas to call on except
their own dangerous ones.

There were interventions by the police and attempts made to connect with the boys by
other adults, but these were generally rejected. The more they became physically, cognitively,
and psychologically cut off from others, the less opportunity they had to receive the diversity
of ideas and support needed to confront false beliefs, promote understanding of others, and
increase responsibility to a larger community. The absence of such diversity of ideas creates
the opportunity for irrational ideas to appear rational, as it did with the shooters in Columbine,
other school shooters, and with suicide victims. Prevention programs fight this process by

emphasizing the expansion of connections between people and groups that will broaden understanding, challenge false beliefs, encourage creative social thinking, and promote a greater sense of trust in the environment.

People who are bullied over time begin losing hope that anyone can help them and that they cannot overcome their situation. The resulting embarrassment over a sense of public inadequacy, lack of obvious supporters, and absence of new ideas to end the torment can lead to homicidal and suicidal thoughts and sometimes actions like those at Columbine (Hazler & Carney, 2000). Most victims of bullies will not turn their worst thoughts into such obviously catastrophic actions, but they will drop out of relationships and make other poor decisions because of the limiting of perceptions and ideas caused by isolation from quality interpersonal interactions.

Continuation of a bullying interaction requires the establishment of isolating situations where others will not step in to better equalize power inequalities, thus further depriving victims of potential support and decreasing a sense of safety for everyone in a community. Bullying can only continue when there are places and times where adults or peers, who could make a difference, are not present or when they choose not to become involved in support of victims. Choosing to reduce victim and situation isolation, by becoming involved, makes adult and peer bystanders critical to the eventual discouragement or encouragement of bullying and harassment (Hazler & Carney, 2000; Salmivalli, 1999).

Successful programs emphasize the need to reduce isolation of people and ideas in numerous ways throughout their socioecological environment. Awareness building is the first step toward infusing new ideas, understandings, and personal connections into people and systems, which each have the tendency to stagnate as they seek the environmental consistency needed for a sense of security. Program aspects like policy development, skill acquisition, collaborative activities, and program assessment are all designed to expand thinking and relationships. The reason these aspects of programs can cause distress among individuals and groups is precisely because they encourage people to move beyond those beliefs and actions with which they have become comfortable.

Reducing isolation of people and ideas is tied directly to the stressful task of making changes in thoughts, beliefs, and behaviors. The best program designs directly address the stressful issue of change by continually encouraging open discussion of ideas, beliefs, and feelings. These programs integrate presentations of positive practices with the encouragement to use creative thinking to identify ways that these and other practices might be implemented in the specific environmental context of those involved. Weaker programs generally provide less direction and encouragement to explore alternative practices, use creative thinking, revise concepts to fit local contexts, or to go beyond the material and ideas presented.

Empathic Involvement

Quality programs recognize that it takes more than knowledge-level awareness to stir people's affective involvement in difficult situations like bullying. Empathy is an essential ingredient in how people view and react to bullying (Espelage & Swearer, 2003). People are more likely to give up valuable time, energy, and even money to help one person or a group of people if they can personally identify with them. An empathic sense for someone also decreases the likelihood of choosing to abuse that person so that it plays a key role in limiting bullying actions. Gaining empathic understanding of others thus becomes a major theme in all phases of bullying prevention programs.

Effective awareness-development techniques highlight empathic awareness that taps emotions and one's personal experience, thereby motivating people to give close attention to others and take personal responsibility for their own actions. Educators are also more hesitant to initiate these types of reactions because the emotions of youth are harder to control than their ability to acquire information. Raising empathic feelings through emotional-awareness activities is therefore a critical first step, but one that is often approached with hesitancy.

Videos, speakers, and discussion formats that prove valuable at the awareness stage focus student attention on the emotions and feelings of all participants in bullying situations and not just the victims. This is not the aspect of the program that identifies things to do or spells out right versus wrong in detail. The attempt is to have people experience the emotions and complexities of the problem from the eyes of victims, bullies, and bystanders. It is from this broad empathic understanding that they are more likely to *feel* the problems and become motivated to work toward finding solutions.

Two examples of videos can serve to provide examples of the difference between creating empathic awareness versus informational awareness. One set of videos (Brown, 1993, 1997, 2004) has few words spoken in them, no direct teaching of lessons, no moderator, lots of time for thinking and feeling, and little time for trying to remember what is said. Designed specifically for students, these videos can stir strong emotions as students identify with the experiences of those in the films. *Don't Laugh at Me* (Operation Respect, 2000) is a video that taps similar emotions in students and even more effectively in adults through musical and visual experiences. These are not the typical videos or activities generally used in schools where there is a direct lesson plan and specific information identified for learning. Videos and other activities like these are instead designed to raise an emotional awareness that promotes creative thinking, discussion, and a desire to take action.

Use of firsthand experiences and current events are another effective awareness building technique emphasized in programs. Newspaper stories of school violence that receive widespread attention or a suicide in a school, although horrific, are good examples of teachable current events that can be used to draw people's attention to the feelings and needs of others. Traumatic circumstances such as these increase emotional investment in a way that cannot be duplicated through any other medium.

Empathic involvement is not just isolated to the initial awareness portion of prevention programs. It is an important continuing component for assuring that the knowledge and skills taught within prevention programs actually get used or applied in positive ways. Knowledge and skills alone can be used for negative as well as positive purposes. It is a sense of empathy toward others that moves people to take actions designed to stop bullying situations (Craig, Henderson, & Murphy, 2000). Consequently, a significant portion of effective prevention programs is time spent gaining understanding of other people's experiences and feelings in relation to one's own experiences and feelings.

SEQUENTIAL PROGRAM STAGES

Initial Awareness Building

The series of events that quickly moved bullying out of the realm of child's play to recognition of its serious consequences were the highly publicized school shootings of the 1990s. Investigations of these and similar, less publicized shootings since the 1980s found that many of the shooters had been victims of bullying over time (Hazler & Carney, 2000; Reddy et al., 2001; Vossekuil, Fein, Reddy, Borum, & Modzeleski, 2002). Suicides related to bullying also received attention (Carney, 2000) that further confirmed to the general public that something needed to be done. Lawsuits, legislation, and the demand for programs on bullying followed, even though bullying is not a new social phenomenon. What created the current demand for action was that people became aware of the potential damage bullying could cause to themselves, their loved ones, and their community. It is a similar type of personalized awareness that all quality programs must build first in order to mobilize such essential support.

Motivating people to take action by creating awareness is the essential first step in a bullying prevention program. Most programs provide written ways to provide initial information and encouragement to administrators, teachers, parents, and students to take part in additional awareness activities. These activities are designed to increase personal recognition of how bullying is a clear and present danger to the wellbeing of students, the school, and the community.

Surveys and associated meetings are informational ways of raising awareness that often work well for adults in particular (e.g., parents, teachers, school boards, etc.). These groups generally desire something better for the young people who they see as needing help, and information can be that starting place. Such information can also be useful for youth, although it probably carries less motivational weight with them. Students are bombarded with information as a part of their daily work in school, so additional information does not provide the uniqueness of presentation that could more effectively spur motivation. Personalized discussions of this information are necessary for both students and adults to turn the general data into personally motivating concepts that demand their immediate attention.

Speakers, videos, books, and other awareness development vehicles can present information in ways that personally connect to adults and youth and promote a more empathic awareness. Their effectiveness depends on helping the audience *see* and *feel* the problem's impact or they will have no more influence than information alone. It is the motivational quality and original accounts that make information more impactful to students in particular because they live with the situation daily, can identify with those feelings in ways that raise the credibility of the presentation. Prevention programs that provide this type of awareness building activity do so in a variety of ways including videotapes, written materials, consultant speakers, or suggestions for how to find speakers.

The focus of these initial awareness building activities is to encourage involvement in program development, to give direction as to what can be done, and to offer confidence that some initial steps are available to start a successful program. It is from this initial push that other activities follow.

Policy Development

Policies regarding rules of behavior are the written statements of a community's social standards and the manner in which those standards are to be enforced. Any good bullying prevention program requires the examination and revision of current policy to clearly demonstrate the official significance given to the problem and how that importance will translate into practical application (Limber & Small, 2003). The importance of these policies demands that they be worked on at the earliest stages of a prevention program in order for other aspects of the program to build on them.

Specific policies against bullying actions have become particularly important parts of prevention programs in the past decade. Changing social norms around bullying have created pressure for inclusion of bullying in disciplinary policies where such a need was not seen in the past (Limber & Small, 2003). Previous policies on school violence generally referred only to fighting and carrying weapons. New recognition of the seriousness of social, sexual, and emotional bullying created a situation where, policy revisions were necessary to more clearly define unacceptable physical, verbal, sexual, and social bullying along with the consequences for those who would violate such policies. These policies serve to guide the actions and reactions of students, staff, parents, and all community members in response to the appropriate and inappropriate behavior of others.

An important element in bullying policy development is the emphasis given by quality programs to the creation of the policies themselves. Most quality programs will only provide general outlines or examples of policy needs and place more emphasis on the process for developing locally appropriate policies. The first of two major reasons for this emphasis on the development aspect is that policies need to reflect the local context of participants that cannot be provided in a program created by a state, national, or international organization (Limber & Small, 2003). For example, following the lead of some state policies like Georgia's three strikes or zero-tolerance policies in other states may not fit with the values of local stakeholders who want more flexibility in such situations. Many believe the policies actually have negative effects (Limber & Small, 2003), such as sending a message to students that their view of events will not be heard (Orpinas et al., 2003). Others point to the fact that there is little evidence to show these policies actually do improve school safety (Skiba & Knesting, 2002).

The second major reason for focusing attention on the policy development is the importance of bringing groups of people together (e.g., teachers, counselors, administrators, parents, community members, and students; Limber & Small, 2003) to realize and work through their diverse views, and come to joint agreement on a set of important issues, values, and the ways to support them in a prevention program. Bullying does not happen in a vacuum, but instead in a complex network (ecology) where bullies and victims are intricately linked with other peers, administrators, teachers, and parents (Rodkin & Hodges, 2003). Truly effective policy can be developed only when members of the local networks work together in a concentrated effort. The overall goal is to create a sense in program participants that it is truly *their* program focused on local issues and run with their local values in mind, not something prescribed to them by a group who does not understand them.

The developmental aspect of policy is normally one that involves more struggle and time than people and organizations would prefer to invest. People invited to participate, who truly do have different views of the issues, must each be heard and their differences worked through if they are to provide effective follow through in support of final policies. Only then can policies offer both the locally appropriate guidelines in combination with the strong backing of critical interest groups necessary for prevention program success.

Skill Development

A central component of anti-bullying programs since the 1990s has been the movement away from punishment of bullying as the primary focus to skill development for everyone in a selected environment. The change was related to letting go of old assumptions that bullies were a handful of problem children for whom punishment was the only way to influence them. New views recognized bullying as a problem experienced by many children, and one that is related to developmental changes, personal perceptions, and social skills. This change in viewpoint made it possible to begin conceptualizing bullying as a developmental issue where teaching and learning could directly lead to improvement, not just for particular problem students, but for everyone in the environment. Teaching on a systemic basis to increase information and skills is what educators and publishers do best, and they have risen to the task of developing and implementing prevention programs built to teach both the children and adults involved.

Universal programs in particular emphasize a variety of skills for victims, bullies, and bystanders designed to produce a community of individuals more likely to think and react in ways that reduce rather than foster abusive situations. None of the skills are exclusive to dealing with bullying situations, but they also promote healthy functioning of individuals who contribute to maintaining a personally caring and supportive society. The most effective prevention programs teach these skills in ways that both emphasize their potential to reduce bullying and also show how they can promote better social experiences for everyone, thereby creating a more productive and safer climate that discourages bullying and other personally harmful actions.

Prevention efforts that focus skill development exclusively on bullying are likely to gain the involvement of fewer people and lose attention of participants more quickly. People have more interest in learning skills when they can see that those skills will help them deal with the multiple situations they experience on a regular basis. They are also more likely to continue using and developing skills that can be applied in multiple contexts. The best programs emphasize this dual model of teaching skills for dealing with bullying while reinforcing how they generalize to other more common situations.

The types of skills taught in prevention programs could be generally categorized as social skills because they are focused on helping students become better citizens who are more able to contribute to a harmonious society. Some of these skills help people to focus on and deal with their internal struggles that influence how they relate to others. Attending to internal feelings and learning productive ways of dealing with them show up early in most programs, because how much one understands oneself influences the ability to understand and react to others. Then there are a range of other interpersonal skills that relate to reading other people's reactions, exploring their thoughts and feelings, and responding to them in ways that will promote understanding and continuing positive contacts. These abilities to recognize the emotions and reactions of oneself and others are essential for making good choices around reacting to potential bullying situations.

Social skills are also essential portions of conflict resolution models that are consistently included in comprehensive bullying prevention programs. The skills needed for reacting in a variety of conflict situations and those that help avoid such situations are important parts of teaching students how to productively intervene in bullying situations. Conflict resolution skills are also part of adult training in comprehensive bullying prevention programs because modeling interactions with students and other adults is a primary technique for promoting the acquisition of assertive and caring interpersonal behaviors that reduce bullying.

The personal, social, and conflict resolution skills taught within a program also serve the function of promoting program initiation and continuation. As people develop and practice more effective ways of overcoming their differences, they gain confidence in the skills and a sense of closeness and common purpose with others. These ingredients are essential to gaining the student and adult investment in bullying prevention that is necessary for program success.

Continuing Involvement

Early prevention models for dealing with issues like drugs, alcohol, smoking, and bullying among others often took the form of a schoolwide assembly, where a presentation highlighted the significance of the problem, identified the reasons for dealing with it, and offered some basics of how to handle it. Somewhat more extensive approaches are to set aside a week or a month to focus on a significant issue. Neither of these approaches is generally effective for more than a short period of time. The models can catch people's attention and provide motivation to act, but without continuing attention, motivation fades, information is no longer used, and skills diminish.

Quality prevention programs set up a system for continuing actions that maintain the involvement of participants in anti-bullying and associated relationship and climate issues (Hazler, 1998). This adds strength by connecting bullying to broader issues of climate, safety, and personal relationships. Continuing to deal with only bullying as a focus would become old to students and adults alike and the better they became at dealing with the specific problem, the less attention it would seem those problems deserve. Such a lessening of attention to the issues then creates the opportunity for bullying to again become a more significant problem in a cycle that can cause people to give up hope of working toward any long-term solutions. Commitment and continuity of effort over time therefore requires the providing of mechanisms for follow-up actions that call repeated attention to how the desired skills and actions improve the general climate as well as reduce bullying.

One common format for implementing continuing involvement is to set aside a short time, preferably daily, for students to talk about problematic peer relationships and other climate concerns. Most often, this model is set up within the school, but it can be copied in the family, youth organizations, and organized recreation activities. Similar models can be set up for teachers, parent groups, or community meetings. The essential aspect of the format is that it serves to offer a regular opportunity to understand changing situation dynamics and to reinforce the use of skills and understandings that were taught in more concentrated portions of the program.

Some programs, like Steps to Respect (Committee for Children, 2002), Bully/Victim Program (Olweus, 1993), or PATHS (Greenberg, 1993), are designed to provide separate activities and goals for different grade levels so that what was learned one year can be built on in the following year. These programs are most often available for elementary and middle schools where students, curriculum, and classes progress in more consistently developmental steps.

Another common ongoing action format utilizes the essential school and community values and behaviors that transcend bullying prevention. Posters, awards, and recognition at extracurricular activities can provide continuing emphases to the important influence such core values and behaviors have on growth, development, quality performance, citizenship, and sportsmanship. The broader and more consistently these core values can be interlaced with school and community activities, the greater are their influence both in bullying prevention success and the associated safer and healthier social climate.

Assessment, Adjustment, and Recycling

Quality prevention programs attend to the evolving nature of people and systems that are influenced by both the program and external conditions. The formal assessment of program activities and outcomes on a planned regular basis is what allows programs to identify their progress, adjust their focus of attention, and revise programmatic efforts for the future. Formative and summative assessments on both the processes and products of prevention programs are used to produce responsible and responsive ongoing activities (Benkofske & Heppner, 1999).

Once socioecological prevention programs are established with recognition that they need to be ongoing and reflective of changing needs, most assessment could be identified as formative in a practical sense. This type of assessment identifies how things have been going within a program for the purpose of evaluating and revising efforts versus summative evaluation, which is generally more of an end-product evaluation. Programs do advocate for evaluating outcomes of separate aspects or phases of programs, but these are generally seen less as end-products and more as formative evaluation for making decisions on how to proceed (Benkofske & Heppner, 1999). Whereas lesser quality programs might suggest finding out whether you have succeeded, better quality programs will emphasize assessment as evaluation for progress and future directions.

Prevention programs of quality emphasize both process and product assessment. Both types of assessment are essential in order to make useful decisions about progress made and adjustments needing attention (Benkofske & Heppner, 1999). The process form of assessment evaluates how well people are effectively carrying out their roles. It addresses the issue of whether people are fulfilling their responsibilities to implement the plan in a timely and effective manner as well as identifying what areas need to be redesigned or techniques revised. It is the portion of the assessment process that gives direction to identification of those needing motivation, training, or other forms of support. It also helps to understand where the system may have accurately predicted, underestimated, or overestimated the ability to implement a given program design within a specific community's unique socioecological environment. Improvement comes not so much from doing things right, the first time, but more so from identifying what is not working and revising efforts based on a solid assessment system.

Product evaluation is an assessment of what outcomes the process produced and is the type of evaluation that funding agencies, school boards, administrators, parents, and so forth most desire. These are the kinds of data that hopefully show less bullying occurring, children feeling safer, discipline referrals dropping, and absenteeism lowering. Even grades and standardized test scores can show expected improvement in a safer feeling environment with more sense of community. This is the type of environment where students can give more concentration time to learning and less to anxiety over social situations. It is an environment where teachers and parents can focus more on learning and less on discipline issues.

Surveys for students and adults are often utilized to identify perceived progress on bullying and general climate issues. School indices such as office referrals, suspensions, and expulsions are also key indicators (Morrison & Skiba, 2001). Evidence for the importance of using school records as continuing assessment of changes in discipline and safety can be found in studies such as the one conducted by Tobin and Sugai (1999), who found that patterns in discipline referrals in sixth grade were associated with referrals for violence in eighth grade. School records can be used to validate information from the more opinion focused surveys. Often interviews, small and large focus group meetings are encouraged for qualitative assessments through discussion rather than other less personal measures (Benkofske & Heppner, 1999).

Many different instrument designs can be used in combination to evaluate individual aspects of the program and community. Here again the emphasis of quality programs is to provide general means and flexible instrumentation for evaluation, while leaving the final design of instrumentation up to the local implementation team in order to create assessments that best reflect the ideas and culture of a community (Benkofske & Heppner, 1999). This local development serves to make instruments more accurately reflect the unique culture, brings people together to form positive working units, and promotes the commitment needed to revise and recycle program efforts.

One example of how assessment is used in a program can be found in *Blueprints for Violence Prevention Book Nine: Bullying Prevention Program* (Olweus et al., 1999). This booklet provides a thorough description of the model for evaluating a recognized program and the reasoning for specific methods used. Another example of how such a Localized Assessment Process might work is the authors' development of a Local Assessment Model. This low-income primarily minority school was understandably wary of being measured by instruments developed on schools made up of mostly White middle-class students, faculty, and parents. Another issue was the desire for the data-gathering instruments and process in general to be a positive experience for all concerned rather than emphasizing the negatives that were the focus of so much outside attention.

It was decided that instead of beginning with traditional measures that seek information on what is wrong, the best starting place would be to explore with students, staff, and parents what behaviors they would expect to see from all concerned at a school with an ideal socioemotional climate for learning. Focus groups from each constituency provided ideas that were later translated into survey instruments that reflected quite traditional expectations of social and academic behaviors as well as the local culture and wording from a positive frame of reference. People accepted and supported use of the survey as their own as opposed to the questioning, resenting, and resisting they often did with other evaluation processes.

Local investment in development and use of the survey instrument lead to interest in the program and the study itself. This interest created its own form of excitement around the program and a desire to make it successful by more people and groups than had previously been involved. It also created more investment by outside groups in the form of volunteer work as well as funding. On the assessment side, other more traditional forms of data were made more readily made available to the researchers. Information such as test scores, grades, attendance, and discipline reports can be very threatening and they become more easily shared when it is clear that outsiders are as understanding of and invested in the welfare of the school as they are in their own agendas.

Assessment, adjustment, and recycling of information are essential for growth and continuing success of prevention program efforts. People make mistakes and environments change. It is local interest and investment in the assessment process that encourages the pride of successes, the identification of potentially valuable changes, and the continuing evolution of a prevention program that keeps it viable in an ever-changing socioecological environment.

CRITIQUE AND LIMITATIONS

An inspirational speaker, film, or other one-time event can fuel the interest of students and adults in a school about a potentially emotional topic like bullying, but gaining a lasting effect depends on a full compliment of bullying program characteristics. Implementation of the major program themes throughout sequential program stages as described in this chapter and summarized in Table 18.1 appear to be the keys to how successful prevention programs turn good intentions into ongoing realities. These basic ingredients are vital portions of comprehensive bullying prevention program designs, regardless of whether those programs are nationally, internationally, or even locally designed and developed. But quality design alone does not create desired outcomes. No matter the source or quality of a program,

TABLE 18.1

Implications for Practice: Characteristics of Effective Bullying Preventions Programs

	Implementation
Program Themes	
Socioecological perspective	Integrate the fullest possible diversity of people and groups into community planning and implementation efforts
Reducing isolation of people and ideas	Reduce physical isolation opportunities and increase social, information, emotional, and ideological inclusion
Empathic involvement	Create and maintain connections between people on the emotional level in addition to knowledge/information level
Sequential Program Stages	
Initial awareness building	Create both knowledge and emotional awareness that promotes understanding, a desire to help, and a press for timely action
Policy development	Create agreed upon values, related rules of behavior, supportive activities, and enforcement procedures involving the fullest possible diversity of school/community participants
Skill development	Teach a wide variety of social skills that encourage abusers, victims, and bystanders alike to assertively implement social/behavioral values and policies
Continuing involvement	Provide regular time for discussions on the school's evolving climate, positive changes, problems, necessary actions, and how to use previously learned skills
Assessment and adjustment	Evaluate progress, identify changing needs, and direct adjustment of efforts

eventual successes are dependent upon the extent and quality of local implementation in their unique socioecological environment (Kallestad & Olweus, 2003; Shinn, 2003). How effectively a program and the community's uniqueness can be combined will make the critical difference.

Each of these program themes and stages requires people to expand their personal and professional boundaries in significant ways (Hazler, 1998). Prevention programs are not designed to dismantle systems, but they do require people to change their ways of thinking and acting. People do not take such steps out of their comfort zones quickly or easily. Program implementation and eventual success, therefore depends on the degree of willingness to change and to implement a program at a speed that matches people's ability to change. Many programs are dropped quickly, not because people refuse to change, but because those who want immediate change are not willing to work with and wait for those who require a slower pace. In the rush to do "something," the power of the larger group support can be lost or even turned into opposition. Conversely, moving too slowly can lose the investment of those who desire more rapid actions. Negotiating the local balance is the key to success.

Prevention programs promote many changes (Benkofske & Heppner, 1999), but they often have less success when the formal changes do not match informal ones. Adults and students may follow one set of non-bullying and victim-supportive guidelines during closely supervised classroom activities, but act very differently at social occasions or during competitive events. These inconsistencies diminish the sense that the teachings of the program are truly universal and promote the idea that they only apply to certain people in selected settings. One of the most difficult yet valuable changes successful programs promote is transferring application of the skills and knowledge developed in a classroom to less organized and unsupervised situations.

Timing is a key factor in the implementation of awareness building, policy creation, skill development, and continuing involvement. One example is that school personnel and other adults are naturally attracted to the quick implementation of knowledge acquisition and skill-building activities so that youth can have them at their disposal. This often results in a rush through the stages of awareness building and comprehensive program development that short changes the emphasis on empathic involvement. The result can be students and adults who do not have the motivation and systemic follow-up necessary to turn good ideas into consistent positive actions. The need for assessment to be given early attention in a program is another example of an important piece of the process (Benkofske & Heppner, 1999) that is often overlooked until late in the process when people begin wishing they had started collecting information earlier. Both these examples reflect the preparation and patience that are essential for successful follow through with a prevention program.

All successful programs involve students, but not all in the same ways. Students may be involved in more passive roles (e.g., gaining awareness, knowledge, or policy follower), supportive roles (e.g., support seeker, caring encourager, mentor, or educator), or more assertive roles (e.g., mediator, policymaker, policy enforcer, or peer counselor; Hazler & Carney, 2002). Communities and individuals are not equally comfortable with students in each of these roles. The better a program matches the willingness of adults to give over certain responsibilities to students to the responsibilities recommended by the program the greater is the likelihood of success.

Successful selection and implementation of a program begins with identifying or creating a design that has all the core themes and stages summarized in Table 18.1 clearly identifiable. With a viable program design in hand, the next question becomes, "What supports the potential success of this design?" Many states provide funding for programs, and a common string often attached to the funding is usually the need for the program to be supported by research and for program outcomes to be evaluated by the local school. The "supported by research" issue is where programs that have invested in research over time such as Bully/Victim Prevention

(Olweus, 1993), Steps to Respect (Committee for Children, 1993), or PATHS (Greenberg, 1993) gain a major advantage over newer programs or programs that have funded development and marketing, but not research. There are no programs that have proven fully successful in all situations (Forgatch, 2003; Shinn, 2003), but the more a local program builds on the research of previous efforts, the greater is the likelihood of choosing a good program or developing one with research to support the various techniques and overall plan to be used.

People deserve the best program available, but finances and time constraints influence what is potentially achievable in a given situation. Purchased or self-developed programs vary widely in the expenses, time, and energy they require of a school system, and if these requirements cannot be met, the expected program outcomes are unlikely to emerge (Limber & Small, 2003). Matching the available budget with program requirements over time is a first and perhaps easier step at this stage. A less concrete step is identifying what kind of time and personnel the program will take and the willingness or ability of the school to support those needs. How much time will be required from a program leader and how much of that person's time can be made available? Can sufficient time be allocated to effectively train staff? How does the time required to be taken from academic or other current school activities match what the school is willing to give?

The effectively selected or designed program needs to match the funds, time, and energy available to make the program work successfully in the local school/community culture. Ignoring these steps or the program themes and stages can lead to half-hearted efforts or discontinuation. Attending to them appropriately produces a program that can effectively integrate quickly into a school system and remain there as an integral part of the development of youth, schools, and community.

REFERENCES

Benkofske, M., & Heppner, C. C. (1999). Program evaluation. In P. P. Heppner, D. M. Kivlighan, Jr., & B. E. Wampold (Eds.), *Research design in counseling* (2nd ed., pp. 488–515). Belmont, CA: Wadsworth.

Brown, T. (Producer). (1993). . . . *Broken toy* [Film]. Warminster, PA: MAR-CO Publishers.

Brown, T. (Producer). (1997). '. . . *but names will never hurt me*' [Film]. Warminster, PA: MAR-CO Publishers.

Brown, T. (Producer). (2004). *SCARS* [Film]. Warminster, PA: MAR-CO Publishers.

Carney, J. V. (2000). Bullied to death: Perceptions of peer abuse and suicidal behavior during adolescence. *School Psychology International, 21*, 44–54.

Carney, J. V., Hazler, R. J., & Higgins J. (2002). Characteristics of school bullies and victims as perceived by public school professionals. *Journal of School Violence, 3*, 91–106.

Committee for Children. (1993). *Second step: A violence prevention curriculum.* Seattle, WA: Author.

Committee for Children. (2002). *Steps to respect: A bullying prevention program.* Seattle, WA: Author.

Craig, W. M., Henderson, K., & Murphy, J. G. (2000). Prospective teachers' attitudes toward bullying and victimization. *School Psychology International, 21*, 5–11.

Craig, W. M., Pepler, D., & Atlas, R. (2000). Observations of bullying in the playground and in the classroom. *School Psychology International, 21*, 22–36.

Demaray, M. K., & Malecki, C. K. (2003). Perceptions of the frequency and importance of social support by students classified as victims, bullies, and bully/victims in an urban middle school. *School Psychology Review, 32*, 471–489.

Dusenbury, L., Falco, M., Lake, A., Brannigan, R., & Bosworth, K. (1997). Nine critical elements of promising violence prevention programs. *Journal of School Health, 67*, 409–414.

Espelage, D. L., & Swearer, S. M. (2003). Research on school bullying and victimization: What have we learned and where do we go from here? *School Psychology Review, 32*, 365–383.

Forgatch, M. S. (2003). Implementation as a second stage in prevention. *Prevention and Treatment, 6*, Article 024c. Available: http://jounrals.apa.org/prevention/volume6/pre0060024c.html

Furlong, M. J., Morrison, G. M., & Greif, J. L. (2003). Reaching an American consensus: Reactions to the special issue on school bullying. *School Psychology Review, 32*, 456–470.

Geffner, R. A., Loring, M., & Young, C. (Eds.). (2001). *Bullying behavior: Current issues, research, and interventions.* New York: Haworth Press.

Greenberg, M. T., & Kusche, C. A. (1993). *Promoting social and emotional development in deaf children: The PATHS project*. Seattle, WA: University of Washington Press.

Greenberg, M. T., Kusche, C. A., Cook, E. T., & Quamma, J. P. (1995). Promoting emotional competence in school-aged children: The effects of the PATHS curriculum. *Development and Psychopathology, 7*, 117–136.

Grossman, D. C., Neckerman, H. J., Koepsell, T. D., & Liu, P. (1997). Effectiveness of a violence prevention curriculum among children in elementary school. *Journal of the American Medical Association, 277*, 1605–1611.

Hazler, R. J. (1996). *Breaking the cycle of violence: Interventions for bullying and victimization*. New York: Taylor & Francis.

Hazler, R. J. (1998). Promoting personal investment is systemic approaches to school violence. *Education, 119*, 222–231.

Hazler, R. J., & Carney, J. V. (2000). When victims turn aggressors: Factors in the development of deadly school violence. *Professional School Counseling, 4*, 105–112.

Hazler, R. J., & Hoover, J. H. (1996). Confronting the bullying problem. *Journal of Emotional and Behavioral Problems, 5*, 2–5.

Hazler, R. J., & Carney, J. V. (2002). Empowering peers to prevent youth violence. *Journal of Humanistic Counseling, Education and Development, 41*, 129–149.

Heartsprings, Inc. (1992). *Creating a peaceful community with Peace Builders*. Tucson: AZ: Author.

Hoover, J., & Hazler, R. J. (1990). Bullies and Victims. *Elementary School Guidance and Counseling, 25*(3), 212–219.

Kallestad, J. H., & Olweus, D. (2003). Predicting teachers' and schools' implementation of the Olweus Bullying Prevention Program: A multilevel study. *Prevention and Treatment, 6*, Article 0021a. Available: http://jounrals.apa.org/prevention/volume6/pre0060021a.html

Kam, C. M., Greenberg, M. T., & Kusche, C. A. (2004). Sustained effects of the PATHS curriculum on the social and psychological adjustment of children in Special Education. *Journal of Emotional and Behavioral Disorders, 12*, 66–78.

Kam, C. M., Greenberg, M. T., & Walls, C. T. (2003). Examining the role of implementation quality in school-based prevention using the PATHS curriculum. *Prevention Science, 4*, 55–63.

Limber, S. P., & Small, M. A. (2003). State laws and policies to address bullying in schools. *School Psychology Review, 32*, 445–455.

Melton, G. B., Limber, S. P., Cunningham, P., Osgood, D.W., Chambers, J., Flerx, V., Henggeler, S., & Nation, M. (1998). *Violence among rural youth*. Final report to the Office of Juvenile Justice and Delinquency Prevention.

Miller, J., Martin, I. R., & Schamess, G. (2003). *School violence and children in crisis: Community and school interventions for social workers and counselors*. Denver, CO: Love Publishing.

Morrison, G. M., & Skiba, R. (2001). Predicting violence from school misbehavior: Promises and perils. *Psychology in the Schools, 38*, 172–184.

Olweus, D. (1993). *Bullying at school: What we know and what we can do*. Cambridge, MA: Blackwell.

Olweus, D., Limber, S., & Mihalic, S. (1999). Bullying prevention program. In D. S. Elliott (Ed.), *Blueprints for violence prevention book nine* (pp. 1–79). Golden, CO: Venture Publishing and C & M Press.

Operation Respect. (2000). *Don't laugh at me*. New York: Author.

Orpinas, P., Horne, A. M., & Staniszewski, D. (2003). School bullying: Changing the problem by changing the school. *School Psychology Review, 32*, 431–444.

Reddy, M., Borum, R., Berglund, J., Vossekuil, B., Fein, R., & Modzeleski, W. (2001). Evaluating risk for targeted violence in schools: Comparing risk assessment, threat assessment, and other approaches. *Psychology in the Schools, 38*, 157–172.

Rigby, K. (1999). Peer victimization at school and the health of secondary students. *British Journal of Educational Psychology, 22*, 28–34.

Rigby, K. (2000). Effects of peer victimization in schools and perceived social support on adolescent well-being. *Journal of Adolescence, 23*, 57–68.

Rigby, K. (2002). *New perspectives on bullying*. Philadelphia, PA: Jessica Kingsley.

Rodkin, P. C., & Hodges, E. B. E. (2003). Bullies and victims in the peer ecology: Four questions for psychologists and school professionals. *School Psychology Review, 32*, 384–400.

Ross, D. (2002). Bullying. In J. Sandoval (Ed.), *Handbook of crisis counseling, intervention, and prevention in the school* (pp. 105–135). Mahwah, NJ: Lawrence Erlbaum Associates.

Salmivalli, C. (1999). Participant role approach to school bullying: Implications for prevention. *Journal of Adolescence, 22*, 453–459.

Samples, F., & Aber, L. (1998). Evaluations of school-based violence prevention programs. In D. S. Elliott, B. A. Hamburg, & K. R. Williams (Eds.), *Violence in American schools* (pp. 217–252). Cambridge, UK: Cambridge University Press.

Scheckner, S. B., & Rollin, S. A. (2003). An elementary school violence prevention program. *Journal of School Violence, 2*, 3–42.

Shinn, M. (2003). Understanding implementation of programs in multilevel systems. Prevention and Treatment, 6, Article022c. Available: http://jounrals.apa.org/prevention/volume6/pre0060022c.html

Skiba, R. J., & Knesting, K. (2002). *Zero tolerance, zero evidence: An analysis of school disciplinary practice.* In R. J. Skiba & G. G. Noam (Eds.), *Zero tolerance: Can suspension and expulsion keep school safe?* (pp.17–43). San Francisco, CA: Jossey-Bass.

Smith, P. K., Morita, Y., Junger-Tas, J., Olweus, D., Catalano, R., & Slee, P. (Eds.). (1999). *The nature of school bullying: A cross-national perspective* (pp. 1–4). New York: Routledge.

Swearer, S. M., & Doll, B. (2001). Bullying in schools: An ecological framework. *Journal of Emotional Abuse*, 2, 7–23.

Tobin, T. J., & Sugai, G. M. (1999). Using sixth-grade school records to predict school violence, chronic discipline problems, and high school outcomes. *Journal of Emotional and Behavioral Disorders, 7,* 40–54.

Tolan, P., & Guerra, N. (1994). *What works in reducing adolescent violence: An empirical review of the field.* Boulder: University of Colorado Press.

U.S. Department of Health and Human Services. (2001). *Youth violence: A report of the Surgeon General.* Rockville, MD: U.S. Department of Health and Human Services, Centers for Disease Control and Prevention, National Center for Injury Prevention, Substance Abuse and Mental Health Services Administration, Center for Mental Health Services, National institute of Health, and National Institute of Mental Health.

Vossekuil, B., Fein, R. A., Reddy, M., Borum, R., & Modzeleski, W. (2002). *The final report and findings of the safe school initiative: Implications for the prevention of school attacks in the United States.* Washington, DC: U.S. Department of Education, Office of Elementary and Secondary Education, Safe and Drug-Free Schools Program and U.S. Secret Service, National Threat Assessment Center.

19

The Olweus Bullying Prevention Program: An Overview of Its Implementation and Research Basis

Susan P. Limber
Clemson University

Although bullying among children and youth is not a recent occurrence, it has received considerable attention in recent years in Europe, the United States, and many other parts of the world. Efforts to reduce and prevent bullying in schools in the United States have become quite popular, but there currently is little research on the effectiveness of various bullying prevention approaches to guide educators and policymakers. The oldest and probably best-researched program is the Olweus Bullying Prevention Program. In this chapter, I describe the conceptual basis for the program, highlight its strategies and components, and summarize existing research related to its implementation and effectiveness. I conclude by noting the limitations of our current knowledge and posing several directions for future research.

BACKGROUND AND IMPORTANCE OF THE ISSUE

Bullying is most commonly defined as repeated aggressive behavior in which there is an imbalance of power or strength between the two parties (Nansel et al., 2001; Olweus, 1993). Bullying behaviors may be direct or overt (e.g., hitting, kicking, name calling, or taunting) or more subtle or indirect in nature (e.g., rumor spreading, social exclusion, friendship manipulation, or cyber-bullying; Olweus, 1993; Rigby, 1996).

Prevalence of Bullying

Olweus (1993) conducted the earliest systematic investigations of the prevalence of bullying by studying more than 150,000 Norwegian and Swedish children ages 8–15 in the 1980s. He found that 15% of students reported being involved in bully–victim problems two to three times per month or more often. Nine percent reported that their peers had bullied them, 7% indicated that they had bullied others, and approximately 2% had bullied others and also had been bullied.

Data from the United States generally has found higher rates of bullying than those in Scandinavia (Melton et al., 1998; Nansel et al., 2001). Using the same questionnaire and definition of bullying as Olweus (1996), Melton and colleagues (1998) found that 23% of fourth to sixth graders in rural South Carolina reported being bullied "several times" or more often within the preceding 3 months, and 20% had bullied others with this frequency. In a nationally representative sample of more than 15,000 students in Grades 6–10, Nansel and colleagues (2001) observed that 17% of children and youth reported having been bullied "sometimes" or more often during the school term and 19% had bullied others. Finally, in a nationally representative telephone study involving children ages 2–17, Finkelhor, Ormond, Turner, and Hamby (2005) interviewed caregivers (for children ages 2–9) or children themselves (children ages 10–17) to assess the extent to which children had experienced a wide range of childhood victimizations, including physical bullying, teasing, and emotional bullying. Physical bullying was assessed by asking participants if other kids had picked on them "by chasing or grabbing your hair or clothes or by making [them] do something [they] didn't want to do" (Finkelhor et al., 2005, p. 21). Teasing and emotional bullying was assessed by asking participants, "In the past year, did you get scared or feel really bad because kids were calling you names, saying mean things about you, or saying they didn't want you around?" (Finkelhor et al., 2005, p. 21). Finkelhor and colleagues found that 22% had been physically bullied in the last year (resulting in a national estimate of 13.7 million children and youth), and 25% had been teased or emotionally bullied within the past year (resulting in a national estimate of 15.7 million children and youth). The highest rates of reported bullying were reported among children ages 6–12 (Finkelhor et al., 2005).

Concerns About Bullying

The culmination of more than a decade of research indicates that bullying may seriously affect the psychosocial functioning, academic work, and the health of children who are targeted (Limber, 2004b). Bully victimization is related to lower self-esteem (Hodges & Perry, 1996; Olweus, 1978; Rigby & Slee, 1993), higher rates of depression (Craig, 1998; Fekkes, Pijpers, & Verloove-Vanhorick, 2003; Hodges & Perry, 1996; Olweus, 1978; Rigby & Slee, 1993; Salmon, James, Cassidy, Janoloyes, & Slee, 1995), loneliness (Kochenderfer & Ladd, 1996; Nansel et al., 2001), anxiety (Craig, 1998; Fekkes et al., 2003; Hodges & Perry, 1996; Olweus, 1978; Rigby & Slee, 1993), and suicidal ideation (Rigby, 1996). Victims are also more likely to report that they want to avoid going to school (Kochenderfer & Ladd, 1996) and have higher school absenteeism rates (Rigby, 1996).

Research also suggests that there is reason to be concerned about children who bully. Children who bully their peers have been found to be more likely than other children and youth to be engaged in antisocial, violent, and/or troubling behavior. Findings from research in the United States and abroad indicate, for example, that children who bully are more likely to engage in fighting (Nansel et al., 2001, Nansel, Overpeck, Haynie, Ruan, & Scheidt, 2003; Olweus, 1993), vandalize property (Olweus, 1993), carry a weapon (Nansel et al., 2003), smoke and drink alcohol (Nansel et al., 2001). They also are more likely than their non-bullying peers to report poorer academic achievement (Nansel et al., 2001), be truant (Byrne, 1994; Olweus, 1993), and drop out of school (Byrne, 1994).

Interest in Bullying Prevention

Interest in bullying prevention has increased dramatically over the last decade among educators, policymakers, and the general public (Limber, 2003, 2004a). In the United States, this increased attention to bullying appears to have been fueled in part by the shootings at Columbine High

School in 1999 (Limber, 2004a), and by subsequent reports by the media, government, and researchers that noted linkages between instances of school shootings and peer bullying of the perpetrators (Anderson et al., 2001; Fein et al., 2004). Numerous school-based programs, curricula, teacher's guides, books, videos, and other materials focused on bullying prevention have been introduced to the marketplace, and several prominent government-sponsored public information campaigns have been launched in the past several years, including National Bullying Prevention Campaign supported by the Health Services and Resources Administration (HRSA) and "Make Time to Listen. Take Time to Talk...About Bullying" supported by the Substance Abuse and Mental Health Services Administration (SAMHSA).

CONCEPTUAL BASIS

Introduction to the Olweus Bullying Prevention Program

Among school-based bullying prevention programs, the best known is probably the Olweus Bullying Prevention Program (Olweus, 1991, 1993; Olweus, Limber, & Mihalic, 1999). Olweus, a psychologist at the University of Bergen in Norway, developed the program. During the mid-1980s, Olweus and colleagues developed, refined, and evaluated the program in 42 schools in Bergen, Norway.

The program was developed to address known risk factors for bullying behavior and to build on protective factors within the child's social ecology. Research suggests that personality characteristics and reaction patterns may place individual children and youth at higher risk of bullying and bully victimization (Olweus et al., 1999). As Olweus and colleagues noted, "at the same time, environmental factors such as the teachers' attitudes, routines, and behaviors play a major role in determining the extent to which the problems will manifest themselves in a larger unit such as the classroom or the school" (p. 16). Environmental-organizational factors (e.g., how break times are scheduled) also may affect rates of bullying among children and youth. As a result, the Olweus Bullying Prevention Program is designed to reduce bullying through a restructuring of the child's social environment at school. This restructuring is intended to reduce the number of opportunities that students have to bully and to reduce the rewards for exhibiting bullying behavior. Additionally, positive, prosocial behaviors are encouraged and rewarded (Olweus et al., 1999)

The Olweus program is built on several key principals: that it is critical to develop a school environment that is characterized by warmth and involvement on the part of adults, where there are clear rules for behavior, where there are consistent and nonhostile sanctions that are consistently applied when rules or norms are violated, and where adults act as authorities and positive role models (Olweus, 1993; Olweus et al., 1999).

DESCRIPTION OF THE APPROACH

The Norwegian Model

The principals noted here have been translated into interventions that are implemented at the schoolwide level, within the classroom, and at the individual level.

Schoolwide Interventions

Key schoolwide interventions include the following: (a) the administration of an anonymous questionnaire, (b) formation of a Bullying Prevention Coordinating Committee, (c) fortification of adult supervision of students in areas where bullying is likely, (d) a school meeting day, (e) meetings with parents, and (f) the development of staff discussion groups (Olweus et al., 1999). The Olweus Bully–Victim Questionnaire is a 39-item self-report measure, administered to students in Grades 3 and higher, that is designed to measure the extent of bully—victim problems within a school, the most common locations for bullying, and student perceptions of and attitudes toward bullying (Olweus, 1996; Solberg & Olweus, 2003). The Bullying Prevention Coordinating Committee is a group of representatives from the school community (e.g., an administrator, a teacher from each grade, a school counselor and/or other school-based mental health professional, a member of the non-teaching staff, and at least one parent) who meet periodically to review data from the student survey, plan for the implementation of the program, and ensure that the effort is integrated into the school's activities and continued over time. These plans typically include a strategy for fortifying adult supervision of students in areas that are believed to be "hot spots" for bullying among students. Findings from the student questionnaire can help educators to identify problematic areas. The school meeting day provides an opportunity for school staff to review the results of their questionnaire, become familiar with the philosophy and approach of the program, and make specific plans for implementation for the school year. Parents are engaged in the program through a variety of strategies, including representation on the school's bullying prevention coordinating committee and through participation in schoolwide (or classroom-level) meetings with school staff, during which they discuss the problem of bullying, the findings from the school's questionnaire, and the school's prevention and intervention plans. Parents also receive printed information about the program and periodic updates through school newsletters and other channels. Finally, in more recent adaptations of the program in Norway, the Olweus program has encouraged the establishment of staff discussion groups within a school. These groups of teachers and other school staff meet regularly and offer staff an opportunity to learn more about the program and to share with each other successes and challenges (Olweus, 2004a).

Classroom Interventions

Core elements of the Olweus program within the classroom include the following: (a) establishing and enforcing rules about bullying; (b) holding regularly scheduled classroom meetings with students to discuss bullying, peer relations, and the relevant class/school rules; and (c) holding classroom-level meetings with parents on the topic of bullying (Olweus, 1993; Olweus et al., 1999). These class meetings are also used to engage students in role-plays and other creative activities designed to help them better understand the harms caused by bullying and effective strategies to deal with it (Olweus et al., 1999).

Individual Interventions

In addition to the school and classroom-level interventions, the program also involves interventions that are targeted at individual students (Olweus, 1993; Olweus et al., 1999). Meetings are held with students who bully and (separately) with students who are bullied, in order to help to ensure that bullying stops and that children get additional support and/or guidance that they may need. School personnel are also encouraged to meet with parents of affected students.

Adaptation in the United States

Limber, Nation, Tracy, Melton, and Flerx (2004), in close consultation with Olweus, conducted the first widescale implementation and evaluation of the Olweus program in the United States. Experiences during that initial project and in subsequent efforts have led to some modifications to the program that reflect some of the unique challenges of implementation in U.S. school systems (Olweus et al., 1999). These modifications include the following:

1. The development of schoolwide rules against bullying. In order to ensure consistency of rules across classroom, it was determined that schoolwide rules about bullying (as opposed to classroom rules) would be developed and enforced. This modification appeared particularly important within the U.S. middle school environment, where students frequently may have five to six teachers and change classes several times throughout the school day.
2. Intensive training of committee members and school staff and ongoing consultation. A system of training has evolved such that members of the Bullying Prevention Coordinating Committee receive an intensive 2-day training from a certified trainer. Committee members (in close consultation with the trainer) provide 1 day of training for the staff in their school. Certified trainers provide ongoing monthly consultation to on-site co-ordinators in each school for at least 1 year.
3. Adaptations of materials used in the Norwegian program and the development of new supportive materials. Several materials used in the Norwegian program (e.g., the student video) were adapted for use in U.S. schools. Additionally, supplemental materials (e.g., suggested topics/lesson plans for classroom meetings) have been developed to support teachers' implementation of the program within the classroom setting.
4. The involvement of community members in bullying prevention activities. Within the U.S. context, we have deemed it important for educators and community members to form partnerships to address bullying problems within the school and within the broader community.

Table 19.1 provides information regarding implications for practice, presenting an overview of the key elements of the Olweus Bullying Prevention Program, as they are introduced to U.S. schools.

TABLE 19.1
Implications for Practice: Overview of Key Elements of the Olweus Bullying Prevention Program,
as Implemented in American Schools

Schoolwide elements	• Administer of anonymous bully–victim questionnaire
	• Form coordinating group
	• Train all staff
	• Introduce the program to staff and students through a school assembly or other events
	• Increase adult supervision
	• Develop schoolwide rules about bullying
	• Develop appropriate positive and negative consequences for students' behavior
	• Hold staff discussion groups on bullying
	• Engage parents in bullying prevention efforts
Classroom elements	• Hold classroom meetings with students
	• Hold classroom-level meetings with parents (where possible)
Individual interventions	• Meet individually with students who are bullied
	• Meet individually with students who bully
	• Meet with parents of affected students
Community involvement	• Engage community members in efforts to support the school's program
	• Help to encourage bullying prevention activities in after-school and community settings

RELEVANT RESEARCH

Over the past two decades, a research base has been growing slowly but steadily, from which one can assess the effectiveness of the Olweus program in diverse cultures and communities. Additionally, recent findings from Norway provide insight into teacher- and school-level variables that predict more complete implementation of the program. Data from several recent U.S. studies shed light on elementary school educators' perceptions of program elements and the ease with which these elements may be implemented in schools.

Outcome Research

Six comprehensive outcome studies of the Olweus Bullying Prevention Program have been conducted in Norway. Additionally, replications (or partial replications) have been conducted in Canada (Pepler, Craig, O'Connell, Atlas, & Charach, 2004), Germany (Hanewinkel, 2004), the United Kingdom (Smith, Sharp, Eslea, & Thompson, 2004; Whitney Rivers, Smith, & Sharp, 1994), and the United States (Limber et al., 2004).

First Bergen Project Against Bullying

The first evaluation of the Olweus program took place in the early-to-mid 1980s and involved approximately 2,500 children in Grades 4–7 from 42 elementary and junior high schools in Bergen, Norway (equivalent to Grades 5–8 in the United States and present-day Norway; Olweus, 1991; Olweus et al., 1999). Using a quasi-experimental (age-cohort) design, Olweus found significant and substantial reductions (by 50% or more for most comparisons by students' age and grade) in self-reported bullying and bully victimization. Peer and teacher ratings of the level of bully–victim problems produced largely similar findings (although the findings were somewhat weaker for teacher ratings). Olweus also observed significant reductions in self-reported vandalism, fighting, theft, alcohol use, and truancy. Significant improvements in the social climate of the classroom were reflected in students' reports of increased satisfaction with school life and schoolwork, improved order and discipline at school, and more positive social relationships (Olweus, 1991, 1993; Olweus et al., 1999). Olweus also observed a dosage–response relationship at the classroom level, such that those classrooms that implemented essential components of the program (including establishment of rules against bullying and classroom meetings) saw greater reductions in bully–victim problems (Olweus, 1991, 1993; Olweus et al., 1999).

More Recent Studies in Norway

In several more recent follow-up studies, Olweus and colleagues have observed similar results (Olweus, 2004). In the New Bergen Project Against Bullying, which took place between 1997 and 1998 (Olweus, 2004a, b; Olweus et al., 1999), Olweus assessed 3,200 students in Grades 5–7 and 9 from 14 intervention and 16 comparison schools. In the interventions schools (where the program had been in place 6 months or less), Olweus observed reductions in bully–victim problems of 21% to 38%. For the comparison schools, there were very small or no significant changes in reports of being bullied and a 35% increase in the level of bullying other students. An evaluation of the Oslo Project Against Bullying, which began in 1999, and which involved 2,300 students in Grades 5–7 and 9, revealed significant decreases in reports of bully–victim problems among students in Grades 5–7. Specifically, Olweus observed reductions in bully victimization of 42% (33% for girls and 48% for boys) and self-reported bullying by 52% (64% for girls and 45% for boys) among fifth to seventh graders within 1 year.

Finally, in three recent studies (2001–2003) comprising the New National Initiative Against Bullying, Olweus (2005), surveyed approximately 21,000 students in grades 4–7 from more than 100 schools. After 8 months of involvement with the Olweus Bullying Prevention Program, significant reductions were observed in bully–victim problems, ranging between 32% and 34% for self-reports of bully victimization, and between 37% and 49% for self-reports of bullying others.

Studies in Canada, Germany, and the United Kingdom

Partial replications of Olweus' approach have been conducted in Toronto, Canada (Pepler, Craig, Ziegler, & Charach, 1994; Pepler et al., 2004), Schleswig-Holstien, Germany (Hanewinkel, 2004), and the Sheffield, England (Smith et al., 2004; Whitney et al., 1994). The German program and its evaluation is described briefly here, as it represents perhaps the closest replication of the three to the original Norwegian program.

In the mid-1990s, the Ministry of Education in Schleswig-Holstein, Germany, supported the implementation and evaluation of a bullying prevention program, which was based on the Olweus model (Hanewinkel, 2004). The program was evaluated using a quasi-experimental design in 37 schools comprising Grades 3–12 (11,052 students). According to school leaders, the primary activities undertaken included restructuring the school yard, establishment of class rules against bullying, training of teachers, regular class discussions about bullying, improved supervision during recess, discussions with parents of involved students, and cooperative learning. The evaluation of the program focused on changes in self-reports of low and high levels of direct and indirect victimization and in self-reported bullying. Low levels were defined as experiencing or engaging in bullying "sometimes" or more often, whereas high levels were defined as experiencing or engaging in bullying "once a week" or more often. Researchers observed that low levels of direct victimization (i.e., reports of being bullied "sometimes" or more often) were reduced in Grades 3–10 to various degrees. Statistically significant reductions in low levels of direct victimization were observed at Grades 3 (15% decrease), 5 (20% decrease), 6 (16% decrease), and 7 (16% decrease). Evaluators did not observe reductions in indirect bullying (measured by students' answers to the question, "How often does it happen that other students don't want to spend recess with you and you end up being alone?" Reductions in self-reports of low-level bullying were found for Grades 4 (decrease of 22%), 5 (decrease of 20%), and 7 (decrease of 19%). Significant reductions in high-level victimization were observed for only one grade (Grade 5, which had a 12% reduction); no reductions were observed for high levels of bullying. From his experience in implementing the program in German schools, Hanewinkel (2004) identified several prerequisites to successful implementation: (a) a committed school leader who is able to motivate his or her staff; (b) a staff consensus about their goals and the desired changes; (c) the establishment of a coordinating group; and (d) concrete and *visible* interventions (e.g., teachers on duty during break times). He also noted the importance of training of staff in program elements and strategies.

Evaluation of the Program in the United States

The first systematic evaluation of the Olweus Bullying Prevention Program in the United States (Limber et al., 2004) was conducted in the mid-1990s, involving 18 middle schools in the South Carolina. After 1 year of implementation, researchers observed large, significant decreases in both boys' and girls' reports of bullying others, and large, significant decreases in boys' reports of being bullied and in boys' reports of social isolation. No significant differences in girls' reports of bully victimization were observed, however, nor did researchers observe significant changes in students' attitudes about bullying.

A more current evaluation of the Olweus program in 12 elementary schools in the Philadelphia area revealed significant reductions in self-reported bullying and victimization and in adults' observations of bullying (in the cafeteria and on the playground) among those schools that had implemented the program with at least moderate fidelity (Black, 2003).

Predictors of Implementation

Both research on the Olweus program and experience in the field confirm that levels of implementation of the program vary substantially among teachers and schools (Kallestad & Olweus, 2003; Olweus, 2004b). Systematic research into the adoption of elements of prevention programs is relatively scarce but critical. As Biglan (1995) emphasized, "the adoption of an effective practice is itself a behavior in need of scientific research" (p. 15). In order to better understand the characteristics of teachers and schools that might explain these differences in program implementation, Kallestad and Olweus (2003) analyzed data from a questionnaire that had been administered to 89 Norwegian teachers at two points in time: October/November of 1983 and May/June of 1984. The 89 teachers were drawn from 37 schools and taught in Grades 6–9. Program implementation was measured by the use of two indices: the Classroom Intervention Measures Index and the Individual Contact Index. The Classroom Intervention Measures Index included seven key program elements (including the establishment of classroom rules against bullying, use of regular classroom meetings and role-playing, and showing and discussing a video depicting bullying among school children) and three questions that assessed the degree to which the teacher had involved him or herself, students, and parents in the implementation of the program. The Individual Contact Index measured the classroom teacher's contact with students and parents of involved students (i.e., children who bullied and children who were bullied). Data were analyzed in a multilevel framework, with schools and teachers nested within schools as the two levels.

Teacher-Level Predictors of Program Implementation

Kallestad and Olweus (2003) found five teacher-level variables to be strong predictors of program implementation. These five predictors accounted for 53% of the variance in the program's implementation. The strongest predictor (with a beta standardized coefficient of .47) was Perceived Staff Importance. Those teachers who viewed themselves, their colleagues, and their schools as important agents for change in addressing bullying among students were more likely to actively implement classroom interventions. A second strong predictor of program implementation was labeled Read Program Information (standardized $\beta = .36$). Those teachers who read the available program materials, which provided research-based knowledge about bullying problems and provided specific strategies to address this problem, were more likely to fully implement the program in their classrooms. As Kallestad and Olweus (2003) note, adequate knowledge about the issue of bullying and about specific program elements appears to be an important prerequisite to implementing the program.

A third predictor of program implementation was Perceived Level of Bullying (standardized $\beta = .25$). Perhaps not surprisingly, teachers who perceived bullying among students in their class were more likely to introduce more elements of the program in their classes. As Olweus (2004b) suggested, "the 'demand characteristics' of the classroom situation...as perceived by the teacher, very likely influenced his or her readiness to do something about the problems (p. 29)." The Olweus Bully–Victim Questionnaire is viewed as an important tool to increase teachers' awareness of bully–victim problems among students in their schools. For those teachers who are not already aware of bullying problems among their students, it may serve as a motivator to address the issue.

Two final variables, Self as a Victimized Child ($\beta = .19$), and Affective Involvement ($\beta = .17$) predicted more complete implementation of the program within the classroom setting. Those teachers who reported having been bullied themselves as children and who reported feeling upset and uncomfortable about bullying among students implemented more of the program components.

Teacher Predictors of Individual Contact With Children and Parents

Kallestad and Olweus (2003) found three variables to be significantly related to a teacher's propensity to make contact with children involved in bullying incidents and their parents. Teachers who perceived bullying problems among their students (Perceived Level of Bullying) and who viewed themselves and colleagues as important agents for change in counteracting bullying problems (Perceived Staff Importance) were more likely to intervene individually with children who bullied, children who were bullied, and parents of involved children. The third significant predictor was, Information About Break Times. Those teachers who were more aware of their students' activities during break times, and who considered such information to be important, tended to be more likely to have contact with students involved in bully–victim problems and with their parents.

Interestingly, neither the teacher's gender, age, or years of experience were related to their implementation of the Olweus program in their classrooms (Kallestad & Olweus, 2003). Contrary to some common assumptions, younger teachers in this study did not appear more open than their older colleagues to implementing new practices in their classrooms.

School-Level Predictors of Program Implementation

Kallestad and Olweus (2003) also examined several school-level predictors of program implementation. They observed that school climate was an important predictor of program implementation within the classroom setting. Those schools that had more openness in communication among teachers (by teacher report) implemented more classroom elements. As Kallestad and Olweus (2003) noted, "openness in collegial communication and a generally positive attitude to change among staff may be important resources" (p. 17) in implementing intervention programs. On the other hand, the researchers also observed a negative correlation between a variable labeled Teacher–Teacher Collaboration and program implementation. Those schools that were characterized by greater collaboration among teachers actually implemented less of the program within classrooms. Although Kallestad and Olweus (2003) urged caution in interpreting this finding, they noted that high satisfaction with working relationships among teachers does not always promote willingness for change in the school environment.

Finally, Kallestad and Olweus (2003) observed that those schools that had implemented more bullying prevention activities for their staff (e.g., had presented results from the bully–victim questionnaire to staff, held an in-service for teachers, encouraged formal and informal staff discussion about bullying) had teachers who implemented more of the program components in their classrooms. It is likely that those schools that implemented more schoolwide activities were more successful in generating interest and motivation among teachers to address bullying in their classrooms.

Perceptions and Practices of School Staff

Experience confirms that no prevention program is appropriate for all schools. In an attempt to better understand the extent to which schools may be prepared to implement a comprehensive program such as the Olweus Bullying Prevention Program, it is useful to assess the current practices and attitudes of school staff. Two recent studies by Dake and colleagues (Dake, Price, Telljohann, & Funk, 2003, 2004) assessed elementary school teachers' and principals' perceptions of a number of several specific aspects of the Olweus program. Each is described briefly.

Teachers' Perceptions and Practices

Dake and colleagues (2003) surveyed a national random sample of 359 elementary school teachers regarding their perceptions and practices of school bullying prevention activities and, in particular, three elements of the Olweus Bullying Prevention Program: (a) involving students in creating classroom rules against bullying, (b) having serious talks with children who bully and with children who are bullied, and (c) setting aside class time for discussions about bullying. As noted earlier, the first of these elements—the creation of rules about bullying—has been modified, particularly in the U.S. context, such that administrators are encouraged to create schoolwide rules against bullying, rather than classroom-specific rules against bullying.

Of the 359 respondents, fewer than one third had received training in violence prevention or bullying prevention. Among the three classroom interventions studied, teachers were most open to having serious talks with bullies and with victims of bullying. Most of the respondents (86%) reported that they currently talked with both bullies and victims when a bullying situation arose. Of these, the vast majority (79%) had done so for 2 or more years. Two thirds of teachers believed that there were no barriers to having discussions with bullies and victims of bullying. Of those who identified barriers, the most common barriers were that bullying was not a problem in their classroom (10%) and that victims of bullying would be reluctant to discuss the issue (10%). Teachers were more likely to hold such discussions if they perceived more bullying at their school and if they perceived fewer barriers.

When asked about the practice of involving students in the development of classroom rules against bullying, a plurality (29%) indicated that they had not seriously thought about doing so. Nearly one quarter (23%) had contemplated involving students in the creation of classroom rules about bullying, 12% were preparing to do so, and 25% had been doing so for 2 or more years. Approximately 50% of the teachers believed that there were barriers to involving students in the development of class rules about bullying. The most commonly cited barriers included the following: (a) students' lack of knowledge about bullying (14%), (b) the perception that bullying was a low priority compared with other problems (13%), and (c) teachers' belief that bullying was not a problem for which to create rules (12%). Teachers were more likely to involve students in creating classroom rules about bullying if they perceived more bullying at their school, if they personally dealt with more bullying problems, if they felt greater confidence in their ability to effectively address bullying, if they received violence or bullying prevention training, and if they perceived fewer barriers this program activity.

Of the three intervention components, teacher-respondents appeared to have the most qualms about setting aside time for class discussions about bullying and bullying prevention. Two thirds were not holding such discussions, although one quarter had done so for the previous 2 years. Nearly 60% perceived that there would be one or more barriers to implementing this program component. Common barriers included a concern that the activity would be too time-consuming (36%), that bullying was not a problem in their classroom (17%), and that bullying was a relatively low priority for them (16%). Teachers were more likely to set aside time for class discussions if they perceived more bullying in U.S. elementary schools or at their own school, if they perceived more violence in the neighborhood surrounding the school, if they felt more confident in their ability to deal with bullying situations, if they perceived fewer barriers, and if they had received training in violence prevention or bullying prevention.

Finally, teachers were asked to rate 14 bullying prevention activities on the basis of their perceived effectiveness. Those activities that were deemed most effective by teachers tended to focus on individual interventions (e.g., contacting parents of bullies, holding a meeting with a bully, victim, and parents), whereas those activities that were more "environmental" (e.g., holding a training day to discuss bullying, establishing a bullying prevention committee) were viewed as less effective. Environmental bullying prevention activities were judged more effective by teachers who perceived more bullying in U.S. elementary schools or at their own school, who perceived greater violence in the neighborhood, who had greater confidence in their ability to deal with bullying situations, and who held a master's degree.

Principals' Perceptions and Practices

In a similar vein, Dake and colleagues (2004) conducted a survey of 378 elementary school principals across the United States to assess their perceptions and practices regarding bullying prevention activities. The questionnaire focused on three particular elements of the Olweus Bullying Prevention Program: (a) administration of a bully–victim questionnaire (b) establishment of a bullying prevention committee to coordinate the school's activities; and (c) having a school "conference day" about bullying prevention that would involve students, parents, and community members to raise awareness of bullying prevention efforts at the school. In current efforts to implement the program in the United States, such a "kick-off" event would take place after the staff had received training in bullying prevention and typically would be relatively short in duration (i.e., it may last 1–2 hours but likely not an entire day). Of these activities, principals were most open to holding a conference day on bullying prevention (only one third had not seriously considered doing so). Half of the principals (51%) reported that they were currently contemplating having such a conference day. A small minority (5%) had already implemented such an activity at the school. More than three quarters of principals perceived barriers to holding a conference day. The most commonly cited barriers included a lack of trained staff (25%), time (18%), funding (22%), and a concern that bullying was a relatively low priority, compared with other concerns (24%).

As noted previously, administration of an anonymous bully–victim questionnaire is a core component of the Olweus program and is viewed as an important tool for raising awareness about bullying problems and developing school-specific prevention activities. Approximately half (47%) of the principals surveyed by Dake and colleagues (2004) had considered administering a survey to students to assess the extent of bullying in the school. One quarter was either contemplating doing so or was currently taking steps to administer a survey, and 18% had already implemented such a survey. Schools that had surveyed students about bullying were more likely to have received training in bullying prevention or to have a bullying prevention program in place. Most principals (57%) perceived at least one barrier to conducting such a survey. The most commonly noted barriers were that bullying was a relatively low priority (25%), that bullying was not a problem in the school (15%), and that they lacked the time (14%) and knowledge to develop and administer a survey to administer a survey (14%).

Particularly in the American context, the bullying prevention coordinating committee has been viewed as an important mechanism for coordinating bullying prevention efforts within a school and helping to ensure that these efforts continue over time (Limber, 2004b; Olweus et al., 1999). Among the principals surveyed by Dake et al. (2004), 60% had not seriously contemplated establishing such a committee at their school. Twenty-one percent had contemplated doing so or were currently taking steps to establish a coordinating committee, and 17% had a committee in place for 1 or more years. Most (59%) principals perceived barriers to the establishment of a bullying prevention coordinating committee. Nearly one third (29%) believed this was a relatively low priority for their school, 28% cited a lack of time for committee meetings, and 21% reported that they lacked funding for such a committee. Those principals who had not seriously considered establishing a coordinating committee differed from their colleagues in several respects. They were less likely to perceive that bullying was a problem in U.S. elementary schools in general and in their own school in particular, they received fewer reports of bullying episodes, and they perceived more barriers to establishing a committee.

TABLE 19.2

Summary of Barriers to and Predictors of Program Implementation

---

Commonly Cited Barriers to Implementing Program Elements

Responses by teachers	Bullying is a relatively low priority[1]
	Bullying is not a problem in classroom[1]
	Program element is too time consuming[1]
Responses by principals	Bullying is a relatively low priority[2]
	Bullying is not a problem in the school[2]
	Program element is too time-consuming[2]
	Limited funding available[2]
	Lack of time[2]
	Lack of training[2]

Predictors of Program (Program Element) Implementation

Teacher-level predictors	Perceived staff importance[3]
	Educated about the program/issue[3]:
	• Read program materials
	• Received training in bullying prevention/violence prevention[1]
	Perceptions of prevalence of bullying
	• Perceived more bullying in class[3]
	• Perceived more bullying in U.S. school or own school[1]
	Felt confident in their ability to deal with bullying[1]
	Personal involvement (as victims of bullying as children)[3]
	Affective involvement with bullying[3]
	Perceived fewer barriers to implementing program component[1]
Principals' predictors	Received training in bullying prevention/violence prevention[2]
	Have a bullying prevention program in place[2]
	Perceive more bullying in U.S. and in own school[2]
	Perceive fewer barriers to implementing program component[2]

---

[1] Dake et al. (2003)
[2] Dake et al. (2004)
[3] Kallestad and Olweus (2003)

When asked to rate the effectiveness of various bullying prevention and intervention activities (most of which were elements of the Olweus program), principals (like teachers) cited post-bullying activities (e.g., meeting with a bully or a victim after a bullying incident, contacting parents of involved students) as most effective and "environmental" activities (e.g., establishing a bullying prevention coordinating committee, establishing rules about bullying, holding parent–teacher meetings to increase awareness about bullying) as least effective. Principals were more likely to rate environmental activities as effective if they had received training in bullying prevention, they perceived more bullying in U.S. schools or in their own school, they perceived more violence in the neighborhood, or there were more reports of bullying at their school.

An understanding of perceived barriers to bullying prevention activities and knowledge of predictors of program implementation are critical for program developers and potential program consumers alike. Program developers and trainers who are involved in helping to disseminate effective practices are wise to keep abreast of concerns that school staff may have about the ease of implementing program components. If too many barriers are perceived, staff members are less likely to attempt to adopt bullying prevention strategies or may be less successful in their attempts. At the same time, knowing which staff- or school-level variables tend to predict program implementation may help school staff members assess how successful they are likely to be in implementing a bullying prevention program. For example, if the majority of teachers at a school perceive that bullying is rare or is a low priority, it may be more difficult to motivate the staff to fully implement a bullying prevention program. Table 19.2 presents a summary of barriers to and predictors of program implementation that have been identified in recent studies by Kallestad and Olweus (2003) and Dake and colleagues (2003, 2004).

LIMITATIONS OF CURRENT KNOWLEDGE AND CONCLUSIONS

Despite the accumulation of research on the Olweus program over the last two decades, additional work will be helpful to assess its implementation and effectiveness in diverse regional settings of the United States (as well as internationally), and among students of different grade levels, gender, and ethnic and cultural groups. Further research also is needed to assess the program's success in (a) reducing various types of bullying among children and youth, (b) influencing other antisocial and/or violent behaviors among children and youth, (c) impacting academic achievement and other measures of school success, and (d) affecting the climates of schools. Recognizing the varying levels of fidelity with which schools implement the program, future work should focus on better understanding those elements of the program that are most critical to its success, as well as variables that predict more faithful implementation of those program elements. Finally, as interest in the program continues to grow, ongoing evaluation of the program's dissemination strategies will be key to ensuring its effective diffusion.

ACKNOWLEDGMENTS

The National Bullying Prevention Campaign ("Take a Stand. Lend a Hand. Stop Bullying Now!") is supported by the Health Resources and Services Administration (www. stopbullyingnow.hrsa.gov). The Substance Abuse and Mental Health Services Administration launched "Make Time to Listen. Take Time to Talk...About Bullying" (www.mentalhealth.samhsa.gov/15plus/aboutbullying.asp).

REFERENCES

Anderson, M., Kaufman, J., Simon, T. R., Barrios, L., Paulozzi, L., Ryan, G., Hammond, R., Modzeleski, W., Feucht, T., Potter, L., & the School-Associated Violent Deaths Study Group (2001). School-associated violent deaths in the United States, 1994–1999. *Journal of the American Medical Association, 286,* 2695–2702.

Biglan, A. (1995). *Changing cultural practices: A contextualist framework for intervention research.* Reno, NV: Context Press.

Black, S. (2003, April). *An ongoing evaluation of the bullying prevention program in Philadelphia schools: Student survey and student observation data.* Paper presented at the Safety in Numbers Conference, Atlanta, GA.

Byrne, B. J. (1994). Bullying in school settings with reference to some Dublin schools. *Irish Journal of Psychology, 15,* 574–586

Craig, W. M. (1998). The relationship among bullying, victimization, depression, anxiety, and aggression in elementary school children. *Personality & Individual Differences, 24,* 123–130.

Dake, J. A., Price, J. H., Telljohann, S. K., & Funk, J. B. (2003). Teacher perceptions and practices regarding school bullying prevention. *Journal of School Health, 73,* 347–355.

Dake, J. A., Price, J. H., Telljohann, S. K., & Funk, J. B. (2004). Principals' perceptions and practices of school bullying prevention activities. *Health Education & Behavior, 31*, 372–387.

Fein, R. A., Vossekuil, B., Pollack, W. S., Borum, R., Modzeleski, W., & Reddy, M. (2002). *Threat assessment in schools: A guide to managing threatening situations and to creating safe school climates.* Washington DC: U.S. Department of Education, Office of Elementary and Secondary Education, Safe and Drug-Free Schools Program and U.S. Secret Service, National Threat Assessment Center.

Fekkes, M., Pijpers, F. I. M., & Verloove-VanHorick, S. P. (2004). Bullying behavior and associations with psychosomatic complaints and depression in victims. *Journal of Pediatrics, 144*, 17–22.

Finkelhor, D., Ormond, R., Turner, H., & Hamby, S. (2005). The victimization of children and youth: A comprehensive, national survey. *Child Maltreatment, 10*, 5–25.

Hanewinkel, R. (2004). Prevention of bullying in German schools: An evaluation of an anti-bullying approach. In P. K. Smith, D. Pepler, & K. Rigby (Eds.), *Bullying in schools: How successful can interventions be?* (pp. 81–97). Cambridge, UK: Cambridge University Press.

Hodges, E. V. E., & Perry, D. G. (1996). Victims of peer abuse: An overview. *Journal of Emotional and Behavioural Problems, 5*, 23–28.

Kallestad, J. H., & Olweus, D. (2003). Predicting teachers' and school's implementation of the Olweus Bullying Prevention Program: A multilevel study. *Prevention & Treatment, 6*, Article 21. Available: http://www.journals.apa.org/prevention/

Kochenderfer, B. J., & Ladd, G. W. (1996). Peer victimization: Cause or consequence of school maladjustment? *Child Development, 67*, 1305–1317.

Limber, S. P. (2003). Efforts to address bullying in U.S. schools. *American Journal of Health Education, 34*, S–23–S–29.

Limber, S. P. (2004a, August). *Bullying prevention and intervention in a post-Columbine era.* Paper presented at the 112th convention of the American Psychological Association. Honolulu, HI.

Limber, S. P. (2004b). Implementation of the Olweus Bullying Prevention Program: Lessons learned from the field. In D. Espelage & S. Swearer (Eds.), *Bullying in American schools: A social-ecological perspective on prevention and intervention* (pp. 351–363). Mahwah, NJ: Lawrence Erlbaum Associates.

Limber, S. P., Nation, M., Tracy, A. J., Melton, G. B., & Flerx, V. (2004). Implementation of the Olweus Bullying Prevention programme in the Southeastern United States. In P. K. Smith, D. Pepler, & K. Rigby (Eds.), *Bullying in schools: How successful can interventions be?* (pp. 55–79). Cambridge, UK: Cambridge University Press.

Melton, G. B., Limber, S. P., Cunningham, P. Osgood, D. W., Chambers, J., Flerx, V., Henggeler, S., & Nation, M. (1998*). Violence among rural youth.* Final report to the Office of Juvenile Justice and Delinquency Prevention. [Available upon request from S. Limber at the Institute on Family & Neighborhood Life, Clemson University, 158 Poole Agricultural Center, Clemson, SC, 29634].

Nansel, T. R., Overpeck, M., Pilla, R. S., Ruan, W. J., Simons-Morton, B., & Scheidt, P. (2001). Bullying behaviors among US youth: Prevalence and association with psychosocial adjustment. *Journal of the American Medical Association, 285*, 2094–2100.

Nansel, T. R., Overpeck, M. D., Haynie, D. L., Ruan, W. J., & Scheidt, P. C. (2003). Relationships between bullying and violence among US youth. *Archives of Pediatric Adolescent Medicine, 157*, 348–353.

Olweus, D. (1978). *Aggression in the schools: Bullies and whipping boys.* Washington, DC: Wiley.

Olweus, D. (1991). bully–victim problems among schoolchildren: Basic facts and effects of a school based intervention program. In D. J. Pepler & K. H. Rubin (Eds.), *The development and treatment of childhood aggression* (pp. 411–448). Hillsdale, NJ: Lawrence Erlbaum Associates.

Olweus, D. (1993). Bullying at school: What we know and what we can do. Cambridge, MA: Blackwell.

Olweus, D. (1996). *The Revised Bully-Victim Questionnaire* (Unpublished material). Bergen, Norway: Research Center for Health Promotin (HIMIL), Chriestiesgate 13, N–5015 Bergen, Norway.

Olweus, D. (2004a). Bullying at school: Prevalence estimation, a useful evaluation design, and a new national initiative in Norway. *Association for Child Psychology and Psychiatry Occasional Papers No. 23*, 5–17.

Olweus, D. (2004b). The Olweus Bullying Prevention Programme: Design and implementation issues and a new national initiative in Norway. In P. K. Smith, D. Pepler, & K. Rigby (Eds.), *Bullying in schools: How successful can interventions be?* (pp. 13–36). Cambridge, UK: Cambridge University Press.

Olweus, D. (2005). A useful evaluation design and effects of the Olweus Bullying Prevention Program. *Psychology, Crime & Law, 11*(4), 1–14.

Olweus, D., Limber, S. P., & Mihalic, S. (1999). *The Bullying Prevention Program: Blueprints for violence prevention, Vol. 10.* Boulder, CO: Center for the Study and Prevention of Violence.

Pepler, D. J., Craig, W., Ziegler, S., & Charach, A. (1994). An evaluation of an anti-bullying intervention in Toronto schools. *Canadian Journal of Community Mental Health, 13*, 95–110.

Pepler, D. J., Craig, W. M., O'Connell, P., Atlas, R., & Charach, A. (2004). Making a difference in bullying: Evaluation of a systemic school-based programme in Canada. In P. K. Smith, D. Pepler, & K. Rigby (Eds.), *Bullying in schools: How successful can interventions be?* (pp. 125–139). Cambridge, UK: Cambridge University Press.

Rigby, K., & Slee, P. T. (1991). Bullying among Australian school children: Reported behavior and attitudes towards victims. *Journal of Social Psychology, 133*, 33–42.

Rigby, K. (1996). *Bullying in schools: And what to do about it.* Bristol, PA: Jessica Kingsley.

Salmon, G., James, A., Casiday, E. L., & Javoloyes, M. A. (2000). Bullying a review: Presentations to an adolescent psychiatric service and within a school for emotionally and behaviourally disturbed children. *Clinical Child Psychology and Psychiatry, 5*, 563–579.

Smith, P. K., Sharp, S., Eslea, M., & Thompson, D. (2004). England: the Sheffield project. In P. K. Smith, D. Pepler, & K. Rigby (Eds.),*Bullying in schools: How successful can interventions be?* (pp. 99–123). Cambridge, UK: Cambridge University Press.

Solberg, M. E., & Olweus, D. (2003). Prevalence estimation of school bullying with the Olweus Bully/Victim Questionnaire. *Aggressive Behavior, 29*, 239–268.

Whitney, I., Rivers, I., Smith, P., & Sharp, S. (1994). The Sheffield project: methodology and findings. In P. Smith & S. Sharp (Eds.), *School bullying: Insights and perspectives* (pp. 20–56). London: Routledge.

20

Promoting Behavior and Beliefs
That Reduce Bullying: The Steps
to Respect[1] Program

Miriam Hirschstein
Karin S. Frey
Committee for Children University of Washington

Bullying in U.S. schools is a chronic and costly problem with far-reaching implications for children's well-being. It is perhaps the most common form of school violence (Batsche, 1997), with most children between the ages of 8 and 11 observed to perpetrate (60.7%) or encourage its perpetration (47.8%) on playgrounds (Frey et al., 2005). Large numbers of U.S. school children also self-report perpetrating (Limber et al., 1997), witnessing (Hoover, Oliver, & Hazler, 1992), and being victimized (Nansel et al., 2001) by bullying behavior. By conservative estimates, 10% of U.S. school children experience chronic bullying (Perry, Kusel, & Perry, 1988), but the true number may be closer to 20% (Pellegrini, Bartini, & Brooks, 1999).

Bullying appears to be a relatively intransigent problem. As the school year progresses, rates of bullying actually increase (Frey et al., 2005). Moreover, there is evidence that students grow more accepting of this coercive process over time (Hymel, Bonanno, Henderson, & McCreith, 2002). Adults report feeling unprepared to deal with bullying problems (Boulton, 1997) and are rarely observed to intervene (Atlas & Pepler, 1998). For these reasons, effective school-based intervention requires a universal and systemic approach.

Bullying behavior occurs within a multilevel, socioecological context (Swearer & Doll, 2001). That is, bullying occurs between students within the contexts of relationships with peers, teachers, other supervisory adults, families, and communities. Appreciation of this has led to consensus in the field that systemic, school-based anti-bullying programs must target multiple levels and mechanisms in order to have an impact (Espelage & Swearer, 2003; Olweus, 1993; Pepler, Craig, & O'Connell, 1999). Use of these whole-school interventions is associated with reductions in student reports of bullying (Olweus, 1991; Whitney, Rivers, Smith, & Sharp, 1994) and their increased willingness to seek adult help (Whitney et al., 1994).

Steps to Respect: A Bullying Prevention Program (Committee for Children, 2001) is a universal, multilevel program designed to reduce bullying problems in elementary school by (a) increasing staff awareness and school responsiveness to bullying, (b) fostering socially

---

[1] Steps to Respect is a registered trademark of Committee for Children.

responsible beliefs among students, (c) teaching students specific skills to solve bullying problems, and (d) promoting acquisition of skills associated with general socioemotional competence. This chapter provides a brief review of the knowledge base regarding harmful outcomes associated with bullying, and then describes conceptual foundations and specific practices found in the Steps to Respect program. This is followed by a summary of evidence of program effectiveness based on a 1-year randomized controlled trial (RCT), as well as a review of findings and issues related to classroom implementation. The chapter concludes with a discussion of program and research limitations, as well as implications for practice.

IMPORTANCE OF ISSUE

Repeated involvement in the process of bullying is associated with numerous risks to the well-being of children and adolescents. Evidence suggests that young people who bully are more likely than other youth to engage in delinquent activities (Olweus, 1991), and become victims of street violence (Andershed, Kerr, & Stattin, 2001). Involvement in bullying is also associated with drug abuse (Pepler et al., 2002) and dating violence (Connolly, Pepler, Craig, & Taradash, 2000).

The impact of bullying on victims appears equally damaging. Victimization by bullying is associated with declines in school attendance (Slee, 1994), academic performance (Schwartz & Gorman, 2003), and feelings of self-worth (Grills & Ollendick, 2002). There is ample evidence of links between chronic victimization and adjustment problems such as aggression, anxiety, depression, and self-inflicted violence (see Hawker & Boulton, 2000, for review). Longitudinal studies show ongoing declines in adjustment when children are chronically victimized by their peers (Hanish & Guerra, 2002; Kochenderfer & Ladd, 1997).

The negative effects of bullying are not limited to those who bully and their victims. Witnessing 85% of bullying episodes (Craig & Pepler, 1995), bystanders are arguably the largest group of students affected. Their intervention efforts tend to halt bullying quickly, but they occur infrequently (Craig, Pepler, & Atlas, 2000), perhaps due to students' fears, confusion about what to do, or the belief that bullying of others is "none of my business." Repeated inaction may lead children to disengage morally (Bandura, 2002) and passively accept injustice (Jeffrey, Miller, & Linn, 2001). Moreover, researchers speculate that seeing bullying "work" may prompt imitation (O'Connell, Pepler, & Craig, 1999).

In addition to the impact of bullying among individual school children, costs to schools and the public are substantial. Bullying may have contributed to student shooting incidents in the late 1990s (Leary, Kowalski, Smith, & Phillips, 2003), prompting passage of legislation to address school bullying in 15 states (Limber & Small, 2003). Legislative efforts to address bullying are laudable. However, programmatic initiatives not grounded in theory, a clear definition of bullying behaviors and empirical evidence may miss the mark (Furlong, Morrison, & Grief, 2003). Specifically, scientific validation with RCTs, as well as consideration of issues related to program implementation, can provide the necessary evidence that school prevention programs are effective.

CONCEPTUAL FOUNDATION OF THE STEPS TO RESPECT PROGRAM

Steps to Respect (Committee for Children, 2001) is a comprehensive elementary school program designed to address bullying at multiple levels. A first step in bullying prevention is to develop shared understanding among all members of a school community about what bullying is. Consistent with the view that bullying is a kind of aggression that involves the use of unequal power and repeated verbal, physical, or socially derogatory behaviors intended to harm others (Atlas & Pepler, 1998; Olweus, 1993; Smith & Brain, 2000), the Steps to Respect program defines bullying as "unfair and one-sided. It happens when someone keeps hurting, frightening, threatening, or leaving someone out on purpose." The program also teaches that bullying may be direct and indirect (Bjorkqvist, Lagerspetz, & Kaukiainen, 1992), the latter being perpetrated "behind the back" via use of gossip, rumors, social exclusion, or other oblique strategies.

Successful implementation of the program entails coordinating a schoolwide environmental intervention with socio cognitive curricula. The environmental intervention aims to provide adults and children with systemic support, procedures, and guidance to impede bullying and motivate prosocial behavior throughout a school. Classroom lessons and instructional practices, designed for use in Grades 3–6, target children's normative beliefs related to bullying (Huesmann & Guerra, 1997), as well as socioemotional skills to counter bullying and promote healthy relationships.

The focus on classroom intervention in Grades 3–6 reflects a desire to intervene before surges in bullying that typically occur toward the end of elementary school and into the middle school years (Pellegrini & Long, 2002). There is evidence that normative beliefs about aggression became stable starting in Grade 4 (Huesman & Guerra, 1997) and that children's views on dealing with aggressive peers also undergo changes around this time (Newman, Murray, & Lussier, 2001). Because behavior, beliefs, and patterns of interaction that are long-standing become increasingly resistant to change (Coie & Dodge, 1998; Huesmann & Guerra, 1997), the Steps to Respect program targets the middle to upper elementary school years as a particularly favorable time to influence bullying-related skills, beliefs, and behavior via classroom lessons.

Environmental Intervention Components

The environmental intervention entails (a) developing and communicating clear schoolwide anti-bullying policy and procedures; (b) increasing adult awareness, responsiveness, and guidance in relation to bullying events; and (c) increasing systemic supports for prosocial behavior. Training related to these components, implemented prior to classroom lessons, aims to provide consistency and to limit student opportunities to benefit socially or materially from bullying (Snell, MacKenzie, & Frey, 2002).

Anti-Bullying Policy and Procedures

Effective intervention requires the development of clear anti-bullying policy and procedures. Policy and procedures provide critical prevention guideposts (Olweus, Limber, & Mihalic, 1999) as they promote shared understanding of (a) the definition of bullying, (b) the consequences and sequence of events associated with bullying events, and (c) adult responsibility for follow-through.

Increasing Adult Awareness and Responsiveness

Adults underestimate both the seriousness and prevalence of school bullying (Atlas & Pepler, 1998). Thus, training and motivating supervisory adults, especially those on the frontline of bullying incidents (e.g., teachers, playground monitors, and bus drivers), to notice and intervene effectively in bullying behavior are key program goals. Training includes providing clear examples of a range of bullying behaviors; discussing myths and empirical findings related to bullying; and teaching adults to monitor, recognize, and respond effectively to students' behaviors and reports.

Active adult guidance for children involved in bullying events is also an important feature of the environmental intervention. Steps to Respect coaching models are intended to provide a safety-focused response to immediate and long-term student needs. Each model (one for students experiencing bullying and the other for those who bully) establishes details and the historical context, asks students to generate solutions to avoid future problems, and includes follow-up. The model for students who bully includes applying consequences. The one for bully victims affirms student feelings and the importance of reporting, and asks them to identify strategies they have tried to solve similar problems in the past.

Based in an educational rather than judicial or punitive approach, the coaching model enables educators to foster student problem solving, perspective taking, and assertiveness skills. Without high-stakes punishment and the consequent need to prove guilt beyond a reasonable doubt, educators can address low-level behaviors before they escalate. Although not ignoring the need to determine facts and apply consequences, this approach places equal emphasis on helping children practice relational and problem-solving skills (Plunk & Frey, in press), enabling educators to discuss norms (e.g., "is that fair?") and collective responsibility for school safety.

Support of Prosocial Behavior

A third aim of the environmental intervention is to support children's motivation to behave prosocially. Consistent with the goal of creating a more respectful and caring school environment, the Steps to Respect program recommends implementing schoolwide procedures for increasing adult recognition of positive social behaviors. One example of this is a principal delivering an outstanding citizenship award to a fourth-grade student who appropriately defended a younger student who was being bullied on the bus. In the face of powerful peer dynamics and the potential pressure to "go along" with bullying behavior, systemwide efforts to call out responsible actions like these may create an important counterinfluence.

Sociocognitive Classroom Curricula

Sociocognitive models (e.g., Bandura, 1986; Crick & Dodge, 1994; Huesmann, 1988) posit that social behavior follows from interactions between skills and beliefs related to norms, self-efficacy, and probable consequences. For these reasons, the Steps to Respect curricula provide multiple pathways to influence behavior: building specific bullying prevention skills, fostering general socioemotional skills, and addressing beliefs and peer-group norms related to bullying.

Bullying Prevention Skills

Specific bullying prevention skills focus on helping students identify bullying behaviors, practice assertive responding to coercive behaviors, and engage in problem solving and risk assessment related to bullying. Students practice reporting bullying incidents, and identify adults in the school they would seek out for help. Newman et al. (2001) discussed the need to actively encourage children, particularly boys in the upper elementary grades, to seek adult help. Lessons also address distinguishing "tattling" (trying to get people into trouble) from "reporting" (telling an adult to keep people safe), a potentially useful tool for both students and teachers.

General Socioemotional Skills

In addition to stopping bullying, intervention efforts should cultivate caring relationships (Espelage & Swearer, 2003). Friendship has been shown to serve as a buffer against bullying in middle childhood (Boulton, Trueman, Chau, Whitehand, & Amatya, 1999; Hodges, Malone, & Perry, 1997). Therefore, initial lessons of the Steps to Respect curriculum focus specifically on friendship skills. Themes that emerge when considering friendship, such as mutuality, respect, and caring for others, reflect (inversely) those found in the dynamics of bullying. In Steps to Respect lessons, children practice skills to help make friends (e.g., joining a group) and maintain existing friendships (e.g., resolving conflicts).

Emotion regulation skills are important in friendships, and may also aid students who are victimized, witness bullying, or bully others. Dysregulation is a strong predictor of rejection and victimization (Perry, Hodges, & Egan, 2001) and harassment by peers clearly can present challenges to maintaining an organized demeanor. Using "self-talk" to cool down, and practicing calm, assertive responses to others may help children avoid the helpless or exaggerated responses of easy targets (Kochenderfer & Ladd, 1997; Schwartz, Dodge, & Coie, 1993).

Similarly, improving emotion regulation skills may enable bystanders to manage emotional distress when viewing victimization, and to channel their concern into helping others rather than ameliorating their own distress (Eisenberg, Wentzel, & Harris, 1998; Snell et al., 2002). Practicing self-regulation skills in conjunction with intervention scripts (e.g., "Stop. That's bullying.") may thus contribute to responsible bystander behavior. Finally, training in emotion regulation may also help some children who bully, particularly those pervasively aggressive children who display self-regulatory deficits (Schwartz, 2000).

It is unlikely, however, that improved socioemotional skills will deter skilled manipulators who use bullying strategically to achieve their ends (Kaukianen et al., 2002). These children appear to have good perspective-taking skills, but are not empathetic. Research shows that empathetic children are less aggressive (Kaukianen et al., 1999) and more prosocial than other children (Eisenberg et al., 1996). For these reasons, Steps to Respect lessons aim to foster children's empathy with activities to recognize feelings, consider perspectives of children in hypothetical situations, and practice caring behaviors.

Beliefs, Norms, and Attitudes

Aggressive youth tend to believe that aggression is justified (Slaby & Guerra, 1988) and leads to positive outcomes (Perry, Perry, & Rasmussen, 1986). Descriptive research suggests that shared antisocial beliefs contribute to a peer climate that condones bullying and discourages responsible bystander behavior (Owens, Slee, & Shute, 2000; Terasahjo & Salmivalli, 2003), particularly when a victim is considered irritating or odd (Oliver, Hoover, & Hazler, 1994; Rigby & Slee, 1991). Even victims may begin to feel deserving of abuse, based on what they come to believe are unique personal defects (Graham & Juvonen, 2001). This perception is challenged in Steps to Respect lessons by increasing student awareness of the prevalence of victimization. Lessons also strongly promote the norm that everyone deserves to be treated respectfully.

Both the environmental intervention and classroom curricula aim to counter the belief that children can bully with impunity by creating a high-profile anti-bullying effort. Strategies to promote this effort includes posting anti-bullying policy throughout a school, talking about bullying prevention at school assemblies, and telling students that all adults in the school have been trained to make the school safer. By increasing children's expectations of adult responsiveness, the program aims to reduce bullying and increase reporting and active defense of those targeted for abuse.

IMPLEMENTING THE STEPS TO RESPECT PROGRAM

Steps to Respect is comprised of a schoolwide program guide, multiple levels of staff training, classroom curricula in Grades 3–5 (or Grades 4–6), and ongoing support for implementation and evaluation. The program guide presents an overview of goals, content, and the research foundation, as well as a blueprint for developing anti-bullying policies and procedures. Included is an example of a yearly introduction letter for parents describing the program and inviting parents to the Steps to Respect Parent Overview, a scripted presentation found in the training manual. Additional materials on communicating with parents, referring children with additional needs, and monitoring program implementation are also provided.

Staff Training

The Steps to Respect training manual provides written and video-based materials for a core instructional session for all school staff, as well as two in-depth training sessions. In Part 1, all staff members receive an overview of program goals and content, including a definition of bullying, descriptions of direct and indirect bullying behaviors, and a model for responding to bullying reports. In Part 2, teachers, counselors, and administrators, are trained to use specific strategies to coach students involved in bullying situations. In Part 3, teachers in Grades 3–6 receive an orientation to the curriculum. The entire training takes approximately 6 hours to complete. Materials for four "booster" staff trainings, conducted throughout the remaining school year, are also included. Staff training may be provided by school personnel, using materials provided, or by professional trainers at the Committee for Children.

In addition to these training materials, a 2-day facilitator training is available to assist in strategic planning during the early phase of program adoption. Facilitator training and materials provided by Committee for Children include step-by-step information about (a) developing a steering committee and timeline for implementation, (b) modeling of the three-part staff training, and (c) hands-on support in designing anti-bullying policy and related procedures. Two training videos; safety guidelines for bus, lunchroom, and playground; and a lesson for children in k–2 are also provided.

Classroom Curriculum

Steps to Respect classroom components are comprised of skill and literature lessons. Classroom teachers first present 10 skill lessons that are divided into three parts, each of which takes 20 to 30 minutes to teach. The three parts of each lesson include discussion, activities, and skill practice, and are designed to be taught within the same week. Classroom teachers have primary responsibility for implementing lessons as well as promoting real-life transfer of skills throughout the day. Normative beliefs, general socioemotional skills, and the recognition, refusal, and reporting of bullying behavior are taught in the context of topics such as being responsible bystanders and "part of the solution," versus "part of the problem," of bullying. Lessons provide examples of positive leadership and courage in the face of coercive behavior.

Following completion of 10 skill lessons, teachers implement a grade-appropriate literature unit comprised of 8 to 10 lessons that are based on existing children's novels (e.g., *The Well*, by Margaret Taylor). Literature lessons integrate socioemotional learning objectives (e.g., empathy) with language arts content, providing further opportunities to discuss issues related to healthy relationships and bullying. Lessons based on *The Well*, for example, focus on issues of racial bullying.

Instructional Materials and Strategies

Curricular materials include lesson cards, videos, and overhead transparencies. Take-home letters for parents outline key skills and concepts, and activities parents may try at home to reinforce program content. Instructional strategies include direct instruction, large- and small-group discussions, modeling, role-plays, games, and writing activities, as these practices support student skill acquisition and generalization (Consortium, 1994).

Because generalization is the ultimate goal of prevention, program materials and training offer numerous activities and strategies to generalize skills and beliefs to real life. First, teachers are encouraged to model program skills, for example by using self-talk to cool down, as well as to use rehearsal, coaching, and feedback in the context of classroom social dynamics (Frey, Hirschstein, & Guzzo, 2000). Teachers who provide students with more guidance in relation to real bullying events are most successful with the program (Edstrom, Hirschstein, Frey, Snell, & MacKenzie, 2004). Second, lessons provide activities that integrate socioemotional and academic content as described in a publication linking federal academic standards and the content and learning strategies found in the Steps to Respect program (Committee for Children, 2005).

Implementation and Evaluation Support

Ongoing implementation support for the Steps to Respect program is available via phone consultation with implementation specialists. Evaluation materials for the program, available via the Web (Steps to Respect Toolkit, located at www.cfchildren.org), provide basic guidelines for evaluation needs, as well as an assortment of process and outcome evaluation measures. These include implementation checklists, student and teacher surveys, guidelines for tracking discipline referrals, a student attitude survey, and information about obtaining other empirically validated resources.

RELEVANT RESEARCH

Examination of program effectiveness has thus far focused on three areas: (a) group differences in student behavior, attitudes, and skills; (b) group differences in teacher attitudes and behavior; and (c) links between teacher behavior and student outcomes. We discuss the first two in detail.

Group Differences in Student Outcomes

Using multisource data, student behaviors, beliefs, and skills were measured using a pre- and a posttest following 1 year of implementation (Frey et al., 2005). We anticipated that the program would (a) reduce bullying and destructive bystander behavior, (b) increase prosocial beliefs related to bullying, and (c) increase social competence. Student skills and attitudes were collected from more than 1,000 students in six schools, via survey and teacher ratings. For 10 weeks in the fall and spring, unbiased coders observed playground behaviors of a random subsample of 544 students. Behaviors (e.g., bullying, bystander encouragement, and agreeable and argumentative social behavior) were coded using a mutually exclusive system of categories. Bullying was coded for aggression involving a discernible power imbalance (e.g., an older child targeting a younger one) and/or repeated aggression toward a nonretaliating peer.

Bullying Behavior

Changes in playground behavior from fall to spring revealed that playground bullying increased in control schools, but not among those receiving the Steps to Respect program. Relative to the control group, intervention students showed a near-significant decline in bystander encouragement of bullying. Effects were strongest among those students displaying these behaviors at pretest. There was also a tendency for intervention students to self-report less victimization, but not less bullying/aggression, than students who did not receive the program.

Interpersonal Skills

There were no differences in teacher ratings of student interpersonal skills as measured on a subscale of the Walker McConnell Scale of Social Competence and School Adjustment (Walker & McConnell, 1995). Playground observations of general social behavior, however, showed a decrease in argumentative interactions and increased agreeable interaction among students in intervention schools, relative to students in control schools.

Beliefs Related to Bullying

Three types of beliefs and attitudes were measured. Following program implementation, intervention students reported a stronger sense of personal responsibility to intervene responsibly as bystanders than did control students. They also reported less tolerance of bullying and aggression than did their control counterparts. Finally, students receiving the program perceived adults as more responsive to bullying problems than did control students.

This study may be unique in its documentation of observed behavioral changes following a bullying intervention. It is also among the first to examine, via observation and student survey, changes in bystander behavior and beliefs.

Group Differences in Teacher Attitudes and Behavior

The extent to which 34 intervention and 35 control teachers perceived bullying as an important problem, and their own sense of preparedness to address it (e.g., "I feel prepared to assess the seriousness of a bullying report"), were also examined. Given that staff in both groups voted to adopt the Steps to Respect program, it was not surprising that the groups ascribed equal importance to the problem, $F < 1$. Intervention teachers, however, reported feeling significantly more prepared to deal with bullying, following staff training, than did control teachers, $F(1, 61) = 13.48, p < .001$. However, a grade-by-group interaction, $F(1, 61) = 3.10 p < .05$, indicated that this confidence was not shared by fifth-grade intervention teachers (other intervention $p^s < .05$).

Monthly self-reports assessed teachers' support for student general socioemotional and bullying prevention skill use outside of lesson instruction. A third scale, measuring teacher coaching of students involved in bullying incidents, was completed by intervention teachers only. Mean level of support was calculated for 2 months before, and 4 months after program onset.

No group differences were found in teacher support for student general socioemotional skills ("I prompted students involved in a conflict to problem solve") before or after program onset, $F < 1$. Neither intervention nor control teachers changed.

Support for student use of bullying prevention skills (e.g., "I prompted student(s) to stand up for someone being picked on") varied by group and time, $F(1, 67) = 8.76, p < .01$. Post hoc analyses indicated equivalent initial levels of support for specific bullying prevention skills among intervention ($M = 1.38$) and control teachers ($M = 1.49$). After the onset of the program, however, control teachers' support for bullying prevention skills declined ($p < .05$, $M = 1.27$) whereas intervention teachers' did not ($M = 1.47$). Among fifth- and sixth-grade intervention students, this kind of support was associated with reduced victimization by aggression on the playground (Edstrom et al., 2004).

Intervention teachers showed a marginal increase, $F(1, 32) = 4.04, p < .06$, in coaching of students involved in bullying incidents after the start of program implementation ($Ms = 0.80$ and 1.02, respectively). Fifth- and sixth-grade teachers who coached bullying participants at least twice a week had students who were less aggressive at posttest than teachers who provided little or no coaching (Edstrom et al, 2004).

These findings suggest teacher support for skill use outside of lesson instruction may be a particularly promising avenue for influencing both norms and behavior related to bullying and playground aggression. Older students, arguably those most at risk for increasing involvement in bullying behavior (Pellegrini & Long, 2002), appeared to be particularly responsive to differences in teacher involvement (Edstrom et al., 2004).

STRENGTHS AND LIMITATIONS
OF THE PROGRAM AND RESEARCH

Adults and Environmental Changes

A number of promising changes in school environments and adult behavior were observed, including development of policy and procedures, parent outreach, training for all staff, improved teacher sense of preparedness to deal with bullying, and teacher support for student skill generalization. Notably, teacher support "in the moment" predicted improvements in students' behaviors.

Despite these promising signs, we were unable to test whether the program promoted true systemic change. Due to the small number of participating schools, school-level effects on program outcomes—factors deemed critical to bullying prevention (Olweus et al., 1999; Pepler et al., 1999; Smith & Sharp, 1994)—were not empirically examined. Additionally, our playground observers provided cautionary anecdotal information about the extent of systemic change after 6 months of program implementation.

Most troubling to us was that adult intervention in playground bullying and aggression was observed too infrequently to measure. The ratio of students to adults on playgrounds (as much as 120 to 1) may have presented logistical problems for adults to monitor and intervene effectively. Research shows that bully–victim problems decrease when the ratio of supervisors to students increases (Olweus, 1993). Coders on the playground, however, also observed supervisory adults brushing off student complaints of victimization. It is possible that this minimization of student distress reflected a "code of silence," taught and maintained by adults (Plunk & Frey, in press), which may have far-reaching implications for program effectiveness and school safety.

To be fair, there appeared to be considerable variation in levels of playground supervision and infrastructure among schools in our study. Some supervisors communicated via walkie-talkies, wore orange vests, and monitored identified regions of the playground. Others clustered close to the school building and were nonresponsive to students. Advancements in measurement related to playground conditions (e.g., Leff, Power, Costigan, & Manz, 2003) may enable researchers to further examine the roles of systemic support, training, and adult responsiveness, in effective responding to bullying problems. Examining contributions of administrators and structural supports to maintaining school safety and staff motivation may be particularly fruitful when viewed over time.

Classroom Lessons

Some investigators have expressed concern that information about specific classroom curricular content, learning objectives, and teaching methodology related to bullying has been limited (Rigby, 2002; Stevens, De Bourdeaudhuij, & Van Oost, 2001). Specificity in these areas is a particular strength of the Steps to Respect program. Research has yet to determine how much of student change is due to classroom curricula as distinguished from larger changes within a school. We note, however, that students' beliefs specifically targeted by classroom lessons were positively influenced, a finding that is consistent with the view that classroom-level intervention may be an important avenue for influencing norms and behavior related to bullying (Olweus et al., 1999).

More specifically, teacher practices employed in the Steps to Respect program are in line with Huesmann and Guerra's (1997) model of normative beliefs development. These practices include direct instruction in values and goals, positive teacher modeling, and reinforcement and coaching "in the moment" as bullying events unfold. Future research conducted with a larger school sample may help to further differentiate the impact of systemic school change, teacher effects, and classroom practices on children's beliefs.

The extent to which student social skill development was influenced by the program is unclear. Although we view emotion regulation as a foundation for performing specific skills (e.g., staying calm and responding assertively to bullying behavior), we did not directly test changes in this area. Reductions in argumentative playground behavior, however, may indicate a decline in anger among intervention students. This interpretation awaits empirical validation.

IMPLICATIONS FOR PRACTICE

We have already touched on a number of issues regarding implementation of the Steps to Respect program in this chapter. We briefly summarize five particularly important ones in the following section. Additionally, implications and recommended activities to support program goals can be found in Table 20.1.

1. Adult myths about bullying may hinder prevention efforts. For example, the belief that children who bully are disliked and disruptive may blind teachers to coercive acts and dynamics involving students who succeed in the classroom. There is evidence that popular students may wield considerable influence through bullying (Rodkin & Hodges, 2003), perhaps because their behaviors go undetected by adults. In our program evaluation, one teacher was concerned we had (randomly) selected the "wrong" students for observing bullying on the playground, as those in her classroom were nondisruptive and well liked. These children were later observed to frequently bully others. This suggests that adult training should provide information about the "democratic" nature of bullying within a school population, as well as helpful hints for discerning problems that may not be readily apparent.

2. There is evidence that teachers' support and coaching for student skill use, outside of lesson instruction, may pay off handsomely. This suggests administrators should create opportunities for staff to discuss and brainstorm strategies to provide ongoing, high levels of this kind of support. Specifically, this may involve increasing adult availability to help coach students in the throes of peer conflict and bullying events.

3. It is important to maintain adult awareness and motivation related to the program. Good practice includes ongoing training and use of strategies to keep a program visible and "acting proud" (Elias et al., 1997). One example we observed was a school reader board that read, "Ask us about the Steps to Respect program."

4. Motivation is strongly influenced by adult perceptions of program effectiveness. The Steps to Respect program was shown to be effective by virtue of having a control group. Many of our first-year findings contrasted deterioration of attitudes and behavior in schools *not* using the program to the maintenance of attitudes and behaviors in intervention schools. School staff members who do not have access to this kind of comparative data may miss important feedback that their efforts are worthwhile. For this reason, it is important that administrators actively sustain staff motivation. One principal used records of previous springtime increases in disciplinary referrals to demonstrate to her staff that a new intervention was working.

TABLE 20.1

Implications for Practice: Activities to Support Steps to Respect Program Goals

Goal	Administrators	Teachers and Other Staff
Develop and disseminate clear anti-bullying policy and procedures	• Post policy throughout school • Send policy to families • Visit classrooms to explain policy and school commitment to student safety • Identify "point people" to carry out specific procedures (e.g., follow up) with students involved in bullying.	• Teachers participate in formulating policy • Teachers post policy in classrooms • Other staff, such as counselors, support anti-bullying procedures (e.g., coaching)
Increase adult awareness monitoring, and guidance	• Enable all staff to attend initial trainings • Enable staff to attend booster trainings • Provide support and resources for effective playground and lunchroom supervision • Present family introduction materials	• Attend to behaviors of all students • Use the reporting model • Provide support of student skill use via coaching and reinforcement • Follow up with students involved in bullying incidents
Support staff and student motivation to prevent bullying	• Acknowledge responsible citizenship • Make program visible (e.g., posters) • Discuss program implementation at staff meetings • Publicize program effects (e.g., reductions in disciplinary incidents)	• Integrate program content with academic areas • Build bridges between program content and real-world world events • Recognize good citizenship
Support implementation integrity	• Use staff meetings to check in with teachers about how lessons are going • Check in regularly with other staff (playground monitors, bus drivers) about bullying and prevention efforts • During teacher evaluations, observe Steps to Respect lessons	• Teach lessons regularly • Model program skills • Support student skill use "in the moment"
Ensure student safety during survey administration	• Monitor student activity and communication • Use visual boundaries to insure privacy • Separate students as necessary • Communicate that participation is voluntary	• Use knowledge of your class to anticipate potential problems • Make sure students have privacy and room • Communicate that honesty is valued
Support evaluation needs	• Identify point person to coordinate evaluation activities • Schedule opportunities for staff and students to complete evaluation materials • Prepare yearly or semi-yearly report on areas for improvement related to program use	• Complete checklists about program implementation • Complete surveys about program

5. Use of student bullying surveys may actually elicit bullying behavior (Austin & Joseph, 1996). We witnessed several incidents when students attempted to coerce peers to refuse the survey or to answer in particular ways. Training related to ethical issues and methods of insuring a safe environment during survey administration may be an important addition to future bullying prevention programs.

CONCLUSION

Given increased concerns about school violence and the damage associated with bullying, there is growing consensus that schools must actively protect students. Because bullying unfolds in the context of peer groups and often goes undetected by adults, intervention poses challenges that require a universal approach that engages students and staff at the level of the individual, the classroom, and the entire school ecology.

Active adult involvement can correct the power imbalances inherent in bullying and bring about changes to increase school safety. Effective policy and procedures are the structural guideposts for making this occur. Additionally, program elements should address student social skills, beliefs, and bystander processes, as these appear to be important loci for change. Classroom-based lessons can provide practice in specific bullying prevention skills as well as general socioemotional skills such as emotion regulation, assertiveness, and empathy. They also provide models of positive leadership and courage, and convey powerful messages about respect and shared responsibility for school safety.

Evidence from a 1-year RCT indicates that the Steps to Respect program successfully reduced bullying and positively influenced student beliefs. Teachers receiving the program felt more prepared to deal effectively with bullying. In line with the conceptual foundations of the program, the beliefs and behaviors of students who received strong support for skill generalization were positively affected. It is our hope that future research may shed more light on the programmatic features and mechanisms that support these kinds of change.

REFERENCES

Andershed, H., Kerr, M., & Stattin, H. (2001). Bullying in school and violence on the streets: Are the same people involved? *Journal of Scandinavian Studies in Criminology and Crime Prevention, 2*, 31–49.

Atlas, R. S., & Pepler, D. J. (1998). Observations of bullying in the classroom. *Journal of Educational Research, 92*, 86–99.

Austin, S., & Joseph, S. (1996). Assessment of bully/victim problems in 8 to 11-year-olds. *British Journal of Educational Psychology, 66*, 447–456.

Bandura, A. (1986). *Social foundations of thought and action: A social cognitive theory*. Englewood, NJ: Prentice Hall.

Bandura, A. (2002). Selective moral disengagement in the exercise of moral agency. *Journal of Moral Education, 2*, 101–119.

Batsche, G. M. (1997). Bullying. In G. G. Bear, K. M. Minke, & A. Thomas (Eds.), *Children's needs II: Development, problems, and alternatives* (pp. 171–179). Bethesda, MD: National Association of School Psychologists.

Bjorkqvist, K., Lagerspetz, K. M., & Kaukiainen, A. (1992). Do girls manipulate and boys fight? Developmental trends in regard to direct and indirect aggression. *Aggressive Behavior, 18*, 117–127.

Boulton, M. J. (1997). Teachers' views on bullying: Definitions, attitudes, and ability to cope. *British Journal of Educational Psychology, 67*, 223–233.

Boulton, M. J., Trueman, M., Chau, C., Whitehand, C., & Amatya, K. (1999). Concurrent and longitudinal links between friendship and peer victimization: Implications for befriending interventions. *Journal of Adolescence, 22*, 461–466.

Coie, J. D., & Dodge, K. A. (1998). The development of aggression and antisocial behavior. In N. Eisenberg (Ed.), *Social, emotional, and personality development* (pp. 779–862). New York: Wiley.

Committee for Children. (2001). *Steps to Respect: A bullying prevention program*. Seattle, WA: Author.

Committee for Children (2005). *Steps to Respect: A bullying prevention program: Alignment with academic content standards*. [Brochure]. Seattle, WA: Author.

Connolly, J., Pepler, D., Craig, W., & Taradash, A. (2000). Dating experiences of bullies in early adolescence. *Child Maltreatment: Journal of the American Professional Society on the Abuse of Children, 5*, 299–310.

Consortium on the School Based Promotion of Social Competence. (1994). The school based promotion of social competence: Theory, research, practice, and policy. In R. J. Haggerty, L. R. Sherrod, N. Garmezy, & M. Rutter (Eds.), *Stress, risk, and resilience in children and adolescents: Processes, mechanisms, and interventions* (pp. 268–316). New York: Cambridge University Press.

Craig, W. M., & Pepler, D. J. (1995). Peer processes in bullying and victimization: An observational study. *Exceptionality Education Canada, 5*, 81–95.

Craig, W. M., & Pepler, D. J. (1997). Observations of bullying and victimization in the schoolyard. *Canadian Journal of School Psychology, 13*, 41–59.

Craig, W. M., Pepler, D., & Atlas, R. (2000). Observations of bullying in the playground and in the classroom. *School Psychology International Special Issue: Bullies and Victims, 21*, 22–36.

Crick, N. R., & Dodge, K. A. (1994). A review and reformulation of social information-processing mechanisms in children's social adjustment. *Psychological Bulletin, 115*, 74–101.

Dodge, K. A., & Coie, J. D. (1987). Social-information-processing factors in reactive and proactive aggression in children's peer groups. *Journal of Personality & Social Psychology, 53*, 1146–1158.

Dodge, K. A., Coie, J. D., Pettit, G. S., & Price, J. M. (1990). Peer status and aggression in boys' groups: Developmental and contextual analyses. *Child Development, 61*, 1289–1309.

Dodge, K. A., Price, J. M., Coie, J. D., & Hristopoulos, C. (1990). On the development of aggressive dyadic relationships in boys peer groups. *Human Development, 33*, 260–270.

Edstrom, L. V., Hirschstein, M., Frey, K., Snell, J. L., & MacKenzie, E. P. (2004, May). *Classroom level influences in school-based bullying prevention: Key program components and implications for instruction*. Paper presented at the annual meeting of the Society for Prevention Research, Quebec City, Canada.

Eisenberg, N., Fabes, R. A., Karbon, M., Murphy, B. C., Carlo, G., & Wosinski, M. (1996). Relations of school children's comforting behavior to empathy-related reactions and shyness. *Social Development, 5*, 330–351.

Eisenberg, N., Fabes, R. A., Shepard, S., Murphy, B. C., Guthrie, I., Jones, S., Friedman, J., Poulin, R., & Maszk, P. (1997). Contemporaneous and longitudinal prediction of children's social functioning from regulation and emotionality. *Child Development, 68*, 642–664.

Eisenberg, N., Wehtzel, M., & Harris, J. D. (1998). The role of emotionality and regulation in empathy-related responding. *School Psychology Review, 27*, 506–521.

Elias, M. J., Zins, J. E., Weissberg, R. P., Frey, K. S., Greenberg, M. T., Haynes, N. M., Kessler, R., Schwab-Stone, M. E., & Shriver, T. P. (1997). *Promoting social and emotional learning: Guidelines for educators*. Alexandria, VA: Association for Supervision and Curriculum Development.

Espelage, D. L., & Swearer, S. M. (2003). Research on school bullying and victimization: What have we learned and where do we go from here? *School Psychology Review, 32*, 365–383.

Frey, K. F., Hirschstein, M. K., & Guzzo, B. A. (2000). Second Step: Preventing aggression by promoting social competence. *Journal of Emotional and Behavioral Disorders, 8*, 102–112.

Frey, K. F., Hirschstein, M. K., Snell, J. L., Van Schoiack-Edstrom, L.V., MacKenzie, E. P., & Broderick, C. J. (2005). Reducing playground bullying and supporting beliefs: An experimental trial of the *Steps to Respect* program. *Developmental Psychology, 41*, 479–491.

Furlong, M. J., Morrison, G. M., & Grief, J. L. (2003). Reaching an American consensus: Reactions to the special issue on school bullying. *School Psychology Review, 32*, 456–470.

Graham, S., & Juvonen, J. (1998). Self-blame and peer victimization in middle school: An attributional analysis. *Developmental Psychology, 32*, 707–716.

Graham, S., & Juvonen, J. (2001). An attributional approach to peer victimization. In S. Graham and J. Juvonen (Eds.), Peer harassment in school: The plight of the vulnerable and victimized (pp. 49–72). New York: Guilford Press.

Grills, A. E., & Ollendick, T. H. (2002). Peer victimization, global self-worth, and anxiety in middle school children. *Journal of Clinical Child and Adolescent Psychology, 31*, 59–68.

Hanish, L. D., & Guerra, N. G. (2002). A longitudinal analysis of patterns of adjustment following peer victimization. *Development and Psychopathology, 14*, 69–89.

Hawker, D. S. J., & Boulton, M. J. (2000). Twenty years' research on peer victimization and psychosocial maladjustment: A meta-analytic review of cross-sectional studies. *Journal of Child Psychology & Psychiatry & Allied Disciplines, 41*, 441–455.

Hodges, E. V., Malone, M. J., Jr., & Perry, D. G. (1997). Individual risk and social risk as interacting determinants of victimization in the peer group. *Developmental Psychology, 33*, 1032–1039.

Hoover, J. H., Oliver, R., & Hazler, R. J. (1992). Bullying: Perceptions of adolescent victims in the Midwestern USA. *School Psychology International, 13*, 5–16.

Huesmann, L. R. (1988). An information processing model for the development of aggression. *Aggressive Behavior, 14*, 13–24.

Huesmann, L. R., & Guerra, N. G. (1997). Children's normative beliefs about aggression and aggressive behavior. *Journal of Personality & Social Psychology, 72*, 408–419.

Hymel, S., Bonanno, R. A., Henderson, N. R., & McCreith, T. (2002). *Moral disengagement & school bullying: An investigation of student attitudes and beliefs.* Paper presented at the International Society for Research on Aggression, Montreal, PQ.

Jeffrey, L. R., Miller, D., & Linn, M. (2001). Middle school and bullying as a context for the development of passive observers for the victimization of others, In R. A. Geffner, M. Loring, & C. Young (Eds.), *Bullying behavior: Current issues, research, and interventions* (pp. 143–156). Binghamton, NY: Haworth Maltreatment and Trauma Press.

Kaukiainen, A., Bjorkqvist, K., Lagerspetz, K., Osterman, K., Salmivalli, C., Rothberg, S., & Ahlbom, A. (1999). The relationships between social intelligence, empathy, and three types of aggression. *Aggressive Behavior, 25*, 81–89.

Kaukiainen, A., Salmivalli, C., Lagerspetz, K., Tamminen, M., Vauras, H. M., & Postkiparta, E. (2002). Learning difficulties, social intelligence, and self concept: Connections to bully-victim problems. *Scandinavian Journal of Psychology, 43*, 269–278.

Kendall, P. C. (1993). Cognitive-behavioral therapies with youth: Guiding theory, current status, and emerging developments. *Journal of Counseling and Clinical Psychology, 61*, 235–247.

Kochenderfer, B. J., & Ladd, G. W. (1997). Victimized children's responses to peers' aggression: Behaviors associated with reduced versus continued victimization. *Development & Psychopathology, 9*, 59–73.

Leary, M. R., Kowalski, R. M., Smith, L., & Phillips, S. (2003). Teasing, rejection, and violence: Case studies of school shootings. *Aggressive Behavior, 29*, 202–214.

Leff, S. S., Power, T. J., Costigan, T. E., & Manz, P. H. (2003). Assessing the climate of the playground and lunchroom: Implications for bullying prevention programming. *School Psychology Review, 32*, 418–430.

Limber, S. P., Cunningham, P., Florx, V., Ivey, J., Nation, M., Chai, S., & Melton, G. (1997, June/July). *Bullying among school children: Preliminary findings from a school-based intervention program.* Paper presented at the fifth International Family Violence Research Conference, Durham, NH.

Limber, S. P., & Small, M. A. (2003). State laws and policies to address bullying in schools. *School Psychology Review, 32*, 445–455.

Nansel, T. R., Overpeck, M., Pilla, R. S., Ruan, W. J., Simons-Morton, B., & Scheidt, P. (2001). Bullying behaviors among US youth: Prevalence and association with psychosocial adjustment. *Journal of the American Medical Association, 285*, 2094–2100.

Newman, R. S., Murray, B., & Lussier, C. (2001). Confrontation with aggressive peers at school: Students' reluctance to seek help from the teacher. *Journal of Educational Psychology, 91*, 398–410.

O'Connell, P., Pepler, D., & Craig, W. (1999). Peer involvement in bullying: Insights and challenges for intervention. *Journal of Adolescence, 22*, 437–452.

Oliver, R., Hoover, J. H., & Hazler, R. (1994). The perceived roles of bullying in small-town midwestern schools. *Journal of Counseling & Development, 72*, 416–420.

Olweus, D. (1991). Bully/victim problems among schoolchildren: Basic facts and effects of a school based intervention program. In D. J. Pepler & K. H. Rubin (Eds.), *The development and treatment of childhood aggression* (pp. 411–448). Hillsdale, NJ: Lawrence Erlbaum Associates.

Olweus, D. (1993). *Bullying at school: What we know and what we can do.* Cambridge, MA: Blackwell.

Olweus, D., Limber, S., & Mihalic, S. (1999). *Blueprints for violence prevention: Bullying prevention program* (Vol. 9). Boulder: Center for the Study and Prevention of Violence, Regents of the University of Colorado.

Owens, L., Slee, P., & Shute, R. (2000). "It hurts a hell of a lot …": The effects of indirect aggression on teenage girls. *School Psychology International, 21*, 359–376.

Pellegrini, A. D. (2001). Sampling instances of victimization in middle school: A methodological comparison. In J. Juvonen & S. Graham (Eds.), *Peer harassment in school: The plight of the vulnerable and victimized* (pp. 125–144). New York: Guilford.

Pellegrini, A. D., Bartini, M., & Brooks, F. (1999). School bullies, victims, and aggressive victims: Factors relating to group affiliation and victimization in early adolescence. *Journal of Educational Psychology, 91*, 216–224.

Pellegrini, A. D., & Long, J. D. (2002). A longitudinal study of bullying, dominance, and victimization during the transition from primary school through secondary school. *British Journal of Developmental Psychology, 20*, 259–280.

Pepler, D. J., Craig, W. M., & Connolly, J., & Henderson, K. (2002). Aggression and substance abuse in early adolescence: My friends made me do it. In C. Werkerle & A. M. Wall (Eds.), *The violence and addiction equation: Theoretical and clinical issues in substance abuse and relationship violence* (pp. 153–168). Philadelphia, PA: Brunner/Mazel.

Pepler, D., Craig, W. M., & O'Connell, P. (1999). Understanding bullying from a dynamic systems perspective. In A. Slater & D. Muir (Eds.), *The Blackwell reader in developmental psychology* (pp. 440–451). Malden, MA: Blackwell.

Perry, D. G., Hodges, E. V. E., & Egan, S. K. (2001). Determinants of chronic victimization by peers: A review and model of family influence. In J. Juvonen & S. Graham (Eds.), *Peer harassment in school: The plight of the vulnerable and victimized* (pp. 73–104). New York: Guilford.

Perry, D. G., Kusel, S. J., & Perry, L. C. (1988). Victims of peer aggression. *Developmental Psychology, 24*, 807–814.

Perry, D. G., Perry, L. C., & Rasmussen, P. (1986). Cognitive social learning mediators of aggression. Child Development, 57, 700–711.

Plunk, S, & Frey, K.S. (in press). Bullying and victimization: Making your school safer. In J. E., Zins & M. J. Elias (Eds.), *Building youth learning capacity and character: A Training and Resource Manual for Educators.*

Rigby, K. (2002). *A meta-evaluation of methods and approaches to reducing bullying in pre–schools and in early primary school in Australia.* Canberra: Commonwealth Attorney-General's Department.

Rigby, K., & Slee, P. T. (1991). Bullying among Australian school children: Reported behavior and attitudes toward victims. *Journal of Social Psychology, 131*, 615–627.

Rodkin, P. C., & Hodges, E. V. E. (2003). Bullies and victims in the peer ecology: Four questions for psychologists and school professionals. *School Psychology Review, 32*, 384–400.

Schwartz, D. (2000). Subtypes of victims and aggressors in children's peer groups. *Journal of Abnormal Child Psychology, 28*, 181–192.

Schwartz, D., Dodge, K. A., & Coie, J. D. (1993). The emergence of chronic peer victimization in boys' play groups. *Child Development, 64*, 1755–1772.

Schwartz, D., & Gorman, A. H. (2003). Community violence exposure and children's academic functioning. *Journal of Educational Psychology, 95*, 163–173.

Slaby, R. G., & Guerra, N. G. (1988). Cognitive mediators of aggression in adolescent offenders: I. Assessment. *Developmental Psychology, 24*, 580–588.

Slee, P. T. (1994). Situational and interpersonal correlates of anxiety associated with peer victimization. *Child Psychiatry and Human Development, 25*, 97–107.

Smith, P. K., & Brain, P. (2000). Bullying in schools: Lessons from two decades of research. *Aggressive Behavior Special Issue: Bullying in the Schools, 26*, 1–9.

Smith, P. K., & Sharp, S. (1994). *Tackling bullying in your school: A practical handbook for teachers.* New York: Routledge.

Snell, J., MacKenzie, E., & Frey, K. (2002). Bullying prevention in elementary schools: The importance of adult leadership, peer group support, and student social-emotional skills. In M. Shinn, H. Walker, & G. Stoner (Eds.), *Interventions for academic and behavior problems II: Preventive and remedial approaches* (pp. 351–372). Bethesda, MD: National Association of School Psychologists.

Stevens, V., De Bourdeaudhuij, I. & Van Oost, P. (2001). Anti-bullying interventions at school: Aspects of programme adaptation and critical issues for further programme development. *Health Promotion International, 16*, 155–167.

Swearer, S. M., & Doll, B. (2001). Bullying in schools: An ecological framework. In R. A. Geffner, M. Loring, & C. Young (Eds.), *Bullying behavior: Current issues, research, and interventions* (pp. 7–23). Binghamton, NY: The Haworth Maltreatment and Trauma Press.

Ter aesahjo, T., & Salmivall, C. (2003) "She is not actually bullied." The discourse of harassment in student groups. *Aggressive Behavior, 29*, 134–154.

Walker, H. M., & McConnell, S. R. (1995). *Walker-McConnell scale of social competence and school adjustment: Elementary version.* San Diego, CA: Singular.

Whitney, I., Rivers, I., Smith, P. K., & Sharp, S. (1994). The Sheffield project: Methodology and findings. In P. K. Smith & S. Sharp (Eds.), *School bullying: Insights and perspectives* (pp. 20–56). London: Routledge.

21

What We Can Learn From Evaluated Studies of School-Based Programs to Reduce Bullying in Schools

Ken Rigby
University of South Australia

The focus in this chapter is on effective programs to reduce bullying in schools. Bullying is not the same thing as aggression in general. Aggressive acts may sometimes be justified, for example, when one is being threatened and there are no alternative ways of responding to prevent oneself or one's friends from being hurt. Under such circumstances one may feel that acting or reacting in an aggressive manner is the only reasonable action. Bullying is a different matter. Typically, the bully is one who is not only in some way more powerful than the target of the aggression but is acting in a manner that is not justified. The unbiased observer, knowing the facts of the case, would reason that the aggression should not have taken place and conclude that the bully is acting in order to feel superior to the person being threatened.

It is also important to keep in mind that not all bullying is physical, as in physical assaults. Some is verbal, as may occur when a person is being repeatedly subjected to ridicule and unpleasant name calling. Bullying can also be indirect, as when a person is continually and unfairly excluded from a group or has nasty and untrue rumours spread about him or her. Often, the target of bullying experiences all three forms of bullying: physical, verbal, and indirect. Often, groups rather than individuals are the perpetrators.

Bullying others and being bullied by others is not, of course, an unusual experience. Most people engage in mild forms of bullying and are bullied occasionally by others at some point in their lives, mostly when they are at school. Of great concern are the extreme forms of bullying, for example, severe physical assaults, constant ridicule from everybody or nearly everybody, and total or near exclusion from being able to interact enjoyably with one's peers. This happens to quite a few children at school. In Australia, it is estimated that one child in six is subjected to bullying on a weekly basis (Rigby, 2002b). The targeted child often suffers a great deal, especially if the bullying treatment goes on for months or even for years.

THE HARM BULLYING DOES

A great deal of research has dealt with the effects of bullying on the mental and physical health of children. (For a comprehensive overview of this research, see Rigby, 2003b.) Suffice here to say that it is commonly observed that severely victimized children typically lose self-esteem, become seriously anxious and depressed, and may become suicidal. Such children may become socially alienated and refuse to go to school. The consequences for the mental health of severely victimized children may extend into the adult years and result in periodic bouts of depression and an inability to trust others and act confidently with people they meet (Rigby, 2003b).

The harm of bullying does not end here. Some children who are bullied seek an opportunity to retaliate. Children who have been assaulted by their peers have been known to attack and kill their oppressor, when the opportunity arose. Children who have become alienated through group rejection have been known to take it out on others, some of whom may not have been involved in the indirect form of bullying. The now infamous Columbine killings were perpetrated by young people who believed they had a grievance against those who had treated them badly or had seemed to collude in their social ostracism.

THE CONTINUUM OF BULLYING

Sometimes it is questioned whether we should be concerned about the relatively mild forms of bullying that go on in every school when there are more serious acts of violence occur. Levels of bullying are on a continuum, from mild to extreme, and by addressing the less extreme forms of bullying (such as name calling, minor episodes of unpleasant and resented pushing and shoving, and periodic exclusion) one is, in fact, making it much less likely that the more serious kinds of bullying will occur.

The intensity of bullying behavior in a school is typically distributed in a skewed manner (see Fig. 21). Data for Fig. 21.1 were taken from a sample of 200 boys and 200 girls between the ages of 10 and 14 years attending Australian co-educational schools in 2003. The students were asked to answer questions about how often they had been bullied at school in each of six ways during the present year. These included physical, verbal, and indirect ways. Students could answer "never," "sometimes" or "often." Scores between 0 and 12 were computed to provide a measure of the level of reported bullying.

It is clear from Fig. 21.1 that being intensively bullied at school by other children is the lot of comparatively few. Most children are bullied relatively infrequently; some not at all. When we look at the other side of the picture, the frequency with which children engage in bullying

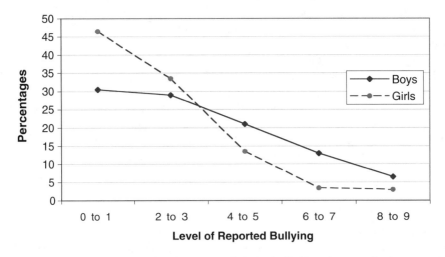

FIG. 21.1.   Frequency levels of reportedly being bullied by others at school.

others at school, we find a similarly skewed distribution. That is, the bulk of children rarely engage in frequently bullying others; a small minority carry out or instigate a great deal of the bullying that occurs.

In the past when school authorities have thought about bullying, they usually concentrated exclusively on the 5% or so of children who constantly bully others: the repeated offenders. It was generally believed that the cause of bullying behavior was located in the dysfunctional personality of the bully and was unaffected by the behavior of others. Increasingly, schools have recognized the role played by other students who may seldom bully others but nevertheless encourage the more "committed bullies" by contributing to an ethos of acceptance of bullying behavior, for example, by engaging in occasional or minor acts of bullying and/or by encouraging and admiring those who impose themselves on others. Hence, schools have increasingly turned their attention to bullying that occurs throughout the whole continuum of bullying and to the social context in which bullying occurs.

EXPLANATIONS FOR BULLYING

Among those who are addressing bullying in schools, a good deal of controversy exists on why bullying occurs. A variety of explanations have been offered. These explanations are important because they have implications for how schools should act to prevent bullying and deal with any cases that occur. Various "explanations" for bullying need to be examined, as far as possible in relation to the available evidence. It may turn out that there is no single "correct" explanation. Each may, in a given context, be useful, and suggest ways of dealing with particular problems. What follows is an overview of proposed explanations.

Bullying as a Developmental Process

According to this perspective, bullying normally begins in early childhood when children begin to assert themselves at the expense of others in order to establish their social dominance. Children tend at first to do so crudely; for instance by hitting out at others in an attempt to intimidate them, especially those less powerful than themselves. This view resonates with evolutionary theory, which argues that domination over others has been, and still is, a primary goal ensuring an individual's survival in a competitive environment. It is seen as the means by which the strongest prevail and the existence of the species is prolonged. However, as Hawley (1999) pointed out, as children develop they gradually discover and begin to employ less socially reprehensible ways of dominating others. Verbal and indirect forms of bullying become more common than physical forms. Judging from the self-reports of children, the kind of behavior that is generally labeled as *bullying* becomes progressively rare (Olweus, 1993; Smith & Sharp, 1994), although, it is fair to say, results based on peer nominations and teacher reports have not confirmed this trend (Salmivalli, 2002). Furthermore, although there is a general diminution in reported victimization over time, when children leave primary school and begin secondary school there is often a temporary upsurge in reported bullying. The new school environment is typically less benign (Rigby, 2002b). Social or contextual factors evidently may outweigh developmental ones.

This developmental view of bullying has appeal to some schools. It suggests that bullying is part of a natural developmental process. This may give comfort to schools in that it suggests that its prevalence does not mean that schools are to blame. This may, unfortunately, lead to schools ignoring the problem. On the positive side, it may motivate some schools to seek to expedite the process according to which children mature and get "beyond" bullying, for example, by encouraging children to behave more responsibly.

Understanding that the nature of bullying changes as children become older may result in teachers becoming more sensitive to the more subtle forms of bullying practiced by older children. These can, in fact, be more devastating than the more obvious and overt forms (Eslea & Rees, 2001; Rigby & Bagshaw, 2001). Teachers may also be encouraged to consider age-appropriate ways of seeking to influence children at different stages of their development.

Bullying as the Outcome of Individual Differences

According to this view, bullying occurs as a result of encounters between children who differ in their personal power. Commonly, the more powerful child is motivated to seek out and oppress the less powerful and to do so repeatedly. In a school there are always considerable imbalances in power between children, related to physical and/or psychological differences. The conjunction of being relatively powerful and also motivated to dominate others is seen as the major reason why bullying occurs in schools.

Much research has been undertaken to identify the physical and psychological factors that are associated with acting in a bullying way and/or being bullied by another person or group of persons at school. It has been reported that children who continually bully others tend to be physically stronger than average, to be generally aggressive, manipulative and low in empathy (Farley, 1999; Olweus, 1993; Sutton & Keogh, 2000). Children who are more often victimized tend to be physically weaker, more introverted, and to have lower self-esteem than others (Mynard & Joseph, 1997; O'Moore & Hillery, 1991; Slee & Rigby, 1993).

At least some of these differences may have genetic bases. It has been reported that identical twins are significantly more likely to be similar in their tendency to bully their peers than fraternal twins (O'Connor, Foch, Todd, & Plomin, 1980). Furthermore, the quality of family life is thought to contribute to a tendency for some children to engage in bullying their peers. Dysfunctional families and oppressive parenting have been implicated in promoting aggressive behavior of children toward their peers (Rigby, 1994).

Although teachers can have only limited influence on the parenting of children who attend their school—and none upon any genetic influences transmitted by parents—this view of the causes of bullying has some practical implications. It draws attention to the importance of identifying individuals who are likely to become "problems," especially children who appear predisposed to act aggressively without concern for the well-being of others, or have characteristics that suggest that they are more likely than others to be victimized. Teachers may be encouraged to seek to modify the behavior of such children by counseling and/or by disciplinary means. Efforts may also be made to help children who are often victimized to become less vulnerable, for example by acquiring relevant social skills, especially greater assertiveness (Field, 1999; Smith & Sharp, 1994).

Bullying as a Sociocultural Phenomenon

A further perspective seeks to explain bullying as an outcome of the existence of social groups that have different levels of power. The focus is typically on differences that may have, at least in part, an historical and cultural basis, for example, gender, race or ethnicity, and social class. Differences due to some children being less "able" or having different religious affiliations may also be included.

Major emphasis has been placed on differences associated with gender. Society is seen as essentially patriarchal. Males are viewed as generally having more power than females as a consequence of pervading social beliefs that they should be the dominant gender. In order to maintain their dominance, boys may feel justified in oppressing girls. Numerous studies have, in fact, indicated that boys are more likely than girls to initiate bullying (Olweus, 1993, Smith

& Sharp, 1994). Moreover, it is clear that boys are more likely to bully girls than vice versa. In a large-scale Australian study of some 38,000 children, a much higher proportion of girls claimed to be bullied exclusively by boys (22.1%) than boys reporting being bullied only by girls (3.4%) (Rigby, 1997). Cross-gender bullying is clearly mostly one-way traffic. This may derive, in part, from the way in which some boys have come to think about how they should behave in the company of girls. Some boys may come to believe that it is acceptable to harass or sexually coerce girls (see Rosenbluth, Whitaker, Sanchez, & Valle, 2004). The process according to which boys come to develop characteristics that lead to them engaging in oppressive behavior is sometimes described as "the construction of hegemonic masculinity" (Connell, 1995; Gilbert & Gilbert, 1998). This is held not only to account largely for boys bullying girls, but also for boys bullying boys who clearly do not possess stereotypical masculine qualities. Such children are commonly referred to as "gay" and may include children whose sexual orientation is homosexual. The use of language with sexual connotations to insult children regarded as "gay" is certainly widely prevalent in schools (Duncan, 1999), although the extent to which it occurs has surprisingly not, as yet, been investigated. Explaining the bullying of girls by girls can invoke the notion of the construction of femininity, with girls deviating from an idealized conception of what it is (or should be) to be feminine.

It is sometimes claimed that bullying tends to be associated with racial or ethnic divides. It is argued that some ethnic groups are more powerful than others and seek to dominate them. Typically, the less powerful are the victims of colonization. For example, indigenous communities in Australia in the late 18th century were subjected to British colonialism. Aboriginal people were seen by many as inferior—this perception still lingers in the minds of people who retain racist beliefs. It is sometimes argued that the "superior" status of the racially or ethnically dominant groups is most threatened among "poor Whites" who are afraid their jobs may be taken by non-Whites. Under such circumstances, hostility and prejudice toward non-Whites are likely to be particularly intense. Through a process of cultural transmission, some non-indigenous children may feel justified in bullying their Aboriginal peers.

To date, however, there is little consistent evidence that racial or ethnic factors render one group more likely to be bullied by outsiders than another. For example, the results of studies conducted in the Netherlands (Junger-Tas, 1999), in Britain (Boulton, 1995), and in Germany (Losel & Bliesener, 1999) failed to support the view that particular ethnic groups were more frequently targeted than others. Nevertheless, an exception has been reported in Australia. In a large-scale study of Australian schoolchildren ($N = 38.684$) Aboriginal children (2% of the sample) reported "being called hurtful names" significantly more often than other ethnic groups. Some 15.9% of Aboriginal children compared with 12.5% of non-Aboriginal children reported experiencing such verbal abuse from others (Rigby, 2002b). This suggests the racial differences in the extent to which children are bullied at school. It is not clear, however, in this study from whom the verbal abuse commonly reported by Aboriginal children originates.

In some accounts of factors affecting bullying, it is suggested that children from families with high social status employ this source of power to bully those who are less privileged. However, studies have so far failed to show that children from lower socioeconomic class homes are more likely to be bullied than children from upper socioeconomic class homes. Olweus (1993) claimed that among boys attending Swedish schools, bullying was unrelated to social class as indicated by indices of parent income level and length of parent education. In studies conducted in Spain, Portugal, and France, bullying has not been found to be related to social class (Almeida, 1999; Duyme, 1990; Ortegas, & Mora-Merchan, 1999).

This perspective providing, as it does, an exclusive or near exclusive reliance on a sociocultural perspective on bullying can have striking implications for how a school approaches the problem of bullying. It directs attention to how a school curriculum can influence children to accept and respect sociocultural differences. It has been suggested that the school curriculum should explicitly and directly address issues related to gender, race or ethnicity, and social class in order to counter prejudice and discrimination. Furthermore, it encourages the view that the mode of delivery of the curricula should indirectly address bullying in the way it promotes cooperative problem solving, emotional sensitivity, and independent critical thinking. The Australian national Website on bullying (http://www.bullyingnoway.com.au/), based mainly on a sociocultural approach to bullying, has placed primary emphasis on this approach (for a more detailed critique of this contribution, see Rigby, 2003a).

Bullying as a Response to Peer Pressures Within the School

This approach has something in common with the sociocultural approach in that it conceives bullying as operating in a social context. However, the context is not simply defined according to sociocultural categories such as gender, race, and class. There is first a broad social context consisting of the behaviors and attitudes of members of the entire school community. This is sometimes called the 'school ethos.' Second, there are smaller groups of peers with whom individuals have relatively closer association. Within a school, such groups are typically formed as a result of perceived common interests and purposes. They provide support for group members, and they may also become a threat to outsiders, sometimes to ex-members, whom they may decide to bully. The motive for doing so may be a grievance or imagined grievance, a prejudice (explicable in sociocultural terms), or simply a desire to have fun at the expense of another person. Importantly, the acts of bullying are seen as typically sustained by a connection with the group (this might be described as peer pressure or allegiance to a group) rather than by individual motives such as personal malevolence.

This view presupposes that bullying is typically a group phenomenon. Early studies of bullying in Scandinavia employed the term *mobbing* suggesting that children are bullied by mobs of children operating in a pack. Although this may sometimes occur, more commonly in schools one or several individuals with the support of others in a group carry out bullying. Often, bullying is carried out in the presence of bystanders. According to a Canadian study, bystanders are present when a child is being bullied at school on about 85% of occasions (Pepler & Craig, 1995). Some of the bystanders reinforce the bullying, either actively or alternatively by providing a noncritical audience. According to Canadian researchers, when a bystander expresses disapproval of the bullying there is a strong possibility that it will stop (Hawkins, Pepler, & Craig, 2001).

The implication for schools is that they should be aware of the roles played by groups as distinct from individuals. They need to identify groups and work with them. Several methods have been devised for working with groups of children who have bullied or are suspected of bullying others. One, the No Blame Approach (Robinson & Maines, 1997), involves a teacher or counselor meeting with the group of children identified as having bullied someone. Some other children who are known to be socially responsible are also invited to attend. The teacher describes to the group the suffering that has been endured by the victim, and the group is expected to consider ways in which the situation can be improved. The "non-bullies" in the group are expected to exert positive peer pressure; that is, influence the "bullies" to act more benevolently toward the victim. An alternative method, generally used with older children, called the Method of Shared Concern (Pikas, 1989, 2002) involves working initially with individuals suspected of being in a group that is bullying someone. The teacher's aim here is to communicate his or her concern for the victim and invite (and then monitor) responsible individual action—and in so doing to lessen the influence the group. At a subsequent stage, bullies and victim are brought together to overcome any unresolved conflict (for a full account and critique of showed concern, see Rigby, K. (2005). Recognition of the importance of the role of bystanders has led some schools, for example in Finland and in Australia (Rigby & Johnson, 2004a, 2004b; Salmivalli, Kaukiainen, Voeten, & Mäntykorpi, 2004).

Bullying From the Perspective of Restorative Justice

This perspective recognizes that some children are more likely than others to be involved in bully–victim problems as a consequence of the kind of character they have developed. Children who bully others typically feel little or no pride in their school and are not well integrated into the community (Morrison, 2002). They mishandle their emotional reactions to the distress they cause by *not* experiencing appropriate feelings of shame; in fact, they tend to attribute unworthy characteristics to those they victimize. By contrast, victims are prone to experience too much inappropriate shame. To some extent, this perspective is one that emphasises individual differences. But in addition, an important role is ascribed to the school community and to significant people who are implicated in the problem. These latter can include family and friends of both bullies and victims: that is, significant others who care about them.

It is believed that appropriate feelings of shame should be engendered in those who bully others and this can be done by exposing them to criticism from those they have offended. This, it is thought, can be done constructively in the presence of those who really care about them. Success is seen as greatly dependent on the support provided by those who care about the perpetrator as a person, while, at the same time, disapproving of his or her past behavior (Morrison, 2002). This approach is concerned with "violations against people" and the restoration of positive relationships rather than applying punishment for breaking rules (Cameron & Thorsborne, 2001).

This view has encouraged some schools to concentrate on promoting values likely to lead to responsible citizenship, such as pride in one's school and an obligation to help others. Addressing problems of bullying is seen as requiring confrontations with perpetrators, the deliberate inducement in them of appropriate shame, and action undertaken by them to restore positive relations with the victim. When serious cases of bullying occur, the use of community conferences is recommended, at which victims are encouraged to express their sense of hurt while perpetrators listen, become contrite, and agree to compensate the victim (see Thorsborne & Vinegrad, 2003).

THE NATURE OF PROGRAMS ADDRESSING BULLYING

Between 1985 and 2001 there has been a substantial number of evaluations of the effectiveness of anti-bullying programs. These have been exhaustively reviewed in Rigby (2002a) and Smith, Pepler, and Rigby (2004). Each of these studies involved measurements of the incidence of children's aggressive or bullying behavior at school or kindergarten before and after an intervention. Mostly, estimates were based on self-reports of students. In some cases, peer nominations were used; in others, teachers or researchers made systematic observations of children's behavior. Some evaluations involved a substantial number of schools, as many as 42; others involved as few as one. In some of the studies, control schools were used, a desirable procedure because pretesting itself can raise awareness of bullying and result in an apparent increase.

1. The programs have typically contained a variety of elements (Rigby, 2003c). This being so, it is generally not possible to identify the crucial factor or factors contributing significantly to the outcome. Most programs have included educational programs aimed in the first place

at improving teacher awareness and understanding of the phenomena of bullying. These have commonly made use of surveys of school bullying followed by discussions of the findings with members of the school community.

2. The development of school anti-bullying policies that receive support from members of the school community, including students and parents.

3. The introduction of relevant curriculum material to raise awareness of bullying among students and promote the acquisition of prosocial values and skills, for example, tolerance for differences, assertiveness—to discourage bullies—and proactive behavior on the part of bystanders.

4. Implement procedures for dealing with actual cases of bullying.

There have been differences in emphases on these elements. For example, some programs have been concerned primarily with developing a positive school or classroom ethos in which certain key values are promoted, such as cooperativeness (Cowie, Smith, Boulton, & Laver, 1994), caring relationships (Ortega & Lera, 2000), respect and consideration for others (Ahmed, Harris, Braithwaite, & Braithwaite, 2001), the appropriate acknowledgment and management of shame (Morrison, 2002), and friendliness (Cross, Hall, Hamilton, Pintabona, & Erceg, 2004).

Emphasis has also been placed on the acceptance of social and cultural differences between students. Central to such programs has been the use of relevant curriculum material and the employment of cooperative teaching strategies. In some programs, specific skills have been taught to make aggressive behavior less likely. For example, in Chicago, in the late 1990s, McMahon, Washburn, Felix, Yakin, and Childrey (2000) introduced into the curriculum for kindergarten children, lessons designed to help them manage their anger, to act assertively rather than aggressively, and to develop greater empathy. Programs have also been devised and implemented to train students to act as mediators and/or positive bystanders when they witness bullying at school, as in a recent program developed by Menesini in Italy, described in Rigby, Smith, and Pepler (2004).

To a large extent, the decision to concentrate more on the production of positive interpersonal relationships as an antidote to bullying has been informed by a view that the social context in which bullying takes place may be more important than the individual personal predispositions of students, for example, the desire to dominate others.

Probably the most conspicuous difference between programs lies in what action needs to be taken when a case of bullying is discovered. On the one hand, there are programs that strongly emphasize the need for clear rules against bullying, a zero tolerance policy, and corresponding sanctions to be administered if the rules are broken. This view is implicit in the programs developed by Olweus (1993), Limber et al. (2004), Alsaker and Valkanover (2001), and Stevens, de Bourdeaudhuij, and Van Oost (2000). This emphasis is also evident in the use of community conferences employed to address severe bully–victim problems from the perspective of restorative justice. Although it cannot be said that these programs have ignored the social context—there is in Olweus's program, for instance, a strong recommendation that teachers work in classes with students to develop acceptable rules of behavior—the emphasis is on discouraging bullying by applying sanctions or procedures that "send a message" to other potential bullies that they could face similar consequences. The sanctions are to be "nonphysical" and parental involvement is seen as very important.

In contrast to the Olweus model, some programs have largely or entirely disavowed the use of such sanctions. For example, a number of programs have incorporated the so-called No-Blame Approach of Robinson and Maines (1997) or the Method of Shared Concern of Pikas (1989, 2002). In place of rules and sanctions, they propose that teachers or counselors can work with students who have bullied others to change their perception of how they should behave. They seek to encourage more positive ways for students to relate to their peers. It should be understood that in neither of these methods is it presumed that the perpetrators have no responsibility for their actions. Rather, it is assumed that changing behavior in a positive direction can best be achieved by taking a *non*-accusatory stance and allowing group processes to influence outcomes—with the skilled connivance of the counselor or mediator! These programs—or adaptations of them—have been used in a number of evaluated programs in England (Smith & Sharp, 1994), in Spain (Ortega & Lera, 2000), Finland (Salmivalli et al., 2004), and Australia (Petersen & Rigby, 1999).

Further differences may be found in the extent to which those who have introduced anti-bullying programs have involved themselves closely in the continued guidance or implementation of school-based interventions. In some programs, close "hands-on" control and/or guidance has been provided by the research team (e.g., Alsaker & Valkanover, 2001; Olweus, 1993). Some others have allowed schools more autonomy in choosing what to do and how to do it (e.g., Ortega & Lera, 2000; Smith & Sharp, 1994).

HOW SUCCESSFUL HAVE THE PROGRAMS BEEN?

Outcomes have been variable. The largest claim of success thus far was an approximate 50% reduction in reported bullying by Dan Olweus in the Bergen area of Norway in the 1980s. Some have had quite small or negligible effect, for instance, the Canadian program introduced in Toronto schools during the 1990s (Pepler, Craig, Ziegler, & Charach, 1994). More typical have been the results of a large-scale intervention in the Sheffield area of England in which an average reduction of 15% of students being bullied was reported for a sample of primary school children (Smith & Sharp, 1994). Most reported reductions have, in fact, been modest in size (see Smith et al., 2004, for a comprehensive account of major intervention outcomes).

It is evident that reductions in bullying following interventions have tended to occur more often among young students than among older students. Furthermore, the reductions have typically occurred more often in the numbers of students being bullied rather than in the number of students bullying others. Finally, reductions were much greater in schools where the programs had been carried out most thoroughly. This was the case in each of the three studies in which measures were taken of the extent to which the programs had actually been implemented in England (Smith & Sharp, 1994), in Spain (Ortega & Lera, 2000), and Finland (Salmivalli et al., 2004).

Broadly, it is possible to differentiate between two kinds of programs, one emphasizing the use of rules and consequences, along the lines suggested by Olweus (1993) and the other relying more on problem-solving approaches to countering bullying. The former has had notable successes, especially when it was implemented in the Bergen area of Norway and more recently in Oslo (Olweus, 2004). Not all applications in Norway have been reported as successful. An analysis of results obtained in Rogaland (south of Bergen) indicated an actual increase in bullying behavior 3 years after the implementation of the Olweus program (Roland, 1993). Generally, results for programs based on the Olweus model outside Norway have been mixed, with none approaching the 50% reduction rate reported in Bergen. When an approach emphasising rules and consequences was implemented among kindergarten children in Switzerland, there were moderate improvements reported on some indices of change, but not on others (Alsaker & Valkanover, 2001). In both Flanders and Schleswig Holstein, it has been reported that a program following the Olweus model reduced bullying minimally in primary schools but not at all in secondary school (Hanewinkel, 2004; Stevens et al., 2000). An implementation of the Olweus Bullying Prevention Program in southeastern United States (Limber et al., 2004) produced disappointing results. Although significant reductions in peer victimization for boys (but not for girls) were reported after 1 year, 2 years later differences from the baseline level of peer victimization were not significant for either boys or girls. Outside Norway, evidence supporting the effectiveness of the Olweus model appears to be sparse.

Programs incorporating problem-solving approaches appear to have been more consistently positive, although in none of the implementations have the reductions in bullying been large. Consistent (although generally small) reductions in the numbers of children being bullied following the implementation of programs using problem-solving method have been reported in studies of the effects of interventions in England (Smith & Sharp, 1994), in Spain (Ortega & Lera, 2000), in Finland (Salmivalli et al., 2004), and in Australia (Petersen & Rigby, 1999). At the same time, it would be premature to suggest that there is clear evidence of the superiority of one approach over another.

A factor in the success or otherwise of anti-bullying programs may be the level of involvement by the initiators in the guidance and implementation of the program. It has been suggested that the close involvement of Olweus in the Norwegian anti-bullying program in the Bergen area may have accounted for its relatively high level of effectiveness in reducing bullying. In contrast, Roland (1993) reported much less successful results in another part of Norway, where the anti-bullying program failed to produce positive outcomes. On the other hand, it seems that involvement by those introducing a program can be too close, and deprive schools of needed autonomy in the work they do in countering bullying (Stevens et al., 2000). The fairly successful anti-bullying initiative headed by Peter Smith in England required that the schools implementing the program fulfill some requirements, for example, develop a school anti-bullying policy, but were free to choose from a range of possible intervention methods suggested by Smith and his team (Smith et al., 1994).

It is now clear that it is important to counter bullying in the early years of schooling. Young children, it seems, be more readily be influenced to become less involved in bullying than older children. Arguably, they are less resistant to adult influence than adolescents. It also seems possible that different methods of dealing with bully–victim cases are needed for adolescent and preadolescent students. Stevens et al. (2000) suggested that punitive methods are less likely to be effective with older students. With them, problem-solving approaches may be more successful. Finally, interventions are evidently more successful in helping children to protect themselves from the bullies than in stopping those who bully. Victimized children are more strongly motivated to learn how to change their behavior than those who bully.

In summary, the results from evaluations of anti-bullying programs have been on the whole, encouraging, especially among younger students. Although the reductions in bullying have typically been modest in size, nearly all the programs have produced some significant results. Thus, it is not possible to state unequivocally what elements should be incorporated in anti-bullying programs to ensure maximum success. Much more research is needed. But it is clear, however, that success is likely to be greater when programs are more thoroughly implemented.

SOME GENERAL CONCLUSIONS

There has been a remarkable rise of interest in the subject of bullying since the 1980s. This has occurred in many countries around the world. In an important book by Smith et al. (1999) reports on countering bullying were featured from Australia, Belgium, Brazil, Cambodia, Canada, Columbia, El Salvador, England, Ethiopia, Finland, France, Germany, Guatemala, Ireland, Italy, Japan, Jordan, Malawi, Malaysia, Netherlands, New Zealand, Nicaragua, Norway, Palestine, Peru, Poland, Portugal, Scotland, Sierra Leone, Spain, Sweden, Switzerland, United

States, and Wales. With increased awareness of the prevalence and harm that bullying does, in many of these countries anti-bullying programs have been developed and implemented in schools.

As we have seen, there has been some notable variation in the ways in which bullying has been understood and explained. These have included the stage of social development of children; individual differences in personality; community prejudices and views about how power should be used (and what constitutes an abuse of power); and the social pressures and influences that affect the way children relate to each other at school. Some programs have especially targeted bullies, some victims, some bystanders, some the entire school community. Some programs have emphasized the use of rules and consequences; some others, the use of problem-solving methods. The proposed explanations and views on how the problem of bullying should be tackled have generated a wide range of anti-bullying initiatives (see Rigby, 2003c; Rigby & Thomas, 2003). However, it is becoming evident that no single explanation covers all cases of bullying. No single method of preventing or dealing with bullying has been shown to be consistently more effective than others. Evaluations of anti-bullying programs around the world indicate that modest reductions in bullying in schools can be achieved with careful planning and diligent implementation of policies and programs. The need to improve our understanding of bullying and how to counter it remains. Meanwhile, an important start has been made, and school educators need to learn from the experience of others and reflect on their own efforts and experiences.

SUMMARY OF IMPLICATIONS FOR PRACTICE: A PERSONAL VIEW

As I argued in this chapter, I do not believe that research into the effectiveness of school anti-bullying programs has provided a blueprint for success. We simply do not know what best practice is. Looking at the research, educational professionals can legitimately come to different conclusions. As a researcher and ex-school teacher who has sought over the last 15 years to make sense of the existing research that has been done to address the problem of bullying, I have opinions for which I think there is some theoretical and empirical support of the kind I have outlined here. These may well change as we accumulate more knowledge and understanding of why children bully at school and how such behavior can be presented. Table 21.1 represents my personal view on what schools should do (a further elaboration may be found in Rigby, 2003c).

TABLE 21.1
Reducing Bullying in the Schools: Implications for Practice

1. Seek to understand the nature, prevalence, and effects of bullying among students in one's school, drawing on survey data.
2. Share the findings with members of the school community in order to raise awareness of the bullying and its effects on children, thereby motivating school authorities to address the problem.
3. Develop an anti-bullying policy, well supported by the entire school community. This should include guidelines to help the school to identify, prevent, and deal with bullying incidents.
4. Work with children in classes to develop an understanding of bullying and its effects, and help children to acquire attitudes, values, and skills that will enable them to protect themselves from being bullied, get help (if needed), and assist others who need their help.
5. Devise and utilize methods of dealing with cases of bullying that are (a) appropriate, given the severity of the offense and the age of the child; (b) well-supported by the school community; and (c) likely to lead to the underlying conflict between children being resolved.

REFERENCES

Ahmed, E., Harris, N., Braithwaite, J., & Braithwaite, V. (2001). *Shame management through reintegration*, Melbourne, Australia: Cambridge University Press.

Almeida, A. (1999). Portugal. In P. K. Smith, Y. Morita, J. Junger-Tas, D. Olweus, R. Catalano, & P. T. Slee (Eds.), *The nature of school bullying: A cross-national perspective* (pp. 174–186). London: Routledge.

Alsaker, F. D., & Valkanover, S. (2001). Early diagnosis and prevention of victimization in kindergarten. In J. Juvonen & S. Graham (Eds.), *Peer harassment in school* (pp. 175–195). New York: Guilford.

Boulton, M. J. (1995). Patterns of bully/victim problems in mixed race groups of children. *Social Development 4*, 277–293.

Cameron, L., & Thorsborne, M. (2001). Restorative justice and school discipline: Mutually exclusive? In J. Braithwaite & H. Strang (Eds.), *Restorative justice and civil society* (pp. 180–194). Cambridge, England: Cambridge University Press, Cambridge.

Connell, R. (1995). *Masculinities*. Sydney: Allen & Unwin.

Cowie, H., Smith, P. K., Boulton, M., & Laver, R. (1994). *Cooperation in the multi-ethnic classroom*. London: David Fulton.

Cross, D., Hall, M., Hamilton, G., Pintabona, Y., & Erceg, E. (2004). Australia: The Friendly Schools Project. In P. K Smith, D. Pepler, & K. Rigby (Eds.), *Bullying in schools: How successful can interventions be?* (pp. 187–221). Cambridge, England: Cambridge University Press.

Duncan, N. (1999). *Sexual bullying: gender conflict and pupil culture in secondary schools*. London: Routledge.

Duyme, M. D. (1990). Antisocial behaviour and postnatal environment: A French adoption study. *Journal of Child Psychology & Psychiatry & Allied Disciplines, 31*, 699–671.

Eslea, M., & Rees, J. (2001). At what age are children most likely to be bullied at school? *Aggressive Behaviour, 27*, 419–429.

Farley, R. L. (1999). *Does a relationship exist between social perception, social intelligence and empathy for students with a tendency to be a bully, a victim or bully/victim?* Unpublished honors thesis, Adelaide Psychology Department, University of Adelaide.

Field, E. M. (1999). *Bully busting*. Lane Cove, NSW: Finch Publishing.

Gilbert, R., & Gilbert, P. (1998). *Masculinity goes to school*. St. Leonards, NSW: Allen & Unwin.

Hanewinkel, R. (2004). Prevention of bullying in German schools: An evaluation of an anti-bullying approach. In P. K. Smith, D. Pepler, & K. Rigby (Eds.), *Bullying in schools: How successful can interventions be* (pp 81–98)? Cambridge, England: Cambridge University Press.

Hawley, P. H. (1999). The ontogenesis of social dominance: a strategy-based evolutionary perspective. *Developmental Review, 19*, 97–132.

Hawkins, D., Pepler, D. J., & Craig, W. M. (2001). Naturalistic observations of peer interventions in bullying. *Social Development, 10*, 512–527.

Junger-Tas, J. (1999). The Netherlands. In P. K Smith, Y. Morita, J. Junger-Tas, D. Olweus, R. Catalano, & P. T. Slee (Eds.), *The nature of school bullying: A cross-national perspective* (pp. 205–223). London: Routledge.

Limber, S. P., Maury, N., Allison J., Tracy, T., Melton, G. B., & Flerx, V. (2004). Implementation of the Olweus Bullying Prevention Program in the southeastern United States. In P. K Smith, D. Pepler, & K., Rigby (Eds.), *Bullying in schools: How successful can interventions be* (pp. 55–80)? Cambridge, England: Cambridge University Press.

Losel, F., & Bliesener, T. (1999). Germany. In P. K. Smith, Y. Morita, J. Junger-Tas, D. Olweus, R. Catalano, & P. T. Slee (Eds.), *The nature of school bullying: A cross-national perspective* (pp. 2242–249). London: Routledge.

McMahon, S. D., Washburn, J., Felix, E. D., Yakin, J., & Childrey, G. (2000). Violence prevention: Program effects on urban pre-school and kindergarten children. *Applied and Preventive Psychology, 9*, 271–281.

Morrison, B. (2002). Bullying and victimization in schools: A restorative justice approach. *Trends and Issues*, 219.

Mynard, H., & Joseph, S. (1997). Bully/victim problems and their association with Eysenck's personality dimensions in 8- to 13-year-olds. *British Journal of Educational Psychology, 66*, 447–456.

O'Connor, M., Foch, T., Todd, S., & Plomin, R. (1980). A twin study of specific behavioural problems of socialisation as viewed by parents. *Journal of Abnormal Child Psychology, 8*, 189–199.

Olweus, D. (1993). *Bullying in schools*. Cambridge, MA: Blackwell.

Olweus, D. (2004). The Olweus Bullying Prevention Programme: Design and implementation issues and a new initiative in Norway. In P. K. Smith, D. Pepler, K. Rigby (eds). *Bullying in schools. How successful can intervntions. pp. 13–36 be*? Cambridge: Cambridge University Press.

O'Moore, A. M., & Hillery, B. (1991). What do teachers need to know? In M. Elliott (Ed.), Bullying: *A practical guide to coping in schools*, (pp. 56–69). Harlow, London: David Fulton.

Ortega, R., & Lera, M. J. (2000). The Seville Anti-Bullying in School Project. *Aggressive Behaviour, 26*, 113–123.

Ortega, R., & Mora-Merchan, J. A. (1999). Spain. In P. K Smith, Y. Morita, J. Junger-Tas, D. Olweus, R. Catalano, & P. T. Slee (Eds.), *The nature of school bullying: A cross-national perspective* (pp.157–173). London: Routledge.

Pepler, D. J., & Craig, W. M. (1995). A peek behind the fence: Naturalistic observations of aggressive children with remote audiovisual recording. *Developmental Psychology, 31*, 548–553.

Pepler, D. J., Craig,W., Ziegler, S., & Charach, A. (1994). An evaluation of an anti-bullying intervention in Toronto schools. *Canadian Journal of Community Mental Health, 13*, 95–110.

Petersen, L., & Rigby, K. (1999). Countering bullying at an Australian secondary school. *Journal of Adolescence, 22*, 481–492.

Pikas, A. (1989). The Common Concern Method for the treatment of mobbing. In E. Roland & E. Munthe (Eds.), *Bullying: an international perspective* (pp. 91–104). London: David Fulton in association with the Professional Development Foundation.

Pikas, A. (2002). New developments of the Shared Concern Method. *School Psychology International, 23*, 307–326

Rigby, K. (1994). Psycho-social functioning in families of Australian adolescent schoolchildren involved in bully/victim problems. *Journal of Family Therapy, 16*, 173–189.

Rigby, K. (1996). Peer victimization and the structure of primary and secondary schooling. *Primary Focus, 10*, 4–5.

Rigby, K. (1997). *Manual for the Peer Relations Questionnaire (PRQ)*. Point Lonsdale, Victoria, Australia: The Professional Reading Guide.

Rigby, K. (2002a). *A meta-evaluation of methods and approaches to reducing bullying in pre-schools and in early primary school in Australia*. Canberra, Australia: Commonwealth Attorney-General's Department.

Rigby K. (2002b). *New perspectives on bullying*. London: Jessica Kingsley

Rigby, K. (2003a). The Bullying No Way Website: A critique. *Educare News, 139*, 24–25.

Rigby, K. (2003b). Consequences of bullying in schools. *The Canadian Journal of Psychiatry, 48*, 583–590.

Rigby, K. (2003c). *Stop the bullying: A handbook for schools: Updated revised edition* Melbourne: Australian Council for Educational Research.

Rigby, K. (2005). The method of showed concern as an intervention technique to address bullying in schools: An overview and appraisal. *Australian Journal of Counselling and Guidance, 15*, 27–34.

Rigby, K., & Bagshaw, D. (2001). The prevalence and hurtfulness of acts of aggression from peers experienced by Australian male and female adolescents at school. *Children Australia, 26*, 36–41.

Rigby, K., & Johnson, B. (2004a, September). Innocent bystanders? *Teacher*, pp. 38–40.

Rigby, K., & Johnson, B. (2004b). Students as bystanders to sexual coercion. How would they react and why. *Youth Studies, Australia, 23*, 11–16.

Rigby, K., & Thomas, E. B. (2003). *How schools counter bullying: Policies and procedures in selected Australian schools*. Geelong, Australia: The Professional Reading Guide.

Robinson, G., & Maines, B. (1997). *Crying for help—the No Blame Approach to Bullying*. Bristol, England: Lucky Duck.

Roland, E. (1993). Bullying: A developing tradition of research and management. In D. P. Tattum (Ed.), *Understanding and managing bullying* (pp. 15–30). Oxford, England: Heinemann Educational.

Rosenbluth, B., Whitaker, D. J., Sanchez, E., & Valle, L. A. (2004). The Expect Respect project: Preventing bullying and harassment in U.S. elementary schools. In P. K. Smith, D. Pepler, & K. Rigby (Eds.), *Bullying in schools: How successful can interventions be?* (pp. 211–250). Cambridge, England: Cambridge University Press.

Salmivalli, C. (2002). Is there an age decline in victimization by peers at school? *Educational Research 44*, 269–277.

Salmivalli C., Kaukiainen, A., Voeten, M., & Mäntykorpi, M. (2004) Targeting the group as a whole: The Finnish anti-bullying intervention. In P. K. Smith, D. Pepler, & K. Rigby (Eds.), *Bullying in schools: How successful can interventions be*? Cambridge, England: Cambridge University Press.

Slee, P. T., & Rigby, K. (1993). The relationship of Eysenck's personality factors and self-esteem to bully/victim behavior in Australian school boys. *Personality and Individual Differences, 14*, 371–373.

Smith, P. K., Morita, J., Junger-Tas, J., Olweus, D., Catalano, R., & Slee, P. T. (Eds). (1999). *The nature of school bullying. A cross-national perspective*. London: Routledge.

Smith, P. K., Pepler, D., & Rigby, K. (2004). *Bullying in schools: How successful can interventions be (pp. 1–12)?* Cambridge, England: Cambridge University Press.

Smith, P. K., & Sharp, S. (Eds.). (1994). *School bullying: Insights and perspectives*. London: Routledge.

Stevens, V., de Bourdeaudhuij, I., & Van Oost, P. (2000). Bullying in Flemish schools: An evaluation of anti-bullying interventions in primary and secondary schools. *British Journal of Educational Psychology, 70*, 195–210.

Stevens, V., Van Oost P., & De Bourdeaudhuij, I. (2004). Interventions against bullying in Flemish schools: Programme development and evaluation. In P. K. Smith, D. Pepler, & K. Rigby (Eds.), *Bullying in schools: How successful can interventions* be? (pp. 141–166). Cambridge, England: Cambridge University Press.

Sutton, J., & Keogh, E . (2000). Social competition in school: Relationships with bullying, Machiavellianism and personality. *British Journal of Educational Psychology, 70*, 443–457.

Thorsborne, M., & Vinegrad, D. (2003).*Restorative practices in schools*. Geelong, Australia: Margaret Thorsborne and Associates.

22

Understanding and Addressing Peer Victimization Among Students

Richard J. DioGuardi
Iona College

Lea A. Theodore
City University of New York, Queens College

Peer victimization may be defined as repeated exposure to physical and verbal aggressive actions by one or more individuals (Olweus, 1991). Victimization is often equated with a power differential, whereby the victim clearly evidences vulnerability in the eyes of the bully. It has been estimated that between 10% and 20% of all school-aged children are the targets of relentless bullying (Kochenderfer-Ladd & Skinner, 2002). More specifically, the prevalence of peer victimization appears to peak during the middle-school years (National Center for Educational Statistics, 1995) and gradually decrease during adolescence. It has been surmised that victimization is more acute during the transition between elementary to middle school, when there is a shift from adult-to peer-focused relationships, increased curriculum demands, reduced teacher attention, and increased social stressors (Nansel, Haynie, & Simons-Morton, 2003). Recent research has found a wide range of variability with respect to the rates of victimization, with estimates ranging from 8.4% to 20% for children bullied several times per week (Limber & Small, 2000; Nansel et al., 2001) and 24.2% (Nansel et al., 2001) to 44.6% (Haynie et al., 2001) for those victimized at some point during the past year. Research has also documented that approximately 33% of special education students report having been victimized (Garrity & Barris, 1996). In light of these estimates, as well as the negative implications stemming from peer victimization, there has been a heightened awareness among researchers, educators, and clinicians concerned about creating a safe environment to enhance the academic and social functioning of children.

VICTIMIZATION AND PSYCHOSOCIAL ADJUSTMENT

In recent years, there has been a growing interest in studying whether victims of peer aggression suffer psychosocial maladjustment, including depression, anxiety, and low self-regard. An increasing number of empirical studies, utilizing cross-sectional designs, have investigated this phenomenon, showing that the experience of being victimized by one's peers is associated with a wide range of social-psychological adjustment difficulties in youth, including generalized and social anxiety (Craig, 1998; Crick & Bigbee, 1998; Crick & Grotpeter, 1996; Grills & Ollendick, 2002; Slee, 1994; Storch, Brassard, & Masia-Warner, 2003; Storch & Masia-Warner, 2004; Storch, Zelman, Sweeney, Danner, & Dove, 2002), depression (Boivin, Hymel, & Bukowski, 1995; Craig, 1998; Crick & Bigbee, 1998; Crick & Grotpeter, 1996; Grills & Ollendick, 2002; Neary & Joseph, 1994; Slee, 1995; Storch et al., 2002), loneliness (Crick & Bigbee, 1998; Crick & Grotpeter, 1996; Ladd & Kochenderfer-Ladd, 2002; Storch et al., 2003; Storch & Masia-Warner, 2004), symptoms of posttraumatic stress (Mynard, Joseph, & Alexander, 2000; Storch & Esposito, 2003), low self-esteem and perceptions of global self-worth and competence in a variety of domains (Boivin & Hymel, 1997; Boulton & Smith, 1994; Callaghan & Joseph, 1995; Egan & Perry, 1998; Grills & Ollendick, 2002; Neary & Joseph, 1994). Victimization has also been related to academic adjustment difficulties, such as avoidance and dislike of school (Kochenderfer & Ladd, 1996) and poor academic performance (Olweus, 1993).

Long-term effects of peer victimization have been linked to low self-esteem and bouts of depression (Olweus, 1992, 1993); poor physical self (Rigby, 1999); self-perceived unpopularity (Khatri, Kupersmidt, & Patterson, 2000); externalizing behavior, attentional difficulties, and neediness (Schwartz, McFadyen-Ketchum, Dodge, Pettit, & Bates, 1998a). Additional psychological sequalae include sociocognitive misperceptions (Dodge, Bates, & Pettit, 1990) and greater likelihood of experiencing loneliness and avoiding school (Kochenderfer & Ladd, 1996).

Peer Rejection

Compounding their own self-appraised maladjustment is the widespread finding that victimized children are frequently rejected by their peer group (Hodges, Malone, & Perry, 1997; Ladd & Kochenderfer-Ladd, 2002; Perry, Kusel, & Perry, 1988) and often have fewer friends (Hodges, Boivin, Vitaro, & Bukowski, 1999). Peer rejection itself is generally associated with poor prosocial behaviors, neediness, immaturity, and attention-seeking behaviors (Bierman, Smoot, & Aumiller, 1993). Other peer relationship difficulties often characterizing the experience of victims are themselves positively correlated with peer victimization (e.g., submissiveness and social withdrawal; Boivin et al., 1995; Boulton & Smith, 1994; Perry et al., 1988; Schwartz, Dodge, & Coie, 1993).

Research has begun to address potential mediating processes that might account for the known associations between victimization and poor adjustment outcomes. Graham and Juvonen (1998) examined how victims construe the reasons for their plight and how these attributions can motivate maladaptive responses. Characterological self-blame, which is esteem-related, stable, perceived as uncontrollable, and associated with the belief that one deserves negative consequences (Schwartz, McFadyen-Ketchum, Dodge, Pettit, & Bates, 1998b), was endorsed more by victims than nonvictims, and this attributional bias was related to more loneliness, social anxiety, and negative self-appraisals. In contrast, attributing victimization to one's specific behavior (i.e., behavioral self-blame), an attribution believed to be unstable and controllable, was unrelated to adjustment problems and was no more highly endorsed by victims than nonvictims.

VICTIM SUBTYPES

Nonaggressive Victims

Research has shown that victims themselves are a heterogeneous population with respect to levels of aggression, with aggressive and nonaggressive victims identified as behaviorally distinct subgroups (Hodges et al., 1997; Pelligrini, 1998; Pellegrini, Bartini, & Brooks, 1999; Perry et al., 1988). Nonaggressive victims, also described as *passive victims*, tend to be characterized as having submissive and passive behavioral styles, and comprise the overwhelming majority of children that are bullied (Schwartz, Proctor, & Chien, 2001). These students tend to be anxious, sensitive, insecure, and cautious. They are more inclined to cry easily, are typically isolated or socially withdrawn, exhibit low self-esteem, and are usually without a single, reliable friendship among their classmates. Olweus (1993) described this subgroup of victims as demonstrating an anxious or *submissive reaction pattern*, which seems to signal insecurity to others, as well as communicate the desire not to retaliate when they are mistreated. Not surprisingly, passive victims are seen as easy targets, likely submit to an aggressor's demands, and perhaps reinforce such behavior (Egan & Perry, 1998; Hodges et al., 1997; Olweus, 1978; Schwartz et al., 1993). Because victims perceive their aggressors as having more power in the relationship, the victims are more apt to acquiesce in the face of intimidation by the bully. This submission may validate the perpetrator's self-appraisal as dominant, invulnerable, and confident in achieving their goal of controlling others. Thus, bully dominance and victim submission are inherently intertwined.

Aggressive Victims

In contrast, aggressive victims, also known as *bully-victims* or *provocative victims*, may be typified as impulsive, demonstrate low frustration tolerance, and evidence behavioral problems (Rubin, Chen, & Hymel, 1993). At greater risk for social rejection than nonaggressive victims, these students are disliked and ostracized by their peers likely due to their antagonistic, unpredictable, and uncontrolled behavior (Perry et al., 1988). As a result of their pragmatic deficits (i.e., difficulty interpreting the social cues of others; Macklem, 2003), there is a greater propensity for aggressive victims to misperceive the intentions of others as being hostile in nature (Schwartz et al., 1998b). Their attention-seeking, confrontational, and disruptive behaviors frequently elicit petulance in others (Perry, Hodges, & Egan, 2001). Similar to the behavior of passive victims, responses of aggressive victims often result in an emotional payoff for the perpetrator. This payoff comes in the form of elevated emotional reactions (Perry, Williard, & Perry, 1990) and excessive hostile retribution (Schwartz et al., 1998b), which reinforce continual victimization. The aggressive and withdrawn behaviors of provocative and passive victims, respectively, have emerged as important correlates of victimization. A distinction between passive and aggressive victims should be underscored in that the overall academic, social, and emotional functioning, as well as long-term psychosocial adjustment and the duration of victimization, may differ between these two groups.

STABILITY OF VICTIMIZATION

Several studies have found victim status to be fairly stable over time (Camodeca, Goossens, Terwogt, & Schuengel, 2002; Hodges et al., 1997; Kochenderfer & Ladd, 1997; Perry et al., 1988), despite a steady decline in the prevalence of victimization between the ages of 8 and 16 (Smith, Shu, & Madson, 2001). Some children victimized at a young age continue to be victimized several years later (Perry et al., 2001), although the form often changes from physical intimidation to that of indirect and/or verbal attacks (Macklem, 2003). In an effort to explain why the reporting of victimization may decline with age in light of evidence showing a general stability of the phenomenon, Smith et al. (2001) suggested that younger children lack the interpersonal skills to deal with aggressive peers. As children grow older, those who develop social competencies are less likely to be subjected to continued assaults, whereas those who fail to acquire these skills or strategies remain victims. Additionally, victimization is likely to be discontinued when the student develops friendships with peers who are less victimized or do not exhibit this type of peer maladjustment (Browning, Cohen, & Warman, 2003).

Behavioral Antecedents of Chronic Victimization

Research on how victims' actions determine the likelihood and course of aggressive attacks against them has identified several risk factors associated with the probability, intensity, and duration of aggression. Victimization increases if the victim is viewed by the aggressor as deliberately provocative (Dodge, 1980), has historically submitted to peers' social initiatives (Schwartz, Dodge, & Coie, 1993) or the demands of the aggressor (Patterson, Littman, & Bricker, 1967), and fails to exhibit behaviors that typically reduce aggressive attacks (Camras, 1980; Ginsburg, Pollman, & Wauson, 1977; Perry & Bussey, 1977; Perry & Perry, 1974). More recently, several studies have shown that not only do some victimized children display high levels of aggression, but also, aggressive behavior is predictive of being victimized (Hodges et al., 1997; Schwartz et al., 1998b; Schwartz, McFadyen-Ketchum, Dodge, Pettit, & Bates, 1999). It is likely that aggressive behavior is annoying to peers, and that those aggressive children, by virtue of this provocative behavior, set themselves up for subsequent retaliation. In contrast, passive victims rarely provoke aggressors directly, but rather they appear to their peers as socially withdrawn, insecure, physically inferior, and depressed. These internalizing symptoms suggest vulnerability, specifically that they are likely apprehensive in asserting themselves and protecting their physical and emotional integrity from assaults. Bullies keenly sense these weaknesses and are successful at exploiting them (Perry et al., 2001). In support of this finding, research indicates that the internalizing difficulties, most salient in passive victims, contribute to chronic victimization (Boulton, 1999; Egan & Perry, 1998; Hodges & Perry, 1999). Finally, characteristics across both victim subtypes, such as poor social skills and peer rejection, promote victimization over time (Egan & Perry, 1998; Hodges & Perry, 1999).

Social Cognitions

In a study focusing on sociocognitive correlates of peer victimization, Schwartz et al. (1998b) found that victims who manifest either a submissive behavioral profile or angry reactive aggression (i.e., an angry retaliatory response to a perceived provocation or frustration) were more likely to have hostile attributional tendencies—tendencies to interpret peer intent as hostile and provocative. Negative expectations for the outcomes of aggressive and assertive behavior were also found to motivate the submissive social behavior associated with frequent receipt of peer aggression. The authors maintain that understanding the sociocognitive mechanisms underlying the maladaptive social behaviors displayed by victimized children could potentially assist in the design of appropriate interventions (see Perry et al., 1988).

Low Self-Esteem

Low self-regard, specifically low self-perceptions of social competence, is yet another vulnerability factor placing one at risk for chronic victimization (Egan & Perry, 1998). The rationale for this includes the following: (a) poor self-esteem is related to one's diminished ability or incentive to effectively assert and defend themselves during confrontations with peers (Egan & Perry, 1998); (b) children with low self-regard anticipate and accept negative social feedback, thus validating their feelings of unworthiness (De La Ronde & Swann, 1993); and (c) children with a minimal sense of worth exhibit depressive symptoms tend to be very circumspect, and demonstrate deficits in affect and behavioral modulation (Baumeister, 1993). Egan and Perry (1998) found that self-perceptions of social competence, rather than global self-regard, promoted victimization over time, as this domain of self-worth is highly relevant in peer interactions. Additionally, behavioral vulnerability, such as anxiety and poor social skills, were more likely to lead to victimization in children with low self-regard.

OVERT AND RELATIONAL VICTIMIZATION

The literature has categorized peer victimization as either overt and direct or relational and indirect, with recent investigators focusing more attention on the distinction between overt and relational forms of victimization and how they may affect victims' sociopsychological adjustment differentially depending on the gender of the victim. Overt victimization involves being the frequent target of peers' direct physical attacks or verbal threats of physical harm. In contrast, relational victimization occurs when the perpetrator attempts to harm the target through the hurtful manipulation of friendships or peer relationships and/or threats of damage to these interpersonal connections (Crick & Grotpeter, 1996). A victim of relational aggression may have friends who threaten to withdraw their affection unless he or she agrees to their demands, may be excluded from important social activities, or may be the subject of malicious rumors spreading throughout the peer group with the goal of encouraging others to reject him or her.

Some research on gender differences in the manifestation of aggression has found that, compared to the overtly aggressive acts that often characterize victimization episodes among boys, maltreatment among girls often involves relationally aggressive behaviors (Bjorkqvist, Lagerspetz, & Kaukiainen, 1992; Crick & Bigbee, 1998; Crick & Grotpeter, 1995; Lagerspetz, Bjorkqvist, & Peltonen, 1988). This finding, however, is not supported by other studies. For instance, some investigations of relational aggression found no significant differences in girls' reports and boys' reports of relational victimization (Crick & Grotpeter, 1996; Paquette & Underwood, 1999; Phelps, 2001). Although findings from studies of gender differences in relational victimization during preschool years, middle childhood and adolescence are mixed, research has demonstrated that, during adolescence, when differences in relational victimization do exist, there is a greater likelihood that girls will be affected (Crick et al., 2001). Additionally, research indicates that relational victimization carries a different meaning for boys than girls. Specifically, girls are more troubled by interpersonal problems, are more likely to respond negatively to perceived relational attacks, and have a propensity to integrate social interactional information into their self-concept (Crick, Grotpeter, & Bigbee, 2002; Galen & Underwood, 1997; Paquette & Underwood, 1999).

The manner in which relational victimization is expressed changes with development. As children mature, increasing complexities in social, emotional, and cognitive functioning underlie the different manifestations of relational victimization (Crick et al., 2001). For instance, during the preschool years, relational victimization may be characterized as direct and focused on preferred activities rather than friendship loyalty. In middle childhood, relational victims face more sophisticated forms of peer harassment, which involve indirect and direct relational attacks. Such tactics include lying, spreading rumors, and excluding the victim. These behaviors persist through adolescence, though they become less obvious and more complex. Relational victimization finds new avenues for expression during this period when romantic relationships and friendships with the opposite gender become more paramount (Crick, Casas, & Nelson, 2002).

PROTECTIVE FACTORS

Protective factors that both buffer the effects of peer victimization and minimize its occurrence include friendships and coping strategies. With respect to friendships, both the quantity of friends and quality of friendships attenuate the effects of victimization (Pellegrini & Long, 2002). Emotional support via friendships is invaluable to children who are victimized (Bryant, 1998). Significantly, the presence of one mutual best friendship mitigates the negative effects of, and decreases risk for, victimization (Hodges et al., 1999). However, the type of friend that a victim has may influence the effects of bullying. That is, friends who are highly regarded by peers, as compared to those with low sociometric status, may result in different outcomes (Schwartz, Dodge, Petit, & Bates, 2000). With regard to the quality of friendship, the willingness of that friend to defend the victim when he or she is attacked or threatened (i.e., high protection) minimizes the relationship between victimization and future behavior problems (Hodges et al., 1999). Similarly, the extent of victimization of that child's friends is equally important in that victims whose friends are also typically the targets of aggression continue to experience maltreatment (Browning et al., 2003). Thus, having a friend who is not only supportive, but also held in high esteem by others, can serve as an important protective factor against an escalating cycle of victimization.

Coping strategies, which may be categorized as either *approach* or *avoidance*, have been implicated in the mediation of peer victimization. Approach tactics involve the student confronting the bullying directly. Both problem solving and searching for social support are approach methods that may be utilized by the individual to stop the harassment (Kochenderfer-Ladd & Skinner, 2002). In contrast, avoidance strategies involve attempts to manage thoughts about and emotional responses to the stressful experience (Fields & Prinz, 1997). Avoidance techniques may be conceptualized as not dealing with or thinking about the stressful situation, worrying or feeling sorry for oneself, and taking out their anger on others (Kochenderfer-Ladd & Skinner, 2002). Although there is research indicating that children's coping strategies are associated with social acceptance (Bijttebier & Vertommen, 1998), more studies are warranted in order to determine the effectiveness of distinct coping strategies as a buffer for victimized students.

INTERVENTIONS FOR VICTIMS OF BULLYING

Effectively addressing the needs of children who are the victims of bullies is a difficult task, particularly because there is a greater propensity for schools to focus on interventions designed specifically for bullies in comparison with their victims (Miller & Rubin, 1998). A recent area of focus has been on developing intervention strategies for victims, as researchers and clinicians are better able to recognize characteristics of victims that may promote continual harassment. Given that victimization impacts and is affected by multiple levels of the school milieu, including the student, peer group, and school climate, it is important to underscore that treatment approaches should be directed towards each of these factors (Hanish, 2000).

Victim Approaches

Generally, when dealing with victimized children, it is imperative that these students are protected from future potential harassment and/or harm (Rigby, 2002). Given the fear and angst surrounding informing an adult of the bullying they have endured, it is important that these students trust the adults who are aiding them. Additionally, it would be prudent to suggest that parents and/or teachers obtain the consent of the victimized child prior to taking any direct action. Not surprisingly, victims typically fear that informing individuals of authority about the problem may exacerbate the situation. However, intervening on a child's behalf takes precedence and the child's best interest systematically outstrips protests made out of fear by the child (Olweus, 1993). Thus, it is crucial that the victim is adequately protected (Olweus, 1993; Rigby, 2002). When an adult who is in a position to intervene is made aware of a bullying situation, the victim should be conferred with first, and an effort should be made to understand the vantage point of the victim. Also, the victim should not be allowed to resolve the situation him or herself as there is usually a power differential between the bully and the victim (Macklem, 2003). Finally, frequent home–school collaboration is a critical component in protecting the victimized student.

Teachers have the potential to play a powerful role in attenuating the cycle of peer harassment. First, teachers may be taught to understand the victim and their role in bully–victim interactions (Horne, Orpinas, Newman-Carlson, & Bartolomucci, 2004). Teachers may also learn the signals of possible victimization such as appearing frightened, developing somatic symptoms, refusing lunch, avoiding school, staying away from the bathroom or certain locations in the classroom, and looking melancholy (Horne et al., 2004). One module within the Bully Busters Program provides classroom activities that may be administered by the teacher to help foster positive beliefs about victimized children, reduce potential blaming of the victim, and enhance empathic responding by peers (Horne et al., 2004). Other strategies that teachers may employ to support victims include establishing a classroom environment where everyone is treated with respect, while providing a process by which peer mediation/conflict resolution can occur, and developing a supportive climate where classmate bystanders can intervene or facilitate in the teacher's absence (Horne et al., 2004).

Social Support

A paucity of research has investigated perceptions of support of bullies, victims, and bully-victims. Notably, three studies provided evidence that victims of peer aggression reported less frequency of perceived social support (Demaray & Malecki, 2003; DioGuardi, Hodges, & Theodore, 2004; Furlong, Chung, Bates, & Morrison, 1995). Demaray and Malecki presented additional evidence that victims and bully-victims valued social support more highly than other student groups. This is a particular concern in that students who place high importance on social support indicated that they are often devoid of this (Malecki & Demaray, 2004). The contextual factor of social support is critical in that it may mediate the association between victimization and psychological adjustment. Specifically, a study by Malecki and Demaray (2002, 2004) found a positive association between level of victimization and overall socio-emotional adjustment. Significantly, when social support was factored into the equation, the experience of being victimized lost much of its predictive power. This finding yields important implications for practice in the schools.

First, teachers may provide support for victimized children by way of engaging classmates as mediators and facilitators, designing opportunities within the classroom to enhance the victim's sociometric status, and collaborating with parents and families to make certain that they are providing ample support (Olweus, Limber, & Mihalic, 1999). Second, teachers have the opportunity to communicate to at-risk students how to seek help. Third, from an ecological perspective, teachers may convey clear requirements for what actions in the school constitute appropriate and inappropriate behaviors. Fourth, creating a committee designed to heighten awareness of bullying at the schoolwide level simultaneously helps to establish a climate of social support.

As mentioned previously, many children who are victimized are socially isolated with few if any friends, and with diminished self-confidence. It would be beneficial to assist these

TABLE 22.1

Implications for Practice: Reducing Peer Victimization

1. Victimization is often equated with a power differential whereby the victim exhibits vulnerability in the eyes of the bully. Furthermore, these children often lack the interpersonal skills to deal with aggressive peers. Programs that aim to improve victims' social skills, assertiveness, and level of social support would help empower the bullied child, enhance their sociometric status, and increase the likelihood that they will radiate behaviors that would potentially ward off future attacks.

2. As intervening bystanders, peers can play a powerful role in reducing victimization. That is, they are critical in determining reinforcement contingencies for bullies. By teaching bystanders (students) to voice disapproval by not becoming an audience, sharing with other students their condemnation of the bullying behavior, and threatening to report the bully if the behavior continues, a bully's assaults may be reduced via weakened social reinforcement. In addition, students may take proactive steps to support victims by including them in conversations and games and regularly inviting them to play.

3. The presence of one mutual best friendship mitigates the negative effects of, and decreases risk for, victimization. By having the teacher restructure cliques and have students work towards a common goal (i.e., employing an interdependent group contingency such as the Good Behavior Game), cooperative behaviors and positive social interactions among all classmates will likely be enhanced.

students in developing and maximizing their strengths while simultaneously forming friendships (Macklem, 2003). Whether it is sports or activities, it is important to foster and enhance talents for students who are victimized so as to develop a sense of empowerment and subsequently improved self-confidence. Consequently, these students may radiate substantially different behaviors, which may result in a new network of friends (Olweus, 1993). The benefits afforded by new friendships are multifold in that students feel supported and cared for (Macklem, 2003). The school psychologist may develop informal support groups for children who are victimized that focus on developing coping strategies, becoming accepted, and providing social support (Macklem, 2003).

Although victims should not be forced to change their identity to avoid harassment, they can learn strategies to enhance their self-esteem and self-efficacy in their ability to protect themselves. Social skills and assertiveness training may be employed to decrease peer aggression by equipping victims with new skills and behaviors to minimize the possibility of becoming targets of future attacks (Horne et al., 2004).

Social Skills Training

Social skills training that specifically addresses effective methods of social interaction is another intervention for school-aged children who are victimized. In this manner, both verbal and nonverbal strategies are taught using role-plays, videos, and incorporating past experiences to not only protect, but to also shift the centralization and focus of attention away from the students themselves (Macklem, 2003). Incorporating instructional strategies that enhance prosocial behavior as well as effective methods of problem solving would be beneficial as well. Recently, a social skills training (SST) program developed by Fox and Boulton (2003a) was investigated to determine its efficacy in supporting victims of bullying. The program's general aim is to improve children's social skills by showing them how to use social problem-solving skills, how to implement relaxation techniques, how to think in a positive manner, how to alter their nonverbal behavior, and how to utilize particular verbal strategies (e.g., fogging and mirroring) to cope with aggressive attacks. Although findings did not indicate any change in victim status, SST participants experienced a significant overall increase in self-esteem (Fox & Boulton, 2003b). Such findings are important in that high self-esteem has been touted as a variable that protects at-risk children from peer victimization (Egan & Perry, 1998).

Assertiveness Training.   Assertiveness training, often a component of SST, improves and enhances self-esteem, sense of competence, and coping skills (Sharp & Cowie, 1994). Learning how to assert themselves and effectively deal with bullies may provide victims with a semblance of control (Macklem, 2003). One such strategy is for students to minimize their emotional response when they are bullied. In this manner, exhibiting nonchalant and indifferent behavior thwarts the bully's emotional payoff and diminishes the likelihood that the student will be victimized in the future (Hazler, 1996; Salmivalli, 1999). The rationale for this is that bullies choose victims who are easy targets; that is, the victims they elect to bully generally evidence minimal confidence in their ability to defend themselves. Hence, bullies back away from individuals who demonstrate more self-confidence as evidenced by their behavior and/or verbal comments (Hazler, 1996). Brusque words or comments, aggressive behavior, and/or helplessness may be interpreted by the bully as a challenge and likely result in continued bullying and harassment (Hazler, 1996; Salmivalli, 1999). Strategies for dealing with bullying behavior in an assertive manner also include techniques such as standing straight, speaking slowly and clearly, and looking the bully in the eyes (Field, 1999; Rigby, 2002; Zarzour, 1999), all of which may be practiced via role-playing with the school psychologist or counselor. Assertiveness training strategies are based on extant literature detailing the characteristics of victims and have yet to be empirically examined.

Peer Approaches

Within the social milieu of the school and classroom, social caste systems or cliques often exist. Students tend to participate in peer networks with individuals who are similar to them. Unfortunately, cliques that are comprised of bullies often reinforce negative behaviors while also developing their own set of social norms (Salmivalli, 1999). Restructuring the cliques and having the class work toward a common goal may aid in the reduction of peer victimization. One method of accomplishing this endeavor is by employing an interdependent group-oriented contingency, such as the Good Behavior Game (Hanish, 2000). The performance of each member of the group contributes to achieving the reward. In this manner, all students need to work together in order to attain a mutual goal, which is administered on an all-or-none basis. The advantages associated with this type of intervention include enhancing student interactions and cooperation among group members.

As intervening bystanders, peers have the potential to play a powerful role in reducing bullying, because they determine the reinforcement contingencies (Macklem, 2003). If bullies observe that their peers socially disapprove of their actions, they may be more apt to change their behavior. Voicing disapproval can be exhibited by not becoming an audience (i.e., turning away), sharing with other students one's condemnation of the bullying behavior, and threatening to report the bully if the behavior continues (Macklem, 2003).

Generally, peer helpers are considered to have a high status among their peers, enjoy healthy self-esteem, and have a positive self-image (Salmivalli, 1999). Given their popularity and peer perceptions of them as positive role models, these students are more likely to win support for their anti-bullying stance and serve as excellent sources of support for students who have been victimized (Salmivalli, 1999). Such students can take proactive steps to support victims such as including them in conversations and games and regularly inviting them to play. Finally, Sharp and Cowie (1994) recommended that conflict resolution, including peer counseling and mediation, be taught to bystanders to help them stop peer aggression.

School Environment Approaches

Concern regarding the deleterious effects of victimization has provided the impetus for the design and implementation of several recent anti-bullying programs to prevent peer victimization. These programs include the Bully Busters Program (Newman, Horne, & Bartolomucci, 2000), the Olweus Bully Prevention Program (Olweus et al., 2003), and Expect Respect (Whitaker, Rosenbluth, Valle, & Sanchez, 2004). An enhanced understanding of individuals who are most likely to be victimized, in addition to the specific processes by which bully–victim difficulties develop within the peer milieu, has aided in the development of such interventions.

Schoolwide policies aimed at increasing awareness of school personnel by describing the prevalence, indicators, and seriousness of bullying in the school is highly recommended (Hanish, 2000). Furthermore, policies developed to foster a nurturing environment for students, employ consistent consequences for bullying, as well as generate supervision in low-structured areas, such as the cafeteria and playground, are critical components for reducing peer victimization.

SUMMARY

In conclusion, this chapter provides an overview of peer victimization with a focus on the forms of aggression experienced by victims, the subtypes of victims, risk and protective factors associated with severity and duration of maltreatment, psychological correlates and long-term outcomes for individuals that are bullied, and interventions. Because the extant literature has focused more on bullies rather than the victim, less is known about those children who suffer harassment and abuse from peers. With an increased awareness of the negative ramifications stemming from peer victimization, as well as factors that promote and protect one from this experience, informed interventions for the victims are more likely to demonstrate success.

REFERENCES

Baumeister, R. F. (1993). Understanding the inner nature of low self-esteem: Uncertain, fragile, protected, and conflicted. In R. F. Baumeister (Ed.), *Self-esteem: The puzzle of low self-regard* (pp. 147–166). New York: Plenum.

Bierman, K. L., Smoot, D. L., & Aumiller, K. (1993). Characteristics of aggressive-rejected, aggressive, (nonrejected), and rejected (nonaggressive) boys. *Child Development, 64,* 139–151.

Bijttebier, P., & Vertommen, H. (1998). Coping with peer arguments in school-age children with bully/victim problems. *British Journal of Educational Psychology, 68,* 387–394.

Bjorkqvist, K., Lagerspetz, K. M. J., & Kaukiainen, A. (1992). Do girls manipulate and boys fight? Developmental trends in regard to direct and indirect aggression. *Aggressive Behavior, 18,* 117–127.

Boivin, M., & Hymel, S. (1997). Peer expectations and social self-perceptions: A sequential model. *Developmental Psychology, 33,* 135–145.

Boivin, M., Hymel, S., & Bukowski, W. M. (1995). The roles of social withdrawal, peer rejection, and victimization by peers in predicting loneliness and depressed mood in childhood. *Development and Psychopathology, 7,* 765–785.

Boulton, M. J. (1999). Concurrent and longitudinal relations between children's playground behavior and social preference, victimization, and bullying. *Child Development, 70,* 944–954.

Boulton, M. J., & Smith, P. K. (1994). Bully/victim problems in middle-school children: Stability, self-perceived competence, peer perceptions and peer acceptance. *British Journal of Developmental Psychology, 12,* 315–329.

Browning, C., Cohen, R., & Warman, D. M. (2003). Peer social competence and the stability of victimization. *Child Study Journal, 33,* 73–90.

Bryant, B. K. (1998). Children's coping at school: The relevance of "failure" and cooperative learning for enduring peer and academic success. In L. H. Meyer, H. Park, M. Grenot-Scheyer, I. S. Schwartz, & B. Harry (Eds.), *Making friends: The influences of culture and development* (pp. 353–366). Baltimore, MD: Paul H. Brookes.

Callaghan, S., & Joseph, S. (1995). Self-concept and peer victimization among school children. *Personality and Individual Differences, 18,* 161–163.

Camodeca, M., Goossens, F. A., Terwogt, M. M., & Schuengel, C. (2002). Bullying and victimization among school-aged children: Stability and links to proactive and reactive aggression. *Social Development, 11,* 332–345.

Camras, L. A. (1980). Children's understanding of facial expressions used during conflict encounters. *Child Development, 51,* 879–885.

Craig, W. M. (1998). The relationship among bullying, victimization, depression, anxiety, and aggression, in elementary school children. *Personality and Individual Differences, 24,* 123–130.

Crick, N. R., & Bigbee, M. A. (1998). Relational and overt forms of peer victimization: A multiinformant approach. *Journal of Consulting and Clinical Psychology, 66,* 337–347.

Crick, N. R., Casas, J. F., & Nelson, D. A. (2002). Toward a more comprehensive understanding of peer maltreatment: Studies of relational victimization. *Current Directions in Psychological Science, 11,* 98–101.

Crick, N. R., & Grotpeter, J. K. (1995). Relational aggression, gender, and social- psychological adjustment. *Child Development, 66,* 710–722.

Crick, N. R., & Grotpeter, J. K. (1996). Children's treatment by peers: Victims of relational and overt aggression. *Development and Psychopathology, 8,* 367–380.

Crick, N. R., Grotpeter, J. K., & Bigbee, M. A. (2002). Relationally and physically aggressive children's intent attributions and feelings of distress for relational and instrumental peer provocations. *Child Development, 73,* 1134–1142.

Crick, N. R., Nelson, D. A., Morales, J. R., Cullerton-Sen, C., Casas, J. F., & Hickman, S. E. (2001). Relational victimization in childhood and adolescence: I hurt you through the grapevine. In J. Juvonen & S. Graham (Eds.), *Peer harassment in school: The plight of the vulnerable and victimized* (pp. 196–214). New York: Guilford Press.

De La Ronde, C., & Swann, W. B. (1993). Caught in the crossfire: Positivity and self-verification strivings among people with low self-esteem. In R. F. Baumeister (Ed.), *Self esteem: The puzzle of low self-regard* (pp. 147–166). New York: Plenum.

Demaray, M. K., & Malecki, C. K. (2003). Perceptions of the frequency and importance of social support by students classified as victims, bullies, and bully/victims in an urban middle school.*School Psychology Review, 32,* 471–489.

DioGuardi, R. A., Hodges, E. V. E., & Theodore, L. A. (2005). *Self-perceptions of social support and mutual best friendships in victims of peer aggression.* Manuscript submitted for publication.

Dodge, K. A. (1980). Social cognition and children's aggressive behavior. *Child Development, 51,* 162–170.

Dodge, K. A., Bates, J. E., & Pettit, G. S. (1990). Mechanisms in the cycle of violence. *Science, 250,* 1678–1683.

Egan, S. K., & Perry, D. G. (1998). Does low self-regard invite victimization? *Developmental Psychology, 34,* 299–309.

Field, E. M. (1999). *Bully busting.* Lane Cove, NSW: Finch Publishing.

Fields, L., & Prinz, R. J. (1997). Coping and adjustment during childhood and adolescence. *Clinical Psychology Review, 17,* 937–976.

Fox, C. L., & Boulton, M. J. (2003a). Evaluating the effectiveness of a social skills training (SST) programme for victims of bullying. *Educational Research, 45,* 231–247.

Fox, C. L., & Boulton, M. J. (2003b, June). A Social Skills Training (SST) Programme for victims of bullying. *Pastoral Care in Education, June,* 19–26.

Furlong, M. J., Chung, A., Bates, M., & Morrison, R. L. (1995). Who are the victims of school violence? A comparison of student, non-victims, and multi-victims. *Education and Treatment of Children, 18,* 282–298.

Galen, B. R., & Underwood, M. K. (1997). A developmental investigation of social aggression among children. *Developmental Psychology, 33,* 589–600.

Garrity, C., & Barris, M. A. (1996). Bullies and victims: A guide for pediatricians. *Contemporary Pediatrics, 13,* 90–114.

Ginsburg, H. J., Pollman, V. A., & Wauson, M. S. (1977). An ethological analysis of nonverbal *inhibitors* of aggressive behavior in male elementary school children. *Developmental Psychology, 13,* 417–418.

Graham, S., & Juvonen, J. (1998). Self-blame and peer victimization in middle school: An attributional analysis. *Developmental Psychology, 34,* 587–599.

Grills, A. E., & Ollendick, T. H. (2002). Peer victimization, global self-worth, and anxiety in middle school children. *Journal of Clinical Child and Adolescent Psychology, 31,* 59–68.

Hanish, L. D. (2000). Children who get victimized at school: What is known? What can be done? *Professional School Counseling, 4,* 113–119.

Haynie, D. L., Nansel, T., Eitel, P., Crump, A. D., Saylor, K., Yu, K., Simmons-Morton , B. (2001). Bullies, victims, and bully/victims: Distinct groups of at-risk youth. *Journal of Early Adolescence, 21,* 29–49.

Hazler, R. J. (1996). *Breaking the cycle of violence: Interventions for bullying and victimization.* Washington, DC: Accelerated Development.

Hodges, E. V. E., Boivin, M., Vitaro, F., & Bukowski, W. M. (1999). The power of friendship: Protection against an escalating cycle of peer victimization. *Developmental Psychology, 35,* 94–101.

Hodges, E. V. E., Malone, M. J., Jr., & Perry, D. G. (1997). Individual risk and social risk as interacting determinants of victimization in the peer group. *Developmental Psychology, 33,* 1032–1039.

Hodges, E. V. E., & Perry, D. G. (1999). Personal and interpersonal antecedents and consequences of victimization by peers. *Journal of Personality and Social Psychology, 76,* 677–685.

Horne, A. M., Orpinas, P., Newman-Carlson, D., & Bartolomucci, C. (2004). Elementary school bully busters program: Understanding why children bully and what to do about it. In D. L. Espelage & S. M. Swearer (Eds.), *Bullying in American schools: A social-ecological perspective on prevention and intervention* (pp. 297–325). Mahwah, NJ: Lawrence Erlbaum Associates.

Khatri, P., Kupersmidt, J. B., & Patterson, C. (2000). Aggression and peer victimization as predictors of self-reported behavioral and emotional adjustment. *Aggressive Behavior, 26,* 345–358.

Kochenderfer, B. J., & Ladd, G. W. (1996). Peer victimization: Cause or consequence of school maladjustment? *Child Development, 67,* 1305–1317.

Kochenderfer, B. J., & Ladd, G. W. (1997). Victimized children's responses to peer's aggression: Behaviors associated with reduced versus continued victimization. *Development and Psychopathology, 9,* 267–283.

Kochenderfer-Ladd, B., & Skinner, K. (2002). Children's coping strategies: Moderators of the effects of peer victimization? *Developmental Psychology, 38,* 267–278.

Ladd, G. W., & Kochenderfer-Ladd, B. (2002). Identifying victims of peer aggression from early to middle childhood: Analysis of cross-informant data for concordance, estimation of relational adjustment, prevalence of victimization, and characteristics of identified victims. *Psychological Assessment, 14,* 74–96.

Lagerspetz, K. M. J., Bjorkqvist, K., & Peltonen, T. (1988). Is indirect aggression typical of females? Gender differences in aggressiveness in 11- to 12-year-old children. *Aggressive Behavior, 14,* 403–414.

Limber, S. P., & Small, M. A. (2000, August). *Self-reports of bully-victimization among primary school students.* Paper presented at the annual meeting of the American Psychological Association, Washington, DC.

Macklem, G. L. (2003). *Bullying and teasing: Social power in children's groups.* New York: Kluwer Academic/Plenum.

Malecki, C. K., & Demaray, M. K. (2002). *Does social support mediate student adjustment for victims of bullying in schools?* Manuscript submitted for publication.

Malecki, C. K., & Demaray, M. K. (2004). The role of social support in the lives of bullies, victims, and bully/victims. In D. L. Espelage & S. M. Swearer (Eds.), *Bullying in American schools: A social-ecological perspective on prevention and intervention* (pp. 211–225). Mahwah, NJ: Lawrence Erlbaum Associates.

Miller, G., & Rubin, K. (1998). Victimization of school-age children: Safe schools strategies for parents and educators. In A. S. Cantor & A. Carroll (Eds.), *Helping children at home and school: Handouts from your school psychologist* (pp. 527–530). Bethesda, MD: National Association of School Psychologists.

Mynard, H., Joseph, S., & Alexander, J. (2000). Peer-victimisation and posttraumatic stress in adolescents. *Personality and Individual Differences, 29,* 815–821.

Nansel, T. R., Haynie, D. L., & Simons-Morton, B. G. (2003). The association of bullying and victimization with middle school adjustment. In M. J. Elias & J. E. Zins (Eds.), *Bullying, peer harassment, and victimization in the schools: The next generation of prevention* (pp. 45–61). New York: Haworth Press.

Nansel, T. R., Overpeck, M., Pilla, R. S., Ruan, W. J., Simons-Morton, B., & Scheidt, P. (2001). Bullying behaviors among US youth: Prevalence and association with psychosocial adjustment. *Journal of the American Medical Association, 285,* 2094–2100.

National Center for Educational Statistics. (1995, October). *Student victimization in schools.* Washington, DC: U.S. Department of Education.

Neary, A., & Joseph, S. (1994). Peer victimization and its relationship to self-concept and depression among Australian schoolgirls. *Personality and Individual Differences, 16,* 183–186.

Newman, D. A., Horne, A. M., & Bartolomucci, C. O. (2000). *Bullybusting: A psychoeducational program for helping bullies and their victims.* Champaign, IL: Research Press.

Olweus, D. (1978). Aggression in the schools: Bullies and whipping boys. Washington, DC: Hemisphere.

Olweus, D. (1991). Bully/victim problems among schoolchildren: Basic facts and effects of a school based intervention program. In D. J. Pepler & K. H. Rubin (Eds.), *The development and treatment of childhood aggression* (pp. 411–448). Hillsdale, NJ: Lawrence Erlbaum Associates.

Olweus, D. (1992). Victimization by peers: Antecedents and long-term outcomes. In K. H. Rubin & J. B. Asendorf (Eds.), *Social withdrawal, inhibition, and shyness in children* (pp. 315–341). Hillsdale, NJ: Lawrence Erlbaum Associates.

Olweus, D. (1993). *Bullying at school: What we know and what we can do.* Oxford, England: Blackwell.

Olweus, D. (1994). Bullying at school: Long-term outcomes for the victims and an effective school-based intervention program. In R. Huesmann (Ed.), *Aggressive behavior: Current perspectives* (pp. 97–130). New York: Plenum.

Olweus, D., Limber, S., & Mihalic, S. F. (1999). *Blueprints for Violence Prevention, Book Nine: Bullying Prevention Program.* Boulder, CO: Center for the Study and Prevention of Violence.

Olweus, D., Limber, S. P., Mullin-Rindler, N., Riese, J., Flerx, V., & Snyder, M. (2003). *Training manual for the Olweus Bullying Prevention Program.* Clemson University: Authors.

Paquette, J. A., & Underwood, M. K. (1999). Gender differences in young adolescents' experiences of peer victim-ization: Social and physical aggression. *Merrill-Palmer Quarterly, 45,* 242–266.

Patterson, G. R., Littman, R. A., & Bricker, W. (1967). Assertive behavior in children: A stop toward a theory of aggression. *Monographs of the Society for Research in Child Development, 32 (5, serial No. 113).*

Pelligrini, A. D. (1998). Bullies and victims in school: A review and call for research. *Journal of Applied Developmental Psychology, 19,* 165–176.

Pellegrini, A. D., Bartini, M., & Brooks, F. (1999). School bullies, victims, and aggressive victims: Factors relating to group affiliation and victimization in early adolescence. *Journal of Educational Psychology, 91,* 216–224.

Pellegrini, A. D., & Long, J. D. (2002). A longitudinal study of bullying, dominance, and victimization during the transition from primary school through secondary school. *British Journal of Developmental Psychology, 20,* 259–280.

Perry, D. G., & Bussey, K. (1977). Self-reinforcement in high- and low-aggressive boys following acts of aggression. *Child Development, 48,* 653–658.

Perry, D. G., Hodges, E. V. E., & Egan, S. K. (2001). Determinants of chronic victimization by peers: A review and a new model of a family influence. In J. Juvonen & S. Graham (Eds.), *Peer harassment in school: The plight of the vulnerable and victimized* (pp. 73–104). New York: Guilford.

Perry, D. G., Kusel, S. J., & Perry, L. C. (1988). Victims of peer aggression. *Developmental Psychology, 24,* 807–814.

Perry, D. G., & Perry, L. C. (1974). Denial of suffering in the victim as a stimulus to violence in aggressive boys. *Child Development, 45,* 55–62.

Perry, D. G., Williard, J. C., & Perry, L. C. (1990). Peers' perceptions of the consequences that victimized children provide aggressors. *Child Development, 61,* 1310–1325.

Phelps, C. E. R. (2001). Children's responses to overt and relational aggression. *Journal of Clinical Child Psychology, 30,* 240–252.

Rigby, K. (1999). Peer victimization at school and the health of secondary school students. *British Journal of Educa-tional Psychology, 69,* 95–104.

Rigby, K. (2002). *New perspectives on bullying.* Philadelphia: Jessica Kingsley.

Rubin, K. H., Chen, X., & Hymel, S. (1993). Socioemotional characteristics of withdrawn and aggressive children. *Merrill-Palmer Quarterly, 39,* 518–534.

Salmivalli, C. (1999). Participant role approach to school bullying: Implications for interventions. *Journal of Adoles-cence, 22,* 453–459.

Schwartz, N. (1999). Self-reports: How the questions shape the answers. *American Psychologist, 54,* 93–105.

Schwartz, D., Dodge, K. A., & Coie, J. D. (1993). The emergence of chronic peer victimization in boys' play groups. *Child Development, 64,* 1755–1772.

Schwartz, D., Dodge, K. A., Petit, G. S., & Bates, J. E. (2000). Friendship as a moderating factor in the pathway between early harsh home environment and later victimization in the peer group. *Developmental Psychology, 36,* 646–662.

Schwartz, D., McFadyen-Ketchum, S., Dodge, K. A., Pettit, G. S., & Bates, J. E. (1998a). Peer group victimization as a predictor of children's behavior problems at home and in school. *Development and Psychopathology, 10,* 87–99.

Schwartz, D., McFadyen-Ketchum, S., Dodge, K. A., Pettit, G. S., & Bates, J. E. (1998b). Social-cognitive and behavioral correlates of aggression and victimization in boys' play groups. *Journal of Abnormal Child Psychology, 26,* 431–440.

Schwartz, D., McFadyen-Ketchum, S., Dodge, K. A., Petit, G. S., & Bates, J. E. (1999). Early behavior problems as a predictor of later peer group victimization: Moderators and mediators in the pathways of social risk. *Journal of Abnormal Child Psychology, 27,* 191–201.

Schwartz, D., Proctor, L. J., & Chien, D. H. (2001). The aggressive victim of bullying: Emotional and behavioral dysregulation as a pathway to victimization by peers. In J. Juvonen & S. Graham (Eds.), *Peer harassment in school: The plight of the vulnerable and victimized* (pp. 147–174). New York: Guilford.

Sharp, S., & Cowie, H. (1994). Empowering pupils to take positive action against bullying. In P. K. Smith & S. Sharp (Eds.), *School bullying: Insights and perspective* (pp. 57–83). London: Routledge.

Slee, P. T. (1994). Situational and interpersonal correlates of anxiety associated with peer victimisation. *Child Psy-chiatry and Human Development, 25,* 97–107.

Slee, P. T. (1995). Peer victimization and its relationship to depression among Australia primary school students. *Personality and Individual Differences, 18,* 57–62.

Smith, P. K., Shu, S., & Madsen, K. (2001). Characteristics of victims of school bullying: Developmental changes in coping strategies and skills. In J. Juvonen & S. Graham (Eds.), *Peer harassment in school: The plight of the vulnerable and victimized* (pp. 332–351). New York: Guilford.

Storch, E. A., Brassard, M. R., & Masia-Warner, C. L. (2003). The relationship of peer victimization to social anxiety and loneliness in adolescence. *Child Study Journal, 33,* 1–18.

Storch, E. A., & Esposito, L. E. (2003). Peer victimization and posttraumatic stress among children. *Child Study Journal, 33,* 91–98.

Storch, E. A., & Masia-Warner, C. (2004). The relationship of peer victimization to social anxiety and loneliness in adolescent females. *Journal of Adolescence, 27,* 351–362.

Storch, E. A., Zelman, E., Sweeney, M., Danner, G., & Dove, S. (2002). Overt and relational victimization and psychosocial adjustment in minority adolescents. *Child Study Journal, 32,* 73–80.

Whitaker, D. J., Rosenbluth, B., Valle, L. A., & Sanchez, E. (2004). Expect Respect: A school-based intervention to promote awareness and effective responses to bullying and sexual harassment. In D. L. Espelage & S. M. Swearer (Eds.), *Bullying in American schools: A social-ecological perspective on prevention and intervention* (pp. 327–350). Mahwah, NJ: Lawrence Erlbaum Associates.

Zarzour, K. (1999). *The schoolyard bully.* Toronto: HarperCollins.

23

Youth Anger Management Treatments for School Violence Prevention

Eva L. Feindler
Scott Weisner
Long Island University, C.W. Post Campus

Anger has long been recognized as a common and natural emotional component of the human experience. However, problems associated with the inappropriate expression of anger and interpersonal aggression are among the most serious concerns of parents, educators, and the mental health community (Debaryshe & Fryxell, 1998). Indeed, the aggressive behavior patterns of children, if left untreated, represent significant clinical concerns as aggression seems stable over time, predicts social adjustment difficulties, and often portends other antisocial behaviors. The development, implementation, and evaluation of both prevention and intervention programs for anger and aggression are imperative and the focus on youth is logical. In fact, a recent analysis of risk factors in school shootings has identified uncontrolled anger and history of aggression as common and lethal individual precursors to violence in school settings (Vossekuil, Fein, Reddy, Borum, & Modzeleski, 2002).

The focus of all anger management intervention is on moderating the intensity, duration, and frequency of anger expression along with facilitating nonaggressive responses to interpersonal issues (Mayne & Ambrose, 1999). Cognitive–behavioral theory (CBT) highlights cognitive processes such as attributions, expectations, interpretations, beliefs, and problem solving as most influential in determining an individual's response to provocation and identifies anger arousal as a mediator of aggressive behavior. Based on the premise that youth exhibit aggressive behavior due to poor anger management, social, and problem-solving skills, Feindler and her colleagues (Feindler & Guttman, 1994; Feindler & Ovens, 1998; Feindler & Scalley, 1998) developed various anger control intervention programs to target these skill deficits. Following a brief discussion of individual risk factors, developmental and contextual influences, this chapter describes these anger management programs, presents an overview of research supporting the implementation in various school and community settings, and highlights current issues in anger management research and practice.

DEVELOPMENTAL AND THEORETICAL FOUNDATIONS

Aggressive Behavior Patterns

Children develop aggressive behavior patterns as a result of a variety of individual, familial, and socioenvironmental risk factors. Sociocognitive theory maintains that an aggressive response to interpersonal dilemmas is not inevitable, but is contingent on aspects of emotion regulation and on specific thoughts and patterns of processing information about the world (Crick & Dodge, 1994). These aggressive responses occur in various contexts that may model, stimulate, and reinforce aggression, thus establishing these responses in a child's sociobehavioral repertoire. Clinical researchers have established categories of aggressive behavior that highlight different precursors and topographies. The distinction between proactive and reactive aggression has important implications for the understanding of the role of anger. Proactive aggression involves aggressive responses that are planned to achieve some goal, require some amount of premeditation, and are reinforced by attainment of the goal (Robbins, 2000). Anger arousal may be a limited aspect, occurring in response to goal-blocking and presenting as frustration. In contrast, reactive aggression emphasizes the emotional response to perceived provocation and in particular focuses on anger arousal as disruptive to prosocial and effective coping or problem-solving responses. Although most youth react with anger to interpersonal triggers and/or misperception of cues in their environment, some are unable to manage this intense emotional arousal, which then may lead to temper outbursts and aggression. These youth will benefit from skills to contain this subjective experience and to respond with effective solutions.

A more recent understanding of aggressive behavior patterns in youth has highlighted some gender differences in expression. Due to hypothesized developmental and socialization processes, research has revealed that boys and girls play differently, relate to others differently, and exhibit aggression differently. According to Underwood (2003), who has compiled much of this research, aggression is a normal aspect of the rough-and-tumble play and competition in which boys engage. Girls engage in less overt aggression and tend to follow display rules more often. Display rules are social conventions for expressing a particular emotion in keeping with the cultural norms. Underwood (2003) concluded that girls seem more responsive to negative adult cues about the expression of overt emotion and aggression and seem in the elementary years to learn some aggression management skills spontaneously. However, girls may develop a pattern of social aggression that is directed at damaging another's self-esteem or social status and is exhibited as rejection, relationship manipulation, or social exclusion (Crick & Grotpeter, 1995). The relationship of anger arousal to these forms of relational aggression has yet to be determined. It may be that anger serves as a motivator and instigator to the relational attack and misperception of social cues or other cognitive distortions may mediate girl's aggressive responding. Recently, developmental scholars have reviewed the developmental framework for gender differences in aggressive behavior (see Putallaz & Bierman, 2004) and suggest that interventions for older girls focus on enhancing relationships and empathic capacity. Clearly, more research is needed to fully understand the role of anger in social aggression and this will certainly have implications for anger management.

Individual and Family Risk Factors

There has been a significant amount of research conducted to help determine specific deficiencies and distortions in the cognitive and emotional processing of aggressive youth. Difficulties encoding appropriate social cues, hostility attributions about the intentionality of provocation, and the misperception of neutral events as direct attacks are characteristic of the social information processing of aggressive individuals. Inferences about other people's goals and evaluation of probable outcome are distorted such that for these youth, aggressive responding is justified (Feindler, 1995; Lochman & Lenhart, 1993). Furthermore, their perceptions and appraisals of trigger events result in an externalization of blame and an egocentric, self-reinforcement of the success of an aggressive response. Nonaggressive or prosocial competence in interpersonal situations would necessitate a more rational and neutral encoding and interpretation of cues and enactment of better coping and problem-solving skills. Aggressive youth typically use impulsive, automatic processing of interpersonal events rather than reflective, deliberate memory-retrieval strategies. Their heightened anger arousal precludes effective solutions (Crick & Dodge, 1994; Feindler & Guttman, 1995). In addition to negative attributional bias in thinking, aggressive youth are more likely than their nonaggressive counterparts to invoke incompetent action-oriented solutions to interpersonal conflicts to generate solutions of retaliation and to approve the instrumental value of being aggressive (Zelli, Dodge, Lochman, & Laird, 1999). Children may believe that aggression will enhance their self-esteem, help avoid a negative image, and lead to positive outcomes. In fact, a recent pilot investigation of adult metacognition of anger experience revealed that rumination or perseverative negative processing of an event, primes selective attention to mood congruent material and heightens that mood (Simpson & Papageorgiu, 2003). Thoughts about retaliation, and the assumptions of hostile motives of others may combine to evoke and justify an aggressive response. Cognitive–behavioral interventions necessarily focus on cognitive restructuring and prosocial self- statements to retrain youth in their appraisals of and responses to provocation.

The understanding of emotion dysregulation will also inform the effectiveness of anger management interventions. Aggressive children appear to have an unusual pattern of affect labeling and over interpret physiological arousal as emanating from an anger experience. Aggressive youth anticipate fewer fear and sadness responses and are less capable of regulating their emotional intensity. Recent research with antisocial youth and emotional temperament has highlighted a unique subset of conduct problem children who evidence a lack of behavioral inhibition and a limited affective component of conscience (Frick et al., 2003; Loney, Frick, Clements, Ellis, & Kerlin, 2003; Oxford, Clavell, & Hughes, 2003). These youth exhibit callous-unemotional traits that relate to lower levels of temperamental fearfulness, lack of responsiveness to punishment cues, and a preference for thrill-seeking activities (Frick et al., 2003). These youth are less concerned about the negative consequences of aggression (being punished, feeling bad about their behavior, and making victims suffer) and instead view aggression as an acceptable way to control and dominate others. From a development perspective, children who have this underresponsive temperament and low behavioral inhibition may miss some of the early precursors to empathic concern that involves emotional arousal evoked by the misfortune and distress of others (Loney et al., 2003). Unlike the impulsive and reactive aggression exhibited by angry youth who cannot regulate emotional intensity, these callous-aggressive responders exhibit social information processes that enhance the positive outcomes and impair the development of appropriate moral reasoning. Another line of emotion research that may relate to empathic capacity and aggressive behavior focuses on the experiences of shame and guilt. Tangney, Wagner, Hill-Barlow, Marschall, and Gramzow (1996) suggested that guilt serves various relationship-enhancing functions, and proneness to "shame-free" guilt inhibits aggressive behavior and influences cognitive reappraisals such that provocations might be viewed as accidental and nonhostile solutions to interpersonal problems might be considered. The role of shame, guilt, and anger as moderators of aggression in your with callous-unemotional traits needs further elaboration and then implications for therapeutic intervention can be considered.

In addition to individual developmental factors, there are a number of contextual factors that establish aggressive behavior in a youth's repertoire. Lochman and Lenhart (1993), in their review of parent behavior, indicated that aversive parenting practices as well as the occurrence of marital aggression witnessed by children are key variables. Indeed, the Vossekuil et al. (2002) review indicated troubled family relationships and lack of parental supervision as common aspects of the school shooter's family environment. A child's difficult temperament, impulsivity, and poor behavioral inhibition can interact with ineffective parenting strategies and can lay the foundation for the cognitive distortions noted in aggressive children (Feindler & Guttman, 1994). However, in investigations of the association between ineffective parenting and conduct disorder in children with callous-unemotional traits, researchers failed to find any "protective" effects of adaptive parenting and suggest that this subset of children will be unresponsive to parental discipline (Oxford et al., 2003; Wootton, Frick, Shelton, & Silverthorn, 1997). Some of the most successful multicomponent anger management programs, such as the Coping Power program described by Lochman and Wells (2003, 2004), include a parent component. Nonetheless, research is still needed on which types of aggressive behavior patterns in children are most impacted by parent psychoeducational components. Clearly, family factors play some role in the development of poor anger management skills, however, whether or not other contextual elements such as teacher/administrator interactions need to be targeted for intervention has not yet been investigated.

In summary, the understanding of the development of inadequate anger management skills in children highlights elements of emotion dysregulation, cognitive distortions, and deficiencies and insufficient prosocial skills. Patterns of aggression hypothesized to be mediated by intense and impulsive anger experiences are related to over attribution of hostile intent, misinterpretation of peer social cues, poor social decision making, high endorsement of beliefs endorsing aggression, low levels of problem-solving and interpersonal skills, and poor consequential thinking. Effective anger management interventions must target each of these skill areas to establish self-control and nonaggressive solutions to provocation for youth. However, a recent meta-analysis of CBT for anger reduction in youth (Sukhodolsky, Kassinove, & Gorman, 2004) concluded that affective psychoeducation treatments (i.e., emotion education, relaxation, and positive imagery) appear less helpful than problem-solving treatments that emphasize cognitive processes. Further research on relational aggression, gender differences, and empathic capacity will only help to tailor the interventions for at risk youth.

ANGER MANAGEMENT TRAINING

Treatment Objectives and Components

The basic program focuses on the control of emotional and impulsive responding to perceived provocation, as well as on the appropriate expression of anger in an assertive and rational manner. By training youth in arousal management skills and through cognitive-restructuring processes, self-control is enhanced and prosocial and conflict-negotiation skills can be exhibited. As each youth builds a repertoire of skills, he or she achieves greater satisfaction from effective communication and problem solving in conflict situations. Increased response options serve to reduce the probabilities of aggressive responding for the youngster as well as the negative consequences for acting-out behavior. Youth are taught to recognize their affect and moderate and regulate their anger and its corresponding cognitive and behavioral components in order to implement prosocial problem-solving actions in response to interpersonal provocations. Some other objectives include enabling these youth to reduce their physiological arousal, aggressive responding, and negative anger sustaining attributions, while increasing the use of self-statements for coping and self-control.

Throughout, the youth are educated about (a) the interaction between the cognitive, physiological, and behavioral components of their anger experience; (b) the adaptive and maladaptive functions of their anger; (c) the situational triggers that provoke their anger; (d) the concept of choice and self-responsibility in their responses to provocations; and (e) the importance of appropriate verbal expression of affect.

Training Methods and Protocol

Cognitive–behavioral anger management programs are generally presented in a psychoeducational skills training format. The three main components—arousal management, cognitive restructuring, and prosocial skills—correspond to hypothesized deficiencies implicated in the development and maintenance of aggressive interpersonal behavior. For each content area, specific skills are presented in a didactic format, modeled by group leaders, rehearsed through repeated role-plays of provocation scenarios, and then applied to the natural environment via homework assignments. Suggested for the school environment, the following 10-session outline contains the key domains of anger management training (AMT) for aggressive youth:

Pre-session: Intake and screening of youth referred for AMT. Treatment readiness to be examined; assessments conducted. Introduce Hassle Log.

Session 1: Orientation to group AMT; rationale for program; affect education and positive–negative aspect of anger; concepts of arousal management; deep breathing and brief relaxation techniques; review hassle logs.

Session 2: Self-assessment of idiosyncratic anger episodes and aggressive behavior patterns. A, B, C sequential analysis and discussion of anger triggers, emotional and behavioral reactions, and consequences.

Session 3: Identification and refuting of aggressive beliefs, reattribution training, understanding the role of cognitive distortions.

Session 4: Assertiveness training, prosocial response to interpersonal conflict and frustration; coping with criticism, moral reasoning, and empathic responding.

Session 5: Self-instruction training, delay of responding tactics, coping self-statements.

Session 6: Continued cognitive restructuring and internalization of self-instructions, rational decision making in choice of response to provocation.

Session 7: Thinking ahead process, anticipatory and consequential cognitions, linking cognitive and arousal management strategies.

Session 8: Self-evaluation processes, metacognitions and objective stance, positive reinforcement, coping statements, and constructive criticism.

Session 9: Problem-solving and effective communication skills, verbal and nonverbal components, identification of best solutions, motivation for implementation.

Session 10: Review of material, individualized anger management plan, preparation for failure, peer feedback, plan for booster sessions.

Detailed session descriptions including expanded topic descriptions, specific role-play scenarios, games and group exercises used in training, homework assignments to promote transfer of skills to the natural environment, as well as materials needed for each session are available in Feindler and Gutman (1994), Feindler and Scalley (1998), and Feindler and Ovens (1998).

Evidence for Treatment Efficacy

Numerous anger management programs have been implemented and/or adapted for specific youth populations across a variety of settings. A focus on outcomes for programs conducted in educational settings reveals, however, limited research for secondary school students. Prominent programs such as Coping Power (Lochman & Wells, 2004), Brain Power (Hudley, et al., 1998), and that reported by Sudhodolsky, Solomon, and Perine (2000) have targeted elementary (Grades 3–6) boys. Evidence from these multicomponent program evaluations in school settings supports the efficacy of the anger management approach to reduction of aggressive behavior, although meta-analysis results suggest that older youth may benefit more from the CBT approach than younger children (Sukhodolsky et al., 2004).

One study, a small group of high school males and females who volunteered to participate in a stress management program received two group and six individual sessions of arousal reduction and cognitive restructuring (Hains, 1994). Decreases in self-reported anger experiences were reported for more than 50% of the treatment subjects who were categorized prior to intervention as having high emotional arousal. Methodological inadequacies, however, limit the interpretations of these results. Hudley et al.'s (1998) Brain Power program focuses on retraining faulty, hostile attributions to reduce peer-directed aggression. A large number of boys in Grades 3–6 were randomly assigned to an attribution retraining, a problem-solving skills, or a no-treatment control group. Treatment participants demonstrated a decrease in hostile attributions and teachers rated them as evidencing greater self-control. Unfortunately, these outcomes were not maintained at a 1-year follow-up (Hudley et al., 1998) and anger experiences were not examined.

Sukhodolsky et al. (2000) conducted a study testing the efficacy of a 10-session program for 33 aggressive fourth- and fifth-grade boys. The intervention techniques used affective education, teaching the children about different emotions in order to increase their emotional vocabulary. Activities were used to help the children become aware of the provocational cues and to learn to monitor their control over anger. The intervention also examined the children's physiological arousal as well as their thoughts during anger-provoking situations. Relaxation techniques were shown to the children to help them control the intensity of their anger. Cognitive skills such as predicting consequences of actions and making proper attributions regarding intent were also taught to help challenge cognitive deficiencies. Finally, the modeling of appropriate behaviors, practicing of alternative behaviors, and role-playing of anger-provoking situations were used to help apply and generalize the new skills. The results showed that compared to the control group, the anger-control intervention was more effective for the reduction of anger-related behaviors as rated by school teachers. Overall, the treatment of anger-related problems in youth has been demonstrated to be effective in both group and individual formats, and when presented with modeling, feedback, and homework strategies.

Lochman and Wells (2004) reported the final results of their Coping Power program as a preventive intervention for boys making the transition from elementary to middle school. High-risk preadolescents identified as disruptive and aggressive by teachers received 8 small-group sessions in the first year and 25 sessions in the second year of AMT. Additionally, parents of these boys participated in 16 sessions focused on improving their discipline and communication strategies. Results from this intensive program emphasized teacher reports of improved school behavior such as an increased ability to resolve problem with peers and teachers and self-reports of lower rates of self-reported covert delinquent behaviors. However, there were no effects for self-reported overt delinquency or in self-report of substance abuse (Lochman & Wells, 2004). Evidence from other studies conducted by Lochman and colleagues (Lochman, Coie, Underwood, & Terry, 1993; Lochman & Lenhart, 1993; Lochman & Wells, 2003) in school setting supports this extensive and multicomponent approach.

The effectiveness of AMT for students in special education settings has also been investigated. Feindler's original anger control program was evaluated for junior high youths in a special program for behavior disorders and multisuspended students (Feindler, Marriott, & Iwata, 1984). More recently, Kellner and Bry (1999) evaluated this anger control program for seven teens in a day school for adolescents with emotional difficulties. Pre–post data for this 10-session intervention revealed a significant decrease on parent and teacher ratings of disruptive behavior. Additionally, physical aggression incidents in the school setting decreased from the 6 months prior to treatment to the 6 months following treatment. A small sample, the absence of a comparison group, and no measurement of the subjective anger experience limit the generalizations of these results. Dwivedi and Gupta (2000) and Sharry and Owens (2000) reported on other small studies with methodological limitations involving adolescent boys with emotional and behavioral difficulties in special education settings. Finally, the anger management approach has been successfully implemented in psychiatric facilities (Feindler, Ecton, Kingsley, & Dubey, 1986; Snyder, Kymisses, & Kessler, 1999), a correctional facility (Guerra & Slaby, 1990), and in residential treatment centers (Dangel, Deschner, & Rasp, 1989; Larson, Calamari, West & Frevert, 1998; Moore & Shannon, 1993; Nugent, Champlin, & Wiinimaki, 1997).

A review of these anger management program evaluations indicates most certainly that angry and aggressive youths benefit from this cognitive–behavioral approach in a variety of settings. Despite the methodological limitations as well as the almost exclusive focus on males, the affect regulation, prosocial, cognitive restructuring, and problem-solving skills training enhances a youth's interpersonal functioning.

However, to date little is known about the exact mechanisms of change, moderators of outcomes, and general viability from clinical research to educational implementation (Sukhodolsky et al., 2004). A recent investigation with boys in an outpatient clinic focused on "dismantling" aspects of the AMT package. Results indicated that cognitive-restructuring strategies were effective in reducing hostile attribution bias, whereas prosocial skills training was effective in improving skills needed to address anger provocation (Sukhodolsky, Golub, Cromwell, & Orban, in press). Additional research on necessary and sufficient treatment components and intervention strategies for both male and female teens is still needed.

Aggression Replacement Training

A complimentary program, which includes anger management as one of three modules, is the aggression replacement training (ART) approach described by Goldstein and Glick (1994). The first module of ART involves "skill streaming," which is designed to teach a broad curriculum of prosocial behavior. The second component consists of anger control training, which empowers the individual to modify his or her own anger. The final section is moral reasoning training, which is aimed to help motivate the individual to employ the skills from the other components.

1. Social skills training objectives: Fifty prosocial skills are taught to the group members. The skills fall into one of six categories of behaviors: beginning skills (e.g., basic conversation skills), advanced social skills (e.g., apologizing and asking for help), skills for dealing with feelings (e.g., expressing affection and dealing with fear), alternatives to aggression (e.g., responding to teasing and negotiating), skills for handling stress (e.g., dealing with being left out or being accused), and planning skills (e.g., goal-setting and decision making).

2. Anger control training objectives: Identify both internal and external triggers that provoke an anger response and identify physiological cues that signal feelings of anger. Self-statements are used to help the individual remain in control of emotional arousal. Other skills such as deep breathing and imagery are also taught to aid in remaining in control. Finally, group members are taught to self-evaluate their performance and reward themselves for remaining in control or at least to begin to learn from their mistakes.

3. Moral reasoning objectives: Designed to raise an individual's level of fairness, justice and concern for the needs and rights of others. Using Kohlberg's research on moral dilemmas as a model, group members are exposed to a moral dilemma designed to arouse cognitive

conflict with the expectation that its resolution will advance the members' level of moral reasoning. Because some aggressive behaviors persist in lieu of the new skills, a values-oriented component was added to push the individual to act in a more socially desirable manner.

As with other anger management programs, the ART small-group sessions are held weekly and each skill is modeled and rehearsed through role-playing activities. Group leaders provide necessary praise, instruction, and feedback, as well as structure other types of learning activities for group members. ART is presented comprehensively in manual format (Goldstein, Glick, & Gibbs, 1998) and can be implemented by a wide variety of educators, mental health professionals, and corrections staff. A training video to accompany the manual is also available (see Research Press, 2002).

Many successful adaptations of ART for violence prevention and intervention with high-risk youth have been described (Goldstein et al., 1998) and several have been evaluated in a systematic way. Data from ART evaluations in a residential correctional facility for males (Goldstein, Glick, Reiner, Zimmerman, & Coultry, 1986) and a runaway shelter for male and female teens (Nugent, Bruley, & Allen, 1998) support its effectiveness. Youth evidenced substantial increases in prosocial behavior and decreases in antisocial behaviors and in-facility, acting-out behaviors. A 1-year follow-up of a small number of teens released from the correctional system indicated that parole officers rated ART youth significantly higher than control youths on community functioning. The only evaluation of the program in a school setting was reported by Jones (1990) and aggressive males receiving ART, compared with two control groups, showed a decrease in aggressive incidents and impulsivity and increases of prosocial and coping skills.

The development of the ART manual with numerous lesson plans, activities, and feedback checklists lends itself to implementation in the school setting. Furthermore, its relevance for females, as well as the opportunity for educators to implement the program, bode well for violence prevention efforts of schools. Because the three components have yet to be evaluated separately, it is unclear how effective the anger management sessions are as stand-alone interventions. What may be most promising given the recent research on the absence of empathic capacity in some youth with conduct disorders is the combination of anger management and moral reasoning skills.

Clinical Issues in Anger Management Training

There are aspects of conduct disorder and characteristics of angry and aggressive youth that may interfere with the success of AMT programs. Howells and Day (2003) provided a good review of individual factors related to "readiness" for AMT. Usually, those referred for AMT have complex issues involving a number of co-morbid problems such as substance abuse, personality disorders, or family problems that need to be addressed in order to increase a client's readiness for anger treatment. Additionally, a client's attitudes and beliefs regarding the legitimacy, justification, or cathartic nature of anger can interfere with treatment. Ethnic, cultural, and gender differences may also interfere by creating different expectations and norms regarding the expression of anger and aggressive behaviors. Therefore, it may be necessary to have leaders of similar ethnicity, gender, or culture who teach and model the intervention. These leaders' example may serve to challenge these socially reinforced norms or expectations. DiGuiseppi (1995) confirms that it is difficult to establish and maintain a therapeutic alliance with angry clients (unless therapist and client agree on treatment goals). These clinical concerns have yet to be discussed relative to adolescents or to a group skills training approach.

Additionally, there may be contextual impediments to program success. The setting in which the intervention occurs can also impede on the readiness of an individual. Settings such as residential treatment centers, juvenile detention centers, and hospitals may create an atmosphere or examples of behaviors that contradict the lessons from the intervention. Furthermore, mandated treatment when a client does not choose the intervention or actively resists the notion of anger control may also create low readiness for treatment.

Perhaps implementation in the school setting will increase treatment acceptability if offered as a complement to other programming. However, the identification of high-risk students, referral, and voluntary participation versus a wide-scale, prevention approach has not been fully examined in terms of response to AMT in youth.

IMPLICATIONS FOR PRACTICE

There are a number of issues relative to implementation of AMT in a school setting that warrant discussion. Some of these have been discussed elsewhere (see Feindler & Scalley, 1998), but few have been researched. Table 23.1 presents the main implications and recommendations for school safety programming that are discussed.

In general, preparation of the school environment prior to implementation of an anger management program is necessary. Securing central and building administrative support, as well as teacher and staff training in the principles and methods of anger management, provides the infrastructure needed to ensure program success and generalization of newly acquired skills. School environments present particular practical and ethical issues related to group treatment or psychoeducational programs and identification of target youth will require careful thought. AMT will help disruptive and aggressive youth to manage their emotions and consider alternate responses to provocation. However, training of youth at risk for aggression due to individual or family variables or training of peers who might be victims or bystanders of interpersonal aggression also seems reasonable. Screening and assessment of youth as well as group composition will vary according to the setting and the treatment objectives.

Often, AMT can be considered as an adjunct program to other types of intervention; however, AMT should be consistent with theoretical orientation and outcomes of other programs.

TABLE 23.1
Implications for Practice: Administrative and Clinical Issues in Anger Management Training
(AMT) for School-Based Prevention

General Program Administration
- Ensure administrative support for structure and implementation of program
- Create guidelines on ethical issues related to screening and identification of group members, consent to treatment and confidentially
- Examine relationship of AMT to other school intervention programs

Structure of AMT Program
- Screening and assessment of youth relative to clinical and risk status and readiness to change
- Group membership: same gender groups, level of risk and/or aggressiveness, readiness for group intervention versus individual treatment, prior relationships with group members
- Selection, training and supervision of group leaders
- Involvement of teachers, staff, and parents

Clinical Issues
- AMT as adjunct clinical treatment
- Overarousal and discharge in role-plays and group discussion
- Ethical issues related to confidentially and group dynamics
- Transfer and generalization of anger management skills; homework compliance, reinforcement procedures and booster sessions

---

It is likely that implementation in conjunction with parent education (Lochman & Wells, 2003, 2004) will produce the greatest impact. However, more research is needed to determine the optimal age for intervention, how the gender differential effects treatment, and which components of AMT delivered in which sequence are most effective. Finally, both AMT and ART programs dovetail wonderfully with the educational setting and can be implemented by a variety of professional staff. Care should be taken to ensure competence of the trainers and treatment validity and ongoing supervision is recommended. All in all, AMT will help youth to appropriately channel their emotions and engage in prosocial problem solving and will help in overall school violence prevention.

REFERENCES

Crick, N. R., & Dodge, D. A. (1994). A review and reformulation of social information-processing mechanisms in children's social adjustment. *Psychological Bulletin, 115*, 74–101.

Crick, N. R., & Grotpeter, J. K. (1995). Relational aggression, gender and social-psychological adjustment. *Child Development, 66*, 710–722.

Dangel, R. F., Deschner, J. P., & Rasp, R. R. (1989). Anger control training for adolescents in residential treatment. *Behavior Modification, 13*, 447–458.

Debaryshe, B. D., & Fryxell, D. (1998). A developmental perspective on anger: Family and peer contexts. *Psychology in the Schools, 35*, 205–216.

DiGiuseppe, R. (1995). Developing the therapeutic alliance with angry clients. In H. Kassinove (Ed.), *Anger disorders: Definitions, diagnosis and treatment* (pp. 131–149). Philadelphia, PA: Taylor & Francis.

Dwivedi, K., & Gupta, A. (2000). "Keeping cool": Anger management through group work *Support for Learning, 15*, 76–81.

Feindler, E. L. (1995). An ideal treatment package for children and adolescents with anger disorders. In H. Kassinove (Ed.), *Anger disorders: Definition, diagnosis, and treatment* (pp. 173–195). Philadelphia, PA: Taylor & Francis.

Feindler, E. L., Ecton, R. B., Kingsley, D., & Dubey, D. (1986). Group anger control training for institutionalized psychiatric male adolescents. *Behavior Therapy, 17*, 109–123.

Feindler, E. L., & Guttman. J. (1994). Cognitive behavioral anger control training for groups of adolescents: A treatment manual. In C. W. LeCroy (Ed.), *Handbook of child and adolescent treatment manuals* (pp. 170-199). New York: Lexington Books.

Feindler, E. L., Marriott, S. A., & Iwata, M. (1984). Group anger control training for junior high school delinquents. *Cognitive Therapy and Research, 8*, 299–311.

Feindler E. L., & Ovens, D. (1998). *Treatment manual: Cognitive-Behavioral Group Anger Management for Youth.* Unpublished manuscript.

Feindler, E. L., & Scalley, M. (1998). Adolescent anger-management groups for violence reduction. In T. Ollendick & K. Storber (Eds.), *Group interventions in the school and community* (pp. 100–118). Needam, MA: Allyn & Bacon.

Frick, P. J., Cornell, A. H., Bodin, S. D., Dave, H. A., Barry, C. T., & Loney, B. R. (2003). Callous-unemotional traits and development pathways to severe conduct problems. *Developmental Psychology, 39*, 246–260.

Goldstein, A. P., & Glick, B. (1994). Aggression replacement training: Curriculum and evaluation. *Simulation and Gaming, 25*, 9–26.

Goldstein, A. P., Glick, B., & Gibbs, J. C. (1998). *Aggression Replacement Training: A comprehensive intervention for aggressive youth.* Champaign, IL: Research Press.

Goldstein, A. P., Glick, B., Reiner, S., Zimmerman, D., & Coultry, T. (1986). *Aggression Replacement Training.* Champaign, IL: Research Press.

Guerra, N. G., & Slaby, R. G. (1990). Cognitive mediators of aggression in adolescent offenders: 2. Intervention. *Developmental Psychology, 26*, 269–277.

Hains, A. A. (1994). The effectiveness of a school-based, cognitive-behavioral stress management program with adolescents reporting high and low levels of emotional arousal. *The School Counselor, 42*, 114–125.

Howells, K., & Day, A. (2003). Readiness for anger management: clinical and theoretical issues. *Clinical Psychology Review, 23*, 319–337.

Hudley, C., Britsch, B., Wakefield, W. D., Smith, F., DeMorat, M., & Cho, S. (1998). An attribution retraining program to reduce aggression in elementary school students. *Psychology in the Schools, 35*, 271–282.

Jones, Y. (1990). *Aggression Replacement Training in a high school setting.* Unpublished manuscript.

Kellner, M. H., & Bry, B. H. (1999). The effects of anger management groups in a day school for emotionally disturbed adolescents. *Adolescence, 34*, 645–651.

Larson, J. D., Calamari, J. E., West, J. G., & Frevert, T. A. (1998). Aggression management with disruptive adolescents in the residential setting: Integration of a cognitive-behavioral component. *Residential Treatment for Children and Youth, 15,* 1–9.

Lochman, J. E., Coie, J. D., Underwood, M. K., & Terry, R. (1993). Effectiveness of a social relations intervention program for aggressive and nonaggressive, rejected children. *Journal of Consulting and Clinical Psychology, 61,* 1053–1058.

Lochman, J. E., & Lenhart, L. A. (1993). Anger coping intervention for aggressive children: Conceptual models and outcome effects. *Clinical Psychology Review, 13,* 785–805.

Lochman, J. E., & Wells, K. C. (2003). Effectiveness of the Coping Power Program and of classroom intervention with aggressive children: Outcomes at a 1-year follow-up. *Behavior Therapy, 34,* 493–515.

Lochman, J. E., & Wells, K. C. (2004). The Coping Power program for preadolescent aggressive boys and their parents: Outcome effect at the 1-year follow-up. *Journal of Consulting and Clinical Psychology, 72,* 571–578.

Loney, B. R., Frick, P. J., Clements, C. B., Ellis, M. C., & Kerlin, K. (2003). Callous-unemotional traits, impulsivity, and emotional processing in adolescents with antisocial behavior problems. *Journal of Clinical Child and Adolescent Psychology, 32,* 66–80.

Mayne, T. J., & Ambrose, T. K. (1999). Research review on anger in psychotherapy. *In Session: Psychotherapy in Practice, 53,* 353–363.

Moore, K. J., & Shannon, K. K. (1993). The development of superstitious beliefs in the effectiveness of treatment of anger: Evidence for the importance of experimental program evaluation in applied settings. *Behavioral Residential Treatment, 8,* 147–161.

Nugent, W. R., Bruley, C., & Allen, P. (1998). The effects of aggression replacement training on antisocial behavior in a runaway shelter. *Research on Social Work Practice, 8,* 637–656.

Nugent, W. R., Champlin, D., & Wiinimaki, L. (1997). The effects of anger control training on adolescent antisocial behavior. *Research on Social Work Practice, 7,* 446–462.

Oxford, M., Cavell, T. A., & Hughes, J. N. (2003). Callous/unemotional traits moderate the relation between ineffective parenting and child externalizing problems: A partial replication and extension. *Journal of Clinical Child and Adolescent Psychology, 32,* 577–586.

Putallaz, M., & Bierman, K. L. (Eds.). (2004). *Aggression, antisocial behavior, and violence among girls.* New York: Guilford.

Robbins, P. R. (2000). *Anger, aggression and violence.* Jefferson, NC: McFarland.

Simpson, C., & Papageorgiu, C. (2003). Metacognitive beliefs about rumination in anger *Cognitive and Behavioral Practice, 10,* 91–94.

Sharry, J., & Owens, C. (2000). "The rules of engagement": A case study of a group with 'angry' adolescents. *Clinical Child Psychology and Psychiatry, 5,* 53–62.

Snyder, K. V., Kymissis, P., & Kessler, K. (1999). Anger management for adolescents: Efficacy of brief group therapy. *Journal of American Academy of Child and Adolescent Psychiatry, 38,* 1409–1416.

Sukhodolsky, D. G., Golub, A., Cromwell, E., & Orban, L. (2005). Dismantling anger control training for children: A randomized pilot study of social problem-solving versus social skills training components. *Behavior Therapy, 36,* 15–23.

Sukhodolsky, D. G., Kassinove, H., & Gorman, B. (2004). Cognitive-behavioral therapy for anger in children and adolescents: A meta-analysis. *Aggression and Violent Behavior, 9,* 247–269.

Sukhodolsky, D. G., Solomon, R. M., & Perine, J. (2000). Cognitive-behavioral, anger-control intervention for elementary school children: A treatment-outcome study *Journal of Child and Adolescent Group Therapy, 10,* 159–170.

Tangney, J. P., Wagner, P. E., Hill-Barlow, D., Marschall, D. E., & Gramzow, R. (1996). Relation of shame and guilt to constructive versus destructive responses to anger across the lifespan. *Journal of Personality and Social Psychology, 70,* 797–809.

Underwood, M. K. (2003). *Social aggression among girls.* New York: Guilford.

Vossekuil, B., Fein, R., Reddy, M., Borum, R., & Modzeleski, W. (2002). *The final report and findings of the Safe School Initiative: Implications for the prevention of school attacks in the United States.* Washington, DC: U.S. Department of Education, Office of Elementary and Secondary Education, Safe and Drug-Free Schools Program and U.S. Secret Service, National Threat Assessment Center.

Wootton, J. M., Frick, P. J., Shelton, K. K., & Silverthorn, P. (1997). Ineffective parenting and childhood conduct problems: The moderating role of callous-unemotional traits. *Journal of Consulting and Clinical Psychology, 65,* 292–300.

Zelli, A., Dodge, K. A., Lochman, J. E., & Laird, R. D. (1999). The distinction between beliefs legitimizing aggression and deviant processing of social cues: Testing measurement validity and the hypothesis that biased processing mediates the effects of beliefs on aggression. *Journal of Personality and Social Psychology, 77,* 150–166.

24

A Critical Analysis of School-Based Anger Management Programs for Youth

Douglas C. Smith
University of Hawaii, Manoa

Jim Larson
DeAnne R. Nuckles
University of Wisconsin, Whitewater

Given recent concerns with increasing levels of youth violence, both in the United States and elsewhere, it is not surprising that anger management interventions have proliferated in public school settings. Despite the intuitive appeal of such strategies for reducing violent behavior, it is far from clear how effective these approaches are with school-age youth. A recent meta-analysis by Del Vecchio and O'Leary (2004), covering 23 studies of anger management with *adults*, resulted in medium to large effect sizes across a wide range of treatment modalities, settings, and service-delivery systems. Reviews by Tafrate (1995) and Beck and Fernandez (1998) provide limited support for anger management interventions with diverse population groups including children, inmates, and child-abusing parents. Finally, a review and meta-analysis by Smith, Larson, DeBaryshe, and Salzman (2000), specifically focusing on anger management with *youth*, found general support for anger management as an intervention strategy, with larger effect sizes evidenced for its impact on angry *affect* as opposed to attitudes or behaviors.

Although anger management as a general intervention appears to offer considerable promise, very little is known at this juncture about specific treatment components most predictive of success or the conditions under which this occurs. Currently, a wide range of treatment strategies fall under the anger management umbrella. These include relaxation training, cognitive-based therapies including cognitive restructuring and social problem solving, and behavioral treatments involving skills training, rehearsal, and feedback (Deffenbacher, McNamara, Stark, & Sabadell, 1990; Deffenbacher, Oetting, Huff, & Thwaites, 1995). An important remaining task is to identify more precisely which treatment components are responsible for the positive outcomes as noted and the specific conditions mediating these effects.

The purpose of this chapter is to provide a detailed description of the variety of interventions that constitute school-based anger management for youth. In so doing, this chapter describes the kinds of students for whom these programs appear best suited, treatment conditions that optimize success, and strategies for improving maintenance and generalization. The description is based on a review and critical analysis of 28 empirical studies evaluating anger management programs in school settings. Results of the analysis form the basis for a set of recommendations for mental health professionals who work with angry and aggressive students in schools.

RATIONALE FOR ANGER MANAGEMENT INTERVENTIONS

Anger is often characterized as a misunderstood human emotion (Tavris, 1989), responsible for a wide range of negative human conditions including physical, behavioral, psychological, and interpersonal problems. Chronically high levels of anger and hostility are cited as risk factors for a variety of health-related concerns including cardiovascular distress, hypertension, gastrointestinal difficulties, and other diseases associated with stress to the immune system (McDermott, Ramsay, & Bray, 2001; Miller, Smith, Turner, Guijarro, & Hallett, 1996; Suinn, 2001). Additionally, uncontrolled anger is thought to contribute to such wide-ranging societal issues as marital and family discord, child abuse, road rage, job loss, and legal difficulties (Deffenbacher, Huff, Lynch, Oetting, & Salvatore, 2000; Del Vecchio & O'Leary, 2004).

Perhaps most importantly to readers of this chapter, frequent and intense anger is clearly related to violent and aggressive behavior, both in children and adults. Dodge and colleagues (Dodge & Coie, 1987; Dodge, Lochman, Harnish, Bates, & Petit, 1997) describe reactive aggression as violent behavior precipitated by physiological arousal such as muscle tension and increased heart rate, often accompanied by hostile appraisals of others. Likewise, Berkowitz (1990, 1993), among others, refers to hostile aggression as violence prompted by emotional upheaval, angry feelings, and negative perceptions of others. In each of these conceptualizations, anger serves as a trigger for ensuing aggression. According to Feindler and Scalley (1998), "anger can act as a determinant of aggressive behavior and will influence the cognitive processes used to mediate one's response to perceived provocation" (p. 104). Based on this view, anger arousal impairs decision making and impulse control, thereby increasing the likelihood of explosive, uninhibited aggressive behavior in the face of adversity.

Additionally, chronically high levels of anger and hostility are frequently cited as risk factors for serious acts of violence at school, that is, school shootings (Dwyer, Osher, & Warger, 1998; O'Toole, 2000). For example, the document *Early Warning, Timely Response* produced by the U.S. Departments of Education and Justice (Dwyer et al., 1998), describes "uncontrolled anger expressed frequently and intently" (p. 15) as one of the key predictors of violence potential at school. Similarly, the American Psychological Association's guide (APA, 1999) to understanding and preventing youth violence lists frequent "loss of temper" as an important trigger for violent behaviors such as fighting, assault, property damage, and so on, as well as more serious and lethal forms of violence.

Given the link between high levels of anger and hostility and aggressive and violent behavior, it is not surprising that comprehensive approaches for violence prevention in schools often include strategies for helping students manage and control their anger. The following section describes the conceptual basis for such programs.

CONCEPTUAL MODELS OF ANGER

Numerous researchers have commented on the lack of clarity in conceptualizing and defining anger (Averill, 1982; Kassinove, 1995; Smith & Furlong, 1994). In many respects, anger is an elusive construct both to define and measure. There is now growing consensus that anger consists of three interrelated domains, which include affective, cognitive, and behavioral components (Spielberger, Reheiser, & Sydeman, 1995).

The emotional or affective component recognizes anger as a fundamental human emotion. Angry feelings can vary in intensity from mild irritation to full-blown rage and can also vary in frequency and/or duration of occurrence. Because these are by and large private events, measurement of angry affect most often relies on self-report. Nelson and Finch (2000), for example, developed the Children's Inventory of Anger (ChIA) to measure intensity of anger experienced across a range of potentially frustrating daily events. Respondents are asked to report how they might feel if these events actually happened to them. Responses are then quantified according to a Likert-type scale ranging from (*I don't care. That situation doesn't even bother me. I don't know why that would make anyone angry or mad*) to (*I can't stand that! I'm furious! I feel like really hurting or killing that person or destroying that thing*). To further clarify response choices, facial icons depicting various levels of angry affect are used to illustrate each response choice. Studies utilizing the ChIA report modest correlations between anger intensity and antisocial behaviors among youth populations (Nelson & Finch, 2000).

A second dimension of anger is cognitive or attitudinal in nature and refers to a set of beliefs about anger-provoking events and, more specifically, the role of others in instigating or exacerbating angry reactions. Researchers have used the term *hostility* to describe a worldview in which the intentions of others are viewed as malevolent and suspicious (Spielberger et al., 1995). The Buss–Durkee Hostility Inventory (BDHI; Buss & Durkee, 1957) was an early attempt to assess such negative thought patterns as resentment, jealousy, suspiciousness, and lack of trust and corresponding behavior patterns including oppositionality, irritability, and verbal and physical aggression. Kazdin, Rodgers, Colbus, and Siegel (1987) subsequently developed the Children's Hostility Inventory (CHI) utilizing the same subscales as the BDHI but relying on parent ratings rather than self-report to assess each item. The CHI is appropriate for use with children ages 6–12 and has been shown to have adequate internal consistency and discriminant validity (Furlong & Smith, 1994).

Finally, anger can be operationalized according to an expressive or behavioral component, which includes not only direct forms of aggression such as physical and verbal assault, but also indirect forms of aggression such as spreading negative rumors or intentionally excluding an individual from a group or activity. Recent research suggests that indirect forms of aggression may be more characteristic of females than males and is often referred to as relational aggression (see Crick, ₁996, for a review). Additionally, anger may be expressed behaviorally utilizing more constructive and socially appropriate skills including assertive negotiation, conflict resolution, positive coping, and other modes of stress reduction.

The Aggression Scale (AS; Orpinas & Frankowski, 2001) is a self-report measure of the frequency of aggressive behavior endorsed by 11- to 14-year-old students. In addition to measuring various forms of overt aggression such as pushing, kicking, hitting, threatening, and teasing, the AS also examines the frequency of angry feelings. In a study of middle school students (Orpinas & Frankowski, 2001; Orpinas, Parcel, McAlister, & Frankowski, 1995), significant positive correlations were found between scores on the AS and teacher ratings of aggression, self-reported fights, and alcohol and marijuana consumption—AS scores were negatively correlated with degree of parental monitoring and with academic achievement.

More recently, there have been attempts to simultaneously assess the three components of anger just described in a single scale. Siegel (1996) developed the Multidimensional Anger Inventory to measure angry feelings, cognitions, and behaviors in adult populations. Smith, Furlong, and colleagues (Furlong, Smith, & Bates, 2002; Smith, Furlong, Bates, & Laughlin, 1998) designed the Multidimensional School Anger Inventory (MSAI) specifically to measure angry affect as a product of potentially frustrating events in school, attitudes toward school and teachers, and both positive coping and negative expressions of anger. Such a conceptualization allows researchers and clinicians to begin to identify various subtypes of anger disorders and to tailor intervention strategies to the specific features of each subtype (Furlong & Smith, 1998).

The three-dimensional model of anger described here is the basis for anger management interventions, both within and outside school settings. All of the interventions reviewed in this chapter included either an affective, cognitive, or behavioral component and many programs included two or more components. Based on our review of the literature, the following sections describe the populations typically served by such programs, the specific intervention components utilized, and factors that appear to enhance treatment generalization.

REVIEW OF ANGER MANAGEMENT LITERATURE

Study Selection Criteria

The studies reviewed in this chapter were obtained through a literature search using PsycINFO. Descriptive terms used in the search were (*anger management*) and (*children*) or (*adolescents*) and (*school*). The search was further restricted to include only articles published between 1980 and 2004. Additionally, the study had to include an intervention effort and anger management, anger regulation, or anger control had to be the primary emphasis of the intervention. Following these criteria, 28 intervention studies were selected for review. Authors and dates of the reviewed studies, participants, settings, meeting frequency, and intervention content are presented in Table 24.1.

Participants and Setting

Of the 28 intervention studies, 16 targeted students in a range that included Grades 4–8. Five were for high school students, and five included younger elementary school students. Eargle, Guerra, and Tolan (1994), had an "early" program and a "late" program, with separate content for elementary school students and middle school students, and Hemphill and Littlefield (2000) examined a program designed for use with an age range of 5- to 14-year-olds. Eight interventions exclusively targeted males, although almost half ($n = 13$) the programs reviewed included both males and females in the treatment groups. Even so, the preponderance of participants in these studies was male. Very little specific data were provided with regard to the ethnic composition of treatment groups, although a sizeable number of studies ($n = 12$) claimed to include more than one ethnic group. Four interventions specifically targeted African-American students and four others utilized only White students. The majority of the interventions reviewed were implemented in small pull-out groups of students. Seven of the programs utilized a classroom environment and two used individual counseling. Most interventions ($n = 13$) were conducted over 6 to 10 sessions, although 12 took place over 10 or more sessions.

Intervention Content

The 28 intervention studies included in this review were examined for treatment content. Given its centrality in the clinical literature since the mid-1970s and the emphasis on short-term, school-based treatment environments, virtually all of the studies employed cognitive–behavioral techniques. Whereas there were variations in the preponderance of one clinical technique over another among the studies, the three major divisions of cognitive–behavioral therapies (CBT) identified by Mahoney and Arnkoff (1978) continue to dominate the anger management literature reviewed here: (a) coping skills therapies, (b) problem-solving therapies, and (c) cognitive-restructuring methods. Many of the interventions also referenced operant components, such as point systems, self-monitoring, or behavioral rehearsal.

Coping skills therapy involves the use of education, therapist modeling, skills rehearsal, and *in vivo* trials so that the student acquires a repertoire of adaptive responses to use in potentially volatile situations. Coping skills are not constrained by any established boundaries and subsume a variety of teachable behaviors. Common among most training programs were skills associated with anger regulation and alternatives to aggressive behavior. A sampling

TABLE 24.1
Summary of Anger Management Studies

Authors	Participants	Setting	Meeting Frequency	Intervention Content	Maintenance and Generalization
Bosworth, Espelage, and Dubay (1998)	• F = 45, M = 36 • 7th grade • Mixed ethnicity	Classroom	Variable over 4 weeks	• Cognitive–behavioral (mc)	• Real-life training examples
Bosworth, Espelage, Dubay Dahlberg, and Daytner (1996)	• N = 558 • 6th–8th grade	Classroom	Variable over 10 weeks	• Psychoeducational using multimedia • Cognitive–behavioral (mc)	• Real-life training examples • Practice modules
Deffenbacher, Lynch, Oetting, and Kemper (1996)	• F = 57, M = 63 • 6th–8th grades • Mixed ethnicity	Small group	9 sessions	• Cognitive–behavioral (mc) • Emotion-focus (relaxation) • Behavioral (positive communication)	• Homework (personal logs) • Real-life training examples
Eargle, Guerra, and Tolan (1994)	• Elementary school • Early program for grades 2nd & 3rd • Late program for grades 5th & 6th	Small group	28 sessions	• Social cognitive (social skills/social problem solving)	• Rewards • Real-life training examples
Feindler, Marriott and Iwata (1984)	• N = 36 (NOT M or F?) • 12–15 years	Small group	10 sessions	• Cognitive–behavioral (mc) • Emotion-focus (mc) • Behavioral	• Homework • Rewards • Real-life training examples
Garrison and Stolberg (1983)	• M = 30 • 3rd–5th grade	Small group	3 sessions	• Emotion-focus (self-awareness)	• None noted

(Continued)

TABLE 24.1
(Continued)

Authors	Participants	Setting	Meeting Frequency	Intervention Content	Maintenance and Generalization
Hains (1994)	• F = 14, M = 5 • 11th grade • Mixed ethnicity	Classroom	8 sessions	• Cognitive (restructuring) • Psychoeducational	• None noted
Hains and Szjakowski (1990)	• M = 21 • 16–17 years • Predominantly white non-Hispanic	Classroom	9 sessions	• Cognitive (restructuring) • Cognitive-behavioral (self-monitoring)	• Follow-up data collected
Hemphill and Littlefield (2000)	• N = 145 • 5–14 years • Mixed ethnicity • Targets students and their parents	Small group	8–10 sessions	• Cognitive-behavioral • Anger management, problem-solving, social skills • Parenting skills, issues of parents • Parent–child interactions	• None noted
Hermann and McWhirter (2003)	• F = 58, M = 149 • 7th–9th grade • 50% Hispanic, 40% Caucasian	Small group	8 weeks	• Cognitive-behavioral (mc) • Anger and aggression management • Emotion focus • Cognitive (self-talk)	• Follow-up data • Anger journal
Hinshaw, Buhrmester, and Heller (1989)	• M = 24 • Mixed ethnicity	Small group	15 sessions	• Cognitive-behavioral (mc) • Pharmacological	• Real-life training examples
	• F = 2, M = 3	Small	6 sessions	• Emotion-focus (self-awareness)	

Study	Sample	Format	Sessions	Approach	Additional components
Horton (1996)	• 6–8 years • Mixed ethnicity	group		• Cognitive (problem-solving) • Behavioral (social skills)	• None noted
Hudley, et al. (1998)	• M = 384 • 3rd–6th grade • Predominantly African-American	Classroom	24 sessions	• Cognitive (restructuring) • Behavioral (expression)	• None noted
Kellner and Tutin (1995)	• F-1, M = 3 • 15–18 years	Small group	5 sessions	• Psychoeducational • Cognitive–behavioral (mc)	• Staff reinforcement • Homework • Incentives
Larson (1992)	• F-15, M = 22 • 7th grade • Mixed ethnicity	Classroom	10 sessions	• Cognitive–behavioral (mc)	• Homework • Review of skills • Reinforcement • Feedback
Lo, Loe, and Cartledge (2002)	• F = 1, M = 4 • 3rd & 4th grade • Urban school • Predominantly African American	Small group	Classroom instruction 3 × week for school year & pull-out 3 × week for school year	• Behavioral (social skills)	
Lochman (1985)	• M = 22 • Mean age = 10.4 year • Mixed ethnicity	Small group	18 sessions	• Cognitive–behavioral (mc) • beghavioral (goal-setting)	• Follow-up data collection
Lochman et al. (1984, 1985)	• M = 76 • 4th–6th grade • Mixed ethnicinty	Small group	12 sessions	• Cognitive–Behavioral (mc) • Behavioral (goal setting)	• None noted
Lochman and Curry (1986)	• M = 20 • 4th & 5th grade • Mixed ethnicity	Small group	18 sessions	• Cognitive–behavioral (mc) Cognitive (self-talk)	• Teacher monitoring

(Continued)

TABLE 24.1
(Continued)

Authors	Participants	Setting	Meeting Frequency	Intervention Content	Maintenance and Generalization
Lochman, Lampron, Gemmer, Harris, and Wyckoff (1989)	• M = 32 • 4th–6th grade • Mixed ethnicity	Small group	18 sessions	• Cognitive–behavioral (mc) • Psychoeducational	• Teacher consultattion
Lochman, Nelson, and Sims (1981)	• F = 1, M = 11 • 7–10 years • African-American	Small group	12 sessions	• Cognitive–behavioral (mc)	• Real-life training examples • Videotape
Massey, Armstrong, and Boroughs (2003)	• M = 42, F = 42 • 9th grade • Majority white, non-Hispanic	Small group	10 sessions	• Cognitive–behavioral (mc)	• Homework
Nickerson (2003)	• 41 (random M & F) • 14–16 years • Predominantly Latino	Classroom	8 sessions	• Cognitive–behavioral (mc)	• None noted
Ninness, Ellis, Miller, Baker, and Rutherford (1995)	• M = 4 • 14.5 years	Small group	50 sessions	• Cognitive–behavioral (self-monitoring) • Behavioral (expression)	• Training in multiple settings

Study	Sample	Format	Dosage	Approach	Incentives/Follow-up
Normand and Robert (1990)	• F = 42 • 4th–5th grade • White, non-Hispanic	Small group	6 sessions	• Behavioral (expression) • Cognitive–behavioral (problem solving and rehearsal)	• Follow-up data collect
Omizo, Hershberger, and Omizo (1988)	• F = 10, F = 14 • 4th–6th grade • N = 78 • 8th grade	Small group	10 sessions	• Psychoeducational • Cognitive–behavioral (mc)	• None noted • Elective course credit
Rollin, Kaiser-Ulrey, Potts, and Creason (2003)	• African–American • School, with community-based mentor	Small group	2 hours/day, 4 days, week	• Behavioral	• Small stipend every 2 weeks, based on performance • Follow-up data collect
Smith, Siegel, Conner, and Thomas (1994)	• F = 1, M = 2 • M = 10.5 years • Mixed ethnicity	Individual	6 sessions	• Cognitive–behavioral (mc)	• Follow-up data collect

Note. M, male; F, female; mc, multiple components, including self-instruction, affective reduction techniques, social problem-solving, and/or cognitive-restructuring.

of selected interventions is summarized here. Feindler, Marriott, and Iwata (1984) and the subsequent adaptations of this intervention (Kellner & Tutin, 1995; Larson, 1992; Massey, Armstrong, & Boroughs, 2003; Nickerson, 2003) taught adolescents coping skills for anger recognition and regulation and alternatives to aggression through developing assertiveness skills. Deffenbacher, Lynch, Oetting, and Kemper (1996) and Lo, Loe, and Cartledge (2002) emphasized social skills training. Lochman and colleagues (Lochman, 1985; Lochman, Burch, Curry, & Lampron, 1984; Lochman & Curry, 1986; Lochman, Lampron, Burch, & Curry, 1985; Lochman, Lampron, Gemmer, Harris, & Wyckoff, 1989; Lochman, Nelson, & Sims, 1981) trained elementary school boys to use self-instruction phrases (e.g., "Cool it. Calm down.") to regulate their level of anger arousal in affectively charged situations. Eargle et al. (1994) trained high-risk urban students in skills to avoid victimization and in how to seek social support through friendships.

Problem-solving procedures generally follow a model that initially trains the student to recognize a problem when it is encountered and then to apply a prescriptive set of problem-solving skills leading toward an effective solution (D'Zurilla & Nezu, 2001). These problem-solving "steps" are typically trained as self-interrogatories such as proposed by Meichenbaum (2001):

1. What is the problem?
2. What are my choices?
3. What are the possible consequences?
4. Which one should I choose?
5. Now do it!
6. How did it work?

Problem-solving training was a substantial component in Feindler et al.'s (1984) anger management intervention with secondary-level students and in the adaptations of that intervention noted earlier. Problem solving was also a significant training element in Lochman and colleagues' anger management training (AMT) with elementary level boys. Hemphill and Littlefield (2001) integrated problem-solving training components in their work with elementary and middle school students with serious externalizing behavior problems. Smith, Siegel, O'Connor, and Thomas (1994) trained three elementary students with high levels of chronic anger and aggression to use the problem-solving mnemonic, ZIPPER, which stood for ". . . Zip your mouth, Identify the problem, Pause, Put yourself in charge, Explore choices, and Reset" (p. 130).

Cognitive-restructuring methods presuppose that anger is, in part, a function of maladaptive thought processes, and interventions focus on challenging and replacing those thoughts with more adaptive cognitions (Dobson & Dozois, 2001). This methodology requires that clients be developmentally able to reflect on their own cognitions; thus, it is typically reserved for older students. Hains (1994) and Hains and Szyjakowski (1990) used cognitive-restructuring techniques in combination with other CBT procedures to help high school students manage problematic anger, anxiety, and depression. With the aid of a prepared self-monitoring sheet, youth were taught to recall, examine, and challenge cognitions that occasioned their emotional arousal. Eargle et al. (1994) assisted high-risk urban students to challenge normative beliefs about aggressive behavior through discussions and reflections about television violence.

The innovative content and training procedures of four studies reviewed here warrants mention. Hudley et al. (1998) focused training on attributional bias of peer intent in a study with aggressive African-American and Latino Grade 3–6 students. Content included training in the ability to accurately detect others' intentions, to increase attribution of negative intent, and to respond with nonaggressive behaviors to ambiguous situations. Presley and

Hughes (2000) trained high school general education peer trainers to conduct social skills instruction with four special education students with high levels of anger-induced behavior problems. The peer trainers used a series of written provocations (e.g., "You let your classmate borrow your Walkman and your favorite tape and he or she refuses to give it back to you" [p. 117]) and then modeled and trained a social skills procedure adapted from Walker et al. (1988, cited in Presley & Hughes, 2000). In this procedure, students were taught to pause and assess the situation (ASSESS), consider the alternatives to angry aggression (AMEND), and then respond (ACT). Rollin, Kaiser-Ulrey, Potts, and Creason (2003) matched high-risk eighth-grade students with community mentors in year-long internships. The students participated in various career-related activities at their mentor sites for 2 hours per day. Finally, the use of computer technology as a means to teach adolescents to manage anger was examined (Bosworth, Espelage, & Dubay, 1998; Bosworth, Espelage, Dubay, Dahlberg, & Daytner, 1996). These authors developed a series of computer modules that train students individually in three primary areas: (a) anger management, (b) dispute resolution, and (c) perspective-taking. The modules use games, simulations, and interactive interviews as training procedures.

Generalization

When a student with anger management problems is taught to enact an anger control skill or coping strategy in the context of the therapy setting, and then the student subsequently employs that skill in the natural setting, generalization has occurred. It is clearly an objective of interventions designed for use in the school to promote behavior change in the greater school setting, not just in the therapy group. Each study in this review was examined for built-in procedures designed to help generalize training to the larger school or home environment. Unfortunately, few of the studies in this sample rose much beyond a "train and hope" standard in which primary effort is focused on the intervention training content and generalization into the natural environment is left to chance. Of the 28 articles selected for this review, 19 indicated at least minimal attention to this aspect (see Table 24.1). The most frequently employed methods were the use of actual incidents from the students' experiences as discussion or role-play scenarios during the training sessions (e.g., Deffenbacher et al., 1996; Feindler et al., 1984) and homework in the form of self-monitoring logs or reflection journals (e.g., Hermann & McWhirter, 2003; Lo et al., 2002). Feindler et al. (1984) took the additional step of preparing youth from the training groups for possible peer antagonism directed at their newly acquired behavioral and cognitive changes. Some of the intervention studies enlisted the active support of classroom teachers as either progress monitors for student goal-setting (e.g., Lochman and colleagues) or facilitators for the completion of self-monitoring logs (e.g., Kellner & Tutin, 1995).

RECOMMENDATIONS FOR PRACTITIONERS

The identification and treatment of students with externalizing behavior and anger control problems within the school setting is an important and continuing service-delivery obligation for supportive services practitioners. As a setting for treatment when viewed in comparison to that of a community-based clinic, schools offer (a) access to children and youth who are at risk, not just those who have been "caught"; (b) more convenient access to them; and (c) the capacity to observe and manipulate the social and academic environment in pursuit of treatment goals (Coie, Underwood, & Lochman, 1991). Quite simply, schools offer practitioners an ideal environment for small-group skills training.

Identification of Treatment Group Members

To identify students in need of treatment, most of the interventions in this review relied on either teacher nomination (e.g., Omizo, Hershberger, & Omizo, 1988) or a combination of teacher nomination and psychometric screening to identify the pool of students (e.g., Eargle et al., 1994; Lochman et al., 1984, 1985; Lo et al., 2002). Hudley and colleagues (1998) added peer nominations to teacher recommendations, and Rollin and associates (2003) relied exclusively on archival records of existing risk factors.

In the applied setting, practitioners need to attend even more carefully to the screening and selection of students for intervention so as to best match skills training with student need. Given the multidimensional nature of anger and related constructs, it is essential that accurate assessment data identify the specific foci of treatment and that intervention efforts be tailored to address these needs (see Furlong & Smith, 1998, for a discussion of anger subtypes).

Virtually all of the intervention studies reviewed here demonstrated a statistically significant level of change on one or more treatment measures. However, school practitioners are seeking authentic behavioral change in the natural environment. Consequently, the selection process must take into account factors such as the following:

1. Comparative severity of the presenting behaviors of potential group members. Students with significant emotional-behavioral disabilities who are included in a group of students with less volatile behaviors can necessitate extraordinary behavior management issues in the group and detract from training effectiveness.
2. Comparative rejection status of group members. The inclusion of a highly rejected peer can increase the possibility for victimization within the group and reduce the social acceptability of the treatment for the other members.
3. Intervention-treatment needs match. Many students present with seriously disruptive discipline problems in the school setting that are secondary to poorly socialized, impulsive, or antisocial influences. A treatment program that focuses on anger control will be of little use to students with externalizing behavior problems that are unrelated to anger.

Practitioners are advised to employ a multiple-gate screening process (e.g., Larson & Lochman, 2001) that includes teacher nomination, archival review, observation, psychometric assessment, and student interview. Beginning an intervention with a group of students with the greatest potential to benefit from the training procedures increases the likelihood of demonstrable outcomes. In addition, data collected from a comprehensive screening assessment will function well as baseline data for program evaluation.

Treatment Content

As noted, the overwhelming number of intervention studies in this review employed CBT designed to train new procedures for cognitively processing volatile or provocative encounters and new behaviors for avoiding problematic responses. No studies were located that supported the effectiveness of simple "talk therapy" in the management of anger-induced, externalizing behavior in the school setting. An effective screening assessment should guide the content and answer the question, "What does this student need to know and be able to do to manage his or her anger-related problem behavior?" Practitioners should then adapt the intervention content to these needs. In this review, two intervention structures received the most support: Feindler et al.'s model for use with adolescents (Feindler et al., 1984; Kellner & Tutin, 1995; Larson, 1992; Massey et al., 2003; Nickerson, 2003) and Lochman and colleagues intervention for students in Grades 3–6 (Lochman, 1985; Lochman, et al., 1984; Lochman et al., 1985; Lochman & Curry, 1986; Lochman et al., 1989; Lochman, Nelson, & Sims, 1981). The adolescent intervention is commercially available as a training component of *Aggression Replacement Training* (Goldstein, Glick, & Gibbs, 1998) and in an adapted version in *Think First: Addressing Aggression in the Secondary Schools* (Larson, 2005). Lochman and colleagues' intervention is commercially available in *Helping Schoolchildren Cope with Anger* (Larson & Lochman, 2001). Practitioners are urged to avoid retrofitting students to the intervention, but rather they should become familiar enough with the manualized training components to effectively identify those students who will potentially benefit. Procedures for screening and identification should involve a collaborative multiple gate nomination process with classroom teachers, comprehensive record review, and student observation and interview. The use of functional behavior assessments (e.g., Watson & Steege, 2003) to identify the potential functional aspects of the student's anger can provide useful information for the identification of training needs and outcomes. Comprehensive discussions of these identification processes with elementary school students can be found in Larson and Lochman (2001) and Walker, Ramsey, and Gresham (2004). Additional procedures for use with secondary level students can be found in Larson (2005).

Generalization

Meichenbaum (2001) noted that the anger management literature abounded with numerous treatment programs that sounded encouraging, but lacked evidence of generalization across settings or maintenance over time. For school practitioners, the overriding objective of AMT is to first produce positive behavior change in the natural school setting. It is difficult enough to help a high-risk student to demonstrate an insight or skill in the context of the therapy setting, however, it is monumentally more difficult to help the student to use it under authentic circumstances in the classroom, hallway, or playground. In the applied setting, generalization is the *sine qua non* of treatment.

In order to increase the probability for generalization, practitioners need to build in procedures and environmental supports at the onset of the training and maintain them as the centerpiece of their entire effort. Classroom teachers, administrators, and parents need to be brought into the training procedures and viewed as true collaborators who can support, monitor, and reinforce training tasks (see Larson & Lochman, 2001, for a discussion). It is not enough to ask and hope for ill-defined cooperation; these individuals need to be trained to engage in identified roles that alter the environmental contingencies to increase the probability of new behavior from the students. Meichenbaum (2001) and Meichenbaum and Beimiller (1998) addressed procedures for assisting students to participate in their own generalization process at the onset, during, and at the conclusion of training activities. Among their many useful recommendations for practitioners is to put trainees in a consultative role in which they demonstrate or teach the skills to others and as a result, acquire greater ownership of the skill.

INDICATIONS FOR FUTURE RESEARCH IN SCHOOL-BASED ANGER MANAGEMENT

The school setting is an ideal context for the treatment of problematic anger. Professionals have ready access to the children and adolescents with needs, teachers and other staff members are available for collaborative support, and the school environment experienced by the students is readily available for systematic management and alteration in pursuit of treatment outcomes. Anger management research within the school setting over the past two decades has advanced the understanding of potentially effective methodologies and provided a solid empirical base for continuing inquiry. However, based on this review of the extant literature examining school-based anger management programs, it is clear that many important questions remain to be addressed, such as the following:

How can school practitioners with multiple other professional obligations identify and effectively treat the most students in the least amount of time? Which students are better served through longer term community interventions? The time and labor allocation problems endemic to the school setting require that research begin to identify the characteristics of student behavior problems that will respond to short-term interventions suitable for the typical academic calendar and the availability of the typical practitioner.

Is the student's primary need related to the identification and processing of angry feelings, to the misunderstanding of social cues or poor problem-solving skills, or to poor regulation of aggressive behavior? There is clearly a need to develop more comprehensive assessment instruments that begin to identify the specific needs of students referred to anger management intervention groups. Anger management intervention strategies have a greater likelihood of long-term success if tailored to the individual needs of students rather than following a "one-size-fits-all" philosophy.

As student populations become increasingly diverse, what adaptations to existing interventions and what practitioner training is necessary to effectively meet the needs of all students? For instance, are there important differential treatment implications for Hispanic students compared with non-Hispanic students? And how can training be modified to address the developmental needs of younger and less competent students?

Finally, in what ways will traditional CBT address relational aggression? How do the treatment needs of girls with anger-induced physical aggression align with or diverge from

TABLE 24.2

Implications for Practitioners: Anger management

- Chronically high level of anger and hostility constitute risk factors for violent behavior at school.
- Anger management training is an important component of comprehensive school violence prevention programs.
- Anger is a multidimensional construct with affective, cognitive, and behavioral components.
- Accurate and specific assessment is a necessary condition for successful anger management interventions.
- It is important to match intervention content to the specific needs of students referred to anger management programs.
- School-based anger management interventions frequently include psychoeducational, emotion-focused, cognitive–behavioral, and social skills training aspects.
- Cognitive–behavioral approaches include problem-solving, cognitive restructuring, and coping skills training.
- Currently, most school-based anger management programs traget male students and are delivered in late elementary through secondary school settings.
- There is a need to develop more early intervention programs and to more specifically address the needs of female students.
- There is a need for better understanding of cultural determinants of anger and hostility and developing appropriate interventions for students of varying ethnic and cultural backgrounds.
- Practitioners should take care to build in generalization procedures including real-life examples, homework assignments, collaborative opportunities with teachers and family members, and other relevant strategies

those of boys? Research needs to address the identification and treatment needs of girls' anger as it is manifested in the school setting.

SUMMARY AND CONCLUSIONS

This chapter reviewed 28 published anger management interventions for children and adolescents conducted in school settings. Based on the review, a number of characteristics of existing programs were identified. These are summarized in Table 24.2. School-based anger management programs typically target male students in upper elementary through secondary settings. Most interventions are delivered in a small group format over six or more sessions. Intervention content can include psychoeducational, emotion-focused, and social skills training but most typically include some type of CBT. More specifically, problem-solving, cognitive restructuring, or coping skills training form the basis of most intervention efforts.

Based on the review, a number of additional points and recommendations for practitioners are presented in Table 24.2. First, anger is a multidimensional construct with affective, cognitive, and behavioral components. Effective interventions need to be intentionally tailored to address the specific needs of students referred for anger management treatment. Second, generalization to the natural school environment is absolutely essential if AMT is to be deemed successful. Care should be taken to provide real-life examples, homework, and opportunities to practice acquired skills in the context of school if this is to occur. Finally, it was noted that there is a need to expand the current repertoire of anger management intervention techniques to address the needs of females, younger students, and students from varying cultural and ethnic backgrounds.

REFERENCES

American Psychological Association. (1999). *Warning signs: A violence prevention guide for youth*. Available: http://helping.apa.org/warningsigns/index.html

Averill, J. R. (1982). *Anger and aggression: An essay on emotion*. New York: Springer-Verlag.

Beck, R., & Fernandez, E. (1998). Cognitive-behavioral therapy in the treatment of anger: A meta-analysis. *Cognitive Therapy and Research, 22*, 63–75.

Berkowitz, L. (1990). On the formation and regulation of anger and aggression: A cognitive-neoassociationistic analysis. *American Psychologist, 45*, 494–503.

Berkowitz, L. (1993). *Aggression: Its causes, consequences, and control*. New York: McGraw-Hill.

Bosworth, K., Espelage, D., & Dubay, T. (1998). A computer-based violence prevention/intervention for young adolescents: Pilot study. *Adolescence, 33*, 785–795.

Bosworth, K., Espelage, D., Dubay, T., Dahlberg, L. L., & Daytner, G. (1996). Using multimedia to teach conflict-resolution skills to young adolescents. *American Journal of Preventive Medicine, 12*, 65–74.

Buss, A. H., & Durkee, A. (1957). An inventory for assessing different kinds of hostility. *Journal of Consulting Psychology, 42*, 155–162.

Coie, J. D., Underwood, M., & Lochman, J. E., (1991). Programmatic intervention with aggressive children in the school setting. In D. J. Pepler & K. H. Rubin (Eds.), *Development and treatment of childhood aggression* (pp. 389–410). Toronto: Lawrence Erlbaum Associates.

Crick, N. R. (1996). The role of overt aggression, relational aggression, and prosocial behavior in the prediction of children's future social adjustment. *Child Development, 67*, 2317–2327.

Deffenbacher, J. L., Lynch, R. S., Oetting, E. R., & Kemper, C. C. (1996). Anger reduction in early adolescents. *Journal of Counseling Psychology, 43*, 149–157.

Deffenbacher, J. L., McNamara, K., Stark, R. S., & Sabadell, P. M. (1990). A comparison of cognitive-behavioral and process-oriented group counseling for general anger reduction. *Journal of Counseling and Development, 69*, 167–172.

Deffenbacher, J. L., Oetting, E. R., Huff, M. H., & Thwaites, G. A. (1995). Fifteen-month follow-up of social skills and cognitive-relaxation approaches to general anger reduction. *Journal of Counseling Psychology, 42*, 400–405.

Del Vecchio, T., & O'Leary, K. D. (2004). The effectiveness of anger treatments for specific anger problems: A meta-analytic review. *Clinical Psychology Review, 24*, 15–34.

Dobson, K. S., & Dozois, D. J. A. (2001). Historical and philosophical bases of the cognitive therapies. In K. S. Dobson (Ed.), *Handbook of cognitive-behavioral therapies* (2nd ed.) (pp. 3–39). New York: Guilford.

Dodge, K. A., & Coie, J. D. (1987). Social-information processing factors in reactive and proactive aggression in children's peer groups. *Journal of Personality and Social Psychology, 53*, 1146–1158.

Dodge, K. A., Lochman, J. E., Harnish, J. D., Bates, J. E., & Petit, G. S. (1997). Reactive and proactive aggression in school children and psychiatrically impaired chronically assaultive youth. *Journal of Abnormal Child Psychology, 106*, 37–51.

Dwyer, K., Osher, D., & Warger, C. (1998). *Early warning, timely response: A guide to safe schools.* Washington, DC: U.S. Department of Education.

D'Zurilla, T., J., & Nezu, A. M. (2001). Problem-solving therapies. In K. S. Dobson (Ed.), *The handbook of cognitive-behavioral therapies* (2nd ed. pp. 211–245). New York: Wiley.

Eargle, A. E., Guerra, N. G., & Tolan, P. H. (1994). Preventing aggression in inner-city children: Small group training to change cognitions, social skills, and behavior. *Journal of Child and Adolescent Group Therapy, 4*, 220–242.

Feindler, E. L., Marriott, S. A., & Iwata, M. (1984). Group anger control training for junior high school delinquents. *Cognitive Therapy and Research, 8*, 299–311.

Feindler, E. L., & Scalley, M. (1998). Adolescent anger-management groups for violence reduction. In K. C. Stoiber & T. R. Kratchowill (Eds.), *Handbook of group intervention for children and families* (pp. 100–119). Needham Heights, MA: Allyn & Bacon.

Furlong, M. J., & Smith, D. C. (1994). Assessment of youth's anger, hostility, and aggression using self-report and rating scales. In M. J. Furlong & D. C. Smith (Eds.), *Anger, hostility, and aggression: Assessment, prevention and intervention strategies for youth* (pp. 167–244). New York: Wiley.

Furlong, M. J., & Smith, D. C. (1998). Raging Rick to tranquil Tom: An empirically-based multidimensional anger typology for adolescent males. *Psychology in the Schools, 35*, 229–245.

Furlong, M. J., Smith, D. C., & Bates, M. P. (2002). Further development of the Multidimensional School Anger Inventory: Construct validation, extension to female adolescents, and preliminary norms. *Journal of Psychoeducational Assessment, 20*, 46–65.

Garrison, S. R., & Stolberg, A. L. (1983). Modification of anger in children by affective imagery training. *Journal of Abnormal Child Psychology, 11*, 115–130

Goldstein, A. P., Glick, B., & Gibbs, J. C. (1998). *Aggression replacement training: A comprehensive program for aggressive youth.* Champaign, IL: Research Press.

Hains, A. A. (1994). The effectiveness of a school-based, cognitive-behavioral stress management program with adolescents reporting high and low levels of emotional arousal. *School Counselor, 42*, 114–125.

Hains, A. A., & Szyjakowski, J. (1990). A cognitive stress-reduction intervention program for adolescents. *Journal of Counseling Psychology, 37*, 79–84.

Hemphill, S. A., & Littlefield, L. (2000). Evaluation of a short-term group therapy program for children with behavior problems and their parents. *Behaviour Research and Therapy, 39*, 823–841.

Hermann, D. S., & McWhirter, J. J. (2003). Anger & aggression management in young adolescents: An experimental validation of the SCARE program. *Education and Treatment of Children, 23*, 273–302.

Hinshaw, S. P., Buhrmester, D., & Heller, T. (1989). Anger control in response to verbal provocation: Effects of stimulant medication for boys with ADHD. *Journal of Abnormal Child Psychology, 17*, 393–407.

Horton, A. (1996). Teaching anger management skills to primary age children. *Teaching and Change, 3*, 281–296.

Hudley, C., Britsch, B., Wakefield, W. D., Smith, T., Demorat, M., & Cho, S-J. (1998). An attribution retraining program to reduce aggression in elementary school students. *Psychology in the Schools, 35*, 271–282.

Kassinove, H. (1995). *Anger disorders: Definition, diagnosis, and treatment.* Washington, DC: Taylor & Francis.

Kazdin, A. E., Rodgers, A., Colbus, D., & Siegel, T. (1987). Children's hostility inventory: Measurement of aggression and hostility in psychiatric inpatient children. *Journal of Clinical Child Psychology, 16*, 320–329.

Kellner M. H., & Tutin, J. (1995). A school-based anger management program for developmentally and emotionally disabled high school students. *Adolescence, 30*, 813–826.

Larson, J. (1992). Anger and aggression management techniques utilizing the Think First curriculum. *Journal of Offender Rehabilitation, 18*, 101–117.

Larson, J. (2005). *Think first: Addressing aggression in the secondary schools.* New York: Guilford.

Larson, J., & Lochman, J. E. (2001). *Helping schoolchildren cope with anger.* New York: Guilford.

Lo, Y., Loe, S., & Cartledge, G. (2002). The effects of social skills instruction on the social behaviors of students at risk for emotional or behavioral disorders. *Behavioral Disorders, 27,* 371–385.

Lochman, J. E. (1985). Effects of different treatment lengths in cognitive-behavioral interventions with aggressive boys. *Child Psychiatry and Human Development, 16,* 45–56.

Lochman, J. E. (1992). Cognitive-behavioral intervention with aggressive boys: Three-year follow-up and preventive effects. *Journal of Consulting and Clinical Psychology, 60,* 426–432.

Lochman, J. E., Burch, P. R., Curry, J. F., & Lampron, L. B. (1984). Treatment and generalization effects of cognitive behavioral and goal setting interventions with aggressive boys. *Journal of Consulting and Clinical Psychology, 52,* 915–916.

Lochman, J. E., & Curry, J. F. (1986). Effects of problem-solving training and self-instruction training with aggressive boys. *Journal of Clinical Child Psychology, 15,* 159–164.

Lochman, J. E., Lampron, L. B., Burch, P. R., & Curry, J. F. (1985). Client characteristics associated with behavior change for treated and untreated aggressive boys. *Journal of Abnormal Psychology, 13,* 527–538.

Lochman, J. E., Lampron, L. B., Gemmer, T. C., Harris, S. R., & Wyckoff, G. M. (1989). Teacher consultation and cognitive-behavioral interventions with aggressive boys. *Psychology in the Schools, 26,* 179–187.

Lochman, J. E., Nelson, W. M., & Sims, J. P. (1981). A cognitive behavioral program for use with aggressive children. *Journal of Clinical Child Psychology, 3,* 146–148.

Mahoney, M. J., & Arnkoff, J. (1978). *Handbook of psychotherapy and behavior change: An empirical analysis* (2nd ed.). New York: Wiley.

Massey, O. T., Armstrong, K. H., & Boroughs, M. (2003). *The Think First anger management curriculum: Effectiveness for secondary students under two conditions of implementation.* Tampa, FL: University of South Florida, Louis de la Parte Florida Mental Health Institute.

McDermott, M. R., Ramsay, J. M. C., & Bray, C. (2001). Components of the anger-hostility complex as risk factors for coronary artery disease severity: A multi-measure study. *Journal of Health Psychology, 6,* 301–311.

Meichenbaum, D. (2001). *Treatment of individuals with anger control problems and aggressive behaviors: A clinical handbook.* Clearwater, FL: Institute Press.

Meichenbaum, D., & Beimiller, A. (1998). *Nurturing independent learners.* Boston: Brookline Books.

Miller, T. Q., Smith, T. W., Turner, C. W., Guijarro, M. L., & Hallett, A. J. (1996). A meta-analytic review of research on hostility and physical health. *Psychological Bulletin, 19,* 322–348.

Nelson, W. M., III, & Finch, A. J., Jr. (2000). *Children's Inventory of Anger: Manual.* Los Angeles: Western Psychological Services.

Nickerson, K. F. (2003). *Anger in adolescents: The effectiveness of a brief cognitive-behavioral anger management training program for reducing attitudinal and behavioral expressions of anger.* Unpublished doctoral dissertation, Cappella University, Minneapolis, MN.

Ninness, H. A., Ellis, J., Miller, W. B., Baker, D., & Rutherford, R. (1995). The effects of a self-management training package on the transfer of aggression control procedures in the absence of supervision. *Behavior Modification, 19,* 464–490.

Normand, D., & Robert, M. (1990). Modeling of anger/hostility control with preadolescent type A girls. *Child Study Journal, 20,* 237–262.

Omizo, M. M., Hershberger, J. M., & Omizo, S. A. (1988). Teaching children to cope with anger. *Elementary School Counseling and Guidance, 22,* 241–245.

Orpinas, P., & Frankowski, R. (2001). The Aggression Scale: A self-report measure of aggressive behavior for young adolescents. *Journal of Early Adolescence, 21,* 50–67.

Orpinas, P., Parcel, G. S., McAlister, A., & Frankowski, R. (1995). Violence prevention in middle schools: A pilot evaluation. *Journal of Adolescent Health, 17,* 360–371.

O'Toole, M. E. (2000). *The school shooter: A threat assessment perspective.* Quantico, VA: Federal Bureau of Investigation, Critical Response Group, National Center for the Analysis of Violent Crime.

Presley, J. A., & Hughes, C. (2000). Peers as teachers of anger management to high school students with behavioral disorders. *Behavioral Disorders, 25,* 114–130.

Rollin, S. A., Kaiser-Ulrey, C., Potts, I., & Creason, A. H. (2003). A school-based violence prevention model for at-risk eighth grade youth. *Psychology in the Schools, 40,* 403–416.

Siegel, J. M. (1996). The Multidimensional Anger Inventory. *Journal of Personality and Social Psychology, 51,* 191–200.

Smith, D. C., & Furlong, M. (1994). Correlates of anger, hostility, and aggression in children and youth. In M. J. Furlong & D.C. Smith (Eds.), *Anger, hostility, and aggression: Assessment, prevention and intervention strategies for youth.* (pp. 15–38). Brandon, VT: Clinical Psychology Press.

Smith, D. C., Furlong, M. J., Bates, M. P., & Laughlin, J. (1998). Development of the Multidimensional School Anger Inventory for males. *Psychology in the Schools, 35,* 1–15.

Smith, D. C., Larson, J. D., DeBaryshe, B., & Salzman, M. (2000). Anger management for youth: What works and for whom? In D. S. Sandhu & C. B. Aspy (Eds.), *Violence in American schools: A practical guide for counselors* (pp. 217–230). Alexandria, VA: American Counseling Association.

Smith, S. W., Siegal, E. M., Conner, A. M., & Thomas, S. B. (1994). Effects of cognitive-behavioral training on angry behavior and aggression of three elementary aged students. *Behavioral Disorders, 19*, 126–135.

Spielberger, C. D., Reheiser, E. C., & Sydeman, S. J. (1995). Measuring the experience, expression, and control of anger. In H. Kassinove (Ed.), *Anger disorders: Definition, diagnosis, and treatment* (pp. 49–67). Washington, DC: Taylor & Francis.

Suinn, R. (2001). The terrible twos—anger and anxiety. *American Psychoologist, 56*, 27–37.

Tafrate, R. C. (1995). Evaluation of treatment strategies for adult anger disorders. In H. Kassinove (Ed.), *Anger disorders: Definition, diagnosis, and treatment* (pp. 109–130). Washington, DC: Taylor & Francis.

Tavris, C. (1989). *Anger: The misunderstood emotion*. New York: Simon & Schuster.

Walker, H. M., Ramsey, E., & Gresham, F. M. (2004). Antisocial behavior in school (2nd ed.). Belmont, CA: Wadworth/Thomson Learning.

Watson, T. S., & Steege, M. W. (2003). *Conducting school-based functional behavioral assessments: A practitioner's guide*. New York: Guilford.

25

Second Step[1]: A Violence Prevention Curriculum

Pam Dell Fitzgerald
Leihua Van Schoiack Edstrom
Committee for Children, Seattle, Washington

Teaching prosocial skills in an effective way actually creates more teachable time. So it does not take time away from—I truly believe it contributes time, and the time it creates is actually much more effective teachable time because the students are in a much better place.
—Patti Peplow (Head Counselor, Mesa Public Schools, personal communication, May 2004)

Second Step: A Violence Prevention Curriculum is a school-based program developed to reduce and prevent aggressive behavior. Three separate age-appropriate curricula are available for preschool through middle school classrooms (preschool/kindergarten level, elementary level, and middle school/junior high level). The curricula are designed to be teacher-friendly and convenient for classroom use. Their primary purpose is to decrease children's aggressive behaviors by helping children develop habits of prosocial behavior and thought. The curricula employ evidence-based strategies that are built on a broad and solid foundation of research. Each of the three curricula have been evaluated and found to reduce aggression and increase social competence (see section on Evidence of Effectiveness).

IMPORTANCE

Research confirms that school and the family are the two most important social and emotional learning environments for children (for a review, see Weissberg, Caplan, & Harwood, 1991). As one of the most important socioemotional learning environments in children's lives, schools have a key impact on their well-being. Prevention programs can help schools comprehensively promote the social and emotional skills that contribute to children's success. At the same time, they can reduce the risk factors that lead to long-term antisocial behavior. Socioemotional prevention programs are most effective when they both reduce risk factors and increase protective factors (Pollard, Hawkins, & Arthur, 1999). To this end, the goals of the *Second Step* curricula are to increase social skills and in doing so, reduce aggression.

---

[1] Second Step is a registered trademark of Committee for Children.

Social skills and aggression have implications for a wide range of developmental outcomes, including effects on peer relations (Coie, Dodge, & Coppotelli, 1982) and school success (e.g., Izard et al., 2001; Wentzel & Wigfield, 1998). In the long run, persistent aggression and social skills deficits are also predictive of substance abuse (for a review, see Hawkins, Catalano, & Miller, 1992), long-term persistent antisocial behavior (for a review, see Moffitt, 1993), and lack of success in the workplace (Spencer & Spencer, 1993).

When children are aggressive and low in social competence, it is clearly harmful to their peer relations. It has long been known that aggressiveness is characteristic of a large proportion of the children who are rejected by their peers (e.g., Coie et al., 1982). However, to understand children's risk for rejection, it is also necessary to consider prosocial skills. In their meta-analysis of social skills studies, Newcomb, Bukowski, and Pattee (1993) confirmed that children could be aggressive without being rejected if they were also high in prosocial skills. Those who were rejected by their peers were characterized as being not only aggressive but also low in prosocial skills—these two characteristics together account for the majority of rejection of children by their peers. Conversely, children who were especially well accepted by their peers were characterized by strong prosocial skills (Newcomb et al., 1993).

Children's social relations, in turn, are related to success in school. Researchers have found that academic performance is higher when children perceive their relationships with people at school to be supportive (for a review, see Zins, Weissberg, Wang, & Walberg, 2004). Students' empathy skills have been found to be related to supportive social behaviors in school (Litvack-Miller, McDougall, & Romney, 1997). Teaching empathy skills to children may improve school climate, giving students a second, indirect benefit from the program. Social skills may contribute to academic success in other ways as well. For example, social skills should contribute to children being able to communicate their needs and get help from teachers and peers. In fact, it may be that poor social skills ultimately have quite serious academic consequences, because early peer rejection predicts later dropping out of school (for a review, see Parker & Asher, 1987).

Research evidence supports the assumption that social skills contribute to academic achievement. Empathy skills of children in kindergarten (Izard et al., 2001) and in 8- to 9-year-old girls (Feshbach & Feshbach, 1987) have predicted later teacher ratings and achievement scores, respectively. Malecki and Elliott (2002) found that social skills of third- and fourth-grade students predicted their scores on the Iowa Test of Basic Skills. In a series of three studies of sixth- and seventh-grade students, Wentzel and her colleagues (Wentzel, 1991, 1993; Wentzel, Weinberger, Ford, & Feldman, 1990) consistently found that social skills were related to children's grades and achievement test scores. In summary, emerging evidence indicates that social skills are related to academic achievement for children from preschool through middle school.

In addition to the impact on their peer relations and academic success, children who are aggressive can be at risk for other serious problems. Excessive and persistent aggressiveness and antisocial behaviors in children put them at risk for long-term antisocial behavior patterns. These risks include substance abuse (for a review, see Hawkins et al., 1992) and criminal behavior (for a review, see Moffitt, 1993). An important distinction to note here is that very early aggression, by itself, is not a strong risk factor. It is when children persist in their aggressiveness throughout childhood that they are at greater risk for poor outcomes in the long run. The *Second Step* curricula are designed as an early intervention and prevention program to reduce aggression, a principal risk factor for long-term antisocial behavior. Because risk factors cannot always be controlled, it is also important to introduce factors that can protect children against long-term harm. Social competence training is an important protective factor (Hawkins et al., 1992).

It is important that these core social and emotional competencies be taught to children in their schools. The social and emotional skills that children learn in school can promote healthy development or cause harm. They can affect not only children's individual development, but also their impact on others. Therefore, it is critical that educators take advantage of the rich opportunities inherent in school settings to teach positive social and emotional skills, rather than leaving to chance the nature of the skills that children learn during the school day. Teaching such competencies forms the foundation of prevention efforts aimed at reducing aggression and is important to the healthy development of all children.

CONCEPTUAL FOUNDATION

Conceptually, the *Second Step* curricula are based on two traditions from developmental research. The first is what is known about the normal development of children's prosocial skills (e.g., Fabes, Eisenberg, Hanish, & Spinrad, 2001). The second is cognitive–behavioral research about the skills that contribute to prosocial behavioral habits (Crick & Dodge, 1994; Lemerise & Arsenio, 2000). The teaching strategies employed in the *Second Step* curricula draw from cognitive–behavioral theory, including behavioral methods and modeling. The program development model entailed teachers and researchers working together to create the *Second Step* curricula. By this method, the curricula were founded on strong evidence of effective strategies. At the same time, implementation is supported by the convenience and relevance of the curricula for classroom use and by ongoing implementation support services.

The social and emotional skills taught in the *Second Step* curricula fall into three broad categories—empathy, problem solving, and emotion management. Empathy skills are key factors in the development of social behavior (e.g., Hastings, Zahn-Waxler, Robinson, Usher, & Bridges, 2000) and acceptance by the peer group (Fabes et al., 2001). Empathy is also integral to children's competence at several other social and emotional skills (for a review, see Lemerise & Arsenio, 2000). For these reasons, in the *Second Step* curricula empathy skills are taught first, to provide a foundation on which the problem-solving and emotion management skills are built.

In subsequent units, children are taught that when they encounter a social conflict, it is useful first to manage their emotions and then to engage in specific, effective problem-solving steps. These strategies are designed to steer children away from the patterns of thinking that characterize aggressive children toward those that characterize children who are nonaggressive and accepted by their peers (Crick & Dodge, 1994).

The problem-solving steps and other social skills taught in the *Second Step* curricula are informed by the cognitive-behavioral tradition. This perspective addresses behaviors, thoughts, and emotions and the interplay amongst them. It focuses on the behavioral triad of the antecedents that cue the behavior, the behavioral responses, and the consequences that result from the behavior. The antecedents, behaviors, and consequences can be emotions, cognitions, or behaviors. For example, in the context of feeling guilty (antecedent), a person may be in the habit of thinking certain kinds of thoughts, such as, "It's really more his fault than mine," (response), and feeling better as a result (consequence). With this reinforcing consequence—feeling better—the person is likely to continue or increase the habit of attributing fault to other people.

The focus of *Second Step* lessons is to foster the skills and habits of constructive thinking that promote prosocial behaviors. This builds a foundation for social interactions that increases the likelihood that children will behave prosocially and decreases the likelihood that children will respond with aggression (Crick & Dodge, 1994; Dodge & Frame, 1982). Additionally, the *Second Step* lessons teach emotion-management strategies and specific behaviors to increase children's repertoire of prosocial behaviors.

Crick and Dodge's (1994) model of social interactions is a useful conceptual framework for the cognitive–behavioral skills addressed by the *Second Step* curricula. Crick and Dodge suggest that children cycle through several steps in social interactions: They (a) encode cues from the people and setting in the interaction, (b) interpret the meaning of the cues, (c) clarify what their goals are in the interaction, (d) examine potential responses from their repertoire, (e) evaluate and select a response, and finally (f) enact a response. Performance of these steps is informed and affected by children's base of knowledge and experience. The *Second Step* curricula teach children prosocial habits for each of these cognitive steps. For example, they teach children to (a) attend to cues about emotions (encode), (b) consider several interpretations of interactions, (c) set goals to avoid causing harm, (d) generate several possible responses, (e) evaluate the consequences of possible responses, and (f) practice prosocial responses.

Lemerise and Arsenio (2000) extended Crick and Dodge's (1994) model to include the influence of emotions at each of their steps. For example, it has long been recognized that strong emotions can interfere with one's ability to respond effectively (for a review, see Campos & Barrett, 1984). In the *Second Step* lessons, children are taught strategies for calming down, and also taught to use upset emotions as cues to develop constructive methods to solve the situation. These emotion-management skills depend on empathy skills.

The skills taught in *Second Step* curricula are interdependent in a variety of ways. Throughout the lessons taught in the *Second Step* curricula, each skill is learned and then incorporated into subsequent lessons. In this way, the complex interactions of emotions, behaviors, and cognitions are addressed. Overall, children learn and practice the behavioral skills and social cognitions that are characteristic of children who succeed in their social interactions.

PROGRAM DESCRIPTION

The *Second Step* curriculum is a commercially available, school-based program for students in preschool through middle school. Designed to teach key social competencies, the program's aims are to decrease children's risk for destructive behavior and increase their potential for success at school (Wentzel & Wigfield, 1998) and in relationships with others (Weissberg & Greenberg, 1997). Since its inception in 1986, the *Second Step* program (Committee for Children, 2002) has been used widely in the United States and Canada and adapted in multiple languages.[2] Long-term application within the classroom has further contributed to refinement of the program and implementation guidelines.

Classroom Lessons

Second Step classroom lessons are developmentally sequenced, building on concepts and skills across grade levels. In general, lessons are taught by classroom teachers, school counselors, or school psychologists who have received program training. The program's developers recommend that classroom teachers take the lead in lesson presentation due to their familiarity with students, ability to adjust lessons accordingly, and capacity for facilitating maintenance and generalization of students' skills (Committee for Children, 2002).

Materials and Format

Curricula for preschool and elementary students consist of 22 to 28 lessons, depending on the grade level. Lessons vary in length from 20 minutes at the preschool level to 45 minutes in Grades 4 and 5. In each lesson, a photograph, written story, puppet, or other prompt depicts a

---

[2]*Second Step* curricula have been translated into Danish, Finnish, German, Greenlandic, Icelandic, Japanese, Lithuanian, Norwegian, Slovakian, Spanish, and Swedish.

social dilemma from which a presentation of the key concepts and objectives extends. Lesson scripts for teachers are provided describing the vignette and outlining lesson activities (e.g., discussion and skill practice). Video clips dramatize and support some of the lessons. The middle school/junior high school curriculum consists of three levels, allowing a comprehensive, multiyear implementation of the program. The lesson format involves group discussion, classroom activities, homework, and use of videos.

Depending on grade level, curriculum materials may include other tools, such as puppets, classroom posters, reproducible homework sheets, and family overview videos. Detailed implementation guides for educators include recommendations for adapting lessons for various populations (e.g., students with disabilities or in multiage or non-school settings). The program's publisher provides gratis technical support to assist program implementation.

Content

Across grade levels, *Second Step* lessons are organized in three skill sets. The first skill set focuses on empathy to provide the affective base for subsequent lessons. This includes: (a) identifying feelings through facial expressions, body language, and situational cues; (b) understanding others' perspectives; and (c) giving emotional support to others. Lesson topics range from recognizing feelings to complex concepts (e.g., fairness).

The problem-solving lessons teach a step-by-step strategy for solving social problems that includes, for example, identifying the problem and evaluating solutions. Students apply the social problem-solving steps to hypothetical situations and to examples from their own lives.

In the emotion-management lessons, students learn to recognize anger cues and "triggers" and to use stress-reduction techniques (e.g., counting backward) to manage or prevent angry feelings. Emotion-management and problem-solving steps are also applied to specific stress-inducing situations typical for students (e.g., bullying or social exclusion).

Instructional and Transfer-of-Learning Strategies

Second Step lessons rely on a range of teaching strategies that facilitate student learning, promote a supportive classroom climate, and encourage the generalization of skills.

Discussion

Group discussion is integral to *Second Step* lessons. The curricula offer several supports to help make discussions engaging and instructive, such as tips to encourage participation and scripted, open-ended questions.

Behavioral Skill Training

Skill training is the second major component of *Second Step* lessons. With teacher guidance, students first generate skill steps for responding to a given social dilemma or situation, such as conversation-making. Next, the teacher models the skill steps and leads students in evaluating his or her performance. Students then have several opportunities to practice the specific behavioral skills with coaching and feedback.

Modeling

Perhaps the most powerful teaching strategy employed in the *Second Step* program, modeling reaches far beyond the confines of lesson instruction. Observing adults' *Second Step* skills "in action" affords students information about effective approaches and demonstrates the values and norms of school staff, setting the stage for prosocial student norms.

Cueing, Coaching, and Reinforcement

School life involves countless opportunities for students to test and refine their skills. Likewise, teachers are presented regularly with "teachable moments" to cue students to use their newly learned skills and coach them in their performance. The curricula offer several specific suggestions for this critical transfer-of-learning step.

Group Problem Solving and Decision Making

Students' participation in solving "real" problems encourages transfer of learning through an active role in situations of intrinsic interest.

Staff Training

The program developers offer *Second Step* training. This entails a 1-day session for teachers and a half-day session for paraprofessional staff. Alternatively, 3-day "training for trainers" sessions are available in which participants learn to conduct staff training for their school or district.

Administrator's Guide

An administrator's guide accompanies curriculum kits for preschool through Grade 5. The guide assists principals or program coordinators in designing a school environment that optimally supports program implementation and integrates social and emotional learning with academic goals.

Family Guide

The family guide is a supplementary module for leading six sessions for caregivers. Participants are introduced to *Second Step* skills and learn how to foster their children's development and use of the skills.

Assessment Tools

An array of assessment tools is available for schools' use in evaluating the *Second Step* program. The process evaluation tools assess features of a school's implementation of the program, such as support for students' transfer of learning and staff and student satisfaction. Outcome tools evaluate students' social and emotional knowledge (preschool through Grade 5), and attitudes linked to aggression and socially competent behavior (Grades 6–8). More information about *Second Step* assessment tools can be found on the Committee for Children website at www.cfchildren.org.

EVIDENCE OF EFFECTIVENESS

Studies performed by multiple research teams demonstrate effectiveness of the *Second Step* curricula with students from a variety of age groups, socioeconomic and racial backgrounds, and geographical regions and settings (i.e., rural, suburban, and urban). Across this research, the *Second Step* curriculum has been linked to student changes in social and emotional knowledge and skills, prosocial attitudes, and behavior, utilizing varied research designs.

The most compelling evidence of program effects comes from a randomized experimental study with second- and third-grade students (Grossman et al., 1997). Nearly 800 children participated from six matched pairs of schools. Behavioral observations of a randomly selected subsample ($n = 588$) revealed decreased physical (but not verbal) aggression for *Second Step* students following implementation, whereas comparison students showed increases in physical aggression. *Second Step* students also demonstrated increases in positive social behavior compared to controls. Across baseline to the 6-month follow-up, coders blind to condition observed mean reductions in physical aggression for program students and not for controls. Parent and teacher ratings did not reflect the changes.

Another experimental study examined 1,253 second- through fifth-grade students from 15 schools with partial random assignment (Frey, Nolen, Edstrom, & Hirschstein, in press). In this study, teachers' implementation was closely monitored and supported by program consultants. After the first year of the program (but not the second year), *Second Step* students were rated as being more socially competent and less antisocial by their teachers than those who did not receive the program. Moreover, the greatest reductions in antisocial behavior were made by *Second Step* students who started out at baseline with the highest ratings of antisocial behavior. Following 2 years of the program, *Second Step* students also were more likely to indicate prosocial goals and reasoning. Unbiased observations revealed that *Second Step* curriculum participants were less aggressive, more cooperative (for girls only), and required less adult intervention in contrived conflict situations with peers.

In an experimental study of the German translation of the *Second Step* curriculum (*Faustlos*), Schick and Cierpka (2003) used a randomized control group design with 325 primary students. Students receiving *Faustlos* were rated by parents as significantly less anxious, depressed, and socially withdrawn, relative to controls. Gender differences in additional treatment effects were noted, with parents indicating more positive intervention benefits for girls than boys. Teacher and student reports did not evince significant group effects, with the exception that *Faustlos* students indicated less anxiety than controls.

Quasi-experimental studies offer additional support. Compared to those in comparison classrooms, *Second Step* students in elementary and middle school show reduced acceptance of physical and relational aggression (Van Schoiack-Edstrom, Frey, & Beland, 2002), more confidence in (Van Schoiack-Edstrom et al., 2002) and increased knowledge of social and emotional skills (Orpinas, Parcel, McAlister, & Frankowski, 1995), and greater social competence and less antisocial behavior as rated by their teachers (Taub, 2002). In a study with a pre-post design and no controls, urban preadolescents indicated increased self-reported empathy, socioemotional knowledge, and teacher-rated prosocial behavior (McMahon & Washburn, 2003). Aggression measures did not show consistent changes pretest to posttest. Interestingly, however, after controlling for pretest ratings, reductions in self-reported aggression were predicted by increases in self-reported empathy. Another study with a similar pre- and posttest only design found observed reductions in aggressive and disruptive behavior in low-income preschool and kindergarten children (McMahon, Washburn, Felix, Yakin, & Childrey, 2000).

In summary, those studies with the most rigorous designs, such as those with the largest sample sizes and behavioral measures by unbiased observers, are also the ones that provide the strongest support for the effectiveness of the *Second Step* program. These studies have shown reductions in aggression and increases in positive skills following use of the *Second Step* curricula. Student measures of goals and attitudes also show promising sensitivity to change. Behavioral ratings by teachers, parents, and students have yielded less consistent results.

It may be that parents and teachers are not sensitive enough to changes in aggression, or are not privy to important settings in which behavioral changes have occurred. It appears that unbiased observational measures may be preferable.

BEST PRACTICES IMPLEMENTATION

To attain expected benefits, the *Second Step* curricula should be implemented with as much fidelity as possible. In our own evaluation research of the *Second Step* program, we have found several aspects of implementation that affect the degree to which children gain from the curricula. These include program dosage (number of lessons taught), the quality of instruction of the lessons, and the degree to which teachers supported their students in generalizing the *Second Step* prosocial skills to real situations. We have found links between the social competence and antisocial behavior of elementary-aged students and the number of *Second Step* lessons taught (Hirschstein, Van Schoiack, & Beretvas, 2000). Moreover, quality of lesson instruction appears to be associated with less endorsement of aggression, and greater empathy and sense of classroom community (Hirschstein, Van Schoiack-Edstrom, Nolen, & Frey, 2001). In addition to explicit instruction in socioemotional skills, we found that teacher support of students' skill practice and generalization was related to more prosocial reasoning and teacher-rated socially competent behavior (Hirschstein et al., 2000; Hirschstein et al., 2001). These preliminary findings offer early evidence of critical implementation ingredients of the *Second Step* program: complete lesson sequencing that addresses the core competencies, effective lesson instruction by teachers who model the skills, and frequent generalization support of students' skills.

The *Second Step* curricula have has the potential to significantly influence students' social and emotional competence and reduce their risk of aggressive behavior and other negative outcomes. However, implementation research like this carries important implications for practice. In order to achieve effective and lasting outcomes in their students, schools using the *Second Step* curriculum must commit to and be supported in thorough and high-quality implementation.

The principles of behavior change provide further guidance for optimal implementation. Children learn skills best and employ them most consistently if the skills are taught and reinforced in a consistent manner, by a wide variety of people, and across a wide variety of settings. Hence, the best implementation procedure is to adopt the *Second Step* curriculum across the whole school. All staff should be trained to support students' use of the *Second Step* skills with consistency throughout the varied settings that children encounter in their school days.

To promote social competence that is lasting, it is important not only to implement social competence curricula across school settings and school personnel, but to implement them across time. School-based socioemotional prevention programs should take place across several years. In a review of home and school prevention programs, Weissberg et al. (1991) concluded that brief classroom-based programs can be expected to produce short-term but not lasting effects. They recommended that programs designed to promote social competence should be implemented across multiple years in order to produce long-term preventive effects. Children are expected to become more competent the longer they are exposed to the program. Additionally, in order to succeed at navigating social interactions as they get older, children need social skills that are more subtle and complex (e.g., Fabes et al., 2001). Multiyear programming is needed to address these changing developmental needs.

Best practices in implementation include excellent training for all school personnel, complete and high-quality lesson implementation, whole-school adoption of the curricula, and

TABLE 25.1

Implications for Practice: Steps Toward Successfully Implementing the *Second Step* Curriculum

Level	Program Conditions and Activities
	Pre-implementation
School	Develop a comprehensive plan for meeting your school's academic, social, and emotional goals
	Involve key stakeholders when choosing the program
	Clearly articulate how the program meets your school's goals
	Form a steering team and designate a program coordinator
	Provide strong leadership for the program (principal and steering team)
	Allocate time and resources with a realistic time line
	Plan for program evaluation as an essential program activity
Classroom	Involve teachers in planning, particularly classroom lesson implementation
	Encourage teachers and other implementers to join steering team
	Implementation delivery
School	Provide *Second Step* training for all staff
	Foster family involvement via curriculum parent letters and family module
	Make the program visible throughout the school
	Provide ongoing support for staff (e.g., consultation, exchange of ideas)
	Maintain practical and social support for the program (particularly by principal)
	Facilitate student use of skills (e.g., cueing, coaching) across settings and throughout the school day
	Collect implementation and outcome data
Classroom	Train teachers in classroom curricula
	Teach classroom lessons in entirety, with fidelity
	Model the program concepts and skills (e.g., respect, empathy)
	Support students' skill development (e.g., cueing, coaching) outside of lessons
	Integrate program concepts throughout the classroom curriculum
Student	Promote individual student skills (e.g., prompting or problem solving)
	Provide additional services as necessary (e.g., individual counseling)
	Post-implementation
School	Summarize process and outcome data
	Use evaluation data to inform planning (e.g., by steering team)
	Share successes with staff, students, and families
	Plan for next year's school implementation, including training and support needs
Classroom	Reflect on implementation successes and obstacles
	Plan classroom implementation for the following year
Student	Consider the need for more intensive services for individual students

Note. The word "teachers" is used to refer to all implementers of the classroom lessons.

sustained *Second Step* lessons across several grade levels. Strong administrative leadership is pivotal to good implementation (Greenberg, Domitrovich, Graczyk, & Zins, 2001; Weissberg & O'Brien, 2004). Other important factors include ongoing evaluation of process and outcomes, integration of the curriculum into the school structure and larger curriculum, and a program coordinator and/or steering team that can help sustain program efforts (see Table 25.1).

To facilitate clients in maximizing the quality of their implementation, the *Second Step* curricula have been developed on the principle of promoting educator comfort with and classroom relevance of the curricula. To achieve the dual goals of program effectiveness and ease of use in the classroom, *Second Step* program development is carried out by teams that include both teachers and researchers. Furthermore, ongoing program implementation support is available free of charge by telephone.

LIMITATIONS AND FUTURE DIRECTIONS

As a universal prevention program, the *Second Step* curricula do not include the kinds of intensive treatment components that might be needed for a few children. On the other hand, the *Second Step* curricula can be important building blocks of a comprehensive prevention strategy that addresses multiple systems and targeted populations (e.g., Sugai, Sprague, & Lewis, this volume). The curricula provide a foundation of basic skills that are beneficial to all children, and provide schoolwide behavioral expectations. These may be necessary components of multicomponent programs that are designed to address the needs of targeted populations. Frey et al. (2005) found that gains from the program were greater among the more antisocial students. This suggests that the program may be a beneficial component of a selected intervention in which students with antisocial behavior patterns are targeted. One approach that we have seen work effectively in practice is to teach *Second Step* lessons to targeted students first within a pull-out group setting and then again in the classroom. This provides students a "double dose" and affords them an opportunity to be "experts" in the material. Research is needed to examine fully how the curricula can be used most effectively with targeted populations.

A related question involves the use of *Second Step* curricula in specially tailored, multi-component, comprehensive programs. They can be used as a basic foundation of social skills, with additional components added that are chosen to meet specific local needs. For example, *Steps to Respect*[3]: *A Bullying Prevention Program*, distributed by the same developers as the *Second Step* curricula (see chapter 26, this volume), was designed to be compatible with *Second Step* curricula.

Second Step curricula have also been included in multicomponent prevention efforts by independent researchers. Sprague and his colleagues (2001) included *Second Step* curricula as one component of a multifaceted approach to promote positive social behavior and improve school safety. Relative to six comparison schools at year's end, intervention schools demonstrated greater overall reductions in discipline referrals and indicated higher staff satisfaction with discipline procedures. Further research is needed about the best way to incorporate *Second Step* curricula into these kinds of multicomponent programs.

Other studies with rigorous experimental designs are also needed, especially studies that examine the differential impacts of the curricula on different groups of children, the causal mechanisms of changes and how program implementation contributes to them, and what the effects are of multiyear implementation. Additionally, attention to a broader range of outcome measures is needed. Researchers have yet to assess the effects of the curricula on whole-school outcomes such as school climate, and on classroom-level outcomes such as classroom management. There is also a strong need for researchers to identify and/or develop effective outcome measures that are feasible for educators to use, and to identify the most effective ways to support implementation.

The *Second Step* curricula are teacher-friendly programs designed to improve children's social competence. They were developed on a foundation of rigorous research. Evaluation studies provide evidence of the effectiveness of *Second Step* curricula in reducing aggression

---

[3] *Steps to Respect* is a registered trademark of Committee for Children.

and increasing social competence. However, more research is needed to add depth to our understanding of social competence training and the *Second Step* curricula specifically.

REFERENCES

Campos, J. J., & Barrett, K. C. (1984). Toward a new understanding of emotions and their development. In C. E. Izard, J. Kagan, & R. Zajonc (Eds.), *Emotions, cognition and behavior* (pp. 229–263). New York: Cambridge University Press.

Coie, J. D., Dodge, K. A., & Coppotelli, H. (1982). Dimensions and types of social status: A cross-age perspective. *Developmental Psychology, 18*, 557–570.

Committee for Children. (1997). *Second Step: A violence prevention curriculum, middle school–junior high.* Seattle, WA: Author.

Committee for Children. (2002). *Second Step: A violence prevention curriculum, preschool/kindergarten–grade* 5 (3rd ed.). Seattle, WA: Author.

Crick, N. R., & Dodge, K. A. (1994). A review and reformulation of social information-processing mechanisms in children's social adjustment. *Psychological Bulletin, 115*, 74–101.

Dodge, K. A., & Frame, C. L. (1982). Social cognitive biases and deficits in aggressive boys. *Child Development, 53*, 620–635.

Fabes, R. A., Eisenberg, N., Hanish, L. D., & Spinrad, T. L. (2001). Preschoolers' spontaneous emotion vocabulary: Relations to likeability. *Early Education and Development, 12*, 11–27.

Feshbach, N. D., & Feshbach, S. (1987). Affective processes and academic achievement. *Child Development, 58*, 1335–1347.

Frey, K. S., Nolen, S. B., Edstrom, L. V., & Hirschstein, M. K. (2005). Effects of a school-based social-emotional competence program: Linking goals, attributions, and behavior. *Journal of Applied Developmental Psychology, 26*, 171–200.

Greenberg, M. T., Domitrovich, C. E., Graczyk, P., & Zins, J. (2001). *A Conceptual Model of Implementation for School-Based Preventive Interventions: Implications for Research, Practice, and Policy.* Report to the Center for Mental Health Services, Substance Abuse and Mental Health Services Administration, U.S. Department of Health and Human Services.

Grossman, D. C., Neckerman, H. J., Koepsell, T. D., Liu, P. Y., Asher, K. N., Beland, K., Frey, K., Rivara, F. P. (1997). Effectiveness of a violence prevention curriculum among children in elementary school: A randomized controlled trial. *Journal of the American Medical Association, 277*, 1605–1611.

Hastings, P. D., Zahn-Waxler, C., Usher, B., Robinson, J., & Bridges, D. (2000). The development of concern for others in children with behavior problems. *Developmental Psychology, 36*, 531–546.

Hawkins, J. D., Catalano, R. F., & Miller, J. Y. (1992). Risk and protective factors for alcohol and other drug problems in adolescence and early adulthood: Implications for substance abuse prevention. *Psychological Bulletin, 112*, 64–105.

Hirschstein, M., Van Schoiack, L., & Beretvas, S. N. (2000, April). *Effects of a social-emotional learning program on student behavior: A multilevel analysis.* Paper presented at the annual meeting of the American Educational Research Association, New Orleans, LA.

Hirschstein, M., Van Schoiack-Edstrom, L., Nolen, S. B., & Frey, K. S. (2001, June). *Second Step: Implementation effects on social goals and perceptions.* Paper presented at the annual conference of the Society for Prevention Research, Washington, DC.

Izard, C., Fine, S., Schultz, D., Mostow, A., Ackerman, B., & Youngstrom, E. (2001). Emotion knowledge as a predictor of social behavior and academic competence in children at risk. *Psychological Science, 12*, 18–23.

Lemerise, E. A., & Arsenio, W. F. (2000). An integrated model of emotion processes and cognition in social information processing. *Child Development, 71*, 107–118.

Litvack-Miller, W., McDougall, D., & Romney, D. M. (1997). The structure of empathy during middle childhood and its relationship to prosocial behavior. *Genetic, Social, and General Psychology Monographs, 123*, 303–324.

Malecki, C. K., & Elliot, S. N. (2002). Children's social behaviors as predictors of academic achievement: A longitudinal analysis. *School Psychology Quarterly, 17*, 1–23.

McMahon, S. D., & Washburn, J. (2003). Violence prevention: An evaluation of program effects with urban African American students. *The Journal of Primary Prevention, 24*, 43–62.

McMahon, S. D., Washburn, J., Felix, E. D., Yakin, J., & Childrey, G. (2000). Violence prevention: Program effects on urban preschool and kindergarten children. *Applied and Preventive Psychology, 9*, 271–281.

Moffitt, T. (1993). Adolescence-limited and life-course-persistent antisocial behavior: A developmental taxonomy. *Psychological Review, 100*, 674–701.

Newcomb, A. F., Bukowski, W. M., & Pattee, L. (1993). Children's peer relations: A meta-analytic review of popular, rejected, neglected, controversial, and average sociometric status. *Psychological Bulletin, 113*, 99–128.

Orpinas, P., Parcel, G. S., McAlister, A., & Frankowski, R. (1995). Violence prevention in middle schools: A pilot evaluation. *Journal of Adolescent Health, 17*, 360–371.

Parker, J. G., & Asher, S. R. (1987). Peer relations and later personal adjustment: Are low-accepted children at risk? *Psychological Bulletin, 102*, 357–389.

Pollard, J. A., Hawkins, D. J., & Arthur, M. W. (1999). Risk and protection: Are both necessary to understand diverse behavioral outcomes in adolescence? *Social Work Research, 23*, 145–158.

Schick, A., & Cierpka, M. (2003). *Faustlos*: Evaluation eines Curriculums zur Forderung sozial-emotionaler Kompetenzen und zur Gewaltpravention in der Grundschule. *Kindheit und Entwicklung, 12*, 100–110.

Spencer, L. M., & Spencer, S. M. (1993). *Competence at work: Models for superior performance.* New York: Wiley.

Sprague, J., Walker, H., Golly, A., White, K., Myers, D. R., & Shannon, T. (2001). Translating research into effective practice: The effects of a universal staff and student intervention on indicators of discipline and school safety. *Education and Treatment of Children, 24*, 495–511.

Taub, J. (2002). Evaluation of the *Second Step* violence prevention program at a rural elementary school. *School Psychology Review 31*, 186–200.

Van Schoiack-Edstrom, L., Frey, K. S., & Beland, K. (2002). Changing adolescents' attitudes about relational and physical aggression: An early evaluation of a school-based intervention. *School Psychology Review, 31*, 201–216.

Weissberg, R. P., Caplan, M., & Harwood, R. L. (1991). Promoting competent young people in competence-enhancing environments: A systems-based perspective on primary prevention. *Journal of Consulting and Clinical Psychology, 59*, 830–841.

Weissberg, R. P., & Greenberg, M. T. (1997). School and community competence-enhancement and prevention programs. In I. E. Siegel & K. A. Renninger (Eds.), *Handbook of child psychology: Vol. 5: Child psychology in practice* (5th ed.) (pp. 45–56). New York: Wiley.

Weissberg, R. P., & O'Brien, M.U. (2004). What works in school-based social and emotional learning programs for positive youth development. *Annals of the American Academy of Political and Social Science, 591*, 86–97.

Wentzel, K. R. (1991). Relations between social competence and academic achievement in early adolescence. *Child Development, 62*, 1066–1078.

Wentzel, K. R. (1993). Does being good make the grade? Social behavior and academic competence in middle school. *Journal of Educational Psychology, 85*, 357–364.

Wentzel, K. R., Weinberger, D. A., Ford, M. E., & Feldman, S. S. (1990). Academic achievement in preadolescence: The role of motivational, affective, and self-regulatory processes. *Journal of Applied Developmental Psychology, 11*, 179–193.

Wentzel, K., & Wigfield, A. (1998). Academic and social motivational influences on students' academic performance *Educational Psychology Review, 10*, 155–175.

Zins, J. E., Weissberg, R. P. Wang, M. C., & Walberg, H. J. (2004). *Building academic success on social and emotional learning.* New York: Teachers College Press.

26

Building Social and Emotional Competence: The PATHS Curriculum

Mark T. Greenberg
Pennsylvania State University

Carol A. Kusché
University of Washington

School and community violence is a substantial problem in modern society. Although there are many levels of approach for reducing violence, important responsibility and possibilities lie with education and the crucial role of schools in increasing protective factors and creating caring and inviting environments in which children can learn about themselves and attain high achievement (Greenberg, Kam, Heinrichs, & Conduct Problems Prevention Research Group, 2003). This chapter provides an overview of the PATHS (Promoting Alternative Thinking Strategies) curriculum (Kusché & Greenberg, 1994), a socioemotional learning program designed for use by teachers in their classrooms. PATHS has been shown to be effective for both prevention and intervention and for use with all elementary and preschool-aged children.

Following an account of the importance of implementing a primary/universal prevention program during childhood, which highlights the significance of emotional development, this chapter continues with a brief discussion of the conceptual models that underlie the PATHS curriculum. A description of PATHS and a review of implementation issues are then provided, as well as the results of five clinical trials conducted over a 20-year period that demonstrate the effectiveness of PATHS in reducing aggression and promoting social competence with both normal and special needs populations of multiple ethnicities in urban and rural schools. This is followed by a discussion of the importance of the quality of implementation, as well as a short review of findings on the relationship between outcome and implementation factors. Recommendations regarding practice, implementation, sustainability, educational goals, and social policy are provided at the conclusion of the chapter.

WHAT IS THE BASIS OF THE PATHS CURRICULUM?

The PATHS curriculum (Kusché & Greenberg, 1994) and Preschool PATHS (Domitrovich, Greenberg, Kusché, & Cortes, 2004) provide a comprehensive program for promoting emotional and social competencies and reducing aggression and behavior problems in preschool and elementary school-aged children, while simultaneously enhancing the educational process in the classroom. PATHS is designed to be used by educators and counselors in a multiyear, universal prevention model. Although primarily focused on the school and classroom settings, information and activities are also included for use with parents.

The PATHS curriculum was developed for use in the classroom setting with all children beginning in the preschool years through the end of elementary school. The first version of PATHS was developed in 1980 and has received ongoing field testing and research for more than 20 years with children in regular education classrooms, Head Start, and a variety of special needs settings (deaf, hearing-impaired, learning disabled, emotionally disturbed, mildly mentally delayed, and gifted). Ideally, Preschool PATHS should begin at entrance to preschool, and K–5 PATHS should be initiated at the beginning of kindergarten and continue through Grade 5. Two examples of classroom applications of K–5 PATHS can be found in Kusché and Greenberg (2001).

The Need for Primary Prevention and Emotional Literacy

The PATHS curriculum was developed to fill the need for a comprehensive, developmentally based curriculum intended to promote social and emotional competence, and prevent or reduce behavior and emotional problems. From its inception, the goal of PATHS was focused on prevention through the development of essential developmental skills in emotional literacy, positive peer relations, and problem solving. Two decades of prior research had indicated an increasing emphasis on the need for universal, school-based curricula for the purposes of both promoting emotional competence and decreasing risk factors related to later aggression, violence, and other forms of maladjustment (Greenberg & Kusché, 1993; Weissberg & Greenberg, 1998). Although these previous studies suggested that such approaches might be especially effective during the elementary school years, most curriculum evaluations were restricted in scope and/or involved programs with considerable limitations (e.g., narrow range of development, short duration, and unreliable and invalid outcome measures).

Although numerous curricula existed by the early 1980s, they generally concentrated on only one component and did not provide a comprehensive paradigm; for example, some models focused primarily on problem solving, others featured humanistic education, and still others emphasized behavioral social skills. In addition to the absence of an overall developmental model, these curricula also lacked a specific and sustained focus on teaching emotional competency, understanding, and awareness. Nevertheless, research at this time strongly suggested that a comprehensive prevention program in the classroom setting had the potential to provide much needed assistance for both normally adjusted and behaviorally at-risk students (Greenberg, Domitrovich, & Bumbarger, 2001).

More recently, the rapid and complex cultural changes of the past few decades, as well as those predicted for the foreseeable future, have made emotional literacy and social competency crucial requirements for optimal achievement and successful functioning of children and for their continuing adaptation as adolescents and adults (Kusché, 2002a). Although socioemotional learning has not been considered a necessary component of education in the past, it has now become as critical for the basic knowledge repertoire of all children as reading, writing, and arithmetic.

As with many of the more recent school-based preventive interventions, PATHS was designed to be taught by regular classroom teachers (initially with support from consultant trainers) as an integrated component of the regular school curriculum. Because teachers typically had little background or established strategies in socioemotional education, it was deemed necessary to provide detailed lessons and instructions, in addition to curricular materials. Moreover, ensuring that students utilized PATHS skills during the entire school day as well as in other contexts was known to be very important for success. Thus, generalization activities and strategies were incorporated for use in (and outside of) the classroom throughout the day. Materials were also included for use with parents.

At the time when the PATHS model was first developed, successful school-based programs that effectively taught socioemotional competence had the following characteristics. They (a) utilized a multigrade level model, (b) synthesized a number of successful approaches, (c) incorporated a developmental model, (d) provided a focus on the role of emotions and emotional development, (e) intentionally emphasized generalization of skills to everyday situations, (f) provided ongoing training and support for implementation, and (g) utilized multiple measures of both process and outcome for assessing program effectiveness. All seven of these critical factors were incorporated into the PATHS curriculum model. Furthermore, as PATHS was utilized with different cohorts and populations over the next 23 years, multiple field tests with extensive feedback from teachers led to expansion and improvements in PATHS. The most recent addition has been the development of the Preschool PATHS curriculum (Domitrovich, Greenberg, et al., 2004).

Theoretical Rationale/Conceptual Framework

The PATHS program is based on five conceptual models. The first, the ABCD (Affective–Behavioral–Cognitive–Dynamic) Model of Development, focuses on the promotion of optimal developmental growth for each individual. The second model incorporates an eco-behavioral systems orientation and emphasizes the manner in which the teacher uses the curriculum model and generalizes the skills to build a healthy classroom atmosphere (i.e., one that supports the children's use and internalization of the material they have been taught). The third model involves the domains of neurobiology and brain structuralization/organization, whereas the fourth paradigm involves psychodynamic education (derived from Developmental Psychodynamic Theory). Finally, the fifth model includes psychological issues related to emotional awareness, or as it is more popularly labeled, emotional intelligence.

The ABCD Model

The ABCD model incorporates aspects of diverse theories of human development including psychodynamic developmental theory, developmental social cognition, cognitive developmental theory, cognitive social-learning theory, and attachment theory. The ABCD model places primary importance on the developmental integration of affect (i.e., emotion, feeling, and mood) and emotion language, behavior, and cognitive understanding to promote social and emotional competence. A basic premise is that a child's coping, as reflected in his or her behavior and internal regulation, is a function of emotional awareness, affective-cognitive control, and sociocognitive understanding. Implicit in the ABCD model is the idea that during the maturational process, emotional development precedes most forms of cognition. That is, young children experience and react on an emotional level long before they can verbalize their experiences. As a result, in early life, affective development is an important precursor of other ways of thinking and later needs to be integrated with cognitive and linguistic abilities, which are slower to develop. Table 26.1 presents a summary of stages in the ABCD model (see Greenberg & Kusché, 1993, for elaboration).

During the first 3 years of life, the entire repertoire of emotional signals develops, and these signals/displays are subsequently used throughout the rest of an individual's lifetime. Thus, by the time children are beginning to utilize language fluently to express internal states of being (e.g., feeling sad, happy, or jealous) most of their emotional responses have already become habitual. By the end of the preschool years, most children have become skilled in both showing and interpreting emotional displays, although there are considerable individual differences in children's emotional profiles. The child also begins to demonstrate affective

TABLE 26.1
ABCD Model (Affective–Behavioral–Cognitive–Developmental),
Stages of Developmental Integration

1. Infancy (birth to 18 months)
  emotion = communication
  arousal and desire = behavior
2. Toddlerhood (18 months to 36 months)
  Language supplements emotion = communication
  Very initial development of emotional labeling
  Arousal and desire = behavior
3. Preschool years (3 to 6 years)
  Language develops powerful role in communication
  Child can recognize/label basic emotions
  Arousal and desire > symbolic mediation > behavior
  Development of role-taking abilities
  Beginning of reflective social planning problem solving
  (generation of alternative plans for behavior)
4. School years (6 to 12–13 years)
  Thinking in language has become habitual
  Increasing ability to reflect on and plan sequences of action
  Developing ability to consider multiple consequences of action
  increasing ability to take multiple perspectives on a situation
5. Adolescence
  Utilize language in the service of hypothetical thought
  Ability to simultaneously consider multiple perspectives

perspective-taking skills (i.e., the ability to differentiate the emotions, needs, and desires of different people in a particular context). The preschooler gradually finds new ways to cope with unpleasant emotions and discovers that internally experienced affects can be directly shared with others through verbal means. Furthermore, the child begins to regulate internal affective states through verbal self-regulation, a critical developmental achievement. An example of this ability is when a preschooler is able to tell someone that he or she is angry instead of showing aggression toward a peer or object.

Between the ages of 5 and 7, children undergo a major developmental transformation that generally includes increases in cognitive-processing skills, as well as changes in brain size and functioning. This transition and the accompanying alterations allow children to undertake major changes in responsibilities, independence, and social roles. During the elementary school years, further developmental integrations occur between affect, behavior, and cognition/language. This integration is of crucial importance in achieving socially competent action and healthy peer relations. For example, in the early elementary years, a child with well-developed socioemotional skills who has been rebuffed when attempting to enter a game with peers might walk away, calm down, and assess how she or he and the other kids are feeling. The child might then think about alternative solutions to the problem such as another strategy for entering the game, finding something else to do, or asking someone else if they want to play. Moreover, for the socially competent child, most of this process will be primarily "automatic" and will not require conscious meta-awareness.

The Eco-Behavioral Systems Model

The second conceptual model incorporates an eco-behavioral systems orientation and examines learning primarily at the level of systems change. School-based programs that focus independently on either the child or the environment are not as effective as those that simultaneously educate the child and instill positive changes in the educational milieu (Elias et al., 1997; Greenberg, Weissberg et al., 2003). Training programs can be considered person-centered when skills are taught in the absence of creating environmental supports for continued skill application in daily interactions. In contrast, ecologically oriented programs emphasize not only the teaching of skills, but also the creation of meaningful real-life opportunities to use these abilities and the establishment of structures to provide reinforcement for effective skill application. Thus, although a central goal of PATHS is to promote the developmental skills of each child by providing learning that integrates affect, cognition, and behavior, another critical ingredient for success is the development of healthy, caring, and responsive classrooms within the context of the school environment.

The extensive generalization procedures, teacher training, and focus on some level of parent participation used in PATHS have the goal of combining classroom instruction with efforts to create environmental support and reinforcement from peers, family members, school personnel, behavioral health professionals, and other concerned community members. Furthermore, training emphasizes the manner in which the teacher uses the curriculum model and generalizes the skills to build a healthy classroom atmosphere (i.e., one that supports the children's use and internalization of the material they have been taught).

Neurobiology and Brain Structuralization/Organization

When PATHS was originally developed, special attention was given to developmental models of brain organization, although these were relatively rudimentary at that time (Kusché, 1984). Subsequent research, however, continued to support the applications of these early conceptual models (see Kusché & Greenberg, 2006, for more detailed information). For example, one crucial characteristic associated with many violent offenders involves difficulty with emotion regulation and impulse control. This, in turn, is now understood to be related to insufficient development of neuronal connections between the prefrontal orbital cortex (the part of the brain located behind our eyes) and the more primitive subcortical limbic areas in the core of the brain (Schore, 1996). Studies with death-row inmates, for example, have shown that most murderers have significant deficits in frontal lobe development and functioning.

The frontal cortex has a unique relationship with the more primitive limbic system because it is the only neocortical site in which information from the limbic system is represented (Damasio, 1994). The unique connections between the frontal lobes and limbic system make it possible for the frontal cortex to "override" or modify commands emanating from the limbic area, much like using the knobs on a stove to turn the heat up or down. Thus, optimal development of the frontal lobes allows them to play a regulatory role in emotional processes, such as guiding our ability to contend with and control emotional expression (Dawson, (1994). Goleman (1995) referred to the frontal lobes as the "emotional manager," due to their apparent executive role in controlling emotion and overriding emotional impulses. He states, "In the neocortex a cascading series of circuits registers and analyzes that information, comprehends it, and through the prefrontal lobes, orchestrates a reaction. If in the process an emotional response is called for, the prefrontal lobes dictate it, working hand-in-hand with the amygdala and other circuits in the emotional brain" (p. 25).

As a child matures, interconnections between the frontal lobes and both the amygdala (in charge of powerful "raw" emotion) and the motor cortex (which controls movement) increase and differentiate. However, these changes are not "automatic," but rather are dependent for growth on experiences and input during childhood. When development goes well, adequate structuralization, along with developments in language and cognition, lead to dramatic changes in emotional maturation (Luria, 1976; White, 1965). Pathways of "vertical control" from the frontal lobes allow for regulation of impulses and action tendencies. The ability to automatically utilize "inner speech" allows for verbal thought to serve as a mediator for behavioral self-control and also enables children to have greater independence, to plan ahead, and to take on greater responsibility.

When development doesn't go well, however, deficits in self-control and emotion regulation are notable. This can result from brain damage, but more often, deficiencies are the result of insufficient socialization (i.e., inadequate input) during childhood. Although these children often perform in the normal range on tests of cognitive functioning (intelligence testing, reading, and mathematics), they nevertheless show marked deficits in social functioning beginning in childhood and continuing throughout the lifespan, primarily in the domains of emotion regulation, adapting to novel situations, and general social behavior. In the area of emotion regulation, limited frustration tolerance, increased impulsivity, poor peer relations, and frequent mood swings are often described. Failure to sustain meaningful relationships, extending across developmental levels, is also common.

Given the crucial importance of the optimal development of "vertical" control, several strategies are utilized in PATHS to teach children self-control in ways that theoretically promote neuronal structuralization and growth between the frontal cortex and limbic system. These paradigms are designed to be developmentally appropriate, beginning with relatively simple motor control in the early years (the "Turtle Technique"), followed by more complex models with increased use of language and cognition (Control Signals Poster, problem solving meetings, and formal problem-solving) that build on one another as the children mature.

Another major area of brain organization incorporated in PATHS involves "horizontal communication" between the left and right cerebral hemisphere. "Horizontal communication" refers to a phenomenon that results from the asymmetry of information processing in the two halves of the cortex (the outermost and evolutionarily newer part of the brain). The left hemisphere is responsible for processing receptive and expressive language as well as the expression of positive affect. The right hemisphere is specialized for processing both comfortable and uncomfortable receptive affect and uncomfortable expressive affect, at least in the majority of English-speaking adults (Bryden & Ley, 1983).

Nonlinguistic information (such as emotion signals) is often processed without awareness (preconscious processing) unless we verbally "think" about it. To verbally label our emotional experiences, and thus become consciously aware of them, this information must be transmitted to the left hemisphere. However, the left and right hemispheres can communicate with one another only via the corpus callosum, a "bridge" that horizontally connects the two sides of the brain. Thus, in order to be truly aware of our emotional experiences, we must utilize both the right and left hemispheres. The language areas on the left side of the brain can also modify and influence affective processing in the right (Davidson, 1998; Sutton & Davidson, 1997).

An interesting situation occurs if for some reason emotion information does not reach the left hemisphere (e.g., an adequate neural network has never developed or interconnections are blocked from intercommunication). When this occurs, an individual will experience emotion, but will not be aware of having done so. Thus, other people can be aware of how the person feels (i.e., by observing facial cues), but the individual will not be aware of having felt the feelings. A frequent illustration of this occurs when a teacher clearly observes a child who is feeling angry, but that child truly has no conscious awareness of feeling that way ("I'm not angry; I feel fine!"). In children, development of the corpus callosum is relatively slow, so that it is only with maturation that optimum hemispheric communication is possible. As with vertical neural networks, the way in which interhemispheric neuronal interconnections develop depends heavily on environmental input during childhood.

Based on this theory of horizontal communication and control, it was hypothesized that verbal identification and labeling, especially of uncomfortable feelings, would powerfully assist with managing these feelings, controlling behavior, and improving hemispheric integration. Thus, PATHS incorporates the use of Feeling Face cards that include the facial drawing of each affect (recognition of which is mediated by the right hemisphere) with the printed label (reading of which is mediated by the left hemisphere). Additionally, a color-coded differentiation of comfortable (yellow) versus uncomfortable (blue) feelings is utilized. These cards facilitate and encourage the verbal discussion of emotional experiences (both at the time they are occurring and in recollection), which further strengthens interhemispheric integration.

In summary, knowledge of the neurobiological development of the brain was heavily influential in the development of PATHS. Research strongly suggests that learning experiences in the context of meaningful relationships during childhood influence the development of neural networks between different areas of the brain, which in turn affects self-control and emotional awareness (Greenberg, Kusché, & Riggs, 2004; Kusché & Greenberg, 2006). Thus, PATHS features strategies to optimize the nature and quality of teacher–child and peer–peer interactions that are likely to impact brain development as well as learning (Greenberg, Kusché, & Speltz, 1991; Greenberg & Snell, 1997). Optimum development of both "vertical" and "horizontal" communication and control during childhood should promote better adaptation in both current and later life.

Psychodynamic Education

Psychodynamic education involves the application of psychoanalytic theory in order to enhance developmental growth, promote mental health, and prevent emotional distress, but it is not treatment (Kusché, 2002a). In this regard, teachers are not therapists and are not expected to act as such. However, teachers are powerful role models (individuals with whom children can identify), and the information they impart is often given the status of absolute truth (i.e., omniscience), especially during the elementary school-age years. When teachers express an interest in children's feelings and emotional experiences and show respect for children's opinions, their students are impacted in a profound manner. As the teacher–student relationships grow increasingly more positive and enriched, learning is enhanced.

Psychodynamic education is derived from a developmental theory and aims to coordinate social, emotional, and cognitive growth (Kusché, Riggs, & Greenberg, 1999). Teachers are encouraged to utilize actual classroom experiences, and the use of children's creative, imaginal processes is emphasized. Students develop a healthy sense of self-esteem from observing the positive reactions of others toward them, not because they are encouraged to parrot simplistic affirmations. Furthermore, teachers play a crucial role by providing clarifications and explanations of emotions and situations.

An important way in which psychodynamic education differs from other models is its emphasis on internalization. Among other important uses, internalization is the primary process utilized in the development of an individual's conscience. When the outcome is positive, the conscience (specialized functioning of neuronal networks in the preorbital frontal lobes) works as a powerful system through which a person can "take ownership" and achieve mastery over his or her own impulses and actions. By promoting the development of internal self-control and self-motivation, along with healthy standards for behavior, children develop autonomy, mature decision-making skills, and the ability to consider the needs and feelings of others. These achievements are crucial for violence prevention and school safety, because they allow individuals to control themselves. There will never be enough police or teachers to provide the external control that is alternatively necessary if internal controls have not been incorporated or are not operative.

PATHS promotes the internalization of prosocial values by helping children to understand why they are important, rather than by simply having them memorize rules. For example, students contemplate and discuss the consequences of having good vs. bad manners and evaluate why good manners are important (e.g., the way we act affects how other people feel), as opposed to merely being taught a list of "good manners" that they are "supposed" to use. In this way, the children come to "own" the concepts as belonging to themselves (i.e., they internalize them), which minimizes resistance and defiance to adopting prosocial values; as a result, children ultimately choose to use good manners voluntarily because that is something they believe is the right thing to do.

In summary, some of the long-range goals of psychodynamic education are for each child to develop a kind, but fair sense of prosocial behavioral control, a positive sense of self, respect for self and others, healthy internal motivation, curiosity, love for learning, and so on, that operate independently of the external environment. This enhances developmental growth, improves school functioning, and optimizes mental health, and at the same time, prevents antisocial tendencies, violent behavior, and substance abuse.

Psychological Issues Related to the Crucial Role of Emotional Awareness.

Research suggests that as children develop more complex and accurate strategies regarding emotions, these plans have a major influence on their social behavior. For example, the ability to think through problem situations and to anticipate their occurrence is critical for socially competent behavior. However, these "cold" cognitive processes are unlikely to be effectively utilized in real-world conditions (e.g., when being teased) unless the child can both accurately process the emotional content of the situation and effectively regulate his or her emotional arousal so that he and she can think through the problem.

Similarly, if children misidentify their own feelings or those of others, they are likely to generate maladaptive solutions to a problem, regardless of their intellectual capacities. In addition to these types of challenges, the child's motivation to engage in the discussion of feelings and to problem solve in interpersonal contexts will be greatly impacted by his or her emotional state, as well as by the modeling and reinforcement of adults and peers. Although emotional awareness and understanding are implicit in many previous models that have been developed to promote social competence, they have rarely been a central or important focus (Kusché & Greenberg, in press-b). Similarly, numerous studies have assessed social problem-solving ability as both a mediator and outcome of intervention without evaluating the role of emotional literacy.

Recently, emotional competence has been subsumed under the new, more popular term, *emotional intelligence* (Goleman, 1995; Mayer & Salovey, 1997), which is defined as the ability to recognize emotional responses in oneself, other people, and situations, and to use this knowledge in effective ways (e.g., in managing one's own emotional responses, to motivate oneself, and to handle relationships effectively). "Self-awareness—recognizing a feeling *as it happens*—is the keystone of emotional intelligence....[T]he ability to monitor feelings from moment to moment is [also] crucial to psychological insight and self-understanding. An inability to notice our true feelings leaves us at their mercy. People with greater certainty about their feelings are better pilots of their lives" (Goleman, 1995, p. 43). Thus, it has been proposed that emotional intelligence may be more important than cognitive intelligence with regard to achieving success and happiness in life.

As such, a central focus of PATHS is to encourage children to discuss feelings, experiences, opinions, and needs that are personally meaningful. In this way, they can feel listened to, supported, and respected by both teachers and peers, which facilitates the internalization of feeling valued, cared for, appreciated, and part of a social group. This, in turn, motivates children to value, care for, and appreciate themselves, their environment, their social groups, other people, and their world.

It can be noted that a sense of belonging is a powerful, biologically based deterrent to the enactment of violent behaviors toward other group members (Kusché, 2002b). However, this does not prevent destructive actions and maltreatment toward members of "other" groups (e.g., the basis of gang warfare and genocide). Thus, in addition to reinforcing inclusion in smaller prosocial groups (e.g., the classroom and the school), we also emphasize an awareness of larger group memberships, such as constituency in the local neighborhood, the global community, and life on our planet.

Summary

The PATHS prevention model contains a number of basic principles that are drawn from the five theories previously discussed. First, to affect significant changes in children's social and emotional competence, it is necessary to take a holistic approach that includes a focus on affect, behavior, and cognitions. Second, the school environment is a fundamental ecology and one that can be a central locus of change. Third, children's ability to understand and discuss emotions is related to their ability to inhibit behavior by utilizing verbal self-control. Fourth, the internalization of prosocial values, impulse control, affect regulation, and motivation promotes autonomy and decreases the need for external supervision. Fifth, children's ability to understand their own and others' emotions is a central component of effective problem solving and social interactions. Finally, developmental models indicate that it is important to build protective factors (e.g., promote reflective thinking, problem solving, and the ability to accurately anticipate and evaluate situations) that reduce maladjustment. These skills, in turn, increase children's access to positive social interactions and provide opportunities for a greater variety of learning experiences. As such, these skills should also contribute to the amelioration of significant underachievement and promote skills that are beneficial to the prevention of other types of future problem behaviors during adolescence (e.g., aggression, substance abuse, and dangerous risk-taking) that contribute to violence and other antisocial consequences.

A BRIEF DESCRIPTION OF PATHS

Due to the fact that ability and needs differ considerably between developmental stages, PATHS was divided into two separate curriculums, one for elementary-age children and one for preschoolers. The K–5 PATHS curriculum (Kusché & Greenberg, 1994) consists of an instructional manual, six volumes of lessons, pictures, photographs, posters, Feeling Faces, and additional materials (see Greenberg & Kusché, 2002, for more detailed information. Free samples of lessons and additional information can be obtained at http://www.channing-bete.com/positiveyouth/pages/PATHS/PATHS.html). Lessons include five conceptual domains: self-control, emotional understanding, positive self-esteem, relationships, and interpersonal problem-solving skills. The development of each of these areas is composed of stages or phases that are marked by increasing differentiation of concepts and skills. Hierarchical integration is also emphasized. A variety of subgoals are targeted for each domain, such as learning to distinguish between feelings and behaviors, practicing perspective-taking skills, decreasing the incidence of teasing, and so on, with attention paid to the particular developmental level and needs of the children receiving instruction. Throughout the lessons, however, a critical focus of PATHS involves facilitating the dynamic relationship between cognitive-affective understanding and real-life situations.

K–5 PATHS is divided into three major units:

1. Readiness and self-control unit: 12 lessons that focus on readiness skills and development of basic self-control.
2. Feelings and relationships unit: 56 lessons that focus on teaching emotional and interpersonal understanding, often referred to as *emotional intelligence.*
3. Interpersonal cognitive problem-solving unit: 33 lessons that cover 11 steps for formal interpersonal problem solving.

Two further areas of focus in PATHS involve building positive self-concept and improving peer communications/relations. Rather than having separate units on these latter two topics, relevant lessons are interspersed throughout the other three units. There is also a supplementary unit containing 30 lessons that reviews and extends PATHS concepts that are covered in the three major units. Pictures and photographs are included for all of the lessons, with smaller graphics provided in the margins of the scripts to make the curriculum more user-friendly. Most of the materials that are needed are included in the PATHS curriculum kit, but supplementary materials can certainly be added as desired.

Although each unit of PATHS focuses on one or more of these skill domains, aspects of all five areas are integrated into each unit. Moreover, certain foci are continually reintroduced to integrate the various themes (e.g., developing a reflective thinking style, increasing self-esteem, encouraging recognition of emotions, emphasizing conflict resolution, etc.), and each new unit builds hierarchically upon and synthesizes the learning that preceded it. Finally, language arts (both reading and writing) are bridged to PATHS in most lessons by including supplementary suggestions for teachers to utilize to reinforce lesson concepts, such as quality children's literature. Further, one of the chapters in the instructional manual provides many ideas for how teachers can directly tie PATHS concepts to language arts, social studies/history, and other subject areas.

K–5 PATHS is designed to be taught three times a week (or more if desired) for 20 to 30 minutes a day (or longer if desired). However, one PATHS lesson can run anywhere from one to five or more PATHS sessions, depending on the developmental level and interest of the class. Thus, K–5 PATHS is an expansive and flexible program that allows for implementation of the 131 lessons over a 5-year period. To encourage generalization to the home environment, parent letters and information are provided periodically in the curricular lessons and can be sent home by the teachers as desired. "Home activity assignments" are also included for children to complete at home with their parents to further facilitate family involvement.

The Preschool PATHS curriculum (Domitrovich, Greenberg, et al., 2004) was adapted from the original K–5 PATHS curriculum. The original concepts were preserved, but the material was modified to be developmentally appropriate for younger children. Preschool PATHS is divided into thematic units that include lessons on such topics as complimenting, sharing, basic and advanced feelings, a self-control strategy called the "Turtle Technique" (Robin, Schneider, & Dolnick, 1976), manners, and problem solving. Various puppets, as well as pictures, photographs, and feeling faces, are used in the lessons to introduce and illustrate the concepts. Additionally, Preschool PATHS is designed to integrate effectively with conventional early childhood programs, and subsequently, with K–5 PATHS.

Preschool PATHS contains 30 lessons that are delivered weekly by early childhood educators during "circle-time" sessions. In each lesson, the teacher introduces new ideas and materials. Over the next few days, the content of that lesson is then practiced through the use of extension activities (e.g., group games, art projects, music, and story time). Some of these generalization strategies are undertaken in a group format, but many are integrated into the existing "center" structure of typical preschool programs. In this way, Preschool PATHS combines the direct teaching of skills with meaningful opportunities to apply and practice them. This paradigm further promotes the establishment of optimal structures in which teachers can provide positive reinforcement for effective skill application.

IMPLEMENTATION, STAFF TRAINING, AND CONSULTATION

When an elementary school implements PATHS for the first time, it is often useful to begin with only a few grades. As PATHS is a developmental model, we suggest using PATHS in Grades K–2 during the first year and expanding by one additional grade each year as the children matriculate. For preschool, we recommend that implementation begin with all of the children enrolled at the center. Teacher and staff training in the use of Preschool PATHS and the K–5 PATHS curriculum, conducted by certified PATHS trainers, can be provided on site. Although training in the use of either curriculum is optional, it is highly recommended before implementation begins. A PATHS training workshop is usually undertaken over 2 consecutive days with up to 30 participants per workshop so as to maximize teacher–trainer interaction. We strongly encourage the attendance of school principals from each site, as our research (see later) has shown a very strong effect for the role of the principal (i.e., the more active the principal in supporting PATHS, the more effective the implementation).

Teachers, personnel, and staff should conceive of training as an ongoing process. Initial orientation to the goals of the curriculum and to the objectives for training usually requires one hour and is best conducted in the spring prior to fall implementation. Ideally, the initial 2-day training workshop then takes place just before the start of the school year for K–5 PATHS or the beginning of new class enrollment for preschool.

If a curriculum consultant is available in a school or preschool, we advise ongoing training that consists of biweekly team meetings with teachers to help them review lessons taught, problem solve on challenges encountered, share experiences, discuss upcoming instruction, and provide mutual support. Additionally, it is helpful for consultants to observe classroom or center lessons on a weekly basis, followed by feedback and discussion with each teacher. Whole-school or center staff discussions (usually on a quarterly basis) regarding curriculum implementation, extension, and so on are also very helpful. If desired, certified PATHS trainers can assist with ongoing training by providing phone support to the on-site curriculum coordinator on a biweekly basis, by revisiting the implementation sites during the beginning of the second year of curriculum use, and by providing a half-day booster/review session for experienced teachers during the second and later years of implementation.

In successive years, experienced teachers and support staff are encouraged to take on the roles of co-trainers for new teachers in the school. Thus, over roughly a 2-year period, local trainers should have assumed control of teacher training and the management of curriculum implementation, supplemented by technical assistance from outside trainers on an as-needed basis. See Greenberg and Kusché (2002) for a more extensive discussion of PATHS and issues in implementation.

Cost estimates for the use of K–5 and Preschool PATHS depend on how existing support personnel (e.g., counselors and head teachers) are utilized in the program. Because either PATHS curriculum is generally taught by classroom or center teachers who are already working and receiving salaries, personnel costs are usually minimal. If a counselor is utilized in the role of curriculum consultant (at least a .5 full time equivalent), curriculum and training costs for the first year of operation for an elementary school are estimated at $12,000, or approximately $25 per student (this includes curriculum costs). Costs in later years would be substantially reduced to about $10 per student, given the expectation of low-to-moderate staff turnover. Thus, the cost over a 3-year period would be approximately $15 per student. In the event that it is necessary to hire an additional staff person to provide teacher consultation, the cost in Year 1 would be approximately $80 per student, but this cost would be reduced by half each subsequent year. Thus, in this case, the cost over a 3-year period would be approximately $45 (see Greenberg & Kusché, 2002, for further information).

EVIDENCE OF PROGRAM EFFECTIVENESS

We have conducted three controlled studies with randomized control versus experimental groups, using 1 year of PATHS implementation with pre-, post-, and follow-up data. These have included three different populations including deaf/hearing impaired, regular education, and special education-classified children (Greenberg & Kusché, 1998, 2004; Greenberg, Kusché, Cook, & Quamma, 1995; Kam, Greenberg, & Kusché, 2004). Findings indicated that PATHS was successful in both increasing protective factors for healthy development and in reducing behavioral and emotional problems.

Increasing Protective Factors

In all three clinical trials, compared to matched control children, the use of the PATHS curriculum significantly increased children's ability to better recognize and understand emotions. Additionally, children receiving PATHS showed improvement in social problem-solving skills. For both regular education and deaf/hearing-impaired children, teachers reported significant improvements in children's prosocial behavior in the following domains: self-control, emotional understanding, and ability to tolerate frustration. Cognitive testing indicated that PATHS resulted in improvements in the following skills: (a) the ability to plan ahead to solve complex tasks was found with normal and special needs children (WISC-R Block Design and the Analogies subtest from the Test of Cognitive Abilities—these were not assessed in the deaf/hearing-impaired group); (b) cognitive flexibility and low impulsivity with nonverbal tasks were evidenced in all three groups (coding subtest from the WISC-R); and (c) improved reading achievement was shown with young deaf children.

Reducing Maladaptive Outcomes

For regular and special needs students, teachers reported significant reductions in aggressive and disruptive behaviors at follow-up. Additionally, among the subgroup of students showing high pretest levels of depression (special needs students), there were significant reductions in depressive symptomatology. Additionally parallel reports from teachers indicated significant reductions in internalizing symptoms (sadness, anxiety, and withdrawal) in these same special needs students.

PATHS Curriculum in the Fast Track Project

Fast Track was a large, randomized trial of a multifaceted intervention designed to reduce serious aggression and conduct problems. It was conducted in four American locations (Seattle, Washington, Nashville, Tennessee, Durham, North Carolina, and rural Pennsylvania), and in each location, there were approximately 14 schools that were randomized equally to intervention versus comparison conditions. PATHS served as the universal intervention and was integrated with five other targeted programs that were designed to be used only with children showing early, significant behavior problems. PATHS (as well as other Fast Track interventions) was conducted in 3 successive years with three cohorts of first graders, resulting in 198 program classrooms and 180 matched comparisons across the three cohorts. These classrooms included approximately 9,000 children. The percentage of children receiving free or reduced lunch was 55% and the mean percentage of ethnic minority children attending the schools was 49%. There were no demographic differences between intervention and control schools. Although there were substantial differences between sites in the degree of risk related to their school locations, there was considerable risk in the average school.

Three types of measures were utilized to assess the effects of the PATHS curriculum: (a) peer sociometric interviews with each child regarding the behavior of each peer in the class, (b) teacher ratings of each child's behavior, and (c) ratings of the classroom atmosphere (10-item rating scale based on an average of 2 hours observations per classroom). Analyses with hierarchical linear models were conducted with the classroom as the unit of analysis.

Findings at the end of Grade 1 indicated that compared to matched comparison schools, there was improved social adaptation in schools in which PATHS was operating as indexed by more positive reports on the following dimensions: lower peer sociometric ratings of aggression and disruptive behavior, lower teacher assessments of disruptive behavior, and improved evaluations by objective observers of positive classroom atmosphere (Conduct Problems Prevention Research Group, 1999). Results at the end of Grade 3 continued to show significant effects in ratings by boys of decreased aggressive behavior in their peers. Furthermore, results indicated that boys who received two or more years of PATHS between Grades 1 and 3 showed more substantial effects than those who only received it in Grade 3 (Greenberg, Kam, et al., 2003).

Effects of Preschool PATHS

The effects of Preschool PATHS were evaluated by using a randomized trial design that included 20 Head Start classrooms located in urban and rural Pennsylvania (Domitrovich, Cortes, & Greenberg, 2004). Following random assignment, half of the teachers implemented the Preschool PATHS curriculum, whereas the other half continued to conduct their classes as usual with the standard Head Start protocol. The evaluation included 248 children from a sample that consisted of 47% African-American, 38% Euro-American, and 10% Hispanic children.

There were four sets of findings. First, it was shown that Head Start teachers, with appropriate support, effectively implemented Preschool PATHS with fidelity. Second, outcome data at the end of 1 year (posttest) indicated that children who received Preschool PATHS had improved outcomes as reported by both teachers and parents. More specifically, children who received Preschool PATHS were described by their teachers and by their parents as more socially skilled than children in the randomly assigned Head Start comparison classrooms. Third, measures collected directly with the children indicated significant improvements in their emotional understanding with regard to both expressive and receptive abilities to identify emotions. Furthermore, the intervention children were less likely to misidentify facial expressions as being angry, that is, they showed less "anger bias." This is significant, as anger bias has been linked to behavior problems (Schultz, Izard, & Ackerman, 2000). Finally, no child characteristics moderated the effects of the intervention, suggesting that Preschool PATHS was equally effective for both genders and at all levels of risk.

WHEN THE RUBBER MEETS THE ROAD: IMPLEMENTING PATHS IN HIGH-IMPACT SCHOOLS

Although most research on PATHS has been conducted using randomized trial designs in which university researchers have managed training and ongoing consultation, recent studies have also examined the effects of PATHS where implementation was administered under local conditions. For example, Kam, Greenberg, and Walls (2003) conducted an "effectiveness" study of a local dissemination of the K–5 PATHS curriculum to a group of inner-city public schools that had very low academic performance and high rates of poverty (90% of children received free and reduced lunch). The findings demonstrated the importance and complex nature of implementation quality in school-based prevention. Both principal support and the quality of teacher implementation at the classroom level were critical factors in determining the success of the program dissemination on child outcomes. In classrooms where teachers implemented with high quality (as observed by others) and where the principal showed strong support for PATHS, there were significant decreases in aggression within the first 4 months of implementation. However, significant intervention effects were only found in those settings where both principal support and teacher implementation were positive. These results underscore the need to study the intricate and multiple facets of the implementation process, including dosage, quality of delivery, teacher commitment, and support from institutional leadership with regard to their degree of influence on disparate factors in different settings (e.g., schools in affluent areas vs. schools in neighborhoods with high rates of poverty).

The complexity of the impact of these types of components is illustrated in a second study (Seifer, Gouley, Miller, & Zakriski, 2004) that similarly examined PATHS implementation in one high-poverty urban school where significant school reform was simultaneously taking place. Although the quality of implementation was not observed, teachers reported feeling overwhelmed and in most cases, having substantial difficulty adding a sufficient number of PATHS lessons to their curriculum. Weak administrative support was noted as an additional problem in this implementation. Nevertheless, despite these serious concerns regarding quality of implementation, significant effects were found in that students who received PATHS evidenced higher social competence.

The Importance of Administrative Leadership

The literature on leadership in educational research supports the finding that principal support can be an important factor in the success of curricular innovation (Hallinger & Heck, 1996; Leithwood & Duke, 1999). It is well known that principals who are effective leaders promote positive social climates that reinforce prosocial norms for behavior throughout the building. Given the important role that administrative leadership appears to play in curricular success, further exploration is needed with regard to the ways in which a principal's vision and action influence implementation and sustainability.

We agree with other researchers that prevention and intervention programs in socioemotional learning, mental health, substance abuse, and so on are unlikely to be effectively undertaken and maintained without forward planning on a school and/or districtwide basis (Weissberg & Elias, 1993). Principals can be very helpful in providing teachers with positive incentives for using a prevention program (e.g., verbal encouragement, clock or credit hours for meetings, access to resource materials, and time for curriculum replication). Additionally, principals are important liaisons in promoting a positive attitude toward the program among parents and the larger community (e.g., with parent orientation meetings and contacts with public officials). Moreover, coordination between classroom teachers and other personnel can be facilitated by an active, pro-intervention administration (e.g., encouraging discussions during staff meetings and coordinating with parent educators and school psychologists). Furthermore, improvements in student behavior can be noted and positively reinforced by administrators, both privately (e.g., during chance observations) and publicly (e.g., at school assemblies). Finally, the principal is the leader of a school, and as such, defines and sets the priorities for teachers to follow.

TABLE 26.2
Implications for Practice: Promoting Alternative Thinking Strategies

1. Evaluate institutional ecology prior to implementation
   a. Are the teachers ready and willing to teach PATHS?
   b. Does the principal or director support the implementation of PATHS?
   c. Is the school district or center committed to PATHS implementation?
   d. Is funding available for implementation? If not, what options are available?
      (e.g., grants or community support)
2. Ascertain school or center implementation and training needs for the first year
   a. Which grades will implement PATHS? (e.g., K–2, schoolwide, entire center, etc.)
   b. Will teacher training be utilized? If so, when will the workshop(s) be held?
   c. Will ongoing technical support from the trainer be arranged? If so, how will the
      time be apportioned?
   d. Will a staff member be utilized as a faculty consultant for PATHS?
      If so, what percentage of time will he or she allocate to PATHS?
   e. Will PATHS teachers attend regular meetings for ongoing support
      and consultation? If so, when and how often will they convene?
   f. How will parents be informed and/or involved?
3. Determine practical considerations for implementation in each classroom
   a. When and how often will PATHS be taught?
   b. How much time will be allocated for each PATHS session?
   c. Where will PATHS charts and posters be displayed in the classroom or
      center?
   d. How will PATHS be integrated with academic or other subjects?
   e. How will each teacher communicate with parents about PATHS?
4. Prepare overall implementation for each classroom
   a. Review table of contents and skim through PATHS for overall perspective.
   b. Determine lessons to be covered during the school year.
   c. Consider ways in which new students entering the class during the school year
      will be integrated into ongoing PATHS lessons.
   d. Reproduce or buy Feeling Faces for all lessons prior to beginning PATHS.
5. Plan ahead for each PATHS session
   a. Read several lessons ahead to attain a sense of continuity.
   b. Read through each lesson at least once prior to teaching it.
   c. Estimate the number of PATHS sessions needed for each lesson.
   d. Refer to the materials section of each lesson for requisite preparation.
   e. Obtain any supplementary material desired for augmenting a lesson.
6. Consider school or center needs after the first year of implementation
   a. Which new grades will receive PATHS in subsequent years?
   b. How will teachers coordinate curricular needs and transitions from
      one year to the next?
   c. How will new teachers be trained?
   d. How will new students be integrated into classes that have previous
      PATHS experience?

Factors That Influence the Quality of Implementation: Implications for Practice

The quantitative research findings previously noted support our clinical experience that there are a number of important dimensions regarding implementation and its support system that can affect the probability of program effectiveness and success (Chen, 1990, 1998; Greenberg, Domitrovich, Graczyk, & Zins, 2004). Some of these factors and their implications for practice are summarized in Table 26.2.

First, the readiness and willingness of schools, centers, and teachers to undertake a new intervention is vitally important. It is essential to obtain principal or director support for the program because it partially determines how well teachers' efforts in program implementation will be supported. Similarly, the long-term institutional commitments of the school district, along with funding availability, are additional factors that can influence curriculum success.

Second, the provision of ongoing technical support and mentoring to teachers and principals dramatically improves the nature of implementation. By providing high-quality and continuous technical support (weekly observations and support for teachers), administrators can maintain better quality control over how the program is utilized. This is also beneficial for helping staff to address and problem-solve challenges in a timely manner. Although these aspects of support result in additional costs for program implementation and require extra pre-utilization planning, without this assistance, it is more difficult to maintain program fidelity.

Third, each teacher needs to determine the practical considerations involved in curriculum implementing, such as when and how often PATHS will be taught, where materials will be located, ways in which PATHS will be integrated with other subjects, and so on. This preparation continues with the fourth factor of overall planning for implementation during the school year. As with any new curriculum, this is especially difficult the first time that PATHS is taught, due to the unfamiliarity of the material, so training and/or assistance from a training consultant can be particularly helpful with this aspect of initiating PATHS. On a special note, reproducing or buying all of the Feeling Faces that will be needed for the classroom during the entire school year, prior to beginning PATHS, greatly simplifies time and effort needed for material preparation.

The fifth area crucial for implementing PATHS involves the ongoing planning and preparation of PATHS lessons. This is particularly time-consuming during the first year when PATHS is new to a teacher. To be effective, the teacher needs to have a sense of the continuity of the topics, as well as familiarity with each specific lesson. Trying to teach lessons without preparation will be difficult, confusing, and ineffective. Experience and practice, of course, play important roles in this regard. Generally, teachers show substantial improvement in administering PATHS, and report that it is considerably easier, during their second year of teaching it. This is even more apparent by Year 3.

Finally, after the first year of implementation, decisions need to be made to coordinate needs and transitions from one year to the next. These include such topics as adding new grades if the implementation did not begin on a schoolwide or entire center basis, training new teachers, integrating new students, and coordinating from one year to the next.

Although the list in Table 26.2 might look intimidating, it is important to remember that although these are guidelines for optimal implementation, no one program is likely to meet all of these criteria. Furthermore, planning ahead to allow sufficient time for problem-solving challenges and issues will minimize the experience of feeling stressed and overwhelmed. Additionally, it should be noted that most of these issues become easier with familiarity after the initial year of implementation.

SUMMARY OF THE PATHS CURRICULUM

K–5 PATHS and Preschool PATHS are comprehensive programs designed to promote emotional literacy, improve social competence, reduce aggression and other behavioral problems, decrease emotional distress, enhance the educational process, and enrich the environments of classrooms, schools, and preschool centers. PATHS incorporates and integrates a number of different theoretical models whose factors are believed to significantly contribute to preventing maladaptive outcomes and to promoting healthy development during childhood, as well as later in adulthood.

In a series of research studies, PATHS has been shown to (a) increase protective factors such as emotional understanding, social-cognition, and social competence; (b) decrease externalizing problems such as aggression (as rated by both peers and teachers); (c) reduce internalizing distress (depressive and anxiety-related symptoms); and (d) promote a more harmonious classroom or center environment. PATHS has also shown positive effects on students' neurocognitive development as well as improvements in indicators of school success.

Careful randomized trials have demonstrated these effects with preschool- and elementary-aged students in both regular and special education. One of our findings also demonstrated the importance of the quality of implementation. More specifically, several factors appear to be central to program success, including (a) active administrative leadership and planning, (b) the integration of academic and socioemotional learning, (c) effective training with teachers and other school or center staff, and (d) ongoing consultation and support. We believe that this combination is optimal for creating high quality school and center environments that can best benefit our students and teachers.

REFERENCES

Bryden, M. P., & Ley, R. G. (1983). Right-hemispheric involvement in the perception and expression of emotion in normal humans. In K. M. Heilman & P. Satz (Eds.), *Neuropsychology of human emotion* (pp. 6–44). New York: Guilford.

Chen, H. T. (1990). *Theory-driven evaluations*. Newbury Park, CA: Sage.

Chen, H. T. (1998). *Theory-driven evaluations. Advances in Educational Productivity, 7*, 15–34.

Conduct Problems Prevention Research Group. (1999). Initial impact of the Fast Track prevention trial for conduct problems: II. Classroom effects. *Journal of Consulting and Clinical Psychology, 67*, 648–657.

Damasio, A. R. (1994). *Descartes' error: Emotion, reason, and the human brain*. New York: Grosset/Putnam.

Davidson, R. J. (1998). Affective style and affective disorders: Perspective from affective neuroscience. *Cognition and Emotion, 12*, 307–330.

Dawson, G. (1994). Frontal electroencephalographic correlates of individual differences in emotion expression in infants: A brain systems perspective on emotion. In N. Fox (Ed.), *Monographs of the society for research in child development: Vol. 59, The development of emotion regulation: Biological and behavioral considerations* (pp. 135–151). Boston: Blackwell.

Domitrovich, C. E., Cortes, R., & Greenberg, M. T. (2004). *Improving young children's social and emotional competence: A randomized trial of the Preschool PATHS Curriculum*. Unpublished manuscript, Prevention Research Center, Pennsylvania State University, University Park, PA.

Domitrovich, C., Greenberg, M. T., Kusché, C. A., & Cortes, R. (2004). *Preschool PATHS*. South Deerfield, MA: Channing-Bete.

Elias, M. J., Zins, J. E., Weissberg, K. S., Greenberg, M. T., Haynes, N. M., Kessler, R., Schwab-Stone, M. E., & Shriver, T. P. (1997). *Promoting social and emotional learning: Guidelines for educators*. Alexandria, VA: Association for Supervision and curriculum Development.

Goleman, D. (1995). *Emotional intelligence*. New York: Bantam Books.

Greenberg, M. T., Domitrovich, C., & Bumbarger, B. (2001). The prevention of mental disorders in school-aged children: Current state of the field. *Prevention and Treatment, Article 1*. Available: http://journals.apa.org/prevention/volume4/pre0040001a.html

Greenberg, M. T., Domitrovich, C., Graczyk, P. A., & Zins, J. E. (2004). *The study of implementation in school-based prevention research: Theory, research and practice*. Report to the Center for Mental Health Services (SAMHSA). Available: www.prevention.psu.edu

Greenberg, M. T., Kam, C., Heinrichs, B., & Conduct Problems Prevention Research Group. (2003, April) *The cumulative effects of the PATHS Curriculum*. Paper presented at the Society for Research in Child Development, Tampa, FL.

Greenberg, M. T., & Kusché, C. A. (1993). *Promoting social and emotional development in deaf children: The PATHS Project*. Seattle: University of Washington Press.

Greenberg, M. T., & Kusché, C. A. (1998). Preventive intervention for school-aged deaf children: The PATHS Curriculum. *Journal of Deaf Studies and Deaf Education, 3*, 49–63.

Greenberg, M. T., & Kusché, C. A. (2002). *Promoting Alternative Thinking Strategies: Blueprint for prevention (book 10), second edition*. Boulder: Institute of Behavioral Sciences, University of Colorado.

Greenberg, M. T., & Kusché, C. A. (2004). *The PATHS curriculum: Follow-up effects and mediational processes*. Unpublished manuscript, Prevention Research Center, Pennsylvania State University, University Park, PA.

Greenberg, M. T., Kusché, C. A., Cook, E. T., & Quamma, J. P. (1995). Promoting emotional competence in school-aged children: The effects of the PATHS Curriculum. *Development and Psychopathology, 7*, 117–136.

Greenberg, M. T., Kusché, C. A., & Riggs, N. (2004). The PATHS curriculum: Theory and research on neuro-cognitive development and school success. In J. E. Zins, R. P. Weissberg, M. C. Wang, & H. J. Walberg (Eds.), *Building academic success on social and emotional learning: What does the research say?* (pp. 170–188). New York: Teachers College Press.

Greenberg, M.T., Kusché, C.A., & Speltz, M. (1991). Emotional regulation, self-control, and psychopathology: The role of relationships in early childhood. In D. Cicchetti & S. L. Toth (Eds.), *Internalizing and externalizing expressions of dysfunction: Rochester Symposium on Developmental Psychopathology* (Vol. 2, pp. 21–55). New York: Cambridge University Press.

Greenberg, M. T., & Snell, J. (1997). The neurological basis of emotional development. In P. Salovey (Ed.), *Emotional development and emotional literacy* (pp. 92–119). New York: Basic Books.

Greenberg, M. T., Weissberg, R. P., Utne O'Brien, M., Zins, J. E., Fredericks, L., Resnik, H., & Elias, M. J. (2003). Enhancing school-based prevention and youth development through coordinated social, emotional, and academic learning, *American Psychologist, 58,* 466–474.

Hallinger, P., & Heck, R. H. (1996). Reassessing the principal's role in school effectiveness: A review of empirical research, 1980–1995. *Educational Administration Quarterly, 32,* 5–44.

Kam, C. M., Greenberg, M. T., & Kusché, C. A. (2004). Sustained effects of the PATHS curriculum on the social and psychological adjustment of children in special education. *Journal of Emotional and Behavioral Disorders, 12,* 66–78.

Kam, C. M., Greenberg, M. T., & Walls, C. T. (2003). Examining the role of implementation quality in school-based prevention using the PATHS curriculum. *Prevention Science, 4,* 55–63.

Kusché, C. A. (1984). *The understanding of emotion concepts by deaf children: An assessment of an affective curriculum.* Unpublished doctoral dissertation. University Microfilms International, DAO 56952. University of Washington Seattle, WA.

Kusché, C. A. (2002a). Psychoanalysis as prevention: Using PATHS to enhance ego development, object relationships, and cortical integration in children. *Journal of Applied Psychoanalytic Studies, 4,* 283–301.

Kusché, C. A. (2002b). *Towards an understanding of violence.* Paper presented at the Alliance Forum, Seattle, WA.

Kusché, C. A., & Greenberg, M. T. (1994). *The PATHS (Promoting Alternative Thinking Strategies) curriculum.* South Deerfield, MA: Channing-Bete.

Kusché, C. A., & Greenberg, M. T. (2001). PATHS in your classroom: Promoting emotional literacy and alleviating emotional distress. In J. Cohen (Ed.), *Caring classrooms/intelligent schools: The socioemotional education of young children* (pp. 140–161). New York: Teachers College Press.

Kusché, C. A., & Greenberg, M. T. (2006). Brain development and social emotional learning: An introduction for educators. In M. Elias & H. Arnold (Eds.), The Educator's Guide to Emotional Intelligence and Academic Achievement. New York: Corwin Press.

Kusché, C. A., & Greenberg, M. T. (2006). Teaching emotional literacy in elementary school classrooms: The PATHS Curriculum. In M. Elias & H. Arnold (Eds.), The Educator's Guide to Emotional Intelligence and Academic Achievement. New York: Corwin Press.

Kusché, C. A., Riggs, R. S., & Greenberg, M. T. (1999). PATHS: Using analytic knowledge to teach emotional literacy. *The American Psychoanalyst, 33,* 20–21.

Leithwood, K. A., & Duke, D. (1999). A century's quest to understand school leadership. In J. Murphy & K. S. Louis (Eds.), *Handbook of research on educational administration* (2nd ed. pp. 45–72). San Francisco: Jossey-Bass.

Luria, A. R. (1976). *Cognitive development: Its cultural and social foundations.* Cambridge, MA: Harvard University Press.

Mayer, J. D., & Salovey, P. (1997). What is emotional intelligence? In P. Salovey (Ed.), *Emotional development and emotional literacy* (pp. 3–31). New York: Basic Books.

Robin, A. L., Schneider, M., & Dolnick, M. (1976). The Turtle Technique: An extended case study of self-control in the classroom. *Psychology in the Schools, 13,* 449–453.

Schore, A. (1996). The experience-dependent maturation of a regulatory system in the orbital prefrontal cortex and the origin of developmental psychopathology. *Developmental Psychopathology, 8,* 59–87.

Schultz, D., Izard, C. E., & Ackerman, B. P. (2000). Children's anger attribution bias: Relations to family environment and social adjustment. *Social Development, 9,* 284–301.

Seifer, R., Gouley, K. K., Miller, A. L., & Zakriski, A. (2004). Implementation of the PATHS curriculum in an urban elementary school. *Early Education and Development, 15,* 471–485.

Sutton, S. K., & Davidson, R. J. (1997). Prefrontal brain asymmetry: A biological substrate of the behavioral approach and inhibition systems. *Psychological Science, 8,* 204–210.

Weissberg, R. P., & Elias, M. J. (1993). Enhancing young people's social competence and health behavior: An important challenge for educators, scientists, policy makers, and funders. *Applied & Preventive Psychology: Current Scientific Perspectives, 3,* 179–190.

Weissberg, R. P., & Greenberg, M. T. (1998). School and community competence-enhancement and prevention programs. In W. Damon (Series Ed.) & I. E. Sigel & K. A. Renninger (Vol. Eds.), *Handbook of child psychology: Vol 4. Child psychology in practice* (5th ed.) (pp. 877–954). New York: Wiley.

White, S. H. (1965). Evidence for a hierarchical arrangement of learning processes. In L. P. Lipsett & C. C. Spiker (Eds.), *Advances in child development and behavior: Vol. 2* (pp. 164–192). New York: Academic Press.

27

Schoolwide Positive
Behavioral Supports

Jeffrey R. Sprague
Robert H. Horner
University of Oregon

To prevent minor, as well as serious, antisocial behavior, educators are turning to a comprehensive and proactive approach to discipline commonly referred to as School Wide Positive Behavior Support (SWPBS; Gresham, Sugai, & Horner, 2001; Osher, Dwyer, & Jackson, 2002; Sprague & Golly, 2004). SWPBS is based on the assumption that when faculty and staff in a school actively teach and acknowledge expected behavior, the proportion of students with serious behavior problems will be reduced and the school's overall climate will improve (Colvin, Kame'enui, & Sugai, 1993; Sugai & Horner, 2002; Sugai, Horner, et al., 2000).

The procedures that define SWPBS are organized around three main themes: prevention, multi-tiered support, and data-based decision making. Investing in prevention of problem behavior involves (a) defining and teaching core behavioral expectations, (b) acknowledging and rewarding appropriate behavior (e.g., compliance to school rules, safe and respectful peer to peer interactions, academic effort/engagement), and (c) establishing a consistent continuum of consequences for problem behavior. The focus is on establishing a positive social climate in which behavioral expectations for students are highly predictable, directly taught, consistently acknowledged, and actively monitored.

Multi-tiered support is available beyond the prevention level for those students with at-risk and antisocial behavior. The greater the student's need for support the more intense the support provided. Within the SWPBS model, emphasis has been on using the principles and procedures of behavior analysis as a foundation for defining behavioral challenges, completing functional behavioral assessments, and using these assessments, in conjunction with person-centered planning, to design effective and efficient procedures for addressing patterns of unacceptable behavior.

Data-based decision making is a theme that is interwoven throughout SWPBS, and builds on the assumption that the faculty, staff, family, and students will be most effective in the design of preventive and reactive supports if they have access to regular, accurate information about the behavior of students. The value of data for decision making is emphasized for both the design of initial supports, and the ongoing assessment and adaptation of support strategies.

The SWPBS approach includes adoption of practical strategies for collecting, summarizing, reporting, and using data on regular cycles.

Evidence suggests that sustained use of SWPBS practices can alter the trajectory of at-risk children toward destructive outcomes, and prevent the onset of risk behavior in typically developing children. It is expected that effective and sustained implementation of SWPBS will create a more responsive school climate that supports the twin goals of schooling for all children: academic achievement and social development (Horner, Sugai, Todd, & Lewis-Palmer, 2005; Walker et al., 1996).

Implementing and sustaining an organized, schoolwide system for behavior support and teaching social behavior is the foundation for effective prevention. In addition to the direct benefit it has on student behavior in school, such a system creates the context for school-based efforts to support effective parenting. When school personnel have a shared vision of the kind of social behavior they want to promote among students and a shared understanding of the type of social environment that is needed to achieve such behavior, they are in a position to inform and support families in creating the same kind of supportive environment at home. When educators are clear about how to use rules, positive reinforcement, and mild, consistent negative consequences to support behavioral development, they are better able to coordinate their efforts with those of parents. As a result, parents will know more about their children's behavior in school and will be able to provide the same supports and consequences that the school is providing.

As of 2005, more than, 2,700 schools across the country are actively implementing SWPBS. These schools are reporting reductions in problem behavior, improved perceptions of school safety, and improved academic outcomes (Horner et al., in press). This chapter describes how to establish and implement a schoolwide positive behavior support system. To first establish the context in which SWPBS is being adopted, we begin by framing the challenge that antisocial behavior presents in schools.

THE CHALLENGE OF ANTISOCIAL BEHAVIOR IN SCHOOLS

Schools in the United States are responding to increasingly serious problem behaviors (e.g., bullying, harassment, victimization, drug and alcohol abuse, the effects of family disruption, poverty; Kingery, 1999). These problem behaviors, and their related challenges (the effects of family disruption, poverty) have created fears about the personal safety of students, teachers, parents, and community members that are very real and need to be addressed in every school.

Although most U.S. schools are relatively safe places for children, youth, and the adults who teach and support them (U.S. Departments of Justice and Education, 1999, 2000), it also is true that some schools have serious antisocial behavior and violence problems. No school is immune from challenging behaviors and the potential for violence. They exist in every school and community, and they always will. The extent of the challenge will vary in intensity and frequency across schools, and the onset and development of antisocial behavior are associated with a variety of school, community, and family risk factors (Sprague, Walker, Sowards, et al., 2002; Walker & Sylwester, 1991). The challenge is to reduce the frequency and intensity of these problems, and to sustain behavioral gains over time.

The social problems noted here compete directly with the instructional mission of schools. The result is decreased academic achievement and a lower quality of life for students and staff alike. The *National Educational Goals Panel Report* (U.S. Department of Education, 1998, 2000) lists five essential areas in which national school performance has declined: (a) reading achievement at Grade 12 has decreased (Goal 3); (b) student drug use has increased (Goal 7); (c) sale of drugs at school in Grades 8, 10, and 12 has increased; (d) threats and injuries to public school teachers have increased (Goal 7); and (e) more teachers are reporting that disruptions in their classroom interfere with their teaching (Goal 7). These outcomes illustrate the clear link between declining school climate, school violence, and academic achievement. It is not possible to achieve national educational goals and meaningful reform without addressing these disturbing conditions (Elias, Zins, Graczyk, & Weissberg, 2003).

School Practices Contribute to the Problem

Many school practices contribute to the development and prevalence of antisocial behavior and the potential for violence. Because of the nearly exclusive emphasis on detecting individual child or youth characteristics that predict antisocial behavior and violence, many important systemic variables are often overlooked as contributors (Colvin et al., 1993; Hawkins, Catalano, Kosterman, Abbott, & Hill, 1999; Mayer, 1995; Walker & Eaton-Walker, 2000; Walker et al., 1996). These include, among others:

1. Ineffective instruction that results in academic failure.
2. Failure to individualize instruction and support to adapt to individual differences (e.g., ethnic and cultural differences, gender, disability).
3. Disagreement and inconsistency of implementation among staff members.
4. Lack of administrator involvement, leadership, and support.
5. Inconsistent and punitive classroom and behavior management practices.
6. Unclear rules and expectations regarding appropriate behavior.
7. Failure to reward compliance to school behavior expectations.
8. Lack of opportunity to learn and practice prosocial interpersonal and self-management skills.
9. Failure to assist students from at-risk (e.g., poverty, racial/ethnic minority members) backgrounds to bond with the schooling process.

Common Response to Behavioral Problems: Turn to Office Referrals, Suspensions, and Expulsions!

Often when a student misbehaves, the first line of response involves increasing monitoring and supervision of the student, restating rules, and delivering sanctions (e.g., referrals to the office, out-of-school suspension, and/or loss of privileges). The administrator may come to a point of frustration and attempt to establish a "bottom line" for disruptive students (usually referral or suspension). Unfortunately, these "get-tough" responses produce immediate, short-lived relief for the school but do not facilitate the progress of the student who may already be disengaged from the schooling process.

Paradoxically, although punishment practices may appear to "work" in the short term, they may merely remove the student for a period of time, thus providing a brief respite. All too often, these practices also can lead some to assign exclusive responsibility for positive change to the student or family and thereby prevent meaningful school engagement and development of solutions. The use of sanctions, without an accompanying program of teaching and recognition for expected positive behavior, may merely displace the problem elsewhere (to the home or the community). There is little evidence of the long-term effect of these practices in reducing antisocial behavior (Irvin, Tobin, Sprague, Sugai, & Vincent, 2004; Skiba & Peterson, 1999). In fact, evidence suggests that schools using punishment practices alone promote more antisocial behavior than those with a firm, but fair discipline system (Mayer, 1995; Skiba & Peterson, 1999). Research shows clearly that schools using only punishment techniques tend to have increased rates of vandalism, aggression, truancy, and ultimately school dropout (Mayer, 1995).

For students with chronic problem behavior these negative practices are more likely to impair child–adult relationships and attachment to schooling rather than reduce the likelihood of problem behavior. Punishment alone, without a balance of support and efforts to restore school engagement, weakens academic outcomes and maintains the antisocial trajectory of at-risk students. Instead, the discipline process should help students accept responsibility, place high value on academic engagement and achievement, teach alternative ways to behave, and focus on restoring a positive environment and social relationships in the school.

If Not Punishment, Then What Is the Solution?

Schools can serve as an ideal setting to organize efforts against the increasing problems of children and youth who display antisocial behavior patterns (Mayer, 1995; Sugai & Horner, 1994; Walker et al., 1996). This practice is sustained by a tendency to try to eliminate the presenting problem quickly by removing the student via suspension or expulsion, or fix a "within-child" deficit rather than focus on the administrative, teaching, and management practices that either contribute to or reduce them (Tobin, Sugai, & Martin, 2000).

CONCEPTUAL BASIS FOR SWPBS

A solid research base exists to guide an analysis of the administrative, teaching, and management practices in a school and design alternatives to ineffective approaches. An important theme from this research is that no single intervention practice should be viewed as meeting all the behavioral challenges in schools. Student behavior is complex and influenced by many variables within the school, within the family/community, and within the student. The behavior support strategies to establish a schoolwide social culture need to be supplemented with classroom interventions and individualized supports for students with chronic and intense patterns of problem behavior. The range of student behavior support needs requires that interventions target both schoolwide and individual student support strategies. Educators in today's schools and classrooms must be supported to adopt and sustain effective; cost-efficient practices in this regard (D. Gottfredson, 1997; G. Gottfredson, Gottfredson, & Czeh, 2000; Walker et al., 1996). A well-developed body of research evidence on school safety indicates that (a) early identification and intervention with at-risk children in schools is feasible; (b) the risk of dropping out of school, delinquency, violence, and other adjustment problems is high unless these children are helped; (c) academic recovery is difficult if early intervention is not provided; and (d) universal interventions need to be combined with interventions targeted to specific problems (G. Gottfredson, 2001; Tolan, Gorman-Smith, & Henry, 2001). Effective schools have shared values regarding the school's mission and purpose, carry out multiple activities designed to promote prosocial behavior and connection to school traditions, and provide a caring nurturing social climate involving collegial relationships among adults and students (Bryk & Driscoll, 1988; G. Gottfredson, Gottfredson, & Czeh, 2000; Scott & Eber, 2003).

Changing School Climate Is an Essential Element

The biggest challenge schools face is to enhance their overall capacity to create and sustain positive and behaviorally effective schools. Schools should provide schoolwide positive behavior supports at the point of school entry and continue implementing through high school (O'Donnell, Hawkins, Catalano, Abbott, & Day, 1995). It is never too late, nor too early to support children and youth in our schools (Loeber & Farrington, 1998). Research indicates that schools can establish clear expectations for learning and positive behavior, while providing firm but fair discipline. Students will be more motivated if they are in environments that are perceived as safe, positive, and predictable. Increased motivation is associated with improved acquisition of skills that will be of value for years following formal education (Katz, 1997).

Thus, the challenge becomes how to give schools the capacity to adopt and sustain the processes, organizational structures, and systems that enable them to carry out these effective interventions (G. Gottfredson et al., 2000). The problem for schools is not the lack of effective programs (those that work), but rather it is one of efficacy (helping typical schools adopt and carry out effective interventions).

Where to Start: No Child Left Behind Principles of Effectiveness

Education professionals may use the U.S. Department of Education's Office of Safe and Drug Free Schools "Principles of Effectiveness" as an organizing framework for planning and implementing whole-school approaches to safety and effectiveness. The principles recommend the following: (a) a local needs assessment of the risk and protective factors affecting the school, families, and the community (including the status of support systems); (b) establishment of measurable goals and objectives by the school that are integrated with school improvement planning; (c) selection of research-based and research-validated curricula and interventions; and (d) implementation of a comprehensive and rigorous evaluation plan, which includes evaluation of inputs (resources, staff, and materials), outputs (actual costs and description of the process of implementation), outcomes (e.g., student behavior change), and impact (overall satisfaction with project products and outcomes). In the next section, SWPBS use and the Principles of Effectiveness as an organizing framework are introduced.

IMPLEMENTING SWPBS

SWPBS is a systems-based approach that promotes safe and orderly schools. Researchers at the University of Oregon (see Sprague, Sugai & Walker, 1998; Sprague, Walker, Golly, et al., 2002; Sugai & Horner, 1999; Taylor-Greene et al., 1997) have field tested the efficacy of SWPBS approaches in reducing school behavior problems and promoting a positive school climate. SWPBS is a multiple system approach to addressing the problems posed by students displaying antisocial behaviors and coping with challenging forms of student behavior. The key practices of SWPBS are as follow:

- Clear definitions of expected appropriate, positive behaviors are provided for students and staff members.
- Clear definitions of problem behaviors and their consequences are defined for students and staff members.
- Regularly scheduled instruction and assistance in desired positive social behaviors is provided that enables students to acquire the necessary skills for the desired behavior change.
- Effective incentives and motivational systems are provided to encourage students to behave differently.
- Staff commitment to staying with the intervention over the long term and to monitor, support, coach, debrief, and provide booster lessons for students as necessary to maintain the achieved gains.
- Staff receives training, feedback, and coaching about effective implementation of the systems.
- Systems for measuring and monitoring the intervention's effectiveness are established and carried out.

Improving Discipline Is a Priority

First, the improvement of school discipline should be one of the top school improvement goals. With competing resources and goals, if work in this area is not a priority, progress will be difficult.

Administrator Leadership

Every school needs a principal committed to SWPBS leadership and participation. In the absence of administrative leadership and district support (e.g., policy and fiscal) it will be difficult to effect broad-based changes. Hallinger and Heck (1998) reviewed the evidence on the principal's contribution to school effectiveness. They concluded that principals exercise a measurable effect on schooling effectiveness and student achievement. Kam, Greenberg, and Walls (2003) reported that the ability of principals to initiate and sustain innovations in their schools is related to successful program implementation. The length of time administrators have spent in the school setting and the leadership characteristics they show in maintaining good relationships with teachers, parents, school boards, site councils, and students also are positively related to successful implementation outcomes. G. Gottfredson et al. (2000) and Ingersoll (2001) showed that high levels of administrative support were also associated with reduced staff turnover.

Commitment to Participate

It is important to secure a commitment to implement the intervention by at least 80% of school staff. Some schools have chosen to use a "vote" to assess this level of commitment. We have found a few approaches that can move a group of colleagues toward program implementation (Embry, 2004).

- Talk about cost and benefit. All adults involved need to know the costs (time and funds) and benefits of working to improve school discipline. For example, presentations by school leaders on the anticipated effects of program adoption (studies indicate that as discipline problems and referrals to the principal's office are dramatically reduced, teaching time is substantially increased; Scott & Barrett, 2004).
- Emphasize the long-term benefits. It also is useful to discuss the "higher good" of prevention and how much your colleagues value such outcomes as better academic achievement, prevention of alcohol, tobacco, and other drug use, and less teacher stress. These discussions may prove to be more powerful and persuasive than simply appealing to authority or law (i.e., We have to do it!).
- "Try before you buy." SWPBS is comprised of many smaller techniques (e.g., reward systems and teaching rules; Embry, 2004) that can be promoted as trial products. You can ask innovators in your building to share their successes, or arrange visits to schools that have already adopted SWPBS practices.
- "Go with the goers." The practice is far more likely to be adopted if you recognize and support people who get on board early, as well as encourage those who are reluctant, or even resistant.

To begin your journey toward establishing a more effective school program, we recommend that you begin by completing the needs assessment presented in Fig. 27.1 (we include only the schoolwide section here). The Assessing Behavior Support in Schools survey developed by Sugai Lewis-Palmer, Todd, and Horner (2000; available for no charge at www.pbis.org) proscribes the essential features of SWPBS at the schoolwide (Fig. 27.1), common area,

---

Effective Behavior Support (EBS) Survey
Assessing and Planning Behavior Support in Schools

Name of school _____   Date _____
District _____   State _____

Person Completing the Survey:

☐ Administrator   ☐ Special Educator   ☐ Parent/Family member
☐ General Educator   ☐ Counselor   ☐ School Psychologist
☐ Educational/Teacher Assistant   ☐ Community member   ☐ Other _____

1. Complete the survey independently.

2. Schedule 20-30 minutes to complete the survey.

3. Base your rating on your individual experiences in the school. If you do not work in classrooms, answer questions that are applicable to you.

    To assess behavior support, first evaluate the <u>status</u> of each system feature (i.e. *in place, partially in place, not in place*; left hand side of survey). Next, examine each feature:

    a. "What is the <u>current status</u> of this feature (i.e., *in place, partially in place, not in place*)?"

    b. For those features rated as partially in place or not in place, "What is the <u>priority for improvement </u> for this feature (i.e., *high, medium, or low*)?"

4. Return your completed survey to _____ by _____

SCHOOL-WIDE SYSTEMS

Current Status			Feature	Priority for Improvement		
In Place	Partial in Place	Not in Place	**School-wide** is defined as involving all students, all staff, & all settings.	High	Med	Low
			1. A small number (e.g., 3-5) of positively & clearly stated student expectations or rules are defined.			
			2. Expected student behaviors are taught directly.			
			3. Expected student behaviors are rewarded regularly.			
			4. Problem behaviors (failure to meet expected student behaviors) are defined clearly.			
			5. Consequences for problem behaviors are defined clearly.			
			6. Distinctions between office vs. classroom managed problem behaviors are clear.			

FIG. 27.1.   Sample needs assessment for planning and evaluating SWPBS. (Continued)

Current Status			Feature	Priority for Improvement		
In Place	Partial in Place	Not in Place	**School-wide** is defined as involving all students, all staff, & all settings.	High	Med	Low
			7. Options exist to allow classroom instruction to continue when problem behavior occurs.			
			8. Procedures are in place to address emergency/dangerous situations.			
			9. A team exists for behavior support planning & problem solving.			
			10. School administrator is an active participant on the behavior support team.			
			11. Data on problem behavior patterns are collected and summarized within an on-going system.			
			12. Patterns of student problem behavior are reported to teams and faculty for active decision-making on a regular basis (e.g., monthly).			
			13. School has formal strategies for informing families about expected student behaviors at school.			
			14. Booster training activities for students are developed, modified, & conducted based on school data.			
			15. School-wide behavior support team has a budget for (a) teaching students, (b) on-going rewards, and (c) annual staff planning.			
			16. All staff are involved directly and/or indirectly in school-wide interventions.			
			17. The school team has access to on-going training and support from district personnel.			
			18. The school is required by the district to report on the social climate, discipline level or student behavior at least annually.			

Name of School _____
Date _____

FIG. 27.1.   (Continued).

classroom, and individual student levels. The survey asks respondents to reflect on whether the practice is in place in their school and to choose which items are priorities for improvement. Your school behavior team will refer to these goals often, and modify them as indicated by a review of key data regarding effectiveness (e.g., office discipline referrals and rates of problem behavior on the playground).

Select Evidence-Based Practices

The SWPBS (Sprague et al., 1998; Sugai & Horner, 1994) approach was developed at the University of Oregon and the National Center on Positive Behavioral Interventions and Supports

TABLE 27.1
What Does SWPBS Look Like?

- Train and support a representative school team (20–30 hours of formal training
  - Principal actively leads and facilitates the process
  - Take time to plan, coach and continuously improve
- Set and promote schoolwide expectations
  - Plan to teach expected behavior
  - Plan to recognize expected behavior and actively supervise
- Use performance-based data for active decision making
  - Office discipline referral patterns (www.swis.org)
  - Discipline survey results
  - Changes in academic performance, attendance
  - Student safety surveys
- How do I know it's working?
  - Expected behaviors taught 20+ times a year
  - Students actively supervised in all school areas
  - Students acknowledged frequently for expected behavior
  - 4:1 positive:negative interactions
  - More than 80% students and adults can describe schoolwide expectations
    Safe, respectful, responsible

(www.pbis.org; an Office of Special Education Programs funded research center). The goal of SWPBS is to facilitate the academic achievement and healthy social development of children and youth in a safe environment conducive to learning. SWPBS involves embedded and ongoing staff development and coaching aimed at improving school and classroom discipline, and associated outcomes such as school violence, and alcohol, tobacco, and other drug use.

SWPBS includes intervention techniques based on more than 30 years of rigorous research regarding school discipline from education, public health, psychology, and criminology disciplines. SWPBS components address whole-school, common area, classroom, and individual student support practices and may be used in combination with other evidence-based prevention programs such as the Second Step Violence Prevention Curriculum (Committee for Children, 2002). Representative school team members are trained to develop and implement positive school rules, direct teaching of rules, positive reinforcement systems, data-based decision making at the school level, effective classroom management methods, curriculum adaptation to prevent problem behavior, and functional behavioral assessment and positive behavioral intervention plans. Teams are also coached to integrate SWPBS systems with other prevention programs to maximize effectiveness.

How Is SWPBS Implemented?

The process for adopting and sustaining SWPBS revolves around a school team typically composed of 5 to 10 individuals that includes an administrator, representative faculty/staff, and local family/community members. Table 27.1 provides a summary of the basic ideas. Although it may seem ideal to train all school staff all the time, it will rarely be feasible or sustainable to provide training at this level due to cost and logistical concerns. However, a representative group of adults, representing all school stakeholders (including students at the secondary level) can learn the key practices of SWPBS and set goals for improvement. The stakeholders can then function as leaders or coaches as they inform their groups of the team activities (e.g., at staff or area meetings) and give support and encouragement during the improvement process. Increasingly, we see district- and statewide initiatives supporting the dissemination of SWPBS training and coaching systems.

While participating in training, and after mastery of the basic material, it is recommended that school discipline teams (building administrator, representative teachers, and other stakeholders) meet approximately once a month to review training content as needed and to set up a regular process of reviewing and refining the school discipline plan (initial goals are developed during training) and other, school site-based activities. A format for these meetings should be specified and each meeting should last between 20 and 60 minutes.

Set and Promote Schoolwide Expectations

A critical first task for the implementation team is to establish schoolwide behavior rule teaching related to student–teacher compliance, peer-to-peer interaction, academic achievement, and academic study skills. It is recommended to use the general framework of "safety," "respect," and "responsibility" and directly teaching lessons throughout the year to establish and maintain the patterns of behavior associated with these personal qualities. Additionally, posting the rules publicly in posters, school newsletters, local media, announcements, assemblies, can be valuable.

Plan to Recognize Expected Behavior and Actively Supervise Students

The school will need to establish a consistent system of enforcement, monitoring, and positive reinforcement to enhance the effect of rule teaching and maintain patterns of desired student behavior. Reinforcement systems may include schoolwide token economies in the form of "tickets" stating each school rule delivered by all adults in the building. These tokens are to be "backed up" with weekly drawings and rewards for the teachers as well. Each school should implement the procedures to fit their school improvement plan and specific discipline needs.

Define and Effectively Correct Problem Behaviors and Their Consequences for Students and Staff Members

As stated earlier, schools using excessive sanctions experience greater levels of vandalism and other forms of misbehavior (Mayer, 1995; Skiba & Peterson, 1999). Positive reinforcement is more effective than punishment because it does not result in the type of counter aggression and withdrawal (fight or flight) that punishment can produce and because it does not focus teachers' attention on detecting and correcting rule violations.

Students should see rules applied fairly. When they feel that rules are unevenly applied, students are more likely to misbehave. Schools with clear rule and reward systems and business-like corrections and sanctions also experience fewer problems. These schools signal appropriate behavior for students and respond to misbehavior predictably. Students in such schools are clear about expected behavior and learn there are consequences for misbehavior. When rules are consistent, students develop a respect for rules and laws, and internalize beliefs that the system of governance works (Bryk & Driscoll, 1988; D. Gottfredson, 1987; D. Gottfredson, Gottfredson, & Hybl, 1993).

Report Data for Active Decision Making

The efficiency of team problem solving is enhanced by providing the team with data-based feedback to schools regarding their implementation of basic SWPBS practices (cf. 'Assessing Behavior Support in Schools' survey; Fig. 27.1) and the impact of implementation on problem behavior as indexed by discipline referral patterns (cf. School-Wide Information System

[SWIS]; Sprague, Sugai, Horner, & Walker, 1999; Sugai, Sprague, Horner, & Walker, 2000). The goal is to use highly efficient data systems that allow teams to ask (a) Are we implementing evidence-based, SWPBS practices? and (b) Are the practices having an effect on the behavior of students? Data on implementation of SWPBS practices typically are collected, summarized, and reported quarterly, and data on student behavior are collected continuously, and reported to the school team weekly, the school faculty monthly, and the school district annually. Irvin et al. (in press) provide an evaluation documenting the value that regular access to student behavioral data has for typical school teams.

Examples of data collection and display tools for assessing implementation of SWPBS can be found on the Internet at www.pbssurveys.org (Boland, Todd, Horner, & Sugai, 2005). Similarly, an example of a Web-based information system designed to help school personnel to use office referral data to design schoolwide and individual student interventions is available at www.swis.org (May et al., 2000). It is anticipated that as schoolwide systems become more common an increasing array of data collection options will become available to schools. A major focus for research on educational systems change lies in the process, and impact of providing teachers, administrators, families and students with regular, accurate information for decision making.

IMPLEMENTING FOR SUSTAINABILITY

Too often, educational innovations, even effective innovations, have been implemented but not maintained (Latham, 1988). If SWPBS is to result in educational change at a scale of practical relevance, schools adopting SWPBS procedures will need to sustain the practices and benefits. An important feature of the SWPBS approach is inclusion of formal strategies for improving the likelihood of sustained implementation. These include (a) the development of training materials at each school that make it "easier" to implement from year to year; (b) the implementation of policies for using SWPBS, and reporting student data; and (c) the training of district-level "coaches" who are available to provide booster training for school teams, initial training for new faculty members, and help with problem solving around more intense challenges. The district coaching role is designed to help a school team sustain effective practices through periodic perturbations in the staffing, organization or fluctuation in student behavior. The issue of sustaining educational innovation is not unique to SWPBS, and remains a worthy focus for research.

WHAT IS THE EVIDENCE FOR SWPBS EFFECTIVENESS?

A number of researchers (see Embry & Flannery, 1994; Knoff & Batsche, 1995; Taylor-Green et al., 1997) have studied SWPBS practices. The effects of the program are documented in a series of studies implemented by researchers at the University of Oregon (Horner et al., in press; Metzler, Biglan, Rusby, & Sprague 2001; Sprague, Walker, Golly, et al., 2002; Taylor-Greene et al., 1997, see also www.pbis.org for the latest research studies and reports). Studies have shown reductions in office discipline referrals of up to 50% a year, with continued improvement over a 3-year period in schools that sustain the intervention (Irvin et al., 2004). In addition, school staff reports show greater satisfaction with their work, compared with schools that did not implement SWPBS. Comparison schools typically show increases or no change in office referrals, along with a general frustration with the school discipline program.

In studies employing the SWPBS components, have documented reductions in antisocial behavior (Sprague, Walker, Golly et al., 2002), vandalism (Mayer, 1995), aggression (Grossman

TABLE 27.2
Implications for Practice: What Educational Professionals Should Do to Enhance Social
and Behavioral Competence in Schools

- Systematically assess the nature, prevalence and effects of antisocial behavior in one's school, using office discipline referral patterns, and other sources of data.
- Share the findings with members of the school community in order to raise awareness of the prevalence of antisocial behavior, thereby motivating school authorities to address the problem.
- Develop clear goals and objectives for improving school discipline, well supported by the entire school community. This should include guidelines to help the school to identify, prevent and deal with incidents of problem behavior.
- Consistently and continuously communicate, teach, and reward schoolwide behavioral expectations (compliance to adult requests, positive peer and teacher interactions, and school effort).
- Provide continuous and ongoing performance-based feedback to staff members regarding the type, location, time, and referring staff persons of office discipline referrals and other indicators of problem behavior. Encourage shared problem solving and recognition of reductions or improvements.

et al., 1997; Lewis, Sugai, & Colvin, 1998), later delinquency (Kellam, Mayer, Rebok, & Hawkins, 1998; O'Donnell et al., 1995), as well as alcohol, tobacco, and other drug use (Biglan, Wang, & Walberg, 2003; O'Donnell et al., 1995). Positive changes in protective factors such as academic achievement (Kellam et al., 1998; O'Donnell et al., 1995) and school engagement (O'Donnell et al., 1995) have been documented using a schoolwide positive behavior support approach such as SWPBS in concert with other prevention interventions.

CONCLUSION

We have described a schoolwide system for positive behavior support, and the implementation steps being used to build both a positive schoolwide social culture, and the capacity to support individual students with more intense behavioral needs. The major messages are as follow: (a) problem behavior in schools is both a significant social challenge and a barrier to effective learning; (b) traditional "get-tough" strategies have not proven effective; (c) the foundation for all behavior support in schools begins with establishing a positive social culture by defining, teaching, and rewarding appropriate behaviors; (d) additional behavior support procedures based on behavior analysis principles are needed for children with more intense behavior support needs; and (e) school personnel are demonstrating both the ability to collect and use quality improvement data systems, and the value of those systems for improving schools. Table 27.2 presents information highlighting implications for practice, indicating what educational professionals should do to enhance social and behavioral competence in schools.

As of mid-2005, randomized controlled research studies were in progress to examine the effects of SWPBS with greater precision and control. Current evaluation results, however, are encouraging. Schools throughout the country are demonstrating the ability to adopt SWPBS practices with fidelity (Horner et al., 2004; Horner et al., in press). When schools adopt SWPBS practices, they are reporting reductions in problem behavior, improved perceptions of school safety, and improved academic performance. Recent Illinois evaluations also report that schools establishing a positive social climate are proving more effective in their implementation of individual, wrap-around support for students with high behavior support needs.

The overall picture is encouraging. Schools are able to improve, and to demonstrate that change is linked to valued student outcomes. If these gains are to become important at a national scale, additional research is needed to demonstrate experimentally controlled effects, strategies for improving efficiency, and strategies for supporting sustained implementation.

REFERENCES

Biglan, A., Wang, M. C., & Walberg, H. J. (2003). Preventing *youth problems*. New York: Kluwer Academic/Plenum.

Boland, J., Todd, A.W., Horner, R.H., & Sugai, G. (2005). *Positive behavior support surveys*. Available: http://www.pbssurveys.org.

Bryk, A. S., & Driscoll, M. E. (1988). *The high school as community: contextual influences, and consequences for students and teachers*. Madison: National Center on Effective Secondary Schools, Wisconsin Center for Education Research, University of Wisconsin-Madison.

Colvin, G., Kame'enui, E. J., & Sugai, G. (1993). School-wide and classroom management: Reconceptualizing the integration and management of students with behavior problems in general education. *Education and Treatment of Children, 16*, 361–381.

Committee for Children. (2002). *Second step violence prevention curriculum*. Seattle, WA: Author.

Elias, M., Zins, J., Graczyk, P., & Weissberg, R. (2003). Implementation, sustainability, and scaling up of social-emotional and academic innovations in public schools. *School Psychology Review 32*, 303–319.

Embry, D. D. (2004). Community-based prevention using simple, low-cost, evidence-based kernels and behavior vaccines. *Journal of Community Psychology 32*, 575–591.

Embry, D. D., & Flannery, D. J. (1994). *Peacebuilders—Reducing youth violence: A working application of cognitive-social-imitative competence research*. Tucson, AZ: Heartsprings.

Gottfredson, D. C. (1997). School-based crime prevention. In L. Sherman, D. Gottfredson, D. Mackenzie, J. Eck, P. Reuter, & S. Bushway (Eds.), *Preventing crime: What works, what doesn't, what's promising* (pp. 5). College Park, MD: Department of Criminology and Criminal Justice.

Gottfredson, D. C. (1987). Developing effective organizations to reduce school disorder. In O. C. Moles (Ed.), *Strategies to reduce student misbehavior* (pp. 87–104). Washington, DC: Office of Educational Research and Improvement.

Gottfredson, D. C., Gottfredson, G. D., & Hybl, L. G. (1993). Managing adolescent behavior: A multiyear, multischool study. *American Educational Research Journal, 30*, 179–215.

Gottfredson, G. (2001). *Delinquency in schools*. New York: Cambridge University Press.

Gottfredson, G., Gottfredson, D., & Czeh, E. (2000). *National study of delinquency prevention in schools*. Ellicott City, MD: Gottfredson Associates.

Grossman, D. C., Neckerman, H. J., Joepsell, T. D., Liu, P., Asher, K. N., Beland, K., Frey, K., & Rivara, F. P. (1997). Effectiveness of a violence prevention curriculum among children in elementary school. *Journal of the American Medical Association, 277*, 1605–1611.

Greenberg, M. T., Domitrovich, C., & Bumbarger, B. (1999) *Preventing mental disorders in school-age children: A review of the effectiveness of prevention programs* (Report submitted to Center for Mental Health Services, Substance Abuse Mental Health Services Administration). Washington, DC: U.S. Department of Health and Human Services.

Gresham, F. M., Sugai, G., & Horner, R.H. (2001). Interpreting outcomes of social skills training for students with high-incidence disabilities. *Exceptional Children, 67*, 331–344.

Hallinger, P., & Heck, R. H. (1998). Exploring the principal's contribution to school effectiveness: 1980–1995. *School Effectiveness and School Improvement, 9*, 157–191.

Hawkins, J. D., Catalano, R. F., Kosterman, R., Abbott, R., & Hill, K. G. (1999). Preventing adolescent health-risk behaviors by strengthening protection during childhood. *Archives of Pediatrics and Adolescent Medicine, 153*, 226–234.

Horner, R., & Sugai, G. (2000). School-wide behavior support: An emerging initiative. *Journal of Positive Behavior Interventions 2*, 231–232.

Horner, R. H., Sugai, G., Todd, A. W., & Lewis-Palmer, T. (2005). School-wide positive behavior support: In L. Bambara & L. Kern (Eds.), *Individualized supports for students with problem behaviors: Designing positive behavior plans* (pp. 359–390). New York: Guilford Press.

Horner, R. H., Todd, A. W., Lewis-Palmer, T., Irvin, L. K., Sugai, G., & Boland, J. B. (2004). The school-wide evaluation tool (SET): A research instrument for assessing school-wide positive behavior support. *Journal of Positive Behavior Interventions, 6*, 3–12.

Ingersoll, R. M. (2001). Teacher turnover and teacher shortages: An organizational analysis. *American Educational Research Journal, 38*, 499–534.

Irvin, L. K., Horner, R. H., Ingram, K., Todd, A. W., Sugai, G., Sampson, N. Q., Boland, J. (in press). Using office discipline referral for decision-making about student behavior in elementary and middle schools: An enpiricay investigation of validity. *Journal of Positive Behavior Interventions*.

Irvin, L. K., Tobin, T. J., Sprague, J. R., Sugai, G., & Vincent, C. G. (2004). Validity of office discipline referrals measures as indices of school-wide behavioral status and effects of school-wide behavioral interventions. *Journal of Positive Behavior Interventions, 6*(3), 131–147.

Kam, C. M., Greenberg, M. T., & Walls, C. T. (2003). Examining the role of implementation quality in school-based prevention using the PATHS curriculum. *Prevention Science, 4*, 55–63.

Katz, M. (1997) *On playing a poor hand well: Insights from the lives of those who have overcome childhood risks and adversities.* New York: Norton.

Kellam, S. G., Mayer, L. S., Rebok, G. W., & Hawkins, W. E. (1998). Effects of improving achievement on aggressive behavior and of improving aggressive behavior on achievement through two preventive interventions: An investigation of causal paths. In B. P. Dohrenwend (Ed.), *Adversity, stress, and psychopathology* (pp. 486–505). New York: Oxford University Press.

Kingery, P. (1999). Suspensions and expulsions: New directions. In *The Hamilton-Fish National Institute on School and Community Violence, Effective violence prevention programs.* Washington, DC: George Washington University.

Knoff, H. M., & Batsche, G. M. (1995). Project ACHIEVE: Analyzing a school reform process for at-risk and underachieving students. *School Psychology Review, 24,* 579–603.

Latham, G. I. (1988). The birth and death cycles of educational innovations. *Principal, 68,* 41–44.

Lewis, T. J., Sugai, G., & Colvin, G. (1998). Reducing problem behavior through a school-side system of effective behavioral support: Investigation of a school-wide social skills training program and contextual interventions. *School Psychology Review, 27,* 446–459.

Loeber, R., & Farrington, D. P. (1998). *Serious and violent juvenile offenders: Risk factors and successful interventions.* Thousand Oaks, CA: Sage.

May, S., Ard, W., III., Todd, A.W., Horner, R. H., Glasgow, A., Sugai, G., & Sprague, J. R. (2000). *School-wide Information System.* Eugene: Educational and Community Supports, University of Oregon.

Mayer, G. R. (1995). Preventing antisocial behavior in the schools. *Journal of Applied Behavior Analysis, 28,* 467–478.

Metzler, C. W., Biglan, A., Rusby, J. C., & Sprague, J. R. (2001). Evaluation of a comprehensive behavior management program to improve school-wide positive behavior support. *Education and Treatment of Children, 24,* 448–479.

O'Donnell, J., Hawkins, J., Catalano, R., Abbott, R., & Day, L. (1995). Preventing school failure, drug use, and delinquency among low-income children: Long-term intervention in elementary schools. *American Journal of Orthopsychiatry, 65,* 87–100.

Osher, D., Dwyer, K., & Jackson, S. (2002). Safe, supportive and successful schools: Step by step. Longmont, CO: Sopris West.

Scott, T. M., & Barrett, S.B. (2004). Using staff and student time engaged in disciplinary procedures to evaluate the impact of school-wide PBS. *Journal of Positive Behavior Interventions, 6*(1) 21–27.

Scott, T. M., & Eber, L. (2003). Functional assessment and wraparound as systemic school processes: Primary, secondary, and tertiary systems examples. *Journal of Positive Behavior Interventions, 5,* 131–143.

Skiba, R., & Peterson, R. (1999). School discipline at a crossroads: From zero tolerance to early reponse. *Exceptional Children 66,* 335–346.

Sprague, J., & Golly, A. (2004). *Best behavior: Building positive behavior supports in schools.* Longmont, CO: Sopris West .

Sprague, J. R., Sugai, G., Horner, R. H., & Walker, H. M. (1999). *Using office discipline referral data to evaluate school-wide discipline and violence prevention interventions.* Oregon School Study Council Bulletin. Eugene: University of Oregon, College of Education.

Sprague, J. R., Sugai, G., & Walker, H. (1998). Antisocial behavior in schools. In T. S. Watson & F. M. Gresham (Eds.), *Handbook of child behavior therapy* (pp. 451–474). New York: Plenum.

Sprague, J., Walker, H., Golly, A., White, K., Myers, D. R., & Shannon, T. (2002). Translating research into effective practice: The effects of a universal staff and student intervention on key indicators of school safety and discipline. *Education and Treatment of Children, 24,* 495–511.

Sprague, J., Walker, H., Sowards, S., Van Bloem, C., Eberhardt, P., & Marshall, B. (2002). Sources of vulnerability to school violence: Systems-level assessment and strategies to improve safety and climate. In M. R. Shinn, G. Stoner, & H. M. Walker (Eds.), *Interventions for academic and behavior problems II: Preventive and remedial approaches* (2nd ed., pp. 295–314). Bethesda, MD: National Association of School Psychologists.

Sugai, G., & Horner, R. (1994). Including students with severe behavior problems in general education settings: Assumptions, challenges, and solutions. *Oregon Conference Monograph, 6,* 102–120.

Sugai, G., & Horner, R. H. (1999). Discipline and behavioral support: Preferred processes and practices. *Effective School Practices, 17,* 10–22.

Sugai, G., & Horner, R. H. (2002). The evolution of discipline practices: School-wide positive behavior supports. *Child & Family Behavior Therapy 24*(1/2), 23–50.

Sugai, G., Horner, R. H., Dunlap, G., Hieneman, M., Lewis, T. J., Nelson, C. M., Scott, T., Liaupsin, C., Sailor, W., Turnbull, A. P., Turnbull, H. R. III., Wickham, D., Reuf, M., & Wilcox, B. (2000). Applying positive behavioral support and functional behavioral assessment in schools. *Journal of Positive Behavioral Interventions, 2,* 131–143.

Sugai, G., Lewis-Palmer, T., Todd, A., & Horner, R. (2000). *Effective Behavior Support (EBS) survey: Assessing and planning behavior support in schools.* Eugene: University of Oregon.

Sugai, G., Sprague, J. R., Horner, R. H., & Walker, H. M. (2000). Preventing school violence: The use of office discipline referrals to assess and monitor school-wide discipline interventions. *Journal of Emotional and Behavioral Disorders, 8,* 94–101.

Taylor-Greene, S., Brown, D., Nelson, L., Longton, J., Gassman, T., Cohen, J., Swartz, J., Horner, R. H., Sugai, G., & Hall, S. (1997). School-wide behavioral support: Starting the year off right. *Journal of Behavioral Education, 7,* 99–112.

Tobin, T., Sugai, G., & Martin, E. (2000). *Final report for Project CREDENTIALS: Current research on educational endeavors to increase at-risk learners' success* (Report submitted to the Office of Professional Technical Education, Oregon Department of Education). Eugene: University of Oregon, College of Education, Behavioral Research and Teaching.

Tolan, P., Gorman-Smith, D., & Henry, D. (2001). New study to focus on efficacy of "whole school" prevention approaches. *Emotional & Behavioral Disorders in Youth, 2,* 5–7.

U.S. Departments of Justice and Education. (1998). *First Annual Report on School Safety.* Washington, DC: Author.

U.S. Departments of Justice and Education. (1999). *Annual Report on School Safety.* Washington, DC: Author.

U.S. Departments of Justice and Education. (2000). *Annual Report on School Safety.* Washington, DC: Author.

Walker, H. M., & Eaton-Walker, J. (2000, March). Key questions about school safety: Critical issues and recommended solutions. *NASSP Bulletin (National Association of Secondary School Principals),* pp. 46–55.

Walker, H. M., Horner, R. H., Sugai, G., Bullis, M., Sprague, J. R., Bricker, D., & Kaufman, M. J. (1996). Integrated approaches to preventing antisocial behavior patterns among school age children and youth. *Journal of Emotional and Behavioral Disorders, 4,* 194–209.

Walker, H. M., & Sylwester, R. (1991). Where is school along the path to prison? *Educational Leadership, 49,* 14–16.

28

How Effective Are School-Based Violence Prevention Programs in Preventing and Reducing Violence and Other Antisocial Behaviors? A Meta-Analysis

Jim Derzon
Pacific Institute for Research and Evaluation

Between 1992 and 2001, attention to youth and school crime and violence fluctuated, and the incidence of school crime and victimizations fell; nonetheless, the fact remains that for many students violence and victimization are indelible features of their lives. During the 1999–2000 school year, approximately 71% of all public schools experienced one or more serious violent crimes (violent crimes included rape, sexual battery other than rape, physical fights/attacks with or without a weapon, threats of such fights and attacks, and robberies with or without a weapon, U.S. Department of Eduction, 2004; National Center for Education Statistics [NCEC], 2004). In 2001, there was one nonfatal (theft plus violent) victimization committed in public schools for every 14 students (U.S. Department of Education, 2004). Out of school, the number dropped to approximately one crime for every 16 students. For each of the 73 per 1,000 student in-school crimes and the 61 per 1,000 out-of-school victimizations in 2001, 28 were for violent or serious violent offenses (U.S. Department of Education, 2004). Taken collectively, these findings indicate that public school students are being exposed to an extraordinary amount of criminal behavior.

Although student crime victimization has fallen in recent years, school bullying has increased. Bullying can contribute to an environment of fear and intimidation in schools (Ericson, 2001). In 2003, 7% of students reported being bullied at school in the previous 6 months (U.S. Department of Education, 2004). The percentage of students who reported being bullied increased between 1999 and 2001, although no increase was detected between 2001 and 2003 (ISCS, 2004).

School violence can make students fearful of the education environment and negatively affect their ability to learn. Because of such violence, many students feel unsafe at school. About 5% of students ages 12 to 18 avoided one or more places at school in 1999 and 2001 (ISCS, 2004). Between 1993 and 2001, the percentage of students being threatened or injured with a weapon (e.g., gun, knife, or club) on school property remained the same (ISCS, 2004). Compounding the alarming findings in schools is the percentage of teachers being physically attacked by students. During the 5-year period between 1998 and 2002, teachers were the victims of approximately 234,000 nonfatal crimes at school, including 144,000 thefts and

90,000 violent crimes (ISCS, 2004). Among the 90,000 violent crimes, there were 11,000 (12% of the total) serious violent crimes, including rape, sexual assault, robbery, and aggravated assault (ISCS, 2004). On average, these data translate into a rate of 32 thefts, 20 violent crimes, and two serious violent crimes per 1,000 teachers annually (ISCS, 2004).

In response to this continuing threat of school violence and because No Child Left Behind requires a local education action plan that uses "evidence-based" programs, many school districts have adopted science- or evidence-based programs to reduce the violence among their students. These programs promise to improve outcomes both for the victims of violence, by creating safe learning environments, and for the perpetrators, by reducing risk for continuing and increasingly adverse outcomes as a result and correlate of their behavior (e.g., Huizinga & Jakob-Chien, 1998; Krug, Brener, Dahlberg, Ryan, & Powell, 1997; Lochman, 1992). Additionally, school-based violence prevention programs have been associated with increased bonding to school and academic success (e.g., Hawkins, Catalano, Kosterman, Abbott, & Hill, 1999).

Although there may well be many important and valuable secondary effects from school-based violence prevention programming, it is worth asking how effective these programs are in reducing the violent and antisocial behaviors they are funded to prevent. This is a reasonable question at several levels. Schools devote significant resources to these interventions. They turn to science to provide evidence of effectiveness so they know their resources are well invested.

Historically, evidence of effectiveness in the social sciences has been defined by significance testing, a probabilistic inference that given an infinite number of trials and the current sample size, the observed difference between the intervention and comparison groups in the trial being tested would not occur more often than that specified by the alpha level (probability [p] value) selected by the researcher. That is, at $p \leq .05$ with a one-tailed test and an infinite number of tests, we would expect to see the result no more often than five times out of every 100 trials if there was no difference at all between the two groups on the tested outcome.

For persons concerned with the practical implications of school safety, however, significance testing is an amalgam of many things, none of which include whether the observed difference is meaningful (Cohen, 1988). Sample size, the true effect of the program in the population, the alpha level, and the sensitivity and accuracy of the measures all influence whether a test detects a significant result. Moreover, in the world of applied science, there are a host of other study vicissitudes and sample idiosyncrasies that may influence a particular test of an intervention (e.g., Derzon, Springer, & Sale, 2005; Wilson & Lipsey, 2001).

Although a program might be branded as effective because of observed statistical significance, the degree to which it should be supported depends, at a minimum, on how effective the program might be, how difficult it is to implement, what the program's direct, indirect, and opportunity costs are, whether the program garners sufficient community and provider support, and other organizational and contextual factors. Being able to estimate the likely effectiveness of a program is essential. For example, if the programs are highly effective in reducing and preventing violence, then committing resources to these programs may be warranted. If programs are only marginally effective, however, then alternative approaches may be appropriate.

Although a seemingly simple question to ask, estimating the effectiveness of school-based violence prevention programs is not straightforward. If a field has relatively few studies and only a few outcomes are of interest, one could list the studies and how they did on each outcome (e.g., Scheckner, Rollin, Kaiser-Ulrey, & Wagner, 2002). If, on the other hand, there are many studies or many outcomes of interest, then listing studies becomes unwieldy, and it becomes necessary to summarize evidence (e.g., Wilson, Gottfredson, & Najaka, 2001). Meta-analysis is a set of procedural and statistical methods for systematically abstracting evidence from summary reports in a form suitable for statistical manipulation. It is, in many respects, akin to survey research, although in the case of meta-analysis, it is summary reports that are being queried and not respondents (Durlak & Lipsey, 1991). Once the evidence has been accumulated into a standardized database, meta-analysis uses statistical methods to summarize and explore relations among the data. In the current study, we describe the overall effectiveness of school-based violence prevention programs in reducing various violent and other antisocial behaviors.

METHOD

Identifying Eligible Reports

A critical step in meta-analysis is identifying the literature appropriate to the study. In this synthesis, we used Boolean logic to search abstracts contained in the DIALOG database for the terms and synonyms of violence, antisocial or aggressive behaviors; evaluation; and school or student. This search of the bibliographic databases ERIC, Social SciSearch, PsycInfo, NCJRS, Dissertation Abstracts International, Mental Health Abstracts, MedLine (performed May 8,1998) yielded more than 2,100 citations and abstracts. These were downloaded and carefully screened for their potential to contribute to the current investigation.

Slightly less than 200 documents were retained from this screen. To assure that no eligible reports were missed, several additional procedures were followed. Review articles and the bibliographies of retrieved studies were carefully examined for additional documents not identified in the original search. In addition, a letter was sent to approximately 160 school-based programs listed on the Partnerships Against Violence Web site (PAVENET) as recommended for reducing violence requesting any appropriate data they might have. Finally, The Hamilton Fish Institute on School and Community Violence provided many documents, including several unpublished reports. These procedures yielded 695 documents potentially eligible for this meta-analysis.

Study Eligibility

Studies are eligible for a meta-analysis when they meet an explicit and detailed set of eligibility criteria. For this meta-analysis, selection criteria were defined to assure some degree of methodological rigor in the eligible studies without being so restrictive that they would exclude a significant proportion of the literature. The criteria applied to this meta-analysis revolved around six principle issues:

1. The intervention should be delivered, at least in part, in a school setting. Schools could be any public or private educational institution, from kindergarten through Grade 12.
2. The intervention could be universal, selected, or indicated as long as the prevention, reduction, treatment, or remediation of violent or antisocial behavior is one of its primary implicit or explicit goals.
3. Students must be between 5 and 18 years of age.
4. Experimental and quasi-experimental designs are both eligible.
5. Quantitative data sufficient for calculating or approximating an effect size must be provided for at least one outcome measure.
6. Although the research may have been conducted prior to 1950, only data published in 1950 or later are eligible.

Applying these criteria to the 695 retrieved documents eliminated 434 reports due to ineligibility. Most reports were dropped because they were either reviews ($n = 123$), did not address violence ($n = 42$), were not school-based ($n = 25$), described a program for which there were no data ($n = 56$), or were not evaluative ($n = 31$). A substantial number of studies did not provide the data necessary to calculate an effect size ($n = 44$). In the end, 261 reports containing data from 83 independent studies of 74 programs were retained for meta-analysis (bibliography available on request).

Coding Procedures

The 83 studies that survived the eligibility screen were subjected to a systematic and thorough coding protocol. In addition to coding effect sizes for each eligible study, information on nearly 100 other items related to study methods and procedures, subject and cohort characteristics, program theory, implementation, and comprehensiveness were coded into a computerized database by carefully trained graduate students. A subset of studies was recoded for reliability. Questions that arose in the course of coding were resolved through group deliberation. Formal weekly meetings were held to discuss coding issues that arose during the week. In all cases, consensus was sought.

Effect sizes provide a common statistical description of the program's effectiveness in reducing violent or antisocial behavior. Although different indices are available to summarize effectiveness, this study defined effectiveness as the difference between the intervention group mean and the comparison group mean at posttest divided by their pooled posttest standard deviation. This may be described algebraically as:

$$d = \frac{TXij - CXij}{SDpooled} \tag{1}$$

This index, known as the d-statistic (Hedges & Olkin, 1985), is a popular index for summarizing effectiveness because various algebraic transformations allow many of the commonly reported indices of relationship to be recoded into this standardized format (Lipsey & Wilson, 2001).

Preparing the Data for Analysis

In meta-analysis, the findings from multiple studies are grouped according to some meaningful clustering strategy and then the studies within those clusters are statistically combined using weighting and variance estimating methods that have been developed specifically for that purpose. The justification for the appropriateness of the grouping strategy is not one of absolute correctness, but of reasonableness and purpose. In meta-analysis, data sets can often be parsed along as many dimensions or levels of aggregation as might be imagined and supported by the available data. It should be emphasized that this was a process of iterative judgments and not an empirical clustering. Different judges might group the measures differently, and different groupings might reasonably be defined for different purposes.

To determine how effective school-based interventions are at reducing violent and antisocial behaviors, studies were grouped and findings were synthesized by ignoring the type of program and pooled findings on type of outcome. For this sorting, an iterative bottom-up sorting of the verbatim descriptions of outcomes was used to develop 10 categories of antisocial and violent behavior. The 10 categories of antisocial and violent behavior are verbal aggression (threatening, teasing, blaming, name calling, and sarcasm); disruptive aggression (acting out/aggressive behaviors, Achenbach's aggression subscale, and Eron's aggressive measure);

aggressively inclined (hostile attribution biases and aggressive fantasies); carried a weapon at school, mixed crimes (self-reported delinquency and police contacts); fights, problem behavior (age-inappropriate behavior and generally inappropriate behaviors and attitudes); suspensions; mixed violence (violent offenses with some nonviolent offenses); and physical violence (violent behavior causing physical injury).

Before the analysis of the effectiveness of these programs across programs was conducted, findings were averaged within each study and outcome so that only one mean estimate from each study was averaged in each outcome. This ensures both statistical independence and keeps studies with multiple findings from overwhelming those that produced only a single finding. In other words, if a study provided multiple outcomes, each representative of a different antisocial behavior, that study's estimates were combined within each outcome prior to synthesis to ensure that each study counted only once in a synthesis. Please note, however, that by this rule a study could contribute different evidence to different outcomes.

Meta-Analytic Procedures

In addition to the decisions just presented, there are several additional procedures that are followed when synthesizing effect sizes across disparate study samples. First, effect sizes based on small samples have been shown to be biased. Therefore, before combining evidence across the studies, we corrected all estimates using the formula provided by Hedges and Olkin (1985):

$$1 - (3/4n - 9) \tag{2}$$

where n is the total sample size (treatment n + control n).

Next, because effect sizes are obtained from summary statistics, those that are obtained from large samples contain less sampling error than those derived from small samples. Therefore, each effect size was weighted by the inverse of the sampling error variance prior to synthesis so that its contribution to the mean estimate was proportionate to its reliability (Hedges & Olkin, 1985). The formula for estimating the sampling error variance for standardized mean difference effect sizes is:

$$\mathrm{var}(d_i) = \frac{n_i^t + n_i^c}{n_i^t n_i^c} + \frac{(d_i)^2}{2(n_i^t + n_i^c)} \tag{3}$$

where n^t is the treatment group sample size for the ith study, n^c is the control group sample size for the ith study, and di is the n-adjusted standardized mean difference effect size for study i.

Third, posttest effect sizes were corrected for pre-existing group differences not attributable to the intervention. Although randomization takes care of many of these differences, when evidence was available on the same measure at pretest and posttest we subtracted the pretest effect size from the posttest effect size so the posttest score was not confounded by pre-existing group differences.

Finally, because d scores are unfamiliar to most, we translated these scores into percent-difference scores, using an index provided by the Binomial Effect Size Display (BESD; Rosenthal, 1994). The BESD converts the observed difference d between the treatment and control groups into a percent difference between the two groups. For example, if 60 out of 100 students in the intervention group and 40 out of 100 students in the control group show improvement, then the difference is equal to 20% improvement attributable to intervention.

The formula for transforming d scores to BESD or "percent improvement" scores is straight forward:

$$BESD = \frac{d}{\sqrt{d^2 + 4}} \qquad (4)$$

FINDINGS

As mentioned previously, 83 study cohorts experienced some test of some unique intervention. A careful reading of these interventions determined that these interventions could be sorted into tests of 74 unique "programs." Although several reports self-identified as replication studies, substantial differences in the intervention—as implemented—meant that very few studies provided actual replications of a program's effectiveness. Nearly 90% of the evidence identified tested some unique program configuration.

Study Features

Table 28.1 provides an accounting of the design, implementation, intervention, and sample characteristics of the 74 programs included in this meta-analysis. Most of the evidence comes from relatively large samples of between 100 and 500 students. More than half of the programs were tested on universal populations of both males and females. These samples were either predominately African American or White and of either low or varied socioeconomic status. Most of the interventions were of moderate intensity and were delivered during regular class time in a classroom setting by teachers who received extensive training. Most programs consisted of one or two sessions per week and were implemented with moderate fidelity. Although most group assignment was done by convenience, pretest group similarity was uniformly rated high. The unit of assignment was typically the student, and attrition rates were low, generally below 5%.

Effectiveness of School-Based Programs in Reducing Antisocial Behavior

As shown in Table 28.2, school-based interventions for reducing and preventing violence were typically successful in reducing antisocial behavior. Thirty-four studies reported findings for aggressive, disruptive behaviors, and these findings were generally positive with a standardized difference score of about 5.4%. The next most frequently reported outcome was for suspensions (14 studies). The effects on this outcome were quite positive, with approximately a 12% difference favoring intervention sites. It should be noted, however, that suspensions are an indirect measure of student behavior. More accurately, it can be described as a school's reaction to student behavior. There were notably strong positive outcomes for the 11 studies reporting criminal behavior outcomes. With a mean effect size of .44 and a standardized difference of 21.4%, these studies are reporting truly stunning effectiveness in reducing criminal behaviors.

Significant positive effects were also observed across the five studies reporting behavioral outcomes for physical violence and the eight studies reporting program effects on student fighting (see Table 28.2). Although the wide confidence interval for physical violence indicates considerable variability in effectiveness across studies, the mean effect of .16 and standardized difference score of approximately 8% is significant and not trivial. Physical violence is, as far as behaviors go, a relatively rare outcome. Detecting program effectiveness for rare events is notoriously difficult, and 8% difference represents a notable program impact.

TABLE 28.1
Study Descriptors

Study Design Features	
Type of control group	
Usual school setting	76%
Wait list	15%
Attention placebo	4%
Minimal contact	3%
Alternate treatment	3%
Unit of assignment	
Student	46%
Class	28%
School	26%
Method of group assignment	
Convenience comparison	37%
Random no matching	20%
Random after matching	15%
Equated at group level	11%
Demographics matched	7%
Matched-person characteristics	4%
Wait-list control group	3%
Pretest scores matched	1%
Purposive selection	1%
Pretest group similarity	
Very high	100%
Attrition rate	
>19%	26%
5–19%	18%
<5%	57%
Implementation	
Frequency of Intervention	
Daily	14%
3–4 × per week	20%
1–2 × per week	42%
1 contact	12%
Continuous	24%
Implementation Quality	
High	42%
Moderate	50%
Low	8%
Characteristics of Treatment	
Treatment site	
Regular class time	35%
Special class	24%
Entire school	14%
Mixed, none predominates	8%
Other	7%
Health class	5%
School office	5%
Cannot tell	1%
Format of treatment sessions	
Classroom group	47%
Mixed format	23%
Student group (not classroom)	14%
Student and provider	10%
School redesign	1%

(Continued)

TABLE 28.1
(Continued)

Study Descriptors	
Who delivered treatment	
Teachers	38%
Various personnel	26%
Intervention specialist	16%
Researcher	15%
Other	5%
Educational aides	3%
Mental health personnel	1%
Training of treatment personnel	
Extensive	39%
Moderate	28%
Brief	23%
Not reported	10%
Intensity of Program	
Very high	15%
High	27%
Moderate	39%
Low	15%
Very low	4%
Sample Characteristics	
Sample Size	
<51	27%
51–100	11%
101–500	35%
<500	27%
Population sampled	
Universal	54%
Selected	19%
Indicated	27%
Primary gender	
>75% male	16%
Mixed gender	58%
>75% female	0%
Cannot tell	26%
Primary race/ethnicity	
African American	38%
White	37%
Mixed	11%
Hispanic	7%
Cannot tell	11%
Primary socioeconomic status	
Middle	8%
Varied	37%
Low	23%
Cannot tell	32%

Programs also had a significant and positive mean effect on the nonbehavioral outcome aggressive inclination (see Table 28.2). Aggressive inclination is characterized not by measures of student's behavior, but of their cognitions. For example, this label contains measures of hostile attribution bias, hostile interpersonal negotiation strategies, and aggressive fantasies. As an aside, it is also the measure most comparable in content to Olweus' (1979) seminal article on the stability of aggressive tendency disorders.

TABLE 28.2
Antisocial Behavior Outcomes

Study Outcome Variables	Effect Size	95% Confidence Interval		BESD	No. of Studies
Aggression, verbal	0.106	−0.002	0.213	5.2%	6
Aggressive, disruptive	0.111	0.075	0.147	5.4%	34
Aggressively inclined	0.132	0.056	0.209	6.4%	6
Carried weapon at school	−0.021	−0.228	0.185	−1.0%	2
Crimes, mixed	0.442	0.397	0.487	21.4%	11
Fights	0.142	0.052	0.232	7.0%	8
Problem behavior	−0.130	−0.224	−0.035	−6.4%	7
Suspensions	0.241	0.198	0.284	12.0%	14
Violence, mixed	−0.183	−0.264	−0.102	−9.0%	5
Violence, physical	0.162	0.012	0.312	8.0%	5

In contrast to program's effectiveness on these outcomes, there were no significant effects for the six independent studies reporting data on verbal aggression or the two studies reporting on weapons carrying at school. More troubling, perhaps, are the significant negative effects for the seven studies reporting data on problem behavior and the two studies reporting outcomes for violence and other antisocial behaviors. These mean effects are significant and negative—youth exposed to these interventions reported greater involvement in problem, antisocial, and violent behaviors than those not exposed to intervention.

Effectiveness of School-Based Programs by Program Strategy

Because it is counterintuitive that youth exposed to interventions would report greater involvement in problem behaviors than those not exposed to the interventions, we re-examined the seven studies on which these effect sizes were based. Although the effect sizes summarized here accurately reflect the data reported in the studies, we believe the findings are driven, at least partially, by reporting error in the primary studies. The hypothesis here is that if programs are successful in making youth more sensitive to recognizing and recalling problem behavior, this could lead to increased reporting of such incidents in the intervention group even if the behavior itself remained unchanged. This increase in reported activity relative to controls would show up as a negative finding. This is, however, only a hypothesis and the fact these pooled findings show iatrogenic effects is disturbing and at this point difficult to readily explain.

DISCUSSION

Meta-analysis offers a procedurally sound method for summarizing a literature. Using methods familiar to social scientists, the meta-analytic process canvasses a population of interest to identify a sample of studies. These studies are then surveyed and information is abstracted and coded into a statistically manageable database, and the evidence abstracted is used to make some knowledge claim about the evidence provided by the studies. In this meta-analysis, we examined whether school-based programs to reduce violence were effective in reducing violent and aggressive behaviors. We undertook a systematic search and uncovered 83 studies of 74 school-based violence prevention programs. From these reports, nearly 2,225 estimates of the effectiveness of various school-based violence prevention programs on 10 different types of aggressive and violent behaviors were coded. From this investigation, several observations emerged.

The first and perhaps most profound observation concerned the depth of knowledge available on the effectiveness of these programs for reducing violent behavior. Of the 261 reports, 50 used the term *violence* in their title. Once the data were coded, however, only five independent study samples presented data on the effectiveness of these programs at preventing or reducing inter personal physical violence. Five studies provided effectiveness estimates on the reduction and prevention of principally violent behaviors, albeit mixed with other antisocial behaviors. Eight additional studies reported estimates on the prevention and reduction in fighting. Even if we assume that these 18 estimates were by independent study samples, this does not appear to represent a wealth of evidence on which to declare that a great deal is known about the effectiveness of school-based programs at reducing and preventing violent behavior.

In fact, the most commonly reported outcome identified concerned the effectiveness of these programs in preventing and reducing aggressive and disruptive behaviors. One third of the evidence summarized in this synthesis concluded that school-based violence prevention programs were effective in reducing aggressive and disruptive behaviors by about 5.5%. Programs were most effective in reducing and preventing criminal behavior, with 11 studies reporting an average reduction in criminal behavior of more than 20%.

Although 11 estimates is certainly more than enough estimates in meta-analysis to declare a robust finding, the category of criminal behavior may be subject to unintended reporting bias by study authors. Because this category captures a variety of delinquent and criminal activities, it is possible that a study's more extreme findings capture an author's attention and those particular items are disproportionately selected for reporting.

With 14 estimates, and an average reduction of 12%, suspensions were another popularly reported outcome. As an indicator of perpetrator activity, however, this outcome is suspect. Suspensions measure an administration's response to student behavior, not the behavior itself. It is not implausible that a school administration might reduce its enforcement of suspension when a perceived valuable service to the students is available. Keeping students in school where they can benefit from intensive prevention programming seems quite reasonable. These programs may also alter the school climate, reducing the perception of need for a severe administrative response to student behavior, since "something [the prevention program] is already being done." These are both benign explanations of a possible response bias that may account for the extraordinary effectives of these programs for reducing suspensions. We do not believe that administrators consciously alter their behavior to demonstrate that prevention programs are working. We do believe, however, that as an outcome, suspensions capture a great deal more than just the behavior of students and are weak indicators of the effectiveness of school-based violence prevention programs.

Two of the mean outcome estimates are negative and significant. For studies that reported outcomes for violence mixed with some other antisocial outcomes and those reporting problem behavior outcomes, the students in the intervention condition reported significantly more negative behaviors than those students in the comparison condition. In addition to the possibility that these programs do, in fact, increase the likelihood of these outcomes, several plausible rival hypotheses exist. For example, for many of these programs, outcomes are based on respondent recall. If the program increases respondent awareness of the outcome, student recall of their or their peer's behaviors may be fundamentally altered over the course of the intervention. If knowledge of the behaviors that constituted the outcome changes and behaviors which at pretest were considered benign are considered problematic at outcome, then the intervention group may report more problem behavior without any real change in activity.

Although these last two outcomes were negative, this meta-analysis provides evidence that school-based violence prevention programs are generally effective at reducing and preventing

TABLE 28.3

Implications for Practice: What Educational Professionals Should Know About the Effectiveness
of School-Based Violence Prevention Programs

- The school-based violence prevention programs included in this analysis are generally effective in reducing or preventing violence and other antisocial behaviors.

- Many studies were identified that claim to be effective in reducing or preventing violence, but they could not be included in this meta-analysis because they were either (a) reviews, (b) not school-based, (c) did not have a violent or antisocial behavior outcome, (d) descriptions of programs for which there were no data, (e) did not have a comparison group, or (f) did not provide the necessary data for calculating an effect size.

- Although effective, these programs do not provide a "cure" for violence and other antisocial behaviors. Although school-based interventions show generally positive and significant impacts in reducing violent and antisocial behaviors, these effects are often modest, possibly leaving much of the behavior unaffected. Thus, an important part of adopting a school-based intervention for reducing and preventing violence and other antisocial behaviors may be expectation management. From the evidence summarized here school-based interventions likely to reduce, but not eliminate, the occurrence of violent and antisocial behaviors.

---

violent and antisocial behaviors. The average difference, across studies, is typically at least 5%, and for some outcomes the average effects are considerably larger. To paraphrase Michael Scriven 1978, 1991, this meta-analysis demonstrates that school-based violence prevention programs have "merit." The question now becomes, do they have worth"?

Scriven distinguished between merit, the intrinsic value of the program (whether the program does what it is intended to do), and worth (whether the program has or provides value to an institution or to society). Effectiveness in reducing antisocial outcomes is a measure of a program's merit, whereas, in addition to effectiveness, direct, indirect, and opportunity costs, implementability, political acceptability, and breadth of coverage all contribute to the assessment of worth. For example, administrators may adopt an intervention at considerable cost if it is wonderfully successful in obtaining a highly desirable outcome. Conversely, an administrator might choose to select a program that may not be particularly effective if it is inexpensive, politically viable, easily implemented, or has broad coverage (e.g., DARE, Ennett, Tobler, Ringwalt, & Flewelling, 1994; mass media trials to reduce substance use; Derzon & Lipsey, 2002).

Although these programs are generally, and in some cases remarkably, effective, knowing that they are worth implementing cannot be determined from the evidence summarized because elements of worth are not generally reported in the research that is included in this meta-analysis. School administrators should therefore use this information to estimate and weigh locally the relative benefits of choosing school-based programs to reduce violence. Table 28.3 provides a brief summary of what educational professionals should know about the effectiveness of school-based violence prevention programs. In addition to estimating worth, administrators may also want to consider the limits of the effectiveness of these programs. None of the programs examined have the technology to make violence or antisocial behaviors disappear. Managing expectations of the amount of violent or antisocial behavior reduced or prevented through adoption of these programs may be a wise strategy.

As a final caution, although this summary provides an accurate representation of the impact of these programs on violent and antisocial behaviors, the absolute effect of these programs on the incidence these behaviors may, in fact, be higher or lower than the evidence summarized suggests. These studies test program effectiveness at the level of the individual. Often only a few individuals are responsible for a majority of criminal activity (White, Moffitt, Earls, Robins, & Silva, 1990, Wolfgang, Figlio, & Sellin, 1972), and this may also be the case with violence (Tremblay, 2000). If a program only deters those least likely to engage in the outcome, then a large effect observed in this analysis frame may produce relatively small reductions in the incidence of violent, antisocial behaviors. If, on the other hand, programs are most effective on those who engage in frequent violent or antisocial behaviors, then the incidence of these behaviors may be reduced well beyond the amount indicated by the effectiveness estimate. Unfortunately, meta-analysis has not yet developed a technology for synthesizing incidence data.

ACKNOWLEDGMENTS

A meta-analysis requires a tremendous amount of work, and this one was no exception. For their tremendous effort in helping identify and collect the studies and coordinating the coding of those studies, I am particularly indebted to my Vanderbilt colleagues Sandra Jo Wilson and Carol Cunningham. My thanks and appreciation also go out to Ajanta, Ann, Gabriella, Jan, Johann, Nustat, Wendy, and Young. Each put in long hours coding and recoding studies. They are as wonderful a team as I have ever had the pleasure to work with. I also thank the editors, Shane R. Jimerson and Michael J. Furlong for their careful read and excellent suggestions for improvements to the manuscript.

REFERENCES

Cohen, J. (1988). *Statistical power analysis for the behavioral sciences* (2nd ed.). Hillsdale, NJ: Lawrence Erlbaum Associates.

Derzon, J. H., & Lipsey, M. W. (2002). A meta-analysis of the effectiveness of mass communication for changing substance use knowledge, attitudes, and behavior. In W. D. Crano (Ed.), *Mass media and drug prevention: Classic and contemporary theories and research* (pp. 231–258). Mahwah, NJ: Lawrence Erlbaum Associates.

Derzon, J. H., Springer, F., Sale, L., & Brounstein, P. (2005). Estimating intervention effectiveness: Synthetic projection of field evaluation results. *Journal of Primary Prevention, 26*, 321–343.

Durlak, J. A., & Lipsey, M. W. (1991). A practitioner's guide to meta-analysis. *American Journal of Community Psychology, 19*, 291–332.

Ennett, S. T., Tobler, N. S., Ringwalt, C. L., & Flewelling, R. L. (1994). How effective is drug abuse resistance education? A meta-analysis of Project DARE outcome evaluations. *American Journal of Public Health, 84*, 1394–1401.

Ericson, N. (2001). *Addressing the problem of juvenile bullying* (OJJDP Fact Sheet no. 27). Washington, DC: U.S. Department of Justice.

Hawkins, J. D., Catalano, R. F., Kosterman, R., Abbott, R., & Hill, K. G. (1999). Preventing adolescent health-risk behaviors by strengthening protection during childhood. *Archives of Pediatric Adolescent Medicine, 153*, 226–234.

Hedges, L. V., & Olkin, I. (1985), *Statistical methods for meta-analysis*. NY: Academic Press.

Huizinga, D., & Jakob-Chien, C. (1998). The contemporaneous co-occurrence of serious and violent juvenile offending and other problem behaviors. In R. Loeber & D. P. Farrington (Eds.), *Serious & violent juvenile offenders: Risk factors and successful interventions* (pp. 47–67). Thousand Oaks, CA: Sage.

Krug, E. G., Brener, N. D., Dahlberg, L. L., Ryan, G. W., & Powell, K. E. (1997). The impact of an elementary school-based violence prevention program on visits to the school nurse. *American Journal of Preventive Medicine, 13*, 459–463.

Lipsey, M. W., & Wilson, D. B. (2001). *Practical Meta-analysis. Applied social Research Methods Series, Vol. 49.* Thousand Oaks, CA: Sage.

Lochman, J. E. (1992). Cognitive-behavioral intervention with aggressive boys: Three-year follow-up and preventive effects. *Journal of Consulting and Clinical Psychology, 60*, 426–432.

National Center for Education Statistics. (2004). *Crime and safety in America's public schools*. Washington, DC: U.S. Department of Education.

Olweus, D. (1979). Stability of aggressive reaction patterns in males: A review. *Psychological Bulletin, 86*, 852–875.

Rosenthal, R. (1994). Statistically describing and combining studies. In H. Cooper & L. V. Hedges (Eds.), *The handbook of research synthesis* (pp. 231–244). New York: Russell Sage.

Scheckner, S., Rollin, S. A., Kaiser-Ulrey, C., & Wagner, R. (2002). School violence in children and adolescents: A meta-analysis of the effectiveness of current interventions. *Journal of School Violence, 1*, 5–32.

Scriven, M. (1978). Merit vs. value. *Evaluation News*, 20–29.

Scriven, M. (1991). *Evaluation thesaurus* (4th Ed.). Newbury Park, CA: Sage.

Tremblay, R. E. (2000). The origins of youth violence. *ISUMA: Canadian Journal of Policy Research, 1*, 19–24.

U.S. Department of Education and U.S. Department of Justice. (2004). *Indicators of School Crime and Safety.* Available: http://nces.ed.gov/pubs2005/2005002.pdf.

Wilson, D. B., Gottfredson, D. C., & Najaka, S. S. (2001). School-based prevention of problem behaviors: A meta-analysis. *Journal of Quantitative Criminology, 17*, 247–272.

Wilson, D. B., & Lipsey, M. W. (2001). The role of method in treatment effectiveness research: Evidence from meta-analysis. *Psychological Methods, 6*, 413–429.

Wolfgang, M., Figlio, R. M., & Sellin, T. (1972). *Delinquency in a birth cohort.* Chicago: University of Chicago Press.

White, J. L., Moffitt, T. E., Earls, F., Robins, L., & Silva, P. A. (1990). How early can we tell? Predictors of childhood conduct disorder and adolescent Delinquency. *Criminology, 28*, 507–528.

29

Preventing, Preparing for, and Responding to School Violence With the National Incident Management System

Stephen E. Brock
California State University, Sacramento

Shane R. Jimerson
University of California, Santa Barbara

Shelley R. Hart
California State University, Sacramento

Extreme acts of violence (e.g., shootings, stabbings, and bomb threats) in schools are rare, however, when these events do occur they affect the physical, emotional, and psychological well-being of students and staff (National Association of School Psychologists, 2000). More common acts of violence and aggression occurring at school include bullying and fighting. Preventing, preparing for, and responding to all of these events involve many different activities, all of which benefit from the direction of a school crisis team. It is important to acknowledge that the establishment of a comprehensive school crisis team can be a daunting task requiring the time, effort, and energy of many different staff members. Furthermore, once a team is established, team maintenance requires that new staff members be trained to provide their specific crisis team roles.

Ideally, a crisis team involves the collaboration and cooperation of educators, parents, students, law enforcement, community leaders, health care providers, and other professionals serving youth (Hester, 2003). The primary responsibility for the development and organization of this team belongs to schools and school districts, and this chapter emphasizes school staff's role in preventing, preparing for, and responding to violence. Selection of the team members of this school crisis team is critical. Although some staff members may typically fill certain roles, consideration should be given to the diverse and complementary nature of the different members' skills, as well as an individual's ability and willingness to commit the required time and effort (Dwyer & Jimerson, 2002; Dwyer & Osher, 2000).

It is also important to acknowledge that crisis events, such as extreme acts of school violence, are not discrete events. Rather they are processes that evolve over time (Vossekuil, Fein, Reddy, Borum, & Modzeleski, 2002); that is, a student does not suddenly wake up one morning and decide to commit an act of school violence. There is usually a series of events and precursors that lead to these, and other school crises. Furthermore, the immediate response to school violence will not likely resolve all crisis issues for all involved students and staff. Typically, the

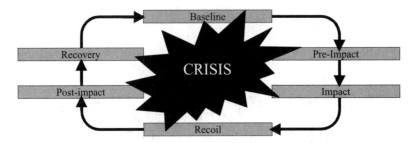

FIG. 29.1.   Illustration of the sequence and phases of a crisis event.

recovery following school violence occurs during subsequent months and years (Brock & Jimerson, 2004). Given this reality, it is essential that comprehensive school crisis teams be prepared for and active during all phases of a crisis (not only during the immediate aftermath of violent acts).

In this chapter the National Incident Management System (NIMS) and its Incident Command System (ICS) are used as a structure for the discussion of comprehensive school crisis teams. The following sections describe the phases of a crisis, the general crisis team activities that should take place during these different crisis phases, the NIMS/ICS model, and suggestions for the specific responsibilities of school crisis team members during each crisis phase.

SCHOOL CRISIS PHASES, ACTIVITIES, AND THE NATIONAL INCIDENT MANAGEMENT SYSTEM

The Phases of a Crisis

Figure 29.1 provides an illustration of the phases of a crisis event. It makes use of a chronology system that divides crises, including acts of violence, into the following five phases:

1. The pre-impact phase, which is the period before the crisis.
2. The impact phase, which is the period when the crisis occurs.
3. The recoil phase, which is the period immediately after the crisis event.
4. The post-impact phase, which are the days to weeks after the crisis event.
5. The recovery and reconstruction phase, which lasts months or years after the event (Valent, 2000).

Comprehensive school crisis teams need to be active during each of these phases.

Crisis Team Activities During Different Crisis Phases

The nature of the crisis determines the nature of the response, however, specific crisis team activities generally correspond to the different phases of a crisis event. The specific activities suggested to be important are (a) crisis prevention, (b) crisis preparedness, (c) crisis response, and (d) crisis recovery (Brock, 2002; U.S. Department of Education, Office of Safe and Drug-Free Schools, 2003). Crisis prevention includes activities designed to reduce the incidence of crisis events. Crisis preparedness ensures response readiness for crises that are not, or cannot be, prevented. Crisis response refers to team activities that minimize crisis damage and restore immediate coping. Finally, crisis recovery refers to the longer term actions that repair crisis damage and return the school to baseline (or pre-crisis) operation/functioning. Figure 29.2 illustrates the relationships between these activities and the phases of a crisis event.

Activity	Phase					
	Baseline	Pre-impact	Impact	Recoil	Post-impact	Recovery
Prevention						
Preparedness						
Response						
Recovery						

FIG. 29.2. Illustration of the relationships among specific crisis team activities and the phases of a crisis.

The National Incident Management System

The NIMS allows all emergency response personnel (including school crisis teams) to respond to any critical incident with clear and consistent organizational structures and strategies. According to U.S. Secretary of Homeland Security, Tom Ridge: "This system will provide a consistent nationwide approach for Federal, State, local, and tribal governments to work effectively and efficiently together to prepare for, prevent, respond to, and recover from domestic incidents, regardless of cause, size, or complexity" (U.S. Department of Homeland Security, 2004, p. iii). Identified as an exemplary practice in emergency management by the Federal Emergency Management Agency (FEMA, 2003), a model almost identical to NIMS (the Standardized Emergency Management System, or SEMS) has been a requirement for all public schools in California since 1992 (California Government Code Section 8607), as well as by all of California's emergency response personnel (e.g., fire departments, law enforcement, emergency medical technicians, and disaster responders). As a result, in California the SEMS provides structure and direction to crisis teams and helps to ensure that when responding to a crisis, school crisis teams and other emergency responders are using common terminology to communicate.

Among the elements of both the SEMS and NIMS is the Incident Command System (ICS). The ICS has traditionally been used to centralize, organize, and coordinate the emergency response to a critical incident (i.e., crisis response). In this chapter, the ICS is used to structure other school crisis team activities (i.e., crisis prevention, preparedness, and recovery). The ICS, which provides overall direction and establishes priorities for use in an emergency, has five functions: (a) management, (b) planning and intelligence, (c) operations, (d) logistics, and (e) finance/administration. It is recommended that under each of these functions school crisis teams pre-assign specific individuals based on their school job assignments (Lockyer & Eastin, 2000).

Figure 29.3 provides a flow chart that illustrates the relationships among the five functions of the ICS. According to the ICS, the Emergency Operations Center Director (at the district level) and/or an Incident Commander (at the school site level) lead school crisis teams. Typically, a school administrator fills this role (e.g., the school principal). However, it is important to note that during a crisis response, which takes place during the impact and recoil phases of a crisis, the nature of the critical incident determines who is the Incident Commander and it may not always be a school staff member. For example, if an act of school violence results in a police emergency, it is likely that a member of law enforcement will be the Incident Commander. However, until this individual arrives at school, and formally assumes this role, a school administrator (typically the principal) is in charge (Thompson, 2004). A school administrator typically fills this role during all other school crisis activities and phases.

The Emergency Operations Center Director (often a Superintendent) and/or the Incident Commander (typically a school principal) are the crisis team "managers." Given the multifaceted nature of school crisis teams, these individuals may designate other "Officers" to assist in the management of the school crisis team. These Officers may include a Public Information

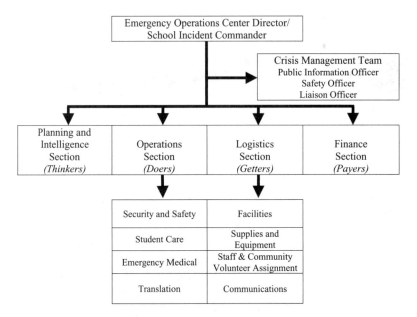

FIG. 29.3. Incident Command System (ICS) hierarchy (adapted from California Governor's Office of Emergency Services, 1998).
Note: This is the hierarchy used by the SEM's ICS. In the NIMS model there is a separate planning section. A separate Intelligence Section is a sixth ICS element operationalized by the Incident Commander depending on the requirements of the situation.

Officer, who is responsible for keeping the public informed about school crisis team activities; a Safety Officer, who is responsible for establishing a safe and secure school environment; and a Liaison Officer, who is responsible for coordinating with crisis management agencies that typically work outside of the school district and/or school (U.S. Department of Education, Office of Safe and Drug-Free Schools, 2003).

The Planning & Intelligence Section ("the thinkers") gathers and assesses information for the crisis team, documents crisis needs and status, and writes evaluations of school crisis team activities. This section relies on a flexible and reliable communication system. According to Lockyer and Eastin (2000), individuals who work in this section "must be able to use communication equipment, gather information in a timely manner and weigh it for significance" (p. 12).

The Operations Section ("the doers") implements the crisis prevention, preparedness, response, and recovery priorities established by crisis team managers. This section includes a Security and Safety Coordinator (typically a school administrator, but ideally a school police officer); a Student Care Coordinator (typically a psychologist, social worker, or counselor); an Emergency Medical Coordinator (typically a school nurse); and a Translation Coordinator (individuals prepared to translate information and materials into primary languages of students, parents, and community members). Working under several of these Coordinators are additional specialists who carry out specific activities. These specialists (whose job titles are descriptive of their ICS functions) are as follows: Facility and Grounds; Search, Rescue, and Accounting; Crowd Management; Traffic Safety; Crisis Intervention; Student Assembly and Release; Shelter, Food, Water, and Supplies; First Aid; and Morgue. The relationships among these members of the Operations Section are summarized in Figure 29.4.

The Logistics Section ("the getters") obtains the resources needed to support all the ICS functions. This Section is composed of a Facilities Coordinator, a Supplies and Equipment

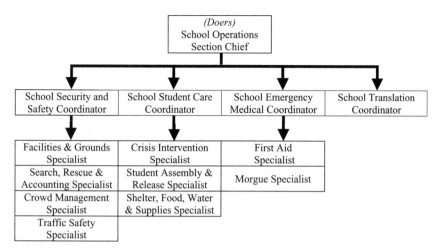

FIG. 29.4.   Operations section hierarchy.

Coordinator, a Staff and Community Volunteer Assignment Coordinator, and a Communications Coordinator. All school staff can assist in this function (Lockyer & Eastin, 2000).

Finally, the Finance Section ("the payers") is responsible for developing a budget, authorizing purchases, and tracking all costs (including personnel costs) associated with the school crisis team. According to Lockyer and Eastin (2000), "Individuals responsible for purchasing, paying bills and balancing books are best suited to this function, which involves planning, purchasing emergency supplies and tracking costs following an emergency" (p. 13).

SCHOOL CRISIS TEAM MEMBER RESPONSIBILITIES

This section examines the specific prevention, preparedness, response, and recovery responsibilities of the five ICS sections of the school crisis team. Working under the leadership of Crisis Management, each section complements and supports the team as a whole.

Crisis Management

Crisis managers are responsible for the organization, delegation, supervision, and evaluation of all violence prevention, preparedness, response, and recovery efforts. Although it is clearly not possible for the crisis managers to independently complete all crisis tasks, it is their job to delegate responsibility and to ensure that others complete these tasks (National Resource Center for Safe Schools, 2000). Additional management responsibilities associated with specific crisis team activities are now discussed.

School Violence Prevention

Crisis management, working collaboratively with the school crisis team, typically sets school violence prevention priorities and then delegates responsibility for the implementation of specific prevention tasks to other school staff members. Additionally, the Public Information Officer may make efforts to inform the school community of the school's or district's violence prevention plan and provide the others with information that may help to prevent acts of school violence. Finally, the Safety Officer may facilitate the development of "safe school plans." The document *Safe Schools: A Planning Guide for Action* (Abbott & Linfor, 2002) may be useful to the crisis manager who is facilitating the development of such plans.

School Violence Preparedness

Crisis management, working collaboratively with the school crisis team, develops the violence preparedness plan and then delegates responsibility for the implementation of specific preparedness tasks to other school staff members. Additionally, to facilitate crisis response, managers should ensure that all crisis team roles are filled, and that contact information for all team members is available. The Public Information Officer should foster relationships with the local media, develop district and/or school policy for how to respond to the media following acts of school violence, prepare press release templates, and make plans for an emergency media center. The Safety Officer should develop a list of resources to ensure student and staff safety during a crisis event. In particular, this individual ensures that staff members are appropriately trained to respond to student violence and law enforcement resources are clearly defined (see chapters 10 and 11 of *Preparing for Crises in the Schools: A Manual for Building School Crisis Response Teams* [Brock, Sandoval, & Lewis, 2001] for specific examples of these tasks). The Liaison Officer fosters relationships with additional emergency response resources and maintains a listing of such. Finally, it is critical that Crisis Management maintains a "Crisis Response Box" and duplicates are made available in various secure locations around each school for easy access (Poland, Pitcher, & Lazarus, 2002). According to Lockyer and Eastin (2000), the primary goal of the Crisis Response Box is to ensure that "school administrators will immediately have the information essential for effective management of a major critical incident" (p. 2). Specific elements of the Crisis Response Box, along with the specific crisis team member to whom responsibility for its inclusion in the box should be delegated, are provided in Table 29.1. Additional materials for those elements marked with an asterisk (*) are provided in the Appendix. The document *Crisis Response Box: A Guide to Help Every School Assemble the Tools and Resources Needed for a Critical Incident Response* (Lockyer & Eastin, 2000) may be a valuable resource for the crisis manager who is facilitating the creation of this box.

School Violence Response

When an act of violence occurs at school, crisis management initiates crisis response procedures (e.g., makes use of a Crisis Response Box) and evaluates the need for assistance from resources located outside of the school (e.g., law enforcement). In addition, the Public Information Officer provides the community with information about the school's crisis response and, if needed, manages the emergency media center. The Safety Officer is responsible for ensuring that all resources necessary for maintaining a safe school environment are available. Finally, the Liaison Officer facilitates communication between the school and any community-based crisis responders (e.g., crisis interveners).

School Violence Recovery

Crisis management, working collaboratively with the school crisis team, typically sets recovery priorities and then delegates responsibility for the implementation of specific recovery tasks to other school staff members. These priorities may be established during daily debriefing meetings held by crisis management; meetings that also offer opportunities for mutual support and a venue for staff to discuss their emotions and reactions to the event (U.S. Department of Education, Office of Safe and Drug-Free Schools, 2003). The Public Information Officer provides the community with information about crisis recovery efforts and resources. The

TABLE 29.1
Crisis Response Box Elements

Element	Responsible Team Member
Crisis Management Team phone numbers	Critical Incident Commander
Crisis Response Team role descriptions	Critical Incident Commander
Media staging area/resources*	Public Information Officer
Media management policy	Public Information Officer
Community emergency resources listing*	Liaison Officer
Emergency response personnel staging area	Safety Officer/Liaison Officer
Structural engineering resources	Safety Officer
Aerial photos of the campus	Intelligence Section
School community map	Intelligence Section
Campus layout (with staging areas indicated)	Intelligence Section
Blueprints of all school buildings	Intelligence Section
Crisis incident log	Intelligence Section
AM/FM battery-operated radio (batteries)	Intelligence Section
Battery-operated weather radio (batteries)	Intelligence Section
Battery-operated laptop (with wireless internet access)	Intelligence Section
Site status report forms	Intelligence Section
Damage documentation tools (e.g., cameras)	Intelligence Section
Keys for all campus facilities	Operations Section (Security & Safety Coord./F&G Sp.)
Fire alarm turn-off procedures	Operations Section (Security & Safety Coord./F&G Sp.)
Sprinkler system turn-off procedures	Operations Section (Security & Safety Coord./F&G Sp.)
Utility shut-off valves/tools	Operations Section (Security & Safety Coord./F&G Sp.)
Gas line and utility layout	Operations Section (Security & Safety Coord./F&G Sp.)
Cable television satellite feed shut-off	Operations Section (Security & Safety Coord./F&G Sp.)
Yellow caution tape	Operations Section (Security & Safety Coord./SRA Sp.)
Search and rescue supplies/equipment*	Operations Section (Security & Safety Coord./SRA Sp.)
Student photos	Operations Section (Security & Safety Coord./SRA Sp.)
Parent center location	Operations Section (Security & Safety Coord./CM Sp.)
Evacuation routes and assembly procedures*	Operations Section (Security & Safety Coord./SAR Sp.)
Evacuations sites	Operations Section (Security & Safety Coord./SAR Sp.)
Student disposition/release forms	Operations Section (Security & Safety Coord./SAR Sp.)
Student release procedures	Operations Section (Security & Safety Coord./SAR Sp.)
Student attendance roster (updated monthly)	Operations Section (Security & Safety Coord./SAR Sp.)
Traffic management plan	Operations Section (Security & Safety Coord./TS Sp.)
Student emergency cards	Operations Section (Student Care Coord./SFW&S Sp.)
Special needs student listing (e.g., medications)	Operations Section (Student Care Coord./SFW&S Sp.)
Crisis codes established	Operations Section (Student Care Coord./CI Sp.)
Lockdown procedures	Operations Section (Student Care Coord./CI Sp.)
Crisis intervention resource listing	Operations Section (Student Care Coord./CI Sp.)
Crisis intervention procedures/resources*	Operations Section (Student Care Coord./CI Sp.)
First aid supplies list and location*	Operations Section (Emergency Medical Coord.)
First aid procedures	Operations Section (Emergency Medical Coord.)
Morgue procedures and supplies*	Operations Section (Emergency Medical Coord.)
Translator listing	Operations Section (Translation Coord.)
Crisis intervention center/service rooms	Logistics Section (Facilities Coord.)
Command post/Staging area signs	Logistics Section (Facilities Coord.)
Care/shelter resource listing (e.g., water, food)*	Logistics Section (Facilities Coord.)
Teacher roster/Assignments	Logistics Section (SCVA Coord.)
Staff roster/Assignments/Crisis duties	Logistics Section (SCVA Coord.)
Staff resources listing/Crisis duties	Logistics Section (SCVA Coord.)
List of key parent/community volunteers	Logistics Section (SCVA Coord.)
Crisis Response Team identification	Logistics Section (SCVA Coord.)

(Continue)

TABLE 29.1
Continuied

Element	Responsible Team Member
Communication resources listing/locations*	Logistics Section (Communications Coord.)
Staff phone tree (with cell phone numbers)	Logistics Section (Communication Coord.)
Phone line use designation listing	Logistics Section (Communications Coord.)
Office supplies	Logistics Section (Supplies & Equipment Coord.)
Flashlights (with extra batteries)	Logistics Section (Supplies & Equipment Coord.)
Emergency resource budget information	Finance Section
Emergency personnel sign-in/sign-out sheet	Finance Section
Purchase order forms	Finance Section
FEMA forms	Finance Section

Adapted from Brock et al. (2001); California Governor's Office of Emergency Services (1998), and Lockyer and Eastin (2000)

*Additional descriptions provided in the Appendix.

F&G Sp., Facilities and Grounds Specialist; SRA SP., Search, Rescue, & Accounting Specialist; CM Sp., Crowd Management Specialist; SAR Sp., Student Assembly and Release Specialist; CI Sp., Crisis Intervention Specialist; TS Sp., Traffic Safety Specialist; SFW&S Sp., Shelter, Food, Water, & Supplies Specialist; SCVA Coordinator., Staff & Community Volunteer Assignment Coordinator.

Safety Officer continues to be responsible for ensuring that all resources necessary to maintain a safe school environment are available. Finally, the Liaison Officer continues to facilitate communication between the school and any community-based crisis responders (e.g., mental health care providers).

Planning and Intelligence

Planning and Intelligence Section members gather and assess information for the crisis team as it conducts violence prevention, preparedness, response, and recovery activities. Specific section responsibilities associated with specific crisis team activities are now discussed. It is essential that the team members meet regularly to discuss planning/intelligence.

School Violence Prevention

The Planning and Intelligence Section's role in violence prevention involves the identification and monitoring of school violence threats (U.S. Department of Education, Office of Safe and Drug-Free Schools, 2003). For example, it might assign a section member to monitor local media for reports of potentially threatening situations. Additionally, section members should strive to maintain contact with local law enforcement for reports of criminal activities (e.g., gang fights) and assess the potential for acts of school violence. Finally, this section may serve as the clearinghouse for all reports of threatening behavior. Given the sensitive nature of such information, especially when it relates to specific students, confidentiality is an important issue to address (Dwyer, Osher, & Warger, 1998).

School Violence Preparedness

To prepare for acts of school violence that either cannot be or are not prevented, the Planning and Intelligence Section acquires and maintains the materials needed to gather information about such an act quickly and efficiently. This includes ensuring the availability of communication tools (e.g., cell phones, computers with Internet access, and two-way radios), and may include monitoring systems, such as closed-circuit video surveillance (Green, 1999). Detailed floor plans are also important to acquire and maintain; if a perpetrator of school violence is on school grounds, these maps will be critical for law enforcement as they attempt to apprehend the individual. Having copies of the detailed floor plans immediately available benefits police and other emergency responders. Preparing for school violence is an ongoing process, not an event. Thus, the comprehensive school crisis management team should engage in regular (at least annual) meetings to continue to update prevention and response plans and activities.

School Violence Response

During the response to an act of school violence, the Planning and Intelligence Section collects facts about the incident and documents all crisis response efforts. Not only does such information help to improve future crisis response efforts, but they may also point to actions that could strengthen the school's violence prevention program (Goldstein & Conoley, 1997). Additionally, this section provides the information crisis managers need to assess the status of the school's response to violence and helps to identify other response needs (e.g., the need for community-based crisis interveners). Annual meetings, near the end of each school year, provide an opportunity to review crisis team response activities and can help to identify challenges, obstacles, and lessons learned.

School Violence Recovery

During crisis recovery, the Planning and Intelligence Section continues to collect facts about the incident and documents all crisis recovery efforts. Additionally, this section provides the information crisis managers need to assess the status of the school's recovery from the crisis and determines other response needs (e.g., the need for community-based mental health assistance).

Operations

Operations Section members implement the crisis prevention, preparedness, response, and recovery priorities established by the crisis team. Specific section responsibilities associated with specific crisis team members and activities are now discussed.

School Violence Prevention

To help prevent acts of school violence the Security and Safety Coordinator ensures that students and staff are provided with the training/education needed to identify and prevent potential acts of violence. In addition to conducting local needs assessments, the document, *Blueprints for Violence Prevention* (Mihalic, Fagan, Irwin, Ballard, & Elliott, 2004), will be helpful for these individuals as they strive to identify needed (and effective) violence prevention programs. Additionally, the Student Care Coordinator ensures that the appropriate guidance services are available to respond to the underlying causes of school violence (e.g., problem-solving deficits and social skills difficulties), as well as helping to ensure the development of a safe school climate (Dwyer & Osher, 2000). It is critical that students identified as being at risk for violent behavior are included in the appropriate school guidance program, and not simply excluded from school (Brock, 1999). Schoolwide data on student behaviors and campus climate should also be considered in preventing school violence.

TABLE 29.2
Operations Section Specialist School Violence Response Responsibilities

Specialist	Responsibilities
Search, Rescue, and Accounting	Following the resolution of an act of school violence, this individual looks for and accounts for all students and staff.
Student Assembly and Release	Oversees the location(s) where students assemble following an act of school violence and supervises parent–student reunification.
Facilities and Grounds	Along with the Safety Officer, ensures that the physical structure of school facilities and grounds are safe.
Crowd Management	Implements procedures designed to manage large crowds (e.g., parents looking for their children).
Traffic Safety	Manages all traffic going to and from the school. In particular, this individual ensures that emergency response vehicles have free movement to and from school grounds.
Crisis Intervention	Conducts psychological triage and addresses the immediate needs of students and staff for psychological first aid.
Shelter, Food, Water, & Supplies	Maintains facilities and as needed distributes basic need supplies.
First Aid Specialist	Maintains and as needed distributes first aid supplies, oversees any first aid activities (at least until emergency medical personnel arrive), and facilitates the work of paramedics.
Morgue	Maintains facilities and supplies to be used to house the deceased until they can be removed.

School Violence Preparedness

To be better prepared for those acts of school violence that cannot be (or are not) prevented, the Security and Safety Coordinator should establish student accounting procedures, establish student assembly and release to parent procedures, and establish crowd control and traffic management procedures (California Governor's Office of Emergency Services, 1998). The Student Care Coordinator develops the school's capacity to provide crisis intervention services, such as psychological triage and first aid [see Brock & Jimerson, [2004], for a discussion of these and other school crisis interventions]. They also develop the capacity to meet the basic needs of students (e.g., shelter, food, and water) in the event that students need to be held at school for a prolonged period of time. The Medical Coordinator develops the school's capacity to meet emergency medical needs (e.g., medical triage and first aid). Finally, the Translation Coordinator ensures that the school has the ability to communicate in all languages spoken in the school community. Typically, this is accomplished by maintaining a listing of translators (both on the school's staff and in the community).

School Violence Response

During the response phase, members of the Operations Section are most likely the most visible members of the crisis team. As a part of the school's response to violence, the Security and Safety Coordinator ensures that all students are accounted for, are evacuated to a safe student assembly area(s) as needed, and then released in a systematic manner to their parents. This Coordinator also manages the large crowds (typically comprised of parents and the media) that may form by sending them to the appropriate waiting/assembly areas, and manages traffic and ensures that emergency response vehicles have access to school grounds. Table 29.2 provides a list of the specific response responsibilities of the Operations Section Specialists.

School Violence Recovery

When helping the school to recover from an act of violence, the Student Care Coordinator ensures that students and staff members who display signs of psychopathology (e.g., Posttraumatic Stress Disorders) are offered appropriate mental health services. This individual should also prepare to provide the supportive crisis teams services and psycho-education that may be required by the anniversary of a crisis event. The Medical Coordinator maintains communication with families of injured students and staff members, and (with the family's permission) maintains contact with medical facilities and provides school crisis team members with medical status updates (Smith, 2001). Knowledge of the medical status of those injured by an act of school violence is critical because the occurrence of fatalities greatly increases the potential of the event to generate psychological trauma (Breslau, 1998), and, as such, significantly affects the recovery environment.

Logistics

Logistics Section members obtain the resources needed to support all school-based crisis team activities. For example, if a member of the Operations Section needs materials to conduct a crisis response activity, the member contacts the Logistics Section, which in turn obtains the necessary materials. Specific section responsibilities associated with specific crisis team activities are now discussed.

School Violence Prevention

The Logistics Section's role in violence prevention involves obtaining crisis prevention-related materials and supplies, this includes assigning an unpublished phone number to facilitate important and necessary staff communications with emergency personnel (Thompson, 2004). Additionally, this section assigns staff and volunteers to specific crisis prevention activities.

School Violence Preparedness

To prepare for acts of school violence, the Logistics Section acquires and maintains all crisis response resources, supplies, and materials. This includes identifying and designating crisis response facilities (e.g., evacuation locations), double checking to make sure that individuals have been identified to fill the various crisis response roles, and ensuring that reliable and redundant communications systems within, to and from school, and from all staff are available.

School Violence Response

During the response to an act of school violence, the Logistics Section makes available all needed crisis response supplies and equipment (California Governor's Office of Emergency Services, 1998). As indicated by the Operations Section, the Logistics Section also obtains additional resources. Additionally, this section directs staff and volunteers to their appropriate crisis response activities, and maintains communications to and from school, and among all school staff members.

School Violence Recovery

As a part of crisis recovery activities the Logistics Section continues to make available all needed crisis response supplies and equipment. Additionally, this section continues to direct staff and volunteers to their appropriate crisis recovery activities, and maintain communications to, from school, and among all school staff members.

Finance

Finance Section members develop the school crisis team budget, authorize, and track all team expenses. Specific section responsibilities associated with specific crisis team activities now are discussed.

School Violence Prevention

The Finance Section's role in violence prevention involves budgeting for and authorizing all crisis prevention-related expenditures. For example, if it was determined that a specific violence prevention curriculum was needed, the Finance Section makes sure that this item was in the crisis team's (or school's) budget and authorizes its purchase.

School Violence Preparedness

To prepare for acts of school violence the Finance Section budgets for and authorizes all crisis preparedness-related expenditures. For example, if it was determined that the school's communication system could not be counted on during the response to school violence, the Finance Section makes sure that this item was in the crisis team's (or school's) budget and authorizes its purchase.

School Violence Response

During the response to an act of school violence, the Finance Section authorizes all crisis response-related expenditures, and records all personnel and material costs. Such activities are especially important if the school hopes to apply for financial relief for crisis related expenditures (U.S. Department of Education, Office of Safe and Drug-Free Schools, 2003).

School Violence Recovery

During the recovery phase the Finance Section continues to authorize all crisis response-related expenditures, obtains emergency financial assistance, and makes the appropriate requests for reimbursement. For example, if it was determined that long-term psychotherapeutic assistance was necessary for a substantial number of students who had been exposed to an act of violence (as documented by the Operations Section), the Finance Section makes sure that this item was in the crisis team's budget and may seek funding to authorize the employment of additional mental health specialists. Alternatively, it may work with community agencies (e.g., victim/witness programs) to provide this support for students.

CONCLUDING COMMENTS

The time to begin crisis planning is not in the midst of the chaos elicited by an act of violence. Preparedness is essential to an effective school crisis team response. However, a plan can be successful only if each member is knowledgeable and prepared for his or her role(s) and understands the comprehensive, interdependent nature of a crisis plan. Therefore, in addition to the development of a plan, the team should periodically (at least annually), review and assess the plan. Educational professionals are encouraged to consider the information provided in this chapter when developing a comprehensive crisis management plan.

Further research is important to determine optimal planning and procedures to prevent, prepare for, and respond to school violence. The NIMS/ICS model described in this chapter offers one strategy for developing an infrastructure for delineating roles and duties of crisis

TABLE 29.3

Implications for Practitioners Preventing, Preparing for, and Responding to School Violence

---

Establishing a comprehensive school crisis management team is important to address (a) crisis prevention, (b) crisis preparedness, (c) crisis response, and (d) crisis recovery

Comprehensive school crisis teams need to be active during each phase of crises: (a) the pre-impact phase, (c) the recoil phase, (d) the post-impact phase, and (e) the recovery and reconstruction phase

Use of the NIMS model provides a valuable structure for establishing a comprehensive school crisis team

Team members should be knowledgeable of the Incident Command System (ICS), which provides overall direction and establishes priorities for use in an emergency, and has five primary functions: (a) management, (b) planning and intelligence, (c) operations, (d) logistics, and (c) finance/administration

When planning for each of the functions of the ICS of the school crisis response team, members should consider specific prevention, preparedness, response, and recovery responsibilities

Preparation and planning is essential in developing effective comprehensive school crisis management teams

---

team members. It is acknowledged that this is not the only possible model for a comprehensive school crisis team. However, our experiences suggest that the NIMS and its ICS does an excellent job of making certain that all important aspects of crisis prevention, preparedness, response and recovery are addressed.

ACKNOWLEDGMENTS

Some of the materials for this article were developed by the first author (Dr. Brock) under a grant awarded to the Hays Unified School District No. 489 in Hays, Kansas, from the Department of Education Office of Safe and Drug Free Schools (CFDA No. 84.184E Emergency Response and Crisis Management Grants). This chapter represents the views of the authors and the contents do not necessarily represent the policy of the Department of Education and endorsement by the Federal Government is not implied and should not be assumed.

APPENDIX: SCHOOL CRISIS TEAM MATERIALS

Media Staging Area/Resources
1. School/District/Community maps (with acetate map covers)
2. Marking pens
3. Easel for display of maps
4. Multiple phones and phone lines
5. Electricity
6. Podium with battery powered public address system
7. Ruled pads or steno notebooks
8. Pens and pencils
9. Scotch/Masking tape
10. Laser pointer
11. Telephone contact list
12. Day-glo sign "All Media Report Here"
13. Lighting for night operations
14. Taperecorders and tapes (to tape all press conferences)
15. Media sign-in sheet
16. Blank press passes
17. AM/FM portable radio
18. Local telephone book
19. Media contact log
20. Overhead projector and Screen
21. Copy machine
22. Computers
23. Press release templates

Community Emergency Resources
1. Emergency Medical Responders
2. Police Department
3. Fire Department
4. Office of Emergency Services
5. Red Cross
6. FEMA
7. Community Mental Health
8. Local hospitals
9. Utilities contacts

Search and Rescue Supplies/Equipment
1. Hard hats
2. Gloves
3. Master key
4. First aid supplies
5. Two-way radio
6. School map
7. Goggles
8. Flashlights
9. Dust mask
10. Pry bar
11. Grease pencil
12. Pencils
13. Duct tape
14. Masking tape
15. Utility shut-off value location/tools
16. Yellow caution tape

First Aid Supplies
1. Stretchers
2. Staff and student medications
3. Forms (first aid care notice, medical treatment log)
4. Marking pens
5. Blankets
6. Quick reference medical guides
7. Ground cover/tarps
8. Supplies
   a. 4×4 compresses: 1,000 per 500 students
   b. 8×10 compresses: 150 per 500 students
   c. Kerlix bandaging: 1 per student
   d. Ace wrap: $2''$: 12 per campus
      $4''$: 12 per campus
   e. Triangular bandage: 24 per campus
   f. Cardboard splints: 24 each, sm, med., lg.
   g. Steri-strip butterfly bandages: 50 per campus
   h. Aqua-Blox (water) cases: $0.016 \times$ students + staff = # of cases (for flushing wounds)
   i. Neosporin: 144 squeeze packs per campus
   j. Hydrogen peroxide: 10 pints per campus
   k. Bleach: 1 small bottle
   l. Paramedic scissors: 4 per campus
   m. Tweezers: 3 assorted per campus
   n. Triage tags: 50 per 500 students
   o. Latex gloves: 100 per 500 students
   p. Oval eye patch: 50 per campus
   q. Tape: $1''$ cloth: 50 rolls per campus
   r. Tape $2''$: 24 per campus
   s. Dust masks: 25 per 100 students
   t. Disposable blanket: 10 per 100 students
   u. Space blankets: 1 per student/staff
   v. First aid books
   w. Heavy duty rubber gloves: 4 pair

Evacuation and Assembly
1. Maps with primary and alternate routes indicated
2. Roll sheets
3. Emergency cards

Crisis Intervention Resources
1. Procedural checklist
2. Referral forms
3. Community resource listings
4. Psycho-educational flyers
5. Triage worksheets
6. Triage summary sheets

Morgue Supplies
1. Tags
2. Pens/Pencils
3. Plastic trash bags
4. Duct tape
5. Vicks Vapo Rub
6. Plastic tarps
7. Stapler
8. $2''$ cloth tape

Care/Shelter Resources
1. Ground cover, tarps
2. Blankets
3. First aid kit
4. Water

5. Food
6. Sanitation supplies
7. Student activities; books games coloring books, etc.
8. Forms: student accounting, notice of first aid care
9. Dust masks

Communication Resources
1. Bull horn
2. Two-way radios
3. Computers with internet access
4. Cell phones (key numbers pre-entered)

Adapted from California Governor's office of Emergency Service (1998).

REFERENCES

Abbott, C., & Linfor, V. (2002). *Safe schools: A planning guide for action.* Sacramento, CA: California Department of Education.

Ballard, P., Elliott, D., Fagan, A., Irwin, K., & Mihalic, S. (2004). *Blueprints for violence prevention.* Washington, DC: Office of Juvenile Justice and Delinquency Prevention. Available: http://www.ncjrs.org/pdffiles1/ojjdp/204274.pdf

Breslau, N. (1998). Epidemiology of trauma and posttraumatic stress disorder. In R. Yehuda (Ed.), *Psychological trauma* (pp. 1–29). Washington, DC: American Psychiatric Press.

Brock, S. E. (1999, Summer). The crisis of youth violence: Dangers and opportunities. *CASP Today: A Quarterly Magazine of the California Association of School Psychologists, 48*(4), 18–20.

Brock, S. E. (2002). Crisis theory: A foundation for the comprehensive crisis prevention and intervention team. In S. E. Brock, P. J. Lazarus, & S. R. Jimerson (Eds.), *Best practices in school crisis prevention and intervention* (pp. 5–17). Bethesda, MD: National Association of School Psychologists.

Brock, S. E., & Jimerson, S. R. (2004). School crisis interventions: Strategies for addressing the consequences of crisis events. In E. R. Gerler Jr. (Ed.), *Handbook of school violence* (pp. 285–332). Binghamton, NY: Haworth Press.

Brock, S. E., Sandoval, J., & Lewis, S. (2001). *Preparing for crises in the schools: A manual for building school crisis response teams* (2nd ed.). New York: Wiley.

California Governor's Office of Emergency Services. (1998, June). *School emergency response: Using SEMS at districts and sites. Guidelines for planning and training in compliance with the Standardized Emergency management System.* Sacramento, CA: Author.

Dwyer, K., & Jimerson S. (2002). Enabling prevention through planning. In S. E. Brock, P. J. Lazarus, & S. R. Jimerson (Eds.), *Best practices in school crisis prevention and intervention* (pp. 23–46). Bethesda, MD: National Association of School Psychologists.

Dwyer, K., & Osher, D. (2000). *Safeguarding our children: An action guide.* Washington, DC: U.S. Departments of Education and Justice, American Institutes for Research.

Dwyer, K., Osher, D., & Warger, C. (1998). *Early warning, timely response: A guide to safe schools.* Washington, DC: U.S. Department of Education.

Federal Emergency Management Agency. (2003, February). *Exemplary practices in emergency management: Standardized Emergency Management System (SEMS).* Available: www.fema.gov/rrr/exp_06.shtm

Goldstein, A. P., & Conoley, J. C. (1997). *School violence intervention: A practical handbook.* New York: Guilford Press.

Green, M. (1999). *The appropriate and effective use of security technologies in U.S. schools: A guide for schools and law enforcement agencies.* Washington, DC: U.S. Department of Justice, Office of Justice Programs.

Hester, J. P. (2003). *Public school safety: A handbook, with a resource guide.* Jefferson, NC: McFarland.

Lockyer, B., & Eastin, D. (2000). *Crisis response box: A guide to help every school assemble the tools and resources needed for a critical incident response.* Sacramento: California Department of Education. Available: http://www.cde.ca.gov/ls/ss/cp/documents/crisisresbox.pdf

National Association of School Psychologists. (2000). *Behavioral interventions: Creating a safe environment in our schools.* Bethesda, MD: Author.

National Resource Center for Safe Schools. (2000). *What school administrators can do about violence.* Washington, DC: U.S. Departments of Education and Justice, American Institutes for Research.

Poland, S., Pitcher, G., & Lazarus, P. M. (2002). Best practices in crisis prevention and management. In A. Thomas & J. Grimes (Eds.), *Best practices in school psychology* (Vol. 4, pp. 1057–1079). Bethesda, MD: National Association of School Psychologists.

Smith, J. (2001). *School crisis management manual* (2nd ed.). Holmes Beach, FL: Learning Publications.

Thompson, R. A. (2004). *Crisis intervention and crisis management: Strategies that work in schools and communities.* New York: Brunner-Routledge.

U.S. Department of Education, Office of Safe and Drug-Free Schools. (2003, May). *Practical information on crisis planning: A guide for schools and communities*. Washington, DC: Author.

U.S. Department of Homeland Security (2004, March 1). *National incident management system*. Available: http://www.dhs.govinterweb/assetlibrary/NIMS-90-web.pdf.

Valent, P. (2000). Disaster syndrome. In G. Fink (Ed.), *Encyclopedia of stress* (Vol. 1, pp.706–709). San Diego, CA: Academic Press.

Vossekuil, B., Fein, R. A., Reddy, M., Borum R., & Modzeleski, W. (2002). *The final report and findings of the safe schools initiative: Implications for the prevention of school attacks in the United States*. Washington, DC: U.S. Government Printing Office. Available: http://www.secretservice.gov/ntac_ssi.shtml

IV

Implementing Comprehensive Safe School Plans

This final section presents valuable knowledge and insights that have emerged through the implementation of comprehensive plans to promote school safety. Chapters in this section include diverse experiences and perspectives from across the United States as well as other regions of the world.

The first three chapters in this section present valuable international insights, including a comprehensive (360-degree) approach to prevent school violence that is used in Australia (chap. 30), a national study of school violence in Israel (chap. 31), and a psychosocial perspective on school violence from the Brazilian perspective (chap. 32). The next five chapters provide a review of efforts to promote safe schools across the United States, including a school, community, and university collaboration to promote safe schools and healthy students in Pennsylvania (chap. 33); the planning, implementation, operation, and sustainability of safe school plans in Florida (chap. 34); the implementation and evaluation of safe school plans in Delaware (chap. 35); a safe schools and healthy students initiative in Kansas (chap. 36); and a school and community mental health partnership in Illlinois to reduce youth violence (chap. 37). The next two chapters both address the implementation of student threat assessment as a strategy to reduce school violence one implemented in Virginia (chap. 38) and a second one with a specific emphasis on the Dallas threat of violence risk assessment (chap. 39). The following chapter in this section provides a case study of a school shooting that shares lessons learned (chap. 40). The final chapter of the book provides a school reform model for implementing best practices in violence prevention (chap. 41).

30

Creating a Safe and Friendly School: Using a 360-Degree Approach

Coosje Griffiths
Tracey Weatherilt
Department of Education and Training, Western Australia

Over the years, greater awareness has developed of the importance of schools being not only physically safe for students, but also psychologically safe, which involves being friendly, inclusive, and responsive to their needs. The *Promotion, Prevention and Early Intervention for Mental Health—A Monograph* (Commonwealth Department of Health and Aged Care, 2000b), the *National Action Plan for Promotion, Prevention and Early Intervention for Mental Health 2000* (Commonwealth Department of Health and Aged Care, 2000a) and Zubrick et al. (1997) have identified schools as key sites for mental health promotion, prevention, and early intervention. There is strong evidence that targeting these approaches to the child and adolescent population results in improved school achievement as well as improved mental health outcomes. The Safe School, Friendly School Framework utilizes the World Health Organization (WHO) Health Promoting Schools Framework, which involves a risk-focused prevention model, and the prevention–intervention spectrum as an effective approach to promotion of health and well-being and prevention of mental health issues in schools (Department of Education, 2001). In order to enhance and recognize school efforts in establishing safe and friendly learning environments the Safe School, Friendly School Framework was developed to provide guidance to schools, through the provision of documented indicators and pointers on how to increase and maintain a safe and friendly school environment. The Safe School, Friendly School Project and Framework are based on the principle that students are better able to achieve educational outcomes and values within an environment of inclusion, friendliness, and safety. The Safe School, Friendly School Project culminated in a self-reflection tool for schools that has now been developed into the manual *Safe School, Friendly School: A Framework for Developing Safe and Friendly Schools* (Griffiths & Weatherilt, 2001).

The project involves schools in a process of working with the school community to ascertain strengths and weaknesses in the school's planning; operations and ethos through surveys for staff, parents, and students; consultation; discussion; and professional development. Once a school considers that it has achieved the criteria, an application is made to go through the process of accreditation. A multiprofessional accreditation team awards Safe School, Friendly School accreditation to schools judged, after a high level of external scrutiny, to have achieved the required standard in safety, inclusivity and customer service. It also provides a framework for schools that aspire to excellence to achieve this goal.

PROJECT PURPOSE

The project aims to (a) support schools in providing a safe and friendly learning and working environment; (b) provide a framework that encompasses the Curriculum Improvement Program, students at educational risk strategies, and other major government schools initiatives; (c) provide a change management tool that assists schools in reflecting on their current practices, examining their strengths and weaknesses, and planning for improvement; (d) identify and share successful school practices; and (e) promote government schools. The promotion of government schools is based on the need to counter the perception that some of the movement of students from government to nongovernment schools is due to safety, discipline, and values education issues, with this perception periodically being reinforced through the media. It is expected that the project would result in enhanced student learning outcomes, student retention in education, school reputation, and customer focus.

The Safe School, Friendly School Framework is based on an overarching vision that schools will be safe and friendly learning environments for all students. It is a vision of quality leadership, inclusion, effective partnerships, student participation, and the provision of quality educational programs within a safe and friendly working environment. It incorporates the values of the *Curriculum Framework* (Curriculum Council, 1999) and enhances schools' ability to achieve the overarching learning outcomes. Schools are increasingly seen as having a significant role in the identification of risk factors in children's development and the provision of preventative strategies to reduce the long-term impact of these risks on their future development. Certain health and well-being issues such as crime and substance abuse, that occur later in life can have their roots in early childhood and the school years (National Committee on Violence, 1990; National Crime Prevention, 1999; Rapp, Carrington, & Nicholson, 1992). The provision of safe and child-friendly organizations is seen as one of the keys to the long-term reduction in the prevalence of these issues.

The Safe School, Friendly School Framework and accreditation process does not envisage schools taking on full responsibility for the well-being of all students or that they must cater for all of the needs of their school community. It is recognized that although parents have primary responsibility for providing care and guidance for their children, schools can support parents in that role (The United Nations, 1989). Schools can provide a strong customer-focused service that encourages parent and student participation in school-based decision making, and can promote their involvement in effective partnerships in assisting all students to achieve the educational outcomes.

Schools have incorporated many significant issues into their delivery of services to students and their school community. Bullying and violence, socioeconomic disadvantage, mental health and well-being, social skills development, multiculturalism, indigenous education, students with disabilities, and child protection issues are now included in school-based planning and programs. There is recognition of the need to provide services and programs for the "whole child," catering for not just the academic, but also the social, emotional, and behavioral needs of all students. It incorporates "a vision of the child as an individual and as a member of family and community, with rights and responsibilities appropriate to his or her age and stage of development. By recognising children's rights in this way, ... the focus is firmly on the whole child" (UNICEF, 1989, Article 28).

From this focus on the whole child, schools have been placing increasing value on the contributions that teachers, students, parents, and external agencies can put into the sometimes difficult task of developing and managing quality educational programs for the benefit of all children. Although the contributions of teachers, parents, and other support agencies have long been a part of school operations, the involvement of students in setting school policy and procedures is a relatively new concept.

This framework empowers the school community to take the initiative in developing workable and sustainable solutions to promote health and well-being and counter issues such as bullying, violence, retention and participation issues, and other factors that place students at educational risk. The Safe School, Friendly School Framework also provides guidance to schools in creating and maintaining a safe and friendly environment, through the provision of pointers that illustrate a safe and friendly school. For a school to be safe and friendly it needs to be inclusive and customer focused, not just have the strategies that promote inclusivity and customer focus.

PROJECT DEVELOPMENT

The project is a culmination of a range of initiatives running in the district including outcomes-focused curriculum, positive peer relations, peer mediation, values-based education, and the challenging and countering bullying in schools professional learning programs. The framework has been developed with extensive consultation and feedback from a range of professional and community groups in national and international contexts.

The response from schools has been positive beyond expectations. The number of schools that responded to the call for nominations was impressive. Their willingness to be scrutinised and reflect on criteria for safety and friendliness proved the projects worth. The education district's directors and student services personnel worked to engage schools, private organizations, and sponsors into a collective partnership to create the accreditation tool and to implement the project.

The development of the indicators, pointers, and the framework involved contributions from a number of administrators in the district and university researchers from Western Australia and overseas. Survey instruments were also developed for schools to gauge their parent, staff, and student beliefs and feelings about the school's safety, curriculum, behavior management, atmosphere, and bullying issues. The survey questions were reviewed by researchers and piloted in schools before being included in the Safe School, Friendly School manual (see Appendices C and D).

THE FRAMEWORK: PRINCIPLES

Characteristics that are evident in safe and friendly schools, and that have been proven to be effective, form the basis of the Safe School, Friendly School Project.

Safe and friendly schools have the following characteristics:

- Quality leadership.
- A solution-focused rather than a problem-focused approach.
- A vision and culture that strives for excellence in learning and teaching.
- Democratic processes that encourage active citizenship.
- An ongoing ethos of review and ongoing planning for improvement.
- Involvement of the whole school community in planning.
- Plans that are comprehensive.

Students
• Increased student participation
• High attendance rates
• Low suspension and exclusion rates
• Improved literacy and numeracy achievements
• Positive perceptions of schooling
• Enhanced perception of the school as a safe and friendly place

Staff
• Improved morale
• Less absenteeism
• Greater participation in decision making
• Positive school perceptions
• Greater job satisfaction
• Pride in their school and the school community

Parents
• Positive perceptions of schooling
• Enhanced perceptions of the school as a safe and friendly place
• Increased participation and a feeling that their participation is encouraged
• Belief that the school communicates with parents in a timely and helpful manner

Administrators
• Provision of quality leadership
• Modeling of positive communication
• Encouragement of school community participation in decision making
• Understanding of and response to school community wishes

Wider Community
• Positive perceptions of the school
• Positive media reports and public relations campaigns
• Partnerships are formed with other agencies and community groups.

FIG. 30.1. Outcome characteristics of a school that is safe and friendly.

• Policies and plans that aim to assist all members of the school community to feel safe and valued.
• A process to collect comprehensive data.
• A range of strategies across all levels of operation: preventative measures, early intervention, and case management.
• Policies and plans that are communicated and applied.
• Strategies that are applied to all settings including the whole school, playground, and the classroom (adapted from Furlong, Morrison, & Clontz, 1993).

OUTCOMES

The data used to classify a school as both *safe* and *friendly* were both qualitative and quantitative. Figure 30.1 illustrates the outcomes considered to be evidence of a school that has developed strategies to create a safe and friendly school environment. The school's success of achieving a safe and friendly environment is not necessarily hindered by risk factors and risk conditions outside the control of the school, such as socioeconomic factors, school location and proximity to risks, and students with challenging behaviors. The school's response to and management of the risks associated with these contextual factors operating in the community is the key to creating a safe and friendly school.

The information schools can use for self-reflection includes existing data available, and the results of surveys and other customer feedback mechanisms utilized by the school. Specific surveys were developed for the process and focus group questions. The following existing information can be gathered and analysed in the self-reflection process:

- School plans related to the Safe School, Friendly School Project.
- School development plans and annual reports.
- School newsletters and communications to parents, students, staff, and other agencies.
- Student data such as attendance, behavior management referrals to school administration, suspensions, exclusions and critical incident reports. Also standards in achievement in literacy and numeracy, class data, students at educational risk identification and profiles, individual student case management, individual education and behavior plans, and student portfolios are highly valuable.
- Evidence that a coordinating committee or task teams are in operation with a focus on safety and friendliness.
- Evidence of interagency collaboration on projects, school-relevant issues, and individual student cases where necessary.
- Surveys or feedback and comment mechanisms are in place to encourage student, staff, and parent participation in school planning and management.
- The school's existing physical environment and plans for improvement.

SCHOOL CHANGE MANAGEMENT

In order to improve school safety at all levels, the school leadership needs to put a range of structures, procedures, and processes in place to ensure whole-school improvement. Figure 30.2 illustrates the steps that are recommended and reflected in current research on change management.

In planning for improvement, schools move through stages that include identification and planning, intervention, and reflection/review in a continuous cycle that builds on attainments and includes setting new improvement goals, as illustrated in Fig. 30.3. Functioning alongside this model is the model focusing on the levels of prevention and risk management necessary to successfully cater for all students in the school.

LEVELS OF OPERATION

The Three-Level Approach to Prevention (Education Department, 2001) illustrates the areas across which all planning and interventions must occur to ensure successful practices and outcomes (see Fig. 30.4). The cone represents the entire school population, with the top level (Level 1) reflecting all students being exposed to whole-school prevention strategies. The narrowing of the cone toward the point indicates that only some students are included in early intervention approaches (Level 2) and that a very small number of students require intensive interventions or individual casework (Level 3).

Level 1: Whole-School Prevention for All Students

At this level, the general resilience of students is promoted by means of whole-school programs designed to promote student participation such as class meetings and student councils, peer mediation/peer support programs, positive behavior management approaches, pastoral care teams/systems, and prosocial skills programs (as described in Prescott, 1995, and Marshall Watt, 1999). Also included are drug and alcohol education, community policing, Aboriginal

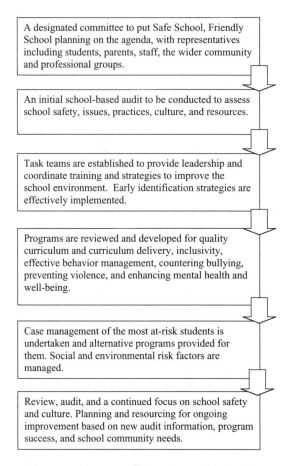

A designated committee to put Safe School, Friendly School planning on the agenda, with representatives including students, parents, staff, the wider community and professional groups.

An initial school-based audit to be conducted to assess school safety, issues, practices, culture, and resources.

Task teams are established to provide leadership and coordinate training and strategies to improve the school environment. Early identification strategies are effectively implemented.

Programs are reviewed and developed for quality curriculum and curriculum delivery, inclusivity, effective behavior management, countering bullying, preventing violence, and enhancing mental health and well-being.

Case management of the most at-risk students is undertaken and alternative programs provided for them. Social and environmental risk factors are managed.

Review, audit, and a continued focus on school safety and culture. Planning and resourcing for ongoing improvement based on new audit information, program success, and school community needs.

FIG. 30.2.   Steps to create a safe and friendly school.

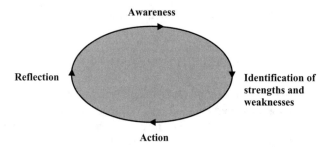

FIG. 30.3.   Planning for ongoing improvement.

and Islander education officer services, positive presentation of the physical environment and programs to promote positive interactions and counter bullying (Griffiths, 2001).

Level 2: Early Intervention for Some Students

This level includes strategies that focus on specific groups who are at risk through, for example, small-group social skills classes, shared concern method (Pikas, 2002), breakfast programs, homework classes, remedial education, education support, extension classes, cultural diversity

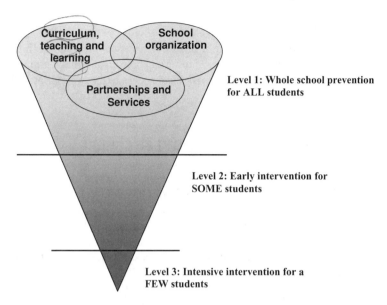

FIG. 30.4.   Three-level approach to prevention, early identification, and intervention. (Adapted from Department of Education, 2001; Dwyer & Osher, 2000).

including racism friendship classes (Griffiths & Hansen, 2001), boys in education approaches (Swan Education District, 2000), and disability/mental health supports.

Level 3: Intensive Intervention for a Few Students

This level focuses specifically on students who are displaying at-risk behaviors and includes case management of students most at risk due to significant emotional, educational, or behavioral concerns, alternative educational, programs or settings, individual counseling services, mentoring, and individual behavior/education plans.

At the top of the cone are three interconnected areas, which are required to effectively implement strategies across the three levels.

Curriculum, Teaching, and Learning

This domain includes pedagogical practice as well as curriculum content that are relevant and engaging to students. It also links to the school culture and values. The key element is the provision of an inclusive and flexible learning environment for students within an outcomes-focused approach.

School Organization and Ethos

This domain involves the school culture, attitudes, and values that translate into making the school a friendly environment where students and staff want to be. School policies and practices need to be developed by the school community to reflect the needs of that community. Organizational structures, such as middle schooling and pastoral care systems, can be implemented to enhance student learning and engagement. Student support teams and other services work collaboratively to create a strong pastoral care system. Provision for the physical safety of students is an essential element.

Partnerships and Services

This domain is concerned with the relationships between school, students, home, and the community. Effective partnerships involving all three can help ensure that learning is practical and relevant, and that students at educational risk have access to the appropriate support from other agencies.

THE FRAMEWORK: EIGHT KEY AREAS

The Safe School, Friendly School Framework groups the characteristics of safe and friendly schools into the following eight key areas: (a) school ethos and culture, (b) school organization and planning processes, (c) school policies and procedures, (d) levels of operation, (e) classroom application, (f) out-of-classroom application, (g) staff training and support, and (h) school physical environment. Each of the key areas has an overarching principle and a set of performance indicators, with associated pointers to assist schools to reflect on their current structures and practices.

The Framework: Indicators

Each of the key areas has a set of graded performance indicators, with associated pointers for excelling performance, to assist schools in reflecting on their current structures and practices. They are set out in a checklist that outlines the characteristics associated with schools that are achieving within one of five developmental levels: (a) excelling, (b) achieving, (c) establishing, (d) developing, and (e) undeveloped. It is expected that schools will be at different stages of development across each of the eight key areas. Schools that have reflected on their practices and consider that they are operating within the top two levels are invited to apply for accreditation as Safe School, Friendly School. Every school that can then successfully demonstrate consistent performance within the achieving or excelling levels are awarded accreditation as a Safe School, Friendly School (see samples in Appendices A and B). Schools that achieve accreditation are expected to continually review their procedures and practices in order to maintain their accreditation status, with a formal review being undertaken by the Safe School, Friendly School Project every 3 years.

ACCREDITATION PROCESSES

The following principles apply in the accreditation process: (a) schools volunteer for the accreditation process; (b) professional development and support is provided for schools to assist in the process of reflection and preparation for accreditation; (c) schools involve the whole-school community in the process of reflection and audit; (d) the accreditation process is rigorous and quality assured; and (e) the accreditation team consists of multiple professionals who are conversant with the framework.

Information Used for Accreditation

Information used for accreditation included existing data available to schools and the district and the results of surveys utilized by the school. Specific surveys were developed for the accreditation process and focus group questions. Schools could use alternative survey instruments for the purposes of accreditation. The following existing information was used in the accreditation process:

- The school's plans related to the framework.
- The school's annual report.
- The school's newsletters.
- Student data available at the district office: attendance, behavior management referrals to administrators, suspensions, exclusions, and critical incident reports.
- Student data available at the school: literacy and numeracy standards and evidence of identification of students at risk as well as evidence of individual student case management, individual education plans (IEPs), individual behavior management plans (IBMPs), and student portfolios;
- Evidence that a coordinating committee is in operation.
- Evidence of interagency collaboration on projects and individual cases.
- Surveys and/or focus groups of students, staff, and parents.
- Student responses to informal questions such as: "What are the school/playground/ classroom rules?" "What do you do when you see someone fighting?" "What do you do if someone is mean to you?"
- Information from parent/community survey.
- The school's physical environment.

Accredited School

It is expected that an accredited school will (a) gain a positive profile in the community through the accreditation process; (b) have an opportunity to celebrate its success in gaining accreditation; (c) be provided with a certificate and school plaque for display in the school foyer; (d) have use of the logo to publicize its accreditation through newsletters and school publicity; (e) provide leadership in the district, by mentoring and supporting other schools; and (f) continue to improve safety and customer focus, by reflecting on practices and planning for ongoing improvement.

THE PROJECT TRIAL

In the initial trial conducted across one district office, a range of schools were initially accredited—a primary school, a school for students with disabilities, a senior high school, a senior campus for postcompulsory students and a language development center. The following is a summary of findings from the accreditation process and provides some insight into the unique ways that schools have achieved a safe and friendly school environment.

School Example 1: Senior Campus

The senior campus is structured to reflect an adult ethos and caters for students from 16 years to mature age, providing an open learning environment for students studying Year 11 and 12 curriculum. A campus council was developed in 2002 and currently a student guild is an integral part of the decision-making processes. Some of the key features of this outstanding school include the flexible time-tabling that allows for the open learning model, collaborative teacher/committee time, and student guild activities. Staff members demonstrated their commitment through flexible teaching times, including running night courses. Their students are drawn from all socioeconomic backgrounds, with students from homeless and refugee backgrounds not uncommon. The school seeks to cater for some of the noneducational needs of their students to improve the educational outcomes for all students. A daily breakfast program opens at 8 a.m. All students are welcome. The school uses a collaborative problem-solving model, where students are assisted in gathering all of those who play a part in their education to develop solutions to pressing issues that may prevent them from achieving their full potential, or even prevent them from continuing in school. The involvement of staff at all levels in a school ethos and culture that values diversity and the concept of "second-chance" education means that the senior campus is able to demonstrate a fully inclusive and flexible approach to education. Students report feeling valued and treated respectfully as equals by staff. Problems that arise are taken seriously and handled sensitively. Consequently, suspensions are rare and students value the school as a safe haven.

School Example 2: Education Support School

The education support school caters to students from kindergarten age to 13 years who have an intellectual disability, with many students also having physical disabilities. As all students are identified as being at risk, policies and procedures have been developed to meet their individual needs. The role of the parents and caregivers is vital and they are involved in all planning with the student's support team. One of the key features of the school is that the physical environment has been carefully planned and developed to assist in meeting the very complex needs of these students. The plants in the junior playground are edible and fragrant, and are therefore both safe and provide the opportunity for the students to both touch and smell. The junior playground incorporates play equipment and settings that allows for stimulation of all their senses. The senior playground is currently undergoing renovations to better meet the advanced social needs of the older students, with more seating and walk areas being developed. Inclusivity and catering for individual differences is embedded in all teaching and learning programs, from the physical school environment to the classroom curriculum and individual education planning.

School Example 3: Primary School

The primary school draws students from a culturally diverse population catering for students from kindergarten to Year 7. Verbal and written communications to parents from non-English-speaking backgrounds are translated to ensure all parents can participate in the development of policies, procedures, and activities run by the school. The primary school has introduced an effective social skills and behavior change program through the establishment of the Personal Best Club. To gain club membership, students self-assess before nominating themselves. Each member wears a membership badge. Student members work toward set achievements and are rewarded with a series of medallions. The medallions represent excellence and personal achievement, which have been well received by all students. The organization of student movement has been modified. All class groups assemble together after each break to set the tone for the next learning session. During the assemblies, students receive recognition for their achievements (academic, social, and behavioral) with the awarding of the Personal Best Club achievements included. Special day programs are regularly organized where the students are grouped vertically and engage in cooperative activities to foster the development of social skills. The following primary school principal's comments illustrate the staff perceptions of the school:

> The Safe Schools, Friendly Schools Project has enabled our school to develop a clear vision for a child-centred, safe, and supportive learning environment. The Safe Schools, Friendly Schools Project addresses physical, emotional, social and curriculum safety at a whole school and class level. The parents and citizens were very eager to become involved as they see its power to forge home/ school partnerships.

Feedback from teachers, parents, and students through surveys and interviews indicated very strong support for the school and a sense of pride in the school's achievements. The school administrators were able to demonstrate a multifaceted and responsive approach to the unique student population where most students felt safe and valued most of the time. When problems arose, parents indicated that the school acted in a timely and effective way where parties involved feel heard and valued.

School Example 4: Language Development Center

The language development center caters to students with significant language disorders from kindergarten to Year 3, with students traveling from all over the district to attend one of the school's three campuses. The school is child-centered with a pastoral care orientation, as all of the students are identified as being at educational risk. Students and parents are actively involved in the educational planning, with both staff and parents attending regular professional development opportunities provided by the school. The social skills program and behavior change mechanisms are an outstanding feature of the school's program, enhancing the inclusiveness of students experiencing significant difficulties in these areas.

The school utilizes social stories, personal goal-setting and conflict resolution strategies to assist their students develop communication and social skills, while also providing for effective behavior change when needed. These strategies provide students with clear visual assistance in developing their skills, with the conflict resolution process involving a floor chart so that the students can "walk" through the steps of problem solving. The integration of relevant curriculum including social skills and behavior management programs has resulted in the North East Metro Language Development Center demonstrating how it has been able to establish a safe and friendly learning environment for students at risk, resulting in marked improvements in their learning, behavior, and social skills.

School Example 5: High School

The senior high school is a medium-sized secondary school in a disadvantaged area. This school systematically reviewed and developed a wide range of policies and procedures concurrently with the Safe School, Friendly School accreditation process. The changes they have implemented are significant and extensive, involving collaboration between staff from all of the faculties, student services, and the school's administration, with student and parent participation also through surveys.

The school had already developed some key strategies to counter bullying and improve peer relations through its Treat Everyone Decently project. The accreditation process enhanced the school's ability to apply for and successfully become a demonstration school in the national MindMatters Plus Project. The school has also reported an increased recognition by the parent body of its efforts to provide a safe learning environment for all students. The school has made extensive use of the Safe School, Friendly School logo on publications, staff badges, and stickers to promote and encourage the positive ethos of the school. The following feedback was provided by the participating high school principal:

> Through the Safe Schools, Friendly Schools Project, the school has reviewed policy and procedures to ensure that they reflect current practice or are in step with current educational thinking. Where gaps have been found, staff have addressed them thereby ensuring that the best possible outcomes are obtained. The survey process has also given the school valuable information about perceptions of the school and concerns that are held. This information has also proved to very useful. The school has been able to plan changes where needed or simply be reassured that it is meeting the needs of the community.

TABLE 30.1

Implications for Practice: What Educational Professionals Should do to Create Safe
and Friendly Schools

- Gain the involvement of the school community in a process of self-reflection and external review on school as a safe, supportive, and inclusive educational community.
- Seek to understand the views of students, parents, and staff regarding their perception of school safety including communication between school and home, quality of relationships, relevant curriculum, behavior management, and countering bullying practices using survey data.
- Utilize the self-evaluation tool to further map the efficacy and inclusiveness of school practices, resulting in a profile of the school's strengths and areas requiring improvement.
- Share the findings with members of the school community in order to raise awareness of areas of strengths and those requiring action.
- Put infrastructures such as a committee into place to implement changes; involve a peer-support principal to assist in the process of reflection and action.
- Develop a range of strategies, systems, and programs to address areas of need including preventative, early intervention, and incident response.
- Maintain a cycle of school improvement including raising awareness, identifying areas of need and action.
- Enter into a process of peer and external review to provide a high level of confidence that the school is operating effectively as a safe and friendly school community.
- Continue to develop a positive school culture while assessing risks and responding to incidents in a timely and effective manner.

PROJECT EVALUATION

Although school principals found the 360-degree approach to the school's reflection and accreditation process daunting, they persisted in the process in order to access rigorous self-reflection processes and those of an external accreditation group. Schools that participated in the Safe School, Friendly School Project reported that the best part of the project was the provision of an effective tool for improving school self-reflection, which enabled them to integrate and respond to system imperatives.

Another feature was that the project brought the school community together in collaborative planning and development of strategies for improvement and reporting to a multidisciplinary accreditation team. The school community also appreciated the recognition of their achievements as well as the outcomes achieved for students. In the participating schools, the positive publicity and community feeling about the school was enhanced, and in some schools correlated with a marked increase in student enrolments following their accreditation. A number of schools were accredited, whereas other participating schools, after reviewing their practice again the framework and the survey outcomes, felt they were not yet ready and delayed their accreditation process to put strategies in place for improvement. The use of a peer administrator assigned to a school engaging in the process of review means that schools felt supported in their efforts to improve school practice. The project achieved a high status among schools and the school community with the official launch and media coverage as well as the presentation of a certificate, brass plaque, posters, badges, and access to the logo for school advertising and publications.

One of the outcomes of the project has been the ability of participating schools is to attract recognition and further community and government support, including funding. For example, a primary school principal of an accredited school credits the Safe School, Friendly School process as a key factor to the school's success in achieving a prestigious national literacy award. One of the accredited secondary schools was chosen as the only school in their state to be a demonstration school for a national project called MindMatters Plus (Commonwealth of Australia, 2000). This project involves resourcing the school to take part in action research into how students with high support needs in the area of mental health can best be supported through school systems, processes, strategies, and evidence-based programs. The principal was able to demonstrate the school's capacity to be involved in such a project through the understandings and data obtained through the Safe School, Friendly School accreditation process.

The project has also drawn interest from other education districts around the state of Western Australia, other Australian states and overseas, with numerous requests for both training on the framework, the accreditation process and the manual. A professor from the United Kingdom participated in the process of accreditation and concluded that the Safe School, Friendly School Project has had a major impact on schools to become more inclusive, as well as addressing issues related to school community safety, bullying, and intimidation (Farrell, 2004). Built on the success of the instrument, the Northern Territory Department of Employment, Education and Training utilized many aspects of the Safe School, Friendly School framework in its systemwide strategy to building relationships and school well-being (Northern Territory Government, 2004). The authors participated in and provided concepts that are reflected in the *National Safe Schools Framework* (Ministerial Council, 2003), which is currently being implemented across Australian jurisdictions.

The Safe School, Friendly School Framework was developed in collaboration with school administrators and researchers at all stages of its development. The project has clearly resulted in schools measuring themselves against best practice in education and has encouraged them to plan for further improvements. It is still in its formative stage and has proven thus far that the Safe School, Friendly School reflection tool and accreditation process not only has merit, but is also able to support school change management in establishing learning and teaching environments that are both safe and friendly for all students.

The development of quality learning environments is a challenge that requires a belief in the ability to make a difference, as well as a willingness to undertake ongoing planning for the full range of students who attend government schools. It is not a process that can be taken on lightly as it requires an understanding of its complexities and the commitment to the process (Bernhardt, 1999).

Over the years, greater awareness has developed of the importance of schools being not only physically safe for students, but also friendly, inclusive, and responsive to their needs. Everyone involved in schools, including staff, has the right to experience a safe working environment and has a responsibility to contribute to its creation. The media have tended to focus on the most negative aspects of schools and in some cases have undermined parent confidence. It is important that each school develop a good working relationship with its whole school community, and that the school community experience and perceive the school as responsive and customer focused. Improvements in public perception will not only enhance working relationships between the schools and their communities, but will also provide an avenue for celebrating their successes.

Finally, much of the research has demonstrated the cost effectiveness of prevention, early intervention and intensive case management for the most at risk students as compared to the costs of crime and end of the line justice responses (National Committee on Violence, 1990; National Crime Prevention, 1999, National Safety Centre, 1990). The 360-degree process of the Safe School, Friendly School Project works at all these levels, utilizing both self- and external feedback systems. It also provides schools with a range of strategies to improve school ethos, practice, and outcomes for students with a focus on establishing safer, friendlier, and more inclusive school community environments.

APPENDIX A: SAFE AND FRIENDLY SCHOOL SAMPLE OF GRADED INDICATORS

Out-of-Class Applications

Excelling

- Students are regularly taught the behavioral expectations of the school and how to demonstrate those behaviors
- Transitions involving the movement of students around the school and out of the school are planned for and managed effectively
- Duty and supervision issues are identified in the school policy and associated procedures are implemented to ensure student safety
- Lunch activities are planned for and implemented to provide opportunities for student participation and to develop prosocial behavior
- Incident response procedures are in place and all staff is trained and able to respond effectively

Achieving

- Students are taught the behavioral expectations of the school and how to demonstrate those behaviors at least each term
- Transitions involving the movement of students around the school and between the breaks and class time are managed at a whole-school level (out-of-school procedures are in place and adhered to)
- Duty and supervision issues are identified and procedures implemented to ensure student safety
- Some lunch activities are planned for and implemented to provide opportunities for student participation and to manage difficult students
- Incident response procedures are in place and most staff trained and able to respond effectively

Establishing

- Students are taught the behavior expectations of the school and how to demonstrate those behaviors at the beginning of each year
- Transitions involving the movement of students around the school and between the breaks and class time are managed at a classroom level (some out of school procedures are in place, with staff adhering to best practice)
- There is a duty roster designed to supervise students on the school grounds and to respond to student needs
- Lunch activities are occasionally planned for and implemented to provide opportunities for student participation and to manage difficult students
- Incident response procedures are in place and key staff-trained and able to respond effectively

Developing

- Students are informed of the behavioral expectations of the school at the beginning of each year
- Transitions involving the movement of students around the school and between the breaks and class time are managed within some classrooms (out-of-school procedures are still being developed, but good practice is generally followed)

- There is a duty roster designed to supervise students in the school grounds
- Some lunch activities are planned for and implemented to manage difficult students
- Incident response procedures are in place and administration staff trained and able to respond effectively

Undeveloped

- Behavior expectations of the school are unclear to students
- Transitions involving the movement of students around the school are not managed (out-of-school procedures are based on the good practice of staff)
- There is a duty roster informed by staffing levels
- Difficult students are confined to specific areas
- Lunchtime activities are not provided generally
- There is no incident response plan (incidents are dealt with as they arise)

APPENDIX B: SAMPLE OF PERFORMANCE INDICATORS AND POINTERS OUT-OF-CLASS APPLICATION: POINTERS FOR EXCELLING PERFORMANCE

Performance Indicators	Pointers
• Students are regularly taught the behavioral expectations of the school and how to demonstrate those behaviors.	• Teaching staff reviews the school's code of conduct and behavioral expectations with their students regularly. • All staff and school support personnel know and can reinforce students in the school's code of conduct and behavioral expectations in out-of-class settings. • Students have access to or are able to engage in social problem-solving strategies for out-of-class settings. • School Managing Information System on Behaviour Management in Schools is analyzed and acted on.
• Transitions involving the movement of students around the school and out of the school are planned for and managed effectively.	• Policies and procedures described: walking/running, lining up areas, students on messages, pathways/walk areas, and supervision. • Excursion procedures and behavior codes are developed and adhered to by all staff. • All staff consistently adheres to stated procedures and reinforces students to follow the procedures. • Documentation concerning the whereabouts of classes and individual students is maintained. • There are formalized communication procedures of the whereabouts of classes and individual students and any changes to these locations.

(Continued)

APPENDIX B

(Continued)

• Duty and supervision issues are identified in the school policy and associated procedures are implemented to ensure student safety.	• Areas that are out of bounds are clearly marked. • Safe areas and "sanctuaries" are provided (e.g., computer room, library, and under cover area). • All staff adhered to the duty roster. • All staff actively supervize students while on duty or in the yard: scanning, approaching groups of students, talking to students, early intervening, and redirecting play/behavior to a appropriate behavior when necessary. • There are set guidelines to responding to inappropriate behavior. • Ongoing information/training of staff is provided in early intervention, observation, and scanning techniques and de-escalation skills.
• Lunch activities are planned for and implemented to provide opportunities for student participation and to develop prosocial behavior.	• Lunch activities are provided, with some supervised or directed activities offered. • Staff members are designated for each task/break period. • Resources are allocated within the school development plan. • A variety of activities are planned to suit the various developmental levels and needs of students. • Student participation maximized with students planning and running some of the activities for themselves or for other groups of students. • Strategies for peer mediation, teaching of game rules, and peer umpiring are in place.
• Incident response procedures are in place and staff members are trained and able to respond effectively.	• Effective procedures in place. • All staff, students, and school support personnel know and can activate the procedures. • The management strategies are applied effectively. • There is communication of the outcomes to all key stakeholders. • Contingency plans for handling severe incidents are in place and known to all staff, students, and school support personnel. • Supports are offered to all individuals involved in severe incidents: debriefing, counseling, relief, and parent involvement.

APPENDIX C: SAFE AND FRIENDLY SCHOOL STUDENT SURVEY

School: [   ]

Year Level: [ ]   **Gender:**   **M** [ ]   **F** [ ]

	Tick the answer that best describes what you think.	*All of the time*	*Nearly all of the time*	*Sometimes*	*Not at all*
1	Do you feel safe at this school **during class time?**				
2	Do you feel safe at this school **during recess and lunch?**				
3	Do you think the **school rules** are **fair**?				
4	If you had a **problem** (e.g., with school work, upset or frightened) do you think you could ask a member of staff for help?				
5	Do you think **teachers listen** to your ideas?				
6	Do you **enjoy coming to school**?				
7	Do you think **bullying** goes on in this school?				
8	Do you think this school **deals well with bullying**?				
9	Do you get **noticed** when you do the **right thing?**				
10	Do you think that students are **disciplined** fairly when they break the school rules?				
11	Do you feel safe **out of school time**?				

What are some things that make this a safe and friendly school (*e.g., safe places to play, teachers on duty, or someone at school to talk to)?*

What would make this school more safe and friendly? (*e.g. more lunchtime activities, duty teachers, different play areas for different year levels*)

APPENDIX D: SAFE AND FRIENDLY SCHOOL STAFF AND PARENT SURVEY

School: [   ]   **Parent** [ ]   **Staff** [ ]

Tick the answer that best describes your view of the school.	*All of the time*	*Nearly all of the time*	*Sometimes*	*Not at all*
1 Do you **feel safe** at this school?				
2 Do you think the this school **communicate** well with the school community?				
3 Do you feel the school rules are **fair**?				
4 Do you think this school would respond well if you had a **concern**?				
5 Do you think this school considers the wishes of the school community in **decision-making**?				
6 To what extent do you think the school **curriculum** is relevant to the students?				
7 Do you think **bullying** goes on in this school?				
8 Do you think this school **deals well with bullying incidents**?				
9 Do you think students get **recognition** for positive behavior?				
10 Do you think that students are **disciplined** fairly when they break the school rules?				
11 Do you think this school encourages **student participation** in a range of school activities?				
12 Do you think this school encourages good **communication** between students and staff?				

What are some things that make this a safe and friendly school?

What would make this school more safe and friendly?

REFERENCES

Bernhardt, V. L. (1999). *The school portfolio: A comprehensive framework for school improvement.* Larchmont: NY: Eye On Education.

Commonwealth of Australia. (2000). *Mind matters.* Melbourne, Victoria: Commonwealth Department of Health and Aged Care Mental Health Branch.

Commonwealth Department of Health and Aged Care. (2000a). *National action plan for promotion, prevention and early intervention for mental health 2000.* Canberra: Mental Health and Special Programs Branch, Commonwealth Department of Health and Aged Care.

Commonwealth Department of Health and Aged Care. (2000b). *Promotion, prevention and early intervention for mental health—A monograph.* Canberra: Mental Health and Special Programs branch, Commonwealth Department of Health and Aged Care.

Conference of Education Systems Chief Executive Officers. (2000). *Racism no way.* Available: http://www.racismnoway.com.au/together/school-education/index

Curriculum Council. (1999). *Curriculum framework for kindergarten to year 12 education in Western Australia.* Osborne Park, Western Australia: Curriculum Council.

Department of Education. (2001). *The student's at educational risk's pathways to health and wellbeing in schools: Focus paper.* Perth, Western Australia: Author.

Dwyer, K., & Osher, D. (2000). *Safeguarding our children: An action guide.* Washington, DC: U.S. Departments of Education and Justice, American Institutes for Research.

Farrell, P. (2004). School psychologists making inclusion a reality for all. *School Psychology International, 25,* 5–18.

Furlong, M., Morrison, R., & Clontz, D. (1993). Planning principles for safe schools. School safety violence prevention: School's newest challenge. *National School Safety Centre News Journal,* 23–27.

Griffiths, C. (Ed.). (2001). *Countering bullying in schools training package.* Perth, Western Australia: Education Department of Western Australia.

Griffiths, C., & Hansen, M. (2001). Friendship classes: Becoming a "No Put Downs" class. In C. Griffiths (Ed.), *Countering bullying in schools: Training package* (pp. 16–18). Perth: WA: Education Department of Western Australia.

Griffiths, C., & Weatherilt. T. (2001). *Safe School, Friendly School: A Framework for Developing Safe and Friendly Schools.* Perth, WA: Education Department of Western Australia.

Marshall, D. J., & Watt, P. (1999). *Child behaviour problems: A literature review of its size and nature and prevention interventions in childhood.* Perth, Western Australia: The Interagency Committee on Children's Futures.

Ministerial Council on Education, Employment, Training and Youth Affairs. (2003). *National safe schools framework.* Carlton South, Victoria: Curriculum Corporation.

National Committee on Violence. (1990). *Violence: Directions for Australia.* Canberra: Australian Institute of Criminology.

National Crime Prevention. (1999). *Pathways to prevention: Developmental and early intervention approaches to crime in Australia.* Canberra: National Crime Prevention, Attorney General's Department.

National Safety Centre. (1990). *School Safety Check Book.* Malibu, CA: Pepperdine University Press.

Northern Territory. (2004) *Building relationships and school well-being.* Darwin, Northern Territories: Department of Employment, Education and Training.

Pikas, A. (2002). New developments of the Shared Concern Method. *School Psychology International, 23,* 307–326.

Prescott, K. (Ed.). (1995). *Teaching prosocial behavior to adolescents: A directory of processes and programs used in Australian schools.* Adelaide, South Australia: Australian Guidance and Counselling Association.

Rapp, J. A., Carrington, F., & Nicholson, G. (1992). *School crime & violence: Victim's rights (Revised).* Malibu, CA: Pepperdine University Press, National Safety Centre.

Swan Education District. (2000). *Making things work for boys in schools.* Perth: WA: Education Department of Western Australia.

The United Nations. (1989). *The United Nations convention on the rights of the child, Article 12.* Available: http://www.untreaty.un.org, Treaty Event 2001: United Nations.

UNICEF (1989). *The United Nations convention on the rights of the child.* Available: http://www.unicef.org/crc/crc.htm, Education Article 28, 29,31.

Zubrick, S. R., Silburn, S. R., Gurrin, L., Teoh, H., Shepherd, C., Carhon, J., & Lawrence, D. (1997). *Western Australian Child Health Survey: Education, health and competence.* Perth, Western Australia: Australian Bureau of Statistic and the TVW Telethon Institute for Child Health Research.

31

A National Study of School Violence in Israel: Implications for Theory, Practice, and Policy

Rami Benbenishty
Hebrew University

Ron Avi Astor
University of Southern California

Roxana Marachi
California State University Northridge

This chapter presents results from a national study of school violence conducted by the first two authors. The study has many implications for research and policymaking in the area of school violence. Our aim is to review research on school violence in Israel while explicating its relevance to theory, practice, and policy. The chapter addresses the following topics: (a) the impact of conducting a series of comprehensive and representative national studies devoted to school violence, (b) the implications of the interplay between methodology and theoretical framework, and (c) how the empirical findings had implications for policy and practice.

The scope of this ongoing study is unique because it reflects a comprehensive and nationally representative profile of school violence. The research design includes systematic collection of multiple layers of socioecological data relevant to school victimization. Methodologically, this is among the few comprehensive studies conducted at a national level that focuses exclusively on the topic of school victimization. This study is the only nested nationally representative research conducted on any non-European or non-Anglo country. The nested sample and design allows us to examine a rather complex and comprehensive set of theoretical questions. The study posits that school victimization is a very broad concept and encompasses many forms of harm, including but not limited to victimization, verbal and physical harm, threats, sexual harassment, and weapon-related threatening and violent behaviors. Our study design could be a model for other countries that are in the process of addressing school violence.

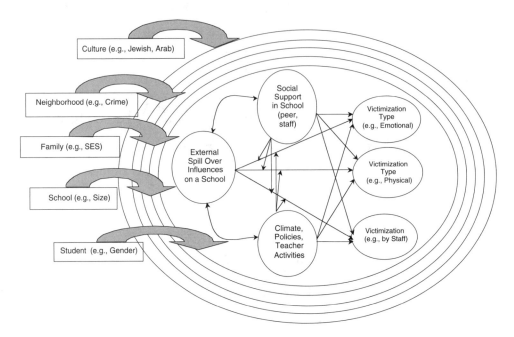

FIG. 31.1.   A model of socioecological influences on student victimization.

The sample in the National Study of School Violence in Israel is stratified by culture (e.g., Arab, Jewish, religious/nonreligious), school type (elementary, junior high, high school), and grade level (4–11). Four waves of data collection were completed, with approximately 70,000 students and samples of their teachers and principals. The students were surveyed with a very detailed questionnaire exclusively devoted to school safety issues. The teachers and principals in the same schools were also surveyed with comparable instruments. Using national databases on schools, neighborhoods, and police records, we assembled aggregated descriptors of the schools, the students' families, and neighborhoods surrounding the schools.

Victimization was also explored as embedded within socioecologically nested contexts. Figure 31.1 represents the influence of the nested contexts on school victimization. It also shows that schools can mediate those effects and generate their own cultures independent but influenced by those contexts. In other words, a major focus of the study was to examine how the rates and structures of victimization experienced by students are influenced by their culture (e.g., ethnicity, religiosity), the school–neighborhood characteristics (e.g., crime, poverty), their family characteristics (e.g., education), the school organization (e.g., school type, size) and climate (e.g., teachers support), and the student's characteristics (e.g., gender and age). These influences may be cumulative. However, they may also interact with each other to influence levels and structures of victimization. The model posits that there are within-school context variables that may mediate and buffer the influences of aspects such as neighborhood and family. Hence, for instance, consistent and appropriate school policies regarding violence may mediate the influences of a violent neighborhood.

This study has many political and social implications for Israel as it attempts to deal with issues of school violence. Thus, this chapter is aimed at providing the reader with a sense of how the study was situated historically, what social conditions helped bring it to fruition, its political outcomes, its design, some major findings, and implications for future studies.

BACKGROUND: HISTORY, SOCIAL CONDITIONS, AND CULTURAL CONTEXT

A study of this complexity does not occur without detailed planning. Many social conditions needed to be in place before the political climate would support such a study. Based on our observations of national school violence policies in different countries over a 20-year period, we believe that the patterns described in Israel are similar to those in other countries that have embarked on systemic school violence programs/studies (e.g., Norway, Sweden, England, New Zealand, and Japan). Given the importance of social and political timing, it is important that the readers have a sense of how the study came to exist.

Within Israel, there has been a longstanding national interest in dealing with youth and school violence. Various aspects of school violence were topics of research in Israeli academia for more than 30 years (e.g., Horowitz & Amir, 1981). Still, until the late 1990s, many Israelis did not believe that school violence was a serious national problem. Discussions in the Israeli mass media commonly conveyed the notion that Israeli schools were much safer than their European or U.S. counterparts. Public sentiment was that any national interest in school violence was conjured up mainly by occasional distorted media coverage on sensational cases. Until the late 1990s, there was no nationally representative data to help define the problem. During this period, whenever a tragic violent event occurred in schools, the Ministry of Education would rely mainly on police youth crime statistics as estimates of school violence (this is common practice in many countries). Thus, Knesset (Israeli Parliament) members, municipal policymakers, and school safety advocates really had no direct estimate of what kinds of school violence problems Israel was facing and subsequently what interventions or laws would work best to address the problems.

This situation persisted with waxing and waning public interest from the late 1970s to the mid- to late 1990s when a series of national and international events co-occurred that impacted the momentum around the issue of school violence in Israeli society. First, and perhaps most importantly, the Israeli mass media began reporting more frequently and more intensely on an array of interpersonal forms of violence including family violence, sexual harassment, child abuse, gangs, and sexual abuse/incest. This process is very similar to the role the media played in raising awareness of these issues in some Western countries a few decades earlier (see Herda-Rapp, 2003; Olweus, 1993; Smith, 2003; Smith et al., 1999, for the role of the media on bullying issues in the United States, Europe, Japan, Australia, and other countries). The intense coverage of these forms of interpersonal violence raised public awareness and created political pressure to deal with this perceived problem.

The second important event that occurred involved a World Health Organization (WHO)-sponsored international health behavior survey in school-aged children that included a handful of youth violence questions. In 1994, Israel participated in this survey (Harel, Kenny, & Rahav, 1997). Released in 1997, the results were quite shocking to the Israeli public. The findings showed that Israel had a measurable youth and school violence problem that was comparable or higher in some respects than many other industrialized countries. The amplified coverage of results created a national environment where school violence issues were talked about by many sectors of Israeli society. There also appeared to be consensus that school violence was indeed a problem that needed to be addressed.

Unfortunately, because of the parameters imposed by the WHO survey, there were only five questions related to youth violence. Moreover, the questions on "youth violence" were not worded directly to highlight the context of the school. Hence, the violence reported could have occurred outside the jurisdiction of the school. Furthermore, the study did not examine primary schools and Arab students were not included. This frustrated many in the Ministry of Education because they could not answer direct questions related to the national school system and issues of school violence. Furthermore, they had limited data on specific school variables that were associated with school victimization.

Then, in the midst of this kind of political atmosphere, several violent events occurred that mobilized the public and politicians to act. In 1998, a series of attempted murders (with knives) on school grounds took place in Israel. These acts coincided with unprecedented intense international media on the rash of school shootings in the United States. These events, along with the international concern in many countries, elevated school safety to the top concern in the Israeli Ministry of Education (as it did in the United States and in many countries in Europe). Along with other academicians from Israel, Ron Astor, who was a visiting scholar at Hebrew University, was invited to the Knesset subcommittee on education to propose next steps in the effort to stem school violence. In that meeting, he suggested that Israel take the international lead in creating a comprehensive national monitoring system that included surveys of students, teachers, and principals. The committee was very receptive to this idea. The model he proposed was very similar to the design of the final study that is described later in this chapter.

Finally, in our opinion, the last important factor that moved Israel to address this issue was a very supportive Minister of Education, Yitzchak Levy, who earlier in his career was a school principal. His wife was a social worker who was professionally trained to deal with violence issues. This personal background with schools and violence was often mentioned as a motivation to press the issue forward. He made it very clear that dealing with school violence from a scientific and accurate national monitoring perspective was his top priority. He was also resolute that he wanted a national monitoring system developed quickly.

During the spring of 1998, the Ministry of Education put out a call for a national study of school violence. Benbenishty, Zeira, Haj-Yahia, and Astor developed a proposal that combined epidemiological aspects to estimate levels of various types of school violence, theoretical questions stemming from an ecological framework of school violence (Benbenishty & Astor, 2005) and the infrastructure for a national monitoring system. The proposal was accepted and four large waves of national studies devoted entirely to school violence have been conducted since then.

ISRAELI NATIONAL STUDY OF SCHOOL VIOLENCE

This chapter is based on an ongoing study that consists of a series of waves of data collection. The first wave was conducted in the fall of 1998 and the last one was conducted winter 2005. Each of these waves utilized similar methodology and instruments. The following sections include a description of the methods and instruments used in these studies. Readers interested in more detail are referred to a recent book (Benbenishty & Astor, 2005).

Method

Sample and Design

Students were given a structured, anonymous questionnaire in classrooms under the guidance of professional monitors. The samples were designed to represent all students in Grades 4–11 in the official public school system supervised by the Israeli Ministry of Education. The probability sampling method was a two-stage stratified cluster sample. In 1998 and 1999 the strata were Jewish/Arab, and primary/junior high/high school. In 2002, a subsample of Bedouin students was added to the study. In the first stage, schools were selected randomly from the sampling frame according to their appropriate strata. The response rate among schools was about 91%, and the response level among the students in these schools was about 95%. In the

TABLE 31.1
Sample Sizes of Three Waves of the National Study of School Violence

Year	Schools	Students	Principals	Homeroom Teachers
1998	232	15,916	—	—
1999	239	16,414	197	1,506
2002	410	21,577	295	595
2005	526	27,316	440	1,861

second stage of sampling, one class was randomly selected from each of the grade levels in the selected schools (in 2002, two classes from two different grade levels were sampled randomly from each school).

The principals of these schools were included in the studies conducted in 1999 and 2002. The response rate among principals was about 85% in 1999 and 66% in 2002. In 1999, all homeroom teachers were sampled in the relevant grade levels (response rate of approximately 60%). In 2002, only the homeroom teachers of the classes participated (response rate of approximately 68%). Table 31.1 shows details of the 4 waves conducted to date.

Instruments

Students. The questionnaires used are an adaptation of the research version of the California School Climate and Safety Survey (Furlong, 1996; Furlong, Morrison, Bates, & Chung, 1998; Rosenblatt & Furlong, 1997; for a recent short form see Furlong et al., 2005). The survey was modified to the Israeli context and to address issues of interest to the researchers. Questionnaires were developed in Hebrew and Arabic, with a shorter version for primary school students and a longer one for secondary school. Changes were made following each of the studies to respond to new needs and issues raised by previous findings. In each of the data collection waves, the research instrument contained more than 100 questions pertaining to several areas: (a) personal victimization by peers, (b) weapons in school, (c) personal victimization by staff, (d) risky peer and staff behaviors in school, (e) feelings and assessments regarding school violence, and (f) school climate.

Principals. The principals' questionnaire was designed specifically for this study and included the following sections: (a) school policies and coping with violence, (b) school climate relevant to violence, (c) report on violent acts in the last month and assessment of the seriousness of the problem, (d) interventions and projects implemented to deal with school violence in the last 2 years, (e) training needs, (f) relationships with and support from others in the school (e.g., PTA) and out of the school (e.g., the police, the central district office), and (h) background information on the school and its staff (such as turnover rates).

Teachers. The teachers responded to a questionnaire that was very similar to the one used with the principals. The questionnaire also included a section on the teachers' feelings and behaviors regarding personal safety in the school.

School Context Information. Several information sources were included to gather data on various aspects of the school and community contexts:

1. Ministry of Education school database: This database provided aggregated information on school characteristics such as number of classes and number of students. It also provided aggregated data on the families of the students, such as percentages of low-income families, low education (less than 8 years of school), family size, and an aggregated socioeconomic status score for the students' families.
2. Census information: Data were extracted for each school's census tracts, including a range of school neighborhood characteristics such as income, education, employment, family size, ethnic/religious heterogeneity, and heterogeneity in terms of new immigrants versus native Israelis.
3. Police data: The police database was used to obtain rates and types of crimes in the school's neighborhood.

ONGOING "MONITORING" VERSUS TRADITIONAL "ONE-TIME" RESEARCH STUDIES

This study is different than many other studies on school violence because it assumes that violence trends have the potential for continual change over time and need to be monitored on a regular basis. It assumes that these changes need to be measured at the site, district, city, state, and national levels. Many studies focus on a single historical time frame and generalize their conclusions over time. The concept of monitoring assumes that research should function much like a social feedback system that continually responds to current needs in an ongoing manner. Monitoring is very similar to the pubic health concept of "surveillance" used by the Centers for Disease Control Prevention. In the United States, the Youth Risk Behavior Survey and Monitoring the Future are examples of such efforts at the national level. Hence, these studies should be considered as a national "snapshot" that should be taken regularly in order to assess and understand change. These kinds of national studies are seen as a source of empirical findings to inform policy and practice. However, these national studies do not inform policy at the local, school site level.

In the current study, Israel is committed to conduct national studies of school violence every 2 to 3 years. Moreover, the ongoing national-level monitoring of school violence is also translated into monitoring at the district and school site levels. This chapter details how the ideas of monitoring can have a major impact on the ways schools and districts address issues of school violence. A national-level monitoring system seems to be an important impetus for creating local monitoring systems that can utilize the national-level instruments and methods and can compare local findings with national ones.

THE IMPLICATIONS OF CONDUCTING A NATIONAL STUDY OF SCHOOL VIOLENCE: CREATING COMMON GROUNDS FOR ESTABLISHING PRIORITIES

When examining the implications and the impact of a study, there is often a focus on its effects on policy, practice, and training. Indeed, as shown later, the findings of this study had such implications. However, it is important to point out that the Israeli National Study of School Violence had a valuable impact on Israeli society and the educational system because it was conducted. The financial investment made by the Ministry of Education was nontrivial. Furthermore, the superintendent of Israeli schools, the minister of education, the chief scientist office, and all regional supervisors made a strong commitment to the study and worked hard to ensure high levels of involvement by all in the educational establishment. These central government efforts sent a very strong signal to the educational system that collecting accurate information to address school violence is a priority. Over time, the Ministry developed means of examining the findings and creating forums to discuss their implications. So, in some ways, the decision to actually collect comprehensive data for the purposes of dealing with these problems started a chain reaction that lead to more substantive changes. As our findings clearly show, the awareness and prevention activities within schools increased dramatically.

Empirical Findings as a Basis for Public and Professional Discourse

In the years since 1998, the findings of the studies have provided a very detailed picture of school violence in Israel. The country now has data on a large number of behaviors in detail for many cultural groups and subgroups, across gender, age, and school types. In our interactions with educators from all levels, we have noted a strong shift from a dynamic of debating personal theories, hunches, and case "examples" to examining representative figures and findings. The focus on the data was also clearly evident in the media. Invariably, when an extremely violent act was reported in the media, it became customary for media outlets to approach Rami Benbenishty (who resides in Israel) and interview him with regard to that event. Rami and others infused into the pubic discussion nationally representative research findings that gave the public an accurate scope of the problem. This limited overgeneralizations made from single cases that were presented in the media. Among the many examples of the impact of having relevant national findings, two studies are illustrated.

Situating the Problem of Students Harming Teachers

Teachers were asked about their feelings of personal safety in school and to what extent students and parents victimized them. Overall, the findings from 1998 indicated that very few of the teachers were physically attacked (many more were verbally abused) and only a very small percentage indicated that they felt unsafe in school. These percentages were even lower in the 2002 study. Nevertheless, within the 1998–2002 time frame, the media started reporting a series of stories about students who physically attacked and injured teachers. It is possible that this trend had to do more with a media campaign of the teachers' union arguing that teachers were not valued (and compensated) enough, than with a real rush of physical victimization of teachers. Although improving teacher compensation is an important goal, the erroneous portrayal of large numbers of students beating up teachers across the country contributed to the unwarranted "demonization" of youth. These kinds of media blitzes helped create public hysteria surrounding the lack of moral values in youth. The data obtained from many teachers in the present study indicated a different picture than what the teacher union presented. During this period, the researchers made a focused effort to encourage public discussion of the findings obtained from the teachers themselves (rather than a media campaign). The data and discourse provided an objective source for the public to understand the scope of the problem, the grades most heavily impacted, which ethnic and religious groups' teachers were most victimized, and the extent of the teacher–student problem when juxtaposed with other more pressing issues of school violence. These discussions helped to provide the public with a more cogent and data-driven understanding of what was needed to support teachers. As a result of these discussions, laws were changed to mandate teacher training on teacher–child violence issues.

Situating the Scope of the Problem and Its Increase or Decrease

Another important illustration of the growing role of empirical findings in the public and professional discourse is the issue of change over time. The heightened awareness to school violence fueled at least partially by our findings in the first waves of the national study, increased the sensitivity to school violence incidents. Hence, when educators and the general public were asked in newspapers polls whether school violence was on the rise, for most the answer was clear: "Yes, and without a doubt." This was also the researchers' experience in many public forums. The general public's perception of an increase in school violence rates was likely due to the increased media reporting of violent events. This dynamic of media influence on public opinion (despite declines in actual rates of violence) is true as well for many countries across the world.

In this context, the empirical findings had a very important role in the public debate. The way to counter the public intuition that violence was on a steep rise, was to continuously present data showing that for most forms of violence there was a marked decrease in student peer victimization. The present research was able to show that the adult populations' subjective views were not "in sync" with the perceptions of youth that attend schools. Most students reported that violence in their schools dropped when compared to prior years. These findings were used extensively in internal discussions in the Ministry of Education and were also brought to all public discussions of school violence, including in the Knesset.

Gathering Information on Staff-Initiated Violence in the Study of School Violence

The Israel National Study of School Violence is the first to integrate staff-initiated violence and peer violence in school. The fact that staff maltreatment of students was included in the surveys had an immediate impact on the Israeli education system. Most discussions of this topic were an immediate "gut response" to well-publicized cases of staff perpetrating extreme physical violence against students, such as a teacher who pulled on the student's ear so hard it was dislodged. For many years, the Israeli National Council for the Child consistently pursued legal and administrative means against teachers who committed serious offenses against children. This advocacy group focused on numerous cases in which, despite being charged and often convicted (mainly in administrative-discipline courts), teachers continued to teach either in the same school or were reinstated in another school. Still, the general public and the general establishment saw this issue as quite marginal. We believe that the approach to teacher–student violence changed once it was made part of a national study and many thousands of students were asked to report whether any staff member maltreated them either emotionally, physically, or sexually in the previous month. The Ministry of Education and the Teacher Union could no longer relate to it as a marginal issue. It changed the perspective and focused on the student's experience and feeling safe both from peer and from staff violence.

The findings of our study made even stronger contributions to bringing this issue to the public eye. Clearly, staff-initiated victimization of students is not a marginal problem experienced by a negligible proportion of students. As reported elsewhere (Benbenishty, Zeira, & Astor, 2002; Benbenishty, Zeira, Astor, & Khoury-Kassabri, 2002), students perceived to be verbally and emotionally maltreated in significant proportions. For instance, one out of four students (27.9%) reported that during the previous month a teacher mocked, insulted, or humiliated him or her, 16.5% reported that a teacher called them "bad names," and 9.7% said that a teacher cursed them. Physical violence was reported less frequently. However, there was disproportional reporting of physical violence by Arab and Bedouin students. For instance, whereas 3% of the Jewish students reported that a staff member kicked or punched them, the percentage among Arab students was 14%. Similarly, 21.3% of Arab students reported being pinched by a staff member compared with 5.6% of Jewish students. Furthermore, our findings indicate that staff physical violence was more prevalent in poor neighborhoods, even when ethnic affiliation was controlled (Benbenishty, Zeira, Astor, & Khoury-Kassabri, 2002).

Our findings on staff-initiated violence raised many theoretical and practical issues. From a theoretical point of view, it became clear that there are several alternative mechanisms that can explain our findings. One explanation is that the teachers do not have the training to handle disruptive students in the class or that they cannot handle a large number of students acting out in a class. Another possibility is that they have the skills, however, they act out of frustration and anger. Finally, teachers may make a deliberate choice to use such violent behaviors toward students because the disciplinary methods are considered acceptable and effective. The findings raise the issue of the extent to which violent behaviors of adults against children are culturally acceptable.

One of the areas that should to be explored further is the role of parents in condoning or objecting to these practices at home and at school. There are reports that some parents condone and even encourage teachers to use physical violence to instill discipline and academic excellence in their children (e.g., see Ellinger & Beckham's, 1997 report of the attitudes of South Korean parents). Currently, parents' views toward corporal punishment in school are rarely incorporated or measured in research or practice on school violence. These issues should be explored and integrated into a larger theoretical and practice framework of how the context, in terms of norms, values, and acceptable childrearing practices impact teacher–student relations in school.

Following the publications of the national studies (Benbenishty, Zeira, & Astor, 2000), we were invited to several forums that addressed the issue of staff-initiated violence. We took part in a series of Knesset committee meetings that examined this issue and in internal discussions in the Ministry of Education in order to draft new national guidelines. Having nationally representative statistics and findings that connected between these statistics and the characteristics of students and contexts (including ethnic affiliation and socioeconomic factors) was a major factor in the impact on these discussions. When the official guidelines were issued at last (after bitter fights with the Teacher Union), the findings of our study were cited extensively.

We believe that our work should encourage policymakers to include this aspect of school violence in future surveys and policy guidelines that relate to student safety. Staff behaviors have an important impact on students, both positively and negatively. Victimization by staff may impact students even more negatively than peer violence. The work by Hyman and colleagues attest to the potential harm that educators can cause (e.g., Hyman, 1990; Hyman & Perone, 1998; Hyman & Snook, 2000). Our study should also encourage scholars of school violence to integrate this type of victimization in comprehensive models of school violence that will include peer violence and the cultural and ideological context in which the school is embedded.

Focusing on the Meanings and Interpretations of Multiple Perspectives: Students, Homeroom Teachers, and Principals

Most school violence studies focus on students, and only a few school violence researchers study teachers and principals. The Israeli studies described here are among the few school violence studies that include multiple respondents (students, teachers, and principals) from the same schools. There are several compelling reasons to include teachers and principals in school violence studies. First, teachers and principals are important actors in the school and their experiences, perceptions, and needs are extremely relevant to understanding how the school community experiences and addresses school violence, and what would be needed to prevent and reduce violence. Two examples from the teachers and principal sections of the study illustrate this point.

Teachers were asked about training in the area of school safety. Their responses were very informative and alarming. Less than one quarter of the homeroom teachers said they had any relevant training during their studies in college or university, only about a one third felt the training was helpful, two thirds said they did not participate in any in-service training on how to deal with school violence, and more than one fourth said they were in need of training. These findings have clear policy and training implications. In fact, some teacher colleges developed training material to respond to this expressed need.

A second example of the importance of hearing the perspective of staff comes from a segment in our survey of principals that focused on their relationships with a series of role partners—parents, support staff, police, supervisors, and the district. In two subsequent waves of data collection the picture was quite clear—principals felt quite alone on the front line of dealing with school safety. They felt that most other partners made very little contribution to their efforts to reduce school violence. The group that was seen as most helpful was the pupil personnel support staff (i.e., counselors and psychologists). Still, only 44% of the principals felt that support staff contributed much or very much to their efforts to reduce school violence and 29% felt they made no contribution or a small one. These findings were communicated to all these role partners through various channels.

In addition to looking separately at each of the multiple perspectives of the members of the school community, the comparisons (similarities or disparities) among them can contribute significantly to research and policy. From a research perspective, the converging or diverging multiple perspectives of school safety in the same school can help validate (or invalidate) the assessments made by each of the members of a particular school community. Although it is expected that students, teachers, and principals would have unique vantage points, it is also likely that there would be similarities between the groups.

In our study, it is impossible to make direct comparisons between students and staff reports of violence. Students report whether they were victimized in the previous month, homeroom teachers report how many times each type of violent behavior occurred in their class, and the principals report on the school as a whole. Nevertheless, one of the interesting findings is that the rank orders of the reports of the three groups are similar. That is, students, homeroom teachers, and principals tend to strongly agree on which violent acts are most frequent and which are the least frequent.

Our findings indicate that the degree of similarity between the three perspectives in the school can reveal how the school is functioning. Large gaps and disagreements between staff and students or between a principal and teachers may indicate that the school does not have a shared mission. For instance, if students assess the school as having a serious violence problem but the teachers and principals do not, one would expect that little will be done to address the students' distress. Thus, exploring the gaps between the multiple perspectives can contribute to our assessment of schools and the identification of schools that show the highest levels of divergence of perspectives.

The findings of all the studies we have conducted suggest that students' subjective evaluations of school safety are more similar to teachers than to principals. Furthermore, the agreement between teachers and students with regard to the level of seriousness of the violence problem in their school was lower for schools with high levels of violence. Thus, in schools that had the lowest level of student victimization, the correlation between teachers and students was $r = 0.75$; this was higher than the second quartile ($r = 0.52$) or the third quartile ($r = 0.48$). In schools that are in the upper quartile (in terms of levels of physical victimization as reported by students), the correlation between students and teachers assessments of the severity of the problem was the lowest ($r = 0.43$).

In contrast, compared to the students, the principals underestimated the seriousness of the problem and the student assessment of the seriousness of the problem. The fact that principals' perspective is quite different than the student perspective may have negative implications for efforts to reduce school violence. Principals may not know accurately what is happening in their schools in terms of violence among students. Coupled with their tendency to underestimate the levels of violence, principals may not act to address issues of school violence. The findings seem to suggest therefore that principals need to become more aware of the students' experiences.

Other Theoretical Implications From Methodological Choices and Study Design

Creating a Focus on the "School" in School Violence

Benbenishty and Astor (2005) argued that even though researchers worldwide have been involved in school violence research, most questions regarding within-school dynamics and their relationships to other social settings such as the family or community have not been explored empirically. Researchers still do not know to what extent and in what ways the school, community, or family contribute to violence on school grounds (Benbenishty & Astor, 2005). The interplay between the context and school violence has not been explored in great detail. Consequently, among the questions that have not been addressed adequately by research is whether the same school factors are at play in different cultures or in different school contexts (primary, junior high, and high schools).

As mentioned earlier in the chapter (see Fig. 31.1), the authors developed a heuristic ecological model that presents school violence within nested contexts (Benbenishty & Astor, 2005). In this model, as suggested by Furlong and Morrison (2000), the school is in the center. School victimization is viewed as being related directly to practices within the school itself, as well as being influenced by factors that "spill over" from outside contexts into the school (e.g., culture, neighborhood, and families). The school policies, procedures, climate, and the reactions of staff and peer group influence student victimization directly and indirectly.

This theoretical model led to a methodological choice to include schools as units of analysis—in addition to students at the individual level. Most of the research literature on school violence has neglected this analytical perspective and focused almost exclusively on student-level views of school victimization. In some ways this is surprising because most of the school safety intervention literature focuses on school-level programs. In order to understand the dynamics of school victimization, assess the need for schoolwide interventions, and examine the outcomes of such programs, it seemed essential to explore victimization from a school unit perspective.

The choice to have the school as a unit of analysis was reflected in (a) the sampling of a large number of schools, each with a large enough number of students to allow reasonable school level estimates; (b) instruments and data collection that included school-level information (e.g., school size, the socioeconomic status of the school neighborhood); and (c) an analytic plan that included multilevel statistical analyses (hierarchical linear modeling; Bryk & Raudenbush, 1992).

This central methodological choice had many implications. First and foremost, it allowed us to explore a comprehensive ecological model that examines how school violence relates to both within- and outside-school contexts. The large sample of schools allowed us to examine the relationships between a series of school context variables and to assess their contribution to levels of school violence, and at the same time to ask how within-school factors, such as school climate, are associated with school violence.

Using schools as a unit of analysis also allows examination of the distribution of school violence for *schools* (rather than for individual students). To illustrate, an intriguing empirical question is whether the distribution of violence in schools follows a normal distribution, in which a few schools have high levels of violence and a few schools have low levels of violence, and the rest are somewhere in the mid range, or perhaps the distribution is skewed and there are a small number of schools that have very high or very low levels of violence that make them stand out as extremes. This issue has implications for policy and practice. Let us assume that 5% of the students report that another student extorted them. From a policy perspective, there is a major difference between the following two situations: (a) most schools have about 5% of the students reporting extortion or (b) in most schools, there are no students reporting extortion and only in a very few schools the levels of extortion are much higher.

To study the form of the distribution we examined (a) a dispersion index that indicates how heterogeneous schools are in terms of their level of violence; and (b) skewness of the distribution, which tells us whether the distribution is normal, or skewed in one direction. A high and positive sign of the skewness index means that there are few schools in which the levels of violence are exceptionally high, and a negative sign indicates that a few schools have very low rates of violence. On examination of this dispersion index, it was found that victimization types that were reported more frequently by the students have a lower dispersion index than victimization types that are less frequent and more severe. The behaviors that showed more variation (the highest dispersion index) were also the rarest. In other words, schools tend to be more similar to each other with regard to the less severe victimization types but differ much more from each other when it comes to the more severe behaviors.

When the skewness of the distribution was examined, a positive skew was found for more severe types of violence—there are few schools with very high levels of severe violence. In about one quarter of the schools, there were no reports of a student cutting another student with a knife or a sharp object, half of the schools had less than 5% of the students making this report, and in more than 80% of the schools the prevalence of this behavior was less than 10%. However, in 5% of the schools, 20% or more of the students reported being cut with a knife or a sharp object, and in 1% of the schools more than one out of four students reported being cut by knife or a sharp object.

From a policy perspective, this pattern strongly suggests that efforts to stem extreme and rare types of violence should be directed to a select few schools, rather than spread thin across many schools. This recommendation implies that levels of school violence be assessed in schools and schools be treated differentially, based on their profile in terms of levels and types of victimization that students experience. The sample design allowed us to explore the characteristics of these schools and recommend targeted interventions that may not be relevant nationwide.

Different Forms of Victimization Needing Unique Explanations and Strategies

Many studies of school violence focus exclusively on bullying behaviors (e.g., Nansel et al., 2001). The Israeli study incorporates a more expansive definition of violence in schools to account for a much wider range of types of school victimization, including verbal violence, exclusion, verbal threats, physical violence (ranging from minor pushing and shoving to needing medical attention due to injuries in a fight), sexual harassment, and staff-initiated emotional, physical and sexual maltreatment. Primary school students reported on their experiences with 25 to 30 different types of victimization and secondary school students reported on 35 to 40 (depending on the data-collection wave). The choice of behaviors to assess had many implications. First, the students' reports of such a wide range of victimization types provided a very rich and detailed picture of what it means to be a student in an Israeli school, and how these experiences differ depending on one's gender, attendance in a religious school, whether one is a Jew, an Arab, or a Bedouin student, or whether one is a primary school or high school student.

When the various types of victimization were examined as they occurred together, we focused on questions surrounding the structure of the different types of victimization (i.e., the relationships among the many victimization types) and how similar or different these structures are among the various groups (culture, age, and gender). This line of inquiry yielded many helpful insights that are discussed in detail elsewhere (Benbenishty & Astor, 2005). This chapter provides two brief illustrations.

Rank Ordering of Different Types of Violence That Occur on School Grounds

Focusing on peer-initiated victimization, we asked, whether all groups experience the same types of victimization in the same order to each other. That is, are certain victimization types consistently more frequent than others, and whether this pattern holds true across school types, cultures, countries, gender, and age? We found that there were significant differences between males and females, Jews and Arabs, and students in primary, junior high, and high school in the base frequency of many of the victimization types. However, although groups differed in their levels of victimization, the order of frequency patterns with types of victimizations appeared to be almost identical. That is, the behaviors that were most frequent for one group were also the most frequent for all other groups. Similarly, certain types of victimization have the lowest frequency in all groups.

When examining the rank order of the frequency of these victimization types in all groups, the patterns were almost identical. In fact, the rank-order correlations among the various groups were higher than $r = 0.90$. Examination of the rank order reveals that frequency and severity (and potential pain) seem to be interrelated. That is, victimization types that are the most severe and have the potential of causing most pain are also the less frequent ones. Thus, the three most frequent victimization types are: "A student cursed you", "A student mocked, insulted, or humiliated you", and "A student seized and shoved you on purpose." The four least frequent victimization types reported by the students were: "Went to doctor or nurse because you were hurt in attack or fight"; "Cut with knife or something sharp by someone trying to hurt you", "Threatened by student with knife and saw the knife", and "Threatened by gun and saw the gun."

With such a strong ordering of behaviors, any "stand out" behavior most likely reflects cultural variations. Thus, in this quite consistent picture, one type of victimization stood out— "Being socially isolated/excluded, by a group of students." This behavior had a higher ranking among female and Arab students, which may serve as an indication that the behavior has a special meaning in certain contexts and cultures. Research on aggression and gender suggests that girls may experience more of these kinds of socially isolating activities than boys (see review in Salmivalli & Kaukiainen, 2004). There is currently no literature that predicts why Arab students would have higher levels of this kind of behavior. This finding has implications for future research exploring the special meaning of this behavior in Arab cultures. These kinds of analyses were made possible because of the large number of behaviors that could be compared with each other across different cultures.

These surprising findings regarding the similarities in rank order among groups in Israel raised the question: Is it possible that the rank order found in Israel will be similar to the rank order in another culture? In order to examine this question, analyses were also conducted on a data set provided by Furlong. The data were collected from about 8,750 students in more than 40 schools in various southern and central counties in California, using a similar instrument. The first issue explored was whether the patterns among boys and girls and Latinos, African American, White/European, Native American, and Asian students in the California sample are similar to each other (see Benbenishty & Astor, 2005, for detailed examples of the cross-cultural comparisions).

We found that the patterns were very similar across the U.S. groups, as well. The most common behaviors were most frequent among boys and girls, Latinos and non-Latinos, and the least common ones had very low frequencies among all groups. Still, as with the prior example on Arab students, certain behaviors deviated from the ranking patterns. Sexual victimization was a much more salient experience for female students[1]. The frequency of sexual harassment was ranked 6th for girls and 14th for boys, and frequency of unwanted physical sexual advances was ranked 10th for girls and 15th for boys. Additionally, for boys, the frequency of being punched and kicked was rank ordered higher than for girls. The patterns of reports made by the different U.S. ethnic groups were very similar. The only difference was that unwanted physical sexual advances were ranked higher by Latino groups.

Given that the California data showed consistent patterns across groups in the United States, we examined whether the rank order might be similar across United States and Israel. The findings clearly showed the similarity in ranking patterns across the two countries. Although there were significant differences in the raw frequencies of the various types of victimization, the rank orders were very similar across the two samples. The only noticeable difference was the higher salience of intimidation by staring in the California sample.

Universality and Cultural Specificity of School Violence Behaviors

Current conceptualizations of violence victimization are classified by conceptually driven content-related domains of behavior (e.g., verbal–social, relational, threats, physical, and sexual). It is possible, however, that in real life being a victim to one type of behavior in a domain increases or decreases the probability of being a victim to another type of violent act from this domain. The findings reported here indicate strongly that victimization types may align along the dimension of severity more than along the content-related categories that are more commonly used (e.g., verbal–emotional, threats, and physical violence). In order to examine this issue further, the following question was asked, "How do different forms of victimization associate with one another, or how they are grouped together in real life?"

We examined this issue from several vantage points. First, victimization types were grouped by their conceptual meaning (e.g., verbal–emotional, threats, and physical violence) and then examined according to how victimization behaviors were associated with gender, age, and cultural/ethnic affiliation. The intent was to determine whether behaviors that were seen as belonging to the same conceptually driven group of behavior actually showed similar patterns of relations.

This initial set of analyses strongly indicated that verbal–emotional types of victimization (e.g., "A student cursed me" or "I was insulted and humiliated by another student") were associated with gender, age, and ethnic/cultural group affiliation very differently than the other two groups of behaviors examined—threats and physical violence. On the other hand, systematic differences did not emerge regarding how threats and physical violence were "behaving" in relation to factors such as gender and age.

In the next step, factor analyses were conducted on all peer-initiated victimization types (not including sexual harassment). These analyses were carried out for the sample as a whole and for each of the 18 groups formed by the intersection of gender (male, female), school type (primary, junior high, and high school) and cultural group (Jewish secular, Jewish religious, and Arabs). The findings indicate that there is a clear tendency for school victimization to be grouped along the dimension of the frequency of the behavior—victimization types that are not frequent belong to one factor, whereas items with higher frequencies are associated with

---

[1]The Israeli study did not include sexual harassment behaviors in these analyses because they belonged to a separate scale.

the second factor. Given that this dimension of frequency is almost identical to the dimension of severity and potential harm, it is evident that being victimized by one type of a moderately violent behavior, such as pushing and shoving, comes together with being victimized by other types of moderate/less severe violent behaviors, such as being threatened. Being victimized by more severe behaviors, such as being cut with a sharp object, comes together with being victimized by other behaviors that reflect more severe consequences, such as being injured in a fight and needing medical attention.

One of the possible theoretical implications of this set of findings regarding the structure of victimization in school is that severity (and possibly pain or potential harm) seems to serve as an organizing mechanism across cultures. Culture seems to have its greatest influence on the frequency of victimization and not necessarily on the way different acts of victimization are experienced. Here, severity and frequency seem to go hand in hand and are more universal.

We think that the fact that culture may not have a huge impact on the ordering of victimization levels or on the grouping of victimization types may have great theoretical implication to fields such as anthropology, psychology, social work, education, public health, and medicine. First, it means that the experiences of violence within each culture are probably hierarchically organized in similar ways according to severity (frequency and severity are two sides of the same coin and cannot be separated). Societal norms do not impact the relative hierarchy within or between cultures but the actual frequency rates of each category of behavior, and within prescribed boundaries created by the overarching hierarchy in that society.

Against the backdrop of what seem to be universal dimensions of pain/severity experienced across genders and cultures, variations and deviations acquire special significance and should lead to further exploration. Hence, if the relative frequency (the rank order) of a certain form of victimization is extremely high or extremely low in a certain group, it suggests that this behavior has special meaning for this group. Consider, for instance, the issue of social exclusion that may rank higher or lower in different cultures. In certain cultures it may be perceived as similar to other types of social–verbal victimization and its frequency would be as high as other forms of victimization, such as spreading rumors. In other cultures, social exclusion may be used only

TABLE 31.2
Implications for Practice: Effective Characteristics of National Efforts to Assess
and Prevent School Violence

---

1. Representative stratified sample by school level and major ethnic/social groups
2. Nested designs that include school, family, neighborhood, and cultural data surrounding the school
3. Multiple perspectives of students, teachers, and principals in the same schools
4. Rich, agreed on instruments that include:
    a. a wide array of behaviors and victimization types both by peers and by staff
    b. indicators of school climate, school organization, and peer-group dynamics
    c. information about specific cultures and languages that is relevant and/or responses that are clearly interpretable in specific cultures
    d. questions that are pertinent to policymakers and district-level policy
5. Use a monitoring perspective to conduct studies repeatedly to continuously inform policy and practice
6. Parallel or mix method studies that target both intercultural commonalities and culturally specific aspects of school violence
7. Research geared at solving theoretical problems targeting cultural issues and violence that may not have immediate practical outcomes but build knowledge of how school victimization patterns relate to each other in different societies (this may facilitate both theory and practice)
8. Replication of the design, concepts, theories, and instruments in many cultures can help create an infrastructure for international mutual learning

in extreme cases of hostility, seen as carrying much more meaningful implications, signifying that the victim is being totally cut off and not part of the peer group. Similarly, differences in the relative frequencies of various forms of sexual victimization between genders will help direct attention to the different meanings that these behaviors have for male and female students. Some researchers have also examined various victim subtype patterns in school violence (see Furlong, Sharma, & Rhee, 2000). An exploration of cultural variation and victim subtypes could be a valuable area for further exploration.

CONCLUDING COMMENTS

School violence is a concern of many countries. Some of the characteristics of school violence may be peculiar and unique to a specific cultural and social context, making generalization to other contexts quite tenuous. Nevertheless, there is much to be learned from research conducted on school violence in other countries. The study described in this chapter can be helpful in the design of similar national studies that can provide the empirical basis for ongoing assessment and improvement of school safety. Table 31.2 includes a summary of suggestions of characteristics for future research on the assessment of school violence on a national scale.

REFERENCES

Benbenishty, R., & Astor R. A. (2005). *School violence in context: Culture, neighborhood, family, school, and gender.* New York: Oxford University Press.

Benbenishty, R., Astor, R. A., & Zeira, A. (2003). Monitoring school violence on the site level: Linking national-, district-, and school-level data over time. *Journal of School Violence, 2,* 29–50.

Benbenishty, R., Zeira, A., & Astor, R. A. (2002). Children's reports of emotional, physical and sexual maltreatment by educational staff in Israel. *Child Abuse & Neglect, 26,* 763–782.

Benbenishty, R., Zeira, A., & Astor, R. A. (2000). *A national study of school violence in Israel—Wave II: Fall 1999.* Jerusalem, Israel: Israeli Ministry of Education.

Benbenishty, R., Zeira, A., Astor, R. A., & Khoury-Kassabri, M. (2002). Maltreatment of primary school students by educational staff in Israel. *Child Abuse and Neglect, 26,* 1291–1309.

Bryk, A. S., & Raudenbush, S. W. (1992). *Hierarchical linear models: Applications and data analysis methods.* Newbury, CA: Sage.

Ellinger, R., & Beckham, G. M. (1997). South Korea: Placing education on top of the family agenda. *Phi Delta Kappan, 78,* 624–625.

Furlong, M. J. (1996). Tools for assessing school violence. In S. Miller, J. Bordine, & T. Miller (Eds.), *Safe by design: Planning for peaceful school communities* (pp. 71–84). Seattle, WA: Committee for Children.

Furlong, M. J., Greif, J. L., Bates, M. P., Whipple, A. D., Jimenez, T. C., & Morrison, R. (2005). Development of the California School Climate and Safety Survey–Short Form. *Psychology in the Schools, 42,* 137–150.

Furlong, M. J., & Morrison, G. (2000). The school in school violence: Definitions and facts. *Journal of Emotional and Behavioral Disorders, 8,* 71–82.

Furlong, M. J., Morrison, R., Bates, M., & Chung, A. (1998). School violence victimization among secondary students in California. *The California School Psychologist, 3,* 71–78.

Furlong, M. J., Sharma, B., & Rhee, S. (2000). Defining school violence victim subtypes: A step toward adapting prevention and intervention programs to match student needs In D. Singh & C. B. Aspy (Eds.), *Violence in American schools: A practical guide for counselors* (pp. 67–88). Washington, DC: American Counseling Association.

Harel, Y., Kenny, D., & Rahav, G. (1997). *Youth in Israel: Social welfare, health and risk behaviors from international perspectives.* Jerusalem: Joint Distribution Committee.

Herda-Rapp, A. (2003). The social construction of local school violence threats by the news media and professional organizations. *Sociological Inquiry, 73,* 545–574.

Horowitz, T., & Amir, M. (1981). *Patterns of coping of the educational system with violence.* Jerusalem: Szald Institute.

Hyman, I. A. (1990). *Reading, writing, and the hickory stick: The appalling story of physical and psychological abuse in American schools.* Lexington: Lexington Books.

Hyman, I. A., & Perone, D. C. (1998). The other side of school violence: Educator policies and practices that may contribute to student misbehavior. *Journal of School Psychology, 36,* 7–27.

Hyman, I. A., & Snook, P. A. (2000). Dangerous schools and what you can do about them. *Phi Delta Kappan, 81*, 489–501.

Nansel, T., Overpeck, M., Pilla, R., Ruan, W. J., Simons-Morton, B., & Scheidt, P. (2001). Bullying behaviors among U.S. youth: Prevalence and association with psychosocial adjustment. *Journal of the American Medical Association, 285*, 2094–2100.

Olweus, D. (1993). *Bullying at school*. Oxford, UK: Blackwell.

Rosenblatt, J. A., & Furlong, M. J. (1997). Assessing the reliability and validity of student self-reports of campus violence. *Journal of Youth and Adolescence, 26*, 187–202.

Salmivalli, C., & Kaukiainen, A. (2004). "Female aggression" revisited: Variable and person-centered approaches to studying gender differences in different types of aggression. *Aggressive Behavior, 30*, 158–163.

Smith, P., Morita, Y., Junger-Tas, J., Olweus, D., Catalano, R., & Slee, P. (1999). *The nature of school bullying: A cross-national perspective*. New York: Routledge.

Smith, P. K. (2003). *Violence in schools: The response in Europe*. London: RoutledgeFalmer.

32

School Violence in Brazil: A Psychosocial Perspective

Raquel Souza Lobo Guzzo
Fernando Lacerda, Jr.
Antonio Euzebios Filho
Pontifical Catholic University of Campinas

This chapter discusses school violence within the context of the Brazilian society, one marked by social and economic inequalities and injustices. A discussion of school violence must consider broader issues including the country's social conditions that constitute the breading ground for school violence. Furthermore, an understanding of some important qualities that shape Brazilian social and educational reality also is needed to understand school violence.

CONTEXTUAL CONSIDERATIONS RELATED TO SCHOOL VIOLENCE IN BRAZIL

Brazil's population of nearly 170 million is distributed over its 8.5 million square kilometers, most within 50 miles of the ocean. Brazil is characterized by profound social and regional inequalities. For example, although the 5,000 richest families in Brazil represent 0.001% of Brazilian families, they control 40% of the national gross domestic product. Additionally, among the 34 million people aged 15 through 24, 40% are in extremely poor families with an average per capita income of half minimum wage or about $60 U.S. per month (Abramovay, 2003; IBGE, 2000; Pochmann, Campos, Amorim, & Silva, 2004). These indicators reflect a society structured by significant social and economic differences.

The Brazilian educational system includes public and private schools. The attendance of which differs by social class. Students from lower class families generally attend public schools and those from middle- and high-class families attend private schools. Initially, the majority of Brazilian students attend public schools. However, as their dropout rate is high, the percentage that attends public schools declines. The Brazilian Institute of Geography and Statistics (IBGE, 2000) reported that among 15- and 16-year-old youth, only 53% attend schools, whereas 22% work and study; 8% only work; 7% study and look for a job; and 10% do not study, do not look for a job, and do not work. These youth are considered to be at high risk because, unless they are in school or employed, their needs and dispositions can result in illicit activities and violence.

In Brazil, school violence is increasing and is having diverse and intense impacts on society and individuals (Candau, 2000).

In a national research with a sample of approximately 300,000 participants it was perceived that violence occurs more frequently in public than in private schools, as can be seen in the following rates of school violence. The frequencies of serious and nonserious violence against students, teachers, and employees in public school Grade 4 was 14.5%, whereas in private schools, the rate was 2.40%. At eighth grade, the rate was 24.3% in elementary public schools compared with 2.6% in private schools. The frequencies of serious and nonserious theft and vandalism at schools also showed some differences: 26.4% for Grade 4 in public elementary schools and 7.8% at the same grade level in private schools, and 37.4% at the eighth-grade level in public elementary schools compared with 7.3% in private elementary schools (Codo & Vasques-Menezes, 2001). This type of violence is more common in schools that have a large physical space, are impersonal, and have a great number of students (Batista & El-moor, 1999).

Brazilian schools, as social institutions, have some responsibility for creating and sustaining inequality. As grade levels progress, fewer children attend school (IBGE, 2000). For example, according to the Brazilian Institute of Geography and Statistics (2000), 95% of all 7-year-old children attend the elementary school, 33% of all children attend high school, and 11% attend college. These statistics reflect the increasing social exclusion. Those who are more prepared academically have increased opportunities for better jobs, whereas those who are not prepared have relatively limited opportunities. These conditions intensify social and economic class differences that hold antagonistic views that contribute to violence in society, which spills over to schools.

The Brazilian constitution entitles everyone the right to a public education. The public school system is characterized by high rates of grade retention, early school withdrawal, and low levels of educational attainment. For example, in 2000, the retention rate for elementary and high school was 21%, and the dropout rate was 4.8%. Approximately 41% of students were older than expected for their grade. Among high school students, 19% were retained, 7% dropped out, and 52% were older than expected for their grade (IBGE, 2000). The Brazilian educational system and the inability of its public schools to adequately educate children from lower class homes has resulted in what many believe to be a public school system that ignores student needs and produces an institutionalized context for violence by creating an educational process that fails to promote learning and thus fails to prepare students for life's realities (Freire, 1973, 2000).

This chapter underscores the following: (a) school violence is embedded in the broader occurrence of violence in Brazilian society; (b) violence is a phenomenon that has structural and cultural dimensions (e.g., its roots are in the conditions of their lives, and not inherent in the people themselves); and (c) schools, as social institutions, reflect the violence and contribute to its occurrence (Batista & El-Moor, 1999; Candau, 2000; Martín-Baró, 2000).

Brazil lacks a scholarly tradition that focuses on school violence (Adorno & Cárdia, 2002). Knowledge about school violence is derived mainly from theoretical and method-ological perspectives about violence in general. Abramovay (2003) noted that there are no governmental statistics or national studies that provide a global picture about school vio-lence in Brazil. There are few academic studies. Between 1980 and 1998, graduate pro-grams in education in Brazil produced 8,667 dissertations and thesis, and only 9 of them were related to school violence. Other publications on this issue were produced by private institutes, isolated researchers, and studies conducted by UNESCO (Abramovay, 2003; Spos-ito, 2001). Thus, a scholarly discussion of school violence in Brazil relies on this existing literature.

CONCEPTUAL FOUNDATION FOR UNDERSTANDING
VIOLENCE IN BRAZIL

An understanding of school violence first requires an understanding of the social contexts of public schools in Brazil. Different authors analyzing school violence have highlighted that several social problems are considered to form the genesis of violence: severe economic differences, injustice, impunity from illegal activities, low educational standards, tendentious media, large and impersonal cities, dismantling of states, and a culture of violence. Violence is not linked to the social inequalities in a linear form. Instead, it is thought to rest on a social structure marked by power and dominance that institutionalize and banalizes violence (Batista & El-moor, 1999; Blanco & Ibáñez, 2003; Buoro, Schilling, Singer, & Soares, 1999; Candau, 2000; Gonçalves & Sposito, 2002; Martín-Baró, 2000; Morais, 1998; Nogueira, 2000; Peralva, 2002; Romano, 2002; Santacruz & Portillo, 1999; Sposito, 2001).

Capitalism and Violence

Prevailing social beliefs link capitalism and violence. Capitalism is thought to generate poverty and promote social exclusion throughout much of Latin America. Capitalism maintains social oppression and thus, contributes to violence (Batista & El-moor, 1999; Blanco & Ibáñez, 2003; Martín-Baró, 2000; Morais, 1998; Nogueira, 2000; Romano, 2002; Santacruz & Portillo, 1999). Evidence of a relationship between capitalism and the maintenance of the oppression and violence can be seen in data that examine social exclusion in Brazil (Pochmann & Amorim, 2004; Pochmann et al., 2004). Social exclusion indicators among Brazilians (e.g., family income, parent education levels, and number of homicides among the young) are clearly linked to the country's geography. Social exclusion is highest in the north and northeastern regions. It is significantly lower in its middle-region, and is lowest in the south. A review of data on educational attainment, unemployment rates, dwelling conditions, and family income led to the conclusion that 42% of Brazilian cities that contain 21% of its population live in conditions of exclusion; that is, they lack adequate education or a dignified life by having work, dwellings, and a family income that is below the poverty line. A primary concern is that the social order is violent and marked by the division between the oppressors and the oppressed (Martín-Baró, 2000; Morais, 1998). Albee (1992) extended this statement, as follows:

> Within the exploitative modern society a small elite maintains its authority and control, by manipulating special groups (teachers and professors, for example) who themselves exploit (or justify the exploitation of) workers, women, minorities, and others. The mass media, and particularly television, owned and controlled by the power elite, constantly explain that this is the way things are and must be, and that anyway there are all kinds of ways to have fun through consumption and waste—bread and circuses, cokes and smokes. (p. 325)

Brazil reproduces the same processes just mentioned, occupying a position of dependence related to the developed countries, and presenting the second largest Gini's coefficient in the world (UNDP, 2003). The Gini's coefficient is an international indicator of social inequality that expresses the degree of concentration (inequality) of wealth's distribution in a country. A Gini's coefficient of 0 means perfect equality in the wealth distribution, whereas a 1 means that the wealth is concentrated in one person only (UNDP, 2003). The Brazilian social context is partially characterized by the synthesis presented by Chaui (2000); Brazil ranks third worldwide in the percentage of unemployment, spends more than $33 billion U.S. on private and public security systems, and the inequality of wealth distribution of Brazil's population is accepted and considered natural and normal.

Defining Violence

The concepts of *violence* and *aggression* often are used synonymously. However, the two are different. Aggression is related to physical processes and human instincts, an intentional act to jeopardize another person and is thought to breed a specific form of violence. In contrast, violence has a broader sense and refers to the excessive use of strength against someone or something. Thus, institutional or structural violence describes those types of violence produced inside schools because schools, like other social institutions, can apply intensive power and authority leading to personal changes (Martín-Baró, 2000; Sá, 1999).

Evaluative Dimension of Violence

Violence can be considered positive or negative. The criteria used to define the value attributed to violence in mainstream psychology are to consider if the violent or aggressive act is for or against the established social order. Schools establish rules to create objective and harmonious relationships between students and teachers. In that sense, violence displayed by teachers toward students, while they are disruptive or in the classroom or do not turn in homework, is considered a positive violence. However, the student's reaction to the teacher is likely to be considered negative.

Intentionality of the Aggressive Act

Many different perspectives in psychology ignore the intentionality of an aggressive act. Intentionality should be considered if the aggressive act is violent. In schools, most violent acts are attributed only to the students and without consideration as to their causes.

Psychosocial Meaning of Violent or Aggressive Actions

Violent or aggressive acts often are justified on the basis of ideological reasoning that has impact on the evaluation of the act or on the intentionality of the act's agent.

As discussed previously, violence and aggression have several forms of manifestation and an historical character that creates the need of comprehension of the context where it is inserted. There are four constitutive dimensions of a violent act.

1. *Formal structure of the act.* Every violent act has a specific configuration that defines its character. That configuration can be distinguished between the instrumental and final violent acts. Instrumental violent acts are those that work to achieve an objective. Final violent acts are those directed to the person without aiming to achieve a secondary objective, it justifies by itself. Instrumental violent acts are much more frequent than the final violent acts.
2. *Personal equation.* Some aspects of a violent act can be explained by the personal traits of the aggressive agent.
3. *Propitious context.* The display of a violent act needs a propitious context that can be broad and mediate, or situational and immediate. The broad and mediate context refers to beliefs, culture and norms. The situational and immediate context is considered the setting existent at the moment of the specific violent act.
4. *Ideological background.* Every violent act is related to socially imposed values, interests, and beliefs, from which emerge the social justifications that may legitimate it. According

to this, the violent act can be considered legal or illegal having as reference a country's specific social order.

Every action to prevent violence in schools should consider the many influences that contribute to violence, including potential violent practices of teachers against students. In Brazilian schools, teachers' positions of authority and control are used to blame students for initiating violence in schools. Because of their authority, teachers and school staff rarely are identified as the source of violence and are protected by their power. The analysis made by different authors about factors related to school failure of elementary school students shows an extensive set of oppressive and authoritarian practices by teachers that take place inside schools (Patto, 1991; Patto, Angelucci, Kalmus, & Paparelli, 2004; Sirino, 2002). Other works reveals oppression, coercion, and prejudice in the school context (Arola, 2003; Collares & Moysés, 1996; Henry, 2000; Mariote, 2005). Thus, individuals rarely are inherently violent or display aggression as a fundamental impulse (Martín-Baró, 2000). Attempts to reduce violence only to emotional factors, personality traits, or learning dimensions in social contexts that are unequal ignore important historical social processes that are inherently a part of a human behavior.

SCHOOL VIOLENCE IN BRAZIL

Educational practices must be understood in light of a country's history and current social conditions (Feracine, 1990; Freire, 1979). Educational institutions fulfill an important social and political function by conveying culture and knowledge, and enhancing personal and social development (Guzzo, 1997). Because schools are deep-rooted social institutions, their qualities are used as one of the important indicators of a country's social development (UNDP, 2003).

School violence can be understood as episodes of violence generated in the pedagogical environment. Violence at school is usually associated with threats, physical and verbal aggressions, drug use by the students, and bullying (Gonçalves & Sposito, 2002). School violence is occasionally viewed narrowly by understanding it only as physical violence between students and by students against teachers. Such a narrow view ignores other elements of school violence such as teachers' lack of commitment, the arbitrary actions of teachers and administrators, and the presence of bars on windows (Henry, 2000). This is why in national research conducted by UNESCO, Abramovay (2003) defined school violence as incorporating different types of violence (verbal, symbolic, institutional, and physical). One may view perpetration of school violence from five levels (Henry, 2000):

Level 1 violence: Student on student, student on teacher, student on school.
Level 2 violence: Teacher on student, administrator on student, administrator on teacher, teacher or administrator on parents, parent on teacher or administrator.
Level 3 violence: School board on school or parent, school district on school or parent, community on school or parent, local political decisions on school and on parent.
Level-4 violence: state and national educational policy on school, state and national juvenile justice policy on student, media and popular culture on student and on administrator, corporate exploitation on student, national and state policies on guns and drugs.
Level-5 violence: harmful social processes and practices that pervade each of the preceding four levels. (pp. 25–26)

Some cognitive processes, moral development, educational practices, and public policies may contribute to violent acts. Additionally, the actions of parents and school officials also impact students.

One way to consider teacher and student relationships can be described as those between an authority figure and the potential object of their authority. Student discipline may result from this relationship. Teachers have institutional authority to exercise their power over students, which can be used positively when they aren't abusive and aim to concretize educational processes. The majority of Brazilian teachers are not prepared to understand or know motivations, emotions, and thoughts present in students' lives that may contribute to their violation of rules imposed by schools or society in general. Some researchers highlight that teachers blend different theoretical conceptions of education and literacy. Consequently, pedagogical practice is guided more by common sense than by techniques and theoretical conceptions, which indicates not only flaws in teacher training in the area of child development, but in the basic notions of learning and teaching (Facci, 2004; Freire & Guimarães, 1982; Patto, 1991; Sirino, 2002; Tomio, 2004).

The consequences of student discipline, apathy, implicit confrontations, and threats of different types contribute to school violence. Schools become violent and unsafe places when they overlook the fact that students often are raised in communities characterized by little or no education, unemployment, poverty, and violence. Brazilian schools have not developed processes to help students address these prevailing conditions in their lives. Additionally, school conditions often ignite the display of violent tendencies. Teachers do not feel competent to understand and take into account many social and emotional problems that students bring to school. Guzzo (2002) noted that the teachers' work could be improved if they could count on support services like counseling, social work, and school psychology, which are nonexistent in almost all of Brazilian public schools.

The impact of violent episodes can be both acute and chronic. The acute effects disrupt the school's daily life because violent acts prohibit planned pedagogical activities. The chronic effects are reflected in the long-term consequences, including mutual mistrust among teachers, students, and their parents (Batista & El-moor, 1999). Chronic violence leads to a culture of violence and violence becomes a natural practice in schools (Candau, 2000).

Relevant Research

Scholarship addressing school violence in Brazil began in the 1980s, a period that marks the country's entrance into a redemocratization process in its political structures. According to Sposito (2001), this scholarship includes school violence and especially focuses on urban violence as an important factor for comprehension of school violence. Two sources have been relied on: those from public agencies and private research institutes or universities, as well as sociological analyses of the occurrence of violence episodes in several Brazilian cities.

Interest in school violence was intensely associated with the country's democratization when violence was seen as a national problem related to public security and the formation of a civil society. Beginning in the 1980s, there was a national consensus about the protection of schools from vandalism. At that time, school violence was characterized by vandalism against public buildings and newcomer's entrance into schools.

During the 1990s, an increase in criminality and a sense of insecurity was felt among the population. These feelings affected school life. At this time, school violence was increasingly observed toward students and was seen as a form of social behavior between peers. Toward the end of the 1990s, and with the growth of left- or center left-wing municipal administration, public initiatives were developed to reduce school violence. These initiatives were thought to evaluate school violence through descriptions made by students about violent situations. The results created quite a different scenario, leading to the increased emergence of physical violence, quarreling, threats, and bullying.

Confrontation within nearby neighborhoods has also been associated with youth violence (Batista & El-moor, 1999). Young people living in environments characterized by insecurity, threats, and fear, recognized that violence was a natural expression in interpersonal relationships. The initiation of violent behaviors became a way to be recognized and to gain power. Research with 52,000 participants (teachers, administrators, and members of school board) from 1,440 public schools throughout Brazil examined three common forms of school violence: theft, vandalism of public buildings, and interpersonal aggression. Vandalism was the most frequent (60% of schools), followed by interpersonal aggression between students (39.4%) and aggression against teachers (16.1%). The incidence of these violent acts was higher in schools in the state capital cities, which have a larger number of students, and a larger physical space compared with most schools in the country. Issues pertaining to school security, theft, and vandalism were a manifestation of external (e.g., neighborhood) or internal agents (e.g., students) at school (Batista & El-moor, 1999). Similar results were found in a 2-year survey about school violence in São Paulo (Nogueira, 2000).

A national study by UNESCO coordinated by Abramovay (2003) and involving 33,655 students in Grades 5–8 and high school throughout state capitals of Brazil, provided some rich information. Among the interviewed students, 33.5% reported drug use in locations near to school. Of these students, 23.1% reported drug use inside school). Thirteen percent reported someone (student, parent, or teacher) carrying a gun in the school, and 25% stated that gangs and drug dealings are the greatest problem areas at school.

Additional research (Candau, 2000) regarding violence in high schools utilized two focus groups of 28 students each. One group was from a public school and the other was from a private school. Public school students expressed the following violence manifestations: gun carrying, domestic violence, trivial violence by media, public corruption, difficulty in interpersonal relationships, and the abuse of power by others (especially family members and teachers). Private school students highlighted their personal experiences as victims of robbery, social violence, and the vulgarization of violence.

Interventions to Address School Violence

In Brazil, there are currently two ways of addressing school violence: (a) through actions that are punitive and repressive and (b) through pedagogical and political measures. In the first way, school violence becomes a public security issue, transferring the responsibility to the police. In the second way, pedagogical and political measures attempt to address issues through comprehensive intervention efforts, including the students as important components in the educative process and characterizing schools as institutions able to develop society and to form critical and responsible citizens (Candau, 2000).

Gonçalves and Sposito (2002) completed a review of public polices intended to decrease school violence in important Brazilian cities. The most frequent episodes of school violence are characterized by verbal and physical aggression, threats, and bullying. The Ministry of Justice initiated programs in response to the high rates of violence involving teenagers and organized crime. According to Abramovay (2003), homicides caused 39.2% of youth deaths. The largest of those programs, Peace in Schools, was developed in 2000 and was carried out in 14 Brazilian states. The program's goal was to decentralize initiatives that address violence in schools, given the knowledge that 56% of the Brazilian schools were affected by violence. The program was grounded on three principles: (a) an ethical urgency, caused by the gravity of the situation involving the majority of Brazilian schools; (b) the need to involve the majority of the population in this effort; and (c) the convergence of goals leading to establishing a culture of peace (Paiva, 2001). All municipalities were encouraged to develop programs that prevented violence. The federal government provided financial support and municipalities were to develop appropriate intervention methods and evaluation. Program activities included mass media campaigns; training sessions involving different topics (conflict resolution techniques, human rights, and ethical questions) with students, teachers, and policemen; and involvement of juvenile participants through the creation of student associations. Unfortunately, since the program's initiation in 2000, little is known about its impact on reducing violence.

Despite these efforts, school violence persists. It has taken different forms and has impacted more of Brazil's population. Current actions create new places that encourage community participation in the school environment in an attempt to neutralize violence that occurred due to the school's isolation from the community. Some schools are open on the weekends to cultural or sports activities involving teachers, students, and community members. Improvements in the quality of relationships between schools and families have improved both the schooling process and community life. These school–community programs have had some negative side effects, including overutilizing limited school resources and difficulty finding human resources to provide extra work without extra wages.

Batista and El-moor (1999) highlighted two kinds of situations employed by the school to face interpersonal aggression, theft, and vandalism: internal security measures (e.g., use of bars on the windows and punishment measures) and public security measures. Internal security measures were adopted by 73% of Brazilian schools, whereas only 30% adopted external security measures. When internal security measures were used, problems such as vandalism, theft, and aggression continued to be present. The initiation of external security measures seemed to be more effective in reducing violence. Additionally, a positive correlation was found between external security and community participation in schools (Batista & El-moor, 1999).

Candau (2000) proposed dealing with school violence through human rights education with the goal to generate new social practices, given the belief that attempts to rescue a student's life requires a permanent reference to an educational process devoted to the creation of different social practices. Through respect for students, knowledge of the prevailing social conditions that impact children, and participation in school decision-making processes, it may be possible to achieve an effective intervention model to reduce school violence (Freire & Guimarães, 1982).

Some programs for dealing with school violence are more coherent with Brazilian society and could contribute to transforming it. These include inclusion of violence prevention and coping programs in a school's curriculum, more public discussion of violence in schools and communities, and initiation of effective participation from all school members in school decision-making processes, thus helping schools to reflect more democratic practices, including critical and participative activities. These actions could serve as models for families and communities, resulting in lower levels of violence. These efforts show promise for overcoming a culture of violence and building a new society. The educational process should extend beyond schools to embrace communities, resulting in improved relationships between teacher and students (Camacho, 2001; Caulfield, 2000; Freire, 1979; Freire & Guimarães, 1982).

IMPLICATIONS FOR PRACTICE

The development of effective school-based interventions presents various challenges that require the serious and continuous involvement of psychologists. Most Brazilian psychologists are prepared to provide clinical (e.g., one-on-one) services and have little preparation to services for work in schools or communities.

Table 32.1 summarizes some possible ways for psychologists to help address school violence in Brazilian public schools. The information in this table is based on previously reviewed scholarship and interventions developed during the past 3 years in the educational and community contexts (Guzzo, 2004). The table includes specific actions for psychologists, school board members, teachers, and staff when dealing with violence. The first column summarizes four levels of action. As noted previously, it is necessary to integrate within the model interventions that include the community, families, school staff, administration, curriculum, teachers, and

TABLE 32.1
Implications for Practice: Applications of School Violence Prevention in Brazil

Actions Level	General Principles and Objectives Involving All School Staff	Psychologist Specific Actions and Responsibilities
Community	• Knowledge of community dynamic • Increasing school and community partnerships • School as a community reference	• Know stories of students and important community agents and bringing incorporate this knowledge into school life • Promote collective organization for participation at school decisions • Create integrated activities between community and school • Know and participate in ways that meet community needs
Curriculum	• Connection with student's everyday life • Curriculum that addresses violence • Discussion of human rights and political polices	• Reflect and respect the needs of students • Participate in teacher's planning activities, suggesting changes as needed in the curriculum based on student needs • Create routine activities related to student's everyday life • Create activities that could mediate and solve interpersonal conflicts
Teachers and school administration	• To know the reality of children's lives through their perceptions • Dialogue between students and adults as a fundamental way to interact • Promote student cohesion • Consider students as active and meaningful participants in their educational process • Decentralize administration	• Participate in teacher training activities • Enhance dialogues between teachers and administration • Development of teacher training programs
Families	• Develop school–family relationships • Encourage active participation by families in school's decisions	• Include families in school's program • Maintain regular contact with families • Provide space for parent discussions and meetings • Include families when developing social polices • Orientation and follow-up
Students	• Develop the critical consciousness of citizenship • Stimulate student's positive involvement in school and community activities • Engage student in school decisions	• Promote peer understanding and acceptance • Encourages peer dialog and expression • Promotes students organizations • Encourages student involvement when making school policy • Recognize and reward student's successes
School staff	• Consider them as educational agents • Encourage their participation in school decisions	• Organize group meetings among all staff

students. The second column summarizes general principles expressed as positive actions for addressing violence involving all school participants. The third column summarizes more specific action for psychologists. Each item has a special form that recognizes school–community partnerships and needs. Intervention efforts incorporating these actions and principles may help to address school violence in Brazil.

ACKNOWLEDGMENTS

We thank Dr. Thomas Oakland for his significant and important support on reviewing this manuscript and developing helpful suggestions. We also thank the handbook editors for their contributions to improving the quality of this manuscript. Finally, we thank the financial support of the National Council of Research (CNPq) of Brazil.

REFERENCES

Abramovay, M. (2003). Enfrentando a violência nas escolas: um informe do Brasil. In M. Abramovay (Ed.), *Violência na escola: América Latina e Caribe* [Violence at school: Latin America and Caribean] (pp. 89–150). Brasília, Brazil: UNESCO.

Adorno, S., & Cárdia, N. (2002). Notas de apresentação: Violência [Presentating notes: Violence]. *Ciência e Cultura, 54*(1), 20–21.

Albee, G. W. (1992). Saving children means social revolution. In G. W. Albee, L. A. Bond, & T. V. C. Monsey (Eds.), *Improving children's lives: global perspectives on prevention* (pp. 311–329). Newbury Park, CA: Sage.

Arola, R. L. (2003). *Educar ou excluir? Questionamentos antropológicos da educação social* [To educate or to exclude? Anthropological questions about social education]. Americana: Centro Universitário Salesiano de São Paulo.

Batista, A. S., & El-moor, P. D. (1999). Violência e agressão [Violence and agression]. In W. Codo (Ed.), *Educação: carinho e trabalho* (pp. 139–160). Petrópolis: Vozes.

Blanco, A., & Ibáñez, L. d. l. C. (2003). Psicología social de la violencia: La perspectiva de Ignacio Martín-Baró [Social psychology of violence: The perspective of Ignacio Martín-Baró]. In A. Blanco & L. d. l. C. Ibáñez (Eds.), *Poder, ideología y violencia* (pp. 9–62). Madrid: Editorial Trotta.

Buoro, A. B., Schilling, F., Singer, H., & Soares, M. (1999). *Violência urbana: Dilemas e desafios* [Urban violence: Dillemas and chalenges]. São Paulo: Editora Atual.

Camacho, L. M. Y. (2001). As sutilezas das faces da violência nas práticas escolares de adolescentes [The subtleties of the faces of violence in the school practices of adolescents]. *Educação e Pesquisa, 27*(1), 123–140.

Candau, V. M. (2000). Direitos humanos, violência e cotidiano escolar [Human rights, violence and school daily life]. In V. M. Candau (Ed.), *Reinventar a escola* (pp. 32–76). Petrópolis, Brazil: Vozes.

Caulfield, S. L. (2000). Creating peaceable schools. *Annals of the American Academy of Political and Social Science, 567,* 170–185.

Chaui, M. (2000). *Brasil: Mito fundador e sociedade autoritária* [Brazil: Founding myth and authoritarian society]. São Paulo: Editora Fundação Perceu Abramo.

Codo, W., & Vasques-Menezes, I. (2001). *As relações entre a escola, a vida e a qualidade de ensino: Relatório realizado pelo Laboratório de Psicologia do Trabalho e pela Confederação Nacional dos Trabalhadores em Educação* [The relations between the school, the life, and the teaching quality: Report made by the Laboratory of Labor Psychology and the National Confederation of Educational Workers]. Brasília: CNTE.

Collares, C. A. L., & Moysés, M. A. A. (1996). *Preconceitos no cotidiano escolar: Ensino e medicalização* [Prejudice at the school daily life: Teaching and medicalization]. São Paulo: Cortez.

Facci, M. G. D. (2004). *Valorização ou esvaziamento do trabalho do professor? Um estudo crítico-comparativo da teria do professor reflexivo, do construtivismo e da psicologia vigotskiana* [Valorization or emptying of teacher's work? A critical-comparative study about reflexive teacher theory, constructivism and vygotskyan psychology]. Campinas: Autores Associados.

Feracine, L. (1990). *O professor como agente de mudança social* [The teacher as agent of social change]. São Paulo: EPU.

Freire, P. (1973). *Uma educação para a liberdade [Education for freedom]* (2nd ed.). Porto, Portugal: Antonio Abreu.

Freire, P., & Guimarães, S. (1982). *Sobre educação: diálogos* [About education: dialogues]. Rio de Janeiro, Brazil: Paz e Terra.

Freire, P. (1979). *Ação cultural para a liberdade e outros escritos [Cultural action for freedom and other texts]* (4th ed.). Rio de Janeiro: Paz e Terra.

Freire, P. (2000). *Pedagogia do oprimido* (29th ed.) [Pedagogy of the opressed]. Rio de Janeiro: Paz e Terra.

Freire, P., & Guimarães, S. (1982). *Sobre educação: diálogos* [About education: dialogues]. Rio de Janeiro, Brazil: Paz e Terra.

Gonçalves, L. A. O., & Sposito, M. P. (2002). Iniciativas públicas de redução da violência escolar no Brasil [Public initiatives for reducing violence in Brazilian schools]. *Cadernos de Pesquisa, 115*, 101–138.

Guzzo, R. S. L. (1997). Avaliação psicológica e planejamento acadêmico: a importância do psicólogo junto ao professor [Psychological assessment and academic planning: The importance of psychologist together with the teacher]. *Psicologia: Teoria, Investigação e Prática, 2*, 99–104.

Guzzo, R. S. L. (2002). Novo paradigma para a formação e atuação do psicólogo escolar no cenário educacional brasileiro [New paradigm for school psychologist training and practice in the Brazilian educational setting]. In R. S. L. Guzzo, *Psicologia escolar: LDB e educação hoje* (2nd ed., pp. 131–144). Campinas: Alínea.

Guzzo, R. S. L. (2004). *Construindo bases para a prevenção primária no Brasil.* [Building bases for the primary prevention in Brazil]. Research report presented at Conselho Nacional de Desenvolvimento Científico e Tecnológico—CNPq.

Henry, S. (2000). What is school violence? An integrated definition. *Annals of the American Academy of Political and Social Science, 567*, 16–29.

Instituto Brasileiro de Geografia e Estatística: (IBGE) (2000). *Censo demográfico 2000* [Demographic Census 2000]. Rio de Janeiro: IBGE.

Mariote, L. E. (2005). *Políticas de inclusão: Compreensão de alunos, pais e professores sobre esse processo* [Inclusion politics: Comprehension of students, parents and teachers about this process]. Unpublished master's dissertation, Pontifícia Universidade Católica de Campinas, Campinas.

Martín-Baró, I. (2000). *Acción e ideología: Psicología social desde centroamérica* [Action and ideology: Social psychology from Central America]. San Salvador: UCA Editores.

Morais, R. D. (1998). *O que é violência urbana?* [What is urban violence?]. São Paulo: Brasiliense.

Nogueira, I. D. S. (2000). A violência nas escolas e o desafio da educação para cidadania [The violence at schools and the challenge of education for citizenship]. In J. Vaidergorn (Ed.), *O direito a ter direitos* (pp. 97–111). Campinas, Brazil: Autores Associados.

Paiva, D. (2001). *Paz na escola: O clamor ético dos nossos tempos* [Peace in schools: The ethical outcry of our times]. Available: http://www.dhnet.org.br/educar/balestreri/inquietude/denise_paiva.htm

Patto, M. H. S. (1991). *A produção do fracasso escolar: Histórias de submissão e rebeldia* [The production of school failure: Stories of submission and insurrection]. São Paulo: T. A. Queiroz.

Patto, M. H. S., Angelucci, C. B., Kalmus, J., & Paparelli, R. (2004). O estado da arte da pesquisa sobre o fracasso escolar (1991–2002): Um estudo introdutório [The state of art in the research about school failure (1991–2002): An introductory study]. *Educação e Pesquisa, 30*(1), 51–72.

Peralva, A. (2002). Violência Brasileira: Entre crescimento da igualdade e fragilidade institucional [Brazilian violence: Between equality growing and institutional fragility]. In D. L. Lévisky (Ed.), *Adolescência e violência: ações comunitárias na prevenção "conhecendo, articulando, intengrando e mutiplicando"* (pp. 25–36). São Paulo: Casa do Psicólogo.

Pochmann, M., & Amorim, R. (2004). *Atlas da exclusão social no Brasil* [Atlas of social exclusion in Brazil]. São Paulo: Cortez.

Pochmann, M., Campos, A., Amorim, R., & Silva, R. (2004). *Atlas da exclusão social no Brasil: Dinâmica e manifestação territorial (Vol. 2)* [Atlas of social exclusion in Brazil: Dynamic and territorial manifestation]. São Paulo: Cortez.

Romano, R. (2002). Violência brasileira: O privado e o público [Brazilian violence: The private and the public]. In D. L. Lévisky (Ed.), *Adolescência e violência: ações comunitárias na prevenção "conhecendo, articulando, intengrando e mutiplicando"* (pp. 37–51). São Paulo: Casa do Psicólogo.

Santacruz, M., & Portillo, N. (1999). *Agresores y agredidos: factores de riesgo de la violencia juvenil en las escuelas* [Agressors and agressed: Risk factors of juvenile violence at schools]. San Salvador: IUDOP.

Sá, A. A. (1999). Algumas questões polêmicas relativas à psicologia da violência [Some polemic questions relative to the psychology of violence]. *Psicologia: Teoria e Prática, 1*(2), 53–63.

Sirino, M. F. (2002). *Repensando o fracasso escolar: Reflexões a partir do discurso da criança-aluno* [Rethinking the school failure: Reflections based on children-student discourse]. Unpublished master's dissertation, Universidade Estadual Paulista, Assis.

Sposito, M. P. (2001). Um breve balanço da pesquisa sobre violência escolar no Brasil [A brief survey of the research on school violence in Brazil]. *Educação e Pesquisa, 27*(1), 87–103.

Tomio, N. A. O. (2004). *Concepções do professor alfabetizador: Uma visão histórico-crítica?* [Conceptions of reading and writing teacher: An historical-critical vision?]. Unpublished master's dissertation, Pontifícia Universidade Católica de Campinas, Campinas.

United Nations Development Programme (UNDP). (2003). *Human Development Report 2003: millennium development goals: a compact among nations to end human poverty.* Available: http://www.undp.org/hdr2003/

33

The Safe Schools, Healthy Students Initiative in Rural Pennsylvania

Janet A. Welsh
Celene E. Domitrovich
Pennsylvania State University

A Safe Schools, Healthy Students (SS/HS) project was implemented in the small community of Tyrone, located in the Appalachian hill country of rural Pennsylvania. The Tyrone Area School District, in collaboration with community organizations and staff at the Prevention Research Center at the Pennsylvania State University (PSU), adopted and implemented comprehensive prevention programming for children, youth, and families during the 3-year period of grant funding, and subsequently sustained a significant proportion of the programming after the grant period ended. This chapter describes the needs and characteristics of this community, the community partners engaged in the project, the types of programming implemented, the evaluation and sustainability strategies adopted for the various programs, and finally the lessons learned from this collaborative experience.

BACKGROUND AND LOCAL NEEDS

The community of Tyrone, Pennsylvania typifies much of rural America, which struggles with high rates of poverty, unemployment, and substance use, and poor health and social services. Despite stereotypes portraying rural life as idyllic and poverty as a primarily urban phenomenon, more than half of the poor children in the United States live in rural areas such as Tyrone (Children's Defense Fund, 1994). Statistics from Blair County, where Tyrone is located, indicated that at the time of the SS/HS initiative, rates of child poverty, child abuse, domestic violence, and adolescent pregnancy exceeded averages for the state of Pennsylvania (Pennsylvania Department of Public Welfare Annual Report, 2002). Tyrone had little industry (much of the previous industrial infrastructure had disappeared) and despite its small population, there were three subsidized housing developments and a low-income trailer park served by the school district. Given that poverty is one of the strongest predictors of child health, mental health, academic success, and IQ (Brooks-Gunn, Duncan, & Aber, 1997; Duncan, Brooks-Gunn, & Klebanov, 1994; Lipman & Offord, 1997; McLoyd, 1990; Montgomery, Kiely, & Pappas, 1996; Pagani, Boulerice, & Tremblay, 1997), it was clear that many young people in Tyrone

511

were at high risk for adjustment difficulties and poor educational outcomes. Data collected by the school district confirmed this. The Communities That Care Survey (CTC; Channing-Bete, 2000), conducted in Tyrone in 2001 with students in Grades 6, 8, and 10, revealed that Tyrone youth scored above Pennsylvania state averages for risk factors including low commitment to school, community disorganization, norms favorable to drugs use and firearms, current drug use, and poor family discipline.

The SS/HS initiative provided a unique opportunity for communities to address complex needs through its emphasis on comprehensive, well-integrated service delivery and its provision of substantial financial and technical resources. However, not all communities were prepared to fully benefit from this opportunity, despite substantial need for the type of integrated and comprehensive services the initiative could potentially support. An emerging literature on the sustainability of community-based prevention initiatives has demonstrated that the mere presence of need is insufficient to support and sustain innovation (Feinberg & Greenberg, 2004). Additional factors include community readiness to engage in the process of collaboration and systems integration. Readiness involves strong leadership capacity, good organizational resources and networks, and positive public and local leadership attitudes toward the initiative (Feinberg, Greenberg, & Osgood, 2004).

Although a typical small town in many ways, the Tyrone community had a number of characteristics that made it particularly ready (compared to many similar communities) to respond to an initiative such as SS/HS. First, the school district had a lengthy history of prior collaboration around implementation and evaluation of evidence-based prevention programming. In 1991, the district became a site for the field evaluation of the FAST Track Project (CPPRG, 1992, 2000). This comprehensive prevention program, which included an integrated system of "best practices" in parent training, child social skills training, academic tutoring, home visiting, and mentoring programs, provided a good fit for the needs of Tyrone youth and families, and was well received within the school district and the larger community. As the cohorts of children involved in FAST Track moved forward, the district institutionalized and sustained the Promoting Alternative Thinking Strategies Curriculum (PATHS; Kusche & Greenberg, 1994), a universal socioemotional curriculum taught by teachers to all children in Grades 1 through 5. The district also obtained state funding to continue targeted FAST Track parent training and social skills groups to a small group of families. Partly as a result of their participation in the FAST Track project, key school district teachers and administrators acquired an excellent level of sophistication in terms of their understanding of research and the value of evidence-based programming. An additional asset of the school district administration was its stability and the widespread respect it enjoyed in the community; as such it was well positioned to follow through with a complex initiative and to accomplish goals established at the outset of the grant period.

RATIONALE AND CONCEPTUAL PRINCIPLES UNDERLYING THE TYRONE SS/HS INITIATIVE

As is the case in many small towns, much of the life of the Tyrone community was organized around the schools. Various community groups used all buildings for extracurricular activities. Given this high level of community engagement, the school district appeared to be a logical "home" for integrated, community-based prevention activities.

The activities of the Tyrone SS/HS initiative were driven by a risk and resilience framework and also shaped by developmental considerations. Given the comprehensive nature of the initiative, an attempt was made to identify both proximal and distal factors associated with risk and resilience for children and youth from early childhood through adolescence, and to select developmentally appropriate and (where possible) evidence-based interventions targeting these risk and protective factors at each age level. Programming was largely, although not exclusively, focused on promoting positive school adjustment, with the distal goal of altering the negative developmental trajectories associated with poverty. As previously mentioned, the prevalent risk pattern in the Tyrone community involved poverty, social isolation, and low educational attainment. Relative to children from middle-class families, poor children who do not receive high-quality early intervention are more likely to exhibit deficits in language, social development, and academic achievement; and to demonstrate aggressive behavior problems (Olds, Robinson, Song, Little, & Hill, 1999; Ramey & Ramey, 1998; Weikart, 1998). As they move through school, children with these skill deficits and behavioral problems are increasingly at risk for peer rejection and academic failure (Catts, Fey, Zhang, & Tomblin, 1999; Patterson, DeBaryshe, & Ramsey, 1989; Redmond & Rice, 1998; Rice, Sell, & Hadley, 1991), which if unchanged, can lead to severe adolescent problems such as alienation from school and community, dropout, substance use, delinquent activity, and early pregnancy (Battistich & Hom, 1997; Hawkins, Catalano, & Miller, 1992). This maladaptive developmental pattern is consistent with the research on early-onset conduct problems (CPPRG, 1992; Reid & Eddy, 1997), and was observed in many high-risk children and youth in Tyrone. Within this developmental framework, programming was organized to create an efficient, integrated, and nonredundant prevention-to-treatment continuum, including universal preventions designed to enhance resilience of all students, targeted programs focused around the needs of specific risk groups, and treatment services for students and families for whom prevention activities alone were deemed insufficient. Finally, as programming was selected, attention was paid to the importance of technical assistance and monitoring around issues of implementation quality, recognizing that programs implemented with low fidelity, no matter how good their previous evidence base, are likely to be ineffective (Domitrovich & Greenberg, 2000).

PROGRAM GOALS AND LEVELS OF INTERVENTION

The Tyrone SS/HS project focused on several key outcome and process goals. These goals are outlined in Table 33.1. Outcome goals included the reduction of violence and problematic behavior, building resilience through the development of adaptive competencies, and the promotion of positive school–family partnerships. Process goals included increasing school–community collaboration to meet the needs of at-risk students and their families, incorporating local law enforcement into delinquency prevention efforts in order to enhance school safety, and strengthening the overall school–community interface. The prevention activities proposed in the grant were selected to address these goals, and specifically addressed identified risk factors in the community that were not targeted by already existing programs. Furthermore, programs were selected and implemented in a manner designed to capitalize on the strengths of already existing partnerships, programs, and internal systems. Additionally, the programming chosen reflected both the developmental model and the prevention-to-treatment framework outlined previously.

CAPACITY BUILDING AND COMMUNITY ENGAGEMENT

As described earlier, Tyrone began its SS/HS initiative with a high level of community readiness. This included openness to innovation; a strong, stable administrative infrastructure within the school district; a history of productive collaboration; and an unusually high level of scientific sophistication regarding adoption of best practices. Additionally, from the outset, school district personnel recognized the importance of monitoring implementation quality and of

TABLE 33.1
Tyrone Safe School/Healthy Student (SS/HS) Goals and Objectives

SS/HS Goal	Specific Objectives
Outcome Goals	
	Reduce violence and problem behavior
	Improve behavioral readiness of at-risk students
	Decrease classroom misbehavior
	Reduce playground aggression
	Improve school safety
	Reduce delinquency and substance use
	Reduce disciplinary actions and suspensions
	Build resilience and enhance competencies
	Expand outreach for families of children ages 0–5
	Enhance readiness skills of pre-kindergarten children
	Improve socioemotional competence of all students
	Improve social skills of at-risk students
	Enhance academic skills of at-risk students
	Enhance school bonding and positive school climate
	Promote family–school partnership
	Increase parent–school involvement
	Improve parenting skills in families at risk
	Increase family access to mental health services
Process Goals	
	Increase school–community collaboration to serve at-risk students
	Create school-based mental health office
	Expand early childhood outreach
	Provide school-based coordinators to link services and families
	Provide summer in-service to all staff
	Increase school–law enforcement collaboration
	Expand School resource officer (SRO) to full-time to participate in development of school safety plan
	Integrate SRO with educational prevention efforts
	Enhance school–community interface
	Develop communications campaign
	Include community members in school-based prevention efforts
	Increase staff capacity to implement and evaluate prevention programming

program evaluation. Nonetheless, in order to execute and sustain an initiative of this scope, it was necessary to develop new administrative structures and capacities, including forging new community partnerships with the county mental health provider and the law enforcement community. Additionally, previous experience with grant-related projects had highlighted the importance of ongoing technical assistance and sustainability planning. This was a consideration from the outset of the initiative. One of the first tasks during the planning phase was the establishment of a staffing infrastructure that included the assistant superintendent as overall project director and individuals appointed as SS/HS programming coordinators at the early childhood, elementary, and secondary levels. This approach reflected the developmental framework of the initiative and the recognition that the salient risk factors and prevention programs would be quite different for children and youth in these different age groups. The coordinators were charged with overseeing project activities in their respective domains and working closely with both the project director and staff from the Pennsylvania State Prevention Research Center, who provided technical assistance for some programming and also conducted the local evaluation. Because the early childhood coordinator's work focused largely on a non-school-based population, this individual was very engaged in outreach activities with the community, including coordination with local primary care physicians, day-care providers, and preschools. Similarly, one of the elementary principals was appointed as communications coordinator and was responsible for engaging and informing parents and various community groups and organizations of SS/HS activities and accomplishments. Beyond the re-deployment of already existing staff to develop the infrastructure necessary to support SS/HS programming, the district also hired and contracted for several new positions. The new district employees hired as part of the SS/HS initiative included two part-time police officers, who served as school resource officers (SROs). The duties of these officers included traditional policing functions such as school security, traffic control, and crisis intervention. SROs also coordinated with guidance staff, teachers, and administrators to participate in educational programming for students of all ages and assisted with extracurricular clubs and enrichment activities for students interested in law enforcement careers. The district also used SS/HS resources to contract with the county mental health authority for the services of two half-time therapists to provide in-house mental health services to Tyrone students and families and one full-time social worker who ran the targeted social skills and parent training program for high-risk children and their families in Grades 1 and 2. In addition to providing traditional mental health services, the mental health staff participated actively in the student assistance program at both the elementary and the secondary schools, and provided consultation to secondary students referred to the in-school suspension program for disciplinary infractions. SS/HS funding was used to purchase program evaluation and technical support services from the Prevention Research Center at PSU. In coordination with the project director and other school district administrators, PSU staff developed evaluation strategies and measures, and oversaw data collection and interpretation. They also provided technical assistance around specific program development and implementation. In Year 2 of the project, the district began making concrete plans to sustain and institutionalize various SS/HS program components, and hired a half-time grant writer to pursue other sources of federal, state, and local funding. The result of this capacity building was the integration of multiple systems, including education, law enforcement, mental health, and research, and the coordination of these multiple skills and talents around the goal of enhancing the adjustment and quality of life of children and youth in the community.

Detailed Description of Program Components

Activities were selected based on their congruence with the developmental model, the school district's educational philosophy, and with the specific goals and objectives of the initiative. Additionally, whenever possible, the programs selected had strong scientific evidence indicating their effectiveness and feasibility in applied settings. Finally, programs were chosen if they seemed sufficiently flexible to allow for multidisciplinary collaboration and coordination. Table 33.2 provides a listing of specific activities for early childhood, elementary, and secondary age groups.

Systemwide components had a number of goals, among them consistency and continuity across developmental levels and the formation of a sustainable infrastructure to support continuation of the programmatic innovations following the end of the grant period. The systemwide components included development of a comprehensive school safety plan, which was conducted by a multidisciplinary, collaborative board that included school, community, and law enforcement personnel. This board met periodically and reviewed and updated the

TABLE 33.2
Tyrone Safe School/Healthy Student Components and Activities

Domain	Program Activity
Systemwide	Comprehensive school safety plan
	Interdisciplinary summer staff development institute
	Early childhood, elementary and secondary coordinators
	School-based mental health services
	School resource officer (SRO)
	Communications campaign
Early childhood	Developmental screening and early referral
	Universal mental health promotion for preschool and kindergarten children
	Transition support services for at-risk children
	Summer enrichment program for at-risk, pre-kindergarten children
Elementary	LIFT Playground Program
	Academic support program
	Olweus Bullying Prevention Program
	Integration of elementary PATHS, SRO activities, peer mediation
	Home visitation and social skills support for at-risk children
Secondary	Motivational resource room
	In-school and after-school academic support
	Transitional support for middle school entry
	Quest Health Education Curriculum

plan as needed. The plan included both routine prevention activities and contingencies for various emergencies, including accidents, natural disasters, and acts of violence. A second systemwide program was a summer staff development institute designed to increase the level of understanding of prevention principles and research, to create a shared philosophy and language among staff from diverse professional backgrounds, and to promote sustainability of SS/HS programming. A third systemwide component was the communications campaign, which kept community stakeholders informed of SS/HS activities and also garnered community support for the initiative. Finally, school-based mental health therapists served families and students of all ages; similarly, the policing and educational duties of the SROs were implemented throughout the school district impacted all students.

At the early childhood level, program activities were chosen with the overall goal of improving early identification and intervention with at-risk children and coordination with other early childhood providers. The SS/HS activities included a developmental screening and early referral system for infants and preschool children and a summer enrichment program for pre-kindergarten children that emphasized socioemotional development, language development, and emergent literacy skills. One goal was to improve coordination and communication with community preschool providers in order to facilitate the transition for children entering kindergarten. Activities included professional development programs for preschool teachers and the implementation of Preschool PATHS (Domitrovich, Greenberg, Kusche, & Cortes, 1999) to promote social and emotional development.

Following the FAST Track trial, some Tyrone teachers continued to implement the PATHS curriculum (Kusche & Greenberg, 1994) at the elementary level, but SS/HS allowed for a re-invigoration of this program. Under SS/HS, PATHS expanded to all elementary teachers, and resources became available to provide the technical support and monitoring necessary to assure high-quality implementation. Additionally, the district re-implemented parent skills training groups, child friendship groups, and home visitation (also components of the FAST Track project) for high-risk children in Grades 1 and 2. An afterschool homework assistance program was established for elementary children experiencing academic difficulty, and the district adopted the playground component of the Linking Interests of Families and Teachers project (LIFT; Reid, Eddy, Fetrow, & Stoolmiller, 1999) in order to reduce aggression and promote prosocial behavior on the playground.

Finally, at the secondary level, the SS/HS initiative included both in-school and after-school academic support for students with academic problems, and an in-school suspension program entitled Motivational Resource Room (MRR), which provided both mental health consultation and academic support services for students experiencing behavioral difficulties. A middle school transition program was developed for entering sixth graders, with components for both typical and special needs students. Additionally, the Quest Health Education Curriculum, an evidence-based health promotion and substance use prevention program, was implemented with seventh graders.

PROGRAM EVALUATION

The complex, multicomponent nature of the SS/HS initiative posed considerable challenges for the research team to design an evaluation that was rigorous enough to answer questions regarding the efficacy of specific programs. This was also hindered by the inability to identify an adequate control or comparison group. Given the limited conclusions that could be drawn from the evaluation regarding individual outcomes of students, the primary focus of the data collection was on gathering implementation and process data. This type of evaluation is critical for initiatives such as Safe Schools/Healthy Students, where communities are required to use evidenced-based interventions. Despite the growing literature base documenting that preventive interventions have the ability to positively impact student outcomes, the majority of these studies have been conducted under controlled conditions and not the "real world" of schools and community settings. In general, very little is known about how these programs transfer between settings because until recently, the majority of program developers did not monitor implementation adequately (Domitrovich & Greenberg, 2000). When interventions are implemented in community settings with diverse populations and under varying conditions, careful monitoring of the intervention and the system is needed to ensure a high degree of program fidelity and overall quality. Using an evidence-based program does not ensure positive outcomes. There are many factors that can undermine the implementation process, which, in turn, causes an "effective" program to "fail" (Greenberg, Domitrovich, Graczyk, & Zins, 2002).

For the Tyrone SS/HS project, monthly implementation and process data were collected on all program components. These allowed the research team to determine how many students received a particular program, how often and how completely the program was implemented (i.e., dosage), and the overall quality with which it was delivered. In some cases, measures of outcomes that were expected to be impacted by the program were also gathered. Although it was impossible to attribute the changes in these outcomes to the specific program, the verification of high quality implementation provided more support for the link than if the program quality had not been monitored at all. For example, twice a semester, observations were conducted in the classrooms where teachers were using the PATHS curriculum (Kusche & Greenberg, 1994). Observers rated the students' overall response to the curriculum and the extent to which they appeared to comprehend the material and remain engaged during lessons. They also rated the extent to which they observed specific activities and generalization practices associated with the curriculum. High-quality implementation was documented across all grades (K–5). Teachers appeared to be using the program appropriately and students were responding positively. Data on the number of disciplinary violations on the playground during the implementation of the LIFT playground program with all elementary students indicated a dramatic decrease in such incidents compared to the pre-LIFT period. Similarly, the implementation of the MRR at the secondary level resulted in a substantial reduction in the number of students suspended out of school, which was a primary goal of this program.

As described, given the applied emphasis of the project, there were few opportunities for rigorous experimental designs. However, an exception to this arose naturally with a summer enrichment program that was part of the initiative. Due to budgetary constraints, not all eligible students could be served. This allowed for an experimental design involving random assignment to condition and comparison of children who received the school-based program to those who received only packets of enrichment activities mailed home. This kindergarten summer enrichment program was developed in response to concern within the district that many children were entering kindergarten unprepared to cope with the academic, social, and behavioral demands of the school setting. The program targeted three critical domains related to successful school adaptation: language development, socioemotional capacities, and emergent literacy skills.

Preliminary findings from this program indicated no significant differences between experimental and control group participants on any indices of school readiness; however, at this time detailed implementation and dosage analyses have not been completed. One speculation on the part of evaluators was that the dosage (6 weeks) was insufficient for the intervention children to consolidate their skill gains. The program originally sought to identify children at kindergarten registration who were at risk for language delays but in actuality, the program ended up being delivered to more of a universal sample of students that included all but the highest functioning. It may be that this type of program needs to be more intensive and individualized to students with the greatest needs.

In addition to straightforward outcome analyses, data collected as part of the kindergarten enrichment program included information from parents regarding their interactive behavior with their pre-kindergarten children (including book reading and discipline style). Analyses revealed systematic relationships between these parenting behaviors and children's language and emergent literacy skills, validating the belief of elementary school personnel that a strong home–school partnership was critical to promoting success for children at school entry (Gest, Freeman, Domitrovich, & Welsh, 2004).

As mentioned previously, a major concern of the Tyrone school district was the high degree of alienation from school and community reported by middle and high school students participating in the CTC youth survey. In order to explore the potential origins of this alienation, as well as to identify possible venues for intervention with vulnerable groups or within particular niches of the school, a developmental study of students' academic and behavioral adjustment, perceptions of school supportiveness, and perceptions of adults in the school was undertaken with students in Grades 3–5. These students completed surveys twice a year for several years, and their patterns of responses were charted across late elementary school and the middle school transition. Data revealed that at the elementary level, students had generally positive views of their relationships with teachers and their perceptions of the school climate and other adults in the school. Nonetheless, there was a small but significant group of highly alienated students that was identifiable as early as third grade, and some developmental trend indicating that this increased across grades, particularly for boys (see Gest, Welsh, & Domitrovich, 2005, for details of these results).

Another central research question was the degree to which students' perceptions of the school environment predict significant adjustment in academic, social, and behavior domains, and the ways in which these perceptions might be affected by a suffusion of prevention programs such as those included in SS/HS. A broad strategy was adopted to evaluate the LIFT program that tracked changes in the students' perceptions of playground safety, in particular, but also the general school environment. For this evaluation, a cohort-sequential design was used. Students received the LIFT evaluation survey in Grades 3–5 in the fall of 2001, prior to the schoolwide implementation of the LIFT program. Students were asked to provide information on playground safety, peer-group affiliation, relationships with teachers and other adults in the school, school commitment, self-perceptions, and general school climate. Additionally, teachers in Grades 3–5 completed ratings of behavior and academic competence for each student in their classrooms. These surveys and rating scales were repeated in the spring of 2002, the fall of 2003, and the fall and spring of 2005. Specifics involving the preliminary findings from this longitudinal, developmental study can be found in Gest et al. (2005).

LESSONS LEARNED: SUCCESSES AND CHALLENGES OF THE SS/HS INITIATIVE IN TYRONE

As the Tyrone community implemented its SS/HS initiative, it faced two major challenges: system integration and sustainability. Despite a generally high level of success at collaboration across the cultures of education, mental health, and law enforcement, some system integration difficulties inevitably arose. Although this problem was anticipated from the outset and the goal of the Summer Staff Institute was to minimize it through development of a common culture, problems with conflicting perspectives, priorities, and procedures did occasionally arise.

Mental Health Lessons

The school-based mental health collaboration was a highly successful component of SS/HS. The provision of these services on school grounds overcame many of the barriers to access of mental health services frequently observed in rural communities, including transportation problems, social stigma, and a lack of appropriate providers (Flaherty, Weist, & Warner, 1996; Kelleher, Taylor, & Rickert, 1992; Weist, 1997). In order to integrate with the educational system and meet the goal of seamless service provision, the referral process for school-based mental health was tied directly into the Student Assistance Program (SAP). The SAP is a state-regulated program that is designed to help identify and provide interventions to students with emotional or behavioral problems that are impacting their school performance. SAP was originally designed for use at the secondary level, but has been adapted for the elementary level as well. At the time of the SS/HS initiative, Tyrone was one of only a few districts in Pennsylvania to have both an elementary and secondary SAP program, and their model has received praise from state educational officials.

Through the SS/HS project, the school-based mental health providers became a part of the SAP team. They conducted additional assessments when necessary and shared the responsibility for case management, which increasingly became an important aspect of the system over time. The mental health providers were also an important link to the community mental health system. They understood the system, particularly the insurance billing process, and knew how to expedite access to intensive services when needed. There were multiple instances when the relationship that developed between a family and the school-based clinician facilitated the family's ability to connect with and benefit from outside services.

According to members of the SAP team and the school-based therapists, the mental health component was a successful aspect of the SS/HS initiative. The providers became an integrated part of the district and filled a significant need. They were able to increase access to interventions and overall volume of services provided to students. Additionally, they were able to increase the speed with which interventions took place, particularly in crisis situations, and they brought a tradition of strong case management skills to a system that benefited from that structure. School-based mental health complimented the guidance and student SAP system and added an important element to the comprehensive model developed by SS/HS. Nonetheless, structural differences between the educational and mental health systems, particularly with regard to billing and reimbursement practices, made it difficult to sustain this valuable service once grant funding had ceased. Additionally, some difficulties arose due to different cultural and procedural characteristics of the two systems. For example, the mental health staff's definition and procedures involving student confidentiality were dictated by their home organization, and sometimes these conflicted with the school's guidelines, causing communication difficulties. Similarly, although overall the mental health program was extremely successful and well integrated into the culture of the school, the targeted social skills and parent training program for high-risk elementary students, which had been fairly successful at engaging parents during the FAST Track project, was relatively unsuccessful as a part of SS/HS. Initially, the reasons for this failure were unclear, but ultimately it appeared that the training model for staff implementing this program had failed to address potential cultural differences between a relatively aggressive, community-based prevention approach and a clinic-based treatment approach that relies on high levels of participant motivation and initiative.

Law Enforcement Lessons

As was the case with the mental health programs, the integration of law enforcement into the school was largely successful. Data collected as part of the developmental study indicated that elementary and middle school students generally felt very positive about the SROs and regarded them as supportive rather than threatening or authoritarian figures. This may have been because these officers performed educational and student outreach functions in addition to traditional policing activities such as school security and criminal investigation. However, there was a down side to this high degree of integration—confusion did arise periodically on the part of the SROs and school administrators regarding prioritization of these multiple responsibilities, and priorities were sometimes inconsistent between the elementary and the secondary schools. Similarly, the district initially lacked clear guidelines and policies for inclusion of the SROs into matters involving student conduct. On several occasions, miscommunication and confusion arose when some school administrators routinely involved the SROs in legal matters involving students, whereas others did not. It was necessary to develop clear guidelines defining the extent of administrative discretion in handling behavioral infractions. Finally, difficulties sometimes occurred because of the differences in definitions and procedures used in law enforcement versus educational settings. School personnel typically interpreted student misbehavior through the lens of school policy, whereas SROs viewed these infractions in legal terms—these views did not always correspond. For example, the school district's definition of "harassment" was different from the legal definition, leading to some confusion and disagreement regarding the disposition of these incidents. Likewise, school policies regarding search and seizure of student property differed from legal guidelines on these matters, resulting at times in disagreements between law enforcement personnel and school staff.

Research Lessons

There were very few systems integration difficulties between the Tyrone Area School District and the PSU research staff that conducted the evaluation and provided technical assistance around various aspects of programming. There were probably several reasons for this. First, school personnel were both familiar and comfortable with research prior to this initiative

TABLE 33.3
Implications for Practice: Key Factors Contributing to Success of the Tyrone Safe School/Healthy
Student (SS/HS) Initiative in Rural Pennsylvania

Key Principles	Implications for Practice
Readiness	Given the challenges of transdisciplinary collaboration and the integration of research into the ongoing activities of the school, openness to innovation, buy-in from key partners (school administrators and staff, school board, agency collaborators, etc.), awareness of research principles, and stability and organization within the school district are important prerequisites for the success of a complex initiative such as SS/HS. Ensuring that early on in the process of implementation, key members of the school staff are involved in the decision-making process can facilitate these conditions. Identify respected and trusted leaders from within the school community and use their endorsement to gain broader support. It is important that staff believe that the problems being targeted by the initiative exist and that there was a research-based rationale for including the different program activities. Providing this type of critical background information may require a communications strategy for the school staff and other members of the community.
Partnership culture	It is critical to recognize that partners from different professional backgrounds (law enforcement, mental health, education, and research) represent different cultures with different priorities, perspectives, and language. These differences must be addressed at the outset through ongoing in-service training in order for collaborations to be maximally productive.
Implementation quality	When implementing evidence-based programs in applied settings, there is significant quality potential for program fidelity to be compromised by "drift" from the intended implementation. Therefore, it is critical to develop an infrastructure for the ongoing monitoring and evaluation of implementation quality. Some program modifications are necessary in community settings in order to adapt programs to the local needs or culture but if possible this should be done with the input of the developer and in a way that maintains the critical components of the intervention.
Evaluation	Rigorous scientific evaluation is difficult in applied settings where many variables cannot be systematically controlled. However, the evaluation can be greatly facilitated by focusing on the process of implementation and targeting research topics of particular importance to the key players and stakeholders (e.g., dropout and suspension rates, academic and behavioral adjustment, etc.). Assessing implementation quality provides the opportunity to link variation in dosage or quality to outcomes which helps explain the mechanisms of change underlying the intervention.
Sustainability	Very few school districts have the resources available to sustain the myriad of services supported by an initiative such as SS/HS. Therefore, planning for sustainability should begin in the early stages of the project and consider a variety of sources, including state, federal, local, private, and foundation funding, as well as school district resources

and did not need convincing regarding the value of evidence-based programming or program evaluation. Similarly, the researchers involved in the SS/HS local evaluation were well known to the district, and there was a high degree of mutual respect and trust based on previous experiences. Specifically, the researchers cultivated this respect and trust through consideration for the schools' priorities, focus on research questions that assisted the schools in meeting the needs of their students, and awareness of community values and dynamics. Additionally, because the researchers provided technical assistance to the district around various aspects of program development and implementation as well as evaluation services, they were regarded as a resource by the district, which further facilitated the collaboration.

CONCLUSIONS AND RECOMMENDATIONS

The SS/HS initiative in Tyrone, Pennsylvania can be regarded as a success in several ways. First, a primary goal of the initiative was integration and coordination of prevention activities across developmental domains and areas of professional expertise (e.g., law enforcement, mental health, education, and research). Tyrone was highly successful at integrating mental health and law enforcement personnel into the ongoing activities of the school system and working through the challenges that this integration of professional cultures inevitably involved. A second goal of improving the efficiency and continuity of prevention and treatment activities for children and youth was also achieved. During the grant period, the district noted that the centralization of resources in the school buildings greatly facilitated access to services for many families who would otherwise not have received them. Students and their families were able to access mental health and early childhood intervention resources without traveling to other communities. Similarly, speed and efficiency of both communication and service delivery was enhanced by the immediate availability of specialists within the educational system. For example, having mental health staff participate directly on the SAP team facilitated a quick and seamless transfer into services for needy students. Having therapists with offices in the building and coverage for the majority of the week allowed mental health services to be delivered across the continuum of need. Mental health staff had the flexibility to provide a strong base of preventive activities but also had the flexibility to respond immediately to crisis situations.

The SS/HS initiative also allowed legal issues involving students to be effectively and efficiently addressed by having an in-house police force. According to the administration at the secondary level, the activities associated with SS/HS initiative were crucial to helping the school promote positive discipline and retain students. The academic support and MRR were proactive discipline options that were more likely to promote student success and less likely to undermine student morale than traditional methods of discipline. These programs combined with school-based mental health and the presence of the SRO created an optimal environment for learning.

The greatest problem facing SS/HS communities is what to do when the grant period ends. Also, there are few models for dissemination of programming from SS/HS sites into other communities. The issue of sustainability is challenging for even the most innovative communities. There is always the option to write for new funds, and utilizing the skills of their professional grant writer, Tyrone has been able to piece together funding sources to cover the cost of some program components that could not be integrated into the general school programming. There are many creative and nontraditional ideas regarding sustainability being generated to address this problem, such as engaging the business community as partners in prevention programming (Small, 2002), but many rely on a financial base that is lacking in many rural communities. The Tyrone Area School District is committed to maintaining its prevention efforts and continuing to increase its capacity to identify, implement and evaluate evidence-based programs. Current sustainability efforts include incorporating teacher volunteers into some of the SS/HS programs, such as academic support. In addition, Tyrone is in the process of strengthening its ties with local- and state-level politicians in the hopes that these partnerships.

REFERENCES

Barnett, W. S. (1995). Long-term effects of early childhood programs on cognitive and social outcomes. *The Future of Children, 5*, 25–50.

Battistich, V., & Hom, A. (1997). The relationship between students' sense of their school as a community and their involvement in problem behaviors. *American Journal of Public Health, 87*, 1997–2001.

Brooks-Dunn, J., & Duncan, G. J. (1997). The effects of poverty on children. *The Future of Children, 7*, 55–71.

Brooks-Dunn, J., Duncan, G. J., & Aber, L. (Eds.). (1997). *Neighborhood poverty: Context and consequences for children*. New York: Russell Sage Foundation.

Catts, H. W., Fey, M. E., Zhang, X., & Tomblin, J. B. (1999). Language basis of reading and reading disabilities: Evidence from a longitudinal investigation. *Scientific Studies of Reading, 34*, 331–361.

Channing-Bete Company, Inc. (2000). *Tyrone Area School District Communities that Care student survey report*. Deerfield, MA: Author.

Children's Defense Fund. (1994). *Wasting America's future: The Children's Defense Fund report on the costs of child poverty*. Boston: Beacon.

Conduct Problems Prevention Research Group (CPPRG). (1992). A developmental and clinical model for the prevention of conduct disorder: The Fast Track Program. *Development and Psychopathology, 4*, 509–527.

Conduct Problems Prevention Research Group (CPPRG). (2000). Merging universal and indicated prevention programs: The Fast Track model. *Addictive Behaviors, 25*, 913–927.

Domitrovich, C. E., Cortes, R., & Greenberg, M. T. (2002). *Preschool PATHS: Promoting social and emotional competence in young children*. Paper presented at the 10th annual meeting of the Society for Prevention Research, March Seattle, WA.

Domitrovich, C., & Greenberg, M. T. (2000). The study of implementation: Current finding from effective programs for school-aged children. *Journal of Educational and Psychological Consultation, 11*, 193–221.

Domitrovich, C. E., Greenberg, M. T., Kusche, C., & Cortes, R. (1999). *The Preschool PATHS Curriculum*. Unpublished curriculum, Pennsylvania State University, University Park, city for PSU?

Duncan, G. J., Brooks-Gunn, J., & Klebanov, P. (1994). Economic deprivation and early-childhood development. *Child Development, 62*, 296–318.

Eddy, M. J., Reid, J. B., & Fetrow, R. A. (2000). An elementary school-based prevention program targeting modifiable antecedents of youth delinquency and violence: Linking the Interests of Families and Teachers (LIFT). *Journal of Emotional and Behavioral Disorders, 8*, 165–176.

Feinberg, M. E., & Greenberg, M. T. (2004). Readiness, functioning, and perceived effectiveness of community prevention coalitions. *American Journal of Community Psychology, 33*, 163–176.

Feinberg, M. E., Greenberg, M. T., & Osgood, W. O. (2004). Technical assistance in prevention programs: Correlates of perceived need in Communities that Care. *Evaluation and Program Planning, 27*, 263–274.

Flaherty, L. T., Weist, M. D., & Warner, B. S. (1996). School-based mental health services in the United States: History, current models and needs. *Community Mental Health Journal, 32*, 341–352.

Gest, S. D., Freeman, N. R. Domitrovich, C. E., & Welsh, J. A. (2004). Parental discipline style as a moderator of the association between shared book reading and language comprehension skills. *Early Childhood Research Quarterly, 19*, 319–336.

Greenberg, M. T., Domitrovich, C. E., Graczyk, P., & Zins, J. (2001). *A conceptual model for the implementation of school-based preventive interventions: Implications for research, practice and policy*. Washington, DC: Report for the Center for Mental Health Services, SAMHSA.

Greenberg, M. T., Domitrovich, C. E., Graczyk, P. A., & Zins, J. E. (2002). *The study of implementation in school-based prevention research: Implications for theory, research, and practice*. Rockville, MD: Center for Mental Health Services, Substance Abuse and Mental Health Services Administration.

Hawkins, J. D., Catalano, R. F., & Miller, J. Y. (1992). Risk and protective factors for alcohol and other drug problems in adolescence and early adulthood: Implications for substance abuse prevention. *Psychological Bulletin, 112*, 64–105.

Institute of Medicine. (1994). *Reducing risks for mental disorders: Frontiers for preventive intervention research*. Washington, DC: National Academy Press.

Kelleher, K. J., Taylor, J. L., & Rickert, V. I. (1992). Mental health services for rural children and adolescents. *Clinical Psychology Review, 12*, 841–852.

Kusche, C. A., & Greenberg, M. T. (1994). *The PATHS Curriculum: Promoting Alternative Thinking Strategies*. Seattle, WA: Developmental Research Programs.

Lipman, E. L., & Offord, D. R. (1997). Psychosocial morbidity among poor children in Ontario. In G. J. Duncan & Brooks-Gunn (Eds.), *Consequences of growing up poor* (pp. 239–287). New York: Russell Sage Foundation.

McLoyd, V. C. (1990). The impact of economic hardship on black families and children: Psychological distress, parenting, and socioemotional development. *Child Development, 61*, 311–346.

Montgomery, L. E., Kiely, J. L., & Pappas, G. (1996). The effects of poverty, race, and family structure on U.S. children's health: Data from the NHIS, 1978–1989 and 1989–1991. *American Journal of Public Health, 86*, 1401–1405.

Olds, D., Robinson, J., Song, N., Little, C., & Hill, P. (1999). *Reducing risks for mental disorders during the first five years of life: A review of preventive interventions*. Washington, DC: Report for the Center for Mental Health Services, SAMHSA.

Ollivier, D. J. (2002). *The state of the child in Pennsylvania: A 2002 guide to child well-being in Pennsylvania. State of the Child in Pennsylvania Fact Book Series*. Harrisburg: Pennsylvania Kids Count.

Pagani, L., Boulerice, B., & Tremblay, R. E. (1997). The influence of poverty on children's classroom placement and behavior problems. In G. J. Duncan & J. Brooks-Gunn (Eds.), *Consequences of growing up poor* (pp. 311–339). New York: Russell Sage Foundation.

Patterson, G. R., DeBaryshe, B. D., & Ramsey, E. (1989). A developmental perspective on antisocial behavior. *American Psychologist, 44*, 329–335.

Pennsylvania Department of Public Welfare. (2002). *Annual report on child abuse*. Harrisburg, PA: Author.

Ramey, C. T., & Ramey, S. L. (1998). Prevention of intellectual disabilities: Early interventions to improve cognitive development. *Preventive Medicine, 27*, 224-232.

Redmond, S. M., & Rice, M. L. (1998). The socioemotional behaviors of children with SLI: Social adaptation or social deviance? *Journal of Speech, Language and Hearing Research, 41*, 688–700.

Reid, J. B., & Eddy, M. J. (1997). The prevention of antisocial behavior: Some considerations in the search for effective interventions. In D. Staff, J. Breiling, & J. D. Maser (Eds.), *Handbook of antisocial behavior* (pp. 343–356). New York: Wiley.

Reid, J. B., Eddy, J. M., Fetrow, R. A., & Stoolmiller, M. (1999). Description and immediate impacts of a preventive intervention for conduct problems. *American Journal of Community Psychology, 27*, 483–517.

Rice, M. L., Sell, M. A., & Hadley, P. A. (1991). Social interactions of speech and language impaired children. *Journal of Speech and Hearing Research, 34*, 1299–1307.

Small, M. (2002). *Developing a sustainability plan: Partnering with businesses and other organizations*. Presentation at the Safe Schools, Healthy Students National Conference, Tysons Corner, VA.

Weikart, D. P. (1998). Changing early childhood development through educational intervention. *Preventive Medicine, 27*, 233–237.

Weist, M. D. (1997). Expanded school mental health services: A national movement in progress. *Advances in Clinical Child Psychology, 19*, 319–352.

34

Implementing Comprehensive Safe School Plans in Pinellas County Schools, Florida: Planning, Implementation, Operation, Sustainability, and Lessons Learned

Kathleen Hague Armstrong
Oliver T. Massey
Michael Boroughs
University of South Florida

This chapter describes the development and implementation of a comprehensive safe school plan that emerged from the implementation and operation of the federal Safe Schools/Health Students Initiative (SS/HSI) in Pinellas County, Florida. The emphasis of this chapter is on practical lessons learned in implementing a wide range of services in one school district, and how the project evolved into a comprehensive plan for improving the health and safety of students. The chapter begins with a description of the federal safe schools effort and a discussion of the local Pinellas County plan and the organization of services for students and staff. The bulk of the discussion describes our experiences in implementing the plan of services including potential strengths and challenges inherent in the organization and development of a working model of services. The comprehensive model of services that emerged as a consequence of efforts to sustain the successes of the 4-year grant effort is also discussed. Finally, lessons learned and implications for other schools and communities wishing to design their own comprehensive plan and build collaborative partnerships that improve the health, safety, and welfare of students are presented.

THE SAFE SCHOOLS/HEALTHY STUDENTS INITIATIVE

In the spring of 1999, the U.S. Departments of Education, Health and Human Services, and Justice announced the SS/HSI. This federal initiative intended to reduce school violence and promote the health and safety of students by comprehensively addressing the social, behavioral, and mental health issues of public school students. The grant program was developed following incidences of extreme violence in schools, cumulating with the series of widely publicized school shootings that were highlighted by national media. The initiative emphasized building collaborations between local school districts and local communities. This grant program was unique in that it (a) involved the cooperation and joint funding of the effort by three federal partners, (b) required the use of comprehensive, evidence-based programs to support the healthy development of students, (c) emphasized ongoing cooperation between school and community providers, and (d) mandated both local and national evaluation of program efforts.

Awards were initially made to 50 sites across the nation, with school districts designated to oversee funds to administer and support collaborative projects along with community providers. The maximum yearly award for SS/HSI grants was $3 million awarded to school districts that were designated as urban communities, with smaller awards provided to communities that were designated as either suburban or rural, based on the population and setting (U.S. Department of Education et al., 1999). The intent of this initiative was to provide schools and communities with an opportunity to come together to problem solve and better address the serious subject of school violence and its impact on the healthy development of children. Another objective was to foster local continuation of successful program elements by creating an atmosphere of cooperation and a positive working relationship between school districts and community partners.

DEVELOPING THE PINELLAS COUNTY MODEL

With its two largest and best known cities being Clearwater and St. Petersburg, Pinellas County is located in west central Florida bordering the Gulf of Mexico and has a population of close to 1 million people (U.S. Census, 2000). The school system is the 23rd largest in the nation, with a student population of more than 111,000 students and 156 schools. It continues to grow as more families relocate to the area (Weitzel & Shockley, 2001). Along with accommodating the rapid growth issues, this school district is challenged by high rates of student mobility (33% annually) and 24,754 students eligible for Exceptional Student Education Programs (ESE; Office of Special Education Programs, 2001). Minority, non-White students comprise 19% of the total student population, yet are disproportionately served in ESE classrooms designated as Educable Mentally Handicapped (57%) and Emotionally Handicapped and Severely Emotionally Disturbed (41%). An additional 12,500 students attend alternative education programs because of their disruptive behavior and poor academic progress (Florida Department of Education, 2000). During the 1999–2000 school year, there were 25,439 out-of-school suspensions and another 1,571 students dropped out of school prior to graduation (Boroughs, Massey & Armstrong, 2004; Weitzel & Shockley, 2001).

Against this backdrop, the Pinellas County school district developed its proposal based on a public health model of violence prevention (Armstrong, Massey, Boroughs, Bailey & LaJoie, 2003). In developing its proposal, the school district capitalized on extensive community resources. The district benefited from long-standing relationships between schools and community service providers. The tradition of local cooperation was further strengthened by a long-standing relationship with a children's services council, known locally as the Juvenile Welfare Board (JWB), established in 1956.

Additional resources were available due to the proximity of the University of South Florida (USF), an acknowledged leader in scholarship in the area of school (Knoff & Batsche, 1995) and mental health reform (Stroul & Friedman, 1994). Representatives from USF were available to assist in writing the grant proposal and served as independent program evaluators for the local SS/HSI effort. As a result of these ongoing relationships, the district supervisor of student services was able to quickly mobilize a grant writing team made up of community collaborators to develop the proposal.

The proposal itself was organized around service system needs documented in the strategic community development plans of the JWB and other local agencies such as juvenile justice, child welfare, and substance abuse advisory boards. These needs assessments were linked to identify service gaps in the school system. Together, the community development plans and school-based needs assessments overwhelmingly demonstrated the need for comprehensive intervention and prevention services in the schools. The resulting service plan was much broader than other school reform initiatives and involved the coordination of school- and community-based programs to prevent school violence. It relied on the provision of services from teams of professions that were drawn from both arenas.

The resulting proposal for Pinellas County incorporated 14 different programs that addressed the six core elements designated by the SS/HSI: (a) school safety and violence prevention, (b) substance abuse, (c) mental health, (d) childhood development, (e) educational reform, and (f) safe school policies. Universal preventions included the establishment of social skills instruction that was implemented across all elementary schools and implementation of violence prevention curriculums such as Second Step (Committee for Children, 1997) in middle and high schools. Parent training programs included home-based instruction for parents of preschool youngsters with challenging behaviors using the Helping the Noncompliant Child curriculum (McMahon & Forehand, 2002). The physical safety of students was to be enhanced through funding additional school resource officers, gang awareness trainers, and drug and weapon interdiction patrols.

Secondary prevention efforts included Families and Schools Together (FAST, McDonald & Frey, 1998), anger management groups at middle and senior high schools using the Think First curriculum (Larson & McBride, 1992), and the On Campus Intervention Program (OCIP; Family Resources, 2002). Efforts to reach out to parents who might feel disenfranchised by the school system were enhanced through the hiring of trained, bilingual advocates. For those students presenting with the most challenging emotional and behavior problems, individualized mental health services were made available including individual and family counseling and wrap-around services.

Integrating these programs into the school system required organizational and resource development and planning, as well as comprehensive and ongoing staff training. School and community partners developed a variety of training opportunities that were offered to teachers, administrators, and other school personnel toward achieving the initiative's goal of creating safer schools. Staff members were given multiple opportunities to learn classroom and schoolwide management strategies intended to prevent or minimize problem behaviors. Individual schools learned to develop their own problem-solving teams to tackle the most challenging problems, following the model described by Project Achieve (Knoff & Batsche, 1995). To boost participation in these training efforts, stipends, materials, and trade days (time off in return for participating in training events) were offered by the school district as incentives.

Practical Experiences in Implementing the SS/HSI Plan

Following the funding of the initiative, the serious work of implementing and operating programs began. Community partners and school staff were faced with working out the details of program operation. Tasks included identifying appropriate sites for service delivery, recruiting and training staff, developing policies and procedures, confirming and strengthening agreements among community and school collaborators, and negotiating responsibilities for program implementation, operation, and feedback. These tasks were not simple decisions that could be addressed once and then forgotten. Although strong existing relationships helped the effort, effective consultation in schools required ongoing communication among partners and true collaboration among school and community stakeholders.

To foster a productive atmosphere for the management of the initiative, a steering committee that met on a monthly basis was organized. This group included representatives from community partners, school and district staff, and local evaluators. Although initially developed for agencies operating within the initiative, the steering committee expanded over time to include representatives from funding boards, state policy advocacy committees, and other community groups.

The immediate concerns of the steering committee centered on identifying appropriate matches between local school needs and the newly available resources and solving problems that arose during program implementation. The steering committee also helped to ensure a continuing recognition and commitment to the needs of the students and helped to reassure the participants of the shared commitment to the goals of the grant. Meetings were used to share information and ideas, keep partners engaged, and make sure that key issues were addressed and desired objectives met. As a result, the steering committee was able to defuse the turf issues that are prone to arise in partnerships.

This steering committee later emerged as the core constituency for ensuring the effective management and long-term sustainability of the plan as well. One of the first lessons learned was the value of such a management group for ensuring continuing cooperation and support among school and community staff. The value of monthly meetings of such a group cannot be over estimated, especially in a reform effort of this magnitude.

A second concern in the implementation of services in schools is how programs can be implemented and operated in each setting, given the unique needs of local stakeholders. Research on school consultation provides evidence that an effective, collaborative partnership is critical for the success of program interventions in schools (Nastasi et al., 2000). Principals, staff, and teachers in each site should be included in the process of program development, and offered shared responsibility for program operation. Pinellas County had the distinct advantage of strong partnerships with community service providers in the county and enthusiasm for the project in schools around the district. Even with these advantages, however, the safe schools effort illustrated the challenges of providing interventions in schools.

In an effort to identify and define successes and problems related to project implementation, providers from each of the 14 distinct programs were invited to attend focus groups that were organized on the basis of whether providers were internal or external providers to the school system and whether their programs were primarily prevention or intervention oriented. Common issues emerged regarding the role and placement of service providers in the schools (Massey, Armstrong, Boroughs, Henson, & McCash, 2005). From their perspective, there seemed to be a lack of communication with the school with regard to roles and expectations and confusion about levels of authority, chains of command, and how to communicate with school personnel. For those providing direct services, there was no clear or consistent manner for obtaining parental permission for individual services.

A second lesson learned was the importance of adopting inclusive strategies and fostering effective communication among school and community partners at the local level. Comprehensive plans are adopted at the district level, but are implemented at the school level. A comprehensive plan for services must take into account the means to foster cooperative relationships among community service partners and schools and should clearly identify the roles and expectations of its partners.

Beyond the need for an ongoing collaboration and communication to organize and manage the comprehensive effort, service plans require ongoing evaluation. In the SS/HSI evaluation consultation served the dual purposes of providing management feedback for continuing program monitoring and improvement, and providing useful evidence of the effectiveness and impact of the program efforts. A comprehensive plan of services requires a continuous feedback process for program monitoring.

The role of evaluation in the unfolding plan included formative evaluations designed to understand the nature of the collaborative relationship and the elements that contributed to successful implementation and operation of programs. Summative-oriented, outcome evaluation activities were also included that would serve to establish the value of programs at the local level. Formative evaluation efforts were centered first in understanding the context of the safe school environment. Understanding the issues that confronted students and teachers in the schools and their needs and expectations for the initiative were important. These data provided valuable feedback about the implementation of programs, their visibility and penetration into schools, and their acceptability to faculty, staff, and students. Even the most well-intended programs were unlikely to be effective if they were not valued by the students and teachers served. In the effort to understand the context of the safe school environment, the evaluation team utilized surveys, focus groups, and the analysis of existing secondary school data such as disciplinary referrals, attendance, and graduation rates. The following section provides a few illustrations of how these streams of information proved to be useful not only for the evaluation of the SS/HSI project, but also more broadly for the eventual development of a comprehensive safe school plan.

DATA INFORMING IMPLEMENTATION OF A COMPREHENSIVE SAFE SCHOOLS PLAN

Surveys and Focus groups

Surveys and focus groups were designed to gain information from the people who would be most affected by this initiative: school staff, students, parents, and providers. These also are key stakeholders in the comprehensive safe schools plan that was subsequently developed. Questions of interest for surveys included the following: (a) What is the nature and meaning of a safe school? (b) What is the status of safety in district schools and what were the biggest needs? (c) What is the most serious safety concerns for students, faculty and staff, and do they share the same concerns? (d) What are the participants' perspectives on the effectiveness of intervention programs and what is their experience with these programs?

Faculty Surveys

Data collected from annual school faculty surveys, which were conducted each year of the 3-year grant, provided a breadth of program implementation information while also being a useful evaluation tool. These surveys identified the school staffs' most serious problems confronting their schools, the perceived value of interventions, and their familiarity with programs operated as part of the larger initiative. Overall, staff reported that they felt safe within their own schools. Staff from schools with students of higher socioeconomic status (SES; based on eligibility for free and reduced lunch), and those from smaller schools with fewer students reported that they felt safer compared with staff from larger schools and lower SES schools. Male staff reported that they felt safer than female staff, and staff who made more referrals for violence felt less safe (Santoro, 2002; Santoro, Massey, & Armstrong, 2002).

Student Surveys

Student surveys were conducted as part of the evaluation. This effort was a unique opportunity for the school district and evaluators to collaborate in what would become both a needs assessment and a measure of evaluative outcomes, not to mention grant impact. The school district had been following a cohort of students each year, since they entered kindergarten, with the Omnibus Survey (Pinellas County, 2001), During the first year of the grant, these students entered high school, which provided the evaluation team with an opportunity to survey them with questions that addressed similar issues to those already being asked of staff. Additional questions were added to the Omnibus Survey with respect to school safety issues and intervention programs that had been put into place as part of the initiative. The district allowed the evaluation team to add questions to this instrument. Students identified bullying and teasing as the major issues that compromised school safety, with 40% of students indicating that bullying occurred on a daily basis in their schools. On the other hand, students did not consider the presence of gangs, drug use, and firearms in schools to be as problematic to their sense of safety.

Consolidating Information Across Sources

A series of focus groups were completed with school staff, parents, and students (Armstrong & Massey, 2002; McCash, 2003). Differences were apparent, depending on the age of the students and school level, but all shared concerns regarding school discipline problems. Elementary school students generally reported feeling safe within their schools, but were more concerned about their safety in traveling to and from school, and after school. From their perspective, older and unsupervised adolescents posed a threat to them, especially when there was no adult supervision. Older students, in contrast, reported daily threats and harassment from their own peers. Although younger students looked to adults to protect them, the older students reported that they thought adults were knowledgeable about these situations, and did nothing to help them.

Students, teachers, and parents identified school discipline problems as challenges affecting safety. Furthermore, all groups identified the lack of parental involvement as a major contributor to discipline problems at school. Elementary students reported that discipline problems often interfered with their daily school activities, and suggested that children needed more discipline from their parents and teachers. Teachers strongly voiced a belief that discipline problems resulted from poor parental supervision and lack of parental involvement with school.

What helped parents and teachers to feel more secure about school safety was strong administrative support. This included clear discipline policies and procedures that were consistently implemented. High school students voiced a need for more counselors to help them deal with their daily challenges.

Surveys and focus groups were very useful toward documenting the effectiveness of safe schools strategies because they provided continuous aggregated feedback from key stakeholders about conditions in the schools. Using surveys with various audiences (i.e., teachers, staff, and students) allowed both evaluators and district administrators to use the data for planning, resource allocation, program implementation modification, program evaluation, and later sustainability. Data derived from surveys also informed administrators about the most critical issues that were reported by those "in the trenches" and these data were reported to the administration in an aggregated and confidential manner. Focus groups allowed for a more individualized approach to information gathering, although it is recommended that they be used in a structured way to maximize the return on the effort. The use of surveys and focus groups were invaluable, in that they teased out critical issues (e.g. bullying and teasing) that might not receive the attention that they deserved in order to be addressed within a comprehensive safe school planning process.

Disciplinary Referrals

Disciplinary referrals are commonly available and frequently used as schoolwide measures of student behavior (Irvin, Tobin, Sprague, Sugai, & Vincent, 2004). They also prove useful as a tool that can be used to assist with program planning, monitor progress with respect to programs implemented in schools to reduce problem behaviors, and assist with sustainability efforts. Whether speaking about serious issues like battery, sexual assault, and drug use, or less serious issues like tardiness or missing detention, tracking referrals allows evaluators the flexibility to measure school behavioral problems and how they change over discreet periods of time. This tracking provided a unique window into program efficacy.

The evaluation of the SS/HSI in Pinellas County schools yielded several interesting findings. Two notable findings included a disproportionately higher rate of referral for disciplinary issues in middle schools compared to either high schools or elementary schools, and a disproportionately higher frequency of referrals was found in lower SES schools.

Middle schools, which had the lowest census of the three school levels, recorded twice the number of disciplinary referrals when compared with either elementary or high schools.

Furthermore, over the 3 years of the grant period, referrals for violence at the middle schools averaged one incident for every 5 students, whereas in high schools and elementary schools; those rates were one to every 27 students. Behaviors that were considered violent included student fighting, battery toward staff, battery of other students, sexual battery, arson, robbery, other sexual offenses, and threats/intimidation. Suspensions for violent behaviors were near quadruple for middle school students compared to the rate of high school students.

SES was the other factor identified as critical through the examination of discipline referrals. Given the myriad of research pointing to SES as a key factor in a variety of social problems, disciplinary referral rates for the top and bottom six schools were compared at all three levels (elementary, middle, and high) in this district of more than 150 schools. Using participation in either a free or reduced-fee lunch program as a indicator of poverty, conspicuous differences in reported behavioral problems in schools were found based on whether they were high (9.1% or less of students participated in a lunch program) or low (50.7% or more of students participated in a lunch program) SES schools. Despite the higher number of students attending the higher SES schools at elementary, middle, and high school levels, low SES schools had four times the number of violent referrals over the 3-year period. In fact, the rate of violent referrals for the 2002 school year at the two low SES middle schools ($N = 626$) was nearly equal to that of the combined number of referrals from all of the other 10 schools (both high and low SES schools) in the study ($N = 661$). Disciplinary data cannot account for why lower SES middle school students have such dramatically different referral patterns, but the results clearly support the importance of using these data before developing and implementing intervention services for students. (Boroughs, Massey, & Armstrong, in press).

The results from analyses of disciplinary referral data highlight their usefulness for implementation of a comprehensive safe schools plan in several ways. First, they helped to identify needs through an objective data source so that resources can be directed appropriately. Second, they helped as an outcome variable because longitudinal changes could be measured and detected downward trends could verify other findings (e.g., survey or focus group results) as useful indicators of program success. Finally, selective findings from referral data helped with program sustainability, documenting when reductions in referrals took place. Disciplinary referral data and other available data sets compiled by school districts are key resources when implementing a comprehensive safe school plan. They provide a broad and comprehensive snapshot of what is taking place districtwide and at the school level, and can be used for program planning, service tracking, evaluating effectiveness, and demonstrating sustainability.

Having a toolbox containing many choices on how to gather information to assess local needs, Pinellas County schools, in conjunction with partners such as evaluators from USF, moved into the next step in implementing a comprehensive safe schools plan. At its most basic level, the goal of implementing this plan meant matching monetary resources with the identified needs.

RESOURCE MAPPING

A strategic resource mapping effort in the district was accomplished in order to develop a unified accounting of the existing programs and resources for students and their families. To achieve the resource mapping effort, a survey of school sites was undertaken founded on the prevention model of services. This resource map identified the availability and distribution of services in each of the districts 156 schools. The survey included identified needs in each school, enumeration of the kinds of services in each school, a listing of community- and school-based service providers in each location, the status of program implementation, and remaining service needs (Bailey & Massey, 2004). School intervention teams had the ability to utilize these resources each month in their efforts to develop services that address the needs of their school. The teams used the prevention model to identify gaps identified in the resource map and to develop a community plan for services. The outcomes of this plan included the following: (a) evidence of the status of resources for each school, (b) a method of integrating school needs with a comprehensive model of services, (c) a standing committee in each school to identify and update service needs on a regular basis, and (d) enumeration of community resources that may be brought to bear on school needs.

SUSTAINABILITY AND THE RESULTING SAFE SCHOOL MODEL

With the successful implementation of programs under the initiative, project staff began to turn to the issue of the sustainability of their efforts. Ideally, sustainability is addressed as part of the initial planning process. However, the practical concerns of implementing and operating programs typically defer questions of sustainability during the early months of a project. Program staff must know that programs can operate in the school and that they produce favorable outcomes with the available resources. As programs began to gain traction, the interests of program staff in both the schools and the community turned to how to ensure the continuation of effective interventions.

Services provided through the initiative were initially organized by agency or systems based programs in the collaborative. However, as the initiative matured, it became more meaningful to think in terms of the types of prevention and intervention efforts that should be available for students and their families, regardless of the source of funding or method of service delivery. Where evidence of effectiveness justified continuation, programs were retained either by securing funding for continuing community-based services, or by retraining existing staff in the school district. However, even with these positive developments, sustainability was not primarily defined as a continuance of funding. Rather, sustainability was operationally defined as the consistent implementation of evidence-based prevention and intervention services that were essential for maintaining and enhancing safe schools. What should be sustained was the comprehensive approach to the identification and delivery of critical services that was initiated by the federal grant process.

These 4 years of experience in designing and implementing new services, developing cooperative relationships, and operating programs provided a rich foundation for the development of a comprehensive plan of services. The plan incorporated the experiences of district staff and community partners and combined their insights and experiences regarding the unique needs of individual schools, the availability of resources, and the process of providing services. The subsequent plan brought together the disparate program efforts into a model of comprehensive services for the health and safety of students. The resulting model, presented in Fig. 34.1, was organized by level of service intensity within a service delivery pyramid.

This model incorporates three levels of programs. The first level, or tier, contains those programs that are the foundation of a safe, nurturing learning environment in which both the

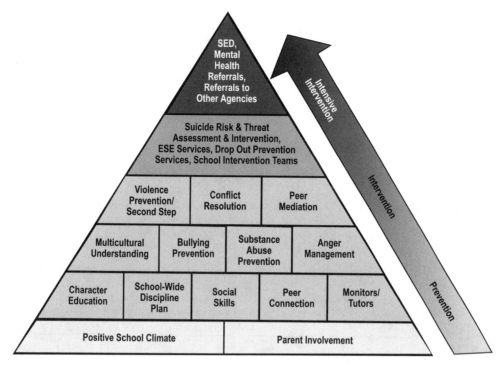

FIG. 34.1.   Safe schools strategic model (Armstrong, Bailey, La Joie, & Massey, 2001).

physical and emotional needs for all students are met. A positive school climate and parent involvement are the base on which other services are built. Services and supports associated with these needs are provided to all students.

Some students will require more interventions in their efforts to overcome academic and social barriers to learning. In the second tier of services, prevention and early intervention services were provided to address student needs. The value of these services was established in the initial grant and includes a number of specific service components. Other services that were either already in place, or identified as meeting specific student needs, were identified as well.

The third tier of services was reserved for those students with significant behavioral and emotional needs. Services in this tier include more intensive interventions that rely on highly skilled school and community professionals. This model has been disseminated districtwide and adopted as the blueprint for schools to follow as they identify gaps in services needed for their students. Staff and faculty have been trained to utilize the model as they develop their annual school improvement plans.

LESSONS LEARNED

Pinellas County's experience in working toward a safe and healthy school environment provided valuable insights regarding the practical development and implementation of services in the schools. Their plan, based on a prevention model, offers schools techniques for identifying critical needs and available resources and a process for developing a system of prevention and intervention to improve school climate and reduce problem behavior.

Summarized in Table 34.1 are a number of implications for practice that should be highlighted. First and foremost, it is essential to establish a foundation of collaboration if reform

TABLE 34.1

Implications for Practice: Lessons Learned From Pinellas County's Experience in Working
Towards Achieving Safe Schools and Healthy Students

Practice Implications	*Outcomes/Results*
Establish a foundation of true collaboration with community leaders and providers	Brings additional knowledge, skills, resources to schools
Provide ongoing staff training	Assures that staff have the knowledge, skills, and resources to promote healthy development
Use data to guide decision making	Identifies needs for program development, guides program improvement, and provides accountability
Support family involvement	Engages family to promote social competencies necessary for school success
Develop a continuum of services from prevention to intervention	Offers support for the chronic, day-to-day challenges that impact school safety, such as bullying, early intervention for minor behavior issues, as well as strategies to engage students with the more extreme behaviors
Promote comprehensive and schoolwide approaches	Enhances successful development of all students, including those presenting the most challenges

is to be accomplished. In Pinellas County, there was already a history of collaboration in the community with respect to children's issues. However, there continued to be a need to bring school and community leaders together, for planning, goal setting, and reviewing progress. The SS/HSI provided much needed opportunities to foster this collaboration. Essential to the success of this complex endeavor was the willingness of school personnel to collaborate with community providers who brought with them additional resources, knowledge, and skills. This team approach had broad representation from school, mental health, and law enforcement members to help address the challenges facing their schools and communities. We also found that it was essential for planning teams to include school and community providers as well as key administrators, to ensure commitment to new programs.

Second, all participants must receive ongoing training and support for their efforts. School faculty, administrators, and other staff need to receive training to gain awareness and encourage their participation and support of programs. They will also gain valuable new knowledge and skills. Well trained staff are not only more supportive of programs that may seem to be somewhat outside of their area of expertise, but may be more willing to implement those strategies themselves. Administrators who are both knowledgeable and involved help to create a culture of safety and support within schools. Providers of services, especially those unfamiliar with schools and their operations need training to gain knowledge about the culture of schools, the curriculum, and their role in the school organization in order to more effectively gain entry and provide successful services.

Third, the use of data to shape decision making is an essential element in safe school planning. Most school districts already have a system in place to track progress in important areas including discipline. From the analysis of disciplinary referral data, middle schools and schools that served students from lower income brackets were most challenged by violence. Had these data been analyzed in the beginning stages of this initiative and used as a needs assessment, resources may have been aimed in a more proactive manner, and progress monitored by tracking these data. Furthermore, resource mapping is a useful technique to locate services within schools, identify needs, and develop strategies to address those needs.

Finally, it was the daily concerns of staff and students that were most problematic, rather than the more extreme issues such as criminal behavior and drug abuse, that resulted in unsafe schools. Unclear disciplinary guidelines and weak administrative support accounted for staff feeling unsafe at their schools. Limited parental involvement further contributed to discipline problems that threatened safety. For students, teasing and bullying resulted in feelings of vulnerability, especially because they felt that adult staff was insensitive and unsupportive of this very significant problem. In this respect, Pinellas County mirrors the rest of the United States, in which research studies have indicated that as many as 30% of school children are victims of bullying each day (Nansel et al., 2001). Both bullies and their victims suffer as a result, and in neither case are able to feel safe or achieve (Armstrong, Scott, & Downes, 2003; Batsche & Knoff, 1994).

Based on our experiences in Pinellas County, we strongly recommend that schools committed to achieving an environment that is safe and supportive for all students consider the implementation of a comprehensive, schoolwide approach such as that recommended by Osher, Dwyer, and Jackson (2003), Horner and Sugai (2000), and the Center for the Study and Prevention of Violence (2001). These approaches recommend conceptualizing schoolwide plans that are comprehensive, and employ a prevention–early intervention model that matches the intensity of the efforts to the overall needs of the school. Furthermore, all significant adults (parents, teachers, and community members) must become involved in the planning process, and staff must be offered the training any support that they need to successfully implement the plan. Finally, all students benefit from learning interpersonal and problem solving skills, and there will always be students who need a more individualized approach and support to be successful.

REFERENCES

American Psychological Association. (1996). *Middle school malaise*. Available: http://helping.apa.org/family/malaise.html

Armstrong, K., Bailey, R., LaJoie, D., & Massey, O. (2000). *Oh the places you'll go! School psychologists lead the way*. Paper presented April at the annual meeting of the National Association of School Psychologists, Washington, DC.

Armstrong, K., & Massey, O. T. (2002). *Building a safe school: Evaluation findings from Clearview Avenue Elementary School*. Tampa: University of South Florida, Louis de la Parte Florida Mental Health Institute, Department of Child and Family Studies.

Armstrong, K., Massey, O. T., Boroughs, M., Bailey, R., & LaJoie, D. (2003). Safe Schools/Healthy Students Initiative: Pinellas County Schools. *Psychology in the Schools, 40*, 489–501.

Armstrong, K., Scott, J., & Downes, K. (2003). Bullies and their victims: A guide for the pediatrician. *Contemporary Pediatrics, 20*, 105–120.

Bailey, R., & Massey, O. T. (2004). *Using resource mapping to sustain programs*. Paper presented in April at Strengthening Our Future: Developing Healthy Children and Youth, Strong Families, and Safe Communities, Kansas City, MO.

Batsche, G., & Knoff, H. (1994). Bullies and their victims: Understanding a pervasive problem in schools. *School Psychology Review, 23*, 165–174.

Boroughs, M., Massey, O. T., & Armstrong, K. (In Press). Socioeconomic Status and Behavior Problems: Addressing the Context for School Safety. *Journal of School Violence*.

Center for the Study of the Prevention of Violence. (2001). *Blueprints for violence prevention*. Available: www.colorado.edu/cspv/blueprints/model/tenbully.htm

Committee for Children. (1997). *Second Step: A violence prevention curriculum*. Available: www.cfchildren.org

Family Resources of Pinellas County. (2002). *On campus intervention program (OCIP)*. Available: www.family-resources.org/asp/ocip.asp

Florida Department of Education. (2000). *Florida schools indicators report*. Available: http://infoe.doe.state.fl.us/fsir2000/school_report.cfm

Horner, R., & Sugai, G. (2000). School-wide behavior support: An emerging initiative. *Journal of Positive Behavior Interventions, 2*, 231–233.

Irvin, L. K., Tobin, T. J., Sprague, J. R., Sugai, G., & Vincent, C. G. (2004). Validity of office disciplinary referral measures as indices of school-wide behavioral status and effects of school-wide behavioral interventions. *Journal of Positive Behavioral Interventions, 6*, 131–147.

Knoff, H., & Batsche, G. (1995). Project Achieve: Analyzing a school reform process for at-risk and underachieving students. *School Psychology Review, 24*, 579–603.

Larson, J. D., & McBride, J. A. (1992). *Think First: Anger and aggression management for secondary level students* (treatment manual). Whitewater, WI: Author.

Massey, O. T., Armstrong, K., Boroughs, M., Henson, K., & McCash, L. (2005). Mental health services in schools: A qualitative analysis of challenges to implementation, operation, and sustainability. *Psychology in the Schools, 42*(4), 361–372.

Massey, O. T., Armstrong, K., & Santoro, R. (2000). *School safety survey.* Tampa: University of South Florida, Louis de la Parte Florida Mental Health Institute, Department of Child and Family Studies.

McCash, L. (2003). *Adolescent behavioral functioning: An examination of exposure to school violence and protective factors.* Unpublished doctoral dissertation. University of South Florida: Tampa.

McDonald, L., & Frey, H. (1998). *Families and schools together: Building relationships.* (Report No. NCI-173423). Washington, DC: Department of Justice, Office of Juvenile Justice and Delinquency Prevention.

McMahon, R., & Forehand, R. (2003). *Helping the noncompliant child: Family-based treatment for oppositional behavior* (2nd ed.). New York: Guilford.

Nansel, T., Overpeck, M., Pilla, R., Ruan, W., Simons-Morton, B., & Sheidt, P. (2001). Bullying behaviors among US youth: Prevalence associated with psychosocial adjustment. *Journal of the American Medical Association, 285*, 2094–2100.

Nastasi, B. K., Varjas, K., Schensul, S. L., Silva, K. T., Schensul, J. J., & Ratnayake, P. (2000). The participatory intervention model: A framework for conceptualizing and promoting intervention acceptability. *School Psychology Quarterly, 15*, 207–232.

Office of Special Education and Rehabilitory Services. (2001). Available: www.ed.gov/offices/OSHERS/OSEP

Osher, D., Dwyer, K., & Jackson, S. (2003). *Safe, supportive and successful schools.* Longmont, CO: Sopris West.

Pinellas County School District. (2001). *The Omnibus Survey.* Available: www.pinellas.k12.org

Santoro, R. (2002). *A validation of the school safety survey.* Unpublished doctoral dissertation, University of South Florida, Tampa.

Santoro, R., Massey, O. T., & Armstrong, K. (2002). *Perceptions of school safety: Year 2 of the School Safety Survey.* Tampa: University of South Florida, Louis de la Parte Florida Mental Health Institute, Department of Child and Family Studies.

Stroul, B., & Friedman, R. (1994). *A system of care for children and youth with severe emotional disturbances.* (Revised edition). Washington, DC: Georgetown University Child Development Center, CASSP Technical Assistance Center.

U.S. Census Bureau. (2000). *Census 2000.* Available: http://factfinder.census.gov

U.S. Departments of Education, Health and Human Services, and Justice. (1999). The Safe Schools/Healthy Students Initiative. Available: www.ed.gov

Weitzel, S., & Shockley, C. (2001). *KIDS count.* Tampa: University of South Florida, Louis de la Parte Florida Mental Health Institute, Department of Child and Family Studies.

35

Beyond Face Fidelity:
When Less Is More

George G. Bear
Susan P. Giancola
University of Delaware

Lindsay Simpson Goetz
Colonial School District, Delaware

Jennifer Parisella Veach
Appoquinimink School District, Delaware

I know what I'm suppose to do. That's not the problem. The big problem is doing it!
—Zach (age 11)

In describing their efforts as external evaluators of a districtwide Safe Schools/Healthy Students (SS/HS) project, referred to herein as Project Blue, Giancola and Bear (2003) began with the above quote by a student with attention deficit/hyperactivity disorder. Zach's statement, made during social skills training with one of the authors, captures the essence of what the evaluators observed during the 3 years of the $4.4 million project. That is, they quickly discovered that the foremost problem faced by the large-scale project, and certainly many others like it, was not the lack of knowledge of "what to do" with respect to preventing school violence, but a failure to translate knowledge into practice. To be sure, the project "looked good," at least on paper, but it lacked true fidelity of implementation. That is, fidelity did not extend beyond face value; there was little evidence of program effectiveness beyond anecdotal reports from those in charge of the project.

The purpose of the first part of this chapter is to summarize the problems, obstacles, and pitfalls that contributed to the project's failure to achieve its goals. The second part of the chapter, presents a contrasting example of successful program development—one involving fewer students (i.e., only one elementary school), a fraction of the resources, fewer and more realistic goals, and a smaller and more practical evaluation design.

PROJECT BLUE

Good Intentions and High Face Fidelity

The goals of Project Blue were to create a comprehensive and coordinated system of services for children, foster resiliency and prosocial behavior, and develop a safe school environment. Similar goals are shared by many SS/HS projects. Each of the project's goals was aligned with specific project activities, (see Table 35.1). Nearly all were evidenced-based activities, in that they had been shown to prevent school violence or targeted factors that have been shown to contribute to school violence (e.g., see Brock, Lazarus, & Jimerson, 2002; Bear, Webster-Stratton, Furlong, & Rhee, 2000; Shinn, Walker, & Staver, 2002). It should be noted that several project activities are not supported by research, but nevertheless were included in the proposal at the request of the administration (or because the federal initiative strongly encouraged its inclusion, as was the case with the hiring of school resource officers [SROs]). Actual action steps not supported by research were part of the administration's emphasis on a zero-tolerance approach to school discipline. Likewise, the project was clearly supported by the good intentions of administrators and staff who desired to achieve the project's goals. However, during both formative and summative evaluations of the project, it became evident that the "big problem is doing it." Indeed, in Project Blue the external evaluators found little evidence that any of the project's goals were ever achieved. Reasons for such failure are summarized here.

The Rush to Get the Money

In the spring of 1999, schools had only a few months to respond to the federal government's request for proposals in the first round of SS/HS grants. Many districts that were able to respond quickly were amply rewarded. Given the press of time, the proposal for Project Blue was written over a 2-week period by the project director, a contracted professional grant writer, and an outside consultant with expertise on research in school discipline (whereas the research consultant drafted much of the project's goals and activities and linked them to necessary activities, this individual was excluded from the preparation of a budget to support project goals and activities). Unfortunately, major stakeholders in the project (e.g., principals, teachers, and school psychologists) were not involved in program planning. Indeed, most of the schools and individuals who were identified by the district as participants should the grant be funded were not made aware of their inclusion during the grant-writing process, but rather were notified after the grant had been approved that they would be participating. Thus, from the very onset, and throughout the project, a critical component of effective project development and systems change was lacking: the involvement of major stakeholders in the planning and decision-making processes (Curtis & Stollar, 2002).

The Rush to Spend the Money

The project's goals were ambitious, perhaps overly so, given the period of time that funding was provided (i.e., 3 years). Of the district's 25 schools, 15 participated in the project, or at least received funding. This included the funding of more than two dozen staff positions, consisting of SROs, school safety liaisons, family crisis therapists, social workers, an educational liaison, and three "additional" school psychologists. Although three new school psychologists were hired, there was no net gain in school psychology positions; thus, the three new school psychologists had to assume responsibilities of the three whom they replaced. Nearly all of these positions ended when the grant did. A major impetus for moving quickly was that it was understood if the funds allocated by the federal government were not spent soon they were likely to be

TABLE 35.1

Project Goals and Proposed Action Steps

Goal 1. Build on the district's existing services to create a comprehensive, integrated system of community services, mental health prevention, treatment, and intervention programs for students and families.

- Increase communication and collaboration between schools, families, and various community agencies that provided mental health and related services.
- Provide a wide range of services through the Wilmington Enterprise Community.
- Provide parent education and family therapy.
- Improve early identification of children with mental health needs.
- Increase availability of site-based consultative and counseling services.
- Improve upon mental health services currently provided in the schools in order to address the individual educational and socioemotional needs of the most challenging children based on risk indicators described earlier.

Goal 2: Develop socioemotional competencies among students and among preschool-age children to foster resilience and prosocial behavior.

- Screen and identify enrolled district children who are in need of additional mental health services that are not being adequately met through the school's prevention program.
- Implement a universal K–12 curriculum (Second Step), with lessons by teachers, school resource officers, and school counselors, designed to teach various socioemotional competencies shown by research to be linked to prosocial behavior, resiliency, and decreased aggression and substance use.
- Implement schoolwide campaigns that (a) reinforce prosocial behavior and close teacher–student relationships and (b) highlight high behavioral and academic expectations and sanctions against aggressive behavior.
- Provide in-service training to staff to enhance teaching competencies related to the development of socioemotional competencies, the identification of early warning signs and effective methods for promoting socioemotional competencies and for responding to discipline and mental health problems.
- Improve the coordination and integration of prevention and intervention components, so that skills taught in one component (such as Project DARE) are reinforced in other components, allowing for greater application of learned skills.
- Based on improved staff capacity to identify at-risk children, increase referrals to the school's student intervention assistance team.
- Increase parent involvement through improved communication and collaboration.

Goal 3: Develop a safe, disruptive-free learning environment that improves academic performance within district schools.

- Hire school resource officers to participate on school intervention teams, to teach resiliency skills, and to provide ongoing consultation and support services to school staff, parents, and community agencies.
- Hire school safety liaisons.
- Conduct a comprehensive review of school policies, security measures, and procedures related to school safety.
- Increase mentoring services.
- Provide staff development to school-based intervention teams for teaching and reinforcing socioemotional skills among children with conduct problems.
- Employ alternative disciplinary interventions to teach positive behavior.
- Fully enforce the district's Code of Student Conduct, including the required reporting of all conduct violations and delivering of negative consequence for all violations.[a]
- Comply with all requirements for reporting school crimes as defined by appropriate local and state regulations and consistent with the district's Local Education Action Plan.[a]
- Continue strong adherence to a "zero-tolerance" policy on the possession, use, or distribution of drugs and alcohol, and possession of firearms and procedures.[a]

[a]The inclusion of these three action steps were not guided by research but were insisted on by the school administration, reflecting its zero-tolerance approach to school discipline.

lost. Thus, when a large surplus of unspent funds was discovered during the second year of the project (note that little money was spent in the first year because of both poor planning and a delay in the release of federal funds), it was arbitrarily decided by the administration to quickly hire six "intervention specialists." These positions were not in the grant's original proposal but creating them was an easy and seemingly reasonable approach to guard against losing federal funds.

The decision to hire intervention specialists was not only an example of poor planning (by both the federal government and the district), but perhaps more importantly it clearly sent a message that was inconsistent with the project's goals—that intervention, reflecting a pervasive zero-tolerance approach, was a much greater priority than prevention and a positive school climate. An additional message was that qualifications and training of staff mattered little in the prevention of school violence. The intervention specialist and other positions were filled as quickly as possible and typically without due consideration of necessary qualifications and job responsibilities. Indeed, as reported by one principal, the intervention specialist in her building was assigned primarily to run the copy room because teachers quickly discovered that the intervention specialist lacked training, special skills, and experience implementing interventions with school-age children. Lacking qualifications to implement the project's proposed activities, many of the newly hired specialists were allowed to establish their own roles and responsibilities or their role was defined for them at the building level. Such roles and responsibilities were often inconsistent with the vision of the grant. Thus, in some cases, staff members were underutilized, whereas in other cases, they devoted considerably more time to correcting behavior problems and enforcing a zero-tolerance agenda endorsed by the superintendent (as well as the state legislature) than to preventing behavior problems and developing prosocial behavior.

Another major component planned for the project was to provide mentoring to approximately 200 students through the Big Brothers/Big Sisters agency. However, this too was a victim of the rush to spend the money. What was overlooked during planning was that this agency was not equipped to provide anywhere near the number of mentors requested. Thus, only a fraction of students identified by teachers and principals as needing mentors ever received them from Big Brothers/Big Sisters. To help fill the void in mentoring services, another local agency was contracted. However, schools quickly complained about such services, noting that they consisted primarily of poorly trained "mentors" taking at-risk students to sports events. As such, the teaching of social problem-solving skills and the value of mentor–student relations, as emphasized in the proposal and supported by research on Big Brothers/Big Sisters (Tierney, Grossman, & Resch, 1995), received little attention.

Another victim of the rush to spend the money, and poor planning, was implementation of the Second Step program, an evidenced-based curriculum for preventing school violence (Grossman et al., 1997; Taub, 2002). Outlined in the proposal as a key grant component for preventing school violence that was to be implemented in every classroom, the curriculum was purchased for each school. Although a trainer-of-trainers model was adopted to train teachers in its implementation, very few teachers were ever trained. It became readily apparent, that time, planning, leadership, and funds for such training were lacking. Interviews by local evaluators at several schools indicated that the project's vision for implementing preventive social and emotional activities in all classrooms was far from being achieved. Indeed, interviews revealed that some project staff were not even aware of this important component and commented that the Second Step curriculum packages were rarely, if ever, used.

A final example of poor planning was the implementation of a parent education program. Research suggests that this component is perhaps the most empirically supported component of comprehensive school violence programs, especially for children with chronic behavior problems (Bear et al., 2000). No parent education activities occurred during the first year, and they were greatly limited during the remaining years. A major obstacle to implementation was an oversight with the family crisis therapists' contracts. The therapists were hired from the state's Division of Family Services to work with families of students at greatest risk; their contract did not allow them to work after school hours, which obviously is when most parents are available. During the course of the 3-year project this issue was resolved, but attempts to institute parent management training continued to fail for this and other reasons. It took more than 1 year for all family crisis therapists to receive the parent management training (the trainer was on the west coast and had limited opportunities to travel to the east). When parent classes were offered, they were offered at only one district school. This school was located in the suburbs, whereas most parents of the district's at-risk students resided in the city.

The rush to spend the money was fostered not only by the fear of losing it but also by the desire to provide others (i.e., school board, SS/HS staff in Washington, and the general public) with evidence that the project was being implemented. This was provided by the highly visible positions of intervention specialists, time-out specialists, SROs, family crisis therapists, and school safety liaisons. Although fidelity of implementation may have appeared high to these constituents, leading a reasonable person to believe that positive outcomes might follow, the evaluators termed the actual implementation as having face fidelity with little chance of anticipated outcomes (Giancola & Bear, 2003). In the rush to enhance evidence of implementation, the prospects for showing positive results were greatly reduced by the hiring of staff who often failed to understand and share the project's proposed goals and who often lacked the necessary skills to achieve them. This major problem may have been addressed not only with better hiring practices but also with in-service training and quality supervision. Unfortunately, such were neither planned nor budgeted, and thus rarely occurred. Consequently, together, the rush to get the money and the rush to spend the money not only consumed considerable time during the first 2 years of the project, but had far more lasting consequences—resulting in the lack of implementation of project activities with fidelity.

The Failure to Persuade

Research shows that lasting systems change is likely to occur when project participants are persuaded that change is worthwhile; such persuasion is most likely to occur through promotion by charismatic leaders, institutional support, professional or social norms, and knowledge/support from experts (Desimone, 2002). Each of these elements was seriously lacking in Project Blue. In contrast to persuasion, Project Blue attempted to influence stakeholders through administering or withholding rewards (i.e., positions)—a strategy that garnered initial cooperation or compliance (until the reward was administered), but did little to persuade others of the importance of the project's goals.

Competing District Goals

Even during Year 1 of the implementation, it readily became apparent that the project was not a serious priority in the district. As often is the case in education, academic achievement was the far greater priority. Likewise, as also is often the case, the administration did not seem to recognize that research shows academic achievement is linked to children's positive social and emotional functioning and to school climate (Malecki & Elliott, 2002). Indeed, accountability, as reflected almost entirely in achievement test scores, was the clear priority of the district. The other major priority was enforcement of zero-tolerance policies. Students with behavioral problems seemed to be viewed as obstacles to gains in academic achievement—obstacles best addressed by their removal via suspension, expulsion, and placement in alternative education programs.

Supported by state legislation that mandated zero-tolerance practices, the district's focus on school safety consisted primarily of developing harsher codes of conduct, requiring name tags among all middle school and high school students (a practice that greatly increased disciplinary referrals because students failed to wear them), hiring time-out specialists for the elementary schools, developing school crisis plans, installing security cameras and other security devices, and eventually hiring (but not with grant funds) the only director of school security in the state. Whereas each of these activities may have bolstered the grant's appearance of "doing something," they were also inconsistent with the vision of the grant. The vision was to foster resiliency and prosocial behavior, to encourage a nurturing school climate, and ultimately to develop a safe and healthy school environment. Contrary to what actually occurred, the vision was not to develop harsher codes of conduct, install security cameras, hire time-out specialists and intervention specialists, and require all students and staff to wear identification.

Lack of Leadership

Given the lack of project planning and the lack of a strong district commitment to project goals, it is perhaps understandable that project leadership was lacking. The district's director of student services served as the project director. For almost 1 year there was no project coordinator. At the start of the project, the project director (who was already serving dual roles) was given the additional responsibility of serving as the principal of one of the district's large high schools. Perhaps understandably, this individual elected to take early retirement before the end of the year. Under pressure from an SS/HS external consultant, the superintendent, who also left the district late in the project, revised the budget to allow the district to contract a project coordinator in the spring of the first year. This project coordinator was with the project less than 1 month. Another project coordinator was contracted, who continued in this position during the remainder of the project. Unfortunately, this individual had little, if any, experience in the areas of prevention, school violence, school administration and supervision, or general education. External to the district, the coordinator also had no administrative authority, and little institutional support.

It should be noted that some principals did assume leadership roles at their individual schools. However, this too was compromised by significant instability in the principals employed. About half of the principals of schools in the original project sites resigned by the end of Year 2. Moreover, during the course of the project a few schools elected to discontinue their participation. Of the schools originally identified as "project schools," few remained as participants in Year 3. As shown in research, change is more likely to occur, and remain, in schools where teachers, administrators, and staff remain stable over time (Desimone, 2002)—such stability was a major problem for Project Blue.

Lack of Coordination and Communication

In light of the above, it is understandable that coordination and communication were major problems. Efforts to address these problems were made but proved largely unsuccessful. The project's proposal did include a 15-member governing board, consisting of parents, students, PTA president, deputy attorney general, and others. The governing board was to coordinate, lead, and make strategic decisions for the project. However, this board was never established. Another oversight board was formed, consisting of the project coordinator, project director, building principals (or their designees, which most often was the case), supervisors of contracted staff (i.e., supervisors of family crisis therapists and school resource officers), and external evaluators. Unfortunately, meetings were used primarily for the district to disseminate information and inform others of decisions that had already been made. As a reflection of their lack of value to the attendees, monthly meetings soon became quarterly meetings, and no meeting was held during the final year of the project.

With the breakdown in communication, most teachers were unaware of the project's goals, much less how they were to achieve them. Likewise, other staff members were provided very little guidance, supervision, and support. Consequently, many activities critical to achieving the project's goals were never implemented, or were implemented without fidelity. For example, interviews with the three school psychologists hired using project funds revealed that they were largely unaware that they were ever part of the project. Not one had altered his or her job roles, but instead continued to engage primarily in assessment instead of activities proposed by the grant (e.g., social skills and anger management training, in-service to teachers on prevention, intervention, team consultation, teaching booster sessions in Second Step for target students, etc.).

Another example of the result of poor communication and coordination was the failure to implement with fidelity a system developed by an external consultant to screen for children who were at risk for social and emotional problems and in need of additional mental health services. Unfortunately, although hundreds of teachers completed a screening checklist on each child in their classroom during Years 1 and 2 of the project, the results were rarely used by intervention teams or support staff. Indeed, interviews in Year 3 of the project revealed that not a single school staff member interviewed was aware of the purpose of the checklist.

Lack of Staff Development and Training

The need for extensive training of project staff was readily apparent throughout the project, but poor planning and coordination were major obstacles to its provision. Few funds were allocated for training (although multiple training activities were proposed). When attempts to provide in-service training to teachers were pursued in Year 2 of the project, it was quickly discovered that the in-service training calendar had already been set for the year, with an emphasis on "accountability," and could not be altered. No training activities were planned for Year 3. Thus, staff members who were hired with little training in prevention, finished the project with little training in prevention and the goal of improving classroom management skills of teachers was never addressed.

Lack of Attention to Evaluation Results

Evaluations of the project by local evaluators were completed during the first 2 years of the project (funding for local evaluation was substantially cut, however, during Year 3). Results documented many of the above problems, leading the local evaluators to make the following six general recommendations:

1. Conduct needs assessments and develop building-level plans that are specific to the goals and proposed activities of the project.
2. Review and specify the roles and responsibilities of all staff members who provide direct and indirect services related to the project's goals and activities.
3. Increase the awareness and coordination of project activities.
4. Develop and implement a comprehensive in-service training program for teachers and project staff.
5. Provide increased opportunities for support staff and teachers to engage in consultation and collaboration.
6. Develop and execute systematic procedures to ensure that program components are being implemented as planned.

A particular concern expressed in the evaluation reports was the project's emphasis on intervention, not prevention. Unfortunately, very few of the recommendations were followed.

Moreover, despite discouraging evaluations and no empirical evidence of success beyond the opinions of project staff (who stood to lose funding or positions if the project was unsuccessful), the district concluded that the project was a great success. For example, the headline of one article published in a state newspaper claimed "Grant Helps Reduce Violence in Schools: District Uses Federal Money for Specialists to Work with Students." To be sure, the district had much evidence to support the second part of the title (i.e., a lot of federal money was used to hire staff).

Most disturbing, however, was that it became clear the local evaluators' reports were not shared with nor requested by the U.S. Department of Education. Nevertheless, as reported by the district, the Department of Education concluded that the project met its performance objectives. What evidence was presented to allow the federal government to draw this conclusion is quite unclear. Thus, one must view with suspicion the validity of a recent report by the U.S. Department of Education that 84% of Safe and Drug-Free and Communities grantees achieve the "results-based goals and objectives that they establish for their programs" (see Objective 8.2 of U.S. Department of Education, n.d., for complete data). In an era of increased accountability, it appears that face fidelity, with an emphasis on intervention and not prevention, is sufficient evidence to demonstrate a project's effectiveness.

Project Blue Discussion

Although 15 schools in the district participated in Project Blue at some time during the 3-year project, none had an implementation like that planned in the proposal and no two schools had an implementation alike. Years 1 and 2 of the Project Blue evaluation yielded voluminous data. Evaluators collected screening checklist data for more than 4,000 students, surveys of about 2,400 elementary and 850 middle school students, more than 200 teacher surveys, and nearly 50 parent interviews. However, survey data revealed few changes between Years 1 and 2 of the project and any meaningful analysis of project impact appeared futile. Hence, during Year 3 of the project, the evaluation team modified the design to gather more in-depth formative information in an effort to better assess the variability and fidelity of project implementation.

The Year 3 evaluation yielded few positive findings and many lessons learned. Several schools had success with the family crisis therapists or school safety liaisons hired through the grant and some felt that the increase in mentoring services had been positive for their students. The Year 3 evaluation also yielded many of the findings discussed earlier—lessons learned primarily in the areas of leadership, communication, in-service training, staff qualifications, and general system change efforts. As noted by Curtis and Stollar (2002), system change efforts do not just happen without proper attention to planning. Planning is difficult if not impossible when leadership, communication, and in-service training are lacking.

FROM BLUE TO GREEN

Clearly, many factors contributed to Project Blue's failure to achieve its goals. Perhaps the greatest shortcoming was the decision to "spread the wealth" throughout the district, rather than planning for the development of one or two "model" schools in which major components of the project could be implemented carefully, deliberately, and with fidelity. Interestingly, an elementary school in a similar school district did choose the latter approach, using primarily school funds and receiving a modest $1,500 in external funding.

Green Elementary School has an enrollment of approximately 750 students in kindergarten through Grade 4. Like the schools in the Project Blue school district, Green is made up of a diverse population of students from both urban and rural areas. Half of Green's students are minority and almost half are eligible for free or reduced lunch. Green Elementary also was similar to Project Blue in pursuing the goals of fostering resiliency and prosocial behavior and developing a positive school climate and safe environment. However, unlike in Project Blue, these goals and the activities for achieving them evolved from within the school, as opposed to being dictated administratively or through the promise of rewards (i.e., new positions). That is, after attending several state-sponsored, in-service workshops on Positive Behavioral Supports (PBS), several staff members persuaded the principal and school staff to develop and implement the school's own version of PBS.

Working together during a 2-day summer workshop, the teachers, administrators, and support staff (including a school psychologist, guidance counselor, nurse, and educational diagnostician) identified four "Koalaty Principles" to guide the program (Green's school mascot is the koala bear and hence the koala theme was carried throughout the program). Students were to: show respect, act responsibly, follow directions, and always do their personal "Koalaty" best. These principles were posted in every classroom and throughout the school; they were taught through the following four program components—components that often characterize effective schoolwide discipline (Bear, 1998, 2005).

1. *Systematic reinforcement of prosocial behavior.* To maintain a schoolwide focus on positive behaviors—teaching students what *to do* rather than what *not to do*—emphasis was placed on "catching students being good." A schoolwide token economy was implemented in which students earned koala paws for exhibiting behaviors reflecting the four Koalaty principles. Whereas receiving a paw was often a reinforcer in and of itself, paws also could be used to obtain items from the teacher and school store, or "big ticket" items such as lunch with a friend, gift certificates from Toys "R" Us, and movie tickets.

2. *Infusion of character education social and emotional learning activities into the general curricula.* Teachers received in-service training on infusing the teaching of values, empathy, moral reasoning, and other social and emotional skills into the general curriculum. Thus, such skills were often highlighted in language arts (via literature and writing assignments) and in social studies.

3. *Direct teaching of specific social and emotional learning skills.* In addition to the infusion of social and emotional learning activities into the general curriculum, teachers used Second Step: A Violence Prevention Curriculum (Committee for Children, 2003) to teach specific problem-solving skills including impulse control, anger management, perspective-taking, empathy, and sensitivity to individual and cultural differences. Teachers also were encouraged to promote generalization of the social and emotional skills taught in the Second Step program, as well as to infuse them in the curriculum by prompting students to apply such skills throughout the day when faced with problem-solving situations and during disciplinary encounters. Also to promote application and generalization of skills taught, the school psychologist and the school counselor implemented a Peer Leader Program in which selected model students were trained as peer leaders and assisted school staff in rewarding students with paws during recess.

4. *Application of a hierarchy of consequences for correcting misbehavior and a system of supports for children with serious and chronic misbehavior.* Based on the four Koalaty principles, the Green oversight team developed and posted clear rules for appropriate behavior in all areas of the building, including halls, cafeteria, recess yard, classroom, and gym. Teachers and staff also developed a hierarchy of consequences to be used by the classroom teacher and a list of behaviors for which it would be appropriate to seek assistance or correction from others (i.e., principal, guidance counselor, school psychologist, time-out specialist). For those students with serious or chronic behavior

problems, "Initial Lines of Inquiry" (i.e., a comprehensive form of functional behavior assessment) were completed, followed by an individualized positive behavior support plan.

These four components did not differ much from program activities that were to be implemented in Project Blue. Perhaps Green was more effective in implementing its program because it included fewer components, but it also is likely that the most critical difference between Project Blue and Green lay not in the components or activities proposed but in the *process* employed to develop and implement the program, as discussed next.

The Proof is in the Process

The Presence of Leaders and the Ability to Persuade

In contrast to the leadership in Project Blue, multiple leaders emerged at Green Elementary, including the school principal, vice principal, school psychologist, several enthusiastic teachers, and a districtwide PBS consultant and special education coordinator. Not only were these leaders strongly committed to the project, but perhaps more importantly nearly all were on site (except for the consultant) and remained together over the 3 years of project planning and implementation. Together, they persuaded teachers and staff to work collaboratively to bring about system change, convincing them that their investment of time and energy in in-service training and project implementation would bring about improved student behavior and a more positive and safe school climate.

Deliberate Planning, Inclusion of Major Stakeholders, and Ongoing Coordination and Communication

Unlike in Project Blue, there was no rush to implement the program or to obtain and spend money. Likewise, the focus was not on adding positions or implementing zero-tolerance policies, but on improving practices and procedures that teachers and staff use to teach responsible behavior and prevent and correct misbehavior. The staff at Green Elementary devoted 1 year to planning prior to implementing system change. Thus, at the onset, and throughout the program's implementation, major stakeholders were directly involved. Indeed, the first step in the schoolwide PBS process was for Green to develop an oversight team consisting of the principal, vice principal, a teacher from each grade level, the school psychologist, school psychology intern, librarian, educational diagnostician, and the district coordinator of special education and PBS. In Year 2 of the project, a parent was added to the team. The team met weekly or biweekly; their deliberations and recommendations were shared and discussed with the entire school staff at weekly staff meetings.

Ongoing Staff Development and Training

Green placed great emphasis on in-service training, a component seriously lacking in Project Blue's implementation. Indeed, more in-service training on preventing behavior problems was provided at Green than any of the Project Blue schools. Using a trainer-of-trainers model, four of the oversight team members attended in-service training sessions, provided approximately every other month, on various topics related to PBS, including functional behavioral assessment, classroom management, interventions for at-risk students, family–school collaboration, individual intervention plans, character education, and wrap-around services. Information was shared with all teachers and staff at weekly faculty meetings and at in-service training workshops held during 2 days in the summer and 3 in-service days during the school year.

Responsiveness to Evaluation Results

With assistance from the University of Delaware's Center for Disabilities' Studies PBS Project, multiple evaluation measures, both formative and summative, were developed and used to evaluate the program's effectiveness. These measures are described here.

Discipline Referrals.   To track infraction-related data, the Green oversight team developed a discipline referral form that was completed by teachers and staff each time a student was sent to the time-out room or to the principal. Data were analyzed and charted using the School Wide Information System (SWIS; May, et al., 2003). Data were reviewed at monthly data meetings by the Green oversight team and specific program areas were identified as needing revision. For example, at the beginning of the school year, data indicated that a large proportion of referrals were made during recess. In response, the team implemented a program in which students could earn paws by engaging in constructive, organized activities during recess. Likewise, largely as the result of data indicating that disrespect was a common problem, the school implemented the character education component during Year 2 of the program.

The SWIS data also allowed the school to view progress and successes. Baseline data were collected during the year prior to the implementation of the program's components. Compared to this baseline, discipline referrals were reduced by more than half from the previous year. Results of the second Year 2 of discipline data showed a continued decline in discipline referrals. After implementing all four program components, the occurrence of disrespectful behaviors decreased nearly 50% over the 2-year period.

Perceptions of School Climate.   School climate surveys developed by the PBS team were administered to teachers, students, and parents at the end of both years of program implementation. Results of both years of the survey indicated that nearly all teachers and staff were satisfied with the school climate and discipline procedures. However, an area of concern was the lack of consistency in the consequences of misbehavior. Only 28% responded that they agreed strongly that consequences were consistent. Teachers were particularly concerned with the discipline procedures used in the time-out room. Many teachers felt that students were rewarded for inappropriate behaviors and that time-out was not a punishment, but a reward. These results prompted Green to provide additional training to time-out staff prior to the second year of PBS implementation. Results also indicated that teachers believed the principal and teachers cared about the students, but that many students did not have the proper care or respect for one another. This information, combined with the discipline referral data discussed previously, were instrumental in the decision to implement the character education component during Year 2.

During both years of the survey, parents and students were overwhelmingly positive with respect to attitudes toward teachers and the school. The only area of concern was that about half of the parents reported some degree of bullying and lack of respect among the students. Like teachers and parents, students at Green were very pleased with the school climate in terms of fairness and safety. However, only 33% agreed that students cared about one another. Some grade-specific weaknesses also were noted. For example, the Year 1 surveys revealed that only about 50% of the fourth graders surveyed felt that paws were rewarding and encouraged them to behave appropriately (this increased to 72%, however, during Year 2). Many also reported that although all students were aware of the school rules and reward system, they nevertheless failed to follow the rules. These results suggested that the token reinforcement system was not working for many students, and provided further support for greater emphasis on character education and social and emotional learning in Year 2. At the end of Year 2, the percent of students who felt that students cared about each other more than doubled (71%).

Fidelity of Implementation.   Green used several measures of implementation fidelity. At the end of Year I, an external evaluation team from the Center for Disabilities' Studies PBS Project used the School-Wide-Evaluation Tool (SET, Horner et al., 2004) to examine fidelity. SET; consists of observations and interviews designed to determine whether or not all essential components of PBS are present in a school, such as the posting of a small number of clearly worded rules, the use of rewards, support for teachers, and so on. A 100% SET score indicates high-implementation fidelity. Results of the SET showed that Green scored above 80% in each of the seven PBS domains (and 100% in four domains). Not surprisingly, district-level support was determined to be the area most in need of improvement. A greatly revised version of the SET (SET-Delaware; University of Delaware Center for Disabilities Studies, 2004) was used in the same manner at the end of Year 2. Unlike the SET, the SET-D included multiple items that tapped facets of PBS beyond behavioral dimensions, such as social and emotional learning and family–school collaboration. Results of the second year were also positive, yielding scores above 80% in all domains. During Year 2, Green made improvements in the areas of teaching behavioral expectations, establishing a reward system, and having a crisis response system. Still, district-level support was determined to be the weakest area of implementation.

To better assess the fidelity of program implementation in individual classrooms, the Classroom Implementation Survey and Observation Form (Bear, Manning, & Goetz, 2004) was developed and used in Year 2 (see Table 35.2). This instrument included questions about the types of reinforcement teachers used for good behavior, how often they asked students to role play or demonstrate appropriate social skills, and the extent to which they taught Second Step, character education, and other social and emotional learning activities. Teachers completed the survey in the fall of Year 2 and again in the spring. A school psychology intern made classroom observations throughout the year. Survey and observation results indicated that teachers were frequently integrating many PBS and character education components into their classrooms.

Discussion of Green's Program

Within 2 years, Green made its schoolwide PBS program an integral component of daily life at school. Many of the implementation components lacking in Project Blue were present in Green's PBS program, including deliberate planning, strong leadership, two-way communication, a commitment to training, and attention to evaluation results. These components were likely responsible for the successful institutionalization of the PBS program into Green's school culture.

CONCLUSIONS

Neither Project Blue nor Green's PBS program had strong evaluation designs. Neither employed a comparison group or controlled interventions. Both evaluation designs would be considered nonexperimental, one-group, descriptive designs. Both evaluation teams relied on the examination of implementation components, multiple indicators, and program logic to establish linkages between program activities and program outcomes. Although Project Blue implemented many program activities at multiple sites, little change was detected in program outcomes. Furthermore, evaluation revealed no evidence of integration or coordination among services to children, a major goal of the grant. Systemic change did not occur; no grant component was institutionalized into school culture and practice. Green focused on what it wanted/could do. Project Blue focused on looking good to the federal government and individual schools did not feel a responsibility to assume leadership.

TABLE 35.2
Classroom Implementation Survey and Observation Form

	How often did you implement this activity during the past month?		
Project Components	*Not at all*	*A few times*	*often*
Spotlighted the behaviors of students and others that are consistent with the key principles of respect, responsibility, following rules, and doing one's personal best.			
Verbally praised specific acts of respect, responsibility, following rules, and doing one's personal best.			
Used paws to reward specific acts of respect, responsibility, following rules, and doing one's personal best. Estimated # of paws given: this week _____ this month _____			
Used other reinforcers when students displayed the key principles. Please list types of reinforcers used:			
Modeled examples of prosocial behavior, thinking skills, or emotions (e.g., models a specific responsible behavior, thinks aloud when modeling how a student might have solved a conflict, voices that you feel good when you see a student do his or her personal best on a given activity).			
Asked students to demonstrate, or role-play, specific social skills or competencies related to the key principles (e.g., asks one or more students to act out and resolve a conflict situation).			
Highlighted WHY certain behaviors are important (e.g., provides justification beyond just saying that an inappropriate behavior is "against the rules," that students "shouldn't do that," or "you should do that to get your paws," etc.).			
Emphasized the effects of students' behavior on others (e.g., "you don't say things like that because it hurts the feelings of others").			
Encouraged class discussion of the emotional, social, and behavioral consequences of inappropriate behavior and the value of prosocial behavior (e.g., asked class to consider why certain behaviors are wrong or right).			
Made instructional and curricular adaptations, as needed and appropriate, to help ensure that individual students are presented with instruction and materials that are developmentally appropriate, motivating and consistent with their achievement level.			

(Continued)

TABLE 35.2
(Continued)

Used specific activities embedded in the general curriculum to highlight or teach respect, responsibility, following rules, and doing one's best. Please list: Writing (e.g., story starter on respect): Class discussion of assignment in general curriculum (e.g., discussed "trust" and "respect" as related to a character in a story): Reading: Other:			
Taught specific lessons from a program that is not part of the general curriculum (e.g., Second Step). Please list curriculum and number of lessons:			

Like Project Blue, Green implemented many, if not all, of its planned project components. However, unlike Project Blue, Green had observable, positive outcomes and a true commitment to continuous program improvement. On closer examination of Green's PBS program, it is clear that the implementation involved true fidelity, with communication, commitment, coordination, training, and leadership, five components that Project Blue struggled with from its

TABLE 35.3
Implications for Practice: Suggestions for Avoiding Mistakes of Project Blue

- Prior to implementing project activities, devote adequate time (e.g., 1 year) to program planning.
- Ensure that program planning and development are based on a comprehensive needs assessment.
- Involve major stakeholders, such as principals, teachers, parents, support staff, in planning, decision-making, development, implementation, and evaluation activities.
- Develop and adopt goals and action steps that are reasonable—not too narrow, nor too broad and ambitious—and that are supported by major stakeholders.
- Implement the project in schools in which there is a commitment to the project's goals.
- Start small: Demonstrate success in a small number of "model" schools before implementing the project districtwide, especially in a large school district.
- Hire project staff who are well trained and qualified and who understand and share the project's vision and goals (e.g., do not hire staff with a harsh zero-tolerance perspective when such a perspective is inconsistent with the prevention-focused goals of the project).
- Hire or appoint strong project leaders and provide them with ample institutional support.
- Match the roles and responsibilities of project staff with the project's goals and action steps.
- Work to ensure that project plans and action steps are implemented with integrity. Develop and execute systematic procedures to help ensure that program components are being implemented as planned.
- Provide ongoing and comprehensive in-service training and professional development activities that match the project's goals.
- Maximize use of internal consultants and supervisors, while seeking knowledge and support from external experts as needed.
- Garner support from others by persuading them that the project's goals are important.
- Emphasize ongoing coordination and communication. For example, hold monthly meetings of stakeholders in which they are active participants in the decision-making process and routinely communicate the project's goals and activities to everyone involved, including teachers, parents, and students.
- Infuse activities for achieving project goals throughout the curriculum, policies, practices, and professional training.
- Adopt a strong evaluation component, including formative and summative components, and attend to the results.

inception. These components are the glue that hold a project together and enable reform, continuous improvement, and ultimately effectiveness. Systemic change is occurring at Green and in just 2 years, many program components already seem to be institutionalized into school culture and practice. Some interesting questions remain, however; questions that cannot be answered through these data and can only be reacted to given what we know and have experienced. With certainty, what accounted for Green's success and Project Blue's lack of success? Does more money result in a more scattered implementation? Do fewer resources force a more focused and deliberate implementation? Could Green have done even more with more funds? Or, is it not about the funding at all, but about the planning, coordinating, and leading? How much of an implementation is school dependent? Would the other schools in Green's district have had the same success with the PBS project? Interestingly, during both years of the evaluation, Green's PBS project measured district-level support as the weakest area. What if the district, and not Green itself, was responsible for PBS? Would the project have had the same success if decisions were made at the district-level? What impact would district-level support have had on Green's PBS implementation? What if the Project Blue schools were given local control and authority of their own program? In Project Blue, commitment and responsibility at the local level were never garnered. Can a project have true commitment and responsibility without local control? Some lessons learned from these two projects are translated into practical suggestions for other programs are listed in Table 35.3. They also are reflected in a comprehensive program implementation checklist, the Delaware PBS Implementation Self-Assessment (Minke & Bear, 2004), which is now used by all PBS projects in Delaware. It is hoped that the lessons learned from Project Blue and Green will aid others in successfully implementing school violence programs in their schools and districts, and it is hoped that the questions remaining will motivate program leaders and staff to pay attention to implementation when planning a project, during active implementation of project components, and while reflecting on post-project performance.

REFERENCES

Bear, G. G. (1998). School discipline in America: Strategies for prevention, correction, and long-term development. *School Psychology Review, 27*, 14–32.

Bear, G. G. (2005). *Developing self-discipline: Preventing and correcting misbehavior.* Boston, MA: Allyn & Bacon.

Bear, G. G., Manning, M., & Goetz, L. (2004). *Classroom Implementation Survey and Observation Form.* Newark, DE: University of Delaware's Center for Disabilities Studies.

Bear, G. G., Webster-Stratton, C., Furlong, M., & Rhee, S. (2000). Preventing aggression and violence. In K. M. Minke & G. G. Bear (Eds.), *Preventing school problems–Promoting school success: Strategies and programs that work* (pp. 1–69). Bethesda, MD: National Association of School Psychologists.

Brock, S. E., Lazarus, P. J., & Jimerson, S. R. (Eds.). (2002). *Best practices in school crisis prevention and intervention.* Bethesda, MD: National Association of School Psychologists.

Curtis, M. J., & Stoller, S. A. (2002). Best practices in system-level change. In A. Thomas & J. Grimes (Eds.), *Best practices in school psychology IV* (Vol. 1, pp. 223–234). Bethesda, MD: National Association of School Psychologists.

Committee for Children. (2003). *Second Step: A violence prevention curriculum.* Seattle, WA: Author.

Desimone, L. (2002). How can comprehensive school reform models be successfully implemented? *Review of Educational Research, 72*, 433–479.

Giancola, S. P., & Bear, G. G. (2003). Face fidelity: Perspectives from a local evaluator. *Psychology in the Schools* (Special issue: *Safe Schools/Healthy Students: National Projects*),*40*, 515–529.

Grossman, D. C., Neckerman, H. J., Koepsell, T. D., Liu, P., Asher, K. N., Beland, K., Frey, K., & Rivara, F. P. (1997). Effectiveness of a violence prevention curriculum among children in elementary school. *Journal of American Medical Association, 277*, 1605–1611.

Horner, R. H., Todd, A. W., Lewis-Palmer, T., Irvin, L. K., & Boland, J. B. (2004). The School-wide Evaluation Tool (SET): A research instrument for assesing school-wide positive behavior support. *Journal of Positive Behavior Interventions, 6*, 3–12.

Lewis, T. J., & Sugai, G. (1999). Effective behavior support: A systems approach to proactive school-wide management. *Focus on Exceptional Children, 31*, 1–24.

Loeber, R., Farrington, D. P., & Waschbusch, D. A. (1998). Serious and violent juvenile offenders. In R. Loeber & D. P. Farrington (Eds.), *Serious & violent juvenile offenders: Risk factors and successful interventions* (pp. 13–29). Thousand Oaks, CA: Sage.

Malecki, C. K., & Elliott, S. (2002). Children's social behaviors as predictors of academic achievement: A longitudinal analysis. *School Psychology Quarterly, 17*, 1–23.

May, S., Ard, W., Todd, A., Horner, R., Glasgow, A., Sugai, G., & Sprague, J. (2003). *School Wide Information System*. Eugene: University of Oregon Center for Positive Behavioral Supports.

Minke, K., & Bear, G. G. (2004). *Delaware Self-Assessment of Implementation of PBS School-Wide Systems*. Newark, DE: University of Delaware's Center for Disabilities Studies.

Shinn, M. R., Walker, H. M., & Stoner, G. (Eds.). (2002). *Interventions for academic and behavior problems II: Preventive and remedial approaches*. Bethesda, MD: National Association of School Psychologists.

Sugai, G., Horner, R. H. (2002). *EBS Self-Assessment Survey version 1.5*. Eugene: University of Oregon, Educational and Community Supports.

Taub, J. (2002). Evaluation of the Second Step Violence Prevention Program at a rural elementary school, *School Psychology Review, 31*, 186–200.

Tierney, J. P., Grossman, J. B., & Resch, N. L. (1995). *Making a difference: An impact study of Big Brothers/Big Sisters*. Philadelphia: Public/Private Ventures.

University of Delaware Center for Disability Studies. (2004). *School Wide Information System–Delaware*. Newark, DE: Author.

U.S. Department of Education. (n.d.). *Safe and Drug-Free School Program—State grants program and national programs—2004*. Available: http://www.ed.gov/about/reports/annual/2004plan/edlite-safeanddrugfree.html

36

Implementing the Safe Schools/Healthy Students Initiative in Kansas

Leslie Z. Paige
Stephen N. Kitzis
Joyce Wolfe
Fort Hays State University

Jennifer Kitson
*The National Center for Mental Health
Promotion and Youth Violence Prevention,
Education Development Center, Inc.*

Rural Underpinnings for Resiliency and Linkages (RURAL) is an example of a Safe Schools/ Healthy Students (SS/HS) project. Co-funded in 1999 by the U.S. Departments of Education, Justice and Health and Human Services, the SS/HS initiative supports prevention, healthy child development, school–community collaboration and evidence-based interventions. The RURAL project was designed to enhance existing partnerships in a rural Kansas county, and included as principal partners three school districts, local private schools, the community mental health center, law enforcement, the regional prevention center, and Fort Hays State University.

A significant number of evidence-based strategies were implemented in the schools and community in a short period of time. RURAL used a public health approach to increase school safety and promote healthy behaviors, with a wide range of services provided to students (preschool through young adults) and their families. RURAL introduced strategies designed to provide universal prevention for the school population, selective interventions for at-risk children and families, and intensive services for those with the greatest needs. Many of the programs designed to prevent violence and to promote the expansion of protective factors are still being implemented despite the cessation of federal funding in 2003. Over the life of the grant, RURAL served 5,500 students in Ellis County.

BACKGROUND AND LOCAL NEEDS

Hays is a small rural community of 28,000 people located in Ellis County, and is the major shopping, medical, and educational center of northwest Kansas, far from metropolitan areas. Settled in the late 1860s, Hays, Kansas earned a well-deserved reputation as one of the most violent communities on the Kansas frontier. A wild and lawless town filled with saloons and dance halls, more than 30 homicides occurred between 1867 and 1873. The first citizens of Hays included many well-known figures of the American west. Later residents were pioneer immigrants who endured the dust bowl and economic downturns, and lived in isolated communities bound to the land, church, and family. Today, their descendants struggle to cope with the declining farm economy and changing demographics.

At the time of RURAL, 91% of children living in Ellis County were non-Hispanic White, 13.7% lived in poverty, and 27% were economically disadvantaged (Census, 2000; Kansas State Department of Education, 2002). Like many isolated rural communities with few resources or funding for programs, the schools provide most of the services and available recreation for children and youth.

The community's heritage left a legacy of ambivalent attitudes toward alcohol and drugs and strong opinions about the right to have firearms. Such attitudes are considered to be risk factors for usage of drugs, alcohol, and firearms in the community.

The Regional Prevention Center and the Ellis County Community Partnership (ECCP; involving schools, social service, mental health, law enforcement, and other organizations) have sponsored annual Communities That Care surveys since 1995. This survey of Grades 6, 8, 10, and 12 evidenced alarming increases since 1995 in the number of youth who use drugs. The county rates of drug and alcohol use among youth are higher than the state averages, with marijuana and methamphetamine use increasingly common (Connect Kansas, 2001). There are low-profile, nearly invisible youth gangs, engaged primarily in weapon and drug sales and petty crimes.

The availability and permissive attitude toward the use of alcohol and illegal drugs is prevalent and further impacted by decreased parent involvement (Connect Kansas, 2001), and increasing rates of crime. In addition to being located on a major interstate route for drug trafficking, illicit methamphetamine labs are easily hidden in abandoned farmsteads and in isolated areas of the county.

Other risk factors are also present. The graduation rate in the school district fell from 95% in 1994 to 91% in 1999 (Kansas State Department of Education, 2002). There have been an increased number of births to single teens, out-of-home placements of children, and increased rates of confirmed child abuse (Kids Count, 2001). Juvenile court filings in the county increased significantly, with approximately 29% of 2001 arrests for driving under the influence in the county involving minors between the ages of 14 and 21. This also reflects a statewide trend as Kansas ranks 14th in the nation for teen deaths, particularly due to car accidents (Kids Count, 2004). In examining these needs, RURAL addressed gaps in services for at-risk and high-risk children and families, as well as the prevention of those factors that could increase risk.

RURAL PARTNERSHIPS AND COALITIONS

Ellis County has enjoyed a long history of collaborations between agencies. School psychologists from the school district and clinical staff from the High Plains Mental Health Center have shared information and collaborated for many years. Prior to seeking the SS/HS federal grant, the school district, mental health center, courts, Social and Rehabilitation Services, and other agencies pooled funding and staff to support an alternative school/partial hospitalization program. The community also has several multidisciplinary teams and coalitions in place that address child abuse, substance abuse, child protection, early childhood, and other issues. The existing agencies in the coalition first came together because of shared goals addressing substance abuse and juvenile crime. The coalition achieved substantial success in sharing funding and personnel, and collaborated to provide families and students with increased treatment and referral options. Other successes served as the impetus for public policy change.

Building on these previous successes, RURAL was a "next step." The RURAL steering committee blended with the ECCP because of the similarity of their missions and membership. As a result of the additional funding and new leadership, community problems were addressed with renewed energy. The RURAL/ECCP committee mapped all community services for children and youth, and helped identify and prioritize service gaps and needs in the community. Task groups developed and implemented strategic plans to resolve community problems.

With the Hays Unified School District acting as lead agency, the partnering agencies provided input into the project's development, as well as substantial in-kind and funding support for implementation. This history of successful partnerships contributed to trust and communication and the partnering agencies communicated frequently, both informally and formally. Partnering agencies include three public school districts, community mental health, law enforcement agencies and the court, juvenile justice agencies, the ECCP, the Regional Prevention Center, Fort Hays State University, the Docking Institute, and others. Coalition members included parochial schools, many youth-serving organizations, the faith community, the local hospital, United Way of Ellis County, parents, youth, and nonprofit agencies.

Quarterly steering committee meetings typically involved 35 to 40 partner or coalition representatives. The steering committee provided input for planning, decision making, resource sharing, community goal-setting, and evaluation.

SPECIFIC STRATEGIES SELECTED

The selection of strategies was determined not only by the risk factors and needs but also by available resources. For example, because Ellis County has very strong early childhood services such as Healthy Start, Head Start, Early Head Start, and Parents as Teachers, adding another program was not necessary. Instead, it was decided to enhance these programs with additional staff training, mental health consultation, and social work services.

Although research-based programs were required by the grant, selecting and utilizing research-based programs was also important because outcomes would be more predictable, programs would be more cost effective, and appropriate programs could be selected based on the needs of the community and community culture. Universal prevention programs were selected based on the quality of their research base, needs of and appropriateness for the population, and recognition by agencies, such as the Center for the Study of Prevention of Violence (Blueprints for Violence Prevention, n.d.). Prevention strategies adopted by RURAL included Life Skills Training (Botvin, 1996), Second Step Violence Prevention (Committee for Children, 1997), Bullying Prevention (Olweus, 1993), and Peer Mediation Training (Schrumpf, Crawford, & Bodine, 1997). Table 36.1 illustrates RURAL project goals and activities.

Other strategies were selected from the literature reflecting strategies to build resilience and protective factors. YouthFriends (YouthFriends, 1999), a school-based mentoring program was chosen based on the established benefits of mentoring, and supported by research conducted by the University of Missouri, Kansas City (Portwood, 2000). Crisis response planning, after-school program support, tutoring services, and youth advisory group development were also selected strategies.

Social work support was needed because of the gap in school–home linkages and the need for early interventions for families struggling with parenting, accessing resources, and other issues. The intent was to prevent more significant problems later. These services targeted very young children and their families, as well as school-age populations. Social work services included individual, family, and group interventions.

In collaboration with the community mental health center, Functional Family Therapy (Alexander et al., 1998) was provided to treat the growing population of juvenile offenders and to address the need for a more effective approach to treating dysfunctional families. Although not intended at the time of proposal development, this decision served to streamline a cumbersome consent process and resulted in other substantial changes at the mental health center.

TABLE 36.1
RURAL Project Goals and Activities

RURAL Goals	Examples of RURAL Activities	SsHS Elements
Provide school services	Second Step Violence Prevention Life Skills Training Bullying Prevention Program YouthFriends Preservice/in-service for teachers After-school program support Summer school program assistance Learning Center	1. Safe school environment 2. Alcohol and other drugs/ violence prevention 3. Educational reform

Provide social services	School social work services
	Early childhood school psychologist
	Parenting groups
	Psychoeducational groups
	Targeted group strategies
		1. Alcohol and other drugs/
		   violence prevention
		2. School/community mental
		   health
		3. Early childhood programs

Provide mental health services	Functional Family Therapy	1. School/community mental health
Decrease substance abuse, violence, and crime	Second Step Violence Prevention Life Skills Training Bullying Prevention Program School resource officer increased role Groups for students (alcohol violations) Peer mediation training	1. Safe school environment 2. Alcohol and other drugs/ violence prevention 3. Safe school policies
Increase school safety	Crisis teams Crisis plans and drills School security strategies Staff identification cards Security equipment	4. Education reform 5. Safe school policies
Revise and adopt school safety policies	Safe schools policy work group School board policy review School handbook reviews Building cadres	1. Education reform 2. Safe school policies
Evaluate RURAL	Data transfer agreements Data collection and analysis Data reporting Collaboration with national evaluators	All SsHS elements
RURAL dissemination activities	Resource library Safe Instead of Sorry conferences RURAL Web site Communications campaign	All SsHS elements

The Learning Center of Ellis County provided dropout prevention and recovery services. Helping to keep students in school, as well as helping those who have dropped out to become more educated and employable, was previously not possible without the SS/HS funding.

DESCRIPTION OF THE PROGRAM

RURAL used a public health model to address community needs. Project functions were divided into prevention, intervention, treatment, community outreach, and evaluation. The public health approach encourages alliances between disciplines, professions, organizations, and community stakeholders, and encourages changes to prioritize health and to use a comprehensive and integrated system of prevention and intervention.

Prevention Components

As recommended by Dwyer and Osher (2000), most resources were allocated to prevention activities. Prevention activities were school-based and targeted to preschool through middle school students because of greater potential for preventing risk behaviors. Rather than attempting to mandate top-down change, RURAL allowed individual schools to choose their preferred level of participation. It was believed that the quality of the programs would be evident once teachers and support staff observed their effectiveness. As a result, the schools would "own" the programs, resulting in improved implementation. This was critical because of the nature of the site-based management in the Hays schools, and sensitivity to the smaller school districts' culture of independence. During proposal development and after the grant was awarded, the project director met with superintendents and principals to reconfirm their commitment and to encourage participation. Although there was some initial hesitancy on the part of a few schools, all schools implemented some of the prevention strategies, and several implemented all prevention strategies in all classrooms.

The role of the prevention team (comprised of school psychologists and a school social worker) was to train and provide technical assistance to school staff to maintain and expand the prevention programs. The prevention team utilized a strategic change process emphasizing awareness, training, support, and sustainability. Teachers could request varying levels of support, such as modeling, handouts, corrective feedback, or consultation. Schools or teachers were able to request additional materials such as posters, videos, or customized handouts to support the new strategies. The prevention team provided ongoing support and secured needed resources. Each school was asked to designate a safety cadre (typically the school psychologist, principal, school counselor, and one or more key teachers). The cadre's responsibility was to (a) assess the safety needs of their school through safety audits provided by the school resource officer; (b) debrief crisis drills; and (c) assess concerns such as communication gaps between the playground and the office, locations prone to discipline issues such as student bathrooms, and the like. Student climate data provided in the form of building reports by the local evaluator were also used by each school to develop plans to address concerns such as bullying, social isolation, and fairness in enforcing rules.

Each school cadre was provided with potential strategies selected by RURAL, and could determine which strategies to adopt. Additionally, each cadre was told at the outset that they would be able to access training and resources for their building over the life of the grant, but that when the federal funding ceased it would be their responsibility to sustain the activities. Cadre members were provided with nominal honoraria and social recognition. Requests for resources and support from RURAL needed to be linked to each school's cadre plan.

YouthFriends school-based mentoring and after-school support programs were highly utilized. Mentoring services from trained adults and high school students were provided to 550 students. After-school supports included training after school staff in safety and positive engagement strategies and providing tutoring services.

Intervention Components

The intervention team was comprised of social work staff assigned to specific schools or programs. The school districts had never before received school-based social work services, not even those typically restricted to children receiving special education services. With SS/HS funding, RURAL developed and implemented a social work program that could be accessed by any child or family. In 1 year alone (2001–2002), 164 students and families accepted services, likely because the services were voluntary, associated with the schools (not Child Protective Services), convenient for the family, and free. Services included individual and/or family social work services, school-based psychoeducational groups, family/parent support groups, targeted school-based groups, parenting education, and consultative and staff development for early childhood programs. Needs assessments were conducted at each school to determine needed school-based services. Individual or family services were provided in the home or school setting, during the school day or in the evening, utilizing family-driven solution focused plans.

Typical issues that needed to be addressed included basic parenting strategies, supervision, boundaries, school attendance, discipline, and resource acquisition. Family issues such as depression, loss, financial stress, divorce, or mental illness were common. Case management and referrals to other services also were available. Parents or teachers referred children to the school psychologist or counselor prior to referral to RURAL to ensure that there was a demonstrated need for services and that the referral was not an attempt to bypass more appropriate referrals to community mental health or special education teams. Unless a parent initiated the referral, the school contacted the parent to decrease barriers to accepting services.

RURAL also provided mental health support to the summer school. A school psychologist worked with teachers and students to resolve learning and behavior problems.

Treatment Components

In partnership with High Plains Mental Health Center, RURAL provided support for Functional Family Therapy (FFT) training, site certification, and supervision training for center clinicians. School psychologists and counselors were invited to participate in the introductory training. During the life of the grant, FFT services were provided free for more than 40 qualifying families.

More than 920 individuals enrolled at the Learning Center between June 2000 and June 2004. The center provides dropout prevention and recovery services, English as a second language instruction, and adult basic education. The curriculum is individualized, self-paced, and uses computer-assisted instruction, videos, CD-ROMS, and print materials. Child-care services and evening hours are used by parents or working students. Individuals who have dropped out of school can enroll in the dropout recovery program. High school diplomas are awarded by one of five high schools once all credits have been earned. Between June 2000 and June 2004, more than 73 individuals have earned their high school diplomas. This is significant because many students enroll with very few high school credits and may only be able to attend for a few hours each week. Dropout prevention services benefited more than 296 students from 2000 to 2004. Students may earn high school credits for failed classes through participation in the Learning Center programs after school or during the summer. The Learning Center is also used as an alternative educational setting.

The Learning Center also provided adult English-language classes. Many participants are recent immigrants. The program served 285 English-language learners between 2000 and 2004.

Community Outreach Activities

RURAL staff and partners provided information and support through newsletters, handouts, community and parent interactions at community fairs, parent–teacher conferences, open houses, and with local media. A yearlong communications campaign, developed by a task group of the RURAL/ECCP committee, with assistance from the national SS/HS communications team, was well accepted by the community. The 'If Children Are the Future, Parents Hold the Key initiative' attempted to address substance abuse and domestic violence issues by increasing awareness of good parenting skills and the availability of community resources. Another collaborative endeavor was the 'Safe Instead of Sorry conferences,' which featured nationally known speakers and local experts on related topics.

Other outreach activities included the RURAL resource library, which provided materials to schools, families, and agencies. RURAL staff provided inservices, workshops, and were present at community fairs, preservice training at the local university, school open houses, and parent–teacher conferences.

EVALUATION OF THE RURAL PROJECT

Overview

In common with other ambitious projects, the goals and objectives of the RURAL project were not simple, isolatable units. The project's goals and objectives involved a large, complex web of interconnecting services, some new and others complementing existing services. Therefore, the first major local evaluation activity was (after achieving familiarity with the project) to identify specific identifiable units for evaluation tracking.

Many of the RURAL project's objectives specified measurable outcome changes across the entire county. This kind of large-scale sociological change seemed rather ambitious for such a relatively short period of time (i.e., 3 years). As attitudinal changes were considered to be a more sensitive measure regarding these outcomes, many survey questions were designed to reveal shifts in attitude that should precede or accompany the desired behavioral changes. Other design concerns were to maintain an overall philosophy of minimal intrusiveness on the target populations, minimizing the total number of instruments created, and asking identical questions of all target populations so that changes in perceptions might be compared directly between different respondent groups.

What resulted was a set of process measures including staff and client satisfaction surveys to assess the perception of program implementation and service delivery, presentation evaluation surveys to assess the satisfaction with trainings and presentations in terms of content, delivery, and utility, and interview protocols which included questions regarding program start-up, implementation challenges and successes, typical client descriptions, and more detailed (anonymous) case studies regarding successful and not-so-successful clients. Because archival data sources alone would not allow detailed analyses and manipulations to sufficiently measure the impact of programs, school and community climate measures were developed. The general structure of the instruments was kept the same, with variations for specific programs or schools as needed to track the varying indicators of project implementation and project impact regardless of the programs.

Taking School and Community Culture into Account

Sensitivity to and respect for school culture was critical. Throughout the process of instrument development, evaluators remained keenly aware of the needs of the local culture so as to avoid situations where misinformation or lack of knowledge would create barriers to sufficient measurement. For example, when conducting climate surveys in the schools, evaluators were cognizant of the time constraints of teachers given the current accountability requirements. With a half dozen or so other "official" surveys that the district schools were required to conduct, it was sometimes difficult to explain why the schools should do "one more survey." To remedy this, teachers were provided student surveys, but were given the freedom to administer them any time during a given week so that they could incorporate the surveying into their classroom schedule. It was hoped that this would increase cooperation, and facilitate understanding and collaboration among school teachers and the project evaluators.

Given that rural communities tend to be concerned with confidentiality and self-disclosure in such areas as mental health and social work (Esters, Cooker, & Ittenbach, 1998; Ginsberg, 1998; New Freedom Commission on Mental Health, 2003), careful consideration was given to the wording of survey questions. Many surveys ask directly about behaviors, (i.e., "How many times have you consumed alcohol in the past 30 days?"), but the evaluators for this project believed that this type of questioning would be perceived as being too intrusive. By asking indirect questions, (i.e., "Have you heard of a student bringing alcohol to school?"), the evaluators assessed the awareness of behaviors in order to evaluate the climate of very small schools.

Although schools collect data associated with suspensions, expulsions, and other incidents, this information is generally unreliable due to nonstandardized procedures for collecting, reporting, and interpreting this kind of data (Griffith, 2000). Behavior that would result in a suspension in one school (or even in an individual classroom) could result in a reprimand or a counseling session in another. Therefore, using suspension, expulsion, and other office referral statistics is not an appropriate measure of school climate. This, combined with the fact that smaller schools tend to have a lower rate of violence compared to larger schools (Klonsky, 2002), makes the measurement of climate in small schools very difficult to achieve.

Therefore, it was thought that measurements of changes in perceptions were the best way to assess school climate, particularly in small schools. Measurement of perceptions associated with safety and awareness of incidents was considered to be the best means to identify changes in climate. The evaluators judged these measures to have a higher likelihood of accuracy and sensitivity to change over time.

Finally, data-sharing was considered an integral part of the evaluation process. It was made clear to each school that this information was not only going to be used for the grant, but would be available for the schools' needs assessments, resource allocation, and program adjustment, based on their building's results. Evaluators provided each school with a baseline report at the beginning of the grant which included data from the first climate survey administration, and a final report which included the results from three years of surveying. These evaluation reports were to be used as tools for data based decision-making so that schools could select the right strategies for addressing their own unique problems.

Outcome Evaluation

Many of the grant's intended outcomes specified that there would be county level improvements in drug, alcohol, and violence indicators, and school performance indicators. Not surprisingly, change at the county level was not evident in just 3 years' time. There was no statistically significant evidence for improvement across the county in terms of student academic performance, student social and emotional skills, juvenile substance abuse rates, juvenile violence rates, or juvenile crime rates.

Although county-level trends were not evident, evaluators found results at lower levels, particularly in school and community climate:

1. The perceptions of adults and students differed greatly on most issues.
2. Students tended to perceive the school environment less positively than adults.

3. There were systematic differences in student perceptions between the start and end of the school year.
4. Middle school climate was more similar to high school than elementary school.
5. Alcohol and drug usage was more of concern in all respondent populations than school violence.
6. Awareness of and willingness to use new RURAL services increased over time.
7. Awareness of school handbooks and crisis plans increased over time.

Changes were also observed at the individual school level. These changes tended to be loosely correlated with the number of new programs embraced by a particular school. That is, more programs implemented at a school tended to be associated with positive trends in school climate, and fewer implemented with negative trends. Although not conclusive (or statistically significant), this seems to suggest that the new programs are having the desired effect.

Process Evaluation

Before long-term changes become visible, process evaluation surveys and qualitative research involving observations or interviews can demonstrate that programs are being implemented as intended, are well liked by staff and clients, and demonstrate outcomes at the individual level. Based on the review of all process evaluation data sources, evaluators determined that all program components were implemented as planned. However, based on interview and survey results, there were some prevention team activities that were a little slow in getting started or accepted at all schools. Otherwise, all of the prevention, intervention, staff development, school policy and planning, and community awareness programs were very active and well utilized. Program staff and client satisfaction ratings were high, and grant-sponsored trainings and presentations were for the most part perceived as being of high quality and containing important and useful information.

Service provider interviews were used to assess both implementation success and individual-level change. The interviews allowed evaluators to determine how the programs were structured, what challenges and barriers to implementation existed, and a general sense for the types of problems that brought clients to their programs. Individual case studies regarding successful and not-so-successful situations allowed the evaluators to get a picture of how administering a program resulted in client improvement.

Informal case studies acquired through interviews with service providers indicated that there were many individual success stories. There were also failures, but most of these could be attributed to the existence of problems well beyond what RURAL programs were designed to address, such as pre-existing severe drug addiction or abuse situations; or lack of buy-in by program participants. It is worth mentioning here that these stories included two cases that seemed to fit all the characteristics of a potentially tragic story ending in a school shooting, including alienation, suicide notes, and playing with bombs or other weapons. For the moment, these cases have apparently happy endings, or at least uneventful endings. In summary, RURAL services appear to have provided the appropriate support at the right time to the right families.

From the point of view of the service providers, their programs were working well and actually were in danger of becoming oversubscribed by demand. Although it was difficult to extrapolate from these interviews the actual impact of these services on the families involved, it did appear that RURAL had touched a large proportion of the community and presumably made a positive effect.

LESSONS LEARNED

Sustained Programs

A critical challenge was the change in the state and national financial picture. In 1999, it was decided that either the school district or other agencies would help support key programs once the federal funding ceased. The current fiscal crisis in Kansas and nationally, plus the impact of 9/11, was not predictable. The last year of SS/HS funding focused on re-evaluating earlier plans and finding ways to continue successful programs in the current fiscal realities.

Sustainability issues focused on the intervention team activities. Mental health services and interventions are costly because they require salaries and funding to support staff. Originally, the school district and the local mental health center had intended to pick up services, but the fiscal crisis made this impossible. As a result, the social work services were abandoned. The model remains in place for the future when funding may once again become available.

Other components have been easier to sustain for several reasons. Because of the focus on capacity building, systems change, and prevention, there was less need to sustain the prevention team, whose responsibilities were designed to end with the grant. The project director and prevention team positions had been designed from the beginning to be temporary. Because of this, the prevention team's efforts were focused primarily on increasing the capacity of teachers and support staff to implement research-based strategies. Another key sustainability factor were the school cadres, which had 3 years of support, encouragement, and technical assistance. They will be key in maintaining the prevention programs, monitoring fidelity, and training new hires in prevention and crisis team activities. Building liaisons were provided the training and information to support key strategies such as Second Step and Life Skills Training.

The Learning Center of Ellis County was provided with critical start-up support. Students enrolled in the center as dropouts generate part of the district's state funding. Affordable class fees are charged for students who have not dropped out, but need to recover credits. Fees are waived for disadvantaged students. Other operating costs have been covered by the district's general fund. The Learning Center generates sufficient revenue to self-sustain.

With key clinicians trained and an on-site certified supervisor, the mental health center continues to utilize FFT. FFT resulted in significant changes in service delivery to the 20 counties in northwest Kansas served by High Plains Mental Health Center.

Other agencies adopted pre-existing RURAL programs, such as the Single Parent Support Group, the Parenting Education Programs, and other activities. The YouthFriends program was so successful that the state YouthFriends agency has covered the expenses of the local coordinator, who works with Ellis County schools and trains other school districts in western Kansas.

The resource library that provides books, videos, and other materials to teachers and parents regarding violence, drugs, parenting, and other childhood issues remains available. The steering committee has evolved into a focused group charged with implementing the Child Youth Development Study in collaboration with the Communities that Care developers, and the Community Mobilization Committee evolved into the Community Action Coalition of Ellis County with a well-defined mission and purpose. The youth empowerment groups have become the Hays Youth Advisory Council, with middle and high school youth working with the local United Way, city commission and other organizations.

Evaluation Lessons

When evaluating a comprehensive project in a short period of time, it is useful to measure both short- and long-term outcomes. It is unrealistic to expect results in a short period of time when the project is multifaceted and the focus is on entire communities. Often, the first available results will be from program implementation and individual-level results.

Especially within rural settings where resources are limited, it was often difficult to find adequate sources of archival data for the outcome evaluation. For those archival sources that were available, many had a lag time that was 1 to 3 years, making much of the data too old to be very useful. Developing local sources of data would have been very helpful for the evaluation, but was difficult to accomplish in such a short period of time, and would have meant convincing existing agencies to drop their current method of data collection. It would have been very useful to have access to juvenile justice agency data reports to track trends in offenses and the movement of juveniles through the system. However, the agencies did not collect data in any sort of standardized manner. Each agency had unique data collection procedures that lacked coordination.

GENERAL CONCLUSIONS

The most positive lesson is that substantial funding in a short amount of time can be a very powerful change agent. Although it is possible that some of these programs could have been introduced to the community over time, the impact would not have been comprehensive. RURAL made a dramatic impact because so much could be accomplished in a short time.

Another lesson was the benefit of funding being tied to research-based programs with clear purposes. This clarified expectations and helped team members emphasize issues such as strategy selection and treatment fidelity.

The hardest lesson learned was that sustainability plans need to be developed and implemented from the initiation of the project. SS/HS sites need to focus on sustaining strategies and essential functions, not the project. From Day 1, SS/HS sites need to plan for the time when federal funding ceases and should emphasize sustainable strategies. And, in today's

TABLE 36.2
Recommended Activities and Strategies for Promoting Safe Schools

---

Communities
Develop a community partnership
1. Identify groups with personnel and skills that are needed to facilitate change
2. Include those with intimate knowledge of agency systems
3. Enhance existing agency relationships
4. Encourage alliances between community agencies and stakeholders

Conduct Community Level Needs Assessment
1. Prioritize concerns and strategies
2. Identify service gaps
3. Identify coordination issues
4. Focus limited resources, eliminate redundancy
5. Identify community strengths and weaknesses

Schools/School Districts
Another Committee!
1. Select key personnel to self-assess school needs
2. Provide evaluation feedback of program outcomes
3. School/district needs assessment
4. Prioritize concerns and strategies
5. Identify service gaps
6. Identify personnel and resources needed
7. Include teachers/staff so they are "on board"
8. Identify programs appropriate to needs
9. Provide support for implementation

---

reality, sustainability plans need to be flexible and develop multiple options to cover operating expenses.

Goals and activities need to be realistic and attainable. Projects should target outcomes that can be achieved in a short period of time. When developing goals and objectives, remember that 3 years of SS/HS funding is a relatively short time to accomplish measurable systems change as a result of new programs.

Implementation can begin rapidly if the project plan is well organized and considers how to recruit, hire, and train staff after the school year has begun. Support from partners and the district stakeholders is essential. One reason for RURAL's rapid start up is that key gatekeepers and stakeholders did not need to be "sold" on the value of the initiative, because they had been asked for input when the grant was written.

Generalization to Other Communities

RURAL could be replicated in other communities for its use of the public health model to address school safety and healthy behaviors in a comprehensive manner. The emphasis on prevention and staff development is also important. The strategies used to enhance and sustain school and community change were apparently effective in a rural community. Table 36.2 provides recommended activities and strategies for other communities and schools interested in replicating a comprehensive school safety strategy.

ACKNOWLEDGMENTS

The project was developed under a grant from the Departments of Education, Justice, and Health and Human Services (CFDA 84: 184L Coordinated Grant to Local Educational Agencies for Safe and Drug-Free Learning Environments, Safe Schools/Healthy Initiative). This chapter represents the view of the authors. The contents do not necessarily represent the federal departments' policy, and endorsement by the federal government should not be assumed. It does not necessarily reflect those of Fort Hays State University. The National Center for Mental Health Promotion and Youth Violence Prevention, Education Development Center, Inc. nor the Hays Unified School District.

REFERENCES

Alexander, J., Barton, C., Gordov, D., Grotpeter, J., Hansson, K., Harrison, R., & et al., (1998). *Blueprints for Violence Prevention, Book Three: Functional Family, Therapy*. Boulder, Co: Center for the study and prevention of violence.

Blueprints for Violence Prevention. (n.d.). University of Colorado, Center for the Study and Prevention of Violence (CSPV). Avalable; http://www.Colorado.EDU/cspv/ blueprints/about/main.htm

Botvin, G. J. (1996). *Life skills training*. Princeton, NJ: Princeton Health Press.

Census 2000. Suitland, MD: U.S. Census Bureau.

Committee for Children. (1997). *Second Step: A violence prevention curriculum*. Seattle, WA: Author. Available: www.cfchildren.org

Connect Kansas. (2001). *Ellis County Communities that Care survey results*. Available: http://216.49.238.48/ ck/portal.php

Dwyer, K., & Osher, D. (2000). *Safeguarding our children: An action guide*. Washington, DC: U.S. Departments of Education and Justice, American Institutes for Research.

Dwyer, K., Osher, D., & Wagner, C. (1998). *Early warning, timely response: A guide to safe schools*. Washington, DC: U.S. Department of Education.

Esters, I. G., Cooker, P. G., & Ittenbach, R. F. (1998). Effects of a unit of instruction in mental health on rural adolescents conceptions of mental illness and attitudes about seeking help. *Adolescence, 33*, 469–476.

Ginsberg, L. H. (1998). *Social work in rural communities.* Alexandria, VA: Council on Social Work Education.

Griffith, J. (2000). School climate as group evaluation and group consensus: Students' and parent perceptions of the elementary school environment. *The Elementary School Journal, 101,* 35–61.

Hawkins, J. D., & Catalano, R. (1992). *Communities that Care: Action for drug abuse prevention.* San Francisco, CA: Jossey-Bass.

Kansas State Department of Education. (2002). *Ellis County statistics.* Available: http://www.ksde.org

Kids Count. (2001). *Ellis County report.* Available: http://www.socwel.ukans.edu /~kidcount/

Klonsky, M. (2002). How smaller schools prevent violence. *Educational Leadership, 59*(5), 65–69.

New Freedom Commission on Mental Health. (2003). *Achieving the promise: Transforming mental health care in America. Final Report.* Rockville, MD: Department of Health and Human Services.

Olweus, D. (1993). *Bullying at school: What we know and what we can do.* Oxford, UK: Blackwell.

Portwood, S. S. (2000). YouthFriends evaluation. Available: http://www.youthfriends.org/ about/evaluation/index.html

Safe Schools/Healthy Students Initiative supports broad-based prevention efforts. (2001). *The Challenge, 10*(1), 1–2.

Schrumpf, F., Crawford, D. K., & Bodine, R. J. (1997). *Peer mediation: Conflict resolution in schools* (rev. ed.). Champaign, IL: Research Press.

YouthFriends. (1999). *YouthFriends operations manual.* Kansas City, MO: author.

37

Implementing Comprehensive Safe School Plans: Effective School and Community Mental Health Collaborations to Reduce Youth Violence

Sharon Telleen
Young Ok Rhee Kim
University of Illinois at Chicago

Helen Stewart-Nava
Community Care Options

Rosario C. Pesce
Susan Maher
Morton High School District

The Safe Schools/Healthy Students (SS/HS) Initiative, (SS/HSI) funded by three federal agencies—the U.S. Department of Education, the U.S. Department of Justice, and the U.S. Department of Health and Human Services—was a nationwide interagency initiative to prevent and reduce youth violence in and around schools. Local educational agencies (LEAs) in partnership with their community's law enforcement, public mental health, and juvenile justice agencies received funding to implement and evaluate community-specific comprehensive plans for youth violence prevention, early intervention, and healthy childhood development. In 1999, the J. Sterling Morton High School District 201 in suburban Cook County Illinois received funding in the first cohort of grantees. Sharon Telleen of the University of Illinois at Chicago was the evaluator to assess the impact of the local initiative.

BACKGROUND AND LOCAL NEEDS

J. Sterling Morton High School District 201 is one of the largest districts in Illinois, serving the Chicago border suburbs of Berwyn, Cicero, Lyons, and Stickney in suburban Cook County. Across the four suburbs there are 32 elementary and middle schools that feed into the high school district. The two high schools in High School District 201—Morton East in Cicero and Morton West in Berwyn—have a combined enrollment of more than 6,000 students. Morton East has the largest Hispanic student body in the state of Illinois (91.5% of its 3,399 students at the start of the initiative in 1999). The students are predominantly Mexican, and 23.9% are limited English-proficient. Many families are recent immigrants or first-generation Mexican Americans. At Morton West, 39% of the students are Hispanic, 4.5% of whom are limited English-proficient. More than 38% of the students in District 201 qualify for free or reduced-fee school lunches. The truancy and dropout rates for District 201 are higher than the state average (State of Illinois, 2002).

In the decade from 1990 to 2000, there was a 70% increase in the number of persons living below the poverty level in Cicero. Families qualifying for public assistance increased by 80% (U.S. Census Bureau, 2000). Few after-school programs existed and opportunities for youth to build social skills were limited.

The town of Cicero, with 85,616 persons, is the largest suburb in District 201. Cicero's population is 77% Latino/a and more than 80% of the population under age 18 is Latino/a (U.S. Census Bureau, 2000). Neighboring Berwyn is a suburb of 54,016 people 38% of whom are Latino. These figures reflect an overall increase in the Chicago region's Latino population—more than 1 million Latinos currently live in the Chicago metropolitan area. According to the Northeastern Illinois Planning Commission (2002), Chicago and its surrounding suburbs have one of the largest Mexican immigrant communities in the country. Metropolitan Chicago ranked second among metropolitan areas after Los Angeles in the number of Mexican immigrants (Northeastern Illinois Planning Council, 2002). The residents' ties to Mexico remain strong, as evidenced by the 2004 trip to the U.S. by Mexico's president, Vincente Fox, who chose to give a major address at Unity Middle School in the Cicero School District.

Needs of the Hispanic Immigrant Community

A recent needs assessment by the Institute for Latino Studies at Notre Dame (2002) found that a general distrust and suspicion exists between the local power structure in Cicero and the Latino community. The town of Cicero has a history from the 1930s as a stronghold of organized crime. Since the 1950s, there have been numerous federal investigations and prosecutions involving town officials, members of the local power structure, and local businessmen (U.S. Department of Justice, 2001).

Mexican and other Hispanic immigrants living in District 201 experience a number of problems. During the 1990s, the town of Cicero was charged by the U.S. Department of Justice with housing discrimination aimed at Latino/as (Institute for Latino Studies, 2002). Currently, the FBI, State of Illinois, and Cook County Board of Elections monitor voting during national, state, and local elections as a result of citizen complaints of voter intimidation and widespread allegations of voting fraud. In 2001, the town president and other officials were indicted on charges of diverting more than $10 million in town funds to their private enterprises (U.S. Department of Justice, 2001); they were convicted in July 2002.

As in most communities, gang activities include drug dealing and the violence that accompanies the drug business. The gangs active in District 201 communities are known to recruit school-aged children. The local police department has identified 22 gangs in Cicero. The adjacent suburbs are concerned that this activity will increasingly spill over into their towns and have worked actively to avoid its spread. Additionally, Cicero is the site of Chicago's major rail and truck yard with goods arriving in cargo containers from Mexico and the Pacific Rim. This provides a major gateway for drugs to enter the Chicago area from Mexico. Rail and truck shipments arriving in Cicero from international ports will require enormous resources to monitor under Homeland Security.

EVOLUTION OF COMMUNITY COLLABORATION FOR YOUTH

A strategy emerged even prior to the SS/HS Initiative to stem the growing influence of gangs, drug dealing, and the number of gang-related violent incidents in the high schools and their communities. In the mid-1990s, Rosario Pesce, in his role as District 201 student assistance program coordinator and school psychologist, developed a collaborative with Interfaith Leadership Project (ILP), a faith-based community action group representing a significant number of local churches. Together, Morton and ILP began conducting community parenting and violence prevention workshops for parents of students. The workshops were designed for Latino immigrant parents and were conducted in both Spanish and English. The teachers who taught the violence prevention and gang resistance curriculum to high school students taught the same content to parents. The parent workshops, however, were held in the churches in the Cicero neighborhoods where most of the parents lived.

Precipitating Events for Collective Action

In 1996, there was a gang-related shooting of a student after school hours within a block of Morton West High School. Students, teachers, and community residents where all shocked and subsequently a well-attended community meeting was held at the high school. As a result of that meeting, the District 201 School Board developed a plan of action to address violence and gang activity throughout the district. This plan included an intervention initiative designed to involve major stakeholders in the community. Just prior to the shooting, Pesce had created a community task force, which was strengthened and became the Morton West Community Violence Prevention Task Force. The school shooting became the catalyst for developing the task force's first action plans. In 1997, a similar task force was established at Morton East. The school, agency, and citizen participation in the community task forces reflected the often stated view that "we don't want this violence here; shootings are not inevitable and we will not accept it as the norm for our community; we can do something about it" (Telleen, Maher & Pesce, 2003).

Regular participants attending the monthly task force meetings included Sharon Telleen, a University of Illinois at Chicago professor, a reporter for the community newspaper, state police gang prevention officers, a Berwyn community policing officer, a Cook County Juvenile Court officer, a town trustee, the ILP, a representative of the Cook County Department of Public Health, local mental health agencies, as well as parents and students. At times, representatives of local businesses (including a bank), the YMCA, youth commissioners, the Berwyn Park District, and the Girl Scouts also attended the monthly meetings.

Each task force identified the current needs of its community, prioritized those needs, and then formed action teams. Each task force member participated in one action team. At the monthly meeting, time was allotted for the action teams to meet. Funding was sought to implement the action plans. Initially, most of the funding came from the Illinois Violence Prevention Authority, then later the U.S. Federal Safe Schools/Healthy Students Initiative.

Goals of the Program: A Particular Model

The District 201 initiative set three primary goals:

1. Provide opportunities for socioemotional learning to enable students to develop the skills and emotional resilience necessary to promote positive mental health, engage in pro-social behavior, and prevent violent behavior and drug use.
2. Ensure that all students attending District 201 and its feeder schools are able to learn in a safe, disciplined, and drug-free environment.
3. Help develop an infrastructure that will institutionalize and sustain integrated services after federal funding ends.

Levels of Intervention: Districtwide, Schoolwide, and Classroom

An integrated, comprehensive, communitywide strategy formed the core of the program's implementation (see Table 37.1). This communitywide approach aimed at ensuring a safe environment in which to learn, thereby fostering healthy child development, preventing the initiation of violent behavior as well as the abuse of alcohol and other drugs, and enhancing the mental health and social services available to at-risk youth and their families. The underlying principles guiding the SS/HS school and community-based violence prevention efforts followed an organizational approach proposed by Furlong, Pavelski, and Saxton (2002)— reaffirm, reconnect, reconstruct, repair, and protect relationships with students at school. The community task force partners reframed their work with youth away from an emphasis on gangs, drugs and violence. They worked toward building community connections for youth (Telleen, Maher & Pesce, 2003), and individualized school connections with students (Flores-Gonzalez, 2002), thereby fostering positive youth development through a prevention approach to youth violence.

Second, the local approach sought to integrate the various services offered within the community. The communitywide collaborative approach used many of the principles identified by Telleen (Telleen & Scott, 2001). SS/HS also sought to integrate and provide role clarity between the juvenile justice system, the schools, and the social service providers; furthermore, it attempted to integrate their efforts. This resulted in a comprehensive communitywide approach, providing programs across the developmental continuum from preschool to high school for each SS/HS goal (Hawkins & Catalano, 1992).

A socioecological/developmental model (Trickett, 1987) was used to guide the development of services within the community, the school district, the school, and within classrooms for children experiencing problems with the law, with gang activity or with emotional/aggressive and academic problems (Dwyer & Osher, 2000). This ecological-developmental model is illustrated in Table 37.1.

SPECIFIC STRATEGIES AND ACTIVITIES SELECTED

To improve student mental health and thereby student academic functioning, school–community based mental health services, in collaboration with local law enforcement, were a major component of the SS/HS in the Morton High School District. One of the goals of the community mental health component was to increase coordination of services among the community mental health agencies. A second goal was to create a bridge between mental health agencies and the schools. This, supported by the increased coordination among the agencies, provided the framework for a seamless entry into services, as well as increased coordination among all services involved in a child's life. This coordination, it was hypothesized, would

TABLE 37.1

Strategies Selected for Safe Schools Intervention

Goal 1. Integrated, Comprehensive Communitywide Strategies to Enhance Social Learning and Prevent Violent Behavior and Drug Use

Level of Strategy	*Level of Intervention*	*Developmental Levels*	*Activities*
Communitywide strategies	Berwyn, IL Cicero, IL	Elementary schools Grades K–12	School resource Officers After-school programs
In-school strategies	*Schoolwide interventions* Cicero, Berwyn, Lyons Berwyn	 Grades 1–6 Grades 7–8	 Cooperative games Olweus Bully Prevention Program (Olweus, 1993)
	Morton East High School –Cicero	Grades 9–12	Stop Gun Violence Art Contest Town vehicle sticker Club-Leaders in full effect-name of club in caps
	Classrom interventions Cicero Cicero Berwyn ann Lyons Cicero	 Preschool 3–5 yrs. Grades 1–6 Grades 4–6	 I Can Problem Solve (Share, 1992) PAX game-classroom management management Classwide peer tutoring
	Targeted individual interventions Mental health case management Truancy prevention Morton-East Cicero	 Grades 1–12 Grades 9–12	 Wraparound case management school outreach worker
	Pregnant and parenting students-Morton-East H.S.	Grades 9–12	Case management, support groups, day care, health care, network of services

Goal 2. Creating a Safe, Disciplined Drug Free Environment

Level of Strategy	*Developmental Level*	*Activities*
Communitywide	Elementary, middle school, high schools All first grades Grades 5–12 Grades 1–9	Police patrols in and around all schools in Cicero and Berwyn Safety Town in Cicero Police summer camp for at-risk youth Summer activity programs
Districtwide	All schools in Cicero, Berwyn Berwyn school districts and police Cicero and Berwyn school personnel	Crisis management plan Emergency preparedness Threat assessment planning
Schoolwide	Elementary and high schools High schools	School facility safety audits Violent incident surveillance reports
Targeted students	G.R.E.A.T. G.A.I.N. Gang Avoidance	Grades 4–5 Grades 9–12

result in improvement in the student's mental health and behavior. Furthermore, previous research found that cooperative learning (Slavin, 1995) and social competence in childhood are predictors of academic achievement (Weissberg, Greenberg, Elias, & Zins, 2000; Wentzel, 1991). Conversely, problem behaviors are negatively predictive of the child's academic achievement (Malecki & Elliott, 2002).

The integrated, comprehensive, communitywide strategy implemented through this program has begun to provide a response to the service gap and increasing demand that existed because there were limited community mental health services to address the needs of families that are struggling with social, economic, and psychological issues. The design of the SS/HS mental health component was intended to prevent aggressive and delinquent behavior and foster healthy child development by enhancing delivery of mental health and social services to at-risk youth and their families (Reddy, Borum, Berglund, Vossekuil, Fein & Modzeleski, 2001). The structure created to intervene in these communities was defined by four distinct factors. First, youth violence had increased in those communities during the previous 5-year period. Second, the fragile connections between the juvenile justice system and the service provider system impeded effective interventions with youth who had significant behavior problems. Third, the lack of clarity and integration between juvenile justice and community service providers in these suburbs resulted in an inconsistent community response to these youth. Fourth, according to the U.S. Surgeon General's Report on Youth Violence (2001), 40% of youth served by the juvenile justice system have been identified as having a mental illness for which there has been no intervention. Nationwide, it is estimated that 75% to 80% of children in need do not receive appropriate and effective mental health services (U.S. Department of Health and Human Services, 2001).

Detailed Description of Program

Coordinated services were developed by four community mental health agencies serving the families in Morton High School District: Community Care Options (Fillmore Center for Human Services), Family Services and Mental Health Center of Cicero, Youth Outreach Services, and Community Family Services of Western Springs. The mental health agencies and schools used an interorganizational collaborative model for coordination between the school social workers and school psychologists and the community mental health providers.

Referral and Intake

Traditionally, in order to access services from any one of the partnering agencies, school staff and/or families had to call each intake department and, at times, be placed on a waiting list for services. The mental health partners sought to create a seamless system of service delivery among the participating mental health agencies to enable better coordination with schools. This was achieved by creating a central point of intake that schools could use. The case management team developed a program-specific referral form that was distributed to all of the schools. The referral form was then completed by the school social worker and faxed directly to the lead case manager, bypassing the agency intake department. Schools were asked to attach a release of information signed by the caretakers ensuring that the family was informed of and agreed with the referral to the program. The lead case manager completed the intake with the assistance of the school social worker and the case was assigned within 48 hours of being referred.

Schools were asked to identify and refer children who were not currently receiving services. The goal was to reach the children who for a variety of reasons had not successfully accessed and engaged any of the existing resources. Children who were actively receiving services in any one of the mental health agencies were not eligible to participate in the program.

Eligibility Criteria

In order to ensure that the program was reaching the intended population, specific eligibility criteria were developed. Children from preschool through high school age who were enrolled in school were eligible. They also needed to meet the following criteria: (a) high risk in one or more of the following: risk for academic failure, truancy, or behavioral problems (aggressive behavior, multiple suspensions or detentions, substance abuse problems, or involvement with law enforcement); (b) multiple obstacles to family involvement; (c) multiproblem families; (d) nonresponsive to existing services, and/or failure to follow through with existing services.

The case managers each had a caseload of 12 families. Each caseload was diverse in gender, age, and presenting problem. The smaller caseload provided the case managers with enough flexibility in their schedule to attend to the diverse and complex needs of each of the families.

Protocol for Case Managers

The case manager contacted caretakers within 24 hours of receiving the referral from the lead case manager. They arranged to meet the parent at a place of the parent's choosing, this included places such as the home, school, or the local fast food outlets. In developing a course of action, the case managers talked to the caretakers and children about their needs. They also sought to involve other key people in the family's life such as relatives or family friends. The case managers included the school staff and other professionals in conversations about the family's strengths and needs.

Each family and its case manager developed an individualized plan based on the needs identified by the family and other key people in their lives. Families were encouraged to involve and access their own natural supports in the process. Over time, the involvement of the case manager lessened as the family took more responsibility for the plan. As case managers accompanied parents and caretakers to public aid, school staffings, or doctor's appointments, they served as models for how to make effective use of resources.

The team collaborated with other providers and agencies in the community. The team's relationship with the local school districts and the local police departments benefited the families, as they were able to make use of these relationships during times of crisis. Team members also developed relationships with key staff at local hospitals, after-school programs, and summer camp providers. In many cases, case managers were able to help resolve misunderstandings between school staff and caretakers, and were instrumental in helping the parents learn to negotiate with larger systems.

The majority of the children were seen in school. Case managers met a minimum of once a week with the identified child and/or the client. As part of the intensive services provided, they spoke regularly with the school staff and the caretakers to ensure open communication and a coordinated service plan.

Intensive individual and family therapy were also a key component of the program. Most of the children entering the program had emotional and/or behavioral problems that were impacting their ability to function. Many came from families with multiple risk factors and longstanding histories of violence, substance abuse, and mental illness. Several children were connected to psychiatric services. This was supported by the ongoing therapy provided by the case managers.

PRINCIPLES UNDERLYING THE PROGRAM

The mental health component of the SS/HS Initiative used a community-based system of care (Duchnowski, Kutash, & Friedman, 2002), a collaborative action research framework

(Kelly, Ryan, Altman, & Satelzner, 2000), and interorganizational collaboration (Telleen & Scott, 2001). The mental health component in the Morton High School District was based on the principles of "wrap-around" case management (Burchard, Burns, & Burchard, 2002). Wrap-around case management helps bridge the gaps between all involved in the life of the child including mental health professionals, education professionals, police and court systems, and community providers. The wrap-around approach is a process rather than a service delivery model. Through this process, families and their case managers can develop individualized, strength-based, needs-driven plans of action within their own communities. The process involves the whole family, rather than the individual child. The process is family-centered, and there is a commitment to unconditional care.

The wrap-around plan brings together the client's family, friends, other service providers and community members, such as clergy to work with the professionals. Together the team, led by the case manager, "wraps" their strengths around the client, providing for an integrated service delivery system. This plan maximizes the child's chances for future success. The team develops individualized plans to help support and meet the needs of each family. These plans seek to involve the community and family supports of each family

Children who are experiencing serious emotional or behavioral problems, such as those served by the SS/HS Initiative, have multiple issues, requiring help from more than one agency to meet their unique needs. The wrap-around process creates a framework for developing partnerships among the different providers in the community so that families get the benefit of the resources of each agency through the work of one case manager. Communication and collaboration between those involved with the children, and the agencies themselves, are enhanced through the work of the case management team and the partnership among the different agencies.

Structures for Interorganizational Collaboration

One of the objectives of the grant was to reach families that were otherwise not receiving services due to difficulties with accessing existing resources. This was accomplished by bringing together four community mental health agencies—Fillmore Center, Community Family Services, Youth Outreach Services, and Family Service and Mental Health Center of Cicero—to work together and form a partnership in order to provide broader and more comprehensive services to high-risk children and families. The model for collaboration used the collaborative principles outlined by Telleen presented in detail in Table 37.2.

The framework for the project's interorganizational collaboration is based on social action system theory (Telleen & Scott, 2001). When two or more organizations form a relationship they create a social action system. Both have collective and self-interest goals, and each has a unique identity separate from each member organization. The goal of a social action system is to attain objectives that are unattainable independently. Goals are attained through structures and processes for organizing activities. The primary activity is resource and information exchange. Collaboration is defined as a joint activity in which two or more organizations work closely, participate in mutual decision making, and share resources and responsibility. The interorganizational structures proposed for successful collaboration appear in Table 37.2. Successful collaboration involves establishing structures for coordination, communication, defined roles, and responsibilities.

Coordination

The goal of the SS/HS Initiative was to support enhanced coordination and resource sharing among mental health and social service providers in schools and other community-based

TABLE 37.2
Implications for Practice: Determinants of Successful Collaboration

Characteristics	Functions
Environmental context	
Governmental guidelines (Polivka, 1996)	• SS/HS funding guidelines
Political climate (Polivka, 1996)	• Amenability of political climate to develop programs of interest
Population characteristics	• Increased incidence of youth violence, increased immigration, increased poverty
Interorganizational structures	
Bases of interaction (Hall &Tolbert, 2004)	• Mandated by government or the funder versus voluntary interaction
Communication (Aiken & Hague, 1968)	• Number and type of meetings per month
Domain consensus (Poole & Van De Ven, 2004)	• Agreement among agencies about goals and resources
Domain similarity (Poole & Van De Ven, 2004)	• Degree of overlap in similarity between organizations
Formalization (Poole & Van De Ven, 2004)	• Rules and regulations governing agreements and contracts
Hierarchical levels (Kloglan, Warren, Winkelpleck, & Paulson 1976)	• Federal, state, and community levels involved
Interpersonal processes	
Building agency capacity (Kelly, Ryan, Altman & Satelzner, 2000)	• Developing community resources Coordination among agency personnel
Coordinating (Alter & Hague, 1988) Awareness (Poole & Van De Ven, 2004)	• Knowledge of systems, goals, personal acquaintances of other agencies
Need for cooperation and trust (Kelly, Ryan, Altman & Satelzner, 2000)	• Perceived need of organizational leaders for cooperation in exchange of resources
Staff characteristics (Aiken & Hague, 1968)	• Staff educational preparation and professional training
Boundary spanning (Poole & Van De Ven 2004)	• Familiarity with competencies and goals of other agencies
Communicating (Poole & Van De Ven, 2004)	• Frequency of communicating about decision-making in the project
Trust (Telleen & Scott, 2001)	• Stable, long term relationship with reciprocity and acknowledgement.

organizations. Each agency had distinct and unique services that benefit children and their families. The hope was to benefit from each agency's resources and make them more accessible to children regardless of the primary agency providing services.

The partnership between the mental health agencies made services to children with serious emotional disturbances better coordinated and integrated. Centralizing the referral and intake process eliminated the added steps of contacting separate intake departments thus delaying access to services. Cases were assigned across agency service areas. The lead case manager provided a central person who was familiar with all the cases and had access to all of the case managers.

Communication

During the planning phase of the grant, the lead case manager met with management representatives from each of the agencies to discuss each agency's involvement in the program. Agency administrators met on more than one occasion to discuss and set the structure of the program. All agency representatives participated in determining caseloads, referral and intake procedures, and theoretical approaches. Prior to being awarded the SS/HS Initiative grant, the local schools and community mental health agencies had developed long-standing relationships through years of working together. Agency and school staff regularly participated in community meetings geared toward improving services for children.

The schools made referrals to the mental health agencies according to mutually defined criteria. After receiving a referral, the lead case manager assigned the cases based on social worker availability and an appropriate match with the family. The five case managers had a weekly staffing meeting with the lead case manager to review cases and coordinate services. The lead case manager represented the group at the monthly SS/HS partner management meetings. Once each semester, the case managers hosted a meeting for the school social workers to give them updates and discuss issues of concern.

Roles and Responsibilities

Roles and responsibilities of the mental health agency social workers and the school social workers were clearly defined and mutually agreed on. The program was developed with the direct involvement of school social workers. They had an active role in determining who would be the target population and what services would be provided. The school staff was invited to participate from the beginning. School personnel, including social workers and psychologists, were asked to be a part of a planning committee that identified key community mental health needs. At a meeting held in June 2000, committee members shared their concerns and needs with the lead case manager and other management staff of the mental health agencies. The primary need identified was a lack of services for families that had traditionally had difficulty engaging in services.

In examining how to provide services for the neediest and most vulnerable families, the committee sought to identify the obstacles that prevent such families from accessing services. Some of the obstacles identified included time limits on length of services, fees, and delays between intake and receipt of services. The school staff also indicated that they wanted to be informed about services provided to families. At the end of the initial meeting, it was agreed that the mental health component of the grant would develop and implement a program that reached out to families who were in need of but not accessing services. The services would not be time limited, there would be no fee for services and the referring schools would be actively involved in the planning and delivery of services to families.

Domain Similarity, Domain Consensus, and Complementary Functions

Domains are functional social systems formed in response to a social problem of common concern (Alter & Hage, 1993). In the SS/HS Initiative, mental health service delivery domain was determined by the partners to be an area that would benefit from interorganizational collaboration, which was possible because the organizations had sufficient domain similarity in the funding (through SS/HS), goals, staff skills, and type of service. Domain consensus is the degree to which the organization's specific goals, services, and populations are agreed on by the collaborating organizations. Complementary functions between the school social workers and the community mental health agencies were critical to successful and effective collaboration.

To ensure complementary functions between schools and mental health agencies, referrals came from the schools. The intention was to create a program that would foster true partnership between the mental heath agencies and the schools. Rather than establishing the community mental health providers as the sole experts, the schools were asked to take an active role in determining who needed intensive services the most, based on their expertise and their interactions with the students. Basic eligibility criteria were developed, but it was left up to each referring school to determine whether they thought a particular student and his or her family would benefit from these services. Initially, each elementary school was given the opportunity to refer two students, whereas the high schools were able to refer four students.

This was done to ensure that each school had equal access to the services, and that no one school would dominate the program. Limiting the referrals to the schools also increased the schools' sense of partnership with the program staff and mental health agencies.

Processes for Interorganizational Collaboration

Processes refer to the flow and exchange of resources and information. There are a number of key processes that must be in place for successful collaboration: communication and coordination, capacity building, staff characteristics of cooperation and trust, and effective organization within each agency.

Communication and Coordination

At the start of the first full year of implementation (Fall, 2000) the case management team hosted a meeting for school principals, social workers, and school psychologists to introduce the new program. The eligibility criteria were explained, as well as the referral and intake processes. The meeting was well attended. All school social workers, were sent the referral form along with instructions on how to access services.

Regular contact with the referring school was required on all cases. This ensured that both the case manager and the school staff had a complete picture of the families' needs. Regular contact with the schools also promoted and fostered the development of strong relationships between the case managers and the individual schools. The case managers became point persons within their own agency for the school social workers, and were able to assist them in accessing a variety of other services outside of the SS/HS program that each agency offers.

Throughout the duration of the grant, the school staff was consistently asked to stay involved and provide feedback about the effectiveness of the program. This increased the schools' ownership and control over the program. The majority of the school social workers were willing to work alongside the case managers and provided space within the schools to see the children. All five districts were responsive to the program. Feedback from the schools was consistently very positive.

Regularly scheduled meetings were held throughout the 3 years of the grant during which school personnel and mental health case managers had an opportunity to share resources, learn about new services, and provide feedback to each other. School social workers, school psychologists, and principals were all invited to attend the meetings.

Building Capacity

One of the goals of the grant was to create a team of bilingual (Spanish–English), bicultural social work case managers who would specialize in working with high-risk children and their families. Initially, this was accomplished by bringing together four community mental health agencies. Each of the agencies hired one bilingual case manager, and Community Care Options had the lead case manager position as well as two additional case managers. The case managers were required to have a master's degree in social work, or counseling or clinical psychology. At the start of the program the social work case managers received extensive training in the wrap-around approach and mental health service delivery assessment.

Staff Characteristics

All five case managers working in Berwyn and Cicero were bilingual and bicultural (Spanish–English). This was particularly important as one of the communities served—Cicero, is largely Latino, primarily of Mexican descent. The goal was not only to hire staff who spoke Spanish, but also who were able to understand and be sensitive to the particular needs of the Latino communities in Berwyn and Cicero.

Intraorganizational Coordination

Historically, families with multiple needs have had to access multiple agencies or providers. It is often difficult for these families to access resources and stay connected to those helping them. At times, they may lack the social or advocacy skills necessary to access the help they need. Often, "helpers" become overwhelmed by the mounting needs of these families and are less effective. In most cases, this results in uncoordinated services that cause more stress and confusion for the family.

The case management team sought to prevent this by blending multiple roles into one position. In this way, the case managers served as coordinators, facilitators, and therapists for the family. The case managers could move seamlessly between roles depending on the unique situation or need of each family. They assisted the family with concrete needs, while also providing skilled mental health services. They communicated regularly with other providers and helped centralize and streamline service delivery for each family.

The case managers focused on helping the families effectively connect to other support sources in the community. The goal was to help the families stabilize and access the resources already available in the community. This was achieved by providing intensive case management and therapeutic services. Services were home- school- and/or community-based. Services included transportation, referral, linkage, advocacy, mediation, individual therapy, and family therapy. Crisis services were also provided to families already involved in the program. This generally involved obtaining emergency assessments, hospitalizations, and follow-up services after hospital discharge. The program embraced the family-centered approach and, as such, addressed the needs of all family members and not just the identified child.

OUTCOMES OF INTERORGANIZATIONAL COLLABORATION

One goal of the program was to serve families who were not receiving services or who had previously dropped out of programs before case closure. More than 85% of the referred families were still receiving services after 3 months. Most of the families who did not continue to receive services after 3 months had moved out of the area or had been referred to other providers for support.

Systems Change

The collaboration among the mental health agencies positively impacted overall child services in the communities. Agencies became more aware of the needs of the most vulnerable children in the community, and efforts were increased to provide appropriate services for them. Communication among the providers also increased and relationships were strengthened.

There was system-level change in the manner of mental health service delivery to school children, reflecting the needs of school personnel and families. This new system of delivery of mental health services is being sustained financially and it is now "part of the culture" of treatment. The theme of the mental health program was to strengthen family connections to the youth as well as school connections with the youth and the family.

The four mental health agencies retained bicultural/bilingual social workers after the SS/HS funding ended. A fifth agency had dropped out of the collaborative after the first year because the SS/HS program did it not fit within the overall agency mission.

Impact on Child Mental Health and Aggression

The university evaluation of the community mental health program consisted of analysis of data collected on 121 children who were followed from intake, and again at 3-, 6-, and 12-months during the middle 18 months of the program (Telleen, Kim, Stewart-Nava, & Maher, 2003). A program description manual, *Community Mental Health: A Safe Schools/ Healthy Students Initiative* (Stewart-Nava & Telleen, 2004) is available from the authors. The case managers collected individual and administrative service data for the evaluation. Parental consent to use agency data for evaluation purposes was obtained by the mental health agencies. Clients were given a choice as to whether they wanted to have the child's data made available for use in an evaluation. Participation in the program services was not contingent on participation in the evaluation. The University of Illinois at Chicago Institutional Review Board approved the project, the UIC evaluators developed the research design, conceptual and statistical framework and conducted the data entry, statistical analyses, and reporting of the results to the community mental health agencies and the schools.

In developing the evaluation component for mental health, the team sought to address different areas in a child's life. For this reason, four standardized measures used by the agency were selected and induced observations from the parent, teacher, and the social worker delivering services:

1. *Child and Adolescent Functioning Assessment Scale* (CAFAS; Hodges, 1997; Hodges & Wotring, 2000): The CAFAS is used by the mental health provider to assess the degree of functional impairment in children and adolescents. All clinicians underwent training and passed a reliability test before administering the CAFAS. CAFAS data were collected at intake and every 3 months thereafter through Month 12 of service. CAFAS has limitations since it is based on clinical judgement (Bates, 2001). Each childhood domain area such as school or home is assessed by the service provider reflecting clinical judgement based on the presence of behaviors.

2. *Child Behavior Checklist/4-18 (CBCL)*: The CBCL is designed to assess children's competencies and mental health symptoms as reported by their parents or parent surrogates (Achenbach, 1991a). This measure is also available in Spanish. At intake and at 6-month intervals the case managers collected the CBCL.

3. *Teacher Report Form* (TRF; Achenbach, 1991b): Teachers rated the child's academic performance and socioemotional functioning.

4. *Demographic scale:* The team was also interested in evaluating whether the targeted population was reached. This was achieved by creating a comprehensive demographic sheet that detailed the identified child's diagnosis and school information, as well as the family's living situation and financial status. Included in the demographic information were both a risk and a strength checklist. These checklists sought to assess the number of risk factors and strengths of the family at intake and reassessed how these changed over time. The case managers completed the demographic scale at intake and at 6-month intervals.

Finally, the team tracked its daily activities on a case management time, activity, and referral log. Through the use of the log, the team was able to track time spent doing specific activities with each family. This allowed the evaluation team to measure the intensity of the intervention and intensity of each component of wrap-around case management (Telleen, 2003).

Mental Health Results

Parent, teacher, and social work case manager reports of child functioning at intake were compared with their reports of child functioning at 3, 6, and 12 months.

The parent reported improvements in the child's behavior as measured by the CBCL (Achenbach, 1991a). After 6 months of family case management, a paired *t*-test analysis at intake and 6 months found that the children's number of aggressive behaviors had decreased significantly,

TABLE 37.3
Analysis of the Child Adolescent Functional Assessment Scale (CAFAS)

Role Performance Function	Assessment Period				Differences Between the Periods Using the Paired T-Test					
	Intake M (SD)	3 mo. M (SD)	6 mo. M (SD)	12 mo. M (SD)	Intake-3 mo.		Intake-6 mo.		Intake-12 mo.	
					t-score (df)	p-value	t-score (df)	p-value	t-score (df)	p-value
School/work	18.48 (10.40)	15.80 (10.69)	13.80 (9.70)	11.75 (9.57)	2.94 (105)	0.004*	6.03 (82)	0.0001**	4.39 (35)	0.0001**
Home	14.92 (10.26)	13.45 (10.20)	12.87 (9.23)	10.75 (7.97)	1.83 (106)	0.070	2.21 (84)	0.030*	2.67 (36)	0.011*
Delinquency in community	3.25 (7.57)	2.05 (5.88)	2.13 (5.46)	1.75 (4.47)	2.26 (107)	0.026*	1.16 (84)	0.251	0.42 (36)	0.676
Behaviors toward others	14.05 (9.05)	13.42 (9.12)	12.02 (9.11)	12.31 (8.42)	0.13 (106)	0.899	1.87 (84)	0.065	1.19 (35)	0.244
Mood/emotion	16.43 (8.90)	14.12 (9.15)	12.90 (9.62)	11.79 (7.91)	2.80 (105)	0.006*	3.06 (83)	0.003*	4.12 (35)	0.0001**
Self-harmful behavior	4.96 (8.99)	2.81 (6.61)	1.28 (4.69)	1.75 (5.00)	1.89 (107)	0.062	2.75 (84)	0.007*	2.53 (36)	0.016*
Substance use	1.59 (5.43)	2.48 (6.62)	1.16 (4.81)	1.22 (4.00)	-2.37 (105)	0.019*	0.28 (85)	0.783	-1.0 (37)	0.324
Thinking	1.43 (4.51)	1.42 (4.16)	1.37 (4.02)	1.25 (4.63)	0.60 (107)	0.551	-1.52 (85)	0.132	-0.81 (36)	0.422

Significance level
* p < .05
** p < .001

$t(70) = 2.55$, $p = .013$. The children's anxious and depressed behaviors as observed by the parent also significantly decreased after 6 months, $t(70) = 2.09$, $p = .04$. Analyses of parent responses to the CBCL using a paired t-test found a significant decrease in internalizing behaviors, such as depression, and in externalizing behaviors, such as aggression toward others as reported in Table 37.4.

Teacher reports showed a statistically significant reduction in the children's social problems at school, $t(65) = 2.17$, $p = .030$, and attention problems at school, $t(64) = 3.28$, $p = .002$, after 6 months of case management. Teachers reported improvements between intake and 12 months with decreases in anxious/depressed behavior, $t(29) = 3.40$, $p = .002$, and in somatic complaints, $t(29) = 3.03$, $p = .005$, and in attention problems, $t(30) = 3.70$, $p = .001$, as reported in Table 37.5.

The social work case managers reported a significant impact on the children's functioning in school as measured by the CAFAS (Hodges, 1997). They rated school functioning as the area with the most problems at intake. Paired t-test analyses of social worker reports of child functioning in school at intake and at 3 months, $t(105) = 2.90$, $p = .004$, at 6 months, $t(82) = 6.03$, $p = .001$, and from intake to 12 months, $t(35) = 4.39$, $p = .001$ showed significant improvement, as seen in Table 37.3. Additionally, the social worker's assessment of the child, as reported on the CAFAS, identified significantly fewer delinquent acts in the community from intake to 3 months, $t(107) = 2.25$, $p = .026$ (see Table 37.3). Finally, case managers, teachers, and parents perceived a reduction of emotional/behavioral symptoms and an improvement in level of functioning as measured by the CAFAS. Students improved to the point that they reduced their use of intensive multiple services and increased their use of outpatient services between intake 6 months and 12 months, (see Fig. 37.1)

System Collaboration Outcomes

The collaborative model developed for the delivery of mental health services was assessed by school social workers in the feeder elementary schools as improving access and efficiency resulting in timely service delivery. Social workers described the program in their evaluation of its effects in the following comments.

- *This is an incredibly valuable, progressive program that fills a serious gap in services by being able to reach out to multi-problem families. The staff is excellent at engaging tough clients. The nontraditional approach (e.g., home visits, in-home therapy, case management that deals with real problems) is one that should be used by more service models.*
- *The ability to be flexible when working with parents (meet in home/school/office, bilingual staff, provide emergency funds, and transportation) have helped parents feel comfortable with the Safe Schools Initiative and willing to participate.*
- *There is an increased ability to provide intensive services to families that have been historically difficult to engage.*
- *Response time is unbelievable. Referral process is easy and brief. I greatly appreciate the feedback and updates from case managers.*
- *They work right in the community. Families do not have to travel very far or to strange areas to reach the caseworker or other resources.*

Sustainability

The interorganizational collaborations and staffing resulted in improved child mental health outcomes. After SS/HS funding ended, the goal was to sustain those interorganizational

TABLE 37.4
Analysis of Child Behavior Check List (Achenbach Parent Scale)

Child's Behavior Problems	Assessment Period			Differences Between the Periods Using the Paired T-Test					
	Intake M (SD)	6 mo. M (SD)	12 mo. M (SD)	Intake–6 mo.		Intake–12 mo.		6 mo.–12 mo.	
				t-score (df)	p-value	t-score (df)	p-value	t-score (df)	p-value
Withdrawn behaviors	4.87 (3.84)	4.29 (3.63)	4.50 (3.61)	1.50 (71)	0.137	1.45 (34)	0.157	1.19 (34)	0.244
Somatic behaviors	2.77 (3.07)	1.93 (2.71)	2.33 (2.96)	2.66 (69)	0.010*	2.80 (34)	0.008*	0.61 (33)	0.545
Anxious/depressed behaviors	8.11 (6.25)	6.81 (5.17)	7.58 (4.91)	2.09 (70)	0.040*	1.86 (34)	0.071	1.44 (33)	0.158
Social problems	3.85 (2.97)	3.68 (3.26)	4.91 (3.36)	0.66 (68)	0.511	-0.77 (30)	0.446	-0.75 (32)	0.456
Thought problems	2.38 (2.47)	1.86 (2.41)	2.27 (2.37)	2.14 (71)	0.036*	2.65 (35)	0.012*	-0.29 (34)	0.772
Attention problems	6.77 (4.38)	5.91 (4.36)	8.03 (4.43)	1.60 (70)	0.121	0 (34)	1.000	-1.58 (34)	0.124
Delinquent problems	4.94 (3.76)	4.23 (3.47)	5.27 (3.28)	1.75 (70)	0.084	0.59 (34)	0.562	-1.15 (34)	0.259
Aggressive problems	15.53 (9.40)	14.09 (9.07)	16.27 (9.55)	2.55 (70)	0.013*	1.16 (34)	0.255	0.05 (34)	0.963
Internalizing/ Withdrawn + Anxious depressed	12.90 (9.67)	10.96 (8.16)	12.17 (8.02)	2.18 (69)	0.030*	1.81 (33)	0.080	1.42 (33)	0.170
Externalizing/ delinquent + Aggressive	20.55 (12.39)	18.29 (11.40)	21.08 (11.74)	2.69 (71)	0.009*	0.97 (33)	0.340	-0.70 (34)	0.490

Significance level
* $p < .05$
** $p < .001$

TABLE 37.5
Analysis of Teachers Report on Child's Problems

| Child's Behavior Problems | Assessment Period | | | Differences Between the Periods Using the Paired T-Test | | | | | |
| | | | | Intake-6 mo. | | Intake-12 mo. | | 6 mo.–12 mo. | |
	Intake	6 mo.	12 mo.	t-score (df)	p-value	t-score (df)	p-value	t-score (df)	p-value
Withdrawn behaviors	4.64 (3.97)	4.36 (4.13)	3.53 (3.27)	1.56 (68)	0.124	3.54 (29)	0.001	1.61 (29)	0.118
Somatic behaviors	1.52 (2.28)	1.54 (2.58)	0.65 (1.01)	0.53 (69)	0.600	3.03 (29)	0.005*	2.16 (29)	0.039*
Anxious/depressed behaviors	6.35 (5.59)	6.09 (5.87)	4.09 (5.12)	1.23 (70)	0.225	3.44 (29)	0.002*	1.88 (30)	0.069
Social problems	4.96 (4.23)	4.49 (4.48)	3.44 (3.42)	2.17 (65)	0.034*	3.40 (29)	0.002*	2.13 (30)	0.042*
Thought problems	1.91 (2.73)	1.43 (2.47)	1.24 (1.69)	2.10 (68)	0.040*	2.48 (29)	0.019*	0.67 (30)	0.511
Attention problems	17.29 (9.94)	15.69 (9.52)	13.97 (9.52)	3.28 (64)	0.002*	3.70 (30)	0.001**	1.87 (28)	0.073
Delinquent problems	3.80 (3.29)	4.57 (4.07)	4.11 (3.86)	-0.71 (61)	0.481	0.64 (30)	0.528	0.72 (28)	0.479
Aggressive problems	13.78 (12.93)	12.18 (12.00)	12.25 (12.12)	1.24 (63)	0.219	1.28 (31)	0.211	0.433 (29)	0.668

Significance level
$* p < .05$
$** p < .001$

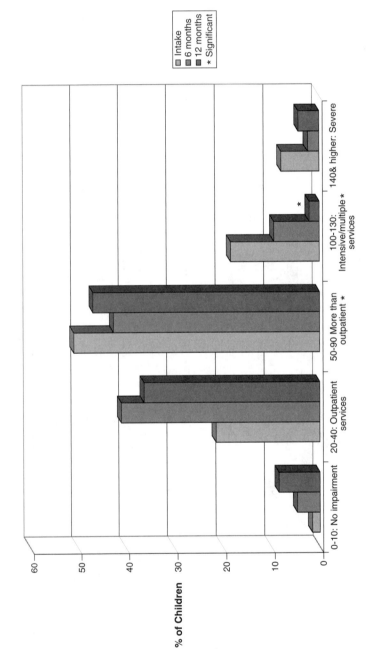

FIG. 37.1. Distribution of CAFAS scores demonstrating overall level of dysfunction at intake, 6-month follow-up, and 12-month follow-up.

structures and processes that had improved service delivery and child mental health. Therefore, the mental health agencies, schools, and other providers continued to collaborate through monthly community meetings such as Berwyn Project Success, Cicero Youth Coalition, and the Local Area Network 58 meeting. The community mental health agencies have allocated funding to maintain the program. For example, Community Care Options has reallocated internal funding to support one position.

Additionally, the elementary school district re-allocated funds to help support the program. This is a model for school districts with school social workers that need to supplement their services with referrals to outside agencies. The Cicero Elementary School District now supports three social work case management positions in two mental health agencies enabling these agencies to accept referrals from the school and work in collaboration with school social workers/psychologists. The Berwyn South District 100 supports the program through funding for services for two families receiving case management services through Community Care Options. Foundation funding supports two case managers at the mental health agency, so they can continue to work with the schools. This foundation requires ongoing program evaluation. It is anticipated that future evaluation efforts will glean additional insights that may be valuable to others attempting to implement school community partnerships to reduce school violence.

ACKNOWLEDGEMENTS

The Morton High School District 201 Safe Schools/Healthy Students initiative in Cicero, IL (1999-2003) was funded by the U.S. Dept. of Education grant no. S184L990380-01. This article represents the work of the authors and does not necessarily represent the official opinion of Morton High School District 201, or the U.S. Dept. of Education.

REFERENCES

Achenbach, T. M. (1991a). *Manual for the Child Behavior Checklist/4-18 and 1991 Profile.* Burlington: University of Vermont Department of Psychiatry.

Achenbach, T. M. (1991b). *Manual for the Teacher's Report Form and 1991 Profile.* Burlington: University of Vermont Department of Psychiatry.

Aiken, M., & Hague, J. (1968). Organizational interdependence and intra-organizational structure. *American Sociological Review, 33*(6), 912–930.

Alter, C. F., & Hage, G. (1993). *Organizations working together.* Newbury Park, CA: Sage.

Bates, M. (2001). The Child and Adolescent Functional Assessment Scale (CAFAS): Review and current status. *Clinical Child and Family Psychology Review, 4*, 63–84.

Brock, S., Lazarus, P., & Jimerson, S. (Eds.). (2002). *Best practices in school crisis prevention and intervention.* Bethesda, MD: National Association of School Psychologists.

Burchard, J., Burns, E., & Burchard, S. (2002). The wraparound approach. In B. Burns & K. Hoagwood (Eds). *Community treatment for youth: Evidence-based interventions for severe emotional and behavioral disorders* (pp. 69–90). New York: Oxford University Press.

Duchnowski, A., Kutash, K., & Friedman, R. (2002). Community-based interventions in a systems of care and outcomes framework. In B. Burns, & K. Hoagwood (Eds.), *Community treatment for youth: Evidence-based interventions for severe emotional and behavioral disorders*(pp. 16–38). New York: Oxford University Press.

Dwyer, K., & Osher, D. (2000). *Safeguarding our children: An action guide.* Washington, DC: U.S. Departments of Education and Justice.

Flores-Gonzalez, N. (2002). *Identify formation of Latino youth.* New York: Columbia Teachers College Press.

Furlong, M., Pavelski, R., & Saxton, J. (2002). Prevention of school violence. In S. Brock, P. Lazarus, & S. Jimerson (Eds.), *Best practices in school crisis prevention and intervention* (pp. 131–150). Bethesda, MD: National Association of School Psychologists.

Hall, R. H., & Tolbert, P. (2004). *Organizations: Structures, processes, and outcomes* (9th ed). Upper Saddle River, NJ: Prentice-Hall.

Hawkins, J. D., & Catalano, R. (1992). *Communities that Care: Action for drug abuse prevention*. San Francisco, CA: Jossey-Bass.

Hodges, K. (1997). *CAFAS Manual for training coordinators, clinical administrators and data managers*. Ann Arbor, MI: Functional Assessment Systems, L.L.C. Self-Training Manual and Blank Scoring Forms.

Hodges, K., & Wotring, J. (2000). Client typology based on functioning across domains using the CAFAS: Implications for service planning. *The Journal of Behavioral Health Services Research, 27*, 257–270.

Institute for Latino Studies, University of Notre Dame. (2002). *Bordering the mainstream: A needs assessment of Latinos in Berwyn and Cicero, Illinois*, Notre Dame, IN: Author.

Kelly, J. G., Ryan, A., Altman, B. E., & Satelzner, S. (2000). Understanding and changing social systems: An ecological view. In J. Rappaport & E. Seidman (Eds.), *Handbook of community psychology* (pp. 133–159). New York: Kluwer Academic/ Plenum.

Kloglan, G. E., Warren, R. D., Winklepleck, J. M., & Paulson, S. K. (1976). Interorganizational measurement in the social services sector: Differences by hierarchical level. *Administrative Science Quarterly, 21*, 675–688.

Malecki, C., & Elliott, S. (2002). Children's social behaviors as predictors of academic achievement: A longitudinal analysis. *School Psychology Quarterly, 17*, 1–23.

Northeastern Illinois Planning Commission. (2002). Census 2000 updates. Available: www.nipc.cog.il.us

Olweus, D. (1993). *Bullying at school: What we know and what we can do*. Oxford, U.K: Blackwell.

Polivka, B.J. (1996). Rural sex education; Assessment of programs and interagency collaboration. *Public Health Nursing, 13*(6), 425.

Poole, M. & Van De Ven, A. (Eds.). (2004). *Handbook of organizational change and innovationt*. New York: Oxford University Press.

Reddy, M., Borum, R., Berglund, J., Vossekuil, B., Fein, R., & Modzeleski, W. (2001). Evaluating risk for targeted violence in schools: Comparing risk assessment, threat assessment, and other approaches. *Psychology in the Schools, 38*, 157–172.

Shure, M. B. (1992). *I can problem solve: An interpersonal cognitive problem solving program*. Champaign, IL: Research Press.

Slavin, R. E. (1995). *Cooperative learning* (2nd ed.). Needhamm Heights, MA: Allyn & Bacon.

Stewart-Nava, H. & Telleen, S. (2004). Community mental health: a Safe School/Healthy Students Initiative. Manual available from the author.

State of Illinois. School Report Card. (2002), Available: www.jsmortonhs.com.

Telleen, S., Kim, Y., Stewart-Nava, H., & Maher, S. (2003, March). *The impact of coordinated community mental health services: Safe Schools/Healthy Students Initiative*. Paper presented at the 15th annual research conference proceeding, A System of Care for Children's Mental Health: Expanding the Research Base.

Telleen, S., Maher, S., & Pesce, R. C. (2003). Building community connections for youth to reduce violence. *Psychology in the Schools, 40*, 549–563.

Telleen, S., & Scott, J. (2001). The infant mortality reduction initiative: Collaborative database design. In M. Sullivan & J. Kelly (Eds.), *Collaborative research: University and community partnership* (pp. 63–84). Washington, DC: American Public Health Association.

Trickett, E. (1987). Community interventions and health psychology: An ecologically oriented perspective. In G. Stone (Ed.), *Health psychology: A discipline and a profession* (pp. 151–164). Chicago: University of Chicago Press.

US.Census 2000. Suitland, MD: U.S. Census Bureau. Available: www.census.gov

U.S. Department of Health and Human Services. (2001). *Youth violence: A report of the Surgeon General*. Rockville, MD: author.

U.S. Department of Justice, United States Attorney, Northern District of Illinois. (2001). Three Cicero officials among 10 indicted in racketeering and fraud scheme to loot town of millions. Press release 15 June 2001, from U.S. Attorney's Office, Northern District of Illinois.

Weissberg, R., Greenberg, M., Elias, M., & Zins, J. (2000). The role of the collaborative to advance social and emotional learning (CASEL) in supporting the implementation of quality school-based prevention programs. *Journal of Educational and Psychological Consultation, 11*, 3–6.

Wentzel, K. R. (1991). Relations between social competence and academic achievement in early adolescence. *Child Development, 62*, 1066–1078.

38

Student Threat Assessment as a Strategy to Reduce School Violence

Dewey Cornell
Farah Williams
University of Virginia

Two months after the 1999 Columbine shooting, the FBI's National Center for the Analysis of Violent Crime held a national conference on school shootings. The conference brought together experts in law enforcement, education, and mental health to identify common factors in school shootings and to propose potential solutions. Although renowned for its expertise in criminal profiling, the FBI cautioned against the use of student profiling to identify potential school shooters (O'Toole, 2000). Instead, the FBI recommended the adoption of a threat assessment approach, consistent with subsequent recommendations of the Secret Service and Department of Education (Fein et al., 2002).

Why did the FBI's own profiling experts advise against a profiling approach? Although it was possible to identify a number of common characteristics of students who carried out school shootings—history of peer mistreatment and bullying, symptoms of depression and suicidality, preoccupation with violent games and fantasies, among others—no list of these characteristics offered sufficient specificity for practical use. Far too many students would be falsely identified as potentially violent (Sewell & Mendelsohn, 2000). One example of this problem was the observation that several school shooters had worn black trench coats to hide their firearms, which prompted some school authorities to view any student wearing a black trench coat with suspicion and even to ban trench coats at school. Conference attendees used the term *black trench coat problem* to refer to all such misguided efforts at profiling potentially dangerous students.

The most promising finding from the FBI's study of school shootings was that the students almost always made threats or communicated their intentions to harm someone before carrying out the shooting. Moreover, the FBI identified a number of cases where school shootings were prevented because authorities investigated a student's threatening statement and found that the student was engaged in plans to carry out the threat. These observations suggested that schools should focus their efforts on the identification and investigation of student threats as a violence prevention strategy.

Unlike black trench coats, student threats can be meaningfully and directly linked to potential violence. Moreover, a threat is an aggressive behavior and, in some circumstances, a criminal act that demands attention. Nevertheless, the FBI report cautioned that the mere observation of a student threat could not be sufficient to identify a violent student—such an approach would be tantamount to profiling (O'Toole, 2000). As conference attendees quipped, "All threats are not created equal." Instead, school authorities must investigate the context and meaning of a student's threat, for the purpose of determining whether the student is engaged in other behaviors that demonstrate intention to carry out the threat. If the investigation indicates that the threat is genuine, the next step would be to take action designed to prevent it from being carried out.

The U.S. Secret Service developed *threat assessment* as an explicit process of threat investigation and intervention in its efforts to protect government officials (Fein, Vossekuil, & Holden, 1995). Reddy and colleagues (Reddy et al., 2001) advocated the application of threat assessment to schools, and in 2002, a joint report of the U.S. Secret Service and Department of Education recommended that schools train threat assessment teams in order to respond to student threats of violence (Fein et al., 2002).

Separate reports by the FBI (O'Toole, 2000) and by the Secret Service and Department of Education (Fein et al., 2002) made a compelling case for schools to establish threat assessment teams that could investigate student threats and carry out interventions appropriate to the seriousness of the threat. Nevertheless, the recommendations of these reports were essentially untried and untested. Could the threat assessment approach used in law enforcement be adapted for schools? How would a school-based threat assessment team operate and what would happen to students subjected to a threat assessment?

The Virginia Youth Violence Project of the Curry School of Education at the University of Virginia took on the task of answering these questions. The challenge was to translate the FBI and Secret Service recommendations into a set of practice guidelines for schools to use in responding to student threats of violence, to train school personnel in the use of these guidelines, and then to field test the guidelines in a sample of schools (Cornell et al., 2004). The first task was to resolve some practical questions, such as who would be on the threat assessment team and who would be in charge. Next, it was important to specify how the team would determine whether a threat was serious and what actions to take if it was. Finally, it was essential to examine what the outcome would be if a school adopted a threat assessment approach. This chapter presents answers to these questions and updates previous reports of what was found when 35 schools field tested the threat assessment approach for one school year (Cornell, 2003, 2004).

THE THREAT ASSESSMENT TEAM

This approach requires each school to form its own threat assessment team rather than rely on an outside team that serves the entire school district. Although a single, divisionwide team would seem to be more efficient, there are strong arguments against it. In particular, threat assessment requires an immediate response. If a student threatens to kill someone, school administrators cannot wait for a team of outside experts to be contacted and assembled. Furthermore, threat assessment requires a careful consideration of contextual and situational factors. A school-based team is more familiar with the school environment, recent events at the school, and the students and others involved in the threat. In most instances, a school principal or counselor will be familiar with the student or students involved in a threat, and may even be familiar with the conflict or problem that preceded the threat. An outside team would spend time and effort gathering background information—and still would not have the nuanced understanding that an on-site team would bring to the incident.

As was expected—and later found to be true—most student threats are not serious enough to warrant the assembly of an outside team. Most student threats involve rash or foolish statements, some made in jest and others in a moment of anger that are easily resolved. Use of an outside team to investigate such threats would not only be an inefficient use of resources, it could magnify the importance of such events. The act of bringing in outside experts to review a student's threatening statement itself alters the context and significance of a student's action, and may influence how the action is perceived by others, including other students and parents.

The use of an external team also has an impact on the authority and responsibility of the school's administrators. Because the principal has primary responsibility for maintaining a safe and orderly school environment, and is ordinarily in charge of discipline, he or she must work closely with the external team. There is potential for divergent perceptions of a student threat, disagreements about the best response to the threat, and ultimately, conflicts in authority that could jeopardize the threat assessment process.

Perhaps the most important reason to have a school-based threat assessment team is that threat assessment should not be limited to an initial assessment, but rather should involve an ongoing process of prevention and intervention. Because the term *threat assessment* might be misconstrued to imply a time-limited procedure, *threat monitoring* or *threat reduction* may be more appropriate labels for this approach. Whoever evaluates the student immediately after the threat should continue to monitor the situation. The danger posed by a threat is not static; it changes in response to events and interactions among students. An effective threat assessment team will not settle for judging the seriousness of a threat at a single point, but will implement a response to a serious threat that is designed to reduce the risk of violence. Viewed from this perspective, it becomes increasingly inefficient for an outside team to assume such responsibilities.

None of these reasons for using an on-site threat assessment team contradicts the use of an outside consultant in some situations. In a complicated case involving a serious threat of violence, the school-based team may want to draw on the expertise of a mental health professional from the community, work closely with law enforcement, or simply consult with authorities in the school division's administration. All of these are appropriate, reasonable, and consistent with the use of a school-based threat assessment team.

The threat assessment teams in the Virginia study reflected staffing patterns at the field test schools. Each team consisted of a principal or assistant principal, school resource officer (SRO), school psychologist, and school counselor (schools with different staffing patterns might need a slightly different team structure, but should be able to cover the same team functions). Primary functions were identified for each team member; however, schools developed variations based on the skills and workloads of their individual team members.

School Principal or Assistant Principal

School principals or assistant principals should lead the threat assessment team because they are responsible for student discipline and safety. Because student threats are usually treated as disciplinary violations, the student can readily be referred to the principal or assistant principal (hereafter simply referred to as "the principal") for both disciplinary and threat assessment purposes. As team leader, the principal conducts a triage evaluation to determine the seriousness of the threat. If the threat is not serious, the principal takes the limited action necessary to resolve the incident, and if the threat is more serious, involves the full team. In all cases, the principal leads the team and makes final decisions about how to respond to the threat. Other team members provide the principal with information and recommendations to consider in making these decisions.

School Resource Officer

SROs are police officers who have been trained to work in schools. In Virginia, sworn law enforcement officers employed by a municipal law enforcement agency may be assigned to work in a public school. There is state-sponsored training on crime prevention and law enforcement for SROs (Virginia Department of Criminal Justice Services, 1999). We followed the recommendations of the FBI (O'Toole, 2000) and Secret Service (Fein et al., 2002) to place a law enforcement officer on every threat assessment team. In schools where there are no SROs, a police liaison officer can be identified from the local police department. Because the participating elementary schools did not have SROs, the officer assigned to the associated middle school served as the liaison.

The SRO performs several functions on the team. First, the SRO responds to emergencies or crises, such as when there is an imminent risk of violence. In such cases, the SRO has the same law enforcement duties and authority that he or she would have in any incident occurring outside of school; for instance, the SRO might arrest a person wielding a weapon or actively threatening to attack someone. In other cases, the SRO might have investigative responsibilities, such as responding to a suspected bomb plot by obtaining a search warrant for a student's home. In these circumstances, the SRO does not act under the authority of the school principal, but rather as an independent law enforcement officer. Because the law enforcement officer has responsibilities that are not entirely under school authority, it is especially important for the principal and the SRO to decide how they will work together, including when the officer will take independent action.

Apart from emergency situations, the SRO can be a consultant on law enforcement and crime prevention. For example, he or she can advise the team whether a student's behavior has violated the law and can instruct students and staff on law enforcement matters. Perhaps most importantly, SROs can be role models and encourage law-abiding behavior by interacting with students and participating in school functions. SROs can have a positive effect on the school climate by maintaining positive, friendly relations with students and becoming confidantes or resources for students. SROs should adopt a problem-solving approach to crime prevention by identifying and monitoring potentially volatile conflicts between students or groups of students.

School Psychologist

The school psychologist has expertise in psychological assessment and intervention that can be useful in ameliorating the interpersonal or emotional difficulties that often underlie a student's threatening behavior (Larson, Smith, & Furlong, 2001). In the most serious cases, the school psychologist conducts a mental health evaluation of the student. This evaluation has two objectives. The first is to screen the student for mental health problems that demand immediate attention, such as psychosis or suicidal ideation. This is consistent with the role that school psychologists already play when a student is suicidal or presents with disturbed behavior that warrants screening and referral for possible hospitalization.

The second objective of the mental health evaluation is to assess why the student made the threat and to gather relevant information about the student's psychological functioning, so that the team can make decisions about the most appropriate mental health and educational interventions. This role is consistent with the function of school psychologists in evaluating student behavior problems and developing behavior plans or other interventions. This objective can be characterized as a risk reduction or risk management approach, as distinguished from a predictive approach (Heilbrun, 1997).

Although it is natural for school personnel to want precise predictions about the likelihood that a student will carry out a threat, such predictions tend to be unreliable and prone to error (Mulvey & Cauffman, 2001). The prediction of violence is complex and difficult, and communications about violence risk are easily misstated or misinterpreted (Borum, 1996). Although psychologists can make reasonably accurate short-term predictions of violence in some situations (Borum, 1996), little is known about the prediction of student violence (Mulvey & Cauffman, 2001). Therefore, the Virginia Youth Violence Project's threat assessment guidelines (Cornell & Sheras, 2006) discourage school psychologists from trying to predict whether a student will carry out the threatened action.

Furthermore, any substantial risk of violence requires that school personnel take protective action. A formal risk assessment estimating that the risk is 30%, 90%, or some other figure is not especially useful and may be subject to misinterpretation. Because risk is a dynamic process that changes in response to interventions and events in the student's daily life, the goal of threat assessment is to reduce risk through interventions aimed at the circumstances that led to the threat.

School Counselor

The school counselor also brings to the team expertise in working with troubled students and helping them resolve conflicts and problems in their relationships. The counselor might identify programs or resources that could serve the student, or take a direct role in implementing an intervention for the student, such as individual counseling for anger management or social skills training to improve the student's peer relationships. The counselor can also lead an effort to resolve a conflict or dispute within a group of students. He or she can serve as the team member who monitors the student's participation in the intervention plan and assesses its impact and continued effectiveness.

There is a large body of evidence that school-based interventions can reduce aggressive behavior. Wilson, Lipsey, and Derzon (2003) conducted a meta-analysis of 221 studies of school-based interventions involving nearly 56,000 students. Each study included pre–post assessment of at least one form of aggressive behavior broadly defined to include fighting, bullying, assault, conduct disorder, and acting out. The researchers found an average effect size of .25 for well-implemented programs, an effect that would eliminate approximately half the incidents of fighting in a typical school year. Examples of effective programs include social competence training, cognitive–behavioral counseling to improve problem-solving skills, and conflict-resolution programs.

School Social Workers and Other Team Members

U.S. schools have varying staffing patterns and staff functions. In some school divisions, social workers can be enlisted as valuable members of the threat assessment team, particularly because of their expertise in working with families, resolving conflicts, and helping students obtain needed assistance. Student assistance professionals, substance abuse counselors, and other mental health professionals can also serve on a threat assessment team. In selecting team members, principals should give greater weight to the skill and experience of the individual staff member than to the individual's specific discipline.

Teachers

Teachers are generally not included as regular members of the threat assessment team because their primary role is instruction. Nevertheless, there may be individual cases or circumstances in which teacher input or participation on the threat assessment team would be useful.

THREAT ASSESSMENT GUIDELINES

How should the team determine the seriousness of a threat? Mindful of the FBI report's admonition that "all threats are not created equal" (O'Toole, 2000, p. 5), each threat must be carefully investigated to determine what danger the student poses to others. Students who

TABLE 38.1
Steps in Student Threat Assessment

Step 1. Evaluate the threat.

The principal investigates a reported threat by interviewing the student who made the threat and any witnesses to the threat. The principal considers the context and meaning of the threat, which is more important than the literal content of the threat.

Step 2. Decide whether the threat is transient or substantive.

A *transient* threat is not a serious threat and can be easily resolved, but a *substantive* threat raises concern of potential injury to others. For transient threats, go to Step 3 and for substantive threats skip to Step 4.

Step 3. Respond to a transient threat.

If the threat is transient, the principal may respond with a reprimand, parental notification, or other actions that are appropriate to the severity and chronicity of the situation. The incident is resolved and no further action is needed.

Step 4. If the threat is substantive, decide whether it is serious or very serious.

If a threat is substantive, the principal must decide how serious the threat is and take appropriate action to protect potential victims. A threat to hit, assault, or beat up someone is serious, whereas a threat to kill, rape, use a weapon, or severely injure someone is considered very serious. For serious threats, go to Step 5 and for very serious threats, skip to Step 6.

Step 5. Respond to a serious substantive threat.

Serious substantive threats require protective action to prevent violence, including notification of potential victims and other actions to address the conflict or problem that generated the threat. The response to serious threats is completed at this step.

Step 6. Respond to a very serious substantive threat.

Very serious threats require immediate protective action, including contact with law enforcement, followed by a comprehensive safety evaluation. The student is suspended from school pending completion of a safety evaluation, which includes a mental health assessment following a prescribed protocol.

Step 7. Implement a safety plan.

The threat assessment team develops and implements an action plan that is designed both to protect potential victims and to meet the student's educational needs. The plan includes provision for monitoring the student and revising the plan as needed.

Note. Reprinted from Cornell and Sheras (2006).

make threats differ in their motivation and capacity to carry out a violent act. The content of the threat—what the student threatens to do—is less important than the context, meaning, and motivation behind the threat. The critical question is not "What did the student threaten to do?" but "Does the student intend to carry out this threat?"

Threat assessment teams followed a seven-step decision tree (see summary in Table 38.1). Each step in the decision tree is accompanied by an extensive set of guidelines and case examples (Cornell & Sheras, 2006). These guidelines recognize that many threats are clearly intended as jokes or rhetorical remarks and that school personnel could not conduct a comprehensive threat assessment every time a student made an inappropriate statement or used seemingly threatening language. Therefore, threat assessment teams need to begin with a triage assessment to determine whether the threat is serious enough to warrant a more comprehensive response.

At Step 1, the leader of the threat assessment team interviews the student who made the threat, using a standard set of questions that can be adapted to the specific situation. The principal should also interview witnesses to the threat and make notes on a standard form. The principal is not concerned simply with the verbal content of the threat, but the context in which the threat was made and what the student meant and intended in making the threat. This approach differs markedly from a zero-tolerance approach, which treats all violations as equal infractions that deserve the same consequence.

At Step 2, the principal must make an important distinction between threats that are serious, in the sense that they pose a continuing risk or danger to others, and those that are not serious because they are readily resolved and do not pose a continuing risk. Less serious threats that are readily resolved, which were termed *transient threats*, are distinguished from *substantive threats*. Transient threats are defined as behaviors that can be readily identified as expressions of anger or frustration—or perhaps inappropriate attempts at humor—but that dissipate quickly when the student has time to reflect on the meaning of what he or she has said. The most important feature of a transient threat is that the student does not have a sustained intention to harm someone.

If the threat is judged to be transient, it is resolved quickly at Step 3 without engaging the full team in a comprehensive threat assessment. The principal may direct the student to apologize or explain to those affected by threat, or take other action to make amends for the student's behavior. The principal may respond with a reprimand or other disciplinary consequence if the behavior was disruptive or violated the school's discipline code. A transient threat may have been sparked by an argument or conflict, and in such cases the principal may involve other team members in helping to address or resolve the problem.

Substantive threats represent a sustained intent to harm someone beyond the immediate incident or argument during which the threat was made. If there is doubt whether a threat is transient or substantive, the threat is regarded as substantive. Several features that are regarded as presumptive indicators may identify substantive threats. The presumptive indicators, derived from the FBI report (O'Toole, 2000), include the following:

- The threat includes plausible details, such as a specific victim, time, place, and method of assault.
- The threat has been repeated over time or communicated to multiple persons.
- The threat is reported as a plan, or planning has taken place.
- The student has accomplices, or has attempted to recruit accomplices.
- The student has invited an audience of peers to watch the threatened event.
- There is physical evidence of intent to carry out the threat, such as a weapon, bomb materials, map, written plan, or list of intended victims.

Although the presence of any one of these features may lead the school administrator to presume the threat is substantive, none are absolute indicators; with additional investigation, other facts could demonstrate that the threat is transient. For example, a student might seek an accomplice to send an angry, threatening letter to a classmate. The threat is transient if the student does not intend to carry out the threat, but only means to frighten the classmate. Such an incident would be handled as a serious disciplinary matter, but not as a serious threat.

The example of a student who frightens a classmate with a transient threat illustrates another important point, which is that threat assessment and discipline are separate processes. In some cases, the disciplinary consequences can be quite severe even if the threat is transient. For example, a false bomb threat is not a substantive threat if the student only intends to disrupt the school, but nonetheless has serious legal consequences. In general, threat assessment is concerned with the risk of future harm to others and what steps should be taken to prevent the threat from being carried out, whereas discipline is concerned with punishing a student as a consequence for his or her actions.

In essence, threat assessment teams must always consider the context of the threat and make reasoned judgments based on all the available information. The team should consider the student's age and capabilities, mental stability, prior history of violent behavior, and other relevant factors. The guidelines assist the team in its investigation, but do not provide a prescription or formula.

If the threat is determined to be a substantive threat, the principal skips Step 3 and proceeds to Step 4. At Step 4, the substantive threat is determined to be serious or very serious. The distinction between serious and very serious threats is based on the intended severity of injury. A *serious* threat is a threat to assault, strike, or beat up someone. A *very serious* threat is a threat to kill, sexually assault, or severely injure someone. A threat involving the use of a weapon is generally considered a threat to severely injure someone.

In the case of a serious substantive threat, the team moves to Step 5. At Step 5, school authorities are obliged to act to protect potential victims. These protective actions depend on the circumstances of the threat, as well as any information indicating how soon and where the threat might be carried out. Immediate protective actions include cautioning the student about the consequences of carrying out the threat and providing supervision so that the student cannot carry out the threat while at school. A team member should contact the student's parents, so that the parents can assume responsibility for supervising the student after school. The parents may be summoned to school so that the student does not leave school without supervision.

The level of supervision should be consistent with the nature and seriousness of the threat. For example, a visibly angry student who threatens to beat up a classmate should be confined to an office or classroom under continuous adult supervision. The school resource officer might meet with the student. More often, however, a student will calm down and can be permitted to return to class, but only on the condition that the student not have any contact with the classmate. As a precaution, the student might be kept from a class attended by the classmate, and the student might be required to report to the office prior to school dismissal, rather than being released to ride the same bus as the classmate. Serious threats are resolved at Step 5.

Very serious threats require the most extensive action by the team. The team skips Step 5 and moves to Steps 6 and 7. At Step 6, the team takes immediate actions in response to the threat, and at Step 7 the team completes a thorough evaluation of the student (termed a *safety evaluation*) and then develops and implements a long-term *safety plan*.

At Step 6, the school administrator takes immediate action to assure that the threat is not carried out. The student should be detained in the principal's office until his or her parents have arrived. Additionally, the law enforcement officer on the team must determine whether the student has violated the law, and if so, what law enforcement action should be taken. A student who threatens someone with a weapon, or is found to be in possession of a weapon is likely to be arrested. The team must notify the intended victim, and if the victim is a student, the victim's parents. The school psychologist should begin a mental health evaluation of the student as soon as possible, with the initial goal of assessing the student's mental state and need for immediate mental health services. The student should be suspended from school, pending a complete assessment of the threat and determination of the most appropriate school placement.

At Step 7, the team completes a safety evaluation that integrates findings from all available sources of information in a written safety plan. The safety plan is designed both to protect potential victims and to address the student's educational needs. The plan includes mental health and counseling recommendations, findings from the law enforcement investigation, and disciplinary consequences. At this point, the principal decides whether the student can return to school or should be placed in an alternative setting. If the student is permitted to return to school, the plan describes the conditions that must be met and the procedures in place to monitor the student when he or she returns.

Threat Victims

The guidelines address threat victim issues in several ways. In all cases, the principal should interview the recipient or target of the threat and consider this person's perspective and his or her understanding of the meaning of the threat. In the case of transient threats, the student making

TABLE 38.2

Implications for Practice: How to Conduct Student Threat Assessments

---

- Each school should have a trained threat assessment team led by the school principal that includes a law enforcement officer, psychologist, and counselor or other mental health professional.
- Teams should give more weight to the context and meaning of a threat than to the student's literal statement, since the critical issue is whether the student poses a threat, not whether the student made a threat.
- Most threats can be quickly resolved as transient threats, whereas more serious, substantive threats require protective action and further investigation.
- Threat assessment, ideally, is a process of risk reduction and threat management, aiming to resolve the underlying problem or conflict that generated the threat.

---

the threat is expected to offer an apology and/or explanation to the person who was threatened. If a threat involves a dispute or conflict, the team will explore the possibility of conflict mediation, provided that both parties are willing to participate. If the threat is substantive, the team has a clear obligation to notify the victim (and if the victim is a student, also that student's parents) for protective purposes. The guidelines indicate when school authorities should break confidentiality in order to notify potential victims and the guidelines include advice on procedures for keeping victims informed later in the process when decisions are made about a student returning to school (Cornell & Sheras, 2006). Key points in conducting a threat assessment are found in Table 38.2.

THREAT ASSESSMENT TRAINING

In order to field test the threat assessment guidelines, teams were trained in each of the 35 schools in the two school divisions. Following consideration of various formats for training and how best to cover all topics, a program of five hour-long sessions was developed (Cornell et al., 2006).

1. Overview of school violence and rationale for threat assessment. In the opening session, facts about the prevalence of violence in schools that contradict the media-generated perception of an epidemic of school violence are presented. The trainer reviews findings and recommendations from the FBI and Secret Service studies of school shootings, and explains why threat assessment is a more flexible and realistic alternative than zero-tolerance policies.

2. Guidelines for threat assessment. In the second session, the threat assessment guidelines are presented, including how the guidelines were developed and how team members use them. The concept of *threat* is defined and each team member's role is explained. Finally, trainees are guided step by step through the decision tree, illustrating the process with case examples of both transient and substantive threats.

3. Law enforcement and administrative issues. The third session covers the legal and administrative issues associated with student threats of violence, including what might constitute reasonable standards for school violence prevention in light of previous court cases and the standards generally applied to mental health professionals. A special emphasis is placed on documenting threats, both for liability protection, and more generally, as a good practice to improve the quality and consistency of the threat assessment process. A form is provided to record a description of the threat, summarize statements by the student and witnesses, and check off actions taken in response to the threat.

4. Mental health assessment and intervention. The fourth session addresses the roles of mental health professionals, usually school psychologists, who conduct evaluations of students

who have made very serious substantive threats. An interview protocol is reviewed, containing the key topics and questions to cover in the evaluation, particularly the student's violence history, access to weapons, and relationship with the intended victim. The trainer describes some of the follow-up interventions that might be undertaken by school counselors, or other school personnel such as student assistance professionals or school social workers, as part of a risk reduction plan.

5. Threat assessment exercises. The final session gives school teams an opportunity to practice using the threat assessment guidelines. Small groups or teams respond to three hypothetical threat scenarios by working their way through the decision tree and devising follow-up plans appropriate to the seriousness of each threat.

At the conclusion of the final session, evaluations of the training are obtained from the participants. In addition to collecting the usual satisfaction ratings, trainees are asked to complete a short quiz on their knowledge and understanding of the guidelines. This was a useful aid for identifying topics that required more attention or careful explanation in future training. In a sample of 500 training participants, 94% agreed that the training "improved my understanding of student violence" and 98% found the training "helpful in responding to student threats of violence." Since the initial work with the field-test schools, more than 20 school divisions have been trained, and a comprehensive 145-page manual that presents the guidelines, case examples, interview protocols, and other training materials has been developed (Cornell & Sheras, 2006).

CASE EXAMPLES

The following three cases demonstrate how the student threat assessment guidelines can be applied to transient, serious, and very serious threats. These are composite cases with details changed to disguise identities and highlight best practices.

Transient Threat

Two middle school boys got into a fight in the hallway. After they were separated by two teachers, one boy shouted to the other, "I'm gonna kill you for that."

Threat Assessment Summary

The principal interviewed the student, who admitted making the statement, but said he made the statement because he was mad and not because he intended to kill anyone. He explained what the other student had done to offend him and how the fight started. The boy was apologetic and agreed to meet with the other boy and try to resolve their conflict. The principal was familiar with both boys and knew their discipline records. The principal consulted with the teachers for any additional information about the conflict between the boys and concluded that the threat was a transient one. Although the threat was transient, the principal suspended both boys for 3 days for fighting, in accord with school discipline policy. Their parents were contacted and the entire situation was reviewed. The SRO met with each boy and pointed out the legal consequences that could follow from fighting and threatening behavior. The boys attended a mediation session to resolve their conflict. After the mediation session, the guidance counselor interviewed each boy to assess whether the conflict had been resolved. The boys were encouraged to contact the guidance counselor if there was renewed conflict.

Serious Substantive Threat

Will and Dan had a history of teasing and mocking one another. One day, Will became so angry with something Dan said that he sent Dan a note, "Meet me at the park tonight at 9 so I can kick your a–." Dan showed the note to a teacher, who in turn contacted the principal. The principal regarded the note as a threat because it expressed intent to harm someone. The fact that the threat was in writing, and specified a time and place for the fight, suggested that it was probably substantive rather than transient.

Threat Assessment Summary

The principal met with Will and then attempted to mediate the dispute by bringing Dan into the meeting. Both boys had a number of complaints and grievances to air. Will was reluctant to apologize, which supported the principal's concern that Will still wanted to fight Dan. At this point, the principal decided that the threat was substantive rather than transient. Because the threat was substantive, the principal was obligated to take some form of protective action. Protective action depends on the nature of the situation. The principal's attempt to mediate the dispute was one form of protective action, and when this did not appear to be effective, she ordered both boys to stay away from one another. She asked the SRO to speak with both boys and to advise them of the legal consequences of threatening, fighting, or injuring one another. The principal also contacted the boys' teachers and made arrangements so that they would not encounter each other between classes or during physical education class. She called both sets of parents to inform them of the situation and followed up with a letter, which offered the services of the school counselor. Will was given after-school detention for writing the note.

Very Serious Substantive Threat

A middle school student named Dennis confided in two of his friends that he was "sick and tired of getting pushed around at the bus stop" by two older boys and that he was going to "bring an equalizer tomorrow and make them pay." The friends understood this to mean that Dennis intended to bring a gun to the bus stop and one of the friends told another student, who in turn told the SRO. The SRO contacted the principal, who decided to investigate the report as a possible threat.

Threat Assessment Summary

The principal interviewed Dennis as well as the student who first heard Dennis make the threat. Dennis at first denied making the statement or having access to a firearm. He did, however, admit that he was upset with two boys who had been bullying him at the bus stop for several weeks. When the principal contacted Dennis's mother, she said that she kept a handgun at home for protection because she was a single parent. Dennis knew that his mother kept the gun in her nightstand. Based on his investigation, the principal decided that the threat could not be regarded as transient, and because it involved a threat to use a weapon, it was a very serious substantive threat. He contacted members of the school threat assessment team, who agreed with this assessment. Dennis was placed on suspension pending completion of a safety evaluation, according to the school's written policy on very serious threats of violence. The principal and school resource officer met with Dennis's mother and reviewed the seriousness of the situation, but also related their plans to investigate the bullying problem.

Following the protocol in the threat assessment guidelines, the school psychologist conducted an initial interview with Dennis that afternoon before he went home. She screened Dennis for psychiatric symptoms that would merit hospitalization, inquired about homicidal and suicidal intention, and obtained information about the bullying he had experienced. The school psychologist met with Dennis' mother and obtained background information about his family history, previous peer relations, and prior aggressive behavior. She assessed the mother's willingness to cooperate with the school in taking actions to prevent Dennis from getting into serious trouble. The mother agreed to let a relative keep the handgun for the foreseeable future.

The school principal contacted the parents of the boys who were the presumed targets of the threat. The principal informed the parents what had happened and that the boy who made the threat had been suspended from school. Because this matter involved a threat of violence, the principal disclosed the name of the student and the actions that were taken for protective purposes. During the next few days, members of the threat assessment team gathered information from Dennis' teachers and also interviewed the bus driver and students who used the same bus stop.

The threat assessment team held a meeting 3 days after the incident and decided on an action plan. Because Dennis had not directly threatened the boys or brought a weapon to the bus stop, he would not be expelled from school and would be permitted to return to school under certain conditions. The first condition was that he was willing to apologize for his threat and expressed understanding that there was a more appropriate way for him to deal with the bullying situation. He accepted the consequence of not being permitted to ride the school bus for the remainder of the school year. Additionally, he agreed to check in with the SRO on a daily basis, and to advise him of any bullying incidents that took place. Dennis also began meeting with the school counselor to talk about his peer relationships. The counselor also met with the two boys who had been teasing Dennis.

FIELD TESTING OF THE THREAT ASSESSMENT GUIDELINES

Threat assessment teams from 35 schools participated in the field-testing project. Methodological details are described in detail elsewhere (Cornell & Sheras, 2006; Cornell et al., 2004). The schools consisted of 4 high schools (Grades 9–12), 6 middle schools (Grades 6–8), 22 elementary schools (Grades K–5), and 3 alternative schools (Grades 7–12). The combined enrollment of these schools was 16,273 students, including 71% Caucasian, 22% African-American, and 7% other groups. Approximately 26% of the students were eligible for free or reduced-fee school meals.

School principals reported cases by completing an electronic form at a secure Web site. The Web site form collected demographic information (age, gender, grade, and race) on the student who made the threat and the intended threat victim, provided space for a description of the threat incident, and presented a checklist of actions taken in response to the threat (e.g., suspending or expelling the student, contacting police, providing counseling services).

A researcher remained in contact with the school principals over the course of the school year to provide consultation on the guidelines and then conducted face-to-face follow-up interviews. Follow-up interviews were conducted during the final weeks of the school year and again the following fall. The follow-up at the end of the school year occurred an average of 148 days after the threat incident and the second follow-up interview occurred an average of 424 days after the threat incident.

Over the course of the school year, the principals reported 188 student threats. This sample represents threats that came to the attention of school authorities. It is recognized that many threats communicated among students are not reported to school authorities, just as many crimes in the community are not reported to the police.

The most common threats were threats to hit or assault someone (41%), followed by threats to kill (15%), shoot (13%), stab (11%) or injure in some other way (5%). Approximately 15%

of threats were too vague to be classified (e.g., "I'm going to get you"). Most threats (76%) were made by boys.

Threats were reported at all grade levels from kindergarten through Grade 12, but the distribution was bimodal. There was a peak at Grades 3 and 4 (each with 27 threats) and then a second peak at Grades 7 and 8 (28 and 24 threats, respectively). Altogether, 56% of the threats took place at these four grade levels.

As anticipated, a large proportion of the threats (70%) were classified as transient threats, whereas the remaining 30% were substantive threats divided between those regarded as serious (23%) and very serious (7%). Threats in the elementary grades were primarily transient threats 85%), whereas threats in the middle school grades were more evenly divided between transient (60%) and substantive (40%) cases. At the high school level, there were 23 (57.5%) transient and 17 (42.5%) substantive cases. A detailed statistical analysis of the field-test data is presented elsewhere (Cornell et al., 2004).

Threat Outcomes

School principals were interviewed to learn what disciplinary consequences were imposed on the students after making the threat. The most common disciplinary consequence was short-term suspension from school. Nearly all of the students who made substantive threats (88%) were suspended from school, with the modal suspension 3 days. In contrast, 34% of students who made transient threats were suspended, with the modal suspension 1 day.

Only 6 of 188 students were arrested. The arrests were based on clearly illegal actions such as weapon possession and assault and battery. Two students who made false bomb threats also were arrested. Only three students were expelled, and all had extensive histories of disciplinary infractions that culminated in the decision to remove them from school.

In follow-up interviews, principals were asked whether the student's behavior had worsened, stayed about the same, or improved since the threat incident. Only 18% of the students were described as worse, 39% were the same, and 43% were improved.

Similarly, principals were asked about the student's relationship with the target of the threat. For this question, the sample size dropped to 126, because for various reasons the principal could not make a judgment (e.g., when either the student or target was no longer in the school). The principals reported that the relationship had worsened in just 5% of the cases, while it remained the same in 63% and improved in 32%.

Finally, principals were asked whether, to their knowledge, the student had carried out the threat. This question focused on what the student did after the threat assessment was conducted, recognizing that some of the students had engaged in a violent act at the time of the threat—for example, some threats were made after a fight. According to the principals, *none* of the threats were carried out. Although it is conceivable that some of the less severe threats (e.g., to hit or strike someone) were carried out without the principal's knowledge, almost certainly none of the more serious threats to shoot, stab, or otherwise severely injure the target were carried out.

FIELD-TESTING LIMITATIONS AND DIRECTIONS FOR FUTURE STUDY

The field-test findings need replication in a controlled study with a comparison group of schools not using threat assessment. Schools using threat assessment should be compared to schools using zero-tolerance policies, a profiling approach, or other systematic practices. The purpose of our project was to develop and field test our guidelines. A field test project is an important step prior to conducting a controlled study, because it provides an opportunity to develop, observe, and refine the procedures and methods that will constitute the proposed intervention.

Additional studies are warranted to confirm the positive outcomes our principals reported. It would be useful to assess threat assessment outcomes using information from multiple sources, and to investigate the relationship between the student and targeted victim in more detail. It may be possible to identify factors associated with successful outcomes. For example, how useful is peer mediation or other conflict resolution strategies when students make threats to harm one another? Although there is evidence in support of certain general forms of youth violence prevention, such as conflict mediation and schoolwide bullying prevention programs (U.S. Surgeon General, 2001), we know of no studies that have examined the impact of such strategies on student conflicts that have resulted in an articulated threat.

It is important to consider the degree to which teams fully implement a threat assessment approach and how skillfully they follow its guidelines. In their landmark meta-analysis of school-based violence prevention programs, Wilson et al. (2003) found that quality of program implementation was critical. Schools that carefully implement and maintain a violence prevention program are more likely to achieve substantial reductions in student aggression and misbehavior than schools that implement programs in a less rigorous manner. It follows that professionals should seek the best methods for training school administrators to implement and maintain a threat assessment approach.

The school principal plays a critical role in leading the threat assessment team. It may be useful to study the role of administrator judgment and decision making. What qualities of the school principal are associated with positive outcomes in the resolution of student threats? In our experience, a fair and reasonable resolution of student threats of violence inevitably relies on the good judgment and skill of the school administrator.

Threat assessment is not a substitute for other violence prevention efforts; it should be implemented in the context of a more comprehensive approach that includes an array of intervention and prevention services (Osher, Dwyer, & Jackson, 2004). Sprague and colleagues (Sprague et al., 2002) investigated the effects of a schoolwide approach that included a schoolwide discipline plan based on Effective Behavioral Support (Sugai & Homer, 1994) and a violence prevention curriculum. They reported both reductions in school discipline referrals and improvement in student knowledge of social skills in nine schools (Sprague et al., 2002). The Olweus Bullying Prevention Program (Olweus, Limber, & Mihalic, 1999) is an especially important intervention because so many student threats are associated with bullying and related peer conflicts.

Our development and field testing of threat assessment guidelines demonstrates that threat assessment is a viable procedure and worthy of further study. Threat assessment is a potentially valuable component of school violence prevention because it uses resources efficiently and targets specific conflicts and disputes before they erupt in violence.

REFERENCES

Borum, R. (1996). Improving the clinical practice of violence risk assessment: Technologies, guidelines and training. *American Psychologist, 51*, 945–956.

Cornell, D. (2003). Guidelines for responding to student threats of violence. *Journal of Educational Administration, 41*, 705–719.

Cornell, D. (2004). Student threat assessment. In E. Gerler (Ed.), *Handbook of school violence* (pp. 115–136). Binghamton, NY: Haworth Press.

Cornell, D., & Sheras, P. (2006). *Guidelines for responding to student threats of violence*. Longmont, CO: Sopris West.

Cornell, D., Sheras, P., Kaplan, S., Levy-Elkon, A., McConville, D. McKnight, L., & Posey, J. (2004). Guidelines for responding to student threats of violence: Field test of a threat assessment approach. In M. J. Furlong, M. P. Bates,

D. C. Smith, & P. M. Kingery (Eds.), *Appraisal and prediction of school violence: Issues, methods, and contexts* (pp. 11–36). Binghamton, NY: Nova Science.

Cornell, D., Sheras, P. Kaplan, S., McConville, D., Posey, J., Levy-Elkon, A., McKnight, L., Branson, C., & Cole, J. (2004). Guidelines for student threat assessment: Field-test findings. *School Psychology Review, 33*, 527–546.

Fein, R. A., Vossekuil, F., & Holden, G. A. (1995). *Threat assessment: An approach to prevent targeted violence*. National Institute of Justice: Research in Action, 1-7 (NCJ 155000), available: http://www.secretservice.gov/ntac.htm.

Fein, R., Vossekuil, B., Pollack, W., Borum, R., Modzeleski, W., & Reddy, M. (2002). *Threat assessment in schools: A guide to managing threatening situations and to creating safe school climates*. Washington, DC: U.S. Secret Service and Department of Education.

Heilbrun, K. (1997). Prediction versus management models relevant to risk assessment: The importance of legal decision–making context. *Law and Human Behavior, 21*, 347–360.

Larson, J., Smith, D. C., & Furlong, M. J. (2001). Best practices in school violence prevention. In A. Thomas & J. Grimes (Eds.), *Best practices in school psychology–IV* (pp. 1081–1097). Washington, DC: National Association of School Psychologists.

Mulvey, E. P., & Cauffman, E. (2001). The inherent limits of predicting school violence. *American Psychologist, 56*, 797–802.

Olweus, D., Limber, S., & Mihalic, S. F. (1999). *Blueprints for violence prevention: Book 9, Bullying Prevention Program*. Boulder, CO: Center for the Study and Prevention of Violence.

Osher, D., Dwyer, K., & Jackson, S. (2004). *Safe, supportive and successful schools: Step by step*. Longmont, CO: Sopris West.

O'Toole, M. E. (2000). *The school shooter: A threat assessment perspective*. Quantico, VA: National Center for the Analysis of Violent Crime, Federal Bureau of Investigation.

Reddy, M., Borum, R., Berglund, J., Vossekuil, B., Fein, R., & Modzeleski, W. (2001). Evaluating risk for targeted violence in schools: Comparing risk assessment, threat assessment, and other approaches. *Psychology in the Schools, 38*, 157–172.

Sewell, K. W., & Mendelsohn, M. (2000). Profiling potentially violent youth: Statistical and conceptual problems. *Children's Services: Social Policy, Research, and Practice, 3*, 147–169.

Sprague, J., Walker, H., Golly, A., White, K., Myers, D., & Shannon, T. (2002). Translating research into effective practice: The effects of a universal staff and student intervention on indicators of discipline and school safety. *Education & Treatment of Children, 24*, 495–511.

Sugai, G., & Horner, R. (1994). Including students with severe behavior problems in general education settings: Assumptions, challenges, and solutions. In J. Marr, G. Sugai, & G. Tindal (Eds.), *The Oregon conference monograph* (Vol 6., pp. 102–120). Eugene: University of Oregon.

U.S. Surgeon General. (2001). *Youth violence: A report of the Surgeon General*. Rockville, MD: U.S. Department of Health and Human Services.

Virginia Department of Criminal Justice Services. (1999). *The Virginia school resource officer program guide*. Available: www.dcjs.virginia.gov/forms/cple/sroguide.pdf

Wilson, S. J., Lipsey, M. W., & Derzon, J. H. (2003). The effects of school-based intervention programs on aggressive behavior: A meta-analysis. *Journal of Consulting and Clinical Psychology, 71*, 136–149.

39

Implementation of the Dallas Threat of Violence Risk Assessment

Russell B. Van Dyke
Panama-Buena Vista Union School District

Jennifer L. Schroeder
Texas A&M University–Commerce

Between 1996 and 1999, numerous multiple-victim school shootings dramatically changed public opinion about the safety of America's schools (U.S. Department of Health and Human Services, 2001). The timing and similarity of these incidents spurred increased media coverage, and prompted many to describe the phenomenon as an "epidemic" (Verlinden, Hersen, & Thomas, 2000). The eight school shootings that occurred between February 1996 and April 1999 impacted public opinion because they differed from more prevalent patterns of violence previously seen in schools—they took place in rural or suburban settings, appeared unrelated to gang or drug activity, and the perpetrators came from primarily middle-class or affluent homes (National School Safety Center [NSSC], 2001; Verlinden et al., 2000). These incidents challenged the common belief that school violence is an urban problem related to gangs, drugs, and poverty (U.S. Department of Health and Human Services, 2001). With news media images of school shootings fresh in their minds, many parents and students questioned the safety of their schools, even though school has consistently been one of the safest places for children (Centers for Disease Control and Prevention [CDC], 2001, 2003; DeVoe et al., 2002; U.S. Department of Health and Human Services, 2001).

With a climate of growing fear and concern, school administrators across the country came under considerable pressure to be proactive in preventing school violence (Fey, Nelson, & Roberts, 2000). Many school districts focused on increasing security by employing police or security officers, and adding metal detectors and surveillance cameras (Lafee, 2000). Some districts adopted a form of profiling advocated by the FBI (Band & Harpold, 1999) in an attempt to identify potentially violent students, particularly those capable of becoming the "next school shooter" (Fey et al., 2000; Lafee, 2000). Schoolwide approaches to student discipline were also advocated as effective methods for reducing and preventing school violence (Dwyer, Osher, & Warger, 1998; Horner, Sugai, & Horner, 2000).

THREAT ASSESSMENT IN THE SCHOOLS

In 2000, the FBI released *The School Shooter: A Threat Assessment Perspective*, a report that presented a systematic procedure for threat assessment and intervention designed for use by educators, mental health professionals, and law enforcement agencies (O'Toole, 2000). The FBI report included general information about threats and described a four-pronged threat assessment model developed by the FBI's National Center for Analysis of Violent Crime (NCAVC). The NCAVC's model is "based on the 'totality of the circumstances' known about the student" (O'Toole, 2000, p. 10) in the areas of personality and behavior, family dynamics, school dynamics, and social dynamics. The report also provided recommendations for developing a schoolwide threat assessment system and for creating a multidisciplinary team as a component of the threat assessment system.

Recently, the U.S. Secret Service and the U.S. Department of Education collaborated on the Safe School Initiative, a systematic analysis of 37 incidents of targeted school shootings and school attacks that occurred between 1974 and 2000. This study examined the thinking, planning, and other pre-attack behaviors of students who carried out school shootings (Vossekuil, Fein, Reddy, Borum, & Modzeleski, 2002). In 2002, the U.S. Secret Service and the U.S. Department of Education released the findings of the Safe School Initiative (Vossekuil et al., 2002) and published a guide for using threat assessment in schools to help create safe school climates (Fein et al., 2002). In addition to the fundamental principles and steps of the threat assessment approach, the U.S. Secret Service recommends three elements essential to a school threat assessment program (Fein et al., 2002). First, schools should have clear policies authorizing school officials to respond to information about potentially threatening situations and to conduct a threat assessment if warranted. Second, schools should establish a threat assessment team trained to respond to potentially threatening situations. The threat assessment team should include (a) an administrator; (b) an investigator, such as a school security officer or other police officer; (c) a mental health professional, such as a school psychologist; and (d) other professionals, such as counselors, teachers, or coaches, who may be able to contribute to the process. Finally, schools must build relationships between individuals and organizations within the school and create policies and procedures for collaboration and co-operation with community organizations concerned with safety and child welfare (Fein et al., 2002).

In the absence of an established method for identifying potentially violent students, many school districts developed their own methods for identifying these students based on the U.S. Secret Service or FBI threat assessment models ("Schools Deploy Programs," 2000; Sheras & Cornell, 2002; Trahant, Olmi, Dubard, & Sterling-Turner, 2003). In response to public concern, the Dallas Independent School District (DISD) formed a committee to develop a districtwide strategy for preventing acts of targeted school violence. The committee originally was formed during the 1997–1998 school year, and included individuals with expertise in psychology, social work, crisis management, school discipline, and the juvenile justice system (Van Dyke, Ryan-Arredondo, Rakowitz, & Torres, 2004). The end result of the committee's work was a districtwide policy for responding to threats of violence and implementation of the Dallas Threat of Violence Risk Assessment (DTVRA). The DTVRA was created to help school personnel systematically assess threats made by students to determine the likelihood of a student following through with a threat. It also provided direction for appropriate intervention strategies to reduce the likelihood of future threats of violence (Ryan-Arredondo et al., 2001; Van Dyke et al., 2004). It is important to recognize that the DTVRA is a minor component of a broader districtwide violence prevention effort and is intended specifically to help school staff address the issue of targeted violence.

DEVELOPING A DISTRICTWIDE POLICY

Response to Threats

Targeted violence is defined as any situation "in which an identifiable (or potentially identifiable) perpetrator poses (or may pose) a threat of violence to a particular individual or group" (Fein, Vossekuil, & Holden, 1995, p. 1). According to the U.S. Secret Service, one important aspect of threat assessment is identifying individuals who pose a threat, regardless of whether the individuals have made a threat (Fein et al., 1995). The DISD committee determined that the first step to identify students who pose a threat is to take all threats seriously. Although various definitions exist for what constitutes a threat, the most widely accepted one among school personnel is "an expression of intent to do harm or act out violently against someone or something" (National Association of School Psychologists [NASP], 2002, p. 2). Threats can be verbal, written, or symbolic. The districtwide policy adopted by the DISD school board states, in part, that "all threats of violence must be reported to the principal.... All threats will be taken seriously" (DISD, 2001).

Seriousness of Threats

The committee also recognized that an important aspect of responding to threats is to differentiate between threats of a more serious nature and those of a less serious nature. The DISD Student Code of Conduct (DISD, 2002) includes the term *terroristic threat* from the Texas Penal Code (1994). In Texas, the police, not school personnel, determine whether or not a terroristic threat has been made. One aspect of a terroristic threat is that a perpetrator places a "person in fear of imminent serious bodily injury" (§ 22.07). The Dallas Police Department's interpretation of "imminent" includes the following: (a) the threat must be direct and verbal (i.e., the targeted person must hear the threat) and (b) the person making the threat must have the means to carry out the threat at that time (D. Smith, personal communication, January 21, 2003). For example, if a student threatens another student by saying, "I'm going to smash your head with a baseball bat," the student must have immediate access to a baseball bat in order for the threat to be considered terroristic. If the student must go home or must leave the immediate vicinity to retrieve a bat, then the criterion for imminent would not be met and the threat would not be considered terroristic. The committee determined that school principals would be responsible for deciding whether or not to call the police when a threat situation appears to match the penal code definition for a terroristic threat. Threats of a less serious nature would be handled by school personnel.

Threat Assessment

Selecting Risk Factors

To assist school personnel in handling threats of violence, the DISD committee developed the DTVRA. Risk factors for the DTVRA were selected based on a review of existing research on youth violence, including information from the NSSC (Ryan-Arredondo et al., 2001). The NSSC began tracking school-associated violent deaths in 1992, and subsequently compiled a checklist of characteristics of students who have caused school-associated violent deaths (NSSC, 1998). The committee used this checklist as a starting point and reviewed the literature on youth violence to evaluate each characteristic on the checklist. Additional risk factors were added based on support from the literature review. The initial version of the DTVRA, first implemented during the 1998–1999 school year, included 18 risk factors. In June 2001, a risk factor addressing emotional stability was added, bringing the total number of risk factors to 19 (see the appendix).

The following 19 risk factors are included in the DTVRA, and are listed with sources and a brief summary of existing research:

1. *Plan: Details* (Borum, Fein, Vossekuil, & Berglund, 1999; Dwyer et al., 1998; Fein et al., 1995; O'Toole, 2000; Verlinden et al., 2000): Detailed and specific threats (i.e., time, place, method) are one of the most reliable indicators of future violence toward self or others, and require immediate intervention by school authorities and possibly law enforcement. In almost all cases that have been analyzed, perpetrators of targeted school shootings planned their attack in advance and shared details of their plan with others.

2. *Plan: Access to weapons* (APA, 1993; Cotton et al., 1994; Huizinga, Loeber, & Thornberry, 1994; NSSC, 1998; Poland, 1993; Valois & McKewon, 1998; Verlinden et al., 2000): Children and adolescents with access to firearms are more likely to be involved in violence, either as a perpetrator or a victim. This is particularly true among youth who may already be at risk for violent behavior.

3. *Plan: Time*: (see *Plan: Details*).

4. *Plan: Viability of plan* (see *Plan: Details*).

5. *Aggressive behavior* (APA, 1993; Dwyer et al., 1998; Hawkins et al., 1998; Lattimore, Visher, & Linster, 1995; NSSC, 1998; Verlinden et al., 2000): Numerous studies have concluded that the best predictor of future violence and aggression is a history of violent and aggressive behavior. Specifically, an early pattern of aggression has been shown to consistently predict later violence.

6. *Discipline record* (Borum, 2000; Dwyer et al., 1998; NSSC, 1998; Verlinden et al., 2000): Chronic behavior and disciplinary problems are related to an increased likelihood of aggression. Students with chronic discipline problems are more likely to be rejected by their peers, become socially isolated, and disengage from school. Social isolation and rejection by peers are strong predictors of delinquency and aggression.

7. *Academic performance* (APA, 1993; Borum, 2000; Dwyer et al., 1998; Farrington, 1989; Huizinga et al., 1994; Lipsey & Derzon, 1998): Low academic achievement, academic failure, and retention are associated with violence and delinquent behavior, particularly among adolescents.

8. *Exposure to violence* (APA, 1993; DuRant, Cadenhead, Pendergrast, Slavens, & Linder, 1994; Singer et al., 1999; Song, Singer, & Anglin, 1998; Verlinden et al., 2000): Numerous studies have validated the assertion that exposure to violence is associated with adolescents' use of violence.

9. *History of previous threats* (Dwyer et al., 1998; Lattimore et al., 1995; NSSC, 1998): Threats of violence toward self or others are associated with future violence, especially among youth who have previously used violence.

10. *Victim of violence or abuse (verbal, sexual, or physical)* (Dwyer et al., 1998; NSSC, 1998; C. Smith & Thornberry, 1995; Thornberry, 1994; Uehara, Chalmers, Jenkins, & Shakoor, 1996; Verlinden et al., 2000; Widom, 1989): Personal victimization and childhood maltreatment, particularly child neglect, have been shown to predict the use of violence among both adults and adolescents.

11. *Exhibits cruelty to animals* (Dwyer et al., 1998; NSSC, 1998; Verlinden et al., 2000): Several perpetrators of school shootings have been involved with cruelty to animals, which may indicate a pattern of aggression toward others.

12. *Victim or perceived victim of discrimination or harassment* (APA, 1993; Dwyer et al., 1998; Kingery, Biafora, & Zimmerman, 1996; NSSC, 1998; Verlinden et al., 2000; Vossekuil et al., 2002): Youth who experience long-standing bullying, harassment, or

discrimination may be more likely to engage in violence, particularly acts of targeted violence.

13. *Gang membership, member of antisocial group or cult* (APA, 1993; Dwyer et al., 1998; Huizinga et al., 1994; Lattimore et al., 1995; NSSC, 1998; U.S. Department of Health and Human Services, 2001; Verlinden et al., 2000): Gang membership greatly increases the risk of violence among adolescents of all ethnic groups.

14. *Family support* (Huizinga et al., 1994; NSSC, 1998; Singer et al., 1999; U.S. Department of Health and Human Services, 2001; Verlinden et al., 2000): Lack of parental supervision and monitoring, low parental involvement, and poor parent–child relations are strong predictors of the development of delinquency and violence in children and adolescents.

15. *Empathy, sympathy, or remorse* (Kingery et al., 1996; NSSC, 1998; Verlinden et al., 2000): Low empathy, as part of low normative values (i.e., little respect for laws and social norms), is a strong predictor of violence among adolescent boys of all ethnicities.

16. *Interpersonal/relationship skills* (Baker, 1998; Dwyer et al., 1998; NSSC, 1998; U.S. Department of Health and Human Services, 2001; Verlinden et al., 2000): Lack of social ties, particularly among adolescents, is a strong predictor of violence. Physically aggressive children are often rejected by peers, which may exacerbate behavior problems, and can lead to further aggression or violence.

17. *Preoccupation with weapons, death, and violent themes* (Dwyer et al., 1998; NSSC, 1998; Singer et al., 1999; Verlinden et al., 2000; Vossekuil et al., 2002): Violent behavior has been linked to a preoccupation with violent themes in many forms, such as violent movies and video games, or an overrepresentation of violence in writings or drawings.

18. *Drugs or alcohol usage; impulsivity* (APA, 1993; Borum, 2000; Dwyer et al., 1998; Huizinga et al., 1994; U.S. Department of Health and Human Services, 2001; Verlinden et al., 2000): Research has consistently shown a strong relationship between substance abuse and violent behavior. There is also a growing body of research indicating that impulsivity, particularly in combination with restlessness and hyperactivity, is associated with aggression and violent behavior among children and adolescents.

19. *Emotional stability* (Borum, 2000; DuRant et al., 1994; National Institute of Mental Health, 2000; Verlinden et al., 2000; Vossekuil et al., 2002): The relationship between depression and violent behavior has been demonstrated among both youth and adults, particularly among boys. Additionally, most perpetrators of school shootings had a history of suicide attempts or suicidal thinking prior to their attacks.

These 19 risk factors are further delineated into three levels: low, medium, and high. Each level describes the extent to which the risk factor is displayed by the student. The low level represents a normal history or an absence of risk factors. The medium level represents the presence of some behaviors or a history related to general youth violence; whereas, the high level represents the presence of risk factors that were found previously in individuals who committed violent acts (Van Dyke et al., 2004). For example, the risk factor Discipline Record defines the low level as "no previous discipline record," the medium level as "record of fighting, harassing, or verbally abusive," and the high level as "has history of disciplinary problems, criminal offenses, or was removed or expelled" (see the appendix). These operational definitions were developed by the committee after careful review of the literature.

Completing Threat Assessment

The format and scoring of the DTVRA worksheet was modeled after the DISD Suicide Risk Assessment worksheet (J. Smith, 1988). Each risk factor is included as a single item on the Threat of Violence Risk Assessment worksheet, for a total of 19 items. The selected risk factors target information that is readily available to school personnel through student, parent, and teacher interviews, and through a review of school records. This allows the DTVRA to be completed without a lengthy investigation. Often, much information is already known about students referred for a threat assessment because many of these students have previously been identified as "at risk," due to either academic or behavioral difficulties.

School counselors usually conduct the threat assessments; however, psychological services personnel are also trained and conduct threat assessments when necessary. To complete the Threat of Violence Risk Assessment worksheet, the counselor uses the information gathered from interviews and review of records to rate the student on each risk factor. The counselor determines which level (low, medium, or high) best describes the student's current circumstances and marks the appropriate level. After all items are completed, the endorsed risk factors at each level are tallied. Next, the total in the low level is multiplied by 1, the total in the medium level is multiplied by 2, and the total in the high level is multiplied by 3 to give greater weight to the more serious risk factors (Van Dyke et al., 2004). It should be noted that this weighting system was developed by the committee without empirical validation. The sum of these weighted scores is divided by 3 to obtain the overall risk assessment score. Based on the overall score, the overall risk level is determined to be low (a score below 9), medium (a score of 9–14), or high (a score above 14). As with the weighting system, these cutoff scores were arbitrarily chosen by the committee without empirical validation. It is recommended that users of such a procedure continuously gather data to evaluate the appropriateness of these threshold values.

An important aspect of conducting a threat assessment is to assess an individual's attack-related behaviors (Borum et al., 1999). Such preparatory behaviors may include selecting and locating a target, securing a weapon, and communicating inappropriate interest in a target or a plan to attack a target (Borum et al., 1999). The first four items on the DTVRA were designed to assess attack-related behaviors. Attack-related behaviors are considered indicative of imminent risk for violence and require immediate action on the part of school personnel (Dwyer et al., 1998). To reflect the serious nature of such a threatening situation, if the first four items of the DTVRA are all marked "high," then the overall risk level is automatically scored high regardless of the overall score.

Action Plan

After the DTVRA is completed, the school staff and parents develop an intervention strategy, called an action plan. The action plan includes both disciplinary action related to the type of threat made and support services deemed necessary to prevent future threats. The Student Code of Conduct (DISD, 2002) includes three offenses related to threats: (a) student-on-student threats, (b) threats by student on personnel and/or facilities, and (c) terroristic threats. Disciplinary action can be as simple as an apology or as serious as expulsion and referral to the Dallas County Juvenile Justice Alternative Education Program. Unless an offense warrants mandatory removal from campus, disciplinary actions are determined by the local campus administrator who follows the guidelines set forth in the Student Code of Conduct.

Support services for students who threaten violence can range from peer mediation to emergency psychiatric services, depending on the results of the DTVRA. In every case a parent conference must be held, although with some low-risk threats, this may be done over the phone. The most common support services included in action plans are (a) individual counseling by the school counselor or psychological services staff, (b) referral to the student support team (SST), and (c) referral to a DISD youth and family center (YFC) or a community agency (Van Dyke, Schroeder, Havsy, & Williams, 2002). The SST is a local campus case management team comprised of an administrator, counselor, nurse, special education teacher, and general education teacher who brainstorm solutions, develop action plans, and monitor the student's progress. The YFCs are low-cost health and mental health clinics on school campuses, a collaborative effort of the DISD and Parkland Health and Hospital System's Community Oriented Primary Care. Each school in the district is served by one of nine YFCs that provide psychiatric, medical, and individual, group, or family therapy services.

The DISD board policy and set of procedures for responding to threats of violence (DISD, 2001) incorporated many of the recommendations outlined by the U.S. Secret Service (Fein et al., 2002). Specifically, the DISD policy (a) authorized school personnel to conduct a threat assessment, (b) defined the behavior that would initiate a threat assessment, (c) designated individuals responsible for gathering and analyzing information, and (d) outlined the steps to be followed from initiation to conclusion of the threat assessment. The board policy and the DTVRA provide clear direction for school personnel when responding to threats of violence.

IMPLEMENTATION OF THE DTVRA

Districtwide Training

Staff from the DISD Psychological Services Department and the DISD Office of Student Discipline conducted districtwide training for all principals and counselors. All training sessions included the same information; however, each group received training tailored to the specific responsibilities they would have in the threat assessment process. Principals' training was focused primarily on the board policy and Student Code of Conduct procedures related to threats of violence. Counselors' training was focused on the threat assessment process and completing the DTVRA. Additionally, all staff of the Psychological Services Department, which includes licensed specialists in school psychology and social workers, received training on how to complete the DTVRA.

Each year, principals receive "refresher" training on the board policy and procedures for responding to threats of violence as part of the districtwide principals' training. Counselors who have previously been trained to use the DTVRA receive refresher training from the psychological services staff member assigned to their school. All new counselors receive in-depth training on the DTVRA from psychological services staff as part of their new counselor training. Each school has an assigned staff member from psychological services who provides assistance and consultation regarding the DTVRA. Schools may also contact a supervising coordinator in the Psychological Services Department for further assistance.

Schoolwide Training

Principals are responsible for training their staff on the board policy regarding threats of violence. The method and extent of this training varies from school to school, and school counselors or psychological services staff may assist with this training. School staff members who are sufficiently trained will know what is expected of them in responding to threats of violence.

Principals are also responsible for informing students of the board policy and creating and maintaining lines of communication between staff members and students. Psychological services staff assists by offering programs targeting bullying and "breaking the code of silence." The code of silence refers to the general reluctance of students to share information with adults about potentially dangerous individuals or situations. The program includes a description of what the code of silence is, a discussion of what information should be shared with adults, and a set of role-plays developed and acted out by students (Haynes, 2003). Additionally, campus-based SSTs, led by school counselors, provide case management and intervention assistance for students referred for making threats of violence.

Portability of the DTVRA

The DTVRA has been used by many school districts as a model for their own threat assessment procedures (B. Rakowitz, personal communication, May 26, 2004). The senior author of this chapter recently took a school psychologist position at a district in California much smaller than the DISD. It is interesting to note that the current policy in this district is modeled after the DTVRA, including the recommended interview format for conducting a threat assessment. Although the reliability and validity of the DTVRA have yet to be established (Van Dyke et al., 2004), the process undertaken by the DISD to develop and implement the DTVRA is a comprehensive model for school districts. The DISD response incorporates the elements recommended by the U.S. Secret Service and the U.S. Department of Education for developing a school threat assessment program.

Implementation Findings and Considerations

Compliance With Board Policy

The DTVRA was first used in the DISD at the beginning of the 1998–1999 school year. Since that time, the Psychological Services Department has tracked the districtwide use of the DTVRA as reported by individual schools. In the 6 years of its use, the number of DTVRAs completed each year increased dramatically, from 148 during 1998–1999 to 639 during 2003–2004. During this same time, the number of students removed to an off-campus disciplinary alternative education program (DAEP) for making threats remained relatively steady (71 in 1998–1999; 82 in 2003–2004). Collectively, these data suggest increased compliance with school board policy rather than indicating an increase in the frequency of threats of violence. However, some unusual variability exists in the number of DTVRAs completed at each school. For example, in 2003–2004, although the majority of schools reported fewer than 5 DTVRAs, several schools reported 10 or more, and two schools reported 25 and 34, respectively. Although the cause of this disparity is unknown, it may be that significant variation exists in administrators' interpretations of and adherence to the board policy. Research has identified similar within-district patterns of inconsistent policy implementation, particularly in large, urban school districts, which has been attributed to lack of training and lack of commitment to implementing the policy (Morrison & Skiba, 2004). Perhaps more in-depth training of administrators is necessary to create a more consistent understanding and application of the board policy.

Reported Risk Levels

Although the number of completed DTVRAs increased each year, the percentage in each overall risk level remained remarkably steady. Of the 639 DTVRAs completed during 2003–2004, 63% were determined to be low risk, 34% medium risk, and 3% high risk. These data are representative of the total number of DTVRAs completed during the past 6 years, and are consistent with the belief that the majority of threats made by students are less serious and that the likelihood is low that these students will follow through with their threats. It also reflects the district policy to take all threats seriously until proven otherwise, or until sufficient information is available to assess the risk level.

Demographic Data

Overall, the majority of DTVRAs were conducted with elementary students (Grades pre-K through 6). However, the percentage of DTVRAs conducted with elementary students rose considerably from 1998–1999 (56%) to 2003–2004 (73%). Given the higher rate of violent incidents among secondary students (Kaufman et al., 2001; Lattimore et al., 1995), it may be that middle and high school students are more capable of hiding threats from adults. Elementary students are generally more closely supervised and may be more willing to report threats to adults. Their acts may also be more impulsive, less thought out, and they may lack the cognitive complexity to be fully aware of the district's threat assessment policy and procedures.

About 20% of the DTVRAs conducted during the 6 years were with students in special education. This percentage is higher than expected based on the overall percentage of special education students in the district. These findings are consistent with research on school discipline showing that students with disabilities tend to be overrepresented in school discipline actions, including expulsions due to zero-tolerance policies (Morrison & D'Incau, 1997; Morrison & Skiba, 2004). Many of these students have chronic emotional and family problems (Morrison & D'Incau, 1997) and may be more likely to become involved in school discipline actions due to poor interpersonal skills and problem-solving abilities. With this in mind, the DTVRA may be a particularly useful tool for identifying needs of students with disabilities in order to develop appropriate interventions for them. Although special education students were overrepresented among those referred for a threat assessment, it should be noted that special education students were less likely than general education students to be sent to an off-campus DAEP, suggesting that the due process rights of special education students were protected.

Another consistent finding is that boys are referred for a threat assessment much more often than girls. During the 6 years from 1998–1999 to 2003–2004, about 85% of DTVRAs were conducted with boys and 15% with girls. These percentages remained stable across the 6 years, and are consistent with the findings of the U.S. Secret Service (Vossekuil et al., 2002) that acts of targeted school violence are committed almost exclusively by males.

CASE STUDY

An illustration of the use of the DTVRA is provided here. The case study presented highlights the steps in the threat assessment process as well as the roles of school personnel in responding to a threat of violence. Issues related to the development of an appropriate action plan are also presented.

A teacher in a Grade 7 computer class overheard several students talking about their plans for the summer. One boy stated he was going to "blow up the school." The teacher reported the incident to the principal who referred the boy to the counselor for a risk assessment. During the interview, the boy admitted making the comment but said he would never really do it. This boy had a history of academic difficulty and received special education services under the category Other Health Impaired, due to an attention deficit hyperactivity disorder. He showed a lack of self-confidence, had difficulty making and keeping friends, and had been disciplined earlier in the year for fighting. He admitted to skipping school and said he recently experimented with marijuana while skipping class with his friend.

Although the threat was vague and there was no evidence of any plans to follow through with the threat, the overall risk level was determined to be medium, due to the presence of several medium-level and two high-level risk factors. The interview with the student revealed that the threat was an expression of dislike for school. The boy stated he wanted to be home-schooled by his mother rather than attend public school. This case illustrates that some threats

TABLE 39.1

Implications for Practice: Developing a School Threat Assessment Program

1. Create a policy approved by the district school board that authorizes school personnel to conduct a threat assessment in response to threats of violence. The school board policy should include the following elements:

(a) The role of school personnel, students, and parents in reporting threats of violence.

(b) The titles of those who may be included on the threat assessment team.

(c) The specific actions that will be taken by school personnel when conducting a threat assessment (e.g., how and when parents will be notified).

(d) The types of recommendations that may be made by school personnel following a threat assessment, including both disciplinary consequences and support services.

2. Involve representatives of community agencies (police departments, community mental health centers, etc.) in the policy development, particularly those agencies with whom collaboration will be most necessary when conducting threat assessments and providing support services to students.

3. Create a procedure for training district personnel who will be involved in conducting threat assessments.

4. Develop a method for compiling data regarding threat assessments conducted in the district. This information can be used to help debrief staff members and to help refine the district policy and procedures as needed.

are less an expression of intent for violence and more a cry for help by students who have unresolved issues. It also highlights the importance of looking beyond the information specific to the threat in order to consider the risk factors, or stressors, at play in the student's life. In this way, it becomes clear that the DTVRA is less about predicting violence and more about preventing violence.

Because the threat was directed at a school facility the disciplinary consequence was mandatory removal to an off-campus DAEP. However, because the boy was a special education student, a manifestation determination meeting was held in which it was decided that his behavior in this incident emanated from the impulsive behavior related to his disability. He remained at his regular school and he and his parents were referred to the YFC for family counseling focused on improving family communication. Additionally, the school psychologist continued to meet regularly with the boy at school to work on improving problem-solving skills.

This case illustrates two important aspects of the DTVRA. First, because the teacher followed the board policy the previously unidentified needs of this boy and his family were revealed during the threat assessment process. Second, school personnel had clear guidance in maintaining the delicate balance of appropriate disciplinary consequences coupled with valuable support services. Additionally, this boy was provided due process as a special education student.

CONCLUSION

Perhaps the best lesson to be learned from the implementation of the DTVRA is that school safety is best achieved through proactive rather than reactive means (see Table 39.1). What began as a reactionary effort to prevent targeted violence has led to confirmation that a school climate of mutual respect and communication between adults and students is essential for such a policy to be effective. Also, efforts to prevent violence and threats of violence must involve a compassionate merger between school discipline and mental health services. Particularly in a district of 165,000 students, success must still be measured one student at a time.

Appendix

THREAT OF VIOLENCE RISK ASSESSMENT
(To be used when a child verbally or non-verbally threatens violence)

Student Name _____   I.D.# _____   School _____   Date _____   Dallas Independent School District

Instructions: **Use as a checklist. See administration questions. Many items require additional contacts with a parent, teacher, counselor or administrator to be able to complete the assessment. Check only one column per item. Do not leave any item without a checkmark. There are 19 items.**

	Low	Medium	High
1. **Plan: Details	vague	some specifics	well thought out, knows when, where, how and who
2. **Plan: Access to weapons	unavailable, difficult to obtain	available, but will have to obtain	have in hand, close by, easy access
3. **Plan: Time	no specific time or in future	within a few hours	immediately
4. **Plan: Viability of plan	plan unrealistic, unlikely to be implemented	some details of plan are plausible	plan realistic
5. Aggressive behavior	when angry does not hurt or threaten to hurt others or property	displays little anger control, considered aggressive, has explosive outbursts, or believes has been treated unfairly	has set fires, has frequent explosive outbursts, or believes in violence to solve problems
6. Discipline record	no previous discipline record	record of fighting, harassing, or verbally abusive	has history of disciplinary problems, criminal offenses, or was removed or expelled
7. Academic performance	no academic difficulties	history of learning difficulties	has been retained or receiving special education services
8. Exposure to violence	exposed to violence only through movies, stories, computer software, video games	has directly witnessed a violent argument or fight at home, in the neighborhood or school	repeated exposure to violence at home, neighborhood or school.
9. History of previous threats	no history of previous threats	friends are aware of threats	has been disciplined in past for terroristic threat
10. Victim of violence or abuse (verbal, sexual or physical)	no evidence that child is a victim of violence or abuse	perceives self as being taken advantage of or a victim but no evidence that abuse has occurred	child has been a victim of violence or abuse, or has been removed from home by Child Protective Services
11. Exhibits cruelty to animals	no tendency to be cruel to animals	discusses cruelty to animals with friends	has tortured or mutilated animals

	Low	Medium	High
12. Victim or perceived victim of discrimination or harassment	no history of discrimination or Harassment	has a history of being teased	documentation of being harassed or discriminated against
13. Gang membership, member of antisocial group or cult	no history of affiliation or interest in becoming a member of a gang, antisocial group, or cult	has past affiliation or has interest in becoming a member of a gang, antisocial group or cult	is currently an active gang member, or cult, sees gang as source of power and protection
14. Family support	Evidence of caring and supportive family relationships	history of neglect	no evidence of early attachment to primary caretaker or little or no parental supervision
15. Empathy, sympathy or remorse	displays normal capacity to feel for others	some indication the development of these feelings are delayed or absent	seems unable to express or feel empathy, sympathy or remorse
16. Interpersonal/relationship skills	has friends, respected among peers and teachers	identified as a bully, has poor interpersonal/relationship skills, or has few friends	others afraid of child, intensely withdrawn, takes advantage of others, or is considered a loner
17. Preoccupation with weapons, death and violent themes	no unusual history of thinking or talking about violence, does not enjoy reading about or watching violence	prefers and enjoys violence on TV or in movies, shows interest in weapons, or talks about violence	preoccupation with violence and death in writings, fantasy, drawings or conversation
18. Drugs or alcohol usage, Impulsivity	does not use drugs or alcohol and is not considered impulsive	some experimentation with drugs or alcohol, 1 or 2 times a month; or somewhat impulsive	heavy use of drugs or alcohol, several times a week; or has little impulse control
19. Emotional stability	emotions similar to peers	depressive and/or manic episodes	history of suicidal threats/attempts
TOTAL CHECKS	LOWER _____	MEDIUM _____	HIGHER _____

Scoring

1. Calculate weighted scores: (x1) = _____   (x2) = _____   (x3) = _____

2. Add weighted scores: = _____

3. Divide by three (÷ 3) = _____   – This is the Final Risk Assessment Score

4. Check the appropriate category at the bottom: Low - below 9
                                                     Medium - 9 through 14
                                                     High - above 14

5. **If items 1-4 (Plan) are ALL marked high, the final risk level is automatically determined to be HIGH.

CHECK FINAL ASSESSMENT   :   LOW _____   MEDIUM _____   HIGH _____   (If high, call Psychological Services)

REFERENCES

American Psychological Association. (1993). *Violence and youth: Psychology's response.* Washington DC: Author.

Baker, J. (1998). Are we missing the forest for the trees? Considering the social context of school violence. *Journal of School Psychology, 30,* 29–44.

Band, S. R., & Harpold, J. A. (1999). School violence: Lessons learned. *FBI Law Enforcement Bulletin, 68*(9), 9–16. Available: http://www.fbi.gov/publications/leb/1999/leb99.htm

Borum, R. (2000). Assessing violence risk among youth. *Journal of Clinical Psychology, 56,* 1263–1288.

Borum, R., Fein, R., Vossekuil, B., & Berglund, J. (1999). Threat assessment: Defining an approach for evaluating risk of targeted violence. *Behavioral Sciences and the Law, 17,* 323–337.

Centers for Disease Control and Prevention (CDC). (2001). *Press release: Study finds school-associated violent deaths rare, fewer events but more deaths per event.* Atlanta, GA: Author. Available: http://www.cdc.gov/od/oc/media/pressrel/r011204.htm

Center for Disease Control and Prevention (CDC). (2003). *Fact sheet: Facts about violence among youth and violence in schools.* Atlanta, GA: Author. Available: http://www.cdc.gov/ncipc/factsheets/schoolvi.htm

Cotton, N. U., Resnick, J., Browne, D. C., Martin, S. L., McCarraher, D. R., & Woods, J. (1994). Aggression and fighting behavior among African-American adolescents: Individual and family factors. *American Journal of Public Health, 84,* 618–622.

Dallas Independent School District (DISD). (2001). *Dallas ISD board policy manual.* Dallas, TX: Author. Available: http://www.tasb.org/policy/pol/private/057905/pol.cfm?DisplayPage=FFE(LOCAL).html

Dallas Independent School District. (2002). *2002–2003 student code of conduct and student handbook.* Dallas, TX: Author. Available: http://www.dallasisd.org/parent_students/ handbooks/code_of_conduct.pdf

DeVoe, J. F., Peter, K., Kaufman, P., Ruddy, S. A., Miller, A. K., Planty, M., Snyder, T . D., Duhart, D. T., & Rand, M. R. (2002). *Indicators of School Crime and Safety: 2002* (NCES 2003-009; NCJ 196753). Washington, DC: U.S. Departments of Education and Justice.

DuRant, R. H., Cadenhead, C., Pendergrast, R. A., Slavens, G., & Linder, C. W. (1994). Factors associated with the use of violence among urban black adolescents. *American Journal of Public Health, 84,* 612–617.

Dwyer, K., Osher, D., & Warger, C.. (1998). *Early warning, timely response: A guide to safe schools: The referenced edition.* Washington, DC: American Institutes for Research.

Farrington, D. P. (1989). Early predictors of adolescent aggression and adult violence. *Violence and Victims, 4,* 79–100.

Fein, R., Vossekuil, B., & Holden, G. (1995, September). *Threat assessment: An approach to prevent targeted violence.* Washington, DC: National Institute of Justice, Research in Action.

Fein, R., Vossekuil, B., Pollack, W., Borum, R., Modzeleski, W., & Reddy, M. (2002). *Threat assessment in schools: A guide to managing threatening situations and to creating safe school climates.* Washington, DC: Department of Education, Office of Elementary and Secondary Education, Safe and Drug-Free Schools Program, and United States Secret Service, National Threat Assessment Center.

Fey, G., Nelson, J. R., & Roberts, M. L. (2000). The perils of profiling. *The School Administrator, 57,* 12–16.

Hawkins, J. D., Herronkohl, T., Farrington, D. P., Brewer, D., Catalano, R. F., & Harachi, T. W. (1998). A review of predictors of youth violence. In R. Loeber & D. P. Farrington (Eds.), *Serious and violent juvenile offenders* (pp. 106–147). Thousand Oaks, CA: Sage.

Haynes, L. (2003). *Breaking the code of silence guidance activities.* Unpublished manuscript, Dallas Independent School District, Dallas, TX.

Horner, R. H, Sugai, G., & Horner, H. F. (2000). A schoolwide approach to student discipline. *The School Administrator, 57,* 20–23.

Huizinga, D., Loeber, R., & Thornberry, T. P. (1994). *Urban delinquency and substance abuse: Initial findings* (NCJ Publication No. 143454). Washington, DC: Office of Juvenile Justice and Delinquency Prevention. Available: www.ncjrs.org/pdffiles/urdel.pdf

Kaufman, P., Chen, X., Choy, S. P., Peter, K., Ruddy, S. A., Miller, A. K., Fleury, J. K., Chandler, K. A., Planty, M. G., & Rand. M. R. (2001). *Indicators of school crime and safety: 2001* (NCES No. 2002-113 / NCJ No. 190075). Washington, DC: U.S. Departments of Education and Justice.

Kingery, P. M., Biafora, F. A., & Zimmerman, R. S. (1996). Risk factors for violent behaviors among ethnically diverse urban adolescents. *School Psychology International, 17,* 171–188.

Lafee, S. (2000). Profiling bad apples. *The School Administrator, 57,* 6–11.

Lattimore, P. K., Visher, C. A., & Linster. R. L. (1995). Predicting rearrest for violence among serious youthful offenders. *Journal of Research in Crime and Delinquency, 32,* 54–83.

Lipsey, M. W., & Derzon, J. H. (1998). Predictors of violent or serious delinquency in adolescence and early adulthood: A synthesis of longitudinal research. In R. Loeber & D. P. Farrington (Eds.), *Serious and violent juvenile offenders* (pp. 86–106). Thousand Oaks, CA: Sage.

Morrison, G. M., & D'Incau, B. (1997). The web of zero-tolerance: Characteristics of students who are recommended for expulsion from school. *Education and Treatment of Children, 20*, 316–335.

Morrison, G. M., & Skiba, R. (2004). School discipline indices and school violence: An imperfect correspondence. In M. J. Furlong, M. P. Bates, D. C. Smith, & P. M. Kingery (Eds.), *Appraisal and prediction of school violence: Methods, issues, and contexts* (pp. 111–134). Hauppauge, NY: Nova Science.

National Association of School Psychologists. (2002). *Threat assessment: Predicting and preventing school violence*. Bethesda, MD: Author. Available: http://www.naspcenter.org/factsheets/threatassess_fs.html

National Institute of Mental Health. (2000). *Fact sheet: Child and adolescent violence research* (NIH Publication No. 00-4706). Bethesda, MD: Author. Available: http://www.nimh.nih.Governing

National School Safety Center (NSSC). (1998). *Checklist of characteristics of youth who have caused school–associated violent deaths*. Westlake Village, CA: Author. Available: http://www.nssc1.org/reporter/checklist.htm

National School Safety Center (NSSC). (2001). *Report on school associated violent deaths*. Westlake Village, CA: Author. Available: http://www.nssc1.org/

O'Toole, M. E. (2000). *The school shooter: A threat assessment perspective*. Quantico, VA: National Center for the Analysis of Violent Crime, Federal Bureau of Investigation. Available: http://www.fbi.gov/publications/school/school2.pdf

Poland, S. (1993). *Crisis manual for the Alaska schools*. Juneau, AK: State Department of Education.

Ryan-Arredondo, K., Renouf, K., Egyed, C., Doxey, M., Dobbins, M., Sanchez, S., & Rakowitz, B. (2001). Threats of violence in schools: The Dallas Independent School District's response. *Psychology in the Schools, 38*, 185–196.

Schools deploy programs to track potentially violent students. (2000, September 21). *Los Angeles Times*.

Sheras, P. L., & Cornell, D. G. (2002, August). *Violence assessment and prevention in the schools*. Paper presented at the ninth annual Institute for Psychology in the Schools, American Psychological Association annual convention, Chicago, IL.

Singer, M. I., Miller, D. B., Guo, S., Flannery, D. J., Frierson, T., & Slovak, K. (1999). Contributors to violent behavior among elementary and middle school children. *Pediatrics, 104*, 878–884.

Smith, C., & Thornberry, T. P. (1995). The relationship between child maltreatment and adolescent involvement in delinquency. *Criminology, 33*, 451–477.

Smith, J. (1988). *Suicide risk assessment worksheet*. Unpublished manuscript. Dallas, TX: Dallas Independent School District.

Song, L., Singer, M. I., & Anglin, T. M. (1998). Violence exposure and emotional trauma as contributors to adolescents' violent behaviors. *Archives of Pediatrics and Adolescent Medicine, 152*, 531–536.

Thornberry, T. (1994). *Fact sheet: Violent families and youth violence* (FS-9421). Washington, DC: U.S. Department of Justice, Office of Juvenile Justice and Delinquency Prevention. Available: http://www.ncjrs.org/txtfiles/fs-9421.txt

Trahant, D. M., Olmi, D. J., Dubard, M., & Sterling-Turner, H. E. (April 2003). *Acceptability and satisfaction for a model of school based threat assessment*. Paper presented at the annual convention of the National Association of School Psychologists, Toronto, Ontario, Canada.

Uehara, E., Chalmers, D., Jenkins, E. J., & Shakoor, B. (1996). African-American youth encounters with violence: Results from the Chicago Community Mental Health Council violence screening project. *Journal of Black Studies, 26*, 768–781.

U.S. Department of Health and Human Services. (2001). *Youth violence: A report of the Surgeon General*. Rockville, MD: U.S. Department of Health and Human Services, Centers for Disease Control and Prevention, National Center for Injury Prevention and Control; Substance Abuse and Mental Health Services Administration, Center for Mental Health Services; and National Institutes of Health, National Institute of Mental Health.

Valois, R., & McKewon, R. (1998). Frequency and correlates of fighting and carrying weapons among public school adolescents. *American Journal of Health Behavior, 22*, 8–17.

Van Dyke, R., Ryan-Arredondo, K., Rakowitz, B., & Torres, J. L. (2004). The Dallas Independent School District's threat assessment procedures: Summary of findings after four years of implementation. In M. J. Furlong, M. P. Bates, D. C. Smith, & P. M. Kingery (Eds.), *Appraisal and prediction of school violence: Methods, issues, and contexts* (pp. 37–62). Hauppauge, NY: Nova Science.

Van Dyke, R. B., Schroeder, J. L., Havsy, L., & Williams, C. (2002). *[Demographic and intervention data from the DTVRA]*. Unpublished raw data.

Verlinden, S., Hersen, M., & Thomas, J. (2000). Risk factors in school shootings. *Clinical Psychology Review, 20*, 3–56.

Vossekuil, B., Fein, R., Reddy, M., Borum, R., & Modzeleski, W. (2002). *The final report and findings of the safe school initiative: Implications for the prevention of school attacks in the United States*. Washington, DC: Department of Education, Office of Elementary and Secondary Education, Safe and Drug-Free Schools Program and United States Secret Service, National Threat Assessment Center.

Widom, C. S. (1989). Child abuse, neglect, and adult behavior: Research design and findings on criminality, violence, and child abuse. *American Journal of Orthopsychiatry, 59*, 355–367.

40

A Case Example of a School Shooting:
Lessons Learned in the Wake
of Tragedy

Laura Delizonna
Ivan Alan
Hans Steiner
Stanford University

This chapter frames the problem of school shootings in the greater context of violence in society. The primary focus is on defining individual factors related to violent behaviors at school and potential interventions. Domains of influence and contextual factors at the school, community, and national levels are highlighted. A case example provides the backdrop for this discussion, because within the details of every school shooting are clues for what went wrong. In the wake of tragedy lies an opportunity for learning what to do differently. It is important to extract from these examples targets of change and to invent prosocial methods to change them.

A SHOOTING AT XY HIGH SCHOOL

Just before 10:50am on Thursday, February 8, 1996, a 16-year-old teenager drove his blue Honda Accord onto the basketball court of his neighborhood high school. He threw bills of large denominations out of the window, apparently trying to lure students in the schoolyard toward his car. Suddenly, he pulled out a handgun and shot randomly at approaching students. Students panicked and sought cover. A 14-year-old student was shot in the leg. Bullets shattered classroom windows but did not hit anyone inside. Shortly after opening fire, the teenager turned the gun on himself. Police secured the area, initially uncertain if there was more than one shooter. Emergency personnel rushed both boys to the hospital. The perpetrator was in very critical condition, while his peer was in stable condition.

School staff hurried the children to their classrooms until the police arrived. Police officers interviewed students who had witnessed the shooting. Students could be seen wandering the halls and huddled in classrooms. Soon teams of media arrived. They canvassed the campus filming in front of bulletin boards and in hallways. In one news report, students were said to have "poked their heads out of classroom doors or through open windows, shouting at members of the press to leave the campus." School administrators closed the campus immediately and sequestered students for the rest of the day in classrooms in an attempt to protect them from unwanted interviews. Mental health professionals from the community and nearby schools talked with the students and staff.

Classes were cancelled the next day. The 16-year-old died in the hospital from his self-inflicted gunshot wound. The other student was discharged from the hospital. Despite being closed, several students dropped by the school. Some were angry, others grieving. The principal commented that some students appeared to be in "free-floating shock." Television and print news portrayed images of the incident over the following days, repeatedly exposing the students as well as members of the community to the traumatic event. School officials called on the school district and county mental health services to provide additional grief and crisis counselors for the students and the staff. Meetings with the parents were held to discuss the incident and its aftermath.

An investigation failed to produce obvious motives but suggested that the perpetrator was emotionally distressed and had planned the shooting. Although the boy was new to the school, the staff was aware that he was having a hard time and was attempting to address his depression. According to other students, he was upset over difficulties with a female friend who, just days before the incident, expressed disinterest in him romantically. Apparently, he had asked classmates about how to acquire a gun, although none of his peers reported supplying him with the weapon. Although he was clearly experiencing difficulties, there were no obvious reasons why he had planned the violent attack on his fellow students. He was not identified as being high risk for homicidal or suicidal behaviors. His hidden desperation must have been intense. Perhaps this was the only way he felt he could escape an intolerable degree of misery.

This incident took place at a suburban high school in the San Francisco bay area in California. The school is referred to in this chapter as *XY* High School. The school was designed to help students who were identified as having difficulty achieving in other schools or who would likely benefit from smaller classes and more individualized attention. It is evident that the school staff were highly committed to helping their students maximize their potential. The majority of the students at this private high school came from well-educated, moderate to high-income families and was Caucasian.

CONCEPTUALIZING THE PROBLEM OF SCHOOL VIOLENCE

Incidents of school violence are not isolated to certain geographic locations or social strata. Furthermore, studies have confirmed that teen violence is not an ethnic or race issue (Kingery, Biafora, & Zimmerman, 1996). No single ethnic or racial group is violent or carries weapons more than another when psychological and behavioral problems are considered. Kingery and colleagues reported that low empathy, stealing, lawbreaking, "normlessness," wanting to quit school, and wanting to leave home—but not race—were predictive of violence and weapon carrying. A study by Hawkins, Pitts, and Steiner (2002) provides evidence that problems with anger, lower parental supervision, drug/alcohol use, and physical abuse are factors bear a strong relationship to weapon carrying regardless of affluence levels.

Although most social scientists would not consider these findings surprising, they may be unexpected to the layperson who is frequently exposed to U.S. media and popular reality TV shows' portrayals of violence and its perpetrators. Rather than a certain subgroup's problem, violence seems to result from a deadly combination of psychological variables, external events, risk factors, and contextual dynamics. Hawkins and colleagues highlighted that multiple domains must be considered when attempting to understand school shootings, from individual factors to family, school, and social dynamics. The pursuit for a comprehensive understanding of the variables that contribute to school shootings requires examinations from biological, psychological, and sociocultural perspectives.

Individual-Level Factors

Commonalities Between School Shooters

Attempts to identify individual factors that uniquely characterize school shooters have failed for the most part. At best, common patterns of behavior may indicate certain personality traits among perpetrators. An FBI study of 18 school shooting cases (O'Toole, 1999) found a range of behaviors and traits common among perpetrators, including anger, various interpersonal difficulties, rigidity, poor coping skills, and emotional and behavioral dysregulation. Additionally, the study highlighted that perpetrators commonly displayed behavior that directly related to an intention to carry out a threat and what the study called "leakage," the intentional or unintentional revealing of clues about feelings, thoughts, fantasies, attitudes, or intentions of an impending violent act. The FBI report concluded that a profile predictive of future violence does not exist. A U.S. Secret Service report (Vossekuil, Fein, Reddy, Brum, & Modzelski, 2002) examined 37 shootings involving 41 attackers, from 1974 to June 2000. It was found that 76% of the shooters were Caucasian with ages ranging from 11 to 21 years. Additionally, nearly 75% of the shooters reported having felt persecuted, bullied, threatened, attacked, or injured by others prior to the incident. Similar to the FBI report (O'Toole, 1999), it was concluded, however, that the background and demographics of the shooters were too diverse to indicate a specific profile. The report emphasized that developing a profile is difficult because these events are inherently unexpected in nature and are rare. Additionally, markers of risk for violence such as impulsivity are highly prevalent and normative in adolescent-stage individuals. Thus, the report concluded that identifying characteristics that predict who will be a perpetrator of a school shooting is quite unreliable (O'Toole, 1999).

Reports indicating that there are not reliably identifiable traits or demographic profiles that distinguish school shooters have significant implications for preventative efforts such as student profiling. Critics of student profiling argue that the probable frequency of false-positives is too damaging to students; proponents urge that the opportunity for preventing a tragedy outweighs the potential costs (see Lumsden, 2000). Because there is no evidence that a student's potential for violence can be reliably identified by his or her behaviors and personal characteristics, it has been recommended that efforts instead focus on student behaviors and communications that may indicate that an attack is being planned (Vossekuil et al., 2002).

Peer Rejection and School Violence

Several researchers have suggested that there may be a relationship between peer rejection and lethal school-based violence. In Gaughan, Cerio, and Myers' (2001) nationwide study, 87% of students stated that they think shootings are motivated by a desire to "get back at those who have hurt them." In this same study, 86% of students attributed the cause of lethal school shootings to be "other kids picking on them, making fun of them or bullying them." Furthermore, in 14 of 16 school-based shootings, Leary, Kowalski, and Smith (2003) found that ostracism, bullying, and/or romantic rejection was present. Several researchers have discussed the relationship between rejection and aggression (e.g., Barnow, Lucht, & Freyberger, 2001; Coie, Dodge, Terry, & Wright, 1991; Marano, 1998; McDougall, Hymel, Vaillancourt, & Mercer, 2001). In a longitudinal study Dodge and colleagues (2003) showed that early rejection predicted future aggression. In a laboratory study, participants in the experimental group were informed that they would end up alone later in life or that other participants had rejected them

(Twenge, Baumeister, Tice, & Stucke, 2001). Compared with the control group, the participants who received the rejection messages behaved more aggressively.

Real or imagined rejection from one's peer group may be a salient factor in peer violence and should be a topic of additional research. Reportedly, the student perpetrators of the Columbine school shooting were "ostracized, taunted, and bullied by other students, particularly athletes" (Leary et al., 2003, p. 207). Although it cannot be confirmed, rejection may have been present in the shooting incident described in the case example. Reports noted that the perpetrator became upset after learning that a female classmate had no romantic interest in him. Additionally, he was new to the school and had recently moved into the area from out of state.

Psychiatric Issues in School Shooters

In the case example provided, there was some evidence suggesting psychiatric difficulties. Staff had identified that the teen was depressed and were attempting to address this issue. It is not known if he actually received evidenced-based mental health treatment. The U.S. Secret Service investigation indicated that many of the perpetrators in school shootings experienced psychological difficulties prior to the violent incident (Vossekuil et al., 2002). In the secret service assessment, 24% of perpetrators had a known history of alcohol or substance abuse and most attackers had past suicidal attempts. In 61% of the perpetrators there appeared to be a history of feeling extreme depression or desperation. Most of the perpetrators were described as having a problem dealing with loss or failure and had experienced a loss or failure prior to the attack. However, the majority of perpetrators had never received a mental health evaluation or had been diagnosed with a mental disorder. These findings are consistent with a growing body of evidence suggesting that major psychological difficulties are characteristic of aggressive youth.

Psychiatric Issues in Aggressive Youth

Given the dearth of information on youth perpetrators involved in school shootings, it may be helpful to consider them as a subpart of the larger population of aggressive youth. Evidence from numerous studies indicate that these youth have a high prevalence of psychiatric disorders and demonstrate general skill deficits in self-regulation and in the ability to flexibly process new information in social situations.

There is a growing consensus that mental health issues are at the core of maladaptive aggression in youth (Cauffman, Feldman, Waterman, & Steiner, 1998; Duclos et al., 1998). Barnow et al. (2001) also found that aggressive boys seem to have more attention deficits, depression, anxiety, delinquency, and social problems. Studies of juvenile offenders have shown that compared to nondelinquent adolescents, youth offenders present with higher prevalence rates of psychiatric morbidity and comorbidity (Aarons, Brown, Hough, Garland, & Wood, 2000; Duclos et al., 1998; Garland et al., 2001). The largest study to date of detained youth reported that 70% of females and 60% of males in the sample had at least one psychiatric disorder (Teplin, Abram, McClelland, Dulcan, & Mericle, 2002). Similar rates of psychiatric disorders were found in incarcerated youth in a study conducted by Steiner and colleagues (2004).

Unequivocal evidence that mental health issues are common in aggressive youth has substantial implications for school-based violence. For example, a student showing an escalation in aggressive behavior should be assessed for psychological difficulties. Furthermore, although many students with psychiatric disorders will not be violent, these disorders must be taken seriously and appropriate actions taken to address them. Evidence-based mental health services, often involving individual or group psychotherapy and/or pharmacotherapy, should be accessible to all students who show symptoms of psychiatric disorders. There has been substantial progress toward establishing effective psychotherapy approaches for antisocial and aggressive youth have been developed (see Kazdin & Weisz, 2003; Steiner, 2004). Furthermore, as a better understanding of the mediators of aggression in youth is gained and as the moderators that predict response to certain treatments are identified, the methods for treating these youth will gain specificity. Knowing who to treat with which treatment—and what exactly to target in that treatment—will lead to more effective interventions. Greater understanding of disorders and mechanisms of action in interventions will lead to more potent technologies in psychotherapy. For example, given that emotional and behavior dysregulation is characteristic of aggressive youth, treatments such as dialectical behavior therapy (DBT), which was developed from a biopsychosocial model of self-dysregulation, may be appropriate (see Miller, Wagner, & Rathus, 2004). Clinicians in some juvenile justice settings have reported positive results with DBT skills groups, which focus directly on improving emotional and behavioral regulation skills; however, only one empirical investigation has been conducted (Trupin, Stewart, Beach, & Boesky, 2002). New innovations await further research in core process variables.

Cognitive Processing in Aggressive Youth

Dodge and Petit (2003) presented a comprehensive biopsychosocial model of the development of chronic conduct disorders in youth. Their model emphasizes the role of cognitive and emotional processes interacting over time with multiple factors such as biological predispositions, sociocultural contexts, and life experiences. Informed by decades of research on the social information-processing patterns of aggressive youth, Dodge and Petit (2003) concluded that aggressive youth develop knowledge structures that include "relational schemas of hostility, aggressive scripts, working models of hostile interpersonal relationships, heuristics involving rapid defensive responding rather than slower reflection, and self defensive goals" (p. 363).

This line of research shows that aggressive youth are typically biased in their processing of social information (see Dodge & Frame, 1982). They rely on prior expectations about social interactions rather than the actual information present in the situation, and although hostile intentions of other boys are "overperceived," they "underperceive" their own aggressiveness in social situations (Lochman & Dodge, 1998). Consistent with research on mindlessness (see Langer, 1989), it seems that there may be a causal relationship between rigid thinking and poor interpersonal effectiveness. Moreover, laboratory research on mindful thinking suggests that mindsets are influenced by contextual variables and that people can think more flexibly with the appropriate prompts (see Langer, 1989; Langer & Moldoveau, 2000). Skill-based interventions should be informed by these findings and evaluated for effectiveness. For example, interventions that process information without an overdependence on mindsets could be helpful. This is an underinvestigated avenue for intervention.

In summary, current understanding of youth aggression has become multidimensional—including biological, psychological, and contextual factors. These factors then interact with sociocultural factors to direct the trajectory of violence (see Dodge, 1990). As Dodge and Petit (2003) stated in their review of conduct problems in youth, proximal mechanisms operate through life experiences and psychological processes. It is through these processes, these researchers contended, that windows of opportunity exist for prevention and intervention. Effective treatments have been established for an array of psychiatric disorders including aggression disorders in youth (see Kazdin & Weisz, 2003; Steiner, 2004), and growing evidence supports that skill deficits are at the core of many psychological difficulties. Although the science of clinical intervention is still generally in its infancy, the understanding of the mediators and moderators of treatment outcomes is improving, as well as the underlying processes that cause psychological and behavioral problems.

School Level Factors and Interventions

Staff Readiness

The staff at *XY* High School was faced with making critical decisions during the crisis while experiencing their own highly emotional reaction to the traumatic event. Inevitably responding to a violent incident will be a tremendous challenge; therefore, staff training and well-planned procedures that are already in place are crucial to guiding the response. Staff must respond quickly—working with law enforcement, calling on emergency personnel, and managing media during and immediately after the crisis. In the aftermath of the traumatic event, many students, parents, school personnel, and the community at large needed assistance to regain a sense of safety, process emotional reactions, and regain a sense of normality. In fact, California law requires all California schools to develop safety and crisis plans. These safety plans should include the evaluation of the present level of safety at each school and should take into consideration the needs and resources of each particular school. In addition, committees are to be developed to work with parents, local education agency plans, local school boards, and the local community in order to develop the plans.

Staff Awareness

Enhancing staff's ability to identify students at high risk for violent outbreaks at school could be helpful adjunct to violence prevention efforts. Although screening instruments are not likely to be helpful in predicting who will be violent, they may be useful in identifying children who are in need of support. Providing school staff with training specific to identifying and responding to students in need or who have made threats of violence is likely to be beneficial. Importantly, research suggests that identifying students who carry weapons is not realistic. In a study conducted after the shooting incident at *XY* High School (Hawkins & Steiner, 1999), even staff who knew the students well had difficulty correctly identifying weapon carriers. Furlong, Pavelski, and Saxton (2004) reported that when examining raw numbers (not proportionately), more weapons were carried to school by students with zero risk factors than students who had all eight risk factors tested present. These authors conclude that weapons are brought to school for many reasons. Assuming that staff "will just know" which students are carrying weapons and/or are contemplating harm is clearly unrealistic.

Schoolwide Programs

School programming has been the topic of extensive research and has been covered extensively in this handbook. It is noteworthy that the Centers for Disease Control and Prevention's (CDC) School Health Policies and Programs Study (1994) identified effective strategies to include school-based curricula that emphasize the development of problem-solving skills, anger management, and other strategies that help students develop social skills. Researchers have emphasized that well-implemented, evidence-derived school-based programs have the potential to be beneficial in a wide range of youth behaviors and development (Greenberg et al., 2003). A meta-analysis of 165 studies of school-based prevention programs suggests that social competency and self-control focused interventions can impact conduct problems and other behavior problems in students (Wilson, SJ, Lipsey MW, Derzon JH. 2003.). Importantly, the findings from this meta-analysis suggest the importance of an ecological perspective when attempting to influence individual behavior. These researchers' results indicate that programs integrating environmental factors within the intervention were most effective. Researchers from the Collaborative for Academic, Social, and Emotional Learning (CASEL) emphasized the importance of teaching social competence in multiyear, multicomponent programs (Greenberg et al., 2003). Greenberg and colleagues contended that socioemotional learning can impact a wide array of social, health, and academic outcomes, including violence (e.g., Grossman et al., 1997). Further studies are needed to determine the most effective components of skills training in a school setting.

School Social Climate

The social climate of a school has been identified as a critical component of preventive efforts targeting student aggression. School characteristics can be modified in an effort to create a more positive learning environment that is less conducive to behavioral problems and potentially violence. Clearly, hostility and humiliation of community members (in this case students) can be either tolerated or discouraged in any institution, as can creative problem solving and proactive use of effective strategies to address conflict.

In a top-down model, an administration can strive to create a climate that pulls for prosocial behavior in its community members. South Dakota, for example, which has been identified as a top performer in state reforms addressing violence prevention, credits its success to schools' fostering a culture where violence is not accepted (Gaughan et al., 2001). Payne, Gottfredson, and Gottfredson (2003) described a communal school organization in which supportive relationships exist between and among teachers, administrators, and students and where there is a common set of goals, norms and a sense of collaboration and involvement. According to these researchers, these schools tend to have more positive student attitudes, better teacher morale, and less severe student problem behaviors. The California Department of Education's School Safety Center (2004b) recommends that administrators and teachers collaborate with students to implement a variety of activities relating to prosocial behaviors. For example, programs to promote student responsibility for safer schools could be initiated.

In publications by Morrison and colleagues, the authors identified several school factors that seem to relate to school violence (Furlong & Morrison, 2000; Morrison & Skiba, 2001). They discussed overly competitive learning environments, a lack of clarity about rules, toleration of abuse, a punitive school disciplinary policy, discriminatory guidance policies, exclusionary practices, expectations and consequences, failure to consider individual differences, low level of academic quality and high rates of academic failure, high teacher to student ratios, and more time spent on discipline than on school climate. The authors posited that the primary characteristics that play a role in school violence are teacher attitudes, administrative centralization, quality of school governance, and teacher perception of student achievement (see Furlong & Morrison, 2000; Morrison & Skiba, 2001).

Schools that foster open communication between students and administration may provide indirect avenues for students to alert officials of potential violent incidents. This could be particularly important in light of the FBI's study (O'Toole, 1999) indicating that many perpetrators in school shootings made comments or gestures indicating their intention prior to committing violence. Following the shooting discussed in the case example, some students stated that they knew their classmate was trying to attain a firearm but did not tell authorities. Although this would be considered normative behavior in adolescents according to a national study in which only half of students said they would alert an adult if they overheard someone talking about shooting someone (Gaughan et al., 2001), open communication may increase the likelihood that students will deviate from the norm and seek help if they become privy to critical information.

SCHOOL VIOLENCE IN ITS LARGER CONTEXT

The shooting at *XY* High School, like other school-based shootings, can be understood in a transactional model, in which the individual both is influenced by and has influence over environmental factors. In this model, incidents of school violence are considered a part of the greater whole. Multiple issues, some of which are far removed from the individual, exert influence on the individual's behavior. Systems, social climate, the media, and sociopolitical attitudes are identified as sources of influence on an individual's responses.

Local Community and National Factors

Procedures and policies at the levels of the school district, county, state, and nation largely determine which resources are available to a school—whether the need is to implement a campus violence prevention program or to de-escalate a crisis. However, schools cannot be expected to adequately address the problem of violence on their campuses without substantial assistance (NGA, 1999), because the problem is embedded within a larger fabric of local and national issues. Bernard (1994) emphasized the magnitude of the problem that schools face by highlighting that schools must provide additional services for aggressive students to compensate for the failures of the juvenile justice system. He described the problem as a system failure that leaves schools without the adequate resources. The consensus among researchers (e.g., Dodge, 2001; Weissberg, Kumfer, & Seligman 2003) and government agencies (e.g., NGA, 1999) is that managing the problem of school violence depends on multimodal, coordinated, and collaborative efforts.

Empirically Informed, Coordinated Interventions and Polices

Unequivocally, programming at all levels of intervention including family, school, community, health care, and policy must be research-informed (Dodge, 2001; Weissberg, Kumfer, & Seligman 2003). Petit and Dodge (2003) urged prevention scientists and policymakers to collaborate and coordinate efforts. They advise social scientists to consider policy issues and prevention findings when developing their research frameworks and designs, and policymakers to draw on research findings in formulating their priorities and policies.

Dodge (2001) outlined the process of bringing violence prevention efforts to full-scale implementation from the perspective of prevention science. He pointed out that few behavioral prevention programs have been implemented at full scale, but there are examples of highly successful ones such as seat belts use and immunization that truly met the public health objectives. The process of dissemination, however, depends on comprehensive evaluation of the impact of widespread implementation of programs shown to be effective in small-scale settings.

A model program on this regard is the Positive Behavior Support (PBS) program. Sugai and colleagues (Sugai & Horner, 2002; Sugai et al., 2000) advocated using PBS programs in the schools. PBS has a strong basis in behavioral science, and its school programs aim to provide behavior support for students who display chronic behavioral problems. PBS promotes a schoolwide response to discipline and problem behaviors (Sugai & Horner, 2002). PBS programs include the creation of teams who develop mission statements and list expected behaviors for their students and procedures that will be used to teach these expectations to their students (Center for Effective Collaboration and Practice, 2005). Additionally, the teams develop procedures and strategies for discouraging rule breaking. The Center for Effective Collaboration and Practice discusses the positive effect that such programs have had on student behavior in a number of Oregon schools in which they were implemented. Such programs can serve as a good example for other schools across the nation, in dealing with student behavioral problems, and potentially in preventing school violence.

Gun Safety and Control

Gaughan and colleagues (2001) reported findings from their nationwide study showing that 61% of respondents said they know students who could bring a gun to school if they wanted to, and 24% said they could "easily get a gun if I wanted to." Improvements in safety technology and controlling access of guns would likely reduce lethal violence. This alone, however, is an overly simplistic answer to the complex problem of school violence. An exhaustive examination at violence in society is crucial. Why, for example, does the United States have a higher annual rate of teen homicide than the 23 wealthiest nations combined (see Blum, 2001)? What may have caused firearm use in violent crimes to decline among persons of all ages between 1993 and 1997 (U.S. Department of Health and Human Services, 2001)? Why did the rates of weapon carrying at schools decrease in the 1990s (U.S. Department of Health and Human Services 2001)?

Media's Role in Framing the Issues

As political scientists Haider-Markel and Joslyn (2001) indicated, the way in which issues are framed and explained directs policy and intervention efforts. They contend that simple-minded blame and attributions of responsibility for tragic events not only prevent accurate understanding of the issues related to violence but also undermine solutions. Extending this perspective, Ogle, Eckman, and Leslie (2003) identified the media as the primary influence on how issues are framed. Providing an example from the Columbine shooting, they argued that media coverage provides the basis for the social construction of the issues surrounding this and other events. Citing that more than 1,000 articles in the Denver metropolitan area were published within 1 year of the Columbine shooting, they contend that the extensive media coverage is a major force in constructing social issues and impacting public policy.

Mindful Progress, Empirically Informed Solutions

In summary, investigations of causal factors and the development of prevention efforts for violence must include individual factors as well as proximal and distal environmental factors (see Table 40.1). With the individual as the center, like concentric circles, there are multiple domains within which the individual exists. The individual is influenced by each of these levels; therefore, a comprehensive understanding of school violence can only be obtained by conducting rigorous investigations that span each of these circles of influences. At each of these levels, there are possibilities for interventions. An FBI report (O'Toole, 1999) emphasizes both the complexity and the potential for intervening, stating that "people do not 'snap'... instead, the path toward violence is an evolutionary one, with signposts along the way" (p. 7). To address the complexity of a problem such as school violence, interventions must be multimodal, coordinated, and comprehensive in that they extend from the individual level to the schools, to the local communities, and to the greater national community (NGA, 1999). Efforts must be coordinated and collaborative to ensure that science, prevention, and public policy work build off one another (Pettit & Dodge, 2003).

Preventing school-based tragedies such as the one at *XY* High School depends on seeking solutions that are informed by science and derived from multiple explanations and mindful, complex thinking. This rigor is a prerequisite for developing real solutions and any proposals or discourses below this standard are unacceptable. Furthermore, as professionals we must conduct our work on violence issues in a manner that bridges the gap between the science of

TABLE 40.1
Implications for Managing Weapon-Related Issues on School Campuses

Level of Influence	
Individual	• Attend and respond to student threats or behaviors that reveal intentions for violence • Provide mental health services when psychiatric distress or disorders are evidenced
School	• Implement school safety plans • Facilitate staff awareness of violence and weapon carrying amongst students (i.e., staff cannot "just know" who is at risk or carrying weapons) • Develop schoolwide violence prevention programs that consider environmental factors • Implement programs that foster positive school social climate and sense of community
Local & National Community	• Mandate that programs and policy are empirically informed • Develop research frameworks and designs that directly inform policy issues and prevention plans • Recognize media's role in constructing social issues and impacting public policy; support expert-informed news reporting policies that draw on research findings • Advocate for strict firearm regulation and control policies • Examine issues complexly (from multiple perspectives) and avoid single-minded solutions

violence prevention and application of interventions. Progress toward building safer schools and a more peaceable society, in general, depends upon collaboration and active coordination between efforts. Social scientists, educators, health care providers, lawmakers and enforcers, political leaders, and others seeking a reduction in aggression must see themselves and each other as team members working toward a common cause.

REFERENCES

Aarons, G. A., Brown, S. A., Hough, R. L., Garland, A. F., & Wood, P. A. (2000). Prevalence of adolescent substance use disorders across five sectors of care. *Journal of the American Academy of Child and Adolescent Psychiatry, 40,* 419–426.

Barnow, S., Lucht, M., & Freyberger, H. J. (2001). Influence of punishment, emotional rejection, child abuse, and broken home on aggression in adolescence: An examination of aggressive adolescents in Germany. *Psychopathology, 34,* 167–173.

Bernard, J. (1994). School violence and the law: The search for suitable tools. *School Psychology Review, 23,* 190–204.

Blum, R. W. (2001). Trends in adolescent health: Perspectives from the United States. *International Journal of Adolescent Medicine and Health, 13,* 287–295.

California Department of Education's National School Safety Center. (2004a). *California Department of Education required actions regarding "persistently dangerous" schools.* Available: www.cde.ca.gov/ls/ss/se/uscoattch3.asp

California Department of Education's National School Safety Center. (2004b). *A contingency plan for school campus emergencies*. Available: www.cde.ca.gov/ls/ss/cp/contplan.asp

California Department of Education's National School Safety Center (2004c). *Unsafe school options provisions*. Available www.cde.ca.gov/ls/ss/se/uscoattch1.asp

Cauffman, E., Feldman, S. S., Waterman, J., & Steiner, H. (1998). Posttraumatic stress disorder among female juvenile offenders. *Journal of the American Academy of Child Adolescent Psychiatry, 31*, 1209–1216.

Center for Disease Control and Prevention. (1999). *Facts about violence among youth and violence in schools*. Atlanta, GA: National Center for Injury Prevention and Control.

Center for Effective Collaboration and Practice. (2005). *Effective behavior support, Second Step: A Violence Prevention Curriculum, First Step to Success, and Lane School, Lane County, Oregon*. Available: http://www.air.org/cecp/resources/safe&drug_free/success_and_lane_school.htm

Coie, J. D., Dodge, K. A., Terry, R., & Wright, V. (1991). The role of aggression in peer relations: An analysis of aggression episodes in boys' play groups. *Child Development, 62*, 812–826.

Cunningham, N. J. (2000). A comprehensive approach to school-community violence prevention. *Professional School Counseling, 4*, 126–134.

Dodge, K. A. (1990). Nature versus nurture in childhood conduct disorder: It's time to ask a different question. *Developmental Psychology, 26*, 698–701.

Dodge, K. A. (2001). The science of youth violence prevention. Progressing from developmental epidemiology to efficacy to effectiveness to public policy. *American Journal of Preventative Medicine, 20*, 63–70.

Dodge, K. A., & Frame, C. L. (1982). Social cognitive biases and deficits in aggressive boys. *Child Development, 53*, 620–635.

Dodge, K. A., Lansford, J. E., Burks, V. S., Bates, J. E., Pettit, G. S., Fontaine, R., & Price, J. E. (2003). Peer Rejection and social information-processing factors in the development of aggressive behavior problems in children. *Child Development, 74*, 374–393.

Dodge, K. A., & Pettit, G. S. (2003). A biopsychosocial model of the development of chronic conduct problems in adolescence. *Developmental Psychology, 39*, 349–371.

Duclos, C. W., Beals, J., Novins, D. K., Martin, C., Jewett, C. S., & Manson, S. M. (1998). Prevalence of common psychiatric disorders among American Indian adolescent detainees. *Journal of the American Academy of Child and Adolescent Psychiatry, 37*, 866–873.

Furlong, M. J., & Morrison, G. M. (1994). Introduction to mini-series: School Violence and safety in perspective. *School Psychology Review, 23*, 139–151.

Furlong, M. J., & Morrison, G. M. (2000). The school in school violence: Definitions and facts. *Journal of Emotional & Behavioral Disorders, 8*, 71–81.

Furlong, M. J., Pavelski, R., & Saxton, J. (2004). Thinking strategically about the prevention of school-site violence. In P. Lazarus & S. Brock (Eds.), *Best practices in crisis prevention* (Chapter 11 pp. 5–1 to 5–10). Washington, DC: National Association of School Psychologists.

Garland, A. F., Hough, R. L., McCabe, K. M., Yeh, M., Wood, P. A., & Aarons, G. A. (2001). Prevalence of psychiatric disorders in youths across five sectors of care. *Journal of the Academy of Child and Adolescent Psychiatry, 40*, 409–418.

Gaughan, E., Cerio, J. D., & Myers, R. A. (2001). *Lethal violence in schools: A national study, final report*. New York: Harris Interactive.

Gottfredson, D. (1997). School-based crime prevention. In L. W. Sherman, D. C. Gottfredson, D. L. MacKenzie, J. Eck, P. Reuter, & S. D. Bushway (Eds.), *Preventing crime: What works, what doesn't, and what's promising*. (pp. 5-1 to 5–101) Washington, DC: National Institute of Justice Research Report. Available: www.ncjrs.org/works/wholedoc.doc

Greenberg, M. T., Weissberg, R. P., O'Brien, M. U., Zins, J. E., Fredericks, L., Resnik, H., & Elias, M. J. (2003). Enhancing school-based prevention and youth development through coordinated social, emotional, and academic learning. *American Psychologist, 58*, 466–474.

Grossman, D. C., Neckerman, H. J., Koepsell, T. D., Liu, P. Y., Asher, K. N., Beland, K., Frey, K. S., & Rivara, F. P. (1997). The effectiveness of a violence prevention curriculum among children in elementary school. *Journal of the American Medical Association, 277*, 1605–1611.

Haider-Markel, D. P., & Joslyn, M. R. (2001). Gun policy, opinion, tragedy, and blame attribution: The conditional influence of issue frames. *Journal of Politics, 63*, 520–543.

Hawkins, S., Pitts, T., & Steiner, H. (2002). Weapons in an affluent suburban school. *Journal of School Violence, 1*, 53–65.

Hawkins, S., & Steiner, H. (1999). Mental health outcomes following a shooting incident on school grounds. *Scientific Proceedings of the Annual Meeting of the American Academy of Child and Adolescent Psychiatry, 15*, 57.

Kachur, S. P., Stennies, G. M., Powell, K .E., Modzeleski, W., Stephens, R., Murphy, R., Kresnow, M., Sleet, D., & Lowry, R. (1996). School-associated violent deaths in the United States, 1992 to 1994. *Journal of the American Medical Association, 275*, 1729–1733.

Kaufman, P., Chen, X., Choy, S. P., Chandler, K. A., Chapman, C. D., Rand, M. R., & Ringel, C. (1998). *Indicators of school crime and safety, 1998.* Washington, DC: U.S. Departments of Education and Justice.

Kazdin, A. E., & Weisz, J. R. (Eds.). (2003). *Evidence-based psychotherapies for children and adolescents.* New York: Guilford.

Kingery, P. M., Biafora, F. A., & Zimmerman, R. S. (1996). Risk factors for violent behaviors among ethnically diverse urban adolescents: Beyond race/ethnicity. *School Psychology International, 17*, 171–188.

Kulig, J., Valentine, J., Griffith, J., & Ruthazer, R. (1998). Predictive model of weapon carrying among urban high school students: Results and validation. *Journal of Adolescent Health, 22*, 312–319.

Langer, E. (1989). *Mindfulness.* Reading, MA: Addison-Wesley.

Langer, E., & Moldoveau, M. (Eds.). (2000, Spring). Mindfulness Theory and social issues. *Journal of Social Issues, 56*(1), 1–9.

Leary, M. R., Kowalski, R. M., Smith, L., & Phillips, S. (2003). Teasing, rejection, and violence: Case studies of school shootings. *Aggressive Behavior, 29*, 202–214.

Lochman, J. E., & Dodge, K. A. (1998). Distorted perceptions in dyadic interactions of aggressive and nonaggressive boys: Effects of prior expectations, context, and boys' age. *Development and Psychopathology, 10*, 495–512.

Lumsden, L. (2000). *Profiling students for violence.* Eugene, OR: ERIC Clearinghouse on Educational Management. Available: http://eric.uoregon.edu/publications/digests/digest139.html

Marano, H. E. (1998). *Why doesn't anybody like me?* New York: Morrow.

McDougall, P., Hymel, S., Vaillancourt, T., & Mercer. L. (2001). The consequences of childhood peer rejection. In M. R. Leary (Ed.), *Interpersonal rejection* (pp. 213–247). New York: Oxford University Press.

Miller, A. L., Wagner, E. E., & Rathus, J. H. (2004). Dialectical Behavior Therapy for suicidal adolescents: An overview. In H. Steiner (Ed.), *Handbook of mental health interventions in children and adolescents: An integrated developmental approach* (pp. 659–684). San Francisco: Jossey-Bass.

Morrison, G. M., & Skiba, R. (2001). Predicting violence from school misbehavior: Promises and perils. *Psychology in the Schools, 38*, 173–185.

National Governors Association (NGA) Center for Best Practices. (1999). Making schools safe. *August Issue Brief*, 1–12.

Ogle, J. P., Eckman, M., & Leslie, C. A. (2003). Appearance cues and the shootings at Columbine High: Construction of a social problem in the print media. *Sociological Inquiry, 73*, 1–27.

Orobio de Castro, B., Slot, N. W., Bosch, J. D., Koops, W., &Veerman, J. W. (2003). Negative feelings exacerbate hostile attributions of intent in highly aggressive boys. *Journal of Clinical Child and Adolescent Psychology, 32*, 56–65.

O'Toole, M. E. (1999). *The school shooter: A threat assessment perspective.* Washington, DC: FBI Academy, National Center for the Analysis of Violent Crime. Available: www.fbi.gov/publications/school/school2.pdf

Payne, A. A., Gottfredson, D. C., & Gottfredson, G. D. (2003). Schools as communities: The relationships among communal school organization, student, bonding, and school disorder. *Criminology, 41*, 749–777.

Peterson, K. S. (1999, May 6). Teens understand how taunts lead to crimes. *Des Moines Register*, p. 3.

Pettit, G. S., & Dodge, K. A. (2003). Violent children: Bridging development, intervention, and public policy. *Developmental Psychology, 39*, 187–188.

Steiner, H. (Ed.). (2004). *Handbook of mental health interventions in children and adolescents: An integrated developmental approach.* San Francisco, CA: Jossey-Bass.

Steiner, H., Delizonna, L. L., Redlich, A., Silverman, M., Britton, L., & Haapanen, R. (2004). *Prevalence of mental disorders in incarcerated youth.* Manuscript in preparation.

Sugai, G., & Horner, R. (2002). Introduction to the special series on positive behavior support in schools. *Journal of Emotional and Behavioral Disorders, 10*, 130–137.

Sugai, G., Horner, R. H., Dunlap, G. Hieneman, M., Lewis, T. J., Nelson, C. M., Scott, T., Liaupsin, C., Sailor, W., Turnbull, A. P., Turnbull, H. R., III, Wickham, D. Reuf, M., & Wilcox, B. (2000). Applying positive behavioral support and functional behavioral assessment in schools. *Journal of Positive Behavioral Interventions, 2*, 131–143.

Teplin, L. A., Abram, K. M., McClelland, G. M., Dulcan, M. K., & Mericle, A. A. (2002). Psychiatric disorders in youth in juvenile detention. *Archives General Psychiatry, 59*, 1133–1143.

Trupin, E. W., Stewart, D. G., Beach, B., & Boesky, L. (2002). Effectiveness of Dialectical Behaviour Therapy program for incarcerated female juvenile offenders. *Child and Adolescent Mental Health, 7*, 121–127.

Twenge, J. M., Baumeister, R. F., Tice, D. M., & Stucke, T. S. (2001). If you can't join them, beat them: Effects of social exclusion on aggressive behavior. *Journal of Personality and Social Psychology, 81*, 1058–1069.

U.S. Department of Health and Human Services. (2001). *Youth violence: A report of the surgeon general.* Washington, DC: Office of the Surgeon General.

Valois, R. F., & Mckewon, R. E. (1998). Frequency and correlates of fighting and carrying weapons among public school adolescents. *American Journal of Health Behavior, 2*, 8–17.

Vossekuil, B., Fein, R. A., Reddy, M., Borum, R., & Modzelski, W. (2002). *The final report and findings of the Safe School Initiative: Implications for the prevention of school attacks in the United States.* Washington, DC: United States Secret Service and United States Department of Education.

Webster, D. W. (1993). The unconvincing case for school-based conflict resolution programs for adolescents. *Health Affairs, 12,* 126–141.

Weissberg, R. P., & Greenberg, M. T. (1998). School and community competence-enhancement and prevention programs. In W. Damon (Series Ed.) & I. E. Sigel & K. A. Renninger (Vol. Eds.), *Handbook of child psychology: Vol. 4. Child psychology in practice* (5th ed., pp. 877–954). New York: Wiley.

Weissberg, R. P., Kumfer, K. L., & Seligman, M. E. P. (2003). Prevention that works for children and youth: An introduction. *American Psychologist, 58,* 425–432.

Weissberg, R. P., Walberg, H. J., O'Brien, M. U., & Kuster C. B. (Eds.). (2003) *Long-term trends in the well-being of children and youth.* Washington, DC: Child Welfare League of America Press.

Wilson, S. J., Lipsey M. W, Derzon J. H. 2003. The effects of school-based intervention programs on aggressive behavior: A meta-analysis. *Journal of Consulting Clinical Psychology, 71*(1), 136–49.

41

The Safe and Responsive Schools Project: A School Reform Model for Implementing Best Practices in Violence Prevention

Russell Skiba
Shana Ritter
Ada Simmons
Indiana University–Bloomington

Reece Peterson
Courtney Miller
University of Nebraska–Lincoln

Multiple victim homicides in U.S. schools in the late 1990s elevated the topic of school discipline from a perennial concern to a national urgency, and made it clear that the threat of school violence cuts across class, locale, and special education status. Although firm, clear limits have a place in maintaining school order in the face of extreme incidents, harsh and punitive discipline cannot in itself foster a school climate that can prevent school violence. This chapter presents evidence supporting the need for a broader perspective, stressing comprehensive planning, prevention, and parent–community involvement is necessary if schools are to develop effective strategies to address the disruptive behavior of all students, including those with disabilities, and prevent further tragedy in our nation's schools.

The Safe and Responsive Schools (SRS) Project was designed to assist schools in implementing a comprehensive and preventive process for addressing school violence, and improving student behavior at school. The model is based on the assumption that an instructional approach (i.e., one based in educational and learning principles) to school discipline will be more effective than a punishment approach in teaching students the skills they need to get along in school and society. In particular, special attention is focused on those students who need explicit instruction and structure to learn the implicit social curriculum of the school. The process is intended to enable schools and school districts to develop a broader perspective on school safety, stressing comprehensive planning, prevention, and parent–community involvement. It incorporates our best knowledge of schoolwide behavior planning in a comprehensive model of systems change in school violence prevention, discipline reform, and behavior change.

BACKGROUND AND RATIONALE

Although the visibility of school shootings in the 1990s created a strong momentum for immediate action to increase the safety of schools, the first responses to those tragedies were not necessarily the most effective. The following sections discuss the complexity of implementing truly effective measures for improving school safety and provide a rationale for the SRS Project.

Promises and Problems in School Violence Prevention

Since the mid-1990s, a number of research efforts and panels on school-based prevention of youth violence have been convened or sponsored by the U.S. government, including a report on youth violence to Congress (Gottfredson, 1997), the Department of Education/Juvenile Justice response to school shootings (e.g., Dwyer, Osher, & Warger, 1998), and the report of the U.S. Surgeon General on violence prevention (Elliott, Hatot, Sirovatka, & Potter, 2001). These panels advanced understanding of what constitutes effective prevention practice by using rigorous methodological criteria to identify effective and promising programs. Their findings are remarkably consistent with each other and with other scholarly reviews (e.g., Gagnon & Leone, 2002) in outlining an emerging conceptual model for school violence prevention, and in identifying programs that appear to be most effective within that model.

Nonetheless, identifying effective school-based interventions for violence prevention does not guarantee implementation of those strategies in schools. Although surveys of school practice have found that prevention programs are beginning to be implemented in schools, the available evidence suggests that the fidelity of implementation of these strategies is typically low (D. Gottfredson, 2001; D. Gottfredson, Gottfredson, & Skroban, 1998; G. Gottfredson, 2000). Shoenwald and Hoagwood (2001) argued that the majority of evidence-based practices in the field of prevention have been developed under "test tube conditions" that fail to mirror the realities of school settings. Such rigorous experimental conditions are critical to demonstrating internal validity, but they do not guarantee that evidence-based procedures will be feasible in real-world settings that typically lack highly trained researchers, graduate assistants, and large amounts of discretionary funds.

Research on school suspension and expulsion has raised serious questions about both the use and effects of traditional school discipline. Data consistently indicate disproportionality in the use of suspension and expulsion for African-American students (Children's Defense Fund, 1974; Costenbader & Markson, 1994; Skiba, Michael, Nardo, & Peterson, 2002). Additionally, the use of suspension and expulsion appear to be associated with a number of negative outcomes, including a less satisfactory school climate (Hellman & Beaton, 1986), increased levels of disruptive behavior over time (Tobin, Sugai, & Colvin, 1996), lower academic achievement (Raffaele-Mendez, Knoff, & Ferron, 2002; Rausch & Skiba, 2004), and school dropout (Ekstrom, Goertz, Pollack, & Rock, 1986). Yet suspension appears to be the single most commonly used disciplinary procedure in both general and special education (Rose, 1988; Skiba, Peterson, & Williams, 1997; Uchitelle, Bartz, & Hillman, 1989), and the popularity of the zero-tolerance paradigm appears to be causing an increase in the use of suspension and expulsion (Wald & Losen, 2003).

The most critical challenge facing alternative approaches to school discipline is to find effective methods for implementing research-based practices in school discipline and school violence prevention. The SRS Project was designed to facilitate the dissemination of best-evidence practices in violence prevention through a process that allows local school districts to adapt those practices to meet their own particular needs. In the following section we describe the goals and underlying model of SRS.

PROGRAM GOALS AND MODEL

The SRS Project was a model development and technical assistance project funded by the U.S. Department of Education Office of Special Education Programs Projects of National Significance Competition (project rationale and description, associated publications, and related resources may be found at the SRS Web sites: www.indiana.edu/~safeschl and www.unl.edu/srs/).

The two overarching goals of the project were to enable schools and school districts to achieve the following:

1. Develop a broader perspective on school violence prevention. The project sought to make information about best practices available to school teams in a way that would be practical and usable by front line educators.
2. Implement more effective strategies for addressing school safety and school discipline. The project sought to develop a needs assessment practice that would enable schools and school districts to adapt information about best practice and tailor school safety planning to meet their local needs.

The fundamental theoretical grounding for the project is a preventive model of behavioral planning emerging as the model most likely to successfully address the complexity of emotional and behavioral problems in schools (APA, 1993; Dwyer & Osher, 2000; Leone, Mayer, Malmgren, & Meisel, 2000; Peterson, Larson, & Skiba, 2001; Pianta, 1990; Walker et al., 1996). Preventive discipline assumes that there is no one simple solution to problems of school disruption. Rather, developing safe and responsive schools requires comprehensive and long-term planning, an array of effective strategies, and a partnership of school, family, and community.

The model involves a comprehensive approach that relies on three components. First, programmatic prevention efforts, such as conflict resolution, can help establish a violence free climate by teaching students alternatives for resolving interpersonal conflict. Second, screening and assessment processes appear to be critical in the early identification of students who may be at risk for violence, and in providing supports to those students before their problems escalate into violence. Finally, schools must have in place carefully planned and effectively delivered responses to disruptive behaviors that do occur.

LEVELS OF INTERVENTION

The project worked with 16 schools in two states to implement a preventive model of school discipline to significantly expand the array of options available to schools in addressing the issue of disruptive behavior. The key level of intervention was schoolwide, mediated by the activities of the SRS teams. In order to increase the likelihood of comprehensive reform, the project implementation also occurred at the district, classroom, and individual levels. To ensure the administrative support so critical to successful school change (Sergiovanni, 1990;

Starratt, 1995; Tewell, 1992), both private meetings and large group kickoff events were held to garner the support of superintendents, principals, and school boards in the participating districts. As the SRS teams developed individual school plans tailored to meet their own local needs, those plans began to be implemented at the classroom level, and at the level of interventions designed to meet individual student needs.

DEVELOPING LOCAL CAPACITY

The SRS model assumes that problems of implementation may come from two sources. First, schools may be unaware of effective alternatives for preventing school violence and promoting school climates conducive to learning. Given the press of daily activities in schools, it is difficult for practitioners to find the time to research best practice alternatives, and especially to judge the effectiveness of various options. Thus, the project sought to provide to school teams materials summarizing the best knowledge of violence prevention in a way that was clear and easily used.

Second, because many best-evidence procedures have been developed with insufficient attention to the realistic constraints of school settings (Schoenwald & Hoagwood, 2001), schools may find existing prevention strategies to be unrealistic or infeasible in their situation. For example, secondary school teams working on the project were fascinated by bullying prevention programs, but frustrated by the lack of such programs validated at the secondary school level. Thus, an important focus of the project was to develop a needs assessment process that could enable school teams to identify their own local needs. School teams were then in a better position to choose among existing programs to meet local needs, or adapt and tailor programs if no extant programs could be identified to meet school needs.

Schools differ in their readiness to implement violence prevention programs or restructure their school disciplinary system. Some programs may be in place, others may be lacking, and the quality of implementation will probably vary considerably from school to school. Needs assessment is thus critical to schools in providing a realistic picture of the resources that are currently available for school safety efforts, and the areas of greatest need.

DESCRIPTION OF THE PROGRAM: STRATEGIES AND ACTIVITIES IN THE SAFE AND RESPONSIVE SCHOOLS MODEL

The SRS Project developed and tested a planning process guiding schools through a needs assessment and strategic planning process that (a) enables school personnel to identify their most central needs, (b) increases awareness of available school-based violence prevention resources, and (c) facilitates strategic planning that allows school-based teams to match available resources with local school safety or violence prevention needs. The following sections describe the implementation of the model in participating schools across the 3 years of project activities.

SRS Strategic Planning Process

At the center of the SRS approach is a strategic planning process. In order to proceed strategically toward a school safety plan that can successfully address key school issues, participating schools engage in a process of structured school planning, typically over the course of a single school year, with implementation of the school plan in the following year. The SRS process guides the school team through four planning phases and an implementation/evaluation phase,

TABLE 41.1
Safe and Responsive Schools' Project Strategic Planning Process: Goals and Activities
Across Planning Phases

Stage	Goals	Activities
Team formation	• To establish a school-based team composed of respected professionals, parents, and students to develop the school plan	• Systematically evaluate and assess strengths and needs • Gather and utilize pertinent information and data • Formulate mission statement and focus • Formulate and implement comprehensive plan to address strengths and needs
Needs assessment	• To identify strengths and limitations of school resources for addressing safety and discipline issues • To identify critical areas of local need in terms of school safety and violence prevention	• School Practices Survey: completed by members of the SRS team in order to better understand current school practices and resources at each of the three intervention levels • SRS Safe School Survey: administered to students, school staff, and parents, assessing areas of climate, incivility and disruption, major safety and delinquency issues, and personal experience of safety
Best practices review	• To increase awareness and knowledge of evidence-based practices relevant to violence prevention and intervention • To assess which strategies best meet local needs	• Series of fact sheets and resource summaries compiled by project staff in areas relevant to each of the three intervention levels • As part of each meeting, teams reviewed one strategy that might be promising in addressing the safety needs of the school • Focus on (a) understanding the strategy, (b) evidence available for that strategy, and (c) the fit between the strategy and local needs
Strategic planning	• To use information from previous phases to craft a comprehensive, preventive plan addressing local needs	• Series of strategic planning worksheets helped guide SRS team • Plans individualized according to school needs • Plans included an overall mission statement, a minimum of three interventions, one at each of the three levels of the model, and procedures for evaluation

described later. A summary of the goals and activities associated with each phase is presented in Table 41.1.

Phase I: Team Formation

In Phase I, participating schools develop a team to carry out the planning activities. To maximize representation, membership on the team is conceptualized broadly as including general and special educators, school psychologists, administrators, parents, and students. Schools carefully select team members to represent important constituencies, or because of their status as respected colleagues. SRS teams meet biweekly, typically for 90 minutes, although teams sometimes choose to combine meetings into half- or whole-day sessions for more intensive work time at some points in the process. In their initial meeting, teams develop a vision statement, providing a long-term guide and a common focus for their work. Subsequent meeting agendas are guided by a comprehensive schedule leading the team through the various stages of the process.

Phase II: Needs Assessment

In the aftermath of serious school violence in the late 1990s, schools were faced with a virtual flood of products designed to address school safety issues, from security to peer mediation to inspirational speakers. With little prior experience with such programs, schools lack a frame of reference for evaluating which strategy, program, or intervention best meets their local needs and concerns.

SRS teams engaged in two needs assessment activities. The team completed the School Practices Survey, designed to assess the extent to which strategies, interventions, or programs to prevent violence or improve school climate are present at their school. For each of the three dimensions in the SRS model, a set of effective or promising practices was identified in the literature. These were framed as questions on which each school team rated their school ("To what extent does your school have a conflict resolution or violence prevention curriculum for all classrooms?" "To what extent does your school have defined procedures for handling threats of violence against staff or students?"). Team members completed the scale individually, then came to consensus as a team in rating each item on a Likert-type scale ranging from 1 (*no awareness*) to 5 (*well-established schoolwide*).

An example of an overall summary of team responses to the School Practices Survey is presented in Table 41.2. In general, school teams rated themselves as having fairly well-developed reactive responses to disruption and violence, such as crisis intervention plans. Most teams saw more pressing school needs and gaps in the areas of primary prevention and community-building programs (e.g., use of social skills/life skills curriculum and peer mediation). More critical than the absolute ratings that teams gave themselves, however, was the momentum created by the process of self-study. Prior to this self-assessment, some team members expressed the sentiment that there were few areas in which they needed to work on school safety. The process of coming to consensus on the School Practices Survey ratings appeared to increase team awareness of significant gaps in their current school discipline and violence prevention systems, and motivation to address those gaps.

Next, each participating team administered the SRS Safe School Survey (see Skiba, Simmons, & Peterson, chap. 11, this volume), a self-report measure tapping the perceptions of students, teachers, and parents in the areas of climate, incivility and disruption, major safety and delinquency issues, and personal experience of safety. In general, both students and staff rated their schools as being safe in terms of personal safety and major safety issues. Ratings tended to be lower in the areas of incivility/disruption, general climate, and belongingness.

Phase III: Best Practices Review

Two-page fact sheets were developed by project staff on a variety of violence prevention strategies, such as bullying prevention, conflict resolution, anger management, early identification strategies, teen courts, and functional assessment. These fact sheets summarized effective strategies in a reader-friendly fashion and were supplemented by Web materials and articles in practitioner-oriented journals (e.g., *Executive Educator* and *Preventing School Failure*).

Each week at their meetings, SRS teams reviewed one of these strategies or interventions for promoting school safety and preventing school violence. Team discussion focused on understanding the details of the strategy, reviewing the evidence available concerning the

TABLE 41.2

Team Responses to School Practices Survey: Mean Scores Across All Participating Schools

Item[a]	Average SRS Team Rating[b]	
	1999–2000	2001–2002
I. Creating a positive climate		
1. Programs for students struggling academically	3.37	3.76
2. Focus on building a sense of community or sense of belonging for students in your school	2.83	3.52
3. A curriculum for all classrooms for teaching social skills or life skills	1.70	3.26
4. Established programs to increase parental involvement (beyond parent–teacher organizations)	2.30	2.86
5. A peer mediation or student conflict manager program	2.44	2.72
6. A conflict resolution or violence prevention curriculum for all classrooms	1.25	2.16
7. A consistent model of classroom management with training for all teachers	1.38	1.96
II. Early identification and intervention		
8. Defined procedures for handling threats of violence against staff or students	3.37	3.36
9. Procedures for identifying students who may be at risk for violence/disruption	1.84	2.73
10. Schoolwide bullying prevention programs	1.31	2.72
11. An adult or cross-age mentoring program	2.02	2.76
12. Counseling or anger management programs for students identified as at risk	2.38	2.70
13. An identified team or staff who serve as a planning and problem-solving team related to student behavior	2.48	2.84
14. A systematic approach for collecting data regarding office referrals and using that data for monitoring students who may be at risk	1.63	2.92
III. Effective responses		
15. A buildingwide behavior/discipline plan	4.29	4.12
16. Individual behavior plans for students who exhibit disruptive behavior, and procedures for designing such plans (e.g., functional assessment)	2.74	3.83
17. A school or district code of conduct that includes an array of consequences (beyond detention, suspension, expulsion) matches levels of offenses with levels of consequences	1.76	3.52
18. Procedures (e.g., a building security audit) to identify and address areas in the building that may be at risk for violence	1.87	2.46
19. An alternative location, school, or program for students who have especially disruptive behavior	3.06	3.56
20. A building crisis or emergency plan	3.20	3.94
21. One or more procedures or drills that are intended to minimize risks in a violent crisis situation	2.15	2.74
22. A strategy for coordinating services and interventions with other community agencies that may be involved with troubled youth and their families	2.32	2.70

[a]Participants rated the extent that their school has the following programs on a scale from 1 (*no awareness*) to 5 (*well-established*).

[b]Based on a sample of 33 team members for the 1999–2000 school year and 25 team members for the 2000–2001 school year.

TABLE 41.3
Summary of SRS Plan Development Process

I. Identifying the focus
A. *Sources of data*
- Survey
- Needs assessment
- Mission statement
- Team discussions/impressions

B. *Questions to consider:*
- What is/are our most critical need(s)?
- What area/s, if we could get them under control, would improve safety/climate the most?
- Does this differ by source? (e.g., parents, teachers, students)
- What should the overall or key focus of this plan be?

II. Selecting plan components
A. *Brainstorm Activities for each of the three components*
- Creating a positive climate
- Early identification and intervention
- Effective responses

B. *Evaluate brainstorms for feasibility and fit*
- Is this strategy practical? Is it something we could do?
- Is this something we are interested in doing?
- Do we have or could we get the resources for doing this?
- Do we have the time and energy to do this?
- Does this strategy address the needs identified in Step 1

C. *Craft most promising strategies into SRS plan*
a. Use voting strategies to identify top choices
b. Develop overall plan
c. Take to faculty meeting for feedback and approval

III. Refining the plan
A. *Description of plan activities: Key features and details*
B. *Scope of the plan: Where will it be implemented and by whom?*
C. *Resources available/needed: What training, staffing or funding are needed?*
D. *Action steps: Time line, presentation, responsibilities, and roles*

---

effectiveness of that strategy, and considering the extent to which that intervention could be expected to fit the needs and context of the school.

Phase IV: Strategic Planning

In the final phase of planning in Year 1, the team, guided by a series of strategic planning worksheets, considered both its needs assessment data and available best-evidence strategies to design an SRS plan. Table 41.3 presents a summary of the steps involved in developing the SRS plan through the strategic planning process. Although the team process had, up until this point, been characterized by biweekly meetings, the majority of school teams chose to develop the rough outline of their SRS plan in a single half-day planning meeting (e.g., by using an existing in-service day for this purpose). Also, teams presented the plan to the rest of the school faculty for their input and approval. At the following meeting, the SRS team completed the last step of Phase IV—defining the details necessary to implement the plan.

Although plans were individualized according to school needs, teams were also required to address three criteria in designing their plan, including (a) an overall mission statement summarizing the identified needs that the plan would respond to; (b) a minimum of three interventions, one at each of the three levels of the model; (c) some assessment measures to provide schools with formative and summative evaluation on school progress during implementation.

Phase V: Implementation and Evaluation

Thus, in the first year of the SRS process, school teams engaged in a strategic planning process resulting in comprehensive and preventive school safety plans tailored to each school's individual needs. During Year 2, participating schools implemented the components they selected as their school plan in the first year. To monitor treatment integrity, project staff conducted observations in participating schools on the consonance between implementation activities and the school plan. Regular presentations of data to the team, school administrators, and the school board allowed monitoring of the effectiveness of newly implemented programs.

Based on feedback from school teams, the process guidelines and evidence-based content were collected into a handbook, the *Safe and Responsive Schools Guide* (Skiba et al., 2001) that could be disseminated to districts seeking to undertake a comprehensive approach to school violence prevention planning. In order to better ensure sustainability and exportability, project technical support was progressively reduced in Years 2 and 3.

Dissemination and Further Testing of the SRS Process

To test the exportability of the *SRS Guide*, five schools in two urban districts and one in a rural district were chosen to replicate the first-year planning process. School-based teams were formed and received copies of the *SRS Guide* for directing a process of disciplinary restructuring. As in initial pilot testing, these additional districts made local decisions about which components to include in their school plans based on assessment needs and available resources. Due to distances involved, replication in the generalization sites necessarily involved lower levels of technical support than the pilot sites, allowing evaluation of the extent to which technical support was necessary to successfully use the *SRS Guide*.

DESCRIPTION OF SPECIFIC SCHOOL PROJECTS

In the first year of the project, 8 out of 10 schools participating in the SRS project developed schoolwide safety plans conforming to the criteria mentioned previously. Two schools failed to complete a plan in Year 1, but formulated plans the following year. Several schools attempted to ensure that their SRS plan would be institutionalized by writing some or all of it into their school's state-mandated school improvement plan.

Table 41.4 briefly summarizes the school plans developed by participating SRS schools. These plans typically include some component of a nationally validated evidence-based program (e.g., PATHS; Greenberg & Kusche, 1998); however, teams also included locally designed activities and strategies that were specifically tailored to address the issues and resource gaps identified in their needs assessment.

An example of a school that made significant progress in addressing its concerns is School A, a large high school in a rural school district. As part of its needs assessment, the team identified as one of its major problems the tremendous numbers of referrals to the office; a large proportion of those referrals appeared to be for minor misbehavior. The team noted that there was a line of chairs in the hall outside the office for students to sit in while waiting to see administrators regarding their referrals. To respond to this concern, the school developed an innovative new program called the Intervention Room. Staffed by both a general and a special education teacher, the Intervention Room functions in part as a resource room for students with disabilities needing academic assistance, but more importantly, also serves as

TABLE 41.4

New Programs Implemented in SRS Schools as a Result of Project Participation

School	Key Components of Safe and Responsive Schools Plan
School A (high school)	• *Intervention Room*: Students are referred to the Intervention Room for classroom behavior problems prior to office referral • *Classroom Management Training*: Workshop before start of school year for all faculty featuring national school discipline • *Pride Day*: Day-long activities for students and faculty on first day of school to kick off new school year and introduce changes
School B (middle school)	• *Safe schools TV show*: Videotaped role-plays, lessons broadcast over school's closed circuit TV system; based on Second Step curriculum; topics include anger management, drugs, and conflict resolution. • *Parent newsletter*: Newsletter sent home once a month detailing activities and events, especially pertaining to school safety
School C (elementary school)	• *Life skills*: Faculty-generated list of 10 key social skills taught to students once a week during class; rewards provided for students who display the life skill of the week • *Promoting Alternative Thinking Strategies (PATHS) Curriculum*: Nationally validated conflict resolution curriculum taught to all students once a week during class
School D (high school)	• *Civility themes*: School activities and events revolve around a selected theme; currently under development • *Alternatives to out-of-school suspension*: Coordinated with local juvenile justice agency, habitually suspended students attend alternative placement during suspension rather than being at home
School E (middle school)	• *Civility code*: Four principles to guide student behavior; students exhibiting code-following behavior receive schoolwide recognition, including postcard sent home and writing their name on "Wall of Fame" • *Civility curriculum*: Curriculum being taught to all students during Home Economics; developed to uphold principles of the code
School F (high school)	• *Out-of-classroom intervention (OCI)*: Cool-down time for students instead of office referral, students complete problem-solving form • *Beatrice After School Education (BASE)*: Behavior management program for students in chronic contact with school discipline
Schools G & H (elementary schools)	• *Bullying prevention*: Nationally renowned bullying expert presented several workshops on the topic of bullying; distributed bullying survey; bullying prevention and awareness week at each school
Schools I & J (elementary schools)	• *Resource book*: Collection of community resources including information on health care, support agencies, and hotlines; copies available at each building • *Mentoring program*: High school students paired with elementary students who may benefit from a mentoring relationship; support and training provided to mentors
School K (elementary school)	• *Code red*: Coordinated several safety drills within their building during the year and helped evaluate and refine their emergency response procedures • *Bullying Awareness Week*: Goals for the week included a focus on education and prevention and working towards establishing a schoolwide common language for problem-solving techniques and behavior frameworks
School L (middle school)	• *Schoolwide organizational plan*: Plan developed in conjunction with Dr. Ron Nelson, at the University of Nebraska-Lincoln, to assist school staff in addressing the student behavior management needs
School M (elementary school)	• *Bullying Awareness Week*: Invited Dr. Swearer to conduct an in-service workshop for staff, an evening workshop for parents, and focus groups with elementary and secondary students; topics addressed included the definition of bullying, effects of bullying, and how to deal with bullying

an option for teachers for disruptive students, both with and without disabilities. Prior to a referral to the office, any teacher may refer a student exhibiting inappropriate or disruptive behavior to the Intervention Room. Relatively minor problems, such as lack of materials, are often quickly resolved and the student returned immediately to his or her classroom. When the referral is based on a more substantial conflict, intervention room teachers attempt to help the student describe the problem, take responsibility for their behavior, and return to the classroom with a plan for avoiding future problems. Other schools made similar changes in their disciplinary and school safety programs. At School F, a medium-size high school in Nebraska, the school developed an out-of-classroom intervention, an after-school program with a mentoring component where students who had been suspended could complete their schoolwork. As a result, out-of-school suspensions dropped from 47% to 16% of disciplinary actions taken during the first year of implementation. Finally, at the elementary school level, changes in disciplinary structure tended to focus less on reactions to student behavior, and more on the implementation of schoolwide prevention programs. For example, at School C (elementary), in response to a needs assessment showing that conflict resolution was the major school issue, the school sought out national programs in conflict resolution and bullying prevention and implemented those in the second and third year of the project, respectively (see quantitative and qualitative data).

EVALUATION: ACCEPTABILITY AND IMPACT OF THE SRS PROCESS

Acceptability of the Process

One important criteria for evaluation of any school-based procedure is social validity (Finn & Sladeczek, 2001; Wolf, 1978), the extent to which those involved in the intervention find the process and outcomes of the intervention worthwhile. Reactions of team members to both the process and outcomes of the SRS Project were, in general, highly favorable. At the completion of the project, SRS team members were asked to complete a 19-item survey assessing team members' perceptions of team functioning. Of the 60 team members asked to complete the survey, 38 responded. The members were asked to evaluate their personal experiences with specific aspects of team functioning in two broad areas: (a) usefulness of various components of the process and (b) personal experience with the change process. Mean results summarized by location are presented in Table 41.5; these data indicate a high level of satisfaction with the SRS process among team members.

Increased Options and Improved Disciplinary Outcomes

The SRS Project was based in part on the hypothesis that schools rely on exclusionary discipline primarily because they perceive few other options for maintaining a safe school climate. Thus, the central evaluation question for the project was whether the introduction of locally responsive intervention alternatives would reduce school use of out-of-school suspension and expulsion.

The SRS process did appear to have increased the options available for schools to address issues of safety and discipline. On 23 out of 24 items on the School Practices Survey regarding options for improving school climate and discipline, SRS team members rated their school as having that option more available at the end of the project than it was at the beginning (see Table 41.1). The greatest improvements were noted in the areas of "A conflict resolution or violence prevention curriculum for all classes" and "A school or district code of conduct."

TABLE 41.5

Final Evaluation of Elements of Safe and Responsive Schools Process by Team Members[a]
School Team Evaluation—Process

	Indiana Schools Mean	Nebraska Schools Mean	Total Mean
Kickoff, orientation meeting	4.03	4.17	4.09
Fact sheets	3.78	4.04	3.89
Needs assessment process	4.21	4.06	4.15
Needs assessment results	4.16	3.95	4.07
SRS survey results	4.29	4.00	4.17
Use of other data in decision making	3.88	3.86	3.87
SRS project staff	4.32	4.25	4.29
Development of a plan	4.42	4.32	4.38
Team discussions/brainstorming	4.45	4.05	4.28
Opportunity to focus on behavior issues	4.33	3.92	4.16

School Team Evaluation—Results	Indiana Schools Mean	Indiana Schools Mean	Total Mean
Clear on purpose of SRS team?	4.57	4.31	4.38
Clear about your role on SRS team?	4.31	3.96	4.16
Time commitment compared to other teams?	3.99	3.78	3.90
Team meeting its goals?	3.06	2.57	2.85
Overall value of SRS team to school?	3.76	3.22	3.53
How many hours spent per month?[b]	8.2	2.00	5.60
Ideal size of team?[c]	7	8.50	7.70

[a]Unless otherwise noted, rating based on paper-and-pencil survey completed by team members at the final official project team meeting, May 2002. Responses based on a scale ranging from 1 (*highly ineffective*) to 5 (*highly effective*).

[b]Team members were asked to estimate how many hours per month they spent in activities related to the Safe and Responsive Schools Project.

[c]Team members were asked to estimate what they felt would be ideal size in terms of number of members for a school safety team.

These shifts in available disciplinary options were accompanied by disciplinary outcome changes. Changes over time in out-of-school suspension and expulsion at Indiana schools in the SRS study were tracked using disciplinary data submitted to the state of Indiana. (No similar data were available at the statewide level in the state of Nebraska, hence disciplinary change data presented in tables represent only the Indiana schools. Where disciplinary data are available for participating Nebraska schools, those are presented.) Table 41.6 shows the change in total suspensions across the 3 years of the project (1999–2000 to 2001–2002), as well as 1-year of generalization (2002–2003) across all students. Table 41.7 provides similar results for students with disabilities. The state of Indiana collects suspension data on students in general education on the basis of incidents, and on students with disabilities by individual. Thus, the absolute numbers across the two tables are not comparable. In general, the implementation of the SRS plans led to an immediate and in some cases dramatic change in school disciplinary

TABLE 41.6
Total Suspensions by School for All Students: 1999–2000 Through 2002–2003 School Years[a]

School	1999–2000	2000–2001	2001–2002	2002–2003	Total % Change[b]
School A (high school)	397	171	330	293	−26%
School B (middle school)	1,293	687	652	295	−77%
School D (high school)	205	179	121	114	−44%
School E (middle school)	577	421	513	413	−28%

[a]Values are the total number of suspensions (in school and out of school) for the entire school year drawn from the Indiana Department of Education Suspension Report. First school year (1999–2000) is baseline, prior to implementation of school plan. 2000–2001 and 2001–2002 represent implementation of schools' SRS plans. 2002–2003 represents generalization year beyond the formal involvement of the Safe and Responsive Schools grant.
[b]Percent change in incidents of total suspension from the 1999–2000 school year to the 2002–2003 school year.

TABLE 41.7
Total Suspensions for Students With Disabilities by School: 1999–2000 Through 2002–2003 School Years[a]

School	1999–2000	2000–2001	2001–2002	2002–2003	Total % Change[b]
School A (high school)	98	31	97	50	−49%
School B (middle school)	39	20	17	0	−100%
School D (high school)	4	6	1	1	−75%
School E (middle school)	28	12	15	20	−29%

[a]Values are the total number of individuals with disabilities suspended (in school and out of school) for the entire school year drawn from the Indiana Department of Education Suspension Report. First school year (1999–2000) is baseline, prior to implementation of school plan. 2000–2001 and 2001–2002 represent implementation of schools' SRS plans. 2002–2003 represents generalization year beyond the formal involvement of the Safe and Responsive Schools grant.
[b]Percent change in number of individuals with disabilities suspended from the 1999–2000 school year to the 2002–2003 school year.

outcomes in the first year of implementation. In some of the schools, the initial reduction in school suspension in the first year was followed by a slight rebound in the third year of the project. But in general, all of the schools showed a declining trend in the use of school suspension that appeared to continue even in the year past the completion of project activities. Similar trends were apparent for school expulsion. Across the same four secondary schools represented in Table 41.6, expulsions dropped from 60 students in the first year of the project, to 16 by the final year of the project.

Finally, Table 41.8 shows the change in the types of infractions that received suspensions from the planning to the implementation year at School A (the high school described previously that implemented the Intervention Room). Note the sharp drop in suspensions for more minor behavior (e.g., disruption, other, and academic consequence) in the 2000–2001 school year, as these more minor infractions began to be dealt with through the Intervention Room.

TABLE 41.8

Changes in Types of Infractions Receiving Suspension From First to Last Year of Project
in One High School (School A)[a]

Incidents	1999–2000		2000–2001	
	Frequency	% of Suspensions	Frequency	% of Suspensions
Disruption	91	22.0%	18	10.3%
Other	75	18.1%	5	2.9%
Attendance	51	12.3%	31	17.7%
Failure to serve consequence	45	10.9%	17	9.7%
Noncompliance/insubordination	33	8.0%	25	14.3%
Physical aggression/assault	30	7.2%	42	24.0
Academic issues	29	7.0%	0	0%
Obscene language/gestures	22	5.3%	6	3.4%
Tobacco	21	5.1%	0	0%
Talking	9	2.2%	0	0%
Vandalism	7	1.7%	6	3.4%
Drugs/alcohol	1	.25%	5	2.9%
Covert behaviors	0	0%	5	2.9%
Harassment	0	0%	1	.6%
Possession of banned items	0	0%	4	2.3%
Threat	0	0%	7	4.0%
Weapons	0	0%	3	1.7%
Total	414	100%	175	100%

[a]Data derived from the office referral electronic database used by the participating high school to record all disciplinary incidents referred to the school office and the consequences for these actions.

In particular, suspensions for lack of materials dropped to zero in the first year of implementation. On an anecdotal level, the team noted important qualitative changes at the school—the number of chairs lined up outside the office gradually declined to zero during the first year of implementation of the intervention room. Finally, these improvements in school climate seem to go along with improvements in school effectiveness in general—during the last year of the project, this school won the prestigious New American High Schools Award for its efforts in promoting a positive and effective learning climate.

Impact of the Project: Participant Reactions

Throughout the project, quantitative data on project outcomes were supplemented by qualitative interview and focus group data. Project team members were interviewed at the end of the 3 years regarding their experiences with the project; several themes that emerged from those exit interviews are worth noting.

As a result of their participation on SRS teams, teachers and staff felt their perceptions of disruptive behavior had shifted markedly, from simple reaction to one of understanding the need for behavior supports. As one team member put it:

> There is always a story behind behavior. It isn't just dismiss them as a rotten kid or a lazy student. . . . Whether or not we can do something about it as a school, or whether it takes a whole

community wraparound type program . . . at least we are becoming more aware of the factors that contribute to the problem.

Additionally, teachers felt the process had made them more aware of what they could do to change behavior. As one high school teacher noted:

I failed to grasp the power that we had to change behavior. I am from the old school, you know "it's a privilege for you to be here with me," and it is amazing when people come together, as this committee has, and worked toward a common goal that has been well understood and well defined, changes that we can enable to happen.

Team members also noticed that the programs in their schools had caught on and made a difference among the students:

It's [Safe Schools videos] opened up a dialogue. You hear kids talking about it, which is good. It's something that makes them think about what they do and how they look at each other.

Some of the teams noted that, despite the progress they saw, the program had not fully generalized to all staff, and that there was clearly more work to be done:

You can't think you are going to start something and have it be awesome and great a month after that. [The success of the newsletter] took 2 years and it is something as simple as a newsletter.

In general, however, the teachers, administrators, and parents who worked on the SRS teams felt their efforts during the 3 years of the project paid off in terms of new programs, and in terms of increased options for keeping students in school:

I just think we work harder with individual students towards keeping them in school and keeping them from dropping out or being expelled. I think that there are other options now that we look at and there's a larger range of opportunities for them to remain in school.

LESSONS LEARNED

Schools involved with the SRS Project have successfully created school plans to address the needs of their schools. In the process, several important lessons were learned, some of which reflect the experience of other school reform efforts.

Needs Assessment Is Central to the Planning Process

School violence researchers sometimes assume that dissemination of best practices is the most important element in the process of change; that is, if schools only knew what to do, they would do it. Yet, the teams clearly placed a priority on the information from the local needs assessment above information about available programs. The information from the needs assessment enabled teams to identify those specific issues that could allow them to tailor specific strategies to meet the unique needs of their school.

Developing a Common Understanding About School Violence Prevention Is Central to Effective School Reform for School Safety

At the outset, some of the school teams had more limited understanding of the meaning and scope of school safety. School safety was defined simply as the presence or absence of weapons and/or school-associated homicides. As the planning process progressed, a more comprehensive perspective on school safety emerged, one that expanded the focus from reaction and response to prevention and early identification/intervention. As the school community began to gain a better understanding of the direct relationship between day-to-day disruption to overall school safety, schools began to see the critical importance to school violence prevention of attending to the issues of climate and civility.

Participants in the Change Process Must Feel That Their Time and Work Is Valued

Strategic planning must be recognized as part of an educator's professional responsibilities and a necessary process in creating the best environment for teaching and learning. Educators repeatedly cite lack of time as a key factor that prevents change. Providing substitutes and teacher release time so that meetings and planning sessions can be held during teacher's working hours, as opposed to meeting before or after the regular school day, offers tangible evidence to teachers that their time and professionalism is valued.

Effective Schools Specialize

The SRS planning process emphasized the development of comprehensive school safety plans, and participating schools succeeded in putting together formal comprehensive plans on paper. In practice, however, it was most typical for schools to implement only some of the components of their plan in the first year. In fact, the most successful schools seemed to be characterized, not by the breadth of their interventions, but by the intensity with which they implemented those components that they chose to focus on. Although in theory the implementation of a wide array of strategies should enable schools to address a broader range of threats to school safety, in practice, the time of front-line educators is limited. Thus, although comprehensive approaches to violence prevention may continue to be the ideal, in practice, a more realistic and successful approach may be to abide by the philosophy of small wins (Weick, 1984). That is, successful schools begin by implementing only as much change as is practical within current resource constraints, and hope that early successes lead to increased enthusiasm and expansion of the program.

The Planning Process Should be Shared With the Entire School Community

Focus groups of students and teachers at participating schools made clear the importance of informing the entire school community about the reform initiative, early in the process. In the beginning of a change process, a small and enthusiastic team can make important progress, but over time, ownership must extend beyond the team to the entire school community, including parents and students. Without that support, enthusiasm among a small and committed team may eventually be replaced by burnout. Schools that succeeded in enlisting the support of all teachers described it as among their most important accomplishments.

Data Collection and Assessment Are Essential

Identifying the right data set for measuring change in school violence prevention is a complex task. Methods for assessing the effectiveness of violence prevention programs must be incorporated into the planning process. However, pinpointing data that can accurately measure and correlate civility and belongingness with school safety, and developing systems to collect these data across school buildings and school district is problematic. Schools do not always have central computer bases on school disciplinary measures, terminology may change frequently, or disciplinary records may not be kept at all. Thus, to ensure school-based measures of the process, the school team and administration should commit at the outset to a standardized system for recording and tracking school disciplinary referrals (see e.g., Morrison, Peterson, O'Farrell, & Redding, 2004). Disciplinary referrals are not the only source of data on school safety, however. Survey data of stakeholders, achievement data, absence and truancy data, even informal focus groups of students, parents, or teachers, can all provide important insights into aspects of the school climate that could predict or prevent violence. These can also be valuable data for evaluating systems change efforts.

IMPLICATIONS FOR PRACTICE, POLICY, AND FUTURE RESEARCH

The SRS Project has had as its goal demonstrating that an alternative, preventive approach to maintaining school discipline and school safety is possible, and that schools can use their own resources to restructure their practices to become more preventive. In order to maximize generalizability and sustainability, project budgets were structured without reliance on massive new influxes of funds to participating schools. We believed that schools could rely on their own resources, in combination with a structured planning process to significantly restructure the way they approached problems of behavior and discipline. The results of the project bear out that faith in the creative problem-solving abilities of school personnel. Table 41.9 presents the implications of the SRS Project for practitioners.

Probably because school violence prevention was an especially salient issue during the years of this project, the SRS Project was actively involved with policymakers during this period. The growth of zero-tolerance school discipline has been to some extent supported by a belief, at the national and state levels, that reactive and exclusionary approaches to discipline are necessary to maintain productive learning climates for students with and without disabilities (Skiba & Knesting, 2002). At the local level, the reliance on school suspension and expulsion as a primary reaction to disciplinary infractions may be not so much a question of philosophy as simply a lack of awareness that other alternatives are available. Yet, the emerging data show that

TABLE 41.9
Implications for Practice: Putting the Safe and Responsive Schools Process Into Action

---

- Develop school-based teams composed of respected representatives of key school and community constituencies, and ensure that the time and accomplishments of that team are valued and recognized.
- Conduct a needs assessment through a variety of means (questionnaires, surveys, team discussion), to identify the school's strengths and resources in school violence prevention as perceived by the school's faculty, students, and parents.
- Using a variety of means (questionnaires, interviews, surveys, and discussion), identify the greatest local needs or concerns with respect to violence, disruption, school discipline, and school climate.
- Review evidence-based practices for addressing violence and disruption at all three levels of prevention to identify promising practices and assess how those practices could be adopted within local resource constraints.
- Utilize all available needs assessment, promising practices, and strategic planning process information to develop a comprehensive plan that addresses local violence prevention needs.
- At each step in the process, seek to expand involvement in the process so as to increase school and community investment in the outcomes.

---

it is possible to maintain a safe school climate that is conducive to learning without removing large numbers of students from the opportunity to learn. This project joins abundant recent research in showing that there are preventive options that can effectively reduce disruption and violence in order to maintain a productive learning climate (Morrison et al., 2002; Osher, Sandler, & Nelson, 2001; Walker et al., 1996).

Finally, this project was intended as a model development project. Further research will be necessary to determine the extent to which the strategic planning process used in this project can be scaled up with a far lower level of technical support than was offered to our participating schools. In particular, despite generally positive results, it is clear that more effort will be required to ensure that violence prevention efforts are truly schoolwide. Unfortunately, the press for academic excellence in our schools may sometimes have the side effect of relegating programming for social behavior to a second-tier status. Furlong and Morrison and their colleagues (Furlong & Morrison, 2000; Morrison, Furlong, & Morrison, 1997) noted that as the field of school violence research has matured, it has moved from attempting to impose a criminal justice model on schools to understanding the unique context of schools as organizational structures. We believe that the next phase of school violence research will be to explore how disciplinary restructuring and school safety planning can be integrated into the core of what schools perceive their mission to be, in order to guarantee that schools will continually seek to implement methods that ensure safe and productive learning climates for all children.

ACKNOWLEDGMENT

The research on which this chapter was based was supported in part under grant no. H325N990009 from the Office of Special Education Programs, Department of Education. However, the opinions expressed herein do not necessarily represent the policy of the Department of Education, and no endorsement by the federal government should be assumed.

REFERENCES

American Psychological Association. (1993). *Violence and youth: Psychology's response*. Washington, DC: Author.

Children's Defense Fund. (1974). *Children out of school in America*. Washington, DC: Author, Washington Research Project.

Costenbader, V. K., & Markson, S. (1994). School suspension: A survey of current policies and practices. *NASSP Bulletin, 78*, 103–107.

Dwyer, K., & Osher, D. (2000). *Safeguarding our children: An action guide*. Washington, DC: U.S. Departments of Education and Justice, and American Institutes for Research.

Dwyer, K., Osher, D., & Warger, C. (1998). *Early warning, timely response: A guide to* safe schools. Washington, DC: U.S. Department of Education.

Ekstrom, R. B., Goertz, M. E., Pollack, J. M., & Rock, D. A. (1986). Who drops out of high school and why?: Findings from a national study. *Teachers College Record, 87*, 357–373.

Elliott, D., Hatot, N. J., Sirovatka, P., & Potter, B. B. (2001). *Youth violence: A report of the Surgeon General*. Washington, DC: U.S. Surgeon General's office.

Finn, C. A., & Sladeczak, I. E. (2001). Assessing the social validity of behavioral intervention: A review of treatment acceptability measures. *School Psychology Quarterly, 16*, 176–206.

Furlong, M. J., & Morrison, G. M. (2000). The school in school violence: Definition and facts. *Journal of Emotional and Behavioral Disorders, 8*, 71–82.

Gagnon, J. C., & Leone, P. E. (2002). Alternative strategies for youth violence prevention. In R. J. Skiba & G. G. Noam (Eds.), *New directions for youth development: no. 92, Zero tolerance: Can suspension and expulsion keep school safe?* (pp. 101–125). San Francisco: Jossey-Bass.

Gottfredson, D. C. (2001). *Schools and delinquency*. New York: Cambridge University Press.

Gottfredson, D. C., Gottfredson, G. D., & Skroban, (1998). Can prevention work where it is needed most? *Evaluation Review, 22*, 315–340.

Gottfredson, D. (1997). School-based crime prevention, In L. Sherman, D. Gottfredson, D. MacKenzie, D. Eck P. Ruter & S. Bushway (Eds.) *Preventing crime: What works, what doesn't what's promising: A report to the United States Congress* (pp. 1–79). Washington DC: U.S. Department of Justice, Office of Justice Programs.

Gottfredson, G. D. (2000). *National study of delinquency prevention in schools: Final report.* Ellicott City, MD: Gottfredson Associates.

Greenberg, M. T., & Kusche, C. A. (1998). Preventive intervention for school-aged deaf children: The PATHS Curriculum. *Journal of Deaf Studies and Deaf Education, 3*, 49–63.

Hellman, D. A., & Beaton, S. (1986). The pattern of violence in urban public schools: The influence of school and community. *Journal of Research in Crime and Delinquency, 23*, 102–127.

Leone, P. E., Mayer, M., Malmgren, K., & Meisel, S. M. (2000). School violence and disruption: Rhetoric, reality, and reasonable balance. *Focus on Exceptional Children, 33*, 1–20.

Morrison, G. M., Furlong, M. J., & Morrison, R. L. (1994). School violence to school safety: Reframing the issue for school psychologists. *School Psychology Review, 23*, 236–256.

Morrison, G. M., Furlong, M. J. & Morrison, R. L. (1997). The safe school: Moving beyond crime prevention to school empowerment. In A. P. Goldstein & J. C. Conoley (Eds.), (1997). *School violence intervention: A practical handbook* (pp. 236–264). New York: Guilford.

Morrison, G. M., Peterson, R., O'Farrell, S., & Redding, M. (2004). Using office referral records in school violence research: Possibilities and limitations. *Journal of School Violence, 3*, 39–61.

Morrison, G. M., Anthony, A., Storino, M. H., Cheng, J. J., Furlong, M. J., & Morrison, R. L. (2002). School expulsion as a process and an event: Before and after effects on children at risk for school discipline. *New Directions for Youth Development, 92*, 45–72.

Osher, D. M., Sandler, S., & Nelson, C. L. (2001). The best approach to safety is to fix schools and support children. *New Directions for Youth Development, 92*, 127–154.

Peterson, R. L., Larson, J., & Skiba, R. (2001). School violence prevention: Current status and policy recommendations. *Law & Policy, 23*, 345–371.

Pianta, R. C. (1990). Widening the debate on educational reform: Prevention as a viable alternative. *Exceptional Children, 56*, 306–313.

Raffaele-Mendez, L. M., Knoff, H. M., & Ferron, J. F. (2002). School demographic variables and out-of-school suspension rates: A quantitative and qualitative analysis of a large, ethnically diverse school district. *Psychology in the Schools, 39*, 259–277.

Rausch, M. K., & Skiba, R. J. (2004). *Unplanned outcomes: Suspensions and expulsions in Indiana.* Bloomington, IN: Center for Evaluation and Education Policy. Available: http://ceep.indiana.edu/ChildrenLeftBehind

Rose, T. L. (1988). Current disciplinary practices with handicapped students: Suspensions and expulsions. *Exceptional Children, 55*, 230–239.

Sergiovanni, T. J. (1990). *Value added leadership.* San Diego, CA: Harcourt Brace Jovanovich.

Sherman, L., Gottfredson, D., MacKenzie, D., Eck, J., Ruter, P., & Bushway, S. (Eds.). (1999). *Preventing crime: What works, what doesn't, what's promising: A report to the United States Congress* (pp. 1–74). Washington, DC: U.S. Department of Justice, Office of Justice Programs.

Schoenwald, S. K., & Hoagwood, K. (2001). Effectiveness, transportability, and dissemination of interventions: What matters when? *Psychiatric Services, 52*, 1190–1197.

Skiba, R. J., & Knesting, K. (2002). Zero tolerance, zero evidence: An analysis of school disciplinary practice, In R. J. Skiba & G. G. Noam (Eds.), *New directions for youth development: no. 92, Zero tolerance: Can suspension and expulsion keep schools safe?* (pp. 17–43). San Francisco: Jossey-Bass.

Skiba, R. J., Michael, R. S., Nardo, A. C., & Peterson, R. (2002). The color of discipline: Sources of racial and gender disproportionality in school punishment. *Urban Review, 34*, 317–342.

Skiba, R., Peterson, R., Boone, K., Miller, C., Ritter, S., & Forde, S. (2001). *Safe and Responsive Schools facilitator's guide.* Bloomington, IN: Center for Evaluation and Education Policy.

Skiba, R. J., Peterson, R. L., & Williams, T. (1997). Office referrals and suspension: Disciplinary intervention in middle schools. *Education and Treatment of Children, 20*, 1–21.

Starratt, R. J. (1995). *Leaders with vision: The quest for school renewal.* Thousand Oaks, CA: Corwin Press.

Tewel, K. J. (1992, April). Preparing for restructuring: A step-by-step approach to building support. *NASSP Bulletin*, 103–113.

Tobin, T., Sugai, G., & Colvin, G. (1996). Patterns in middle school discipline records. *Journal of Emotional and Behavioral Disorders, 4*, 82–94.

Uchitelle, S., Bartz, D., & Hillman, L. (1989). Strategies for reducing suspensions. *Urban Education, 24*, 163–176.

Wald, J., & Losen, D. (2003). Defining and redirecting a school-to-prison pipeline. *New Directions in Youth Development, 99*, 9–15.

Walker, H. M., Horner, R. H., Sugai, G., Bullis, M., Sprague, J. R., Bricker, D., & Kaufman, M. J. (1996). Integrated approaches to preventing antisocial behavior patterns among school-age children and youth. *Journal of Emotional and Behavioral Disorders, 4*, 194–209.

Wolf, M. M. (1978). Social validity: The case for subjective measurement or how applied behavior analysis is finding its heart. *Journal of Applied Behavior Analysis, 11*, 203–214.

Weick, K. E. (1984). Small wins: Redefining the scale of social problems. *American Psychologist, 39*, 40–49.

Author Index

Ruan, W. J., 21, *29*, 191, 196, *208*, *232*, 293, 294, *306*, 309, *322*, 339, *350*, 492, *497*, 535, *536*
Rubin, K. H., 7, *18*, 341, 344, *350*, *351*
Ruddy, S. A., 243, *253*, 603, 611, *615*
Rumberger, R. W., 4, *18*
Rusby, J. C., 423, *426*
Russo, M. F., 5, *18*
Ruter, P., *649*
Ruthazer, R., 249, *253*, *628*
Rutherford, R., 372, *381*
Rutherford, R. B., Jr., 57, 63, *66*, *68*
Rutter, M., 4, 11, 12, *17*, *18*, 55, *69*
Rutter, R. A., 57, 60, *70*
Ryan, A., 58, *69*, 574, 575, *586*
Ryan, G., 295, *305*
Ryan, G. W., 430, *440*
Ryan, J. A. M., 54, 55, *65*
Ryan, R. M., 12, *18*
Ryan-Arredondo, K., 604, 605, 607, 610, *616*

S

Sá, A. A., 502, *509*
Sabadell, P. M., 365, 366, *379*
Sack, K., 226, *233*
Sackett, D. L., 176, *189*
Safran, S., 14, *18*
Sager, N., 191, 198, *207*
Sailor, W., 56, 63, *70*, 187, *190*, 413, *426*, 624, *628*
Salas, L. M., 109, 115, *117*
Sale, L., 430, *440*
Salleh, N. M., 111, 113, *116*
Salmivalli, C., 109, *117*, 202, *209*, 259, 260, *273*, 280, *290*, 313, *322*, *323*, 327, 331, 333, 334, *337*, 347, *351*, 493, *497*
Salmon, G., 294, *307*
Salonen, J. T., 136, *144*
Salonen, R., 136, *144*
Salovey, P., 402, *412*
Salzman, M., 365, *382*
Samara, M. M., 261, *273*
Samdal, O., 104, 108, 109, 112, *116*
Sameroff, A. J., 9, *18*, 52, 54, *69*
Samples, F., 276, 277, *290*
Sampson, N. Q., 423, *425*
Sanchez, E., 191, *209*, 329, *337*, 348, *352*
Sanchez, S., 604, 605, *616*
Sandler, I. N., 54, *65*
Sandler, S., 25, *29*, 55, 56, *68*, 648, *649*
Sandoval, J., 89, *100*, 448, 450, *457*
Sanftner, J., 138, 139, *145*
Santacruz, M., 501, *509*
Santoro, R., 529, *536*
Sarvela, P. D., *252*
Satelzner, S., 574, 575, *586*
Saxton, J., 22, 23, *28*, 570, 585, 622, *627*
Sayger, T., 62, *68*
Saylor, K., 339, *349*
Scales, P. C., 61, *69*

Scalley, M., 353, 357, 361, *362*, 366, *380*
Schachar, R., 5, *19*
Schamess, G., 276, *290*
Schaps, E., 57, 61, *70*
Scheckner, S. B., 275, *290*, 430, *440*
Scheerens, J., 13, *18*
Scheidt, P. C., 21, *29*, 191, 196, *208*, *232*, 293, 294, *306*, 309, *322*, 339, *350*, 492, *497*
Schensul, J. J., 528, *536*
Schensul, S. L., 528, *536*
Schick, A., 389, *394*
Schilling, F., 501, *508*
Schinke, S., 171, 179, *189*
Schiraldi, V., 148, *155*, 212, *219*
Schmader, T., 260, *272*
Schmidt, F. L., 183, *189*
Schmuck, R., 159, *169*
Schneider, B., 14, *15*, 52, 56, *65*
Schneider, B. H., 191, *209*
Schneider, M., 402, *412*
Schneider, R. H., 136, *144*
Schoenwald, S. K., 175, 176, 182, 183, *188*, *189*, 632, 634, *649*
Schore, A., 399, *412*
Schreck, C. J., 24, 25, *29*
Schroeder, J. L., 608, *616*
Schrumpf, F., 555, *565*
Schuengel, C., 341, *349*
Schuerman, J., 181, *190*
Schultz, D., 384, *393*, 407, *412*
Schulz, A. J., 23, *28*
Schulz, K. F., 181, *189*
Schwab-Stone, M. E., 318, *321*, 399, *411*
Schwartz, D., 204, *209*, 261, *273*, 310, 313, *323*, 340, 341, 342, 344, *351*
Schwartz, N., 128, 129, *134*, *351*
Scott, J., 535, 570, 574, 575, *586*
Scott, T. M., 12, 13, *18*, 23, 25, *29*, 56, 63, *69*, *70*, 80, 87, 187, *190*, 213, *220*, 413, 415, 418, *426*, 624, *628*
Scriven, M., 439, *441*
Sealand, N., 262, 264, *271*
Seifer, R., 408, *412*
Seligman, M. E. P., 624, *629*
Sell, M. A., 513, *524*
Sellin, T., 439, *441*
Sells, S. B., 12, *18*
Sergiovanni, T. J., 633, *649*
Settertobulte, W., 104, 108, 109, 112, *116*
Sewell, K. W., 149, 150, 153, *156*, 587, *601*
Shaheen, T. A., 159, *169*
Shakoor, B., 606, *616*
Shannon, K. K., 359, *363*
Shannon, T., 57, *70*, 392, *394*, 417, 423, *426*, 600, *601*
Shapiro, J. P., 202, *209*, 249, *253*
Sharkey, J. D., 77, *87*, 121, 123, 125, 126, 128, 130, 131, *133*, 198, *207*, 235, 237, 242, 249, 250, *252*
Sharma, B., 246, *252*, 496, *496*
Sharp, S., 222, *233*, 298, 299, *307*, 309, 317, *323*, 327, 328–329, 333, 334, *337*, 347, *351*

Subject Index

C